J. R. M Jones

January 8th

THALBERT INVOKING THE WHITE LADY.

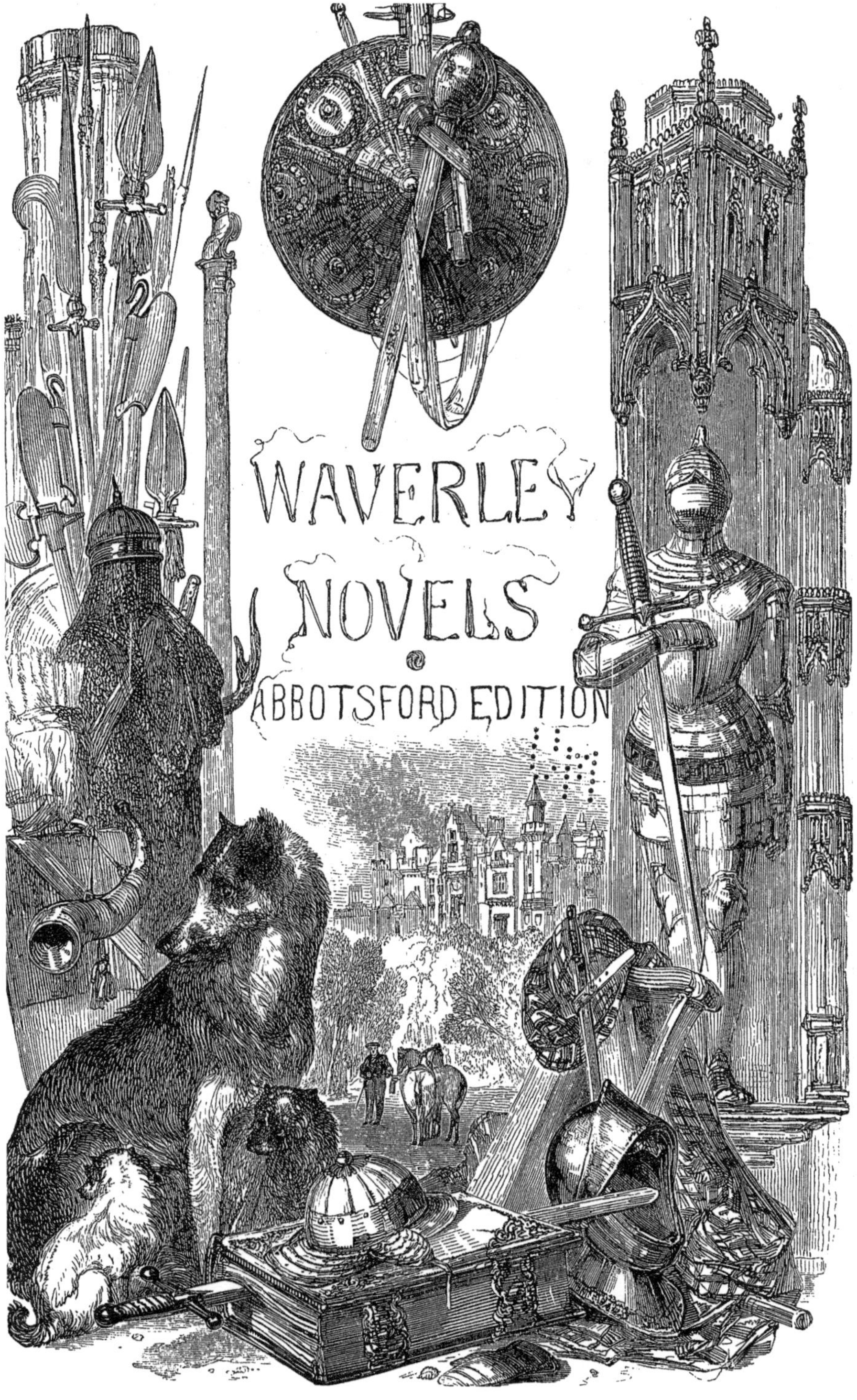
WAVERLEY
NOVELS
ABBOTSFORD EDITION

Abbotsford Edition.

THE

WAVERLEY NOVELS,

BY

SIR WALTER SCOTT.

COMPLETE

IN TWELVE VOLUMES.

PRINTED

From the latest English Editions,

EMBRACING

THE AUTHOR'S LAST CORRECTIONS, PREFACES, AND NOTES.

VOL. V.

THE MONASTERY—THE ABBOT.

PHILADELPHIA:
J. B. LIPPINCOTT & CO.
1856.

THE MONASTERY.

THE MONASTERY.

INTRODUCTION — (1830.)

It would be difficult to assign any good reason why the author of Ivanhoe, after using, in that work, all the art he possessed to remove the personages, action, and manners of the tale, to a distance from his own country, should choose for the scene of his next attempt the celebrated ruins of Melrose, in the immediate neighbourhood of his own residence. But the reason, or caprice, which dictated his change of system, has entirely escaped his recollection, nor is it worth while to attempt recalling what must be a matter of very little consequence.

The general plan of the story was, to conjoin two characters in that bustling and contentious age, who, thrown into situations which gave them different views on the subject of the Reformation, should, with the same sincerity and purity of intention, dedicate themselves, the one to the support of the sinking fabric of the Catholic Church, the other to the establishment of the Reformed doctrines. It was supposed that some interesting subjects for narrative might be derived from opposing two such enthusiasts to each other in the path of life, and contrasting the real worth of both with their passions and prejudices. The localities of Melrose suited well the scenery of the proposed story; the ruins themselves form a splendid theatre for any tragic incident which might be brought forward; joined to the vicinity of the fine river, with all its tributary streams, flowing through a country which has been the scene of so much fierce fighting, and is rich with so many recollections of former times, and lying almost under the immediate eye of the author, by whom they were to be used in composition.

The situation possessed farther recommendations. On the opposite bank of the Tweed might be seen the remains of ancient enclosures, surrounded by sycamores and ash-trees of considerable size. These had once formed the crofts or arable ground of a village, now reduced to a single hut, the abode of a fisherman, who also manages a ferry. The cottages, even the church which once existed there, have sunk into vestiges hardly to be traced without visiting the spot, the inhabitants having gradually withdrawn to the more prosperous town of Galashiels, which has risen into consideration, within two miles of their neighbourhood. Superstitious eld, however, has tenanted the deserted groves with aerial beings, to supply the want of the mortal tenants who have deserted it. The ruined and abandoned churchyard of Boldside has been long believed to be haunted by the Fairies, and the deep broad current of the Tweed, wheeling in moonlight round the foot of the steep bank, with the number of trees originally planted for shelter round the fields of the cottagers, but now presenting the effect of scattered and detached groves, fill up the idea which one would form in imagination for a scene that Oberon and Queen Mab might love to revel in.

There are evenings when the spectator might believe, with Father Chaucer, that the

— Queen of Faery,
With harp, and pipe, and symphony,
Were dwelling in the place.

Another, and even a more familiar refuge of the elfin race, (if tradition is to be trusted,) is the glen of the river, or rather brook, named the Allen, which falls into the Tweed from the northward, about a quarter of a mile above the present bridge. As the streamlet finds its way behind Lord Sommerville's hunting-seat, called the Pavilion, its valley has been popularly termed the Fairy Dean, or rather the Nameless Dean, because of the supposed ill luck attached by the popular faith of ancient times, to any one who might name or allude to the race, whom our fathers distinguished as the Good Neighbours, and the Highlanders called Daoine Shie, or Men of Peace; rather by way of compliment, than on account of any particular idea of friendship or pacific relation which either Highlander or Borderer entertained towards the irritable beings whom they thus distinguished, or supposed them to bear to humanity.*

In evidence of the actual operations of the fairy people even at this time, little pieces of calcareous matter are found in the glen after a flood, which either the labours of those tiny artists, or the eddies of the brook among the stones, have formed into a fantastic resemblance of cups, saucers, basins, and the like, in which children who gather them pretend to discern fairy utensils.

Besides these circumstances of romantic locality, *mea paupera regna* (as Captain Dalgetty denominates his territory of Drumthwacket) are bounded by a small but deep lake, from which eyes that yet look on the light are said to have seen the waterbull ascend, and shake the hills with his roar.

Indeed, the country around Melrose, if possessing less of romantic beauty than some other scenes in Scotland, is connected with so many associations of a fanciful nature, in which the imagination takes delight, as might well induce one even less attached to the spot than the author, to accommodate, after a general manner, the imaginary scenes he was framing to the localities to which he was partial. But it would be a misapprehension to suppose, that, because Melrose may in general pass for Kennaquhair, or because it agrees with scenes of the Monastery in the circumstances of the drawbridge, the milldam, and other points of resemblance, that therefore an accurate or perfect local similitude is to be found in all the particulars of the picture. It was not the purpose of the author to present a landscape copied from nature, but a piece of composition, in which a real scene, with which he is familiar, had afforded him some leading outlines. Thus the resemblance of the imaginary Glendearg with the real vale of the Allen, is far from being minute, nor did the author aim at identifying them. This must appear plain to all who know the actual character of the Glen of Allen, and have taken the trouble to read the account of the imaginary Glendearg. The stream in the latter case is described as wandering down a romantic little valley, shifting itself, after the fashion of such a brook, from one side to the other, as it can most easily find its passage, and touching nothing in its progress that gives token of cultivation. It rises near a solitary tower, the abode of a supposed church vassal, and the scene of several incidents in the Romance.

The real Allen, on the contrary, after traversing the romantic ravine called the Nameless Dean, thrown off from side to side alternately, like a billiard ball repelled by the sides of the table on which it has been played, and in that part of its course resembling the stream which pours down Glendearg, may be traced upwards into a more open country, where the banks retreat farther from each other, and the vale exhibits a good deal of

* See Rob. Roy, Note, p. 202.

dry ground, which has not been neglected by the active cultivators of the district. It arrives, too, at a sort of termination, striking in itself, but totally irreconcilable with the narrative of the Romance. Instead of a single peel-house, or border tower of defence, such as Dame Glendinning is supposed to have inhabited, the head of the Allen, about five miles above its junction with the Tweed, shows three ruins of Border houses, belonging to different proprietors, and each, from the desire of mutual support so natural to troublesome times, situated at the extremity of the property of which it is the principal messuage. One of these is the ruinous mansion-house of Hillslap, formerly the property of the Cairncrosses, and now of Mr. Innes of Stow; a second the tower of Colmslie, an ancient inheritance of the Borthwick family, as is testified by their crest, the Goat's Head, which exists on the ruin;* a third, the house of Langshaw, also ruinous, but near which the proprietor, Mr. Baillie of Jerviswood and Mellerstain, has built a small shooting box.

All these ruins, so strangely huddled together in a very solitary spot, have recollections and traditions of their own, but none of them bear the most distant resemblance to the descriptions in the Romance of the Monastery; and as the author could hardly have erred so grossly regarding a spot within a morning's ride of his own house, the inference is, that no resemblance was intended. Hillslap is remembered by the humours of the last inhabitants, two or three elderly ladies, of the class of Miss Raynalds, in the Old Manor House, though less important by birth and fortune. Colmslie is commemorated in song:—

Colmslie stands on Colmslie hill,
The water it flows round Colmslie mill;
The mill and the kiln gang bonnily,
And it's up with the whippers of Colmslie.

Langshaw, although larger than the other mansions assembled at the head of the supposed Glendearg, has nothing about it more remarkable than the inscription of the present proprietor over his shooting lodge—*Utinam hanc etiam viris impleam amicis*—a modest wish, which I know no one more capable of attaining upon an extended scale, than the gentleman who has expressed it upon a limited one.

Having thus shown that I could say something of these desolated towers, which the desire of social intercourse, or the facility of mutual defence, had drawn together at the head of this Glen, I need not add any farther reason to show, that there is no resemblance between them and the solitary habitation of Dame Elspeth Glendinning. Beyond these dwellings are some remains of natural wood, and a considerable portion of morass and bog; but I would not advise any who may be curious in localities, to spend time in looking for the fountain and holly-tree of the White Lady.

While I am on the subject I may add, that Captain Clutterbuck, the imaginary editor of the Monastery, has no real prototype in the village of Melrose or neighbourhood, that ever I saw or heard of. To give some individuality to this personage, he is described as a character which sometimes occurs in actual society—a person who, having spent his life within the necessary duties of a technical profession, from which he has been at length emancipated, finds himself without any occupation whatever, and is apt to become the prey of ennui, until he discerns some petty subject of investigation commensurate to his talents, the study of which gives him employment

* It appears that Sir Walter Scott's memory was not quite accurate on these points. John Borthwick, Esq., in a note to the publisher, (June 14, 1843,) says that *Colmslie* belonged to Mr. Innes of Stow, while *Hillslap* forms part of the estate of Crookston. He adds—"In proof that the tower of Hillslap, which I have taken measures to preserve from injury, was chiefly in his head, as the tower of *Glendearg*, when writing the Monastery, I may mention that, on one of the occasions when I had the honour of being a visiter at Abbotsford, the stables then being full, I sent a pony to be put up at our tenant's at Hillslap:—'Well,' said Sir Walter, 'if you do that, you must trust for its not being *lifted* before to-morrow, to the protection of Halbert Glendinning against Christie of the Clintshill.' At page 58, vol. iii., the first edition, the '*winding* stair' which the monk ascended is described. The winding stone stair is still to be seen in Hillslap, but not in either of the other two towers." It is, however, probable, from the Goat's-Head crest on Colmslie, that that tower also had been of old a possession of the Borthwicks.

in solitude; while the conscious possession of information peculiar to himself, adds to his consequence in society. I have often observed, that the lighter and trivial branches of antiquarian study are singularly useful in relieving vacuity of such a kind, and have known them serve many a Captain Clutterbuck to retreat upon; I was therefore a good deal surprised, when I found the antiquarian Captain identified with a neighbour and friend of my own, who could never have been confounded with him by any one who had read the book, and seen the party alluded to. This erroneous identification occurs in a work entitled, "Illustrations of the Author of Waverley, being Notices and Anecdotes of real Characters, Scenes, and Incidents, supposed to be described in his works, by Robert Chambers." This work was, of course, liable to many errors, as any one of the kind must be, whatever may be the ingenuity of the author, which takes the task of explaining what can be only known to another person. Mistakes of place or inanimate things referred to, are of very little moment; but the ingenious author ought to have been more cautious of attaching real names to fictitious characters. I think it is in the Spectator we read of a rustic wag, who, in a copy of "The Whole Duty of Man," wrote opposite to every vice the name of some individual in the neighbourhood, and thus converted that excellent work into a libel on a whole parish.

The scenery being thus ready at the author's hand, the reminiscences of the country were equally favourable. In a land where the horses remained almost constantly saddled, and the sword seldom quitted the warrior's side — where war was the natural and constant state of the inhabitants, and peace only existed in the shape of brief and feverish truces—there could be no want of the means to complicate and extricate the incidents of his narrative at pleasure. There was a disadvantage, notwithstanding, in treading this Border district, for it had been already ransacked by the author himself, as well as others; and unless presented under a new light, was likely to afford ground to the objection of *Crambe bis cocta.*

To attain the indispensable quality of novelty, something, it was thought, might be gained by contrasting the character of the vassals of the church with those of the dependants of the lay barons, by whom they were surrounded. But much advantage could not be derived from this. There were, indeed, differences betwixt the two classes, but, like tribes in the mineral and vegetable world, which, resembling each other to common eyes, can be sufficiently well discriminated by naturalists, they were yet too similar, upon the whole, to be placed in marked contrast with each other.

Machinery remained — the introduction of the supernatural and marvellous; the resort of distressed authors since the days of Horace, but whose privileges as a sanctuary have been disputed in the present age, and well-nigh exploded. The popular belief no longer allows the possibility of existence to the race of mysterious beings which hovered betwixt this world and that which is invisible. The fairies have abandoned their moonlight turf; the witch no longer holds her black orgies in the hemlock dell; and

> Even the last lingering phantom of the brain,
> The churchyard ghost, is now at rest again.

From the discredit attached to the vulgar and more common modes in which the Scottish superstition displays itself, the author was induced to have recourse to the beautiful, though almost forgotten, theory of astral spirits, or creatures of the elements, surpassing human beings in knowledge and power, but inferior to them, as being subject, after a certain space of years, to a death which is to them annihilation, as they have no share in the promise made to the sons of Adam. These spirits are supposed to be of four distinct kinds, as the elements from which they have their origin, and are known, to those who have studied the cabalistical philosophy, by the names of Sylphs, Gnomes, Salamanders, and Naiads, as they belong to the elements of Air, Earth, Fire, or Water. The general reader will find an entertaining account of these elementary spirits in the French book entitled, "Entretiens de Compte du Gabalis." The ingenious Compte de la Motte Fouqué composed, in German, one of the most successful productions of his fertile brain, where a beautiful and even afflicting effect is produced by the introduction of a water-nymph, who loses the privilege of immortality by consenting to become accessible to human feelings, and uniting her lot with that of a mortal, who treats her with ingratitude.

In imitation of an example so successful, the White Lady of Avenel was introduced into the following sheets. She is represented as connected with the family of Avenel by one of those mystic ties, which, in ancient times, were supposed to exist, in certain circumstances, between the creatures of the elements and the children of men. Such instances of mysterious union are recognized in Ireland, in the real Milesian families, who are possessed of a Banshie; and they are known among the traditions of the Highlands, which, in many cases, attached an immortal being or spirit to the service of particular families or tribes. These demons, if they are to be called so, announced good or evil fortune to the families connected with them; and though some only condescended to meddle with matters of importance, others, like the May Mollach, or Maid of the Hairy Arms, condescended to mingle in ordinary sports, and even to direct the Chief how to play at draughts.

There was, therefore, no great violence in supposing such a being as this to have existed, while the elementary spirits were believed in; but it was more difficult to describe or imagine its attributes and principles of action. Shakspeare, the first of authorities in such a case, has painted Ariel, that beautiful creature of his fancy, as only approaching so near to humanity as to know the nature of that sympathy which the creatures of clay felt for each other, as we learn from the expression—"Mine would, if I were human." The inferences from this are singular, but seem capable of regular deduction. A being, however superior to man in length of life—in power over the elements—in certain perceptions respecting the present, the past, and the future, yet still incapable of human passions, of sentiments of moral good and evil, of meriting future rewards or punishments, belongs rather to the class of animals, than of human creatures, and must therefore be presumed to act more from temporary benevolence or caprice, than from anything approaching to feeling or reasoning. Such a being's superiority in power can only be compared to that of the elephant or lion, who are greater in strength than man, though inferior in the scale of creation. The partialities which we suppose such spirits to entertain must be like those of the dog; their sudden starts of passion, or the indulgence of a frolic, or mischief, may be compared to those of the numerous varieties of the cat. All these propensities are, however, controlled by the laws which render the elementary race subordinate to the command of man—liable to be subjected by his science, (so the sect of Gnostics believed, and on this turned the Rosicrucian philosophy,) or to be overpowered by his superior courage and daring, when it set their illusions at defiance.

It is with reference to this idea of the supposed spirits of the elements, that the White Lady of Avenel is represented as acting a varying, capricious, and inconsistent part in the pages assigned to her in the narrative; manifesting interest and attachment to the family with whom her destinies are associated, but evincing whim, and even a species of malevolence, towards other mortals, as the Sacristan, and the Border robber, whose incorrect life subjected them to receive petty mortifications at her hand. The White Lady is scarcely supposed, however, to have possessed either the power or the inclination to do more than inflict terror or create embarrassment, and is also subjected by those mortals, who, by virtuous resolution, and mental energy, could assert superiority over her. In these particulars she seems to constitute a being of a middle class, between the *esprit follet* who places its pleasure in misleading and tormenting mortals, and the benevolent Fairy of the East, who uniformly guides, aids, and supports them.

Either, however, the author executed his purpose indifferently, or the public did not approve of it; for the White Lady of Avenel was far from being popular. He does not now make the present statement, in the view of arguing readers into a more favourable opinion on the subject, but merely with the purpose of exculpating himself from the charge of having wantonly intruded into the narrative a being of inconsistent powers and propensities.

In the delineation of another character, the author of the Monastery failed, where he hoped for some success. As nothing is so successful a subject for ridicule as the fashionable follies of the time, it occurred to him that the more serious scenes of his narrative might be relieved by the humour of a cavaliero of the age of Queen Elizabeth. In every period, the attempt to gain and maintain the highest rank of society, has depended on the power of assuming and supporting a certain fashionable kind of affectation, usually connected with some vivacity of talent and energy of character, but distinguished at the same time by a transcendent flight, beyond sound reason and common sense; both faculties too vulgar to be admitted into the estimate of one who claims to be esteemed "a choice spirit of the age." These, in their different phases, constitute the gallants of the day, whose boast it is to drive the whims of fashion to extremity.

On all occasions, the manners of the sovereign, the court, and the time, must give the tone to the peculiar description of qualities by which those who would attain the height of fashion must seek to distinguish themselves. The reign of Elizabeth, being that of a maiden queen, was distinguished by the decorum of the courtiers, and especially the affectation of the deepest deference to the sovereign. After the acknowledgment of the Queen's matchless perfections, the same devotion was extended to beauty as it existed among the lesser stars in her court, who sparkled, as it was the mode to say, by her reflected lustre. It is true, that gallant knights no longer vowed to Heaven, the peacock, and the ladies, to perform some feat of extravagant chivalry, in which they endangered the lives of others as well as their own; but although their chivalrous displays of personal gallantry seldom went farther in Elizabeth's days than the tilt-yard, where barricades, called barriers, prevented the shock of the horses, and limited the display of the cavalier's skill to the comparatively safe encounter of their lances, the language of the lovers to their ladies was still in the exalted terms which Amadis would have addressed to Oriana, before encountering a dragon for her sake. This tone of romantic gallantry found a clever but conceited author, to reduce it to a species of constitution and form, and lay down the courtly manner of conversation, in a pedantic book, called Euphues and his England. Of this, a brief account is given in the text, to which it may now be proper to make some additions.

The extravagance of Euphuism, or a symbolical jargon of the same class, predominates in the romances of Calprenade and Scuderi, which were read for the amusement of the fair sex of France during the long reign of Louis XIV., and were supposed to contain the only legitimate language of love and gallantry. In this reign they encountered the satire of Molière and Boileau. A similar disorder, spreading into private society, formed the ground of the affected dialogue of the *Précieuses*, as they were styled, who formed the coterie of the Hotel de Rambouillet, and afforded Molière matter for his admirable comedy, *Les Précieuses Ridicules*. In England, the humour does not seem to have long survived the accession of James I.

The author had the vanity to think that a character, whose peculiarities should turn on extravagances which were once universally fashionable, might be read in a fictitious story with a good chance of affording amusement to the existing generation, who, fond as they are of looking back on the actions and manners of their ancestors, might be also supposed to be sensible of their absurdities. He must fairly acknowledge that he was disappointed, and that the Euphuist, far from being accounted a well drawn and humorous character of the period, was condemned as unnatural and absurd.

It would be easy to account for this failure, by supposing the defect to arise from the author's want of skill, and, probably, many readers may not be inclined to look farther. But as the author himself can scarcely be supposed willing to acquiesce in this final cause, if any other can be alleged, he has been led to suspect, that, contrary to what he originally supposed, his subject was injudiciously chosen, in which, and not in his mode of treating it, lay the source of the want of success.

The manners of a rude people are always founded on nature, and therefore the feelings of a more polished generation immediately sympathize with them. We need no numerous notes, no antiquarian dissertations, to enable the most ignorant to recognize the sentiments and diction of the characters of Homer; we have but, as Lear says, to strip off our lendings — to set aside the factitious principles and adornments which we have received from our comparatively artificial system of society, and our natural feelings are in unison with those of the bard of Chios and the heroes who live in his verses. It is the same with a great part of the narratives of my friend Mr. Cooper. We sympathize with his Indian chiefs and back-woodsmen, and acknowledge, in the characters which he presents to us, the same truth of human nature by which we should feel ourselves influenced if placed in the same condition. So much is this the case, that, though it is difficult, or almost impossible, to reclaim a savage, bred from his youth to war and the chase, to the restraints and the duties of civilized life, nothing is more easy or common than to find men who have been educated in all the habits and comforts of improved society, willing to exchange them for the wild labours of the hunter and the fisher. The very amusements most pursued and relished by men of all ranks, whose constitutions permit active exercise, are hunting, fishing, and, in some instances, war, the natural and necessary business of the savage of Dryden, where his hero talks of being

> —"As free as nature first made man,
> When wild in woods the noble savage ran."

But although the occupations, and even the sentiments, of human beings in a primitive state, find access and interest in the minds of the more civilized part of the species, it does not therefore follow, that the national tastes, opinions, and follies of one civilized period, should afford either the same interest or the same amusement to those of another. These generally, when driven to extravagance, are founded, not upon any natural taste proper to the species, but upon the growth of some peculiar cast of affectation, with which mankind in general, and succeeding generations in particular, feel no common interest or sympathy. The extravagances of coxcombry in manners and apparel are indeed the legitimate and often the successful objects of satire, during the time when they exist. In evidence of this, theatrical critics may observe how many dramatic *jeux d' esprit* are well received every season, because the satirist levels at some well-known or fashionable absurdity; or, in the dramatic phrase, "shoots folly as it flies." But when the peculiar kind of folly keeps the wing no longer, it is reckoned but waste of powder to pour a discharge of ridicule on what has ceased to exist; and the pieces in which such forgotten absurdities are made the subject of ridicule, fall quietly into oblivion with the follies which gave them fashion, or only continue to exist on the scene, because they contain some other more permanent interest than that which connects them with manners and follies of a temporary character.

This, perhaps, affords a reason why the comedies of Ben Jonson, founded upon system, or what the age termed humours, — by which was meant factitious and affected characters, superinduced on that which was common to the rest of their race, — in spite of acute satire, deep scholarship, and strong sense, do not now afford general pleasure, but are confined to the closet of the antiquary, whose studies have assured him that the personages of the dramatist were once, though they are now no longer, portraits of existing nature.

Let us take another example of our hypothesis from Shakspeare himself, who, of all authors, drew his portraits for all ages. With the whole sum of the idolatry which affects us at his name, the mass of readers peruse, without amusement, the characters formed on the extravagances of temporary fashion; and the Euphuist Don Armado, the pedant Holofernes, even Nym and Pistol, are read with little pleasure by the mass of the public, being portraits of which we cannot recognize the humour, because the originals no longer exist. In like manner, while the distresses of Romeo and Juliet continue to interest every bosom, Mercutio, drawn as an accurate representation of the finished fine gentleman of the period, and as such received by the unanimous approbation of contemporaries, has so little to interest the present age, that, stripped of all his puns, and quirks of verbal wit, he only retains his place in the scene, in virtue of his fine and fanciful speech upon dreaming, which belongs to no particular age, and because he is a personage whose presence is indispensable to the plot.

We have already prosecuted perhaps too far an argument, the tendency of which is to prove, that the introduction of an humorist, acting like Sir Piercie Shafton, upon some forgotten and obsolete model of folly, once fashionable, is rather likely to awaken the disgust of the reader, as unnatural, than find him food for laughter. Whether owing to this theory, or whether to the more simple and probable cause of the author's failure in the delineation of the subject he had proposed to himself, the formidable objection of *incredulus odi* was applied to the Euphuist, as well as to the White Lady of Avenel; and the one was denounced as unnatural, while the other was rejected as impossible.

There was little in the story to atone for these failures in two principal points. The incidents were inartificially huddled together. There was no part of the intrigue to which deep interest was found to apply; and the conclusion was brought about, not by incidents arising out of the story itself, but in consequence of public transactions, with which the narrative has little connexion, and which the reader had little opportunity to become acquainted with.

This, if not a positive fault, was yet a great defect in the Romance. It is true, that not only the practice of some great authors in this department, but even the general course of human life itself, may be quoted in favour of this more obvious and less artificial practice of arranging a narrative. It is seldom that the same circle of personages who have surrounded an individual at his first outset in life, continue to have an interest in his career till his fate comes to a crisis. On the contrary, and more especially if the events of his life be of a varied character, and worth communicating to others, or to the world, the hero's later connexions are usually totally separated from those with whom he began the voyage, but whom the individual has outsailed, or who have drifted astray, or foundered on the passage. This hackneyed comparison holds good in another point. The numerous vessels of so many different sorts, and destined for such different purposes, which are launched in the same mighty ocean, although each endeavours to pursue its own course, are in every case more influenced by the winds and tides, which are common to the element which they all navigate, than by their own separate exertions. And it is thus in the world, that, when human prudence has done its best, some general, perhaps national, event, destroys the schemes of the individual, as the casual touch of a more powerful being sweeps away the web of the spider.

Many excellent romances have been composed in this view of human life, where the hero is conducted through a variety of detached scenes, in which various agents appear and disappear, without, perhaps, having any permanent influence on the progress of the story. Such is the structure of Gil Blas, Roderick Random, and the lives and adventures of many other heroes, who are described as running through different stations of life, and encountering various adventures, which are only connected with each other by having happened to be witnessed by the same individual, whose identity unites them together, as the string of a necklace links the beads, which are otherwise detached.

But though such an unconnected course of adventures is what most fre quently occurs in nature, yet the province of the romance writer being arti ficial, there is more required from him than a mere compliance with the simplicity of reality,—just as we demand from the scientific gardener, that he shall arrange, in curious knots and artificial parterres, the flowers which "nature boon" distributes freely on hill and dale. Fielding, accordingly, in most of his novels, but especially in Tom Jones, his *chef-d'œuvre*, has set the distinguished example of a story regularly built and consistent in all its parts, in which nothing occurs, and scarce a personage is introduced, that has not some share in tending to advance the catastrophe.

To demand equal correctness and felicity in those who may follow in the track of that illustrious novelist, would be to fetter too much the power of giving pleasure, by surrounding it with penal rules; since of this sort of light literature it may be especially said—*tout genre est permis, hors le genre ennuyeux*. Still, however, the more closely and happily the story is combined, and the more natural and felicitous the catastrophe, the nearer such a composition will approach the perfection of the novelist's art; nor can an author neglect this branch of his profession, without incurring proportional censure.

For such censure the Monastery gave but too much occasion. The intrigue of the Romance, neither very interesting in itself, nor very happily detailed, is at length finally disentangled by the breaking out of national hostilities between England and Scotland, and the as sudden renewal of the truce. Instances of this kind, it is true, cannot in reality have been uncommon, but the resorting to such, in order to accomplish the catastrophe, as by a *tour de force*, was objected to as inartificial, and not perfectly intelligible to the general reader.

Still the Monastery, though exposed to severe and just criticism, did not fail, judging from the extent of its circulation, to have some interest for the public. And this, too, was according to the ordinary course of such matters; for it very seldom happens that literary reputation is gained by a single effort, and still more rarely is it lost by a solitary miscarriage.

The author, therefore, had his days of grace allowed him, and time, if he pleased, to comfort himself with the burden of the old Scots song,

"If it isna weel bobbit,
We'll bob it again."

ABBOTSFORD,
1st *November*, 1830.

INTRCDUCTORY EPISTLE

FROM CAPTAIN CLUTTERBUCK, LATE OF HIS MAJESTY'S —— REGIMENT OF INFANTRY, TO THE AUTHOR OF WAVERLEY.

SIR,

ALTHOUGH I do not pretend to the pleasure of your personal acquaintance, like many whom I believe to be equally strangers to you, I am nevertheless interested in your publications, and desire their continuance;—not that I pretend to much taste in fictitious composition, or that I am apt to be interested in your grave scenes, or amused by those which are meant to be lively. I will not disguise from you, that I have yawned over the last interview of MacIvor and his sister, and fell fairly asleep while the schoolmaster was reading the humours of Dandie Dinmont. You see, sir, that I scorn to solicit your favour in a way to which you are no stranger. If the papers I enclose you are worth nothing, I will not endeavour to recommend them by personal flattery, as a bad cook pours rancid butter upon stale fish. No, sir! what I respect in you is the light you have occasionally thrown on national antiquities, a study which I have commenced rather late in life, but to which I am attached with the devotions of a first love, because it is the only study I ever cared a farthing for.

You shall have my history, sir, (it will not reach to three volumes,) before that of my manuscript; and as you usually throw out a few lines of verse (by way of skirmishers, I suppose) at the head of each division of prose, I have had the luck to light upon a stanza in the schoolmaster's copy of Burns which describes me exactly. I love it the better, because it was originally designed for Captain Grose, an excellent antiquary, though, like yourself, somewhat too apt to treat with levity his own pursuits:

'Tis said he was a soldier bred,
And ane wad rather fa'en than fled;
But now he's quit the spurtle blade,
And dog-skin wallet,
And ta'en the—antiquarian trade,
I think they call it.

I never could conceive what influenced me, when a boy, in the choice of a profession. Military zeal and ardour it was not, which made me stand out for a commission in the Scots Fusiliers, when my tutors and curators wished to bind me apprentice to old David Stiles, Clerk to his Majesty's Signet. I say, military zeal it was *not;* for I was no fighting boy in my own person, and cared not a penny to read the history of the heroes who turned the world upside down in former ages. As for courage, I had, as I have since discovered, just as much of it as served my turn, and not one grain of surplus. I soon found out, indeed, that in action there was more danger in running away than in standing fast; and besides, I could not afford to lose my commission, which was my chief means of support. But, as for that overboiling valour, which I have heard many of *ours* talk of, though I seldom observed that it influenced them in the actual affair—that exuberant zeal, which courts Danger as a bride,—truly my courage was of a complexion much less ecstatical.

Again, the love of a red coat, which, in default of all other aptitudes to the profession, has made many a bad soldier and some good ones, was an utter stranger to my disposition. I cared not a "bodle" for the company of the misses: Nay, though there was a boarding-school in the village, and though we used to meet with its fair inmates at Simon Lightfoot's weekly Practising, I cannot recollect any strong emotions being excited on these occasions, excepting the infinite regret with which I went through the polite ceremonial of presenting my partner with an orange, thrust into my pocket by my aunt for this special purpose, but which, had I dared, I certainly would have secreted for my own personal use. As for vanity, or love of finery for itself, I was such a stranger to it, that the difficulty was great to make me brush my coat, and appear in proper trim upon parade. I shall never forget the rebuke of my old Colonel on a morning when the King reviewed a brigade of which ours made part. "I am no friend to extravagance, Ensign Clutterbuck," said he; "but, on the day when we are to pass before the Sovereign of the kingdom, in the name of God I would have at least shown him an inch of clean linen."

Thus, a stranger to the ordinary motives which lead young men to make the army their choice, and without the least desire to become either a hero or a dandy, I really do not know what determined my thoughts that way, unless it were the happy state of half-pay indolence enjoyed by Captain Doolittle, who had set up his staff of rest in my native village. Every other person had, or seemed to have, something to do, less or more. They did not, indeed, precisely go to school and learn tasks, that last of evils in my estimation; but it did not escape my boyish observation, that they were all bothered with something or other like duty or labour — all but the happy Captain Doolittle. The minister had his parish to visit, and his preaching to prepare, though perhaps he made more fuss than he needed about both. The laird had his farming and improving operations to superintend; and, besides, he had to attend trustee meetings, and lieutenancy meetings, and head-courts, and meetings of justices, and what not—was as early up, (that I detested,) and as much in the open air, wet and dry, as his own grieve. The shopkeeper (the village boasted but one of eminence) stood indeed pretty much at his ease behind his counter, for his custom was by no means overburdensome; but still he enjoyed his *status*, as the Bailie calls it, upon condition of tumbling all the wares in his booth over and over, when any one chose to want a yard of muslin, a mousetrap, an ounce of caraways, a paper of pins, the Sermons of Mr. Peden, or the Life of Jack the Giant-Queller, (not Killer, as usually erroneously written and pronounced. — See my essay on the true history of this worthy, where real facts have in a peculiar degree been obscured by fable.) In short, all in the village were under the necessity of doing something which they would rather have left undone, excepting Captain Doolittle, who walked every morning in the open street, which formed the high mall of our village, in a blue coat with a red neck, and played at whist the whole evening, when he could make up a party. This happy vacuity of all employment appeared to me so delicious, that it became the primary hint, which, according to the system of Helvetius, as the minister says, determined my infant talents towards the profession I was destined to illustrate.

But who, alas! can form a just estimate of their future prospects in this deceitful world? I was not long engaged in my new profession, before I discovered, that if the independent indolence of half-pay was a paradise, the officer must pass through the purgatory of duty and service in order to gain admission to it. Captain Doolittle might brush his blue coat with the red neck, or leave it unbrushed, at his pleasure; but Ensign Clutterbuck had no such option. Captain Doolittle might go to bed at ten o'clock, if he had a mind; but the Ensign must make the rounds in his turn. What was worse, the Captain might repose under the tester of his tent-bed until noon, if he was so pleased; but the Ensign, God help him, had to appear upon parade at peep of day. As for duty, I made that as easy as I could, had the sergeant to whisper to me the words of command, and bustled through as other folks did. Of service, I saw enough for an indolent man — was buffeted up and down the world, and visited both the East and West Indies, Egypt, and other distant places, which my youth had scarce dreamed of. The French I saw, and felt too; witness two fingers on my right hand, which one of their cursed hussars took off with his sabre as neatly as an hospital surgeon. At length, the death of an old aunt, who left me some fifteen hundred pounds, snugly vested in the three per cents, gave me the long-wished-for opportunity of retiring, with the prospect of enjoying a clean shirt and a guinea four times a-week at least.

For the purpose of commencing my new way of life, I selected for my residence the village of Kennaquhair, in the south of Scotland, celebrated for the ruins of its magnificent Monastery, intending there to lead my future life in the *otium cum dignitate* of half-pay and annuity. I was not long, however, in making the grand discovery, that in order to enjoy leisure, it is absolutely necessary it should be preceded by occupation. For some time, it was delightful to wake at daybreak, dreaming of the reveillé — then to recollect my happy emancipation from the slavery that doomed me to start at a piece of clattering parchment, turn on my other side, damn the parade, and go to sleep again. But even this enjoyment had its termination; and time, when it became a stock entirely at my own disposal, began to hang heavy on my hand.

I angled for two days, during which time I lost twenty hooks, and several scores of yards of gut and line, and caught not even a minnow. Hunting was out of the question, for the stomach of a horse by no means agrees with the half-pay establishment. When I shot, the shepherds, and ploughmen, and my very dog, quizzed me every time that I missed, which was, generally speaking, every time I fired. Besides, the country gentlemen in this quarter like their game, and began to talk of prosecutions and interdicts. I did not give up fighting the French to commence a domestic war with the "pleasant men of Teviotdale," as the song calls them; so I e'en spent three days (very agreeably) in cleaning my gun, and disposing it upon two hooks over my chimney-piece.

The success of this accidental experiment set me on trying my skill in the mechanical arts. Accordingly I took down and cleaned my landlady's cuckoo-clock, and in so doing, silenced that companion of the spring for ever and a day. I mounted a turning-lathe, and in attempting to use it, I very nearly cribbed off, with an inch-and-half former, one of the fingers which the hussar had left me.

Books I tried, both those of the little circulating library, and of the more rational subscription collection maintained by this intellectual people. But neither the light reading of the one, nor the heavy artillery of the other, suited my purpose. I always fell asleep at the fourth or fifth page of history or disquisition; and it took me a month's hard reading to wade through a half-bound trashy novel, during which I was pestered with applications to return the volumes, by every half-bred milliner's miss about the place. In short, during the time when all the town besides had something to do, I had nothing for it, but to walk in the church-yard, and whistle till it was dinner-time.

During these promenades, the ruins necessarily forced themselves on my attention, and, by degrees, I found myself engaged in studying the more minute ornaments, and at length the general plan, of this noble structure. The old sexton aided my labours, and gave me his portion of traditional lore. Every day added something to my stock of knowledge respecting the ancient state of the building; and at length I made discoveries concerning the purpose of several detached and very ruinous portions of it, the use of which had hitherto been either unknown altogether or erroneously explained.

The knowledge which I thus acquired I had frequent opportunities of retailing to those visiters whom the progress of a Scottish tour brought to visit this celebrated spot. Without encroaching on the privilege of my friend the sexton, I became gradually an assistant Cicerone in the task of description and explanation, and often (seeing a fresh party of visiters arrive) has he turned over to me those to whom he had told half his story, with the flattering observation, "What needs I say ony mair about it? There's the Captain kens mair anent it than I do, or any man in the town." Then would I salute the strangers courteously, and expatiate to their astonished minds upon crypts and chancels, and naves, arches, Gothic and Saxon architraves, mullions and flying buttresses. It not unfrequently happened, that an acquaintance which commenced in the Abbey concluded in the inn, which served to relieve the solitude as well as the monotony of my landlady's shoulder of mutton, whether roast, cold, or hashed.

By degrees my mind became enlarged; I found a book or two which enlightened me on the subject of Gothic architecture, and I read now with pleasure, because I was interested in what I read about. Even my character began to dilate and expand. I spoke with more authority at the club, and was listened to with deference, because on one subject, at least, I possessed more information than any of its members. Indeed, I found that even my stories about Egypt, which, to say truth, were somewhat threadbare, were now listened to with more respect than formerly. "The Captain," they said, "had something in him after a',—there were few folk kend sae muckle about the Abbey."

With this general approbation waxed my own sense of self-importance, and my feeling of general comfort. I ate with more appetite, I digested with more ease, I lay down at night with joy, and slept sound till morning, when I arose with a sense of busy importance, and hied me to measure, to examine, and to compare the various parts of this interesting structure. I lost all sense and consciousness of certain unpleasant sensations of a nondescript nature, about my head and stomach, to which I had been in the habit of attending, more for the benefit of the village apothecary than my own, for the pure want of something else to think about. I had found out an occupation unwittingly, and was happy because I had something to do. In a word, I had commenced local antiquary, and was not unworthy of the name.

Whilst I was in this pleasing career of busy idleness, for so it might at best be called, it happened that I was one night sitting in my little parlour, adjacent to the closet which my landlady calls my bedroom, in the act of preparing for an early retreat to the realms of Morpheus. Dugdale's Monasticon, borrowed from the library at A——, was lying on the table before me, flanked by some excellent Cheshire cheese, (a present, by the way, from an honest London citizen, to whom I had explained the difference between a Gothic and a Saxon arch,) and a glass of Vanderhagen's best ale. Thus armed at all points against my old enemy Time, I was leisurely and deliciously preparing for bed—now reading a line of old Dugdale—now sipping my ale, or munching my bread and cheese—now undoing the strings at my breeches' knees, or a button or two of my waistcoat, until the village clock should strike ten, before which time I make it a rule never to go to bed. A loud knocking, however, interrupted my ordinary process on this occasion, and the voice of my honest landlord of the George was heard vociferating,* "What the deevil, Mrs. Grimslees, the Captain is no in his bed? and a gentleman at our house has ordered a fowl and minced collops, and a bottle of sherry, and has sent to ask him to supper, to tell him all about the Abbey."

"Na," answered Luckie Grimslees, in the true sleepy tone of a Scottish matron when ten o'clock is going to strike, "he's no in his bed, but I'se warrant him no gae out at this time o' night to keep folks sitting up waiting for him—the Captain's a decent man."

* The George was, and is, the principal inn in the village of Kennaquhair, or Melrose. But the landlord of the period was not the same civil and quiet person by whom the inn is now kept. David Kyle, a Melrose proprietor of no little importance, a first-rate person of consequence in whatever belonged to the business of the town, was the original owner and landlord of the inn. Poor David, like many other busy men, took so much care of public affairs, as in some degree to neglect his own. There are persons still alive at Kennaquhair who can recognise him and his peculiarities in the following sketch of mine Host of the George.

I plainly perceived this last compliment was made for my hearing, by way both of indicating and of recommending the course of conduct which Mrs. Grimslees desired I should pursue. But I had not been knocked about the world for thirty years and odd, and lived a bluff bachelor all the while, to come home and be put under petticoat government by my landlady. Accordingly I opened my chamber-door, and desired my old friend David to walk up stairs.

"Captain," said he, as he entered, "I am as glad to find you up as if I had hooked a twenty pound saumon. There's a gentleman up yonder that will not sleep sound in his bed this blessed night unless he has the pleasure to drink a glass of wine with you."

"You know, David," I replied, with becoming dignity, "that I cannot with propriety go out to visit strangers at this time of night, or accept of invitations from people of whom I know nothing."

David swore a round oath, and added, "Was ever the like heard of? He has ordered a fowl and egg sauce, a pancake and minced collops and a bottle of sherry—D'ye think I wad come and ask you to go to keep company with ony bit English rider that sups on toasted cheese, and a cheerer of rum-toddy? This is a gentleman every inch of him, and a virtuoso, a clean virtuoso—a sad-coloured stand of claithes, and a wig like the curled back of a mug-ewe. The very first question he speered was about the auld drawbrig that has been at the bottom of the water these twal score years—I have seen the fundations when we were sticking saumon—And how the deevil suld he ken ony thing about the old drawbrig, unless he were a virtuoso?"*

David being a virtuoso in his own way, and moreover a landholder and heritor, was a qualified judge of all who frequented his house, and therefore I could not avoid again tying the strings of my knees.

"That's right, Captain," vociferated David; "you twa will be as thick as three in a bed an ance ye forgather. I haena seen the like o' him my very sell since I saw the great Doctor Samuel Johnson on his tower through Scotland, whilk tower is lying in my back parlour for the amusement of my guests, wi' the twa boards torn aff."

"Then the gentleman is a scholar, David?"

"I'se uphaud him a scholar," answered David: "he has a black coat on, or a brown ane, at ony rate."

"Is he a clergyman?"

"I am thinking no, for he looked after his horse's supper before he spoke o' his ain," replied mine host.

"Has he a servant?" demanded I.

"Nae servant," answered David; "but a grand face o' his ain, that wad gar ony body be willing to serve him that looks upon him."

"And what makes him think of disturbing me? Ah, David, this has been some of your chattering; you are perpetually bringing your guests on my shoulders, as if it were my business to entertain every man who comes to the George."

"What the deil wad ye hae me do, Captain?" answered mine host; "a gentleman lights down, and asks me in a most earnest manner, what man of sense and learning there is about our town, that can tell him about the antiquities of the place, and specially about the auld Abbey—ye wadna hae me tell the gentleman a lee? and ye ken weel eneugh there is naebody in the town can say a reasonable word about it, be it no yoursell, except the bedral, and he is as fou as a piper by this time. So, says I, there's Captain Clutterbuck, that's a very civil gentleman, and has little to do forby telling a' the auld cracks about the Abbey, and dwells just hard by. Then says the gentleman to me, 'Sir,' says he, very civilly, 'have the goodness to

* There is more to be said about this old bridge hereafter. See Note, p. 57.

step to Captain Clutterbuck with my compliments, and say I am a stranger, who have been led to these parts chiefly by the fame of these Ruins, and that I would call upon him, but the hour is late.' And mair he said that I have forgotten, but I weel remember it ended,—'And, landlord, get a bottle of your best sherry, and supper for two.'—Ye wadna have had me refuse to do the gentleman's bidding, and me a publican?"

"Well, David," said I, "I wish your virtuoso had taken a fitter hour—but as you say he is a gentleman——"

"I'se uphaud him that—the order speaks for itsell—a bottle of sherry—minched collops and a fowl—that's speaking like a gentleman, I trow?—That's right, Captain, button weel up, the night's raw—but the water's clearing for a' that; we'll be on't neist night wi' my Lord's boats, and we'll hae ill luck if I dinna send you a kipper to relish your ale at e'en."*

In five minutes after this dialogue, I found myself in the parlour of the George, and in the presence of the stranger.

He was a grave personage, about my own age, (which we shall call about fifty,) and really had, as my friend David expressed it, something in his face that inclined men to oblige and to serve him. Yet this expression of authority was not at all of the cast which I have seen in the countenance of a general of brigade, neither was the stranger's dress at all martial. It consisted of a uniform suit of iron-gray clothes, cut in rather an old-fashioned form. His legs were defended with strong leathern gambadoes, which, according to an antiquarian contrivance, opened at the sides, and were secured by steel clasps. His countenance was worn as much by toil and sorrow as by age, for it intimated that he had seen and endured much. His address was singularly pleasing and gentlemanlike, and the apology which he made for disturbing me at such an hour, and in such a manner, was so well and handsomely expressed, that I could not reply otherwise than by declaring my willingness to be of service to him.

"I have been a traveller to-day, sir," said he, "and I would willingly defer the little I have to say till after supper, for which I feel rather more appetized than usual."

We sate down to table, and notwithstanding the stranger's alleged appetite, as well as the gentle preparation of cheese and ale which I had already laid aboard, I really believe that I of the two did the greater honour to my friend David's fowl and minced collops.

When the cloth was removed, and we had each made a tumbler of negus, of that liquor which hosts call Sherry, and guests call Lisbon, I perceived that the stranger seemed pensive, silent, and somewhat embarrassed, as if he had something to communicate which he knew not well how to introduce. To pave the way for him, I spoke of the ancient ruins of the Monastery, and of their history. But, to my great surprise, I found I had met my match with a witness. The stranger not only knew all that I could tell him, but a great deal more; and, what was still more mortifying, he was ble, by reference to dates, charters, and other evidence of facts, that, as Burns says, "downa be disputed," to correct many of the vague tales which I had adopted on loose and vulgar tradition, as well as to confute more than one of my favourite theories on the subject of the old monks and their dwellings, which I had sported freely in all the presumption of superior information. And here I cannot but remark, that much of the stranger's arguments and inductions rested upon the authority of Mr. Deputy Register of Scotland,† and his lucubrations; a gentleman whose indefatigable research into the national records is like to destroy my trade, and that of

* The nobleman whose boats are mentioned in the text, is the late kind and amiable Lord Sommerville, an intimate friend of the author. David Kyle was a constant and privileged attendant when Lord Sommerville had a party for spearing salmon; on such occasions, eighty or a hundred fish were often killed between Gleamer and Leaderfoot.

† Thomas Thomson, Esq., whose well-deserved panegyric ought to be found on another page than one written by an intimate friend of thirty years' standing.

all local antiquaries, by substituting truth instead of legend and romance. Alas! I would the learned gentleman did but know how difficult it is for us dealers in petty wares of antiquity to—

> Pluck from our memories a rooted "legend,"
> Raze out the written records of our brain,
> Or cleanse our bosoms of that perilous stuff—

and so forth. It would, I am sure, move his pity to think how many old dogs he hath set to learn new tricks, how many venerable parrots he hath taught to sing a new song, how many gray heads he hath addled by vain attempts to exchange their old *Mumpsimus* for his new *Sumpsimus.* But let it pass. *Humana perpessi sumus*— All changes round us, past, present, and to come; that which was history yesterday becomes fable to-day, and the truth of to-day is hatched into a lie by to-morrow.

Finding myself like to be overpowered in the Monastery, which I had hitherto regarded as my citadel, I began, like a skilful general, to evacuate that place of defence, and fight my way through the adjacent country. I had recourse to my acquaintance with the families and antiquities of the neighbourhood, ground on which I thought I might skirmish at large without its being possible for the stranger to meet me with advantage. But I was mistaken.

The man in the iron-gray suit showed a much more minute knowledge of these particulars than I had the least pretension to. He could tell the very year in which the family of De Haga first settled on their ancient barony.* Not a Thane within reach but he knew his family and connexions, how many of his ancestors had fallen by the sword of the English, how many in domestic brawl, and how many by the hand of the executioner for march-treason. Their castles he was acquainted with from turret to foundation-stone; and as for the miscellaneous antiquities scattered about the country, he knew every one of them, from a *cromlech* to a *cairn,* and could give as good an account of each as if he had lived in the time of the Danes or Druids.

I was now in the mortifying predicament of one who suddenly finds himself a scholar when he came to teach, and nothing was left for me but to pick up as much of his conversation as I could, for the benefit of the next company. I told, indeed, Allan Ramsay's story of the Monk and Miller's Wife, in order to retreat with some honour under cover of a parting volley. Here, however, my flank was again turned by the eternal stranger.

"You are pleased to be facetious, sir," said he; "but you cannot be ignorant that the ludicrous incident you mentioned is the subject of a tale much older than that of Allan Ramsay."

I nodded, unwilling to acknowledge my ignorance, though, in fact, I knew no more what he meant than did one of my friend David's post-horses.

"I do not allude," continued my omniscient companion, "to the curious poem published by Pinkerton from the Maitland Manuscript, called the Fryars of Berwick, although it presents a very minute and amusing picture of Scottish manners during the reign of James V.; but rather to the Italian novelist, by whom, so far as I know, the story was first printed, although unquestionably he first took his original from some ancient *fabliau.*"†

"It is not to be doubted," answered I, not very well understanding, however, the proposition to which I gave such unqualified assent.

"Yet," continued my companion, "I question much, had you known my

---

* The family of De Haga, modernized into Haig, of Bemerside, is of the highest antiquity, and is the subject of one of the prophecies of Thomas the Rhymer:—

> Betide, betide, whate'er betide,
> Haig shall be Haig of Bemerside.

† It is curious to remark at how little expense of invention successive ages are content to receive amusement. The same story which Ramsay and Dunbar have successively handled, forms also the subject of the modern farce, No Song, no Supper.

situation and profession, whether you would have pitched upon this precise anecdote for my amusement."

This observation he made in a tone of perfect good-humour. I pricked up my ears at the hint, and answered as politely as I could, that my ignorance of his condition and rank could be the only cause of my having stumbled on anything disagreeable; and that I was most willing to apologize for my unintentional offence, so soon as I should know wherein it consisted.

"Nay, no offence, sir," he replied; "offence can only exist where it is taken. I have been too long accustomed to more severe and cruel misconstructions, to be offended at a popular jest, though directed at my profession."

"Am I to understand, then," I answered, "that I am speaking with a Catholic clergyman?"

"An unworthy monk of the order of Saint Benedict," said the stranger, "belonging to a community of your own countrymen, long established in France, and scattered unhappily by the events of the Revolution."

"Then," said I, "you are a native Scotchman, and from this neighbourhood?"

"Not so," answered the monk; "I am a Scotchman by extraction only, and never was in this neighbourhood during my whole life."

"Never in this neighbourhood, and yet so minutely acquainted with its history, its traditions, and even its external scenery! You surprise me, sir," I replied.

"It is not surprising," he said, "that I should have that sort of local information, when it is considered, that my uncle, an excellent man, as well as a good Scotchman, the head also of our religious community, employed much of his leisure in making me acquainted with these particulars; and that I myself, disgusted with what has been passing around me, have for many years amused myself, by digesting and arranging the various scraps of information which I derived from my worthy relative, and other aged brethren of our order."

"I presume, sir," said I, "though I would by no means intrude the question, that you are now returned to Scotland with a view to settle amongst your countrymen, since the great political catastrophe of our time has reduced your corps?"

"No, sir," replied the Benedictine, "such is not my intention. A European potentate, who still cherishes the Catholic faith, has offered us a retreat within his dominions, where a few of my scattered brethren are already assembled, to pray to God for blessings on their protector, and pardon to their enemies. No one, I believe, will be able to object to us under our new establishment, that the extent of our revenues will be inconsistent with our vows of poverty and abstinence; but, let us strive to be thankful to God, that the snare of temporal abundance is removed from us."

"Many of your convents abroad, sir," said I, "enjoyed very handsome incomes — and yet, allowing for times, I question if any were better provided for than the Monastery of this village. It is said to have possessed nearly two thousand pounds in yearly money-rent, fourteen chalders and nine bolls of wheat, fifty-six chalders five bolls barley, forty-four chalders and ten bolls oats, capons and poultry, butter, salt, carriage and arriage, peats and kain, wool and ale."

"Even too much of all these temporal goods, sir," said my companion, "which, though well intended by the pious donors, served only to make the establishment the envy and the prey of those by whom it was finally devoured."

"In the meanwhile, however," I observed, "the monks had an easy life of it, and, as the old song goes,

——made gude kale
On Fridays when they fasted."

"I understand you, sir," said the Benedictine; "it is difficult, saith the proverb, to carry a full cup without spilling. Unquestionably the wealth of the community, as it endangered the safety of the establishment by exciting the cupidity of others, was also in frequent instances a snare to the brethren themselves. And yet we have seen the revenues of convents expended, not only in acts of beneficence and hospitality to individuals, but in works of general and permanent advantage to the world at large. The noble folio collection of French historians, commenced in 1737, under the inspection and at the expense of the community of Saint Maur, will long show that the revenues of the Benedictines were not always spent in self-indulgence, and that the members of that order did not uniformly slumber in sloth and indolence, when they had discharged the formal duties of their rule."

As I knew nothing earthly at the time about the community of St. Maur, and their learned labours, I could only return a mumbling assent to this proposition. I have since seen this noble work in the library of a distinguished family, and I must own I am ashamed to reflect, that, in so wealthy a country as ours, a similar digest of our historians should not be undertaken, under the patronage of the noble and the learned, in rivalry of that which the Benedictines of Paris executed at the expense of their own conventual funds.

"I perceive," said the ex-Benedictine, smiling, "that your heretical prejudices are too strong to allow us poor brethren any merit, whether literary or spiritual."

"Far from it, sir," said I; "I assure you I have been much obliged to monks in my time. When I was quartered in a Monastery in Flanders, in the campaign of 1793, I never lived more comfortably in my life. They were jolly fellows, the Flemish Canons, and right sorry was I to leave my good quarters, and to know that my honest hosts were to be at the mercy of the Sans-Culottes. But *fortune de la guerre!*"

The poor Benedictine looked down and was silent. I had unwittingly awakened a train of bitter reflections, or rather I had touched somewhat rudely upon a chord which seldom ceased to vibrate of itself. But he was too much accustomed to this sorrowful train of ideas to suffer it to overcome him. On my part, I hastened to atone for my blunder. "If there was any object of his journey to this country in which I could, with propriety, assist him, I begged to offer him my best services." I own I laid some little emphasis on the words "with propriety," as I felt it would ill become me, a sound Protestant, and a servant of government so far as my half-pay was concerned, to implicate myself in any recruiting which my companion might have undertaken in behalf of foreign seminaries, or in any similar design for the advancement of Popery, which, whether the Pope be actually the old lady of Babylon or no, it did not become me in any manner to advance or countenance.

My new friend hastened to relieve my indecision. "I was about to request your assistance, sir," he said, "in a matter which cannot but interest you as an antiquary, and a person of research. But I assure you it relates entirely to events and persons removed to the distance of two centuries and a half. I have experienced too much evil from the violent unsettlement of the country in which I was born, to be a rash labourer in the work of innovation in that of my ancestors."

I again assured him of my willingness to assist him in anything that was not contrary to my allegiance or religion.

"My proposal," he replied, "affects neither. — May God bless the reigning family in Britain! They are not, indeed, of that dynasty to restore which my ancestors struggled and suffered in vain; but the Providence who has conducted his present Majesty to the throne, has given him the virtues necessary to his time—firmness and intrepidity—a true love of his country, and an enlightened view of the dangers by which she is surrounded.—For the religion of these realms, I am contented to hope that the great Power, whose mysterious dispensation has rent them from the bosom of the church, will, in his own good time and manner, restore them to its holy pale. The efforts of an individual, obscure and humble as myself, might well retard, but could never advance, a work so mighty."

"May I then inquire, sir," said I, "with what purpose you seek this country?"

Ere my companion replied, he took from his pocket a clasped paper book, about the size of a regimental orderly-book, full, as it seemed, of memoranda; and, drawing one of the candles close to him, (for David, as a strong proof of his respect for the stranger, had indulged us with two,) he seemed to peruse the contents very earnestly.

"There is among the ruins of the western end of the Abbey church," said he, looking up to me, yet keeping the memorandum-book half open, and occasionally glancing at it, as if to refresh his memory, "a sort of recess or chapel beneath a broken arch, and in the immediate vicinity of one of those shattered Gothic columns which once supported the magnificent roof, whose fall has now encumbered that part of the building with its ruins."

"I think," said I, "that I know whereabouts you are. Is there not in the side wall of the chapel, or recess, which you mention, a large carved stone, bearing a coat of arms, which no one hitherto has been able to decipher?"

"You are right," answered the Benedictine; and again consulting his memoranda, he added, "the arms on the dexter side are those of Glendinning, being a cross parted by a cross indented and countercharged of the same; and on the sinister three spur-rowels for those of Avenel; they are two ancient families, now almost extinct in this country—the arms *part y per pale.*"

"I think," said I, "there is no part of this ancient structure with which you are not as well acquainted as was the mason who built it. But if your information be correct, he who made out these bearings must have had better eyes than mine."

"His eyes," said the Benedictine, "have long been closed in death; probably when he inspected the monument it was in a more perfect state, or he may have derived his information from the tradition of the place."

"I assure you," said I, "that no such tradition now exists. I have made several reconnoissances among the old people, in hopes to learn something of the armorial bearings, but I never heard of such a circumstance. It seems odd that you should have acquired it in a foreign land."

"These trifling particulars," he replied, "were formerly looked upon as more important, and they were sanctified to the exiles who retained recollection of them, because they related to a place dear indeed to memory, but which their eyes could never again behold. It is possible, in like manner, that on the Potomac or Susquehannah, you may find traditions current concerning places in England, which are utterly forgotten in the neighbourhood where they originated. But to my purpose. In this recess, marked by the armorial bearings, lies buried a treasure, and it is in order to remove it that I have undertaken my present journey."

"A treasure!" echoed I, in astonishment.

"Yes," replied the monk, "an inestimable treasure, for those who know how to use it rightly."

I own my ears did tingle a little at the word treasure, and that a handsome tilbury, with a neat groom in blue and scarlet livery, having a smart cockade on his glazed hat, seemed as it were to glide across the room before my eyes, while a voice, as of a crier, pronounced in my ear, "Captain Clutterbu:k's tilbury — drive up." But I resisted the devil, and he fled from me.

"I believe," said I, "all hidden treasure belongs either to the king or the lord of the soil; and as I have served his majesty, I cannot concern myself in any adventure which may have an end in the Court of Exchequer."

"The treasure I seek," said the stranger, smiling, "will not be envied by princes or nobles, — it is simply the heart of an upright man."

"Ah! I understand you," I answered; "some relic, forgotten in the confusion of the Reformation. I know the value which men of your persuasion put upon the bodies and limbs of saints. I have seen the Three Kings of Cologne."

"The relics which I seek, however," said the Benedictine, "are not precisely of that nature. The excellent relative whom I have already mentioned, amused his leisure hours with putting into form the traditions of his family, particularly some remarkable circumstances which took place about the first breaking out of the schism of the church in Scotland. He became so much interested in his own labours, that at length he resolved that the heart of one individual, the hero of his tale, should rest no longer in a land of heresy, now deserted by all his kindred. As he knew where it was deposited, he formed the resolution to visit his native country for the purpose of recovering this valued relic. But age, and at length disease, interfered with his resolution, and it was on his deathbed that he charged me to undertake the task in his stead. The various important events which have crowded upon each other, our ruin and our exile, have for many years obliged me to postpone this delegated duty. Why, indeed, transfer the relics of a holy and worthy man to a country, where religion and virtue are become the mockery of the scorner? I have now a home, which I trust may be permanent, if any thing in this earth can be termed so. Thither will I transport the heart of the good father, and beside the shrine which it shall occupy, I will construct my own grave."

"He must, indeed, have been an excellent man," replied I, "whose memory, at so distant a period, calls forth such strong marks of regard."

"He was, as you justly term him," said the ecclesiastic, "indeed excellent — excellent in his life and doctrine — excellent, above all, in his self-denied and disinterested sacrifice of all that life holds dear to principle and to friendship. But you shall read his history. I shall be happy at once to gratify your curiosity, and to show my sense of your kindness, if you will have the goodness to procure me the means of accomplishing my object."

I replied to the Benedictine, that, as the rubbish amongst which he proposed to search was no part of the ordinary burial-ground, and as I was on the best terms with the sexton, I had little doubt that I could procure him the means of executing his pious purpose.

With this promise we parted for the night; and on the ensuing morning I made it my business to see the sexton, who, for a small gratuity, readily granted permission of search, on condition, however, that he should be present himself, to see that the stranger removed nothing of intrinsic value.

"To banes, and skulls, and hearts, if he can find ony, he shall be welcome," said this guardian of the ruined Monastery, "there's plenty a' about, an he's curious of them; but if there be ony picts" (meaning perhaps *pyx*) "or chalishes, or the like of such Popish veshells of gold and silver, deil hae me an I conneve at their being removed."

The sexton also stipulated, that our researches should take place at night, being unwilling to excite observation, or give rise to scandal.

My new acquaintance and I spent the day as became lovers of hoar antiquity. We visited every corner of these magnificent ruins again and again during the forenoon; and, having made a comfortable dinner at David's, we walked in the afternoon to such places in the neighbourhood as ancient tradition or modern conjecture had rendered markworthy. Night found us in the interior of the ruins, attended by the sexton, who carried a dark lantern, and stumbling alternately over the graves of the dead, and the fragments of that architecture, which they doubtless trusted would have canopied their bones till doomsday."

I am by no means particularly superstitious, and yet there was that in the present service which I did not very much like. There was something awful in the resolution of disturbing, at such an hour, and in such a place, the still and mute sanctity of the grave. My companions were free from this impression—the stranger from his energetic desire to execute the purpose for which he came — and the sexton from habitual indifference. We soon stood in the aisle, which, by the account of the Benedictine, contained the bones of the family of Glendinning, and were busily employed in removing the rubbish from a corner which the stranger pointed out. If a half-pay Captain could have represented an ancient Border-knight, or an ex-Benedictine of the nineteenth century a wizard monk of the sixteenth, we might have aptly enough personified the search after Michael Scott's lamp and book of magic power. But the sexton would have been *de trop* in the group.*

Ere the stranger, assisted by the sexton in his task, had been long at work, they came to some hewn stones, which seemed to have made part of a small shrine, though now displaced and destroyed.

"Let us remove these with caution, my friend," said the stranger, "lest we injure that which I come to seek."

"They are prime stanes," said the sexton, "picked free every ane of them;—warse than the best wad never serve the monks, I'se warrant."

A minute after he had made this observation, he exclaimed, "I hae fund something now that stands again' the spade, as if it were neither earth nor stane."

The stranger stooped eagerly to assist him.

"Na, na, haill o' my ain," said the sexton; "nae halves or quarters;"—and he lifted from amongst the ruins a small leaden box.

"You will be disappointed, my friend," said the Benedictine, "if you expect any thing there but the mouldering dust of a human heart, closed in an inner case of porphyry."

I interposed as a neutral party, and taking the box from the sexton, reminded him, that if there were treasure concealed in it, still it could not become the property of the finder. I then proposed, that as the place was too dark to examine the contents of the leaden casket, we should adjourn to David's, where we might have the advantage of light and fire while carrying on our investigation. The stranger requested us to go before, assuring us that he would follow in a few minutes.

I fancy that old Mattocks suspected these few minutes might be employed in effecting farther discoveries amongst the tombs, for he glided back through a side-aisle to watch the Benedictine's motions, but presently returned, and told me in a whisper that "the gentleman was on his knees amang the cauld stanes, praying like ony saunt."

I stole back, and beheld the old man actually employed as Mattocks had informed me. The language seemed to be Latin; and as the whispered, yet solemn accent, glided away through the ruined aisles, I could not help reflecting how long it was since they had heard the forms of that religion, for the exercise of which they had been reared at such cost of time, taste, labour, and expense. "Come away, come away," said I; "let us leave him to himself, Mattocks; this is no business of ours."

* This is one of those passages which must now read awkwardly, since every one knows that the Novelist and the author of the Lay of the Minstrel, is the same person. But before the avowal was made, the author was forced into this and similar offences against good taste, to meet an argument, often repeated, that there was something very mysterious in the Author of Waverley's reserve concerning Sir Walter Scott, an author sufficiently voluminous at least. I had a great mind to remove the passages from this edition, but the more candid way is to explain how they came there.

"My certes, no, Captain," said Mattocks; "ne'ertheless, it winna be amiss to keep an ee on him. My father, rest his saul, was a horse-couper, and used to say he never was cheated in a naig in his life, saving by a west-country whig frae Kilmarnock, that said a grace ower a dram o' whisky. But this gentleman will be a Roman, I'se warrant?"

"You are perfectly right in that, Saunders," said I.

"Ay, I have seen twa or three of their priests that were chased ower here some score o' years syne. They just danced like mad when they looked on the friars' heads, and the nuns' heads, in the cloister yonder; they took to them like auld acquaintance like.—Od, he is not stirring yet, mair than he were a through-stane!* I never kend a Roman, to say kend him, but ane—mair by token, he was the only ane in the town to ken—and that was auld Jock of the Pend. It wad hae been lang ere ye fand Jock praying in the Abbey in a thick night, wi' his knees on a cauld stane. Jock likit a kirk wi' a chimley in't. Mony a merry ploy I hae had wi' him down at the inn yonder; and when he died, decently I wad hae earded him; but, or I gat his grave weel howkit, some of the quality, that were o' his ain unhappy persuasion, had the corpse whirried away up the water, and buried him after their ain pleasure, doubtless—they kend best. I wad hae made nae great charge. I wadna hae excised Johnnie, dead or alive.—Stay, see—the strange gentleman is coming."

"Hold the lantern to assist him, Mattocks," said I.—"This is rough walking, sir."

"Yes," replied the Benedictine; "I may say with a poet, who is doubtless familiar to you——"

I should be surprised if he were, thought I internally.

The stranger continued:

"Saint Francis be my speed! how oft to-night
Have my old feet stumbled at graves!"

"We are now clear of the churchyard," said I, "and have but a short walk to David's, where I hope we shall find a cheerful fire to enliven us after our night's work."

We entered, accordingly, the little parlour, into which Mattocks was also about to push himself with sufficient effrontery, when David, with a most astounding oath, expelled him by head and shoulders, d—ning his curiosity, that would not let gentlemen be private in their own inn. Apparently mine host considered his own presence as no intrusion, for he crowded up to the table on which I had laid down the leaden box. It was frail and wasted, as might be guessed, from having lain so many years in the ground. On opening it, we found deposited within, a case made of porphyry, as the stranger had announced to us.

"I fancy," he said, "gentlemen, your curiosity will not be satisfied,—perhaps I should say that your suspicions will not be removed,—unless I undo this casket; yet it only contains the mouldering remains of a heart, once the seat of the noblest thoughts."

He undid the box with great caution; but the shrivelled substance which it contained bore now no resemblance to what it might once have been, the means used having been apparently unequal to preserve its shape and colour, although they were adequate to prevent its total decay. We were quite satisfied, notwithstanding, that it was, what the stranger asserted, the remains of a human heart; and David readily promised his influence in the village, which was almost co-ordinate with that of the bailie himself, to silence all idle rumours. He was, moreover, pleased to favour us with his company to supper; and having taken the lion's share of two bottles of sherry, he not only sanctioned with his plenary authority the stranger's removal of the heart, but, I believe, would have authorized the removal of

* A tombstone.

the Abbey itself, were it not that it happens considerably to advantage the worthy publican's own custom.

The object of the Benedictine's visit to the land of his forefathers being now accomplished, he announced his intention of leaving us early in the ensuing day, but requested my company to breakfast with him before his departure. I came accordingly, and when we had finished our morning's meal, the priest took me apart, and pulling from his pocket a large bundle of papers, he put them into my hands. "These," said he, "Captain Clutterbuck, are genuine Memoirs of the sixteenth century, and exhibit in a singular, and, as I think, an interesting point of view, the manners of that period. I am induced to believe that their publication will not be an unacceptable present to the British public; and willingly make over to you any profit that may accrue from such a transaction."

I stared a little at this annunciation, and observed, that the hand seemed too modern for the date he assigned to the manuscript.

"Do not mistake me, sir," said the Benedictine; "I did not mean to say the Memoirs were written in the sixteenth century, but only, that they were compiled from authentic materials of that period, but written in the taste and language of the present day. My uncle commenced this book; and I, partly to improve my habit of English composition, partly to divert melancholy thoughts, amused my leisure hours with continuing and concluding it. You will see the period of the story where my uncle leaves off his narrative, and I commence mine. In fact, they relate in a great measure to different persons, as well as to a different period."

Retaining the papers in my hand, I proceeded to state to him my doubts, whether, as a good Protestant, I could undertake or superintend a publication written probably in the spirit of Popery.

"You will find," he said, "no matter of controversy in these sheets, nor any sentiments stated, with which, I trust, the good in all persuasions will not be willing to join. I remembered I was writing for a land unhappily divided from the Catholic faith; and I have taken care to say nothing which, justly interpreted, could give ground for accusing me of partiality. But if, upon collating my narrative with the proofs to which I refer you — for you will find copies of many of the original papers in that parcel — you are of opinion that I have been partial to my own faith, I freely give you leave to correct my errors in that respect. I own, however, I am not conscious of this defect, and have rather to fear that the Catholics may be of opinion, that I have mentioned circumstances respecting the decay of discipline which preceded, and partly occasioned, the great schism, called by you the Reformation, over which I ought to have drawn a veil. And indeed, this is one reason why I choose the papers should appear in a foreign land, and pass to the press through the hands of a stranger."

To this I had nothing to reply, unless to object my own incompetency to the task the good father was desirous to impose upon me. On this subject he was pleased to say more, I fear, than his knowledge of me fully warranted —more, at any rate, than my modesty will permit me to record. At length he ended, with advising me, if I continued to feel the diffidence which I stated, to apply to some veteran of literature, whose experience might supply my deficiencies. Upon these terms we parted, with mutual expressions of regard, and I have never since heard of him.

After several attempts to peruse the quires of paper thus singularly conferred on me, in which I was interrupted by the most inexplicable fits of yawning, I at length, in a sort of despair, communicated them to our village club, from whom they found a more favourable reception than the unlucky conformation of my nerves had been able to afford them. They unanimously pronounced the work to be exceedingly good, and assured me I would be guilty of the greatest possible injury to our flourishing village, if

I should suppress what threw such an interesting and radiant light upon the history of the ancient Monastery of Saint Mary.

At length, by dint of listening to their opinion, I became dubious of my own; and, indeed, when I heard passages read forth by the sonorous voice of our worthy pastor, I was scarce more tired than I have felt myself at some of his own sermons. Such, and so great is the difference betwixt reading a thing one's self, making toilsome way through all the difficulties of manuscript, and, as the man says in the play, "having the same read to you;"—it is positively like being wafted over a creek in a boat, or wading through it on your feet, with the mud up to your knees. Still, however, there remained the great difficulty of finding some one who could act as editor, corrector at once of the press and of the language, which, according to the schoolmaster, was absolutely necessary.

Since the trees walked forth to choose themselves a king, never was an honour so bandied about. The parson would not leave the quiet of his chimney-corner—the bailie pleaded the dignity of his situation, and the approach of the great annual fair, as reasons against going to Edinburgh to make arrangements for printing the Benedictine's manuscript. The schoolmaster alone seemed of malleable stuff; and, desirous perhaps of emulating the fame of Jedediah Cleishbotham, evinced a wish to undertake this momentous commission. But a remonstrance from three opulent farmers, whose sons he had at bed, board, and schooling, for twenty pounds per annum a-head, came like a frost over the blossoms of his literary ambition, and he was compelled to decline the service.

In these circumstances, sir, I apply to you, by the advice of our little council of war, nothing doubting you will not be disinclined to take the duty upon you, as it is much connected with that in which you have distinguished yourself. What I request is, that you will review, or rather revise and correct, the enclosed packet, and prepare it for the press, by such alterations, additions, and curtailments, as you think necessary. Forgive my hinting to you, that the deepest well may be exhausted, — the best corps of grenadiers, as our old general of brigade expressed himself, may be *used up*. A few hints can do you no harm; and, for the prize-money, let the battle be first won, and it shall be parted at the drum-head. I hope you will take nothing amiss that I have said. I am a plain soldier, and little accustomed to compliments. I may add, that I should be well contented to march in the front with you — that is, to put my name with yours on the title-page. I have the honour to be, SIR,

Your unknown humble Servant,

CUTHBERT CLUTTERBUCK.

VILLAGE OF KENNAQUHAIR,
—— *of April*, 18—

For the Author of "Waverley," &c.
care of Mr. John Ballantyne,
Hanover Street, Edinburgh.

ANSWER BY "THE AUTHOR OF WAVERLEY,"

TO THE FOREGOING LETTER FROM CAPTAIN CLUTTERBUCK.

DEAR CAPTAIN,

Do not admire, that, notwithstanding the distance and ceremony of your address, I return an answer in the terms of familiarity. The truth is, your origin and native country are better known to me than even to yourself. You derive your respectable parentage, if I am not greatly mistaken, from a land which has afforded much pleasure, as well as profit, to those who have traded to it successfully,—I mean that part of the *terra incognita* which is called the province of Utopia. Its productions, though censured by many (and some who use tea and tobacco without scruple) as idle and unsubstantial luxuries, have nevertheless, like many other luxuries, a general acceptation, and are secretly enjoyed even by those who express the greatest scorn and dislike of them in public. The dram-drinker is often the first to be shocked at the smell of spirits — it is not unusual to hear old maiden ladies declaim against scandal — the private book-cases of some grave-seeming men would not brook decent eyes — and many, I say not of the wise and learned, but of those most anxious to seem such, when the spring-lock of their library is drawn, their velvet cap pulled over their ears, their feet insinuated into their turkey slippers, are to be found, were their retreats suddenly intruded upon, busily engaged with the last new novel.

I have said, the truly wise and learned disdain these shifts, and will open the said novel as avowedly as they would the lid of their snuff-box. I will only quote one instance, though I know a hundred. Did you know the celebrated Watt of Birmingham, Captain Clutterbuck? I believe not, though, from what I am about to state, he would not have failed to have sought an acquaintance with you. It was only once my fortune to meet him, whether in body or in spirit it matters not. There were assembled about half a score of our Northern Lights, who had amongst them, Heaven knows how, a well-known character of your country, Jedediah Cleishbotham. This worthy person, having come to Edinburgh during the Christmas vacation, had become a sort of lion in the place, and was lead in leash from house to house along with the guisards, the stone-eater, and other amusements of the season, which "exhibited their unparalleled feats to private family-parties, if required." Amidst this company stood Mr. Watt, the man whose genius discovered the means of multiplying our national resources to a degree perhaps even beyond his own stupendous powers of calculation and combination; bringing the treasures of the abyss to the summit of the earth — giving the feeble arm of man the momentum of an Afrite — commanding manufactures to arise, as the rod of the prophet produced water in the desert — affording the means of dispensing with that time and tide which wait for no man, and of sailing without that wind which defied the commands and threats of Xerxes himself.* This potent commander of the elements — this abridger of time and space — this magician, whose cloudy machinery has produced a change on the world, the effects of which, extraordinary as they are, are perhaps only now beginning to be felt — was not only the most profound man of science, the most successful combiner of powers and calculator of numbers as adapted to practical purposes, — was

---

* Probably the ingenious author alludes to the national adage:

The king said sail,
But the wind said no.

Our schoolmaster (who is also a land surveyor) thinks this whole passage refers to Mr. Watt's improvements on the steam engine.—*Note by Captain Clutterbuck.*

not only one of the most generally well-informed, — but one of the best and kindest of human beings.

There he stood, surrounded by the little band I have mentioned of Northern literati, men not less tenacious, generally speaking, of their own fame and their own opinions, than the national regiments are supposed to be jealous of the high character which they have won upon service. Methinks I yet see and hear what I shall never see or hear again. In his eighty-fifth year, the alert, kind, benevolent old man, had his attention alive to every one's question, his information at every one's command.

His talents and fancy overflowed on every subject. One gentleman was a deep philologist — he talked with him on the origin of the alphabet as if he had been coeval with Cadmus; another a celebrated critic, — you would have said the old man had studied political economy and belles-lettres all his life, — of science it is unnecessary to speak, it was his own distinguished walk. And yet, Captain Clutterbuck, when he spoke with your countryman Jedediah Cleishbotham, you would have sworn he had been coeval with Claver'se and Burley, with the persecutors and persecuted, and could number every shot the dragoons had fired at the fugitive Covenanters. In fact, we discovered that no novel of the least celebrity escaped his perusal, and that the gifted man of science was as much addicted to the productions of your native country, (the land of Utopia aforesaid,) in other words, as shameless and obstinate a peruser of novels, as if he had been a very milliner's apprentice of eighteen. I know little apology for troubling you with these things, excepting the desire to commemorate a delightful evening, and a wish to encourage you to shake off that modest diffidence which makes you afraid of being supposed connected with the fairy-land of delusive fiction. I will requite your tag of verse, from Horace himself, with a paraphrase for your own use, my dear Captain, and for that of your country club, excepting in reverence the clergyman and schoolmaster: —

Ne sit ancillæ tibi amor pudori, &c.

Take thou no scorn
Of fiction born,
Fair fiction's muse to woo;
Old Homer's theme
Was but a dream,
Himself a fiction too.

Having told you your country, I must next, my dear Captain Clutterbuck, make free to mention your own immediate descent. You are not to suppose your land of prodigies so little known to us as the careful concealment of your origin would seem to imply. But you have it in common with many of your country, studiously and anxiously to hide any connexion with it. There is this difference, indeed, betwixt your countrymen and those of our more material world, that many of the most estimable of them, such as an old Highland gentleman called Ossian, a monk of Bristol called Rowley, and others, are inclined to pass themselves off as denizens of the land of reality, whereas most of our fellow-citizens who deny their country are such as that country would be very willing to disclaim. The especial circumstances you mention relating to your life and services, impose not upon us. We know the versatility of the unsubstantial species to which you belong permits them to assume all manner of disguises; we have seen them apparelled in the caftan of a Persian, and the silken robe of a Chinese,* and are prepared to suspect their real character under every disguise. But how can we be ignorant of your country and manners, or deceived by the evasion of its inhabitants, when the voyages of discovery which have been made to it rival in number those recorded by Purchas or by Hackluyt?† And to show the skill and perseverance of your navigators and travellers, we have only to name Sindbad, Aboulfouaris, and Robinson Crusoe. These were the men for discoveries. Could we have sent Captain

* See the Persian Letters, and the Citizen of the World.

† See Les Voyages Imaginaires.

Greenland to look out for the north-west passage, or Peter Wilkins to examine Baffin's Bay, what discoveries might we not have expected? But there are feats, and these both numerous and extraordinary, performed by the inhabitants of your country, which we read without once attempting to emulate.

I wander from my purpose, which was to assure you, that I know you as well as the mother who *did* not bear you, for MacDuff's peculiarity sticks to your whole race. You are not born of woman, unless, indeed, in that figurative sense, in which the celebrated Maria Edgeworth may, in her state of single blessedness, be termed mother of the finest family in England. You belong, sir, to the Editors of the land of Utopia, a sort of persons for whom I have the highest esteem. How is it possible it should be otherwise, when you reckon among your corporation the sage Cid Hamet Benengeli, the short-faced president of the Spectator's Club, poor Ben Silton, and many others, who have acted as gentlemen-ushers to works which have cheered our heaviest, and added wings to our lightest hours?

What I have remarked as peculiar to Editors of the class in which I venture to enrol you, is the happy combination of fortuitous circumstances which usually put you in possession of the works which you have the goodness to bring into public notice. One walks on the sea-shore, and a wave casts on land a small cylindrical trunk or casket, containing a manuscript much damaged with sea-water, which is with difficulty deciphered, and so forth.* Another steps into a chandler's shop, to purchase a pound of butter, and, behold! the waste-paper on which it is laid is the manuscript of a cabalist.† A third is so fortunate as to obtain from a woman who lets lodgings, the curious contents of an antique bureau, the property of a deceased lodger.‡ All these are certainly possible occurrences; but, I know not how, they seldom occur to any Editors save those of your country. At least I can answer for myself, that in my solitary walks by the sea, I never saw it cast ashore any thing but dulse and tangle, and now and then a deceased star-fish; my landlady never presented me with any manuscript save her cursed bill; and the most interesting of my discoveries in the way of waste-paper, was finding a favourite passage of one of my own novels wrapt round an ounce of snuff. No, Captain, the funds from which I have drawn my power of amusing the public, have been bought otherwise than by fortuitous adventure. I have buried myself in libraries to extract from the nonsense of ancient days new nonsense of my own. I have turned over volumes, which, from the pot-hooks I was obliged to decipher, might have been the cabalistic manuscripts of Cornelius Agrippa, although I never saw "the door open and the devil come in."§ But all the domestic inhabitants of the libraries were disturbed by the vehemence of my studies:—

From my research the boldest spider fled,
And moths, retreating, trembled as I read.

From this learned sepulchre I emerged like the Magician in the Persian Tales, from his twelve-month's residence in the mountain, not like him to soar over the heads of the multitude, but to mingle in the crowd, and to elbow amongst the throng, making my way from the highest society to the lowest, undergoing the scorn, or, what is harder to brook, the patronizing condescension of the one, and enduring the vulgar familiarity of the other, — and all, you will say, for what? — to collect materials for one of those manuscripts with which mere chance so often accommodates your countrymen; in other words, to write a successful novel. — "O Athenians, how hard we labour to deserve your praise!"

I might stop here, my dear Clutterbuck; it would have a touching effect, and the air of proper deference to our dear Public. But I will not be false

* See the History of Automathes. † Adventures of a Guinea. ‡ Adventures of an Atom.
§ See Southey's Ballad on the Young Man who read in a Conjuror's Books.

with you,—(though falsehood is—excuse the observation—the current coin of your country,) the truth is, I have studied and lived for the purpose of gratifying my own curiosity, and passing my own time; and though the result has been, that, in one shape or other, I have been frequently before the Public, perhaps more frequently than prudence warranted, yet I cannot claim from them the favour due to those who have dedicated their ease and leisure to the improvement and entertainment of others.

Having communicated thus freely with you, my dear Captain, it follows, of course, that I will gratefully accept of your communication, which, as your Benedictine observed, divides itself both by subject, manner, and age, into two parts. But I am sorry I cannot gratify your literary ambition, by suffering your name to appear upon the title-page; and I will candidly tell you the reason.

The Editors of your country are of such a soft and passive disposition, that they have frequently done themselves great disgrace by giving up the coadjutors who first brought them into public notice and public favour, and suffering their names to be used by those quacks and impostors who live upon the ideas of others. Thus I shame to tell how the sage Cid Hamet Benengeli was induced by one Juan Avellaneda to play the Turk with the ingenious Miguel Cervantes, and to publish a Second Part of the adventures of his hero the renowned Don Quixote, without the knowledge or co-operation of his principal aforesaid. It is true, the Arabian sage returned to his allegiance, and thereafter composed a genuine continuation of the Knight of La Mancha, in which the said Avellaneda of Tordesillas is severely chastised. For in this you pseudo-editors resemble the juggler's disciplined ape, to which a sly old Scotsman likened James I., "if you have Jackoo in your hand, you can make him bite me; if I have Jackoo in my hand, I can make him bite you." Yet, notwithstanding the *amende honorable* thus made by Cid Hamet Benengeli, his temporary defection did not the less occasion the decease of the ingenious Hidalgo Don Quixote, if he can be said to die, whose memory is immortal. Cervantes put him to death, lest he should again fall into bad hands. Awful, yet just consequence of Cid Hamet's defection!

To quote a more modern and much less important instance. I am sorry to observe my old acquaintance Jedediah Cleishbotham has misbehaved himself so far as to desert his original patron, and set up for himself. I am afraid the poor pedagogue will make little by his new allies, unless the pleasure of entertaining the public, and, for aught I know, the gentlemen of the long robe, with disputes about his identity.* Observe, therefore, Captain Clutterbuck, that, wise by these great examples, I receive you as a partner, but a sleeping partner only. As I give you no title to employ or use the firm of the copartnery we are about to form, I will announce my property in my title-page, and put my own mark on my own chattels, which the attorney tells me it will be a crime to counterfeit, as much as it would to imitate the autograph of any other empiric—a crime amounting, as advertisements upon little vials assure to us, to nothing short of felony. If, therefore, my dear friend, your name should hereafter appear in any title-page without mine, readers will know what to think of you. I scorn to use either arguments or threats; but you cannot but be sensible, that, as you owe your literary existence to me on the one hand, so, on the other, your very all is at my disposal. I can at pleasure cut off your annuity,

---

* I am since more correctly informed, that Mr. Cleishbotham died some months since at Gandercleuch, and that the person assuming his name is an impostor. The real Jedediah made a most Christian and edifying end; and, as I am credibly informed, having sent for a Cameronian clergyman when he was *in extremis*, was so fortunate as to convince the good man, that, after all, he had no wish to bring down on the scattered remnant of Mountain folks, "the bonnets of Bonny Dundee." Hard that the speculators in print and paper will not allow a good man to rest quiet in his grave.

This note, and the passages in the text, were occasioned by a London bookseller having printed, as a speculation, an additional collection of Tales of My Landlord, which was not so fortunate as to succeed in passing on the world as genuine.

strike your name from the half-pay establishment, nay, actually put you to death, without being answerable to any one. These are plain words to a gentleman who has served during the whole war; but, I am aware, you will take nothing amiss at my hands.

And now, my good sir, let us address ourselves to our task, and arrange, as we best can, the manuscript of your Benedictine, so as to suit the taste of this critical age. You will find I have made very liberal use of his permission, to alter whatever seemed too favourable to the Church of Rome, which I abominate, were it but for her fasts and penances.

Our reader is doubtless impatient, and we must own, with John Bunyan,

> We have too long detain'd him in the porch,
> And kept him from the sunshine with a torch.

Adieu, therefore, my dear Captain — remember me respectfully to the parson, the schoolmaster, and the bailie, and all friends of the happy club in the village of Kennaquhair. I have never seen, and never shall see, one of their faces; and notwithstanding, I believe that as yet I am better acquainted with them than any other man who lives. — I shall soon introduce you to my jocund friend, Mr. John Ballantyne of Trinity Grove, whom you will find warm from his match at single-stick with a brother Publisher.* Peace to their differences! It is a wrathful trade, and the *irritabile genus* comprehends the bookselling as well as the book-writing species. — Once more adieu!

THE AUTHOR OF WAVERLEY.

* In consequence of the pseudo *Tales of My Landlord* printed in London, as already mentioned, the late Mr. John Ballantyne, the author's publisher, had a controversy with the interloping bibliopolist, each insisting that his Jedediah Cleishbotham was the real Simon Pure.

THE MONASTERY.

Chapter the First.

O ay! the Monks, the Monks they did the mischief!
Theirs all the grossness, all the superstition
Of a most gross and superstitious age—
May He be praised that sent the healthful tempest
And scatter'd all these pestilential vapours!
But that we owed them *all* to yonder Harlot
Throned on the seven hills with her cup of gold,
I will as soon believe, with kind Sir Roger,
That old Moll White took wing with cat and broomstick,
And raised the last night's thunder.

OLD PLAY.

THE village described in the Benedictine's manuscript by the name of Kennaquhair, bears the same Celtic termination which occurs in Traquhair, Caquhair, and other compounds. The learned Chalmers derives this word Quhair, from the winding course of a stream; a definition which coincides, in a remarkable degree, with the serpentine turns of the river Tweed near the village of which we speak. It has been long famous for the splendid Monastery of Saint Mary, founded by David the First of Scotland, in whose reign were formed, in the same county, the no less splendid establishments of Melrose, Jedburgh, and Kelso. The donations of land with which the King endowed these wealthy fraternities procured him from the Monkish historians the epithet of Saint, and from one of his impoverished descendants the splenetic censure, "that he had been a sore saint for the Crown."

It seems probable, notwithstanding, that David, who was a wise as well as a pious monarch, was not moved solely by religious motives to those great acts of munificence to the church, but annexed political views to his pious generosity. His possessions in Northumberland and Cumberland became precarious after the loss of the Battle of the Standard; and since the comparatively fertile valley of Teviot-dale was likely to become the frontier of his kingdom, it is probable he wished to secure at least a part of these valuable possessions by placing them in the hands of the monks, whose property was for a long time respected, even amidst the rage of a frontier war. In this manner alone had the King some chance of ensuring protection and security to the cultivators of the soil; and, in fact, for several ages the possessions of these Abbeys were each a sort of Goshen, enjoying the calm light of peace and immunity, while the rest of the country, occupied by wild clans and marauding barons, was one dark scene of confusion, blood, and unremitted outrage.

But these immunities did not continue down to the union of the crowns. Long before that period the wars betwixt England and Scotland had lost their original character of international hostilities, and had become on the part of the English a struggle for subjugation, on that of the Scots a desperate and infuriated defence of their liberties. This introduced on both sides a degree of fury and animosity unknown to the earlier period of their history; and as religious scruples soon gave way to national hatred spurred by a love of plunder, the patrimony of the Church was no longer sacred from incursions on either side. Still, however, the tenants and vassals of the great Abbeys had many advantages over those of the lay barons, who were harassed by constant military duty, until they became desperate, and lost all relish for the arts of peace. The vassals of the church, on the other hand, were only liable to be called to arms on general occasions, and at other times were permitted in comparative quiet to possess their farms and feus.* They of course exhibited superior skill in every thing that related to the cultivation of the soil, and were therefore both wealthier and better informed than the military retainers of the restless chiefs and nobles in their neighbourhood.

The residence of these church vassals was usually in a small village or hamlet, where, for the sake of mutual aid and protection, some thirty or forty families dwelt together. This was called the Town, and the land belonging to the various families by whom the Town was inhabited, was called the Township. They usually possessed the land in common, though in various proportions, according to their several grants. The part of the Township properly arable, and kept as such continually under the plough, was called *in-field*. Here the use of quantities of manure supplied in some degree the exhaustion of the soil, and the feuars raised tolerable oats and bear,† usually sowed on alternate ridges, on which the labour of the whole community was bestowed without distinction, the produce being divided after harvest, agreeably to their respective interests.

There was, besides, *out-field* land, from which it was thought possible to extract a crop now and then, after which it was abandoned to the "skiey influences," until the exhausted powers of vegetation were restored. These out-field spots were selected by any feuar at his own choice, amongst the sheep-walks and hills which were always annexed to the Township, to serve as pasturage to the community. The trouble of cultivating these patches of out-field, and the precarious chance that the crop would pay the labour, were considered as giving a right to any feuar, who chose to undertake the adventure, to the produce which might result from it.

There remained the pasturage of extensive moors, where the valleys often afforded good grass, and upon which the whole cattle belonging to the community fed indiscriminately during the summer, under the charge of the Town-herd, who regularly drove them out to pasture in the morning, and brought them back at night, without which precaution they would have fallen a speedy prey to some of the Snatchers in the neighbourhood. These are things to make modern agriculturists hold up their hands and stare; but the same mode of cultivation is not yet entirely in desuetude in some distant parts of North Britain, and may be witnessed in full force and exercise in the Zetland Archipelago.

The habitations of the church-feuars were not less primitive than their agriculture. In each village or town were several small towers, having battlements projecting over the side walls, and usually an advanced angle or two with shot-holes for flanking the door-way, which was always defended by a strong door of oak, studded with nails, and often by an exterior grated door of iron. These small peel-houses were ordinarily inhabited by the principal feuars and their families; but, upon the alarm of approaching danger, the whole inhabitants thronged from their own miserable cottages,

* Small possessions conferred upon vassals and their heirs, held for a small quit-rent, or a moderate proportion of the produce. This was a favourite manner, by which the churchmen peopled the patrimony of their convents; and many descendants of such *feuars*, as they are called, are still to be found in possession of their family inheritances in the neighbourhood of the great Monasteries of Scotland.

† Or bigg, a kind of coarse barley.

which were situated around, to garrison these points of defence. It was then no easy matter for a hostile party to penetrate into the village, for the men were habituated to the use of bows and fire-arms, and the towers being generally so placed, that the discharge from one crossed that of another, it was impossible to assault any of them individually.

The interior of these houses was usually sufficiently wretched, for it would have been folly to have furnished them in a manner which could excite the avarice of their lawless neighbours. Yet the families themselves exhibited in their appearance a degree of comfort, information, and independence, which could hardly have been expected. Their in-field supplied them with bread and home-brewed ale, their herds and flocks with beef and mutton (the extravagance of killing lambs or calves was never thought of). Each family killed a mart, or fat bullock, in November, which was salted up for winter use, to which the good wife could, upon great occasions, add a dish of pigeons or a fat capon,—the ill-cultivated garden afforded "lang-cale,"—and the river gave salmon to serve as a relish during the season of Lent.

Of fuel they had plenty, for the bogs afforded turf; and the remains of the abused woods continued to give them logs for burning, as well as timber for the usual domestic purposes. In addition to these comforts, the good-man would now and then sally forth to the greenwood, and mark down a buck of season with his gun or his cross-bow; and the Father Confessor seldom refused him absolution for the trespass, if duly invited to take his share of the smoking haunch. Some, still bolder, made, either with their own domestics, or by associating themselves with the moss-troopers, in the language of shepherds, "a start and overloup;" and the golden ornaments and silken head-gear worn by the females of one or two families of note, were invidiously traced by their neighbours to such successful excursions. This, however, was a more inexplicable crime in the eyes of the Abbot and Community of Saint Mary's, than the borrowing one of the "gude king's deer;" and they failed not to discountenance and punish, by every means in their power, offences which were sure to lead to severe retaliation upon the property of the church, and which tended to alter the character of their peaceful vassalage.

As for the information possessed by those dependents of the Abbacies, they might have been truly said to be better fed than taught, even though their fare had been worse than it was. Still, however, they enjoyed opportunities of knowledge from which others were excluded. The monks were in general well acquainted with their vassals and tenants, and familiar in the families of the better class among them, where they were sure to be received with the respect due to their twofold character of spiritual father and secular landlord. Thus it often happened, when a boy displayed talents and inclination for study, one of the brethren, with a view to his being bred to the church, or out of good-nature, in order to pass away his own idle time, if he had no better motive, initiated him into the mysteries of reading and writing, and imparted to him such other knowledge as he himself possessed. And the heads of these allied families, having more time for reflection, and more skill, as well as stronger motives for improving their small properties, bore amongst their neighbours the character of shrewd, intelligent men, who claimed respect on account of their comparative wealth, even while they were despised for a less warlike and enterprising turn than the other Borderers. They lived as much as they well could amongst themselves, avoiding the company of others, and dreading nothing more than to be involved in the deadly feuds and ceaseless contentions of the secular landholders.

Such is a general picture of these communities. During the fatal wars in the commencement of Queen Mary's reign, they had suffered dreadfully by the hostile invasions. For the English, now a Protestant people, were so far from sparing the church-lands, that they forayed them with more unrelenting severity than even the possessions of the laity. But the peace of 1550 had restored some degree of tranquillity to those distracted and harassed regions, and matters began again gradually to settle upon the former footing. The monks repaired their ravaged shrines — the feuar again roofed his small fortalice which the enemy had ruined — the poor labourer rebuilt his cottage — an easy task, where a few sods, stones, and some pieces of wood from the next copse, furnished all the materials necessary. The cattle, lastly, were driven out of the wastes and thickets in which the remnant of them had been secreted; and the mighty bull moved at the head of his seraglio and their followers, to take possession of their wonted pastures. There ensued peace and quiet, the state of the age and nation considered, to the Monastery of Saint Mary, and its dependencies, for several tranquil years.

Chapter the Second.

In yon lone vale his early youth was bred,
Not solitary then—the bugle-horn
Of fell Alecto often waked its windings,
From where the brook joins the majestic river,
To the wild northern bog, the curlew's haunt,
Where oozes forth its first and feeble streamlet.
OLD PLAY.

WE have said, that most of the feuars dwelt in the village belonging to their townships. This was not, however, universally the case. A lonely tower, to which the reader must now be introduced, was at least one exception to the general rule.

It was of small dimensions, yet larger than those which occurred in the village, as intimating that, in case of assault, the proprietor would have to rely upon his own unassisted strength. Two or three miserable huts, at the foot of the fortalice, held the bondsmen and tenants of the feuar. The site was a beautiful green knoll, which started up suddenly in the very throat of a wild and narrow glen, and which, being surrounded, except on one side, by the winding of a small stream, afforded a position of considerable strength.

But the great security of Glendearg, for so the place was called, lay in its secluded, and almost hidden situation. To reach the tower, it was necessary to travel three miles up the glen, crossing about twenty times the little stream, which, winding through the narrow valley, encountered at every hundred yards the opposition of a rock or precipitous bank on the one side, which altered its course, and caused it to shoot off in an oblique direction to the other. The hills which ascend on each side of this glen are very steep, and rise boldly over the stream, which is thus imprisoned within their barriers. The sides of the glen are impracticable for horse, and are only to be traversed by means of the sheep-paths which lie along their sides. It would not be readily supposed that a road so hopeless and so difficult could lead to any habitation more important than the summer shealing of a shepherd.

Yet the glen, though lonely, nearly inaccessible, and sterile, was not then absolutely void of beauty. The turf which covered the small portion of level ground on the sides of the stream, was as close and verdant as if it had occupied the scythes of a hundred gardeners once a-fortnight; and it was garnished with an embroidery of daisies and wild flowers, which the scythes would certainly have destroyed. The little brook, now confined betwixt closer limits, now left at large to choose its course through the narrow valley, danced carelessly on from stream to pool, light and unturbid, as that better class of spirits who pass their way through life, yielding to insurmountable obstacles, but as far from being subdued by them as the sailor who meets by chance with an unfavourable wind, and shapes his course so as to be driven back as little as possible.

The mountains, as they would have been called in England, *Scotticè* the steep *braes*, rose abruptly over the little glen, here presenting the gray face of a rock, from which the turf had been peeled by the torrents, and there displaying patches of wood and copse, which had escaped the waste of the cattle and the sheep of the feuars, and which, feathering naturally up the beds of empty torrents, or occupying the concave recesses of the bank, gave at once beauty and variety to the landscape. Above these scattered woods rose the hill, in barren, but purple majesty; the dark rich hue, particularly in autumn, contrasting beautifully with the thickets of oak and birch, the mountain ashes and thorns, the alders and quivering aspens, which checquered and varied the descent, and not less with the dark-green and velvet turf, which composed the level part of the narrow glen.

Yet, though thus embellished, the scene could neither be strictly termed sublime nor beautiful, and scarcely even picturesque or striking. But its extreme solitude pressed on the heart; the traveller felt that uncertainty whither he was going, or in what so wild a path was to terminate, which, at times, strikes more on the imagination than the grand features of a show-scene, when you know the exact distance of the inn where your dinner is bespoke, and at the moment preparing. These are ideas, however, of a far later age; for at the time we treat of, the picturesque, the beautiful, the sublime, and all their intermediate shades, were ideas absolutely unknown to the inhabitants and occasional visiters of Glendearg.

These had, however, attached to the scene feelings fitting the time. Its name, signifying the Red Valley, seems to have been derived, not only from the purple colour of the heath, with which the upper part of the rising banks was profusely clothed, but also from the dark red colour of the rocks, and of the precipitous earthen banks, which in that country are called *scaurs*. Another glen, about the head of Ettrick, has acquired the same name from similar circumstances; and there are probably more in Scotland to which it has been given.

As our Glendearg did not abound in mortal visitants, superstition, that it might not be absolutely destitute of inhabitants, had peopled its recesses with beings belonging to another world. The savage and capricious Brown Man of the Moors, a being which seems the genuine descendant of the northern dwarfs, was supposed to be seen there frequently, especially after the autumnal equinox, when the fogs were thick, and objects not easily distinguished. The Scottish fairies, too, a whimsical, irritable, and mischievous tribe, who, though at times capriciously benevolent, were more frequently adverse to mortals, were also supposed to have formed a residence in a particularly wild recess of the glen, of which the real name was, in allusion to that circumstance, *Corrie nan Shian*, which, in corrupted Celtic, signifies the Hollow of the Fairies. But the neighbours were more cautious in speaking about this place, and avoided giving it a name, from an idea common then throughout all the British and Celtic provinces of Scotland, and still retained in many places, that to speak either good or ill of this capricious race of imaginary beings, is to provoke their resentment, and that secrecy and silence is what they chiefly desire from those who may intrude upon their revels, or discover their haunts.

A mysterious terror was thus attached to the dale, which afforded access from the broad valley of the Tweed, up the little glen we have described, to the fortalice called the Tower of Glendearg. Beyond the knoll, where, as we have said, the tower was situated, the hills grew more steep, and narrowed on the slender brook, so as scarce to leave a footpath; and there the glen terminated in a wild waterfall, where a slender thread of water dashed in a precipitous line of foam over two or three precipices. Yet farther in the same direction, and above these successive cataracts, lay a wild and extensive morass, frequented only by waterfowl, wide, waste, apparently almost interminable, and serving in a great measure to separate the inhabitants of the glen from those who lived to the northward.

To restless and indefatigable moss-troopers, indeed, these morasses were well known, and sometimes afforded a retreat. They often rode down the glen—called at this tower—asked and received hospitality—but still with a sort of reserve on the part of its more peaceful inhabitants, who entertained them as a party of North-American Indians might be received by a new European settler, as much out of fear as hospitality, while the uppermost wish of the landlord is the speedy departure of the savage guests.

This had not always been the current of feeling in the little valley and its tower. Simon Glendinning, its former inhabitant, boasted his connexion by blood to that ancient family of Glendonwyne, on the western border. He used to narrate, at his fireside, in the autumn evenings, the feats of the family to which he belonged, one of whom fell by the side of the brave Earl of Douglas at Otterbourne. On these occasions Simon usually held upon his knee an ancient broadsword, which had belonged to his ancestors before any of the family had consented to accept a fief under the peaceful dominion of the monks of St. Mary's. In modern days, Simon might have lived at ease on his own estate, and quietly murmured against the fate that had doomed him to dwell there, and cut off his access to martial renown. But so many opportunities, nay so many calls there were for him, who in those days spoke big, to make good his words by his actions, that Simon Glendinning was soon under the necessity of marching with the men of the Halidome, as it was called, of St. Mary's, in that disastrous campaign which was concluded by the battle of Pinkie.

The Catholic clergy were deeply interested in that national quarrel, the principal object of which was, to prevent the union of the infant Queen Mary, with the son of the heretical Henry VIII. The Monks had called out their vassals, under an experienced leader. Many of themselves had taken arms, and marched to the field, under a banner representing a female, supposed to personify the Scottish Church, kneeling in the attitude of prayer, with the legend, *Afflictæ Sponsæ ne obliviscaris.**

The Scots, however, in all their wars, had more occasion for good and cautious generals, than for excitation, whether political or enthusiastic. Their headlong and impatient courage uniformly induced them to rush into action without duly weighing either their own situation, or that of their enemies, and the inevitable consequence was frequent defeat. With the dolorous slaughter of Pinkie we have nothing to do, excepting that, among ten thousand men of low and high degree, Simon Glendinning, of the Tower of Glendearg, bit the dust, no way disparaging in his death that ancient race from which he claimed his descent.

When the doleful news, which spread terror and mourning through the whole of Scotland, reached the Tower of Glendearg, the widow of Simon, Elspeth Brydone by her family name, was alone in that desolate habitation, excepting a hind or two, alike past martial and agricultural labour, and the helpless widows and families of those who had fallen with their master. The feeling of desolation was universal;—but what availed it? The monks, their patrons and protectors, were driven from their Abbey by the English forces, who now overran the country, and enforced at least an appearance of submission on the part of the inhabitants. The Protector, Somerset, formed a strong camp among the ruins of the ancient Castle of Roxburgh,

* Forget not the afflicted spouse.

and compelled the neighbouring country to come in, pay tribute, and take assurance from him, as the phrase then went. Indeed, there was no power of resistance remaining; and the few barons, whose high spirit disdained even the appearance of surrender, could only retreat into the wildest fastnesses of the country, leaving their houses and property to the wrath of the English, who detached parties everywhere to distress, by military exaction, those whose chiefs had not made their submission. The Abbot and his community having retreated beyond the Forth, their lands were severely forayed, as their sentiments were held peculiarly inimical to the alliance with England.

Amongst the troops detached on this service was a small party, commanded by Stawarth Bolton, a captain in the English army, and full of the blunt and unpretending gallantry and generosity which has so often distinguished that nation. Resistance was in vain. Elspeth Brydone, when she descried a dozen of horsemen threading their way up the glen, with a man at their head, whose scarlet cloak, bright armour, and dancing plume, proclaimed him a leader, saw no better protection for herself than to issue from the iron grate, covered with a long mourning veil, and holding one of her two sons in each hand, to meet the Englishman — state her deserted condition—place the little tower at his command—and beg for his mercy. She stated, in a few brief words, her intention, and added, "I submit, because I have nae means of resistance."

"And I do not ask your submission, mistress, for the same reason," replied the Englishman. "To be satisfied of your peaceful intentions is all I ask; and, from what you tell me, there is no reason to doubt them."

"At least, sir," said Elspeth Brydone, "take share of what our spence and our garners afford. Your horses are tired — your folk want refreshment."

"Not a whit — not a whit," answered the honest Englishman; "it shall never be said we disturbed by carousal the widow of a brave soldier, while she was mourning for her husband.—Comrades, face about.—Yet stay," he added, checking his war-horse, "my parties are out in every direction; they must have some token that your family are under my assurance of safety. —Here, my little fellow," said he, speaking to the eldest boy, who might be about nine or ten years old, "lend me thy bonnet."

The child reddened, looked sulky, and hesitated, while the mother, with many a *fye* and *nay pshaw*, and such sarsenet chidings as tender mothers give to spoiled children, at length succeeded in snatching the bonnet from him, and handing it to the English leader.

Stawarth Bolton took his embroidered red cross from his barret-cap, and putting it into the loop of the boy's bonnet, said to the mistress, (for the title of lady was not given to dames of her degree,) "By this token, which all my people will respect, you will be freed from any importunity on the part of our forayers."* He placed it on the boy's head; but it was no sooner there, than the little fellow, his veins swelling, and his eyes shooting fire through tears, snatched the bonnet from his head, and, ere his mother could interfere, skimmed it into the brook. The other boy ran instantly to fish it out again, threw it back to his brother, first taking out the cross, which, with great veneration, he kissed and put into his bosom. The Englishman was half diverted, half surprised, with the scene.

---

* As gallantry of all times and nations has the same mode of thinking and acting, so it often expresses itself by the same symbols. In the civil war 1745-6, a party of Highlanders, under a Chieftain of rank, came to Rose Castle, the seat of the Bishop of Carlisle, but then occupied by the family of Squire Dacre of Cumberland. They demanded quarters, which of course were not to be refused to armed men of a strange attire and unknown language. But the domestic represented to the captain of the mountaineers, that the lady of the mansion had been just delivered of a daughter, and expressed her hope, that, under these circumstances, his party would give as little trouble as possible. "God forbid," said the gallant chief, "that I or mine should be the means of adding to a lady's inconvenience at such a time. May I request to see the infant?" The child was brought, and the Highlander, taking his cockade out of his bonnet, and pinning it on the child's breast, "That will be a token," he said, "to any of our people who may come hither, that Donald M'Donald of Kinloch-Moidart, has taken the family of Rose Castle under his protection." The lady who received in infancy this gage of Highland protection, is now Mary, Lady Clerk of Pennycuik; and on the 10th of June still wears the cockade which was pinned on her breast, with a white rose as a kindred decoration.

"What mean ye by throwing away Saint George's red cross?" said he to the elder boy, in a tone betwixt jest and earnest.

"Because Saint George is a southern saint," said the child, sulkily.

"Good"—said Stawarth Bolton.—"And what did you mean by taking it out of the brook again, my little fellow?" he demanded of the younger.

"Because the priest says it is the common sign of salvation to all good Christians."

"Why, good again!" said the honest soldier. "I protest unto you, mistress, I envy you these boys. Are they both yours?"

Stawarth Bolton had reason to put the question, for Halbert Glendinning, the elder of the two, had hair as dark as the raven's plumage, black eyes, large, bold, and sparkling, that glittered under eyebrows of the same complexion; a skin deep embrowned, though it could not be termed swarthy, and an air of activity, frankness, and determination, far beyond his age. On the other hand, Edward, the younger brother, was light-haired, blue-eyed, and of fairer complexion, in countenance rather pale, and not exhibiting that rosy hue which colours the sanguine cheek of robust health. Yet the boy had nothing sickly or ill-conditioned in his look, but was, on the contrary, a fair and handsome child, with a smiling face, and mild, yet cheerful eye.

The mother glanced a proud motherly glance, first at the one, and then at the other, ere she answered the Englishman, "Surely, sir, they are both my children."

"And by the same father, mistress?" said Stawarth; but, seeing a blush of displeasure arise on her brow, he instantly added, "Nay, I mean no offence; I would have asked the same question at any of my gossips in merry Lincoln.—Well, dame, you have two fair boys; I would I could borrow one, for Dame Bolton and I live childless in our old hall.—Come, little fellows, which of you will go with me?"

The trembling mother, half-fearing as he spoke, drew the children towards her, one with either hand, while they both answered the stranger. "I will not go with you," said Halbert, boldly, "for you are a false-hearted Southern; and the Southerns killed my father; and I will war on you to the death, when I can draw my father's sword."

"God-a-mercy, my little levin-bolt," said Stawarth, "the goodly custom of deadly feud will never go down in thy day, I presume.—And you, my fine white-head, will you not go with me, to ride a cock-horse?"

"No," said Edward, demurely, "for you are a heretic."

"Why, God-a-mercy still!" said Stawarth Bolton. "Well, dame, I see I shall find no recruits for my troop from you; and yet I do envy you these two little chubby knaves." He sighed a moment, as was visible, in spite of gorget and corslet, and then added, "And yet, my dame and I would but quarrel which of the knaves we should like best; for I should wish for the black-eyed rogue—and she, I warrant me, for that blue-eyed, fair-haired darling. Natheless, we must brook our solitary wedlock, and wish joy to those that are more fortunate. Sergeant Brittson, do thou remain here till recalled—protect this family, as under assurance—do them no wrong, and suffer no wrong to be done to them, as thou wilt answer it.—Dame, Brittson is a married man, old and steady; feed him on what you will, but give him not over much liquor."

Dame Glendinning again offered refreshments, but with a faltering voice, and an obvious desire her invitation should not be accepted. The fact was, that, supposing her boys as precious in the eyes of the Englishman as in her own, (the most ordinary of parental errors,) she was half afraid, that the admiration he expressed of them in his blunt manner might end in his actually carrying off one or other of the little darlings whom he appeared to covet so much. She kept hold of their hands, therefore, as if her feeble strength could have been of service, had any violence been intended, and saw with joy she could not disguise, the little party of horse countermarch, in order to descend the glen. Her feelings did not escape Bolton: "I forgive you, dame," he said, "for being suspicious that an English falcon was hovering over your Scottish moor-brood. But fear not—those who have fewest children have fewest cares; nor does a wise man covet those of another household. Adieu, dame; when the black-eyed rogue is able to drive a foray from England, teach him to spare women and children, for the sake of Stawarth Bolton."

"God be with you, gallant Southern!" said Elspeth Glendinning, but not till he was out of hearing, spurring on his good horse to regain the head of his party, whose plumage and armour were now glancing and gradually disappearing in the distance, as they winded down the glen.

"Mother," said the elder boy, "I will not say amen to a prayer for a Southern."

"Mother," said the younger, more reverentially, "is it right to pray for a heretic?"

"The God to whom I pray only knows," answered poor Elspeth; "but these two words, Southern and heretic, have already cost Scotland ten thousand of her best and bravest, and me a husband, and you a father; and, whether blessing or banning, I never wish to hear them more.—Follow me to the Place, sir," she said to Brittson, "and such as we have to offer you shall be at your disposal."

Chapter the Third.

They lighted down on Tweed water
And blew their coals sae het,
And fired the March and Teviotdale,
All in an evening late.

AULD MAITLAND.

THE report soon spread through the patrimony of Saint Mary's and its vicinity, that the Mistress of Glendearg had received assurance from the English Captain, and that her cattle were not to be driven off, or her corn burned. Among others who heard this report, it reached the ears of a lady, who, once much higher in rank than Elspeth Glendinning, was now by the same calamity reduced to even greater misfortune.

She was the widow of a brave soldier, Walter Avenel, descended of a very ancient Border family, who once possessed immense estates in Eskdale. These had long since passed from them into other hands, but they still enjoyed an ancient Barony of considerable extent, not very far from the patrimony of Saint Mary's, and lying upon the same side of the river with the narrow vale of Glendearg, at the head of which was the little tower of the Glendinnings. Here they had lived, bearing a respectable rank amongst the gentry of their province, though neither wealthy nor powerful. This general regard had been much augmented by the skill, courage, and enterprise which had been displayed by Walter Avenel, the last Baron.

When Scotland began to recover from the dreadful shock she had sustained after the battle of Pinkie-Cleuch, Avenel was one of the first who, assembling a small force, set an example in those bloody and unsparing skirmishes, which showed that a nation, though conquered and overrun by invaders, may yet wage against them such a war of detail as shall in the end become fatal to the foreigners. In one of these, however, Walter Avenel fell, and the news which came to the house of his fathers was followed by the distracting intelligence, that a party of Englishmen were coming to plunder the mansion and lands of his widow, in order, by this act of terror, to prevent others from following the example of the deceased.

The unfortunate lady had no better refuge than the miserable cottage of a shepherd among the hills, to which she was hastily removed, scarce conscious where or for what purpose her terrified attendants were removing her and her infant daughter from her own house. Here she was tended with all the duteous service of ancient times by the shepherd's wife, Tibb Tacket, who in better days had been her own bowerwoman. For a time the lady was unconscious of her misery; but when the first stunning effect of grief was so far passed away that she could form an estimate of her own situation, the widow of Avenel had cause to envy the lot of her husband in his dark and silent abode. The domestics who had guided her to her place of refuge, were presently obliged to disperse for their own safety, or to seek for necessary subsistence; and the shepherd and his wife, whose poor cottage she shared, were soon after deprived of the means of affording their late mistress even that coarse sustenance which they had gladly shared with her. Some of the English forayers had discovered and driven off the few sheep which had escaped the first researches of their avarice. Two cows shared the fate of the remnant of their stock; they had afforded the family almost their sole support, and now famine appeared to stare them in the face.

"We are broken and beggared now, out and out," said old Martin the shepherd—and he wrung his hands in the bitterness of agony, "the thieves, the harrying thieves! not a cloot left of the haill hirsel!"

"And to see poor Grizzie and Crumbie," said his wife, "turning back their necks to the byre, and routing while the stony-hearted villains were brogging them on wi' their lances!"

"There were but four of them," said Martin, "and I have seen the day forty wad not have ventured this length. But our strength and manhood is gane with our puir maister."

"For the sake of the holy rood, whisht, man," said the goodwife, "our leddy is half gane already, as ye may see by that fleightering of the ee-lid—a word mair and she's dead outright."

"I could almost wish," said Martin, "we were a' gane, for what to do passes my puir wit. I care little for mysell, or you, Tibb,—we can make a fend—work or want—we can do baith, but she can do neither."

They canvassed their situation thus openly before the lady, convinced by the paleness of her look, her quivering lip, and dead-set eye, that she neither heard nor understood what they were saying.

"There is a way," said the shepherd, "but I kenna if she could bring her heart to it,—there's Simon Glendinning's widow of the glen yonder, has had assurance from the Southern loons, and nae soldier to steer them for one cause or other. Now, if the leddy could bow her mind to take quarters with Elspeth Glendinning till better days cast up, nae doubt it wad be doing an honour to the like of her, but——"

"An honour," answered Tibb, "ay, by my word, sic an honour as wad be pride to her kin mony a lang year after her banes were in the mould. Oh! gudeman, to hear ye even the Lady of Avenel to seeking quarters wi' a Kirk-vassal's widow!"

"Loath should I be to wish her to it," said Martin; "but what may we do?—to stay here is mere starvation; and where to go, I'm sure I ken nae mair than ony tup I ever herded."

"Speak no more of it," said the widow of Avenel, suddenly joining in the conversation, "I will go to the tower.—Dame Elspeth is of good folk, a widow, and the mother of orphans,—she will give us house-room until something be thought upon. These evil showers make the low bush better than no bield."

"See there, see there," said Martin, "you see the leddy has twice our sense."

"And natural it is," said Tibb, "seeing that she is convent-bred, and can lay silk broidery, forby white-seam and shell-work."

"Do you not think," said the lady to Martin, still clasping her child to her bosom and making it clear from what motives she desired the refuge, "that Dame Glendinning will make us welcome?"

"Blithely welcome, blithely welcome, my leddy," answered Martin, cheerily, "and we shall deserve a welcome at her hand. Men are scarce now, my leddy, with these wars; and gie me a thought of time to it, I can do as good a day's darg as ever I did in my life, and Tibb can sort cows with ony living woman."

"And muckle mair could I do," said Tibb, "were it ony feasible house; but there will be neither pearlins to mend, nor pinners to busk up, in Elspeth Glendinning's."

"Whisht wi' your pride, woman," said the shepherd; "eneugh you can do, baith outside and inside, an ye set your mind to it; and hard it is if we twa canna work for three folk's meat, forby my dainty wee leddy there. Come awa, come awa, nae use in staying here langer; we have five Scots miles over moss and muir, and that is nae easy walk for a leddy born and bred."

Household stuff there was little or none to remove or care for; an old pony which had escaped the plunderers, owing partly to its pitiful appearance, partly from the reluctance which it showed to be caught by strangers, was employed to carry the few blankets and other trifles which they possessed. When Shagram came to his master's well-known whistle, he was surprised to find the poor thing had been wounded, though slightly, by an arrow, which one of the forayers had shot off in anger after he had long chased it in vain.

"Ay, Shagram," said the old man, as he applied something to the wound, "must you rue the lang-bow as weel as all of us?"

"What corner in Scotland rues it not!" said the Lady of Avenel.

"Ay, ay, madam," said Martin, "God keep the kindly Scot from the cloth-yard shaft, and he will keep himself from the handy stroke. But let us go our way; the trash that is left I can come back for. There is nae ane to stir it but the good neighbours, and they——"

"For the love of God, goodman," said his wife, in a remonstrating tone, "haud your peace! Think what ye're saying, and we hae sae muckle wild land to go over before we win to the girth gate."

The husband nodded acquiescence; for it was deemed highly imprudent to speak of the fairies, either by their title of *good neighbours* or by any other, especially when about to pass the places which they were supposed to haunt.*

---

* This superstition continues to prevail, though one would suppose it must now be antiquated. It is only a year or two since an itinerant puppet show-man, who, disdaining to acknowledge the profession of Gines de Passamonte, called himself an artist from Vauxhall, brought a complaint of a singular nature before the author, as Sheriff of Selkirkshire. The singular dexterity with which the show-man had exhibited the machinery of his little stage, had, upon a Selkirk fair-day, excited the eager curiosity of some mechanics of Galashiels. These men, from no worse motive that could be discovered than a thirst after knowledge beyond their sphere, committed a burglary upon the barn in which the puppets had been consigned to repose, and carried them off in the nook of their plaids, when returning from Selkirk to their own village.

"But with the morning cool reflection came."

The party found, however, they could not make Punch dance, and that the whole troop were equally intractable; they had also, perhaps, some apprehensions of the Rhadamauth of the district; and, willing to be quit of their booty, they left the puppets seated in a grove by the side of the Ettrick, where they were sure to be touched by the first beams of the rising sun. Here a shepherd, who was on foot with sunrise to pen his master's sheep on a field of turnips, to his utter astonishment, saw this train, profusely gay, sitting in the little grotto. His examination proceeded thus:—

Sheriff. You saw these gay-looking things? what did you think they were?
Shepherd. Ou, I am no that free to say what I might think they were.
Sheriff. Come, lad, I must have a direct answer—who did you think they were?
Shepherd. Ou, sir, troth I am no that free to say that I mind wha I might think they were.
Sheriff. Come, come sir! I ask you distinctly, did you think they were the fairies you saw?
Shepherd. Indeed, sir, and I winna say but I might think it was the Good Neighbours.

Thus unwillingly was he brought to allude to the irritable and captious inhabitants of fairy land.

They set forward on their pilgrimage on the last day of October. "This is thy birthday, my sweet Mary," said the mother, as a sting of bitter recollection crossed her mind. "Oh, who could have believed that the head, which, a few years since, was cradled amongst so many rejoicing friends, may perhaps this night seek a cover in vain!"

The exiled family then set forward,—Mary Avenel, a lovely girl between five and six years old, riding gipsy fashion upon Shagram, betwixt two bundles of bedding; the Lady of Avenel walking by the animal's side; Tibb leading the bridle, and old Martin walking a little before, looking anxiously around him to explore the way.

Martin's task as guide, after two or three miles' walking, became more difficult than he himself had expected, or than he was willing to avow. It happened that the extensive range of pasturage, with which he was conversant, lay to the west, and to get into the little valley of Glendearg he had to proceed easterly. In the wilder districts of Scotland, the passage from one vale to another, otherwise than by descending that which you leave, and reascending the other, is often very difficult. — Heights and hollows, mosses and rocks intervene, and all those local impediments which throw a traveller out of his course. So that Martin, however sure of his general direction, became conscious, and at length was forced reluctantly to admit, that he had missed the direct road to Glendearg, though he insisted they must be very near it. "If we can but win across this wide bog," he said, "I shall warrant ye are on the top of the tower."

But to get across the bog was a point of no small difficulty. The farther they ventured into it, though proceeding with all the caution which Martin's experience recommended, the more unsound the ground became, until, after they had passed some places of great peril, their best argument for going forward came to be, that they had to encounter equal danger in returning.

The Lady of Avenel had been tenderly nurtured, but what will not a woman endure when her child is in danger? Complaining less of the dangers of the road than her attendants, who had been inured to such from their infancy, she kept herself close by the side of the pony, watching its every footstep, and ready, if it should flounder in the morass, to snatch her little Mary from its back. At length they came to a place where the guide greatly hesitated, for all around him was broken lumps of heath, divided from each other by deep sloughs of black tenacious mire. After great consideration, Martin, selecting what he thought the safest path, began himself to lead forward Shagram, in order to afford greater security to the child. But Shagram snorted, laid his ears back, stretched his two feet forward, and drew his hind feet under him, so as to adopt the best possible posture for obstinate resistance, and refused to move one yard in the direction indicated. Old Martin, much puzzled, now hesitated whether to exert his absolute authority, or to defer to the contumacious obstinacy of Shagram, and was not greatly comforted by his wife's observation, who, seeing Shagram stare with his eyes, distend his nostrils, and tremble with terror, hinted that "he surely saw more than they could see."

In this dilemma, the child suddenly exclaimed — "Bonny leddy signs to us to come yon gate." They all looked in the direction where the child pointed, but saw nothing, save a wreath of rising mist, which fancy might form into a human figure; but which afforded to Martin only the sorrowful conviction, that the danger of their situation was about to be increased by a heavy fog. He once more essayed to lead forward Shagram; but the animal was inflexible in its determination not to move in the direction Martin recommended. "Take your awn way for it, then," said Martin, "and let us see what you can do for us."

Shagram, abandoned to the discretion of his own free-will, set off boldly in the direction the child had pointed. There was nothing wonderful in this, nor in its bringing them safe to the other side of the dangerous morass; for the instinct of these animals in traversing bogs is one of the most curious parts of their nature, and is a fact generally established. But it was remarkable, that the child more than once mentioned the beautiful lady and her signals, and that Shagram seemed to be in the secret, always moving in the same direction which she indicated. The Lady of Avenel took little notice at the time, her mind being probably occupied by the instant danger; but her attendants changed expressive looks with each other more than once.

"All-Hallow Eve!" said Tibb, in a whisper to Martin.

"For the mercy of Our Lady, not a word of that now!" said Martin in reply. "Tell your beads, woman, if you cannot be silent."

When they got once more on firm ground, Martin recognized certain land-marks, or cairns, on the tops of the neighbouring hills, by which he was enabled to guide his course, and ere long they arrived at the Tower of Glendearg.

It was at the sight of this little fortalice that the misery of her lot pressed hard on the poor Lady of Avenel. When by any accident they had met at church, market, or other place of public resort, she remembered the distant and respectful air with which the wife of the warlike baron was addressed by the spouse of the humble feuar. And now, so much was her pride humbled, that she was to ask to share the precarious safety of the same feuar's widow, and her pittance of food, which might perhaps be yet more precarious. Martin probably guessed what was passing in her mind, for he looked at her with a wistful glance, as if to deprecate any change of resolution; and answering to his looks, rather than his words, she said, while the sparkle of subdued pride once more glanced from her eye, "If it were for myself alone, I could but die—but for this infant—the last pledge of Avenel——"

"True, my lady," said Martin, hastily; and, as if to prevent the possibility of her retracting, he added, "I will step on and see Dame Elspeth—I kend her husband weel, and have bought and sold with him, for as great a man as he was."

Martin's tale was soon told, and met all acceptance from her companion in misfortune. The Lady of Avenel had been meek and courteous in her prosperity; in adversity, therefore, she met with the greatest sympathy. Besides, there was a point of pride in sheltering and supporting a woman of such superior birth and rank; and, not to do Elspeth Glendinning injustice, she felt sympathy for one whose fate resembled her own in so many points, yet was so much more severe. Every species of hospitality was gladly and respectfully extended to the distressed travellers, and they were kindly requested to stay as long at Glendearg as their circumstances rendered necessary, or their inclination prompted.

Chapter the Fourth.

Ne'er be I found by thee unawed,
On that thrice hallow'd eve abroad,
When goblins haunt from flood and fen,
The steps of men.

COLLINS'S *Ode to Fear.*

As the country became more settled, the Lady of Avenel would have willingly returned to her husband's mansion. But that was no longer in her power. It was a reign of minority, when the strongest had the best right, and when acts of usurpation were frequent amongst those who had much power and little conscience.

Julian Avenel, the younger brother of the deceased Walter, was a person of this description. He hesitated not to seize upon his brother's house and lands, so soon as the retreat of the English permitted him. At first, he occupied the property in the name of his niece; but when the lady proposed to return with her child to the mansion of its fathers, he gave her to understand, that Avenel, being a male fief, descended to the brother, instead of the daughter, of the last possessor. The ancient philosopher declined a dispute with the emperor who commanded twenty legions, and the widow of Walter Avenel was in no condition to maintain a contest with the leader of twenty moss-troopers. Julian was also a man of service, who could back a friend in case of need, and was sure, therefore, to find protectors among the ruling powers. In short, however clear the little Mary's right to the possessions of her father, her mother saw the necessity of giving way, at least for the time, to the usurpation of her uncle.

Her patience and forbearance were so far attended with advantage, that Julian, for very shame's sake, could no longer suffer her to be absolutely dependant on the charity of Elspeth Glendinning. A drove of cattle and a bull (which were probably missed by some English farmer) were driven to the pastures of Glendearg; presents of raiment and household stuff were sent liberally, and some little money, though with a more sparing hand: for those in the situation of Julian Avenel could come more easily by the goods, than the representing medium of value, and made their payments chiefly in kind.

In the meantime, the widows of Walter Avenel and Simon Glendinning had become habituated to each other's society, and were unwilling to part. The lady could hope no more secret and secure residence than in the Tower of Glendearg, and she was now in a condition to support her share of the mutual housekeeping. Elspeth, on the other hand, felt pride, as well as pleasure, in the society of a guest of such distinction, and was at all times willing to pay much greater deference than the Lady of Walter Avenel could be prevailed on to accept.

Martin and his wife diligently served the united family in their several vocations, and yielded obedience to both mistresses, though always considering themselves as the especial servants of the Lady of Avenel. This distinction sometimes occasioned a slight degree of difference between Dame Elspeth and Tibb; the former being jealous of her own consequence, and the latter apt to lay too much stress upon the rank and family of her mistress. But both were alike desirous to conceal such petty squabbles from the lady, her hostess scarce yielding to her old domestic in respect for her person. Neither did the difference exist in such a degree as to interrupt the general harmony of the family, for the one wisely gave way as she saw the other become warm; and Tibb, though she often gave the first provocation, had generally the sense to be the first in relinquishing the argument.

The world which lay beyond was gradually forgotten by the inhabitants of this sequestered glen, and unless when she attended mass at the Monastery Church upon some high holiday, Alice of Avenel almost forgot that she once held an equal rank with the proud wives of the neighbouring barons and nobles who on such occasions crowded to the solemnity. The recollection gave her little pain. She loved her husband for himself, and in his inestimable loss all lesser subjects of regret had ceased to interest her. At times, indeed, she thought of claiming the protection of the Queen Regent (Mary of Guise) for her little orphan, but the fear of Julian Avenel always came between. She was sensible that he would have neither scruple nor difficulty in spiriting away the child, (if he did not proceed farther,) should he once consider its existence as formidable to his interest. Besides, he led a wild and unsettled life, mingling in all feuds and forays, wherever there was a spear to be broken; he evinced no purpose of marrying, and the fate which he continually was braving might at length remove him from his usurped inheritance. Alice of Avenel, therefore, judged it wise to check all ambitious thoughts for the present, and remain quiet in the rude, but peaceable retreat, to which Providence had conducted her.

It was upon an All-Hallow's eve, when the family had resided together for the space of three years, that the domestic circle was assembled round the blazing turf-fire, in the old narrow hall of the Tower of Glendearg. The idea of the master or mistress of the mansion feeding or living apart from their domestics, was at this period never entertained. The highest end of the board, the most commodious settle by the fire, — these were the only marks of distinction; and the servants mingled, with deference indeed, but unreproved and with freedom, in whatever conversation was going forward. But the two or three domestics, kept merely for agricultural purposes, had retired to their own cottages without, and with them a couple of wenches, usually employed within doors, the daughters of one of the hinds.

After their departure, Martin locked, first, the iron grate; and, secondly, the inner door of the tower, when the domestic circle was thus arranged. Dame Elspeth sate pulling the thread from her distaff; Tibb watched the progress of scalding the whey, which hung in a large pot upon the *crook*, a chain terminated by a hook, which was suspended in the chimney to serve the purpose of the modern crane. Martin, while busied in repairing some of the household articles, (for every man in those days was his own carpenter and smith, as well as his own tailor and shoemaker,) kept from time to time a watchful eye upon the three children.

They were allowed, however, to exercise their juvenile restlessness by running up and down the hall, behind the seats of the elder members of the family, with the privilege of occasionally making excursions into one or two small apartments which opened from it, and gave excellent opportunity to play at hide-and-seek. This night, however, the children seemed not disposed to avail themselves of their privilege of visiting these dark regions, but preferred carrying on their gambols in the vicinity of the light.

In the meanwhile, Alice of Avenel, sitting close to an iron candlestick, which supported a misshapen torch of domestic manufacture, read small detached passages from a thick clasped volume, which she preserved with the greatest care. The art of reading the lady had acquired by her residence in a nunnery during her youth, but she seldom, of late years, put it to any other use than perusing this little volume, which formed her whole library. The family listened to the portions which she selected, as to some good thing which there was a merit in hearing with respect, whether it was fully understood or no. To her daughter, Alice of Avenel had determined to impart their mystery more fully, but the knowledge was at that period attended with personal danger, and was not rashly to be trusted to a child.

The noise of the romping children interrupted, from time to time, the voice of the lady, and drew on the noisy culprits the rebuke of Elspeth.

"Could they not go farther a-field, if they behoved to make such a din, and disturb the lady's good words?" And this command was backed with the threat of sending the whole party to bed if it was not attended to punctually. Acting under the injunction, the children first played at a greater distance from the party, and more quietly, and then began to stray into the adjacent apartments, as they became impatient of the restraint to which they were subjected. But, all at once, the two boys came open-mouthed into the hall, to tell that there was an armed man in the spence.

"It must be Christie of Clint-hill," said Martin, rising; "what can have brought him here at this time?"

"Or how came he in?" said Elspeth.

"Alas! what can he seek?" said the Lady of Avenel, to whom this man, a retainer of her husband's brother, and who sometimes executed his commissions at Glendearg, was an object of secret apprehension and suspicion. "Gracious heavens!" she added, rising up, "where is my child?" All rushed to the spence, Halbert Glendinning first arming himself with a rusty sword, and the younger seizing upon the lady's book. They hastened to the spence, and were relieved of a part of their anxiety by meeting Mary at the door of the apartment. She did not seem in the slightest degree alarmed, or disturbed. They rushed into the spence, (a sort of interior apartment in which the family ate their victuals in the summer season,) but there was no one there.

"Where is Christie of Clint-hill?" said Martin.

"I do not know," said little Mary; "I never saw him."

"And what made you, ye misleard loons," said Dame Elspeth to her two boys, "come yon gate into the ha', roaring like bullsegs, to frighten the leddy, and her far frae strong?" The boys looked at each other in silence and confusion, and their mother proceeded with her lecture. "Could ye find nae night for daffin but Hallowe'en, and nae time but when the leddy was reading to us about the holy Saints? May ne'er be in my fingers, if I dinna sort ye baith for it!" The eldest boy bent his eyes on the ground, the younger began to weep, but neither spoke; and the mother would have proceeded to extremities, but for the interposition of the little maiden.

"Dame Elspeth, it was *my* fault—I did say to them, that I saw a man in the spence."

"And what made you do so, child," said her mother, "to startle us all thus?"

"Because," said Mary, lowering her voice, "I could not help it."

"Not help it, Mary!—you occasioned all this idle noise, and you could not help it? How mean you by that, minion?"

"There really was an armed man in this spence," said Mary; "and because I was surprised to see him, I cried out to Halbert and Edward——"

"She has told it herself," said Halbert Glendinning, "or it had never been told by me."

"Nor by me neither," said Edward, emulously.

"Mistress Mary," said Elspeth, "you never told us anything before that was not true; tell us if this was a Hallowe'en cantrip, and make an end of it." The Lady of Avenel looked as if she would have interfered, but knew not how; and Elspeth, who was too eagerly curious to regard any distant hint, persevered in her inquiries. "Was it Christie of the Clint-hill?—I would not for a mark that he were about the house, and a body no ken whare."

"It was not Christie," said Mary; "it was—it was a gentleman—a gentleman with a bright breastplate, like what I hae seen langsyne, when we dwelt at Avenel——"

"What like was he?" continued Tibb, who now took share in the investigation.

"Black-haired, black-eyed, with a peaked black beard," said the child; "and many a fold of pearling round his neck, and hanging down his breast ower his breastplate; and he had a beautiful hawk, with silver bells, standing on his left hand, with a crimson silk hood upon its head——"

"Ask her no more questions, for the love of God," said the anxious menial to Elspeth, "but look to my leddy!" But the Lady of Avenel, taking Mary in her hand, turned hastily away, and, walking into the hall, gave them no opportunity of remarking in what manner she received the child's communication, which she thus cut short. What Tibb thought of it appeared from her crossing herself repeatedly, and whispering into Elspeth's ear, "Saint Mary preserve us!—the lassie has seen her father!"

When they reached the hall, they found the lady holding her daughter on her knee, and kissing her repeatedly. When they entered, she again arose, as if to shun observation, and retired to the little apartment where her child and she occupied the same bed.

The boys were also sent to their cabin, and no one remained by the hall fire save the faithful Tibb and dame Elspeth, excellent persons both, and as thorough gossips as ever wagged a tongue.

It was but natural that they should instantly resume the subject of the supernatural appearance, for such they deemed it, which had this night alarmed the family.

"I could hae wished it had been the deil himself — be good to and preserve us! — rather than Christie o' the Clint-hill," said the matron of the mansion, "for the word runs rife in the country, that he is ane of the maist masterfu' thieves ever lap on horse."

"Hout-tout, Dame Elspeth," said Tibb, "fear ye naething frae Christie; tods keep their ain holes clean. You kirk-folk make sic a fasherie about men shifting a wee bit for their living! Our Border-lairds would ride with few men at their back, if a' the light-handed lads were out o' gate."

"Better they rade wi' nane than distress the country-side the gate they do," said Dame Elspeth.

"But wha is to haud back the Southron, then," said Tibb, "if ye take away the lances and broadswords? I trow we auld wives couldna do that wi' rock and wheel, and as little the monks wi' bell and book."

"And sae weel as the lances and broadswords hae kept them back, I trow!—I was mair beholden to ae Southron, and that was Stawarth Bolton, than to a' the border-riders ever wore Saint Andrew's cross—I reckon their skelping back and forward, and lifting honest men's gear, has been a main cause of a' the breach between us and England, and I am sure that cost me a kind goodman. They spoke about the wedding of the Prince and our Queen, but it's as like to be the driving of the Cumberland folk's stocking that brought them down on us like dragons." Tibb would not have failed in other circumstances to answer what she thought reflections disparaging to her country folk; but she recollected that Dame Elspeth was mistress of the family, curbed her own zealous patriotism, and hastened to change the subject.

"And is it not strange," she said, "that the heiress of Avenel should have seen her father this blessed night?"

"And ye think it was her father, then?" said Elspeth Glendinning.

"What else can I think?" said Tibb.

"It may hae been something waur, in his likeness," said Dame Glendinning.

"I ken naething about that," said Tibb, — "but his likeness it was, that I will be sworn to, just as he used to ride out a-hawking; for having enemies in the country, he seldom laid off the breast-plate; and for my part," added Tibb, "I dinna think a man looks like a man unless he has steel on his breast, and by his side too."

"I have no skill of your harness on breast or side either," said Dame Glendinning; "but I ken there is little luck in Hallowe'en sights, for I have had ane mysell."

"Indeed, Dame Elspeth?" said old Tibb, edging her stool closer to the huge elbow-chair occupied by her friend, "I should like to hear about that."

"Ye maun ken, then, Tibb," said Dame Glendinning, "that when I was a hempie of nineteen or twenty, it wasna my fault if I wasna at a' the merry-makings time about."

"That was very natural," said Tibb; "but ye hae sobered since that, or ye wadna haud our braw gallants sae lightly."

"I have had that wad sober me or ony ane," said the matron. "Aweel, Tibb, a lass like me wasna to lack wooers, for I wasna sae ill-favoured that the tikes wad bark after me."

"How should that be," said Tibb, "and you sic a weel-favoured woman to this day?"

"Fie, fie, cummer," said the matron of Glendearg, hitching her seat of honour, in her turn, a little nearer to the cuttie-stool on which Tibb was seated; "weel-favoured is past my time of day; but I might pass then, for I wasna sae tocherless but what I had a bit land at my breast-lace. My father was portioner of Little-dearg."

"Ye hae tell'd me that before," said Tibb; "but anent the Hallowe'en?"

"Aweel, aweel, I had mair joes than ane, but I favoured nane o' them; and sae, at Hallowe'en, Father Nicolas the cellarer—he was cellarer before this father, Father Clement, that now is—was cracking his nuts and drinking his brown beer with us, and as blithe as might be, and they would have me try a cantrip to ken wha suld wed me: and the monk said there was nae ill in it, and if there was, he would assoil me for it. And wha but I into the barn to winnow my three weights o' naething—sair, sair my mind misgave me for fear of wrang-doing and wrang-suffering baith; but I had aye a bauld spirit. I had not winnowed the last weight clean out, and the moon was shining bright upon the floor, when in stalked the presence of my dear Simon Glendinning, that is now happy. I never saw him plainer in my life than I did that moment; he held up an arrow as he passed me, and I swarf'd awa wi' fright. Muckle wark there was to bring me to mysell again, and sair they tried to make me believe it was a trick of Father Nicolas and Simon between them, and that the arrow was to signify Cupid's shaft, as the Father called it; and mony a time Simon wad threep it to me after I was married—gude man, he liked not it should be said that he was seen out o' the body!—But mark the end o' it, Tibb; we were married, and the gray-goose wing was the death o' him after a'!"

"As it has been of ower mony brave men," said Tibb; "I wish there wasna sic a bird as a goose in the wide warld, forby the clecking that we hae at the burn-side."

"But tell me, Tibb," said Dame Glendinning, "what does your leddy aye do reading out o' that thick black book wi' the silver clasps?—there are ower mony gude words in it to come frae ony body but a priest—An it were about Robin Hood, or some o' David Lindsay's ballants, ane wad ken better what to say to it. I am no misdoubting your mistress nae way, but I wad like ill to hae a decent house haunted wi' ghaists and gyre-carlines."

"Ye hae nae reason to doubt my leddy, or ony thing she says or does, Dame Glendinning," said the faithful Tibb, something offended; "and touching the bairn, it's weel kend she was born on Hallowe'en, was nine years gane, and they that are born on Hallowe'en whiles see mair than ither folk."

"And that wad be the cause, then, that the bairn didna mak muckle din about what it saw?—if it had been my Halbert himself, forby Edward, who is of softer nature, he wad hae yammered the haill night of a constancy. But it's like Mistress Mary hae sic sights mair natural to her."

"That may weel be," said Tibb; "for on Hallowe'en she was born, as I tell ye, and our auld parish priest wad fain hae had the night ower, and All-Hallow day begun. But for a' that, the sweet bairn is just like ither bairns, as ye may see yourself; and except this blessed night, and ance before when we were in that weary bog on the road here, I kenna that it saw mair than ither folk."

"But what saw she in the bog, then," said Dame Glendinning, "forby moor-cocks and heather-blutters?"

"The wean saw something like a white leddy that weised us the gate," said Tibb; "when we were like to hae perished in the moss-hags—certain it was that Shagram reisted, and I ken Martin thinks he saw something."

"And what might the white leddy be?" said Elspeth; "have ye ony guess o' that?"

"It's weel kend that, Dame Elspeth," said Tibb; "if ye had lived under grit folk, as I hae dune, ye wadna be to seek in that matter."

"I hae aye keepit my ain ha' house abune my head," said Elspeth, not without emphasis, "and if I havena lived wi' grit folk, grit folk have lived wi' me."

"Weel, weel, dame," said Tibb, "your pardon's prayed, there was nae offence meant. But ye maun ken the great ancient families canna be just served wi' the ordinary saunts, (praise to them!) like Saunt Anthony, Saunt Cuthbert, and the like, that come and gang at every sinner's bidding, but they hae a sort of saunts or angels, or what not, to themsells; and as for the White Maiden of Avenel, she is kend ower the haill country. And she is aye seen to yammer and wail before ony o' that family dies, as was weel kend by twenty folk before the death of Walter Avenel, haly be his cast!"

"If she can do nae mair than that," said Elspeth, somewhat scornfully, "they needna make mony vows to her, I trow. Can she make nae better fend for them than that, and has naething better to do than wait on them?"

"Mony braw services can the White Maiden do for them to the boot of that, and has dune in the auld histories," said Tibb, "but I mind o' naething in my day, except it was her that the bairn saw in the bog."

"Aweel, aweel, Tibb," said Dame Glendinning, rising and lighting the iron lamp, "these are great privileges of your grand folk. But our Lady and Saunt Paul are good eneugh saunts for me, and I'se warrant them never leave me in a bog that they can help me out o', seeing I send four waxen candles to their chapels every Candlemas; and if they are not seen to weep at my death, I'se warrant them smile at my joyful rising again, whilk Heaven send to all of us, Amen."

"Amen," answered Tibb, devoutly; "and now it's time I should hap up the wee bit gathering turf, as the fire is ower low."

Busily she set herself to perform this duty. The relict of Simon Glendinning did but pause a moment to cast a heedful and cautious glance all around the hall, to see that nothing was out of its proper place; then, wishing Tibb good-night, she retired to repose.

"The deil's in the carline," said Tibb to herself, "because she was the wife of a cock-laird, she thinks herself grander, I trow, than the bower-woman of a lady of that ilk!" Having given vent to her suppressed spleen in this little ejaculation, Tibb also betook herself to slumber.

Chapter the Fifth.

A priest, ye cry, a priest! — lame shepherds they,
How shall they gather in the straggling flock?
Dumb dogs which bark not — how shall they compel
The loitering vagrants to the Master's fold?
Fitter to bask before the blazing fire,
And snuff the mess neat-handed Phillis dresses,
Than on the snow-wreath battle with the wolf.

REFORMATION.

THE health of the Lady of Avenel had been gradually decaying ever since her disaster. It seemed as if the few years which followed her husband's death had done on her the work of half a century. She lost the fresh elasticity of form, the colour and the mien of health, and became wasted, wan, and feeble. She appeared to have no formed complaint; yet it was evident to those who looked on her, that her strength waned daily. Her lips at length became blenched and her eye dim; yet she spoke not of any desire to see a priest, until Elspeth Glendinning in her zeal could not refrain from touching upon a point which she deemed essential to salvation. Alice of Avenel received her hint kindly, and thanked her for it.

"If any good priest would take the trouble of such a journey," she said, "he should be welcome; for the prayers and lessons of the good must be at all times advantageous."

This quiet acquiescence was not quite what Elspeth Glendinning wished or expected. She made up, however, by her own enthusiasm, for the lady's want of eagerness to avail herself of ghostly counsel, and Martin was despatched with such haste as Shagram would make, to pray one of the religious men of Saint Mary's to come up to administer the last consolations to the widow of Walter Avenel.

When the Sacristan had announced to the Lord Abbot, that the Lady of the umquhile Walter de Avenel was in very weak health in the Tower of Glendearg, and desired the assistance of a father confessor, the lordly monk paused on the request.

"We do remember Walter de Avenel," he said; "a good knight and a valiant; he was dispossessed of his lands, and slain by the Southron—May not the lady come hither to the sacrament of confession? the road is distant and painful to travel."

"The lady is unwell, holy father," answered the Sacristan, "and unable to bear the journey."

"True—ay,—yes—then must one of our brethren go to her—Knowest thou if she hath aught of a jointure from this Walter de Avenel?"

"Very little, holy father," said the Sacristan; "she hath resided at Glendearg since her husband's death, well-nigh on the charity of a poor widow, called Elspeth Glendinning."

"Why, thou knowest all the widows in the country-side!" said the Abbot. "Ho! ho! ho!" and he shook his portly sides at his own jest.

"Ho! ho! ho!" echoed the Sacristan, in the tone and tune in which an inferior applauds the jest of his superior.—Then added, with a hypocritical shuffle, and a sly twinkle of his eye, "It is our duty, most holy father, to comfort the widow—He! he! he!"

This last laugh was more moderate, until the Abbot should put his sanction on the jest.

"Ho! ho!" said the Abbot; "then, to leave jesting, Father Philip, take thou thy riding gear, and go to confess this Dame Avenel."

"But," said the Sacristan——

"Give me no *Buts;* neither But nor If pass between monk and Abbot, Father Philip; the bands of discipline must not be relaxed—heresy gathers force like a snow-ball—the multitude expect confessions and preachings from the Benedictine, as they would from so many beggarly friars—and we may not desert the vineyard, though the toil be grievous unto us."

"And with so little advantage to the holy monastery," said the Sacristan.

"True, Father Philip; but wot you not that what preventeth harm doth good? This Julian de Avenel lives a light and evil life, and should we neglect the widow of his brother, he might foray our lands, and we never able to show who hurt us—moreover it is our duty to an ancient family, who, in their day, have been benefactors to the Abbey. Away with thee instantly, brother; ride night and day, an it be necessary, and let men see how diligent Abbot Boniface and his faithful children are in the execution of their spiritual duty—toil not deterring them, for the glen is five miles in length—fear not withholding them, for it is said to be haunted of spectres—nothing moving them from pursuit of their spiritual calling; to the confusion of calumnious heretics, and the comfort and edification of all true and faithful sons of the Catholic Church. I wonder what our brother Eustace will say to this?"

Breathless with his own picture of the dangers and toil which he was to encounter, and the fame which he was to acquire, (both by proxy,) the Abbot moved slowly to finish his luncheon in the refectory, and the Sacristan, with no very good will, accompanied old Martin in his return to Glendearg; the greatest impediment in the journey being the trouble of restraining his pampered mule, that she might tread in something like an equal pace with poor jaded Shagram.

After remaining an hour in private with his penitent, the monk returned moody and full of thought. Dame Elspeth, who had placed for the honoured guest some refreshment in the hall, was struck with the embarrassment which appeared in his countenance. Elspeth watched him with great anxiety. She observed there was that on his brow which rather resembled a person come from hearing the confession of some enormous crime, than the look of a confessor who resigns a reconciled penitent, not to earth, but to heaven. After long hesitating, she could not at length refrain from hazarding a question. She was sure, she said, the leddy had made an easy shrift. Five years had they resided together, and she could safely say, no woman lived better.

"Woman," said the Sacristan, sternly, "thou speakest thou knowest not what—What avails clearing the outside of the platter, if the inside be foul with heresy?"

"Our dishes and trenchers are not so clean as they could be wished, holy father," said Elspeth, but half understanding what he said, and beginning with her apron to wipe the dust from the plates, of which she supposed him to complain.

"Forbear, Dame Elspeth," said the monk; "your plates are as clean as wooden trenchers and pewter flagons can well be; the foulness of which I speak is of that pestilential heresy which is daily becoming ingrained in this our Holy Church of Scotland, and as a canker-worm in the rose-garland of the Spouse."

"Holy Mother of Heaven!" said Dame Elspeth, crossing herself, "have I kept house with a heretic?"

"No, Elspeth, no," replied the monk; "it were too strong a speech for me to make of this unhappy lady, but I would I could say she is free from heretical opinions. Alas! they fly about like the pestilence by noon-day, and infect even the first and fairest of the flock! For it is easy to see of this dame, that she hath been high in judgment as in rank."

"And she can write and read, I had almost said, as weel as your reverence," said Elspeth.

"Whom doth she write to, and what doth she read?" said the monk, eagerly.

"Nay," replied Elspeth, "I cannot say I ever saw her write at all, but her maiden that was—she now serves the family—says she can write—And for reading, she has often read to us good things out of a thick black volume with silver clasps."

"Let me see it," said the monk, hastily, "on your allegiance as a true vassal—on your faith as a Catholic Christian—instantly—instantly let me see it."

The good woman hesitated, alarmed at the tone in which the confessor took up her information; and being moreover of opinion, that what so good a woman as the Lady of Avenel studied so devoutly, could not be of a tendency actually evil. But borne down by the clamour, exclamations, and something like threats used by Father Philip, she at length brought him the fatal volume. It was easy to do this without suspicion on the part of the owner, as she lay on her bed exhausted with the fatigue of a long conference with her confessor, and as the small *round*, or turret closet, in which was the book and her other trifling property, was accessible by another door. Of all her effects the book was the last she would have thought of securing, for of what use or interest could it be in a family who neither read themselves, nor were in the habit of seeing any who did? so that Dame Elspeth had no difficulty in possessing herself of the volume, although her heart all the while accused her of an ungenerous and an inhospitable part towards her friend and inmate. The double power of a landlord and a feudal superior was before her eyes; and to say truth, the boldness, with which she might otherwise have resisted this double authority, was, I grieve to say it, much qualified by the curiosity she entertained, as a daughter of Eve, to have some explanation respecting the mysterious volume which the lady cherished with so much care, yet whose contents she imparted with such caution. For never had Alice of Avenel read them any passage from the book in question until the iron door of the tower was locked, and all possibility of intrusion prevented. Even then she had shown, by the selection of particular passages, that she was more anxious to impress on their minds the principles which the volume contained, than to introduce them to it as a new rule of faith.

When Elspeth, half curious, half remorseful, had placed the book in the monk's hands, he exclaimed, after turning over the leaves, "Now, by mine order, it is as I suspected!—My mule, my mule!—I will abide no longer here—well hast thou done, dame, in placing in my hands this perilous volume."

"Is it then witchcraft or devil's work?" said Dame Elspeth, in great agitation.

"Nay, God forbid!" said the monk, signing himself with the cross, "it is the Holy Scripture. But it is rendered into the vulgar tongue, and therefore, by the order of the Holy Catholic Church, unfit to be in the hands of any lay person."

"And yet is the Holy Scripture communicated for our common salvation," said Elspeth. "Good Father, you must instruct mine ignorance better; but lack of wit cannot be a deadly sin, and truly, to my poor thinking, I should be glad to read the Holy Scripture."

"I dare say thou wouldst," said the monk; "and even thus did our mother Eve seek to have knowledge of good and evil, and thus Sin came into the world, and Death by Sin."

"I am sure, and it is true," said Elspeth. "Oh, if she had dealt by the counsel of Saint Peter and Saint Paul!"

"If she had reverenced the command of Heaven," said the monk, "which, as it gave her birth, life, and happiness, fixed upon the grant such conditions as best corresponded with its holy pleasure. I tell thee, Elspeth, *the Word slayeth*—that is, the text alone, read with unskilled eye and unhallowed lips, is like those strong medicines which sick men take by the advice of the learned. Such patients recover and thrive; while those dealing in them at their own hand, shall perish by their own deed."

"Nae doubt, nae doubt," said the poor woman, "your reverence knows best."

"Not I," said Father Philip, in a tone as deferential as he thought could possibly become the Sacristan of Saint Mary's,—"Not I, but the Holy Father of Christendom, and our own holy father, the Lord Abbot, know best. I, the poor Sacristan of Saint Mary's, can but repeat what I hear from others my superiors. Yet of this, good woman, be assured,—the Word, the mere Word, slayeth. But the church hath her ministers to gloze and to expound the same unto her faithful congregation; and this I say, not so much, my beloved brethren—I mean my beloved sister," (for the Sacristan had got into the end of one of his old sermons,)—"This I speak not so much of the rectors, curates, and secular clergy, so called because they live after the fashion of the *seculum* or age, unbound by those ties which sequestrate us from the world; neither do I speak this of the mendicant friars, whether black or gray, whether crossed or uncrossed; but of the monks, and especially of the monks Benedictine, reformed on the rule of Saint Bernard of Clairvaux, thence called Cistercian, of which monks, Christian brethren — sister, I would say — great is the happiness and glory of the country in possessing the holy ministers of Saint Mary's, whereof I, though an unworthy brother, may say it hath produced more saints, more bishops, more popes — may our patrons make us thankful! — than any holy foundation in Scotland. Wherefore——But I see Martin hath my mule in readiness, and I will but salute you with the kiss of sisterhood, which maketh not ashamed, and so betake me to my toilsome return, for the glen is of bad reputation for the evil spirits which haunt it. Moreover, I may arrive too late at the bridge, whereby I may be obliged to take to the river, which I observed to be somewhat waxen."

Accordingly, he took his leave of Dame Elspeth, who was confounded by the rapidity of his utterance, and the doctrine he gave forth, and by no means easy on the subject of the book, which her conscience told her she should not have communicated to any one, without the knowledge of its owner.

Notwithstanding the haste which the monk as well as the mule made to return to better quarters than they had left at the head of Glendearg; notwithstanding the eager desire Father Philip had to be the very first who should acquaint the Abbot that a copy of the book they most dreaded had been found within the Halidome, or patrimony of the Abbey; notwithstanding, moreover, certain feelings which induced him to hurry as fast as possible through the gloomy and evil-reputed glen, still the difficulties of the road, and the rider's want of habitude of quick motion, were such, that twilight came upon him ere he had nearly cleared the narrow valley.

It was indeed a gloomy ride. The two sides of the vale were so near, that at every double of the river the shadows from the western sky fell upon, and totally obscured, the eastern bank; the thickets of copsewood seemed to wave with a portentous agitation of boughs and leaves, and the very crags and scaurs seemed higher and grimmer than they had appeared to the monk while he was travelling in daylight, and in company. Father Philip was heartily rejoiced, when, emerging from the narrow glen, he gained the open valley of the Tweed, which held on its majestic course from current to pool, and from pool stretched away to other currents, with a dignity peculiar to itself amongst the Scottish rivers; for whatever may have been the drought of the season, the Tweed usually fills up the space between its banks, seldom leaving those extensive sheets of shingle which deform the margins of many of the celebrated Scottish streams.

The monk, insensible to beauties which the age had not regarded as deserving of notice, was, nevertheless, like a prudent general, pleased to find himself out of the narrow glen in which the enemy might have stolen upon him unperceived. He drew up his bridle, reduced his mule to her natural and luxurious amble, instead of the agitating and broken trot at which, to his no small inconvenience, she had hitherto proceeded, and, wiping his brow, gazed forth at leisure on the broad moon, which, now mingling with the lights of evening, was rising over field and forest, village and fortalice, and, above all, over the stately Monastery, seen far and dim amid the yellow light.

The worst part of the magnificent view, in the monk's apprehension, was, that the Monastery stood on the opposite side of the river, and that of the many fine bridges which have since been built across that classical stream, not one then existed. There was, however, in recompense, a bridge then standing which has since disappeared, although its ruins may still be traced by the curious.

It was of a very peculiar form. Two strong abutments were built on either side of the river, at a part where the stream was peculiarly contracted. Upon a rock in the centre of the current was built a solid piece of masonry, constructed like the pier of a bridge, and presenting, like a pier, an angle to the current of the stream. The masonry continued solid until the pier rose to a level with the two abutments upon either side, and from thence the building rose in the form of a tower. The lower story of this tower consisted only of an archway or passage through the building, over either entrance to which hung a drawbridge with counterpoises, either of which, when dropped, connected the archway with the opposite abutment, where the farther end of the drawbridge rested. When both bridges were thus lowered, the passage over the river was complete.

The bridge-keeper, who was the dependant of a neighbouring baron, resided with his family in the second and third stories of the tower, which, when both drawbridges were raised, formed an insulated fortalice in the midst of the river. He was entitled to a small toll or custom for the passage, concerning the amount of which disputes sometimes arose between him and the passengers. It is needless to say, that the bridge-ward had usually the better in these questions, since he could at pleasure detain the traveller on the opposite side; or, suffering him to pass half way, might keep him prisoner in his tower till they were agreed on the rate of pontage.*

But it was most frequently with the Monks of Saint Mary's that the warder had to dispute his perquisites. These holy men insisted for, and at length obtained, a right of gratuitous passage to themselves, greatly to the discontent of the bridge-keeper. But when they demanded the same immunity for the numerous pilgrims who visited the shrine, the bridge-keeper waxed restive, and was supported by his lord in his resistance. The controversy grew animated on both sides; the Abbot menaced excommunication, and the keeper of the bridge, though unable to retaliate in kind, yet made each individual monk who had to cross and recross the river, endure a sort of purgatory, ere he would accommodate them with a passage. This was a great inconvenience, and would have proved a more serious one, but that the river was fordable for man and horse in ordinary weather.

It was a fine moonlight night, as we have already said, when Father Philip approached this bridge, the singular construction of which gives a curious idea of the insecurity of the times. The river was not in flood, but it was above its ordinary level — *a heavy water*, as it is called in that country, through which the monk had no particular inclination to ride, if he could manage the matter better.

"Peter, my good friend," cried the Sacristan, raising his voice; "my very excellent friend, Peter, be so kind as to lower the drawbridge. Peter, I say, dost thou not hear?—it is thy gossip, Father Philip, who calls thee."

Peter heard him perfectly well, and saw him into the bargain; but as he had considered the Sacristan as peculiarly his enemy in his dispute with

* A bridge of the very peculiar construction described in the text, actually existed at a small hamlet about a mile and a half above Melrose, called from the circumstance Bridge-end. It is thus noticed in Gordon's *Iter Septentrionale*:—

"In another journey through the south parts of Scotland, about a mile and a half from Melrose, in the shire of Teviotdale, I saw the remains of a curious bridge over the river Tweed, consisting of three octangular pillars, or rather towers, standing within the water, without any arches to join them. The middle one, which is the most entire, has a door towards the north, and I suppose another opposite one toward the south, which I could not see without crossing the water. In the middle of this tower is a projection or cornice surrounding it: the whole is hollow from the door upwards, and now open at the top, near which is a small window. I was informed that not long ago a countryman and his family lived in this tower—and got his livelihood by laying out planks from pillar to pillar, and conveying passengers over the river. Whether this be ancient or modern, I know not; but as it is singular in its kind I have thought fit to exhibit it."

The vestiges of this uncommon species of bridge still exist, and the author has often seen the foundations of the columns when drifting down the Tweed at night for the purpose of killing salmon by torch-light. Mr. John Mercer of Bridge-end recollects, that about fifty years ago the pillars were visible above water; and the late Mr. David Kyle, of the George Inn, Melrose, told the author that he saw a stone taken from the river bearing this inscription:—

"I, Sir John Pringle of Palmer stede,
Give an hundred markis of gowd sae reid,
To help to bigg my brigg ower Tweed."

Pringle of Galashiels, afterwards of Whytbank, was the Baron to whom the bridge belonged.

the convent, he went quietly to bed, after reconnoitring the monk through his loop-hole, observing to his wife, that "riding the water in a moonlight night would do the Sacristan no harm, and would teach him the value of a brig the neist time, on whilk a man might pass high and dry, winter and summer, flood and ebb."

After exhausting his voice in entreaties and threats, which were equally unattended to by Peter of the Brig, as he was called, Father Philip at length moved down the river to take the ordinary ford at the head of the next stream. Cursing the rustic obstinacy of Peter, he began, nevertheless, to persuade himself that the passage of the river by the ford was not only safe, but pleasant. The banks and scattered trees were so beautifully reflected from the bosom of the dark stream, the whole cool and delicious picture formed so pleasing a contrast to his late agitation, to the warmth occasioned by his vain endeavours to move the relentless porter of the bridge, that the result was rather agreeable than otherwise.

As Father Philip came close to the water's edge, at the spot where he was to enter it, there sat a female under a large broken scathed oak-tree, or rather under the remains of such a tree, weeping, wringing her hands, and looking earnestly on the current of the river. The monk was struck with astonishment to see a female there at that time of night. But he was, in all honest service,—and if a step farther, I put it upon his own conscience,—a devoted squire of dames. After observing the maiden for a moment, although she seemed to take no notice of his presence, he was moved by her distress, and willing to offer his assistance. "Damsel," said he, "thou seemest in no ordinary distress; peradventure, like myself, thou hast been refused passage at the bridge by the churlish keeper, and thy crossing may concern thee either for performance of a vow, or some other weighty charge."

The maiden uttered some inarticulate sounds, looked at the river, and then in the face of the Sacristan. It struck Father Philip at that instant, that a Highland chief of distinction had been for some time expected to pay his vows at the shrine of Saint Mary's; and that possibly this fair maiden might be one of his family, travelling alone for accomplishment of a vow, or left behind by some accident, to whom, therefore, it would be but right and prudent to use every civility in his power, especially as she seemed unacquainted with the Lowland tongue. Such at least was the only motive the Sacristan was ever known to assign for his courtesy; if there was any other, I once more refer it to his own conscience.

To express himself by signs, the common language of all nations, the cautious Sacristan first pointed to the river, then to his mule's crupper, and then made, as gracefully as he could, a sign to induce the fair solitary to mount behind him. She seemed to understand his meaning, for she rose up as if to accept his offer; and while the good monk, who, as we have hinted, was no great cavalier, laboured, with the pressure of the right leg and the use of the left rein, to place his mule with her side to the bank in such a position that the lady might mount with ease, she rose from the ground with rather portentous activity, and at one bound sate behind the monk upon the animal, much the firmer rider of the two. The mule by no means seemed to approve of this double burden; she bounded, bolted, and would soon have thrown Father Philip over her head, had not the maiden with a firm hand detained him in the saddle.

At last the restive brute changed her humour; and, from refusing to budge off the spot, suddenly stretched her nose homeward, and dashed into the ford as fast as she could scamper. A new terror now invaded the monk's mind—the ford seemed unusually deep, the water eddied off in strong ripple from the counter of the mule, and began to rise upon her side. Philip lost his presence of mind, which was at no time his most ready attribute, the mule yielded to the weight of the current, and as the rider was not attentive to keep her head turned up the river, she drifted downward, lost the ford and her footing at once, and began to swim with her head down the stream. And what was sufficiently strange, at the same moment, notwithstanding the extreme peril, the damsel began to sing, thereby increasing, if anything could increase, the bodily fear of the worthy Sacristan.

I.

Merrily swim we, the moon shines bright,
Both current and ripple are dancing in light.
We have roused the night raven, I heard him croak,
As we plashed along beneath the oak
That flings its broad branches so far and so wide,
Their shadows are dancing in midst of the tide.
"Who wakens my nestlings," the raven he said,
"My beak shall ere morn in his blood be red.
For a blue swoln corpse is a dainty meal,
And I'll have my share with the pike and the eel."

II.

Merrily swim we, the moon shines bright,
There's a golden gleam on the distant height;
There's a silver shower on the alders dank,
And the drooping willows that wave on the bank.
I see the abbey, both turret and tower,
It is all astir for the vesper hour;
The monks for the chapel are leaving each cell,
But where's Father Philip, should toll the bell?

III.

Merrily swim we, the moon shines bright,
Downward we drift through shadow and light,
Under yon rock the eddies sleep,
Calm and silent, dark and deep,
The Kelpy has risen from the fathomless pool,
He has lighted his candle of death and of dool.
Look, Father, look, and you'll laugh to see
How he gapes and glares with his eyes on thee.

IV.

Good luck to your fishing, whom watch ye to-night?
A man of mean, or a man of might?
Is it layman or priest that must float in your cove,
Or lover who crosses to visit his love?
Hark! heard ye the Kelpy reply, as we pass'd,—
"God's blessing on the warder, he lock'd the bridge fast!
All that come to my cove are sunk,
Priest or layman, lover or monk."

How long the damsel might have continued to sing, or where the terrified monk's journey might have ended, is uncertain. As she sung the last stanza, they arrived at, or rather in, a broad tranquil sheet of water, caused by a strong wear or damhead, running across the river, which dashed in a broad cataract over the barrier. The mule, whether from choice, or influenced by the suction of the current, made towards the cut intended to supply the convent mills, and entered it half swimming half wading, and pitching the unlucky monk to and fro in the saddle at a fearful rate.

As his person flew hither and thither, his garment became loose, and in an effort to retain it, his hand lighted on the volume of the Lady of Avenel which was in his bosom. No sooner had he grasped it, than his companion pitched him out of the saddle into the stream, where, still keeping her hand on his collar, she gave him two or three good souses in the watery fluid, so as to ensure that every other part of him had its share of wetting, and then quitted her hold when he was so near the side that by a slight effort (of a great one he was incapable) he might scramble on shore. This accordingly he accomplished, and turning his eyes to see what had become of his extraordinary companion, she was nowhere to be seen; but still he heard, as if from the surface of the river, and mixing with the noise of the water breaking over the damhead, a fragment of her wild song, which seemed to run thus:—

Landed—landed! the black book hath won,
Else had you seen Berwick with morning sun!
Sain ye, and save ye, and blithe mot ye be,
For seldom they land that go swimming with me.

The ecstasy of the monk's terror could be endured no longer; his head grew dizzy, and, after staggering a few steps onward and running himself against a wall, he sunk down in a state of insensibility.

Chapter the Sixth.

Now let us sit in conclave. That these weeds
Be rooted from the vineyard of the church,
That these foul tares be severed from the wheat,
We are, I trust, agreed.—Yet how to do this,
Nor hurt the wholesome crop and tender vine-plants,
Craves good advisement.

THE REFORMATION.

THE vesper-service in the Monastery Church of Saint Mary's was now over. The Abbot had disrobed himself of his magnificent vestures of ceremony, and resumed his ordinary habit, which was a black gown, worn over a white cassock, with a narrow scapulary; a decent and venerable dress, which was calculated to set off to advantage the portly mien of Abbot Boniface.

In quiet times no one could have filled the state of a mitred Abbot, for such was his dignity, more respectably than this worthy prelate. He had, no doubt, many of those habits of self-indulgence which men are apt to acquire who live for themselves alone. He was vain, moreover; and when boldly confronted, had sometimes shown symptoms of timidity, not very consistent with the high claims which he preferred as an eminent member of the church, or with the punctual deference which he exacted from his religious brethren, and all who were placed under his command. But he was hospitable, charitable, and by no means of himself disposed to proceed with severity against any one. In short, he would in other times have slumbered out his term of preferment with as much credit as any other "purple Abbot," who lived easily, but at the same time decorously — slept soundly, and did not disquiet himself with dreams.

But the wide alarm spread through the whole Church of Rome by the progress of the reformed doctrines, sorely disturbed the repose of Abbot Boniface, and opened to him a wide field of duties and cares which he had never so much as dreamed of. There were opinions to be combated and refuted — practices to be inquired into — heretics to be detected and punished—the fallen off to be reclaimed—the wavering to be confirmed—scandal to be removed from the clergy, and the vigour of discipline to be re-established. Post upon post arrived at the Monastery of Saint Mary's — horses reeking, and riders exhausted — this from the Privy Council, that from the Primate of Scotland, and this other again from the Queen Mother, exhorting, approving, condemning, requesting advice upon this subject, and requiring information upon that.

These missives Abbot Boniface received with an important air of helplessness, or a helpless air of importance, whichever the reader may please to term it, evincing at once gratified vanity, and profound trouble of mind.

The sharp-witted Primate of Saint Andrews had foreseen the deficiencies of the Abbot of St. Mary's, and endeavoured to provide for them by getting admitted into his Monastery as Sub-Prior a brother Cistercian, a man of parts and knowledge, devoted to the service of the Catholic Church, and very capable not only to advise the Abbot on occasions of difficulty, but to make him sensible of his duty in case he should, from good-nature or timidity, be disposed to shrink from it.

Father Eustace played the same part in the Monastery as the old general who, in foreign armies, is placed at the elbow of the Prince of the Blood, who nominally commands in chief, on condition of attempting nothing without the advice of his dry-nurse; and he shared the fate of all such dry-nurses, being heartily disliked as well as feared by his principal. Still, however, the Primate's intention was fully answered. Father Eustace became the constant theme and often the bugbear of the worthy Abbot, who hardly dared to turn himself in his bed without considering what Father Eustace would think of it. In every case of difficulty, Father Eustace was summoned, and his opinion asked; and no sooner was the embarrassment removed, than the Abbot's next thought was how to get rid of his adviser. In every letter which he wrote to those in power, he recommended Father Eustace to some high church preferment, a bishopric or an abbey; and as they dropped one after another, and were otherwise conferred, he began to think, as he confessed to the Sacristan in the bitterness of his spirit, that the Monastery of St. Mary's had got a life-rent lease of their Sub-Prior.

Yet more indignant he would have been, had he suspected that Father Eustace's ambition was fixed upon his own mitre, which, from some attacks of an apoplectic nature, deemed by the Abbot's friends to be more serious than by himself, it was supposed might be shortly vacant. But the confidence which, like other dignitaries, he reposed in his own health, prevented Abbot Boniface from imagining that it held any concatenation with the motions of Father Eustace.

The necessity under which he found himself of consulting with his grand adviser, in cases of real difficulty, rendered the worthy Abbot particularly desirous of doing without him in all ordinary cases of administration, though not without considering what Father Eustace would have said of the matter. He scorned, therefore, to give a hint to the Sub-Prior of the bold stroke by which he had dispatched Brother Philip to Glendearg; but when the vespers came without his re-appearance he became a little uneasy, the more as other matters weighed upon his mind. The feud with the warder or keeper of the bridge threatened to be attended with bad consequences, as the man's quarrel was taken up by the martial baron under whom he served; and pressing letters of an unpleasant tendency had just arrived from the Primate. Like a gouty man, who catches hold of his crutch while he curses the infirmity that induces him to use it, the Abbot, however reluctant, found himself obliged to require Eustace's presence, after the service was over, in his house, or rather palace, which was attached to, and made part of, the Monastery.

Abbot Boniface was seated in his high-backed chair, the grotesque carved back of which terminated in a mitre, before a fire where two or three large logs were reduced to one red glowing mass of charcoal. At his elbow, on an oaken stand, stood the remains of a roasted capon, on which his reverence had made his evening meal, flanked by a goodly stoup of Bordeaux of excellent flavour. He was gazing indolently on the fire, partly engaged in meditation on his past and present fortunes, partly occupied by endeavouring to trace towers and steeples in the red embers.

"Yes," thought the Abbot to himself, "in that red perspective I could fancy to myself the peaceful towers of Dundrennan, where I passed my life ere I was called to pomp and to trouble. A quiet brotherhood we were, regular in our domestic duties; and when the frailties of humanity prevailed over us, we confessed, and were absolved by each other, and the most formidable part of the penance was the jest of the convent on the culprit. I can almost fancy that I see the cloister garden, and the pear-trees which I grafted with my own hands. And for what have I changed all this, but to be overwhelmed with business which concerns me not, to be called My Lord Abbot, and to be tutored by Father Eustace? I would these towers were the Abbey of Aberbrothwick, and Father Eustace the Abbot,—or I would he were in the fire on any terms, so I were rid of him! The Primate says our Holy Father the Pope hath an adviser—I am sure he could not live a week with such a one as mine. Then there is no learning what Father Eustace thinks till you confess your own difficulties—No hint will bring forth his opinion—he is like a miser, who will not unbuckle his purse to bestow a farthing, until the wretch who needs it has owned his excess of poverty, and wrung out the boon by importunity. And thus I am dishonoured in the eyes of my religious brethren, who behold me treated like a child which hath no sense of its own — I will bear it no longer! — Brother Bennet," — (a lay brother answered to his call) — "tell Father Eustace that I need not his presence."

"I came to say to your reverence, that the holy father is entering even now from the cloisters."

"Be it so," said the Abbot, "he is welcome, — remove these things — or rather, place a trencher, the holy father may be a little hungry — yet, no — remove them, for there is no good fellowship in him — Let the stoup of wine remain, however, and place another cup."

The lay brother obeyed these contradictory commands in the way he judged most seemly — he removed the carcass of the half-sacked capon, and placed two goblets beside the stoup of Bourdeaux. At the same instant entered Father Eustace.

He was a thin, sharp-faced, slight-made little man, whose keen grey eyes seemed almost to look through the person to whom he addressed himself. His body was emaciated not only with the fasts which he observed with rigid punctuality, but also by the active and unwearied exercise of his sharp and piercing intellect; —

A fiery soul, which working out its way,
Fretted the puny body to decay,
And o'er-informed the tenement of clay.

He turned with conventual reverence to the Lord Abbot; and as they stood together, it was scarce possible to see a more complete difference of form and expression. The good-natured rosy face and laughing eye of the Abbot, which even his present anxiety could not greatly ruffle, was a wonderful contrast to the thin pallid cheek and quick penetrating glance of the monk, in which an eager and keen spirit glanced through eyes to which it seemed to give supernatural lustre.

The Abbot opened the conversation by motioning to his monk to take a stool, and inviting to a cup of wine. The courtesy was declined with respect, yet not without a remark, that the vesper service was past.

"For the stomach's sake, brother," said the Abbot, colouring a little — "You know the text."

"It is a dangerous one," answered the monk, "to handle alone, or at late hours. Cut off from human society, the juice of the grape becomes a perilous companion of solitude, and therefore I ever shun it."

Abbot Boniface had poured himself out a goblet which might hold about half an English pint; but, either struck with the truth of the observation, or ashamed to act in direct opposition to it, he suffered it to remain untasted before him, and immediately changed the subject.

"The Primate hath written to us," said he, "to make strict search within our bounds after the heretical persons denounced in this list, who have withdrawn themselves from the justice which their opinions deserve. It is deemed probable that they will attempt to retire to England by our Borders, and the Primate requireth me to watch with vigilance, and what not."

"Assuredly," said the monk, "the magistrate should not bear the sword in vain — those be they that turn the world upside down — and doubtless your reverend wisdom will with due diligence second the exertions of the Right Reverend Father in God, being in the peremptory defence of the Holy Church."

"Ay, but how is this to be done?" answered the Abbot; "Saint Mary aid us! The Primate writes to me as if I were a temporal baron — a man under command, having soldiers under him! He says, send forth — scour the country—guard the passes—Truly these men do not travel as those who would give their lives for nothing—the last who went south passed the dry-march at the Riding-burn with an escort of thirty spears, as our reverend brother the Abbot of Kelso did write unto us. How are cowls and scapularies to stop the way?"

"Your bailiff is accounted a good man at arms, holy father," said Eustace; "your vassals are obliged to rise for the defence of the Holy Kirk — it is the tenure on which they hold their lands — if they will not come forth for the Church which gives them bread, let their possessions be given to others."

"We shall not be wanting," said the Abbot, collecting himself with importance, "to do whatever may advantage Holy Kirk — thyself shall hear the charge to our Bailiff and our officials—but here again is our controversy with the warden of the bridge and the Baron of Meigallot — Saint Mary! vexations do so multiply upon the House, and upon the generation, that a man wots not where to turn to! Thou didst say, Father Eustace, thou wouldst look into our evidents touching this free passage for the pilgrims?"

"I have looked into the Chartulary of the House, holy father," said Eustace, "and therein I find a written and formal grant of all duties and customs payable at the drawbridge of Brigton, not only by ecclesiastics of this foundation, but by every pilgrim truly designed to accomplish his vows at this House, to the Abbot Ailford, and the monks of the House of Saint Mary in Kennaquhair, from that time and for ever. The deed is dated on Saint Bridget's Even, in the year of Redemption, 1137, and bears the sign and seal of the granter, Charles of Meigallot, great-great-grandfather of this baron, and purports to be granted for the safety of his own soul, and for the weal of the souls of his father and mother, and of all his predecessors and successors, being Barons of Meigallot."

"But he alleges," said the Abbot, "that the bridge-wards have been in possession of these dues, and have rendered them available for more than fifty years — and the baron threatens violence — meanwhile, the journey of the pilgrims is interrupted, to the prejudice of their own souls and the diminution of the revenues of Saint Mary. The Sacristan advised us to put on a boat; but the warden, whom thou knowest to be a godless man, has sworn the devil tear him, but that if they put on a boat on the laird's stream, he will rive her board from board — and then some say we should compound the claim for a small sum in silver." Here the Abbot paused a moment for a reply, but receiving none, he added, "But what thinkest thou, Father Eustace? why art thou silent?"

"Because I am surprised at the question which the Lord Abbot of Saint Mary's asks at the youngest of his brethren."

"Youngest in time of your abode with us, Brother Eustace," said the Abbot, "not youngest in years, or I think in experience. Sub-Prior also of this convent."

"I am astonished," continued Eustace, "that the Abbot of this venerable house should ask of any one whether he can alienate the patrimony of our holy and divine patroness, or give up to an unconscientious, and perhaps, a heretic baron, the rights conferred on this church by his devout progenitor. Popes and councils alike prohibit it—the honour of the living, and the weal of departed souls, alike forbid it — it may not be. To force, if he dare use it, we must surrender; but never by our consent should we see the goods of the church plundered, with as little scruple as he would drive off a herd of English beeves. Rouse yourself, Reverend father, and doubt nothing but that the good cause shall prevail. Whet the spiritual sword, and direct it against the wicked who would usurp our holy rights. Whet the temporal sword, if it be necessary, and stir up the courage and zeal of your loyal vassals."

The Abbot sighed deeply. "All this," he said, "is soon spoken by him who hath to act it not; but——" He was interrupted by the entrance of Bennet rather hastily. "The mule on which the Sacristan had set out in the morning had returned," he said, "to the convent stable all over wet, and with the saddle turned round beneath her belly."

"Sancta Maria!" said the Abbot, "our dear brother hath perished by the way!"

"It may not be," said Eustace, hastily—"let the bell be tolled—cause the brethren to get torches—alarm the village—hurry down to the river—I myself will be the foremost."

The real Abbot stood astonished and agape, when at once he beheld his office filled, and saw all which he ought to have ordered, going forward at the dictates of the youngest monk in the convent. But ere the orders of Eustace, which nobody dreamed of disputing, were carried into execution, the necessity was prevented by the sudden apparition of the Sacristan, whose supposed danger excited all the alarm.

Chapter the Seventh.

Raze out the written troubles of the brain,
Cleanse the foul bosom of the perilous stuff
That weighs upon the heart.

MACBETH.

WHAT betwixt cold and fright the afflicted Sacristan stood before his Superior, propped on the friendly arm of the convent miller, drenched with water, and scarce able to utter a syllable.

After various attempts to speak, the first words he uttered were,

"Swim we merrily—the moon shines bright."

"Swim we merrily!" retorted the Abbot, indignantly; "a merry night have ye chosen for swimming, and a becoming salutation to your Superior!"

"Our brother is bewildered," said Eustace;—"speak, Father Philip, how is it with you?"

"Good luck to your fishing,"

continued the Sacristan, making a most dolorous attempt at the tune of his strange companion.

"Good luck to your fishing!" repeated the Abbot, still more surprised than displeased; "by my halidome he is drunken with wine, and comes to our presence with his jolly catches in his throat! If bread and water can cure this folly——"

"With your pardon, venerable father," said the Sub-Prior, "of water our brother has had enough; and methinks, the confusion of his eye, is rather that of terror, than of aught unbecoming his profession. Where did you find him, Hob Miller?"

"An it please your reverence, I did but go to shut the sluice of the mill—and as I was going to shut the sluice, I heard something groan near to me; but judging it was one of Giles Fletcher's hogs—for so please you he never shuts his gate—I caught up my lever, and was about—Saint Mary forgive me!—to strike where I heard the sound, when, as the saints would have it, I heard the second groan just like that of a living man. So I called up my knaves, and found the Father Sacristan lying wet and senseless under the wall of our kiln. So soon as we brought him to himself a bit, he prayed to be brought to your reverence, but I doubt me his wits have gone a bell-wavering by the road. It was but now that he spoke in somewhat better form."

"Well!" said Brother Eustace, "thou hast done well, Hob Miller; only begone now, and remember a second time to pause, ere you strike in the dark."

"Please your reverence, it shall be a lesson to me," said the miller, "not to mistake a holy man for a hog again, so long as I live." And, making a bow, with profound humility, the miller withdrew.

"And now that this churl is gone, Father Philip," said Eustace, "wilt thou tell our venerable Superior what ails thee? art thou *vino gravatus*, man? if so we will have thee to thy cell."

"Water! water! not wine," muttered the exhausted Sacristan.

"Nay," said the monk, "if that be thy complaint, wine may perhaps cure thee;" and he reached him a cup, which the patient drank off to his great benefit.

"And now," said the Abbot, "let his garments be changed, or rather let him be carried to the infirmary; for it will prejudice our health, should we hear his narrative while he stands there, steaming like a rising hoar-frost."

"I will hear his adventure," said Eustace, "and report it to your reverence." And, accordingly, he attended the Sacristan to his cell. In about half an hour he returned to the Abbot.

"How is it with Father Philip?" said the Abbot; "and through what came he into such a state?"

"He comes from Glendearg, reverend sir," said Eustace; "and for the rest, he telleth such a legend, as has not been heard in this Monastery for many a long day." He then gave the Abbot the outlines of the Sacristan's adventures in the homeward journey, and added, that for some time he was inclined to think his brain was infirm, seeing he had sung, laughed, and wept all in the same breath.

"A wonderful thing it is to us," said the Abbot, "that Satan has been permitted to put forth his hand thus far on one of our sacred brethren!"

"True," said Father Eustace; "but for every text there is a paraphrase; and I have my suspicions, that if the drenching of Father Philip cometh of the Evil one, yet it may not have been altogether without his own personal fault."

"How!" said the Father Abbot; "I will not believe that thou makest doubt that Satan, in former days, hath been permitted to afflict saints and holy men, even as he afflicted the pious Job?"

"God forbid I should make question of it," said the monk, crossing himself; "yet, where there is an exposition of the Sacristan's tale, which is less than miraculous, I hold it safe to consider it at least, if not to abide by it. Now, this Hob the Miller hath a buxom daughter. Suppose — I say only suppose — that our Sacristan met her at the ford on her return from her uncle's on the other side, for there she hath this evening been — suppose, that, in courtesy, and to save her stripping hose and shoon, the Sacristan brought her across behind him—suppose he carried his familiarities farther than the maiden was willing to admit; and we may easily suppose, farther, that this wetting was the result of it."

"And this legend invented to deceive us!" said the Superior, reddening with wrath; "but most strictly shall it be sifted and inquired into; it is not upon us that Father Philip must hope to pass the result of his own evil practices for doings of Satan. To-morrow cite the wench to appear before us—we will examine, and we will punish."

"Under your reverence's favour," said Eustace, "that were but poor policy. As things now stand with us, the heretics catch hold of each flying report which tends to the scandal of our clergy. We must abate the evil, not only by strengthening discipline, but also by suppressing and stifling the voice of scandal. If my conjectures are true, the miller's daughter will be silent for her own sake; and your reverence's authority may also impose silence on her father, and on the Sacristan. If he is again found to afford room for throwing dishonour on his order, he can be punished with severity, but at the same time with secrecy. For what say the

Decretals! *Facinora ostendi dum punientur, flagitia autem abscondi debent.*"

A sentence of Latin, as Eustace had before observed, had often much influence on the Abbot, because he understood it not fluently, and was ashamed to acknowledge his ignorance. On these terms they parted for the night.

The next day, Abbot Boniface strictly interrogated Philip on the real cause of his disaster of the previous night. But the Sacristan stood firm to his story; nor was he found to vary from any point of it, although the answers he returned were in some degree incoherent, owing to his intermingling with them ever and anon snatches of the strange damsel's song, which had made such deep impression on his imagination, that he could not prevent himself from imitating it repeatedly in the course of his examination. The Abbot had compassion with the Sacristan's involuntary frailty, to which something supernatural seemed annexed, and finally became of opinion, that Father Eustace's more natural explanation was rather plausible than just. And, indeed, although we have recorded the adventure as we find it written down, we cannot forbear to add that there was a schism on the subject in the convent, and that several of the brethren pretended to have good reason for thinking that the miller's black-eyed daughter was at the bottom of the affair after all. Whichever way it might be interpreted, all agreed that it had too ludicrous a sound to be permitted to get abroad, and therefore the Sacristan was charged, on his vow of obedience, to say no more of his ducking; an injunction which, having once eased his mind by telling his story, it may be well conjectured that he joyfully obeyed.

The attention of Father Eustace was much less forcibly arrested by the marvellous tale of the Sacristan's danger, and his escape, than by the mention of the volume which he had brought with him from the Tower of Glendearg. A copy of the Scriptures, translated into the vulgar tongue, had found its way even into the proper territory of the church, and had been discovered in one of the most hidden and sequestered recesses of the Halidome of Saint Mary's.

He anxiously requested to see the volume. In this the Sacristan was unable to gratify him, for he had lost it, as far as he recollected, when the supernatural being, as he conceived her to be, took her departure from him. Father Eustace went down to the spot in person, and searched all around it, in hopes of recovering the volume in question; but his labour was in vain. He returned to the Abbot, and reported that it must have fallen into the river or the mill-stream; "for I will hardly believe," he said, "that Father Philip's musical friend would fly off with a copy of the Holy Scriptures."

"Being," said the Abbot, "as it is, an heretical translation, it may be thought that Satan may have power over it."

"Ay!" said Father Eustace, "it is indeed his chiefest magazine of artillery, when he inspireth presumptuous and daring men to set forth their own opinions and expositions of Holy Writ. But though thus abused, the Scriptures are the source of our salvation, and are no more to be reckoned unholy, because of these rash men's proceedings, than a powerful medicine is to be contemned, or held poisonous, because bold and evil leeches have employed it to the prejudice of their patients. With the permission of your reverence, I would that this matter were looked into more closely. I will myself visit the Tower of Glendearg ere I am many hours older, and we shall see if any spectre or white woman of the wild will venture to interrupt my journey or return. Have I your reverend permission and your blessing?" he added, but in a tone that appeared to set no great store by either.

"Thou hast both, my brother," said the Abbot; but no sooner had Eustace left the apartment, than Boniface could not help breaking on the willing ear of the Sacristan his sincere wish, that any spirit, black, white, or gray. would read the adviser such a lesson, as to cure him of his presumption in esteeming himself wiser than the whole community.

"I wish him no worse lesson," said the Sacristan, "than to go swimming merrily down the river with a ghost behind, and Kelpies, night-crows, and mud-eels, all waiting to have a snatch at him.

Merrily swim we, the moon shines bright!
Good luck to your fishing, whom watch you to-night?"

"Brother Philip," said the Abbot, "we exhort thee to say thy prayers, compose thyself, and banish that foolish chant from thy mind;—it is but a deception of the devil's."

"I will essay, reverend Father," said the Sacristan, "but the tune hangs by my memory like a bur in a beggar's rags; it mingles with the psalter—the very bells of the convent seem to repeat the words, and jingle to the tune; and were you to put me to death at this very moment, it is my belief I should die singing it—'Now swim we merrily'—it is as it were a spell upon me."

He then again began to warble

"Good luck to your fishing.

And checking himself in the strain with difficulty, he exclaimed, "It is too certain—I am but a lost priest! Swim we merrily—I shall sing it at the very mass—Wo is me! I shall sing all the remainder of my life, and yet never be able to change the tune!"

The honest Abbot replied, "he knew many a good fellow in the same condition;" and concluded the remark with "ho! ho! ho!" for his reverence, as the reader may partly have observed, was one of those dull folks who love a quiet joke.

The Sacristan, well acquainted with his Superior's humour, endeavoured to join in the laugh, but his unfortunate canticle came again across his imagination, and interrupted the hilarity of his customary echo.

"By the rood, Brother Philip," said the Abbot, much moved, "you become altogether intolerable! and I am convinced that such a spell could not subsist over a person of religion, and in a religious house, unless he were under mortal sin. Wherefore, say the seven penitentiary psalms—make diligent use of thy scourge and hair-cloth—refrain for three days from all food, save bread and water—I myself will shrive thee, and we will see if this singing devil may be driven out of thee; at least I think Father Eustace himself could devise no better exorcism."

The Sacristan sighed deeply, but knew remonstrance was vain. He retired therefore to his cell, to try how far psalmody might be able to drive off the sounds of the syren tune which haunted his memory.

Meanwhile, Father Eustace proceeded to the drawbridge, in his way to the lonely valley of Glendearg. In a brief conversation with the churlish warder, he had the address to render him more tractable in the controversy betwixt him and the convent. He reminded him that his father had been a vassal under the community; that his brother was childless; and that their possession would revert to the church on his death, and might be either granted to himself the warder, or to some greater favourite of the Abbot, as matters chanced to stand betwixt them at the time. The Sub-Prior suggested to him also, the necessary connexion of interests betwixt the Monastery and the office which this man enjoyed. He listened with temper to his rude and churlish answers; and by keeping his own interest firm pitched in his view, he had the satisfaction to find that Peter gradually softened his tone, and consented to let every pilgrim who travelled upon foot pass free of exaction until Pentecost next; they who travelled on horseback or otherwise, contenting to pay the ordinary custom. Having thus accommodated a matter in which the weal of the convent was so deeply interested, Father Eustace proceeded on his journey.

Chapter the Eighth.

Nay, dally not with time, the wise man's treasure,
Though fools are lavish on't — the fatal Fisher
Hooks souls, while we waste moments.

OLD PLAY.

A NOVEMBER mist overspread the little valley, up which slowly but steadily rode the Monk Eustace. He was not insensible to the feeling of melancholy inspired by the scene and by the season. The stream seemed to murmur with a deep and oppressed note, as if bewailing the departure of autumn. Among the scattered copses which here and there fringed its banks, the oak-trees only retained that pallid green that precedes their russet hue. The leaves of the willows were most of them stripped from the branches, lay rustling at each breath, and disturbed by every step of the mule; while the foliage of other trees, totally withered, kept still precarious possession of the boughs, waiting the first wind to scatter them.

The monk dropped into the natural train of pensive thought which these autumnal emblems of mortal hopes are peculiarly calculated to inspire. "There," he said, looking at the leaves which lay strewed around, "lie the hopes of early youth, first formed that they may soonest wither, and loveliest in spring to become most contemptible in winter; but you, ye lingerers," he added, looking to a knot of beeches which still bore their withered leaves, "you are the proud plans of adventurous manhood, formed later, and still clinging to the mind of age, although it acknowledges their inanity! None lasts — none endures, save the foliage of the hardy oak, which only begins to show itself when that of the rest of the forest has enjoyed half its existence. A pale and decayed hue is all it possesses, but still it retains that symptom of vitality to the last. — So be it with Father Eustace! The fairy hopes of my youth I have trodden under foot like those neglected rustlers — to the prouder dreams of my manhood I look back as to lofty chimeras, of which the pith and essence have long since faded; but my religious vows, the faithful profession which I have made in my maturer age, shall retain life while aught of Eustace lives. Dangerous it may be — feeble it must be — yet live it shall, the proud determination to serve the Church of which I am a member, and to combat the heresies by which she is assailed." Thus spoke, at least thus thought, a man zealous according to his imperfect knowledge, confounding the vital interests of Christianity with the extravagant and usurped claims of the Church of Rome, and defending his cause with an ardour worthy of a better.

While moving onward in this contemplative mood, he could not help thinking more than once, that he saw in his path the form of a female dressed in white, who appeared in the attitude of lamentation. But the impression was only momentary, and whenever he looked steadily to the point where he conceived the figure appeared, it always proved that he had mistaken some natural object, a white crag, or the trunk of a decayed birch-tree with its silver bark, for the appearance in question.

Father Eustace had dwelt too long in Rome to partake the superstitious feelings of the more ignorant Scottish clergy; yet he certainly thought it extraordinary, that so strong an impression should have been made on his mind by the legend of the Sacristan. "It is strange," he said to himself, "that this story, which doubtless was the invention of Brother Philip to cover his own impropriety of conduct, should run so much in my head, and disturb my more serious thoughts — I am wont, I think, to have more command over my senses. I will repeat my prayers, and banish such folly from my recollection."

The monk accordingly began with devotion to tell his beads, in pursuance of the prescribed rule of his order, and was not again disturbed by any wanderings of the imagination, until he found himself beneath the little fortalice of Glendearg.

Dame Glendinning, who stood at the gate, set up a shout of surprise and joy at seeing the good father. "Martin," she said, "Jasper, where be a' the folk?—help the right reverend Sub-Prior to dismount, and take his mule from him.—O father! God has sent you in our need—I was just going to send man and horse to the convent, though I ought to be ashamed to give so much trouble to your reverences."

"Our trouble matters not, good dame," said Father Eustace; "in what can I pleasure you? I came hither to visit the Lady of Avenel."

"Well-a-day!" said Dame Alice, "and it was on her part that I had the boldness to think of summoning you, for the good lady will never be able to wear over the day!—Would it please you to go to her chamber?"

"Hath she not been shriven by Father Philip?" said the monk.

"Shriven she was," said the Dame of Glendearg, "and by Father Philip, as your reverence truly says—but—I wish it may have been a clean shrift—Methought Father Philip looked but moody upon it—and there was a book which he took away with him, that——" She paused as if unwilling to proceed.

"Speak out, Dame Glendinning," said the Father; "with us it is your duty to have no secrets."

"Nay, if it please your reverence, it is not that I would keep anything from your reverence's knowledge, but I fear I should prejudice the lady in your opinion; for she is an excellent lady—months and years has she dwelt in this tower, and none more exemplary than she; but this matter, doubtless, she will explain it herself to your reverence."

"I desire first to know it from you, Dame Glendinning," said the monk; "and I again repeat, it is your duty to tell it to me."

"This book, if it please your reverence, which Father Philip removed from Glendearg, was this morning returned to us in a strange manner," said the good widow.

"Returned!" said the monk; "how mean you?"

"I mean," answered Dame Glendinning, "that it was brought back to the tower of Glendearg, the saints best know how—that same book which Father Philip carried with him but yesterday. Old Martin, that is my tasker and the lady's servant, was driving out the cows to the pasture—for we have three good milk-cows, reverend father, blessed be Saint Waldave, and thanks to the holy Monastery——"

The monk groaned with impatience; but he remembered that a woman of the good dame's condition was like a top, which, if you let it spin on untouched, must at last come to a pause; but, if you interrupt it by flogging, there is no end to its gyrations. "But, to speak no more of the cows, your reverence, though they are likely cattle as ever were tied to a stake, the tasker was driving them out, and the lads, that is my Halbert and my Edward, that your reverence has seen at church on holidays, and especially Halbert,—for you patted him on the head and gave him a brooch of Saint Cuthbert, which he wears in his bonnet,—and little Mary Avenel, that is the lady's daughter, they ran all after the cattle, and began to play up and down the pasture as young folk will, your reverence. And at length they lost sight of Martin and the cows; and they began to run up a little cleugh which we call *Corri-nan-Shian*, where there is a wee bit stripe of a burn, and they saw there—Good guide us!—a White Woman sitting on the burnside wringing her hands—so the bairns were frighted to see a strange woman sitting there, all but Halbert, who will be sixteen come Whitsuntide; and, besides, he never feared ony thing—and when they went up to her—behold she was passed away!"

"For shame, good woman!" said Father Eustace; "a woman of your sense to listen to a tale so idle! — the young folk told you a lie, and that was all."

"Nay, sir, it was more than that," said the old dame; "for, besides that they never told me a lie in their lives, I must warn you that on the very ground where the White Woman was sitting, they found the Lady of Avenel's book, and brought it with them to the tower."

"That is worthy of mark at least," said the monk. "Know you no other copy of this volume within these bounds?"

"None, your reverence," returned Elspeth; "why should there? — no one could read it were there twenty."

"Then you are sure it is the very same volume which you gave to Father Philip?" said the monk.

"As sure as that I now speak with your reverence."

"It is most singular!" said the monk; and he walked across the room in a musing posture.

"I have been upon nettles to hear what your reverence would say," continued Dame Glendinning, "respecting this matter — There is nothing I would not do for the Lady of Avenel and her family, and that has been proved, and for her servants to boot, both Martin and Tibb, although Tibb is not so civil sometimes as altogether I have a right to expect; but I cannot think it beseeming to have angels, or ghosts, or fairies, or the like, waiting upon a leddy when she is in another woman's house, in respect it is no ways creditable. Ony thing she had to do was always done to her hand, without costing her either pains or pence, as a country body says; and besides the discredit, I cannot but think that there is no safety in having such unchancy creatures about ane. But I have tied red thread round the bairns's throats," (so her fondness still called them,) "and given ilka ane of them a riding-wand of rowan-tree, forby sewing up a slip of witch-elm into their doublets; and I wish to know of your reverence if there be ony thing mair that a lone woman can do in the matter of ghosts and fairies? — Be here! that I should have named their unlucky names twice ower!"

"Dame Glendinning," answered the monk, somewhat abruptly, when the good woman had finished her narrative, "I pray you, do you know the miller's daughter?"

"Did I know Kate Happer?" replied the widow; "as well as the beggar knows his dish — a canty quean was Kate, and a special cummer of my ain maybe twenty years syne."

"She cannot be the wench I mean," said Father Eustace; "she after whom I inquire is scarce fifteen, a black-eyed girl — you may have seen her at the kirk."

"Your reverence must be in the right; and she is my cummer's niece, doubtless, that you are pleased to speak of: but I thank God I have always been too duteous in attention to the mass, to know whether young wenches have black eyes or green ones."

The good father had so much of the world about him, that he was unable to avoid smiling, when the dame boasted her absolute resistance to a temptation, which was not quite so liable to beset her as those of the other sex.

"Perhaps, then," he said, "you know her usual dress, Dame Glendinning?"

"Ay, ay, father," answered the dame readily enough, "a white kirtle the wench wears, to hide the dust of the mill, no doubt — and a blue hood, that might weel be spared, for pridefulness."

"Then, may it not be she," said the father, "who has brought back this book, and stepped out of the way when the children came near her?"

The dame paused — was unwilling to combat the solution suggested by the monk — but was at a loss to conceive why the lass of the mill should come so far from home into so wild a corner merely to leave an old book with three children, from whose observation she wished to conceal herself.

Above all, she could not understand why, since she had acquaintances in the family, and since the Dame Glendinning had always paid her multure and knaveship duly, the said lass of the mill had not come in to rest herself and eat a morsel, and tell her the current news of the water.

These very objections satisfied the monk that his conjectures were right. "Dame," he said, "you must be cautious in what you say. This is an instance — I would it were the sole one — of the power of the Enemy in these days. The matter must be sifted with a curious and a careful hand."

"Indeed," said Elspeth, trying to catch and chime in with the ideas of the Sub-Prior, "I have often thought the miller's folk at the Monastery-mill were far over careless in sifting our melder, and in bolting it too — some folk say they will not stick at whiles to put in a handful of ashes amongst Christian folk's corn-meal."

"That shall be looked after also, dame," said the Sub-Prior, not displeased to see that the good old woman went off on a false scent; "and now, by your leave, I will see this lady — do you go before, and prepare her to see me."

Dame Glendinning left the lower apartment accordingly, which the monk paced in anxious reflection, considering how he might best discharge, with humanity as well as with effect, the important duty imposed on him. He resolved to approach the bedside of the sick person with reprimands, mitigated only by a feeling for her weak condition — he determined, in case of her reply, to which late examples of hardened heretics might encourage her, to be prepared with answers to the customary scruples. High fraught, also, with zeal against her unauthorized intrusion into the priestly function, by study of the Sacred Scriptures, he imagined to himself the answers which one of the modern school of heresy might return to him — the victorious refutation which should lay the disputant prostrate at the Confessor's mercy — and the healing, yet awful exhortation, which, under pain of refusing the last consolations of religion, he designed to make to the penitent, conjuring her, as she loved her own soul's welfare, to disclose to him what she knew of the dark mystery of iniquity, by which heresies were introduced into the most secluded spots of the very patrimony of the Church herself — what agents they had who could thus glide, as it were unseen, from place to place, bring back the volume which the Church had interdicted to the spots from which it had been removed under her express auspices; and, who, by encouraging the daring and profane thirst after knowledge forbidden and useless to the laity, had encouraged the fisher of souls to use with effect his old bait of ambition and vain-glory.

Much of this premeditated disputation escaped the good father, when Elspeth returned, her tears flowing faster than her apron could dry them, and made him a signal to follow her. "How," said the monk, "is she then so near her end? — nay, the Church must not break or bruise, when comfort is yet possible;" and forgetting his polemics, the good Sub-Prior hastened to the little apartment, where, on the wretched bed which she had occupied since her misfortunes had driven her to the Tower of Glendearg, the widow of Walter Avenel had rendered up her spirit to her Creator. "My God!" said the Sub-Prior, "and has my unfortunate dallying suffered her to depart without the Church's consolation! Look to her, dame," he exclaimed, with eager impatience; "is there not yet a sparkle of the life left? — may she not be recalled — recalled but for a moment? — Oh! would that she could express, but by the most imperfect word — but by the most feeble motion, her acquiescence in the needful task of penitential prayer! — Does she not breathe? — Art thou sure she doth not?"

"She will never breathe more," said the matron. "Oh! the poor fatherless girl — now motherless also — Oh, the kind companion I have had these many years, whom I shall never see again! But she is in heaven for certain, if ever woman went there; for a woman of better life——"

"Wo to me," said the good monk, "if indeed she went not hence in good assurance — wo to the reckless shepherd, who suffered the wolf to carry a choice one from the flock, while he busied himself with trimming his sling and his staff to give the monster battle! Oh! if in the long Hereafter, aught but weal should that poor spirit share, what has my delay cost?—the value of an immortal soul!"

He then approached the body, full of the deep remorse natural to a good man of his persuasion, who devoutly believed the doctrines of the Catholic Church. "Ay," said he, gazing on the pallid corpse, from which the spirit had parted so placidly as to leave a smile upon the thin blue lips, which had been so long wasted by decay that they had parted with the last breath of animation without the slightest convulsive tremor — "Ay," said Father Eustace, "there lies the faded tree, and, as it fell, so it lies—awful thought for me, should my neglect have left it to descend in an evil direction!" He then again and again conjured Dame Glendinning to tell him what she knew of the demeanour and ordinary walk of the deceased.

All tended to the high honour of the deceased lady; for her companion, who admired her sufficiently while alive, notwithstanding some trifling points of jealousy, now idolized her after her death, and could think of no attribute of praise with which she did not adorn her memory.

Indeed, the Lady of Avenel, however she might privately doubt some of the doctrines announced by the Church of Rome, and although she had probably tacitly appealed from that corrupted system of Christianity to the volume on which Christianity itself is founded, had nevertheless been regular in her attendance on the worship of the Church, not, perhaps, extending her scruples so far as to break off communion. Such indeed was the first sentiment of the earlier reformers, who seemed to have studied, for a time at least, to avoid a schism, until the violence of the Pope rendered it inevitable.

Father Eustace, on the present occasion, listened with eagerness to everything which could lead to assure him of the lady's orthodoxy in the main points of belief; for his conscience reproached him sorely, that, instead of protracting conversation with the Dame of Glendearg, he had not instantly hastened where his presence was so necessary. "If," he said, addressing the dead body, "thou art yet free from the utmost penalty due to the followers of false doctrine—if thou dost but suffer for a time, to expiate faults done in the body, but partaking of mortal frailty more than of deadly sin, fear not that thy abode shall be long in the penal regions to which thou mayest be doomed—if vigils—if masses—if penance—if maceration of my body, till it resembles that extenuated form which the soul hath abandoned, may assure thy deliverance. The Holy Church—the godly foundation—our blessed Patroness herself, shall intercede for one whose errors were counterbalanced by so many virtues.—Leave me, dame—here, and by her bed-side, will I perform those duties which this piteous case demands!"

Elspeth left the monk, who employed himself in fervent and sincere, though erroneous prayers, for the weal of the departed spirit. For an hour he remained in the apartment of death, and then returned to the hall, where he found the still weeping friend of the deceased.

But it would be injustice to Mrs. Glendinning's hospitality, if we suppose her to have been weeping during this long interval, or rather if we suppose her so entirely absorbed by the tribute of sorrow which she paid frankly and plentifully to her deceased friend, as to be incapable of attending to the rights of hospitality due to the holy visiter—who was confessor at once, and Sub-Prior—mighty in all religious and secular considerations, so far as the vassals of the Monastery were interested.

Her barley-bread had been toasted — her choicest cask of home-brewed ale had been broached — her best butter had been placed on the hall-table, along with her most savoury ham, and her choicest cheese, ere she aban doned herself to the extremity of sorrow; and it was not till she had arranged her little repast neatly on the board, that she sat down in the chimney corner, threw her checked apron over her head, and gave way to the current of tears and sobs. In this there was no grimace or affectation. The good dame held the honours of her house to be as essential a duty, especially when a monk was her visitant, as any other pressing call upon her conscience; nor until these were suitably attended to did she find herself at liberty to indulge her sorrow for her departed friend.

When she was conscious of the Sub-Prior's presence, she rose with the same attention to his reception; but he declined all the offers of hospitality with which she endeavoured to tempt him. Not her butter, as yellow as gold, and the best, she assured him, that was made in the patrimony of St. Mary — not the barley scones, which "the departed saint, God sain her! used to say were so good" — not the ale, nor any other cates which poor Elspeth's stores afforded, could prevail on the Sub-Prior to break his fast.

"This day," he said, "I must not taste food until the sun go down, happy if, in so doing, I can expiate my own negligence — happier still, if my sufferings of this trifling nature, undertaken in pure faith and singleness of heart, may benefit the soul of the deceased. Yet, dame," he added, I may not so far forget the living in my cares for the dead, as to leave behind me that book, which is to the ignorant what, to our first parents, the tree of Knowledge of Good and Evil unhappily proved—excellent indeed in itself, but fatal because used by those to whom it is prohibited."

"Oh, blithely, reverend father," said the widow of Simon Glendinning, "will I give you the book, if so be I can while it from the bairns; and indeed, poor things, as the case stands with them even now, you might take the heart out of their bodies, and they never find it out, they are sae begrutten."*

"Give them this missal instead, good dame," said the father, drawing from his pocket one which was curiously illuminated with paintings, "and I will come myself, or send one at a fitting time, and teach them the meaning of these pictures."

"The bonny images!" said Dame Glendinning, forgetting for an instant her grief in her admiration, "and weel I wot," added she, "it is another sort of a book than the poor Lady of Avenel's; and blessed might we have been this day, if your reverence had found the way up the glen, instead of Father Philip, though the Sacristan is a powerful man too, and speaks as if he would ger the house fly abroad, save that the walls are gey thick. Simon's forebears (may he and they be blessed!) took care of that."

The monk ordered his mule, and was about to take his leave; and the good dame was still delaying him with questions about the funeral, when a horseman, armed and accoutred, rode into the little court-yard which surrounded the Keep.

* *Begrutten* — over-weeped.

Chapter the Ninth.

For since they rode among our doors
With splent on spauld and rusty spurs,
There grows no fruit into our furs;
Thus said John Up-on-land.
BANNATYNE MS.

THE Scottish laws, which were as wisely and judiciously made as they were carelessly and ineffectually executed, had in vain endeavoured to restrain the damage done to agriculture, by the chiefs and landed proprietors retaining in their service what were called jack-men, from the *jack*, or doublet quilted with iron which they wore as defensive armour. These military retainers conducted themselves with great insolence towards the industrious part of the community—lived in a great measure by plunder, and were ready to execute any commands of their master, however unlawful. In adopting this mode of life, men resigned the quiet hopes and regular labours of industry, for an unsettled, precarious, and dangerous trade, which yet had such charms for those once accustomed to it, that they became incapable of following any other. Hence the complaint of John Upland, a fictitious character, representing a countryman, into whose mouth the poets of the day put their general satires upon men and manners.

They ride about in such a rage,
By forest, frith, and field,
With buckler, bow, and brand.
Lo! where they ride out through the rye!
The Devil mot save the company,
Quoth John Up-on-land.

Christie of the Clinthill, the horseman who now arrived at the little Tower of Glendearg, was one of the hopeful company of whom the poet complains, as was indicated by his "splent on spauld," (iron-plates on his shoulder,) his rusted spurs, and his long lance. An iron skull-cap, none of the brightest, bore for distinction a sprig of the holly, which was Avenel's badge. A long two-edged straight sword, having a handle made of polished oak, hung down by his side. The meagre condition of his horse, and the wild and emaciated look of the rider, showed their occupation could not be accounted an easy or a thriving one. He saluted Dame Glendinning with little courtesy, and the monk with less; for the growing disrespect to the religious orders had not failed to extend itself among a class of men of such disorderly habits, although it may be supposed they were tolerably indifferent alike to the new or the ancient doctrines.

"So, our lady is dead, Dame Glendinning?" said the jack-man; "my master has sent you even now a fat bullock for her mart—it may serve for her funeral. I have left him in the upper cleugh, as he is somewhat kenspeckle,* and is marked both with cut and birn—the sooner the skin is off, and he is in saultfat, the less like you are to have trouble—you understand me? Let me have a peck of corn for my horse, and beef and beer for myself, for I must go on to the Monastery—though I think this monk here might do mine errand."

"Thine errand, rude man!" said the Sub-Prior, knitting his brows——

"For God's sake!" cried poor Dame Glendinning, terrified at the idea of a quarrel between them,—"O Christie!—it is the Sub-Prior—O reverend sir, it is Christie of the Clinthill, the laird's chief jack-man; ye know that little havings can be expected from the like o' them."

"Are you a retainer of the Laird of Avenel?" said the monk, addressing

* *Kenspeckle*—that which is easily recognized by the eye.

himself to the horseman, "and do you speak thus rudely to a brother of Saint Mary's, to whom thy master is so much beholden?"

"He means to be yet more beholden to your house, Sir Monk," answered the fellow; "for hearing his sister-in-law, the widow of Walter of Avenel, was on her death-bed, he sent me to say to the Father Abbot and the brethren, that he will hold the funeral-feast at their convent, and invites himself thereto, with a score of horse and some friends, and to abide there for three days and three nights, — having horse-meat and men's-meat at the charge of the community; of which his intention he sends due notice, that fitting preparation may be timeously made."

"Friend," said the Sub-Prior, "believe not that I will do to the Father Abbot the indignity of delivering such an errand.—Think'st thou the goods of the church were bestowed upon her by holy princes and pious nobles, now dead and gone, to be consumed in revelry by every profligate layman who numbers in his train more followers than he can support by honest means, or by his own incomings? Tell thy master, from the Sub-Prior of Saint Mary's, that the Primate hath issued his commands to us that we submit no longer to this compulsory exaction of hospitality on slight or false pretences. Our lands and goods were given to relieve pilgrims and pious persons, not to feast bands of rude soldiers."

"This to me!" said the angry spearman, "this to me and to my master — Look to yourself then, Sir Priest, and try if *Ave* and *Credo* will keep bullocks from wandering, and hay-stacks from burning."

"Dost thou menace the Holy Church's patrimony with waste and fire-raising," said the Sub-Prior, "and that in the face of the sun? I call on all who hear me to bear witness to the words this ruffian has spoken. Remember how the Lord James drowned such as you by scores in the black pool at Jeddart.—To him and to the Primate will I complain." The soldier shifted the position of his lance, and brought it down to a level with the monk's body.

Dame Glendinning began to shriek for assistance. "Tibb Tacket! Martin! where be ye all? — Christie, for the love of God, consider he is a man of Holy Kirk!"

"I care not for his spear," said the Sub-Prior; "if I am slain in defending the rights and privileges of my community, the Primate will know how to take vengeance."

"Let him look to himself," said Christie, but at the same time depositing his lance against the wall of the tower; "if the Fife men spoke true who came hither with the Governor in the last raid, Norman Leslie has him at feud, and is like to set him hard. We know Norman a true bloodhound, who will never quit the slot. But I had no design to offend the holy father," he added, thinking perhaps he had gone a little too far; "I am a rude man, bred to lance and stirrup, and not used to deal with book-learned men and priests; and I am willing to ask his forgiveness — and his blessing, if I have said aught amiss."

"For God's sake! your reverence," said the widow of Glendearg apart to the Sub-Prior, "bestow on him your forgiveness — how shall we poor folk sleep in security in the dark nights, if the convent is at feud with such men as he is?"

"You are right, dame," said the Sub-Prior, "your safety should, and must be, in the first instance consulted. — Soldier, I forgive thee, and may God bless thee and send thee honesty."

Christie of the Clinthill made an unwilling inclination with his head, and muttered apart, "that is as much as to say, God send thee starvation. But now to my master's demand, Sir Priest? What answer am I to return?"

"That the body of the widow of Walter of Avenel," answered the Father, "shall be interred as becomes her rank, and in the tomb of her valiant husband. For your master's proffered visit of three days, with such a company and retinue, I have no authority to reply to it; you must intimate your Chief's purpose to the Reverend Lord Abbot."

"That will cost me a farther ride," said the man, "but it is all in the day's work. — How now, my lad," said he to Halbert, who was handling the long lance which he had laid aside; "how do you like such a plaything? — will you go with me and be a moss-trooper?"

"The Saints in their mercy forbid!" said the poor mother; and then, afraid of having displeased Christie by the vivacity of her exclamation, she followed it up by explaining, that since Simon's death she could not look on a spear or a bow, or any implement of destruction without trembling.

"Pshaw!" answered Christie, "thou shouldst take another husband, dame, and drive such follies out of thy thoughts — what sayst thou to such a strapping lad as I? Why, this old tower of thine is fensible enough, and there is no want of cleuchs, and crags, and bogs, and thickets, if one was set hard; a man might bide here and keep his half-score of lads, and as many geldings, and live on what he could lay his hand on, and be kind to thee, old wench."

"Alas! Master Christie," said the matron, "that you should talk to a lone woman in such a fashion, and death in the house besides!"

"Lone woman! — why, that is the very reason thou shouldst take a mate. Thy old friend is dead, why, good — choose thou another of somewhat tougher frame, and that will not die of the pip like a young chicken. — Better still — Come, dame, let me have something to eat, and we will talk more of this."

Dame Elspeth, though she well knew the character of the man, whom in fact she both disliked and feared, could not help simpering at the personal address which he thought proper to make to her. She whispered to the Sub-Prior, "ony thing just to keep him quiet," and went into the tower to set before the soldier the food he desired, trusting betwixt good cheer and the power of her own charms, to keep Christie of the Clinthill so well amused, that the altercation betwixt him and the holy father should not be renewed.

The Sub-Prior was equally unwilling to hazard any unnecessary rupture between the community and such a person as Julian of Avenel. He was sensible that moderation, as well as firmness, was necessary to support the tottering cause of the Church of Rome; and that, contrary to former times, the quarrels betwixt the clergy and laity had, in the present, usually terminated to the advantage of the latter. He resolved, therefore, to avoid farther strife by withdrawing, but failed not, in the first place, to possess himself of the volume which the Sacristan carried off the evening before, and which had been returned to the glen in such a marvellous manner.

Edward, the younger of Dame Elspeth's boys, made great objections to the book's being removed, in which Mary would probably have joined, but that she was now in her little sleeping-chamber with Tibb, who was exerting her simple skill to console the young lady for her mother's death. But the younger Glendinning stood up in defence of her property, and, with a positiveness which had hitherto made no part of his character, declared, that now the kind lady was dead, the book was Mary's, and no one but Mary should have it.

"But if it is not a fit book for Mary to read, my dear boy," said the father, gently, "you would not wish it to remain with her?"

"The lady read it," answered the young champion of property; "and so it could not be wrong — it shall not be taken away. — I wonder where Halbert is? — listening to the bravading tales of gay Christie, I reckon, — he is always wishing for fighting, and now he is out of the way."

"Why, Edward, you would not fight with me, who am both a priest and an old man?"

"If you were as good a priest as the Pope," said the boy, "and as old as the hills to boot, you shall not carry away Mary's book without her leave. I will do battle for it."

"But see you, my love," said the monk, amused with the resolute friendship manifested by the boy, "I do not take it; I only borrow it; and I leave in its place my own gay missal, as a pledge I will bring it again."

Edward opened the missal with eager curiosity, and glanced at the pictures with which it was illustrated. "Saint George and the dragon — Halbert will like that; and Saint Michael brandishing his sword over the head of the Wicked One — and that will do for Halbert too. And see the Saint John leading his lamb in the wilderness, with his little cross made of reeds, and his scrip and staff — that shall be my favourite; and where shall we find one for poor Mary? — here is a beautiful woman weeping and lamenting herself."

"This is Saint Mary Magdalen repenting of her sins, my dear boy," said the father.

"That will not suit *our* Mary; for she commits no faults, and is never angry with us, but when we do something wrong."

"Then," said the father, "I will show you a Mary, who will protect her and you, and all good children. See how fairly she is represented, with her gown covered with golden stars."

The boy was lost in wonder at the portrait of the Virgin, which the Sub-Prior turned up to him.

"This," he said, "is really like our sweet Mary; and I think I will let you take away the black book, that has no such goodly shows in it, and leave this for Mary instead. But you must promise to bring back the book, good father — for now I think upon it, Mary may like that best which was her mother's."

"I will certainly return," said the monk, evading his answer, "and perhaps I may teach you to write and read such beautiful letters as you see there written, and to paint them blue, green, and yellow, and to blazon them with gold."

"Ay, and to make such figures as these blessed Saints, and especially these two Marys?" said the boy.

"With their blessing," said the Sub-Prior, "I can teach you that art too, so far as I am myself capable of showing, and you of learning it."

"Then," said Edward, "will I paint Mary's picture—and remember you are to bring back the black book; that you must promise me."

The Sub-Prior, anxious to get rid of the boy's pertinacity, and to set forward on his return to the convent, without having any further interview with Christie the galloper, answered by giving the promise Edward required, mounted his mule, and set forth on his return homeward.

The November day was well spent ere the Sub-Prior resumed his journey; for the difficulty of the road, and the various delays which he had met with at the tower, had detained him longer than he proposed. A chill easterly wind was sighing among the withered leaves, and stripping them from the hold they had yet retained on the parent trees.

"Even so," said the monk, "our prospects in this vale of time grow more disconsolate as the stream of years passes on. Little have I gained by my journey, saving the certainty that heresy is busy among us with more than his usual activity, and that the spirit of insulting religious orders, and plundering the Church's property, so general in the eastern districts of Scotland, has now come nearer home."

The tread of a horse which came up behind him, interrupted his reverie, and he soon saw he was mounted by the same wild rider whom he had left at the tower.

"Good even, my son, and benedicite," said the Sub-Prior as he passed; but the rude soldier scarce acknowledged the greeting, by bending his head; and dashing the spurs into his horse, went on at a pace which soon left the monk and his mule far behind. And there, thought the Sub-Prior, goes another plague of the times — a fellow whose birth designed him to cultivate the earth, but who is perverted by the unhallowed and unchristian divisions of the country, into a daring and dissolute robber. The barons of Scotland are now turned masterful thieves and ruffians, oppressing the poor by violence, and wasting the Church, by extorting free-quarters from abbeys and priories, without either shame or reason. I fear me I shall be too late to counsel the Abbot to make a stand against these daring *sorners** — I must make haste." He struck his mule with his riding wand accordingly; but, instead of mending her pace, the animal suddenly started from the path, and the rider's utmost efforts could not force her forward.

"Art thou, too, infected with the spirit of the times?" said the Sub-Prior; "thou wert wont to be ready and serviceable, and art now as restive as any wild jack-man or stubborn heretic of them all."

While he was contending with the startled animal, a voice, like that of a female, chanted in his ear, or at least very close to it,

"Good evening, Sir Priest, and so late as you ride,
With your mule so fair, and your mantle so wide;
But ride you through valley, or ride you o'er hill,
There is one that has warrant to wait on you still.
Back, back,
The volume black!
I have a warrant to carry it back."

The Sub-Prior looked around, but neither bush nor brake was near which could conceal an ambushed songstress. "May Our Lady have mercy on me!" he said; "I trust my senses have not forsaken me — yet how my thoughts should arrange themselves into rhymes which I despise, and music which I care not for, or why there should be the sound of a female voice in ears, in which its melody has been so long indifferent, baffles my comprehension, and almost realizes the vision of Philip the Sacristan. Come, good mule, betake thee to the path, and let us hence while our judgment serves us."

But the mule stood as if it had been rooted to the spot, backed from the point to which it was pressed by its rider, and by her ears laid close into her neck, and her eyes almost starting from their sockets, testified that she was under great terror.

While the Sub-Prior, by alternate threats and soothing, endeavoured to reclaim the wayward animal to her duty, the wild musical voice was again heard close beside him.

"What, ho! Sub-Prior, and came you but here
To conjure a book from a dead woman's bier?
Sain you, and save you, be wary and wise,
Ride back with the book, or you'll pay for your prize.
Back, back,
There's death in the track!
In the name of my master I bid thee bear back."

"In the name of MY Master," said the astonished monk, "that name before which all things created tremble, I conjure thee to say what thou art that hauntest me thus?"

The same voice replied,

"That which is neither ill nor well,
That which belongs not to Heaven nor to hell,
A wreath of the mist, a bubble of the stream,
'Twixt a waking thought and a sleeping dream;
A form that men spy
With the half-shut eye,
In the beams of the setting sun, am I."

"This is more than simple fantasy," said the Sub-Prior, rousing himself; though, notwithstanding the natural hardihood of his temper, the

* To *sorne*, in Scotland, is to exact free quarters against the will of the landlord. It is declared equivalent to theft, by a statute passed in the year 1445. The great chieftains oppressed the monasteries very much by exactions of this nature. The community of Aberbrothwick complained of an Earl of Angus, I think, who was in the regular habit of visiting them once a-year, with a train of a thousand horse, and abiding till the whole winter provisions of the convent were exhausted.

sensible presence of a supernatural being so near him, failed not to make his blood run cold, and his hair bristle. "I charge thee," he said aloud, "be thine errand what it will, to depart and trouble me no more! False spirit, thou canst not appal any save those who do the work negligently."

The voice immediately answered:

> Vainly, Sir Prior, wouldst thou bar me my right!
> Like the star when it shoots, I can dart through the night;
> I can dance on the torrent and ride on the air,
> And travel the world with the bonny night-mare.
> Again, again,
> At the crook of the glen,
> Where bickers the burnie, I'll meet thee again."

The road was now apparently left open; for the mule collected herself, and changed from her posture of terror to one which promised advance, although a profuse perspiration, and general trembling of the joints, indicated the bodily terror she had undergone.

"I used to doubt the existence of Cabalists and Rosicrucians," thought the Sub-Prior, "but, by my Holy Order, I know no longer what to say! — My pulse beats temperately — my hand is cool — I am fasting from everything but sin, and possessed of my ordinary faculties—Either some fiend is permitted to bewilder me, or the tales of Cornelius Agrippa, Paracelsus, and others who treat of occult philosophy, are not without foundation.—At the crook of the glen? I could have desired to avoid a second meeting, but I am on the service of the Church, and the gates of hell shall not prevail against me."

He moved around accordingly, but with precaution, and not without fear; for he neither knew the manner in which, or the place where his journey might be next interrupted by his invisible attendant. He descended the glen without interruption for about a mile farther, when, just at the spot where the brook approached the steep hill, with a winding so abrupt as to leave scarcely room for a horse to pass, the mule was again visited with the same symptoms of terror which had before interrupted her course. Better acquainted than before with the cause of her restiveness, the Priest employed no effort to make her proceed, but addressed himself to the object, which he doubted not was the same that had formerly interrupted him, in the words of solemn exorcism prescribed by the Church of Rome on such occasions.

In reply to his demand, the voice again sung;—

> "Men of good are bold as sackless,*
> Men of rude are wild and reckless,
> Lie thou still
> In the nook of the hill,
> For those be before thee that wish thee ill."

While the Sub-Prior listened, with his head turned in the direction from which the sounds seemed to come, he felt as if something rushed against him; and ere he could discover the cause, he was pushed from his saddle with gentle but irresistible force. Before he reached the ground his senses were gone, and he lay long in a state of insensibility; for the sunset had not ceased to gild the top of the distant hill when he fell, — and when he again became conscious of existence, the pale moon was gleaming on the landscape. He awakened in a state of terror, from which, for a few minutes, he found it difficult to shake himself free. At length he sate upon the grass, and became sensible, by repeated exertion, that the only personal injury which he had sustained was the numbness arising from extreme cold. The motion of something near him made the blood again run to his heart, and by a sudden effort he started up, and, looking around, saw to his relief that the noise was occasioned by the footsteps of his own mule. The peaceable animal had remained quietly beside her master during his trance, browsing on the grass which grew plentifully in that sequestered nook.

* *Sackless* — Innocent.

With some exertion he collected himself, remounted the animal, and meditating upon his wild adventure, descended the glen till its junction with the broader valley through which the Tweed winds. The drawbridge was readily dropped at his first summons; and so much had he won upon the heart of the churlish warden, that Peter appeared himself with a lantern to show the Sub-Prior his way over the perilous pass.

"By my sooth, sir," he said, holding the light up to Father Eustace's face, "you look sorely travelled and deadly pale—but a little matter serves to weary out you men of the cell. I now who speak to you—I have ridden —before I was perched up here on this pillar betwixt wind and water—it may be thirty Scots miles before I broke my fast, and have had the red of a bramble rose in my cheek all the while—But will you taste some food, or a cup of distilled waters?"

"I may not," said Father Eustace, "being under a vow; but I thank you for your kindness, and pray you to give what I may not accept to the next poor pilgrim who comes hither pale and fainting, for so it shall be the better both with him here, and with you hereafter."

"By my faith, and I will do so," said Peter Bridge-Ward, "even for thy sake—It is strange now, how this Sub-Prior gets round one's heart more than the rest of these cowled gentry, that think of nothing but quaffing and stuffing!—Wife, I say—wife, we will give a cup of distilled waters and a crust of bread unto the next pilgrim that comes over; and ye may keep for the purpose the grunds of the last greybeard,* and the ill-baked bannock which the bairns couldna eat."

While Peter issued these charitable, and, at the same time, prudent injunctions, the Sub-Prior, whose mild interference had awakened the Bridge-Ward to such an act of unwonted generosity, was pacing onward to the Monastery. In the way, he had to commune with and subdue his own rebellious heart, an enemy, he was sensible, more formidable than any which the external powers of Satan could place in his way.

Father Eustace had indeed strong temptation to suppress the extraordinary incident which had befallen him, which he was the more reluctant to confess, because he had passed so severe a judgment upon Father Philip, who, as he was not unwilling to allow, had, on his return from Glendearg, encountered obstacles somewhat similar to his own. Of this the Sub-Prior was the more convinced, when, feeling in his bosom for the Book which he had brought off from the Tower of Glendearg, he found it was amissing, which he could only account for by supposing it had been stolen from him during his trance.

"If I confess this strange visitation," thought the Sub-Prior, "I become the ridicule of all my brethren—I whom the Primate sent hither to be a watch, as it were, and a check upon their follies. I give the Abbot an advantage over me which I shall never again recover, and Heaven only knows how he may abuse it, in his foolish simplicity, to the dishonour and loss of Holy Kirk.—But then, if I make not true confession of my shame, with what face can I again presume to admonish or restrain others?—Avow, proud heart," continued he, addressing himself, "that the weal of Holy Church interests thee less in this matter than thine own humiliation—Yes, Heaven has punished thee even in that point in which thou didst deem thyself most strong, in thy spiritual pride and thy carnal wisdom. Thou hast laughed at and derided the inexperience of thy brethren—stoop thyself in turn to their derision—tell what they may not believe—affirm that which they will ascribe to idle fear, or perhaps to idle falsehood—sustain the disgrace of a silly visionary, or a wilful deceiver.—Be it so, I will do my duty, and make ample confession to my Superior. If the discharge of this duty destroys my usefulness in this house, God and Our Lady will send me where I can better serve them."

---

* An old-fashioned name for an earthen jar for holding spirits.

There was no little merit in the resolution thus piously and generously formed by Father Eustace. To men of any rank the esteem of their order is naturally most dear; but in the monastic establishment, cut off, as the brethren are, from other objects of ambition, as well as from all exterior friendship and relationship, the place which they hold in the opinion of each other is all in all.

But the consciousness how much he should rejoice the Abbot and most of the other monks of Saint Mary's, who were impatient of the unauthorized, yet irresistible control, which he was wont to exercise in the affairs of the convent, by a confession which would put him in a ludicrous, or perhaps even in a criminal point of view, could not weigh with Father Eustace in comparison with the task which his belief enjoined.

As, strong in his feelings of duty, he approached the exterior gate of the Monastery, he was surprised to see torches gleaming, and men assembled around it, some on horseback, some on foot, while several of the monks, distinguished through the night by their white scapularies, were making themselves busy among the crowd. The Sub-Prior was received with a unanimous shout of joy, which at once made him sensible that he had himself been the object of their anxiety.

"There he is! there he is! God be thanked—there he is, hale and fear!" exclaimed the vassals; while the monks exclaimed, "*Te Deum laudamus*—the blood of thy servants is precious in thy sight!"

"What is the matter, children? what is the matter, my brethren?" said Father Eustace, dismounting at the gate.

"Nay, brother, if thou know'st not, we will not tell thee till thou art in the refectory," answered the monks; "suffice it that the Lord Abbot had ordered these, our zealous and faithful vassals, instantly to set forth to guard thee from imminent peril—Ye may ungirth your horses, children, and dismiss; and to-morrow, each who was at this rendezvous may send to the convent kitchen for a quarter of a yard of roast beef, and a black-jack full of double ale."*

The vassals dispersed with joyful acclamation, and the monks, with equal jubilee, conducted the Sub-Prior into the refectory.

Chapter the Tenth.

Here we stand——
Woundless and well, may Heaven's high name be bless'd for't!
As erst, ere treason couch'd a lance against us.

DECKER.

No sooner was the Sub-Prior hurried into the refectory by his rejoicing companions, than the first person on whom he fixed his eye proved to be Christie of the Clinthill. He was seated in the chimney-corner, fettered and guarded, his features drawn into that air of sulky and turbid resolution with which those hardened in guilt are accustomed to view the approach of punishment. But as the Sub-Prior drew near to him, his face assumed a more wild and startled expression, while he exclaimed—"The devil! the devil himself, brings the dead back upon the living!"

"Nay," said a monk to him, "say rather that Our Lady foils the attempts of the wicked on her faithful servants—our dear brother lives and moves."

* It was one of the few reminiscences of Old Parr, or Henry Jenkins, I forget which, that, at some convent in the veteran's neighbourhood, the community, before the dissolution, used to dole out roast-beef by the measure of feet and yards.

"Lives and moves!" said the ruffian, rising and shuffling towards the Sub-Prior as well as his chains would permit; "nay, then, I will never trust ashen shaft and steel point more — It is even so," he added, as he gazed on the Sub-Prior with astonishment; "neither wem nor wound—not as much as a rent in his frock!"

"And whence should my wound have come?" said Father Eustace.

"From the good lance that never failed me before," replied Christie of the Clinthill.

"Heaven absolve thee for thy purpose!" said the Sub-Prior; "wouldst thou have slain a servant of the altar?"

"To choose!" answered Christie; "the Fifemen say, an the whole pack of ye were slain, there were more lost at Flodden."

"Villain! art thou heretic as well as murderer?"

"Not I, by Saint Giles," replied the rider; "I listened blithely enough to the Laird of Monance, when he told me ye were all cheats and knaves; but when he would have had me go hear one Wiseheart, a gospeller as they call him, he might as well have persuaded the wild colt that had flung one rider to kneel down and help another into the saddle."

"There is some goodness about him yet," said the Sacristan to the Abbot, who at that moment entered—"He refused to hear a heretic preacher."

"The better for him in the next world," answered the Abbot. "Prepare for death, my son, — we deliver thee over to the secular arm of our bailie, for execution on the Gallow-hill by peep of light."

"Amen!" said the ruffian; "'tis the end I must have come by sooner or later — and what care I whether I feed the crows at Saint Mary's or at Carlisle?"

"Let me implore your reverend patience for an instant," said the Sub-Prior; "until I shall inquire——"

"What!" exclaimed the Abbot, observing him for the first time—"Our dear brother restored to us when his life was unhoped for!—nay, kneel not to a sinner like me—stand up—thou hast my blessing. When this villain came to the gate, accused by his own evil conscience, and crying out he had murdered thee, I thought that the pillar of our main aisle had fallen — no more shall a life so precious be exposed to such risks as occur in this border country; no longer shall one beloved and rescued of Heaven hold so low a station in the church as that of a poor Sub-Prior—I will write by express to the Primate for thy speedy removal and advancement."

"Nay, but let me understand," said the Sub-Prior; "did this soldier say he had slain me?"

"That he had transfixed you," answered the Abbot, "in full career with his lance — but it seems he had taken an indifferent aim. But no sooner didst thou fall to the ground mortally gored, as he deemed, with his weapon, than our blessed Patroness appeared to him, as he averred——"

"I averred no such thing," said the prisoner; "I said a woman in white interrupted me, as I was about to examine the priest's cassock, for they are usually well lined—she had a bulrush in her hand, with one touch of which she struck me from my horse, as I might strike down a child of four years old with an iron mace — and then, like a singing fiend as she was, she sung to me.

'Thank the holly-bush
 That nods on thy brow;
Or with this slender rush
 I had strangled thee now.'

I gathered myself up with fear and difficulty, threw myself on my horse, and came hither like a fool to get myself hanged for a rogue."

"Thou seest, honoured brother," said the Abbot to the Sub-Prior, "in what favour thou art with our blessed Patroness, that she herself becomes the guardian of thy paths—Not since the days of our blessed founder hath she shown such grace to any one. All unworthy were we to hold spiritual superiority over thee, and we pray thee to prepare for thy speedy removal to Aberbrothwick."

"Alas! my lord and father," said the Sub-Prior, "your words pierce my very soul. Under the seal of confession will I presently tell thee why I conceive myself rather the baffled sport of a spirit of another sort, than the protected favourite of the heavenly powers. But first let me ask this unhappy man a question or two."

"Do as ye list," replied the Abbot—"but you shall not convince me that it is fitting you remain in this inferior office in the convent of Saint Mary."

"I would ask of this poor man," said Father Eustace, "for what purpose he nourished the thought of putting to death one who never did him evil?"

"Ay! but thou didst menace me with evil," said the ruffian, "and no one but a fool is menaced twice. Dost thou not remember what you said touching the Primate and Lord James, and the black pool of Jedwood? Didst thou think me fool enough to wait till thou hadst betrayed me to the sack and the fork! There were small wisdom in that, methinks — as little as in coming hither to tell my own misdeeds — I think the devil was in me when I took this road — I might have remembered the proverb, 'Never Friar forgot feud.'"

"And it was solely for that — for that only hasty word of mine, uttered in a moment of impatience, and forgotten ere it was well spoken?" said Father Eustace.

"Ay! for that, and—for the love of thy gold crucifix," said Christie of the Clinthill.

"Gracious Heaven! and could the yellow metal — the glittering earth—so far overcome every sense of what is thereby represented?—Father Abbot, I pray, as a dear boon, you will deliver this guilty person to my mercy."

"Nay, brother," interposed the Sacristan, "to your doom, if you will, not to your mercy — Remember, we are not all equally favoured by our blessed Lady, nor is it likely that every frock in the Convent will serve as a coat of proof when a lance is couched against it."

"For that very reason," said the Sub-Prior, "I would not that for my worthless self the community were to fall at feud with Julian of Avenel, this man's master."

"Our Lady forbid!" said the Sacristan, "he is a second Julian the Apostate."

"With our reverend father the Abbot's permission, then," said Father Eustace, "I desire this man be freed from his chains, and suffered to depart uninjured; — and here, friend," he added, giving him the golden crucifix, "is the image for which thou wert willing to stain thy hands with murder. View it well, and may it inspire thee with other and better thoughts than those which referred to it as a piece of bullion! Part with it, nevertheless, if thy necessities require, and get thee one of such coarse substance that Mammon shall have no share in any of the reflections to which it gives rise. It was the bequest of a dear friend to me; but dearer service can it never do than that of winning a soul to Heaven."

The Borderer, now freed from his chains, stood gazing alternately on the Sub-Prior, and on the golden crucifix. "By Saint Giles," said he, "I understand ye not! — An ye give me gold for couching my lance at thee, what would you give me to level it at a heretic?"

"The Church," said the Sub-Prior, "will try the effect of her spiritual censures to bring these stray sheep into the fold, ere she employ the edge of the sword of Saint Peter."

"Ay, but," said the ruffian, "they say the Primate recommends a little strangling and burning in aid of both censure and of sword. But fare ye weel, I owe you a life, and it may be I will not forget my debt."

The bailie now came bustling in, dressed in his blue coat and bandaliers, and attended by two or three halberdiers. "I have been a thought too late in waiting upon your reverend lordship. I am grown somewhat fatter since the field of Pinkie, and my leathern coat slips not on so soon as it was won't; but the dungeon is ready, and though, as I said, I have been somewhat late——"

Here his intended prisoner walked gravely up to the officer's nose, to his great amazement.

"You have been indeed somewhat late, bailie," said he, "and I am greatly obligated to your buff-coat, and to the time you took to put it on. If the secular arm had arrived some quarter of an hour sooner, I had been out of the reach of spiritual grace; but as it is, I wish you good even, and a safe riddance out of your garment of durance, in which you have much the air of a hog in armour."

Wroth was the bailie at this comparison, and exclaimed in ire — "An it were not for the presence of the venerable Lord Abbot, thou knave——"

"Nay, an thou wouldst try conclusions," said Christie of the Clinthill, "I will meet thee at day-break by Saint Mary's Well."

"Hardened wretch!" said Father Eustace, "art thou but this instant delivered from death, and dost thou so soon morse thoughts of slaughter?"

"I will meet with thee ere it be long, thou knave," said the bailie, "and teach thee thine Oremus."

"I will meet thy cattle in a moonlight night before that day," said he of the Clinthill.

"I will have thee by the neck one misty morning, thou strong thief," answered the secular officer of the Church.

"Thou art thyself as strong a thief as ever rode," retorted Christie; "and if the worms were once feasting on that fat carcass of thine I might well hope to have thine office, by favour of these reverend men."

"A cast of their office, and a cast of mine," answered the bailie; "a cord and a confessor, that is all thou wilt have from us."

"Sirs," said the Sub-Prior, observing that his brethren began to take more interest than was exactly decorous in this wrangling betwixt justice and iniquity, "I pray you both to depart—Master Bailie, retire with your halberdiers, and trouble not the man whom we have dismissed.—And thou, Christie, or whatever be thy name, take thy departure, and remember thou owest thy life to the Lord Abbot's clemency."

"Nay, as to that," answered Christie, "I judge that I owe it to your own; but impute it to whom ye list, I owe a life among ye, and there is an end." And whistling as he went, he left the apartment, seeming as if he held the life which he had forfeited not worthy further thanks.

"Obstinate even to brutality!" said Father Eustace; "and yet who knows but some better ore may lie under so rude an exterior?"

"Save a thief from the gallows," said the Sacristan—"you know the rest of the proverb; and admitting, as may Heaven grant, that our lives and limbs are safe from this outrageous knave, who shall insure our meal and our malt, our herds and our flocks?"

"Marry, that will I, my brethren," said an aged monk. "Ah, brethren, you little know what may be made of a repentant robber. In Abbot Ingilram's days—ay, and I remember them as it were yesterday—the freebooters were the best welcome men that came to Saint Mary's. Ay, they paid tithe of every drove that they brought over from the South, and because they were something lightly come by, I have known them make the tithe a seventh — that is, if their confessor knew his business — ay, when we saw from the tower a score of fat bullocks, or a drove of sheep, coming down the valley, with two or three stout men-at-arms behind them with their glittering steel caps, and their black-jacks, and their long lances, the good Lord Abbot Ingilram was wont to say—he was a merry man—there come the tithes of the spoilers of the Egyptians! Ay, and I have seen the famous John the Armstrang — a fair man he was and a goodly, the more pity that hemp was ever heckled for him — I have seen him come into the Abbey-church with nine tassels of gold in his bonnet, and every tassel made of nine English nobles, and he would go from chapel to chapel, and from image to image, and from altar to altar, on his knees — and leave here a tassel, and there a noble, till there was as little gold on his bonnet as on my hood—you will find no such Border thieves now!"

"No, truly, Brother Nicolas," answered the Abbot; "they are more apt to take any gold the Church has left, than to bequeath or bestow any—and for cattle, beshrew me if I think they care whether beeves have fed on the meadows of Lanercost Abbey or of Saint Mary's!"

"There is no good thing left in them," said Father Nicolas; "they are clean naught — Ah, the thieves that I have seen! — such proper men! and as pitiful as proper, and as pious as pitiful!"

"It skills not talking of it, Brother Nicolas," said the Abbot; "and I will now dismiss you, my brethren, holding your meeting upon this our inquisition concerning the danger of our reverend Sub-Prior, instead of the attendance on the lauds this evening — Yet let the bells be duly rung for the edification of the laymen without, and also that the novices may give due reverence. — And now, benedicite, brethren! The cellarer will bestow on each a grace-cup and a morsel as ye pass the buttery, for ye have been turmoiled and anxious, and dangerous it is to fall asleep in such case with empty stomach."

"*Gratias agimus quam maximas, Domine reverendissime,*" replied the brethren, departing in their due order.

But the Sub-Prior remained behind, and falling on his knees before the Abbot, as he was about to withdraw, craved him to hear under the seal of confession the adventures of the day. The reverend Lord Abbot yawned, and would have alleged fatigue; but to Father Eustace, of all men, he was ashamed to show indifference in his religious duties. The confession, therefore, proceeded, in which Father Eustace told all the extraordinary circumstances which had befallen him during the journey. And being questioned by the Abbot, whether he was not conscious of any secret sin, through which he might have been subjected for a time to the delusions of evil spirits, the Sub-Prior admitted, with frank avowal, that he thought he might have deserved such penance for having judged with unfraternal rigour of the report of Father Philip the Sacristan.

"Heaven," said the penitent, "may have been willing to convince me, not only that he can at pleasure open a communication betwixt us and beings of a different, and, as we word it, supernatural class, but also to punish our pride of superior wisdom, or superior courage, or superior learning."

It is well said that virtue is its own reward; and I question if duty was ever more completely recompensed, than by the audience which the reverend Abbot so unwillingly yielded to the confession of the Sub-Prior. To find the object of his fear shall we say, or of his envy, or of both, accusing himself of the very error with which he had so tacitly charged him, was a corroboration of the Abbot's judgment, a soothing of his pride, and an allaying of his fears. The sense of triumph, however, rather increased than diminished his natural good-humour; and so far was Abbot Boniface from being disposed to tyrannize over his Sub-Prior in consequence of this discovery, that in his exhortation he hovered somewhat ludicrously betwixt the natural expression of his own gratified vanity, and his timid reluctance to hurt the feelings of Father Eustace.

"My brother," said he, *ex cathedra*, "it cannot have escaped your judicious observation, that we have often declined our own judgment in favour of your opinion, even about those matters which most nearly concerned the community. Nevertheless, grieved would we be, could you think that we did this, either because we deemed our own opinion less pregnant, or our wit more shallow, than that of our brethren. For it was done exclusively

H

to give our younger brethren, such as your much esteemed self, my dearest brother, that courage which is necessary to a free deliverance of your opinion,—we ofttimes setting apart our proper judgment, that our inferiors, and especially our dear brother the Sub-Prior, may be comforted and encouraged in proposing valiantly his own thoughts. Which our deference and humility may, in some sort, have produced in your mind, most reverend brother, that self-opinion of parts and knowledge, which hath led unfortunately to your over-estimating your own faculties, and thereby subjecting yourself, as is but too visible, to the japes and mockeries of evil spirits. For it is assured that Heaven always holdeth us in the least esteem when we deem of ourselves most highly, and also, on the other hand, it may be that we have somewhat departed from what became our high seat in this Abbey, in suffering ourselves to be too much guided, and even, as it were, controlled, by the voice of our inferior. Wherefore," continued the Lord Abbot, "in both of us such faults shall and must be amended—you hereafter presuming less upon your gifts and carnal wisdom, and I taking heed not so easily to relinquish mine own opinion for that of one lower in place and in office. Nevertheless, we would not that we should thereby lose the high advantage which we have derived, and may yet derive, from your wise counsels, which hath been so often recommended to us by our most reverend Primate. Wherefore, on affairs of high moment, we will call you to our presence in private, and listen to your opinion, which, if it shall agree with our own, we will deliver to the Chapter as emanating directly from ourselves; thus sparing you, dearest brother, that seeming victory which is so apt to engender spiritual pride, and avoiding ourselves the temptation of falling into that modest facility of opinion, whereby our office is lessened and our person (were that of consequence) rendered less important in the eyes of the community over which we preside."

Notwithstanding the high notions which, as a rigid Catholic, Father Eustace entertained of the sacrament of confession, as his Church calls it, there was some danger that a sense of the ridiculous might have stolen on him, when he heard his Superior, with such simple cunning, lay out a little plan for availing himself of the Sub-Prior's wisdom and experience, while he should take the whole credit to himself. Yet his conscience immediately told him he was right.

"I should have thought more," he reflected, "of the spiritual Superior, and less of the individual. I should have spread my mantle over the frailties of my spiritual father, and done what I might to support his character, and, of course, to extend his utility among the brethren, as well as with others. The Abbot cannot be humbled, but what the community must be humbled in his person. Her boast is, that over all her children, especially over those called to places of distinction, she can diffuse those gifts which are necessary to render them illustrious."

Actuated by these sentiments, Father Eustace frankly assented to the charge which his Superior, even in that moment of authority, had rather intimated than made, and signified his humble acquiescence in any mode of communicating his counsel which might be most agreeable to the Lord Abbot, and might best remove from himself all temptation to glory in his own wisdom. He then prayed the reverend Father to assign him such penance as might best suit his offence, intimating, at the same time, that he had already fasted the whole day.

"And it is that I complain of," answered the Abbot, instead of giving him credit for his abstinence; "it is these very penances, fasts, and vigils, of which we complain; as tending only to generate airs and fumes of vanity, which, ascending from the stomach into the head, do but puff us up with vain-glory and self-opinion. It is meet and beseeming that novices should undergo fasts and vigils; for some part of every community must fast, and young stomachs may best endure it. Besides, in them it abates wicked thoughts, and the desire of worldly delights. But, reverend brother, for those to fast who are dead and mortified to the world, as I and thou, is work of supererogation, and is but the matter of spiritual pride. Wherefore, I enjoin thee, most reverend brother, go to the buttery and drink two cups at least of good wine, eating withal a comfortable morsel, such as may best suit thy taste and stomach. And in respect that thine opinion of thy own wisdom hath at times made thee less conformable to, and companionable with, the weaker and less learned brethren, I enjoin thee, during the said repast, to choose for thy companion, our reverend brother Nicolas, and without interruption or impatience, to listen for a stricken hour to his narration, concerning those things which befel in the times of our venerable predecessor, Abbot Ingilram, on whose soul may Heaven have mercy! And for such holy exercises as may farther advantage your soul, and expiate the faults whereof you have contritely and humbly avowed yourself guilty, we will ponder upon that matter, and announce our will unto you the next morning.

It was remarkable, that after this memorable evening, the feelings of the worthy Abbot towards his adviser were much more kindly and friendly than when he deemed the Sub-Prior the impeccable and infallible person, in whose garment of virtue and wisdom no flaw was to be discerned. It seemed as if this avowal of his own imperfections had recommended Father Eustace to the friendship of the Superior, although at the same time this increase of benevolence was attended with some circumstances, which, to a man of the Sub-Prior's natural elevation of mind and temper, were more grievous than even undergoing the legends of the dull and verbose Father Nicolas. For instance, the Abbot seldom mentioned him to the other monks, without designing him our beloved Brother Eustace, poor man! — and now and then he used to warn the younger brethren against the snares of vain-glory and spiritual pride, which Satan sets for the more rigidly righteous, with such looks and demonstrations as did all but expressly designate the Sub-Prior as one who had fallen at one time under such delusions. Upon these occasions, it required all the votive obedience of a monk, all the philosophical discipline of the schools, and all the patience of a Christian, to enable Father Eustace to endure the pompous and patronizing parade of his honest, but somewhat thick-headed Superior. He began himself to be desirous of leaving the Monastery, or at least he manifestly declined to interfere with its affairs, in that marked and authoritative manner, which he had at first practised.

Chapter the Eleventh.

You call this education, do you not?
Why 'tis the forced march of a herd of bullocks
Before a shouting drover. The glad van
Move on at ease, and pause a while to snatch
A passing morsel from the dewy greensward,
While all the blows, the oaths, the indignation,
Fall on the croupe of the ill-fated laggard
That cripples in the rear.

OLD PLAY.

Two or three years glided on, during which the storm of the approaching alteration in church government became each day louder and more perilous. Owing to the circumstances which we have intimated in the end of the last chapter, the Sub-Prior Eustace appeared to have altered considerably his habits of life. He afforded, on all extraordinary occasions, to the Abbot, whether privately, or in the assembled Chapter, the support of his wisdom and experience; but in his ordinary habits he seemed now to live more for himself, and less for the community, than had been his former practice.

He often absented himself for whole days from the convent; and as the adventure of Glendearg dwelt deeply on his memory, he was repeatedly induced to visit that lonely tower, and to take an interest in the orphans who had their shelter under its roof. Besides, he felt a deep anxiety to know whether the volume which he had lost, when so strangely preserved from the lance of the murderer, had again found its way back to the Tower of Glendearg. "It was strange," he thought, "that a spirit," for such he could not help judging the being whose voice he had heard, "should, on the one side, seek the advancement of heresy, and, on the other, interpose to save the life of a zealous Catholic priest."

But from no inquiry which he made of the various inhabitants of the Tower of Glendearg could he learn that the copy of the translated Scriptures, for which he made such diligent inquiry, had again been seen by any of them.

In the meanwhile, the good father's occasional visits were of no small consequence to Edward Glendinning and to Mary Avenel. The former displayed a power of apprehending and retaining whatever was taught him, which filled Father Eustace with admiration. He was at once acute and industrious, alert and accurate; one of those rare combinations of talent and industry, which are seldom united.

It was the earnest desire of Father Eustace that the excellent qualities thus early displayed by Edward should be dedicated to the service of the Church, to which he thought the youth's own consent might be easily obtained, as he was of a calm, contemplative, retired habit, and seemed to consider knowledge as the principal object, and its enlargement as the greatest pleasure, in life. As to the mother, the Sub-Prior had little doubt that, trained as she was to view the monks of Saint Mary's with such profound reverence, she would be but too happy in an opportunity of enrolling one of her sons in its honoured community. But the good Father proved to be mistaken in both these particulars.

When he spoke to Elspeth Glendinning of that which a mother best loves to hear—the proficiency and abilities of her son—she listened with a delighted ear. But when Father Eustace hinted at the duty of dedicating to the service of the Church, talents which seemed fitted to defend and adorn it, the dame endeavoured always to shift the subject; and when pressed farther, enlarged on her own incapacity, as a lone woman, to manage the feu; on the advantage which her neighbours of the township were often taking of her unprotected state, and on the wish she had that Edward might fill his father's place, remain in the tower, and close her eyes.

On such occasions the Sub-Prior would answer, that even in a worldly point of view the welfare of the family would be best consulted by one of the sons entering into the community of Saint Mary's, as it was not to be supposed that he would fail to afford his family the important protection which he could then easily extend towards them. What could be a more pleasing prospect than to see him high in honour? or what more sweet than to have the last duties rendered to her by a son, reverend for his holiness of life and exemplary manners? Besides, he endeavoured to impress upon the dame, that her eldest son, Halbert, whose bold temper and headstrong indulgence of a wandering humour, rendered him incapable of learning, was, for that reason, as well as that he was her eldest born, fittest to bustle through the affairs of the world, and manage the little fief.

Elspeth durst not directly dissent from what was proposed, for fear of giving displeasure, and yet she always had something to say against it.

Halbert, she said, was not like any of the neighbour boys—he was taller by the head, and stronger by the half, than any boy of his years within the Halidome. But he was fit for no peaceful work that could be devised. If he liked a book ill, he liked a plough or a pattle worse. He had scoured his father's old broadsword—suspended it by a belt round his waist, and seldom stirred without it. He was a sweet boy and a gentle if spoken fair, but cross him and he was a born devil. "In a word," she said, bursting into tears, "deprive me of Edward, good father, and ye bereave my house of prop and pillar; for my heart tells me that Halbert will take to his father's gates, and die his father's death."

When the conversation came to this crisis, the good-humoured monk was always content to drop the discussion for the time, trusting some opportunity would occur of removing her prejudices, for such he thought them, against Edward's proposed destination.

When, leaving the mother, the Sub-Prior addressed himself to the son, animating his zeal for knowledge, and pointing out how amply it might be gratified should he agree to take holy orders, he found the same repugnance which Dame Elspeth had exhibited. Edward pleaded a want of sufficient vocation to so serious a profession—his reluctance to leave his mother, and other objections, which the Sub-Prior treated as evasive.

"I plainly perceive," he said one day, in answer to them, "that the devil has his factors as well as Heaven, and that they are equally, or, alas! the former are perhaps more active, in bespeaking for their master the first of the market. I trust, young man, that neither idleness, nor licentious pleasure, nor the love of worldly gain and worldly grandeur, the chief baits with which the great Fisher of souls conceals his hook, are the causes of your declining the career to which I would incite you. But above all I trust—above all I hope—that the vanity of superior knowledge—a sin with which those who have made proficiency in learning are most frequently beset—has not led you into the awful hazard of listening to the dangerous doctrines which are now afloat concerning religion. Better for you that you were as grossly ignorant as the beasts which perish, that that the pride of knowledge should induce you to lend an ear to the voice of heretics." Edward Glendinning listened to the rebuke with a downcast look, and failed not, when it was concluded, earnestly to vindicate himself from the charge of having pushed his studies into any subjects which the Church inhibited; and so the monk was left to form vain conjectures respecting the cause of his reluctance to embrace the monastic state.

It is an old proverb, used by Chaucer, and quoted by Elizabeth, that "the greatest clerks are not the wisest men;" and it is as true as if the poet had not rhymed, or the queen reasoned on it. If Father Eustace had not had his thoughts turned so much to the progress of heresy, and so little to what was passing in the tower, he might have read, in the speaking eyes of Mary Avenel, now a girl of fourteen or fifteen, reasons which might disincline her youthful companion towards the monastic vows. I have said, that she also was a promising pupil of the good father, upon whom her innocent and infantine beauty had an effect of which he was himself, perhaps, unconscious. Her rank and expectations entitled her to be taught the arts of reading and writing;—and each lesson which the monk assigned her was conned over in company with Edward, and by him explained and re-explained, and again illustrated, until she became perfectly mistress of it.

In the beginning of their studies, Halbert had been their school companion. But the boldness and impatience of his disposition soon quarrelled with an occupation in which, without assiduity and unremitted attention, no progress was to be expected. The Sub-Prior's visits were at regular intervals, and often weeks would intervene between them, in which case Halbert was sure to forget all that had been prescribed for him to learn, and much which he had partly acquired before. His deficiencies on these occasions gave him pain, but it was not of that sort which produces amendment.

For a time, like all who are fond of idleness, he endeavoured to detach the attention of his brother and Mary Avenel from their task, rather than to learn his own, and such dialogues as the following would ensue:

"Take your bonnet, Edward, and make haste — the Laird of Colmslie is at the head of the glen with his hounds."

"I care not, Halbert," answered the younger brother; "two brace of dogs may kill a deer without my being there to see them, and I must help Mary Avenel with her lesson."

"Ay! you will labour at the monk's lessons till you turn monk yourself," answered Halbert.—"Mary, will you go with me, and I will show you the cushat's nest I told you of?"

"I cannot go with you, Halbert," answered Mary, "because I must study this lesson — it will take me long to learn it — I am sorry I am so dull, for if I could get my task as fast as Edward, I should like to go with you."

"Should you indeed?" said Halbert; "then I will wait for you — and, what is more, I will try to get my lesson also."

With a smile and a sigh he took up the primer, and began heavily to con over the task which had been assigned him. As if banished from the society of the two others, he sat sad and solitary in one of the deep window-recesses, and after in vain struggling with the difficulties of his task, and his disinclination to learn it, he found himself involuntarily engaged in watching the movements of the other two students, instead of toiling any longer.

The picture which Halbert looked upon was delightful in itself, but somehow or other it afforded very little pleasure to him. The beautiful girl, with looks of simple, yet earnest anxiety, was bent on disentangling those intricacies which obstructed her progress to knowledge, and looking ever and anon to Edward for assistance, while, seated close by her side, and watchful to remove every obstacle from her way, he seemed at once to be proud of the progress which his pupil made, and of the assistance which he was able to render her. There was a bond betwixt them, a strong and interesting tie, the desire of obtaining knowledge, the pride of surmounting difficulties.

Feeling most acutely, yet ignorant of the nature and source of his own emotions, Halbert could no longer endure to look upon this quiet scene, but, starting up, dashed his book from him, and exclaimed aloud, "To the fiend I bequeath all books, and the dreamers that make them! — I would a score of Southrons would come up the glen, and we should learn how little all this muttering and scribbling is worth."

Mary Avenel and his brother started, and looked at Halbert with surprise, while he went on with great animation, his features swelling, and the tears starting into his eyes as he spoke. — "Yes, Mary — I wish a score of Southrons came up the glen this very day; and you should see one good hand, and one good sword, do more to protect you, than all the books that were ever opened, and all the pens that ever grew on a goose's wing."

Mary looked a little surprised and a little frightened at his vehemence, but instantly replied affectionately, "You are vexed, Halbert, because you do not get your lesson so fast as Edward can; and so am I, for I am as stupid as you—But come, and Edward shall sit betwixt us and teach us."

"He shall not teach *me*," said Halbert, in the same angry mood; "I never can teach *him* to do any thing that is honourable and manly, and he shall not teach *me* any of his monkish tricks.—I hate the monks, with their drawling nasal tone like so many frogs, and their long black petticoats like so many women, and their reverences, and their lordships, and their lazy vassals that do nothing but peddle in the mire with plough and harrow from Yule to Michaelmas. I will call none lord, but him who wears a sword to make his title good; and I will call none man, but he that can bear himself manlike and masterful."

"For Heaven's sake, peace, brother!" said Edward; "if such words were taken up and reported out of the house, they would be our mother's ruin."

"Report them yourself, then, and they will be *your* making, and nobody's marring save mine own. Say that Halbert Glendinning will never be vassal to an old man with a cowl and shaven crown, while there are twenty barons who wear casque and plume that lack bold followers. Let them grant you these wretched acres, and much meal may they bear you to make your *brachan.*" He left the room hastily, but instantly returned, and continued to speak with the same tone of quick and irritated feeling. "And you need not think so much, neither of you, and especially you, Edward, need not think so much of your parchment book there, and your cunning in reading it. By my faith, I will soon learn to read as well as you; and—for I know a better teacher than your grim old monk, and a better book than his printed breviary; and since you like scholarcraft so well, Mary Avenel, you shall see whether Edward or I have most of it." He left the apartment, and came not again.

"What can be the matter with him?" said Mary, following Halbert with her eyes from the window, as with hasty and unequal steps he ran up the wild glen—"Where can your brother be going, Edward?—what book?—what teacher does he talk of?"

"It avails not guessing," said Edward. "Halbert is angry, he knows not why, and speaks of he knows not what; let us go again to our lessons, and he will come home when he has tired himself with scrambling among the crags as usual."

But Mary's anxiety on account of Halbert seemed more deeply rooted. She declined prosecuting the task in which they had been so pleasingly engaged, under the excuse of a headach; nor could Edward prevail upon her to resume it again that morning.

Meanwhile Halbert, his head unbonneted, his features swelled with jealous anger, and the tear still in his eye, sped up the wild and upper extremity of the little valley of Glendearg with the speed of a roebuck, choosing, as if in desperate defiance of the difficulties of the way, the wildest and most dangerous paths, and voluntarily exposing himself a hundred times to dangers which he might have escaped by turning a little aside from them. It seemed as if he wished his course to be as straight as that of the arrow to its mark.

He arrived at length in a narrow and secluded *cleuch*, or deep ravine, which ran down into the valley, and contributed a scanty rivulet to the supply of the brook with which Glendearg is watered. Up this he sped with the same precipitate haste which had marked his departure from the tower, nor did he pause and look around until he had reached the fountain from which the rivulet had its rise.

Here Halbert stopt short, and cast a gloomy, and almost a frightened glance around him. A huge rock rose in front, from a cleft of which grew a wild holly-tree, whose dark green branches rustled over the spring which arose beneath. The banks on either hand rose so high, and approached each other so closely, that it was only when the sun was at its meridian height, and during the summer solstice, that its rays could reach the bottom of the chasm in which he stood. But it was now summer, and the hour was noon, so that the unwonted reflection of the sun was dancing in the pellucid fountain.

"It is the season and the hour," said Halbert to himself; "and now I——I might soon become wiser than Edward with all his pains! Mary should see whether he alone is fit to be consulted, and to sit by her side, and hang over her as she reads, and point out every word and every letter. And she loves me better than him—I am sure she does—for she comes of noble blood, and scorns sloth and cowardice.—And do I myself not stand here slothful and cowardly as any priest of them all?—Why should I fear to call upon this form—this shape?—Already have I endured the vision, and why not again? What can it do to me, who am a man of lith and limb, and have by my side my father's sword? Does my heart beat—do my hairs bristle, at the thought of calling up a painted shadow, and how should I face a band of Southrons in flesh and blood? By the soul of the first Glendinning, I will make proof of the charm!"

He cast the leathern brogue or buskin from his right foot, planted himself in a firm posture, unsheathed his sword, and first looking around to collect his resolution, he bowed three times deliberately towards the holly-tree, and as often to the little fountain, repeating at the same time, with a determined voice, the following rhyme:

"Thrice to the holly brake—
Thrice to the well:—
I bid thee awake,
White Maid of Avenel!

"Noon gleams on the Lake—
Noon glows on the Fell—
Wake thee, O wake,
White Maid of Avenel!"

These lines were hardly uttered, when there stood the figure of a female clothed in white, within three steps of Halbert Glendinning.

"I guess 'twas frightful there to see
A lady richly clad as she—
Beautiful exceedingly."*

Chapter the Twelfth.

There's something in that ancient superstition,
Which, erring as it is, our fancy loves.
The spring that, with its thousand crystal bubbles,
Bursts from the bosom of some desert rock
In secret solitude, may well be deem'd
The haunt of something purer, more refined,
And mightier than ourselves.

OLD PLAY.

YOUNG Halbert Glendinning had scarcely pronounced the mystical rhymes, than, as we have mentioned in the conclusion of the last chapter, an appearance, as of a beautiful female, dressed in white, stood within two yards of him. His terror for the moment overcame his natural courage, as well as the strong resolution which he had formed, that the figure which he had now twice seen should not a third time daunt him. But it would seem there is something thrilling and abhorrent to flesh and blood, in the consciousness that we stand in presence of a being in form like to ourselves, but so different in faculties and nature, that we can neither understand its purposes, nor calculate its means of pursuing them.

Halbert stood silent and gasped for breath, his hairs erecting themselves on his head—his mouth open—his eyes fixed, and, as the sole remaining sign of his late determined purpose, his sword pointed towards the apparition. At length with a voice of ineffable sweetness, the White Lady, for by that name we shall distinguish this being, sung, or rather chanted, the following lines:—

"Youth of the dark eye, wherefore didst thou call me?
Wherefore art thou here, if terrors can appal thee?
He that seeks to deal with us must know no fear nor failing!
To coward and churl our speech is dark, our gifts are unavailing.
The breeze that brought me hither now, must sweep Egyptian ground,
The fleecy cloud on which I ride for Araby is bound;
The fleecy cloud is drifting by, the breeze sighs for my stay,
For I must sail a thousand miles before the close of day."

* Coleridge's Christabelle.

The astonishment of Halbert began once more to give way to his resolution, and he gained voice enough to say, though with a faltering accent, "In the name of God, what art thou?" The answer was in melody of a different tone and measure: —

"What I am I must not show—
What I am thou couldst not know—
Something betwixt heaven and hell—
Something that neither stood nor fell—
Something that through thy wit or will
May work thee good—may work thee ill.
Neither substance quite nor shadow,
Haunting lonely moor and meadow,
Dancing by the haunted spring,
Riding on the whirlwind's wing;
Aping in fantastic fashion
Every change of human passion,
While o'er our frozen minds they pass,
Like shadows from the mirror'd glass.
Wayward, fickle is our mood,
Hovering betwixt bad and good,
Happier than brief-dated man,
Living twenty times his span;
Far less happy, for we have
Help nor hope beyond the grave!
Man awakes to joy or sorrow;
Ours the sleep that knows no morrow.
This is all that I can show—
This is all that thou mayest know."

The White Lady paused, and appeared to await an answer; but, as Halbert hesitated how to frame his speech, the vision seemed gradually to fade, and became more and more incorporeal. Justly guessing this to be a symptom of her disappearance, Halbert compelled himself to say, —"Lady, when I saw you in the glen, and when you brought back the black book of Mary Avenel, thou didst say I should one day learn to read it."

The White Lady replied,

"Ay! and I taught thee the word and the spell,
To waken me here by the Fairies' Well,
But thou hast loved the heron and hawk,
More than to seek my haunted walk;
And thou hast loved the lance and the sword,
More than good text and holy word;
And thou hast loved the deer to track,
More than the lines and the letters black;
And thou art a ranger of moss and of wood,
And scornest the nurture of gentle blood."

"I will do so no longer, fair maiden," said Halbert; "I desire to learn; and thou didst promise me, that when I did so desire, thou wouldst be my helper; I am no longer afraid of thy presence, and I am no longer regardless of instruction." As he uttered these words, the figure of the White Maiden grew gradually as distinct as it had been at first; and what had well-nigh faded into an ill-defined and colourless shadow, again assumed an appearance at least of corporeal consistency, although the hues were less vivid, and the outline of the figure less distinct and defined — so at least it seemed to Halbert — than those of an ordinary inhabitant of earth. "Wilt thou grant my request," he said, "fair Lady, and give to my keeping the holy book which Mary of Avenel has so often wept for?"

The White Lady replied:

"Thy craven fear my truth accused,
Thine idlehood my trust abused;
He that draws to harbour late,
Must sleep without, or burst the gate.
There is a star for thee which burn'd,
Its influence wanes, its course is turn'd;
Valour and constancy alone
Can bring thee back the chance that's flown."

"If I have been a loiterer, Lady," answered young Glendinning, "thou shalt now find me willing to press forward with double speed. Other thoughts have filled my mind, other thoughts have engaged my heart, within a brief period — and by Heaven, other occupations shall henceforward fill up my time. I have lived in this day the space of years — I came hither a boy — I will return a man — a man, such as may converse not only with his own kind, but with whatever God permits to be visible to him. I will learn the contents of that mysterious volume — I will learn why the Lady of Avenel loved it — why the priests feared, and would have stolen it — why thou didst twice recover it from their hands. — What mystery is wrapt in it? — Speak, I conjure thee!" The lady assumed an air peculiarly sad and solemn, as drooping her head, and folding her arms on her bosom, she replied:

"Within that awful volume lies
The mystery of mysteries!
Happiest they of human race,
To whom God has granted grace
To read, to fear, to hope, to pray,
To lift the latch, and force the way;
And better had they ne'er been born,
Who read to doubt, or read to scorn."

"Give me the volume, Lady," said young Glendinning. "They call me idle — they call me dull — in this pursuit my industry shall not fail, nor, with God's blessing, shall my understanding. Give me the volume." The apparition again replied:

"Many a fathom dark and deep
I have laid the book to sleep;
Ethereal fires around it glowing—
Ethereal music ever flowing—
The sacred pledge of Heav'n
All things revere,
Each in his sphere,
Save man for whom 'twas giv'n:
Lend thy hand, and thou shalt spy
Things ne'er seen by mortal eye."

Halbert Glendinning boldly reached his hand to the White Lady.

"Fearest thou to go with me?" she said, as his hand trembled at the soft and cold touch of her own—

"Fearest thou to go with me?
Still it is free to thee
A peasant to dwell;
Thou mayst drive the dull steer,
And chase the king's deer,
But never more come near
This haunted well."

"If what thou sayest be true," said the undaunted boy, "my destinies are higher than thine own. There shall be neither well nor wood which I dare not visit. No fear of aught, natural or supernatural, shall bar my path through my native valley."

He had scarce uttered the words, when they both descended through the earth with a rapidity which took away Halbert's breath and every other sensation, saving that of being hurried on with the utmost velocity. At length they stopped with a shock so sudden, that the mortal journeyer through this unknown space must have been thrown down with violence, had he not been upheld by his supernatural companion.

It was more than a minute, ere, looking around him, he beheld a grotto, or natural cavern, composed of the most splendid spars and crystals, which returned in a thousand prismatic hues the light of a brilliant flame that glowed on an altar of alabaster. This altar, with its fire, formed the central point of the grotto, which was of a round form, and very high in the roof, resembling in some respects the dome of a cathedral. Corresponding to the four points of the compass, there went off four long galleries, or arcades, constructed of the same brilliant materials with the dome itself, and the termination of which was lost in darkness.

No human imagination can conceive, or words suffice to describe, the glorious radiance which, shot fiercely forth by the flame, was returned from so many hundred thousand points of reflection, afforded by the sparry pillars and their numerous angular crystals. The fire itself did not remain steady and unmoved, but rose and fell, sometimes ascending in a brilliant pyramid of condensed flame half way up the lofty expanse, and again fading into a softer and more rosy hue, and hovering, as it were, on the surface of the altar to collect its strength for another powerful exertion. There was no visible fuel by which it was fed, nor did it emit either smoke or vapour of any kind.

What was of all the most remarkable, the black volume so often mentioned lay not only unconsumed, but untouched in the slightest degree, amid this intensity of fire, which, while it seemed to be of force sufficient to melt adamant, had no effect whatever on the sacred book thus subjected to its utmost influence.

The White Lady, having paused long enough to let young Glendinning take a complete survey of what was around him, now said in her usual chant,

"Here lies the volume thou boldly hast sought;
Touch it, and take it,—'twill dearly be bought!"

Familiarized in some degree with marvels, and desperately desirous of showing the courage he had boasted, Halbert plunged his hand, without hesitation, into the flame, trusting to the rapidity of the motion, to snatch out the volume before the fire could greatly affect him. But he was much disappointed. The flame instantly caught upon his sleeve, and though he withdrew his hand immediately, yet his arm was so dreadfully scorched, that he had well-nigh screamed with pain. He suppressed the natural expression of anguish, however, and only intimated the agony which he felt by a contortion and a muttered groan. The White Lady passed her cold hand over his arm, and, ere she had finished the following metrical chant, his pain had entirely gone, and no mark of the scorching was visible:

"Rash thy deed,
Mortal weed
To immortal flames applying;
Rasher trust
Has thing of dust,
On his own weak worth relying:
Strip thee of such fences vain,
Strip, and prove thy luck again."

Obedient to what he understood to be the meaning of his conductress, Halbert bared his arm to the shoulder, throwing down the remains of his sleeve, which no sooner touched the floor on which he stood than it collected itself together, shrivelled itself up, and was without any visible fire reduced to light tinder, which a sudden breath of wind dispersed into empty space. The White Lady, observing the surprise of the youth, immediately repeated—

"Mortal warp and mortal woof,
Cannot brook this charmed roof;
All that mortal art hath wrought,
In our cell returns to nought.
The molten gold returns to clay,
The polish'd diamond melts away.
All is alter'd, all is flown,
Nought stands fast but truth alone.
Not for that thy quest give o'er:
Courage! prove thy chance once more."

Imboldened by her words, Halbert Glendinning made a second effort, and, plunging his bare arm into the flame, took out the sacred volume without feeling either heat or inconvenience of any kind. Astonished, and almost terrified at his own success, he beheld the flame collect itself, and shoot up into one long and final stream, which seemed as if it would ascend to the very roof of the cavern, and then, sinking as suddenly, became totally extinguished. The deepest darkness ensued; but Halbert had no time to consider his situation, for the White Lady had already caught his hand, and they ascended to upper air with the same velocity with which they had sunk into the earth.

They stood by the fountain in the Corri-nan-shian when they emerged from the bowels of the earth; but on casting a bewildered glance around him, the youth was surprised to observe, that the shadows had fallen far to the east, and that the day was well-nigh spent. He gazed on his conductress for explanation, but her figure began to fade before his eyes—her cheeks grew paler, her features less distinct, her form became shadowy, and blended itself with the mist which was ascending the hollow ravine. What had late the symmetry of form, and the delicate, yet clear hues of feminine beauty, now resembled the flitting and pale ghost of some maiden who has died for love, as it is seen indistinctly and by moonlight, by her perjured lover.

"Stay, spirit!" said the youth, imboldened by his success in the subterranean dome, "thy kindness must not leave me, as one encumbered with a weapon he knows not how to wield. Thou must teach me the art to read, and to understand this volume; else what avails it me that I possess it?"

But the figure of the White Lady still waned before his eye, until it became an outline as pale and indistinct as that of the moon, when the winter morning is far advanced, and ere she had ended the following chant, she was entirely invisible:—

"Alas! alas!
Not ours the grace
These holy characters to trace:
Idle forms of painted air,
Not to us is given to share
The boon bestow'd on Adam's race!
With patience bide,
Heaven will provide
The fitting time, the fitting guide."

The form was already gone, and now the voice itself had melted away in melancholy cadence, softening, as if the Being who spoke had been slowly wafted from the spot where she had commenced her melody.

It was at this moment that Halbert felt the extremity of the terror which he had hitherto so manfully suppressed. The very necessity of exertion had given him spirit to make it, and the presence of the mysterious Being, while it was a subject of fear in itself, had nevertheless given him the sense of protection being near to him. It was when he could reflect with composure on what had passed, that a cold tremor shot across his limbs, his hair bristled, and he was afraid to look around lest he should find at his elbow something more frightful than the first vision. A breeze arising suddenly, realized the beautiful and wild idea of the most imaginative of our modern bards*—

It fann'd his cheek, it raised his hair,
Like a meadow gale in spring;
It mingled strangely with his fears,
Yet it fell like a welcoming.

The youth stood silent and astonished for a few minutes. It seemed to him that the extraordinary Being he had seen, half his terror, half his protectress, was still hovering on the gale which swept past him, and that she might again make herself sensible to his organs of sight. "Speak!" he said, wildly tossing his arms, "speak yet again—be once more present, lovely vision!—thrice have I now seen thee, yet the idea of thy invisible presence around or beside me, makes my heart beat faster than if the earth yawned and gave up a demon."

But neither sound nor appearance indicated the presence of the White Lady, and nothing preternatural beyond what he had already witnessed, was again audible or visible. Halbert, in the meanwhile, by the very exertion of again inviting the presence of this mysterious Being, had recovered his natural audacity. He looked around once more, and resumed his solitary path down the valley into whose recesses he had penetrated.

Nothing could be more strongly contrasted than the storm of passion with which he had bounded over stock and crag, in order to plunge himself into the Corri-nan-shian, and the sobered mood in which he now returned homeward, industriously seeking out the most practicable path, not from a wish to avoid danger, but that he might not by personal toil distract his attention, deeply fixed on the extraordinary scene which he had witnessed. In the former case, he had sought by hazard and bodily exertion to indulge at once the fiery excitation of passion, and to banish the cause of the excitement from his recollection; while now he studiously avoided all interruption to his contemplative walk, lest the difficulty of the way should interfere with, or disturb, his own deep reflections. Thus slowly pacing forth his course, with the air of a pilgrim rather than of a deer-hunter, Halbert about the close of the evening regained his paternal tower.

* Coleridge.

Chapter the Thirteenth.

> *The Miller was of manly make,*
> *To meet him was na mows;*
> *There durst na ten come him to take,*
> *Sae noited he their pows.*
>
> CHRIST'S KIRK ON THE GREEN.

It was after sunset, as we have already stated, when Halbert Glendinning returned to the abode of his father. The hour of dinner was at noon, and that of supper about an hour after sunset at this period of the year. The former had passed without Halbert's appearing; but this was no uncommon circumstance, for the chase, or any other pastime which occurred, made Halbert a frequent neglecter of hours; and his mother, though angry and disappointed when she saw him not at table, was so much accustomed to his occasional absence, and knew so little how to teach him more regularity, that a testy observation was almost all the censure with which such omissions were visited.

On the present occasion, however, the wrath of good Dame Elspeth soared higher than usual. It was not merely on account of the special tup's-head and trotters, the haggis and the side of mutton, with which her table was set forth, but also because of the arrival of no less a person than Hob Miller, as he was universally termed, though the man's name was Happer.

The object of the Miller's visit to the Tower of Glendearg was like the purpose of those embassies which potentates send to each other's courts, partly ostensible, partly politic. In outward show, Hob came to visit his friends of the Halidome, and share the festivity common among country folk, after the barn-yard has been filled, and to renew old intimacies by new conviviality. But in very truth he also came to have an eye upon the contents of each stack, and to obtain such information respecting the extent of the crop reaped and gathered in by each feuar, as might prevent the possibility of *abstracted multures.*

All the world knows that the cultivators of each barony or regality, temporal or spiritual, in Scotland, are obliged to bring their corn to be grinded at the mill of the territory, for which they pay a heavy charge, called the *intown multures.* I could speak to the thirlage of *invecta et illata* too, but let that pass. I have said enough to intimate that I talk not without book. Those of the *Sucken,* or enthralled ground, were liable in penalties, if, deviating from this thirlage, (or thraldom,) they carried their grain to another mill. Now such another mill, erected on the lands of a lay-baron, lay within a tempting and convenient distance of Glendearg; and the Miller was so obliging, and his charges so moderate, that it required Hob Miller's utmost vigilance to prevent evasions of his right of monopoly.

The most effectual means he could devise was this show of good fellowship and neighbourly friendship,—under colour of which he made his annual cruise through the barony—numbered every corn-stack, and computed its contents by the boll, so that he could give a shrewd hint afterwards whether or not the grist came to the right mill.

Dame Elspeth, like her compeers, was obliged to take these domiciliary visits in the sense of politeness; but in her case they had not occurred since her husband's death, probably because the Tower of Glendearg was distant, and there was but a trifling quantity of arable or *infield* land attached to it. This year there had been, upon some speculation of old Martin's, several bolls sown in the out-field, which, the season being fine, had ripened remarkably well. Perhaps this circumstance occasioned the honest Miller's including Glendearg, on this occasion, in his annual round

Dame Glendinning received with pleasure a visit which she used formerly only to endure with patience; and she had changed her view of the matter chiefly, if not entirely, because Hob had brought with him his daughter Mysie, of whose features she could give so slight an account, but whose dress she had described so accurately to the Sub-Prior.

Hitherto this girl had been an object of very trifling consideration in the eyes of the good widow; but the Sub-Prior's particular and somewhat mysterious inquiries had set her brains to work on the subject of Mysie of the Mill; and she had here asked a broad question, and there she had thrown out an innuendo, and there again she had gradually led on to a conversation on the subject of poor Mysie. And from all inquiries and investigations she had collected, that Mysie was a dark-eyed, laughter-loving wench, with cherry-cheeks, and a skin as white as her father's finest bolted flour, out of which was made the Abbot's own wastel-bread. For her temper, she sung and laughed from morning to night; and for her fortune, a material article, besides that which the Miller might have amassed by means of his proverbial golden thumb, Mysie was to inherit a good handsome lump of land, with a prospect of the mill and mill-acres descending to her husband on an easy lease, if a fair word were spoken in season to the Abbot, and to the Prior, and to the Sub-Prior, and to the Sacristan, and so forth.

By turning and again turning these advantages over in her own mind, Elspeth at length came to be of opinion, that the only way to save her son Halbert from a life of "spur, spear, and snaffle," as they called that of the border-riders, from the dint of a cloth-yard shaft, or the loop of an inch-cord, was, that he should marry and settle, and that Mysie Happer should be his destined bride.

As if to her wish, Hob Miller arrived on his strong-built mare, bearing on a pillion behind him the lovely Mysie, with cheeks like a peony-rose, (if Dame Glendinning had ever seen one,) spirits all afloat with rustic coquetry, and a profusion of hair as black as ebony. The *beau-idéal* which Dame Glendinning had been bodying forth in her imagination, became unexpectedly realized in the buxom form of Mysie Happer, whom, in the course of half an hour, she settled upon as the maiden who was to fix the restless and untutored Halbert. True, Mysie, as the dame soon saw, was like to love dancing round a May-pole as well as managing a domestic establishment, and Halbert was like to break more heads than he would grind stacks of corn. But then a miller should always be of manly make, and has been described so since the days of Chaucer and James I.* Indeed, to be able to outdo and bully the whole *Sucken*, (once more we use this barbarous phrase,) in all athletic exercises, was one way to render easy the collection of dues which men would have disputed with a less formidable champion. Then, as to the deficiencies of the miller's wife, the dame was of opinion that they might be supplied by the activity of the miller's mother. "I will keep house for the young folk myself, for the tower is grown very lonely," thought Dame Glendinning, "and to live near the kirk will be mair comfortable in my auld age — and then Edward may agree with his brother about the feu, more especially as he is a favourite with the Sub-Prior, and then he may live in the auld tower like his worthy father before him — and wha kens but Mary Avenel, high-blood as she is, may e'en draw in her stool to the chimney-nook, and sit down here for good and a'? — It's true

---

* The verse we have chosen for a motto, is from a poem imputed to James I. of Scotland. As for the Miller who figures among the Canterbury pilgrims, besides his sword and buckler, he boasted other attributes, all of which, but especially the last, show that he relied more on the strength of the outside than that of the inside of his skull.

The miller was a stout carl for the nones,
Full big he was of brawn, and eke of bones;
That proved well, for wheresoe'r he cam,
At wrestling he wold bear away the ram;
He was short shoulder'd, broad, a thick gnar;
There n'as no door that he n'old heave of bar,
Or break it at a running with his head, &c.

she has no tocher, but the like of her for beauty and sense ne'er crossed my een; and I have kend every wench in the Halidome of St. Mary's — ay, and their mothers that bore them — ay, she is a sweet and a lovely creature as ever tied snood over brown hair — ay, and then, though her uncle keeps her out of her ain for the present time, yet it is to be thought the gray-goose shaft will find a hole in his coat of proof, as, God help us! it has done in many a better man's — And, moreover, if they should stand on their pedigree and gentle race, Edward might say to them, that is, to her gentle kith and kin, 'whilk o' ye was her best friend, when she came down the glen to Glendearg in a misty evening, on a beast mair like a cuddie than aught else?' — And if they tax him with churl's blood, Edward might say, that, forby the old proverb, how

Gentle deed
Makes gentle bleid;

yet, moreover, there comes no churl's blood from Glendinning or Brydone; for, says Edward——"

The hoarse voice of the Miller at this moment recalled the dame from her reverie, and compelled her to remember that if she meant to realize her airy castle, she must begin by laying the foundation in civility to her guest and his daughter, whom she was at that moment most strangely neglecting, though her whole plan turned on conciliating their favour and good opinion, and that, in fact, while arranging matters for so intimate a union with her company, she was suffering them to sit unnoticed, and in their riding gear, as if about to resume their journey. "And so I say, dame," concluded the Miller, (for she had not marked the beginning of his speech,) "an ye be so busied with your housekep, or ought else, why, Mysie and I will trot our way down the glen again to Johnnie Broxmouth's, who pressed us right kindly to bide with him."

Starting at once from her dream of marriages and intermarriages, mills, mill-lands, and baronies, Dame Elspeth felt for a moment like the milk-maid in the fable, when she overset the pitcher, on the contents of which so many golden dreams were founded. But the foundation of Dame Glendinning's hopes was only tottering, not overthrown, and she hastened to restore its equilibrium. Instead of attempting to account for her absence of mind and want of attention to her guests, which she might have found something difficult, she assumed the offensive, like an able general when he finds it necessary, by a bold attack, to disguise his weakness.

A loud exclamation she made, and a passionate complaint she set up against the unkindness of her old friend, who could for an instant doubt the heartiness of her welcome to him and to his hopeful daughter; and then to think of his going back to Johnny Broxmouth's, when the auld tower stood where it did, and had room in it for a friend or two in the worst of times — and he too a neighbour that his umquhile gossip Simon, blessed be his cast, used to think the best friend he had in the Halidome! And on she went, urging her complaint with so much seriousness, that she had well-nigh imposed on herself as well as upon Hob Miller, who had no mind to take any thing in dudgeon; and as it suited his plans to pass the night at Glendearg, would have been equally contented to do so even had his reception been less vehemently hospitable.

To all Elspeth's expostulations on the unkindness of his proposal to leave her dwelling, he answered composedly, "Nay, dame, what could I tell? ye might have had other grist to grind, for ye looked as if ye scarce saw us— or what know I? ye might bear in mind the words Martin and I had about the last barley ye sawed—for I ken dry multures* will sometimes stick in the throat. A man seeks but his awn, and yet folk shall hold him for both miller and miller's man, that is millar and knave,† all the country over."

* Dry multures were a fine, or compensation in money, for not grinding at the mill of the thirl. It was, and is, accounted a vexatious exaction.

† The under miller is, in the language of thirlage, called the knave, which, indeed, signified originally his

"Alas, that you will say so, neighbour Hob," said Dame Elspeth, "or that Martin should have had any words with you about the mill-dues! I will chide him roundly for it, I promise you, on the faith of a true widow. You know full well that a lone woman is sore put upon by her servants."

"Nay, dame," said the miller, unbuckling the broad belt which made fast his cloak, and served, at the same time, to suspend by his side a swinging Andrea Ferrara, "bear no grudge at Martin, for I bear none—I take it on me as a thing of mine office, to maintain my right of multure, lock, and gowpen.* And reason good, for as the old song says,

I live by my mill, God bless her,
She's parent, child, and wife.

The poor old slut, I am beholden to her for my living, and bound to stand by her, as I say to my mill knaves, in right and in wrong. And so should every honest fellow stand by his bread-winner.—And so, Mysie, ye may doff your cloak since our neighbour is so kindly glad to see us—why, I think, we are as blithe to see her—not one in the Halidome pays their multures more duly, sequels, arriage, and carriage, and mill-services, used and wont."

With that the Miller hung his ample cloak without farther ceremony upon a huge pair of stag's antlers, which adorned at once the naked walls of the tower, and served for what we vulgarly call cloak-pins.

In the meantime Dame Elspeth assisted to disembarrass the damsel whom she destined for her future daughter-in-law, of her hood, mantle, and the rest of her riding gear, giving her to appear as beseemed the buxom daughter of the wealthy Miller, gay and goodly, in a white kirtle, the seams of which were embroidered with green silken lace or fringe, entwined with some silver thread. An anxious glance did Elspeth cast upon the good-humoured face, which was now more fully shown to her, and was only obscured by a quantity of raven black hair, which the maid of the mill had restrained by a snood of green silk, embroidered with silver, corresponding to the trimmings of her kirtle. The countenance itself was exceedingly comely—the eyes black, large, and roguishly good-humoured—the mouth was small—the lips well formed, though somewhat full—the teeth were pearly white—and the chin had a very seducing dimple in it. The form belonging to this joyous face was full and round, and firm and fair. It might become coarse and masculine some years hence, which is the common fault of Scottish beauty; but in Mysie's sixteenth year she had the shape of a Hebe. The anxious Elspeth, with all her maternal partiality, could not help admitting within herself, that a better man than Halbert might go farther and fare worse. She looked a little giddy, and Halbert was not nineteen; still it was time he should be settled, for to that point the dame always returned; and here was an excellent opportunity.

The simple cunning of Dame Elspeth now exhausted itself in commendations of her fair guest, from the snood, as they say, to the single-soled shoe. Mysie listened and blushed with pleasure for the first five minutes; but ere ten had elapsed, she began to view the old lady's compliments rather as subjects of mirth than of vanity, and was much more disposed to laugh at than to be flattered with them, for Nature had mingled the good-humour with which she had endowed the damsel with no small portion of shrewdness. Even Hob himself began to tire of hearing his daughter's praises, and broke in with, "Ay, ay, she is a clever quean enough; and, were she five years older, she shall lay a loaded sack on an *aver*† with e'er a lass in

---

lad, (*Knabe*—German,) but by degrees came to be taken in a worse sense. In the old translation of the Bible, Paul is made to term himself the knave of our Saviour. The allowance of meal taken by the miller's servant was called knave-ship.

* The multure was the regular exaction for grinding the meal. The *lock*, signifying a small quantity, and the *gowpen*, a handful, were additional perquisites demanded by the miller, and submitted to or resisted by the *Suckener* as circumstances permitted. These and other petty dues were called in general the *Sequels*.

† *Aver*—properly a horse of labour.

the Halidome. But I have been looking for your two sons, dame. Men say downby that Halbert's turned a wild springald, and that we may have word of him from Westmoreland one moonlight night or another."

"God forbid, my good neighbour; God, in his mercy, forbid!" said Dame Glendinning, earnestly; for it was touching the very key-note of her apprehensions, to hint any probability that Halbert might become one of the marauders so common in the age and country. But, fearful of having betrayed too much alarm on this subject, she immediately added, "That though, since the last rout at Pinkiecleuch, she had been all of a tremble when a gun or a spear was named, or when men spoke of fighting; yet, thanks to God and our Lady, her sons were like to live and die honest and peaceful tenants to the Abbey, as their father might have done, but for that awful hosting which he went forth to with mony a brave man that never returned."

"Ye need not tell me of it, dame," said the Miller, "since I was there myself, and made two pair of legs (and these were not mine, but my mare's,) worth one pair of hands. I judged how it would be, when I saw our host break ranks, with rushing on through that broken ploughed field, and so as they had made a pricker of me, I e'en pricked off with myself while the play was good."

"Ay, ay, neighbour," said the dame, "ye were aye a wise and a wary man; if my Simon had had your wit, he might have been here to speak about it this day; but he was aye cracking of his good blood and his high kindred, and less would not serve him than to bide the bang to the last, with the earls, and knights, and squires, that had no wives to greet for them, or else had wives that cared not how soon they were widows; but that is not for the like of us. But touching my son Halbert, there is no fear of him; for if it should be his misfortune to be in the like case, he has the best pair of heels in Halidome, and could run almost as fast as your mare herself."

"Is this he, neighbour?" quoth the Miller.

"No," replied the mother; "that is my youngest son, Edward, who can read and write like the Lord Abbot himself, if it were not a sin to say so."

"Ay," said the Miller; "and is that the young clerk the Sub-Prior thinks so much of? they say he will come far ben that lad; wha kens but he may come to be Sub-Prior himself?—as broken a ship has come to land."

"To be a Prior, neighbour Miller," said Edward, "a man must first be a priest, and for that I judge I have little vocation."

"He will take to the pleugh-pettle, neighbour," said the good dame; "and so will Halbert too, I trust. I wish you saw Halbert.—Edward, where is your brother?"

"Hunting, I think," replied Edward; "at least he left us this morning to join the Laird of Colmslie and his hounds. I have heard them baying in the glen all day."

"And if I had heard that music," said the Miller, "it would have done my heart good, ay, and may be taken me two or three miles out of my road. When I was the Miller of Morebattle's knave, I have followed the hounds from Eckford to the foot of Hounam-law—followed them on foot, Dame Glendinning, ay, and led the chase when the Laird of Cessford and his gay riders were all thrown out by the mosses and gills. I brought the stag on my back to Hounam Cross, when the dogs had pulled him down. I think I see the old gray knight, as he sate so upright on his strong war-horse, all white with foam; and 'Miller,' said he to me, 'an thou wilt turn thy back on the mill, and wend with me, I will make a man of thee.' But I chose rather to abide by clap and happer, and the better luck was mine; for the proud Percy caused hang five of the Laird's henchmen at Alnwick for burning a rickle of houses some gate beyond Fowberry, and it might have been my luck as well as another man's."

"Ah, neighbour, neighbour," said Dame Glendinning, "you were aye wise and wary; but if you like hunting, I must say Halbert's the lad to please you. He hath all those fair holiday terms of hawk and hound as ready in his mouth as Tom with the tod's tail, that is the Lord Abbot's ranger."

"Ranges he not homeward at dinner-time, dame," demanded the Miller; "for we call noon the dinner-hour at Kennaquhair?"

The widow was forced to admit that, even at this important period of the day, Halbert was frequently absent; at which the Miller shook his head, intimating, at the same time, some allusion to the proverb of MacFarlane's geese, which "liked their play better than their meat."*

That the delay of dinner might not increase the Miller's disposition to prejudge Halbert, Dame Glendinning called hastily on Mary Avenel to take her task of entertaining Mysie Happer, while she herself rushed to the kitchen, and, entering at once into the province of Tibb Tacket, rummaged among trenchers and dishes, snatched pots from the fire, and placed pans and gridirons on it, accompanying her own feats of personal activity with such a continued list of injunctions to Tibb, that Tibb at length lost patience, and said, "Here was as muckle wark about meating an auld miller, as if they had been to banquet the blood of Bruce." But this, as it was supposed to be spoken aside, Dame Glendinning did not think it convenient to hear.

Chapter the Fourteenth.

Nay, let me have the friends who eat my victuals,
As various as my dishes.—The feast's naught,
Where one huge plate predominates. John Plaintext,
He shall be mighty beef, our English staple;
The worthy Alderman, a butter'd dumpling;
Yon pair of whisker'd Cornets, ruffs and rees:
Their friend the Dandy, a green goose in sippets,
And so the board is spread at once and fill'd
On the same principle—Variety.

NEW PLAY.

"AND what brave lass is this?" said Hob Miller, as Mary Avenel entered the apartment to supply the absence of Dame Elspeth Glendinning.

"The young Lady of Avenel, father," said the Maid of the Mill, dropping as low a curtsy as her rustic manners enabled her to make. The Miller, her father, doffed his bonnet, and made his reverence, not altogether so low perhaps as if the young lady had appeared in the pride of rank and riches, yet so as to give high birth the due homage which the Scotch for a length of time scrupulously rendered to it.

Indeed, from having had her mother's example before her for so many years, and from a native sense of propriety and even of dignity, Mary Avenel had acquired a demeanour, which marked her title to consideration, and effectually checked any attempt at familiarity on the part of those who might be her associates in her present situation, but could not be well termed her equals. She was by nature mild, pensive, and contemplative, gentle

* A brood of wild-geese, which long frequented one of the uppermost islands in Loch-Lomond, called Inch-Tavoe, were supposed to have some mysterious connexion with the ancient family of MacFarlane of that ilk, and it is said were never seen after the ruin and extinction of that house. The MacFarlanes had a house and garden upon that same island of Inch-Tavoe. Here James VI. was, on one occasion, regaled by the chieftain. His Majesty had been previously much amused by the geese pursuing each other on the Loch. But, when one which was brought to table, was found to be tough and ill fed, James observed—"that MacFarlane's geese liked their play better than their meat," a proverb which has been current ever since.

in disposition, and most placable when accidentally offended; but still she was of a retired and reserved habit, and shunned to mix in ordinary sports, even when the rare occurrence of a fair or wake gave her an opportunity of mingling with companions of her own age. If at such scenes she was seen for an instant, she appeared to behold them with the composed indifference of one to whom their gaiety was a matter of no interest, and who seemed only desirous to glide away from the scene as soon as she possibly could.

Something also had transpired concerning her being born on All-hallow Eve, and the powers with which that circumstance was supposed to invest her over the invisible world. And from all these particulars combined, the young men and women of the Halidome used to distinguish Mary among themselves by the name of the Spirit of Avenel, as if the fair but fragile form, the beautiful but rather colourless cheek, the dark blue eye, and the shady hair, had belonged rather to the immaterial than the substantial world. The general tradition of the White Lady, who was supposed to wait on the fortunes of the family of Avenel, gave a sort of zest to this piece of rural wit. It gave great offence, however, to the two sons of Simon Glendinning; and when the expression was in their presence applied to the young lady, Edward was wont to check the petulance of those who used it by strength of argument, and Halbert by strength of arm. In such cases Halbert had this advantage, that although he could render no aid to his brother's argument, yet when circumstances required it, he was sure to have that of Edward, who never indeed himself commenced a fray, but, on the other hand, did not testify any reluctance to enter into combat in Halbert's behalf or in his rescue.

But the zealous attachment of the two youths, being themselves, from the retired situation in which they dwelt, comparative strangers in the Halidome, did not serve in any degree to alter the feelings of the inhabitants towards the young lady, who seemed to have dropped amongst them from another sphere of life. Still, however, she was regarded with respect, if not with fondness; and the attention of the Sub-Prior to the family, not to mention the formidable name of Julian Avenel, which every new incident of those tumultuous times tended to render more famous, attached to his niece a certain importance. Thus some aspired to her acquaintance out of pride while the more timid of the feuars were anxious to inculcate upon their children the necessity of being respectful to the noble orphan. So that Mary Avenel, little loved because little known, was regarded with a mysterious awe, partly derived from fear of her uncle's moss-troopers, and partly from her own retired and distant habits, enhanced by the superstitious opinions of the time and country.

It was not without some portion of this awe, that Mysie felt herself left alone in company with a young person so distant in rank, and so different in bearing, from herself; for her worthy father had taken the first opportunity to step out unobserved, in order to mark how the barnyard was filled, and what prospect it afforded of grist to the mill. In youth, however, there is a sort of free-masonry, which, without much conversation, teaches young persons to estimate each other's character, and places them at ease on the shortest acquaintance. It is only when taught deceit by the commerce of the world, that we learn to shroud our character from observation, and to disguise our real sentiments from those with whom we are placed in communion.

Accordingly, the two young women were soon engaged in such objects of interest as best became their age. They visited Mary Avenel's pigeons, which she nursed with the tenderness of a mother; they turned over her slender stores of finery, which yet contained some articles that excited the respect of her companion, though Mysie was too good-humoured to nourish envy. A golden rosary, and some female ornaments marking superior rank, had been rescued in the moment of their utmost adversity, more by

Tibb Tacket's presence of mind, than by the care of their owner, who was at that sad period too much sunk in grief to pay any attention to such circumstances. They struck Mysie with a deep impression of veneration; for, excepting what the Lord Abbot and the convent might possess, she did not believe there was so much real gold in the world as was exhibited in these few trinkets, and Mary, however sage and serious, was not above being pleased with the admiration of her rustic companion.

Nothing, indeed, could exhibit a stronger contrast than the appearance of the two girls; — the good-humoured laughter-loving countenance of the Maid of the Mill, who stood gazing with unrepressed astonishment on whatever was in her inexperienced eye rare and costly, and with an humble, and at the same time cheerful acquiescence in her inferiority, asking all the little queries about the use and value of the ornaments, while Mary Avenel, with her quiet composed dignity and placidity of manner, produced them one after another for the amusement of her companion.

As they became gradually more familiar, Mysie of the Mill was just venturing to ask, why Mary Avenel never appeared at the May-pole, and to express her wonder when the young lady said she disliked dancing, when a trampling of horses at the gate of the tower interrupted their conversation.

Mysie flew to the shot-window in the full ardour of unrestrained female curiosity. "Saint Mary! sweet lady! here come two well-mounted gallants; will you step this way to look at them?"

"No," said Mary Avenel, "you shall tell me who they are."

"Well, if you like it better," said Mysie—"but how shall I know them? —Stay, I do know one of them, and so do you, lady; he is a blithe man, somewhat light of hand, they say, but the gallants of these days think no great harm of that. He is your uncle's henchman, that they call Christie of the Clinthill; and he has not his old green jerkin and the rusty black-jack over it, but a scarlet cloak, laid down with silver lace three inches broad, and a breast-plate you might see to dress your hair in, as well as in that keeking-glass in the ivory frame that you showed me even now. Come, dear lady, come to the shot-window and see him."

"If it be the man you mean, Mysie," replied the orphan of Avenel, "I shall see him soon enough, considering either the pleasure or comfort the sight will give me."

"Nay, but if you will not come to see gay Christie," replied the Maid of the Mill, her face flushed with eager curiosity, "come and tell me who the gallant is that is with him, the handsomest, the very lovesomest young man I ever saw with sight."

"It is my foster-brother, Halbert Glendinning," said Mary, with apparent indifference; for she had been accustomed to call the sons of Elspeth her foster-brethren, and to live with them as if they had been brothers in earnest.

"Nay, by Our Lady, that it is not," said Mysie; "I know the favour of both the Glendinnings well, and I think this rider be not of our country. He has a crimson velvet bonnet, and long brown hair falling down under it, and a beard on his upper lip, and his chin clean and close shaved, save a small patch on the point of the chin, and a sky-blue jerkin slashed and lined with white satin, and trunk-hose to suit, and no weapon but a rapier and dagger—Well, if I was a man, I would never wear weapon but the rapier! it is so slender and becoming, instead of having a cartload of iron at my back, like my father's broad-sword with its great rusty basket-hilt. Do you not delight in the rapier and poniard, lady?"

"The best sword," answered Mary, "if I must needs answer a question of the sort, is that which is drawn in the best cause, and which is best used when it is out of the scabbard."

"But can you not guess who this stranger should be?" said Mysie.

"Indeed, I cannot even attempt it; but to judge by his companion, it is no matter how little he is known," replied Mary.

"My benison on his bonny face," said Mysie, "if he is not going to alight here! Now, I am as much pleased as if my father had given me the silver earrings he has promised me so often; — nay, you had as well come to the window, for you must see him by and by whether you will or not."

I do not know how much sooner Mary Avenel might have sought the point of observation, if she had not been scared from it by the unrestrained curiosity expressed by her buxom friend; but at length the same feeling prevailed over her sense of dignity, and satisfied with having displayed all the indifference that was necessary in point of decorum, she no longer thought herself bound to restrain her curiosity.

From the outshot or projecting window, she could perceive that Christie of the Clinthill was attended on the present occasion by a very gay and gallant cavalier, who, from the nobleness of his countenance and manner, his rich and handsome dress, and the showy appearance of his horse and furniture, must, she agreed with her new friend, be a person of some consequence.

Christie also seemed conscious of something, which made him call out with more than his usual insolence of manner, "What, ho! so ho! the house! Churl peasants, will no one answer when I call? — Ho! Martin, — Tibb, — Dame Glendinning! — a murrain on you, must we stand keeping our horses in the cold here, and they steaming with heat, when we have ridden so sharply?"

At length he was obeyed, and old Martin made his appearance. "Ha!" said Christie, "art thou there, old Truepenny? here, stable me these steeds, and see them well bedded, and stretch thine old limbs by rubbing them down; and see thou quit not the stable till there is not a turned hair on either of them."

Martin took the horses to the stable as commanded, but suppressed not his indignation a moment after he could vent it with safety. "Would not any one think," he said to Jasper, an old ploughman, who, in coming to his assistance, had heard Christie's imperious injunctions, "that this loon, this Christie of the Clinthill, was laird or lord at least of him? No such thing, man! I remember him a little dirty turnspit boy in the house of Avenel, that every body in a frosty morning like this warmed his fingers by kicking or cuffing! and now he is a gentleman, and swears, d—n him and renounce him, as if the gentlemen could not so much as keep their own wickedness to themselves, without the like of him going to hell in their very company, and by the same road. I have as much a mind as ever I had to my dinner, to go back and tell him to sort his horse himself, since he is as able as I am."

"Hout tout, man!" answered Jasper, "keep a calm sough; better to fleech a fool than fight with him."

Martin acknowledged the truth of the proverb, and, much comforted therewith, betook himself to cleaning the stranger's horse with great assiduity, remarking, it was a pleasure to handle a handsome nag, and turned over the other to the charge of Jasper. Nor was it until Christie's commands were literally complied with that he deemed it proper, after fitting ablutions, to join the party in the spence; not for the purpose of waiting upon them, as a mere modern reader might possibly expect, but that he might have his share of dinner in their company.

In the meanwhile, Christie had presented his companion to Dame Glendinning as Sir Piercie Shafton, a friend of his and of his master, come to spend three or four days with little din in the tower. The good dame could not conceive how she was entitled to such an honour, and would fain have pleaded her want of every sort of convenience to entertain a guest of that quality. But, indeed, the visiter, when he cast his eyes round the bare walls, eyed the huge black chimney, scrutinized the meagre and broken furniture of the apartment, and beheld the embarrassment of the mistress of the family, intimated great reluctance to intrude upon Dame Glendinning a visit, which could scarce, from all appearances, prove otherwise than an inconvenience to her, and a penance to himself.

But the reluctant hostess and her guest had to do with an inexorable man, who silenced all expostulations with, "such was his master's pleasure. And, moreover," he continued, "though the Baron of Avenel's will must, and ought to prove law to all within ten miles around him, yet here, dame," he said, "is a letter from your petticoated baron, the lord-priest yonder, who enjoins you, as you regard his pleasure, that you afford to this good knight such decent accommodation as is in your power, suffering him to live as privately as he shall desire.—And for you, Sir Piercie Shafton," continued Christie, "you will judge for yourself, whether secrecy and safety is not more your object even now, than soft beds and high cheer. And do not judge of the dame's goods by the semblance of her cottage; for you will see by the dinner she is about to spread for us, that the vassal of the kirk is seldom found with her basket bare." To Mary Avenel, Christie presented the stranger, after the best fashion he could, as to the niece of his master the baron.

While he thus laboured to reconcile Sir Piercie Shafton to his fate, the widow, having consulted her son Edward on the real import of the Lord Abbot's injunction, and having found that Christie had given a true exposition, saw nothing else left for her but to make that fate as easy as she could to the stranger. He himself also seemed reconciled to his lot by some feeling probably of strong necessity, and accepted with a good grace the hospitality which the dame offered with a very indifferent one.

In fact, the dinner, which soon smoked before the assembled guests, was of that substantial kind which warrants plenty and comfort. Dame Glendinning had cooked it after her best manner; and, delighted with the handsome appearance which her good cheer made when placed on the table, forgot both her plans and the vexations which interrupted them, in the hospitable duty of pressing her assembled visiters to eat and drink, watching every trencher as it waxed empty, and loading it with fresh supplies ere the guest could utter a negative.

In the meanwhile, the company attentively regarded each other's motions, and seemed endeavouring to form a judgment of each other's character. Sir Piercie Shafton condescended to speak to no one but to Mary Avenel, and on her he conferred exactly the same familiar and compassionate, though somewhat scornful sort of attention, which a pretty fellow of these days will sometimes condescend to bestow on a country miss, when there is no prettier or more fashionable woman present. The manner indeed was different, for the etiquette of those times did not permit Sir Piercie Shafton to pick his teeth, or to yawn, or to gabble like the beggar whose tongue (as he says) was cut out by the Turks, or to affect deafness or blindness, or any other infirmity of the organs. But though the embroidery of his conversation was different, the groundwork was the same, and the high-flown and ornate compliments with which the gallant knight of the sixteenth century interlarded his conversation, were as much the offspring of egotism and self-conceit, as the jargon of the coxcombs of our own days.

The English knight was, however, something daunted at finding that Mary Avenel listened with an air of indifference, and answered with wonderful brevity, to all the fine things which ought, as he conceived, to have dazzled her with their brilliancy, and puzzled her by their obscurity. But if he was disappointed in making the desired, or rather the expected impression, upon her whom he addressed, Sir Piercie Shafton's discourse was marvellous in the ears of Mysie the Miller's daughter, and not the less so that she did not comprehend the meaning of a single word which he uttered. Indeed, the gallant knight's language was far too courtly to be understood by persons of much greater acuteness than Mysie's.

It was about this period, that the "only rare poet of his time, the witty, comical, facetiously-quick, and quickly-facetious, John Lylly — he that sate at Apollo's table, and to whom Phœbus gave a wreath of his own bays without snatching"*—he, in short, who wrote that singularly coxcomical work, called *Euphues and his England,* was in the very zenith of his absurdity and his reputation. The quaint, forced, and unnatural style which he introduced by his "Anatomy of Wit," had a fashion as rapid as it was momentary—all the court ladies were his scholars, and to *parler Euphuisme,* was as necessary a qualification to a courtly gallant, as those of understanding how to use his rapier, or to dance a measure.

It was no wonder that the Maid of the Mill was soon as effectually blinded by the intricacies of this erudite and courtly style of conversation, as she had ever been by the dust of her father's own meal-sacks. But there she sate with her mouth and eyes as open as the mill-door and the two windows, showing teeth as white as her father's bolted flour, and endeavouring to secure a word or two for her own future use out of the pearls of rhetoric which Sir Piercie Shafton scattered around him with such bounteous profusion.

For the male part of the company, Edward felt ashamed of his own manner and slowness of speech, when he observed the handsome young courtier, with an ease and volubility of which he had no conception, run over all the commonplace topics of high-flown gallantry. It is true the good sense and natural taste of young Glendinning soon informed him that the gallant cavalier was speaking nonsense. But, alas! where is the man of modest merit, and real talent, who has not suffered from being outshone in conversation and outstripped in the race of life, by men of less reserve, and of qualities more showy, though less substantial? and well constituted must the mind be, that can yield up the prize without envy to competitors more worthy than himself.

Edward Glendinning had no such philosophy. While he despised the jargon of the gay cavalier, he envied the facility with which he could run on, as well as the courtly tone and expression, and the perfect ease and elegance with which he offered all the little acts of politeness to which the duties of the table gave opportunity. And if I am to speak truth, I must own that he envied those qualities the more as they were all exercised in Mary Avenel's service, and, although only so far accepted as they could not be refused, intimated a wish on the stranger's part to place himself in her good graces, as the only person in the room to whom he thought it worth while to recommend himself. His title, rank, and very handsome figure, together with some sparks of wit and spirit which flashed across the cloud of nonsense which he uttered, rendered him, as the words of the old song say, "a lad for a lady's viewing;" so that poor Edward, with all his real worth and acquired knowledge, in his home-spun doublet, blue cap, and deerskin trowsers, looked like a clown beside the courtier, and, feeling the full inferiority, nourished no good-will to him by whom he was eclipsed.

Christie, on the other hand, as soon as he had satisfied to the full a commodious appetite, by means of which persons of his profession could, like the wolf and eagle, gorge themselves with as much food at one meal as might serve them for several days, began also to feel himself more in the back-ground than he liked to be. This worthy had, amongst his other good qualities, an excellent opinion of himself; and, being of a bold and forward disposition, had no mind to be thrown into the shade by any one. With an impudent familiarity which such persons mistake for graceful ease, he

* Such, and yet more extravagant, are the compliments paid to this author by his editor, Blount. Notwithstanding all exaggeration, Lylly was really a man of wit and imagination, though both were deformed by the most unnatural affectation that ever disgraced a printed page.

broke in upon the knight's finest speeches with as little remorse as he would have driven the point of his lance through a laced doublet.

Sir Piercie Shafton, a man of rank and high birth, by no means en couraged or endured this familiarity, and requited the intruder either with total neglect, or such laconic replies as intimated a sovereign contempt for the rude spearman, who affected to converse with him upon terms of equality.

The Miller held his peace; for, as his usual conversation turned chiefly on his clapper and toll-dish, he had no mind to brag of his wealth in presence of Christie of the Clinthill, or to intrude his discourse on the English cavalier.

A little specimen of the conversation may not be out of place, were it but to show young ladies what fine things they have lost by living when Euphuism is out of fashion.

"Credit me, fairest lady," said the knight, "that such is the cunning of our English courtiers, of the hodiernal strain, that, as they have infinitely refined upon the plain and rusticial discourse of our fathers, which, as I may say, more beseemed the mouths of country roisterers in a May-game than that of courtly gallants in a galliard, so I hold it ineffably and unutterably impossible, that those who may succeed us in that garden of wit and courtesy shall alter or amend it. Venus delighted but in the language of Mercury, Bucephalus will stoop to no one but Alexander, none can sound Apollo's pipe but Orpheus."

"Valiant sir," said Mary, who could scarcely help laughing, "we have but to rejoice in the chance which hath honoured this solitude with a glimpse of the sun of courtesy, though it rather blinds than enlightens us."

"Pretty and quaint, fairest lady," answered the Euphuist. "Ah, that I had with me my Anatomy of Wit—that all-to-be-unparalleled volume—that quintessence of human wit—that treasury of quaint invention—that exquisitively-pleasant-to-read, and inevitably-necessary-to-be-remembered manual, of all that is worthy to be known — which indoctrines the rude in civility, the dull in intellectuality, the heavy in jocosity, the blunt in gentility, the vulgar in nobility, and all of them in that unutterable perfection of human utterance, that eloquence which no other eloquence is sufficient to praise, that art which, when we call it by its own name of Euphuism, we bestow on it its richest panegyric."

"By Saint Mary," said Christie of the Clinthill, "if your worship had told me that you had left such stores of wealth as you talk of at Prudhoe Castle, Long Dickie and I would have had them off with us if man and horse could have carried them; but you told us of no treasure I wot of, save the silver tongs for turning up your mustachoes."

The knight treated this intruder's mistake—for certainly Christie had no idea that all these epithets which sounded so rich and splendid, were lavished upon a small quarto volume—with a stare, and then turning again to Mary Avenel, the only person whom he thought worthy to address, he proceeded in his strain of high-flown oratory, "Even thus," said he, "do hogs contemn the splendour of Oriental pearls; even thus are the delicacies of a choice repast in vain offered to the long-eared grazer of the common, who turneth from them to devour a thistle. Surely as idle is it to pour forth the treasures of oratory before the eyes of the ignorant, and to spread the dainties of the intellectual banquet before those who are, morally and metaphysically speaking, no better than asses."

"Sir Knight, since that is your quality," said Edward, "we cannot strive with you in loftiness of language; but I pray you in fair courtesy, while you honour my father's house with your presence, to spare us such vile comparisons."

"Peace, good villagio," said the knight, gracefully waving his hand, "I prithee peace, kind rustic; and you, my guide, whom I may scarce call honest, let me prevail upon you to imitate the laudable taciturnity of that honest yeoman, who sits as mute as a mill-post, and of that comely damsel, who seems as with her ears she drank in what she did not altogether comprehend, even as a palfrey listening to a lute, whereof, howsoever, he knoweth not the gamut."

"Marvellous fine words," at length said Dame Glendinning, who began to be tired of sitting so long silent, "marvellous fine words, neighbour Happer, are they not?"

"Brave words—very brave words—very exceeding pyet words," answered the Miller; "nevertheless, to speak my mind, a lippy of bran were worth a bushel of them."

"I think so too, under his worship's favour," answered Christie of the Clinthill. "I well remember that at the race of Morham, as we call it, near Berwick, I took a young Southern fellow out of saddle with my lance, and cast him, it might be, a gad's length from his nag; and so, as he had some gold on his laced doublet, I deemed he might ha' the like on it in his pocket too, though that is a rule that does not aye hold good — So I was speaking to him of ransom, and out he comes with a handful of such terms as his honour there hath gleaned up, and craved me for mercy, as I was a true son of Mars, and such like."

"And obtained no mercy at thy hand, I dare be sworn," said the knight, who deigned not to speak Euphuism excepting to the fair sex.

"By my troggs," replied Christie, "I would have thrust my lance down his throat, but just then they flung open that accursed postern-gate, and forth pricked old Hunsdon, and Henry Carey, and as many fellows at their heels as turned the chase northward again. So I e'en pricked Bayard with the spur, and went off with the rest; for a man should ride when he may not wrestle, as they say in Tynedale."

"Trust me," said the knight, again turning to Mary Avenel, "if I do not pity you, lady, who, being of noble blood, are thus in a manner compelled to abide in the cottage of the ignorant, like the precious stone in the head of the toad, or like a precious garland on the brow of an ass. — But soft, what gallant have we here, whose garb savoureth more of the rustic than doth his demeanour, and whose looks seem more lofty than his habit; even as——"

"I pray you, Sir Knight," said Mary, "to spare your courtly similitudes for refined ears, and give me leave to name unto you my foster-brother, Halbert Glendinning."

"The son of the good dame of the cottage, as I opine," answered the English knight; "for by some such name did my guide discriminate the mistress of this mansion, which you, madam, enrich with your presence.— And yet, touching this juvenal, he hath that about him which belongeth to higher birth, for all are not black who dig coals——"

"Nor all white who are millers," said honest Happer, glad to get in a word, as they say, edgeways.

Halbert, who had sustained the glance of the Englishman with some impatience, and knew not what to make of his manner and language, replied with some asperity, "Sir Knight, we have in this land of Scotland an ancient saying, 'Scorn not the bush that bields you'—you are a guest of my father's house to shelter you from danger, if I am rightly informed by the domestics. Scoff not its homeliness, nor that of its inmates—ye might long have abidden at the court of England, ere we had sought your favour, or cumbered you with our society. Since your fate has sent you hither amongst us, be contented with such fare and such converse as we can afford you, and scorn us not for our kindness; for the Scots wear short patience and long daggers."

All eyes were turned on Halbert while he was thus speaking, and there was a general feeling that his countenance had an expression of intelligence, and his person an air of dignity, which they had never before observed. Whether it were that the wonderful Being with whom he had so lately held communication, had bestowed on him a grace and dignity of look and bearing which he had not before, or whether the being conversant in high matters, and called to a destiny beyond that of other men, had a natural effect in giving becoming confidence to his language and manner, we pretend not to determine. But it was evident to all, that, from this day, young Halbert was an altered man; that he acted with the steadiness, promptitude, and determination, which belonged to riper years, and bore himself with a manner which appertained to higher rank.

The knight took the rebuke with good humour. "By my mine honour," he said, "thou hast reason on thy side, good juvenal—nevertheless, I spoke not as in ridicule of the roof which relieves me, but rather in your own praise, to whom, if this roof be native, thou mayst nevertheless rise from its lowliness; even as the lark, which maketh its humble nest in the furrow, ascendeth towards the sun, as well as the eagle which buildeth her eyry in the cliff."

This high-flown discourse was interrupted by Dame Glendinning, who, with all the busy anxiety of a mother, was loading her son's trencher with food, and dinning in his ear her reproaches on account of his prolonged absence. "And see," she said, "that you do not one day get such a sight while you are walking about among the haunts of them that are not of our flesh and bone, as befell Mungo Murray when he slept on the greensward ring of the Auld Kirkhill at sunset, and wakened at daybreak in the wild hills of Breadalbane. And see that, when you are looking for deer, the red stag does not gall you as he did Diccon Thorburn, who never overcast the wound that he took from a buck's horn. And see, when you go swaggering about with a long broadsword by your side, whilk it becomes no peaceful man to do, that you dinna meet with them that have broadsword and lance both — there are enow of rank riders in this land, that neither fear God nor regard man."

Here her eye "in a fine frenzy rolling," fell full upon that of Christie of the Clinthill, and at once her fears for having given offence interrupted the current of maternal rebuke, which, like rebuke matrimonial, may be often better meant than timed. There was something of sly and watchful significance in Christie's eye, an eye gray, keen, fierce, yet wily, formed to express at once cunning, and malice, which made the dame instantly conjecture she had said too much, while she saw in imagination her twelve goodly cows go lowing down the glen in a moonlight night, with half a score of Border spearsmen at their heels.

Her voice, therefore, sunk from the elevated tone of maternal authority into a whimpering apologetic sort of strain, and she proceeded to say, "It is no that I have ony ill thoughts of the Border riders, for Tibb Tacket there has often heard me say that I thought spear and bridle as natural to a Borderman as a pen to a priest, or a feather-fan to a lady; and — have you not heard me say it, Tibb?"

Tibb showed something less than her expected alacrity in attesting her mistress's deep respect for the freebooters of the southland hills; but, thus conjured, did at length reply, "Hout ay, mistress, I'se warrant I have heard you say something like that."

"Mother!" said Halbert, in a firm and commanding tone of voice, "what or whom is it that you fear under my father's roof? — I well hope that it harbours not a guest in whose presence you are afraid to say your pleasure to me or my brother? I am sorry I have been detained so late, being ignorant of the fair company which I should encounter on my return. — I pray you let this excuse suffice: and what satisfies you, will, I trust, be nothing less than acceptable to your guests."

An answer calculated so justly betwixt the submission due to his parent, and the natural feeling of dignity in one who was by birth master of the mansion, excited universal satisfaction. And as Elspeth herself confessed to Tibb on the same evening, "She did not think it had been in the callant. Till that night, he took pets and passions if he was spoke to, and lap through the house like a four-year-auld at the least word of advice that was minted at him. but now he spoke as grave and as douce as the Lord Abbot himself. She kendna," she said, "what might be the upshot of it, but it was like he was a wonderfu' callant even now."

The party then separated, the young men retiring to their apartments, the elder to their household cares. While Christie went to see his horse properly accommodated, Edward betook himself to his book, and Halbert, who was as ingenious in employing his hands as he had hitherto appeared imperfect in mental exertion, applied himself to constructing a place of concealment in the floor of his apartment by raising a plank, beneath which he resolved to deposit that copy of the Holy Scriptures which had been so strangely regained from the possession of men and spirits.

In the meanwhile Sir Piercie Shafton sate still as a stone, in the chair in which he had deposited himself, his hands folded on his breast, his legs stretched straight out before him and resting upon the heels, his eyes cast up to the ceiling as if he had meant to count every mesh of every cobweb with which the arched roof was canopied, wearing at the same time a face of as solemn and imperturbable gravity, as if his existence had depended on the accuracy of his calculation.

He could scarce be roused from his listless state of contemplative absorption so as to take some supper, a meal at which the younger females appeared not. Sir Piercie stared around twice or thrice as if he missed something; but he asked not for them, and only evinced his sense of a proper audience being wanting, by his abstraction and absence of mind, seldom speaking until he was twice addressed, and then replying, without trope or figure, in that plain English which nobody could speak better when he had a mind.

Christie, finding himself in undisturbed possession of the conversation, indulged all who chose to listen with details of his own wild and inglorious warfare, while Dame Elspeth's curch bristled with horror, and Tibb Tacket, rejoiced to find herself once more in the company of a jackman, listened to his tales, like Desdemona to Othello's, with undisguised delight. Meantime the two young Glendinnings were each wrapped up in his own reflections, and only interrupted in them by the signal to move bedward.

Chapter the Fifteenth.

He strikes no coin, 'tis true, but coins new phrases,
And vends them forth as knaves vend gilded counters,
Which wise men scorn, and fools accept in payment.

OLD PLAY.

In the morning Christie of the Clinthill was nowhere to be seen. As this worthy personage did seldom pique himself on sounding a trumpet before his movements, no one was surprised at his moonlight departure, though some alarm was excited lest he had not made it empty-handed. So, in the language of the national ballad,

Some ran to cupboard, and some to kist,
But nought was away that could be mist.

All was in order, the key of the stable left above the door, and that of the iron-grate in the inside of the lock. In short, the retreat had been made with scrupulous attention to the security of the garrison, and so far Christie left them nothing to complain of.

The safety of the premises was ascertained by Halbert, who instead of catching up a gun or cross-bow, and sallying out for the day as had been his frequent custom, now, with a gravity beyond his years, took a survey of all around the tower, and then returned to the spence, or public apartment, in which, at the early hour of seven, the morning meal was prepared.

There he found the Euphuist in the same elegant posture of abstruse calculation which he had exhibited on the preceding evening, his arms folded in the same angle, his eyes turned up to the same cobwebs, and his heels resting on the ground as before. Tired of this affectation of indolent importance, and not much flattered with his guest's persevering in it to the last, Halbert resolved at once to break the ice, being determined to know what circumstance had brought to the tower of Glendinning a guest at once so supercilious and so silent.

"Sir Knight," he said with some firmness, "I have twice given you good morning, to which the absence of your mind hath, I presume, prevented you from yielding attention, or from making return. This exchange of courtesy is at your pleasure to give or withhold—But, as what I have further to say concerns your comfort and your motions in an especial manner, I will entreat you to give me some signs of attention, that I may be sure I am not wasting my words on a monumental image."

At this unexpected address, Sir Piercie Shafton opened his eyes, and afforded the speaker a broad stare; but as Halbert returned the glance without either confusion or dismay, the knight thought proper to change his posture, draw in his legs, raise his eyes, fix them on young Glendinning, and assume the appearance of one who listens to what is said to him. Nay, to make his purpose more evident, he gave voice to his resolution in these words, "Speak! we do hear."

"Sir Knight," said the youth, "it is the custom of this Halidome, or patrimony of St. Mary's, to trouble with inquiries no guests who receive our hospitality, providing they tarry in our house only for a single revolution of the sun. We know that both criminals and debtors come hither for sanctuary, and we scorn to extort from the pilgrim, whom chance may make our guest, an avowal of the cause of his pilgrimage and penance. But when one so high above our rank as yourself, Sir Knight, and especially one to whom the possession of such pre-eminence is not indifferent, shows his determination to be our guest for a longer time, it is our usage to inquire of him whence he comes, and what is the cause of his journey?"

The English knight gaped twice or thrice before he answered, and then replied in a bantering tone, "Truly, good villagio, your question hath in it somewhat of embarrassment, for you ask me of things concerning which I am not as yet altogether determined what answer I may find it convenient to make. Let it suffice thee, kind juvenal, that thou hast the Lord Abbot's authority for treating me to the best of that power of thine, which, indeed, may not always so well suffice for my accommodation as either of us would desire."

"I must have a more precise answer than this, Sir Knight," said the young Glendinning.

"Friend," said the knight, "be not outrageous. It may suit your northern manners thus to press harshly upon the secrets of thy betters; but believe me, that even as the lute, struck by an unskilful hand, doth produce discords, so——" At this moment the door of the apartment opened, and Mary Avenel presented herself—"But who can talk of discords," said the knight, assuming his complimentary vein and humour, "when the soul of harmony descends upon us in the presence of surpassing beauty! For even as foxes, wolves, and other animals void of sense and reason, do fly from the presence of the resplendent sun of heaven when he arises in his glory, so do strife, wrath, and all ireful passions retreat, and, as it were, scud away, from the face which now beams upon us, with power to compose our angry passions, illuminate our errors and difficulties, soothe our wounded minds, and lull to rest our disorderly apprehensions; for as the heat and warmth of the eye of day is to the material and physical world, so is the eye which I now bow down before to that of the intellectual microcosm."

He concluded with a profound bow; and Mary Avenel, gazing from one to the other, and plainly seeing that something was amiss, could only say, "For heaven's sake, what is the meaning of this?"

The newly-acquired tact and intelligence of her foster-brother was as yet insufficient to enable him to give an answer. He was quite uncertain how he ought to deal with a guest, who preserving a singularly high tone of assumed superiority and importance, seemed nevertheless so little serious in what he said, that it was quite impossible to discern with accuracy whether he was in jest or earnest.

Forming, however, the internal resolution to bring Sir Piercie Shafton to a reckoning at a more fit place and season, he resolved to prosecute the matter no farther at present; and the entrance of his mother with the damsel of the Mill, and the return of the honest Miller from the stack-yard, where he had been numbering and calculating the probable amount of the season's grist, rendered farther discussion impossible for the moment.

In the course of the calculation it could not but strike the man of meal and grindstones, that after the church's dues were paid, and after all which he himself could by any means deduct from the crop, still the residue which must revert to Dame Glendinning could not be less than considerable. I wot not if this led the honest Miller to nourish any plans similar to those adopted by Elspeth; but it is certain that he accepted with grateful alacrity an invitation which the dame gave to his daughter, to remain a week or two as her guest at Glendearg.

The principal persons being thus in high good humour with each other, all business gave place to the hilarity of the morning repast; and so much did Sir Piercie appear gratified by the attention which was paid to every word that he uttered by the nut-brown Mysie, that, notwithstanding his high birth and distinguished quality, he bestowed on her some of the more ordinary and second-rate tropes of his elocution.

Mary Avenel, when relieved from the awkwardness of feeling the full weight of his conversation addressed to herself, enjoyed it much more; and the good knight, encouraged by those conciliating marks of approbation from the sex, for whose sake he cultivated his oratorical talents, made speedy intimation of his purpose to be more communicative than he had shown himself in his conversation with Halbert Glendinning, and gave them to understand, that it was in consequence of some pressing danger that he was at present their involuntary guest.

The conclusion of the breakfast was a signal for the separation of the company. The Miller went to prepare for his departure; his daughter to arrange matters for her unexpected stay; Edward was summoned to consultation by Martin concerning some agricultural matter, in which Halbert could not be brought to interest himself; the dame left the room upon her household concerns, and Mary was in the act of following her, when she suddenly recollected, that if she did so, the strange knight and Halbert must be left alone together, at the risk of another quarrel.

The maiden no sooner observed this circumstance, than she instantly returned from the door of the apartment, and, seating herself in a small stone window-seat, resolved to maintain that curb which she was sensible her presence imposed on Halbert Glendinning, of whose quick temper she had some apprehensions.

The stranger marked her motions, and, either interpreting them as inviting his society, or obedient to those laws of gallantry which permitted him not to leave a lady in silence and solitude, he instantly placed himself near to her side and opened the conversation as follows:—

"Credit me, fair lady," he said, addressing Mary Avenel, "it much rejoiceth me, being, as I am, a banished man from the delights of mine own country, that I shall find here in this obscure and silvan cottage of the north, a fair form and a candid soul, with whom I may explain my mutual sentiments. And let me pray you in particular, lovely lady, that, according to the universal custom now predominant in our court, the garden of superior wits, you will exchange with me some epithet whereby you may mark my devotion to your service. Be henceforward named, for example, my Protection, and let me be your Affability."

"Our northern and country manners, Sir Knight, do not permit us to exchange epithets with those to whom we are strangers," replied Mary Avenel.

"Nay, but see now," said the knight, "how you are startled! even as the unbroken steed, which swerves aside from the shaking of a handkerchief, though he must in time encounter the waving of a pennon. This courtly exchange of epithets of honour, is no more than the compliments which pass between valour and beauty, wherever they meet, and under whatever circumstances. Elizabeth of England herself calls Philip Sydney her Courage, and he in return calls that princess his Inspiration. Wherefore, my fair Protection, for by such epithet it shall be mine to denominate you——"

"Not without the young lady's consent, sir!" interrupted Halbert; "most truly do I hope your courtly and quaint breeding will not so far prevail over the more ordinary rules of civil behaviour."

"Fair tenant of an indifferent copyhold," replied the knight, with the same coolness and civility of mien, but in a tone somewhat more lofty than he used to the young lady, "we do not in the southern parts, much intermingle discourse, save with those with whom we may stand on some footing of equality; and I must, in all discretion, remind you, that the necessity which makes us inhabitants of the same cabin, doth not place us otherwise on a level with each other."

"By Saint Mary," replied young Glendinning, "it is my thought that it does; for plain men hold, that he who asks the shelter is indebted to him who gives it; and so far, therefore, is our rank equalized while this roof covers us both."

"Thou art altogether deceived," answered Sir Piercie; "and that thou mayst fully adapt thyself to our relative condition, know that I account not myself thy guest, but that of thy master, the Lord Abbot of Saint Mary's, who, for reasons best known to himself and me, chooseth to administer his hospitality to me through the means of thee, his servant and vassal, who art, therefore, in good truth, as passive an instrument of my accommodation as this ill-made and rugged joint-stool on which I sit, or as the wooden trencher from which I eat my coarse commons. Wherefore," he added, turning to Mary, "fairest mistress, or rather, as I said before, most lovely Protection*——"

Mary Avenel was about to reply to him, when the stern, fierce, and resentful expression of voice and countenance with which Halbert exclaimed,

* There are many instances to be met with in the ancient dramas of this whimsical and conceited custom of persons who formed an intimacy, distinguishing each other by some quaint epithet. In *Every Man out of his Humour*, there is a humorous debate upon names most fit to bind the relation betwixt Sogliardo and Cavaliero Shift, which ends by adopting those of Countenance and Resolution. What is more to the point is in the speech of Hedon, a voluptuary and a courtier in *Cynthia's Revels*. "You know that I call Madam Pliantia my *Honour*, and she calls me her *Ambition*. Now, when I meet her in the presence, anon, I will come to her and say, 'Sweet Honour, I have hitherto contented my sense with the lilies of your hand, and now I will taste the roses of your lip.' To which she cannot but blushing answer, 'Nay, now you are too ambitious;' and then do I reply, 'I cannot be too ambitious of Honour, sweet lady. Wilt not be good?'"—I think there is some remnant of this foppery preserved in masonic lodges, where each brother is distinguished by a name in the Lodge, signifying some abstract quality as Discretion, or the like. See the poems of Gavin Wilson.

"not from the King of Scotland, did he live, would I brook such terms!" induced her to throw herself between him and the stranger, exclaiming, "for God's sake, Halbert, beware what you do!"

"Fear not, fairest Protection," replied Sir Piercie, with the utmost serenity, "that I can be provoked by this rustical and mistaught juvenal to do aught misbecoming your presence or mine own dignity; for as soon shall the gunner's linstock give fire unto the icicle, as the spark of passion inflame my blood, tempered as it is to serenity by the respect due to the presence of my gracious Protection."

"You may well call her your protection, Sir Knight," said Halbert; "by Saint Andrew, it is the only sensible word I have heard you speak! But we may meet where her protection shall no longer afford you shelter."

"Fairest Protection," continued the courtier, not even honouring with a look, far less with a direct reply, the threat of the incensed Halbert, "doubt not that thy faithful Affability will be more commoved by the speech of this rudesby, than the bright and serene moon is perturbed by the baying of the cottage-cur, proud of the height of his own dunghill, which, in his conceit, lifteth him nearer unto the majestic luminary."

To what lengths so unsavoury a simile might have driven Halbert's indignation, is left uncertain; for at that moment Edward rushed into the apartment with the intelligence that two most important officers of the Convent, the Kitchener and Refectioner, were just arrived with a sumpter-mule, loaded with provisions, announcing that the Lord Abbot, the Sub-Prior, and the Sacristan, were on their way thither. A circumstance so very extraordinary had never been recorded in the annals of Saint Mary's, or in the traditions of Glendearg, though there was a faint legendary report that a certain Abbot had dined there in old days, after having been bewildered in a hunting expedition amongst the wilds which lie to the northward. But that the present Lord Abbot should have taken a voluntary journey to so wild and dreary a spot, the very Kamtschatka of the Halidome, was a thing never dreamt of; and the news excited the greatest surprise in all the members of the family saving Halbert alone.

This fiery youth was too full of the insult he had received to think of anything as unconnected with it. "I am glad of it," he exclaimed; "I am glad the Abbot comes hither. I will know of him by what right this stranger is sent hither to domineer over us under our father's roof, as if we were slaves and not freemen. I will tell the proud priest to his beard——"

"Alas! alas! my brother," said Edward, "think what these words may cost thee!"

"And what will, or what can they cost me," said Halbert, "that I should sacrifice my human feelings and my justifiable resentment to the fear of what the Abbot can do?"

"Our mother—our mother!" exclaimed Edward; "think, if she is de prived of her home, expelled from her property, how can you amend what your rashness may ruin?"

"It is too true, by Heaven!" said Halbert, striking his forehead. Then, stamping his foot against the floor to express the full energy of the passion to which he dared no longer give vent, he turned round and left the apartment.

Mary Avenel looked at the stranger knight, while she was endeavouring to frame a request that he would not report the intemperate violence of her foster-brother to the prejudice of his family, in the mind of the Abbot. But Sir Piercie, the very pink of courtesy, conjectured her meaning from her embarrassment, and waited not to be entreated.

"Credit me, fairest Protection," said he, "your Affability is less than capable of seeing or hearing, far less of reciting or reiterating, aught of an unseemly nature which may have chanced while I enjoyed the Elysium of your presence. The winds of idle passion may indeed rudely agitate the bosom of the rude; but the heart of the courtier is polished to resist them. As the frozen lake receives not the influence of the breeze, even so——"

The voice of Dame Glendinning, in shrill summons, here demanded Mary Avenel's attendance, who instantly obeyed, not a little glad to escape from the compliments and similes of this courtlike gallant. Nor was it apparently less a relief on his part; for no sooner was she past the threshold of the room, than he exchanged the look of formal and elaborate politeness which had accompanied each word he had uttered hitherto, for an expression of the utmost lassitude and ennui; and after indulging in one or two portentous yawns, broke forth into a soliloquy.

"What the foul fiend sent this wench hither? As if it were not sufficient plague to be harboured in a hovel that would hardly serve for a dog's kennel in England, baited by a rude peasant-boy, and dependent on the faith of a mercenary ruffian, but I cannot even have time to muse over my own mishap, but must come aloft, frisk, fidget, and make speeches, to please this pale hectic phantom, because she has gentle blood in her veins? By mine honour, setting prejudice aside, the mill-wench is the more attractive of the two — But patienza, Piercie Shafton; thou must not lose thy well-earned claim to be accounted a devout servant of the fair sex, a witty-brained, prompt, and accomplished courtier. Rather thank heaven, Piercie Shafton, which hath sent thee a subject, wherein, without derogating from thy rank, (since the honours of the Avenel family are beyond dispute,) thou mayest find a whetstone for thy witty compliments, a strop whereon to sharpen thine acute engine, a butt whereat to shoot the arrows of thy gallantry. For even as a Bilboa blade, the more it is rubbed, the brighter and the sharper will it prove, so——But what need I waste my stock of similitudes in holding converse with myself?—Yonder comes the monkish retinue, like some half score of crows winging their way slowly up the valley — I hope, a'gad, they have not forgotten my trunk-mails of apparel amid the ample provision they have made for their own belly-timber—Mercy, a'gad, I were finely holped up if the vesture has miscarried among the thievish Borderers!"

Stung by this reflection, he ran hastily down stairs, and caused his horse to be saddled, that he might, as soon as possible, ascertain this important point, by meeting the Lord Abbot and his retinue as they came up the glen. He had not ridden a mile before he met them advancing with the slowness and decorum which became persons of their dignity and profession. The knight failed not to greet the Lord Abbot with all the formal compliments with which men of rank at that period exchanged courtesies. He had the good fortune to find that his mails were numbered among the train of baggage which attended upon the party; and, satisfied in that particular, he turned his horse's head, and accompanied the Abbot to the Tower of Glendearg.

Great, in the meanwhile, had been the turmoil of the good Dame Elspeth and her coadjutors, to prepare for the fitting reception of the Father Lord Abbot and his retinue. The monks had indeed taken care not to trust too much to the state of her pantry; but she was not the less anxious to make such additions as might enable her to claim the thanks of her feudal lord and spiritual father. Meeting Halbert, as, with his blood on fire, he returned from his altercation with her guest, she commanded him instantly to go forth to the hill, and not to return without venison; reminding him that he was apt enough to go thither for his own pleasure, and must now do so for the credit of the house.

The Miller, who was now hastening his journey homewards, promised to send up some salmon by his own servant. Dame Elspeth, who by this time thought she had guests enough, had begun to repent of her invitation to poor Mysie, and was just considering by what means, short of giving offence, she could send off the Maid of the Mill behind her father, and adjourn all her own aerial architecture till some future opportunity, when this unexpected generosity on the part of the sire rendered any present attempt to return his daughter on his hands too highly ungracious to be farther thought on. So the Miller departed alone on his homeward journey.

Dame Elspeth's sense of hospitality proved in this instance its own reward; for Mysie had dwelt too near the Convent to be altogether ignorant of the noble art of cookery, which her father patronized to the extent of consuming on festival days such dainties as his daughter could prepare in emulation of the luxuries of the Abbot's kitchen. Laying aside, therefore, her holiday kirtle, and adopting a dress more suitable to the occasion, the good-humored maiden bared her snowy arms above the elbows; and, as Elspeth acknowledged, in the language of the time and country, took "entire and aefauld part with her" in the labours of the day; showing unparalleled talent, and indefatigable industry, in the preparation of *mortreux*, *blanc-manger*, and heaven knows what delicacies besides, which Dame Glendinning, unassisted by her skill, dared not even have dreamt of presenting.

Leaving this able substitute in the kitchen, and regretting that Mary Avenel was so brought up, that she could intrust nothing to her care, unless it might be seeing the great chamber strewed with rushes, and ornamented with such flowers and branches as the season afforded, Dame Elspeth hastily donned her best attire, and with a beating heart presented herself at the door of her little tower, to make her obeisance to the Lord Abbot as he crossed her humble threshold. Edward stood by his mother, and felt the same palpitation, which his philosophy was at a loss to account for. He was yet to learn how long it is ere our reason is enabled to triumph over the force of external circumstances, and how much our feelings are affected by novelty, and blunted by use and habit.

On the present occasion, he witnessed with wonder and awe the approach of some half-score of riders, sober men upon sober palfreys, muffled in their long black garments, and only relieved by their white scapularies, showing more like a funeral procession than aught else, and not quickening their pace beyond that which permitted easy conversation and easy digestion. The sobriety of the scene was indeed somewhat enlivened by the presence of Sir Piercie Shafton, who, to show that his skill in the manege was not inferior to his other accomplishments, kept alternately pressing and checking his gay courser, forcing him to piaffe, to caracole, to passage, and to do all the other feats of the school, to the great annoyance of the Lord Abbot, the wonted sobriety of whose palfrey became at length discomposed by the vivacity of its companion, while the dignitary kept crying out in bodily alarm, "I do pray you — Sir Knight — good now, Sir Piercie — Be quiet, Benedict, there is a good steed—soh, poor fellow!" and uttering all the other precatory and soothing exclamations by which a timid horseman usually bespeaks the favour of a frisky companion, or of his own unquiet nag, and concluding the bead-roll with a sincere *Deo gratias* so soon as he alighted in the court-yard of the Tower of Glendearg.

The inhabitants unanimously knelt down to kiss the hand of the Lord Abbot, a ceremony which even the monks were often condemned to. Good Abbot Boniface was too much fluttered by the incidents of the latter part of his journey, to go through this ceremony with much solemnity, or indeed with much patience. He kept wiping his brow with a snow-white handkerchief with one hand, while another was abandoned to the homage of his vassals; and then signing the cross with his outstretched arm, and exclaiming, "Bless ye — bless ye, my children!" he hastened into the house, and murmured not a little at the darkness and steepness of the rugged winding stair, whereby he at length scaled the spence destined for his entertainment, and, overcome with fatigue, threw himself, I do not say into an easy chair, but into the easiest the apartment afforded.

Chapter the Sixteenth.

A courtier extraordinary, who by diet
Of meats and drinks, his temperate exercise,
Choice music, frequent bath, his horary shifts
Of shirts and waistcoats, means to immortalize
Mortality itself, and makes the essence
Of his whole happiness the trim of court.
MAGNETIC LADY.

WHEN the Lord Abbot had suddenly and superciliously vanished from the eyes of his expectant vassals, the Sub-Prior made amends for the negligence of his principal, by the kind and affectionate greeting which he gave to all the members of the family, but especially to Dame Elspeth, her foster-daughter, and her son Edward. "Where," he even condescended to inquire, "is that naughty Nimrod, Halbert? — He hath not yet, I trust, turned, like his great prototype, his hunting-spear against man!"

"O no, an it please your reverence," said Dame Glendinning, "Halbert is up at the glen to get some venison, or surely he would not have been absent when such a day of honour dawned upon me and mine."

"Oh, to get savoury meat, such as our soul loveth," muttered the Sub-Prior; "it has been at times an acceptable gift. — I bid you good morrow, my good dame, as I must attend upon his lordship the Father Abbot."

"And O, reverend sir," said the good widow, detaining him, "if it might be your pleasure to take part with us if there is any thing wrong; and if there is any thing wanted, to say that it is just coming, or to make some excuses your learning best knows how. Every bit of vassail and silver work have we been spoiled of since Pinkie Cleuch, when I lost poor Simon Glendinning, that was the warst of a'."

"Never mind — never fear," said the Sub-Prior, gently extricating his garment from the anxious grasp of Dame Elspeth, "the Refectioner has with him the Abbot's plate and drinking cups; and I pray you to believe that whatever is short in your entertainment will be deemed amply made up in your good-will."

So saying, he escaped from her and went into the spence, where such preparations as haste permitted were making for the noon collation of the Abbot and the English knight. Here he found the Lord Abbot, for whom a cushion, composed of all the plaids in the house, had been unable to render Simon's huge elbow-chair a soft or comfortable place of rest.

"Benedicite!" said Abbot Boniface, "now marry fie upon these hard benches with all my heart — they are as uneasy as the *scabella* of our novices. Saint Jude be with us, Sir Knight, how have you contrived to pass over the night in this dungeon? An your bed was no softer than your seat, you might as well have slept on the stone couch of Saint Pacomius. After trotting a full ten miles, a man needs a softer seat than has fallen to my hard lot."

With sympathizing faces, the Sacristan and the Refectioner ran to raise the Lord Abbot, and to adjust his seat to his mind, which was at length accomplished in some sort, although he continued alternately to bewail his fatigue, and to exult in the conscious sense of having discharged an arduous duty. "You errant cavaliers," said he, addressing the knight, "may now perceive that others have their travail and their toils to undergo as well as your honoured faculty. And this I will say for myself and the soldiers of Saint Mary, among whom I may be termed captain, that it is not our wont to flinch from the heat of the service, or to withdraw from the good fight. No, by Saint Mary! — no sooner did I learn that you were here, and dared not for certain reasons come to the Monastery, where, with as good will, and with more convenience, we might have given you a better reception, than, striking the table with my hammer, I called a brother — Timothy, said I, let them saddle Benedict — let them saddle my black palfrey, and bid the Sub-Prior and some half-score of attendants be in readiness to-morrow after matins — we would ride to Glendearg. — Brother Timothy stared, thinking, I imagine, that his ears had scarce done him justice—but I repeated my commands, and said, Let the Kitchener and Refectioner go before to aid the poor vassals to whom the place belongs in making a suitable collation. So that you will consider, good Sir Piercie, our mutual incommodities, and forgive whatever you may find amiss."

"By my faith," said Sir Piercie Shafton, "there is nothing to forgive — If you spiritual warriors have to submit to the grievous incommodities which your lordship narrates, it would ill become me, a sinful and secular man, to complain of a bed as hard as a board, of broth which relished as if made of burnt wool, of flesh, which, in its sable and singed shape, seemed to put me on a level with Richard Cœur-de-Lion, when he ate up the head of a Moor carbonadoed, and of other viands savouring rather of the rusticity of this northern region."

"By the good Saints, sir," said the Abbot, somewhat touched in point of his character for hospitality, of which he was in truth a most faithful and zealous professor, "it grieves me to the heart that you have found our vassals no better provided for your reception—Yet I crave leave to observe, that if Sir Piercie Shafton's affairs had permitted him to honour with his company our poor house of Saint Mary's, he might have had less to complain of in respect of easements."

"To give your lordship the reasons," said Sir Piercie Shafton, "why I could not at this present time approach your dwelling, or avail myself of its well-known and undoubted hospitality, craves either some delay, or," looking around him, "a limited audience."

The Lord Abbot immediately issued his mandate to the Refectioner: "Hie thee to the kitchen, Brother Hilarius, and there make inquiry of our brother the Kitchener, within what time he opines that our collation may be prepared, since sin and sorrow it were, considering the hardships of this noble and gallant knight, no whit mentioning or weighing those we ourselves have endured, if we were now either to advance or retard the hour of refection beyond the time when the viands are fit to be set before us."

Brother Hilarius parted with an eager alertness to execute the will of his Superior, and returned with the assurance, that punctually at one afternoon would the collation be ready.

"Before that time," said the accurate Refectioner, "the wafers, flamms, and pastry-meat, will scarce have had the just degree of fire which learned pottingers prescribe as fittest for the body; and if it should be past one o'clock, were it but ten minutes, our brother the Kitchener opines, that the haunch of venison would suffer in spite of the skill of the little turn-broche whom he has recommended to your holiness by his praises."

"How!" said the Abbot, "a haunch of venison! — from whence comes that dainty? I remember not thou didst intimate its presence in thy hamper of vivers."

"So please your holiness and lordship," said the Refectioner, "he is a son of the woman of the house who has shot it and sent it in — killed but now; yet, as the animal heat hath not left the body, the Kitchener undertakes it shall eat as tender as a young chicken — and this youth hath a special gift in shooting deer, and never misses the heart or the brain; so that the blood is not driven through the flesh, as happens too often with us. It is a hart of grease — your holiness has seldom seen such a haunch."

"Silence, Brother Hilarius," said the Abbot, wiping his mouth; "it is not beseeming our order to talk of food so earnestly, especially as we must oft have our animal powers exhausted by fasting, and be accessible (as being ever mere mortals) to those signs of longing" (he again wiped his mouth) "which arise on the mention of victuals to an hungry man. — Minute down, however, the name of that youth — it is fitting merit should be rewarded, and he shall hereafter be a *frater ad succurrendum* in the kitchen and buttery."

"Alas! reverend Father and my good lord," replied the Refectioner, "I did inquire after the youth, and I learn he is one who prefers the casque to the cowl, and the sword of the flesh to the weapons of the spirit."

"And if it be so," said the Abbot, "see that thou retain him as a deputy-keeper and man-at-arms, and not as a lay brother of the Monastery — for old Tallboy, our forester, waxes dim-eyed, and hath twice spoiled a noble buck, by hitting him unwarily on the haunch. Ah! 'tis a foul fault, the abusing by evil-killing, evil-dressing, evil-appetite, or otherwise, the good creatures indulged to us for our use. Wherefore, secure us the service of this youth, Brother Hilarius, in the way that may best suit him. — And now, Sir Piercie Shafton, since the fates have assigned us a space of well-nigh an hour, ere we dare hope to enjoy more than the vapour or savour of our repast, may I pray you, of your courtesy, to tell me the cause of this visit; and, above all, to inform us, why you will not approach our more pleasant and better furnished *hospitium?*"

"Reverend Father, and my very good lord," said Sir Piercie Shafton, "it is well known to your wisdom, that there are stone walls which have ears, and that secrecy is to be looked to in matters which concern a man's head."

The Abbot signed to his attendants, excepting the Sub-Prior, to leave the room, and then said, "Your valour, Sir Piercie, may freely unburden yourself before our faithful friend and counsellor Father Eustace, the benefits of whose advice we may too soon lose, inasmuch as his merits will speedily recommend him to an higher station, in which we trust he may find the blessing of a friend and adviser as valuable as himself, since I may say of him, as our claustral rhyme goeth,*

'Dixit Abbas ad Prioris,
Tu es homo boni moris,
Quia semper sanioris
Mihi das concilia.'

Indeed," he added, "the office of Sub-Prior is altogether beneath our dear brother; nor can we elevate him unto that of Prior, which, for certain reasons, is at present kept vacant amongst us. Howbeit, Father Eustace is fully possessed of my confidence, and worthy of yours, and well may it be said of him, *Intravit in secretis nostris.*"

Sir Piercie Shafton bowed to the reverend brethren, and, heaving a sigh, as if he would burst his steel cuirass, he thus commenced his speech: —

"Certes, reverend sirs, I may well heave such a suspiration, who have, as it were, exchanged heaven for purgatory, leaving the lightsome sphere of the royal court of England for a remote nook in this inaccessible desert — quitting the tilt-yard, where I was ever ready among my compeers to splinter a lance, either for the love of honour, or for the honour of love, in order to couch my knightly spear against base and pilfering besognios and marauders — exchanging the lighted halls, wherein I used nimbly to pace the swift coranto, or to move with a loftier grace in the stately galliard, for this rugged and decayed dungeon of rusty-coloured stone — quitting the gay theatre, for the solitary chimney-nook of a Scottish dog-house — bartering the sounds of the soul-ravishing lute, and the love-awaking viol-de-gamba, for the discordant squeak of a northern bagpipe — above all, exchanging the smiles of those beauties, who form a gay galaxy around the throne of England, for the cold courtesy of an untaught damsel, and the bewildered

* The rest of this doggerel rhyme may be found in Fosbrooke's learned work on British Monachism.

stare of a miller's maiden. More might I say of the exchange of the conversation of gallant knights and gay courtiers of mine own order and capacity, whose conceits are bright and vivid as the lightning, for that of monks and churchmen — but it were discourteous to urge that topic."

The Abbot listened to this list of complaints with great round eyes, which evinced no exact intelligence of the orator's meaning; and when the knight paused to take breath, he looked with a doubtful and inquiring eye at the Sub-Prior, not well knowing in what tone he should reply to an exordium so extraordinary. The Sub-Prior accordingly stepped in to the relief of his principal.

"We deeply sympathize with you, Sir Knight, in the several mortifications and hardships to which fate has subjected you, particularly in that which has thrown you into the society of those, who, as they were conscious they deserved not such an honour, so neither did they at all desire it. But all this goes little way to expound the cause of this train of disasters, or, in plainer words, the reason which has compelled you into a situation having so few charms for you."

"Gentle and reverend sir," replied the knight, "forgive an unhappy person, who, in giving a history of his miseries, dilateth upon them extremely, even as he who, having fallen from a precipice, looketh upward to measure the height from which he hath been precipitated."

"Yea, but," said Father Eustace, "methinks it were wiser in him to tell those who come to lift him up, which of his bones have been broken."

"You, reverend sir," said the knight, "have, in the encounter of our wits, made a fair attaint; whereas I may be in some sort said to have broken my staff across.* Pardon me, grave sir, that I speak in the language of the tilt-yard, which is doubtless strange to your reverend years. — Ah! brave resort of the noble, the fair and the gay! — Ah! throne of love, and citadel of honour! — Ah! celestial beauties, by whose bright eyes it is graced! Never more shall Piercie Shafton advance, as the centre of your radiant glances, couch his lance, and spur his horse at the sound of the spirit-stirring trumpets, nobly called the voice of war — never more shall he baffle his adversary's encounter boldly, break his spear dexterously, and ambling around the lovely circle, receive the rewards with which beauty honours chivalry!"

Here he paused, wrung his hands, looked upwards, and seemed lost in contemplation of his own fallen fortunes.

"Mad, very mad," whispered the Abbot to the Sub-Prior; "I would we were fairly rid of him; for, of a truth, I expect he will proceed from raving to mischief—Were it not better to call up the rest of the brethren?"

But the Sub-Prior knew better than his Superior how to distinguish the jargon of affectation from the ravings of insanity, and although the extremity of the knight's passion seemed altogether fantastic, yet he was not ignorant to what extravagancies the fashion of the day can conduct its votaries.

Allowing, therefore, two minutes' space to permit the knight's enthusiastic feelings to exhaust themselves, he again gravely reminded him that the Lord Abbot had taken a journey, unwonted to his age and habits, solely to learn in what he could serve Sir Piercie Shafton—that it was altogether impossible he could do so without his receiving distinct information of the situation in which he had now sought refuge in Scotland.—"The day wore on," he observed, looking at the window; "and if the Abbot should be obliged to return to the Monastery without obtaining the necessary intelligence, the regret might be mutual, but the inconvenience was like to be all on Sir Piercie's own side."

The hint was not thrown away.

---

* *Attaint* was a term of tilting used to express the champion's having *attained* his mark, or, in other words, struck his lance straight and fair against the helmet or breast of his adversary. Whereas to break the lance across, intimated a total failure in directing the point of the weapon on the object of his aim.

"O, goddess of courtesy!" said the knight, "can I so far have forgotten thy behests as to make this good prelate's ease and time a sacrifice to my vain complaints! Know, then, most worthy, and not less worshipful, that I, your poor visitor and guest, am by birth nearly bound to the Piercie of Northumberland, whose fame is so widely blown through all parts of the world where English worth hath been known. Now, this present Earl of Northumberland, of whom I propose to give you the brief history——"

"It is altogether unnecessary," said the Abbot; "we know him to be a good and true nobleman, and a sworn upholder of our Catholic faith, in the spite of the heretical woman who now sits upon the throne of England. And it is specially as his kinsman, and as knowing that ye partake with him in such devout and faithful belief and adherence to our holy Mother Church, that we say to you, Sir Piercie Shafton, that ye be heartily welcome to us, and that, and we wist how, we would labour to do you good service in your extremity."

"For such kind offer I rest your most humble debtor," said Sir Piercie, "nor need I at this moment say more than that my Right Honourable Cousin of Northumberland, having devised with me and some others, the choice and picked spirits of the age, how and by what means the worship of God, according to the Catholic Church, might be again introduced into this distracted kingdom of England, (even as one deviseth, by the assistance of his friend, to catch and bridle a runaway steed,) it pleased him so deeply to intrust me in those communications, that my personal safety becomes, as it were, entwined or complicated therewith. Natheless, as we have had sudden reason to believe, this Princess Elizabeth, who maintaineth around her a sort of counsellors skilful in tracking whatever schemes may be pursued for bringing her title into challenge, or for erecting again the discipline of the Catholic Church, has obtained certain knowledge of the trains which we had laid before we could give fire unto them. Wherefore, my Right Honourable Cousin of Northumberland, thinking it best belike that one man should take both blame and shame for the whole, did lay the burden of all this trafficking upon my back; which load I am the rather content to bear, in that he hath always shown himself my kind and honourable kinsman, as well as that my estate, I wot not how, hath of late been somewhat insufficient to maintain the expense of those braveries, wherewith it is incumbent on us, who are chosen and selected spirits, to distinguish ourselves from the vulgar."

"So that possibly," said the Sub-Prior, "your private affairs rendered a foreign journey less incommodious to you than it might have been to the noble earl, your right worthy cousin?"

"You are right, reverend sir," answered the courtier; "*rem acu*—you have touched the point with a needle—My cost and expenses had been indeed somewhat lavish at the late triumphs and tourneys, and the flat-capp'd citizens had shown themselves unwilling to furnish my pocket for new gallantries for the honour of the nation, as well as for mine own peculiar glory—and, to speak truth, it was in some part the hope of seeing these matters amended that led me to desire a new world in England."

"So that the miscarriage of your public enterprise, with the derangement of your own private affairs," said the Sub-Prior, "have induced you to seek Scotland as a place of refuge?"

"*Rem acu*, once again," said Sir Piercie; and not without good cause, since my neck, if I remained, might have been brought within the circumstances of a halter—and so speedy was my journey northward, that I had but time to exchange my peach-coloured doublet of Genoa velvet, thickly laid over with goldsmith's work, for this cuirass, which was made by Bonamico of Milan, and travelled northward with all speed, judging that I might do well to visit my Right Honourable Cousin of Northumberland, at one of his numerous castles. But as I posted towards Alnwick, even with the speed of a star, which, darting from its native sphere, shoots wildly downwards, I was met at Northallerton by one Henry Vaughan, a servant of my right honourable kinsman, who showed me, that as then I might not with safety come to his presence, seeing that, in obedience to orders from his court, he was obliged to issue out letters for my incarceration."

"This," said the Abbot, "seems but hard measure on the part of your honourable kinsman."

"It might be so judged, my lord," replied Sir Piercie; "nevertheless, I will stand to the death for the honour of my Right Honourable Cousin of Northumberland. Also, Henry Vaughan gave me, from my said cousin, a good horse, and a purse of gold, with two Border-prickers, as they are called, for my guides, who conducted me, by such roads and by-paths as have never been seen since the days of Sir Lancelot and Sir Tristrem, into this kingdom of Scotland, and to the house of a certain baron, or one who holds the style of such, called Julian Avenel, with whom I found such reception as the place and party could afford."

"And that," said the Abbot, "must have been right wretched; for to judge from the appetite which Julian showeth when abroad, he hath not, I judge, over-abundant provision at home."

"You are right, sir—your reverence is in the right," continued Sir Piercie; "we had but lenten fare, and, what was worse, a score to clear at the departure; for though this Julian Avenel called us to no reckoning, yet he did so extravagantly admire the fashion of my poniard—the *poignet* being of silver exquisitely hatched, and indeed the weapon being altogether a piece of exceeding rare device and beauty—that in faith I could not for very shame's sake but pray his acceptance of it; words which he gave me not the trouble of repeating twice, before he had stuck it into his greasy buff-belt, where, credit me, reverend sir, it showed more like a butcher's knife than a gentleman's dagger."

"So goodly a gift might at least have purchased you a few days' hospitality," said Father Eustace.

"Reverend sir," said Sir Piercie, "had I abidden with him, I should have been complimented out of every remnant of my wardrobe—actually flayed, by the hospitable gods I swear it! Sir, he secured my spare doublet, and had a pluck at my galligaskins—I was enforced to beat a retreat before I was altogether unrigged. That Border knave, his serving man, had a pluck at me too, and usurped a scarlet cassock and steel cuirass belonging to the page of my body, whom I was fain to leave behind me. In good time I received a letter from my Right Honourable Cousin, showing me that he had written to you in my behalf, and sent to your charge two mails filled with wearing apparel—namely, my rich crimson silk doublet, slashed out and lined with cloth of gold, which I wore at the last revels, with baldric and trimmings to correspond—also two pair black silk slops, with hanging garters of carnation silk—also the flesh-coloured silken doublet, with the trimmings of fur, in which I danced the salvage man at the Gray's-Inn mummery—also ——"

"Sir Knight," said the Sub-Prior, "I pray you to spare the farther inventory of your wardrobe. The monks of Saint Mary's are no free-booting barons, and whatever part of your vestments arrived at our house, have been this day faithfully brought hither, with the mails which contained them. I may presume from what has been said, as we have indeed been given to understand by the Earl of Northumberland, that your desire is to remain for the present as unknown and as unnoticed, as may be consistent with your high worth and distinction?"

"Alas, reverend father!" replied the courtier, "a blade when it is in the scabbard cannot give lustre, a diamond when it is in the casket cannot give light, and worth, when it is compelled by circumstances to obscure itself, cannot draw observation — my retreat can only attract the admiration of those few to whom circumstances permit its displaying itself."

"I conceive now, my venerable father and lord," said the Sub-Prior, "that your wisdom will assign such a course of conduct to this noble knight, as may be alike consistent with his safety, and with the weal of the community. For you wot well, that perilous strides have been made in these audacious days, to the destruction of all ecclesiastical foundations, and that our holy community has been repeatedly menaced. Hitherto they have found no flaw in our raiment; but a party, friendly as well to the Queen of England, as to the heretical doctrines of the schismatical church, or even to worse and wilder forms of heresy, prevails now at the court of our sovereign, who dare not yield to her suffering clergy the protection she would gladly extend to them."

"My lord, and reverend sir," said the knight, "I will gladly relieve you of my presence, while ye canvass this matter at your freedom; and to speak truly, I am desirous to see in what case the chamberlain of my noble kinsman hath found my wardrobe, and how he hath packed the same, and whether it has suffered from the journey — there are four suits of as pure and elegant device as ever the fancy of a fair lady doated upon, every one having a treble, and appropriate change of ribbons, trimmings, and fringes, which, in case of need, may as it were renew each of them, and multiply the four into twelve. — There is also my sad-coloured riding-suit, and three cut-work shirts with falling bands — I pray you, pardon me — I must needs see how matters stand with them without farther dallying."

Thus speaking, he left the room; and the Sub-Prior, looking after him significantly, added, "Where the treasure is will the heart be also."

"Saint Mary preserve our wits!" said the Abbot, stunned with the knight's abundance of words; "were man's brains ever so stuffed with silk and broadcloth, cut-work, and I wot not what besides! And what could move the Earl of Northumberland to assume for his bosom counsellor, in matters of death and danger, such a feather-brained coxcomb as this?"

"Had he been other than what he is, venerable father," said the Sub-Prior, "he had been less fitted for the part of scape-goat, to which his Right Honourable Cousin had probably destined him from the commencement, in case of their plot failing. I know something of this Piercie Shafton. The legitimacy of his mother's descent from the Piercie family, the point on which he is most jealous, hath been called in question. If hairbrained courage, and an outrageous spirit of gallantry, can make good his pretensions to the high lineage he claims, these qualities have never been denied him. For the rest, he is one of the ruffling gallants of the time, like Rowland Yorke, Stukely,* and others, who wear out their fortunes, and endanger their lives, in idle braveries, in order that they may be esteemed the only choice gallants of the time; and afterwards endeavour to repair their

---

* "Yorke," says Camden, "was a Londoner, a man of loose and dissolute behaviour, and desperately audacious — famous in his time amongst the common bullies and swaggerers, as being the first that, to the great admiration of many at his boldness, brought into England the bold and dangerous way of fencing with the rapier in duelling. Whereas, till that time, the English used to fight with long swords and bucklers, striking with the edge, and thought it no part of man either to push or strike beneath the girdle.

Having a command in the Low Countries, Yorke revolted to the Spaniards, and died miserably, poisoned, as was supposed, by his new allies. Three years afterwards, his bones were dug up and gibbeted by the command of the States of Holland.

Thomas Stukely, another distinguished gallant of the time, was bred a merchant, being the son of a rich clothier in the west. He wedded the daughter and heiress of a wealthy alderman of London, named Curtis, after whose death he squandered the riches he thus acquired in all manner of extravagance. His wife, whose fortune supplied his waste, represented to him that he ought to make more of her. Stukely replied, "I will make as much of thee, believe me, as it is possible for any to do;" and he kept his word in one sense, having stripped her even of her wearing apparel, before he finally ran away from her.

Having fled to Italy, he contrived to impose upon the Pope, with a plan of invading Ireland, for which he levied soldiers, and made some preparations, but ended by engaging himself and his troops in the service of King Sebastian of Portugal. He sailed with that prince on his fatal voyage to Barbary, and fell with him at the battle of Alcazar.

Stukely, as one of the first gallants of the time, has had the honour to be chronicled in song, in Evans' Old Ballads, vol. iii. edition 1810. His fate is also introduced in a tragedy, by George Peel, as has been supposed, called the Battle of Alcazar, from which play Dryden is alleged to have taken the idea of Don Sebastian; if so, it is surprising he omitted a character so congenial to King Charles the Second's time as the witty, brave, and profligate Thomas Stukely.

estate, by engaging in the desperate plots and conspiracies which wiser heads have devised. To use one of his own conceited similitudes, such courageous fools resemble hawks, which the wiser conspirator keeps hooded and blinded on his wrist until the quarry is on the wing, and who are then flown at them."

"Saint Mary," said the Abbot, "he were an evil guest to introduce into our quiet household. Our young monks make bustle enough, and more than is beseeming God's servants, about their outward attire already — this knight were enough to turn their brains, from the *Vestiarius* down to the very scullion boy."

"A worse evil might follow," said the Sub-Prior: "in these bad days, the patrimony of the church is bought and sold, forfeited and distrained, as if it were the unhallowed soil appertaining to a secular baron. Think what penalty awaits us, were we convicted of harbouring a rebel to her whom they call the Queen of England! There would neither be wanting Scottish parasites to beg the lands of the foundation, nor an army from England to burn and harry the Halidome. The men of Scotland were once Scotsmen, firm and united in the love of their country, and throwing every other consideration aside when the frontier was menaced — now they are — what shall I call them—the one part French, the other part English, considering their dear native country merely as a prize-fighting stage, upon which foreigners are welcome to decide their quarrels."

"Benedictine!" replied the Abbot, "they are indeed slippery and evil times."

"And therefore," said Father Eustace, "we must walk warily—we must not, for example, bring this man—this Sir Piercie Shafton, to our house of Saint Mary's."

"But how then shall we dispose of him?" replied the Abbot; "bethink thee that he is a sufferer for holy Church's sake — that his patron, the Earl of Northumberland, hath been our friend, and that, lying so near us, he may work us weal or wo according as we deal with his kinsman."

"And, accordingly," said the Sub-Prior, "for these reasons, as well as for discharge of the great duty of Christian charity, I would protect and relieve this man. Let him not go back to Julian Avenel—that unconscientious baron would not stick to plunder the exiled stranger—Let him remain here—the spot is secluded, and if the accommodation be beneath his quality, discovery will become the less likely. We will make such means for his convenience as we can devise."

"Will he be persuaded, thinkest thou?" said the Abbot; "I will leave my own travelling bed for his repose, and send up a suitable easy-chair."

"With such easements," said the Sub-Prior, "he must not complain; and then, if threatened by any sudden danger, he can soon come down to the sanctuary, where we will harbour him in secret until means can be devised of dismissing him in safety."

"Were we not better," said the Abbot, "send him on to the court, and get rid of him at once?"

"Ay, but at the expense of our friends — this butterfly may fold his wings, and lie under cover in the cold air of Glendearg; but were he at Holyrood, he would, did his life depend on it, expand his spangled drapery in the eyes of the queen and court — Rather than fail of distinction, he would sue for love to our gracious sovereign — the eyes of all men would be upon him in the course of three short days, and the international peace of the two ends of the island endangered for a creature, who, like a silly moth, cannot abstain from fluttering round a light."

"Thou hast prevailed with me, Father Eustace," said the Abbot, "and it will go hard but I improve on thy plan — I will send up in secret, not only household stuff, but wine and wassell-bread. There is a young swankie here who shoots venison well. I will give him directions to see that the knight lacks none."

"Whatever accommodation he can have, which infers not a risk of discovery," said the Sub-Prior, "it is our duty to afford him."

"Nay," said the Abbot, "we will do more, and will instantly despatch a servant express to the keeper of our revestiary to send us such things as he may want, even this night. See it done, good father."

"I will," answered Father Eustace; "but I hear the gull clamorous for some one to truss his points.* He will be fortunate if he lights on any one here who can do him the office of groom of the chamber."

"I would he would appear," said the Abbot, "for here comes the Refectioner with the collation — By my faith, the ride hath given me a sharp appetite!"

Chapter the Seventeenth.

I'll seek for other aid — Spirits, they say,
Flit round invisible, as thick as motes
Dance in the sunbeam. If that spell
Or necromancer's sigil can compel them,
They shall hold council with me.

James Duff.

The reader's attention must be recalled to Halbert Glendinning, who had left the Tower of Glendearg immediately after his quarrel with its new guest, Sir Piercie Shafton. As he walked with a rapid pace up the glen, Old Martin followed him, beseeching him to be less hasty.

"Halbert," said the old man, "you will never live to have white hair, if you take fire thus at every spark of provocation."

"And why should I wish it, old man," said Halbert, "if I am to be the butt that every fool may aim a shaft of scorn against? — What avails it, old man, that you yourself move, sleep, and wake, eat thy niggard meal, and repose on thy hard pallet?—Why art thou so well pleased that the morning should call thee up to daily toil, and the evening again lay thee down a wearied-out wretch? Were it not better sleep and wake no more, than to undergo this dull exchange of labour for insensibility and of insensibility for labour?"

"God help me," answered Martin, "there may be truth in what thou sayest — but walk slower, for my old limbs cannot keep pace with your young legs — walk slower, and I will tell you why age, though unlovely, is yet endurable."

"Speak on then," said Halbert, slackening his pace, "but remember we must seek venison to refresh the fatigues of these holy men, who will this morning have achieved a journey of ten miles; and if we reach not the Brocksburn head we are scarce like to see an antler."

"Then know, my good Halbert," said Martin, "whom I love as my own son, that I am satisfied to live till death calls me, because my Maker wills it. Ay, and although I spend what men call a hard life, pinched with cold in winter, and burnt with heat in summer, though I feed hard and sleep hard, and am held mean and despised, yet I bethink me, that were I of no use on the face of this fair creation, God would withdraw me from it."

* The points were the strings of cord or ribbon, (so called, because *pointed* with metal like the laces of women's stays,) which attached the doublet to the hose. They were very numerous, and required assistance to tie them properly, which was called *trussing*.

"Thou poor old man," said Halbert, "and can such a vain conceit as this of thy fancied use, reconcile thee to a world where thou playest so poor a part?"

"My part was nearly as poor," said Martin, "my person nearly as much despised, the day that I saved my mistress and her child from perishing in the wilderness."

"Right, Martin," answered Halbert; "there, indeed, thou didst what might be a sufficient apology for a whole life of insignificance."

"And do you account it for nothing, Halbert, that I should have the power of giving you a lesson of patience, and submission to the destinies of Providence? Methinks there is use for the grey hairs on the old scalp, were it but to instruct the green head by precept and by example."

Halbert held down his face, and remained silent for a minute or two, and then resumed his discourse: "Martin, seest thou aught changed in me of late?"

"Surely," said Martin. "I have always known you hasty, wild, and inconsiderate, rude, and prompt to speak at the volley and without reflection; but now, methinks, your bearing, without losing its natural fire, has something in it of force and dignity which it had not before. It seems as if you had fallen asleep a carle, and awakened a gentleman."

"Thou canst judge, then, of noble bearing?" said Halbert.

"Surely," answered Martin, "in some sort I can; for I have travelled through court, and camp, and city, with my master, Walter Avenel, although he could do nothing for me in the long run, but give me room for two score of sheep on the hill — and surely even now, while I speak with you, I feel sensible that my language is more refined than it is my wont to use, and that—though I know not the reason—the rude northern dialect, so familiar to my tongue, has given place to a more town-bred speech."

"And this change in thyself and me, thou canst by no means account for?" said young Glendinning.

"Change!" replied Martin, "by our Lady it is not so much a change which I feel, as a recalling and renewing sentiments and expressions which I had some thirty years since, ere Tibb and I set up our humble household. It is singular, that your society should have this sort of influence over me, Halbert, and that I should never have experienced it ere now."

"Thinkest thou," said Halbert, "thou seest in me aught that can raise me from this base, low, despised state, into one where I may rank with those proud men, who now despise my clownish poverty?"

Martin paused an instant, and then answered, "Doubtless you may, Halbert; as broken a ship has come to land. Heard ye never of Hughie Dun, who left this Halidome some thirty-five years gone by? A deliverly fellow was Hughie—could read and write like a priest, and could wield brand and buckler with the best of the riders. I mind him — the like of him was never seen in the Halidome of Saint Mary's, and so was seen of the preferment that God sent him."

"And what was that?" said Halbert, his eyes sparkling with eagerness.

"Nothing less," answered Martin, "than body-servant to the Archbishop of Saint Andrews!"

Halbert's countenance fell.—"A servant—and to a priest? Was this all that knowledge and activity could raise him to?"

Martin, in his turn, looked with wistful surprise in the face of his young friend. "And to what could fortune lead him farther?" answered he. "The son of a kirk-feuar is not the stuff that lords and knights are made of. Courage and school craft cannot change churl's blood into gentle blood, I trow. I have heard, forby, that Hughie Dun left a good five hundred punds of Scots money to his only daughter, and that she married the Bailie of Pittenweem."

At this moment, and while Halbert was embarrassed with devising a suitable answer, a deer bounded across their path. In an instant the cross-bow was at the youth's shoulder, the bolt whistled, and the deer, after giving one bound upright, dropt dead on the green sward.

"There lies the venison our dame wanted," said Martin; "who would have thought of an out-lying stag being so low down the glen at this season?—And it is a hart of grease too, in full season, and three inches of fat on the brisket. Now this is all your luck, Halbert, that follows you, go where you like. Were you to put in for it, I would warrant you were made one of the Abbot's yeoman-prickers, and ride about in a purple doublet as bold as the best."

"Tush, man," answered Halbert, "I will serve the Queen or no one. Take thou care to have down the venison to the Tower, since they expect it. I will on to the moss. I have two or three bird-bolts at my girdle, and it may be I shall find wild-fowl."

He hastened his pace, and was soon out of sight. Martin paused for a moment, and looked after him. "There goes the making of a right gallant stripling, an ambition have not the spoiling of him—Serve the Queen! said he. By my faith, and she hath worse servants, from all that I e'er heard of him. And wherefore should he not keep a high head? They that ettle to the top of the ladder will at least get up some rounds. They that mint* at a gown of gold, will always get a sleeve of it. But come, sir, (addressing the stag,) you shall go to Glendearg on my two legs somewhat more slowly than you were frisking it even now on your own four nimble shanks. Nay, by my faith, if you be so heavy, I will content me with the best of you, and that's the haunch and the nombles, and e'en heave up the rest on the old oak-tree yonder, and come back for it with one of the yauds."†

While Martin returned to Glendearg with the venison, Halbert prosecuted his walk, breathing more easily since he was free of his companion. "The domestic of a proud and lazy priest—body-squire to the Archbishop of Saint Andrews," he repeated to himself; "and this, with the privilege of allying his blood with the Bailie of Pittenween, is thought a preferment worth a brave man's struggling for;—nay more, a preferment which, if allowed, should crown the hopes, past, present, and to come, of the son of a Kirk-vassal! By Heaven, but that I find in me a reluctance to practise their acts of nocturnal rapine, I would rather take the jack and lance, and join with the Border-riders.—Something I will do. Here, degraded and dishonoured, I will not live the scorn of each whiffling stranger from the South, because, forsooth, he wears tinkling spurs on a tawney boot. This thing—this phantom, be it what it will, I will see it once more. Since I spoke with her, and touched her hand, thoughts and feelings have dawned on me, of which my former life had not even dreamed; but shall I, who feel my father's glen too narrow for my expanding spirit, brook to be bearded in it by this vain gewgaw of a courtier, and in the sight too of Mary Avenel? I will not stoop to it, by Heaven!"

As he spoke thus, he arrived in the sequestered glen of Corri-nan-shian, as it verged upon the hour of noon. A few moments he remained looking upon the fountain, and doubting in his own mind with what countenance the White Lady might receive him. She had not indeed expressly forbidden his again evoking her; but yet there was something like such a prohibition implied in the farewell, which recommended him to wait for another guide.

Halbert Glendinning did not long, however, allow himself to pause. Hardihood was the natural characteristic of his mind; and under the expansion and modification which his feelings had lately undergone, it had been augmented rather than diminished. He drew his sword, undid the buskin from his foot, bowed three times with deliberation towards the

* *Mint*—aim at.

† *Yauds*—horses; more particularly horses of labour.

fountain, and as often towards the tree, and repeated the same rhyme as formerly,—

"Thrice to the holy brake—
Thrice to the well:—
I bid thee awake,
White Maid of Avenel!

Noon gleams on the lake—
Noon glows on the fell—
Wake thee, O wake,
White Maid of Avenel!"

His eye was on the holly bush as he spoke the last line; and it was not without an involuntary shuddering that he saw the air betwixt his eye and that object become more dim, and condense, as it were, into the faint appearance of a form, through which, however, so thin and transparent was the first appearance of the phantom, he could discern the outline of the bush, as through a veil of fine crape. But, gradually, it darkened into a more substantial appearance, and the White Lady stood before him with displeasure on her brow. She spoke, and her speech was still song, or rather measured chant; but, as if now more familiar, it flowed occasionally in modulated blank-verse, and at other times in the lyrical measure which she had used at their former meeting.

"This is the day when the fairy kind
Sits weeping alone for their hopeless lot,
And the wood-maiden sighs to the sighing wind,
And the mer-maiden weeps in her crystal grot:
For this is the day that a deed was wrought,
In which we have neither part nor share,
For the children of clay was salvation bought,
But not for the forms of sea or air!
And ever the mortal is most forlorn,
Who meeteth our race on the Friday morn."

"Spirit," said Halbert Glendinning, boldly, "it is bootless to threaten one who holds his life at no rate. Thine anger can but slay; nor do I think thy power extendeth, or thy will stretcheth, so far. The terrors which your race produce upon others, are vain against me. My heart is hardened against fear, as by a sense of despair. If I am, as thy words infer, of a race more peculiarly the care of Heaven than thine, it is mine to call, it must be thine to answer. I am the nobler being."

As he spoke, the figure looked upon him with a fierce and ireful countenance, which, without losing the similitude of that which it usually exhibited, had a wilder and more exaggerated cast of features. The eyes seemed to contract and become more fiery, and slight convulsions passed over the face, as if it was about to be transformed into something hideous. The whole appearance resembled those faces which the imagination summons up when it is disturbed by laudanum, but which do not remain under the visionary's command, and, beautiful in their first appearance, become wild and grotesque ere we can arrest them.

But when Halbert had concluded his bold speech, the White Lady stood before him with the same pale, fixed, and melancholy aspect, which she usually bore. He had expected the agitation which she exhibited would conclude in some frightful metamorphosis. Folding her arms on her bosom, the phantom replied,—

"Daring youth! for thee it is well,
Here calling me in haunted dell,
That thy heart has not quail'd,
Nor thy courage fail'd,
And that thou couldst brook
The angry look
Of Her of Avenel.

Did one limb shiver,
Or an eyelid quiver,
Thou wert lost for ever.
Though I am form'd from the ether blue,
And my blood is of the unfallen dew,
And thou art framed of mud and dust,
'Tis thine to speak, reply I must."

"I demand of thee, then," said the youth, "by what charm it is that I am thus altered in mind and in wishes—that I think no longer of deer or dog, of bow or bolt—that my soul spurns the bounds of this obscure glen—that my blood boils at an insult from one by whose stirrup I would some days since have run for a whole summer's morn, contented and honoured by the notice of a single word? Why do I now seek to mate me with princes, and knights, and nobles?—Am I the same, who but yesterday, as it were, slumbered in contented obscurity, but who am to-day awakened to glory and ambition? — Speak — tell me, if thou canst, the meaning of this change?—Am I spell-bound?—or have I till now been under the influence of a spell, that I feel as another being, yet am conscious of remaining the same? Speak and tell me, is it to thy influence that the change is owing?"

The White Lady replied,—

"A mightier wizard far than I
Wields o'er the universe his power;
Him owns the eagle in the sky,
The turtle in the bower.
Changeful in shape, yet mightiest still,
He wields the heart of man at will,
From ill to good, from good to ill,
In cot and castle-tower."

"Speak not thus darkly," said the youth, colouring so deeply, that face, neck, and hands were in a sanguine glow; "make me sensible of thy purpose."

The spirit answered,—

"Ask thy heart, whose secret cell
Is fill'd with Mary Avenel!
Ask thy pride, why scornful look
In Mary's view it will not brook?
Ask it, why thou seek'st to rise
Among the mighty and the wise?—
Why thou spurn'st thy lowly lot?—
Why thy pastimes are forgot?
Why thou wouldst in bloody strife
Mend thy luck or lose thy life?
Ask thy heart, and it shall tell,
Sighing from its secret cell,
'Tis for Mary Avenel."

"Tell me, then," said Halbert, his cheek still deeply crimsoned, "thou who hast said to me that which I dared not say to myself, by what means shall I urge my passion—by what means make it known?"

The White Lady replied,—

"Do not ask me;
On doubts like these thou canst not task me.
We only see the passing show
Of human passions' ebb and flow;
And view the pageant's idle glance
As mortals eye the northern dance,
When thousand streamers, flashing bright,
Career it o'er the brow of night,
And gazers mark their changeful gleams,
But feel no influence from their beams."

"Yet thine own fate," replied Halbert, "unless men greatly err, is linked with that of mortals?"

The phantom answered,

"By ties mysterious link'd, our fated race
Holds strange connexion with the sons of men.
The star that rose upon the House of Avenel,
When Norman Ulric first assumed the name,
That star, when culminating in its orbit,
Shot from its sphere a drop of diamond dew,
And this bright font received it — and a Spirit
Rose from the fountain, and her date of life
Hath co-existence with the House of Avenel,
And with the star that rules it."

"Speak yet more plainly," answered young Glendinning; "of this I can understand nothing. Say, what hath forged thy wierded* link of destiny with the House of Avenel? Say, especially, what fate now overhangs that house?"

The White Lady replied,—

"Look on my girdle — on this thread of gold —
'Tis fine as web of lightest gossamer,
And, but there is a spell on't, would not bind,
Light as they are, the folds of my thin robe.
But when 'twas donn'd, it was a massive chain,
Such as might bind the champion of the Jews,

---

* *Wierded* — fated.

Even when his locks were longest — it hath dwindled,
Hath minish'd in its substance and its strength,
As sunk the greatness of the House of Avenel.
When this frail thread gives way, I to the elements
Resign the principles of life they lent me.
Ask me no more of this! — the stars forbid it."

"Then canst thou read the stars," answered the youth; "and mayest tell me the fate of my passion, if thou canst not aid it?"

The White Lady again replied,—

"Dim burns the once bright star of Avenel,
Dim as the beacon when the morn is nigh,
And the o'er-wearied warder leaves the light-house;
There is an influence sorrowful and fearful,
That dogs its downward course. Disastrous passion,
Fierce hate and rivalry, are in the aspect
That lowers upon its fortunes."

"And rivalry?" repeated Glendinning; "it is, then, as I feared! — But shall that English silkworm presume to beard me in my father's house, and in the presence of Mary Avenel?—Give me to meet him, spirit—give me to do away the vain distinction of rank on which he refuses me the combat. Place us on equal terms, and gleam the stars with what aspect they will, the sword of my father shall control their influences."

She answered as promptly as before,—

"Complain not of me, child of clay,
If to thy harm I yield the way.
We, who soar thy sphere above,
Know not aught of hate or love:
As will or wisdom rules thy mood,
My gifts to evil turn, or good."

"Give me to redeem my honour," said Halbert Glendinning — "give me to retort on my proud rival the insults he has thrown on me, and let the rest fare as it will. If I cannot revenge my wrong, I shall sleep quiet, and know nought of my disgrace."

The phantom failed not to reply,—

"When Piercie Shafton boasteth high,
Let this token meet his eye.
The sun is westering from the dell,
Thy wish is granted — fare thee well!"

As the White Lady spoke or chanted these last words, she undid from her locks a silver bodkin around which they were twisted, and gave it to Halbert Glendinning; then shaking her dishevelled hair till it fell like a veil around her, the outlines of her form gradually became as diffuse as her flowing tresses, her countenance grew pale as the moon in her first quarter, her features became indistinguishable, and she melted into the air.

Habit inures us to wonders; but the youth did not find himself alone by the fountain without experiencing, though in a much less degree, the revulsion of spirits which he had felt upon the phantom's former disappearance. A doubt strongly pressed upon his mind, whether it were safe to avail himself of the gifts of a spirit which did not even pretend to belong to the class of angels, and might, for aught he knew, have a much worse lineage than that which she was pleased to avow. "I will speak of it," he said, "to Edward, who is clerkly learned, and will tell me what I should do. And yet, no—Edward is scrupulous and wary.—I will prove the effect of her gift on Sir Piercie Shafton, if he again braves me, and by the issue, I will be myself a sufficient judge whether there is danger in resorting to her counsel. Home, then, home — and we shall soon learn whether that home shall longer hold me; for not again will I brook insult, with my father's sword by my side, and Mary for the spectator of my disgrace."

Chapter the Eighteenth.

I give thee eighteenpence a-day,
 And my bow shalt thou bear,
And over all the north country,
 I make thee the chief rydere.
And I thirteenpence a-day, quoth the queen,
 By God and by my faye,
Come fetch thy payment when thou wilt,
 No man shall say thee nay.
WILLIAM OF CLOUDESLEY.

THE manners of the age did not permit the inhabitants of Glendearg to partake of the collation which was placed in the spence of that ancient tower, before the Lord Abbot and his attendants, and Sir Piercie Shafton. Dame Glendinning was excluded, both by inferiority of rank and by sex, for (though it was a rule often neglected) the Superior of Saint Mary's was debarred from taking his meals in female society. To Mary Avenel the latter, and to Edward Glendinning the former, incapacity attached; but it pleased his lordship to require their presence in the apartment, and to say sundry kind words to them upon the ready and hospitable reception which they had afforded him.

The smoking haunch now stood upon the table; a napkin, white as snow, was, with due reverence, tucked under the chin of the Abbot by the Refectioner; and nought was wanting to commence the repast, save the presence of Sir Piercie Shafton, who at length appeared, glittering like the sun, in a carnation-velvet doublet, slashed and puffed out with cloth of silver, his hat of the newest block, surrounded by a hatband of goldsmith's work, while around his neck he wore a collar of gold, set with rubies and topazes so rich, that it vindicated his anxiety for the safety of his baggage from being founded upon his love of mere finery. This gorgeous collar or chain, resembling those worn by the knights of the highest orders of chivalry, fell down on his breast, and terminated in a medallion.

"We waited for Sir Piercie Shafton," said the Abbot, hastily assuming his place in the great chair which the Kitchener advanced to the table with ready hand.

"I pray your pardon, reverend father, and my good lord," replied that pink of courtesy; "I did but wait to cast my riding slough, and to transmew myself into some civil form meeter for this worshipful company."

"I cannot but praise your gallantry, Sir Knight," said the Abbot, "and your prudence, also, for choosing the fitting time to appear thus adorned. Certes, had that goodly chain been visible in some part of your late progress, there was risk that the lawful owner might have parted company therewith."

"This chain, said your reverence?" answered Sir Piercie; "surely it is but a toy, a trifle, a slight thing which shows but poorly with this doublet—marry, when I wear that of the murrey-coloured double-piled Genoa velvet, puffed out with ciprus, the gems, being relieved and set off by the darker and more grave ground of the stuff, show like stars giving a lustre through dark clouds."

"I nothing doubt it," said the Abbot, "but I pray you to sit down at the board."

But Sir Piercie had now got into his element, and was not easily interrupted —"I own," he continued, "that slight as the toy is, it might perchance have had some captivation for Julian — Santa Maria!" said he, interrupting himself; "what was I about to say, and my fair and beauteous Protection, or shall I rather term her my Discretion, here in presence! — Indiscreet hath it been in your Affability, O most lovely Discretion, to suffer a stray word to have broke out of the penfold of his mouth, that might overleap the fence of civility, and trespass on the manor of decorum."

"Marry!" said the Abbot, somewhat impatiently, "the greatest discretion that I can see in the matter is, to eat our victuals being hot—Father Eustace, say the Benedicite, and cut up the haunch."

The Sub-Prior readily obeyed the first part of the Abbot's injunction, but paused upon the second—"It is Friday, most reverend," he said in Latin, desirous that the hint should escape, if possible, the ears of the stranger.

"We are travellers," said the Abbot, in reply, "and *viatoribus licitum est* —You know the canon—a traveller must eat what food his hard fate sets before him. I grant you all a dispensation to eat flesh this day, conditionally that you, brethren, say the Confiteor at curfew time, that the knight give alms to his ability, and that all and each of you fast from flesh on such day within the next month that shall seem most convenient; wherefore fall to and eat your food with cheerful countenances, and you, Father Refectioner, *da mixtus*."

While the Abbot was thus stating the conditions on which his indulgence was granted, he had already half finished a slice of the noble haunch, and now washed it down with a flagon of Rhenish, modestly tempered with water.

"Well is it said," he observed, as he required from the Refectioner another slice, "that virtue is its own reward; for though this is but humble fare, and hastily prepared, and eaten in a poor chamber, I do not remember me of having had such an appetite since I was a simple brother in the Abbey of Dundrennan, and was wont to labour in the garden from morning until nones, when our Abbot struck the *Cymbalum*. Then would I enter keen with hunger, parched with thirst, (*da mihi vinum quæso, et merum sit,*) and partake with appetite of whatever was set before us, according to our rule; feast or fast day, *caritas* or *penitentia*, was the same to me. I had no stomach complaints then, which now crave both the aid of wine and choice cookery, to render my food acceptable to my palate, and easy of digestion."

"It may be, holy father," said the Sub-Prior, "an occasional ride to the extremity of Saint Mary's patrimony, may have the same happy effect on your health as the air of the garden at Dundrennan."

"Perchance, with our patroness's blessing, such progresses may advantage us," said the Abbot; "having an especial eye that our venison is carefully killed by some woodsman that is master of his craft."

"If the Lord Abbot will permit me," said the Kitchener, "I think the best way to assure his lordship on that important point, would be to retain as a yeoman-pricker, or deputy-ranger, the eldest son of this good woman, Dame Glendinning, who is here to wait upon us. I should know by mine office what belongs to killing of game, and I can safely pronounce, that never saw I, or any other *coquinarius*, a bolt so justly shot. It has cloven the very heart of the buck."

"What speak you to us of one good shot, father?" said Sir Piercie; "I would advise you that such no more maketh a shooter, than doth one swallow make a summer—I have seen this springald of whom you speak, and if his hand can send forth his shafts as boldly as his tongue doth utter presumptuous speeches, I will own him as good an archer as Robin Hood."

"Marry," said the Abbot, "and it is fitting we know the truth of this matter from the dame herself; for ill advised were we to give way to any rashness in this matter, whereby the bounties which Heaven and our patroness provide might be unskilfully mangled, and rendered unfit for worthy men's use.—Stand forth, therefore, dame Glendinning, and tell to us, as thy liege lord and spiritual Superior, using plainness and truth, without either fear or favour, as being a matter wherein we are deeply interested,

Doth this son of thine use his bow as well as the Father Kitchener avers to us?"

"So please your noble fatherhood," answered Dame Glendinning with a deep curtsy, "I should know somewhat of archery to my cost, seeing my husband — God assoilzie him! — was slain in the field of Pinkie with an arrow-shot, while he was fighting under the Kirk's banner, as became a liege vassal of the Halidome. He was a valiant man, please your reverence, and an honest; and saving that he loved a bit of venison, and shifted for his living at a time as Border-men will sometimes do, I wot not of sin that he did. And yet, though I have paid for mass after mass to the matter of a forty shilling, besides a quarter of wheat and four firlocks of rye, I can have no assurance yet that he has been delivered from purgatory."

"Dame," said the Lord Abbot, "this shall be looked into heedfully; and since thy husband fell, as thou sayest, in the Kirk's quarrel, and under her banner, rely upon it that we will have him out of purgatory forthwith — that is, always provided he be there. — But it is not of thy husband whom we now devise to speak, but of thy son; not of a shot Scotsman, but of a shot deer — Wherefore, I say, answer me to the point, is thy son a practised archer, ay or no?"

"Alack! my reverend lord," replied the widow, "and my croft would be better tilled, if I could answer your reverence that he is not. — Practised archer! — marry, holy sir, I would he would practise something else — cross-bow and long-bow, hand-gun and hack-but, falconet and saker, he can shoot with them all. And if it would please this right honourable gentleman, our guest, to hold out his hat at the distance of a hundred yards, our Halbert shall send shaft, bolt, or bullet through it, (so that right honourable gentleman swerve not, but hold out steady,) and I will forfeit a quarter of barley if he touch but a knot of his ribands. I have seen our old Martin do as much, and so has our right reverend the Sub-Prior, if he be pleased to remember it."

"I am not like to forget it, dame," said Father Eustace; "for I knew not which most to admire, the composure of the young marksman, or the steadiness of the old mark. Yet I presume not to advise Sir Piercie Shafton to subject his valuable beaver, and yet more valuable person, to such a risk, unless it should be his own special pleasure."

"Be assured it is not," said Sir Piercie Shafton, something hastily; "be well assured, holy father, that it is not. I dispute not the lad's qualities, for which your reverence vouches. But bows are but wood, strings are but flax, or the silk-worm excrement at best; archers are but men, fingers may slip, eyes may dazzle, the blindest may hit the butt, the best marker may shoot a bow's length beside. Therefore will we try no perilous experiments."

"Be that as you will, Sir Piercie," said the Abbot; "meantime we will name this youth bow-bearer in the forest granted to us by good King David, that the chase might recreate our wearied spirits, the flesh of the deer improve our poor commons, and the hides cover the books of our library; thus tending at once to the sustenance of body and soul."

"Kneel down, woman, kneel down," said the Refectioner and the Kitchener, with one voice, to Dame Glendinning, "and kiss his lordship's hand, for the grace which he has granted to thy son."

They then, as if they had been chanting the service and the responses, set off in a sort of duetto, enumerating the advantages of the situation.

"A green gown and a pair of leathern galligaskins every Pentecost," said the Kitchener.

"Four marks by the year at Candlemas," answered the Refectioner.

"A hogshead of ale at Martlemas, of the double strike, and single ale at pleasure, as he shall agree with the Cellarer——"

"Who is a reasonable man," said the Abbot, "and will encourage an active servant of the convent."

"A mess of broth and a dole of mutton or beef, at the Kitchener's, on each high holiday," resumed the Kitchener.

"The gang of two cows and a palfrey on our Lady's meadow," answered his brother officer.

"An ox-hide to make buskins of yearly, because of the brambles," echoed the Kitchener.

"And various other perquisites, *quæ nunc præscribere longum*," said the Abbot, summing, with his own lordly voice, the advantages attached to the office of conventional bow-bearer.

Dame Glendinning was all this while on her knees, her head mechanically turning from the one church officer to the other, which, as they stood one on each side of her, had much the appearance of a figure moved by clock-work, and so soon as they were silent, most devotedly did she kiss the munificent hand of the Abbot. Conscious, however, of Halbert's intractability in some points, she could not help qualifying her grateful and reiterated thanks for the Abbot's bountiful proffer, with a hope that Halbert would see his wisdom, and accept of it.

"How," said the Abbot, bending his brows, "accept of it?—Woman, is thy son in his right wits?"

Elspeth, stunned by the tone in which this question was asked, was altogether unable to reply to it. Indeed, any answer she might have made could hardly have been heard, as it pleased the two office-bearers of the Abbot's table again to recommence their alternate dialogue.

"Refuse!" said the Kitchener.

"Refuse!" answered the Refectioner, echoing the other's word in a tone of still louder astonishment.

"Refuse four marks by the year!" said the one.

"Ale and beer—broth and mutton—cow's grass and palfrey's!" shouted the Kitchener.

"Gown and galligaskins!" responded the Refectioner.

"A moment's patience, my brethren," answered the Sub-Prior, "and let us not be thus astonished before cause is afforded of our amazement. This good dame best knoweth the temper and spirit of her son—this much I can say, that it lieth not towards letters or learning, of which I have in vain endeavoured to instil into him some tincture. Nevertheless, he is a youth of no common spirit, but much like those (in my weak judgment) whom God raises up among a people when he meaneth that their deliverance shall be wrought out with strength of hand and valour of heart. Such men we have seen marked with a waywardness, and even an obstinacy of character, which hath appeared intractability and stupidity to those among whom they walked and were conversant, until the very opportunity hath arrived in which it was the will of Providence that they should be the fitting instrument of great things."

"Now, in good time hast thou spoken, Father Eustace," said the Abbot; "and we will see this swankie before we decide upon the means of employing him.—How say you, Sir Piercie Shafton, is it not the court fashion to suit the man to the office, and not the office to the man?"

"So please your reverence and lordship," answered the Northumbrian knight, "I do partly, that is, in some sort, subscribe to what your wisdom hath delivered—Nevertheless, under reverence of the Sub-Prior, we do not look for gallant leaders and national deliverers in the hovels of the mean common people. Credit me, that if there be some flashes of martial spirit about this young person, which I am not called upon to dispute, (though I have seldom seen that presumption and arrogance were made good upon the upshot by deed and action,) yet still these will prove insufficient to distinguish him, save in his own limited and lowly sphere—even as the glowworm, which makes a goodly show among the grass of the field, would be of little avail if deposited in a beacon-grate."

"Now, in good time," said the Sub-Prior, "and here comes the young huntsman to speak for himself;" for, being placed opposite to the window, he could observe Halbert as he ascended the little mound on which the tower was situated.

"Summon him to our presence," said the Lord Abbot; and with an obedient start the two attendant monks went off with emulous alertness. Dame Glendinning sprung away at the same moment, partly to gain an instant to recommend obedience to her son, partly to prevail with him to change his apparel before coming in presence of the Abbot. But the Kitchener and Refectioner, both speaking at once, had already seized each an arm, and were leading Halbert in triumph into the apartment, so that she could only ejaculate, "His will be done; but an he had but had on him his Sunday's hose!"

Limited and humble as this desire was, the fates did not grant it, for Halbert Glendinning was hurried into the presence of the Lord Abbot and his party without a word of explanation, and without a moment's time being allowed to assume his holiday hose, which, in the language of the time, implied both breeches and stockings.

Yet, though thus suddenly presented amid the centre of all eyes, there was something in Halbert's appearance which commanded a certain degree of respect from the company into which he was so unceremoniously intruded, and the greater part of whom were disposed to consider him with hauteur if not with absolute contempt. But his appearance and reception we must devote to another chapter.

Chapter the Nineteenth.

Now choose thee, gallant, betwixt wealth and honour;
There lies the pelf, in sum to bear thee through
The dance of youth, and the turmoil of manhood,
Yet leave enough for age's chimney-corner;
But an thou grasp to it, farewell ambition,
Farewell each hope of bettering thy condition,
And raising thy low rank above the churls
That till the earth for bread.

OLD PLAY.

It is necessary to dwell for some brief space on the appearance and demeanour of young Glendinning, ere we proceed to describe his interview with the Abbot of St. Mary's, at this momentous crisis of his life.

Halbert was now about nineteen years old, tall and active rather than strong, yet of that hardy conformation of limb and sinew, which promises great strength when the growth shall be complete, and the system confirmed. He was perfectly well made, and, like most men who have that advantage, possessed a grace and natural ease of manner and carriage, which prevented his height from being the distinguished part of his external appearance. It was not until you had compared his stature with that of those amongst or near to whom he stood, that you became sensible that the young Glendinning was upwards of six feet high. In the combination of unusual height with perfect symmetry, ease, and grace of carriage, the young heir of Glendearg, notwithstanding his rustic birth and education, had greatly the advantage even of Sir Piercie Shafton himself, whose stature was lower, and his limbs, though there was no particular point to object to, were on the whole less exactly proportioned. On the other hand, Sir Piercie's very handsome countenance afforded him as decided an advantage over the Scotsman, as regularity of features and brilliance of complexion could give over traits which were rather strongly marked than beautiful, and upon whose complexion the "skyey influences," to which he was constantly exposed, had blended the red and white into the purely nut-brown hue, which coloured alike cheeks, neck, and forehead, and blushed only in a darker glow upon the former.—Halbert's eyes supplied a marked and distinguished part of his physiognomy. They were large and of a hazel colour, and sparkled in moments of animation with such uncommon brilliancy, that it seemed as if they actually emitted light. Nature had closely curled the locks of dark-brown hair, which relieved and set off the features, such as we have described them, displaying a bold and animated disposition, much more than might have been expected from his situation, or from his previous manners, which hitherto had seemed bashful, homely, and awkward.

Halbert's dress was certainly not of that description which sets off to the best advantage a presence of itself prepossessing. His jerkin and hose were of coarse rustic cloth, and his cap of the same. A belt round his waist served at once to sustain the broad-sword which we have already mentioned, and to hold five or six arrows and bird-bolts, which were stuck into it on the right side, along with a large knife hilted with buck-horn, or, as it was then called, a dudgeon-dagger. To complete his dress, we must notice his loose buskins of deer's hide, formed so as to draw up on the leg as high as the knee, or at pleasure to be thrust down lower than the calves. These were generally used at the period by such as either had their principal occupation, or their chief pleasure, in silvan sports, as they served to protect the legs against the rough and tangled thickets into which the pursuit of game frequently led them.—And these trifling particulars complete his external appearance.

It is not easy to do justice to the manner in which young Glendinning's soul spoke through his eyes when ushered so suddenly into the company of those whom his earliest education had taught him to treat with awe and reverence. The degree of embarrassment, which his demeanor evinced, had nothing in it either meanly servile, or utterly disconcerted. It was no more than became a generous and ingenuous youth of a bold spirit, but totally inexperienced, who should for the first time be called upon to think and act for himself in such society and under such disadvantageous circumstances. There was not in his carriage a grain either of forwardness or of timidity, which a friend could have wished away.

He kneeled and kissed the Abbot's hand, then rose, and retiring two paces, bowed respectfully to the circle around, smiling gently as he received an encouraging nod from the Sub-Prior, to whom alone he was personally known, and blushing as he encountered the anxious look of Mary Avenel, who beheld with painful interest the sort of ordeal to which her foster-brother was about to be subjected. Recovering from the transient flurry of spirits into which the encounter of her glance had thrown him, he stood composedly awaiting till the Abbot should express his pleasure.

The ingenuous expression of countenance, noble form, and graceful attitude of the young man, failed not to prepossess in his favor the churchmen in whose presence he stood. The Abbot looked round, and exchanged a gracious and approving glance with his counsellor Father Eustace, although probably the appointment of a ranger, or bow-bearer, was one in which he might have been disposed to proceed without the Sub-Prior's advice, were it but to show his own free agency. But the good mien of the young man now in nomination was such, that he rather hastened to exchange congratulation on meeting with so proper a subject of promotion, than to indulge any other feeling. Father Eustace enjoyed the pleasure which a well-constituted mind derives from seeing a benefit light on a deserving object; for as he had not seen Halbert since circumstances had made so material a change in his manner and feelings, he scarce doubted that the proffered appointment would, notwithstanding his mother's uncertainty, suit the disposition of a youth who had appeared devoted to woodland sports, and a foe alike to sedentary or settled occupation of any kind. The Refectioner and Kitchener were so well pleased with Halbert's prepossessing appearance, that they seemed to think that the salary, emoluments, and perquisites, the dole, the grazing, the gown, and the galligaskins, could scarce be better bestowed than on the active and graceful figure before them.

Sir Piercie Shafton, whether from being more deeply engaged in his own cogitations, or that the subject was unworthy of his notice, did not seem to partake of the general feeling of approbation excited by the young man's presence. He sate with his eyes half shut, and his arms folded, appearing to be wrapped in contemplations of a nature deeper than those arising out of the scene before him. But, notwithstanding his seeming abstraction and absence of mind, there was a flutter of vanity in Sir Piercie's very handsome countenance, an occasional change of posture from one striking attitude (or what he conceived to be such) to another, and an occasional stolen glance at the female part of the company, to spy how far he succeeded in riveting their attention, which gave a marked advantage, in comparison, to the less regular and more harsh features of Halbert Glendinning, with their composed, manly, and deliberate expression of mental fortitude.

Of the females belonging to the family of Glendearg, the Miller's daughter alone had her mind sufficiently at leisure to admire, from time to time, the graceful attitudes of Sir Piercie Shafton; for both Mary Avenel and Dame Glendinning were waiting in anxiety and apprehension the answer which Halbert was to return to the Abbot's proposal, and fearfully anticipating the consequences of his probable refusal. The conduct of his brother Edward, for a lad constitutionally shy, respectful, and even timid, was at once affectionate and noble. This younger son of Dame Elspeth had stood unnoticed in a corner, after the Abbot, at the request of the Sub-Prior, had honoured him with some passing notice, and asked him a few common-place questions about his progress in Donatus, and in the *Promptuarium Parvulorum*, without waiting for the answers. From his corner he now glided round to his brother's side, and keeping a little behind him, slid his right hand into the huntsman's left, and by a gentle pressure, which Halbert instantly and ardently returned, expressed at once his interest in his situation, and his resolution to share his fate.

The group was thus arranged, when, after the pause of two or three minutes, which he employed in slowly sipping his cup of wine, in order that he might enter on his proposal with due and deliberate dignity, the Abbot at length expressed himself thus: —

"My son — we your lawful Superior, and the Abbot, under God's favour, of the community of Saint Mary's, have heard of your manifold good gifts — a-hem — especially touching wood-craft — and the huntsman-like fashion in which you strike your game, truly and as a yeoman should, not abusing Heaven's good benefits by spoiling the flesh, as is too often seen in careless rangers — a-hem." He made here a pause, but observing that Glendinning only replied to his compliment by a bow, he proceeded, — "My son, we commend your modesty; nevertheless, we will that thou shouldst speak freely to us touching that which we have premeditated for thine advancement, meaning to confer on thee the office of bow-bearer and ranger, as well over the chases and forests wherein our house hath privilege by the gifts of pious kings and nobles, whose souls now enjoy the fruits of their bounties to the Church as to those which belong to us in exclusive right of property and perpetuity. Thy knee, my son — that we may, with our own hand, and without loss of time, induct thee into office."

"Kneel down," said the Kitchener on the one side; and "Kneel down," said the Refectioner on the other.

But Halbert Glendinning remained standing.

"Were it to show gratitude and good-will for your reverend lordship's noble offer, I could not," he said, "kneel low enough, or remain long enough kneeling. But I may not kneel to take investure of your noble gift, my Lord Abbot, being a man determined to seek my fortune otherwise."

"How is that, sir?" said the Abbot, knitting his brows; "do I hear you speak aright? and do you, a born vassal of the Halidome, at the moment when I am destining to you such a noble expression of my good-will, propose exchanging my service for that of any other?"

"My lord," said Halbert Glendinning, "it grieves me to think you hold me capable of undervaluing your gracious offer, or of exchanging your service for another. But your noble proffer doth but hasten the execution of a determination which I have long since formed."

"Ay, my son," said the Abbot, "is it indeed so? — right early have you learned to form resolutions without consulting those on whom you naturally depend. But what may it be, this sagacious resolution, if I may so far pray you?"

"To yield up to my brother and mother," answered Halbert, "mine interest in the fief of Glendearg, lately possessed by my father, Simon Glendinning: and having prayed your lordship to be the same kind and generous master to them, that your predecessors, the venerable Abbots of Saint Mary's, have been to my fathers in times past; for myself, I am determined to seek my fortune where I may best find it."

Dame Glendinning here ventured, emboldened by maternal anxiety, to break silence with an exclamation of "O my son!" Edward clinging to his brother's side, half spoke, half whispered, a similar ejaculation, of "Brother! brother!"

The Sub-Prior took up the matter in a tone of grave reprehension, which, as he conceived, the interest he had always taken in the family at Glendearg required at his hand.

"Wilful young man," he said, "what folly can urge thee to push back the hand that is stretched out to aid thee? What visionary aim hast thou before thee, that can compensate for the decent and sufficient independence which thou art now rejecting with scorn?"

"Four marks by the year, duly and truly," said the Kitchener.

"Cow's-grass, doublet, and galligaskins," responded the Refectioner.

"Peace, my brethren," said the Sub-Prior; "and may it please your lordship, venerable father, upon my petition, to allow this headstrong youth a day for consideration, and it shall be my part so to indoctrinate him, as to convince him what is due on this occasion to your lordship, and to his family, and to himself."

"Your kindness, reverend father," said the youth, "craves my dearest thanks — it is the continuance of a long train of benevolence towards me, for which I give you my gratitude, for I have nothing else to offer. It is my mishap, not your fault, that your intentions have been frustrated. But my present resolution is fixed and unalterable. I cannot accept the generous offer of the Lord Abbot; my fate calls me elsewhere, to scenes where I shall end it or mend it."

"By our Lady," said the Abbot, "I think the youth be mad indeed — or that you, Sir Piercie, judged of him most truly, when you prophesied that he would prove unfit for the promotion we designed him — it may be you knew something of this wayward humour before?"

"By the mass, not I," answered Sir Piercie Shafton, with his usual indifference. "I but judged of him by his birth and breeding; for seldom doth a good hawk come out of a kite's egg."

"Thou art thyself a kite, and kestrel to boot," replied Halbert Glendinning, without a moment's hesitation.

"This in our presence, and to a man of worship?" said the Abbot, the blood rushing to his face.

"Yes, my lord," answered the youth; "even in your presence I return to this gay man's face, the causeless dishonour which he has flung on my name. My brave father, who fell in the cause of his country, demands that justice at the hands of his son!"

"Unmannered boy!" said the Abbot.

"Nay, my good lord," said the knight, "praying pardon for the coarse interruption, let me entreat you not to be wroth with this rustical—Credit me, the north wind shall as soon puff one of your rocks from its basis, as aught which I hold so slight and inconsiderate as the churlish speech of an untaught churl, shall move the spleen of Piercie Shafton."

"Proud as you are, Sir Knight," said Halbert, "in your imagined superiority, be not too confident that you cannot be moved."

"Faith, by nothing that thou canst urge," said Sir Piercie.

"Knowest thou, then, this token?" said young Glendinning, offering to him the silver bodkin he had received from the White Lady.

Never was such an instant change, from the most contemptuous serenity, to the most furious state of passion, as that which Sir Piercie Shafton exhibited. It was the difference between a cannon lying quiet in its embrasure, and the same gun when touched by the linstock. He started up, every limb quivering with rage, and his features so inflamed and agitated by passion, that he more resembled a demoniac, than a man under the regulation of reason. He clenched both his fists, and thrusting them forward, offered them furiously at the face of Glendinning, who was even himself startled at the frantic state of excitation which his action had occasioned. The next moment he withdrew them, struck his open palm against his own forehead, and rushed out of the room in a state of indescribable agitation. The whole matter had been so sudden, that no person present had time to interfere.

When Sir Piercie Shafton had left the apartment, there was a moment's pause of astonishment; and then a general demand that Halbert Glendinning should instantly explain by what means he had produced such a violent change in the deportment of the English cavalier.

"I did nought to him," answered Halbert Glendinning, "but what you all saw—am I to answer for his fantastic freaks of humour?"

"Boy," said the Abbot, in his most authoritative manner, "these subterfuges shall not avail thee. This is not a man to be driven from his temperament without some sufficient cause. That cause was given by thee, and must have been known to thee. I command thee, as thou wilt save thyself from worse measure, to explain to me by what means thou hast moved our friend thus—We choose not that our vassals shall drive our guests mad in our very presence, and we remain ignorant of the means whereby that purpose is effected."

"So may it please your reverence, I did but show him this token," said Halbert Glendinning, delivering it at the same time to the Abbot, who looked at it with much attention, and then, shaking his head, gravely delivered it to the Sub-Prior, without speaking a word.

Father Eustace looked at the mysterious token with some attention; and then addressing Halbert in a stern and severe voice, said, "Young man, if thou wouldst not have us suspect thee of some strange double-dealing in this matter, let us instantly know whence thou hadst this token, and how it possesses an influence on Sir Piercie Shafton?"—It would have been extremely difficult for Halbert, thus hard pressed, to have either evaded or answered so puzzling a question. To have avowed the truth might, in those times, have occasioned his being burnt at a stake, although, in ours, his confession would have only gained for him the credit of a liar beyond all rational credibility. He was fortunately relieved by the return of Sir Piercie Shafton himself, whose ear caught, as he entered, the sound of the Sub-Prior's question.

Without waiting until Halbert Glendinning replied, he came forward, whispering to him as he passed, "Be secret — thou shalt have the satisfaction thou hast dared to seek for."

When he returned to his place, there were still marks of discomposure on his brow; but, becoming apparently collected and calm, he looked around him, and apologized for the indecorum of which he had been guilty, which he ascribed to sudden and severe indisposition. All were silent, and looked on each other with some surprise.

The Lord Abbot gave orders for all to retire from the apartment, save himself, Sir Piercie Shafton, and the Sub-Prior. "And have an eye," he added, "on that bold youth, that he escape not; for if he hath practised by charm, or otherwise, on the health of our worshipful guest, I swear by the alb and mitre which I wear, that his punishment shall be most exemplary."

"My lord and venerable father," said Halbert, bowing respectfully, "fear not but that I will abide my doom. I think you will best learn from the worshipful knight himself, what is the cause of his distemperature, and how slight my share in it has been."

"Be assured," said the knight, without looking up, however, while he spoke, "I will satisfy the Lord Abbot."

With these words the company retired, and with them young Glendinning.

When the Abbot, the Sub-Prior, and the English knight were left alone, Father Eustace, contrary to his custom, could not help speaking the first. "Expound unto us, noble sir," he said, "by what mysterious means the production of this simple toy could so far move your spirit, and overcome your patience, after you had shown yourself proof to all the provocation offered by this self-sufficient and singular youth?"

The knight took the silver bodkin from the good father's hand, looked at it with great composure, and, having examined it all over, returned it to the Sub-Prior, saying at the same time, "In truth, venerable father, I cannot but marvel, that the wisdom implied alike in your silver hairs, and in your eminent rank, should, like a babbling hound, (excuse the similitude,) open thus loudly on a false scent. I were, indeed, more slight to be moved than the leaves of the aspen-tree, which wag at the least breath of heaven, could I be touched by such a trifle as this, which in no way concerns me more than if the same quantity of silver were stricken into so many groats. Truth is, that from my youth upward, I have been subjected to such a malady as you saw me visited with even now — a cruel and searching pain, which goeth through nerve and bone, even as a good brand in the hands of a brave soldier sheers through limb and sinew—but it passes away speedily, as you yourselves may judge."

"Still," said the Sub-Prior, "this will not account for the youth offering to you this piece of silver, as a token by which you were to understand something, and, as we must needs conjecture, something disagreeable."

"Your reverence is to conjecture what you will," said Sir Piercie; "but I cannot pretend to lay your judgment on the right scent when I see it at fault. I hope I am not liable to be called upon to account for the foolish actions of a malapert boy?"

"Assuredly," said the Sub-Prior, "we shall prosecute no inquiry which is disagreeable to our guest. Nevertheless," said he, looking to his Superior, "this chance may, in some sort, alter the plan your lordship had formed for your worshipful guest's residence for a brief term in this tower, as a place alike of secrecy and of security; both of which, in the terms which we now stand on with England, are circumstances to be desired."

"In truth," said the Abbot, "and the doubt is well thought on, were it as well removed; for I scarce know in the Halidome so fitting a place of refuge, yet see I not how to recommend it to our worshipful guest, considering the unrestrained petulance of this headstrong youth."

"Tush! reverend sirs — what would you make of me?" said Sir Piercie

Shafton. "I protest, by mine honour, I would abide in this house were I to choose. What! I take no exceptions at the youth for showing a flash of spirit, though the spark may light on mine own head. I honour the lad for it. I protest I will abide here, and he shall aid me in striking down a deer. I must needs be friends with him, and he be such a shot: and we will speedily send down to my lord Abbot a buck of the first head, killed so artificially as shall satisfy even the reverend Kitchener."

This was said with such apparent ease and good-humour, that the Abbot made no farther observation on what had passed, but proceeded to acquaint his guest with the details of furniture, hangings, provisions, and so forth, which he proposed to send up to the Tower of Glendearg for his accommodation. This discourse, seasoned with a cup or two of wine, served to prolong the time until the reverend Abbot ordered his cavalcade to prepare for their return to the Monastery.

"As we have," he said, "in the course of this our toilsome journey, lost our meridian,* indulgence shall be given to those of our attendants who shall, from very weariness, be unable to attend the duty at prime,† and this by way of misericord or *indulgentia*."‡

Having benevolently intimated a boon to his faithful followers, which he probably judged would be far from unacceptable, the good Abbot, seeing all ready for his journey, bestowed his blessing on the assembled household — gave his hand to be kissed by Dame Glendinning — himself kissed the cheek of Mary Avenel, and even of the Miller's maiden, when they approached to render him the same homage — commanded Halbert to rule his temper, and to be aiding and obedient in all things to the English Knight — admonished Edward to be *discipulus impiger atque strenuus* — then took a courteous farewell of Sir Piercie Shafton, advising him to lie close, for fear of the English borderers, who might be employed to kidnap him; and having discharged these various offices of courtesy, moved forth to the court-yard, followed by the whole establishment. Here, with a heavy sigh, approaching to a groan, the venerable father heaved himself upon his palfrey, whose dark purple housings swept the ground; and, greatly comforted that the discretion of the animal's pace would be no longer disturbed by the gambadoes of Sir Piercie and his prancing war-horse, he set forth at a sober and steady trot upon his return to the Monastery.

When the Sub-Prior had mounted to accompany his principal, his eye sought out Halbert, who, partly hidden by a projection of the outward wall of the court, stood apart from, and gazing upon the departing cavalcade, and the group which assembled around them. Unsatisfied with the explanation he had received concerning the mysterious transaction of the silver bodkin, yet interesting himself in the youth, of whose character he had formed a favourable idea, the worthy monk resolved to take an early opportunity of investigating that matter. In the meanwhile, he looked upon Halbert with a serious and warning aspect, and held up his finger to him as he signed farewell. He then joined the rest of the churchmen, and followed his Superior down the valley.

---

* The hour of repose at noon, which, in the middle ages, was employed in slumber, and which the monastic rules of nocturnal vigils rendered necessary.

† *Prime* was the midnight service of the monks.

‡ *Misericord*, according to the learned work of Fosbrooke on British Monachism, meant not only an indulgence, or exoneration from particular duties, but also a particular apartment in a convent, where the monks assembled to enjoy such indulgences or allowances as were granted beyond the rule.

Chapter the Twentieth.

I hope you'll give me cause to think you noble,
And do me right with your sword, sir, as becomes
One gentleman of honour to another;
All this is fair, sir—let us make no days on't,
I'll lead your way.

LOVE'S PILGRIMAGE.

THE look and sign of warning which the Sub-Prior gave to Halbert Glendinning as they parted, went to his heart; for although he had profited much less than Edward by the good man's instructions, he had a sincere reverence for his person; and even the short time he had for deliberation tended to show him he was embarked in a perilous adventure. The nature of the provocation which he had given to Sir Piercie Shafton he could not even conjecture; but he saw that it was of a mortal quality, and he was now to abide the consequences.

That he might not force these consequences forward by any premature renewal of their quarrel, he resolved to walk apart for an hour, and consider on what terms he was to meet this haughty foreigner. The time seemed propitious for his doing so without having the appearance of wilfully shunning the stranger, as all the members of the little household were dispersing either to perform such tasks as had been interrupted by the arrival of the dignitaries, or to put in order what had been deranged by their visit.

Leaving the tower, therefore, and descending, unobserved as he thought, the knoll on which it stood, Halbert gained the little piece of level ground which extended betwixt the descent of the hill, and the first sweep made by the brook after washing the foot of the eminence on which the tower was situated, where a few straggling birch and oak-trees served to secure him from observation. But scarcely had he reached the spot, when he was surprised to feel a smart tap upon the shoulder, and, turning around, he perceived he had been closely followed by Sir Piercie Shafton.

When, whether from our state of animal spirits, want of confidence in the justice of our cause, or any other motive, our own courage happens to be in a wavering condition, nothing tends so much altogether to disconcert us, as a great appearance of promptitude on the part of our antagonist. Halbert Glendinning, both morally and constitutionally intrepid, was nevertheless somewhat troubled at seeing the stranger, whose resentment he had provoked, appear at once before him, and with an aspect which boded hostility. But though his heart might beat somewhat thicker, he was too high-spirited to exhibit any external signs of emotion. — "What is your pleasure, Sir Piercie?" he said to the English knight, enduring without apparent discomposure all the terrors which his antagonist had summoned into his aspect.

"What is my pleasure?" answered Sir Piercie; "a goodly question after the part you have acted towards me! — Young man, I know not what infatuation has led thee to place thyself in direct and insolent opposition to one who is a guest of thy liege-lord the Abbot, and who, even from the courtesy due to thy mother's roof, had a right to remain there without meeting insult. Neither do I ask, or care, by what means thou hast become possessed of the fatal secret by which thou hast dared to offer me open shame. But I must now tell thee, that the possession of it has cost thee thy life."

"Not, I trust, if my hand and sword can defend it," replied Halbert, boldly.

"True," said the Englishman, "I mean not to deprive thee of thy fair chance of self-defence. I am only sorry to think, that, young and country-bred as thou art, it can but little avail thee. But thou must be well aware, that in this quarrel I shall use no terms of quarter."

"Rely on it, proud man," answered the youth, "that I shall ask none; and although thou speakest as if I lay already at thy feet, trust me, that as I am determined never to ask thy mercy, so I am not fearful of needing it."

"Thou wilt, then," said the knight, "do nothing to avert the certain fate which thou hast provoked with such wantonness?"

"And how were that to be purchased?" replied Halbert Glendinning, more with the wish of obtaining some farther insight into the terms on which he stood with this stranger, than to make him the submission which he might require.

"Explain to me instantly," said Sir Piercie, "without equivocation or delay, by what means thou wert enabled to wound my honour so deeply—and shouldst thou point out to me by so doing an enemy more worthy of my resentment, I will permit thine own obscure insignificance to draw a veil over thine insolence."

"This is too high a flight," said Glendinning, fiercely, "for thine own presumption to soar without being checked. Thou hast come to my father's house, as well as I can guess, a fugitive and an exile, and thy first greeting to its inhabitants has been that of contempt and injury. By what means I have been able to retort that contempt, let thine own conscience tell thee. Enough for me that I stand on the privilege of a free Scotchman, and will brook no insult unreturned, and no injury unrequited."

"It is well, then," said Sir Piercie Shafton; "we will dispute this matter to-morrow morning with our swords. Let the time be daybreak, and do thou assign the place. We will go forth as if to strike a deer."

"Content," replied Halbert Glendinning: "I will guide thee to a spot where an hundred men might fight and fall without any chance of interruption."

"It is well," answered Sir Piercie Shafton. "Here then we part.—Many will say, that in thus indulging the right of a gentleman to the son of a clod-breaking peasant, I derogate from my sphere, even as the blessed sun would derogate should he condescend to compare and match his golden beams with the twinkle of a pale, blinking, expiring, gross-fed taper. But no consideration of rank shall prevent my avenging the insult thou hast offered me. We bear a smooth face, observe me, Sir Villagio, before the worshipful inmates of yonder cabin, and to-morrow we try conclusions with our swords." So saying, he turned away towards the tower.

It may not be unworthy of notice, that in the last speech only, had Sir Piercie used some of those flowers of rhetoric which characterized the usual style of his conversation. Apparently, a sense of wounded honour, and the deep desire of vindicating his injured feelings, had proved too strong for the fantastic affectation of his acquired habits. Indeed, such is usually the influence of energy of mind, when called forth and exerted, that Sir Piercie Shafton had never appeared in the eyes of his youthful antagonist half so much deserving of esteem and respect as in this brief dialogue, by which they exchanged mutual defiance. As he followed him slowly to the tower, he could not help thinking to himself, that, had the English knight always displayed this superior tone of bearing and feeling, he would not probably have felt so earnestly disposed to take offence at his hand. Mortal offence, however, had been exchanged, and the matter was to be put to mortal arbitrement.

The family met at the evening meal, when Sir Piercie Shafton extended the benignity of his countenance and the graces of his conversation far more generally over the party than he had hitherto condescended to do. The greater part of his attention was, of course, still engrossed by his divine and inimitable Discretion, as he chose to term Mary Avenel; but, nevertheless, there were interjectional flourishes to the Maid of the Mill, under the title of Comely Damsel, and to the Dame, under that of Worthy Matron. Nay, lest he should fail to excite their admiration by the graces of his rhetoric, he generously, and without solicitation, added those of his voice; and after regretting bitterly the absence of his viol-de-gamba, he regaled them with a song, "which," said he, "the inimitable Astrophel, whom mortals call Philip Sidney, composed in the nonage of his muse, to show the world what they are to expect from his riper years, and which will one day see the light in that not-to-be-paralleled perfection of human wit, which he has addressed to his sister, the matchless Parthenope, whom men call Countess of Pembroke; a work," he continued, "whereof his friendship hath permitted me, though unworthy, to be an occasional partaker, and whereof I may well say, that the deep afflictive tale which awakeneth our sorrows, is so relieved with brilliant similitudes, dulcet descriptions, pleasant poems, and engaging interludes, that they seem as the stars of the firmament, beautifying the dusky robe of night. And though I wot well how much the lovely and quaint language will suffer by my widowed voice, widowed in that it is no longer matched by my beloved viol-de-gamba, I will essay to give you a taste of the ravishing sweetness of the poesy of the un-to-be-imitated Astrophel."

So saying, he sung without mercy or remorse about five hundred verses, of which the two first and the four last may suffice for a specimen—

"What tongue can her perfections tell,
On whose each part all pens may dwell.
* * * * *
Of whose high praise and praiseful bliss,
Goodness the pen, Heaven paper is;
The ink immortal fame doth send,
As I began so I must end."

As Sir Piercie Shafton always sung with his eyes half shut, it was not until, agreeably to the promise of poetry, he had fairly made an end, that looking round, he discovered that the greater part of his audience had, in the meanwhile, yielded to the charms of repose. Mary Avenel, indeed, from a natural sense of politeness, had contrived to keep awake through all the perplexities of the divine Astrophel; but Mysie was transported in dreams back to the dusty atmosphere of her father's mill. Edward himself, who had given his attention for some time, had at length fallen fast asleep; and the good dame's nose, could its tones have been put in regulation, might have supplied the bass of the lamented viol-de-gamba. Halbert, however, who had no temptation to give way to the charms of slumber, remained awake with his eyes fixed on the songster; not that he was better entertained with the words, or more ravished with the execution, than the rest of the company, but rather because he admired, or perhaps envied, the composure, which could thus spend the evening in interminable madrigals, when the next morning was to be devoted to deadly combat. Yet it struck his natural acuteness of observation, that the eye of the gallant cavalier did now and then, furtively as it were, seek a glance of his countenance, as if to discover how he was taking the exhibition of his antagonist's composure and serenity of mind.

He shall read nothing in my countenance, thought Halbert, proudly, that can make him think my indifference less than his own.

And taking from the shelf a bag full of miscellaneous matters collected for the purpose, he began with great industry to dress hooks, and had finished half-a-dozen of flies (we are enabled, for the benefit of those who admire the antiquities of the gentle art of angling, to state that they were brown hackles) by the time that Sir Piercie had arrived at the conclusion of his long-winded strophes of the divine Astrophel. So that he also testified a magnanimous contempt of that which to-morrow should bring forth.

As it now waxed late, the family of Glendearg separated for the evening; Sir Piercie first saying to the dame, that "her son Albert——"

"Halbert," said Elspeth, with emphasis, "Halbert, after his goodsire, Halbert Brydone."

"Well, then, I have prayed your son, Halbert, that we may strive to-morrow, with the sun's earliness, to wake a stag from his lair, that I may see whether he be as prompt at that sport as fame bespeaks him."

"Alas! sir," answered Dame Elspeth, "he is but too prompt, an you talk of promptitude, at any thing that has steel at one end of it, and mischief at the other. But he is at your honourable disposal, and I trust you will teach him how obedience is due to our venerable father and lord, the Abbot, and prevail with him to take the bow-bearer's place in fee; for, as the two worthy monks said, it will be a great help to a widow-woman."

"Trust me, good dame," replied Sir Piercie, "it is my purpose so to indoctrinate him, touching his conduct and bearing towards his betters, that he shall not lightly depart from the reverence due to them.—We meet, then, beneath the birch-trees in the plain," he said, looking to Halbert, "so soon as the eye of day hath opened its lids."—Halbert answered with a sign of acquiescence, and the knight proceeded, "And now, having wished to my fairest Discretion those pleasant dreams which wave their pinions around the couch of sleeping beauty, and to this comely damsel the bounties of Morpheus, and to all others the common good-night, I will crave you leave to depart to my place of rest, though I may say with the poet,

'Ah rest!—no rest but change of place and posture:
Ah sleep!—no sleep but worn-out Nature's swooning;
Ah bed!—no bed but cushion fill'd with stones:
Rest, sleep, nor bed, await not on an exile.'"

With a delicate obeisance he left the room, evading Dame Glendinning, who hastened to assure him he would find his accommodations for repose much more agreeable than they had been the night before, there having been store of warm coverlets, and a soft feather-bed, sent up from the Abbey. But the good knight probably thought that the grace and effect of his exit would be diminished, if he were recalled from his heroics to discuss such sublunary and domestic topics, and therefore hastened away without waiting to hear her out.

"A pleasant gentleman," said Dame Glendinning; "but I will warrant him an humorous*—And sings a sweet song, though it is somewhat of the longest.—Well, I make mine avow he is goodly company—I wonder when he will go away."

Having thus expressed her respect for her guest, not without intimation that she was heartily tired of his company, the good dame gave the signal for the family to disperse, and laid her injunctions on Halbert to attend Sir Piercie Shafton at daybreak, as he required.

When stretched on his pallet by his brother's side, Halbert had no small cause to envy the sound sleep which instantly settled on the eyes of Edward, but refused him any share of its influence. He saw now too well what the spirit had darkly indicated, that, in granting the boon which he had asked so unadvisedly, she had contributed more to his harm than his good. He was now sensible, too late, of the various dangers and inconveniences with which his dearest friends were threatened, alike by his discomfiture or his success in the approaching duel. If he fell, he might say personally, "good-night all." But it was not the less certain that he should leave a dreadful legacy of distress and embarrassment to his mother and family,—an anticipation which by no means tended to render the front of death, in itself a grisly object, more agreeable to his imagination. The vengeance of the Abbot, his conscience told him, was sure to descend on his mother and brother, or could only be averted by the generosity of the victor—And Mary Avenel—he should have shown himself, if he succumbed in the present

* *Humorous*—full of whims—thus Shakspeare, "Humorous as winter."—The vulgar word humorsome comes nearest to the meaning.

combat, as inefficient in protecting her, as he had been unnecessarily active in bringing disaster on her, and on the house in which she had been protected from infancy. And to this view of the case were to be added all those imbittered and anxious feelings with which the bravest men, even in a better or less doubtful quarrel, regard the issue of a dubious conflict, the first time when it has been their fate to engage in an affair of that nature.

But however disconsolate the prospect seemed in the event of his being conquered, Halbert could expect from victory little more than the safety of his own life, and the gratification of his wounded pride. To his friends — to his mother and brother — especially to Mary Avenel — the consequences of his triumph would be more certain destruction than the contingency of his defeat and death. If the English knight survived, he might in courtesy extend his protection to them; but if he fell, nothing was likely to screen them from the vindictive measures which the Abbot and convent would surely adopt against the violation of the peace of the Halidome, and the slaughter of a protected guest by one of their own vassals, within whose house they had lodged him for shelter. These thoughts, in which neither view of the case augured aught short of ruin to his family, and that ruin entirely brought on by his own rashness, were thorns in Halbert Glendinning's pillow, and deprived his soul of peace and his eyes of slumber.

There appeared no middle course, saving one which was marked by degradation, and which, even if he stooped to it, was by no means free of danger. He might indeed confess to the English knight the strange circumstances which led to his presenting him with that token which the White Lady (in her displeasure as it now seemed) had given him, that he might offer it to Sir Piercie Shafton. But to this avowal his pride could not stoop, and reason, who is wonderfully ready to be of counsel with pride on such occasions, offered many arguments to show it would be useless as well as mean so far to degrade himself. "If I tell a tale so wonderful," thought he, "shall I not either be stigmatized as a liar, or punished as a wizard? — Were Sir Piercie Shafton generous, noble, and benevolent, as the champions of whom we hear in romance, I might indeed gain his ear, and, without demeaning myself, escape from the situation in which I am placed. But as he is, or at least seems to be, self-conceited, arrogant, vain, and presumptuous—I should but humble myself in vain—and I will not humble myself!" he said, starting out of bed, grasping his broadsword, and brandishing it in the light of the moon, which streamed through the deep niche that served them as a window; when, to his extreme surprise and terror, an airy form stood in the moonlight, but intercepted not the reflection on the floor. Dimly as it was expressed, the sound of the voice soon made him sensible he saw the White Lady.

At no time had her presence seemed so terrific to him; for when he had invoked her, it was with the expectation of the apparition, and the determination to abide the issue. But now she had come uncalled, and her presence impressed him with a sense of approaching misfortune, and with the hideous apprehension that he had associated himself with a demon, over whose motions he had no control, and of whose powers and quality he had no certain knowledge. He remained, therefore, in mere terror, gazing on the apparition, which chanted or recited in cadence the following lines—

"He whose heart for vengeance sued,
Must not shrink from shedding blood:
The knot that thou hast tied with word,
Thou must loose by edge of sword."

"Avaunt thee, false Spirit!" said Halbert Glendinning; "I have bought thy advice too dearly already—Begone in the name of God!"

The Spirit laughed; and the cold unnatural sound of her laughter had something in it more fearful than the usually melancholy tones of her voice. She then replied,—

"You have summon'd me once—you have summon'd me twice,
And without e'er a summons I come to you thrice;
Unask'd for, unsued for, you came to my glen;
Unsued and unask'd I am with you again."

Halbert Glendinning gave way for a moment to terror, and called on his brother, "Edward! waken, waken, for Our Lady's sake!"

Edward awaked accordingly, and asked what he wanted.

"Look out," said Halbert, "look up! seest thou no one in the room?"

"No, upon my good word," said Edward, looking out.

"What! seest thou nothing in the moonshine upon the floor there?"

"No, nothing," answered Edward, "save thyself resting on thy naked sword. I tell thee, Halbert, thou shouldst trust more to thy spiritual arms, and less to those of steel and iron. For this many a night hast thou started and moaned, and cried out of fighting, and of spectres, and of goblins—thy sleep hath not refreshed thee—thy waking hath been a dream.—Credit me, dear Halbert, say the *Pater* and *Credo*, resign thyself to the protection of God, and thou wilt sleep sound and wake in comfort."

"It may be," said Halbert slowly, and having his eye still bent on the female form which to him seemed distinctly visible,—"it may be—But tell me, dear Edward, seest thou no one on the chamber floor but me?"

"No one," answered Edward, raising himself on his elbow; "dear brother, lay aside thy weapon, say thy prayers, and lay thee down to rest."

While he thus spoke, the Spirit smiled at Halbert as if in scorn; her wan cheek faded in the wan moonlight even before the smile had passed away, and Halbert himself no longer beheld the vision to which he had so anxiously solicited his brother's attention. "May God preserve my wits!" he said, as, laying aside his weapon, he again threw himself on his bed.

"Amen! my dearest brother," answered Edward; "but we must not provoke that Heaven in our wantonness which we invoke in our misery.—Be not angry with me, my dear brother—I know not why you have totally of late estranged yourself from me—It is true, I am neither so athletic in body, nor so alert in courage, as you have been from your infancy; yet, till lately, you have not absolutely cast off my society—Believe me, I have wept in secret, though I forbore to intrude myself on your privacy. The time has been when you held me not so cheap; and when, if I could not follow the game so closely, or mark it so truly as you, I could fill up our intervals of pastime with pleasant tales of the olden times, which I had read or heard, and which excited even your attention as we sate and ate our provision by some pleasant spring—but now I have, though I know not why, lost thy regard and affection.—Nay, toss not thy arms about thee thus wildly," said the younger brother; "from thy strange dreams, I fear some touch of fever hath affected thy blood—let me draw closer around thee thy mantle."

"Forbear," said Halbert—"your care is needless—your complaints are without reason—your fears on my account are in vain."

"Nay, but hear me, brother," said Edward. "Your speech in sleep, and now even your waking dreams, are of beings which belong not to this world, or to our race—Our good Father Eustace says, that howbeit we may not do well to receive all idle tales of goblins and spectres, yet there is warrant from holy Scripture to believe, that the fiends haunt waste and solitary places; and that those who frequent such wildernesses alone, are the prey, or the sport, of these wandering demons. And therefore, I pray thee, brother, let me go with you when you go next up the glen, where, as you well know, there be places of evil reputation—Thou carest not for my escort; but, Halbert, such dangers are more safely encountered by the wise in judgment, than by the bold in bosom; and though I have small cause to boast of my own wisdom, yet I have that which ariseth from the written knowledge of elder times."

There was a moment during this discourse, when Halbert had well-nigh come to the resolution of disburdening his own breast, by intrusting Edward with all that weighed upon it. But when his brother reminded him that this was the morning of a high holiday, and that, setting aside all other business or pleasure, he ought to go to the Monastery and shrive himself before Father Eustace, who would that day occupy the confessional, pride stepped in and confirmed his wavering resolution. "I will not avow," he thought, "a tale so extraordinary, that I may be considered as an impostor or something worse — I will not fly from this Englishman, whose arm and sword may be no better than my own. My fathers have faced his betters, were he as much distinguished in battle as he is by his quaint discourse."

Pride, which has been said to save man, and woman too, from falling, has yet a stronger influence on the mind when it embraces the cause of passion, and seldom fails to render it victorious over conscience and reason. Halbert, once determined, though not to the better course, at length slept soundly, and was only awakened by the dawn of day.

Chapter the Twenty-First.

Indifferent, but indifferent — pshaw, he doth it not
Like one who is his craft's master — ne'er the less
I have seen a clown confer a bloody coxcomb
On one who was a master of defence.

OLD PLAY.

WITH the first gray peep of dawn, Halbert Glendinning arose and hastened to dress himself, girded on his weapon, and took a cross-bow in his hand, as if his usual sport had been his sole object. He groped his way down the dark and winding staircase, and undid, with as little noise as possible, the fastenings of the inner door, and of the exterior iron grate. At length he stood free in the court-yard, and looking up to the tower, saw a signal made with a handkerchief from the window. Nothing doubting that it was his antagonist, he paused, expecting him. But it was Mary Avenel, who glided like a spirit from under the low and rugged portal.

Halbert was much surprised, and felt, he knew not why, like one caught in the act of a meditated trespass. The presence of Mary Avenel had till that moment never given him pain. She spoke, too, in a tone where sorrow seemed to mingle with reproach, while she asked him with emphasis, "What he was about to do?"

He showed his cross-bow, and was about to express the pretext he had meditated, when Mary interrupted him.

"Not so, Halbert — that evasion were unworthy of one whose word has hitherto been truth. You meditate not the destruction of the deer — your hand and your heart are aimed at other game — you seek to do battle with this stranger."

"And wherefore should I quarrel with our guest?" answered Halbert, blushing deeply.

"There are, indeed, many reasons why you should not," replied the maiden, "nor is there one of avail wherefore you should—yet nevertheless, such a quarrel you are now searching after."

"Why should you suppose so, Mary?" said Halbert, endeavouring to hide his conscious purpose—"he is my mother's guest—he is protected by the Abbot and the community, who are our masters—he is of high degree also, — and wherefore should you think that I can, or dare, resent a hasty word, which he has perchance thrown out against me more from the wantonness of his wit, than the purpose of his heart?"

"Alas!" answered the maiden, "the very asking that question puts your resolution beyond a doubt. Since your childhood you were ever daring, seeking danger rather than avoiding it — delighting in whatever had the air of adventure and of courage: and it is not from fear that you will now blench from your purpose — Oh, let it then be from pity! — from pity, Halbert, to your aged mother, whom your death or victory will alike deprive of the comfort and stay of her age."

"She has my brother Edward," said Halbert, turning suddenly from her.

"She has indeed," said Mary Avenel, "the calm, the noble-minded, the considerate Edward, who has thy courage, Halbert, without thy fiery rashness, — thy generous spirit, with more of reason to guide it. He would not have heard his mother, would not have heard his adopted sister, beseech him in vain not to ruin himself, and tear up their future hopes of happiness and protection."

Halbert's heart swelled as he replied to this reproach. "Well — what avails it speaking? — you have him that is better than me — wiser, more considerate—braver, for aught I know—you are provided with a protector, and need care no more for me."

Again he turned to depart, but Mary Avenel laid her hand on his arm so gently that he scarce felt her hold, yet felt that it was impossible for him to strike it off. There he stood, one foot advanced to leave the court-yard, but so little determined on departure, that he resembled a traveller arrested by the spell of a magician, and unable either to quit the attitude of motion, or to proceed on his course.

Mary Avenel availed herself of his state of suspense. "Hear me," she said, "hear me, Halbert! — I am an orphan, and even Heaven hears the orphan — I have been the companion of your infancy, and if *you* will not hear me for an instant, from whom may Mary Avenel claim so poor a boon?"

"I hear you," said Halbert Glendinning, "but be brief, dear Mary—you mistake the nature of my business — it is but a morning of summer sport which we propose."

"Say not thus," said the maiden, interrupting him, "say not thus to me — others thou mayst deceive, but me thou canst not — There has been that in me from the earliest youth, which fraud flies from, and which imposture cannot deceive. For what fate has given me such a power I know not; but bred an ignorant maiden, in this sequestered valley, mine eyes can too often see what man would most willingly hide—I can judge of the dark purpose, though it is hid under the smiling brow, and a glance of the eye says more to me than oaths and protestations do to others."

"Then," said Halbert, "if thou canst so read the human heart, — say, dear Mary—what dost thou see in mine?—tell me that—say that what thou seest—what thou readest in this bosom, does not offend thee—say but *that*, and thou shalt be the guide of my actions, and mould me now and henceforward to honour or to dishonour at thy own free will!"

Mary Avenel became first red, and then deadly pale, as Halbert Glendinning spoke. But when, turning round at the close of his address, he took her hand, she gently withdrew it, and replied, "I cannot read the heart, Halbert, and I would not of my will know aught of yours, save what beseems us both — I only can judge of signs, words, and actions of little outward import, more truly than those around me, as my eyes, thou knowest, have seen objects not presented to those of others."

"Let them gaze then on one whom they shall never see more," said Halbert, once more turning from her, and rushing out of the court-yard without again looking back.

Mary Avenel gave a faint scream, and clasped both her hands firmly on her forehead and eyes. She had been a minute in this attitude, when she was thus greeted by a voice from behind: "Generously done, my most clement Discretion, to hide those brilliant eyes from the far inferior beams which even now begin to gild the eastern horizon—Certes, peril there were that Phœbus, outshone in splendour, might in very shamefacedness turn back his car, and rather leave the world in darkness, than incur the disgrace of such an encounter—Credit me, lovely Discretion——"

But as Sir Piercie Shafton (the reader will readily set down these flowers of eloquence to the proper owner) attempted to take Mary Avenel's hand, in order to proceed in his speech, she shook him abruptly off, and regarding him with an eye which evinced terror and agitation, rushed past him into the tower.

The knight stood looking after her with a countenance in which contempt was strongly mingled with mortification. "By my knighthood!" he ejaculated, "I have thrown away upon this rude rustic Phidelé a speech, which the proudest beauty at the court of Felicia (so let me call the Elysium from which I am banished!) might have termed the very matins of Cupid. Hard and inexorable was the fate that sent thee thither, Piercie Shafton, to waste thy wit upon country wenches, and thy valour upon hob-nailed clowns! But that insult — that affront — had it been offered to me by the lowest plebeian, he must have died for it by my hand, in respect the enormity of the offence doth countervail the inequality of him by whom it is given. I trust I shall find this clownish roisterer not less willing to deal in blows than in taunts."

While he held this conversation with himself, Sir Piercie Shafton was hastening to the little tuft of birch-trees which had been assigned as the place of meeting. He greeted his antagonist with a courtly salutation, followed by this commentary: "I pray you to observe, that I doff my hat to you, though so much my inferior in rank, without derogation on my part, inasmuch as my having so far honoured you in receiving and admitting your defiance, doth, in the judgment of the best martialists, in some sort and for the time, raise you to a level with me — an honour which you may and ought to account cheaply purchased, even with the loss of your life, if such should chance to be the issue of this duello."

"For which condescension," said Halbert, "I have to thank the token which I presented to you."

The knight changed colour, and grinded his teeth with rage—"Draw your weapon!" said he to Glendinning.

"Not in this spot," answered the youth; "we should be liable to interruption — Follow me, and I will bring you to a place where we shall encounter no such risk."

He proceeded to walk up the glen, resolving that their place of combat should be in the entrance of the Corri-nan-shian; both because the spot, lying under the reputation of being haunted, was very little frequented, and also because he regarded it as a place which to him might be termed fated, and which he therefore resolved should witness his death or victory.

They walked up the glen for some time in silence, like honourable enemies who did not wish to contend with words, and who had nothing friendly to exchange with each other. Silence, however, was always an irksome state with Sir Piercie, and, moreover, his anger was usually a hasty and short-lived passion. As, therefore, he went forth, in his own idea, in all love and honour towards his antagonist, he saw not any cause for submitting longer to the painful restraint of positive silence. He began by complimenting Halbert on the alert activity with which he surmounted the obstacles and impediments of the way.

"Trust me," said he, "worthy rustic, we have not a lighter or a firmer step in our courtlike revels, and if duly set forth by a silk hose, and trained unto that stately exercise, your leg would make an indifferent good show in a pavin or a galliard. And I doubt nothing," he added, "that you have availed yourself of some opportunity to improve yourself in the art of fence, which is more akin than dancing to our present purpose?"

"I know nothing more of fencing," said Halbert, "than hath been taught me by an old shepherd of ours, called Martin, and at whiles a lesson from Christie of the Clinthill — for the rest, I must trust to good sword, strong arm, and sound heart."

"Marry and I am glad of it, young Audacity, (I will call you my Audacity, and you will call me your Condescension, while we are on these terms of unnatural equality,) I am glad of your ignorance with all my heart. For we martialists proportion the punishments which we inflict upon our opposites, to the length and hazard of the efforts wherewith they oppose themselves to us. And I see not why you, being but a tyro, may not be held sufficiently punished for your outrecuidance, and orgillous presumption, by the loss of an ear, an eye, or even a finger, accompanied by some flesh-wound of depth and severity, suited to your error—whereas, had you been able to stand more effectually on your defence, I see not how less than your life could have atoned sufficiently for your presumption."

"Now, by God and Our Lady," said Halbert, unable any longer to restrain himself, "thou art thyself over-presumptuous, who speakest thus daringly of the issue of a combat which is not yet even begun — Are you a god, that you already dispose of my life and limbs? or are you a judge in the justice-air, telling at your ease and without risk, how the head and quarters of a condemned criminal are to be disposed of?"

"Not so, O thou, whom I have well permitted to call thyself my Audacity. I, thy Condescension, am neither a god to judge the issue of the combat before it is fought, nor a judge to dispose at my ease and in safety of the limbs and head of a condemned criminal; but I am an indifferent good master of fence, being the first pupil of the first master of the first school of fence that our royal England affords, the said master being no other than the truly noble, and all-unutterably skilful Vincentio Saviola, from whom I learned the firm step, quick eye, and nimble hand — of which qualities thou, O my most rustical Audacity, art full like to reap the fruits so soon as we shall find a piece of ground fitting for such experiments."

They had now reached the gorge of the ravine, where Halbert had at first intended to stop; but when he observed the narrowness of the level ground, he began to consider that it was only by superior agility that he could expect to make up his deficiency in the science, as it was called, of defence. He found no spot which afforded sufficient room to traverse for this purpose, until he gained the well-known fountain, by whose margin, and in front of the huge rock from which it sprung, was an amphitheatre of level turf, of small space indeed, compared with the great height of the cliffs with which it was surrounded on every point save that from which the rivulet issued forth, yet large enough for their present purpose.

When they had reached this spot of ground, fitted well by its gloom and sequestered situation to be a scene of mortal strife, both were surprised to observe that a grave was dug close by the foot of the rock with great neatness and regularity, the green turf being laid down upon the one side, and the earth thrown out in a heap upon the other. A mattock and shovel lay by the verge of the grave.

Sir Piercie Shafton bent his eye with unusual seriousness upon Halbert Glendinning, as he asked him sternly, "Does this bode treason, young man? And have you purpose to set upon me here as in an emboscata or place of vantage?"

"Not on my part, by Heaven!" answered the youth: "I told no one of our purpose, nor would I for the throne of Scotland take odds against a single arm."

"I believe thou wouldst not, mine Audacity," said the knight, resuming the affected manner which was become a second nature to him; "nevertheless this fosse is curiously well shaped, and might be the masterpiece of Nature's last bed-maker, I would say the sexton — Wherefore, let us be thankful to chance or some unknown friend, who hath thus provided for one of us the decencies of sepulture, and let us proceed to determine which shall have the advantage of enjoying this place of undisturbed slumber."

So saying, he stripped off his doublet and cloak, which he folded up with great care, and deposited upon a large stone, while Halbert Glendinning, not without some emotion, followed his example. Their vicinity to the favourite haunt of the White Lady led him to form conjectures concerning the incident of the grave — "It must have been her work!" he thought: "the Spirit foresaw and has provided for the fatal event of the combat — I must return from this place a homicide, or I must remain here for ever!"

The bridge seemed now broken down behind him, and the chance of coming off honourably without killing or being killed, (the hope of which issue has cheered the sinking heart of many a duellist,) seemed now altogether to be removed. Yet the very desperation of his situation gave him, on an instant's reflection, both firmness and courage, and presented to him one sole alternative, conquest, namely, or death.

"As we are here," said Sir Piercie Shafton, "unaccompanied by any patrons or seconds, it were well you should pass your hands over my sides, as I shall over yours; not that I suspect you to use any quaint device of privy armour, but in order to comply with the ancient and laudable custom practised on all such occasions."

While, complying with his antagonist's humour, Halbert Glendinning went through this ceremony, Sir Piercie Shafton did not fail to solicit his attention to the quality and fineness of his wrought and embroidered shirt — "In this very shirt," said he, "O mine Audacity! — I say in this very garment, in which I am now to combat a Scottish rustic like thyself, it was my envied lot to lead the winning party at that wonderous match at ballon, made betwixt the divine Astrophel, (our matchless Sidney,) and the right honourable my very good lord of Oxford. All the beauties of Felicia (by which name I distinguish our beloved England) stood in the gallery, waving their kerchiefs at each turn of the game, and cheering the winners by their plaudits. After which noble sport we were refreshed by a suitable banquet, whereat it pleased the noble Urania (being the unmatched Countess of Pembroke) to accommodate me with her fan for the cooling my somewhat too much inflamed visage, to requite which courtesy, I said, casting my features into a smiling, yet melancholy fashion, O divinest Urania! receive again that too fatal gift, which not like the Zephyr cooleth, but like the hot breath of the Sirocco, heateth yet more that which is already inflamed. Whereupon, looking upon me somewhat scornfully, yet not so but what the experienced courtier might perceive a certain cast of approbative affection——"

Here the knight was interrupted by Halbert, who had waited with courteous patience for some little time, till he found, that far from drawing to a close, Sir Piercie seemed rather inclined to wax prolix in his reminiscences.

"Sir Knight," said the youth, "if this matter be not very much to the purpose, we will, if you object not, proceed to that which we have in hand. You should have abidden in England had you desired to waste time in words, for here we spend it in blows."

"I crave your pardon, most rusticated Audacity," answered Sir Piercie; "truly I become oblivious of every thing beside, when the recollections of the divine court of Felicia press upon my wakened memory, even as a saint is dazzled when he bethinks him of the beatific vision. Ah, felicitous Feliciana! delicate nurse of the fair, chosen abode of the wise, the birth-place and cradle of nobility, the temple of courtesy, the fane of sprightly chivalry — Ah, heavenly court, or rather courtly heaven! cheered with dances, lulled asleep with harmony, wakened with sprightly sports and tourneys, decored with silks and tissues, glittering with diamonds and jewels, standing on end with double-piled velvets, satins, and satinettas!"

"The token, Sir Knight, the token!" exclaimed Halbert Glendinning, who, impatient of Sir Piercie's interminable oratory, reminded him of the ground of their quarrel, as the best way to compel him to the purpose of their meeting.

And he judged right; for Sir Piercie Shafton no sooner heard him speak, than he exclaimed, "Thy death-hour has struck — betake thee to thy sword —Via!"

Both swords were unsheathed, and the combatants commenced their engagement. Halbert became immediately aware, that, as he had expected, he was far inferior to his adversary in the use of his weapon. Sir Piercie Shafton had taken no more than his own share of real merit, when he termed himself an absolutely good fencer; and Glendinning soon found that he should have great difficulty in escaping with life and honour from such a master of the sword. The English knight was master of all the mystery of the *stoccata*, *imbrocata*, *punto-reverso*, *incartata*, and so forth, which the Italian masters of defence had lately introduced into general practice. But Glendinning, on his part, was no novice in the principles of the art, according to the old Scottish fashion, and possessed the first of all qualities, a steady and collected mind. At first, being desirous to try the skill, and become acquainted with the play of his enemy, he stood on his defence, keeping his foot, hand, eye, and body, in perfect unison, and holding his sword short, and with the point towards his antagonist's face, so that Sir Piercie, in order to assail him, was obliged to make actual passes, and could not avail himself of his skill in making feints; while, on the other hand, Halbert was prompt to parry these attacks, either by shifting his ground or with the sword. The consequence was, that after two or three sharp attempts on the part of Sir Piercie, which were evaded or disconcerted by the address of his opponent, he began to assume the defensive in his turn, fearful of giving some advantage by being repeatedly the assailant. But Halbert was too cautious to press on a swordsman whose dexterity had already more than once placed him within a hair's breadth of death, which he had only escaped by uncommon watchfulness and agility.

When each had made a feint or two, there was a pause in the conflict, both as if by one assent dropping their swords' point, and looking on each other for a moment without speaking. At length Halbert Glendinning, who felt perhaps more uneasy on account of his family than he had done before he had displayed his own courage, and proved the strength of his antagonist, could not help saying, "Is the subject of our quarrel, Sir Knight, so mortal, that one of our two bodies must needs fill up that grave? or may we with honour, having proved ourselves against each other, sheathe our swords and depart friends?"

"Valiant and most rustical Audacity," said the Southron knight, "to no man on earth could you have put a question on the code of honour, who was more capable of rendering you a reason. Let us pause for the space of one venue, until I give you my opinion on this dependence,* for certain it is, that brave men should not run upon their fate like brute and furious wild beasts, but should slay each other deliberately, decently, and with reason. Therefore, if we coolly examine the state of our dependence, we may the better apprehend whether the sisters three have doomed one of us to expiate the same with his blood — Dost thou understand me?"

"I have heard Father Eustace," said Halbert, after a moment's recollection, "speak of the three furies, with their thread and their shears."

* *Dependence*—A phrase among the brethren of the sword for an existing quarrel.

"Enough — enough,"— interrupted Sir Piercie Shafton, crimsoning with a new fit of rage, "the thread of thy life is spun!"

And with these words he attacked with the utmost ferocity the Scottish youth, who had but just time to throw himself into a posture of defence. But the rash fury of the assailant, as frequently happens, disappointed its own purpose; for, as he made a desperate thrust, Halbert Glendinning avoided it, and ere the knight could recover his weapon, requited him (to use his own language) with a resolute stoccata, which passed through his body, and Sir Piercie Shafton fell to the ground.

Chapter the Twenty-Second.

Yes, life hath left him — every busy thought,
Each fiery passion, every strong affection,
All sense of outward ill and inward sorrow,
Are fled at once from the pale trunk before me;
And I have given that which spoke and moved,
Thought, acted, suffer'd as a living man,
To be a ghastly form of bloody clay,
Soon the foul food for reptiles.

OLD PLAY.

I BELIEVE few successful duellists (if the word successful can be applied to a superiority so fatal) have beheld their dead antagonist stretched on the earth at their feet, without wishing they could redeem with their own blood that which it has been their fate to spill. Least of all could such indifference be the lot of so young a man as Halbert Glendinning, who, unused to the sight of human blood, was not only struck with sorrow, but with terror, when he beheld Sir Piercie Shafton lie stretched on the green-sward before him, vomiting gore as if impelled by the strokes of a pump. He threw his bloody sword on the ground, and hastened to kneel and support him, vainly striving, at the same time, to stanch his wound, which seemed rather to bleed inwardly than externally.

The unfortunate knight spoke at intervals, when the syncope would permit him, and his words, so far as intelligible, partook of his affected and conceited, yet not ungenerous character.

"Most rustical youth," he said, "thy fortune hath prevailed over knightly skill — and Audacity hath overcome Condescension, even as the kite hath sometimes hawked at and struck down the falcon-gentle.—Fly and save thyself!—Take my purse—it is in the nether pocket of my carnation-coloured hose — and is worth a clown's acceptance. See that my mails, with my vestments, be sent to the Monastery of Saint Mary's"—(here his voice grew weak, and his mind and recollection seemed to waver) — "I bestow the cut velvet jerkin, with close breeches conforming—for—oh!—the good of my soul."

"Be of good comfort, sir," said Halbert, half distracted with his agony of pity and remorse. "I trust you shall yet do well — Oh for a leech!"

"Were there twenty physicians, O most generous Audacity, and that were a grave spectacle — I might not survive, my life is ebbing fast. — Commend me to the rustical nymph whom I called my Discretion — O Claridiana! — true empress of this bleeding heart—which now bleedeth in sad earnest!—Place me on the ground at my length, most rustical victor, born to quench the pride of the burning light of the most felicitous court of Feliciana — O saints and angels — knights and ladies — masques and theatres — quaint devices — chain-work and broidery — love, honour, and beauty!——"

While muttering these last words, which slid from him, as it were unawares, while doubtless he was calling to mind the glories of the English court, the gallant Sir Piercie Shafton stretched out his limbs — groaned deeply, shut his eyes, and became motionless.

The victor tore his hair for very sorrow, as he looked on the pale countenance of his victim. Life, he thought, had not utterly fled, but without better aid than his own, he saw not how it could be preserved.

"Why," he exclaimed in vain penitence, "why did I provoke him to an issue so fatal! Would to God I had submitted to the worst insult man could receive from man, rather than be the bloody instrument of this bloody deed — and doubly cursed be this evil-boding spot, which, haunted as I knew it to be by a witch or a devil, I yet chose for the place of combat! In any other place, save this, there had been help to be gotten by speed of foot, or by uplifting of voice — but here there is no one to be found by search, no one to hear my shouts, save the evil spirit who has counselled this mischief. It is not her hour—I will essay the spell howsoever; and if she can give me aid, she *shall* do it, or know of what a madman is capable even against those of another world!"

He spurned his bloody shoe from his foot, and repeated the spell with which the reader is well acquainted; but there was neither voice, apparition, nor signal of answer. The youth, in the impatience of his despair, and with the rash hardihood which formed the basis of his character, shouted aloud, "Witch—Sorceress—Fiend!—art thou deaf to my cries of help, and so ready to appear and answer those of vengeance? Arise and speak to me, or I will choke up thy fountain, tear down thy hollybush, and leave thy haunt as waste and bare as thy fatal assistance has made me waste of comfort and bare of counsel!"—This furious and raving invocation was suddenly interrupted by a distant sound, resembling a hollo, from the gorge of the ravine. "Now may Saint Mary be praised," said the youth, hastily fastening his sandal, "I hear the voice of some living man, who may give me counsel and help in this fearful extremity."

Having donned his sandal, Halbert Glendinning, hallooing at intervals, in answer to the sound which he had heard, ran with the speed of a hunted buck down the rugged defile, as if paradise had been before him, hell and all her furies behind, and his eternal happiness or misery had depended upon the speed which he exerted. In a space incredibly short for any one but a Scottish mountaineer having his nerves strung by the deepest and most passionate interest, the youth reached the entrance of the ravine, through which the rill that flows down Corri-nan-shian discharges itself, and unites with the brook that waters the little valley of Glendearg.

Here he paused, and looked around him upwards and downwards through the glen, without perceiving a human form. His heart sank within him. But the windings of the glen intercepted his prospect, and the person, whose voice he had heard, might therefore, be at no great distance, though not obvious to his sight. The branches of an oak-tree, which shot straight out from the face of a tall cliff, proffered to his bold spirit, steady head, and active limbs, the means of ascending it as a place of out-look, although the enterprise was what most men would have shrunk from. But by one bound from the earth, the active youth caught hold of the lower branch, and swung himself up into the tree, and in a minute more gained the top of the cliff, from which he could easily descry a human figure descending the valley. It was not that of a shepherd, or of a hunter, and scarcely any others used to traverse this deserted solitude, especially coming from the north, since the reader may remember that the brook took its rise from an extensive and dangerous morass which lay in that direction.

But Halbert Glendinning did not pause to consider who the traveller might be, or what might be the purpose of his journey. To know that he saw a human being, and might receive, in the extremity of his distress, the countenance and advice of a fellow-creature, was enough for him at the moment. He threw himself from the pinnacle of the cliff once more into the arms of the projecting oak-tree, whose boughs waved in middle air, anchored by the roots in a huge rift or chasm of the rock. Catching at the branch which was nearest to him, he dropped himself from that height upon the ground; and such was the athletic springiness of his youthful sinews, that he pitched there as lightly, and with as little injury, as the falcon stooping from her wheel.

To resume his race at full speed up the glen, was the work of an instant; and as he turned angle after angle of the indented banks of the valley, without meeting that which he sought, he became half afraid that the form which he had seen at such a distance had already melted into thin air, and was either a deception of his own imagination, or of the elementary spirits by which the valley was supposed to be haunted.

But to his inexpressible joy, as he turned round the base of a huge and distinguished crag, he saw, straight before and very near to him, a person, whose dress, as he viewed it hastily, resembled that of a pilgrim.

He was a man of advanced life, and wearing a long beard, having on his head a large slouched hat, without either band or brooch. His dress was a tunic of black serge, which, like those commonly called hussar-cloaks, had an upper part, which covered the arms and fell down on the lower; a small scrip and bottle, which hung at his back, with a stout staff in his hand, completed his equipage. His step was feeble, like that of one exhausted by a toilsome journey.

"Save ye, good father!" said the youth. "God and Our Lady have sent you to my assistance."

"And in what, my son, can so frail a creature as I am, be of service to you?" said the old man, not a little surprised at being thus accosted by so handsome a youth, his features discomposed by anxiety, his face flushed with exertion, his hands and much of his dress stained with blood.

"A man bleeds to death in the valley here, hard by. Come with me — come with me! You are aged — you have experience — you have at least your senses—and mine have well nigh left me."

"A man — and bleeding to death — and here in this desolate spot!" said the stranger.

"Stay not to question it, father," said the youth, "but come instantly to his rescue. Follow me,—follow me, without an instant's delay."

"Nay, but, my son," said the old man, "we do not lightly follow the guides who present themselves thus suddenly in the bosom of a howling wilderness. Ere I follow thee, thou must expound to me thy name, thy purpose, and thy cause."

"There is no time to expound any thing," said Halbert; "I tell thee a man's life is at stake, and thou must come to aid him, or I will carry thee thither by force!"

"Nay, thou shalt not need," said the traveller; "if it indeed be as thou sayest, I will follow thee of free-will — the rather that I am not wholly unskilled in leech-craft, and have in my scrip that which may do thy friend a service—Yet walk more slowly, I pray thee, for I am already well-nigh forespent with travel."

With the indignant impatience of the fiery steed when compelled by his rider to keep pace with some slow drudge upon the highway, Halbert accompanied the wayfarer, burning with anxiety which he endeavoured to subdue, that he might not alarm his companion, who was obviously afraid to trust him. When they reached the place where they were to turn off the wider glen into the Corri, the traveller made a doubtful pause, as if unwilling to leave the broader path—"Young man," he said, "if thou meanest aught but good to these gray hairs, thou wilt gain little by thy cruelty—I have no earthly treasure to tempt either robber or murderer."

"And I," said the youth, "am neither — and yet — God of Heaven! — I *may* be a murderer, unless your aid comes in time to this wounded wretch!"

"Is it even so," said the traveller; "and do human passions disturb the breast of nature, even in her deepest solitude? — Yet why should I marvel that where darkness abides the works of darkness should abound? — By its fruits is the tree known — Lead on, unhappy youth — I follow thee!"

And with better will to the journey than he had evinced hitherto, the stranger exerted himself to the uttermost, and seemed to forget his own fatigue in his efforts to keep pace with his impatient guide.

What was the surprise of Halbert Glendinning, when, upon arriving at the fatal spot, he saw no appearance of the body of Sir Piercie Shafton! The traces of the fray were otherwise sufficiently visible. The knight's cloak had indeed vanished as well as his body, but his doublet remained where he had laid it down, and the turf on which he had been stretched was stained with blood in many a dark crimson spot.

As he gazed round him in terror and astonishment, Halbert's eyes fell upon the place of sepulture which had so lately appeared to gape for a victim. It was no longer open, and it seemed that earth had received the expected tenant; for the usual narrow hillock was piled over what had lately been an open grave, and the green sod was adjusted over all with the accuracy of an experienced sexton. Halbert stood aghast. The idea rushed on his mind irresistibly, that the earth-heap before him enclosed what had lately been a living, moving, and sentient fellow-creature, whom, on little provocation, his fell act had reduced to a clod of the valley, as senseless and as cold as the turf under which he rested. The hand that scooped the grave had completed its word; and whose hand could it be save that of the mysterious being of doubtful quality, whom his rashness had invoked, and whom he had suffered to intermingle in his destinies?

As he stood with clasped hands and uplifted eyes, bitterly ruing his rashness, he was roused by the voice of the stranger, whose suspicions of his guide had again been awakened by finding the scene so different from what Halbert had led him to expect. — "Young man," he said, "hast thou baited thy tongue with falsehood to cut perhaps only a few days from the life of one whom Nature will soon call home, without guilt on thy part to hasten his journey?"

"By the blessed Heaven! — by our dear Lady!" ejaculated Halbert——

"Swear not at all!" said the stranger, interrupting him, "neither by Heaven, for it is God's throne, nor by earth, for it is his footstool — nor by the creatures whom he hath made, for they are but earth and clay as we are. Let thy yea be yea, and thy nay, nay. Tell me in a word, why and for what purpose thou hast feigned a tale, to lead a bewildered traveller yet farther astray?"

"As I am a Christian man," said Glendinning, "I left him here bleeding to death — and now I nowhere spy him, and much I doubt that the tomb that thou seest has closed on his mortal remains!"

"And who is he for whose fate thou art so anxious?" said the stranger; "or how is it possible that this wounded man could have been either removed from, or interred in, a place so solitary?"

"His name," said Halbert, after a moment's pause, "is Piercie Shafton — there, on that very spot I left him bleeding; and what power has conveyed him hence, I know no more than thou dost."

"Piercie Shafton?" said the stranger; "Sir Piercie Shafton of Wilverton, a kinsman, as it is said, of the great Piercie of Northumberland? If thou hast slain him, to return to the territories of the proud Abbot is to give thy neck to the gallows. He is well known, that Piercie Shafton; the meddling tool of wiser plotters — a harebrained trafficker in treason — a champion of the Pope, employed as a forlorn hope by those more politic heads, who have more will to work mischief, than valour to encounter danger. — Come with me, youth, and save thyself from the evil consequences of this deed—Guide me to the Castle of Avenel, and thy reward shall be protection and safety."

Again Halbert paused, and summoned his mind to a hasty council. The vengeance with which the Abbot was likely to visit the slaughter of Shafton, his friend, and in some measure his guest, was likely to be severe; yet, in the various contingencies which he had considered previous to their duel, he had unaccountably omitted to reflect what was to be his line of conduct in case of Sir Piercie falling by his hand. If he returned to Glendearg, he was sure to draw on his whole family, including Mary Avenel, the resentment of the Abbot and community, whereas it was possible that flight might make him be regarded as the sole author of the deed, and might avert the indignation of the monks from the rest of the inhabitants of his paternal tower. Halbert recollected also the favour expressed for the household, and especially for Edward, by the Sub-Prior; and he conceived that he could, by communicating his own guilt to that worthy ecclesiastic, when at a distance from Glendearg, secure his powerful interposition in favour of his family. These thoughts rapidly passed through his mind, and he determined on flight. The stranger's company and his promised protection came in aid of that resolution; but he was unable to reconcile the invitation which the old man gave him to accompany him for safety to the Castle of Avenel, with the connexions of Julian, the present usurper of that inheritance. "Good father," he said, "I fear that you mistake the man with whom you wish me to harbour. Avenel guided Piercie Shafton into Scotland, and his henchman, Christie of the Clinthill, brought the Southron hither."

"Of that," said the old man, "I am well aware. Yet if thou wilt trust to me, as I have shown no reluctance to confide in thee, thou shalt find with Julian Avenel welcome, or at least safety."

"Father," replied Halbert, "though I can ill reconcile what thou sayest with what Julian Avenel hath done, yet caring little about the safety of a creature so lost as myself, and as thy words seem those of truth and honesty, and finally, as thou didst render thyself frankly up to my conduct, I will return the confidence thou hast shown, and accompany thee to the Castle of Avenel by a road which thou thyself couldst never have discovered." He led the way, and the old man followed for some time in silence.

Chapter the Twenty-Third.

'Tis when the wound is stiffening with the cold,
The warrior first feels pain—'tis when the heat
And fiery fever of his soul is pass'd,
The sinner feels remorse.

OLD PLAY.

THE feelings of compunction with which Halbert Glendinning was visited upon this painful occasion, were deeper than belonged to an age and country in which human life was held so cheap. They fell far short certainly of those which might have afflicted a mind regulated by better religious precepts, and more strictly trained under social laws; but still they were deep and severely felt, and divided in Halbert's heart even the regret with which he parted from Mary Avenel and the tower of his fathers.

The old traveller walked silently by his side for some time, and then addressed him.—"My son, it has been said that sorrow must speak or die—Why art thou so much cast down?—Tell me thy unhappy tale, and it may be that my gray head may devise counsel and aid for your young life."

"Alas!" said Halbert Glendinning, "can you wonder why I am cast down?—I am at this instant a fugitive from my father's house, from my mother, and from my friends, and I bear on my head the blood of a man who injured me but in idle words, which I have thus bloodily requited. My heart now tells me I have done evil—it were harder than these rocks if it could bear unmoved the thought, that I have sent this man to a long account, unhousled and unshrieved!"

"Pause there, my son," said the traveller. "That thou hast defaced God's image in thy neighbour's person—that thou hast sent dust to dust in idle wrath or idler pride, is indeed a sin of the deepest dye—that thou hast cut short the space which Heaven might have allowed him for repentance, makes it yet more deadly—but for all this there is balm in Gilead."

"I understand you not, father," said Halbert, struck by the solemn tone which was assumed by his companion.

The old man proceeded. "Thou hast slain thine enemy—it was a cruel deed: thou hast cut him off perchance in his sins—it is a fearful aggravation. Do yet by my counsel, and in lieu of him whom thou hast perchance consigned to the kingdom of Satan, let thine efforts wrest another subject from the reign of the Evil One."

"I understand you, father," said Halbert; "thou wouldst have me atone for my rashness by doing service to the soul of my adversary—But how may this be? I have no money to purchase masses, and gladly would I go barefoot to the Holy Land to free his spirit from purgatory, only that——"

"My son," said the old man, interrupting him, "the sinner for whose redemption I entreat you to labour, is not the dead but the living. It is not for the soul of thine enemy I would exhort thee to pray—that has already had its final doom from a Judge as merciful as he is just; nor, wert thou to coin that rock into ducats, and obtain a mass for each one, would it avail the departed spirit. Where the tree hath fallen, it must lie. But the sapling, which hath in it yet the vigour and juice of life, may be bended to the point to which it ought to incline."

"Art thou a priest, father?" said the young man, "or by what commission dost thou talk of such high matters?"

"By that of my Almighty Master," said the traveller, "under whose banner I am an enlisted soldier."

Halbert's acquaintance with religious matters was no deeper than could be derived from the Archbishop of Saint Andrew's Catechism, and the pamphlet called the Twapennie Faith, both which were industriously circulated and recommended by the monks of Saint Mary's. Yet, however indifferent and superficial a theologian, he began to suspect that he was now in company with one of the gospellers, or heretics, before whose influence the ancient system of religion now tottered to the very foundation. Bred up, as may well be presumed, in a holy horror against these formidable sectaries, the youth's first feelings were those of a loyal and devoted church vassal. "Old man," he said, "wert thou able to make good with thy hand the words that thy tongue hath spoken against our Holy Mother Church, we should have tried upon this moor which of our creeds hath the better champion."

"Nay," said the stranger, "if thou art a true soldier of Rome, thou wilt not pause from thy purpose because thou hast the odds of years and of strength on thy side. Hearken to me, my son. I have showed thee how to make thy peace with Heaven, and thou hast rejected my proffer. I will now show thee how thou shalt make thy reconciliation with the powers of this world. Take this gray head from the frail body which supports it, and carry it to the chair of proud Abbot Boniface; and when thou tellest him thou hast slain Piercie Shafton, and his ire rises at the deed, lay the head of Henry Warden at his foot, and thou shalt have praise instead of censure."

Halbert Glendinning stepped back in surprise. "What! are you that Henry Warden so famous among the heretics, that even Knox's name is scarce more frequently in their mouths? Art thou he, and darest thou to approach the Halidome of Saint Mary's?"

"I am Henry Warden, of a surety," said the old man, "far unworthy to be named in the same breath with Knox, but yet willing to venture on whatever dangers my master's service may call me to."

"Hearken to me, then," said Halbert; "to slay thee, I have no heart—to make thee prisoner, were equally to bring thy blood on my head—to leave thee in this wild without a guide, were little better. I will conduct thee, as I promised, in safety to the Castle of Avenel; but breathe not, while we are on the journey, a word against the doctrines of the holy church of which I am an unworthy—but though an ignorant, a zealous member.—When thou art there arrived, beware of thyself—there is a high price upon thy head, and Julian Avenel loves the glance of gold bonnet-pieces."*

"Yet thou sayest not," answered the Protestant preacher, for such he was, "that for lucre he would sell the blood of his guest?"

"Not if thou comest an invited stranger, relying on his faith," said the youth; "evil as Julian may be, he dare not break the rites of hospitality; for, loose as we on these marches may be in all other ties, these are respected amongst us even to idolatry, and his nearest relations would think it incumbent on them to spill his blood themselves, to efface the disgrace such treason would bring upon their name and lineage. But if thou goest self-invited, and without assurance of safety, I promise thee thy risk is great."

"I am in God's hand," answered the preacher; "it is on His errand that I traverse these wilds amidst dangers of every kind; while I am useful for my master's service, they shall not prevail against me, and when, like the barren fig-tree, I can no longer produce fruit, what imports it when or by whom the axe is laid to the root?"

"Your courage and devotion," said Glendinning, "are worthy of a better cause."

"That," said Warden, "cannot be—mine is the very best."

They continued their journey in silence, Halbert Glendinning tracing with the utmost accuracy the mazes of the dangerous and intricate morasses and hills which divided the Halidome from the barony of Avenel. From time to time he was obliged to stop, in order to assist his companion to cross the black intervals of quaking bog, called in the Scottish dialect *hags*, by which the firmer parts of the morass were intersected.

"Courage, old man," said Halbert, as he saw his companion almost exhausted with fatigue, "we shall soon be upon hard ground. And yet soft as this moss is, I have seen the merry falconers go through it as light as deer when the quarry was upon the flight."

"True, my son," answered Warden, "for so I will still call you, though you term me no longer father; and even so doth headlong youth pursue its pleasures, without regard to the mire and the peril of the paths through which they are hurried."

"I have already told thee," answered Halbert Glendinning, sternly, "that I will hear nothing from thee that savours of doctrine."

"Nay, but, my son," answered Warden, "thy spiritual father himself would surely not dispute the truth of what I have now spoken for your edification!"

Glendinning stoutly replied, "I know not how that may be—but I wot

* A gold coin of James V., the most beautiful of the Scottish series; so called because the effigy of the sovereignty is represented wearing a bonnet.

well it is the fashion of your brotherhood to bait your hook with fair discourse, and to hold yourselves up as angels of light, that you may the better extend the kingdom of darkness."

"May God," replied the preacher, "pardon those who have thus reported of his servants! I will not offend thee, my son, by being instant out of season — thou speakest but as thou art taught — yet sure I trust that so goodly a youth will be still rescued, like a brand from the burning."

While he thus spoke, the verge of the morass was attained, and their path lay on the declivity. Green-sward it was, and, viewed from a distance, chequered with its narrow and verdant line the dark-brown heath which it traversed, though the distinction was not so easily traced when they were walking on it.* The old man pursued his journey with comparative ease; and, unwilling again to awaken the jealous zeal of his young companion for the Roman faith, he discoursed on other matters. The tone of his conversation was still grave, moral, and instructive. He had travelled much, and knew both the language and manners of other countries, concerning which Halbert Glendinning, already anticipating the possibility of being obliged to leave Scotland for the deed he had done, was naturally and anxiously desirous of information. By degrees he was more attracted by the charms of the stranger's conversation than repelled by the dread of his dangerous character as a heretic, and Halbert had called him father more than once, ere the turrets of Avenel Castle came in view.

The situation of this ancient fortress was remarkable. It occupied a small rocky islet in a mountain lake, or *tarn*, as such a piece of water is called in Westmoreland. The lake might be about a mile in circumference, surrounded by hills of considerable height, which, except where old trees and brushwood occupied the ravines that divided them from each other, were bare and heathy. The surprise of the spectator was chiefly excited by finding a piece of water situated in that high and mountainous region, and the landscape around had features which might rather be termed wild, than either romantic or sublime; yet the scene was not without its charms. Under the burning sun of summer, the clear azure of the deep unruffled lake refreshed the eye, and impressed the mind with a pleasing feeling of deep solitude. In winter, when the snow lay on the mountains around, these dazzling masses appeared to ascend far beyond their wonted and natural height, while the lake, which stretched beneath, and filled their bosom with all its frozen waves, lay like the surface of a darkened and broken mirror around the black and rocky islet, and the walls of the gray castle with which it was crowned.

As the castle occupied, either with its principal buildings, or with its flanking and outward walls, every projecting point of rock, which served as its site, it seemed as completely surrounded by water as the nest of a wild swan, save where a narrow causeway extended betwixt the islet and the shore. But the fortress was larger in appearance than in reality; and of the buildings which it actually contained, many had become ruinous and uninhabitable. In the times of the grandeur of the Avenel family, these had been occupied by a considerable garrison of followers and retainers, but they were now in a great measure deserted; and Julian Avenel would probably have fixed his habitation in a residence better suited to his diminished fortunes, had it not been for the great security which the situation of the old castle afforded to a man of his precarious and perilous mode of life. Indeed, in this respect, the spot could scarce have been more happily chosen, for it could be rendered almost completely inaccessible at the pleasure of the inhabitant. The distance betwixt the nearest shore and the islet was not indeed above an hundred yards; but then the causeway which con-

* This sort of path, visible when looked at from a distance, but not to be seen when you are upon it, is called on the Border by the significant name of a Blind-road.

nected them was extremely narrow, and completely divided by two cuts, one in the mid-way between the islet and shore, and another close under the outward gate of the castle. These formed a formidable, and almost insurmountable interruption to any hostile approach. Each was defended by a drawbridge, one of which, being that nearest to the castle, was regularly raised at all times during the day, and both were lifted at night.*

The situation of Julian Avenel, engaged in a variety of feuds, and a party to almost every dark and mysterious transaction which was on foot in that wild and military frontier, required all these precautions for his security. His own ambiguous and doubtful course of policy had increased these dangers; for as he made professions to both parties in the state, and occasionally united more actively with either the one or the other, as chanced best to serve his immediate purpose, he could not be said to have either firm allies and protectors, or determined enemies. His life was a life of expedients and of peril; and while, in pursuit of his interest, he made all the doubles which he thought necessary to attain his object, he often overran his prey, and missed that which he might have gained by observing a straighter course.

Chapter the Twenty-Fourth.

I'll walk on tiptoe; arm my eye with caution,
My heart with courage, and my hand with weapon,
Like him who ventures on a lion's den.

OLD PLAY.

WHEN, issuing from the gorge of a pass which terminated upon the lake, the travellers came in sight of the ancient castle of Avenel, the old man looked with earnest attention upon the scene before him. The castle was, as we have said, in many places ruinous, as was evident, even at this distance, by the broken, rugged, and irregular outline of the walls and of the towers. In others it seemed more entire, and a pillar of dark smoke, which ascended from the chimneys of the donjon, and spread its long dusky pennon through the clear ether, indicated that it was inhabited. But no corn-fields or enclosed pasture-grounds on the side of the lake showed that provident attention to comfort and subsistence which usually appeared near the houses of the greater, and even of the lesser barons. There were no cottages with their patches of infield, and their crofts and gardens, surrounded by rows of massive sycamores; no church with its simple tower in the valley; no herds of sheep among the hills; no cattle on the lower ground; nothing which intimated the occasional prosecution of the arts of peace and of industry. It was plain that the inhabitants, whether few or numerous, must be considered as the garrison of the castle, living within its defended precincts, and subsisting by means which were other than peaceful.

Probably it was with this conviction that the old man, gazing on the castle, muttered to himself, "*Lapis offensionis et petra scandali!*" and then, turning to Halbert Glendinning, he added, "We may say of yonder fort as King

* It is in vain to search near Melrose for any such castle as is here described. The lakes at the head of the Yarrow, and those at the rise of the water of Ale, present no object of the kind. But in Yetholm Loch, (a romantic sheet of water, in the dry march, as it is called,) there are the remains of a fortress called Lochside Tower, which, like the supposed Castle of Avenel, is built upon an island, and connected with the land by a causeway. It is much smaller than the Castle of Avenel is described, consisting only of a single ruinous tower.

James did of another fastness in this province, that he who built it was a thief in his heart."*

"But it was not so," answered Glendinning; "yonder castle was built by the old lords of Avenel, men as much beloved in peace as they were respected in war. They were the bulwark of the frontiers against foreigners, and the protectors of the natives from domestic oppression. The present usurper of their inheritance no more resembles them, than the night-prowling owl resembles a falcon, because she builds on the same rock."

"This Julian Avenel, then, holds no high place in the love and regard of his neighbours?" said Warden.

"So little," answered Halbert, "that besides the jack-men and riders with whom he has associated himself, and of whom he has many at his disposal, I know of few who voluntarily associate with him. He has been more than once outlawed both by England and Scotland, his lands declared forfeited, and his head set at a price. But in these unquiet times, a man so daring as Julian Avenel has ever found some friends willing to protect him against the penalties of the law, on condition of his secret services."

"You describe a dangerous man," replied Warden.

"You may have experience of that," replied the youth, "if you deal not the more warily;—though it may be that he also has forsaken the community of the church, and gone astray in the path of heresy."

"What your blindness terms the path of heresy," answered the reformer, "is indeed the straight and narrow way, wherein he who walks turns not aside, whether for worldly wealth or for worldly passions. Would to God this man were moved by no other and no worse spirit than that which prompts my poor endeavours to extend the kingdom of Heaven! This Baron of Avenel is personally unknown to me, is not of our congregation or of our counsel; yet I bear to him charges touching my safety, from those whom he must fear if he does not respect them, and upon that assurance I will venture upon his hold—I am now sufficiently refreshed by these few minutes of repose."

"Take then this advice for your safety," said Halbert, "and believe that it is founded upon the usage of this country and its inhabitants. If you can better shift for yourself, go not to the Castle of Avenel—if you do risk going thither, obtain from him, if possible, his safe conduct, and beware that he swears it by the Black Rood—And lastly, observe whether he eats with you at the board, or pledges you in the cup; for if he gives you not these signs of welcome, his thoughts are evil towards you."

"Alas!" said the preacher, "I have no better earthly refuge for the present than these frowning towers, but I go thither trusting to aid which is not of this earth—But thou, good youth, needest thou trust thyself in this dangerous den?"

"I," answered Halbert, "am in no danger. I am well known to Christie of the Clinthill, the henchman of this Julian Avenel; and, what is a yet better protection, I have nothing either to provoke malice or to tempt plunder."

The tramp of a steed, which clattered along the shingly banks of the loch, was now heard behind them; and, when they looked back, a rider was visible, his steel cap and the point of his long lance glancing in the setting sun, as he rode rapidly towards them.

Halbert Glendinning soon recognized Christie of the Clinthill, and made his companion aware that the henchman of Julian Avenel was approaching.

"Ha, youngling!" said Christie to Halbert, as he came up to them, "thou hast made good my word at last, and come to take service with my noble master, hast thou not? Thou shalt find a good friend and a true; and ere Saint Barnaby come round again, thou shalt know every pass betwixt Mill-

* It was of Lochwood, the hereditary fortress of the Johnstones of Annandale, a strong castle situated in the centre of a quaking bog, that James VI. made this remark.

burn Plain and Netherby, as if thou hadst been born with a jack on thy back, and a lance in thy hand.—What old carle hast thou with thee?—He is not of the brotherhood of Saint Mary's—at least he has not the buist* of these black cattle."

"He is a wayfaring man," said Halbert, "who has concerns with Julian of Avenel. For myself, I intend to go to Edinburgh to see the court and the Queen, and when I return hither we will talk of your proffer. Meantime, as thou hast often invited me to the castle, I crave hospitality there to-night for myself and my companion."

"For thyself and welcome, young comrade," replied Christie; "but we harbour no pilgrims, nor aught that looks like a pilgrim."

"So please you," said Warden, "I have letters of commendation to thy master from a sure friend, whom he will right willingly oblige in higher matters than in affording me a brief protection.—And I am no pilgrim, but renounce the same, with all its superstitious observances."

He offered his letters to the horseman, who shook his head.

"These," he said, "are matters for my master, and it will be well if he can read them himself; for me, sword and lance are my book and psalter, and have been since I was twelve years old. But I will guide you to the castle, and the Baron of Avenel will himself judge of your errand."

By this time the party had reached the causeway, along which Christie advanced at a trot, intimating his presence to the warders within the castle by a shrill and peculiar whistle. At this signal the farther drawbridge was lowered. The horseman passed it, and disappeared under the gloomy portal which was beyond it.

Glendinning and his companion advancing more leisurely along the rugged causeway, stood at length under the same gateway, over which frowned, in dark red freestone, the ancient armorial bearings of the house of Avenel, which represented a female figure shrouded and muffled, which occupied the whole field. The cause of their assuming so singular a device was uncertain, but the figure was generally supposed to represent the mysterious being called the White Lady of Avenel.† The sight of this mouldering shield awakened in the mind of Halbert the strange circumstances which had connected his fate with that of Mary Avenel, and with the doings of the spiritual being who was attached to her house, and whom he saw here represented in stone, as he had before seen her effigy upon the seal-ring of Walter Avenel, which, with other trinkets formerly mentioned, had been saved from pillage, and brought to Glendearg, when Mary's mother was driven from her habitation.

"You sigh, my son," said the old man, observing the impression made on his youthful companion's countenance, but mistaking the cause; "if you fear to enter, we may yet return."

"That can ye not," said Christie of the Clinthill, who emerged at that instant from the side-door under the archway. "Look yonder, and choose whether you will return skimming the water like a wild-duck, or winging the air like a plover."

They looked, and saw that the drawbridge which they had just crossed was again raised, and now interposed its planks betwixt the setting sun and the portal of the castle, deepening the gloom of the arch under which they stood. Christie laughed and bid them follow him, saying, by way of encouragement, in Halbert's ear, "Answer boldly and readily to whatever the Baron asks you. Never stop to pick your words, and above all show no fear of him—the devil is not so black as he is painted."

As he spoke thus, he introduced them into the large stone hall, at the upper end of which blazed a huge fire of wood. The long oaken table,

* *Buist*—The brand, or mark, set upon sheep or cattle, by their owners.

† There is an ancient English family, I believe, which bears, or did bear, a ghost or spirit passant sable in a field argent. This seems to have been a device of a punning or *canting* herald.

which, as usual, occupied the midst of the apartment, was covered with rude preparations for the evening meal of the Baron and his chief domestics, five or six of whom, strong, athletic, savage-looking men, paced up and down the lower end of the hall, which rang to the jarring clang of their long swords that clashed as they moved, and to the heavy tramp of their high-heeled jack-boots. Iron jacks, or coats of buff, formed the principal part of their dress, and steel-bonnets, or large slouched hats with Spanish plumes drooping backwards, were their head attire.

The Baron of Avenel was one of those tall, muscular, martial figures, which are the favourite subjects of Salvator Rosa. He wore a cloak which had been once gaily trimmed, but which, by long wear and frequent exposure to the weather, was now faded in its colours. Thrown negligently about his tall person, it partly hid, and partly showed, a short doublet of buff, under which was in some places visible that light shirt of mail which was called a *secret*, because worn instead of more ostensible armour to protect against private assassination. A leathern belt sustained a large and heavy sword on one side, and on the other that gay poniard which had once called Sir Piercie Shafton master, of which the hatchments and gildings were already much defaced, either by rough usage or neglect.

Notwithstanding the rudeness of his apparel, Julian Avenel's manner and countenance had far more elevation than those of the attendants who surrounded him. He might be fifty or upwards, for his dark hair was mingled with gray, but age had neither tamed the fire of his eye nor the enterprise of his disposition. His countenance had been handsome, for beauty was an attribute of the family; but the lines were roughened by fatigue and exposure to the weather, and rendered coarse by the habitual indulgence of violent passions.

He seemed in deep and moody reflection, and was pacing at a distance from his dependents along the upper end of the hall, sometimes stopping from time to time to caress and feed a gos-hawk, which sat upon his wrist, with its jesses (*i. e.* the leathern straps fixed to its legs) wrapt around his hand. The bird, which seemed not insensible to its master's attention, answered his caresses by ruffling forward its feathers, and pecking playfully at his finger. At such intervals the Baron smiled, but instantly resumed the darksome air of sullen meditation. He did not even deign to look upon an object, which few could have passed and repassed so often without bestowing on it a transient glance.

This was a woman of exceeding beauty, rather gaily than richly attired, who sat on a low seat close by the huge hall chimney. The gold chains round her neck and arms,—the gay gown of green which swept the floor,—the silver embroidered girdle, with its bunch of keys, depending in housewifely pride by a silver chain,—the yellow silken *couvrechef* (Scotticè, *curch*) which was disposed around her head, and partly concealed her dark profusion of hair, — above all, the circumstance so delicately touched in the old ballad, that "the girdle was too short," the "gown of green all too strait," for the wearer's present shape, would have intimated the Baron's lady. But then the lowly seat, — the expression of deep melancholy, which was changed into a timid smile whenever she saw the least chance of catching the eye of Julian Avenel,—the subdued look of grief, and the starting tear for which that constrained smile was again exchanged when she saw herself entirely disregarded, — these were not the attributes of a wife, or they were those of a dejected and afflicted female, who had yielded her love on less than legitimate terms.

Julian Avenel, as we have said, continued to pace the hall without paying any of that mute attention which is rendered to almost every female either by affection or courtesy. He seemed totally unconscious of her presence, or of that of his attendants, and was only roused from his own dark reflections by the notice he paid to the falcon, to which, however, the lady seemed to attend, as if studying to find either an opportunity of speaking to the Baron, or of finding something enigmatical in the expressions which he used to the bird. All this the strangers had time enough to remark; for no sooner had they entered the apartment than their usher, Christie of the Clinthill, after exchanging a significant glance with the menials or troopers at the lower end of the apartment, signed to Halbert Glendinning and to his companion to stand still near the door, while he himself, advancing nearer the table, placed himself in such a situation as to catch the Baron's observation when he should be disposed to look around, but without presuming to intrude himself on his master's notice. Indeed, the look of this man, naturally bold, hardy, and audacious, seemed totally changed when he was in presence of his master, and resembled the dejected and cowering manner of a quarrelsome dog when rebuked by his owner, or when he finds himself obliged to deprecate the violence of a superior adversary of his own species.

In spite of the novelty of his own situation, and every painful feeling connected with it, Halbert felt his curiosity interested in the female, who sate by the chimney unnoticed and unregarded. He marked with what keen and trembling solicitude she watched the broken words of Julian, and how her glance stole towards him, ready to be averted upon the slightest chance of his perceiving himself to be watched.

Meantime he went on with his dalliance with his feathered favourite, now giving, now withholding, the morsel with which he was about to feed the bird, and so exciting its appetite and gratifying it by turns. "What! more yet? — thou foul kite, thou wouldst never have done — give thee part thou wilt have all — Ay, prune thy feathers, and prink thyself gay — much thou wilt make of it now — dost think I know thee not? — dost think I see not that all that ruffling and pluming of wing and feathers is not for thy master, but to try what thou canst make of him, thou greedy gled?—well—there—take it then, and rejoice thyself—little boon goes far with thee, and with all thy sex—and so it should."

He ceased to look on the bird, and again traversed the apartment. Then taking another small piece of raw meat from the trencher, on which it was placed ready cut for his use, he began once again to tempt and tease the bird, by offering and withdrawing it, until he awakened its wild and bold disposition. "What! struggling, fluttering, aiming at me with beak and single?* So la! So la! wouldst mount? wouldst fly? the jesses are round thy clutches, fool—thou canst neither stir nor soar but by my will—Beware thou come to reclaim, wench, else I will wring thy head off one of these days—Well, have it then, and well fare thou with it.—So ho, Jenkin!" One of the attendants stepped forward—"Take the foul gled hence to the mew —or, stay; leave her, but look well to her casting and to her bathing—we will see her fly to-morrow.—How now, Christie, so soon rêturned?"

Christie advanced to his master, and gave an account of himself and his journey, in the way in which a police-officer holds communication with his magistrate, that is, as much by signs as by words.

"Noble sir," said that worthy satellite, "the Laird of——," he named no place, but pointed with his finger in a south-western direction,—"may not ride with you the day he purposed, because the Lord Warden has threatened that he will——"

Here another blank, intelligibly enough made up by the speaker touching his own neck with his left fore-finger, and leaning his head a little to one side.

"Cowardly caitiff!" said Julian; "by Heaven! the whole world turns sheer naught—it is not worth a brave man's living in—ye may ride a day and night, and never see a feather wave or hear a horse prance—the spirit of our fathers is dead amongst us — the very brutes are degenerated — the

* In the *kindly* language of hawking, as Lady Juliana Berners terms it, hawks' talons are called their *singles*.

cattle we bring at our life's risk are mere carrion—our hawks are riflers*—our hounds are turnspits and trindle-tails—our men are women—and our women are——"

He looked at the female for the first time, and stopped short in the midst of what he was about to say, though there was something so contemptuous in the glance, that the blank might have been thus filled up—"Our women are such as she is."

He said it not, however, and as if desirous of attracting his attention at all risks, and in whatever manner, she rose and came forward to him, but with a timorousness ill-disguised by affected gaiety.—"Our women, Julian—what would you say of the women?"

"Nothing," answered Julian Avenel, "at least nothing but that they are kind-hearted wenches like thyself, Kate." The female coloured deeply, and returned to her seat. —"And what strangers hast thou brought with thee, Christie, that stand yonder like two stone statues?" said the Baron.

"The taller," answered Christie, "is, so please you, a young fellow called Halbert Glendinning, the eldest son of the old widow at Glendearg."

"What brings him here?" said the Baron; "hath he any message from Mary Avenel?"

"Not as I think," said Christie; "the youth is roving the country—he was always a wild slip, for I have known him since he was the height of my sword."

"What qualities hath he?" said the Baron.

"All manner of qualities," answered his follower—"he can strike a buck, track a deer, fly a hawk, halloo to a hound—he shoots in the long and cross-bow to a hair's-breadth—wields a lance or sword like myself nearly—backs a horse manfully and fairly—I wot not what more a man need to do to make him a gallant companion."

"And who," said the Baron, "is the old miser† who stands beside him?"

"Some cast of a priest as I fancy—he says he is charged with letters to you."

"Bid them come forward," said the Baron; and no sooner had they approached him more nearly, than, struck by the fine form and strength displayed by Halbert Glendinning, he addressed him thus: "I am told, young Swankie, that you are roaming the world to seek your fortune,—if you will serve Julian Avenel, you may find it without going farther."

"So please you," answered Glendinning, "something has chanced to me that makes it better I should leave this land, and I am bound for Edinburgh."

"What!—thou hast stricken some of the king's deer, I warrant,—or lightened the meadows of Saint Mary's of some of their beeves—or thou hast taken a moonlight leap over the border?"

"No, sir," said Halbert, "my case is entirely different."

"Then I warrant thee," said the Baron, "thou hast stabbed some brother churl in a fray about a wench—thou art a likely lad to wrangle in such a cause."

Ineffably disgusted at his tone and manner, Halbert Glendinning remained silent, while the thought darted across his mind, what would Julian Avenel have said, had he known the quarrel of which he spoke so lightly, had arisen on account of his own brother's daughter! "But be thy cause of flight what it will," said Julian, in continuation, "dost thou think the law or its emissaries can follow thee into this island, or arrest thee under the standard of Avenel?—Look at the depth of the lake, the strength of the walls, the length of the causeway—look at my men, and think if they are

---

* So called when they only caught their prey by the feathers.

† Miser, used in the sense in which it often occurs in Spenser, and which is indeed its literal import—"wretched old man."

likely to see a comrade injured, or if I, their master, am a man to desert a faithful follower, in good or evil. I tell thee it shall be an eternal day of truce betwixt thee and justice, as they call it, from the instant thou hast put my colours into thy cap — thou shalt ride by the Warden's nose as thou wouldst pass an old market-woman, and ne'er a cur which follows him shall dare to bay at thee!"

"I thank you for your offers, noble sir," replied Halbert, "but I must answer in brief, that I cannot profit by them — my fortunes lead me elsewhere."

"Thou art a self-willed fool for thy pains," said Julian, turning from him; and signing Christie to approach, he whispered in his ear, "there is promise in that young fellow's looks, Christie, and we want men of limbs and sinews so compacted — those thou hast brought to me of late are the mere refuse of mankind, wretches scarce worth the arrow that ends them: this youngster is limbed like Saint George. Ply him with wine and wassail —let the wenches weave their meshes about him like spiders—thou understandest?" Christie gave a sagacious nod of intelligence, and fell back to a respectful distance from his master. — "And thou, old man," said the Baron, turning to the elder traveller, "hast thou been roaming the world after fortune too? — it seems not she has fallen into thy way."

"So please you," replied Warden, "I were perhaps more to be pitied than I am now, had I indeed met with that fortune, which, like others, I have sought in my greener days."

"Nay, understand me, friend," said the Baron; "if thou art satisfied with thy buckram gown and long staff, I also am well content thou shouldst be as poor and contemptible as is good for the health of thy body and soul — All I care to know of thee is, the cause which hath brought thee to my castle, where few crows of thy kind care to settle. Thou art, I warrant thee, some ejected monk of a suppressed convent, paying in his old days the price of the luxurious idleness in which he spent his youth.—Ay, or it may be some pilgrim with a budget of lies from Saint James of Compostella, or Our Lady of Loretto; or thou mayest be some pardoner with his budget of relics from Rome, forgiving sins at a penny a-dozen, and one to the tale.—Ay, I guess why I find thee in this boy's company, and doubtless thou wouldst have such a strapping lad as he to carry thy wallet, and relieve thy lazy shoulders; but by the mass I will cross thy cunning. I make my vow to sun and moon, I will not see a proper lad so misleard as to run the country with an old knave like Simmie and his brother.* Away with thee!" he added, rising in wrath, and speaking so fast as to give no opportunity of answer, being probably determined to terrify the elder guest into an abrupt flight—"Away with thee, with thy clouted coat, scrip, and scallop-shell, or, by the name of Avenel, I will have them loose the hounds on thee."

Warden waited with the greatest patience until Julian Avenel, astonished that the threats and violence of his language made no impression on him, paused in a sort of wonder, and said in a less imperious tone, "Why the fiend dost thou not answer me?"

"When you have done speaking," said Warden, in the same composed manner, "it will be full time to reply."

"Say on man, in the devil's name—but take heed—beg not here—were it but for the rinds of cheese, the refuse of the rats, or a morsel that my dogs would turn from—neither a grain of meal, nor the nineteenth part of a gray groat, will I give to any feigned limmer of thy coat."

"It may be," answered Warden, "that you would have less quarrel with my coat if you knew what it covers. I am neither a friar nor mendicant, and would be right glad to hear thy testimony against these foul deceivers

* Two *quæstionarii*, or begging friars, whose accoutrements and roguery make the subject of an old Scottish satirical poem

of God's church, and usurpers of his rights over the Christian flock, were it given in Christian charity."

"And who or what art thou, then," said Avenel, "that thou comest to this Border land, and art neither monk, nor soldier, nor broken man?"

"I am an humble teacher of the holy word," answered Warden. "This letter from a most noble person will speak why I am here at this present time."

He delivered the letter to the Baron, who regarded the seal with some surprise, and then looked on the letter itself, which seemed to excite still more. He then fixed his eyes on the stranger, and said, in a menacing tone, "I think thou darest not betray me or deceive me?"

"I am not the man to attempt either," was the concise reply.

Julian Avenel carried the letter to the window, where he perused, or at least attempted to peruse it more than once, often looking from the paper and gazing on the stranger who had delivered it, as if he meant to read the purport of the missive in the face of the messenger. Julian at length called to the female,—"Catherine, bestir thee, and fetch me presently that letter which I bade thee keep ready at hand in thy casket, having no sure lockfast place of my own."

Catherine went with the readiness of one willing to be employed; and as she walked, the situation which requires a wider gown and a longer girdle, and in which woman claims from man a double portion of the most anxious care, was still more visible than before. She soon returned with the paper, and was rewarded with a cold—"I thank thee, wench; thou art a careful secretary."

This second paper he also perused and reperused more than once, and still. as he read it, bent from time to time a wary and observant eye upon Henry Warden. This examination and re-examination, though both the man and the place were dangerous, the preacher endured with the most composed and steady countenance, seeming, under the eagle, or rather the vulture eye of the baron, as unmoved as under the gaze of an ordinary and peaceful peasant. At length Julian Avenel folded both papers, and having put them into the pocket of his cloak, cleared his brow, and, coming forward, addressed his female companion. "Catherine," said he, "I have done this good man injustice, when I mistook him for one of the drones of Rome. He is a preacher, Catherine—a preacher of the—the new doctrine of the Lords of the Congregation."

"The doctrine of the blessed Scriptures," said the preacher, "purified from the devices of men."

"Sayest thou?" said Julian Avenel—"Well, thou mayest call it what thou lists; but to me it is recommended, because it flings off all those sottish dreams about saints and angels and devils, and unhorses lazy monks that have ridden us so long, and spur-galled us so hard. No more masses and corpse-gifts—no more tithes and offerings to make men poor—no more prayers or psalms to make men cowards—no more christenings and penances, and confessions and marriages."

"So please you," said Henry Warden, "it is against the corruptions, not against the fundamental doctrines, of the church, which we desire to renovate, and not to abolish."

"Prithee, peace, man," said the Baron; "we of the laity care not what you set up, so you pull merrily down what stands in our way. Specially it suits well with us of the Southland fells; for it is our profession to turn the world upside down, and we live ever the blithest life when the downer side is uppermost."

Warden would have replied; but the Baron allowed him not time, striking the table with the hilt of his dagger, and crying out,—"Ha! you loitering knaves, bring our supper-meal quickly. See you not this holy man is exhausted for lack of food? heard ye ever of priest or preacher that devoured not his five meals a-day?"

The attendants bustled to and fro, and speedily brought in several large smoking platters filled with huge pieces of beef, boiled and roasted, but without any variety whatsoever; without vegetables, and almost without bread, though there was at the upper end a few oat-cakes in a basket. Julian Avenel made a sort of apology to Warden.

"You have been commended to our care, Sir Preacher, since that is your style, by a person whom we highly honour."

"I am assured," said Warden, "that the most noble Lord——"

"Prithee, peace, man," said Avenel; "what need of naming names, so we understand each other? I meant but to speak in reference to your safety and comfort, of which he desires us to be chary. Now, for your safety, look at my walls and water. But touching your comfort, we have no corn of our own, and the meal-girnels of the south are less easily transported than their beeves, seeing they have no legs to walk upon. But what though? a stoup of wine thou shalt have, and of the best — thou shalt sit betwixt Catherine and me at the board-end.—And, Christie, do thou look to the young springald, and call to the cellarer for a flagon of the best."

The Baron took his wonted place at the upper end of the board; his Catherine sate down, and courteously pointed to a seat betwixt them for their reverend guest. But notwithstanding the influence both of hunger and fatigue, Henry Warden retained his standing posture.

Chapter the Twenty-Fifth.

When lovely woman stoops to folly,
And finds too late that men betray——
* * * *

JULIAN Avenel saw with surprise the demeanour of the reverend stranger. "Beshrew me," he said, "these new-fashioned religioners have fast-days, I warrant me—the old ones used to confer these blessings chiefly on the laity."

"We acknowledge no such rule," said the preacher—"We hold that our faith consists not in using or abstaining from special meats on special days; and in fasting we rend our hearts, and not our garments."

"The better — the better for yourselves, and the worse for Tom Tailor," said the Baron; "but come, sit down, or, if thou needs must e'en give us a cast of thy office, mutter thy charm."

"Sir Baron," said the preacher, "I am in a strange land, where neither mine office nor my doctrine are known, and where, it would seem, both are greatly misunderstood. It is my duty so to bear me, that in my person, however unworthy, my Master's dignity may be respected, and that sin may take not confidence from relaxation of the bonds of discipline."

"Ho la! halt there," said the Baron; "thou wert sent hither for thy safety, but not, I think, to preach to me, or control me. What is it thou wouldst have, Sir Preacher? Remember thou speakest to one somewhat short of patience, who loves a short health and a long draught."

"In a word, then," said Henry Warden, "that lady——"

"How?" said the Baron, starting — "what of her? — what hast thou to say of that dame?"

"Is she thy house-dame?" said the preacher, after a moment's pause, in which he seemed to seek for the best mode of expressing what he had to say—"Is she, in brief, thy wife?"

The unfortunate young woman pressed both her hands on her face, as if to hide it, but the deep blush which crimsoned her brow and neck, showed that her cheeks were also glowing; and the bursting tears, which found their way betwixt her slender fingers, bore witness to her sorrow, as well as to her shame.

"Now, by my father's ashes!" said the Baron, rising and spurning from him his footstool with such violence, that it hit the wall on the opposite side of the apartment—then instantly constraining himself, he muttered, "What need to run myself into trouble for a fool's word?"—then resuming his seat, he answered coldly and scornfully—"No, Sir Priest or Sir Preacher, Catherine is not my wife—Cease thy whimpering, thou foolish wench—she is not my wife, but she is handfasted with me, and that makes her as honest a woman."

"Handfasted?"—repeated Warden.

"Knowest thou not that rite, holy man?" said Avenel, in the same tone of derision; "then I will tell thee. We Border-men are more wary than your inland clowns of Fife and Lothian—no jump in the dark for us—no clenching the fetters around our wrists till we know how they will wear with us—we take our wives, like our horses, upon trial. When we are handfasted, as we term it, we are man and wife for a year and day—that space gone by, each may choose another mate, or, at their pleasure, may call the priest to marry them for life—and this we call handfasting."*

"Then," said the preacher, "I tell thee, noble Baron, in brotherly love to thy soul, it is a custom licentious, gross, and corrupted, and, if persisted in, dangerous, yea, damnable. It binds thee to the frailer being while she is the object of desire—it relieves thee when she is most the subject of pity—it gives all to brutal sense, and nothing to generous and gentle affection. I say to thee, that he who can meditate the breach of such an engagement, abandoning the deluded woman and the helpless offspring, is worse than the birds of prey; for of them the males remain with their mates until the nestlings can take wing. Above all, I say it is contrary to the pure Christian doctrine, which assigns woman to man as the partner of his labour, the soother of his evil, his helpmate in peril, his friend in affliction; not as the toy of his looser hours, or as a flower, which, once cropped, he may throw aside at pleasure."

"Now, by the Saints, a most virtuous homily!" said the Baron; "quaintly conceived and curiously pronounced, and to a well-chosen congregation. Hark ye, Sir Gospeller! trow ye to have a fool in hand? Know I not that your sect rose by bluff Harry Tudor, merely because ye aided him to change *his* Kate; and wherefore should I not use the same Christian liberty with *mine?* Tush, man! bless the good food, and meddle not with what concerns thee not—thou hast no gull in Julian Avenel."

"He hath gulled and cheated himself," said the preacher, "should he even incline to do that poor sharer of his domestic cares the imperfect justice that remains to him. Can he now raise her to the rank of a pure and uncontaminated matron?—Can he deprive his child of the misery of owing birth to a mother who has erred? He can indeed give them both the rank, the state of married wife and of lawful son; but, in public opinion, their names will be smirched and sullied with a stain which his tardy efforts cannot entirely efface. Yet render it to them, Baron of Avenel, render to them this late and imperfect justice. Bid me bind you together for ever, and celebrate the day of your bridal, not with feasting or wassail, but with

* This custom of handfasting actually prevailed in the upland days. It arose partly from the want of priests. While the convents subsisted, monks were detached on regular circuits through the wilder districts, to marry those who had lived in this species of connexion. A practice of the same kind existed in the Isle of Portland.

sorrow for past sin, and the resolution to commence a better life. Happy then will have the chance been that has drawn me to this castle, though I come driven by calamity, and unknowing where my course is bound, like a leaf travelling on the north wind."

The plain, and even coarse features, of the zealous speaker, were warmed at once and ennobled by the dignity of his enthusiasm; and the wild Baron, lawless as he was, and accustomed to spurn at the control whether of religious or moral law, felt, for the first time perhaps in his life, that he was under subjection to a mind superior to his own. He sat mute and suspended in his deliberations, hesitating betwixt anger and shame, yet borne down by the weight of the just rebuke thus boldly fulminated against him.

The unfortunate young woman, conceiving hopes from her tyrant's silence and apparent indecision, forgot both her fear and shame in her timid expectation that Avenel would relent; and fixing upon him her anxious and beseeching eyes, gradually drew near and nearer to his seat, till at length, laying a trembling hand on his cloak, she ventured to utter, "O noble Julian, listen to the good man!"

The speech and the motion were ill-timed, and wrought on that proud and wayward spirit the reverse of her wishes.

The fierce Baron started up in a fury, exclaiming, "What! thou foolish callet, art thou confederate with this strolling vagabond, whom thou hast seen beard me in my own hall! Hence with thee, and think that I am proof both to male and female hypocrisy!"

The poor girl started back, astounded at his voice of thunder and looks of fury, and, turning pale as death, endeavoured to obey his orders, and tottered towards the door. Her limbs failed in the attempt, and she fell on the stone floor in a manner which her situation might have rendered fatal —The blood gushed from her face.—Halbert Glendinning brooked not a sight so brutal, but, uttering a deep imprecation, started from his seat, and laid his hand on his sword, under the strong impulse of passing it through the body of the cruel and hard-hearted ruffian. But Christie of the Clinthill, guessing his intention, threw his arms around him, and prevented him from stirring to execute his purpose.

The impulse to such an act of violence was indeed but momentary, as it instantly appeared that Avenel himself, shocked at the effects of his violence, was lifting up and endeavouring to soothe in his own way the terrified Catherine.

"Peace," he said, "prithee, peace, thou silly minion—why, Kate, though I listen not to this tramping preacher, I said not what might happen an thou dost bear me a stout boy. There—there—dry thy tears—Call thy women. —So ho!—where be these queans?—Christie—Rowley—Hutcheon—drag them hither by the hair of the head!"

A half dozen of startled wild-looking females rushed into the room, and bore out her who might be either termed their mistress or their companion. She showed little sign of life, except by groaning faintly and keeping her hand on her side.

No sooner had this luckless female been conveyed from the apartment, than the Baron, advancing to the table, filled and drank a deep goblet of wine; then, putting an obvious restraint on his passions, turned to the preacher, who stood horror-struck at the scene he had witnessed, and said, "You have borne too hard on us, Sir Preacher—but coming with the commendations which you have brought me, I doubt not but your meaning was good. But we are a wilder folk than you inland men of Fife and Lothian. Be advised, therefore, by me—Spur not an unbroken horse—put not your ploughshare too deep into new land—Preach to us spiritual liberty, and we will hearken to you.—But we will give no way to spiritual bondage.—Sit, therefore, down, and pledge me in old sack, and we will talk over these matters."

"It is *from* spiritual bondage," said the preacher, in the same tone of admonitory reproof, "that I came to deliver you — it is from a bondage more fearful than than that of the heaviest earthly gyves — it is from your own evil passions."

"Sit down," said Avenel, fiercely; "sit down while the play is good — else by my father's crest and my mother's honour!——"

"Now," whispered Christie of the Clinthill to Halbert, "if he refuse to sit down, I would not give a gray groat for his head."

"Lord Baron," said Warden, "thou hast placed me in extremity. But if the question be, whether I am to hide the light which I am commanded to show forth, or to lose the light of this world, my choice is made. I say to thee, like the Holy Baptist to Herod, it is not lawful for thee to have this woman; and I say it though bonds and death be the consequence, counting my life as nothing in comparison of the ministry to which I am called."

Julian Avenel, enraged at the firmness of this reply, flung from his right hand the cup in which he was about to drink to his guest, and from the other cast off the hawk, which flew wildly through the apartment. His first motion was to lay hand upon his dagger. But, changing his resolution, he exclaimed, "To the dungeon with this insolent stroller!—I will hear no man speak a word for him—Look to the falcon, Christie, thou fool—an she escape, I will despatch you after her every man—Away with that hypocritical dreamer — drag him hence if he resist!"

He was obeyed in both points. Christie of the Clinthill arrested the hawk's flight, by putting his foot on her jesses, and so holding her fast, while Henry Warden was led off, without having shown the slightest symptoms of terror, by two of the Baron's satellites. Julian Avenel walked the apartment for a short time in sullen silence, and despatching one of his attendants with a whispered message, which probably related to the health of the unfortunate Catherine, he said aloud, "These rash and meddling priests — By Heaven! they make us worse than we would be without them." *

The answer which he presently received seemed somewhat to pacify his angry mood, and he took his place at the board, commanding his retinue to the like. All sat down in silence, and began the repast.

During the meal Christie in vain attempted to engage his youthful companion in carousal, or, at least, in conversation. Halbert Glendinning pleaded fatigue, and expressed himself unwilling to take any liquor stronger

---

* If it were necessary to name a prototype for this brutal, licentious and cruel Border chief, in an age which showed but too many such, the Laird of Black Ormiston might be selected for that purpose. He was a friend and confidant of Bothwell, and an agent in Henry Darnley's murder. At his last stage, he was, like other great offenders, a seeming penitent; and, as his confession bears, divers gentlemen and servants being in the chamber, he said, "For God's sake, sit down and pray for me, for I have been a great sinner otherwise," (that is, besides his share in Darnley's death,) "for the which God is this day punishing me; for of all men on the earth, I have been one of the proudest, and most high-minded, and most unclean of my body. But specially I have shed the innocent blood of one Michael Hunter with my own hands. Alas, therefore! because the said Michael, having me lying on my back, having a fork in his hand, might have slain me if he had pleased, and did it not, which of all things grieves me most in conscience. Also, in a rage, I hanged a poor man for a horse; — with many other wicked deeds, for whilk I ask my God mercy. It is not marvel I have been wicked, considering the wicked company that ever I have been in, but specially within the seven years by-past, in which I never saw two good men or one good deed, but all kind of wickedness, and yet God would not suffer me to be lost." — See the whole confession in the State Trials.

Another worthy of the Borders, called Geordy Bourne, of somewhat subordinate rank, was a similar picture of profligacy. He had fallen into the hands of Sir Robert Carey, then Warden of the English East Marches, who gives the following account of his prisoner's confession:—

"When all things were quiet, and the watch set at night, after supper, about ten of the clock, I took one of my men's liveries, and put it about me, and took two other of my servants with me in their liveries; and we three, as the Warden's men, came to the Provost Marshal's where Bourne was, and were let into his chamber. We sate down by him, and told him that we were desirous to see him, because we heard he was stout and valiant, and true to his friend, and that we were sorry our master could not be moved to save his life. He voluntarily of himself said, that he had lived long enough to do so many villanies as he had done; and withal told us, that he had lain with above forty men's wives, what in England what in Scotland; and that he had killed seven Englishmen with his own hands, cruelly murdering them; and that he had spent his whole time in whoring, drinking, stealing, and taking deep revenge for slight offences. He seemed to be very penitent, and much desired a minister for the comfort of his soul. We promised him to let our master know his desire, who, we knew would promptly grant it. We took leave of him; and presently I took order that Mr. Selby, a very honest preacher, should go to him, and not stir from him till his execution the next morning; for after I had heard his own confession, I was resolved no conditions should save his life, and so took order, that at the gates opening the next morning, he should be carried to execution, which accordingly was performed."— *Memoirs of Sir Robert Carey, Earl of Monmouth.*

than the heather ale, which was at that time frequently used at meals. Thus every effort at jovialty died away, until the Baron, striking his hand against the table, as if impatient of the long unbroken silence, cried out aloud, "What, ho! my masters—are ye Border-riders, and sit as mute over your meal as a mess of monks and friars? — Some one sing, if no one list to speak. Much eaten without either mirth or music is ill of digestion. — Louis," he added, speaking to one of the youngest of his followers, "thou art ready enough to sing when no one bids thee."

The young man looked first at his master, then up to the arched roof of the hall, then drank off the horn of ale, or wine, which stood beside him, and with a rough, yet not unmelodious voice, sung the following ditty to the ancient air of "Blue bonnets over the Border."

I.

March, march, Ettrick and Teviotdale,
Why the deil dinna ye march forward in order?
March, march, Eskdale and Liddesdale,
All the Blue Bonnets are bound for the Border
Many a banner spread,
Flutters above your head,
Many a crest that is famous in story;
Mount and make ready then,
Sons of the mountain glen,
Fight for the Queen and the old Scottish glory!

II.

Come from the hills where the hirsels are grazing,
Come from the glen of the buck and the roe;
Come to the crag where the beacon is blazing,
Come with the buckler, the lance, and the bow.
Trumpets are sounding,
War-steeds are bounding,
Stand to your arms then, and march in good order;
England shall many a day
Tell of the bloody fray,
When the Blue Bonnets came over the Border!

The song, rude as it was, had in it that warlike character which at any other time would have roused Halbert's spirit; but at present the charm of minstrelsy had no effect upon him. He made it his request to Christie to suffer him to retire to rest, a request with which that worthy person, seeing no chance of making a favourable impression on his intended proselyte in his present humour, was at length pleased to comply. But no Sergeant Kite, who ever practised the profession of recruiting, was more attentive that his object should not escape him, than was Christie of the Clinthill. He indeed conducted Halbert Glendinning to a small apartment overlooking the lake, which was accommodated with a truckle bed. But before quitting him, Christie took special care to give a look to the bars which crossed the outside of the window, and when he left the apartment, he failed not to give the key a double turn; circumstances which convinced young Glendinning that there was no intention of suffering him to depart from the Castle of Avenel at his own time and pleasure. He judged it, however, most prudent to let these alarming symptoms pass without observation.

No sooner did he find himself in undisturbed solitude, than he ran rapidly over the events of the day in his recollection, and to his surprise found that his own precarious fate, and even the death of Piercie Shafton, made less impression on him than the singularly bold and determined conduct of his companion, Henry Warden. Providence, which suits its instruments to the end they are to achieve, had awakened in the cause of Reformation in Scotland, a body of preachers of more energy than refinement, bold in spirit, and strong in faith, contemners of whatever stood betwixt them and their principal object, and seeking the advancement of the great cause in which they laboured by the roughest road, provided it were the shortest. The soft breeze may wave the willow, but it requires the voice of the tempest to agitate the boughs of the oak; and, accordingly, to milder hearers, and in a less rude age, their manners would have been ill-adapted, but they were singularly successful in their mission to the rude people to whom it was addressed.

Owing to these reasons, Halbert Glendinning, who had resisted and repelled the arguments of the preacher, was forcibly struck by the firmness of his demeanour in the dispute with Julian Avenel. It might be discour teous, and most certainly it was incautious, to choose such a place and such an audience, for upbraiding with his transgressions a baron, whom both manners and situation placed in full possession of independent power. But the conduct of the preacher was uncompromising, firm, manly, and obviously grounded upon the deepest conviction which duty and principle could afford; and Glendinning, who had viewed the conduct of Avenel with the deepest abhorrence, was proportionally interested in the brave old man, who had ventured life rather than withhold the censure due to guilt. This pitch of virtue seemed to him to be in religion what was demanded by chivalry of her votaries in war; an absolute surrender of all selfish feelings, and a combination of every energy proper to the human mind, to discharge the task which duty demanded.

Halbert was at the period when youth was most open to generous emotions, and knows best how to appreciate them in others, and he felt, although he hardly knew why, that, whether catholic or heretic, the safety of this man deeply interested him. Curiosity mingled with the feeling, and led him to wonder what the nature of those doctrines could be, which stole their votary so completely from himself, and devoted him to chains or to death as their sworn champion. He had indeed been told of saints and martyrs of former days, who had braved for their religious faith the extremity of death and torture. But their spirit of enthusiastic devotion had long slept in the ease and indolent habits of their successors, and their adventures, like those of knights-errant, were rather read for amusement than for edification. A new impulse had been necessary to rekindle the energies of religious zeal, and that impulse was now operating in favour of a purer religion, with one of whose steadiest votaries the youth had now met for the first time.

The sense that he himself was a prisoner, under the power of this savage chieftain, by no means diminished Halbert's interest in the fate of his fellow sufferer, while he determined at the same time so far to emulate his fortitude, that neither threats nor suffering should compel him to enter into the service of such a master. The possibility of escape next occurred to him, and though with little hope of effecting it in that way, Glendinning proceeded to examine more particularly the window of the apartment. The apartment was situated in the first story of the castle; and was not so far from the rock on which it was founded, but that an active and bold man might with little assistance descend to a shelf of rock which was immediately below the window, and from thence either leap or drop himself down into the lake which lay before his eye, clear and blue in the placid light of a full summer's moon.—"Were I once placed on that ledge," thought Glendinning, "Julian Avenel and Christie had seen the last of me." The size of the window favoured such an attempt, but the stanchions or iron bars seemed to form an insurmountable obstacle.

While Halbert Glendinning gazed from the window with that eagerness of hope which was prompted by the energy of his character and his determination not to yield to circumstances, his ear caught some sounds from below, and listening with more attention, he could distinguish the voice of the preacher engaged in his solitary devotions. To open a correspondence with him became immediately his object, and failing to do so by less marked sounds, he at length ventured to speak, and was answered from beneath—"Is it thou, my son?" The voice of the prisoner now sounded more distinctly than when it was first heard, for Warden had approached the small aperture, which, serving his prison for a window, opened just betwixt the wall and the rock, and admitted a scanty portion of light through a wall of immense thickness. This *soupirail* being placed exactly under Halbert's window, the contiguity permitted the prisoners to converse in a low tone, when Halbert declared his intention to escape, and the possibility he saw of achieving his purpose, but for the iron stanchions of the window—"Prove thy strength, my son, in the name of God!" said the preacher. Halbert obeyed him more in despair than hope, but to his great astonishment, and somewhat to his terror, the bar parted asunder near the bottom, and the longer part being easily bent outwards, and not secured with lead in the upper socket, dropt out into Halbert's hand. He immediately whispered, but as energetically as a whisper could be expressed — "By Heaven, the bar has given way in my hand!"

"Thank Heaven, my son, instead of swearing by it," answered Warden from his dungeon.

With little effort Halbert Glendinning forced himself through the opening thus wonderfully effected, and using his leathern sword-belt as a rope to assist him, let himself safely drop on the shelf of rock upon which the preacher's window opened. But through this no passage could be effected, being scarce larger than a loop-hole for musketry, and apparently constructed for that purpose.

"Are there no means by which I can assist your escape, my father?" said Halbert.

"There are none, my son," answered the preacher; "but if thou wilt ensure my safety, that may be in thy power."

"I will labour earnestly for it," said the youth.

"Take then a letter which I will presently write, for I have the means of light and writing materials in my scrip — Hasten towards Edinburgh, and on the way thou wilt meet a body of horse marching southwards—Give this to their leader, and acquaint him of the state in which thou hast left me. It may hap that thy doing so will advantage thyself."

In a minute or two the light of a taper gleamed through the shot-hole, and very shortly after, the preacher, with the assistance of his staff, pushed a billet to Glendinning through the window.

"God bless thee, my son," said the old man, "and complete the marvellous work which he has begun."

"Amen!" answered Halbert, with solemnity, and proceeded on his enterprise.

He hesitated a moment whether he should attempt to descend to the edge of the water; but the steepness of the rock, and darkness of the night, rendered the enterprise too dangerous. He clasped his hands above his head and boldly sprung from the precipice, shooting himself forward into the air as far as he could for fear of sunken rocks, and alighted on the lake, head foremost, with such force as sunk him for a minute below the surface. But strong, long-breathed, and accustomed to such exercise, Halbert, even though encumbered with his sword, dived and rose like a sea-fowl, and swam across the lake in the northern direction. When he landed and looked back on the castle, he could observe that the alarm had been given, for lights glanced from window to window, and he heard the drawbridge lowered, and the tread of horses' feet upon the causeway. But, little alarmed for the consequence of a pursuit during the darkness, he wrung the water from his dress, and, plunging into the moors, directed his course to the north-east by the assistance of the polar star

Chapter the Twenty-Sixth.

Why, what an intricate impeach is this!
I think you all have drank of Circe's cup.
If here you housed him, here he would have been;
If he were mad, he would not plead so coldly.
COMEDY OF ERRORS.

THE course of our story, leaving for the present Halbert Glendinning to the guidance of his courage and his fortune, returns to the Tower of Glendearg, where matters in the meanwhile fell out, with which it is most fitting that the reader should be acquainted.

The meal was prepared at noontide with all the care which Elspeth and Tibb, assisted by the various accommodations which had been supplied from the Monastery, could bestow on it. Their dialogue ran on as usual in the intervals of their labour, partly as between mistress and servant, partly as maintained by gossips of nearly equal quality.

"Look to the minced meat, Tibb," said Elspeth; "and turn the broach even, thou good-for-nothing Simmie, — thy wits are harrying birds' nests, child. — Weel, Tibb, this is a fasheous job, this Sir Piercie lying leaguer with us up here, and wha kens for how lang?"

"A fasheous job indeed," answered her faithful attendant, "and little good did the name ever bring to fair Scotland. Ye may have your hands fuller of them than they are yet. Mony a sair heart have the Piercies given to Scots wife and bairns with their pricking on the Borders. There was Hotspur and many more of that bloody kindred, have sate in our skirts since Malcolm's time, as Martin says!"

"Martin should keep a well-scrapit tongue in his head," said Elspeth, "and not slander the kin of any body that quarters at Glendearg; forby, that Sir Piercie Shafton is much respected with the holy fathers of the community, and they will make up to us ony fasherie that we may have with him, either by good word or good deed, I'se warrant them. He is a considerate lord the Lord Abbot."

"And weel he likes a saft seat to his hinder end," said Tibb; "I have seen a belted baron sit on a bare bench, and find nae fault. But an ye are pleased, mistress, I am pleased."

"Now, in good time, here comes Mysie of the Mill.—And where hae ye been, lass for a's gane wrang without you?" said Elspeth.

"I just gaed a blink up the burn," said Mysie, "for the young lady has been down on her bed, and is no just that weel—So I gaed a gliff up the burn."

"To see the young lads come hame frae the sport, I will warrant you," said Elspeth. "Ay, ay, Tibb, that's the way the young folk guide us, Tibbie — leave us to do the wark, and out to the play themsells."

"Ne'er a bit of that, mistress," said the Maid of the Mill, stripping her round pretty arms, and looking actively and good-humouredly round for some duty that she could discharge, "but just — I thought ye might like to ken if they were coming back, just to get the dinner forward."

"And saw ye ought of them then?" demanded Elspeth.

"Not the least tokening," said Mysie, "though I got to the head of a knowe, and though the English knight's beautiful white feather could have been seen over all the bushes in the Shaw."

"The knight's white feather!" said Dame Glendinning; "ye are a silly hempie — my Halbert's high head will be seen farther than his feather, let it be as white as it like, I trow."

Mysie made no answer, but began to knead dough for wastel-cake with all despatch, observing that Sir Piercie had partaken of that dainty, and commended it upon the preceding day. And presently, in order to place on the fire the *girdle*, or iron plate on which these cates were to be baked, she displaced a stew-pan in which one of Tibb's delicacies were submitted to the action of the kitchen fire. Tibb muttered betwixt her teeth — "And it is the broth for my sick bairn, that maun make room for the dainty Southron's wastel-bread. It was a blithe time in Wight Wallace's day, or good King Robert's, when the pock-puddings gat naething here but hard straiks and bloody crowns. But we will see how it will a' end."

Elspeth did not think it proper to notice these discontented expressions of Tibbie, but they sunk into her mind; for she was apt to consider her as a sort of authority in matters of war and policy, with which her former experience as bower-woman at Avenel Castle made her better acquainted than were the peaceful inhabitants of Halidome. She only spoke, however, to express her surprise that the hunters did not return.

"An they come not back the sooner," said Tibb, "they will fare the waur, for the meat will be roasted to a cinder—and there is poor Simmie that can turn the spit nae langer: the bairn is melting like an icicle in warm water —Gang awa, bairn, and take a mouthful of the caller air, and I will turn the broach till ye come back."

"Rin up to the bartizan at the tower-head, callant," said Dame Glendinning, "the air will be callerer there than ony gate else, and bring us word if our Halbert and the gentleman are coming down the glen."

The boy lingered long enough to allow his substitute, Tibb Tacket, heartily to tire of her own generosity, and of his cricket-stool by the side of a huge fire. He at length returned with the news that he had seen nobody.

The matter was not so remarkable as far as Halbert Glendinning was concerned, for, patient alike of want and of fatigue, it was no uncommon circumstance for him to remain in the wilds till curfew time. But nobody had given Sir Piercie Shafton credit for being so keen a sportsman, and the idea of an Englishman preferring the chase to his dinner was altogether inconsistent with their preconceptions of the national character. Amidst wondering and conjecturing, the usual dinner-hour passed long away; and the inmates of the tower, taking a hasty meal themselves, adjourned their more solemn preparations until the hunters' return at night, since it seemed now certain that their sport had either carried them to a greater distance, or engaged them for a longer time than had been expected.

About four hours after noon, arrived, not the expected sportsmen, but an unlooked for visitant, the Sub-Prior from the Monastery. The scene of the preceding day had dwelt on the mind of Father Eustace, who was of that keen and penetrating cast of mind which loves not to leave unascertained whatever of mysterious is subjected to its inquiry. His kindness was interested in the family of Glendearg, which he had now known for a long time; and besides, the community was interested in the preservation of the peace betwixt Sir Piercie Shafton and his youthful host, since whatever might draw public attention on the former, could not fail to be prejudicial to the Monastery, which was already threatened by the hand of power. He found the family assembled, all but Mary Avenel, and was informed that Halbert Glendinning had accompanied the stranger on a day's sport. So far was well. They had not returned; but when did youth and sport conceive themselves bound by set hours? and the circumstance excited no alarm in his mind.

While he was conversing with Edward Glendinning touching his progress in the studies he had pointed out to him, they were startled by a shriek from Mary Avenel's apartment, which drew the whole family thither in headlong haste. They found her in a swoon in the arms of old Martin, who was bitterly accusing himself of having killed her; so indeed it seemed, for her pale features and closed eyes argued rather a dead corpse than a living person. The whole family were instantly in tumult. Snatching her from Martin's arms with the eagerness of affectionate terror, Edward bore her to the casement, that she might receive the influence of the open air; the Sub-Prior, who, like many of his profession, had some knowledge of medicine, hastened to prescribe the readiest remedies which occurred to him, and the terrified females contended with, and impeded each other, in their rival efforts to be useful.

"It has been ane of her weary ghaists," said Dame Glendinning.

"It's just a trembling on her spirits, as her blessed mother used to have," said Tibb.

"It's some ill news has come ower her," said the miller's maiden; while burnt feathers, cold water, and all the usual means of restoring suspended animation, were employed alternately, and with little effect.

At length a new assistant, who had joined the group unobserved, tendered his aid in the following terms:—"How is this, my most fair Discretion?

What cause hath moved the ruby current of life to rush back to the citadel of the heart, leaving pale those features in which it should have delighted to meander for ever?—Let me approach her," he said, "with this sovereign essence, distilled by the fair hands of the divine Urania, and powerful to recall fugitive life, even if it were trembling on the verge of departure."

Thus speaking, Sir Piercie Shafton knelt down, and most gracefully presented to the nostrils of Mary Avenel a silver pouncet-box, exquisitely chased, containing a sponge dipt in the essence which he recommmended so highly. Yes, gentle reader, it was Sir Piercie Shafton himself who thus unexpectedly proffered his good offices! his cheeks, indeed, very pale, and some part of his dress stained with blood, but not otherwise appearing different from what he was on the preceding evening. But no sooner had Mary Avenel opened her eyes, and fixed them on the figure of the officious courtier, than she screamed faintly, and exclaimed,—"Secure the murderer!"

Those present stood aghast with astonishment, and none more so than the Euphuist, who found himself so suddenly and so strangely accused by the patient whom he was endeavouring to succour, and who repelled his attempts to yield her assistance with all the energy of abhorrence.

"Take him away!" she exclaimed—"take away the murderer!"

"Now, by my knighthood," answered Sir Piercie, "your lovely faculties either of mind or body are, O my most fair Discretion, obnubilated by some strange hallucination. For either your eyes do not discern that it is Piercie Shafton, your most devoted Affability, who now stands before you, or else, your eyes discerning truly, your mind hath most erroneously concluded that he hath been guilty of some delict or violence to which his hand is a stranger. No murder, O most scornful Discretion, hath been this day done, saving but that which your angry glances are now performing on your most devoted captive."

He was here interrupted by the Sub-Prior, who had, in the meantime, been speaking with Martin apart, and had received from him an account of the circumstances, which, suddenly communicated to Mary Avenel, had thrown her into this state. "Sir Knight," said the Sub-Prior, in a very solemn tone, yet with some hesitation, "circumstances have been communicated to us of a nature so extraordinary, that, reluctant as I am to exercise such authority over a guest of our venerable community, I am constrained to request from you an explanation of them. You left this tower early in the morning, accompanied by a youth, Halbert Glendinning, the eldest son of this good dame, and you return hither without him. Where, and at what hour, did you part company from him?"

The English knight paused for a moment, and then replied,—"I marvel that your reverence employs so grave a tone to enforce so light a question. I parted with the villagio whom you call Halbert Glendinning some hour or twain after sunrise."

"And at what place, I pray you?" said the monk.

"In a deep ravine, where a fountain rises at the base of a huge rock; an earth-born Titan, which heaveth up its gray head, even as——"

"Spare us farther description," said the Sub-Prior; "we know the spot. But that youth hath not since been heard of, and it will fall on you to account for him."

"My bairn! my bairn!" exclaimed Dame Glendinning. "Yes, holy father, make the villain account for my bairn!"

"I swear, good woman, by bread and by water, which are the props of our life——"

"Swear by wine and wastel-bread, for these are the props of *thy* life, thou greedy Southron!" said Dame Glendinning;—"a base belly-god, to come here to eat the best, and practise on our lives that give it to him!"

"I tell thee, woman," said Sir Piercie Shafton, "I did but go with thy son to the hunting."

"A black hunting it has been to him, poor bairn," replied Tibb; "and sae I said it wad prove since I first saw the false Southron snout of thee. Little good comes of a Piercie's hunting, from Chevy Chase till now."

"Be silent, woman," said the Sub-Prior, "and rail not upon the English knight; we do not yet know of any thing beyond suspicion."

"We will have his heart's blood!" said Dame Glendinning; and, seconded by the faithful Tibbie, she made such a sudden onslaught on the unlucky Euphuist, as must have terminated in something serious, had not the monk, aided by Mysie Happer, interposed to protect him from their fury. Edward had left the apartment the instant the disturbance broke out, and now entered, sword in hand, followed by Martin and Jasper, the one having a hunting spear in his hand, the other a cross-bow.

"Keep the door," he said to his two attendants; "shoot him or stab him without mercy, should he attempt to break forth; if he offers an escape, by Heaven he shall die!"

"How now, Edward," said the Sub-Prior; "how is this that you so far forget yourself? meditating violence to a guest, and in my presence, who represent your liege lord?"

Edward stepped forward with his drawn sword in his hand. "Pardon me, reverend father," he said, "but in this matter the voice of nature speaks louder and stronger than yours. I turn my sword's point against this proud man, and I demand of him the blood of my brother—the blood of my father's son — of the heir of our name! If he denies to give me a true account of him, he shall not deny me vengeance."

Embarrassed as he was, Sir Piercie Shafton showed no personal fear. "Put up thy sword," he said, "young man; not in the same day does Piercie Shafton contend with two peasants."

"Hear him! he confesses the deed, holy father," said Edward.

"Be patient, my son," said the Sub-Prior, endeavouring to soothe the feelings which he could not otherwise control, "be patient — thou wilt attain the ends of justice better through my means than thine own violence — And you, women, be silent—Tibb, remove your mistress and Mary Avenel."

While Tibb, with the assistance of the other females of the household, bore the poor mother and Mary Avenel into separate apartments, and while Edward, still keeping his sword in his hand, hastily traversed the room, as if to prevent the possibility of Sir Piercie Shafton's escape, the Sub-Prior insisted upon knowing from the perplexed knight the particulars which he knew respecting Halbert Glendinning. His situation became extremely embarrassing, for what he might with safety have told of the issue of their combat was so revolting to his pride, that he could not bring himself to enter into the detail; and of Halbert's actual fate he knew, as the reader is well aware, absolutely nothing.

The father in the meanwhile pressed him with remonstrances, and prayed him to observe, he would greatly prejudice himself by declining to give a full account of the transactions of the day. "You cannot deny," he said, "that yesterday you seemed to take the most violent offence at this unfortunate youth; and that you suppressed your resentment so suddenly as to impress us all with surprise. Last night you proposed to him this day's hunting party, and you set out together by break of day. You parted, you said, at the fountain near the rock, about an hour or twain after sunrise, and it appears that before you parted you had been at strife together."

"I said not so," replied the knight. "Here is a coil indeed about the absence of a rustical bondsman, who, I dare say, hath gone off (if he be gone) to join the next rascally band of freebooters! Ye ask me, a knight of the Piercie's lineage, to account for such an insignificant fugitive, and I answer,—let me know the price of his head, and I will pay it to your convent treasurer."

"You admit, then, that you have slain my brother?" said Edward, interfering once more; "I will presently show you at what price we Scots rate the lives of our friends."

"Peace, Edward, peace—I entreat—I command thee," said the Sub-Prior. "And you, Sir Knight, think better of us than to suppose you may spend Scottish blood, and reckon for it as for wine spilt in a drunken revel. This youth was no bondsman—thou well knowest, that in thine own land thou hadst not dared to lift thy sword against the meanest subject of England, but her laws would have called thee to answer for the deed. Do not hope it will be otherwise here, for you will but deceive yourself."

"You drive me beyond my patience," said the Euphuist, "even as the over-driven ox is urged into madness!—What can I tell you of a young fellow whom I have not seen since the second hour after sunrise?"

"But can you explain in what circumstances you parted with him?" said the monk.

"What *are* the circumstances, in the devil's name, which you desire should be explained?—for although I protest against this constraint as alike unworthy and inhospitable, yet would I willingly end this fray, provided that by words it may be ended," said the knight.

"If these end it not," said Edward, "blows shall, and that full speedily."

"Peace, impatient boy!" said the Sub-Prior; "and do you, Sir Piercie Shafton, acquaint me why the ground is bloody by the verge of the fountain in Corri-nan-shian, where, as you say yourself, you parted from Halbert Glendinning?"

Resolute not to avow his defeat if possibly he could avoid it, the knight answered in a haughty tone, that he supposed it was no unusual thing to find the turf bloody where hunters had slain a deer.

"And did you bury your game as well as kill it?" said the monk. "We must know from you who is the tenant of that grave, that newly-made grave, beside the very fountain whose margin is so deeply crimsoned with blood?—thou seest thou canst not evade me; therefore be ingenuous, and tell us the fate of this unhappy youth, whose body is doubtless lying under that bloody turf."

"If it be," said Sir Piercie, "they must have buried him alive; for I swear to thee, reverend father, that this rustic juvenal parted from me in perfect health. Let the grave be searched, and if his body be found, then deal with me as ye list."

"It is not my sphere to determine thy fate, Sir Knight, but that of the Lord Abbot, and the right reverend Chapter. It is but my duty to collect such information as may best possess their wisdom with the matters which have chanced."

"Might I presume so far, reverend father," said the knight, "I should wish to know the author and evidence of all these suspicions, so unfoundedly urged against me?"

"It is soon told," said the Sub-Prior; "nor do I wish to disguise it, if it can avail you in your defence. This maiden, Mary Avenel, apprehending that you nourished malice against her foster-brother under a friendly brow, did advisedly send up the old man, Martin Tacket, to follow your footsteps and to prevent mischief. But it seems that your evil passions had outrun precaution: for when he came to the spot, guided by your footsteps upon the dew, he found but the bloody turf and the new covered grave; and after long and vain search through the wilds after Halbert and yourself, he brought back the sorrowful news to her who had sent him."

"Saw he not my doublet, I pray you?" said Sir Piercie; "for when I came to myself, I found that I was wrapped in my cloak, but without my under garment as your reverence may observe."

So saying, he opened his cloak, forgetting, with his characteristical inconsistency, that he showed his shirt stained with blood.

"How! cruel man," said the monk, when he observed this confirmation of his suspicions; "wilt thou deny the guilt, even while thou bearest on thy person the blood thou hast shed?—Wilt thou longer deny that thy rash hand has robbed a mother of a son, our community of a vassal, the Queen of Scotland of a liege subject? and what canst thou expect, but that, at the least, we deliver thee up to England, as undeserving our farther protection?"

"By the Saints!" said the knight, now driven to extremity, "if this blood be the witness against me, it is but rebel blood, since this morning at sunrise it flowed within my own veins."

"How were that possible, Sir Piercie Shafton," said the monk, "since I see no wound from whence it can have flowed?"

"That," said the knight, "is the most mysterious part of the transaction —See here!"

So saying, he undid his shirt collar, and, opening his bosom, showed the spot through which Halbert's sword had passed, but already cicatrized, and bearing the appearance of a wound lately healed.

"This exhausts my patience, Sir Knight," said the Sub-Prior, "and is adding insult to violence and injury. Do you hold me for a child or an idiot, that you pretend to make me believe that the fresh blood with which your shirt is stained, flowed from a wound which has been healed for weeks or months? Unhappy mocker, thinkest thou thus to blind us? Too well do we know that it is the blood of your victim, wrestling with you in the desperate and mortal struggle, which has thus dyed your apparel."

The knight, after a moment's recollection, said in reply, "I will be open with you, my father — bid these men stand out of ear-shot, and I will tell you all I know of this mysterious business; and muse not, good father, though it may pass thy wit to expound it, for I avouch to you it is too dark for mine own."

The monk commanded Edward and the two men to withdraw, assuring the former that his conference with the prisoner should be brief, and giving him permission to keep watch at the door of the apartment; without which allowance he might, perhaps, have had some difficulty in procuring his absence. Edward had no sooner left the chamber, than he despatched messengers to one or two families of the Halidome, with whose sons his brother and he sometimes associated, to tell them that Halbert Glendinning had been murdered by an Englishman, and to require them to repair to the Tower of Glendearg without delay. The duty of revenge in such cases was held so sacred, that he had no reason to doubt they would instantly come with such assistance as would ensure the detention of the prisoner. He then locked the doors of the tower, both inner and outer, and also the gate of the court-yard. Having taken these precautions, he made a hasty visit to the females of the family, exhausting himself in efforts to console them, and in protestations that he would have vengeance for his murdered brother.

Chapter the Twenty-Seventh.

Now, by Our Lady, Sheriff, 'tis hard reckoning,
That I, with every odds of birth and barony
Should be detain'd here for the casual death
Of a wild forester, whose utmost having
Is but the brazen buckle of the belt
In which he sticks his hedge-knife.

OLD PLAY.

WHILE Edward was making preparations for securing and punishing the supposed murderer of his brother, with an intense thirst for vengeance, which had not hitherto shown itself as part of his character, Sir Piercie Shafton made such communications as it pleased him to the Sub-Prior, who listened with great attention, though the knight's narrative was none of the clearest, especially as his self-conceit led him to conceal or abridge the details which were necessary to render it intelligible.

"You are to know," he said, "reverend father, that this rustical juvenal having chosen to offer me, in the presence of your venerable Superior, yourself, and other excellent and worthy persons, besides the damsel, Mary Avenel, whom I term my Discretion in all honour and kindness, a gross insult, rendered yet more intolerable by the time and place, my just resentment did so gain the mastery over my discretion, that I resolved to allow him the privileges of an equal, and to indulge him with the combat."

"But, Sir Knight," said the Sub-Prior, "you still leave two matters very obscure. First, why the token he presented to you gave you so much offence, as I with others witnessed; and then again, how the youth, whom you then met for the first, or, at least, the second time, knew so much of your history as enabled him so greatly to move you."

The knight coloured very deeply.

"For your first query," he said, "most reverend father, we will, if you please, pretermit it as nothing essential to the matter in hand; and for the second—I protest to you that I know as little of his means of knowledge as you do, and that I am well-nigh persuaded he deals with Sathanas, of which more anon.—Well, sir—In the evening, I failed not to veil my purpose with a pleasant brow, as is the custom amongst us martialists, who never display the bloody colours of defiance in our countenance until our hand is armed to fight under them. I amused the fair Discretion with some canzonettes, and other toys, which could not but be ravishing to her inexperienced ears. I arose in the morning, and met my antagonist, who, to say truth, for an inexperienced villagio, comported himself as stoutly as I could have desired.—So, coming to the encounter, reverend sir, I did try his mettle with some half-a-dozen of downright passes, with any one of which I could have been through his body, only that I was loth to take so fatal an advantage, but rather, mixing mercy with my just indignation, studied to inflict upon him some flesh-wound of no very fatal quality. But, sir, in the midst of my clemency, he, being instigated, I think, by the devil, did follow up his first offence with some insult of the same nature. Whereupon, being eager to punish him, I made an estramazone, and my foot slipping at the same time,—not from any fault of fence on my part, or any advantage of skill on his, but the devil having, as I said, taken up the matter in hand, and the grass being slippery,—ere I recovered my position I encountered his sword, which he had advanced, with my undefended person, so that, as I think, I was in some sort run through the body. My juvenal, being beyond measure appalled at his own unexpected and unmerited success in this strange encounter, takes the flight and leaves me there, and I fall into a dead swoon for the lack of the blood I had lost so foolishly — and when I awake, as from a sound sleep, I find myself lying, an it like you, wrapt up in my cloak at the foot of one of the birch-trees which stand together in a clump near to this place. I feel my limbs, and experience little pain, but much weakness—I put my hand to the wound—it was whole and skinned over as you now see it — I rise and come hither; and in these words you have my whole day's story."

"I can only reply to so strange a tale," answered the monk, "that it is scarce possible that Sir Piercie Shafton can expect me to credit it. Here is a quarrel, the cause of which you conceal,—a wound received in the morning, of which there is no recent appearance at sunset, — a grave filled up, in which no body is deposited — the vanquished found alive and well — the victor departed no man knows whither. These things, Sir Knight, hang not so well together, that I should receive them as gospel."

"Reverend father," answered Sir Piercie Shafton, "I pray you in the first place to observe, that if I offer peaceful and civil justification of that which I have already averred to be true, I do so only in devout deference to your dress and to your order, protesting, that to any other opposite, saving a man of religion, a lady or my liege prince, I would not deign to support that which I had once attested, otherwise than with the point of my good sword. And so much being premised, I have to add, that I can but gage my honour as a gentleman, and my faith as a Catholic Christian, that the things which I have described to you have happened to me as I have described them, and not otherwise."

"It is a deep assertion, Sir Knight," answered the Sub-Prior; "yet, bethink you, it is only an assertion, and that no reason can be alleged why things should be believed which are so contrary to reason. Let me pray you to say whether the grave, which has been seen at your place of combat, was open or closed when your encounter took place?"

"Reverend father," said the knight, "I will veil from you nothing, but show you each secret of my bosom; even as the pure fountain revealeth the smallest pebble which graces the sand at the bottom of its crystal mirror, and as——"

"Speak in plain terms, for the love of heaven!" said the monk; "these holiday phrases belong not to solemn affairs—Was the grave open when the conflict began?"

"It was," answered the knight, "I acknowledge it; even as he that acknowledgeth——"

"Nay, I pray you, fair son, forbear these similitudes, and observe me. On yesterday at even no grave was found in that place, for old Martin chanced, contrary to his wont, to go thither in quest of a strayed sheep. At break of day, by your own confession, a grave was opened in that spot, and there a combat was fought — only one of the combatants appears, and he is covered with blood, and to all appearance woundless." — Here the knight made a gesture of impatience.—"Nay, fair son, hear me but one moment—the grave is closed and covered by the sod—what can we believe, but that it conceals the bloody corpse of the fallen duellist?"

"By Heaven, it cannot!" said the knight, "unless the juvenal hath slain himself and buried himself, in order to place me in the predicament of his murderer."

"The grave shall doubtless be explored, and that by to-morrow's dawn," said the monk; "I will see it done with mine own eyes."

"But," said the prisoner, "I protest against all evidence which may arise from its contents, and do insist beforehand, that whatever may be found in that grave shall not prejudice me in my defence. I have been so haunted by diabolical deceptions in this matter, that what do I know but that the devil may assume the form of this rustical juvenal, in order to procure me farther vexation? — I protest to you, holy father, it is my very thought that there is witchcraft in all that hath befallen me. Since I entered into this northern land, in which men say that sorceries do abound, I, who am held in awe and regard even by the prime gallants in the court of Feliciana, have been here bearded and taunted by a clod-treading clown. I, whom Vincentio Saviola termed his nimblest and most agile disciple, was, to speak briefly, foiled by a cow-boy, who knew no more of fence than is used at every country wake. I am run, as it seemed to me, through the body, with a very sufficient stoccata, and faint on the spot; and yet, when I recover, I find myself without either wem or wound, and, lacking nothing of my apparel, saving my murrey-coloured doublet, slashed with satin, which I will pray may be inquired after, lest the devil, who transported me, should have dropped it in his passage among some of the trees or bushes—it being a choice and most fanciful piece of raiment, which I wore for the first time at the Queen's pageant in Southwark."

"Sir Knight," said the monk, "you do again go astray from this matter. I inquire of you respecting that which concerns the life of another man, and it may be, touches your own also, and you answer me with the tale of an old doublet!"

"Old!" exclaimed the knight; "now, by the gods and saints, if there be a gallant at the British Court more fancifully considerate, and more considerately fanciful, but quaintly curious, and more curiously quaint, in frequent changes of all rich articles of vesture, becoming one who may be accounted point-de-vice a courtier, I will give you leave to term me a slave and a liar."

The monk thought, but did not say, that he had already acquired right to doubt the veracity of the Euphuist, considering the marvellous tale which he had told. Yet his own strange adventure, and that of Father Philip, rushed on his mind, and forbade his coming to any conclusion. He contented himself, therefore, with observing, that these were certainly strange incidents, and requested to know if Sir Piercie Shafton had any other reason for suspecting himself to be in a manner so particularly selected for the sport of sorcery and witchcraft.

"Sir Sub-Prior," said the Euphuist, "the most extraordinary circumstance remains behind, which alone, had I neither been bearded in dispute, nor foiled in combat, nor wounded and cured in the space of a few hours, would nevertheless of itself, and without any other corroborative, have compelled me to believe myself the subject of some malevolent fascination. Reverend sir, it is not to your ears that men should tell tales of love and gallantry, nor is Sir Piercie Shafton one who, to any ears whatsoever, is wont to boast of his fair acceptance with the choice and prime beauties of the court; insomuch that a lady, none of the least resplendent constellations which revolve in that hemisphere of honour, pleasure, and beauty, but whose name I here pretermit, was wont to call me her Taciturnity. Nevertheless truth must be spoken; and I cannot but allow, as the general report of the court, allowed in camps, and echoed back by city and country, that in the alacrity of the accost, the tender delicacy of the regard, the facetiousness of the address, the adopting and pursuing of the fancy, the solemn close and the graceful fall-off, Piercie Shafton was accounted the only gallant of the time, and so well accepted among the choicer beauties of the age, that no silk-hosed reveller of the presence-chamber, or plumed jouster of the tilt-yard, approached him by a bow's length in the ladies' regard, being the mark at which every well-born and generous juvenal aimeth his shaft. Nevertheless, reverend sir, having found in this rude place something which by blood and birth might be termed a lady, and being desirous to keep my gallant humour in exercise, as well as to show my sworn devotion to the sex in general, I did shoot off some arrows of compliment at this Mary Avenel, terming her my Discretion, with other quaint and well-imagined courtesies, rather bestowed out of my bounty than warranted by her merit, or perchance like unto the boyish fowler, who, rather than not exercise his bird-piece, will shoot at crows or magpies for lack of better game ——"

"Mary Avenel is much obliged by your notice," answered the monk; "but to what does all this detail of past and present gallantry conduct us?"

"Marry, to this conclusion," answered the knight; "that either this my Discretion, or I myself, am little less than bewitched; for, instead of receiving my accost with a gratifying bow, answering my regard with a suppressed smile, accompanying my falling off or departure with a slight sigh—honours with which I protest to you the noblest dancers and proudest beauties in Feliciana have graced my poor services — she hath paid me as little and as cold regard as if I had been some hob-nailed clown of these bleak mountains! Nay, this very day, while I was in the act of kneeling at her feet to render her the succours of this pungent quintessence, of purest spirit distilled by the fairest hands of the court of Feliciana, she pushed me from her with looks which savoured of repugnance, and, as I think, thrust at me with her foot as if to spurn me from her presence. These things, reverend father, are strange, portentous, unnatural, and befall not in the current of mortal affairs, but are symptomatic of sorcery and fascination. So that, having given to your reverence a perfect, simple, and plain account of all that I know concerning this matter, I leave it to your wisdom to solve what may be found soluble in the same, it being my purpose to-morrow, with the peep of dawn, to set forward towards Edinburgh."

"I grieve to be an interruption to your designs, Sir Knight," said the monk, "but that purpose of thine may hardly be fulfilled."

"How, reverend father!" said the knight, with an air of the utmost surprise; "if what you say respects my departure, understand that it *must* be, for I have so resolved it."

"Sir Knight," reiterated the Sub-Prior, "I must once more repeat, this *cannot* be, until the Abbot's pleasure be known in the matter."

"Reverend sir," said the knight, drawing himself up with great dignity, "I desire my hearty and thankful commendations to the Abbot; but in this matter I have nothing to do with his reverend pleasure, designing only to consult my own."

"Pardon me," said the Sub-Prior; "the Lord Abbot hath in this matter a voice potential."

Sir Piercie Shafton's colour began to rise—"I marvel," he said, "to hear your reverence talk thus — What! will you, for the imagined death of a rude, low-born frampler and wrangler, venture to impinge upon the liberty of the kinsman of the house of Piercie?"

"Sir Knight," returned the Sub-Prior, civilly, "your high lineage and your kindling anger will avail you nothing in this matter — You shall not come here to seek a shelter, and then spill our blood as if it were water."

"I tell you," said the knight, "once more, as I have told you already, that there was no blood spilled but mine own!"

"That remains to be proved," replied the Sub-Prior; "we of the community of Saint Mary's of Kennaquhair, use not to take fairy tales in exchange for the lives of our liege vassals."

"We of the house of Piercie," answered Shafton, "brook neither threats nor restraint — I say I will travel to-morrow, happen what may!"

"And I," answered the Sub-Prior, in the same tone of determination, "say that I will break your journey, come what may!"

"Who shall gainsay me," said the knight, "if I make my way by force?"

"You will judge wisely to think ere you make such an attempt," answered the monk, with composure; "there are men enough in the Halidome to vindicate its rights over those who dare infringe them."

"My cousin of Northumberland will know how to revenge this usage to a beloved kinsman so near to his blood," said the Englishman.

"The Lord Abbot will know how to protect the rights of his territory, both with the temporal and spiritual sword," said the monk. "Besides, consider, were we to send you to your kinsman at Alnwick or Warkworth to-morrow, he dare do nothing but transmit you in fetters to the Queen of England. Bethink, Sir Knight, that you stand on slippery ground, and will act most wisely in reconciling yourself to be a prisoner in this place until the Abbot shall decide the matter. There are armed men enow to countervail all your efforts at escape. Let patience and resignation, therefore, arm you to a necessary submission."

So saying, he clapped his hands, and called aloud. Edward entered, accompanied by two young men who had already joined him, and were well armed.

"Edward," said the Sub-Prior, "you will supply the English Knight here in this spence with suitable food and accommodation for the night, treating him with as much kindness as if nothing had happened between you. But you will place a sufficient guard, and look carefully that he make not his escape. Should he attempt to break forth, resist him to the death; but in no other case harm a hair of his head, as you shall be answerable."

Edward Glendinning replied, — "That I may obey your commands, reverend sir, I will not again offer myself to this person's presence; for shame it were to me to break the peace of the Halidome, but not less shame to leave my brother's death unavenged."

As he spoke, his lips grew livid, the blood forsook his cheek, and he was about to leave the apartment, when the Sub-Prior recalled him and said in a solemn tone, — "Edward, I have known you from infancy — I have done what lay within my reach to be of use to you — I say nothing of what you owe to me as the representative of your spiritual Superior — I say nothing of the duty from the vassal to the Sub-Prior — But Father Eustace expects from the pupil whom he has nurtured — he expects from Edward Glendinning, that he will not by any deed of sudden violence, however justified in his own mind by the provocation, break through the respect due to public justice, or that which he has an especial right to claim from him."

"Fear nothing, my reverend father, for so in an hundred senses may I well term you," said the young man; "fear not, I would say, that I will in any thing diminish the respect I owe to the venerable community by whom we have so long been protected, far less that I will do aught which can be personally less than respectful to you. But the blood of my brother must not cry for vengeance in vain — your reverence knows our Border creed."

"'Vengeance is mine, saith the Lord, and I will requite it,'" answered the monk. "The heathenish custom of deadly feud which prevails in this land, through which each man seeks vengeance at his own hand when the death of a friend or kinsman has chanced, hath already deluged our vales with the blood of Scottish men, spilled by the hands of countrymen and kindred. It were endless to count up the fatal results. On the Eastern Border, the Homes are at feud with the Swintons and Cockburns; in our Middle Marches, the Scotts and Kerrs have spilled as much brave blood in domestic feud as might have fought a pitched field in England, could they have but forgiven and forgotten a casual rencounter that placed their names in opposition to each other. On the west frontier, the Johnstones are at war with the Maxwells, the Jardines with the Bells, drawing with them the flower of the country, which should place their breasts as a bulwark against England, into private and bloody warfare, of which it is the only end to waste and impair the forces of the country, already divided in itself. Do not, my dear son Edward, permit this bloody prejudice to master your mind. I cannot ask you to think of the crime supposed as if the blood spilled had been less dear to you — Alas! I know that is impossible. But I do require you, in proportion to your interest in the supposed sufferer, (for as yet the whole is matter of supposition,) to bear on your mind the evidence on which the guilt of the accused person must be tried. He hath spoken with me, and I confess his tale is so extraordinary, that I should have, without a moment's hesitation, rejected it as incredible, but that an affair which chanced to myself in this very glen — More of that another time — Suffice it for the present to say, that from what I have myself experienced, I deem it possible, that, extraordinary as Sir Piercie Shafton's story may seem, I hold it not utterly impossible."

"Father," said Edward Glendinning, when he saw that his preceptor paused, unwilling farther to explain upon what grounds he was inclined to give a certain degree of credit to Sir Piercie Shafton's story, while he admitted it as improbable — "Father to me you have been in every sense. You know that my hand grasped more readily to the book than to the sword; and that I lacked utterly the ready and bold spirit which distinguished——" Here his voice faltered, and he paused for a moment, and then went on with resolution and rapidity — "I would say, that I was unequal to Halbert in promptitude of heart and of hand; but Halbert is gone, and I stand his representative, and that of my father — his successor in all his rights," (while he said this his eyes shot fire,) "and bound to assert and maintain them as he would have done — therefore I am a changed man, increased in courage as in my rights and pretensions. And, reverend father, respectfully, but plainly and firmly do I say, his blood, if it has been shed by this man, shall be atoned — Halbert shall not sleep neglected in his lonely grave, as if with him the spirit of my father had ceased forever. His blood flows in my veins, and while his has been poured forth unrequited, mine will permit me no rest. My poverty and meanness of rank shall not avail the lordly murderer. My calm nature and peaceful studies shall not be his protection. Even the obligations, holy father, which I acknowledge to you, shall not be his protection. I wait with patience the judgment of the Abbot and Chapter, for the slaughter of one of their most anciently descended vassals. If they do right to my brother's memory, it is well. But mark me, father, if they shall fail in rendering me that justice, I bear a heart and a hand which, though I love not such extremities, are capable of remedying such an error. He who takes up my brother's succession must avenge his death."

The monk perceived with surprise, that Edward, with his extreme diffidence, humility, and obedient assiduity, for such were his general characteristics, had still boiling in his veins the wild principles of those from whom he was descended, and by whom he was surrounded. His eyes sparkled, his frame was agitated, and the extremity of his desire for vengeance seemed to give a vehemence to his manner resembling the restlessness of joy.

"May God help us," said Father Eustace, "for, frail wretches as we are, we cannot help ourselves under sudden and strong temptation. — Edward, I will rely on your word that you do nothing rashly."

"That will I not," said Edward, — "that, my better than father, I surely will not. But the blood of my brother, — the tears of my mother — and — and — and of Mary Avenel, shall not be shed in vain. I will not deceive you, father — if this Piercie Shafton hath slain my brother, he dies, if the whole blood of the whole house of Piercie were in his veins."

There was a deep and solemn determination in the utterance of Edward Glendinning expressive of a rooted resolution. The Sub-Prior sighed deeply, and for the moment yielded to circumstances, and urged the acquiescence of his pupil no farther. He commanded lights to be placed in the lower chamber, which for a time he paced in silence.

A thousand ideas, and even differing principles, debated with each other in his bosom. He greatly doubted the English knight's account of the duel, and of what had followed it. Yet the extraordinary and supernatural circumstances which had befallen the Sacristan and himself in that very glen, prevented him from being absolutely incredulous on the score of the wonderful wound and recovery of Sir Piercie Shafton, and prevented him from at once condemning as impossible that which was altogether improbable. Then he was at a loss how to control the fraternal affections of Edward, with respect to whom he felt something like the keeper of a wild animal, a lion's whelp or tiger's cub, which he has held under his command from infancy, but which, when grown to maturity, on some sudden provocation displays his fangs and talons, erects his crest, resumes his savage nature, and bids defiance at once to his keeper and to all mankind.

How to restrain and mitigate an ire which the universal example of the times rendered deadly and inveterate, was sufficient cause of anxiety to Father Eustace. But he had also to consider the situation of his community, dishonoured and degraded by submitting to suffer the slaughter of a vassal to pass unavenged; a circumstance which of itself might in those times have afforded pretext for a revolt among their wavering adherents, or, on the other hand, exposed the community to imminent danger, should they proceed against a subject of England of high degree, connected with the house of Northumberland, and other northern families of high rank, who, as they possessed the means, could not be supposed to lack inclination, to wreak upon the patrimony of Saint Mary of Kennaquhair, any violence which might be offered to their kinsman.

In either case, the Sub-Prior well knew that the ostensible cause of feud, insurrection, or incursion, being once afforded, the case would not be ruled either by reason or by evidence, and he groaned in spirit when, upon counting up the chances which arose in this ambiguous dilemma, he found he had only a choice of difficulties. He was a monk, but he felt also as a man, indignant at the supposed slaughter of young Glendinning by one skilful in all the practice of arms, in which the vassal of the Monastery was most likely to be deficient; and to aid the resentment which he felt for the loss of a youth whom he had known from infancy, came in full force the sense of dishonour arising to his community from passing over so gross an insult unavenged. Then the light in which it might be viewed by those who at present presided in the stormy Court of Scotland, attached as they were to the Reformation, and allied by common faith and common interest with Queen Elizabeth, was a formidable subject of apprehension. The Sub-Prior well knew how they lusted after the revenues of the Church, (to express it in the ordinary phrase of the religious of the time,) and how readily they would grasp at such a pretext for encroaching on those of Saint Mary's, as would be afforded by the suffering to pass unpunished the death of a native Scottishman by a Catholic Englishman, a rebel to Queen Elizabeth.

On the other hand, to deliver up to England, or, which was nearly the same thing, the Scottish administration, an English knight leagued with the Piercie by kindred and political intrigue, a faithful follower of the Catholic Church, who had fled to the Halidome for protection, was, in the estimation of the Sub-Prior, an act most unworthy in itself, and meriting the malediction of Heaven, besides being, moreover, fraught with great temporal risk. If the government of Scotland was now almost entirely in the hands of the Protestant party, the Queen was still a Catholic, and there was no knowing when, amid the sudden changes which agitated that tumultuous country, she might find herself at the head of her own affairs, and able to protect those of her own faith. Then, if the Court of England and its Queen were zealously Protestant, the northern counties, whose friendship or enmity were of most consequence in the first instance to the community of Saint Mary's, contained many Catholics, the heads of whom were able, and must be supposed willing, to avenge any injury suffered by Sir Piercie Shafton.

On either side, the Sub-Prior, thinking, according to his sense of duty, most anxiously for the safety and welfare of his Monastery, saw the greatest risk of damage, blame, inroad, and confiscation. The only course on which he could determine, was to stand by the helm like a resolute pilot, watch every contingence, do his best to weather each reef and shoal, and commit the rest to heaven and his patroness.

As he left the apartment, the knight called after him, beseeching he would order his trunk-mails to be sent into his apartment, understanding he was to be guarded there for the night, as he wished to make some alteration in his apparel.*

"Ay, ay," said the monk, muttering as he went up the winding stair, "carry him his trumpery with all despatch. Alas! that man, with so many noble objects of pursuit, will amuse himself like a jackanape, with a laced jerkin and a cap and bells!—I must now to the melancholy work of consoling that which is well-nigh inconsolable, a mother weeping for her first-born."

Advancing, after a gentle knock, into the apartment of the women, he found that Mary Avenel had retired to bed, extremely indisposed, and that Dame Glendinning and Tibb were indulging their sorrows by the side of a decaying fire, and by the light of a small iron lamp, or cruize, as it was termed. Poor Elspeth's apron was thrown over her head, and bitterly did she sob and weep for "her beautiful, her brave, — the very image of her dear Simon Glendinning, the stay of her widowhood and the support of her old age."

---

* Sir Piercie Shafton's extreme love of dress was an attribute of the coxcombs of this period. The display made by their forefathers was in the numbers of their retinue; but as the actual influence of the nobility began to be restrained both in France and England by the increasing power of the crown, the indulgence of vanity in personal display became more inordinate. There are many allusions to this change of custom in Shakspeare and other dramatic writers, where the reader may find mention made of

"Bonds enter'd into
For gay apparel against the triumph day."

Jonson informs us, that for the first entrance of a gallant, "'twere good you turned four or five hundred acres of your best land into two or three trunks of apparel." — *Every Man out of his Humour.*

In the Memorie of the Somerville family, a curious instance occurs of this fashionable species of extravagance. In the year 1537, when James V. brought over his shortlived bride from France, the Lord Somerville of the day was so profuse in the expense of his apparel, that the money which he borrowed on the occasion was compensated by a perpetual annuity of threescore pounds Scottish, payable out of the barony of Carnwarth till doomsday, which was assigned by the creditor to Saint Magdalen's Chapel. By this deep expense the Lord Somerville had rendered himself so glorious in apparel, that the King, who saw so brave a gallant enter the gate of Holyrood, followed by only two pages, called upon several of the courtiers to ascertain who it could be who was so richly dressed and so slightly attended, and he was not recognised until he entered the presence-chamber. "You are very brave, my lord," said the King, as he received his homage; "but where are all your men and attendants?" The Lord Somerville readily answered, "If it please your Majesty, here they are," pointing to the lace that was on his own and his pages' clothes; whereat the King laughed heartily, and having surveyed the finery more nearly, bade him have away with it all, and let him have his stout band of spears again.

There is a scene in Jonson's "Every Man out of his Humour," (Act IV. Scene 6,) in which a Euphuist of the time gives an account of the effects of a duel on the clothes of himself and his opponent, and never departs a syllable from the catalogue of his wardrobe. We shall insert it in evidence that the foppery of our ancestors was not inferior to that of our own time.

"*Fastidius.* Good faith, Signior, now you speak of a quarrel, I'll acquaint you with a difference that happened between a gallant and myself, Sir Puntarvolo. You know him if I should name him—Signor Luculento

"*Punt.* Luculento! What inauspicious chance interposed itself to your two lives?

"*Fast.* Faith, sir, the same that sundered Agamemnon, and great Thetis' son; but let the cause escape sir. He sent me a challenge, mixt with some few braves, which I restored; and, in fine, we met. Now indeed, sir, I must tell you, he did offer at first very desperately, but without judgment; for look you, sir, I cast myself into this figure; now he came violently on, and withal advancing his rapier to strike, I thought to have took his arm, for he had left his body to my election, and I was sure he could not recover his guard. Sir, I mist my purpose in his arm, rashed his doublet sleeves, ran him close by the left cheek and through his hair. He, again, light me here — I had on a gold cable hat-band, then new come up, about a murrey French hat I had; cuts my hat-band, and yet it was massy goldsmith's work, cuts my brim, which, by good fortune, being thick embroidered with gold twist and spangles, disappointed the force of the blow; nevertheless it grazed on my shoulder, takes me away six purls of an Italian cut-work band I wore, cost me three pounds in the Exchange but three days before.

"*Punt.* This was a strange encounter.

"*Fast.* Nay, you shall hear, sir. With this, we both fell out and breathed. Now, upon the second sign of his assault, I betook me to my former manner of defence; he, on the other side, abandoned his body to the same danger as before, and follows me still with blows; but I, being loath to take the deadly advantage that lay before me of his left side, made a kind of stramazoun, ran him up to the hilt through the doublet, through the shirt, and yet missed the skin. He, making a reverse blow, falls upon my embossed girdle,—I had thrown off the hangers a little before,—strikes off a skirt of a thick-laced satin doublet I had, lined with four taffetas, cuts off two panes embroidered with pearl, rends through the drawings-out of tissue, enters the linings, and spiks the flesh.

"*Car.* I wonder he speaks not of his wrought shirt.

"*Fast.* Here, in the opinion of mutual damage, we paused. But, ere I proceed, I must tell you, signior, that in the last encounter, not having leisure to put off my silver spurs, one of the rowels catched hold of the ruffles of my boot, and, being Spanish leather and subject to tear, overthrows me, rends me two pair of silk stockings that I put on, being somewhat of a raw morning, a peach colour and another, and strikes me some half-inch deep into the side of the calf: He, seeing the blood come, presently takes horse and away; I having bound up my wound with a piece of my wrought shirt——

"*Car.* O, comes it in there.

"*Fast.* Ride after him, and, lighting at the court gate both together, embraced, and marched hand in hand up into the presence. Was not this business well carried?

"*Maci.* Well! yes; and by this we can guess what apparel the gentleman wore.

"*Punt.* 'Fore valour! it was a designment begun with much resolution, maintained with as much prowess, and ended with more humanity."

The faithful Tibb echoed her complaints, and, more violently clamorous, made deep promises of revenge on Sir Piercie Shafton, "if there were a man left in the south who could draw a whinger, or a woman that could thraw a rape." The presence of the Sub-Prior imposed silence on these clamours. He sate down by the unfortunate mother, and essayed, by such topics as his religion and reason suggested, to interrupt the current of Dame Glendinning's feelings; but the attempt was in vain. She listened, indeed, with some little interest, while he pledged his word and his influence with the Abbot, that the family which had lost their eldest-born by means of a guest received at his command, should experience particular protection at the hands of the community; and that the fief which belonged to Simon Glendinning should, with extended bounds and added privileges, be conferred on Edward.

But it was only for a very brief space that the mother's sobs were apparently softer, and her grief more mild. She soon blamed herself for casting a moment's thought upon world's gear while poor Halbert was lying stretched in his bloody shirt. The Sub-Prior was not more fortunate, when he promised that Halbert's body "should be removed to hallowed ground, and his soul secured by the prayers of the Church in his behalf." Grief would have its natural course, and the voice of the comforter was wasted in vain.

Chapter the Twenty-Eighth.

He is at liberty, I have ventured for him!
—————————— if the law
Find and condemn me for't, some living wenches,
Some honest-hearted maids will sing my dirge,
And tell to memory my death was noble,
Dying almost a martyr.

THE TWO NOBLE KINSMEN.

THE Sub-Prior of Saint Mary's, in taking his departure from the spence in which Sir Piercie Shafton was confined, and in which some preparations were made for his passing the night as the room which might be most conveniently guarded, left more than one perplexed person behind him. There was connected with this chamber, and opening into it, a small *outshot*, or projecting part of the building, occupied by a sleeping apartment, which upon ordinary occasions, was that of Mary Avenel, and which, in the unusual number of guests who had come to the tower on the former evening, had also accommodated Mysie Happer, the Miller's daughter; for anciently, as well as in the present day, a Scottish house was always rather too narrow and limited for the extent of the owner's hospitality, and some shift and contrivance was necessary, upon any unusual occasion, to ensure the accommodation of all the guests.

The fatal news of Halbert Glendinning's death had thrown all former arrangements into confusion. Mary Avenel, whose case required immediate attention, had been transported into the apartment hitherto occupied by Halbert and his brother, as the latter proposed to watch all night, in order to prevent the escape of the prisoner. Poor Mysie had been altogether overlooked, and had naturally enough betaken herself to the little apartment which she had hitherto occupied, ignorant that the spence, through which lay the only access to it, was to be the sleeping chamber of Sir Piercie Shafton. The measures taken for securing him there had been so sudden, that she was not aware of it, until she found that the other females had been removed from the spence by the Sub-Prior's direction, and having once missed the opportunity of retreating along with them; bashfulness, and the high respect which she was taught to bear to the monks, prevented her venturing forth alone, and intruding herself on the presence of Father Eustace, while in secret conference with the Southron. There appeared no remedy but to wait till their interview was over; and, as the door was thin, and did not shut very closely, she could hear every word that passed betwixt them.

It thus happened, that without any intended intrusion on her part, she became privy to the whole conversation of the Sub-Prior and the English knight, and could also observe from the window of her little retreat, that more than one of the young men summoned by Edward arrived successively at the tower. These circumstances led her to entertain most serious apprehension that the life of Sir Piercie Shafton was in great and instant peril.

Woman is naturally compassionate, and not less willingly so when youth and fair features are on the side of him who claims her sympathy. The handsome presence, elaborate dress and address, of Sir Piercie Shafton, which had failed to make any favorable impression on the grave and lofty character of Mary Avenel, had completely dazzled and bewildered the poor Maid of the Mill. The knight had perceived this result, and, flattered by seeing that his merit was not universally underrated, he had bestowed on Mysie a good deal more of his courtesy than in his opinion her rank warranted. It was not cast away, but received with a devout sense of his condescension, and with gratitude for his personal notice, which, joined to her fears for his safety, and the natural tenderness of her disposition, began to make wild work in her heart.

"To be sure it was very wrong in him to slay Halbert Glendinning," (it was thus she argued the case with herself,) "but then he was a gentleman born, and a soldier, and so gentle and courteous withal, that she was sure the quarrel had been all of young Glendinning's own seeking; for it was well known that both these lads were so taken up with that Mary Avenel, that they never looked at another lass in the Halidome, more than if they were of a different degree. And then Halbert's dress was as clownish as his manners were haughty; and this poor young gentleman, (who was habited like any prince,) banished from his own land, was first drawn into a quarrel by a rude brangler, and then persecuted and like to be put to death by his kin and allies."

Mysie wept bitterly at the thought, and then her heart rising against such cruelty and oppression to a defenceless stranger, who dressed with so much skill, and spoke with so much grace, she began to consider whether she could not render him some assistance in this extremity.

Her mind was now entirely altered from its original purpose. At first her only anxiety had been to find the means of escaping from the interior apartment, without being noticed by any one; but now she began to think that Heaven had placed her there for the safety and protection of the persecuted stranger. She was of a simple and affectionate, but at the same time an alert and enterprising character, possessing more than female strength of body, and more than female courage, though with feelings as capable of being bewildered with gallantry of dress and language, as a fine gentleman of any generation would have desired to exercise his talents upon. "I will save him," she thought, "that is the first thing to be resolved — and then I wonder what he will say to the poor Miller's maiden, that has done for him what all the dainty dames in London or Holyrood would have been afraid to venture upon."

Prudence began to pull her sleeve as she indulged speculations so hazardous, and hinted to her that the warmer Sir Piercie Shafton's gratitude might prove, it was the more likely to be fraught with danger to his benefactress. Alas! poor Prudence, thou mayest say with our moral teacher,

"I preach for ever, but I preach in vain."

The Miller's maiden, while you pour your warning into her unwilling bosom, has glanced her eye on the small mirror by which she has placed her little lamp, and it returns to her a countenance and eyes, pretty and sparkling at all times, but ennobled at present with the energy of expression proper to those who have dared to form, and stand prepared to execute, deeds of generous audacity. "Will these features — will these eyes, joined to the benefit I am about to confer upon Sir Piercie Shafton, do nothing towards removing the distance of rank between us?"

Such was the question which female vanity asked of fancy; and though even fancy dared not answer in a ready affirmative, a middle conclusion was adopted — "Let me first succour the gallant youth, and trust to fortune for the rest."

Banishing, therefore, from her mind every thing that was personal to herself, the rash but generous girl turned her whole thoughts to the means of executing this enterprise.

The difficulties which interposed were of no ordinary nature. The vengeance of the men of that country, in cases of deadly feud, that is, in cases of a quarrel excited by the slaughter of any of their relations, was one of their most marked characteristics; and Edward, however gentle in other respects, was so fond of his brother, that there could be no doubt that he would be as signal in his revenge as the customs of the country authorized. There were to be passed the inner door of the apartment, the two gates of the tower itself, and the gate of the court-yard, ere the prisoner was at liberty; and then a guide and means of flight were to be provided, otherwise ultimate escape was impossible. But where the will of woman is strongly bent on the accomplishment of such a purpose, her wit is seldom baffled by difficulties, however embarrassing.

The Sub-Prior had not long left the apartment, ere Mysie had devised a scheme for Sir Piercie Shafton's freedom, daring, indeed, but likely to be successful, if dexterously conducted. It was necessary, however, that she should remain where she was till so late an hour, that all in the tower should have betaken themselves to repose, excepting those whose duty made them watchers. The interval she employed in observing the movements of the person in whose service she was thus boldly a volunteer.

She could hear Sir Piercie Shafton pace the floor to and fro, in reflection doubtless on his own untoward fate and precarious situation. By and by she heard him making a rustling among his trunks, which, agreeable to the order of the Sub-Prior, had been placed in the apartment to which he was confined, and which he was probably amusing more melancholy thoughts by examining and arranging. Then she could hear him resume his walk through the room, and, as if his spirits had been somewhat relieved and elevated by the survey of his wardrobe, she could distinguish that at one turn he half recited a sonnet, at another half whistled a galliard, and at the third hummed a saraband. At length she could understand that he extended himself on the temporary couch which had been allotted to him, after muttering his prayers hastily, and in a short time she concluded he must be fast asleep.

She employed the moment which intervened in considering her enterprise under every different aspect; and dangerous as it was, the steady review which she took of the various perils accompanying her purpose, furnished her with plausible devices for obviating them. Love and generous compassion, which give singly such powerful impulse to the female heart, were in this case united, and championed her to the last extremity of hazard.

It was an hour past midnight. All in the tower slept sound but those who had undertaken to guard the English prisoner; or if sorrow and suffering drove sleep from the bed of Dame Glendinning and her foster-daughter, they were too much wrapt in their own griefs to attend to external sounds. The means of striking light were at hand in the small apartment, and thus the Miller's maiden was enabled to light and trim a small lamp. With a trembling step and throbbing heart, she undid the door which separated her from the apartment in which the Southron knight was confined, and almost flinched from her fixed purpose, when she found herself in the same room with the sleeping prisoner. She scarcely trusted herself to look upon him, as he lay wrapped in his cloak, and fast asleep upon the pallet bed, but turned her eyes away while she gently pulled his mantle with no more force than was just equal to awaken him. He moved not until she had twitched his cloak a second and a third time, and then at length looking up, was about to make an exclamation in the suddenness of his surprise.

Mysie's bashfulness was conquered by her fear. She placed her fingers on her lips, in token that he must observe the most strict silence, and then pointed to the door to intimate that it was watched.

Sir Piercie Shafton now collected himself and sat upright on his couch. He gazed with surprise on the graceful figure of the young woman who stood before him; her well-formed person, her flowing hair, and the outline of her features, showed dimly, and yet to advantage, by the partial and feeble light which she held in her hand. The romantic imagination of the gallant would soon have coined some compliment proper for the occasion, but Mysie left him not time.

"I come," she said, "to save your life, which is else in great peril — if you answer me, speak as low as you can, for they have sentinelled your door with armed men."

"Comeliest of miller's daughters," answered Sir Piercie, who by this time was sitting upright on his couch, "dread nothing for my safety. Credit me, that, as in very truth, I have not spilled the red puddle (which these villagios call the blood) of their most uncivil relation, so I am under no apprehension whatever for the issue of this restraint, seeing that it cannot but be harmless to me. Natheless, to thee, O most Molendinar beauty, I return the thanks which thy courtesy may justly claim."

"Nay, but, Sir Knight," answered the maiden, in a whisper as low as it was tremulous, "I deserve no thanks unless you will act by my counsel. Edward Glendinning hath sent for Dan of the Howlet-hirst, and young Adie of Aikenshaw, and they are come with three men more, and with bow, and jack, and spear, and I heard them say to each other, and to Edward, as they alighted in the court, that they would have amends for the death of their kinsman, if the monk's cowl should smoke for it — And the vassals are so wilful now, that the Abbot himself dare not control them, for fear they turn heretics, and refuse to pay their feu-duties."

"In faith," said Sir Piercie Shafton, "it may be a shrewd temptation, and perchance the monks may rid themselves of trouble and cumber, by handing me over the march to Sir John Foster or Lord Hundson, the English wardens, and so make peace with their vassals and with England at once. Fairest Molinara, I will for once walk by thy rede, and if thou dost contrive to extricate me from this vile kennel, I will so celebrate thy wit and beauty, that the Baker's nymph of Raphael d'Urbino shall seem but a gipsey in comparison of my Molinara."

"I pray you, then, be silent," said the Miller's daughter; "for if your speech betrays that you are awake, my scheme fails utterly, and it is Heaven's mercy and Our Lady's that we are not already overheard and discovered."

"I am silent," replied the Southron, "even as the starless night — but yet — if this contrivance of thine should endanger thy safety, fair and no less kind than fair damsel, it were utterly unworthy of me to accept it at thy hand."

"Do not think of me," said Mysie, hastily; "I am safe — I will take thought for myself, if I once saw you out of this dangerous dwelling — if you would provide yourself with any part of your apparel or goods, lose no time."

The knight *did*, however, lose some time, ere he could settle in his own mind what to take and what to abandon of his wardrobe, each article of which seemed endeared to him by recollection of the feasts and revels at which it had been exhibited. For some little while Mysie left him to make his selections at leisure, for she herself had also some preparations to make for flight. But when, returning from the chamber into which she had retired, with a small bundle in her hand, she found him still indecisive, she insisted in plain terms, that he should either make up his baggage for the enterprise, or give it up entirely. Thus urged, the disconsolate knight hastily made up a few clothes into a bundle, regarded his trunk-mails with a mute expression of parting sorrow, and intimated his readiness to wait upon his kind guide.

She led the way to the door of the apartment, having first carefully extinguished her lamp, and motioning to the knight to stand close behind her, tapped once or twice at the door. She was at length answered by Edward Glendinning, who demanded to know who knocked within, and what was desired.

"Speak low," said Mysie Happer, "or you will awaken the English knight. It is I, Mysie Happer, who knock — I wish to get out — you have locked me up — and I was obliged to wait till the Southron slept."

"Locked you up!" replied Edward, in surprise.

"Yes," answered the Miller's daughter, "you have locked me up into this room — I was in Mary Avenel's sleeping apartment."

"And can you not remain there till morning," replied Edward, "since it has so chanced?"

"What!" said the Miller's daughter, in a tone of offended delicacy, "I remain here a moment longer than I can get out without discovery!—I would not, for all the Halidome of St. Mary's, remain a minute longer in the neighbourhood of a man's apartment than I can help it—For whom, or for what do you hold me? I promise you my father's daughter has been better brought up than to put in peril her good name."

"Come forth then, and get to thy chamber in silence," said Edward.

So saying, he undid the bolt. The staircase without was in utter darkness, as Mysie had before ascertained. So soon as she stept out, she took hold of Edward as if to support herself, thus interposing her person betwixt him and Sir Piercie Shafton, by whom she was closely followed. Thus screened from observation, the Englishman slipped past on tiptoe, unshod and in silence, while the damsel complained to Edward that she wanted a light.

"I cannot get you a light," said he, "for I cannot leave this post; but there is a fire below."

"I will sit below till morning," said the Maid of the Mill; and, tripping down stairs, heard Edward bolt and bar the door of the now tenantless apartment with vain caution.

At the foot of the stair which she descended, she found the object of her care waiting her farther directions. She recommended to him the most absolute silence, which, for once in his life, he seemed not unwilling to observe, conducted him, with as much caution as if he were walking on cracked ice, to a dark recess, used for depositing wood, and instructed him to ensconce himself behind the fagots. She herself lighted her lamp once more at the kitchen fire, and took her distaff and spindle, that she might not seem to be unemployed, in case any one came into the apartment.

From time to time, however, she stole towards the window on tiptoe, to catch the first glance of the dawn, for the farther prosecution of her adventurous project. At length she saw, to her great joy, the first peep of the morning brighten upon the gray clouds of the east, and, clasping her hands together, thanked Our Lady for the sight, and implored protection during the remainder of her enterprise. Ere she had finished her prayer, she started at feeling a man's arm across her shoulder, while a rough voice spoke in her ear—"What! menseful Mysie of the Mill so soon at her prayers?—now, benison on the bonny eyes that open so early!—I'll have a kiss for good morrow's sake."

Dan of the Howlet-hirst, for he was the gallant who paid Mysie this compliment, suited the action with the word, and the action, as is usual in such cases of rustic gallantry, was rewarded with a cuff, which Dan received as a fine gentleman receives a tap with a fan, but which, delivered by the energetic arm of the Miller's maiden, would have certainly astonished a less robust gallant.

"How now, Sir Coxcomb!" said she, "and must you be away from your guard over the English knight, to plague quiet folks with your horse-tricks!"

"Truly you are mistaken, pretty Mysie," said the clown, "for I have not yet relieved Edward at his post; and were it not a shame to let him stay any longer, by my faith, I could find it in my heart not to quit you these two hours."

"Oh, you have hours and hours enough to see any one," said Mysie; "but you must think of the distress of the household even now, and get Edward to sleep for a while, for he has kept watch this whole night."

"I will have another kiss first," answered Dan of the Howlet-hirst.

But Mysie was now on her guard, and, conscious of the vicinity of the wood-hole, offered such strenuous resistance, that the swain cursed the nymph's bad humour with very unpastoral phrase and emphasis, and ran up stairs to relieve the guard of his comrade. Stealing to the door, she heard the new sentinel hold a brief conversation with Edward, after which the latter withdrew, and the former entered upon the duties of his watch.

Mysie suffered him to walk there a little while undisturbed, until the dawning became more general, by which time she supposed he might have digested her coyness, and then presenting herself before the watchful sentinel, demanded of him "the keys of the outer tower, and of the court-yard gate."

"And for what purpose?" answered the warder.

"To milk the cows, and drive them out to their pasture," said Mysie; "you would not have the poor beasts kept in the byre a' morning, and the family in such distress, that there is na ane fit to do a turn but the byre-woman and myself?"

"And where is the byre-woman?" said Dan.

"Sitting with me in the kitchen, in case these distressed folks want any thing."

"There are the keys, then, Mysie Dorts," said the sentinel.

"Many thanks, Dan Ne'er-do-weel," answered the Maid of the Mill, and escaped down stairs in a moment.

To hasten to the wood-hole, and there to robe the English knight in a short gown and petticoat, which she had provided for the purpose, was the work of another moment. She then undid the gates of the tower, and made towards the byre, or cow-house, which stood in one corner of the court-yard. Sir Piercie Shafton remonstrated against the delay which this would occasion.

"Fair and generous Molinara," he said, "had we not better undo the outward gate, and make the best of our way hence, even like a pair of sea-mews who make towards shelter of the rocks as the storm waxes high?"

"We must drive out the cows first," said Mysie, "for a sin it were to spoil the poor widow's cattle, both for her sake and the poor beasts' own; and I have no mind any one shall leave the tower in a hurry to follow us. Besides, you must have your horse, for you will need a fleet one ere all be done."

So saying, she locked and double-locked both the inward and outward door of the tower, proceeded to the cow-house, turned out the cattle, and, giving the knight his own horse to lead, drove them before her out at the court-yard gate, intending to return for her own palfrey. But the noise attending the first operation caught the wakeful attention of Edward, who, starting to the bartizan, called to know what the matter was.

Mysie answered with great readiness, that "she was driving out the cows, for that they would be spoiled for want of looking to."

"I thank thee, kind maiden," said Edward—"and yet," he added, after a moment's pause, "what damsel is that thou hast with thee?"

Mysie was about to answer, when Sir Piercie Shafton, who apparently did not desire that the great work of his liberation should be executed without the interposition of his own ingenuity, exclaimed from beneath, "I am she, O most bucolical juvenal, under whose charge are placed the milky mothers of the herd."

"Hell and darkness!" exclaimed Edward, in a transport of fury and astonishment, "it is Piercie Shafton—What! treason! treason!—ho!—Dan—Jasper—Martin—the villain escapes!"

"To horse! to horse!" cried Mysie, and in an instant mounted behind the knight, who was already in the saddle.

Edward caught up a cross-bow, and let fly a bolt, which whistled so near Mysie's ear, that she called to her companion,—"Spur—spur, Sir Knight! —the next will not miss us.—Had it been Halbert instead of Edward who bent that bow, we had been dead."

The knight pressed his horse, which dashed past the cows, and down the knoll on which the tower was situated. Then taking the road down the valley, the gallant animal, reckless of its double burden, soon conveyed them out of hearing of the tumult and alarm with which their departure filled the Tower of Glendearg.

Thus it strangely happened, that two men were flying in different directions at the same time, each accused of being the other's murderer.

Chapter the Twenty-Ninth.

————Sure he cannot
Be so unmanly as to leave me here;
If he do, maids will not so easily
Trust men again.

THE TWO NOBLE KINSMEN.

THE knight continued to keep the good horse at a pace as quick as the road permitted, until they had cleared the valley of Glendearg, and entered upon the broad dale of the Tweed, which now rolled before them in crystal beauty, displaying on its opposite bank the huge gray Monastery of St. Mary's, whose towers and pinnacles were scarce yet touched by the newly-risen sun, so deeply the edifice lies shrouded under the mountains which rise to the southward.

Turning to the left, the knight continued his road down to the northern bank of the river, until they arrived nearly opposite to the weir, or dam-dike, where Father Philip concluded his extraordinary aquatic excursion.

Sir Piercie Shafton, whose brain seldom admitted more than one idea at a time, had hitherto pushed forward without very distinctly considering where he was going. But the sight of the Monastery so near to him, reminded him that he was still on dangerous ground, and that he must necessarily provide for his safety by choosing some settled plan of escape. The situation of his guide and deliverer also occurred to him, for he was far from being either selfish or ungrateful. He listened, and discovered that the Miller's daughter was sobbing and weeping bitterly as she rested her head on his shoulder.

"What ails thee," he said, "my generous Molinara?—is there aught that Piercie Shafton can do which may show his gratitude to his deliverer?" Mysie pointed with her finger across the river, but ventured not to turn her eyes in that direction. "Nay, but speak plain, most generous damsel," said the knight, who, for once, was puzzled as much as his own elegance of speech was wont to puzzle others, "for I swear to you that I comprehend nought by the extension of thy fair digit."

"Yonder is my father's house," said Mysie, in a voice interrupted by the increased burst of her sorrow.

"And I was carrying thee discourteously to a distance from thy habitation?" said Shafton, imagining he had found out the source of her grief. "Wo worth the hour that Piercie Shafton, in attention to his own safety, neglected the accommodation of any female, far less of his most beneficent liberatrice! Dismount, then, O lovely Molinara, unless thou wouldst rather that I should transport thee on horseback to the house of thy molendinary father, which, if thou sayest the word, I am prompt to do, defying all dangers which may arise to me personally, whether by monk or miller."

Mysie suppressed her sobs, and with considerable difficulty muttered her desire to alight, and take her fortune by herself. Sir Piercie Shafton, too devoted a squire of dames to consider the most lowly as exempted from a respectful attention, independent of the claims which the Miller's maiden possessed over him, dismounted instantly from his horse, and received in his arms the poor girl, who still wept bitterly, and, when placed on the ground, seemed scarce able to support herself, or at least still clung, though, as it appeared, unconsciously, to the support he had afforded. He carried her to a weeping birch tree, which grew on the green-sward bank around which the road winded, and, placing her on the ground beneath it, exhorted her to compose herself. A strong touch of natural feeling struggled with, and half overcame, his acquired affectation, while he said, "Credit me, most generous damsel, the service you have done to Piercie Shafton he would have deemed too dearly bought, had he foreseen it was to cost you these tears and singults. Show me the cause of your grief, and if I can do aught to remove it, believe that the rights you have acquired over me will make your commands sacred as those of an empress. Speak, then, fair Molinara, and command him whom fortune hath rendered at once your debtor and your champion. What are your orders?"

"Only that you will fly and save yourself," said Mysie, mustering up her utmost efforts to utter these few words.

"Yet," said the knight, "let me not leave you without some token of remembrance." Mysie would have said there needed none, and most truly would she have spoken, could she have spoken for weeping. "Piercie Shafton is poor," he continued, "but let this chain testify he is not ungrateful to his deliverer."

He took from his neck the rich chain and medallion we have formerly mentioned, and put it into the powerless hand of the poor maiden, who neither received nor rejected it, but, occupied with more intense feelings, seemed scarce aware of what he was doing.

"We shall meet again," said Sir Piercie Shafton, "at least I trust so; meanwhile, weep no more, fair Molinara, an thou lovest me."

The phrase of conjuration was but used as an ordinary commonplace expression of the time, but bore a deeper sense to poor Mysie's ear. She dried her tears; and when the knight, in all kind and chivalrous courtesy, stooped to embrace her at their parting, she rose humbly up to receive the proffered honour in a posture of more deference, and meekly and gratefully accepted the offered salute. Sir Piercie Shafton mounted his horse, and began to ride off, but curiosity, or perhaps a stronger feeling, soon induced him to look back, when he beheld the Miller's daughter standing still motionless on the spot where they had parted, her eyes turned after him, and the unheeded chain hanging from her hand.

It was at this moment that a glimpse of the real state of Mysie's affections, and of the motive from which she had acted in the whole matter, glanced on Sir Piercie Shafton's mind. The gallants of that age, disinterested, aspiring, and lofty-minded, even in their coxcombry, were strangers to those degrading and mischievous pursuits which are usually termed low amours. They did not "chase the humble maidens of the plain," or degrade their own rank, to deprive rural innocence of peace and virtue. It followed, of course, that as conquests in this class were no part of their ambition, they were in most cases totally overlooked and unsuspected, left unimproved, as a modern would call it, where, as on the present occasion, they were casually made. The companion of Astrophel, and flower of the tilt-yard of Feliciana, had no more idea that his graces and good parts could attach the love of Mysie Happer, than a first-rate beauty in the boxes dreams of the fatal wound which her charms may inflict on some attorney's romantic apprentice in the pit. I suppose, in any ordinary case, the pride of rank and distinction would have pronounced on the humble admirer the doom which Beau Fielding denounced against the whole female world, "Let them look and die;" but the obligations under which he lay to the enamoured maiden, miller's daughter as she was, precluded the possibility of Sir Piercie's treating the matter *en cavalier*, and, much embarrassed, yet a little flattered at the same time, he rode back to try what could be done for the damsel's relief.

The innate modesty of poor Mysie could not prevent her showing too obvious signs of joy at Sir Piercie Shafton's return. She was betrayed by the sparkle of the rekindling eye, and a caress which, however timidly bestowed, she could not help giving to the neck of the horse which brought back the beloved rider

"What farther can I do for you, kind Molinara?" said Sir Piercie Shafton, himself hesitating and blushing; for, to the grace of Queen Bess's age be it spoken, her courtiers wore more iron on their breasts than brass on their foreheads, and even amid their vanities preserved still the decaying spirit of chivalry, which inspired of yore the very gentle Knight of Chaucer,

> Who in his port was modest as a maid.

Mysie blushed deeply, with her eyes fixed on the ground, and Sir Piercie proceeded in the same tone of embarrassed kindness. "Are you afraid to return home alone, my kind Molinara?—would you that I should accompany you?"

"Alas!" said Mysie, looking up, and her cheek changing from scarlet to pale, "I have no home left."

"How! no home!" said Shafton; "says my generous Molinara she hath no home, when yonder stands the house of her father, and but a crystal stream between?"

"Alas!" answered the Miller's maiden, "I have no longer either home or father. He is a devoted servant to the Abbey—I have offended the Abbot, and if I return home my father will kill me."

"He dare not injure thee, by Heaven!" said Sir Piercie; "I swear to thee, by my honour and knighthood, that the forces of my cousin of Northumberland shall lay the Monastery so flat, that a horse shall not stumble as he rides over it, if they should dare to injure a hair of your head! Therefore be hopeful and content, kind Mysinda, and know you have obliged one who can and will avenge the slightest wrong offered to you."

He sprung from his horse as he spoke, and, in the animation of his argument, grasped the willing hand of Mysie, (or Mysinda as he had now christened her.) He gazed too upon full black eyes, fixed upon his own with an expression which, however subdued by maidenly shame, it was impossible to mistake, on cheeks where something like hope began to restore the natural colour, and on two lips which, like double rosebuds, were kept a little apart by expectation, and showed within a line of teeth as white as pearl. All this was dangerous to look upon, and Sir Piercie Shafton, after repeating with less and less force his request that the fair Mysinda would allow him to carry her to her father's, ended by asking the fair Mysinda to go along with him—"At least," he added, "until I shall be able to conduct you to a place of safety."

Mysie Happer made no answer; but blushing scarlet betwixt joy and shame, mutely expressed her willingness to accompany the Southron Knight, by knitting her bundle closer, and preparing to resume her seat *en croupe*. "And what is your pleasure that I should do with this?" she said, holding up the chain as if she had been for the first time aware that it was in her hand.

"Keep it, fairest Mysinda, for my sake," said the Knight.

"Not so, sir," answered Mysie, gravely; "the maidens of my country take no such gifts from their superiors, and I need no token to remind me of this morning."

Most earnestly and courteously did the Knight urge her acceptance of the proposed guerdon, but on this point Mysie was resolute; feeling, perhaps, that to accept of any thing bearing the appearance of reward, would be to place the service she had rendered him on a mercenary footing. In short, she would only agree to conceal the chain, lest it might prove the means of detecting the owner, until Sir Piercie should be placed in perfect safety.

They mounted and resumed their journey, of which Mysie, as bold and sharp-witted in some points as she was simple and susceptible in others, now took in some degree the direction, having only inquired its general destination, and learned that Sir Piercie Shafton desired to go to Edinburgh, where he hoped to find friends and protection. Possessed of this information, Mysie availed herself of her local knowledge to get as soon as possible out of the bounds of the Halidome, and into those of a temporal baron, supposed to be addicted to the reformed doctrines, and upon whose limits, at least, she thought their pursuers would not attempt to hazard any violence. She was not indeed very apprehensive of a pursuit, reckoning with some confidence that the inhabitants of the Tower of Glendearg would find it a matter of difficulty to surmount the obstacles arising from their own bolts and bars, with which she had carefully secured them before setting forth on the retreat.

They journeyed on, therefore, in tolerable security, and Sir Piercie Shafton found leisure to amuse the time in high-flown speeches and long anecdotes of the court of Feliciana, to which Mysie bent an ear not a whit less attentive, that she did not understand one word out of three which was uttered by her fellow-traveller. She listened, however, and admired upon trust, as many a wise man has been contented to treat the conversation of a handsome but silly mistress. As for Sir Piercie, he was in his element; and, well assured of the interest and full approbation of his auditor, he went on spouting Euphuism of more than usual obscurity, and at more than usual length. Thus passed the morning, and noon brought them within sight of a winding stream, on the side of which arose an ancient baronial castle, surrounded by some large trees. At a small distance from the gate of the mansion, extended, as in those days was usual, a straggling hamlet, having a church in the centre.

"There are two hostelries in this Kirk-town," said Mysie, "but the worst is best for our purpose; for it stands apart from the other houses, and I ken the man weel, for he has dealt with my father for malt."

This *causa scientiæ*, to use a lawyer's phrase, was ill chosen for Mysie's purpose; for Sir Piercie Shafton had, by dint of his own loquacity, been talking himself all this while into a high esteem for his fellow-traveller, and, pleased with the gracious reception which she afforded to his powers of conversation, had well-nigh forgotten that she was not herself one of those high-born beauties of whom he was recounting so many stories, when this unlucky speech at once placed the most disadvantageous circumstances attending her lineage under his immediate recollection. He said nothing, however. What indeed could he say? Nothing was so natural as that a miller's daughter should be acquainted with publicans who dealt with her father for malt, and all that was to be wondered at was the concurrence of events which had rendered such a female the companion and guide of Sir Piercie Shafton of Wilverton, kinsman of the great Earl of Northumberland, whom princes and sovereigns themselves termed cousin, because of the Piercie blood.* He felt the disgrace of strolling through the country with a miller's maiden on the crupper behind him, and was even ungrateful enough to feel some emotions of shame, when he halted his horse at the door of the little inn.

But the alert intelligence of Mysie Happer spared him farther sense of derogation, by instantly springing from his horse, and cramming the ears of mine host, who came out with his mouth agape to receive a guest of the knight's appearance, with an imagined tale, in which circumstance on circumstance were huddled so fast, as to astonish Sir Piercie Shafton, whose own invention was none of the most brilliant. She explained to the publican that this was a great English knight travelling from the Monastery to the court of Scotland, after having paid his vows to Saint Mary, and that she had been directed to conduct him so far on the road; and that Ball, her palfrey, had fallen by the way, because he had been over-wrought with carrying home the last melder of meal to the portioner of Langhope; and that she had turned in Ball to graze in the Tasker's park, near Cripplecross, for he had stood as still as Lot's wife with very weariness; and that the knight had courteously insisted she should ride behind him, and that she had brought him to her kend friend's hostelry rather than to proud Peter Peddie's, who got his malt at the Mellerstane mills; and that he must get the best that the house afforded, and that he must get it ready in a moment of time, and that she was ready to help in the kitchen.

All this ran glibly off the tongue without pause on the part of Mysie Happer, or doubt on that of the landlord. The guest's horse was conducted to the stable, and he himself installed in the cleanest corner and best seat which the place afforded. Mysie, ever active and officious, was at once engaged in preparing food, in spreading the table, and in making all the better arrangements which her experience could suggest, for the honour and comfort of her companion. He would fain have resisted this; for while it was impossible not to be gratified with the eager and alert kindness which was so active in his service, he felt an undefinable pain in seeing

* Froissart tells us somewhere, (the readers of romances are indifferent to accurate reference,) that the King of France called one of the Piercies cousin, because of the blood of Northumberland.

Mysinda engaged in these menial services, and discharging them, moreover, as one to whom they were but too familiar. Yet this jarring feeling was mixed with, and perhaps balanced by, the extreme grace with which the neat-handed maiden executed these tasks, however mean in themselves, and gave to the wretched corner of a miserable inn of the period, the air of a bower, in which an enamoured fairy, or at least a shepherdess of Arcadia, was displaying, with unavailing solicitude, her designs on the heart of some knight, destined by fortune to higher thoughts, and a more splendid union.

The lightness and grace with which Mysie covered the little round table with a snow-white cloth, and arranged upon it the hastily-roasted capon, with its accompanying stoup of Bourdeaux, were but plebeian graces in themselves; but yet there were very flattering ideas excited by each glance. She was so very well made, agile at once and graceful, with her hand and arm as white as snow, and her face in which a smile contended with a blush, and her eyes which looked ever at Shafton when he looked elsewhere, and were dropped at once when they encountered his, that she was irresistible! In fine, the affectionate delicacy of her whole demeanour, joined to the promptitude and boldness she had so lately evinced, tended to ennoble the services she had rendered, as if some

> ——— sweet engaging Grace
> Put on some clothes to come abroad,
> And took a waiter's place.

But, on the other hand, came the damning reflection, that these duties were not taught her by Love, to serve the beloved only, but arose from the ordinary and natural habits of a miller's daughter, accustomed, doubtless, to render the same service to every wealthier churl who frequented her father's mill. This stopped the mouth of vanity, and of the love which vanity had been hatching, as effectually as a peck of literal flour would have done.

Amidst this variety of emotions, Sir Piercie Shafton forgot not to ask the object of them to sit down and partake the good cheer which she had been so anxious to provide and to place in order. He expected that this invitation would have been bashfully, perhaps, but certainly most thankfully, accepted; but he was partly flattered, and partly piqued, by the mixture of deference and resolution with which Mysie declined his invitation. Immediately after, she vanished from the apartment, leaving the Euphuist to consider whether he was most gratified or displeased by her disappearance.

In fact, this was a point on which he would have found it difficult to make up his mind, had there been any necessity for it. As there was none, he drank a few cups of claret, and sang (to himself) a strophe or two of the canzonettes of the divine Astrophel. But in spite both of wine and of Sir Philip Sidney, the connexion in which he now stood, and that which he was in future to hold, with the lovely Molinara, or Mysinda, as he had been pleased to denominate Mysie Happer, recurred to his mind. The fashion of the times (as we have already noticed) fortunately coincided with his own natural generosity of disposition, which indeed amounted almost to extravagance, in prohibiting, as a deadly sin, alike against gallantry, chivalry, and morality, his rewarding the good offices he had received from this poor maiden, by abusing any of the advantages which her confidence in his honour had afforded. To do Sir Piercie justice, it was an idea which never entered into his head; and he would probably have dealt the most scientific *imbroccata, stoccata*, or *punto reverso*, which the school of Vincent Saviola had taught him, to any man who had dared to suggest to him such selfish and ungrateful meanness. On the other hand, he was a man, and foresaw various circumstances which might render their journey together in this intimate fashion a scandal and a snare. Moreover, he was a coxcomb and a courtier, and felt there was something ridiculous in travelling the land with a miller's daughter behind his saddle, giving rise to suspicions not very creditable to either, and to ludicrous constructions, so far as he himself was concerned.

"I would," he said half aloud, "that if such might be done without harm or discredit to the too-ambitious, yet too-well-distinguishing Molinara, she and I were fairly severed, and bound on our different courses; even as we see the goodly vessel bound for the distant seas hoist sails and bear away into the deep, while the humble fly-boat carries to shore those friends, who, with wounded hearts and watery eyes, have committed to their higher destinies the more daring adventurers by whom the fair frigate is manned."

He had scarce uttered the wish when it was gratified; for the host entered to say that his worshipful knighthood's horse was ready to be brought forth as he had desired; and on his inquiry for "the—the damsel—that is—the young woman——"

"Mysie Happer," said the landlord, "has returned to her father's; but she bade me say, you could not miss the road for Edinburgh, in respect it was neither far way nor foul gate."

It is seldom we are exactly blessed with the precise fulfilment of our wishes at the moment when we utter them; perhaps, because Heaven wisely withholds what, if granted, would be often received with ingratitude. So at least it chanced in the present instance; for when mine host said that Mysie was returned homeward, the knight was tempted to reply, with an ejaculation of surprise and vexation, and a hasty demand, whither and when she had departed? The first emotions his prudence suppressed, the second found utterance.

"Where is she gane?" said the host, gazing on him, and repeating his question—"She is gane hame to her father's, it is like—and she gaed just when she gave orders about your worship's horse, and saw it well fed, (she might have trusted me, but millers and millers' kin think a' body as thief-like as themselves,) an' she's three miles on the gate by this time."

"Is she gone then?" muttered Sir Piercie, making two or three hasty strides through the narrow apartment—"Is she gone?—Well, then, let her go. She could have had but disgrace by abiding by me, and I little credit by her society. That I should have thought there was such difficulty in shaking her off! I warrant she is by this time laughing with some clown she has encountered; and my rich chain will prove a good dowry.—And ought it not to prove so? and has she not deserved it, were it ten times more valuable?—Piercie Shafton! Piercie Shafton! dost thou grudge thy deliverer the guerdon she hath so dearly won? The selfish air of this northern land hath infected thee, Piercie Shafton! and blighted the blossoms of thy generosity, even as it is said to shrivel the flowers of the mulberry.—Yet I thought," he added, after a moment's pause, "that she would not so easily and voluntarily have parted from me. But it skills not thinking of it.—Cast my reckoning, mine host, and let your groom lead forth my nag."

The good host seemed also to have some mental point to discuss, for he answered not instantly, debating perhaps whether his conscience would bear a double charge for the same guests. Apparently his conscience replied in the negative, though not without hesitation, for he at length replied—"It's daffing to lee; it winna deny that the lawing is clean paid. Ne'ertheless, if your worshipful knighthood pleases to give aught for increase of trouble——"

"How!" said the knight; "the reckoning paid? and by whom, I pray you?"

"E'en by Mysie Happer, if truth maun be spoken, as I said before," answered the honest landlord, with as many compunctious visitings for telling the verity as another might have felt for making a lie in the circumstances—"And out of the moneys supplied for your honour's journey by the Abbot, as she tauld to me. And laith were I to surcharge any gentleman that darkens my doors." He added in the confidence of honesty which his frank avowal entitled him to entertain, "Nevertheless, as I said before, if it pleases your knighthood of free good-will to consider extraordinary trouble——"

The knight cut short his argument, by throwing the landlord a rose-noble, which probably doubled the value of a Scottish reckoning, though it would have defrayed but a half one at the Three Cranes or the Vintry. The bounty so much delighted mine host, that he ran to fill the stirrup-cup (for which no charge was ever made) from a butt yet charier than that which he had pierced for the former stoup. The knight paced slowly to horse, partook of his courtesy, and thanked him with the stiff condescension of the court of Elizabeth; then mounted and followed the northern path, which was pointed out as the nearest to Edinburgh, and which, though very unlike a modern highway, bore yet so distinct a resemblance to a public and frequented road as not to be easily mistaken.

"I shall not need her guidance it seems," said he to himself, as he rode slowly onward; "and I suppose that was one reason of her abrupt departure, so different from what one might have expected.—Well, I am well rid of her. Do we not pray to be liberated from temptation? Yet that she should have erred so much in estimation of her own situation and mine, as to think of defraying the reckoning! I would I saw her once more, but to explain to her the solecism of which her inexperience hath rendered her guilty. And I fear," he added, as he emerged from some straggling trees, and looked out upon a wild moorish country, composed of a succession of swelling lumpish hills, "I fear I shall soon want the aid of this Ariadne, who might afford me a clew through the recesses of yonder mountainous labyrinth."

As the Knight thus communed with himself, his attention was caught by the sound of a horse's footsteps; and a lad, mounted on a little gray Scottish nag, about fourteen hands high, coming along a path which led from behind the trees, joined him on the high-road, if it could be termed such.

The dress of the lad was completely in village fashion, yet neat and handsome in appearance. He had a jerkin of gray cloth slashed and trimmed, with black hose of the same, with deer-skin rullions or sandals, and handsome silver spurs. A cloak of a dark mulberry colour was closely drawn round the upper part of his person, and the cape in part muffled his face, which was also obscured by his bonnet of black velvet cloth, and its little plume of feathers.

Sir Piercie Shafton, fond of society, desirous also to have a guide, and, moreover, prepossessed in favour of so handsome a youth, failed not to ask him whence he came, and whither he was going. The youth looked another way, as he answered, that he was going to Edinburgh, "to seek service in some nobleman's family."

"I fear me you have run away from your last master," said Sir Piercie, "since you dare not look me in the face while you answer my question."

"Indeed, sir, I have not," answered the lad, bashfully, while, as if with reluctance, he turned round his face, and instantly withdrew it. It was a glance, but the discovery was complete. There was no mistaking the dark full eye, the cheek in which much embarrassment could not altogether disguise an expression of comic humour, and the whole figure at once betrayed, under her metamorphosis, the Maid of the Mill. The recognition was joyful, and Sir Piercie Shafton was too much pleased to have regained his companion to remember the very good reasons which had consoled him for losing her.

To his questions respecting her dress, she answered that she had obtained it in the Kirktown from a friend; it was the holiday suit of a son of hers, who had taken the field with his liege-lord, the baron of the land. She had borrowed the suit under pretence she meant to play in some mumming or rural masquerade. She had left, she said, her own apparel in exchange, which was better worth ten crowns than this was worth four.

"And the nag, my ingenious Molinara," said Sir Piercie, "whence comes the nag?"

"I borrowed him from our host at the Gled's-Nest," she replied; and added, half stifling a laugh, "he has sent to get, instead of it, our Ball, which I left in the Tasker's Park at Cripplecross. He will be lucky if he find it there."

"But then the poor man will lose his horse, most argute Mysinda," said Sir Piercie Shafton, whose English notions of property were a little startled at a mode of acquisition more congenial to the ideas of a miller's daughter (and he a Border miller to boot) than with those of an English person of quality.

"And if he does lose his horse," said Mysie, laughing, "surely he is not the first man on the marches who has had such a mischance. But he will be no loser, for I warrant he will stop the value out of moneys which he has owed my father this many a day."

"But then your father will be the loser," objected yet again the pertinacious uprightness of Sir Piercie Shafton.

"What signifies it now to talk of my father?" said the damsel, pettishly; then instantly changing to a tone of deep feeling, she added, "my father has this day lost that which will make him hold light the loss of all the gear he has left."

Struck with the accents of remorseful sorrow in which his companion uttered these few words, the English knight felt himself bound both in honour and conscience to expostulate with her as strongly as he could, on the risk of the step which she had now taken, and on the propriety of her returning to her father's house. The matter of his discourse, though adorned with many unnecessary flourishes, was honourable both to his head and heart.

The Maid of the Mill listened to his flowing periods with her head sunk on her bosom as she rode, like one in deep thought or deeper sorrow. When he had finished, she raised up her countenance, looked full on the knight, and replied with great firmness — "If you are weary of my company, Sir Piercie Shafton, you have but to say so, and the Miller's daughter will be no farther cumber to you. And do not think I will be a burden to you, if we travel together to Edinburgh; I have wit enough and pride enough to be a willing burden to no man. But if you reject not my company at present, and fear not it will be burdensome to you hereafter, speak no more to me of returning back. All that you can say to me I have said to myself; and that I am now here, is a sign that I have said it to no purpose. Let this subject, therefore, be forever ended betwixt us. I have already, in some small fashion, been useful to you, and the time may come I may be more so; for this is not your land of England, where men say justice is done with little fear or favour to great and to small; but it is a land where men do by the strong hand, and defend by the ready wit, and I know better than you the perils you are exposed to."

Sir Piercie Shafton was somewhat mortified to find that the damsel conceived her presence useful to him as a protectress as well as guide, and said something of seeking protection of nought save his own arm and his good sword. Mysie answered very quietly, that she nothing doubted his bravery; but it was that very quality of bravery which was most likely to involve him in danger. Sir Piercie Shafton, whose head never kept very long in any continued train of thinking, acquiesced without much reply, resolving in his own mind that the maiden only used this apology to disguise her real motive, of affection to his person. The romance of the situation flattered his vanity and elevated his imagination, as placing him in the situation of one of those romantic heroes of whom he had read the histories, where similar transformations made a distinguished figure.

He took many a sidelong glance at his page, whose habits of country sport and country exercise had rendered her quite adequate to sustain the character she had assumed. She managed the little nag with dexterity, and even with grace; nor did any thing appear that could have betrayed her disguise, except when a bashful consciousness of her companion's eye being fixed on her, gave her an appearance of temporary embarrassment, which greatly added to her beauty.

The couple rode forward as in the morning, pleased with themselves and with each other, until they arrived at the village where they were to repose for the night, and where all the inhabitants of the little inn, both male and female, joined in extolling the good grace and handsome countenance of the English knight, and the uncommon beauty of his youthful attendant.

It was here that Mysie Happer first made Sir Piercie Shafton sensible of the reserved manner in which she proposed to live with him. She announced him as her master, and, waiting upon him with the reverent demeanour of an actual domestic, permitted not the least approach to familiarity, not even such as the knight might with the utmost innocence have ventured upon. For example, Sir Piercie, who, as we know, was a great connoisseur in dress, was detailing to her the advantageous change which he proposed to make in her attire as soon as they should reach Edinburgh, by arraying her in his own colours of pink and carnation. Mysie Happer listened with great complacency to the unction with which he dilated upon welts, laces, slashes, and trimmings, until, carried away by the enthusiasm with which he was asserting the superiority of the falling band over the Spanish ruff, he approached his hand, in the way of illustration, towards the collar of his page's doublet. She instantly stepped back and gravely reminded him that she was alone and under his protection.

"You cannot but remember the cause which has brought me here," she continued; "make the least approach to any familiarity which you would not offer to a princess surrounded by her court, and you have seen the last of the Miller's daughter — She will vanish as the chaff disappears from the shieling-hill * when the west wind blows."

"I do protest, fair Molinara," said Sir Piercie Shafton — but the fair Molinara had disappeared before his protest could be uttered. "A most singular wench," said he to himself; "and by this hand, as discreet as she is fair-featured — Certes, shame it were to offer her scathe or dishonour! She makes similes too, though somewhat savouring of her condition. Had she but read Euphues, and forgotten that accursed mill and shieling-hill, it is my thought that her converse would be broidered with as many and as choice pearls of compliment, as that of the most rhetorical lady in the court of Feliciana. I trust she means to return to bear me company."

But that was no part of Mysie's prudential scheme. It was then drawing to dusk, and he saw her not again until the next morning, when the horses were brought to the door that they might prosecute their journey.

But our story here necessarily leaves the English knight and his page, to return to the Tower of Glendearg.

---

* The place where corn was winnowed, while that operation was performed by the hand, was called in Scotland the Shieling-hill.

Chapter the Thirtieth.

> You call it an ill angel—it may be so,
> But sure I am, among the ranks which fell,
> 'Tis the first fiend e'er counsell'd man to rise,
> And win the bliss the sprite himself had forfeited.
>
> OLD PLAY.

WE must resume our narrative at the period when Mary Avenel was conveyed to the apartment which had been formerly occupied by the two Glendinnings, and when her faithful attendant, Tibbie, had exhausted herself in useless attempts to compose and to comfort her. Father Eustace also dealt forth with well-meant kindness those apophthegms and dogmata of consolation, which friendship almost always offers to grief, though they are uniformly offered in vain. She was at length left to indulge in the desolation of her own sorrowful feelings. She felt as those who, loving for the first time, have lost what they loved, before time and repeated calamity have taught them that every loss is to a certain extent reparable or endurable.

Such grief may be conceived better than it can be described, as is well known to those who have experienced it. But Mary Avenel had been taught by the peculiarity of her situation, to regard herself as the Child of Destiny; and the melancholy and reflecting turn of her disposition gave to her sorrows a depth and breadth peculiar to her character. The grave—and it was a bloody grave—had closed, as she believed, over the youth to whom she was secretly, but most warmly attached; the force and ardour of Halbert's character bearing a singular correspondence to the energy of which her own was capable. Her sorrow did not exhaust itself in sighs and tears, but when the first shock had passed away, concentrated itself with deep and steady meditation, to collect and calculate, like a bankrupt debtor, the full amount of her loss. It seemed as if all that connected her with earth, had vanished with this broken tie. She had never dared to anticipate the probability of an ultimate union with Halbert, yet now his supposed fall seemed that of the only tree which was to shelter her from the storm. She respected the more gentle character, and more peaceful attainments, of the younger Glendinning; but it had not escaped her (what never indeed escaped woman in such circumstances) that he was disposed to place himself in competition with what she, the daughter of a proud and warlike race, deemed the more manly qualities of his elder brother; and there is no time when a woman does so little justice to the character of a surviving lover, as when comparing him with the preferred rival of whom she has been recently deprived.

The motherly, but coarse kindness of Dame Glendinning, and the doating fondness of her old domestic, seemed now the only kind feeling of which she formed the object; and she could not but reflect how little these were to be compared with the devoted attachment of a high-souled youth, whom the least glance of her eye could command, as the high-mettled steed is governed by the bridle of the rider. It was when plunged among these desolating reflections, that Mary Avenel felt the void of mind, arising from the narrow and bigoted ignorance in which Rome then educated the children of her church. Their whole religion was a ritual, and their prayers were the formal iteration of unknown words, which, in the hour of affliction, could yield but little consolation to those who from habit resorted to them. Unused to the practice of mental devotion, and of personal approach to the Divine Presence by prayer, she could not help exclaiming in her distress, "There is no aid for me on earth, and I know not how to ask it from Heaven!"

As she spoke thus in an agony of sorrow, she cast her eyes into the apartment, and saw the mysterious Spirit, which waited upon the fortunes of her house, standing in the moonlight in the midst of the room. The same form, as the reader knows, had more than once offered itself to her sight; and either her native boldness of mind, or some peculiarity attached to her from her birth, made her now look upon it without shrinking. But the White Lady of Avenel was now more distinctly visible, and more closely present, than she had ever before seemed to be, and Mary was appalled by her presence. She would, however, have spoken; but there ran a tradition, that though others who had seen the White Lady had asked questions and received answers, yet those of the house of Avenel who had ventured to speak to her, had never long survived the colloquy. The figure, besides, as sitting up in her bed, Mary Avenel gazed on it intently, seemed by its gestures to caution her to keep silence, and at the same time to bespeak attention.

The White Lady then seemed to press one of the planks of the floor with her foot, while, in her usual low, melancholy, and musical chant, she repeated the following verses:

"Maiden, whose sorrows wail the Living Dead,
 Whose eyes shall commune with the Dead Alive,
Maiden, attend! Beneath my foot lies hid
 The Word, the Law, the Path, which thou dost strive
To find and canst not find.—Could spirits shed
 Tears for their lot, it were my lot to weep,
Showing the road which I shall never tread,
 Though my foot points it.—Sleep, eternal sleep,
Dark, long, and cold forgetfulness my lot!—
 But do not thou at human ills repine,
Secure there lies full guerdon in this spot
 For all the woes that wait frail Adam's line—
Stoop, then, and make it yours—I may not make it mine!"

The phantom stooped towards the floor as she concluded, as if with the intention of laying her hand on the board on which she stood. But ere she had completed that gesture, her form became indistinct, was presently only like the shade of a fleecy cloud, which passed betwixt earth and the moon, and was soon altogether invisible.

A strong impression of fear, the first which she had experienced in her life to any agitating extent, seized upon the mind of Mary Avenel, and for a minute she felt a disposition to faint. She repelled it, however, mustered her courage, and addressed herself to saints and angels, as her church recommended. Broken slumbers at length stole on her exhausted mind and frame, and she slept until the dawn was about to rise, when she was awakened by the cry of "Treason! treason! follow, follow!" which arose in the tower, when it was found that Piercie Shafton had made his escape.

Apprehensive of some new misfortune, Mary Avenel hastily arranged the dress which she had not laid aside, and, venturing to quit her chamber, learned from Tibb, who, with her gray hairs dishevelled like those of a sibyl, was flying from room to room, that the bloody Southron villain had made his escape, and that Halbert Glendinning, poor bairn, would sleep unrevenged and unquiet in his bloody grave. In the lower apartments, the young men were roaring like thunder, and venting in oaths and exclamations against the fugitives the rage which they experienced in finding themselves locked up within the tower, and debarred from their vindictive pursuit by the wily precautions of Mysie Happer. The authoritative voice of the Sub-Prior commanding silence was next heard; upon which Mary Avenel, whose tone of feeling did not lead her to enter into counsel or society with the rest of the party, again retired to her solitary chamber.

The rest of the family held counsel in the spence, Edward almost beside himself with rage, and the Sub-Prior in no small degree offended at the effrontery of Mysie Happer in attempting such a scheme, as well as at the mingled boldness and dexterity with which it had been executed. But neither surprise nor anger availed aught. The windows, well secured with iron bars for keeping assailants out, proved now as effectual for detaining the inhabitants within. The battlements were open, indeed; but without ladder or ropes to act as a substitute for wings, there was no possibility of descending from them. They easily succeeded in alarming the inhabitants of the cottages beyond the precincts of the court; but the men had been called in to strengthen the guard for the night, and only women and children remained who could contribute nothing in the emergency, except their useless exclamations of surprise, and there were no neighbours for miles around. Dame Elspeth, however, though drowned in tears, was not so unmindful of external affairs, but that she could find voice enough to tell the women and children without, to "leave their skirling, and look after the cows that she couldna get minded, what wi' the awfu' distraction of her mind, what wi' that fause slut having locked them up in their ain tower as fast as if they had been in the Jeddart tolbooth."

Meanwhile, the men finding other modes of exit impossible, unanimously concluded to force the doors with such tools as the house afforded for the purpose. These were not very proper for the occasion, and the strength of the doors was great. The interior one, formed of oak, occupied them for three mortal hours, and there was little prospect of the iron door being forced in double the time.

While they were engaged in this ungrateful toil, Mary Avenel had with much less labour acquired exact knowledge of what the Spirit had intimated in her mystic rhyme. On examining the spot which the phantom had indicated by her gestures, it was not difficult to discover that a board had been loosened, which might be raised at pleasure. On removing this piece of plank, Mary Avenel was astonished to find the Black Book, well remembered by her as her mother's favourite study, of which she immediately took possession, with as much joy as her present situation rendered her capable of feeling.

Ignorant in a great measure of its contents, Mary Avenel had been taught from her infancy to hold this volume in sacred veneration. It is probable that the deceased Lady of Walter Avenel only postponed initiating her daughter into the mysteries of the Divine Word, until she should be better able to comprehend both the lessons which it taught, and the risk at which, in those times, they were studied. Death interposed, and removed her before the times became favourable to the reformers, and before her daughter was so far advanced in age as to be fit to receive religious instruction of this deep import. But the affectionate mother had made preparations for the earthly work which she had most at heart. There were slips of paper inserted in the volume, in which, by an appeal to, and a comparison of, various passages in holy writ, the errors and human inventions with which the Church of Rome had defaced the simple edifice of Christianity, as erected by its divine architect, were pointed out. These controversial topics were treated with a spirit of calmness and Christian charity, which might have been an example to the theologians of the period; but they were clearly, fairly, and plainly argued, and supported by the necessary proofs and references. Other papers there were which had no reference whatever to polemics, but were the simple effusions of a devout mind communing with itself. Among these was one frequently used, as it seemed from the state of the manuscript, on which the mother of Mary had transcribed and placed together those affecting texts to which the heart has recourse, in affliction, and which assures us at once of the sympathy and protection afforded to the children of the promise. In Mary Avenel's state of mind, these attracted her above all the other lessons, which, coming from a hand so dear, had reached her at a time so critical, and in a manner so touching. She read the affecting promise, "I will never leave thee nor forsake thee," and the consoling exhortation, "Call upon me in the day of trouble, and I will deliver thee." She read them, and her heart acquiesced in the conclusion Surely this is the word of God!

There are those to whom a sense of religion has come in storm and tempest; there are those whom it has summoned amid scenes of revelry and idle vanity; there are those, too, who have heard its "still small voice" amid rural leisure and placid contentment. But perhaps the knowledge which causeth not to err, is most frequently impressed upon the mind during seasons of affliction; and tears are the softened showers which cause the seed of Heaven to spring and take root in the human breast. At least it was thus with Mary Avenel. She was insensible to the discordant noise which rang below, the clang of bars and the jarring symphony of the levers which they used to force them, the measured shouts of the labouring inmates as they combined their strength for each heave, and gave time with their voices to the exertion of their arms, and their deeply muttered vows of revenge on the fugitives who had bequeathed them at their departure a task so toilsome and difficult. Not all this din, combined in hideous concert, and expressive of aught but peace, love, and forgiveness, could divert Mary Avenel from the new course of study on which she had so singularly entered. "The serenity of Heaven," she said, "is above me; the sounds which are around are but those of earth and earthly passion."

Meanwhile the noon was passed, and little impression was made on the iron grate, when they who laboured at it received a sudden reinforcement by the unexpected arrival of Christie of the Clinthill. He came at the head of a small party, consisting of four horsemen, who bore in their caps the sprig of holly, which was the badge of Avenel.

"What, ho!—my masters," he said, "I bring you a prisoner."

"You had better have brought us liberty," said Dan of the Howlet-hirst.

Christie looked at the state of affairs with great surprise. "An I were to be hanged for it," he said, "as I may for as little a matter, I could not forbear laughing at seeing men peeping through their own bars like so many rats in a rat-trap, and he with the beard behind, like the oldest rat in the cellar."

"Hush, thou unmannered knave," said Edward, "it is the Sub-Prior; and this is neither time, place, nor company, for your ruffian jests."

"What, ho! is my young master malapert?" said Christie; "why, man, were he my own carnal father, instead of being father to half the world, I would have my laugh out. And now it is over, I must assist you, I reckon, for you are setting very greenly about this gear — put the pinch nearer the staple, man, and hand me an iron crow through the grate, for that's the fowl to fly away with a wicket on its shoulders. I have broke into as many grates as you have teeth in your young head — ay, and broke out of them too, as the captain of the Castle of Lochmaben knows full well."

Christie did not boast more skill than he really possessed; for, applying their combined strength, under the direction of that experienced engineer, bolt and staple gave way before them, and in less than half an hour, the grate, which had so long repelled their force, stood open before them.

"And now," said Edward, "to horse, my mates, and pursue the villain Shafton!"

"Halt, there," said Christie of the Clinthill; "pursue your guest, my master's friend and my own?—there go two words to that bargain. What the foul fiend would you pursue him for?"

"Let me pass," said Edward, vehemently, "I will be staid by no man—the villain has murdered my brother!"

"What says he?" said Christie, turning to the others; "murdered? who is murdered, and by whom?"

"The Englishman, Sir Piercie Shafton," said Dan of the Howlet-hirst, "has murdered young Halbert Glendinning yesterday morning, and we have all risen to the fray."

"It is a bedlam business, I think," said Christie. "First I find you all locked up in your own tower, and next I am come to prevent you revenging a murder that was never committed!"

"I tell you," said Edward, "that my brother was slain and buried yesterday morning by this false Englishman."

"And I tell you," answered Christie, "that I saw him alive and well last night. I would I knew his trick of getting out of the grave; most men find it more hard to break through a green sod than a grated door."

Every body now paused, and looked on Christie in astonishment, until the Sub-Prior, who had hitherto avoided communication with him, came up and required earnestly to know, whether he meant really to maintain that Halbert Glendinning lived.

"Father," he said, with more respect than he usually showed to any one save his master, "I confess I may sometimes jest with those of your coat, but not with you; because, as you may partly recollect, I owe you a life. It is certain as the sun is in heaven, that Halbert Glendinning supped at the house of my master the Baron of Avenel last night, and that he came thither in company with an old man, of whom more anon."

"And where is he now?"

"The devil only can answer that question," replied Christie, "for the devil has possessed the whole family, I think. He took fright, the foolish lad, at something or other which our Baron did in his moody humour, and so he jumped into the lake and swam ashore like a wild-duck. Robin of Redcastle spoiled a good gelding in chasing him this morning."

"And why did he chase the youth?" said the Sub-Prior; "what harm had he done?"

"None that I know of," said Christie; "but such was the Baron's order, being in his mood, and all the world having gone mad, as I have said before."

"Whither away so fast, Edward?" said the monk.

"To Corri-nan-shian, Father," answered the youth. — "Martin and Dan, take pickaxe and mattock, and follow me if you be men!"

"Right," said the monk, "and fail not to give us instant notice what you find."

"If you find aught there like Halbert Glendinning," said Christie, hallooing after Edward, "I will be bound to eat him unsalted. — 'T is a sight to see how that fellow takes the bent! — It is in the time of action men see what lads are made of. Halbert was aye skipping up and down like a roe, and his brother used to sit in the chimney nook with his book and sic-like trash—But the lad was like a loaded hackbut, which will stand in the corner as quiet as an old crutch until ye draw the trigger, and then there is nothing but flash and smoke. — But here comes my prisoner; and, setting other matters aside, I must pray a word with you, Sir Sub-Prior, respecting him. I came on before to treat about him, but I was interrupted with this fasherie."

As he spoke, two more of Avenel's troopers rode into the court-yard, leading betwixt them a horse, on which, with his hands bound to his side, sate the reformed preacher, Henry Warden.

Chapter the Thirty-First.

At school I knew him—a sharp-witted youth,
Grave, thoughtful, and reserved among his mates,
Turning the hours of sport and food to labour,
Starving his body to inform his mind.

OLD PLAY.

THE Sub-Prior, at the Borderer's request, had not failed to return to the tower, into which he was followed by Christie of the Clinthill, who, shutting the door of the apartment, drew near, and began his discourse with great confidence and familiarity.

"My master," he said, "sends me with his commendations to you, Sir Sub-Prior, above all the community of Saint Mary's, and more specially than even to the Abbot himself; for though he be termed my lord, and so forth, all the world knows that you are the tongue of the trump."

"If you have aught to say to me concerning the community," said the Sub-Prior, "it were well you proceeded in it without farther delay. Time presses, and the fate of young Glendinnning dwells on my mind."

"I will be caution for him, body for body," said Christie. "I do protest to you, as sure as I am a living man, so surely is he one."

"Should I not tell his unhappy mother the joyful tidings?" said Father Eustace, — "and yet better wait till they return from searching the grave. Well, Sir Jackman, your message to me from your master?"

"My lord and master," said Christie, "hath good reason to believe that, from the information of certain back friends, whom he will reward at more leisure, your reverend community hath been led to deem him ill attached to Holy Church, allied with heretics and those who favour heresy, and a hungerer after the spoils of your Abbey."

"Be brief, good henchman," said the Sub-Prior, "for the devil is ever most to be feared when he preacheth."

"Briefly, then — my master desires your friendship; and to excuse himself from the maligner's calumnies, he sends to your Abbot that Henry Warden, whose sermons have turned the world upside down, to be dealt with as Holy Church directs, and as the Abbot's pleasure may determine."

The Sub-Prior's eyes sparkled at the intelligence; for it had been accounted a matter of great importance that this man should be arrested, possessed, as he was known to be, of so much zeal and popularity, that scarcely the preaching of Knox himself had been more awakening to the people, and more formidable to the Church of Rome.

In fact, that ancient system, which so well accommodated its doctrines to the wants and wishes of a barbarous age, had, since the art of printing, and the gradual diffusion of knowledge, lain floating like some huge Leviathan, into which ten thousand reforming fishers were darting their harpoons. The Roman Church of Scotland, in particular, was at her last gasp, actually blowing blood and water, yet still with unremitted, though animal exertions, maintaining the conflict with the assailants, who on every side were plunging their weapons into her bulky body. In many large towns, the monasteries had been suppressed by the fury of the populace; in other places, their possessions had been usurped by the power of the reformed nobles; but still the hierarchy made a part of the common law of the realm, and might claim both its property and its privileges wherever it had the means of asserting them. The community of Saint Mary's of Kennaquhair was considered as being particularly in this situation. They had retained, undiminished, their territorial power and influence; and the great barons in the neighbourhood, partly from their attachment to the party in the state who still upheld the old system of religion, partly because each grudged the share of the prey which the others must necessarily claim, had as yet abstained from despoiling the Halidome. The Community was also understood to be protected by the powerful Earls of Northumberland and Westmoreland, whose zealous attachment to the Catholic faith caused at a later period the great rebellion of the tenth of Elizabeth.

Thus happily placed, it was supposed by the friends of the decaying cause of the Roman Catholic faith, that some determined example of courage and resolution, exercised where the franchises of the church were yet entire, and her jurisdiction undisputed, might awe the progress of the new opinions into activity; and, protected by the laws which still existed, and by the favour of the sovereign, might be the means of securing the territory which Rome yet preserved in Scotland, and perhaps of recovering that which she had lost.

The matter had been considered more than once by the northern Catholics of Scotland, and they had held communication with those of the south. Father Eustace, devoted by his public and private vows, had caught the flame, and had eagerly advised that they should execute the doom of heresy on the first reformed preacher, or, according to his sense, on the first heretic of eminence, who should venture within the precincts of the Halidome. A heart, naturally kind and noble, was, in this instance, as it has been in many more, deceived by its own generosity. Father Eustace would have been a bad administrator of the inquisitorial power of Spain, where that power was omnipotent, and where judgment was exercised without danger to those who inflicted it. In such a situation his rigour might have relented in favour of the criminal, whom it was at his pleasure to crush or to place at freedom. But in Scotland, during this crisis, the case was entirely different. The question was, whether one of the spirituality dared, at the hazard of his own life, to step forward to assert and exercise the rights of the church. Was there any who would venture to wield the thunder in her cause, or must it remain like that in the hand of a painted Jupiter, the object of derision instead of terror? The crisis was calculated to awake the soul of Eustace; for it comprised the question, whether he dared, at all hazards to himself, to execute with stoical severity a measure which, according to the general opinion, was to be advantageous to the church, and, according to ancient law, and to his firm belief, was not only justifiable but meritorious.

While such resolutions were agitated amongst the Catholics, chance placed a victim within their grasp. Henry Warden had, with the animation proper to the enthusiastic reformers of the age, transgressed, in the vehemence of his zeal, the bounds of the discretional liberty allowed to his sect so far, that it was thought the Queen's personal dignity was concerned in bringing him to justice. He fled from Edinburgh, with recommendations, however, from Lord James Stewart, afterwards the celebrated Earl of Murray, to some of the Border chieftains of inferior rank, who were privately conjured to procure him safe passage into England. One of the principal persons to whom such recommendation was addressed, was Julian Avenel; for as yet, and for a considerable time afterwards, the correspondence and interest of Lord James lay rather with the subordinate leaders than with the chiefs of great power, and men of distinguished influence upon the Border. Julian Avenel had intrigued without scruple with both parties—yet bad as he was, he certainly would not have practised aught against the guest whom Lord James had recommended to his hospitality, had it not been for what he termed the preacher's officious intermeddling in his family affairs. But when he had determined to make Warden rue the lecture he had read him, and the scene of public scandal which he had caused in his hall, Julian resolved, with the constitutional shrewdness of his disposition, to combine his vengeance with his interest. And therefore, instead of doing violence on the person of Henry Warden within his own castle, he determined to deliver him up to the Community of Saint Mary's, and at once make them the instruments of his own revenge, and found a claim of personal recompense, either in money, or in a grant of Abbey lands at a low quit-rent, which last began now to be the established form in which the temporal nobles plundered the spirituality.

The Sub-Prior, therefore, of Saint Mary's, unexpectedly saw the steadfast, active, and inflexible enemy of the church delivered into his hand, and felt himself called upon to make good his promises to the friends of the Catholic faith, by quenching heresy in the blood of one of its most zealous professors.

To the honour more of Father Eustace's heart than of his consistency, the communication that Henry Warden was placed within his power, struck him with more sorrow than triumph; but his next feelings were those of exultation. "It is sad," he said to himself, "to cause human suffering; it is awful to cause human blood to be spilled; but the judge to whom the sword of Saint Paul, as well as the keys of Saint Peter, are confided, must not flinch from his task. Our weapon returns into our own bosom, if not wielded with a steady and unrelenting hand against the irreconcilable enemies of the Holy Church. *Pereat iste!* It is the doom he has incurred, and were all the heretics in Scotland armed and at his back, they should not prevent its being pronounced, and, if possible, enforced.—Bring the heretic before me," he said, issuing his commands aloud, and in a tone of authority.

Henry Warden was led in, his hands still bound, but his feet at liberty.

"Clear the apartment," said the Sub-Prior, "of all but the necessary guard on the prisoner."

All retired except Christie of the Clinthill, who, having dismissed the inferior troopers whom he commanded, unsheathed his sword, and placed himself beside the door, as if taking upon him the character of sentinel.

The judge and the accused met face to face, and in that of both was enthroned the noble confidence of rectitude. The monk was about, at the utmost risk to himself and his community, to exercise what in his ignorance he conceived to be his duty. The preacher, actuated by a better-informed, yet not a more ardent zeal, was prompt to submit to execution for God's sake, and to seal, were it necessary, his mission with his blood. Placed at such a distance of time as better enables us to appreciate the tendency of the principles on which they severally acted, we cannot doubt to which the palm ought to be awarded. But the zeal of Father Eustace was as free from passion and personal views as if it had been exerted in a better cause.

They approached each other, armed each and prepared for intellectual conflict, and each intently regarding his opponent, as if either hoped to spy out some defect, some chasm in the armour of his antagonist.—As they gazed on each other, old recollections began to awake in either bosom, at the sight of features long unseen and much altered, but not forgotten. The brow of the Sub-Prior dismissed by degrees its frown of command, the look of calm yet stern defiance gradually vanished from that of Warden, and both lost for an instant that of gloomy solemnity. They had been ancient and intimate friends in youth at a foreign university, but had been long separated from each other; and the change of name, which the preacher had adopted from motives of safety, and the monk from the common custom of the convent, had prevented the possibility of their hitherto recognizing each other in the opposite parts which they had been playing in the great polemical and political drama. But now the Sub-Prior exclaimed, "Henry Wellwood!" and the preacher replied, "William Allan!" —and, stirred by the old familiar names, and never-to-be-forgotten recollections of college studies and college intimacy, their hands were for a moment locked in each other.

"Remove his bonds," said the Sub-Prior, and assisted Christie in performing that office with his own hands, although the prisoner scarcely would consent to be unbound, repeating with emphasis, that he rejoiced in the cause for which he suffered shame. When his hands were at liberty, however, he showed his sense of the kindness by again exchanging a grasp and a look of affection with the Sub-Prior.

The salute was frank and generous on either side, yet it was but the friendly recognition and greeting which are wont to take place betwixt adverse champions, who do nothing in hate but all in honour. As each felt the pressure of the situation in which they stood, he quitted the grasp of the other's hand, and fell back, confronting each other with looks more calm and sorrowful than expressive of any other passion. The Sub-Prior was the first to speak.

"And is this, then, the end of that restless activity of mind, that bold and indefatigable love of truth that urged investigation to its utmost limits, and seemed to take heaven itself by storm — is this the termination of Wellwood's career? — And having known and loved him during the best years of our youth, do we meet in our old age as judge and criminal?"

"Not as judge and criminal," said Henry Warden, — for to avoid confusion we describe him by his later and best known name — "Not as judge and criminal do we meet, but as a misguided oppressor and his ready and devoted victim. I, too, may ask, are these the harvest of the rich hopes excited by the classical learning, acute logical powers, and varied knowledge of William Allan, that he should sink to be the solitary drone of a cell, graced only above the swarm with the high commission of executing Roman malice on all who oppose Roman imposture?"

"Not to thee," answered the Sub-Prior, "be assured—not unto thee, nor unto mortal man, will I render an account of the power with which the church may have invested me. It was granted but as a deposit for her welfare — for her welfare it shall at every risk be exercised, without fear and without favour."

"I expected no less from your misguided zeal," answered the preacher; "and in me have you met one on whom you may fearlessly exercise your authority, secure that his mind at least will defy your influence, as the snows of that Mont Blanc which we saw together, shrink not under the heat of the hottest summer sun."

"I do believe thee," said the Sub-Prior, "I do believe that thine is indeed metal unmalleable by force. Let it yield then to persuasion. Let us debate these matters of faith, as we once were wont to conduct our scholastic disputes, when hours, nay, days, glided past in the mutual exercise of our intellectual powers. It may be thou mayest yet hear the voice of the shepherd, and return to the universal fold."

"No, Allan," replied the prisoner, "this is no vain question, devised by dreaming scholiasts, on which they may whet their intellectual faculties until the very metal be wasted away. The errors which I combat are like those fiends which are only cast out by fasting and prayer. Alas! not many wise, not many learned are chosen; the cottage and the hamlet shall in our days bear witness against the schools and their disciples. Thy very wisdom, which is foolishness, hath made thee, as the Greeks of old, hold as foolishness that which is the only true wisdom."

"This," said the Sub-Prior, sternly, "is the mere cant of ignorant enthusiasm, which appealeth from learning and from authority, from the sure guidance of that lamp which God hath afforded us in the Councils and in the Fathers of the Church, to a rash, self-willed, and arbitrary interpretation of the Scriptures, wrested according to the private opinion of each speculating heretic."

"I disdain to reply to the charge," replied Warden. "The question at issue between your Church and mine, is, whether we will be judged by the

Holy Scriptures, or by the devices and decisions of men not less subject to error than ourselves, and who have defaced our holy religion with vain devices, reared up idols of stone and wood, in form of those, who, when they lived, were but sinful creatures, to share the worship due only to the Creator —established a toll-house betwixt heaven and hell, that profitable purgatory of which the Pope keeps the keys, like an iniquitous judge commutes punishment for bribes, and ——"

"Silence, blasphemer," said the Sub-Prior, sternly, "or I will have thy blatant obloquy stopped with a gag!"

"Ay," replied Warden, "such is the freedom of the Christian conference to which Rome's priests so kindly invite us! — the gag — the rack — the axe — is the *ratio ultima Romæ*. But know thou, mine ancient friend, that the character of thy former companion is not so changed by age, but that he still dares to endure for the cause of truth all that thy proud hierarchy shall dare to inflict."

"Of that," said the monk, "I nothing doubt — Thou wert ever a lion to turn against the spear of the hunter, not a stag to be dismayed at the sound of his bugle."—He walked through the room in silence. "Wellwood," he said at length, "we can no longer be friends. Our faith, our hope, our anchor on futurity, is no longer the same."

"Deep is my sorrow that thou speakest truth. May God so judge me," said the Reformer, "as I would buy the conversion of a soul like thine with my dearest heart's blood."

"To thee, and with better reason, do I return the wish," replied the Sub-Prior; "it is such an arm as thine that should defend the bulwarks of the Church, and it is now directing the battering-ram against them, and rendering practicable the breach through which all that is greedy, and all that is base, and all that is mutable and hot-headed in this innovating age, already hope to advance to destruction and to spoil. But since such is our fate, that we can no longer fight side by side as friends, let us at least act as generous enemies. You cannot have forgotten,

'O gran bonta dei cavalieri antiqui!
Erano nemici, eran' de fede diversa'—

Although, perhaps," he added, stopping short in his quotation, "your new faith forbids you to reserve a place in your memory, even for what high poets have recorded of loyal faith and generous sentiment."

"The faith of Buchanan," replied the preacher, "the faith of Buchanan and of Beza, cannot be unfriendly to literature. But the poet you have quoted affords strains fitter for a dissolute court than for a convent."

"I might retort on your Theodore Beza," said the Sub-Prior, smiling; "but I hate the judgment that, like the flesh-fly, skims over whatever is sound, to detect and settle upon some spot which is tainted. But to the purpose. If I conduct thee or send thee a prisoner to St. Mary's, thou art to-night a tenant of the dungeon, to-morrow a burden to the gibbet-tree. If I were to let thee go hence at large, I were thereby wronging the Holy Church, and breaking mine own solemn vow. Other resolutions may be adopted in the capital, or better times may speedily ensue. Wilt thou remain a true prisoner upon thy parole, rescue or no rescue, as is the phrase amongst the warriors of this country? Wilt thou solemnly promise that thou wilt do so, and at my summons thou wilt present thyself before the Abbot and Chapter at Saint Mary's, and that thou wilt not stir from this house above a quarter of a mile in any direction? Wilt thou, I say, engage me thy word for this? and such is the sure trust which I repose in thy good faith, that thou shalt remain here unharmed and unsecured, a prisoner at large, subject only to appear before our court when called upon."

The preacher paused — "I am unwilling," he said, "to fetter my native liberty by any self-adopted engagement. But I am already in your power, and you may bind me to my answer. By such promise, to abide within a certain limit, and to appear when called upon, I renounce not any liberty which I at present possess, and am free to exercise; but, on the contrary, being in bonds, and at your mercy, I acquire thereby a liberty which I at present possess not. I will therefore accept of thy proffer, as what is courteously offered on thy part, and may be honourably accepted on mine."

"Stay yet," said the Sub-Prior; "one important part of thy engagement is forgotten—thou art farther to promise, that while thus left at liberty, thou wilt not preach or teach, directly or indirectly, any of those pestilent heresies by which so many souls have been in this our day won over from the kingdom of light to the kingdom of darkness."

"There we break off our treaty," said Warden, firmly—"Wo unto me if I preach not the Gospel!"

The Sub-Prior's countenance became clouded, and he again paced the apartment, and muttered, "A plague upon the self-willed fool!" then stopped short in his walk, and proceeded in his argument.—"Why, by thine own reasoning, Henry, thy refusal here is but peevish obstinacy. It is in my power to place you where your preaching can reach no human ear; in promising therefore to abstain from it, you grant nothing which you have it in your power to refuse."

"I know not that," replied Henry Warden; "thou mayest indeed cast me into a dungeon, but can I foretell that my Master hath not task-work for me to perform even in that dreary mansion? The chains of saints have, ere now, been the means of breaking the bonds of Satan. In a prison, holy Paul found the jailor whom he brought to believe the word of salvation, he and all his house."

"Nay," said the Sub-Prior, in a tone betwixt anger and scorn, "if you match yourself with the blessed Apostle, it were time we had done—prepare to endure what thy folly, as well as thy heresy, deserves.—Bind him, soldier."

With proud submission to his fate, and regarding the Sub-Prior with something which almost amounted to a smile of superiority, the preacher placed his arms so that the bonds could be again fastened round him.

"Spare me not," he said to Christie; for even that ruffian hesitated to draw the cord straitly.

The Sub-Prior, meanwhile, looked at him from under his cowl, which he had drawn over his head, and partly over his face, as if he wished to shade his own emotions. They were those of a huntsman within point-blank shot of a noble stag, who is yet too much struck with his majesty of front and of antler to take aim at him. They were those of a fowler, who, levelling his gun at a magnificent eagle, is yet reluctant to use his advantage when he sees the noble sovereign of the birds pruning himself in proud defiance of whatever may be attempted against him. The heart of the Sub-Prior (bigoted as he was) relented, and he doubted if he ought to purchase, by a rigorous discharge of what he deemed his duty, the remorse he might afterwards feel for the death of one so nobly independent in thought and character, the friend, besides, of his own happiest years, during which they had, side by side, striven in the noble race of knowledge, and indulged their intervals of repose in the lighter studies of classical and general letters.

The Sub-Prior's hand pressed his half-o'ershadowed cheek, and his eye, more completely obscured, was bent on the ground, as if to hide the workings of his relenting nature.

"Were but Edward safe from the infection," he thought to himself—"Edward, whose eager and enthusiastic mind presses forward in the chase of all that hath even the shadow of knowledge, I might trust this enthusiast with the women, after due caution to them that they cannot, without guilt, attend to his reveries."

As the Sub-Prior revolved these thoughts, and delayed the definitive order which was to determine the fate of the prisoner, a sudden noise at the entrance of the tower diverted his attention for an instant, and, his cheek and brow inflamed with all the glow of heat and determination, Edward Glendinning rushed into the room.

Chapter the Thirty-Second.

Then in my gown of sober gray
  Along the mountain path I'll wander,
And wind my solitary way
  To the sad shrine that courts me yonder.

There, in the calm monastic shade,
  All injuries may be forgiven;
And there for thee, obdurate maid,
  My orisons shall rise to heaven.

THE CRUEL LADY OF THE MOUNTAINS.

THE first words which Edward uttered were,—"My brother is safe, reverend father—he is safe, thank God, and lives!—There is not in Corri-nan-shian a grave, nor a vestige of a grave. The turf around the fountain has neither been disturbed by pick-axe, spade, nor mattock, since the deer's-hair first sprang there. He lives as surely as I live!"

The earnestness of the youth—the vivacity with which he looked and moved—the springy step, outstretched hand, and ardent eye, reminded Henry Warden of Halbert, so lately his guide. The brothers had indeed a strong family resemblance, though Halbert was far more athletic and active in his person, taller and better knit in the limbs, and though Edward had, on ordinary occasions, a look of more habitual acuteness and more profound reflection. The preacher was interested as well as the Sub-Prior.

"Of whom do you speak, my son?" he said, in a tone as unconcerned as if his own fate had not been at the same instant trembling in the balance, and as if a dungeon and death did not appear to be his instant doom—"Of whom, I say, speak you? If of a youth somewhat older than you seem to be—brown-haired, open-featured, taller and stronger than you appear, yet having much of the same air and of the same tone of voice—if such a one is the brother whom you seek, it may be I can tell you news of him."

"Speak, then, for Heaven's sake," said Edward—"life or death lies on thy tongue!"

The Sub-Prior joined eagerly in the same request, and, without waiting to be urged, the preacher gave so minute an account of the circumstances under which he met the elder Glendinning, with so exact a description of his person, that there remained no doubt as to his identity. When he mentioned that Halbert Glendinning had conducted him to a dell in which they found the grass bloody, and a grave newly closed, and told how the youth accused himself of the slaughter of Sir Piercie Shafton, the Sub-Prior looked on Edward with astonishment.

"Didst thou not say, even now," he said, "that there was no vestige of a grave in that spot?"

"No more vestige of the earth having been removed than if the turf had grown there since the days of Adam," replied Edward Glendinning. "It is true," he added, "that the adjacent grass was trampled and bloody."

"These are delusions of the Enemy," said the Sub-Prior, crossing himself.—"Christian men may no longer doubt of it."

"But an it be so," said Warden, "Christian men might better guard themselves by the sword of prayer than by the idle form of a cabalistical spell."

"The badge of our salvation," said the Sub-Prior, "cannot be so term d—the sign of the cross disarmeth all evil spirits."

"Ay," answered Henry Warden, apt and armed for controversy, "but it should be borne in the heart, not scored with the fingers in the air. That very impassive air, through which your hand passes, shall as soon bear the imprint of your action, as the external action shall avail the fond bigot who substitutes vain motions of the body, idle genuflections, and signs of the cross, for the living and heart-born duties of faith and good works."

"I pity thee," said the Sub-Prior, as actively ready for polemics as himself,—"I pity thee, Henry, and reply not to thee. Thou mayest as well winnow forth and measure the ocean with a sieve, as mete out the power of holy words, deeds, and signs, by the erring gauge of thine own reason."

"Not by mine own reason would I mete them," said Warden; "but by His holy Word, that unfading and unerring lamp of our paths, compared to which human reason is but as a glimmering and fading taper, and your boasted tradition only a misleading wildfire. Show me your Scripture warrant for ascribing virtue to such vain signs and motions!"

"I offered thee a fair field of debate," said the Sub-Prior, "which thou didst refuse. I will not at present resume the controversy."

"Were these my last accents," said the reformer, "and were they uttered at the stake, half-choked with smoke, and as the fagots kindled into a blaze around me, with that last utterance I would testify against the superstitious devices of Rome."

The Sub-Prior suppressed with pain the controversial answer which arose to his lips, and, turning to Edward Glendinning, he said, "there could be now no doubt that his mother ought presently to be informed that her son lived."

"I told you that two hours since," said Christie of the Clinthill, "an you would have believed me. But it seems you are more willing to take the word of an old gray sorner, whose life has been spent in pattering heresy, than mine, though I never rode a foray in my life without duly saying my paternoster."

"Go then," said Father Eustace to Edward; "let thy sorrowing mother know that her son is restored to her from the grave, like the child of the widow of Zarephath; at the intercession," he added, looking at Henry Warden, "of the blessed Saint whom I invoked in his behalf."

"Deceived thyself," said Warden, instantly, "thou art a deceiver of others. It was no dead man, no creature of clay, whom the bless d Tishbite invoked, when, stung by the reproach of the Shunamite woman, he prayed that her son's soul might come into him again."

"It was by his intercession, however," repeated the Sub-Prior; "for what says the Vulgate? Thus it is written: '*Et exaudivit Dominus vocem Helie; et reversa est anima pueri intra eum, et revixit;*'—and thinkest thou the intercession of a glorified saint is more feeble than when he walks on earth, shrouded in a tabernacle of clay, and seeing but with the eye of flesh?"

During this controversy Edward Glendinning appeared restless and impatient, agitated by some internal feeling, but whether of joy, grief, or expectation, his countenance did not expressly declare. He took now the unusual freedom to break in upon the discourse of the Sub-Prior, who, notwithstanding his resolution to the contrary, was obviously kindling in the spirit of controversy, which Edward diverted by conjuring his reverence to allow him to speak a few words with him in private.

"Remove the prisoner," said the Sub-Prior to Christie; "look to him carefully that he escape not; but for thy life do him no injury."

His commands being obeyed, Edward and the monk were left alone, when the Sub-Prior thus addressed him:

"What hath come over thee, Edward, that thy eye kindles so wildly, and thy cheek is thus changing from scarlet to pale? Why didst thou break in so hastily and unadvisedly upon the argument with which I was prostrating yonder heretic? And wherefore dost thou not tell thy mother that her son is restored to her by the intercession, as Holy Church well warrants us to believe, of Blessed Saint Benedict, the patron of our Order? For if ever my prayers were put forth to him with zeal, it hath been in behalf of this house, and thine eyes have seen the result — go tell it to thy mother."

"I must tell her then," said Edward, "that if she has regained one son, another is lost to her."

"What meanest thou, Edward? what language is this?" said the Sub Prior.

"Father," said the youth, kneeling down to him, "my sin and my shame shall be told thee, and thou shalt witness my penance with thine own eyes."

"I comprehend thee not," said the Sub-Prior. "What canst thou have done to deserve such self-accusation? — Hast thou too listened," he added, knitting his brows, "to the demon of heresy, ever most effectual tempter of those, who, like yonder unhappy man, are distinguished by their love of knowledge?"

"I am guiltless in that matter," answered Glendinning, "nor have presumed to think otherwise than thou, my kind father, hast taught me, and than the Church allows."

"And what is it then, my son," said the Sub-Prior, kindly, "which thus afflicts thy conscience? speak it to me, that I may answer thee in the words of comfort; for the Church's mercy is great to those obedient children who doubt not her power."

"My confession will require her mercy," replied Edward. "My brother Halbert—so kind, so brave, so gentle, who spoke not, thought not, acted not, but in love to me, whose hand had aided me in every difficulty, whose eye watched over me like the eagle's over her nestlings, when they prove their first flight from the eyry — this brother, so kind, so gently affectionate — I heard of his sudden, his bloody, his violent death, and I rejoiced — I heard of his unexpected restoration, and I sorrowed!"

"Edward," said the father, "thou art beside thyself — what could urge thee to such odious ingratitude? — In your hurry of spirits you have mistaken the confused tenor of your feelings — Go, my son, pray and compose thy mind — we will speak of this another time."

"No, father, no," said Edward, vehemently, "now or never! — I will find the means to tame this rebellious heart of mine, or I will tear it out of my bosom — Mistake its passions? —No, father, grief can ill be mistaken for joy — All wept, all shrieked around me — my mother — the menials — she too, the cause of my crime — all wept — and I — I could hardly disguise my brutal and insane joy under the appearance of revenge — Brother, I said, I cannot give thee tears, but I will give thee blood — Yes, father, as I counted hour after hour, while I kept watch upon the English prisoner, and said, I am an hour nearer to hope and to happiness——"

"I understand thee not, Edward," said the monk, "nor can I conceive in what way thy brother's supposed murder should have affected thee with such unnatural joy — Surely the sordid desire to succeed him in his small possessions——"

"Perish the paltry trash!" said Edward, with the same emotion. "No, father, it was rivalry—it was jealous rage—it was the love of Mary Avenel, that rendered me the unnatural wretch I confess myself!"

"Of Mary Avenel!" said the Priest—"of a lady so high above either of you in name and in rank? How dared Halbert — how dared you, to presume to lift your eye to her but in honour and respect, as a superior of another degree from yours?"

"When did love wait for the sanction of heraldry?" replied Edward; "and in what but a line of dead ancestors was Mary, our mother's guest and foster-child, different from us, with whom she was brought up?—Enough, we loved — we both loved her! But the passion of Halbert was requited. He knew it not, he saw it not—but I was sharper-eyed. I saw that even when I was more approved, Halbert was more beloved. With me she would sit for hours at our common task with the cold simplicity and indifference of a sister, but with Halbert she trusted not herself. She changed colour, she was fluttered when he approached her; and when he left her, she was sad, pensive, and solitary. I bore all this—I saw my rival's advancing progress in her affections—I bore it, father, and yet I hated him not—I could not hate him!"

"And well for thee that thou didst not," said the father; "wild and head-strong as thou art, wouldst thou hate thy brother for partaking in thine own folly?"

"Father," replied Edward, "the world esteems thee wise, and holds thy knowledge of mankind high; but thy question shows that thou hast never loved. It was by an effort that I saved myself from hating my kind and affectionate brother, who, all unsuspicious of my rivalry, was perpetually loading me with kindness. Nay, there were moods of my mind, in which I could return that kindness for a time with energetic enthusiasm. Never did I feel this so strongly as on the night which parted us. But I could not help rejoicing when he was swept from my path—could not help sorrowing when he was again restored to be a stumbling-block in my paths."

"May God be gracious to thee, my son!" said the monk; "this is an awful state of mind. Even in such evil mood did the first murderer rise up against his brother, because Abel's was the more acceptable sacrifice."

"I will wrestle with the demon which has haunted me, father," replied the youth, firmly—"I will wrestle with him, and I will subdue him. But first I must remove from the scenes which are to follow here. I cannot endure that I should see Mary Avenel's eyes again flash with joy at the restoration of her lover. It were a sight to make indeed a second Cain of me! My fierce, turbid, and transitory joy discharged itself in a thirst to commit homicide, and how can I estimate the frenzy of my despair?"

"Madman!" said the Sub-Prior, "at what dreadful crime does thy fury drive?"

"My lot is determined, father," said Edward, in a resolute tone; "I will embrace the spiritual state which you have so oft recommended. It is my purpose to return with you to Saint Mary's, and, with the permission of the Holy Virgin and of Saint Benedict, to offer my profession to the Abbot."

"Not now, my son," said the Sub-Prior, "not in this distemperature of mind. The wise and good accept not gifts which are made in heat of blood, and which may be after repented of; and shall we make our offerings to wisdom and to goodness itself with less of solemn resolution and deep devotion of mind, than is necessary to make them acceptable to our own frail companions in this valley of darkness? This I say to thee, my son, not as meaning to deter thee from the good path thou art now inclined to prefer, but that thou mayst make thy vocation and thine election sure."

"There are actions, father," returned Edward, "which brook no delay, and this is one. It must be done this very *now;* or it may never be done. Let me go with you; let me not behold the return of Halbert into this house. Shame, and the sense of the injustice I have already done him, will join with these dreadful passions which urge me to do him yet farther wrong. Let me then go with you."

"With me, my son," said the Sub-Prior, "thou shalt surely go; but our rule, as well as reason and good order, require that you should dwell a space with us as a probationer, or novice, before taking upon thee those final vows, which, sequestering thee for ever from the world, dedicate thee to the service of Heaven."

"And when shall we set forth, father?" said the youth, as eagerly as if the journey which he was now undertaking led to the pleasures of a summer holiday.

"Even now, if thou wilt," said the Sub-Prior, yielding to his impetuosity—"go, then, and command them to prepare for our departure.—Yet stay," he said, as Edward, with all the awakened enthusiasm of his character, hastened from his presence, "come hither, my son, and kneel down."

Edward obeyed, and kneeled down before him. Notwithstanding his slight figure and thin features, the Sub-Prior could, from the energy of his tone, and the earnestness of his devotional manner, impress his pupils and his penitents with no ordinary feelings of personal reverence. His heart always was, as well as seemed to be, in the duty which he was immediately performing; and the spiritual guide who thus shows a deep conviction of the importance of his office, seldom fails to impress a similar feeling upon his hearers. Upon such occasions as the present, his puny body seemed to assume more majestic stature—his spare and emaciated countenance bore a bolder, loftier, and more commanding port — his voice, always beautiful, trembled as labouring under the immediate impulse of the Divinity — and his whole demeanour seemed to bespeak, not the mere ordinary man, but the organ of the Church in which she had vested her high power for delivering sinners from their load of iniquity.

"Hast thou, my fair son," said he, "faithfully recounted the circumstances which have thus suddenly determined thee to a religious life?"

"The sins I have confessed, my father," answered Edward, "but I have not yet told of a strange appearance, which, acting in my mind, hath, I think, aided to determine my resolution."

"Tell it, then, now," returned the Sub-Prior; "it is thy duty to leave me uninstructed in nought, so that thereby I may understand the temptation that besets thee."

"I tell it with unwillingness," said Edward; "for although, God wot, I speak but the mere truth, yet even while my tongue speaks it as truth, my own ears receive it as fable."

"Yet say the whole," said Father Eustace; "neither fear rebuke from me, seeing I may know reasons for receiving as true that which others might regard as fabulous."

"Know, then, father," replied Edward, "that betwixt hope and despair — and, heavens! what a hope! — the hope to find the corpse mangled and crushed hastily in amongst the bloody clay which the foot of the scornful victor had trod down upon my good, my gentle, my courageous brother,— I sped to the glen called Corri-nan-shian; but, as your reverence has been already informed, neither the grave, which my unhallowed wishes had in spite of my better self longed to see, nor any appearance of the earth having been opened, was visible in the solitary spot where Martin had, at morning yesterday, seen the fatal hillock. You know your dalesmen, father. The place hath an evil name, and this deception of the sight inclined them to leave it. My companions became affrighted, and hastened down the glen as men caught in trespass. My hopes were too much blighted, my mind too much agitated, to fear either the living or the dead. I descended the glen more slowly than they, often looking back, and not ill pleased with the poltroonery of my companions, which left me to my own perplexed and moody humour, and induced them to hasten into the broader dale. They were already out of sight, and lost amongst the windings of the glen, when, looking back, I saw a female form standing beside the fountain——"

"How, my fair son?" said the Sub-Prior, "beware you jest not with your present situation!"

"I jest not, father," answered the youth; "it may be I shall never jest again—surely not for many a day. I saw, I say, the form of a female clad in white, such as the Spirit which haunts the house of Avenel is supposed to be. Believe me, my father, for, by heaven and earth, I say nought but what I saw with these eyes!"

"I believe thee, my son," said the monk; "proceed in thy strange story."

"The apparition," said Edward Glendinning, "sung, and thus ran her lay; for, strange as it may seem to you, her words abide by my remembrance as if they had been sung to me from infancy upward:—

'Thou who seek'st my fountain lone,
With thoughts and hopes thou dar'st not own;
Whose heart within leap'd wildly glad
When most his brow seem'd dark and sad;
Hie thee back, thou find'st not here
Corpse or coffin, grave or bier;
The Dead Alive is gone and fled—
Go thou, and join the Living Dead!

'The Living Dead, whose sober brow
Oft shrouds such thoughts as thou hast now,
Whose hearts within are seldom cured
Of passions by their vows abjured;
Where, under sad and solemn show,
Vain hopes are nursed, wild wishes glow.
Seek the convent's vaulted room,
Prayer and vigil be thy doom;
Doff the green, and don the gray,
To the cloister hence away!'"

"'Tis a wild lay," said the Sub-Prior, "and chanted, I fear me, with no good end. But we have power to turn the machinations of Satan to his shame. Edward, thou shalt go with me as thou desirest; thou shalt prove the life for which I have long thought thee best fitted—thou shalt aid, my son, this trembling hand of mine to sustain the Holy Ark, which bold unhallowed men press rashly forward to touch and to profane.—Wilt thou not first see thy mother?"

"I will see no one," said Edward, hastily; "I will risk nothing that may shake the purpose of my heart. From Saint Mary's they shall learn my destination—all of them shall learn it. My mother—Mary Avenel—my restored and happy brother—they shall all know that Edward lives no longer to the world to be a clog on their happiness. Mary shall no longer need to constrain her looks and expressions to coldness because I am nigh. She shall no longer——"

"My son," said the Sub-Prior, interrupting him, "it is not by looking back on the vanities and vexations of this world, that we fit ourselves for the discharge of duties which are not of it. Go, get our horses ready, and, as we descend the glen together, I will teach thee the truths through which the fathers and wise men of old had that precious alchemy, which can convert suffering into happiness."

Chapter the Thirty-Third.

Now, on my faith, this gear is all entangled,
Like to the yarn-clew of the drowsy knitter,
Dragg'd by the frolic kitten through the cabin,
While the good dame sits nodding o'er the fire!
Masters, attend; 'twill crave some skill to clear it.

OLD PLAY.

Edward, with the speed of one who doubts the steadiness of his own resolution, hastened to prepare the horses for their departure, and at the same time thanked and dismissed the neighbours who had come to his assistance, and who were not a little surprised both at the suddenness of his proposed departure, and at the turn affairs had taken.

"Here's cold hospitality," quoth Dan of the Howlet-hirst to his comrades; "I trow the Glendinnings may die and come alive right oft, ere I put foot in stirrup again for the matter."

Martin soothed them by placing food and liquor before them. They ate sullenly, however, and departed in bad humour.

The joyful news that Halbert Glendinning lived, was quickly communicated through the sorrowing family. The mother wept and thanked Heaven alternately; until her habits of domestic economy awakening as her feelings became calmer, she observed, "It would be an unco task to mend the yetts, and what were they to do while they were broken in that fashion? At open doors dogs come in."

Tibb remarked, "She aye thought Halbert was ower gleg at his weapon to be killed sae easily by ony Sir Piercie of them a'. They might say of these Southrons as they liked; but they had not the pith and wind of a canny Scot, when it came to close grips."

On Mary Avenel the impression was inconceivably deeper. She had but newly learned to pray, and it seemed to her that her prayers had been instantly answered—that the compassion of Heaven, which she had learned to implore in the words of Scripture, had descended upon her after a manner almost miraculous, and recalled the dead from the grave at the sound of her lamentations. There was a dangerous degree of enthusiasm in this strain of feeling, but it originated in the purest devotion.

A silken and embroidered muffler, one of the few articles of more costly attire which she possessed, was devoted to the purpose of wrapping up and concealing the sacred volume, which henceforth she was to regard as her chiefest treasure, lamenting only that, for want of a fitting interpreter, much must remain to her a book closed and a fountain sealed. She was unaware of the yet greater danger she incurred, of putting an imperfect or even false sense upon some of the doctrines which appeared most comprehensible. But Heaven had provided against both these hazards.

While Edward was preparing the horses, Christie of the Clinthill again solicited his orders respecting the reformed preacher, Henry Warden, and again the worthy monk laboured to reconcile in his own mind the compassion and esteem which, almost in spite of him, he could not help feeling for his former companion, with the duty which he owed to the Church. The unexpected resolution of Edward had removed, he thought, the chief objection to his being left at Glendearg.

"If I carry this Well-wood, or Warden, to the Monastery," he thought, "he must die—die in his heresy—perish body and soul. And though such a measure was once thought advisable, to strike terror into the heretics, yet such is now their daily increasing strength, that it may rather rouse them to fury and to revenge. True, he refuses to pledge himself to abstain from sowing his tares among the wheat; but the ground here is too barren to receive them. I fear not his making impression on these poor women, the vassals of the Church, and bred up in due obedience to her behests. The keen, searching, inquiring, and bold disposition of Edward, might have afforded fuel to the fire; but that is removed, and there is nothing left which the flame may catch to.—Thus shall he have no power to spread his evil doctrines abroad, and yet his life shall be preserved, and it may be his soul rescued as a prey from the fowler's net. I will myself contend with him in argument; for when we studied in common, I yielded not to him, and surely the cause for which I struggle will support me, were I yet more weak than I deem myself. Were this man reclaimed from his errors, an hundred-fold more advantage would arise to the Church from his spiritual regeneration, than from his temporal death."

Having finished these meditations, in which there was at once goodness of disposition and narrowness of principle, a considerable portion of self-opinion, and no small degree of self-delusion, the Sub-Prior commanded the prisoner to be brought into his presence.

"Henry," he said, "whatever a rigid sense of duty may demand of me, ancient friendship and Christian compassion forbid me to lead thee to assured death. Thou wert wont to be generous, though stern and stubborn in thy resolves; let not thy sense of what thine own thoughts term duty, draw thee farther than mine have done. Remember, that every sheep whom thou shalt here lead astray from the fold, will be demanded in time and through eternity of him who hath left thee the liberty of doing such evil. I ask no engagement of thee, save that thou remain a prisoner on thy word at this tower, and wilt appear when summoned."

"Thou hast found an invention to bind my hands," replied the preacher, "more sure than would have been the heaviest shackles in the prison of thy convent. I will not rashly do what may endanger thee with thy unhappy superiors, and I will be the more cautious, because, if we had farther opportunity of conference, I trust thine own soul may yet be rescued as a brand from the burning, and that, casting from thee the livery of Anti-Christ, that trader in human sins and human souls, I may yet assist thee to lay hold on the Rock of Ages."

The Sub-Prior heard the sentiment, so similar to that which had occurred to himself, with the same kindly feelings with which the game-cock hears and replies to the challenge of his rival.

"I bless God and Our Lady," said he, drawing himself up, "that my faith is already anchored on that Rock on which Saint Peter founded his Church."

"It is a perversion of the text," said the eager Henry Warden, "grounded on a vain play upon words—a most idle paronomasia."

The controversy would have been rekindled, and in all probability — for what can insure the good temper and moderation of polemics?—might have ended in the preacher's being transported a captive to the Monastery, had not Christie of the Clinthill observed that it was growing late, and that he, having to descend the glen, which had no good reputation, cared not greatly for travelling there after sunset. The Sub-Prior, therefore, stifled his desire of argument, and again telling the preacher, that he trusted to his gratitude and generosity, he bade him farewell.

"Be assured, my old friend," replied Warden, "that no willing act of mine shall be to thy prejudice. But if my Master shall place work before me, I must obey God rather than man."

These two men, both excellent from natural disposition and acquired knowledge, had more points of similarity than they themselves would have admitted. In truth, the chief distinction betwixt them was, that the Catholic, defending a religion which afforded little interest to the feelings, had, in his devotion to the cause he espoused, more of the head than of the heart, and was politic, cautious, and artful; while the Protestant, acting under the strong impulse of more lately-adopted conviction, and feeling, as he justly might, a more animated confidence in his cause, was enthusiastic, eager, and precipitate in his desire to advance it. The priest would have been contented to defend, the preacher aspired to conquer; and, of course, the impulse by which the latter was governed, was more active and more decisive. They could not part from each other without a second pressure of hands, and each looked in the face of his old companion, as he bade him adieu, with a countenance strongly expressive of sorrow, affection, and pity.

Father Eustace then explained briefly to Dame Glendinning, that this person was to be her guest for some days, forbidding her and her whole household, under high spiritual censures, to hold any conversation with him on religious subjects, but commanding her to attend to his wants in all other particulars.

"May Our Lady forgive me, reverend father," said Dame Glendinning, somewhat dismayed at this intelligence, "but I must needs say, that ower mony guests have been the ruin of mony a house, and I trow they will bring down Glendearg. First came the Lady of Avenel — (her soul be at rest — she meant nae ill) — but she brought with her as mony bogles and fairies, as hae kept the house in care ever since, sae that we have been living as it were in a dream. And then came that English knight, if it please you, and if he hasna killed my son outright, he has chased him aff the gate, and it may be lang eneugh ere I see him again—forby the damage done to outer door and inner door. And now your reverence has given me the charge of a heretic, who, it is like, may bring the great horned devil himself down upon us all; and they say that it is neither door nor window will serve him, but he will take away the side of the auld tower along with him. Nevertheless, reverend father, your pleasure is doubtless to be done to our power."

"Go to, woman," said the Sub-Prior; "send for workmen from the clachan, and let them charge the expense of their repairs to the Community, and I will give the treasurer warrant to allow them. Moreover, in settling the rental mails, and feu-duties, thou shalt have allowance for the trouble and charges to which thou art now put, and I will cause strict search to be made after thy son."

The dame curtsied deep and low at each favourable expression; and when the Sub-Prior had done speaking, she added her farther hope that the Sub-Prior would hold some communing with her gossip the Miller, concerning the fate of his daughter, and expound to him that the chance had by no means happened through any negligence on her part.

"I sair doubt me, father," she said, "whether Mysie finds her way back to the Mill in a hurry; but it was all her father's own fault that let her run lamping about the country, riding on bare-backed naigs, and never settling to do a turn of wark within doors, unless it were to dress dainties at dinner-time for his ain kyte."

"You remind me, dame, of another matter of urgency," said Father Eustace; "and, God knows, too many of them press on me at this moment. This English knight must be sought out, and explanation given to him of these most strange chances. The giddy girl must also be recovered. If she hath suffered in reputation by this unhappy mistake, I will not hold myself innocent of the disgrace. Yet how to find them out I know not."

"So please you," said Christie of the Clinthill, "I am willing to take the chase, and bring them back by fair means or foul; for though you have always looked as black as night at me, whenever we have forgathered, yet I have not forgotten that had it not been for you, my neck would have kend the weight of my four quarters. If any man can track the tread of them, I will say in the face of both Merse and Teviotdale, and take the Forest to boot, I am that man. But first I have matters to treat of on my master's score, if you will permit me to ride down the glen with you."

"Nay, but my friend," said the Sub-Prior, "thou shouldst remember I have but slender cause to trust thee for a companion through a place so solitary."

"Tush! tush!" said the Jackman, "fear me not; I had the worst too surely to begin that sport again. Besides, have I not said a dozen of times, I owe you a life? and when I owe a man either a good turn or a bad, I never fail to pay it sooner or later. Moreover, beshrew me if I care to go alone down the glen, or even with my troopers, who are, every loon of them, as much devil's bairns as myself; whereas, if your reverence, since that is the word, take beads and psalter, and I come along with jack and spear, you will make the devils take the air, and I will make all human enemies take the earth."

Edward here entered, and told his reverence that his horse was prepared. At this instant his eye caught his mother's, and the resolution which he had so strongly formed was staggered when he recollected the necessity of bidding her farewell. The Sub-Prior saw his embarrassment, and came to his relief.

"Dame," said he, "I forgot to mention that your son Edward goes with me to Saint Mary's, and will not return for two or three days."

"You'll be wishing to help him to recover his brother? May the saints reward your kindness!"

The Sub-Prior returned the benediction which, in this instance, he had not very well deserved, and he and Edward set forth on their route. They were presently followed by Christie, who came up with his followers at such a speedy pace, as intimated sufficiently that his wish to obtain spiritual convoy through the glen, was extremely sincere. He had, however, other matters to stimulate his speed, for he was desirous to communicate to the Sub-Prior a message from his master Julian, connected with the delivery of the prisoner Warden; and having requested the Sub-Prior to ride with him a few yards before Edward, and the troopers of his own party, he thus addressed him, sometimes interrupting his discourse in a manner testifying that his fear of supernatural beings was not altogether lulled to rest by his confidence in the sanctity of his fellow-traveller.

"My master," said the rider, "deemed he had sent you an acceptable gift in that old heretic preacher; but it seems, from the slight care you have taken of him, that you make small account of the boon."

"Nay," said the Sub-Prior, "do not thus judge of it. The Community must account highly of the service, and will reward it to thy master in goodly fashion. But this man and I are old friends, and I trust to bring him back from the paths of perdition."

"Nay," said the moss-trooper, "when I saw you shake hands at the beginning I counted that you would fight it all out in love and honour, and that there would be no extreme dealings betwixt ye—however it is all one to my master—Saint Mary! what call you yon, Sir Monk?"

"The branch of a willow streaming across the path betwixt us and the sky."

"Beshrew me," said Christie, "if it looked not like a man's hand holding a sword.—But touching my master, he, like a prudent man, hath kept himself aloof in these broken times, until he could see with precision what footing he was to stand upon. Right tempting offers he hath had from the Lords of Congregation, whom you call heretics; and at one time he was minded, to be plain with you, to have taken their way—for he was assured that the Lord James* was coming this road at the head of a round body of cavalry. And accordingly Lord James did so far reckon upon him, that he sent this man Warden, or whatsoever be his name, to my master's protection, as an assured friend; and, moreover, with tidings that he himself was marching hitherward at the head of a strong body of horse."

"Now, Our Lady forfend!" said the Sub-Prior.

"Amen!" answered Christie, in some trepidation, "did your reverence see aught?"

"Nothing whatever," replied the monk; "it was thy tale which wrested from me that exclamation."

"And it was some cause," replied he of the Clinthill, "for if Lord James should come hither, your Halidome would smoke for it. But be of good cheer—that expedition is ended before it was begun. The Baron of Avenel had sure news that Lord James has been fain to march westward with his merry-men, to protect Lord Semple against Cassilis and the Kennedies. By my faith, it will cost him a brush; for wot ye what they say of that name,—

'Twixt Wigton and the town of Ayr,
Portpatrick and the cruives of Cree,
No man need think for to bide there,
Unless he court Saint Kennedie.'"

"Then," said the Sub-Prior, "the Lord James's purpose of coming south

* Lord James Stewart, afterwards the Regent Murray.

wards being broken, cost this person, Henry Warden, a cold reception at Avenel Castle."

"It would not have been altogether so rough a one," said the moss-trooper; "for my master was in heavy thought what to do in these unsettled times, and would scarce have hazarded misusing a man sent to him by so terrible a leader as the Lord James. But, to speak the truth, some busy devil tempted the old man to meddle with my master's Christian liberty of hand-fasting with Catherine of Newport. So that broke the wand of peace between them, and now ye may have my master, and all the force he can make, at your devotion, for Lord James never forgave wrong done to him; and if he come by the upper hand, he will have Julian's head if there were never another of the name, as it is like there is not, excepting the bit slip of a lassie yonder. And now I have told you more of my master's affairs than he would thank me for; but you have done me a frank turn once, and I may need one at your hands again."

"Thy frankness," said the Sub-Prior, "shall surely advantage thee; for much it concerns the Church in these broken times to know the purposes and motives of those around us. But what is it that thy master expects from us in reward of good service? for I esteem him one of those who are not willing to work without their hire."

"Nay, that I can tell you flatly; for Lord James had promised him, in case he would be of his faction in these parts, an easy tack of the teind-sheaves of his own Barony of Avenel, together with the lands of Cranberry-moor, which lie intersected with his own. And he will look for no less at your hand."

"But there is old Gilbert of Cranberry-moor," said the Sub-Prior; "what are we to make of him? The heretic Lord James may take on him to dispone upon the goods and lands of the Halidome at his pleasure, because, doubtless, but for the protection of God, and the baronage which yet remain faithful to their creed, he may despoil us of them by force; but while they are the property of the Community, we may not take steadings from ancient and faithful vassals, to gratify the covetousness of those who serve God only from the lucre of gain."

"By the mass," said Christie, "it is well talking, Sir Priest; but when ye consider that Gilbert has but two half-starved cowardly peasants to follow him, and only an auld jaded aver to ride upon, fitter for the plough than for manly service; and that the Baron of Avenel never rides with fewer than ten jackmen at his back, and oftener with fifty, bodin in all that effeirs to war as if they were to do battle for a kingdom, and mounted on nags that nicker at the clash of the sword as if it were the clank of the lid of a corn-chest—I say, when ye have computed all this, ye may guess what course will best serve your Monastery."

"Friend," said the monk, "I would willingly purchase thy master's assistance on his own terms, since times leave us no better means of defence against sacrilegious spoliation of heresy; but to take from a poor man his patrimony——"

"For that matter," said the rider, "his seat would scarce be a soft one, if my master thought that Gilbert's interest stood betwixt him and what he wishes. The Halidome has land enough, and Gilbert may be quartered elsewhere."

"We will consider the possibility of so disposing the matter," said the monk, "and will expect in consequence your master's most active assistance, with all the followers he can make, to join in the defence of the Halidome, against any force by which it may be threatened."

"A man's hand and a mailed glove on that,"* said the jackman. "They

* As some atonement for their laxity of morals on most occasions, the Borderers were severe observers of the faith which they had pledged, even to an enemy. If any person broke his word so plighted, the individual to whom faith had not been observed, used to bring to the next Border-meeting a glove hung on the point of

call us marauders, thieves, and what not; but the side we take we hold by. —And I will be blithe when my Baron comes to a point which side he will take, for the castle is a kind of hell, (Our Lady forgive me for naming such a word in this place!) while he is in his mood, studying how he may best advantage himself. And now, Heaven be praised, we are in the open valley, and I may swear a round oath, should aught happen to provoke it."

"My friend," said the Sub-Prior, "thou hast little merit in abstaining from oaths or blasphemy, if it be only out of fear of evil spirits."

"Nay, I am not quite a Church vassal yet," said the jackman, "and if you link the curb too tight on a young horse, I promise you he will rear — Why, it is much for me to forbear old customs on any account whatever."

The night being fine, they forded the river at the spot where the Sacristan met with his unhappy encounter with the spirit. As soon as they arrived at the gate of the Monastery, the porter in waiting eagerly exclaimed, "Reverend father, the Lord Abbot is most anxious for your presence."

"Let these strangers be carried to the great hall," said the Sub-Prior, "and be treated with the best by the cellarer; reminding them, however, of that modesty and decency of conduct which becometh guests in a house like this."

"But the Lord Abbot demands you instantly, my venerable brother," said Father Philip, arriving in great haste. "I have not seen him more discouraged or desolate of counsel since the field of Pinkie-cleugh was stricken."

"I come, my good brother, I come," said Father Eustace. "I pray thee, good brother, let this youth, Edward Glendinning, be conveyed to the Chamber of the Novices, and placed under their instructor. God hath touched his heart, and he proposeth laying aside the vanities of the world, to become a brother of our holy order; which, if his good parts be matched with fitting docility and humility, he may one day live to adorn."

"My very venerable brother," exclaimed old Father Nicholas, who came hobbling with a third summons to the Sub-Prior, "I pray thee to hasten to our worshipful Lord Abbot. The holy patroness be with us! never saw I Abbot of the House of St. Mary's in such consternation; and yet I remember me well when Father Ingelram had the news of Flodden-field."

"I come, I come, venerable brother," said Father Eustace —And having repeatedly ejaculated "I come!" he at last went to the Abbot in good earnest.

Chapter the Thirty-Fourth.

It is not texts will do it—Church artillery
Are silenced soon by real ordnance,
And canons are but vain opposed to cannon.
Go, coin your crosier, melt your church plate down
Bid the starved soldier banquet in your halls,
And quaff your long-saved hogsheads—Turn them out
Thus primed with your good cheer, to guard your wall,
And they will venture for't.——

OLD PLAY.

THE Abbot received his counsellor with a tremulous eagerness of welcome, which announced to the Sub-Prior an extreme agitation of spirits, and the

a spear, and proclaim to Scots and English the name of the defaulter. This was accounted so great a disgrace to all connected with him, that his own clansmen sometimes destroyed him, to escape the infamy he had brought on them.

Constable, a spy engaged by Sir Ralph Sadler, talks of two Border thieves, whom he used as his guides:— 'That they would not care to steal, and yet that they would not betray any man that trusts in them, for all the gold in Scotland or in France. They are my guides and outlaws. If they would betray me they might get their pardons, and cause me to be hanged; but I have tried them ere this."—*Sadler's Letters during the Northern Insurrection.*

utmost need of good counsel. There was neither mazer-dish nor standing-cup upon the little table, at the elbow of his huge chair of state; his beads alone lay there, and it seemed as if he had been telling them in his extremity of distress. Beside the beads was placed the mitre of the Abbot, of an antique form, and blazing with precious stones, and the rich and highly-embossed crosier rested against the same table.

The Sacristan and old Father Nicholas had followed the Sub-Prior into the Abbot's apartment, perhaps with the hope of learning something of the important matter which seemed to be in hand.—They were not mistaken: for, after having ushered in the Sub-Prior, and being themselves in the act of retiring, the Abbot made them a signal to remain.

"My brethren," he said, "it is well known to you with what painful zeal we have overseen the weighty affairs of this house committed to our unworthy hand—your bread hath been given to you, and your water hath been sure—I have not wasted the revenues of the Convent on vain pleasures, as hunting or hawking, or in change of rich cope or alb, or in feasting idle bards and jesters, saving those who, according to old wont, were received in time of Christmas and Easter. Neither have I enriched either mine own relations nor strange women, at the expense of the Patrimony."

"There hath not been such a Lord Abbot," said Father Nicholas, "to my knowledge, since the days of Abbot Ingelram, who——"

At that portentous word, which always preluded a long story, the Abbot broke in.

"May God have mercy on his soul!—we talk not of him now.—What I would know of ye, my brethren, is, whether I have, in your mind, faithfully discharged the duties of mine office?"

"There has never been subject of complaint," answered the Sub-Prior.

The Sacristan, more diffuse, enumerated the various acts of indulgence and kindness which the mild government of Abbot Boniface had conferred on the brotherhood of Saint Mary's—the *indulgentiæ*—the *gratias*—the *biberes*—the weekly mess of boiled almonds—the enlarged accommodation of the refectory—the better arrangement of the cellarage—the improvement of the revenue of the Monastery—the diminution of the privations of the brethren.

"You might have added, my brother," said the Abbot, listening with melancholy acquiescence to the detail of his own merits, "that I caused to be built that curious screen, which secureth the cloisters from the north-east wind.—But all these things avail nothing—As we read in holy Maccabee, *Capta est civitas per voluntatem Dei.* It hath cost me no little thought, no common toil, to keep these weighty matters in such order as you have seen them—there was both barn and binn to be kept full—Infirmary, dormitory, guest-hall, and refectory, to be looked to—processions to be made, confessions to be heard, strangers to be entertained, *veniæ* to be granted or refused; and I warrant me, when every one of you was asleep in your cell, the Abbot hath lain awake for a full hour by the bell, thinking how these matters might be ordered seemly and suitably."

"May we ask, reverend my lord," said the Sub-Prior, "what additional care has now been thrown upon you, since your discourse seems to point that way?"

"Marry, this it is," said the Abbot. "The talk is not now of *biberes*,*

* The *biberes, caritas*, and boiled almonds, of which Abbot Boniface speaks, were special occasions for enjoying luxuries, afforded to the monks by grants from different sovereigns, or from other benefactors to the convent. There is one of these charters called *De Pitancia Centum Librarum.* By this charter, which is very curious, our Robert Bruce, on the 10th January, and in the twelfth year of his reign, assigns, out of the customs of Berwick, and failing them, out of the customs of Edinburgh or Haddington, the sum of one hundred pounds, at the half-yearly terms of Pentecost and Saint Martin's in winter, to the abbot and community of the monks of Melrose. The precise purpose of this annuity is to furnish to each of the monks of the said monastery, while placed at food in the refectory, an extra mess of rice boiled with milk, or of almonds, or peas, or other pulse of that kind which could be procured in the country. This addition to their commons is to be entitled the King's Mess. And it is declared, that although any monk should, from some honest apology, want appetite or inclination to eat of the king's mess, his share should, nevertheless, be placed on

or of *caritas*, or of boiled almonds, but of an English band coming against us from Hexham, commanded by Sir John Foster; nor is it of the screening us from the east wind, but how to escape Lord James Stewart, who cometh to lay waste and destroy with his heretic soldiers."

"I thought that purpose had been broken by the feud between Semple and the Kennedies," said the Sub-Prior, hastily.

"They have accorded that matter at the expense of the church as usual," said the Abbot; "the Earl of Cassilis is to have the teind-sheaves of his lands, which were given to the house of Crossraguel, and he has stricken hands with Stewart, who is now called Murray.—*Principes convenerunt unum adversus Dominum.*—There are the letters."

The Sub-Prior took the letters, which had come by an express messenger from the Primate of Scotland, who still laboured to uphold the tottering fabric of the system under which he was at length buried, and, stepping towards the lamp, read them with an air of deep and settled attention—the Sacristan and Father Nicholas looked as helplessly at each other, as the denizens of the poultry-yard when the hawk soars over it. The Abbot seemed bowed down with the extremity of sorrowful apprehension, but kept his eye timorously fixed on the Sub-Prior, as if striving to catch some comfort from the expression of his countenance. When at length he beheld that, after a second intent perusal of the letters, he remained still silent and full of thought, he asked him in an anxious tone, "What is to be done?"

---

the table with those of his brethren, and afterwards carried to the gate and given to the poor. "Neither is it our pleasure," continues the bountiful sovereign, "that the dinner, which is or ought to be served up to the said monks according to their ancient rule, should be diminished in quantity, or rendered inferior in quality, on account of this our mess, so furnished as aforesaid." It is, moreover, provided, that the abbot, with the consent of the most sage of his brethren, shall name a prudent and decent monk for receiving, directing, and expending, all matters concerning this annuity for the benefit of the community, agreeably to the royal desire and intention, rendering a faithful account thereof to the abbot and superiors of the same convent. And the same charter declares the king's farther pleasure, that the said men of religion should be bound yearly and for ever, in acknowledgment of the above donation, to clothe fifteen poor men at the feast of Saint Martin in winter, and to feed them on the same day, delivering to each of them four ells of large or broad, or six ells of narrow cloth, and to each also a new pair of shoes or sandals, according to their order; and if the said monks shall fail in their engagements or any of them, it is the king's will that the fault shall be redeemed by a double performance of what has been omitted, to be executed at the sight of the chief forester of Ettrick for the time being, and before the return of Saint Martin's day succeeding that on which the omission has taken place.

Of this charter, respecting the pittance of 100*l* assigned to furnish the monks of Melrose with a daily mess of boiled rice, almonds, or other pulse, to mend their commons, the antiquarian reader will be pleased, doubtless, to see the original.

CARTA REGIS ROBERTI I. ABBATI ET CONVENTUI DE MELROSS.

Carta de Pitancia Centum Librarum.

Robertus Dei gracia Rex Scottorum omnibus probis hominibus tocius terre sue Salutem. Sciatis nos pro salute anime nostre et pro salute animarum antecessorum et successorum nostrorum Regum Scocie Dedisse Concessisse et hac presenti Carta nostra confirmasse Deo et Beate Marie virgini et Religiosis viris Abbati et Conventui de Melross et eorum successoribus in perpetuum Centum Libras Sterlingorum Annui Redditus singulis annis percipiendas de firmis nostris Burgi Berwici super. Twedam ad terminos Pentecostis et Sancti Martini in hyeme pro equali portione vel de nova Custuma nostra Burgi predicti si firme nostre predicte ad dictam summam pecunie sufficere non poterunt vel de nova Custuma nostra Burgorum nostrorum de Edenburg et de Hadington Si firme nostre et Custuma nostra ville Berwici aliquo casu contingente ad hoc forte non sufficiant. Ita quod dicta summa pecunie Centum Librarum eis annuatim integre et absque contradictione aliqua plenarie persolvatur pre cunctis aliis quibuscunque assignacionibus per nos factis seu faciendis ad inveniendum in perpetuum singulis diebus cuilibet monacho monasterii predicti comedenti in Refectorio unum sufficiens ferculum risarum factarum cum lacte, amigdalarum vel pisarum sive aliorum ciborum consimilis condicionis inventorum in patria et illud ferculum ferculum Regis vocabitur in eternum. Et si aliquis monachus ex aliqua causa honesta de dicto ferculo comedere noluerit vel refici non poterit non minus attamen sibi de dicto ferculo ministretur et ad portam pro pauperibus deportetur. Nec volumus quod occasione ferculi nostri predicti prandium dicti Conventus de quo antiquitus communiter eis deserviri s re ministrari solebat in aliquo pejoretur seu diminuatur. Volum us insuper et ordinamus quod Abbas ejusdem monasterii qui pro tempore fuerit de consensu saniorum de Conventu specialiter constituat unum monachum providum et discretum ad recipiendum ordinandum et expendendum totam summam pecunie memorate pro utilitate conventus secundum votum et intencionem mentis nostre superius annotatum et ad reddendum fidele compotum coram Abbate et Maioribus de Conventu singulis annis de pecunia sic recepta. Et volumus quod dicti religiosi teneantur annuatim in perpetuum pro predicta donacione nostra ad perpetuam nostri memoriam vestire quindecim pauperes ad festum Sancti Martini in hieme et eosdem cibare eodem die liberando eorum cuilibet quatuor ulnas panni grossi et lati vel sex ulnas panni stricti et eorum cuilibet unum novum par sotularium de ordine suo. Et si dicti religiosi in premissis vel aliquo premissorum aliquo anno defecerint volumus quod illud quod minus perimpletum fuerit dupplicetur diebus magis necessariis per visum capitalis forestarii nostri de Selkirk, qui pro tempore fuerit. Et quod dicta dupplicatio fiat ante natale domini proximo sequens festum Sancti Martini predictum. In cujus rei testimonium presenti Carte nostre sigillum nostrum precipimus apponi. Testibus venerabilibus in Christo patribus Willielmo, Johanne, Willielmo et David Sancti Andree, Glasguensis, Dunkeldensis et Moraviensis ecclesiarum dei gracia episcopis Bernardo Abbate de Abirbrothock Cancellario, Duncano, Malisio, et Hugone de Fyf de Strathin et de Ross, Comitibus Waltero Senescallo Scocie. Jacobo domini de Duglas et Alexandro Fraser Camerario nostre Socie militibus. Apud Abirbrothock, decimo die Januarij. Anno Regni nostri vicesimo.

"Our duty must be done," answered the Sub-Prior, "and the rest is in the hands of God."

"Our duty — our duty?" answered the Abbot, impatiently; "doubtless we are to do our duty; but what is that duty? or how will it serve us? — Will bell, book, and candle, drive back the English heretics? or will Murray care for psalms and antiphonars? or can I fight for the Halidome, like Judas Maccabeus, against those profane Nicanors? or send the Sacristan against this new Holofernes, to bring back his head in a basket?"

"True, my Lord Abbot," said the Sub-Prior, "we cannot fight with carnal weapons, it is alike contrary to our habit and vow; but we can die for our Convent and for our Order. Besides, we can arm those who will and can fight. The English are but few in number, trusting, as it would seem, that they will be joined by Murray, whose march has been interrupted. If Foster, with his Cumberland and Hexham bandits, ventures to march into Scotland, to pillage and despoil our House, we will levy our vassals, and, I trust, shall be found strong enough to give him battle."

"In the blessed name of Our Lady," said the Abbot, "think you that I am Petrus Eremita, to go forth the leader of an host?"

"Nay," said the Sub-Prior, "let some man skilled in war lead our people —there is Julian Avenel, an approved soldier."

"But a scoffer, a debauched person, and, in brief, a man of Belial," quoth the Abbot.

"Still," said the monk, "we must use his ministry in that to which he has been brought up. We can guerdon him richly, and indeed I already know the price of his service. The English, it is expected, will presently set forth, hoping here to seize upon Piercie Shafton, whose refuge being taken with us, they make the pretext of this unheard-of inroad."

"Is it even so?" said the Abbot; "I never judged that his body of satin and his brain of feathers boded us much good."

"Yet we must have his assistance, if possible," said the Sub-Prior; "he may interest in our behalf the great Piercie, of whose friendship he boasts, and that good and faithful Lord may break Foster's purpose. I will despatch the jackman after him with all speed. — Chiefly, however, I trust to the military spirit of the land, which will not suffer peace to be easily broken on the frontier. Credit me, my lord, it will bring to our side the hands of many, whose hearts may have gone astray after strange doctrines. The great chiefs and barons will be ashamed to let the vassals of peaceful monks fight unaided against the old enemies of Scotland."

"It may be," said the Abbot, "that Foster will wait for Murray, whose purpose hitherward is but delayed for a short space."

"By the rood, he will not," said the Sub-Prior; "we know this Sir John Foster — a pestilent heretic, he will long to destroy the church — born a Borderer, he will thirst to plunder her of her wealth—a Border-warden, he will be eager to ride in Scotland. There are too many causes to urge him on. If he joins with Murray, he will have at best but an auxiliary's share of the spoil — if he comes hither before him, he will reckon on the whole harvest of depredation as his own. Julian Avenel also has, as I have heard, some spite against Sir John Foster; they will fight, when they meet, with double determination. — Sacristan, send for our bailiff.—Where is the roll of fencible men liable to do suit and service to the Halidome? — Send off to the Baron of Meigallot; he can raise threescore horse and better — Say to him the Monastery will compound with him for the customs of his bridge, which have been in controversy, if he will show himself a friend at such a point. — And now, my lord, let us compute our possible numbers, and those of the enemy, that human blood be not spilled in vain — Let us therefore calculate——"

"My brain is dizzied with the emergency," said the poor Abbot—"I am not, I think, more a coward than others, so far as my own person is concerned; but speak to me of marching and collecting soldiers, and calculating forces, and you may as well tell of it to the youngest novice of a nunnery. But my resolution is taken.—Brethren," he said, rising up, and coming forward with that dignity which his comely person enabled him to assume, "hear for the last time the voice of your Abbot Boniface. I have done for you the best that I could; in quieter times I had perhaps done better, for it was for quiet that I sought the cloister, which has been to me a place of turmoil, as much as if I had sate in the receipt of custom, or ridden forth as leader of an armed host. But now matters turn worse and worse, and I, as I grow old, am less able to struggle with them. Also, it becomes me not to hold a place, whereof the duties, through my default or misfortune, may be but imperfectly filled by me. Wherefore I have resolved to demit this mine high office, so that the order of these matters may presently devolve upon Father Eustatius here present, our well-beloved Sub-Prior; and I now rejoice that he hath not been provided according to his merits elsewhere, seeing that I well hope he will succeed to the mitre and staff which it is my present purpose to lay down."

"In the name of Our Lady, do nothing hastily, my lord!" said Father Nicholas—"I do remember that when the worthy Abbot Ingelram, being in his ninetieth year—for I warrant you he could remember when Benedict the Thirteenth was deposed—and being ill at ease and bed-rid, the brethren rounded in his ear that he were better resign his office. And what said he, being a pleasant man? marry, that while he could crook his little finger he would keep hold of the crosier with it."

The Sacristan also strongly remonstrated against the resolution of his Superior, and set down the insufficiency he pleaded to the native modesty of his disposition. The Abbot listened in downcast silence; even flattery could not win his ear.

Father Eustace took a nobler tone with his disconcerted and dejected Superior. "My Lord Abbot," he said, "if I have been silent concerning the virtues with which you have governed this house, do not think that I am unaware of them. I know that no man ever brought to your high office a more sincere wish to do well to all mankind; and if your rule has not been marked with the bold lines which sometimes distinguished your spiritual predecessors, their faults have equally been strangers to your character."

"I did not believe," said the Abbot, turning his looks to Father Eustace with some surprise, "that you, father, of all men, would have done me this justice."

"In your absence," said the Sub-Prior, "I have even done it more fully. Do not lose the good opinion which all men entertain of you, by renouncing your office when your care is most needed."

"But, my brother," said the Abbot, "I leave a more able in my place."

"That you do not," said Eustace; "because it is not necessary you should resign, in order to possess the use of whatever experience or talent I may be accounted master of. I have been long enough in this profession to know that the individual qualities which any of us may have, are not his own, but the property of the Community, and only so far useful when they promote the general advantage. If you care not in person, my lord, to deal with this troublesome matter, let me implore you to go instantly to Edinburgh, and make what friends you can in our behalf, while I in your absence will, as Sub-Prior, do my duty in defence of the Halidome. If I succeed, may the honour and praise be yours, and if I fail, let the disgrace and shame be mine own."

The Abbot mused for a space, and then replied,—"No, Father Eustatius, you shall not conquer me by your generosity. In times like these, this house must have a stronger pilotage than my weak hands afford; and he who steers the vessel must be chief of the crew. Shame were it to accept the praise of other men's labours; and, in my poor mind, all the praise which can be bestowed on him who undertakes a task so perilous and perplexing, is a meed beneath his merits. Misfortune to him would deprive him of an iota of it! Assume, therefore, your authority to-night, and proceed in the preparations you judge necessary. Let the Chapter be summoned to-morrow after we have heard mass, and all shall be ordered as I have told you. Benedicite, my brethren!—peace be with you! May the new Abbot-expectant sleep as sound as he who is about to resign his mitre."

They retired, affected even to tears. The good Abbot had shown a point of his character to which they were strangers. Even Father Eustace had held his spiritual Superior hitherto as a good-humoured, indolent, self-indulgent man, whose chief merit was the absence of gross faults; so that this sacrifice of power to a sense of duty, even if a little alloyed by the meaner motives of fear and apprehended difficulties, raised him considerably in the Sub-Prior's estimation. He even felt an aversion to profit by the resignation of the Abbot Boniface, and in a manner to rise on his ruins; but this sentiment did not long contend with those which led him to recollect higher considerations. It could not be denied that Boniface was entirely unfit for his situation in the present crisis; and the Sub-Prior felt that he himself, acting merely as a delegate, could not well take the decisive measures which the time required; the weal of the Community therefore demanded his elevation. If, besides, there crept in a feeling of a high dignity obtained, and the native exultation of a haughty spirit called to contend with the imminent dangers attached to a post of such distinction, these sentiments were so cunningly blended and amalgamated with others of a more disinterested nature, that, as the Sub-Prior himself was unconscious of their agency, we, who have a regard for him, are not solicitous to detect it.

The Abbot elect carried himself with more dignity than formerly, when giving such directions as the pressing circumstances of the times required; and those who approached him could perceive an unusual kindling of his falcon eye, and an unusual flush upon his pale and faded cheek. With briefness and precision he wrote and dictated various letters to different barons, acquainting them with the meditated invasion of the Halidome by the English, and conjuring them to lend aid and assistance as in a common cause. The temptation of advantage was held out to those whom he judged less sensible of the cause of honour, and all were urged by the motives of patriotism and ancient animosity to the English. The time had been when no such exhortations would have been necessary. But so essential was Elizabeth's aid to the reformed party in Scotland, and so strong was that party almost every where, that there was reason to believe a great many would observe neutrality on the present occasion, even if they did not go the length of uniting with the English against the Catholics.

When Father Eustace considered the number of the immediate vassals of the church whose aid he might legally command, his heart sunk at the thoughts of ranking them under the banner of the fierce and profligate Julian Avenel.

"Were the young enthusiast Halbert Glendinning to be found," thought Father Eustace in his anxiety, "I would have risked the battle under his leading, young as he is, and with better hope of God's blessing. But the bailiff is now too infirm, nor know I a chief of name whom I might trust in this important matter better than this Avenel."—He touched a bell which stood on the table, and commanded Christie of the Clinthill to be brought before him.—"Thou owest me a life," said he to that person on his entrance, "and I may do thee another good turn if thou be'st sincere with me."

Christie had already drained two standing-cups of wine, which would, on another occasion, have added to the insolence of his familiarity. But at present there was something in the augmented dignity of manner of Father Eustace, which imposed a restraint on him. Yet his answers partook of his usual character of undaunted assurance. He professed himself willing to return a true answer to all inquiries.

"Has the Baron (so styled) of Avenel any friendship with Sir John Foster, Warden of the West Marches of England?"

"Such friendship as is between the wild-cat and the terrier," replied the rider.

"Will he do battle with him should they meet?"

"As surely," answered Christie, "as ever cock fought on Shrovetide-even."

"And would he fight with Foster in the Church's quarrel?"

"On any quarrel, or upon no quarrel whatever," replied the jackman.

"We will then write to him, letting him know, that if upon occasion of an apprehended incursion by Sir John Foster, he will join his force with ours, he shall lead our men, and be gratified for doing so to the extent of his wish. — Yet one word more — Thou didst say thou couldst find out where the English knight Piercie Shafton has this day fled to?"

"That I can, and bring him back too, by fair means or force, as best likes your reverence."

"No force must be used upon him. Within what time wilt thou find him out?"

"Within thirty hours, so he have not crossed the Lothian firth — If it is to do you a pleasure, I will set off directly, and wind him as a sleuth-dog tracks the moss-trooper," answered Christie.

"Bring him hither then, and thou wilt deserve good at our hands, which I may soon have free means of bestowing on thee."

"Thanks to your reverence, I put myself in your reverence's hands. We of the spear and snaffle walk something recklessly through life; but if a man were worse than he is, your reverence knows he must live, and that's not to be done without shifting, I trow."

"Peace, sir, and begone on thine errand — thou shalt have a letter from us to Sir Piercie."

Christie made two steps towards the door; then turning back and hesitating, like one who would make an impertinent pleasantry if he dared, he asked what he was to do with the wench Mysie Happer whom the Southron knight had carried off with him.

"Am I to bring her hither, please your reverence?"

"Hither, you malapert knave?" said the churchman; "remember you to whom you speak?"

"No offence meant," replied Christie; "but if such is not your will, I would carry her to Avenel Castle, where a well-favoured wench was never unwelcome.

"Bring the unfortunate girl to her father's and break no scurril jests here," said the Sub-Prior — "See that thou guide her in all safety and honour."

"In safety, surely," said the rider, "and in such honour as her outbreak has left her. — I bid your reverence farewell, I must be on horse before cock-crow."

"What, in the dark! — how knowest thou which way to go?"

"I tracked the knight's horse-tread as far as near to the ford, as we rode along together," said Christie, "and I observed the track turn to the northward. He is for Edinburgh, I will warrant you — so soon as daylight comes I will be on the road again. It is a kenspeckle hoof-mark, for the shoe was made by old Eckie of Cannobie — I would swear to the curve of the caulker." So saying, he departed.

"Hateful necessity," said Father Eustace, looking after him, "that obliges us to use such implements as these! But assailed as we are on all sides, and by all conditions of men, what alternative is left us? — But now let me to my most needful task."

The Abbot elect accordingly sate down to write letters, arrange orders, and take upon him the whole charge of an institution which tottered to its fall, with the same spirit of proud and devoted fortitude wherewith the commander of a fortress, reduced nearly to the last extremity, calculates what means remain to him to protract the fatal hour of successful storm. In the meanwhile Abbot Boniface, having given a few natural sighs to the downfall of the pre-eminence he had so long enjoyed amongst his brethren, fell fast asleep, leaving the whole cares and toils of office to his assistant and successor.

Chapter the Thirty-Fifth.

And when he came to broken briggs,
He slacked his bow and swam;
And when he came to grass growing,
Set down his feet and run.
GIL MORRICE.

WE return to Halbert Glendinning, who, as our readers may remember, took the high road to Edinburgh. His intercourse with the preacher, Henry Warden, from whom he received a letter at the moment of his deliverance, had been so brief, that he had not even learned the name of the nobleman to whose care he was recommended. Something like a name had been spoken indeed, but he had only comprehended that he was to meet the chief advancing towards the south, at the head of a party of horse. When day dawned on his journey he was in the same uncertainty. A better scholar would have been informed by the address of the letter, but Halbert had not so far profited by Father Eustace's lessons as to be able to decipher it. His mother-wit taught him that he must not, in such uncertain times, be too hasty in asking information of any one; and when, after a long day's journey, night surprised him near a little village, he began to be dubious and anxious concerning the issue of his journey.

In a poor country, hospitality is generally exercised freely, and Halbert, when he requested a night's quarters, did nothing either degrading or extraordinary. The old woman, to whom he made this request, granted it the more readily, that she thought she saw some resemblance between Halbert and her son Saunders, who had been killed in one of the frays so common in the time. It is true, Saunders was a short square-made fellow, with red hair and a freckled face, and somewhat bandy-legged, whereas the stranger was of a brown complexion, tall, and remarkably well-made. Nevertheless, the widow was clear that there existed a general resemblance betwixt her guest and Saunders, and kindly pressed him to share of her evening cheer. A pedlar, a man of about forty years old, was also her guest, who talked with great feeling of the misery of pursuing such a profession as his in the time of war and tumult.

"We think much of knights and soldiers," said he; "but the pedder-coffe who travels the land has need of more courage than them all. I am sure he maun face mair risk, God help him. Here have I come this length, trusting the godly Earl of Murray would be on his march to the Borders, for he was to have guestened with the Baron of Avenel; and instead of that comes news that he has gone westlandways about some tuilzie in Ayrshire. And what to do I wot not; for if I go to the south without a safeguard, the next bonny rider I meet might ease me of sack and pack, and maybe of my life to boot; and then, if I try to strike across the moors, I may be as ill off before I can join myself to that good Lord's company."

No one was quicker at catching a hint than Halbert Glendinning. He said he himself had a desire to go westward. The pedlar looked at him with a very doubtful air, when the old dame, who perhaps thought her young guest resembled the umquhile Saunders, not only in his looks, but in a certain pretty turn to sleight-of-hand, which the defunct was supposed to have possessed, tipped him the wink, and assured the pedlar he need have no doubt that her young cousin was a true man.

"Cousin!" said the pedlar, "I thought you said this youth had been a stranger."

"Ill hearing makes ill rehearsing," said the landlady; "he is a stranger to me by eye-sight, but that does not make him a stranger to me by blood, more especially seeing his likeness to my son Saunders, poor bairn."

The pedlar's scruples and jealousies being thus removed, or at least silenced, the travellers agreed that they would proceed in company together the next morning by daybreak, the pedlar acting as a guide to Glendinning, and the youth as a guard to the pedlar, until they should fall in with Murray's detachment of horse. It would appear that the lady never doubted what was to be the event of this compact, for, taking Glendinning aside, she charged him, "to be moderate with the puir body, but at all events, not to forget to take a piece of black say, to make the auld wife a new rokelay." Halbert laughed and took his leave.

It did not a little appal the pedlar, when, in the midst of a black heath, the young man told him the nature of the commission with which their hostess had charged him. He took heart, however, upon seeing the open, frank, and friendly demeanor of the youth, and vented his exclamations on the ungrateful old traitress. "I gave her," he said, "yesterday-e'en nae farther gane, a yard of that very black say, to make her a couvre-chef; but I see it is ill done to teach the cat the way to the kirn."

Thus set at ease on the intentions of his companion (for in those happy days the worst was always to be expected from a stranger), the pedlar acted as Halbert's guide over moss and moor, over hill and many a dale, in such a direction as might best lead them towards the route of Murray's party. At length they arrived upon the side of an eminence, which commanded a distant prospect over a tract of savage and desolate moorland, marshy and waste—an alternate change of shingly hill and level morass, only varied by blue stagnant pools of water. A road scarcely marked winded like a serpent through the wilderness, and the pedlar, pointing to it, said—"The road from Edinburgh to Glasgow. Here we must wait, and if Murray and his train be not already passed by, we shall soon see trace of them, unless some new purpose shall have altered their resolution; for in these blessed days no man, were he the nearest the throne, as the Earl of Murray may be, knows when he lays his head on his pillow at night where it is to lie upon the following even."

They paused accordingly and sat down, the pedlar cautiously using for a seat the box which contained his treasures, and not concealing from his companion that he wore under his cloak a pistolet hanging at his belt in case of need. He was courteous, however, and offered Halbert a share of the provisions which he carried about him for refreshment. They were of the coarsest kind—oat-bread baked in cakes, oatmeal slaked with cold water, an onion or two, and a morsel of smoked ham completed the feast. But such as it was, no Scotsman of the time, had his rank been much higher than that of Glendinning, would have refused to share in it, especially as the pedlar produced, with a mysterious air, a tup's horn, which he carried slung from his shoulders, and which, when its contents were examined, produced to each party a clam-shell-full of excellent usquebaugh—a liquor strange to Halbert, for the strong waters known in the south of Scotland came from France, and in fact such were but rarely used. The pedlar recommended it as excellent, said he had procured it in his last visit to the braes of Doune, where he had securely traded under the safe-conduct of the Laird of Buchanan. He also set an example to Halbert, by devoutly emptying the cup "to the speedy downfall of Anti-Christ."

Their conviviality was scarce ended, ere a rising dust was seen on the road of which they commanded the prospect, and half a score of horsemen were dimly descried advancing at considerable speed, their casques glancing, and the points of their spears twinkling as they caught a glimpse of the sun.

"These," said the pedlar, "must be the out-scourers of Murray's party; let us lie down in the peat-hag, and keep ourselves out of sight."

"And why so?" said Halbert; "let us rather go down and make a signal to them."

"God forbid!" replied the pedlar; "do you ken so ill the customs of our Scottish nation? That plump of spears that are spurring on so fast are doubtless commanded by some wild kinsman of Morton, or some such daring fear-nothing as neither regards God nor man. It is their business, if they meet with any enemies, to pick quarrels and clear the way of them; and the chief knows nothing of what happens, coming up with his more discreet and moderate friends, it may be a full mile in the rear. Were we to go near these lads of the laird's belt, your letter would do you little good, and my pack would do me muckle black ill; they would tirl every steek of claithes from our back, fling us into a moss-hag with a stone at our heels, naked as the hour that brought us into this cumbered and sinful world, and neither Murray nor any other man ever the wiser. But if he did come to ken of it, what might he help it? — it would be accounted a mere mistake, and there were all the moan made. O credit me, youth, that when men draw cold steel on each other in their native country, they neither can nor may dwell deeply on the offences of those whose swords are useful to them."

They suffered, therefore, the vanguard, as it might be termed, of the Earl of Murray's host to pass forward; and it was not long until a denser cloud of dust began to arise to the northward.

"Now," said the pedlar, "let us hurry down the hill; for to tell the truth," said he, dragging Halbert along earnestly, "a Scottish noble's march is like a serpent — the head is furnished with fangs, and the tail hath its sting; the only harmless point of access is the main body."

"I will hasten as fast as you," said the youth; "but tell me why the rearward of such an army should be as dangerous as the van?"

"Because, as the vanguard consists of their picked wild desperates, resolute for mischief, such as neither fear God nor regard their fellow-creatures, but understand themselves bound to hurry from the road whatever is displeasing to themselves, so the rear-guard consists of misproud serving-men, who, being in charge of the baggage, take care to amend by their exactions upon travelling-merchants and others, their own thefts on their master's property. You will hear the advanced *enfans perdus*, as the French call them, and so they are indeed, namely, children of the fall, singing unclean and fulsome ballads of sin and harlotrie. And then will come on the middle-ward, when you will hear the canticles and psalms sung by the reforming nobles, and the gentry, and honest and pious clergy, by whom they are accompanied. And last of all, you will find in the rear a legend of godless lackies, palfreniers, and horse-boys, talking of nothing but dicing, drinking, and drabbing."

As the pedlar spoke, they had reached the side of the high-road, and Murray's main body was in sight, consisting of about three hundred horse, marching with great regularity, and in a closely compacted body. Some of the troopers wore the liveries of their masters, but this was not common. Most of them were dressed in such colours as chance dictated. But the majority, being clad in blue cloth, and the whole armed with cuirass and back-plate, with sleeves of mail, gauntlets, and poldroons, and either mailed hose or strong jack-boots, they had something of a uniform appearance.

Many of the leaders were clad in complete armour, and all in a certain half-military dress, which no man of quality in those disturbed times ever felt himself sufficiently safe to abandon.

The foremost of this party immediately rode up to the pedlar and to Hal bert Glendinning, and demanded of them who they were. The pedlar told his story, the young Glendinning exhibited his letter, which a gentleman carried to Murray. In an instant after, the word "Halt!" was given through the squadron, and at once the onward heavy tramp, which seemed the most distinctive attribute of the body, ceased, and was heard no more. The command was announced that the troop should halt here for an hour to refresh themselves and their horses. The pedlar was assured of safe protection, and accommodated with the use of a baggage horse. But at the same time he was ordered into the rear; a command which he reluctantly obeyed, and not without wringing pathetically the hand of Halbert as he separated from him.

The young heir of Glendearg was in the meanwhile conducted to a plot of ground more raised, and therefore drier than the rest of the moor. Here a carpet was flung on the ground by way of table-cloth, and around it sat the leaders of the party, partaking of an entertainment as coarse, with relation to their rank, as that which Glendinning had so lately shared. Murray himself rose as he came forward, and advanced a step to meet him.

This celebrated person had in his appearance, as well as in his mind, much of the admirable qualities of James V. his father. Had not the stain of illegitimacy rested upon his birth, he would have filled the Scottish throne with as much honour as any of the Stewart race. But History, while she acknowledges his high talents, and much that was princely, nay, royal, in his conduct, cannot forget that ambition led him farther than honour or loyalty warranted. Brave amongst the bravest, fair in presence and in favour, skilful to manage the most intricate affairs, to attach to himself those who were doubtful, to stun and overwhelm, by the suddenness and intrepidity of his enterprises, those who were resolute in resistance, he attained, and as to personal merit certainly deserved, the highest place in the kingdom. But he abused, under the influence of strong temptation, the opportunities which his sister Mary's misfortunes and imprudence threw in his way; he supplanted his sovereign and benefactress in her power, and his history affords us one of those mixed characters, in which principle was so often sacrificed to policy, that we must condemn the statesman while we pity and regret the individual. Many events in his life gave likelihood to the charge that he himself aimed at the crown; and it is too true, that he countenanced the fatal expedient of establishing an English, that is a foreign and a hostile interest, in the councils of Scotland. But his death may be received as an atonement for his offences, and may serve to show how much more safe is the person of a real patriot, than that of the mere head of a faction, who is accounted answerable for the offences of his meanest attendants.

When Murray approached, the young rustic was naturally abashed at the dignity of his presence. The commanding form and the countenance to which high and important thoughts were familiar, the features which bore the resemblance of Scotland's long line of kings, were well calculated to impress awe and reverence. His dress had little to distinguish him from the high-born nobles and barons by whom he was attended. A buff-coat, richly embroidered with silken lace, supplied the place of armour; and a massive gold chain, with its medal, hung round his neck. His black velvet bonnet was decorated with a string of large and fair pearls, and with a small tufted feather; a long heavy sword was girt to his side, as the familiar companion of his hand. He wore gilded spurs on his boots, and these completed his equipment.

"This letter," he said, "is from the godly preacher of the word, Henry

Warden, young man? is it not so?" Halbert answered in the affirmative. "And he writes to us, it would seem, in some strait, and refers us to you for the circumstances. Let us know, I pray you, how things stand with him."

In some perturbation Halbert Glendinning gave an account of the circumstances which had accompanied the preacher's imprisonment. When he came to the discussion of the *handfasting* engagement, he was struck with the ominous and displeased expression of Murray's brows, and, contrary to all prudential and politic rule, seeing something was wrong, yet not well aware what that something was, had almost stopped short in his narrative.

"What ails the fool?" said the Earl, drawing his dark-red eyebrows together, while the same dusky glow kindled on his brow — "Hast thou not learned to tell a true tale without stammering?"

"So please you," answered Halbert, with considerable address, "I have never before spoken in such a presence."

"He seems a modest youth," said Murray, turning to his next attendant, "and yet one who in a good cause will neither fear friend nor foe. — Speak on, friend, and speak freely."

Halbert then gave an account of the quarrel betwixt Julian Avenel and the preacher, which the Earl, biting his lip the while, compelled himself to listen to as a thing of indifference. At first he appeared even to take the part of the Baron.

"Henry Warden," he said, "is too hot in his zeal. The law both of God and man maketh allowance for certain alliances, though not strictly formal, and the issue of such may succeed."

This general declaration he expressed, accompanying it with a glance around upon the few followers who were present at this interview. The most of them answered—"There is no contravening that;" but one or two looked on the ground, and were silent. Murray then turned again to Glendinning, commanding him to say what next chanced, and not to omit any particular. When he mentioned the manner in which Julian had cast from him his concubine, Murray drew a deep breath, set his teeth hard, and laid his hand on the hilt of his dagger. Casting his eyes once more around the circle, which was now augmented by one or two of the reformed preachers, he seemed to devour his rage in silence, and again commanded Halbert to proceed. When he came to describe how Warden had been dragged to a dungeon, the Earl seemed to have found the point at which he might give vent to his own resentment, secure of the sympathy and approbation of all who were present. "Judge you," he said, looking to those around him, "judge you, my peers, and noble gentlemen of Scotland, betwixt me and this Julian Avenel — he hath broken his own word, and hath violated my safe-conduct — and judge you also, my reverend brethren, he hath put his hand forth upon a preacher of the gospel, and perchance may sell his blood to the worshippers of Anti-Christ!"

"Let him die the death of a traitor," said the secular chiefs, "and let his tongue be struck through with the hangman's fiery iron to avenge his perjury!"

"Let him go down to his place with Baal's priests," said the preachers, "and be his ashes cast into Tophet!"

Murray heard them with the smile of expected revenge; yet it is probable that the brutal treatment of the female, whose circumstances somewhat resembled those of the Earl's own mother, had its share in the grim smile which curled his sun-burnt cheek and its haughty lip. To Halbert Glendinning, when his narrative was finished, he spoke with great kindness.

"He is a bold and gallant youth," said he to those around, "and formed of the stuff which becomes a bustling time. There are periods when men's spirits shine bravely through them. I will know something more of him."

He questioned him more particularly concerning the Baron of Avenel's probable forces — the strength of his castle — the dispositions of his next heir, and this brought necessarily forward the sad history of his brother's daughter, Mary Avenel, which was told with an embarrassment that did not escape Murray.

"Ha! Julian Avenel," he said, "and do you provoke my resentment, when you have so much more reason to deprecate my justice! I knew Walter Avenel, a true Scotsman and a good soldier. Our sister, the Queen, must right his daughter; and were her land restored, she would be a fitting bride to some brave man who may better merit our favour than the traitor Julian." — Then looking at Halbert, he said, "Art thou of gentle blood, young man?"

Halbert, with a faltering and uncertain voice, began to speak of his distant pretensions to claim a descent from the ancient Glendonwynes of Galloway, when Murray interrupted him with a smile.

"Nay — nay — leave pedigrees to bards and heralds. In our days, each man is the son of his own deeds. The glorious light of reformation hath shone alike on prince and peasant; and peasant as well as prince may be illustrated by fighting in its defence. It is a stirring world, where all may advance themselves who have stout hearts and strong arms. Tell me frankly why thou hast left thy father's house."

Halbert Glendinning made a frank confession of his duel with Piercie Shafton, and mentioned his supposed death.

"By my hand," said Murray, "thou art a bold sparrow-hawk, to match thee so early with such a kite as Piercie Shafton. Queen Elizabeth would give her glove filled with gold crowns to know that meddling coxcomb to be under the sod.—Would she not, Morton?"

"Ay, by my word, and esteem her glove a better gift than the crowns," replied Morton, "which few Border lads like this fellow will esteem just valuation."

"But what shall we do with this young homicide?" said Murray; "what will our preachers say?"

"Tell them of Moses and of Benaiah," said Morton; "it is but the smiting of an Egyptian when all is said out."

"Let it be so," said Murray, laughing; "but we will bury the tale, as the prophet did the body, in the sand. I will take care of this swankie. — Be near to us, Glendinning, since that is thy name. We retain thee as a squire of our household. The master of our horse will see thee fully equipped and armed."

During the expedition which he was now engaged in, Murray found several opportunities of putting Glendinning's courage and presence of mind to the test, and he began to rise so rapidly in his esteem, that those who knew the Earl considered the youth's fortune as certain. One step only was wanting to raise him to a still higher degree of confidence and favour — it was the abjuration of the Popish religion. The ministers who attended upon Murray and formed his chief support amongst the people, found an easy convert in Halbert Glendinning, who, from his earliest days, had never felt much devotion towards the Catholic faith, and who listened eagerly to more reasonable views of religion. By thus adopting the faith of his master, he rose higher in his favour, and was constantly about his person during his prolonged stay in the west of Scotland, which the intractability of those whom the Earl had to deal with, protracted from day to day, and week to week.

Chapter the Thirty-Sixth.

Faint the din of battle bray'd
  Distant down the hollow wind;
War and terror fled before,
  Wounds and death were left behind.
PENROSE.

THE autumn of the year was well advanced, when the Earl of Morton, one morning, rather unexpectedly, entered the antechamber of Murray, in which Halbert Glendinning was in waiting.

"Call your master, Halbert," said the Earl; "I have news for him from Teviotdale; and for you too, Glendinning. — News! news! my Lord of Murray!" he exclaimed at the door of the Earl's bedroom; "come forth instantly." The Earl appeared, and greeted his ally, demanding eagerly his tidings.

"I have had a sure friend with me from the south," said Morton; "he has been at Saint Mary's Monastery, and brings important tidings."

"Of what complexion?" said Murray, "and can you trust the bearer?"

"He is faithful, on my life," said Morton; "I wish all around your Lordship may prove equally so."

"At what, and whom, do you point?" demanded Murray.

"Here is the Egyptian of trusty Halbert Glendinning, our Southland Moses, come alive again, and flourishing, gay and bright as ever, in that Teviotdale Goshen, the Halidome of Kennaquhair."

"What mean you, my lord?" said Murray.

"Only that your new henchman has put a false tale upon you. Piercie Shafton is alive and well; by the same token that the gull is thought to be detained there by love to a miller's daughter, who roamed the country with him in disguise."

"Glendinning," said Murray, bending his brow into his darkest frown, "thou hast not, I trust, dared to bring me a lie in thy mouth, in order to win my confidence?"

"My lord," said Halbert, "I am incapable of a lie. I should choke on one were my life to require that I pronounced it. I say, that this sword of my father was through the body—the point came out behind his back—the hilt pressed upon his breast-bone. And I will plunge it as deep in the body of any one who shall dare to charge me with falsehood."

"How, fellow!" said Morton, "wouldst thou beard a nobleman?"

"Be silent, Halbert," said Murray, "and you, my Lord of Morton, forbear him. I see truth written on his brow."

"I wish the inside of the manuscript may correspond with the superscription," replied his more suspicious ally. "Look to it, my lord, you will one day lose your life by too much confidence."

"And you will lose your friends by being too readily suspicious," answered Murray. "Enough of this—let me hear thy tidings."

"Sir John Foster," said Morton, "is about to send a party into Scotland to waste the Halidome."

"How! without waiting my presence and permission?" said Murray—"he is mad—will he come as an enemy into the Queen's country?"

"He has Elizabeth's express orders," answered Morton, "and they are not to be trifled with. Indeed, his march has been more than once projected and laid aside during the time we have been here, and has caused much alarm at Kennaquhair. Boniface, the old Abbot, has resigned, and whom think you they have chosen in his place?"

"No one surely," said Murray; "they would presume to hold no election until the Queen's pleasure and mine were known?"

Morton shrugged his shoulders—"They have chosen the pupil of old Cardinal Beatoun, that wily determined champion of Rome, the bosom-friend of our busy Primate of Saint Andrews. Eustace, late the Sub-Prior of Kennaquhair, is now its Abbot, and, like a second Pope Julius, is levying men and making musters to fight with Foster if he comes forward."

"We must prevent that meeting," said Murray, hastily; "whichever party wins the day, it were a fatal encounter for us—Who commands the troop of the Abbot?"

"Our faithful old friend, Julian Avenel, nothing less," answered Morton.

"Glendinning," said Murray, "sound trumpets to horse directly, and let all who love us get on horseback without delay—Yes, my lord, this were indeed a fatal dilemma. If we take part with our English friends, the country will cry shame on us—the very old wives will attack us with their rocks and spindles—the very stones of the street will rise up against us—we cannot set our face to such a deed of infamy. And my sister, whose confidence I already have such difficulty in preserving, will altogether withdraw it from me. Then, were we to oppose the English Warden, Elizabeth would call it a protecting of her enemies and what not, and we should lose her."

"The she-dragon," said Morton, "is the best card in our pack; and yet I would not willingly stand still and see English blades carve Scots flesh—What say you to loitering by the way, marching far and easy for fear of spoiling our horses? They might then fight dog fight bull, fight Abbot fight archer, and no one could blame us for what chanced when we were not present."

"All would blame us, James Douglas," replied Murray; "we should lose both sides—we had better advance with the utmost celerity, and do what we can to keep the peace betwixt them.—I would the nag that brought Piercie Shafton hither had broken his neck over the highest heuch in Northumberland!—He is a proper coxcomb to make all this bustle about, and to occasion perhaps a national war!"

"Had we known in time," said Douglas, "we might have had him privily waited upon as he entered the Borders; there are strapping lads enough would have rid us of him for the lucre of his spur-whang.* But to the saddle, James Stewart, since so the phrase goes. I hear your trumpets sound to horse and away—we shall soon see which nag is best breathed."

Followed by a train of about three hundred well-mounted men-at-arms, these two powerful barons directed their course to Dumfries, and from thence eastward to Teviotdale, marching at a rate which, as Morton had foretold, soon disabled a good many of their horses, so that when they approached the scene of expected action, there were not above two hundred of their train remaining in a body, and of these most were mounted on steeds which had been sorely jaded.

They had hitherto been amused and agitated by various reports concerning the advance of the English soldiers, and the degree of resistance which the Abbot was able to oppose to them. But when they were six or seven miles from Saint Mary's of Kennaquhair, a gentleman of the country, whom Murray had summoned to attend him, and on whose intelligence he knew he could rely, arrived at the head of two or three servants, "bloody with spurring, fiery red with haste." According to his report, Sir John Foster, after several times announcing, and as often delaying, his intended incursion, had at last been so stung with the news that Piercie Shafton was openly residing within the Halidome, that he determined to execute the commands of his mistress, which directed him, at every risk, to make himself master of the Euphuist's person. The Abbot's unceasing exertions

* *Spur-whang*—Spur-leather.

had collected a body of men almost equal in number to those of the English Warden, but less practised in arms. They were united under the command of Julian Avenel, and it was apprehended they would join battle upon the banks of a small stream which forms the verge of the Halidome.

"Who knows the place?" said Murray.

"I do, my lord," answered Glendinning.

"'Tis well," said the Earl; "take a score of the best-mounted horse—make what haste thou canst, and announce to them that I am coming up instantly with a strong power, and will cut to pieces, without mercy, whichever party strikes the first blow.—Davidson," said he to the gentleman who brought the intelligence, "thou shalt be my guide.—Hie thee on, Glendinning—Say to Foster, I conjure him, as he respects his mistress's service, that he will leave the matter in my hands. Say to the Abbot, I will burn the Monastery over his head, if he strikes a stroke till I come—Tell the dog, Julian Avenel, that he hath already one deep score to settle with me—I will set his head on the top of the highest pinnacle of Saint Mary's, if he presume to open another. Make haste, and spare not the spur for fear of spoiling horse-flesh."

"Your bidding shall be obeyed, my lord," said Glendinning; and choosing those whose horses were in best plight to be his attendants, he went off as fast as the jaded state of their cavalry permitted. Hill and hollow vanished from under the feet of the chargers.

They had not ridden half the way, when they met stragglers coming off from the field, whose appearance announced that the conflict was begun. Two supported in their arms a third, their elder brother, who was pierced with an arrow through the body. Halbert, who knew them to belong to the Halidome, called them by their names, and questioned them of the state of the affray; but just then, in spite of their efforts to retain him in the saddle, their brother dropped from the horse, and they dismounted in haste to receive his last breath. From men thus engaged, no information was to be obtained. Glendinning, therefore, pushed on with his little troop, the more anxiously, as he perceived other stragglers, bearing Saint Andrew's cross upon their caps and corslets, flying apparently from the field of battle. Most of these, when they were aware of a body of horsemen approaching on the road, held to the one hand or the other, at such a distance as precluded coming to speech of them. Others, whose fear was more intense, kept the onward road, galloping wildly as fast as their horses could carry them, and when questioned, only glared without reply on those who spoke to them, and rode on without drawing bridle. Several of these were also known to Halbert, who had therefore no doubt, from the circumstances in which he met them, that the men of the Halidome were defeated. He became now unspeakably anxious concerning the fate of his brother, who, he could not doubt, must have been engaged in the affray. He therefore increased the speed of his horse, so that not above five or six of his followers could keep up with him. At length he reached a little hill, at the descent of which, surrounded by a semi-circular sweep of a small stream, lay the plain which had been the scene of the skirmish.

It was a melancholy spectacle. War and terror, to use the expression of the poet, had rushed on to the field, and left only wounds and death behind them. The battle had been stoutly contested, as was almost always the case with these Border skirmishes, where ancient hatred, and mutual injuries, made men stubborn in maintaining the cause of their conflict. Towards the middle of the plain, there lay the bodies of several men who had fallen in the very act of grappling with the enemy; and there were seen countenances which still bore the stern expression of unextinguishable hate and defiance, hands which clasped the hilt of the broken falchion, or strove in vain to pluck the deadly arrow from the wound. Some were wounded, and, cowed of the courage they had lately shown, were begging aid, and craving water, in a tone of melancholy depression, while others tried to teach the faltering tongue to pronounce some half-forgotten prayer, which, even when first learned, they had but half understood. Halbert, uncertain what course he was next to pursue, rode through the plain to see if, among the dead or wounded, he could discover any traces of his brother Edward. He experienced no interruption from the English. A distant cloud of dust announced that they were still pursuing the scattered fugitives, and he guessed, that to approach them with his followers, until they were again under some command, would be to throw away his own life, and that of his men, whom the victors would instantly confound with the Scots, against whom they had been successful. He resolved, therefore, to pause until Murray came up with his forces, to which he was the more readily moved, as he heard the trumpets of the English Warden sounding the retreat, and recalling from the pursuit. He drew his men together, and made a stand in an advantageous spot of ground, which had been occupied by the Scots in the beginning of the action, and most fiercely disputed while the skirmish lasted.

While he stood here, Halbert's ear was assailed by the feeble moan of a woman, which he had not expected to hear amid that scene, until the retreat of the foes had permitted the relations of the slain to approach, for the purpose of paying them the last duties. He looked with anxiety, and at length observed, that by the body of a knight in bright armour, whose crest, though soiled and broken, still showed the marks of rank and birth, there sat a female wrapped in a horseman's cloak, and holding something pressed against her bosom, which he soon discovered to be a child. He glanced towards the English. They advanced not, and the continued and prolonged sound of their trumpets, with the shouts of the leaders, announced that their powers would not be instantly re-assembled. He had, therefore, a moment to look after this unfortunate woman. He gave his horse to a spearman as he dismounted, and, approaching the unhappy female, asked her, in the most soothing tone he could assume, whether he could assist her in her distress. The mourner made him no direct answer; but endeavouring, with a trembling and unskilful hand, to undo the springs of the visor and gorget, said, in a tone of impatient grief, "Oh, he would recover instantly could I but give him air—land and living, life and honour, would I give for the power of undoing these cruel iron platings that suffocate him!" He that would soothe sorrow must not argue on the vanity of the most deceitful hopes. The body lay as that of one whose last draught of vital air had been drawn, and who must never more have concern with the nether sky. But Halbert Glendinning failed not to raise the visor and cast loose the gorget, when, to his great surprise, he recognized the pale face of Julian Avenel. His last fight was over, the fierce and turbid spirit had departed in the strife in which it had so long delighted.

"Alas! he is gone," said Halbert, speaking to the young woman, in whom he had now no difficulty of knowing the unhappy Catherine.

"Oh, no, no, no!" she reiterated, "do not say so — he is not dead — he is but in a swoon. I have lain as long in one myself — and then his voice would arouse me, when he spoke kindly, and said, Catherine, look up for my sake—And look up, Julian, for mine!" she said, addressing the senseless corpse; "I know you do but counterfeit to frighten me, but I am not frightened," she added, with an hysterical attempt to laugh; and then instantly changing her tone, entreated him to "speak, were it but to curse my folly. Oh, the rudest word you ever said to me would now sound like the dearest you wasted on me before I gave you all. Lift him up," she said, "lift him up, for God's sake!—have you no compassion? He promised to wed me if I bore him a boy, and this child is so like to its father!—How shall he keep his word, if you do not help me to awaken him?—Christie of the Clinthill,

Rowley, Hutcheon! ye were constant at his feast, but ye fled from him at the fray, false villains as ye are!"

"Not I, by Heaven!" said a dying man, who made some shift to raise himself on his elbow, and discovered to Halbert the well-known features of Christie; "I fled not a foot, and a man can but fight while his breath lasts —mine is going fast.—So, youngster," said he, looking at Glendinning, and seeing his military dress, "thou hast ta'en the basnet at last? it is a better cap to live in than die in. I would chance had sent thy brother here instead—there was good in him — but thou art as wild, and wilt soon be as wicked as myself."

"God forbid!" said Halbert, hastily.

"Marry, and amen, with all my heart," said the wounded man, "there will be company enow without thee where I am going. But God be praised I had no hand in that wickedness," said he, looking to poor Catherine; and with some exclamation in his mouth, that sounded betwixt a prayer and a curse, the soul of Christie of the Clinthill took wing to the last account.

Deeply wrapt in the painful interest which these shocking events had excited, Glendinning forgot for a moment his own situation and duties, and was first recalled to them by a trampling of horse, and the cry of Saint George for England, which the English soldiers still continued to use. His handful of men, for most of the stragglers had waited for Murray's coming up, remained on horseback, holding their lances upright, having no command either to submit or resist.

"There stands our Captain," said one of them, as a strong party of English came up, the vanguard of Foster's troop.

"Your Captain! with his sword sheathed, and on foot in the presence of his enemy? a raw soldier, I warrant him," said the English leader. "So! ho! young man, is your dream out, and will you now answer me if you will fight or fly?"

"Neither," answered Halbert Glendinning, with great tranquillity.

"Then throw down thy sword and yield thee," answered the Englishman.

"Not till I can help myself no otherwise," said Halbert, with the same moderation of tone and manner.

"Art thou for thine own hand, friend, or to whom dost thou owe service?" demanded the English Captain.

"To the noble Earl of Murray."

"Then thou servest," said the Southron, "the most disloyal nobleman who breathes—false both to England and Scotland."

"Thou liest," said Glendinning, regardless of all consequences.

"Ha! art thou so hot now, and wert so cold but a minute since? I lie, do I? Wilt thou do battle with me on that quarrel?"

"With one to one — one to two — or two to five, as you list," said Halbert Glendinning; "grant me but a fair field."

"That thou shalt have. — Stand back, my mates," said the brave Englishman. "If I fall, give him fair play, and let him go off free with his people."

"Long life to the noble Captain!" cried the soldiers, as impatient to see the duel, as if it had been a bull-baiting.

"He will have a short life of it, though," said the sergeant, "if he, an old man of sixty, is to fight, for any reason, or for no reason, with every man he meets, and especially the young fellows he might be father to. — And here comes the Warden besides to see the sword-play."

In fact, Sir John Foster came up with a considerable body of his horsemen, just as his Captain, whose age rendered him unequal to the combat with so strong and active a youth as Glendinning, was deprived of his sword.

"Take it up for shame, old Stawarth Bolton," said the English Warden; "and thou, young man, tell me who and what thou art?"

"A follower of the Earl of Murray, who bore his will to your honour," answered Glendinning, — "but here he comes to say it himself; I see the van of his horsemen come over the hills."

"Get into order, my masters," said Sir John Foster to his followers; "you that have broken your spears, draw your swords. We are something unprovided for a second field, but if yonder dark cloud on the hill edge bring us foul weather, we must bear as bravely as our broken cloaks will bide it. Meanwhile, Stawarth, we have got the deer we have hunted for — here is Piercie Shafton hard and fast betwixt two troopers."

"Who, that lad?" said Bolton; "he is no more Piercie Shafton than I am. He hath his gay cloak indeed — but Piercie Shafton is a round dozen of years older than that slip of roguery. I have known him since he was thus high. Did you never see him in the tilt-yard or in the presence?"

"To the devil with such vanities!" said Sir John Foster; "when had I leisure for them or any thing else? During my whole life has she kept me to this hangman's office, chasing thieves one day and traitors another, in daily fear of my life; the lance never hung up in the hall, the foot never out of the stirrup, the saddles never off my nags' backs; and now, because I have been mistaken in the person of a man I never saw, I warrant me, the next letters from the Privy Council will rate me as I were a dog — a man were better dead than thus slaved and harassed."

A trumpet interrupted Foster's complaints, and a Scottish pursuivant who attended, declared "that the noble Earl of Murray desired, in all honour and safety, a personal conference with Sir John Foster, midway between their parties, with six of company in each, and ten free minutes to come and go."

"And now," said the Englishman, "comes another plague. I must go speak with yonder false Scot, and he knows how to frame his devices, to cast dust in the eyes of a plain man, as well as ever a knave in the north. I am no match for him in words, and for hard blows we are but too ill provided.— Pursuivant, we grant the conference — and you, Sir Swordsman," (speaking to young Glendinning,) "draw off with your troopers to your own party — march — attend your Earl's trumpet. — Stawarth Bolton, put our troop in order, and be ready to move forward at the wagging of a finger. — Get you gone to your own friends, I tell you, Sir Squire, and loiter not here."

Notwithstanding this peremptory order, Halbert Glendinning could not help stopping to cast a look upon the unfortunate Catherine, who lay insensible of the danger and of the trampling of so many horses around her, insensible, as the second glance assured him, of all and forever. Glendinning almost rejoiced when he saw that the last misery of life was over, and that the hoofs of the war-horses, amongst which he was compelled to leave her, could only injure and deface a senseless corpse. He caught the infant from her arms, half ashamed of the shout of laughter which rose on all sides, at seeing an armed man in such a situation assume such an unwonted and inconvenient burden.

"Shoulder your infant!" cried a harquebusier.

"Port your infant!" said a pikeman.

"Peace, ye brutes," said Stawarth Bolton, "and respect humanity in others if you have none yourselves. I pardon the lad having done some discredit to my gray hairs, when I see him take care of that helpless creature, which ye would have trampled upon as if ye had been littered of bitch-wolves, not born of women."

While this passed, the leaders on either side met in the neutral space betwixt the forces of either, and the Earl accosted the English Warden: "Is this fair or honest usage, Sir John, or for whom do you hold the Earl of Morton and myself, that you ride in Scotland with arrayed banner, fight, slay, and make prisoners at your own pleasure? Is it well done, think you, to spoil our land and shed our blood, after the many proofs we have given to your mistress of our devotion due to her will, saving always the allegiance due to our own sovereign?"

"My Lord of Murray," answered Foster, "all the world knows you to be a man of quick ingine and deep wisdom, and these several weeks you have held me in hand with promising to arrest my sovereign mistress's rebel, this Piercie Shafton of Wilverton, and you have never kept your word, alleging turmoils in the west, and I wot not what other causes of hinderance. Now, since he has had the insolence to return hither, and live openly within ten miles of England, I could no longer, in plain duty to my mistress and queen, tarry upon your successive delays, and therefore I have used her force to take her rebel, by the strong hand, wherever I can find him."

"And is Piercie Shafton in your hands, then?" said the Earl of Murray. "Be aware that I may not, without my own great shame, suffer you to remove him hence without doing battle."

"Will you, Lord Earl, after all the advantages you have received at the hands of the Queen of England, do battle in the cause of her rebel?" said Sir John Foster.

"Not so, Sir John," answered the Earl, "but I will fight to the death in defence of the liberties of our free kingdom of Scotland."

"By my faith," said Sir John Foster, "I am well content — my sword is not blunted with all it has done yet this day."

"By my honour, Sir John," said Sir George Heron of Chipchase, "there is but little reason we should fight these Scottish Lords e'en now, for I hold opinion with old Stawarth Bolton, and believe yonder prisoner to be no more Piercie Shafton than he is the Earl of Northumberland; and you were but ill advised to break the peace betwixt the countries for a prisoner of less consequence than that gay mischief-maker."

"Sir George," replied Foster, "I have often heard you herons are afraid of hawks — Nay, lay not hand on sword, man — I did but jest; and for this prisoner, let him be brought up hither, that we may see who or what he is — always under assurance, my Lords," he continued, addressing the Scots.

"Upon our word and honour," said Morton, "we will offer no violence."

The laugh turned against Sir John Foster considerably, when the prisoner, being brought up, proved not only a different person from Sir Piercie Shafton, but a female in man's attire.

"Pluck the mantle from the quean's face, and cast her to the horse-boys," said Foster; "she has kept such company ere now, I warrant."

Even Murray was moved to laughter, no common thing with him, at the disappointment of the English Warden; but he would not permit any violence to be offered to the fair Molinara, who had thus a second time rescued Sir Piercie Shafton at her own personal risk.

"You have already done more mischief than you can well answer," said the Earl to the English Warden, "and it were dishonour to me should I permit you to harm a hair of this young woman's head."

"My lord," said Morton, "if Sir John will ride apart with me but for one moment, I will show him such reasons as shall make him content to depart, and to refer this unhappy day's work to the judgment of the Commissioners nominated to try offences on the Border."

He then led Sir John Foster aside, and spoke to him in this manner:— "Sir John Foster, I much marvel that a man who knows your Queen Elizabeth as you do, should not know that, if you hope any thing from her, it must be for doing her useful service, not for involving her in quarrels with her neighbours without any advantage. Sir Knight, I will speak frankly what I know to be true. Had you seized the true Piercie Shafton by this ill-advised inroad; and had your deed threatened, as most likely it might, a breach betwixt the countries, your politic princess and her politic council would rather have disgraced Sir John Foster than entered into war in his behalf. But now that you have stricken short of your aim, you may rely on it you will have little thanks for carrying the matter farther. I will work thus far on the Earl of Murray, that he will undertake to dismiss Sir

Piercie Shafton from the realm of Scotland.—Be well advised, and let the matter now pass off—you will gain nothing by farther violence, for if we fight, you as the fewer and the weaker through your former action, will needs have the worse."

Sir John Foster listened with his head declining on his breast-plate.

"It is a cursed chance," he said, "and I shall have little thanks for my day's work."

He then rode up to Murray, and said, that, in deference to his Lordship's presence and that of my Lord of Morton, he had come to the resolution of withdrawing himself, with his power, without farther proceedings.

"Stop there, Sir John Foster," said Murray; "I cannot permit you to retire in safety, unless you leave some one who may be surety to Scotland, that the injuries you have at present done us may be fully accounted for—you will reflect, that by permitting your retreat, I become accountable to my Sovereign, who will demand a reckoning of me for the blood of her subjects, if I suffer those who shed it to depart so easily."

"It shall never be told in England," said the Warden, "that John Foster gave pledges like a subdued man, and that on the very field on which he stands victorious.—But," he added, after a moment's pause, "if Stawarth Bolton wills to abide with you on his own free choice, I will say nothing against it; and, as I bethink me, it were better he should stay to see the dismissal of this same Piercie Shafton."

"I receive him as your hostage, nevertheless, and shall treat him as such," said the Earl of Murray. But Foster, turning away as if to give directions to Bolton and his men, affected not to hear this observation.

"There rides a faithful servant of his most beautiful and Sovereign Lady," said Murray aside to Morton. "Happy man! he knows not whether the execution of her commands may not cost him his head; and yet he is most certain that to leave them unexecuted will bring disgrace and death without reprieve. Happy are they who are not only subjected to the caprices of Dame Fortune, but held bound to account and be responsible for them, and that to a sovereign as moody and fickle as her humorous ladyship herself!"

"We also have a female Sovereign, my lord," said Morton.

"We have so, Douglas," said the Earl, with a suppressed sigh; "but it remains to be seen how long a female hand can hold the reins of power in a realm so wild as ours. We will now go on to Saint Mary's, and see ourselves after the state of that House.—Glendinning, look to that woman, and protect her.—What the fiend, man, hast thou got in thine arms?—an infant as I live!—where couldst thou find such a charge, at such a place and moment?"

Halbert Glendinning briefly told the story. The Earl rode forward to the place where the body of Julian Avenel lay, with his unhappy companion's arms wrapped around him like the trunk of an uprooted oak borne down by the tempest with all its ivy garlands. Both were cold dead. Murray was touched in an unwonted degree, remembering, perhaps, his own birth. "What have they to answer for, Douglas," he said, "who thus abuse the sweetest gifts of affection?"

The Earl of Morton, unhappy in his marriage, was a libertine in his amours.

"You must ask that question of Henry Warden, my lord, or of John Knox—I am but a wild counsellor in women's matters."

"Forward to Saint Mary's," said the Earl; "pass the word on—Glendinning, give the infant to this same female cavalier, and let it be taken charge of. Let no dishonour be done to the dead bodies, and call on the country to bury or remove them.—Forward, I say, my masters!"

Chapter the Thirty-Seventh.

Gone to be married?—Gone to swear a peace!
KING JOHN.

THE news of the lost battle, so quickly carried by the fugitives to the village and convent, had spread the greatest alarm among the inhabitants. The Sacristan and other monks counselled flight; the Treasurer recommended that the church plate should be offered as a tribute to bribe the English officer; the Abbot alone was unmoved and undaunted.

"My brethren," he said, "since God has not given our people victory in the combat, it must be because he requires of us, his spiritual soldiers, to fight the good fight of martyrdom, a conflict in which nothing but our own faint-hearted cowardice can make us fail of victory. Let us assume, then, the armour of faith, and prepare, if it be necessary, to die under the ruin of these shrines, to the service of which we have devoted ourselves. Highly honoured are we all in this distinguished summons, from our dear brother Nicholas, whose gray hairs have been preserved until they should be surrounded by the crown of martyrdom, down to my beloved son Edward, who, arriving at the vineyard at the latest hour of the day, is yet permitted to share its toils with those who have laboured from the morning. Be of good courage, my children. I dare not, like my sainted predecessors, promise to you that you shall be preserved by miracle—I and you are alike unworthy of that especial interposition, which, in earlier times, turned the sword of sacrilege against the bosom of tyrants by whom it was wielded, daunted the hardened hearts of heretics with prodigies, and called down hosts of angels to defend the shrine of God and of the Virgin. Yet, by heavenly aid, you shall this day see that your Father and Abbot will not disgrace the mitre which sits upon his brow. Go to your cells, my children, and exercise your private devotions. Array yourselves also in alb and cope, as for our most solemn festivals, and be ready, when the tolling of the largest bell announces the approach of the enemy, to march forth to meet them in solemn procession. Let the church be opened to afford such refuge as may be to those of our vassals, who, from their exertion in this day's unhappy battle, or the cause, are particularly apprehensive of the rage of the enemy. Tell Sir Piercie Shafton, if he has escaped the fight——"

"I am here, most venerable Abbot," replied Sir Piercie; "and if it so seemeth meet to you, I will presently assemble such of the men as have escaped this escaramouche, and will renew the resistance, even unto the death. Certes, you will learn from all, that I did my part in this unhappy matter. Had it pleased Julian Avenel to have attended to my counsel, specially in somewhat withdrawing of his main battle, even as you may have marked the heron eschew the stoop of the falcon, receiving him rather upon his beak than upon his wing, affairs, as I do conceive, might have had a different face, and we might then, in a more bellacose manner, have maintained that affray. Nevertheless, I would not be understood to speak any thing in disregard of Julian Avenel, whom I saw fall fighting manfully with his face to his enemy, which hath banished from my memory the unseemly term of 'meddling coxcomb,' with which it pleased him something rashly to qualify my advice, and for which, had it pleased Heaven and the saints to have prolonged the life of that excellent person, I had it bound upon my soul to have put him to death with my own hand."

"Sir Piercie," said the Abbot, at length interrupting him, "our time allows brief leisure to speak what might have been."

"You are right, most venerable Lord and Father," replied the incorrigible Euphuist; "the preterite, as grammarians have it, concerns frail mortality less than the future mood, and indeed our cogitations respect chiefly the present. In a word, I am willing to head all who will follow me, and offer such opposition as manhood and mortality may permit, to the advance of the English, though they be my own countrymen; and be assured, Piercie Shafton will measure his length, being five feet ten inches, on the ground as he stands, rather than give two yards in retreat, according to the usual motion in which we retrograde."

"I thank you, Sir Knight," said the Abbot, "and I doubt not that you would make your words good; but it is not the will of Heaven that carnal weapons should rescue us. We are called to endure, not to resist, and may not waste the blood of our innocent commons in vain—Fruitless opposition becomes not men of our profession; they have my commands to resign the sword and the spear,—God and Our Lady have not blessed our banner."

"Bethink you, reverend lord," said Piercie Shafton, very eagerly, "ere you resign the defence that is in your power—there are many posts near the entry of this village, where brave men might live or die to the advantage; and I have this additional motive to make defence,—the safety, namely, of a fair friend, who, I hope, hath escaped the hands of the heretics."

"I understand you, Sir Piercie," said the Abbot—"you mean the daughter of our Convent's miller?"

"Reverend my lord," said Sir Piercie, not without hesitation, "the fair Mysinda is, as may be in some sort alleged, the daughter of one who mechanically prepareth corn to be manipulated into bread, without which we could not exist, and which is therefore an employment in itself honourable, nay necessary. Nevertheless, if the purest sentiments of a generous mind, streaming forth like the rays of the sun reflected by a diamond, may ennoble one, who is in some sort the daughter of a molendinary mechanic——"

"I have no time for all this, Sir Knight," said the Abbot; "be it enough to answer, that with our will we war no longer with carnal weapons. We of the spirituality will teach you of the temporality how to die in cold blood, our hands not clenched for resistance, but folded for prayer—our minds not filled with jealous hatred, but with Christian meekness and forgiveness—our ears not deafened, nor our senses confused, by the sound of clamorous instruments of war; but, on the contrary, our voices composed to Halleluiah, Kyrie-Eleison, and Salve Regina, and our blood temperate and cold, as those who think upon reconciling themselves with God, not of avenging themselves of their fellow-mortals."

"Lord Abbot," said Sir Piercie, "this is nothing to the fate of my Molinara, whom I beseech you to observe, I will not abandon, while golden hilt and steel blade bide together on my falchion. I commanded her not to follow us to the field, and yet methought I saw her in her page's attire amongst the rear of the combatants."

"You must seek elsewhere for the person in whose fate you are so deeply interested," said the Abbot; "and at present I will pray of your knighthood to inquire concerning her at the church, in which all our more defenceless vassals have taken refuge. It is my advice to you, that you also abide by the horns of the altar; and, Sir Piercie Shafton," he added, "be of one thing secure, that if you come to harm, it will involve the whole of this brotherhood; for never, I trust, will the meanest of us buy safety at the expense of surrendering a friend or a guest. Leave us, my son, and may God be your aid!"

When Sir Piercie Shafton had departed, and the Abbot was about to betake himself to his own cell, he was surprised by an unknown person anxiously requiring a conference, who, being admitted, proved to be no other than Henry Warden. The Abbot started as he entered, and exclaimed, angrily,—"Ha! are the few hours that fate allows him who may last wear the mitre of this house, not to be excused from the intrusion of heresy?

Dost thou come," he said, "to enjoy the hopes which fate holds out to thy demented and accursed sect, to see the bosom of destruction sweep away the pride of old religion — to deface our shrines,—to mutilate and lay waste the bodies of our benefactors, as well as their sepulchres — to destroy the pinnacles and carved work of God's house, and Our Lady's?"

"Peace, William Allan!" said the Protestant preacher, with dignified composure; "for none of these purposes do I come. I would have these stately shrines deprived of the idols which, no longer simply regarded as the effigies of the good and of the wise, have become the objects of foul idolatry. I would otherwise have its ornaments subsist, unless as they are, or may be, a snare to the souls of men; and especially do I condemn those ravages which have been made by the heady fury of the people, stung into zeal against will-worship by bloody persecution. Against such wanton devastations I lift my testimony."

"Idle distinguisher that thou art!" said the Abbot Eustace, interrupting him; "what signifies the pretext under which thou dost despoil the house of God? and why at this present emergence will thou insult the master of it by thy ill-omened presence?"

"Thou art unjust, William Allan," said Warden; "but I am not the less settled in my resolution. Thou hast protected me some time since at the hazard of thy rank, and what I know thou holdest still dearer, at the risk of thy reputation with thine own sect. Our party is now uppermost, and, believe me, I have come down the valley, in which thou didst quarter me for sequestration's sake, simply with the wish to keep my engagements to thee."

"Ay," answered the Abbot, "and it may be, that my listening to that worldly and infirm compassion which pleaded with me for thy life, is now avenged by this impending judgment. Heaven hath smitten, it may be, the erring shepherd, and scattered the flock."

"Think better of the Divine judgments," said Warden. "Not for thy sins, which are those of thy blended education and circumstances; not for thine own sins, William Allan, art thou stricken, but for the accumulated guilt which thy mis-named Church hath accumulated on her head, and those of her votaries, by the errors and corruption of ages."

"Now, by my sure belief in the Rock of Peter," said the Abbot, "thou dost rekindle the last spark of human indignation for which my bosom has fuel — I thought I might not again have felt the impulse of earthly passion, and it is thy voice which once more calls me to the expression of human anger! yes, it is thy voice that comest to insult me in my hour of sorrow, with these blasphemous accusations of that church which hath kept the light of Christianity alive from the times of the Apostles till now."

"From the times of the Apostles?" said the preacher, eagerly. "*Negatur, Gulielme Allan* — the primitive church differed as much from that of Rome, as did light from darkness, which, did time permit, I should speedily prove. And worse dost thou judge, in saying, I come to insult thee in thy hour of affliction, being here, God wot, with the Christian wish of fulfilling an engagement I had made to my host, and of rendering myself to thy will while it had yet power to exercise aught upon me, and if it might so be, to mitigate in thy behalf the rage of the victors whom God hath sent as a scourge to thy obstinacy."

"I will none of thy intercession," said the Abbot, sternly; "the dignity to which the church has exalted me, never should have swelled my bosom more proudly in the time of the highest prosperity, than it doth at this crisis — I ask nothing of thee, but the assurance that my lenity to thee hath been the means of perverting no soul to Satan, that I have not given to the wolf any of the stray lambs whom the Great Shepherd of souls had intrusted to my charge."

"William Allan," answered the Protestant, "I will be sincere with thee. What I promised I have kept — I have withheld my voice from speaking even good things. But it has pleased Heaven to call the maiden Mary Avenel to a better sense of faith than thou and all the disciples of Rome can teach. Her I have aided with my humble power — I have extricated her from the machinations of evil spirits to which she and her house were exposed during the blindness of their Romish superstition, and, praise be to my Master, I have not reason to fear she will again be caught in thy snares."

"Wretched man!" said the Abbot, unable to suppress his rising indignation, "is it to the Abbot of St. Mary's that you boast having misled the soul of a dweller in Our Lady's Halidome into the paths of foul error and damning heresy? — Thou dost urge me, Wellwood, beyond what it becomes me to bear, and movest me to employ the few moments of power I may yet possess, in removing from the face of the earth one whose qualities, given by God, have been so utterly perverted as thine to the service of Satan."

"Do thy pleasure," said the preacher; "thy vain wrath shall not prevent my doing my duty to advantage thee, where it may be done without neglecting my higher call. I go to the Earl of Murray."

Their conference, which was advancing fast into bitter disputation, was here interrupted by the deep and sullen toll of the largest and heaviest bell of the Convent, a sound famous in the chronicles of the Community, for dispelling of tempests, and putting to flight demons, but which now only announced danger, without affording any means of warding against it. Hastily repeating his orders, that all the brethren should attend in the choir, arrayed for solemn procession, the Abbot ascended to the battlements of the lofty Monastery, by his own private staircase, and there met the Sacristan, who had been in the act of directing the tolling of the huge bell, which fell under his charge.

"It is the last time I shall discharge mine office, most venerable Father and Lord," said he to the Abbot, "for yonder come the Philistines; but I would not that the large bell of Saint Mary's should sound for the last time, otherwise than in true and full tone — I have been a sinful man for one of our holy profession," added he, looking upward, "yet may I presume to say, not a bell hath sounded out of tune from the tower of the house, while Father Philip had the superintendence of the chime and the belfry."

The Abbot, without reply, cast his eyes towards the path, which, winding around the mountain, descends upon Kennaquhair, from the south-east. He beheld at a distance a cloud of dust, and heard the neighing of many horses, while the occasional sparkle of the long line of spears, as they came downwards into the valley, announced that the band came thither in arms.

"Shame on my weakness!" said Abbot Eustace, dashing the tears from his eyes; "my sight is too much dimmed to observe their motions — look, my son Edward," for his favourite novice had again joined him, "and tell me what ensigns they bear."

"They are Scottish men, when all is done!" exclaimed Edward — "I see the white crosses—it may be the Western Borderers, or Ferniehurst and his clan."

"Look at the banner," said the Abbot; "tell me, what are the blazonries?"

"The arms of Scotland," said Edward, "the lion and its tressure, quartered, as I think, with three cushions—Can it be the royal standard?"

"Alas! no," said the Abbot, "it is that of the Earl of Murray. He hath assumed with his new conquest the badge of the valiant Randolph, and hath dropt from his hereditary coat the bend which indicates his own base birth—would to God he may not have blotted it also from his memory, and aim as well at possessing the name, as the power, of a king."

"At least, my father," said Edward, "he will secure us from the violence of the Southron."

"Ay, my son, as the shepherd secures a silly lamb from the wolf, which he destines in due time to his own banquet. Oh my son, evil days are on us! A breach has been made in the walls of our sanctuary—thy brother hath fallen from the faith. Such news brought my last secret intelligence—Murray hath already spoken of rewarding his services with the hand of Mary Avenel."

"Of Mary Avenel!" said the novice, tottering towards and grasping hold of one of the carved pinnacles which adorned the proud battlement.

"Ay, of Mary Avenel, my son, who has also abjured the faith of her fathers. Weep not, my Edward, weep not, my beloved son! or weep for their apostasy, and not for their union—Bless God, who hath called thee to himself, out of the tents of wickedness; but for the grace of Our Lady and Saint Benedict, thou also hadst been a castaway."

"I endeavour, my father," said Edward, "I endeavour to forget; but what I would now blot from my memory has been the thought of all my former life—Murray dare not forward a match so unequal in birth."

"He dares do what suits his purpose—The Castle of Avenel is strong, and needs a good castellan, devoted to his service; as for the difference of their birth, he will mind it no more than he would mind defacing the natural regularity of the ground, were it necessary he should erect upon it military lines and intrenchments. But do not droop for that—awaken thy soul within thee, my son. Think you part with a vain vision, an idle dream, nursed in solitude and inaction.—I weep not, yet what am I now like to lose?—Look at these towers, where saints dwelt, and where heroes have been buried—Think that I, so briefly called to preside over the pious flock, which has dwelt here since the first light of Christianity, may be this day written down the last father of this holy community—Come, let us descend, and meet our fate. I see them approach near to the village."

The Abbot descended, the novice cast a glance around him; yet the sense of the danger impending over the stately structure, with which he was now united, was unable to banish the recollection of Mary Avenel.—"His brother's bride!" he pulled the cowl over his face, and followed his Superior.

The whole bells of the Abbey now added their peal to the death-toll of the largest which had so long sounded. The monks wept and prayed as they got themselves into the order of their procession for the last time, as seemed but too probable.

"It is well our Father Boniface hath retired to the inland," said Father Philip; "he could never have put over this day—it would have broken his heart!"

"God be with the soul of Abbot Ingelram!" said old Father Nicholas, "there were no such doings in his days.—They say we are to be put forth of the cloisters; and how I am to live any where else than where I have lived for these seventy years, I wot not—the best is, that I have not long to live any where."

A few moments after this the great gate of the Abbey was flung open, and the procession moved slowly forward from beneath its huge and richly-adorned gateway. Cross and banner, pix and chalice, shrines containing relics, and censers steaming with incense, preceded and were intermingled with the long and solemn array of the brotherhood, in their long black gowns and cowls, with their white scapularies hanging over them, the various officers of the convent each displaying his proper badge of office. In the centre of the procession came the Abbot, surrounded and supported by his chief assistants. He was dressed in his habit of high solemnity, and appeared as much unconcerned as if he had been taking his usual part in some ordinary ceremony. After him came the inferior persons of the convent; the novices in their albs or white dresses, and the lay brethren distinguished by their beards, which were seldom worn by the Fathers. Women and children, mixed with a few men, came in the rear, bewailing the apprehended desolation of their ancient sanctuary. They moved, however, in order, and restrained the marks of their sorrow to a low wailing sound, which rather mingled with than interrupted the measured chant of the monks.

In this order the procession entered the market-place of the village of Kennaquhair, which was then, as now, distinguished by an ancient cross of curious workmanship, the gift of some former monarch of Scotland. Close by the cross, of much greater antiquity, and scarcely less honoured, was an immensely large oak-tree, which perhaps had witnessed the worship of the Druids, ere the stately Monastery to which it adjoined had raised its spires in honour of the Christian faith. Like the Bentang-tree of the African villages, or the Plaistow-oak mentioned in White's Natural History of Selborne, this tree was the rendezvous of the villagers, and regarded with peculiar veneration; a feeling common to most nations, and which perhaps may be traced up to the remote period when the patriarch feasted the angels under the oak at Mamre.*

The monks formed themselves each in their due place around the cross, while under the ruins of the aged tree crowded the old and the feeble, with others who felt the common alarm. When they had thus arranged themselves, there was a deep and solemn pause. The monks stilled their chant, the lay populace hushed their lamentations, and all awaited in terror and silence the arrival of those heretical forces, whom they had been so long taught to regard with fear and trembling.

A distant trampling was at length heard, and the glance of spears was seen to shine through the trees above the village. The sounds increased, and became more thick, one close continuous rushing sound, in which the tread of hoofs was mingled with the ringing of armour. The horsemen soon appeared at the principal entrance which leads into the irregular square or market-place which forms the centre of the village. They entered two by two, slowly, and in the greatest order. The van continued to move on, riding round the open space, until they had attained the utmost point, and then turning their horses' heads to the street, stood fast; their companions followed in the same order, until the whole market-place was closely surrounded with soldiers; and the files who followed, making the same manœuvre, formed an inner line within those who had first arrived, until the place was begirt with a quadruple file of horsemen closely drawn up. There was now a pause, of which the Abbot availed himself, by commanding the brotherhood to raise the solemn chant *De profundis clamavi.* He looked around the armed ranks, to see what impression the solemn sounds made on them. All were silent, but the brows of some had an expression of contempt, and almost all the rest bore a look of indifference; their course had been too long decided to permit past feelings of enthusiasm to be anew awakened by a procession or by a hymn.

"Their hearts are hardened," said the Abbot to himself in dejection, but not in despair; "it remains to see whether those of their leaders are equally obdurate."

The leaders, in the meanwhile, were advancing slowly, and Murray, with Morton, rode in deep conversation before a chosen band of their most distinguished followers, amongst whom came Halbert Glendinning. But the preacher Henry Warden, who, upon leaving the Monastery, had instantly joined them, was the only person admitted to their conference.

"You are determined, then," said Morton to Murray, "to give the heiress of Avenel, with all her pretensions, to this nameless and obscure young man?"

"Hath not Warden told you," said Murray, "that they have been bred together, and are lovers from their youth upward?"

"And that they are both," said Warden, "by means which may be

---

* It is scarcely necessary to say, that in Melrose, the prototype of Kennaquhair, no such oak ever existed.

almost termed miraculous, rescued from the delusions of Rome, and brought within the pale of the true church. My residence at Glendearg hath made me well acquainted with these things. Ill would it beseem my habit and my calling, to thrust myself into match-making and giving in marriage, but worse were it in me to see your lordships do needless wrong to the feelings which are proper to our nature, and which, being indulged honestly and under the restraints of religion, become a pledge of domestic quiet here, and future happiness in a better world. I say, that you will do ill to rend those ties asunder, and to give this maiden to the kinsman of Lord Morton, though Lord Morton's kinsman he be."

"These are fair reasons, my Lord of Murray," said Morton, "why you should refuse me so simple a boon as to bestow this silly damsel upon young Bennygask. Speak out plainly, my lord; say you would rather see the Castle of Avenel in the hands of one who owes his name and existence solely to your favour, than in the power of a Douglas, and of my kinsman."

"My Lord of Morton," said Murray, "I have done nothing in this matter which should aggrieve you. This young man Glendinning has done me good service, and may do me more. My promise was in some degree passed to him, and that while Julian Avenel was alive, when aught beside the maiden's lily hand would have been hard to come by; whereas, you never thought of such an alliance for your kinsman, till you saw Julian lie dead yonder on the field, and knew his land to be a waif free to the first who could seize it. Come, come, my lord, you do less than justice to your gallant kinsman, in wishing him a bride bred up under the milk-pail; for this girl is a peasant wench in all but the accident of birth. I thought you had more deep respect for the honour of the Douglasses."

"The honour of the Douglasses is safe in my keeping," answered Morton, haughtily; "that of other ancient families may suffer as well as the name of Avenel, if rustics are to be matched with the blood of our ancient barons."

"This is but idle talking," answered Lord Murray; "in times like these, we must look to men and not to pedigrees. Hay was but a rustic before the battle of Loncarty—the bloody yoke actually dragged the plough ere it was emblazoned on a crest by the herald. Times of action make princes into peasants, and boors into barons. All families have sprung from one mean man; and it is well if they have never degenerated from his virtue who raised them first from obscurity."

"My Lord of Murray will please to except the house of Douglas," said Morton, haughtily; "men have seen it in the tree, but never in the sapling—have seen it in the stream, but never in the fountain.* In the earliest of

* The late excellent and laborious antiquary, Mr. George Chalmers, has rebuked the vaunt of the House of Douglas, or rather of Hume of Godscroft, their historian, but with less than his wonted accuracy. In the first volume of his Caledonia, he quotes the passage in Godscroft for the purpose of confuting it.

The historian (of the Douglasses) cries out, "We do not know them in the fountain, but in the stream; not in the root, but in the stem; for we know not which is the mean man that did rise above the vulgar." This assumption Mr. Chalmers conceives ill-timed, and alleges, that if the historian had attended more to research than to declamation, he might easily have seen the first mean man of this renowned family. This he alleges to have been one Theobaldus Flammaticus, or Theobald the Fleming, to whom Arnold, Abbot of Kelso, between the year 1147 and 1160, granted certain lands on Douglas water, by a deed which Mr. Chalmers conceives to be the first link of the chain of title-deeds to Douglasdale. Hence, he says, the family must renounce their family domain, or acknowledge this obscure Fleming as their ancestor. Theobald the Fleming, it is acknowledged, did not himself assume the name of Douglas; "but," says the antiquary, "his son William, who inherited his estate, called himself, and was named by others, De Duglas;" and he refers to the deeds in which he is so designed. Mr. Chalmers' full argument may be found in the first volume of his Caledonia, p. 579.

This proposition is one which a Scotsman will admit unwillingly, and only upon undeniable testimony: and as it is liable to strong grounds of challenge, the present author, with all the respect to Mr. Chalmers which his zealous and effectual researches merit, is not unwilling to take this opportunity to state some plausible grounds for doubting that Theobaldus Flammaticus was either the father of the first William de Douglas, or in the slightest degree connected with the Douglas family.

It must first be observed, that there is no reason whatever for concluding Theobaldus Flammaticus to be the father of William de Douglas, except that they both held lands upon the small river of Douglas; and that there are two strong presumptions to the contrary. For, first, the father being named Fleming, there seems no good reason why the son should have assumed a different designation: secondly, there does not occur a single instance of the name of Theobald during the long line of the Douglas pedigree, an omission very unlikely to take place had the original father of the race been so called. These are secondary con

our Scottish annals, the Black Douglas was powerful and distinguished as now."

"I bend to the honours of the house of Douglas," said Murray, somewhat ironically; "I am conscious we of the Royal House have little right to compete with them in dignity—What though we have worn crowns and carried sceptres for a few generations, if our genealogy moves no farther back than to the humble *Alanus Dapifer!*"*

Morton's cheek reddened as he was about to reply; but Henry Warden availed himself of the liberty which the Protestant clergy long possessed, and exerted it to interrupt a discussion which was becoming too eager and personal to be friendly.

"My lords," he said, "I must be bold in discharging the duty of my Master. It is a shame and scandal to hear two nobles, whose hands have been so forward in the work of reformation, fall into discord about such vain follies as now occupy your thoughts. Bethink you how long you have thought with one mind, seen with one eye, heard with one ear, confirmed by your union the congregation of the Church, appalled by your joint authority the congregation of Anti-Christ; and will you now fall into discord, about an old decayed castle and a few barren hills, about the loves and likings of an humble spearman, and a damsel bred in the same obscurity, or about the still vainer questions of idle genealogy?"

"The good man hath spoken right, noble Douglas," said Murray, reaching him his hand, "our union is too essential to the good cause to be broken off upon such idle terms of dissension. I am fixed to gratify Glendinning in this matter—my promise is passed. The wars, in which I have had my share, have made many a family miserable; I will at least try if I may not make one happy. There are maids and manors enow in Scotland.——I promise you, my noble ally, that young Bennygask shall be richly wived."

"My lord," said Warden, "you speak nobly, and like a Christian. Alas! this is a land of hatred and bloodshed—let us not chase from thence the few traces that remain of gentle and domestic love.—And be not too eager for wealth to thy noble kinsman, my Lord of Morton, seeing contentment in the marriage state no way depends on it."

"If you allude to my family misfortune," said Morton, whose Countess, wedded by him for her estate and honours, was insane in her mind, "the habit you wear, and the liberty, or rather license, of your profession, protect you from my resentment."

"Alas! my lord," replied Warden, "how quick and sensitive is our self-love! When pressing forward in our high calling, we point out the errors of the Sovereign, who praises our boldness more than the noble Morton? But touch we upon his own sore, which most needs lancing, and he shrinks from the faithful chirurgeon in fear and impatient anger!"

---

siderations indeed; but they are important, in so far as they exclude any support of Mr. Chalmers' system, except from the point which he has rather assumed than proved, namely, that the lands granted to Theobald the Fleming were the same which were granted to William de Douglas, and which constituted the original domain of which we find this powerful family lords.

Now, it happens, singularly enough, that the lands granted by the Abbot of Kelso to Theobaldus Flammaticus are not the same of which William de Douglas was in possession. Nay, it would appear, from comparing the charter granted to Theobaldus Flammaticus, that, though situated on the water of Douglas, they never made a part of the barony of that name, and therefore cannot be the same with those held by William de Douglas in the succeeding generation. But if William de Douglas did not succeed Theobaldus Flammaticus, there is no more reason for holding these two persons to be father and son than if they had lived in different provinces; and we are still as far from having discovered the first mean man of the Douglas family as Hume of Godscroft was in the 16th century. We leave the question to antiquaries and genealogists.

* To atone to the memory of the learned and indefatigable Chalmers for having ventured to impeach his genealogical proposition concerning the descent of the Douglasses, we are bound to render him our grateful thanks for the felicitous light which he has thrown on that of the House of Stewart, still more important to Scottish history.

The acute pen of Lord Hailes, which, like the spear of Ithuriel, conjured so many shadows from Scottish history, had dismissed among the rest those of Banquo and Fleance, the rejection of which fables left the illustrious family of Stewart without an ancestor beyond Walter the son of Allan, who is alluded to in the text. The researches of our late learned antiquary detected in this Walter, the descendant of Allan, the son of Flaald, who obtained from William the Conqueror the Castle of Oswestry in Shropshire, and was the father of an illustrious line of English nobles, by his first son, William, and by his second son, Walter, the progenitor of the royal family of Stewart.

"Enough of this, good and reverend sir," said Murray; "you transgress the prudence yourself recommended even now.—We are now close upon the village, and the proud Abbot is come forth at the head of his hive. Thou hast pleaded well for him, Warden, otherwise I had taken this occasion to pull down the nest, and chase away the rooks."

"Nay, but do not so," said Warden; "this William Allan, whom they call the Abbot Eustatius, is a man whose misfortunes would more prejudice our cause than his prosperity. You cannot inflict more than he will endure; and the more that he is made to bear, the higher will be the influence of his talents and his courage. In his conventual throne he will be but coldly looked on — disliked, it may be, and envied. But turn his crucifix of gold into a crucifix of wood — let him travel through the land, an oppressed and impoverished man, and his patience, his eloquence, and learning, will win more hearts from the good cause, than all the mitred abbots of Scotland have been able to make prey of during the last hundred years."

"Tush! tush! man," said Morton, "the revenues of the Halidome will bring more men, spears, and horses, into the field in one day, than his preaching in a whole lifetime. These are not the days of Peter the Hermit, when monks could march armies from England to Jerusalem; but gold and good deeds will still do as much or more than ever. Had Julian Avenel had but a score or two more men this morning, Sir John Foster had not missed a worse welcome. I say, confiscating the monk's revenues is drawing his fang-teeth."

"We will surely lay him under contribution," said Murray; "and, moreover, if he desires to remain in his Abbey, he will do well to produce Piercie Shafton."

As he thus spoke, they entered the market-place, distinguished by their complete armour and their lofty plumes, as well as by the number of followers bearing their colours and badges. Both these powerful nobles, but more especially Murray, so nearly allied to the crown, had at that time a retinue and household not much inferior to that of Scottish royalty. As they advanced into the market-place, a pursuivant, pressing forward from their train, addressed the monks in these words: — "The Abbot of Saint Mary's is commanded to appear before the Earl of Murray."

"The Abbot of Saint Mary's," said Eustace, "is, in the patrimony of his Convent, superior to every temporal lord. Let the Earl of Murray, if he seeks him, come himself to his presence."

On receiving this answer, Murray smiled scornfully, and, dismounting from his lofty saddle, he advanced, accompanied by Morton, and followed by others, to the body of monks assembled around the cross. There was an appearance of shrinking among them at the approach of the heretic lord, so dreaded and so powerful. But the Abbot, casting on them a glance of rebuke and encouragement, stepped forth from their ranks like a courageous leader, when he sees that his personal valour must be displayed to revive the drooping courage of his followers. "Lord James Stewart," he said, "or Earl of Murray, if that be thy title, I, Eustatius, Abbot of Saint Mary's, demand by what right you have filled our peaceful village, and surrounded our brethren, with these bands of armed men? If hospitality is sought, we have never refused it to courteous asking — if violence be meant against peaceful churchmen, let us know at once the pretext and the object?"

"Sir Abbot," said Murray, "your language would better have become another age, and a presence inferior to ours. We come not here to reply to your interrogations, but to demand of you why you have broken the peace, collecting your vassals in arms, and convocating the Queen's lieges, whereby many men have been slain, and much trouble, perchance breach of amity with England, is likely to arise?"

"*Lupus in fabula,*" answered the Abbot, scornfully. "The wolf accused the sheep of muddying the stream when he drank in it above her — but it served as a pretext for devouring her. Convocate the Queen's lieges! I did so to defend the Queen's land against foreigners. I did but my duty; and I regret I had not the means to do it more effectually."

"And was it also a part of your duty to receive and harbour the Queen of England's rebel and traitor; and to inflame a war betwixt England and Scotland?" said Murray.

"In my younger days, my lord," answered the Abbot, with the same intrepidity, "a war with England was no such dreaded matter; and not merely a mitred abbot, bound by his rule to show hospitality and afford sanctuary to all, but the poorest Scottish peasant, would have been ashamed to have pleaded fear of England as the reason for shutting his door against a persecuted exile. But in those olden days, the English seldom saw the face of a Scottish nobleman, save through the bars of his visor."

"Monk!" said the Earl of Morton, sternly, "this insolence will little avail thee; the days are gone by when Rome's priests were permitted to brave noblemen with impunity. Give us up this Piercie Shafton, or by my father's crest I will set thy Abbey in a bright flame!"

"And if thou dost, Lord of Morton, its ruins will tumble above the tombs of thine own ancestors. Be the issue as God wills, the Abbot of Saint Mary's gives up no one whom he hath promised to protect."

"Abbot!" said Murray, "bethink thee ere we are driven to deal roughly—the hands of these men," he said, pointing to the soldiers, "will make wild work among shrines and cells, if we are compelled to undertake a search for this Englishman."

"Ye shall not need," said a voice from the crowd; and, advancing gracefully before the Earls, the Euphuist flung from him the mantle in which he was muffled. "Via the cloud that shadowed Shafton!" said he; "behold, my lords, the Knight of Wilverton, who spares you the guilt of violence and sacrilege."

"I protest before God and man against any infraction of the privileges of this house," said the Abbot, "by an attempt to impose violent hands upon the person of this noble knight. If there be yet spirit in a Scottish Parliament, we will make you hear of this elsewhere, my lords!"

"Spare your threats," said Murray; "it may be, my purpose with Sir Piercie Shafton is not such as thou dost suppose—Attach him, pursuivant, as our prisoner, rescue or no rescue."

"I yield myself," said the Euphuist, "reserving my right to defy my Lord of Murray and my Lord of Morton to single duel, even as one gentleman may demand satisfaction of another."

"You shall not want those who will answer your challenge, Sir Knight," replied Morton, "without aspiring to men above thine own degree."

"And where am I to find these superlative champions," said the English knight, "whose blood runs more pure than that of Piercie Shafton?"

"Here is a flight for you, my lord!" said Murray.

"As ever was flown by a wild-goose," said Stawarth Bolton, who had now approached to the front of the party.

"Who dared to say that word?" said the Euphuist, his face crimson with rage.

"Tut! man," said Bolton, "make the best of it, thy mother's father was but a tailor, old Overstitch of Holderness—Why, what! because thou art a misproud bird, and despiseth thine own natural lineage, and rufflest in unpaid silks and velvets, and keepest company with gallants and cutters, must we lose our memory for that? Thy mother, Moll Overstitch, was the prettiest wench in those parts—she was wedded by wild Shafton of Wilverton, who men say, was akin to the Piercie on the wrong side of the blanket."

"Help the knight to some strong waters," said Morton; "he hath fallen from such a height, that he is stunned with the tumble."

In fact, Sir Piercie Shafton looked like a man stricken by a thunderbolt, while, notwithstanding the seriousness of the scene hitherto, no one of those present, not even the Abbot himself, could refrain from laughing at the rueful and mortified expression of his face.

"Laugh on," he said at length, "laugh on, my masters," shrugging his shoulders; "it is not for me to be offended—yet would I know full fain from that squire who is laughing with the loudest, how he had discovered this unhappy blot in an otherwise spotless lineage, and for what purpose he hath made it known?"

"*I* make it known?" said Halbert Glendinning, in astonishment,—for to him this pathetic appeal was made,—"I never heard the thing till this moment."*

"Why, did not that old rude soldier learn it from thee?" said the knight, in increasing amazement.

"Not I, by Heaven!" said Bolton; "I never saw the youth in my life before."

"But you *have* seen him ere now, my worthy master," said Dame Glendinning, bursting in her turn from the crowd. "My son, this is Stawarth Bolton, he to whom we owe life, and the means of preserving it—if he be a prisoner, as seems most likely, use thine interest with these noble lords to be kind to the widow's friend."

"What, my Dame of the Glen!" said Bolton, "thy brow is more withered, as well as mine, since we met last, but thy tongue holds the touch better than my arm. This boy of thine gave me the foil sorely this morning. The Brown Varlet has turned as stout a trooper as I prophesied; and where is White Head?"

"Alas!" said the mother, looking down, "Edward has taken orders, and become a monk of this Abbey."

"A monk and a soldier!—Evil trades both, my good dame. Better have made one a good master fashioner, like old Overstitch, of Holderness. I sighed when I envied you the two bonny children, but I sigh not now to call either the monk or the soldier mine own. The soldier dies in the field, the monk scarce lives in the cloister."

"My dearest mother," said Halbert, "where is Edward—can I not speak with him?"

"He has just left us for the present," said Father Philip, "upon a message from the Lord Abbot."

"And Mary, my dearest mother?" said Halbert.—Mary Avenel was not far distant, and the three were soon withdrawn from the crowd, to hear and relate their various chances of fortune.

While the subordinate personages thus disposed of themselves, the Abbot held serious discussion with the two Earls, and, partly yielding to their demands, partly defending himself with skill and eloquence, was enabled to make a composition for his Convent, which left it provisionally in no worse situation than before. The Earls were the more reluctant to drive matters to extremity, since he protested, that if urged beyond what his conscience would comply with, he would throw the whole lands of the Monastery into the Queen of Scotland's hands, to be disposed of at her

* The contrivance of provoking the irritable vanity of Sir Piercie Shafton, by presenting him with a bodkin, indicative of his descent from a tailor, is borrowed from a German romance, by the celebrated Tieck, called Das Peter Manchem, *i. e.* The Dwarf Peter. The being who gives name to the tale, is the Burg-geist, or castle spectre, of a German family, whom he aids with his counsel, as he defends their castle by his supernatural power. But the Dwarf Peter is so unfortunate an adviser, that all his counsels, though producing success in the immediate results, are in the issue attended with mishap and with guilt. The youthful baron, the owner of the haunted castle, falls in love with a maiden, the daughter of a neighbouring count, a man of great pride, who refuses him the hand of the young lady, on account of his own superiority of descent. The lover, repulsed and affronted, returns to take counsel with the Dwarf Peter, how he may silence the count, and obtain the victory in the argument, the next time they enter on the topic of pedigree. The dwarf gives his patron or pupil a horse-shoe, instructing him to give it to the count when he is next giving himself superior airs on the subject of his family. It has the effect accordingly. The count, understanding it as an allusion to a misalliance of one of his ancestors with the daughter of a blacksmith, is thrown into a dreadful passion with the young lover, the consequences of which are the seduction of the young lady, and the slaughter of her father.

If we suppose the dwarf to represent the corrupt part of human nature,—that "law in our members which wars against the law of our minds,"—the work forms an ingenious allegory.

pleasure. This would not have answered the views of the Earls, who were contented, for the time, with a moderate sacrifice of money and lands. Matters being so far settled, the Abbot became anxious for the fate of Sir Piercie Shafton, and implored mercy in his behalf.

"He is a coxcomb," he said, "my lords, but he is a generous, though a vain fool; and it is my firm belief you have this day done him more pain than if you had run a poniard into him."

"Run a needle into him you mean, Abbot," said the Earl of Morton; "by mine honour, I thought this grandson of a fashioner of doublets was descended from a crowned head at least!"

"I hold with the Abbot," said Murray; "there were little honour in surrendering him to Elizabeth, but he shall be sent where he can do her no injury. Our pursuivant and Bolton shall escort him to Dunbar, and ship him off for Flanders. — But soft, here he comes, and leading a female, as I think."

"Lords and others," said the English knight with great solemnity, "make way for the Lady of Piercie Shafton — a secret which I listed not to make known, till fate, which hath betrayed what I vainly strove to conceal, makes me less desirous to hide that which I now announce to you."

"It is Mysie Happer, the Miller's daughter, on my life!" said Tibb Tacket. "I thought the pride of these Piercies would have a fa'."

"It is indeed the lovely Mysinda," said the knight, "whose merits towards her devoted servant deserved higher rank than he had to bestow."

"I suspect, though," said Murray, "that we should not have heard of the Miller's daughter being made a lady, had not the knight proved to be the grandson of a tailor."

"My lord," said Piercie Shafton, "it is poor valour to strike him that cannot smite again; and I hope you will consider what is due to a prisoner by the law of arms, and say nothing more on this odious subject. When I am once more mine own man, I will find a new road to dignity."

"*Shape* one, I presume," said the Earl of Morton.

"Nay, Douglas, you will drive him mad," said Murray; "besides, we have other matter in hand—I must see Warden wed Glendinning with Mary Avenel, and put him in possession of his wife's castle without delay. It will be best done ere our forces leave these parts."

"And I," said the Miller, "have the like grist to grind; for I hope some one of the good fathers will wed my wench with her gay bridegroom."

"It needs not," said Shafton; "the ceremonial hath been solemnly performed."

"It will not be the worse of another bolting," said the Miller; "it is always best to be sure, as I say when I chance to take multure twice from the same meal-sack."

"Stave the miller off him," said Murray, "or he will worry him dead. The Abbot, my lord, offers us the hospitality of the Convent; I move we should repair hither, Sir Piercie and all of us. I must learn to know the Maid of Avenel — to-morrow I must act as her father — All Scotland shall see how Murray can reward a faithful servant."

Mary Avenel and her lover avoided meeting the Abbot, and took up their temporary abode in a house of the village, where next day their hands were united by the Protestant preacher in presence of the two Earls. On the same day Piercie Shafton and his bride departed, under an escort which was to conduct him to the sea-side, and see him embark for the Low Countries. Early on the following morning the bands of the Earls were under march to the Castle of Avenel, to invest the young bridegroom with the property of his wife, which was surrendered to them without opposition.

But not without those omens which seemed to mark every remarkable event which befell the fated family, did Mary take possession of the ancient castle of her forefathers. The same warlike form which had appeared more than once at Glendearg, was seen by Tibb Tacket and Martin, who returned with their young mistress to partake her altered fortunes. It glided before the cavalcade as they advanced upon the long causeway, paused at each drawbridge, and flourished its hand, as in triumph, as it disappeared under the gloomy archway, which was surmounted by the insignia of the house of Avenel. The two trusty servants made their vision only known to Dame Glendinning, who, with much pride of heart, had accompanied her son to see him take his rank among the barons of the land. "Oh, my dear bairn!" she exclaimed, when she heard the tale, "the castle is a grand place to be sure, but I wish ye dinna a' desire to be back in the quiet braes of Glendearg before the play be played out." But this natural reflection, springing from maternal anxiety, was soon forgotten amid the busy and pleasing task of examining and admiring the new habitation of her son.

While these affairs were passing, Edward had hidden himself and his sorrows in the paternal Tower of Glendearg, where every object was full of matter for bitter reflection. The Abbot's kindness had despatched him thither upon pretence of placing some papers belonging to the Abbey in safety and secrecy; but in reality to prevent his witnessing the triumph of his brother. Through the deserted apartments, the scene of so many bitter reflections, the unhappy youth stalked like a discontented ghost, conjuring up around him at every step new subjects for sorrow and for self-torment. Impatient, at length, of the state of irritation and agonized recollection in which he found himself, he rushed out and walked hastily up the glen, as if to shake off the load which hung upon his mind. The sun was setting when he reached the entrance of Corri-nan-shian, and the recollection of what he had seen when he last visited that haunted ravine, burst on his mind. He was in a humour, however, rather to seek out danger than to avoid it.

"I will face this mystic being," he said; "she foretold the fate which has wrapt me in this dress,—I will know whether she has aught else to tell me of a life which cannot but be miserable."

He failed not to see the White Spirit seated by her accustomed haunt, and singing in her usual low and sweet tone. While she sung, she seemed to look with sorrow on her golden zone, which was now diminished to the fineness of a silken thread.

'Fare thee well, thou Holly green,
Thou shalt seldom now be seen,
With all thy glittering garlands bending,
As to greet my slow descending,
Startling the bewilder'd hind,
Who sees thee wave without a wind.

"Farewell, Fountain! now not long
Shalt thou murmur to my song,
While thy crystal bubbles glancing,
Keep the time in mystic dancing,
Rise and swell, are burst and lost,
Like mortal schemes by fortune crost.

"The knot of fate at length is tied,
The Churl is Lord, the Maid is bride.
Vainly did my magic sleight
Send the lover from her sight;
Wither bush, and perish well,
Fall'n is lofty Avenel!"

The vision seemed to weep while she sung; and the words impressed on Edward a melancholy belief, that the alliance of Mary with his brother might be fatal to them both.

Here terminates the First Part of the Benedictine's Manuscript. I have in vain endeavoured to ascertain the precise period of the story, as the dates cannot be exactly reconciled with those of the most accredited histories. But it is astonishing how careless the writers of Utopia are upon these important subjects. I observe that the learned Mr. Laurence Templeton, in his late publication entitled IVANHOE, has not only blessed the bed of

Edward the Confessor with an offspring unknown to history, with sundry other solecisms of the same kind, but has inverted the order of nature, and feasted his swine with acorns in the midst of summer. All that can be alleged by the warmest admirer of this author amounts to this,—that the circumstances objected to are just as true as the rest of the story; which appears to me (more especially in the matter of the acorns) to be a very imperfect defence, and that the author will do well to profit by Captain Absolute's advice to his servant, and never tell him more lies than are indispensably necessary.

END OF THE MONASTERY.

R. GRÆME AND CATHARINE SETON BEFORE QUEEN MARY.

THE ABBOT.

THE ABBOT;

BEING THE SEQUEL TO THE MONASTERY.

INTRODUCTION—(1831.)

From what is said in the Introduction to the Monastery, it must necessarily be inferred, that the Author considered that romance as something very like a failure. It is true, the booksellers did not complain of the sale, because, unless on very felicitous occasions, or on those which are equally the reverse, literary popularity is not gained or lost by a single publication. Leisure must be allowed for the tide both to flow and ebb. But I was conscious that, in my situation, not to advance was in some degree to recede, and being naturally unwilling to think that the principle of decay lay in myself, I was at least desirous to know of a certainty, whether the degree of discountenance which I had incurred, was now owing to an ill-managed story, or an ill-chosen subject.

I was never, I confess, one of those who are willing to suppose the brains of an author to be a kind of milk, which will not stand above a single creaming, and who are eternally harping to young authors to husband their efforts, and to be chary of their reputation, lest it grow hackneyed in the eyes of men. Perhaps I was, and have always been, the more indifferent to the degree of estimation in which I might be held as an author, because I did not put so high a value as many others upon what is termed literary reputation in the abstract, or at least upon the species of popularity which had fallen to my share; for though it were worse than affectation to deny that my vanity was satisfied at my success in the department in which chance had in some measure enlisted me, I was, nevertheless, far from thinking that the novelist or romance-writer stands high in the ranks of literature. But I spare the reader farther egotism on this subject, as I have expressed my opinion very fully in the Introductory Epistle to the Fortunes of Nigel, first edition; and, although it be composed in an imaginary character, it is as sincere and candid as if it had been written "without my gown and band."

In a word, when I considered myself as having been unsuccessful in the Monastery, I was tempted to try whether I could not restore, even at the risk of totally losing, my so-called reputation, by a new hazard—I looked round my library, and could not but observe, that, from the time of Chaucer to that of Byron, the most popular authors had been the most prolific. Even the aristarch Johnson allowed that the quality of readiness and profusion had a merit in itself, independent of the intrinsic value of the composition. Talking of Churchill, I believe, who had little merit in his prejudiced eyes, he allowed him that of fertility, with some such qualification as this, "A crab-apple can bear but crabs after all; but there is a great difference in favour of that which bears a large quantity of fruit, however indifferent, and that which produces only a few."

Looking more attentively at the patriarchs of literature, whose career was as long as it was brilliant, I thought I perceived that in the busy and prolonged course of exertion, there were no doubt occasional failures, but that still those who were favourites of their age triumphed over these miscarriages. By the new efforts which they made, their errors were obliterated, they became identified with the literature of their country, and after having long received law from the critics, came in some degree to impose it. And when such a writer was at length called from the scene, his death first made the public sensible what a large share he had occupied in their attention. I recollected a passage in Grimm's Correspondence, that while the unexhausted Voltaire sent forth tract after tract to the very close of a long life, the first impression made by each as it appeared, was, that it was inferior to its predecessors; an opinion adopted from the general idea that the Patriarch of Ferney must at last find the point from which he was to decline. But the opinion of the public finally ranked in succession the last of Voltaire's Essays on the same footing with those which had formerly charmed the French nation. The inference from this and similar facts seemed to me to be, that new works were often judged of by the public, not so much from their own intrinsic merit, as from extrinsic ideas which readers had previously formed with regard to them, and over which a writer might hope to triumph by patience and by exertion. There is risk in the attempt;

"If he fall in, good night, or sink or swim."

But this is a chance incident to every literary attempt, and by which men of a sanguine temper are little moved.

I may illustrate what I mean, by the feelings of most men in travelling. If we have found any stage particularly tedious, or in an especial degree interesting, particularly short, or much longer than we expected, our imaginations are so apt to exaggerate the original impression, that, on repeating the journey, we usually find that we have considerably over-rated the predominating quality, and the road appears to be duller or more pleasant, shorter or more tedious, than what we expected, and, consequently, than what is actually the case. It requires a third or fourth journey to enable us to form an accurate judgment of its beauty, its length, or its other attributes.

In the same manner, the public, judging of a new work, which it receives perhaps with little expectation, if surprised into applause, becomes very often ecstatic, gives a great deal more approbation than is due, and elevates the child of its immediate favour to a rank which, as it affects the author, it is equally difficult to keep, and painful to lose. If, on this occasion, the author trembles at the height to which he is raised, and becomes afraid of the shadow of his own renown, he may indeed retire from the lottery with the prize which he has drawn, but, in future ages, his honour will be only in proportion to his labours. If, on the contrary, he rushes again into the lists, he is sure to be judged with severity proportioned to the former favour of the public. If he be daunted by a bad reception on this second occasion, he may again become a stranger to the arena. If, on the contrary, he can keep his ground, and stand the shuttlecock's fate, of being struck up and down, he will probably, at length, hold with some certainty the level in public opinion which he may be found to deserve; and he may perhaps boast of arresting the general attention, in the same manner as the Bachelor Samson Carrasco, of fixing the weathercock La Giralda of Seville for weeks, months, or years, that is, for as long as the wind shall uniformly blow from one quarter. To this degree of popularity the author had the hardihood to aspire, while, in order to attain it, he assumed the daring resolution to keep himself in the view of the public by frequent appearances before them.

It must be added, that the author's incognito gave him greater courage to renew his attempts to please the public, and an advantage similar to that which Jack the Giant-killer received from his coat of darkness. In sending the Abbot forth so soon after the Monastery, he had used the well-known practice recommended by Bassanio: —

"In my school days, when I had lost one shaft,
I shot another of the self-same flight,
The self-same way, with more advised watch,
To find the other forth."

And, to continue the simile, his shafts, like those of the lesser Ajax, were discharged more readily that the archer was as inaccessible to criticism, personally speaking, as the Grecian archer under his brother's sevenfold shield.

Should the reader desire to know upon what principles the Abbot was expected to amend the fortune of the Monastery, I have first to request his attention to the Introductory Epistle addressed to the imaginary Captain Clutterbuck; a mode by which, like his predecessors in this walk of fiction, the real author makes one of his *dramatis personæ* the means of communicating his own sentiments to the public, somewhat more artificially than by a direct address to the readers. A pleasing French writer of fairy tales, Monsieur Pajon, author of the History of Prince Soly, has set a diverting example of the same machinery, where he introduces the presiding Genius of the land of Romance conversing with one of the personages of the tale.

In this Introductory Epistle, the author communicates, in confidence, to Captain Clutterbuck, his sense that the White Lady had not met the taste of the times, and his reason for withdrawing her from the scene. The author did not deem it equally necessary to be candid respecting another alteration. The Monastery was designed, at first, to have contained some supernatural agency, arising out of the fact, that Melrose had been the place of deposit of the great Robert Bruce's heart. The writer shrunk, however, from filling up, in this particular, the sketch as it was originally traced; nor did he venture to resume, in continuation, the subject which he had left unattempted in the original work. Thus, the incident of the discovery of the heart, which occupies the greater part of the Introduction to the Monastery, is a mystery unnecessarily introduced, and which remains at last very imperfectly explained. In this particular, I was happy to shroud myself by the example of the author of "Caleb Williams," who never condescends to inform us of the actual contents of that Iron Chest which makes such a figure in his interesting work, and gives the name to Mr. Colman's drama.

The public had some claim to inquire into this matter, but it seemed indifferent policy in the author to give the explanation. For, whatever praise may be due to the ingenuity which brings to a general combination all the loose threads of a narrative, like the knitter at the finishing of her stocking, I am greatly deceived if in many cases a superior advantage is not attained, by the air of reality which the deficiency of explanation attaches to a work written on a different system. In life itself, many things befall every mortal, of which the individual never knows the real cause or origin; and were we to point out the most marked distinction between a real and a fictitious narrative, we would say, that the former in reference to the remote causes of the events it relates, is obscure, doubtful, and mysterious; whereas, in the latter case, it is a part of the author's duty to afford satisfactory details upon the causes of the separate events he has recorded, and, in a word, to account for every thing. The reader, like Mungo in the Padlock, will not be satisfied with hearing what he is not made fully to comprehend.

I omitted, therefore, in the Introduction to the Abbot, any attempt to explain the previous story, or to apologize for unintelligibility.

Neither would it have been prudent to have endeavoured to proclaim, in the Introduction to the Abbot, the real spring, by which I hoped it might attract a greater degree of interest than its immediate predecessor. A taking title, or the announcement of a popular subject, is a recipe for success much in favour with booksellers, but which authors will not always find efficacious. The cause is worth a moment's examination.

There occur in every country some peculiar historical characters, which are, like a spell or charm, sovereign to excite curiosity and attract attention, since every one in the slightest degree interested in the land which they belong to, has heard much of them, and longs to hear more. A tale turning on the fortunes of Alfred or Elizabeth in England, or of Wallace or Bruce in Scotland, is sure by the very announcement to excite public curiosity to a considerable degree, and ensure the publisher's being relieved of the greater part of an impression, even before the contents of the work are known. This is of the last importance to the bookseller, who is at once, to use a technical phrase, "brought home," all his outlay being repaid. But it is a different case with the author, since it cannot be denied that we are apt to feel least satisfied with the works of which we have been induced, by titles and laudatory advertisements, to entertain exaggerated expectations. The intention of the work has been anticipated, and misconceived or misrepresented, and although the difficulty of executing the work again reminds us of Hotspur's task of "o'er-walking a current roaring loud," yet the adventurer must look for more ridicule if he fails, than applause if he executes, his undertaking.

Notwithstanding a risk, which should make authors pause ere they adopt a theme which, exciting general interest and curiosity, is often the preparative for disappointment, yet it would be an injudicious regulation which should deter the poet or painter from attempting to introduce historical portraits, merely from the difficulty of executing the task in a satisfactory manner. Something must be trusted to the generous impulse, which often thrusts an artist upon feats of which he knows the difficulty, while he trusts courage and exertion may afford the means of surmounting it.

It is especially when he is sensible of losing ground with the public, that an author may be justified in using with address, such selection of subject or title as is most likely to procure a rehearing. It was with these feelings of hope and apprehension, that I venture to awaken, in a work of fiction, the memory of Queen Mary, so interesting by her wit, her beauty, her misfortunes, and the mystery which still does, and probably always will, overhang her history. In doing so, I was aware that failure would be a conclusive disaster, so that my task was something like that of an enchanter who raises a spirit over whom he is uncertain of possessing an effectual control; and I naturally paid attention to such principles of composition, as I conceived were best suited to the historical novel.

Enough has been already said to explain the purpose of composing the Abbot. The historical references are, as usual, explained in the notes. That which relates to Queen Mary's escape from Lochleven Castle, is a more minute account of that romantic adventure, than is to be found in the histories of the period.

ABBOTSFORD,
1st *January*, 1831.

INTRODUCTORY EPISTLE.

FROM THE AUTHOR OF "WAVERLEY," TO CAPTAIN CLUTTERBUCK, LATE OF HIS MAJESTY'S —— REGIMENT OF INFANTRY.

DEAR CAPTAIN:

I AM sorry to observe, by your last favour, that you disapprove of the numerous retrenchments and alterations which I have been under the necessity of making on the Manuscript of your friend, the Benedictine, and I willingly make you the medium of apology to many, who have honoured me more than I deserve.

I admit that my retrenchments have been numerous, and leave gaps in the story, which, in your original manuscript, would have run well-nigh to a fourth volume, as my printer assures me. I am sensible, besides, that, in consequence of the liberty of curtailment you have allowed me, some parts of the story have been huddled up without the necessary details. But, after all, it is better that the travellers should have to step over a ditch, than to wade through a morass—that the reader should have to suppose what may easily be inferred, than be obliged to creep through pages of dull explanation. I have struck out, for example, the whole machinery of the White Lady, and the poetry by which it is so ably supported, in the original manuscript. But you must allow that the public taste gives little encouragement to those legendary superstitions, which formed alternately the delight and the terror of our predecessors. In like manner, much is omitted illustrative of the impulse of enthusiasm in favour of the ancient religion in Mother Magdalen and the Abbot. But we do not feel deep sympathy at this period with what was once the most powerful and animating principle in Europe, with the exception of that of the Reformation, by which it was successfully opposed.

You rightly observe, that these retrenchments have rendered the title no longer applicable to the subject, and that some other would have been more suitable to the Work, in its present state, than that of THE ABBOT, who made so much greater figure in the original, and for whom your friend, the Benedictine, seems to have inspired you with a sympathetic respect. I must plead guilty to this accusation, observing, at the same time, in manner of extenuation, that though the objection might have been easily removed, by giving a new title to the Work, yet, in doing so, I should have destroyed the necessary cohesion between the present history, and its predecessor THE MONASTERY, which I was unwilling to do, as the period, and several of the personages, were the same.

After all, my good friend, it is of little consequence what the work is called, or on what interest it turns, provided it catches the public attention; for the quality of the wine (could we but insure it) may, according to the old proverb, render the bush unnecessary, or of little consequence.

I congratulate you upon your having found it consistent with prudence to establish your Tilbury, and approve of the colour, and of your boy's livery, (subdued green and pink.)—As you talk of completing your descriptive poem on the "Ruins of Kennaquhair, with notes by an Antiquary," I hope you have procured a steady horse.—I remain, with compliments to all friends, dear Captain, very much

Yours, &c. &c. &c.

THE AUTHOR OF WAVERLEY.

THE ABBOT.

Chapter the First.

Domum mansit—lanam fecit.
Ancient Roman Epitaph.

She keepit close the hous, and birlit at the quhele.
GAWAIN DOUGLAS.

THE time which passes over our heads so imperceptibly, makes the same gradual change in habits, manners, and character, as in personal appearance. At the revolution of every five years we find ourselves another, and yet the same—there is a change of views, and no less of the light in which we regard them ; a change of motives as well as of actions. Nearly twice that space had glided away over the head of Halbert Glendinning and his lady, betwixt the period of our former narrative, in which they played a distinguished part, and the date at which our present tale commences.

Two circumstances only had imbittered their union, which was otherwise as happy as mutual affection could render it. The first of these was indeed the common calamity of Scotland, being the distracted state of that unhappy country, where every man's sword was directed against his neighbour's bosom. Glendinning had proved what Murray expected of him, a steady friend, strong in battle, and wise in counsel, adhering to him, from motives of gratitude, in situations where by his own unbiassed will he would either have stood neuter, or have joined the opposite party. Hence, when danger was near—and it was seldom far distant—Sir Halbert Glendinning, for he now bore the rank of knighthood, was perpetually summoned to attend his patron on distant expeditions, or on perilous enterprises, or to assist him with his counsel in the doubtful intrigues of a half-barbarous court. He was thus frequently, and for a long space, absent from his castle and from his lady; and to this ground of regret we must add, that their union had not been blessed with children, to occupy the attention of the Lady of Avenel, while she was thus deprived of her husband's domestic society.

On such occasions she lived almost entirely secluded from the world, within the walls of her paternal mansion. Visiting amongst neighbors was a matter entirely out of the question, unless on occasions of solemn festival, and then it was chiefly confined to near kindred. Of these the Lady of Avenel had none who survived, and the dames of the neighbouring barons affected to regard her less as the heiress of the house of Avenel than as the wife of a peasant, the son of a church-vassal, raised up to mushroom eminence by the capricious favour of Murray.

The pride of ancestry, which rankled in the bosom of the ancient gentry, was more openly expressed by their ladies, and was, moreover, imbittered not a little by the political feuds of the time, for most of the Southern chiefs were friends to the authority of the Queen, and very jealous of the power of Murray. The Castle of Avenel was, therefore, on all these accounts, as melancholy and solitary a residence for its lady as could well be imagined. Still it had the essential recommendation of great security. The reader is already aware that the fortress was built upon an islet on a small lake, and was only accessible by a causeway, intersected by a double ditch, defended by two draw-bridges, so that without artillery, it might in those days be considered as impregnable. It was only necessary, therefore, to secure against surprise, and the service of six able men within the castle was sufficient for that purpose. If more serious danger threatened, an ample garrison was supplied by the male inhabitants of a little hamlet, which, under the auspices of Halbert Glendinning, had arisen on a small piece of level ground, betwixt the lake and the hill, nearly adjoining to the spot where the causeway joined the mainland. The Lord of Avenel had found it an easy matter to procure inhabitants, as he was not only a kind and beneficent overlord, but well qualified, both by his experience in arms, his high character for wisdom and integrity, and his favour with the powerful Earl of Murray, to protect and defend those who dwelt under his banner. In leaving his castle for any length of time, he had, therefore, the consolation to reflect, that this village afforded, on the slightest notice, a band of thirty stout men, which was more than sufficient for its defence; while the families of the villagers, as was usual on such occasions, fled to the recesses of the mountains, drove their cattle to the same places of shelter, and left the enemy to work their will on their miserable cottages.

One guest only resided generally, if not constantly, at the Castle of Avenel. This was Henry Warden, who now felt himself less able for the stormy task imposed on the reforming clergy; and having by his zeal given personal offence to many of the leading nobles and chiefs, did not consider himself as perfectly safe, unless when within the walls of the strong mansion of some assured friend. He ceased not, however, to serve his cause as eagerly with his pen, as he had formerly done with his tongue, and had engaged in a furious and acrimonious contest, concerning the sacrifice of the mass, as it was termed, with the Abbot Eustatius, formerly the Sub-Prior of Kennaquhair. Answers, replies, duplies, triplies, quadruplies, followed thick upon each other, and displayed, as is not unusual in controversy, fully as much zeal as Christian charity. The disputation very soon became as celebrated as that of John Knox and the Abbot of Crosraguel, raged nearly as fiercely, and, for aught I know, the publications to which it gave rise may be as recious in the eyes of bibliographers.* But the engrossing nature of his cupation rendered the theologian not the most interesting companion for a solitary female; and his grave, stern, and absorbed deportment, which seldom showed any interest, except in that which concerned his religious profession, made his presence rather add to than diminish the gloom which hung over the Castle of Avenel. To superintend the tasks of numerous female domestics, was the principal part of the Lady's daily employment; her spindle and distaff, her Bible, and a solitary walk upon the battlements of the castle, or upon the causeway, or occasionally, but more seldom, upon the banks of the little lake, consumed the rest of the day. But so great was the insecurity of the period, that when she ventured to extend her walk beyond the hamlet, the warder on the watch-tower was directed to keep a sharp look-out in every direction, and four or five men held themselves in readiness to mount and sally forth from the castle on the slightest appearance of alarm.

Thus stood affairs at the castle, when, after an absence of several weeks, the Knight of Avenel, which was now the title most frequently given to Sir Halbert Glendinning, was daily expected to return home. Day after day, however, passed away, and he returned not. Letters in those days were rarely written, and the Knight must have resorted to a secretary to express

* The tracts which appeared in the Disputation between the Scottish Reformer and Quentin Kennedy Abbot of Crosraguel, are among the scarcest in Scottish Bibliography. See M'Crie's *Life of Knox*, p. 258.

his intentions in that manner; besides, intercourse of all kinds was precarious and unsafe, and no man cared to give any public intimation of the time and direction of a journey, since, if his route were publicly known, it was always likely he might in that case meet with more enemies than friends upon the road. The precise day, therefore, of Sir Halbert's return, was not fixed, but that which his lady's fond expectation had calculated upon in her own mind had long since passed, and hope delayed began to make the heart sick.

It was upon the evening of a sultry summer's day, when the sun was half-sunk behind the distant western mountains of Liddesdale, that the Lady took her solitary walk on the battlements of a range of buildings, which formed the front of the castle, where a flat roof of flag-stones presented a broad and convenient promenade. The level surface of the lake, undisturbed except by the occasional dipping of a teal-duck, or coot, was gilded with the beams of the setting luminary, and reflected, as if in a golden mirror, the hills amongst which it lay embossed. The scene, otherwise so lonely, was occasionally enlivened by the voices of the children in the village, which, softened by distance, reached the ear of the Lady, in her solitary walk, or by the distant call of the herdsman, as he guided his cattle from the glen in which they had pastured all day, to place them in greater security for the night, in the immediate vicinity of the village. The deep lowing of the cows seemed to demand the attendance of the milk-maidens, who, singing shrilly and merrily, strolled forth, each with her pail on her head, to attend to the duty of the evening. The Lady of Avenel looked and listened; the sounds which she heard reminded her of former days, when her most important employment, as well as her greatest delight, was to assist Dame Glendinning and Tibb Tackett in milking the cows at Glendearg. The thought was fraught with melancholy.

"Why was I not," she said, "the peasant girl which in all men's eyes I seemed to be? Halbert and I had then spent our life peacefully in his native glen, undisturbed by the phantoms either of fear or of ambition. His greatest pride had then been to show the fairest herd in the Halidome; his greatest danger to repel some pilfering snatcher from the Border; and the utmost distance which would have divided us, would have been the chase of some outlying deer. But, alas! what avails the blood which Halbert has shed, and the dangers which he encounters, to support a name and rank, dear to him because he has it from me, but which we shall never transmit to our posterity! with me the name of Avenel must expire."

She sighed as the reflections arose, and, looking towards the shore of the lake, her eye was attracted by a group of children of various ages, assembled to see a little ship, constructed by some village artist, perform its first voyage on the water. It was launched amid the shouts of tiny voices and the clapping of little hands, and shot bravely forth on its voyage with a favouring wind, which promised to carry it to the other side of the lake. Some of the bigger boys ran round to receive and secure it on the farther shore, trying their speed against each other as they sprang like young fawns along the shingly verge of the lake. The rest, for whom such a journey seemed too arduous, remained watching the motions of the fairy vessel from the spot where it had been launched. The sight of their sports pressed on the mind of the childless Lady of Avenel.

"Why are none of these prattlers mine?" she continued, pursuing the tenor of her melancholy reflections. "Their parents can scarce find them the coarsest food — and I, who could nurse them in plenty, I am doomed never to hear a child call me mother!"

The thought sunk on her heart with a bitterness which resembled envy, so deeply is the desire of offspring implanted in the female breast. She pressed her hands together as if she were wringing them in the extremity of her desolate feeling, as one whom Heaven had written childless. A large stag-hound of the greyhound species approached at this moment, and attracted perhaps by the gesture, licked her hands and pressed his large head against them. He obtained the desired caresses in return, but still the sad impression remained.

"Wolf," she said, as if the animal could have understood her complaints, "thou art a noble and beautiful animal; but, alas! the love and affection that I long to bestow, is of a quality higher than can fall to thy share, though I love thee much."

And, as if she were apologizing to Wolf for withholding from him any part of her regard, she caressed his proud head and crest, while, looking in her eyes, he seemed to ask her what she wanted, or what he could do to show his attachment. At this moment a shriek of distress was heard on the shore, from the playful group which had been lately so jovial. The Lady looked, and saw the cause with great agony.

The little ship, the object of the children's delighted attention, had stuck among some tufts of the plant which bears the water-lily, that marked a shoal in the lake about an arrow-flight from the shore. A hardy little boy, who had taken the lead in the race round the margin of the lake, did not hesitate a moment to strip off his *wylie-coat*, plunge into the water, and swim towards the object of their common solicitude. The first movement of the Lady was to call for help; but she observed that the boy swam strongly and fearlessly, and as she saw that one or two villagers, who were distant spectators of the incident, seemed to give themselves no uneasiness on his account, she supposed that he was accustomed to the exercise, and that there was no danger. But whether, in swimming, the boy had struck his breast against a sunken rock, or whether he was suddenly taken with cramp, or whether he had over-calculated his own strength, it so happened, that when he had disembarrassed the little plaything from the flags in which it was entangled, and sent it forward on its course, he had scarce swam a few yards in his way to the shore, than he raised himself suddenly from the water, and screamed aloud, clapping his hands at the same time with an expression of fear and pain.

The Lady of Avenel, instantly taking the alarm, called hastily to the attendants to get the boat ready. But this was an affair of some time. The only boat permitted to be used on the lake, was moored within the second cut which intersected the canal, and it was several minutes ere it could be unmoored and got under way. Meantime, the Lady of Avenel, with agonizing anxiety, saw that the efforts that the poor boy made to keep himself afloat, were now exchanged for a faint struggling, which would soon have been over, but for aid equally prompt and unhoped-for. Wolf, who, like some of that large species of greyhound, was a practised water-dog, had marked the object of her anxiety, and, quitting his mistress's side, had sought the nearest point from which he could with safety plunge into the lake. With the wonderful instinct which these noble animals have so often displayed in the like circumstances, he swam straight to the spot where his assistance was so much wanted, and seizing the child's under-dress in his mouth, he not only kept him afloat, but towed him towards the causeway. The boat having put off with a couple of men, met the dog half-way, and relieved him of his burden. They landed on the causeway, close by the gates of the castle, with their yet lifeless charge, and were there met by the Lady of Avenel, attended by one or two of her maidens, eagerly waiting to administer assistance to the sufferer.

He was borne into the castle, deposited upon a bed, and every mode of recovery resorted to, which the knowledge of the times, and the skill of Henry Warden, who professed some medical science, could dictate. For some time it was all in vain, and the Lady watched, with unspeakable earnestness, the pallid countenance of the beautiful child. He seemed about ten years old. His dress was of the meanest sort, but his long curled hair, and the noble cast of his features, partook not of that poverty of appearance. The proudest noble in Scotland might have been yet prouder could he have called that child his heir. While, with breathless anxiety, the Lady of Avenel gazed on his well-formed and expressive features, a slight shade of colour returned gradually to the cheek; suspended animation became restored by degrees, the child sighed deeply, opened his eyes, which to the human countenance produces the effect of light upon the natural landscape, stretched his arms towards the Lady, and muttered the word "Mother," that epithet, of all others, which is dearest to the female ear.

"God, madam," said the preacher, "has restored the child to your wishes; it must be yours so to bring him up, that he may not one day wish that he had perished in his innocence."

"It shall be my charge," said the Lady; and again throwing her arms around the boy, she overwhelmed him with kisses and caresses, so much was she agitated by the terror arising from the danger in which he had been just placed, and by joy at his unexpected deliverance.

"But you are not my mother," said the boy, recovering his recollection, and endeavouring, though faintly, to escape from the caresses of the Lady of Avenel; "you are not my mother,—alas! I have no mother—only I have dreamt that I had one."

"I will read the dream for you, my love," answered the Lady of Avenel; "and I will be myself your mother. Surely God has heard my wishes, and, in his own marvellous manner, hath sent me an object on which my affections may expand themselves." She looked towards Warden as she spoke. The preacher hesitated what he should reply to a burst of passionate feeling, which, perhaps, seemed to him more enthusiastic than the occasion demanded. In the meanwhile, the large stag-hound, Wolf, which, dripping wet as he was, had followed his mistress into the apartment, and had sat by the bedside, a patient and quiet spectator of all the means used for resuscitation of the being whom he had preserved, now became impatient of remaining any longer unnoticed, and began to whine and fawn upon the Lady with his great rough paws.

"Yes," she said, "good Wolf, and you shall be remembered also for your day's work; and I will think the more of you for having preserved the life of a creature so beautiful."

But Wolf was not quite satisfied with the share of attention which he thus attracted; he persisted in whining and pawing upon his mistress, his caresses rendered still more troublesome by his long shaggy hair being so much and thoroughly wetted, till she desired one of the domestics, with whom he was familiar, to call the animal out of the apartment. Wolf resisted every invitation to this purpose, until his mistress positively commanded him to be gone, in an angry tone; when, turning towards the bed on which the body still lay, half awake to sensation, half drowned in the meanders of fluctuating delirium, he uttered a deep and savage growl, curled up his nose and lips, showing his full range of white and sharpened teeth, which might have matched those of an actual wolf, and then, turning round, sullenly followed the domestic out of the apartment.

"It is singular," said the Lady, addressing Warden; "the animal is not only so good-natured to all, but so particularly fond of children. What can ail him at the little fellow whose life he has saved?"

"Dogs," replied the preacher, "are but too like the human race in their foibles, though their instinct be less erring than the reason of poor mortal man when relying upon his own unassisted powers. Jealousy, my good lady, is a passion not unknown to them, and they often evince it, not only with respect to the preferences which they see given by their masters to individuals of their own species, but even when their rivals are children. You have caressed that child much and eagerly, and the dog considers himself as a discarded favourite."

"It is a strange instinct," said the Lady; "and from the gravity with which you mention it, my reverend friend, I would almost say that you supposed this singular jealousy of my favourite Wolf, was not only well founded, but justifiable. But perhaps you speak in jest?"

"I seldom jest," answered the preacher; "life was not lent to us to be expended in that idle mirth which resembles the crackling of thorns under the pot. I would only have you derive, if it so please you, this lesson from what I have said, that the best of our feelings, when indulged to excess, may give pain to others. There is but one in which we may indulge to the utmost limit of vehemence of which our bosom is capable, secure that excess cannot exist in the greatest intensity to which it can be excited—I mean the love of our Maker."

"Surely," said the Lady of Avenel, "we are commanded by the same authority to love our neighbour?"

"Ay, madam," said Warden, "but our love to God is to be unbounded—we are to love him with our whole heart, our whole soul, and our whole strength. The love which the precept commands us to bear to our neighbour, has affixed to it a direct limit and qualification—we are to love our neighbour as ourself; as it is elsewhere explained by the great commandment, that we must do unto him as we would that he should do unto us. Here there is a limit, and a bound, even to the most praiseworthy of our affections, so far as they are turned upon sublunary and terrestrial objects. We are to render to our neighbour, whatever be his rank or degree, that corresponding portion of affection with which we could rationally expect we should ourselves be regarded by those standing in the same relation to us. Hence, neither husband nor wife, neither son nor daughter, neither friend nor relation, are lawfully to be made the objects of our idolatry. The Lord our God is a jealous God, and will not endure that we bestow on the creature that extremity of devotion which He who made us demands as his own share. I say to you, Lady, that even in the fairest, and purest, and most honourable feelings of our nature, there is that original taint of sin which ought to make us pause and hesitate, ere we indulge them to excess."

"I understand not this, reverend sir," said the Lady; "nor do I guess what I can have now said or done, to draw down on me an admonition which has something a taste of reproof."

"Lady," said Warden, "I crave your pardon, if I have urged aught beyond the limits of my duty. But consider, whether in the sacred promise to be not only a protectress, but a mother, to this poor child, your purpose may meet the wishes of the noble knight your husband. The fondness which you have lavished on the unfortunate, and, I own, most lovely child, has met something like a reproof in the bearing of your household dog.—Displease not your noble husband. Men, as well as animals, are jealous of the affections of those they love."

"This is too much, reverend sir," said the Lady of Avenel, greatly offended. "You have been long our guest, and have received from the Knight of Avenel and myself that honour and regard which your character and profession so justly demand. But I am yet to learn that we have at any time authorized your interference in our family arrangements, or placed you as a judge of our conduct towards each other. I pray this may be forborne in future."

"Lady," replied the preacher, with the boldness peculiar to the clergy of his persuasion at that time, "when you weary of my admonitions—when I see that my services are no longer acceptable to you, and the noble knight your husband, I shall know that my Master wills me no longer to abide here; and, praying for a continuance of his best blessings on your family I will then, were the season the depth of winter, and the hour midnight, walk out on yonder waste, and travel forth through these wild mountains, as lonely and unaided, though far more helpless, than when I first met your husband in the valley of Glendearg. But while I remain here, I will not see you err from the true path, no, not a hair's-breadth, without making the old man's voice and remonstrance heard."

"Nay, but," said the Lady, who both loved and respected the good man, though sometimes a little offended at what she conceived to be an exuberant degree of zeal, "we will not part this way, my good friend. Women are quick and hasty in their feelings; but, believe me, my wishes and my purposes towards this child are such as both my husband and you will approve of." The clergyman bowed, and retreated to his own apartment.

Chapter the Second.

How steadfastly he fix'd his eyes on me—
His dark eyes shining through forgotten tears—
Then stretch'd his little arms, and call'd me mother!
What could I do? I took the bantling home—
I could not tell the imp he had no mother.

COUNT BASIL.

WHEN Warden had left the apartment, the Lady of Avenel gave way to the feelings of tenderness which the sight of the boy, his sudden danger, and his recent escape, had inspired; and no longer awed by the sternness, as she deemed it, of the preacher, heaped with caresses the lovely and interesting child. He was now, in some measure, recovered from the consequences of his accident, and received passively, though not without wonder, the tokens of kindness with which he was thus loaded. The face of the lady was strange to him, and her dress different and far more sumptuous than any he remembered. But the boy was naturally of an undaunted temper; and indeed children are generally acute physiognomists, and not only pleased by that which is beautiful in itself, but peculiarly quick in distinguishing and replying to the attentions of those who really love them. If they see a person in company, though a perfect stranger, who is by nature fond of children, the little imps seem to discover it by a sort of freemasonry, while the awkward attempts of those who make advances to them for the purpose of recommending themselves to the parents, usually fail in attracting their reciprocal attention. The little boy, therefore, appeared in some degree sensible of the lady's caresses, and it was with difficulty she withdrew herself from his pillow, to afford him leisure for necessary repose.

"To whom belongs our little rescued varlet?" was the first question which the Lady of Avenel put to her handmaiden Lilias, when they had retired to the hall.

"To an old woman in the hamlet," said Lilias, "who is even now come so far as the porter's lodge to inquire concerning his safety. Is it your pleasure that she be admitted?"

"Is it my pleasure?" said the Lady of Avenel, echoing the question with a strong accent of displeasure and surprise; "can you make any doubt of it? What woman but must pity the agony of the mother, whose heart is throbbing for the safety of a child so lovely!"

"Nay, but, madam," said Lilias, "this woman is too old to be the mother of the child; I rather think she must be his grandmother, or some more distant relation."

"Be she who she will, Lilias," replied the Lady, "she must have an aching heart while the safety of a creature so lovely is uncertain. Go instantly and bring her hither. Besides, I would willingly learn something concerning his birth."

Lilias left the hall, and presently afterwards returned, ushering in a tall female very poorly dressed, yet with more pretension to decency and cleanliness than was usually combined with such coarse garments. The Lady of Avenel knew her figure the instant she presented herself. It was the fashion of the family, that upon every Sabbath, and on two evenings in the week besides, Henry Warden preached or lectured in the chapel at the castle. The extension of the Protestant faith was, upon principle, as well as in good policy, a primary object with the Knight of Avenel. The inhabitants of the village were therefore invited to attend upon the instructions of Henry Warden, and many of them were speedily won to the doctrine which their master and protector approved. These sermons, homilies, and lectures, had made a great impression on the mind of the Abbot Eustace, or Eustatius, and were a sufficient spur to the severity and sharpness of his controversy with his old fellow-collegiate; and, ere Queen Mary was dethroned, and while the Catholics still had considerable authority in the Border provinces, he more than once threatened to levy his vassals, and assail and level with the earth that stronghold of heresy the Castle of Avenel. But notwithstanding the Abbot's impotent resentment, and notwithstanding also the disinclination of the country to favour the new religion, Henry Warden proceeded without remission in his labours, and made weekly converts from the faith of Rome to that of the reformed church. Amongst those who gave most earnest and constant attendance on his ministry, was the aged woman, whose form, tall, and otherwise too remarkable to be forgotten, the Lady had of late observed frequently as being conspicuous among the little audience. She had indeed more than once desired to know who that stately-looking woman was, whose appearance was so much above the poverty of her vestments. But the reply had always been, that she was an Englishwoman, who was tarrying for a season at the hamlet, and that no one knew more concerning her. She now asked her after her name and birth.

"Magdalen Græme is my name," said the woman; "I come of the Græmes of Heathergill, in Nicol Forest,* a people of ancient blood."

"And what make you," continued the Lady, "so far distant from your home?"

"I have no home," said Magdalen Græme, "it was burnt by your Border-riders — my husband and my son were slain — there is not a drop's blood left in the veins of any one which is of kin to mine."

"That is no uncommon fate in these wild times, and in this unsettled land," said the Lady; "the English hands have been as deeply dyed in our blood as ever those of Scotsmen have been in yours."

"You have right to say it, Lady," answered Magdalen Græme; "for men tell of a time when this castle was not strong enough to save your father's life, or to afford your mother and her infant a place of refuge. And why ask ye me, then, wherefore I dwell not in mine own home, and with mine own people?"

"It was indeed an idle question," answered the Lady, "where misery so often makes wanderers; but wherefore take refuge in a hostile country?"

"My neighbours were Popish and mass-mongers," said the old woman; "it has pleased Heaven to give me a clearer sight of the gospel, and I have tarried here to enjoy the ministry of that worthy man Henry Warden, who, to the praise and comfort of many, teacheth the Evangel in truth and in sincerity."

"Are you poor?" again demanded the Lady of Avenel.

"You hear me ask alms of no one," answered the Englishwoman.

---

* A district of Cumberland, lying close to the Scottish Border.

Here there was a pause. The manner of the woman was, if not disrespectful, at least much less than gracious; and she appeared to give no encouragement to farther communication. The Lady of Avenel renewed the conversation on a different topic.

"You have heard of the danger in which your boy has been placed?"

"I have, Lady, and how by an especial providence he was rescued from death. May Heaven make him thankful, and me!"

"What relation do you bear to him?"

"I am his grandmother, lady, if it so please you; the only relation he hath left upon earth to take charge of him."

"The burden of his maintenance must necessarily be grievous to you in your deserted situation?" pursued the Lady.

"I have complained of it to no one," said Magdalen Græme, with the same unmoved, dry, and unconcerned tone of voice, in which she had answered all the former questions.

"If," said the Lady of Avenel, "your grandchild could be received into a noble family, would it not advantage both him and you?"

"Received into a noble family!" said the old woman, drawing herself up, and bending her brows until her forehead was wrinkled into a frown of unusual severity; "and for what purpose, I pray you? — to be my lady's page, or my lord's jackman, to eat broken victuals, and contend with other menials for the remnants of the master's meal? Would you have him to fan the flies from my lady's face while she sleeps, to carry her train while she walks, to hand her trencher when she feeds, to ride before her on horseback, to walk after her on foot, to sing when she lists, and to be silent when she bids? — a very weathercock, which, though furnished in appearance with wings and plumage, cannot soar into the air — cannot fly from the spot where it is perched, but receives all its impulse, and performs all its revolutions, obedient to the changeful breath of a vain woman? When the eagle of Helvellyn perches on the tower of Lanercost, and turns and changes his place to show how the wind sits, Roland Græme shall be what you would make him.

The woman spoke with a rapidity and vehemence which seemed to have in it a touch of insanity; and a sudden sense of the danger to which the child must necessarily be exposed in the charge of such a keeper, increased the Lady's desire to keep him in the castle if possible.

"You mistake me, dame," she said, addressing the old woman in a soothing manner; "I do not wish your boy to be in attendance on myself, but upon the good knight my husband. Were he himself the son of a belted earl, he could not better be trained to arms, and all that befits a gentleman, than by the instructions and discipline of Sir Halbert Glendinning."

"Ay," answered the old woman, in the same style of bitter irony, "I know the wages of that service; — a curse when the corslet is not sufficiently brightened, — a blow when the girth is not tightly drawn, — to be beaten because the hounds are at fault, — to be reviled because the foray is unsuccessful, — to stain his hands for the master's bidding in the blood alike of beast and of man, — to be a butcher of harmless deer, a murderer and defacer of God's own image, not at his own pleasure, but at that of his lord, — to live a brawling ruffian, and a common stabber — exposed to heat, to cold, to want of food, to all the privations of an anchoret, not for the love of God, but for the service of Satan, — to die by the gibbet, or in some obscure skirmish, — to sleep out his brief life in carnal security, and to awake in the eternal fire, which is never quenched."

"Nay," said the Lady of Avenel, "but to such unhallowed course of life your grandson will not be here exposed. My husband is just and kind to those who live under his banner; and you yourself well know, that youth have here a strict as well as a good preceptor in the person of our chaplain."

The old woman appeared to pause.

"You have named," she said, "the only circumstance which can move me. I must soon onward, the vision has said it — I must not tarry in the same spot — I must on, — I must on, it is my weird. — Swear, then, that you will protect the boy as if he were your own, until I return hither and claim him, and I will consent for a space to part with him. But especially swear, he shall not lack the instruction of the godly man who hath placed the gospel-truth high above those idolatrous shavelings, the monks and friars."

"Be satisfied, dame," said the Lady of Avenel; "the boy shall have as much care as if he were born of my own blood. Will you see him now?"

"No," answered the old woman sternly; "to part is enough. I go forth on my own mission. I will not soften my heart by useless tears and wailings, as one that is not called to a duty."

"Will you not accept of something to aid you in your pilgrimage?" said the Lady of Avenel, putting into her hands two crowns of the sun. The old woman flung them down on the table.

"Am I of the race of Cain," she said, "proud Lady, that you offer me gold in exchange for my own flesh and blood?"

"I had no such meaning," said the Lady, gently; "nor am I the proud woman you term me. Alas! my own fortunes might have taught me humility, even had it not been born with me."

The old woman seemed somewhat to relax her tone of severity.

"You are of gentle blood," she said, "else we had not parleyed thus long together. — You are of gentle blood, and to such," she added, drawing up her tall form as she spoke, "pride is as graceful as is the plume upon the bonnet. But for these pieces of gold, lady, you must needs resume them. I need not money. I am well provided; and I may not care for myself, nor think how, or by whom, I shall be sustained. Farewell, and keep your word. Cause your gates to be opened, and your bridges to be lowered. I will set forward this very night. When I come again, I will demand from you a strict account, for I have left with you the jewel of my life! Sleep will visit me but in snatches, food will not refresh me, rest will not restore my strength, until I see Roland Græme. Once more, farewell."

"Make your obeisance, dame," said Lilias to Magdalen Græme, as she retired, "make your obeisance to her ladyship, and thank her for her goodness, as is but fitting and right."

The old woman turned short around on the officious waiting-maid. "Let her make her obeisance to me then, and I will return it. Why should I bend to her? — is it because her kirtle is of silk, and mine of blue lockeram? — Go to, my lady's waiting-woman. Know that the rank of the man rates that of the wife, and that she who marries a churl's son, were she a king's daughter, is but a peasant's bride."

Lilias was about to reply in great indignation, but her mistress imposed silence on her, and commanded that the old woman should be safely conducted to the mainland.

"Conduct her safe!" exclaimed the incensed waiting-woman, while Magdalen Græme left the apartment; "I say, duck her in the loch, and then we will see whether she is witch or not, as every body in the village of Lochside will say and swear. I marvel your ladyship could bear so long with her insolence." But the commands of the Lady were obeyed, and the old dame, dismissed from the castle, was committed to her fortune. She kept her word, and did not long abide in that place, leaving the hamlet on the very night succeeding the interview, and wandering no one asked whither. The Lady of Avenel inquired under what circumstances she had appeared among them, but could only learn that she was believed to be the widow of some man of consequence among the Græmes who then inhabited the Debateable Land, a name given to a certain portion of territory which was the frequent subject of dispute betwixt Scotland and England — that she had suffered great wrong in some of the frequent forays by which that unfortunate district was wasted, and had been driven from her dwelling-place. She had arrived in the hamlet no one knew for what purpose, and was held by some to be a witch, by others a zealous Protestant, and by others again a Catholic devotee. Her language was mysterious, and her manners repulsive; and all that could be collected from her conversation seemed to imply that she was under the influence either of a spell or of a vow, — there was no saying which, since she talked as one who acted under a powerful and external agency.

Such were the particulars which the Lady's inquiries were able to collect concerning Magdalen Græme, being far too meagre and contradictory to authorize any satisfactory deduction. In truth, the miseries of the time, and the various turns of fate incidental to a frontier country, were perpetually chasing from their habitations those who had not the means of defence or protection. These wanderers in the land were too often seen, to excite much attention or sympathy. They received the cold relief which was extorted by general feelings of humanity; a little excited in some breasts, and perhaps rather chilled in others, by the recollection that they who gave the charity to-day might themselves want it to-morrow. Magdalen Græme, therefore, came and departed like a shadow from the neighbourhood of Avenel Castle.

The boy whom Providence, as she thought, had thus strangely placed under her care, was at once established a favourite with the Lady of the castle. How could it be otherwise? He became the object of those affectionate feelings, which, finding formerly no object on which to expand themselves, had increased the gloom of the castle, and imbittered the solitude of its mistress. To teach him reading and writing as far as her skill went, to attend to his childish comforts, to watch his boyish sports, became the Lady's favourite amusement. In her circumstances, where the ear only heard the lowing of the cattle from the distant hills, or the heavy step of the warder as he walked upon his post, or the half-envied laugh of her maiden as she turned her wheel, the appearance of the blooming and beautiful boy gave an interest which can hardly be conceived by those who live amid gayer and busier scenes. Young Roland was to the Lady of Avenel what the flower, which occupies the window of some solitary captive, is to the poor wight by whom it is nursed and cultivated,—something which at once excited and repaid her care; and in giving the boy her affection, she felt, as it were, grateful to him for releasing her from the state of dull apathy in which she had usually found herself during the absence of Sir Halbert Glendinning.

But even the charms of this blooming favourite were unable to chase the recurring apprehensions which arose from her husband's procrastinated return. Soon after Roland Græme became a resident at the castle, a groom, despatched by Sir Halbert, brought tidings that business still delayed the Knight at the Court of Holyrood. The more distant period which the messenger had assigned for his master's arrival at length glided away, summer melted into autumn, and autumn was about to give place to winter, and yet he came not.

Chapter the Third.

The waning harvest-moon shone broad and bright,
The warder's horn was heard at dead of night,
And while the portals wide were flung,
With trampling hoofs the rocky pavement rung.
LEYDEN.

"AND you, too, would be a soldier, Roland?" said the Lady of Avenel to her young charge, while, seated on a stone chair at one end of the battlements, she saw the boy attempt, with a long stick, to mimic the motions of the warder, as he alternately shouldered, or ported, or sloped pike.

"Yes, Lady," said the boy,—for he was now familiar, and replied to her questions with readiness and alacrity,—"a soldier will I be; for there ne'er was gentleman but who belted him with the brand."

"Thou a gentleman!" said Lilias, who, as usual, was in attendance; "such a gentleman as I would make of a bean-cod with a rusty knife."

"Nay, chide him not, Lilias," said the Lady of Avenel, "for, beshrew me, but I think he comes of gentle blood—see how it musters in his face at your injurious reproof."

"Had I my will, madam," answered Lilias, "a good birchen wand should make his colour muster to better purpose still."

"On my word, Lilias," said the Lady, "one would think you had received harm from the poor boy—or is he so far on the frosty side of your favour because he enjoys the sunny side of mine?"

"Over heavens forbode, my Lady!" answered Lilias; "I have lived too long with gentles, I praise my stars for it, to fight with either follies or fantasies, whether they relate to beast, bird, or boy."

Lilias was a favourite in her own class, a spoiled domestic, and often accustomed to take more licence than her mistress was at all times willing to encourage. But what did not please the Lady of Avenel, she did not choose to hear, and thus it was on the present occasion. She resolved to look more close and sharply after the boy, who had hitherto been committed chiefly to the management of Lilias. He must, she thought, be born of gentle blood; it were shame to think otherwise of a form so noble, and features so fair;—the very wildness in which he occasionally indulged, his contempt of danger, and impatience of restraint, had in them something noble;—assuredly the child was born of high rank. Such was her conclusion, and she acted upon it accordingly. The domestics around her, less jealous, or less scrupulous than Lilias, acted as servants usually do, following the bias, and flattering, for their own purposes, the humour of the Lady; and the boy soon took on him those airs of superiority, which the sight of habitual deference seldom fails to inspire. It seemed, in truth, as if to command were his natural sphere, so easily did he use himself to exact and receive compliance with his humours. The chaplain, indeed, might have interposed to check the air of assumption which Roland Græme so readily indulged, and most probably would have willingly rendered him that favour; but the necessity of adjusting with his brethren some disputed points of church discipline had withdrawn him for some time from the castle, and detained him in a distant part of the kingdom.

Matters stood thus in the castle of Avenel, when a winded bugle sent its shrill and prolonged notes from the shore of the lake, and was replied to cheerily by the signal of the warder. The Lady of Avenel knew the sounds of her husband, and rushed to the window of the apartment in which she was sitting. A band of about thirty spearmen, with a pennon displayed before them, winded along the indented shores of the lake, and approached the causeway. A single horseman rode at the head of the party, his bright arms catching a glance of the October sun as he moved steadily along. Even at that distance, the Lady recognized the lofty plume, bearing the mingled colours of her own liveries and those of Glendonwyne, blended with the holly-branch; and the firm seat and dignified demeanour of the rider, joined to the stately motion of the dark-brown steed, sufficiently announced Halbert Glendinning.

The Lady's first thought was that of rapturous joy at her husband's return — her second was connected with a fear which had sometimes intruded itself, that he might not altogether approve the peculiar distinction with which she had treated her orphan ward. In this fear there was implied a consciousness, that the favour she had shown him was excessive; for Halbert Glendinning was at least as gentle and indulgent, as he was firm and rational in the intercourse of his household; and to her in particular, his conduct had ever been most affectionately tender.

Yet she did fear, that, on the present occasion, her conduct might incur Sir Halbert's censure; and hastily resolving that she would not mention the anecdote of the boy until the next day, she ordered him to be withdrawn from the apartment by Lilias.

"I will not go with Lilias, madam," answered the spoiled child, who had more than once carried his point by perseverance, and who, like his betters, delighted in the exercise of such authority, — "I will not go to Lilias's gousty room — I will stay and see that brave warrior who comes riding so gallantly along the drawbridge."

"You must not stay, Roland," said the Lady, more positively than she usually spoke to her little favourite.

"I will," reiterated the boy, who had already felt his consequence, and the probable chance of success.

"You *will*, Roland!" answered the Lady, "what manner of word is that? I tell you, you must go."

"*Will*," answered the forward boy, "is a word for a man, and *must* is no word for a lady."

"You are saucy, sirrah," said the Lady — "Lilias, take him with you instantly."

"I always thought," said Lilias, smiling, as she seized the reluctant boy by the arm, "that my young master must give place to my old one."

"And you, too, are malapert, mistress!" said the Lady; "hath the moon changed, that ye all of you thus forget yourselves?"

Lilias made no reply, but led off the boy, who, too proud to offer unavailing resistance, darted at his benefactress a glance, which intimated plainly, how willingly he would have defied her authority, had he possessed the power to make good his point.

The Lady of Avenel was vexed to find how much this trifling circumstance had discomposed her, at the moment when she ought naturally to have been entirely engrossed by her husband's return. But we do not recover composure by the mere feeling that agitation is mistimed. The glow of displeasure had not left the Lady's cheek, her ruffled deportment was not yet entirely composed, when her husband, unhelmeted, but still wearing the rest of his arms, entered the apartment. His appearance banished the thoughts of every thing else; she rushed to him, clasped his iron-sheathed frame in her arms, and kissed his martial and manly face with an affection which was at once evident and sincere. The warrior returned her embrace and her caress with the same fondness; for the time which had passed since their union had diminished its romantic ardour, perhaps, but it had rather increased its rational tenderness, and Sir Halbert Glendinning's long and frequent absences from his castle had prevented affection from degenerating by habit into indifference.

When the first eager greetings were paid and received, the Lady gazed fondly on her husband's face as she remarked, "You are altered, Halbert--you have ridden hard and far to-day, or you have been ill?"

"I have been well, Mary," answered the Knight, "passing well have I been; and a long ride is to me, thou well knowest, but a thing of constant custom. Those who are born noble may slumber out their lives within the walls of their castles and manor-houses; but he who hath achieved nobility by his own deeds must ever be in the saddle, to show that he merits his advancement."

While he spoke thus, the Lady gazed fondly on him, as if endeavouring to read his inmost soul; for the tone in which he spoke was that of melancholy depression.

Sir Halbert Glendinning was the same, yet a different person from what he had appeared in his early years. The fiery freedom of the aspiring youth had given place to the steady and stern composure of the approved soldier and skilful politician. There were deep traces of care on those noble features, over which each emotion used formerly to pass, like light clouds across a summer sky. That sky was now, not perhaps clouded, but still and grave, like that of the sober autumn evening. The forehead was higher and more bare than in early youth, and the locks which still clustered thick and dark on the warrior's head, were worn away at the temples, not by age, but by the constant pressure of the steel cap, or helmet. His beard, according to the fashion of the time, grew short and thick, and was turned into mustaches on the upper lip, and peaked at the extremity. The cheek, weather-beaten and embrowned, had lost the glow of youth, but showed the vigorous complexion of active and confirmed manhood. Halbert Glendinning was, in a word, a knight to ride at a king's right hand, to bear his banner in war, and to be his counsellor in time of peace; for his looks expressed the considerate firmness which can resolve wisely and dare boldly. Still, over these noble features, there now spread an air of dejection, of which, perhaps, the owner was not conscious, but which did not escape the observation of his anxious and affectionate partner.

"Something has happened, or is about to happen," said the Lady of Avenel; "this sadness sits not on your brow without cause — misfortune, national or particular, must needs be at hand."

"There is nothing new that I wot of," said Halbert Glendinning; "but there is little of evil which can befall a kingdom, that may not be apprehended in this unhappy and divided realm."

"Nay, then," said the Lady, "I see there hath really been some fatal work on foot. My Lord of Murray has not so long detained you at Holyrood, save that he wanted your help in some weighty purpose."

"I have not been at Holyrood, Mary," answered the Knight; "I have been several weeks abroad."

"Abroad! and sent me no word?" replied the Lady.

"What would the knowledge have availed, but to have rendered you unhappy, my love?" replied the Knight; "your thoughts would have converted the slightest breeze that curled your own lake, into a tempest raging in the German ocean."

"And have you then really crossed the sea?" said the Lady, to whom the very idea of an element which she had never seen conveyed notions of terror and of wonder, — "really left your own native land, and trodden distant shores, where the Scottish tongue is unheard and unknown?"

"Really, and really," said the Knight, taking her hand in affectionate playfulness, "I have done this marvellous deed — have rolled on the ocean for three days and three nights, with the deep green waves dashing by the side of my pillow, and but a thin plank to divide me from it."

"Indeed, my Halbert," said the Lady, "that was a tempting of Divine Providence. I never bade you unbuckle the sword from your side, or lay the lance from your hand — I never bade you sit still when your honour called you to rise and ride; but are not blade and spear dangers enough for one man's life, and why would you trust rough waves and raging seas?"

"We have in Germany, and in the Low Countries, as they are called," answered Glendinning, "men who are united with us in faith, and with whom it is fitting we should unite in alliance. To some of these I was despatched on business as important as it was secret. I went in safety, and I returned in security; there is more danger to a man's life betwixt this and Holyrood, than are in all the seas that wash the lowlands of Holland."

"And the country, my Halbert, and the people," said the Lady, "are they like our kindly Scots? or what bearing have they to strangers?"

"They are a people, Mary, strong in their wealth, which renders all other nations weak, and weak in those arts of war by which other nations are strong."

"I do not understand you," said the Lady.

"The Hollander and the Fleming, Mary, pour forth their spirit in trade, and not in war; their wealth purchases them the arms of foreign soldiers, by whose aid they defend it. They erect dikes on the sea-shore to protect the land which they have won, and they levy regiments of the stubborn Switzers and hardy Germans to protect the treasures which they have amassed. And thus they are strong in their weakness; for the very wealth which tempts their masters to despoil them, arms strangers in their behalf."

"The slothful hinds!" exclaimed Mary, thinking and feeling like a Scotswoman of the period; "have they hands, and fight not for the land which bore them? They should be notched off at the elbow!"

"Nay, that were but hard justice," answered her husband; "for their hands serve their country, though not in battle, like ours. Look at these barren hills, Mary, and at that deep winding vale by which the cattle are even now returning from their scanty browse. The hand of the industrious Fleming would cover these mountains with wood, and raise corn where we now see a starved and scanty sward of heath and ling. It grieves me, Mary, when I look on that land, and think what benefit it might receive from such men as I have lately seen — men who seek not the idle fame derived from dead ancestors, or the bloody renown won in modern broils, but tread along the land, as preservers and improvers, not as tyrants and destroyers."

"These amendments would here be but a vain fancy, my Halbert," answered the Lady of Avenel; "the trees would be burned by the English foemen, ere they ceased to be shrubs, and the grain that you raised would be gathered in by the first neighbour that possessed more riders than follow your train. Why should you repine at this? The fate that made you Scotsman by birth, gave you head, and heart, and hand, to uphold the name as it must needs be upheld."

"It gave *me* no name to uphold," said Halbert, pacing the floor slowly; "my arm has been foremost in every strife — my voice has been heard in every council, nor have the wisest rebuked me. The crafty Lethington, the deep and dark Morton, have held secret council with me, and Grange and Lindsay have owned, that in the field I did the devoir of a gallant knight— but let the emergence be passed when they need my head and hand, and they only know me as son of the obscure portioner of Glendearg."

This was a theme which the Lady always dreaded; for the rank conferred on her husband, the favour in which he was held by the powerful Earl of Murray, and the high talents by which he vindicated his right to that rank and that favour, were qualities which rather increased than diminished the envy which was harboured against Sir Halbert Glendinning among a proud aristocracy, as a person originally of inferior and obscure birth, who had risen to his present eminence solely by his personal merit. The natural firmness of his mind did not enable him to despise the ideal advantages of a higher pedigree, which were held in such universal esteem by all with whom he conversed; and so open are the noblest minds to jealous inconsistencies, that there were moments in which he felt mortified that his lady should possess those advantages of birth and high descent which he himself did not enjoy, and regretted that his importance as the proprietor of Avenel was qualified by his possessing it only as the husband of the heiress. He was not so unjust as to permit any unworthy feelings to retain permanent possession of his mind, but yet they recurred from time to time, and did not escape his lady's anxious observation.

"Had we been blessed with children," she was wont on such occasions to say to herself, "had our blood been united in a son who might have joined my advantages of descent with my husband's personal worth, these painful and irksome reflections had not disturbed our union even for a moment. But the existence of such an heir, in whom our affections, as well as our pretensions, might have centred, has been denied to us."

With such mutual feelings, it cannot be wondered that it gave the Lady pain to hear her husband verging towards this topic of mutual discontent. On the present, as on other similar occasions, she endeavoured to divert the knight's thoughts from this painful channel.

"How can you," she said, "suffer yourself to dwell upon things which profit nothing? Have you indeed no name to uphold? You, the good and the brave, the wise in council, and the strong in battle, have you not to support the reputation your own deeds have won, a reputation more honourable than mere ancestry can supply? Good men love and honour you, the wicked fear, and the turbulent obey you; and is it not necessary you should exert yourself to ensure the endurance of that love, that honour, and wholesome fear, and that necessary obedience?"

As she thus spoke, the eye of her husband caught from hers courage and comfort, and it lightened as he took her hand and replied, "It is most true, my Mary, and I deserve thy rebuke, who forget what I am, in repining because I am not what I cannot be. I am now what the most famed ancestors of those I envy were, the mean man raised into eminence by his own exertions; and sure it is a boast as honourable to have those capacities which are necessary to the foundation of a family, as to be descended from one who possessed them some centuries before. The Hay of Loncarty, who bequeathed his bloody yoke to his lineage,—the 'dark gray man,' who first founded the house of Douglas, had yet less of ancestry to boast than I have. For thou knowest, Mary, that my name derives itself from a line of ancient warriors, although my immediate forefathers preferred the humble station in which thou didst first find them; and war and counsel are not less proper to the house of Glendonwyne, even in its most remote descendants, than to the proudest of their baronage."*

He strode across the hall as he spoke; and the Lady smiled internally to observe how much his mind dwelt upon the prerogatives of birth, and endeavoured to establish his claims, however remote, to a share in them, at the very moment when he affected to hold them in contempt. It will easily be guessed, however, that she permitted no symptom to escape her that could show she was sensible of the weakness of her husband, a perspicacity which perhaps his proud spirit could not very easily have brooked.

As he returned from the extremity of the hall, to which he had stalked while in the act of vindicating the title of the house of Glendonwyne in its

* This was a house of ancient descent and superior consequence, including persons who fought at Bannockburn and Otterburn, and closely connected by alliance and friendship with the great Earls of Douglas. The Knight in the story argues as most Scotsmen would do in his situation, for all of the same clan are popularly considered as descended from the same stock, and as having a right to the ancestral honour of the chief branch. This opinion, though sometimes ideal, is so strong, even at this day of innovation, that it may be observed as a national difference between my countrymen and the English. If you ask an Englishman of good birth, whether a person of the same name be connected with him, he answers, (if *in dubio*,) "No—he is a mere namesake." Ask a similar question of a Scot, (I mean a Scotsman,) he replies—"He is one of our clan; I daresay there is a relationship, though I do not know how distant." The Englishman thinks of discountenancing a species of rivalry in society; the Scotsman's answer is grounded on the ancient idea of strengthening the clan.

most remote branches to the full privileges of aristocracy, "Where," he said, "is Wolf? I have not seen him since my return, and he was usually the first to welcome my home-coming."

"Wolf," said the Lady, with a slight degree of embarrassment, for which perhaps, she would have found it difficult to assign any reason even to herself, "Wolf is chained up for the present. He hath been surly to my page."

"Wolf chained up — and Wolf surly to your page!" answered Sir Halbert Glendinning; "Wolf never was surly to any one; and the chain will either break his spirit or render him savage — So ho, there — set Wolf free directly."

He was obeyed; and the huge dog rushed into the hall, disturbing, by his unwieldy and boisterous gambols, the whole economy of reels, rocks, and distaffs, with which the maidens of the household were employed when the arrival of their lord was a signal to them to withdraw, and extracting from Lilias, who was summoned to put them again in order, the natural observation, "That the Laird's pet was as troublesome as the lady's page."

"And who is this page, Mary?" said the Knight, his attention again called to the subject by the observation of the waiting-woman, — "Who is this page, whom every one seems to weigh in the balance with my old friend and favourite, Wolf? — When did you aspire to the dignity of keeping a page, or who is the boy?"

"I trust, my Halbert," said the Lady, not without a blush, "you will not think your wife entitled to less attendance than other ladies of her quality?"

"Nay, Dame Mary," answered the Knight, "it is enough you desire such an attendant. — Yet I have never loved to nurse such useless menials — a lady's page — it may well suit the proud English dames to have a slender youth to bear their trains from bower to hall, fan them when they slumber, and touch the lute for them when they please to listen; but our Scottish matrons were wont to be above such vanities, and our Scottish youth ought to be bred to the spear and the stirrup."

"Nay, but, my husband," said the Lady, "I did but jest when I called this boy my page; he is in sooth a little orphan whom we saved from perishing in the lake, and whom I have since kept in the castle out of charity. — Lilias, bring little Roland hither."

Roland entered accordingly, and, flying to the Lady's side, took hold of the plaits of her gown, and then turned round, and gazed with an attention not unmingled with fear, upon the stately form of the Knight. — "Roland," said the Lady, "go kiss the hand of the noble Knight, and ask him to be thy protector." — But Roland obeyed not, and, keeping his station, continued to gaze fixedly and timidly on Sir Halbert Glendinning. — "Go to the Knight, boy," said the Lady; "what dost thou fear, child? Go, kiss Sir Halbert's hand."

"I will kiss no hand save yours, Lady," answered the boy.

"Nay, but do as you are commanded, child," replied the Lady. — "He is dashed by your presence," she said, apologizing to her husband; "but is he not a handsome boy?"

"And so is Wolf," said Sir Halbert, as he patted his huge four-footed favourite, "a handsome dog; but he has this double advantage over your new favourite, that he does what he is commanded, and hears not when he is praised."

"Nay, now you are displeased with me," replied the Lady; "and yet why should you be so? There is nothing wrong in relieving the distressed orphan, or in loving that which is in itself lovely and deserving of affection. But you have seen Mr. Warden at Edinburgh, and he has set you against the poor boy."

"My dear Mary," answered her husband, "Mr. Warden better knows his place than to presume to interfere either in your affairs or mine. I neither blame your relieving this boy, nor your kindness for him. But, I think, considering his birth and prospects, you ought not to treat him with injudicious fondness, which can only end in rendering him unfit for the humble situation to which Heaven has designed him."

"Nay, but, my Halbert, do but look at the boy," said the Lady, "and see whether he has not the air of being intended by Heaven for something nobler than a mere peasant. May he not be designed, as others have been, to rise out of a humble situation into honour and eminence?"

Thus far had she proceeded, when the consciousness that she was treading upon delicate ground at once occurred to her, and induced her to take the most natural, but the worst of all courses in such occasions, whether in conversation or in an actual bog, namely, that of stopping suddenly short in the illustration which she had commenced. Her brow crimsoned, and that of Sir Halbert Glendinning was slightly overcast. But it was only for an instant; for he was incapable of mistaking his lady's meaning, or supposing that she meant intentional disrespect to him.

"Be it as you please, my love," he replied; "I owe you too much to contradict you in aught which may render your solitary mode of life more endurable. Make of this youth what you will, and you have my full authority for doing so. But remember he is your charge, not mine—remember he hath limbs to do man's service, a soul and a tongue to worship God; breed him, therefore, to be true to his country and to Heaven; and for the rest, dispose of him as you list—it is, and shall rest, your own matter."

This conversation decided the fate of Roland Græme, who from thenceforward was little noticed by the master of the mansion of Avenel, but indulged and favoured by its mistress.

This situation led to many important consequences, and, in truth, tended to bring forth the character of the youth in all its broad lights and deep shadows. As the Knight himself seemed tacitly to disclaim alike interest and control over the immediate favourite of his lady, young Roland was, by circumstances, exempted from the strict discipline to which, as the retainer of a Scottish man of rank, he would otherwise have been subjected, according to all the rigour of the age. But the steward, or master of the household—such was the proud title assumed by the head domestic of each petty baron—deemed it not advisable to interfere with the favourite of the Lady, and especially since she had brought the estate into the present family. Master Jasper Wingate was a man experienced, as he often boasted, in the ways of great families, and knew how to keep the steerage even when the wind and tide chanced to be in contradiction.

This prudent personage winked at much, and avoided giving opportunity for farther offence, by requesting little of Roland Græme beyond the degree of attention which he was himself disposed to pay; rightly conjecturing, that however lowly the place which the youth might hold in the favour of the Knight of Avenel, still to make an evil report of him would make an enemy of the Lady, without securing the favour of her husband. With these prudential considerations, and doubtless not without an eye to his own ease and convenience, he taught the boy as much, and only as much, as he chose to learn, readily admitting whatever apology it pleased his pupil to allege in excuse for idleness or negligence. As the other persons in the castle, to whom such tasks were delegated, readily imitated the prudential conduct of the major-domo, there was little control used towards Roland Græme, who, of course, learned no more than what a very active mind, and a total impatience of absolute idleness led him to acquire upon his own account, and by dint of his own exertions. The latter were especially earnest, when the Lady herself condescended to be his tutress, or to examine his progress.

It followed also from his quality as my Lady's favourite, that Roland was viewed with no peculiar good-will by the followers of the Knight, many of whom, of the same age, and apparently similar origin, with the fortunate page, were subjected to severe observance of the ancient and rigorous discipline of a feudal retainer. To these, Roland Græme was of course an object of envy, and, in consequence, of dislike and detraction; but the youth possessed qualities which it was impossible to depreciate. Pride, and a sense of early ambition, did for him what severity and constant instruction did for others. In truth, the youthful Roland displayed that early flexibility both of body and mind, which renders exercise, either mental or bodily, rather matter of sport than of study; and it seemed as if he acquired accidentally, and by starts, those accomplishments, which earnest and constant instruction, enforced by frequent reproof and occasional chastisement, had taught to others. Such military exercises, such lessons of the period, as he found it agreeable or convenient to apply to, he learned so perfectly, as to confound those who were ignorant how often the want of constant application is compensated by vivacity of talent and ardent enthusiasm. The lads, therefore, who were more regularly trained to arms, to horsemanship, and to other necessary exercises of the period, while they envied Roland Græme the indulgence or negligence with which he seemed to be treated, had little reason to boast of their own superior acquirements; a few hours, with the powerful exertion of a most energetic will, seemed to do for him more than the regular instruction of weeks could accomplish for others.

Under these advantages, if, indeed, they were to be termed such, the character of young Roland began to develope itself. It was bold, peremptory, decisive, and overbearing; generous, if neither withstood nor contradicted; vehement and passionate, if censured or opposed. He seemed to consider himself as attached to no one, and responsible to no one, except his mistress, and even over her mind he had gradually acquired that species of ascendancy which indulgence is so apt to occasion. And although the immediate followers and dependents of Sir Halbert Glendinning saw his ascendancy with jealousy, and often took occasion to mortify his vanity, there wanted not those who were willing to acquire the favour of the Lady of Avenel by humouring and taking part with the youth whom she protected; for although a favourite, as the poet assures us, has no friend, he seldom fails to have both followers and flatterers.

The partisans of Roland Græme were chiefly to be found amongst the inhabitants of the little hamlet on the shore of the lake. These villagers, who were sometimes tempted to compare their own situation with that of the immediate and constant followers of the Knight, who attended him on his frequent journeys to Edinburgh and elsewhere, delighted in considering and representing themselves as more properly the subjects of the Lady of Avenel than of her husband. It is true, her wisdom and affection on all occasions discountenanced the distinction which was here implied; but the villagers persisted in thinking it must be agreeable to her to enjoy their peculiar and undivided homage, or at least in acting as if they thought so; and one chief mode by which they evinced their sentiments, was by the respect they paid to young Roland Græme, the favourite attendant of the descendant of their ancient lords. This was a mode of flattery too pleasing to encounter rebuke or censure; and the opportunity which it afforded the youth to form, as it were, a party of his own within the limits of the ancient barony of Avenel, added not a little to the audacity and decisive tone of a character, which was by nature bold, impetuous, and incontrollable.

Of the two members of the household who had manifested an early jealousy of Roland Græme, the prejudices of Wolf were easily overcome; and in process of time the noble dog slept with Bran, Luath, and the celebrated hounds of ancient days. But Mr. Warden, the chaplain, lived, and retained his dislike to the youth. That good man, single-minded and benevolent as he really was, entertained rather more than a reasonable idea of the respect due to him as a minister, and exacted from the inhabitants of the castle more deference than the haughty young page, proud of his mis tress's favour, and petulant from youth and situation, was at all times willing to pay. His bold and free demeanour, his attachment to rich dress and decoration, his inaptitude to receive instruction, and his hardening himself against rebuke, were circumstances which induced the good old man, with more haste than charity, to set the forward page down as a vessel of wrath, and to presage that the youth nursed that pride and haughtiness of spirit which goes before ruin and destruction. On the other hand, Roland evinced at times a marked dislike, and even something like contempt, of the chaplain. Most of the attendants and followers of Sir Halbert Glendinning entertained the same charitable thoughts as the reverend Mr. Warden; but while Roland was favoured by their lady, and endured by their lord, they saw no policy in making their opinions public.

Roland Græme was sufficiently sensible of the unpleasant situation in which he stood; but in the haughtiness of his heart he retorted upon the other domestics the distant, cold, and sarcastic manner in which they treated him, assumed an air of superiority which compelled the most obstinate to obedience, and had the satisfaction at least to be dreaded, if he was heartily hated.

The chaplain's marked dislike had the effect of recommending him to the attention of Sir Halbert's brother, Edward, who now, under the conventual appellation of Father Ambrose, continued to be one of the few monks who, with the Abbot Eustatius, had, notwithstanding the nearly total downfall of their faith under the regency of Murray, been still permitted to linger in the cloisters at Kennaquhair. Respect to Sir Halbert had prevented their being altogether driven out of the Abbey, though their order was now in a great measure suppressed, and they were interdicted the public exercise of their ritual, and only allowed for their support a small pension out of their once splendid revenues. Father Ambrose, thus situated, was an occasional, though very rare visitant, at the Castle of Avenel, and was at such times observed to pay particular attention to Roland Græme, who seemed to return it with more depth of feeling than consisted with his usual habits.

Thus situated, years glided on, during which the Knight of Avenel continued to act a frequent and important part in the convulsions of his distracted country; while young Græme anticipated, both in wishes and personal accomplishments, the age which should enable him to emerge from the obscurity of his present situation.

Chapter the Fourth.

Amid their cups that freely flow'd,
Their revelry and mirth,
A youthful lord tax'd Valentine
With base and doubtful birth.
VALENTINE AND ORSON.

WHEN Roland Græme was a youth about seventeen years of age, he chanced one summer morning to descend to the mew in which Sir Halbert Glendinning kept his hawks, in order to superintend the training of an eyas, or young hawk, which he himself, at the imminent risk of neck and limbs, had taken from the celebrated eyry in the neighborhood, called Gledscraig. As he was by no means satisfied with the attention which had been bestowed on his favourite bird, he was not slack in testifying his displeasure to the falconer's lad, whose duty it was to have attended upon it.

"What, ho! sir knave," exclaimed Roland, "is it thus you feed the eyas with unwashed meat, as if you were gorging the foul brancher of a worthless hoodie-crow? by the mass, and thou hast neglected its castings also for these two days! Think'st thou I ventured my neck to bring the bird down from the crag, that thou shouldst spoil him by thy neglect?" And to add force to his remonstrances, he conferred a cuff or two on the negligent attendant of the hawks, who, shouting rather louder than was necessary under all the circumstances, brought the master falconer to his assistance.

Adam Woodcock, the falconer of Avenel, was an Englishman by birth, but so long in the service of Glendinning, that he had lost much of his notional attachment in that which he had formed to his master. He was a favourite in his department, jealous and conceited of his skill, as masters of the game usually are; for the rest of his character he was a jester and a parcel poet, (qualities which by no means abated his natural conceit,) a jolly fellow, who, though a sound Protestant, loved a flagon of ale better than a long sermon, a stout man of his hands when need required, true to his master, and a little presuming on his interest with him.

Adam Woodcock, such as we have described him, by no means relished the freedom used by young Græme, in chastising his assistant. "Hey, hey, my Lady's page," said he, stepping between his own boy and Roland, "fair and softly, an it like your gilt jacket — hands off is fair play — if my boy has done amiss, I can beat him myself, and then you may keep your hands soft."

"I will beat him and thee too," answered Roland, without hesitation, "an you look not better after your business. See how the bird is cast away between you. I found the careless lurdane feeding him with unwashed flesh, and she an eyas."*

"Go to," said the falconer, "thou art but an eyas thyself, child Roland. — What knowest thou of feeding? I say that the eyas should have her meat unwashed, until she becomes a brancher — 'twere the ready way to give her the frounce, to wash her meat sooner, and so knows every one who knows a gled from a falcon."

"It is thine own laziness, thou false English blood, that dost nothing but drink and sleep," retorted the page, "and leaves that lither lad to do the work, which he minds as little as thou."

"And am I so idle then," said the falconer, "that have three cast of hawks to look after, at perch and mew, and to fly them in the field to boot? — and is my Lady's page so busy a man that he must take me up short?—and am I of false English blood? — I marvel what blood thou art — neither Englander nor Scot — fish nor flesh — a bastard from the Debateable Land, without either kith, kin, or ally! — Marry, out upon thee, foul kite, that would fain be a tercel gentle!"

The reply to this sarcasm was a box on the ear, so well applied, that it overthrew the falconer into the cistern in which water was kept for the benefit of the hawks. Up started Adam Woodcock, his wrath no way appeased by the cold immersion, and seizing on a truncheon which stood by, would have soon requited the injury he had received, had not Roland laid his hand on his poniard, and sworn by all that was sacred, that if he offered a stroke towards him, he would sheath the blade in his bowels. The noise was now so great, that more than one of the household came in, and amongst others the major-domo, a grave personage, already mentioned, whose gold chain and white wand intimated his authority. At the appearance of this dignitary, the strife was for the present appeased. He embraced, however, so favourable an opportunity, to read Roland Græme a shrewd lecture on the impropriety of his deportment to his fellow-menials, and to assure him, that, should he communicate this fray to his master, (who, though now on

* There is a difference amongst authorities how long the nestling hawk should be fed with flesh which has previously been washed.

one of his frequent expeditions, was speedily expected to return,) which but for respect to his Lady he would most certainly do, the residence of the culprit in the Castle of Avenel would be but of brief duration. "But, however," added the prudent master of the household, "I will report the matter first to my Lady."

"Very just, very right, Master Wingate," exclaimed several voices together; "my Lady will consider if daggers are to be drawn on us for every idle word, and whether we are to live in a well-ordered household, where there is the fear of God, or amidst drawn dirks and sharp knives."

The object of this general resentment darted an angry glance around him, and suppressing with difficulty the desire which urged him to reply in furious or in contemptuous language, returned his dagger into his scabbard, looked disdainfully around upon the assembled menials, turned short upon his heel, and pushing aside those who stood betwixt him and the door, left the apartment.

"This will be no tree for my nest," said the falconer, "if this cock-sparrow is to crow over us as he seems to do."

"He struck me with his switch yesterday," said one of the grooms, "because the tail of his worship's gelding was not trimmed altogether so as suited his humour."

"And I promise you," said the laundress, "my young master will stick nothing to call an honest woman slut and quean, if there be but a speck of soot upon his band-collar."

"If Master Wingate do not his errand to my Lady," was the general result, "there will be no tarrying in the same house with Roland Græme."

The master of the household heard them all for some time, and then, motioning for universal silence, he addressed them with all the dignity of Malvolio himself.—"My masters,—not forgetting you, my mistresses,—do not think the worse of me that I proceed with as much care as haste in this matter. Our master is a gallant knight, and will have his sway at home and abroad, in wood and field, in hall and bower, as the saying is. Our Lady, my benison upon her, is also a noble person of long descent, and rightful heir of this place and barony, and she also loves her will; as for that matter, show me the woman who doth not. Now, she hath favoured, doth favour, and will favour, this jack-an-ape,—for what good part about him I know not, save that as one noble lady will love a messan dog, and another a screaming popinjay, and a third a Barbary ape, so doth it please our noble dame to set her affections upon this stray elf of a page, for nought that I can think of, save that she was the cause of his being saved (the more's the pity) from drowning." And here Master Wingate made a pause.

"I would have been his caution for a gray groat against salt water or fresh," said Roland's adversary, the falconer; "marry, if he crack not a rope for stabbing or for snatching, I will be content never to hood hawk again."

"Peace, Adam Woodcock," said Wingate, waving his hand; "I prithee, peace man—Now, my Lady liking this springald, as aforesaid, differs therein from my Lord, who loves never a bone in his skin. Now, is it for me to stir up strife betwixt them, and put as 'twere my finger betwixt the bark and the tree, on account of a pragmatical youngster, whom, nevertheless, I would willingly see whipped forth of the barony? Have patience, and this boil will break without our meddling. I have been in service since I wore a beard on my chin, till now that that beard is turned gray, and I have seldom known any one better themselves, even by taking the lady's part against the lord's; but never one who did not dirk himself, if he took the lord's against the lady's."

"And so," said Lilias, "we are to be crowed over, every one of us, men and women, cock and hen, by this little upstart?—I will try titles with him first, I promise you.—I fancy, Master Wingate, for as wise as you look, you will be pleased to tell what you have seen to-day, if my lady commands you?"

"To speak the truth when my lady commands me," answered the prudential major-domo, "is in some measure my duty, Mistress Lilias; always providing for and excepting those cases in which it cannot be spoken without breeding mischief and inconvenience to myself or my fellow-servants; for the tongue of a tale-bearer breaketh bones as well as Jeddart-staff."*

"But this imp of Satan is none of your friends or fellow-servants," said Lilias; "and I trust you mean not to stand up for him against the whole family besides?"

"Credit me, Mrs. Lilias," replied the senior, "should I see the time fitting, I would with right good-will give him a lick with the rough side of my tongue."

"Enough said, Master Wingate," answered Lilias; "then trust me his song shall soon be laid. If my mistress does not ask me what is the matter below stairs before she be ten minutes of time older, she is no born woman, and my name is not Lilias Bradbourne."

In pursuance of her plan, Mistress Lilias failed not to present herself before her mistress with all the exterior of one who is possessed of an important secret,—that is, she had the corners of her mouth turned down, her eyes raised up, her lips pressed as fast together as if they had been sewed up, to prevent her babbling, and an air of prim mystical importance diffused over her whole person and demeanour, which seemed to intimate, "I know something which I am resolved not to tell you!"

Lilias had rightly read her mistress's temper, who, wise and good as she was, was yet a daughter of grandame Eve, and could not witness this mysterious bearing on the part of her waiting-woman without longing to ascertain the secret cause. For a space, Mrs. Lilias was obdurate to all inquiries, sighed, turned her eyes up higher yet to heaven, hoped for the best, but had nothing particular to communicate. All this, as was most natural and proper, only stimulated the Lady's curiosity; neither was her importunity to be parried with,—"Thank God, I am no makebate—no tale-bearer,—thank God, I never envied any one's favour, or was anxious to propale their misdemeanour—only, thank God, there has been no bloodshed and murder in the house—that is all."

"Bloodshed and murder!" exclaimed the Lady, "what does the quean mean?—if you speak not plain out, you shall have something you will scarce be thankful for."

"Nay, my Lady," answered Lilias, eager to disburden her mind, or, in Chaucer's phrase, to "unbuckle her mail," "if you bid me speak out the truth, you must not be moved with what might displease you—Roland Græme has dirked Adam Woodstock—that is all."

"Good Heaven!" said the Lady, turning pale as ashes, "is the man slain?"

"No, madam," replied Lilias, "but slain he would have been, if there had not been ready help; but may be, it is your Ladyship's pleasure that this young esquire shall poniard the servants, as well as switch and baton them."

"Go to, minion," said the Lady, "you are saucy—tell the master of the household to attend me instantly."

Lilias hastened to seek out Mr. Wingate, and hurry him to his lady's presence, speaking as a word in season to him on the way, "I have set the stone a-trowling, look that you do not let it stand still."

The steward, too prudential a person to commit himself otherwise, answered by a sly look and a nod of intelligence, and presently after stood

* A species of battle-axe, so called as being in especial use in that ancient burgh, whose armorial bearings still represent an armed horseman brandishing such a weapon.

in the presence of the Lady of Avenel, with a look of great respect for his lady, partly real, partly affected, and an air of great sagacity, which inferred no ordinary conceit of himself.

"How is this, Wingate," said the Lady, "and what rule do you keep in the castle, that the domestics of Sir Halbert Glendinning draw the dagger on each other, as in a cavern of thieves and murderers? — is the wounded man much hurt? and what — what hath become of the unhappy boy?"

"There is no one wounded as yet, madam," replied he of the golden chain; "it passes my poor skill to say how many may be wounded before Pasche,* if some rule be not taken with this youth—not but the youth is a fair youth," he added, correcting himself, "and able at his exercise; but somewhat too ready with the ends of his fingers, the butt of his riding-switch, and the point of his dagger."

"And whose fault is that," said the Lady, "but yours, who should have taught him better discipline, than to brawl or to draw his dagger."

"If it please your Ladyship so to impose the blame on me," answered the steward, "it is my part, doubtless, to bear it — only I submit to your consideration, that unless I nailed his weapon to the scabbard, I could no more keep it still, than I could fix quicksilver, which defied even the skill of Raymond Lullius."

"Tell me not of Raymond Lullius," said the Lady, losing patience, "but send me the chaplain hither. You grow all of you too wise for me, during your lord's long and repeated absences. I would to God his affairs would permit him to remain at home and rule his own household, for it passes my wit and skill!"

"God forbid, my Lady!" said the old domestic, "that you should sincerely think what you are now pleased to say: your old servants might well hope, that after so many years' duty, you would do their service more justice than to distrust their gray hairs, because they cannot rule the peevish humour of a green head, which the owner carries, it may be, a brace of inches higher than becomes him."

"Leave me," said the Lady; "Sir Halbert's return must now be expected daily, and he will look into these matters himself — leave me, I say, Wingate, without saying more of it. I know you are honest, and I believe the boy is petulant; and yet I think it is my favour which hath set all of you against him."

The steward bowed and retired, after having been silenced in a second attempt to explain the motives on which he acted.

The chaplain arrived; but neither from him did the Lady receive much comfort. On the contrary, she found him disposed, in plain terms, to lay to the door of her indulgence all the disturbances which the fiery temper of Roland Græme had already occasioned, or might hereafter occasion, in the family. "I would," he said, "honoured Lady, that you had deigned to be ruled by me in the outset of this matter, sith it is easy to stem evil in the fountain, but hard to struggle against it in the stream. You, honoured madam, (a word which I do not use according to the vain forms of this world, but because I have ever loved and honoured you as an honourable and elect lady,)—you, I say, madam, have been pleased, contrary to my poor but earnest counsel, to raise this boy from his station, into one approaching to your own."

"What mean you, reverend sir?" said the Lady; "I have made this youth a page — is there aught in my doing so that does not become my character and quality?"

"I dispute not, madam," said the pertinacious preacher, "your benevolent purpose in taking charge of this youth, or your title to give him this idle character of page, if such was your pleasure; though what the educa-

* Easter.

tion of a boy in the train of a female can tend to, save to ingraft foppery and effeminacy on conceit and arrogance, it passes my knowledge to discover. But I blame you more directly for having taken little care to guard him against the perils of his condition, or to tame and humble a spirit naturally haughty, overbearing, and impatient. You have brought into your bower a lion's cub; delighted with the beauty of his fur, and the grace of his gambols, you have bound him with no fetters befitting the fierceness of his disposition. You have let him grow up as unawed as if he had been still a tenant of the forest, and now you are surprised, and call out for assistance, when he begins to ramp, rend, and tear, according to his proper nature."

"Mr. Warden," said the Lady, considerably offended, "you are my husband's ancient friend, and I believe your love sincere to him and to his household. Yet let me say, that when I asked you for counsel, I expected not this asperity of rebuke. If I have done wrong in loving this poor orphan lad more than others of his class, I scarce think the error merited such severe censure; and if stricter discipline were required to keep his fiery temper in order, it ought, I think, to be considered, that I am a woman, and that if I have erred in this matter, it becomes a friend's part rather to aid than to rebuke me. I would these evils were taken order with before my lord's return. He loves not domestic discord or domestic brawls; and I would not willingly that he thought such could arise from one whom I favoured—What do you counsel me to do?"

"Dismiss this youth from your service, madam," replied the preacher.

"You cannot bid me do so," said the Lady; "you cannot, as a Christian and a man of humanity, bid me turn away an unprotected creature against whom my favour, my injudicious favour if you will, has reared up so many enemies."

"It is not necessary you should altogether abandon him, though you dismiss him to another service, or to a calling better suiting his station and character," said the preacher; "elsewhere he may be an useful and profitable member of the commonweal—here he is but a makebate, and a stumbling-block of offence. The youth has snatches of sense and of intelligence, though he lacks industry. I will myself give him letters commendatory to Olearius Schinderhausen, a learned professor at the famous university of Leyden, where they lack an under-janitor—where, besides gratis instruction, if God give him the grace to seek it, he will enjoy five merks by the year, and the professor's cast-off suit, which he disparts with biennially."

"This will never do, good Mr. Warden," said the Lady, scarce able to suppress a smile; "we will think more at large upon this matter. In the meanwhile, I trust to your remonstrances with this wild boy and with the family, for restraining these violent and unseemly jealousies and bursts of passion; and I entreat you to press on him and them their duty in this respect towards God, and towards their master."

"You shall be obeyed, madam," said Warden. "On the next Thursday I exhort the family, and will, with God's blessing, so wrestle with the demon of wrath and violence, which hath entered into my little flock, that I trust to hound the wolf out of the fold, as if he were chased away with bandogs."

This was the part of the conference from which Mr. Warden derived the greatest pleasure. The pulpit was at that time the same powerful engine for affecting popular feeling which the press has since become, and he had been no unsuccessful preacher, as we have already seen. It followed as a natural consequence, that he rather over-estimated the powers of his own oratory, and, like some of his brethren about the period, was glad of an opportunity to handle any matters of importance, whether public or private, the discussion of which could be dragged into his discourse. In that rude age the delicacy was unknown which prescribed time and place to personal exhortations; and as the court-preacher often addressed the King individually, and dictated to him the conduct he ought to observe in matters of state, so the nobleman himself, or any of his retainers, were, in the chapel of the feudal castle, often incensed or appalled, as the case might be, by the discussion of their private faults in the evening exercise, and by spiritual censures directed against them, specifically, personally, and by name.

The sermon, by means of which Henry Warden purposed to restore concord and good order to the Castle of Avenel, bore for text the well-known words, "*He who striketh with the sword shall perish by the sword,*" and was a singular mixture of good sense and powerful oratory with pedantry and bad taste. He enlarged a good deal on the word striketh, which he assured his hearers comprehended blows given with the point as well as with the edge, and more generally, shooting with hand-gun, cross-bow, or long-bow, thrusting with a lance, or doing any thing whatever by which death might be occasioned to the adversary. In the same manner, he proved satisfactorily, that the word *sword* comprehended all descriptions, whether backsword or basket-hilt, cut-and-thrust or rapier, falchion, or scimitar. "But if," he continued, with still greater animation, "the text includeth in its anathema those who strike with any of those weapons which man hath devised for the exercise of his open hostility, still more doth it comprehend such as from their form and size are devised rather for the gratification of privy malice by treachery, than for the destruction of an enemy prepared and standing upon his defence. Such," he proceeded, looking sternly at the place where the page was seated on a cushion at the feet of his mistress, and wearing in his crimson belt a gay dagger with a gilded hilt,—"such, more especially, I hold to be those implements of death, which, in our modern and fantastic times, are worn not only by thieves and cut-throats, to whom they most properly belong, but even by those who attend upon women, and wait in the chambers of honourable ladies. Yes, my friends,—every species of this unhappy weapon, framed for all evil and for no good, is comprehended under this deadly denunciation, whether it be a stillet, which we have borrowed from the treacherous Italian, or a dirk, which is borne by the savage Highlandman, or a whinger, which is carried by our own Border thieves and cut-throats, or a dudgeon-dagger, all are alike engines invented by the devil himself, for ready implements of deadly wrath, sudden to execute, and difficult to be parried. Even the common sword-and-buckler brawler despises the use of such a treacherous and malignant instrument, which is therefore fit to be used, not by men or soldiers, but by those who, trained under female discipline, become themselves effeminate hermaphrodites, having female spite and female cowardice added to the infirmities and evil passions of their masculine nature."

The effect which this oration produced upon the assembled congregation of Avenel cannot very easily be described. The lady seemed at once embarrassed and offended; the menials could hardly contain, under an affectation of deep attention, the joy with which they heard the chaplain lanch his thunders at the head of the unpopular favourite, and the weapon which they considered as a badge of affectation and finery. Mrs. Lilias crested and drew up her head with all the deep-felt pride of gratified resentment; while the steward, observing a strict neutrality of aspect, fixed his eyes upon an old scutcheon on the opposite side of the wall, which he seemed to examine with the utmost accuracy, more willing, perhaps, to incur the censure of being inattentive to the sermon, than that of seeming to listen with marked approbation to what appeared so distasteful to his mistress.

The unfortunate subject of the harangue, whom nature had endowed with passions which had hitherto found no effectual restraint, could not disguise the resentment which he felt at being thus directly held up to the scorn, as well as the censure, of the assembled inhabitants of the little world in which he lived. His brow grew red, his lip grew pale, he set his teeth, he clenched his hand, and then with mechanical readiness grasped the weapon of which the clergyman had given so hideous a character; and at length, as the preacher heightened the colouring of his invective, he felt his rage become so ungovernable, that, fearful of being hurried into some deed of desperate violence, he rose up, traversed the chapel with hasty steps, and left the congregation.

The preacher was surprised into a sudden pause, while the fiery youth shot across him like a flash of lightning, regarding him as he passed, as if he had wished to dart from his eyes the same power of blighting and of consuming. But no sooner had he crossed the chapel, and shut with violence behind him the door of the vaulted entrance by which it communicated with the castle, than the impropriety of his conduct supplied Warden with one of those happier subjects for eloquence, of which he knew how to take advantage for making a suitable impression on his hearers. He paused for an instant, and then pronounced, in a slow and solemn voice, the deep anathema: "He hath gone out from us because he was not of us—the sick man hath been offended at the wholesome bitter of the medicine — the wounded patient hath flinched from the friendly knife of the surgeon — the sheep hath fled from the sheepfold and delivered himself to the wolf, because he could not assume the quiet and humble conduct demanded of us by the great Shepherd. Ah! my brethren, beware of wrath — beware of pride — beware of the deadly and destroying sin which so often shows itself to our frail eyes in the garments of light! What is our earthly honour? Pride, and pride only — What our earthly gifts and graces? Pride and vanity. Voyagers speak of Indian men who deck themselves with shells, and anoint themselves with pigments, and boast of their attire as we do of our miserable carnal advantages — Pride could draw down the morning-star from Heaven even to the verge of the pit — Pride and self-opinion kindled the flaming sword which waves us off from Paradise — Pride made Adam mortal, and a weary wanderer on the face of the earth, which he had else been at this day the immortal lord of — Pride brought amongst us sin, and doubles every sin it has brought. It is the outpost which the devil and the flesh most stubbornly maintain against the assaults of grace; and until it be subdued, and its barriers levelled with the very earth, there is more hope of a fool than of the sinner. Rend, then, from your bosoms this accursed shoot of the fatal apple; tear it up by the roots, though it be twisted with the chords of your life. Profit by the example of the miserable sinner that has passed from us, and embrace the means of grace while it is called today — ere your conscience is seared as with a fire-brand, and your ears deafened like those of the adder, and your heart hardened like the nether mill-stone. Up, then, and be doing—wrestle and overcome; resist, and the enemy shall flee from you — Watch and pray, lest ye fall into temptation, and let the stumbling of others be your warning and your example. Above all, rely not on yourselves, for such self-confidence is even the worst symptom of the disorder itself. The Pharisee, perhaps, deemed himself humble while he stooped in the Temple, and thanked God that he was not as other men, and even as the publican. But while his knees touched the marble pavement, his head was as high as the topmost pinnacle of the Temple. Do not, therefore, deceive yourselves, and offer false coin, where the purest you can present is but as dross — think not that such will pass the assay of Omnipotent Wisdom. Yet shrink not from the task, because, as is my bounden duty, I do not disguise from you its difficulties. Self-searching can do much — Meditation can do much — Grace can do all."

And he concluded with a touching and animating exhortation to his hearers to seek divine grace, which is perfected in human wakness.

The audience did not listen to this address without being considerably affected; though it might be doubted whether the feelings of triumph, excited by the disgraceful retreat of the favourite page, did not greatly qualify in the minds of many the exhortations of the preacher to charity and to humility. And, in fact, the expression of their countenances much resembled the satisfied triumphant air of a set of children, who, having just seen a companion punished for a fault in which they had no share, con their task with double glee, both because they themselves are out of the scrape, and because the culprit is in it.

With very different feelings did the Lady of Avenel seek her own apartment. She felt angry at Warden having made a domestic matter, in which she took a personal interest, the subject of such public discussion. But this she knew the good man claimed as a branch of his Christian liberty as a preacher, and also that it was vindicated by the universal custom of his brethren. But the self-willed conduct of her protegé afforded her yet deeper concern. That he had broken through in so remarkable a degree, not only the respect due to her presence, but that which was paid to religious admonition in those days with such peculiar reverence, argued a spirit as untameable as his enemies had represented him to possess. And yet so far as he had been under her own eye, she had seen no more of that fiery spirit than appeared to her to become his years and his vivacity. This opinion might be founded in some degree on partiality; in some degree, too, it might be owing to the kindness and indulgence which she had always extended to him; but still she thought it impossible that she could be totally mistaken in the estimate she had formed of his character. The extreme of violence is scarce consistent with a course of continued hypocrisy, (although Lilias charitably hinted, that in some instances they were happily united,) and therefore she could not exactly trust the report of others against her own experience and observation. The thoughts of this orphan boy clung to her heartstrings with a fondness for which she herself was unable to account. He seemed to have been sent to her by Heaven, to fill up those intervals of languor and vacuity which deprived her of much enjoyment. Perhaps he was not less dear to her, because she well saw that he was a favourite with no one else, and because she felt, that to give him up was to afford the judgment of her husband and others a triumph over her own; a circumstance not quite indifferent to the best of spouses of either sex.

In short, the Lady of Avenel formed the internal resolution, that she would not desert her page while her page could be rationally protected; and, with a view of ascertaining how far this might be done, she caused him to be summoned to her presence.

Chapter the Fifth.

> ——— In the wild storm,
> The seaman hews his mast down, and the merchant
> Heaves to the billows wares he once deem'd precious;
> So prince and peer, 'mid popular contentions,
> Cast off their favourites.
>
> OLD PLAY.

IT was some time ere Roland Græme appeared. The messenger (his old friend Lilias) had at first attempted to open the door of his little apartment with the charitable purpose, doubtless, of enjoying the confusion, and marking the demeanour of the culprit. But an oblong bit of iron, ycleped a bolt, was passed across the door on the inside, and prevented her benign intentions. Lilias knocked and called at intervals. "Roland—Roland Græme—*Master* Roland Græme," (an emphasis on the word Master,) "will you be pleased to undo the door?—What ails you?—are you at your prayers in private, to complete the devotion which you left unfinished in public?—Surely we must have a screened seat for you in the chapel, that your gentility may be free from the eyes of common folks!" Still no whisper was heard in reply. "Well, master Roland," said the waiting-maid, "I must tell my mistress, that if she would have an answer, she must either come herself, or send those on errand to you who can beat the door down."

"What says your Lady?" answered the page from within.

"Marry, open the door, and you shall hear," answered the waiting-maid. "I trow it becomes my Lady's message to be listened to face to face; and I will not for your idle pleasure, whistle it through a key-hole."

"Your mistress's name," said the page, opening the door, "is too fair a cover for your impertinence—What says my Lady?"

"That you will be pleased to come to her directly, in the withdrawing-room," answered Lilias. "I presume she has some directions for you concerning the forms to be observed in leaving chapel in future."

"Say to my Lady, that I will directly wait on her," answered the page; and returning into his apartment, he once more locked the door in the face of the waiting-maid.

"Rare courtesy!" muttered Lilias; and, returning to her mistress, acquainted her that Roland Græme would wait on her when it suited his convenience.

"What, is that his addition, or your own phrase, Lilias?" said the Lady, coolly.

"Nay, madam," replied the attendant, not directly answering the question, "he looked as if he could have said much more impertinent things than that, if I had been willing to hear them.—But here he comes to answer for himself."

Roland Græme entered the apartment with a loftier mien, and somewhat a higher colour than his wont; there was embarrassment in his manner, but it was neither that of fear nor of penitence.

"Young man," said the Lady, "what trow you I am to think of your conduct this day?"

"If it has offended you, madam, I am deeply grieved," replied the youth.

"To have offended me alone," replied the Lady, "were but little—You have been guilty of conduct which will highly offend your master—of violence to your fellow-servants, and of disrespect to God himself, in the person of his ambassador."

"Permit me again to reply," said the page, "that if I have offended my only mistress, friend, and benefactress, it includes the sum of my guilt, and deserves the sum of my penitence—Sir Halbert Glendinning calls me not servant, nor do I call him master—he is not entitled to blame me for chastising an insolent groom—nor do I fear the wrath of Heaven for treating with scorn the unauthorized interference of a meddling preacher."

The Lady of Avenel had before this seen symptoms in her favourite of boyish petulance, and of impatience of censure or reproof. But his present demeanour was of a graver and more determined character, and she was for a moment at a loss how she should treat the youth, who seemed to have at once assumed the character not only of a man, but of a bold and determined one. She paused an instant, and then assuming the dignity which was natural to her, she said, "Is it to me, Roland, that you hold this language? Is it for the purpose of making me repent the favour I have shown you, that you declare yourself independent both of an earthly and a Heavenly master? Have you forgotten what you were, and to what the loss of my protection would speedily again reduce you?"

"Lady," said the page, "I have forgot nothing, I remember but too much. I know, that but for you, I should have perished in yon blue waves," pointing, as he spoke, to the lake, which was seen through the window, agitated by the western wind. "Your goodness has gone farther, madam—you have protected me against the malice of others, and against my own folly. You are free, if you are willing, to abandon the orphan you have reared. You have left nothing undone by him, and he complains of nothing. And yet, Lady, do not think I have been ungrateful—I have endured something on my part, which I would have borne for the sake of no one but my benefactress."

"For my sake!" said the Lady; "and what is it that I can have subjected you to endure, which can be remembered with other feelings than those of thanks and gratitude?"

"You are too just, madam, to require me to be thankful for the cold neglect with which your husband has uniformly treated me—neglect not unmingled with fixed aversion. You are too just, madam, to require me to be grateful for the constant and unceasing marks of scorn and malevolence with which I have been treated by others, or for such a homily as that with which your reverend chaplain has, at my expense, this very day regaled the assembled household."

"Heard mortal ears the like of this!" said the waiting-maid, with her hands expanded and her eyes turned up to heaven; "he speaks as if he were son of an earl, or of a belted knight the least penny!"

The page glanced on her a look of supreme contempt, but vouchsafed no other answer. His mistress, who began to feel herself seriously offended, and yet sorry for the youth's folly, took up the same tone.

"Indeed, Roland, you forget yourself so strangely," said she, "that you will tempt me to take serious measures to lower you in your own opinion by reducing you to your proper station in society."

"And that," added Lilias, "would be best done by turning him out the same beggar's brat that your ladyship took him in."

"Lilias speaks too rudely," continued the Lady, "but she has spoken the truth, young man; nor do I think I ought to spare that pride which hath so completely turned your head. You have been tricked up with fine garments, and treated like the son of a gentleman, until you have forgot the fountain of your churlish blood."

"Craving your pardon, most honourable madam, Lilias hath *not* spoken truth, nor does your ladyship know aught of my descent, which should entitle you to treat it with such decided scorn. I am no beggar's brat—my grandmother begged from no one, here nor elsewhere—she would have perished sooner on the bare moor. We were harried out and driven from our home—a chance which has happed elsewhere, and to others. Avenel Castle, with its lake and its towers, was not at all times able to protect its inhabitants from want and desolation."

"Hear but his assurance!" said Lilias, "he upbraids my Lady with the distresses of her family!"

"It had indeed been a theme more gratefully spared," said the Lady, affected nevertheless with the allusion.

"It was necessary, madam, for my vindication," said the page, "or I had not even hinted at a word that might give you pain. But believe, honoured Lady, I am of no churl's blood. My proper descent I know not; but my only relation has said, and my heart has echoed it back and attested the truth, that I am sprung of gentle blood, and deserve gentle usage."

"And upon an assurance so vague as this," said the Lady, "do you propose to expect all the regard, all the privileges, befitting high rank and distinguished birth, and become a contender for concessions which are only due to the noble? Go to, sir, know yourself, or the master of the household shall make you know you are liable to the scourge as a malapert boy. You have tasted too little the discipline fit for your age and station."

"The master of the household shall taste of my dagger, ere I taste of his discipline," said the page, giving way to his restrained passion. "Lady, I have been too long the vassal of a pantoufle, and the slave of a silver whistle. You must henceforth find some other to answer your call; and let him be of birth and spirit mean enough to brook the scorn of your menials, and to call a church vassal his master."

"I have deserved this insult," said the Lady, colouring deeply, "for so long enduring and fostering your petulance. Begone, sir. Leave this castle to-night—I will send you the means of subsistence till you find some honest mode of support, though I fear your imaginary grandeur will be above all others, save those of rapine and violence. Begone, sir, and see my face no more."

The page threw himself at her feet in an agony of sorrow. "My dear and honoured mistress," he said, but was unable to bring out another syllable.

"Arise, sir," said the Lady, "and let go my mantle—hypocrisy is a poor cloak for ingratitude."

"I am incapable of either, madam," said the page, springing up with the hasty start of passion which belonged to his rapid and impetuous temper. "Think not I meant to implore permission to reside here; it has been long my determination to leave Avenel, and I will never forgive myself for having permitted you to say the word *begone*, ere I said, 'I leave you.' I did but kneel to ask your forgiveness for an ill-considered word used in the height of displeasure, but which ill became my mouth, as addressed to you. Other grace I asked not—you have done much for me—but I repeat, that you better know what you yourself have done, than what I have suffered."

"Roland," said the Lady, somewhat appeased, and relenting towards her favourite, "you had me to appeal to when you were aggrieved. You were neither called upon to suffer wrong, nor entitled to resent it, when you were under my protection."

"And what," said the youth, "if I sustained wrong from those you loved and favoured, was I to disturb your peace with idle tale-bearings and eternal complaints? No, madam; I have borne my own burden in silence, and without disturbing you with murmurs; and the respect with which you accuse me of wanting, furnishes the only reason why I have neither appealed to you, nor taken vengeance at my own hand in a manner far more effectual. It is well, however, that we part. I was not born to be a stipendiary, favoured by his mistress, until ruined by the calumnies of others. May Heaven multiply its choicest blessings on your honoured head; and, for your sake, upon all that are dear to you!"

He was about to leave the apartment, when the Lady called upon him to return. He stood still, while she thus addressed him: "It was not my intention, nor would it be just, even in the height of my displeasure, to dismiss you without the means of support; take this purse of gold."

"Forgive me, Lady," said the boy, "and let me go hence with the consciousness that I have not been degraded to the point of accepting alms. If my poor services can be placed against the expense of my apparel and my maintenance, I only remain debtor to you for my life, and that alone is a debt which I can never repay; put up then that purse, and only say, instead, that you do not part from me in anger."

"No, not in anger," said the Lady, "in sorrow rather for your wilfulness; but take the gold, you cannot but need it."

"May God evermore bless you for the kind tone and the kind word! but the gold I cannot take. I am able of body, and do not lack friends so wholly as you may think; for the time may come that I may yet show myself more thankful than by mere words." He threw himself on his knees, kissed the hand which she did not withdraw, and then hastily left the apartment.

Lilias, for a moment or two, kept her eye fixed on her mistress, who looked so unusually pale, that she seemed about to faint; but the Lady instantly recovered herself, and declining the assistance which her attendant offered her, walked to her own apartment.

Chapter the Sixth.

Thou hast each secret of the household, Francis.
I dare be sworn thou hast been in the buttery,
Steeping thy curious humour in fat ale,
And in thy butler's tattle—ay, or chatting
With the glib waiting-woman o'er her comfits—
These bear the key to each domestic mystery.
OLD PLAY.

UPON the morrow succeeding the scene we have described, the disgraced favourite left the castle; and at breakfast-time the cautious old steward and Mrs. Lilias sat in the apartment of the latter personage, holding grave converse on the important event of the day, sweetened by a small treat of comfits, to which the providence of Mr. Wingate had added a little flask of racy canary.

"He is gone at last," said the abigail, sipping her glass; "and here is to his good journey."

"Amen," answered the steward, gravely; "I wish the poor deserted lad no ill."

"And he is gone like a wild-duck, as he came," continued Mrs. Lilias; "no lowering of drawbridges, or pacing along causeways, for him. My master has pushed off in the boat which they call the little Herod, (more shame to them for giving the name of a Christian to wood and iron,) and has rowed himself by himself to the farther side of the loch, and off and away with himself, and left all his finery strewed about his room. I wonder who is to clean his trumpery out after him—though the things are worth lifting, too."

"Doubtless, Mistress Lilias," answered the master of the household, "in the which case, I am free to think, they will not long cumber the floor."

"And now tell me, Master Wingate," continued the damsel, "do not the very cockles of your heart rejoice at the house being rid of this upstart whelp, that flung us all into shadow?"

"Why, Mistress Lilias," replied Wingate, "as to rejoicing—those who have lived as long in great families as has been my lot, will be in no hurry to rejoice at any thing. And for Roland Græme, though he may be a good riddance in the main, yet what says the very sooth proverb, 'Seldom comes a better.'"

"Seldom comes a better, indeed!" echoed Mrs. Lilias. "I say, never can come a worse, or one half so bad. He might have been the ruin of our poor dear mistress," (here she used her kerchief,) "body and soul, and estate too; for she spent more coin on his apparel than on any four servants about the house."

"Mistress Lilias," said the sage steward, "I do opine that our mistress requireth not this pity at your hands, being in all respects competent to take care of her own body, soul, and estate into the bargain."

"You would not mayhap have said so," answered the waiting-woman, "had you seen how like Lot's wife she looked when young master took his leave. My mistress is a good lady, and a virtuous, and a well-doing lady, and a well-spoken of — but I would not Sir Halbert had seen her last evening for two and a plack."

"Oh, foy! foy! foy!" reiterated the steward; "servants should hear and see, and say nothing. Besides that, my lady is utterly devoted to Sir Halbert, as well she may, being, as he is, the most renowned knight in these parts."

"Well, well," said the abigail, "I mean no more harm; but they that seek least renown abroad, are most apt to find quiet at home, that's all; and my Lady's lonesome situation is to be considered, that made her fain to take up with the first beggar's brat that a dog brought her out of the loch."

"And, therefore," said the steward, "I say, rejoice not too much, or too hastily, Mistress Lilias; for if your Lady wished a favourite to pass away the time, depend upon it, the time will not pass lighter now that he is gone. So she will have another favourite to choose for herself; and be assured, if she wishes such a toy, she will not lack one."

"And where should she choose one, but among her own tried and faithful servants," said Mrs. Lilias, "who have broken her bread, and drunk her drink, for so many years? I have known many a lady as high as she is, that never thought either of a friend or favourite beyond their own waiting-woman — always having a proper respect, at the same time, for their old and faithful master of the household, Master Wingate."

"Truly, Mistress Lilias," replied the steward, "I do partly see the mark at which you shoot, but I doubt your bolt will fall short. Matters being with our Lady as it likes you to suppose, it will neither be your crimped pinners, Mrs. Lilias, (speaking of them with due respect,) nor my silver hair, or golden chain, that will fill up the void which Roland Græme must needs leave in our Lady's leisure. There will be a learned young divine with some new doctrine — a learned leech with some new drug — a bold cavalier, who will not be refused the favour of wearing her colours at a running at the ring — a cunning harper that could harp the heart out of woman's breast, as they say Signor David Rizzio did to our poor Queen; — these are the sort of folk who supply the loss of a well-favoured favourite, and not an old steward, or a middle-aged waiting-woman."

"Well," replied Lilias, "you have experience, Master Wingate, and truly I would my master would leave off his picking hither and thither, and look better after the affairs of his household. There will be a papestrie among us next, for what should I see among master's clothes but a string of gold beads! I promise you, *aves* and *credos* both! — I seized on them like a falcon."

"I doubt it not, I doubt it not," said the steward, sagaciously nodding his head; "I have often noticed that the boy had strange observances which savoured of popery, and that he was very jealous to conceal them. But you will find the Catholic under the Presbyterian cloak as often as the knave under the Friar's hood—what then? we are all mortal—Right proper beads they are," he added, looking attentively at them, "and may weigh four ounces of fine gold."

"And I will have them melted down presently," she said, "before they be the misguiding of some poor blinded soul."

"Very cautious, indeed, Mistress Lilias," said the steward, nodding his head in assent.

"I will have them made," said Mrs. Lilias, "into a pair of shoe-buckles; I would not wear the Pope's trinkets, or whatever has once borne the shape of them, one inch above my instep, were they diamonds instead of gold — But this is what has come of Father Ambrose coming about the castle, as demure as a cat that is about to steal cream."

"Father Ambrose is our master's brother," said the steward gravely.

"Very true, Master Wingate," answered the Dame; "but is that a good reason why he should pervert the king's liege subjects to papistrie?"

"Heaven forbid, Mistress Lilias," answered the sententious major-domo; "but yet there are worse folk than the Papists."

"I wonder where they are to be found," said the waiting-woman, with some asperity; "but I believe, Master Wingate, if one were to speak to you about the devil himself, you would say there were worse people than Satan."

"Assuredly I might say so," replied the steward, "supposing that I saw Satan standing at my elbow."

The waiting-woman started, and having exclaimed, "God bless us!" added, "I wonder, Master Wingate, you can take pleasure in frightening one thus."

"Nay, Mistress Lilias, I had no such purpose," was the reply; "but look you here—the Papists are but put down for the present, but who knows how long this word *present* will last? There are two great Popish earls in the north of England, that abominate the very word reformation; I mean the Northumberland and Westmoreland Earls, men of power enough to shake any throne in Christendom. Then, though our Scottish king be, God bless him, a true Protestant, yet he is but a boy; and here is his mother that was our queen—I trust there is no harm to say, God bless her too—and she is a Catholic; and many begin to think she has had but hard measure, such as the Hamiltons in the west, and some of our Border clans here, and the Gordons in the north, who are all wishing to see a new world; and if such a new world should chance to come up, it is like that the Queen will take back her own crown, and that the mass and the cross will come up, and then down go pulpits, Geneva-gowns, and black silk skull-caps."

"And have you, Master Jasper Wingate, who have heard the word, and listened unto pure and precious Mr. Henry Warden, have you, I say, the patience to speak, or but to think, of popery coming down on us like a storm, or of the woman Mary again making the royal seat of Scotland a throne of abomination? No marvel that you are so civil to the cowled monk, Father Ambrose, when he comes hither with his downcast eyes that he never raises to my Lady's face, and with his low sweet-toned voice, and his benedicites, and his benisons; and who so ready to take them kindly as Master Wingate?"

"Mistress Lilias," replied the butler, with an air which was intended to close the debate, "there are reasons for all things. If I received Father Ambrose debonairly, and suffered him to steal a word now and then with this same Roland Græme, it was not that I cared a brass bodle for his benison or malison either, but only because I respected my master's blood. And who can answer, if Mary come in again, whether he may not be as stout a tree to lean to as ever his brother hath proved to us? For down goes the Earl of Murray when the Queen comes by her own again; and good is his luck if he can keep the head on his own shoulders. And down goes our Knight, with the Earl, his patron; and who so like to mount into his empty saddle as this same Father Ambrose? The Pope of Rome can so soon dispense with his vows, and then we should have Sir Edward the soldier, instead of Ambrose the priest."

Anger and astonishment kept Mrs. Lilias silent, while her old friend, in his self-complacent manner, was making known to her his political speculations. At length her resentment found utterance in words of great ire and scorn. "What, Master Wingate! have you eaten my mistress's bread, to say nothing of my master's, so many years, that you could live to think of her being dispossessed of her own Castle of Avenel, by a wretched monk, who is not a drop's blood to her in the way of relation? I, that am but a woman, would try first whether my rock or his cowl was the better metal. Shame on you, Master Wingate! If I had not held you as so old an acquaintance, this should have gone to my Lady's ears though I had been called pickthank and tale-pyet for my pains, as when I told of Roland Græme shooting the wild swan."

Master Wingate was somewhat dismayed at perceiving, that the details which he had given of his far-sighted political views had produced on his hearer rather suspicion of his fidelity, than admiration of his wisdom, and endeavoured, as hastily as possible, to apologize and to explain, although internally extremely offended at the unreasonable view, as he deemed it, which it had pleased Mistress Lilias Bradbourne to take of his expressions; and mentally convinced that her disapprobation of his sentiments arose solely out of the consideration, that though Father Ambrose, supposing him to become the master of the castle, would certainly require the services of a steward, yet those of a waiting-woman would, in the supposed circumstances, be altogether superfluous.

After his explanation had been received as explanations usually are, the two friends separated; Lilias to attend the silver whistle which called her to her mistress's chamber, and the sapient major-domo to the duties of his own department. They parted with less than their usual degree of reverence and regard; for the steward felt that his worldly wisdom was rebuked by the more disinterested attachment of the waiting-woman, and Mistress Lilias Bradbourne was compelled to consider her old friend as something little better than a time-server.

Chapter the Seventh.

When I hae a saxpence under my thumb,
Then I get credit in ilka town;
But when I am puir they bid me gae by—
Oh, poverty parts good company!

OLD SONG.

WHILE the departure of the page afforded subject for the conversation which we have detailed in our last chapter, the late favourite was far advanced on his solitary journey, without well knowing what was its object, or what was likely to be its end. He had rowed the skiff in which he left the castle, to the side of the lake most distant from the village, with the desire of escaping from the notice of the inhabitants. His pride whispered, that he would be, in his discarded state, only the subject of their wonder and compassion; and his generosity told him, that any mark of sympathy which his situation should excite, might be unfavourably reported at the castle. A trifling incident convinced him he had little to fear for his friends on the latter score. He was met by a young man some years older than himself, who had on former occasions been but too happy to be permitted to share in his sports in the subordinate character of his assistant. Ralph Fisher approached to greet him, with all the alacrity of an humble friend.

"What, Master Roland, abroad on this side, and without either hawk or hound?"

"Hawk or hound," said Roland, "I will never perhaps hollo to again. I have been dismissed—that is, I have left the castle."

Ralph was surprised. "What! you are to pass into the Knight's service, and take the black jack and the lance?"

"Indeed," replied Roland Græme, "I am not—I am now leaving the service of Avenel for ever."

"And whither are you going, then?" said the young peasant.

"Nay, that is a question which it craves time to answer — I have that matter to determine yet," replied the disgraced favourite.

"Nay, nay," said Ralph, "I warrant you it is the same to you which way you go — my Lady would not dismiss you till she had put some lining into the pouches of your doublet."

"Sordid slave!" said Roland Græme, "dost thou think I would have accepted a boon from one who was giving me over a prey to detraction and to ruin, at the instigation of a canting priest and a meddling serving-woman? The bread that I had bought with such an alms would have choked me at the first mouthful."

Ralph looked at his quondam friend with an air of wonder not unmixed with contempt. "Well," he said, at length, "no occasion for passion — each man knows his own stomach best — but, were I on a black moor at this time of day, not knowing whither I was going, I should be glad to have a broad piece or two in my pouch, come by them as I could. — But perhaps you will go with me to my father's — that is, for a night, for to-morrow we expect my uncle Menelaus and all his folk; but, as I said, for one night——"

The cold-blooded limitation of the offered shelter to one night only, and that tendered most unwillingly, offended the pride of the discarded favourite.

"I would rather sleep on the fresh heather, as I have done many a night on less occasion," said Roland Græme, "than in the smoky garret of your father, that smells of peat smoke and usquebaugh like a Highlander's plaid."

"You may choose, my master, if you are so nice," replied Ralph Fisher; "you may be glad to smell a peat-fire, and usquebaugh too, if you journey long in the fashion you propose. You might have said God-a-mercy for your proffer, though — it is not every one that will put themselves in the way of ill-will by harbouring a discarded serving-man."

"Ralph," said Roland Græme, "I would pray you to remember that I have switched you before now, and this is the same riding-wand which you have tasted."

Ralph, who was a thickset clownish figure, arrived at his full strength, and conscious of the most complete personal superiority, laughed contemptuously at the threats of the slight-made stripling.

"It may be the same wand," he said, "but not the same hand; and that is as good rhyme as if it were in a ballad. Look you, my Lady's page that was, when your switch was up, it was no fear of you, but of your betters, that kept mine down — and I wot not what hinders me from clearing old scores with this hazel rung, and showing you it was your Lady's livery-coat which I spared, and not your flesh and blood, Master Roland."

In the midst of his rage, Roland Græme was just wise enough to see, that by continuing this altercation, he would subject himself to very rude treatment from the boor, who was so much older and stronger than himself; and while his antagonist, with a sort of jeering laugh of defiance, seemed to provoke the contest, he felt the full bitterness of his own degraded condition, and burst into a passion of tears, which he in vain endeavoured to conceal with both his hands.

Even the rough churl was moved with the distress of his quondam companion.

"Nay, Master Roland," he said, "I did but as 'twere jest with thee — I would not harm thee, man, were it but for old acquaintance sake. But ever look to a man's inches ere you talk of switching — why, thine arm, man, is but like a spindle compared to mine. — But hark, I hear old Adam Woodcock hollowing to his hawk — Come along, man, we will have a merry afternoon, and go jollily to my father's in spite of the peat-smoke and usquebaugh to boot. Maybe we may put you into some honest way of winning your bread, though it's hard to come by in these broken times."

The unfortunate page made no answer, nor did he withdraw his hands from his face, and Fisher continued in what he imagined a suitable tone of comfort.

"Why, man, when you were my Lady's minion, men held you proud, and some thought you a Papist, and I wot not what; and so, now that you have no one to bear you out, you must be companionable and hearty, and wait on the minister's examinations, and put these things out of folk's head; and if he says you are in fault, you must jouk your head to the stream; and if a gentleman, or a gentleman's gentleman, give you a rough word, or a light blow, you must only say, thank you for dusting my doublet, or the like, as I have done by you.—But hark to Woodcock's whistle again. Come, and I will teach you all the trick on't as we go on."

"I thank you," said Roland Græme, endeavouring to assume an air of indifference and of superiority; "but I have another path before me, and were it otherwise, I could not tread in yours."

"Very true, Master Roland," replied the clown; "and every man knows his own matters best, and so I will not keep you from the path, as you say. Give us a grip of your hand, man, for auld lang syne.—What! not clap palms ere we part?—well, so be it—a wilful man will have his way, and so farewell, and the blessing of the morning to you."

"Good-morrow—good-morrow," said Roland, hastily; and the clown walked lightly off, whistling as he went, and glad, apparently, to be rid of an acquaintance, whose claims might be troublesome, and who had no longer the means to be serviceable to him.

Roland Græme compelled himself to walk on while they were within sight of each other, that his former intimate might not augur any vacillation of purpose, or uncertainty of object, from his remaining on the same spot; but the effort was a painful one. He seemed stunned, as it were, and giddy; the earth on which he stood felt as if unsound, and quaking under his feet like the surface of a bog; and he had once or twice nearly fallen, though the path he trode was of firm greensward. He kept resolutely moving forward, in spite of the internal agitation to which these symptoms belonged, until the distant form of his acquaintance disappeared behind the slope of a hill, when his heart failed at once; and, sitting down on the turf, remote from human ken, he gave way to the natural expressions of wounded pride, grief, and fear, and wept with unrestrained profusion and unqualified bitterness.

When the first violent paroxysm of his feelings had subsided, the deserted and friendless youth felt that mental relief which usually follows such discharges of sorrow. The tears continued to chase each other down his cheeks, but they were no longer accompanied by the same sense of desolation; an afflicting yet milder sentiment was awakened in his mind, by the recollection of his benefactress, of the unwearied kindness which had attached her to him, in spite of many acts of provoking petulance, now recollected as offences of a deep dye, which had protected him against the machinations of others, as well as against the consequences of his own folly, and would have continued to do so, had not the excess of his presumption compelled her to withdraw her protection.

"Whatever indignity I have borne," he said, "has been the just reward of my own ingratitude. And have I done well to accept the hospitality, the more than maternal kindness, of my protectress, yet to detain from her the knowledge of my religion?—but she shall know that a Catholic has as much gratitude as a Puritan—that I have been thoughtless, but not wicked—that in my wildest moments I have loved, respected, and honoured her—and that the orphan boy might indeed be heedless, but was never ungrateful!"

He turned, as these thoughts passed through his mind, and began hastily to retread his footsteps towards the castle. But he checked the first eagerness of his repentant haste, when he reflected on the scorn and contempt with which the family were likely to see the return of the fugitive, humbled, as they must necessarily suppose him, into a supplicant, who requested pardon for his fault, and permission to return to his service. He slackened his pace, but he stood not still.

"I care not," he resolutely determined; "let them wink, point, nod, sneer, speak of the conceit which is humbled, of the pride which has had a fall—I care not; it is a penance due to my folly, and I will endure it with patience. But if she also, my benefactress, if she also should think me sordid and weak-spirited enough to beg, not for her pardon alone, but for a renewal of the advantages which I derived from her favour — *her* suspicion of my meanness I cannot—I will not brook."

He stood still, and his pride rallying with constitutional obstinacy against his more just feeling, urged that he would incur the scorn of the Lady of Avenel, rather than obtain her favour, by following the course which the first ardour of his repentant feelings had dictated to him.

"If I had but some plausible pretext," he thought, "some ostensible reason for my return, some excuse to allege which might show I came not as a degraded supplicant, or a discarded menial, I might go thither—but as I am, I cannot—my heart would leap from its place and burst."

As these thoughts swept through his mind, something passed in the air so near him as to dazzle his eyes, and almost to brush the plume in his cap. He looked up — it was the favourite falcon of Sir Halbert, which, flying around his head, seemed to claim his attention, as that of a well-known friend. Roland extended his arm, and gave the accustomed whoop, and the falcon instantly settled on his wrist, and began to prune itself, glancing at the youth from time to time an acute and brilliant beam of its hazel eye, which seemed to ask why he caressed it not with his usual fondness.

"Ah, Diamond!" he said, as if the bird understood him, "thou and I must be strangers henceforward. Many a gallant stoop have I seen thee make, and many a brave heron strike down; but that is all gone and over, and there is no hawking more for me!"

"And why not, Master Roland," said Adam Woodcock the falconer, who came at that instant from behind a few alder bushes which had concealed him from view, "why should there be no more hawking for you? Why, man, what were our life without our sports? — thou know'st the jolly old song —

"And rather would Allan in dungeon lie,
Than live at large where the falcon cannot fly;
And Allan would rather lie in Sexton's pound,
Than live where he followed not the merry hawk and hound."

The voice of the falconer was hearty and friendly, and the tone in which he half-sung half-recited his rude ballad, implied honest frankness and cordiality. But remembrance of their quarrel, and its consequences, embarrassed Roland, and prevented his reply. The falconer saw his hesitation, and guessed the cause.

"What now," said he, "Master Roland? do you, who are half an Englishman, think that I, who am a whole one, would keep up anger against you, and you in distress? That were like some of the Scots, (my master's reverence always excepted,) who can be fair and false, and wait their time, and keep their mind, as they say, to themselves, and touch pot and flagon with you, and hunt and hawk with you, and, after all, when time serves, pay off some old feud with the point of the dagger. Canny Yorkshire has no memory for such old sores. Why, man, an you had hit me a rough blow, maybe I would rather have taken it from you, than a rough word from another; for you have a good notion of falconry, though you stand up for washing the meat for the eyases. So give us your hand, man, and bear no malice."

Roland, though he felt his proud blood rebel at the familiarity of honest Adam's address, could not resist its downright frankness. Covering his face with the one hand, he held out the other to the falconer, and returned with readiness his friendly grasp.

"Why, this is hearty now," said Woodcock; "I always said you had a kind heart, though you have a spice of the devil in your disposition, that is certain. I came this way with the falcon on purpose to find you, and yon half-bred lubbard told me which way you took flight. You ever thought too much of that kestril-kite, Master Roland, and he knows nought of sport after all, but what he caught from you. I saw how it had been betwixt you, and I sent him out of my company with a wanion — I would rather have a rifler on my perch than a false knave at my elbow—and now, Master Roland, tell me what way wing ye?"

"That is as God pleases," replied the page, with a sigh which he could not suppress.

"Nay, man, never droop a feather for being cast off," said the falconer; "who knows but you may soar the better and fairer flight for all this yet? —Look at Diamond there, 'tis a noble bird, and shows gallantly with his hood, and bells, and jesses; but there is many a wild falcon in Norway that would not change properties with him — And that is what I would say of you. You are no longer my Lady's page, and you will not clothe so fair, or feed so well, or sleep so soft, or show so gallant—What of all that? if you are not her page, you are your own man, and may go where you will, without minding whoop or whistle. The worst is the loss of the sport, but who knows what you may come to? They say that Sir Halbert himself, I speak with reverence, was once glad to be the Abbot's forester, and now he has hounds and hawks of his own, and Adam Woodcock for a falconer to the boot."

"You are right, and say well, Adam," answered the youth, the blood mantling in his cheeks, "the falcon will soar higher without his bells than with them, though the bells be made of silver."

"That is cheerily spoken," replied the falconer; "and whither now?"

"I thought of going to the Abbey of Kennaquhair," answered Roland Græme, "to ask the counsel of Father Ambrose."

"And joy go with you," said the falconer, "though it is likely you may find the old monks in some sorrow; they say the commons are threatening to turn them out of their cells, and make a devil's mass of it in the old church, thinking they have forborne that sport too long; and troth I am clear of the same opinion."

"Then will Father Ambrose be the better of having a friend beside him!" said the page, manfully.

"Ay, but, my young fearnought," replied the falconer, "the friend will scarce be the better of being beside Father Ambrose—he may come by the redder's lick, and that is ever the worst of the battle."

"I care not for that," said the page, "the dread of a lick should not hold me back; but I fear I may bring trouble between the brothers by visiting Father Ambrose. I will tarry to-night at Saint Cuthbert's cell, where the old priest will give me a night's shelter; and I will send to Father Ambrose to ask his advice before I go down to the convent."

"By Our Lady," said the falconer, "and that is a likely plan—and now," he continued, exchanging his frankness of manner for a sort of awkward embarrassment, as if he had somewhat to say that he had no ready means to bring out—"and now, you wot well that I wear a pouch for my hawk's meat,* and so forth; but wot you what it is lined with, Master Roland?"

"With leather, to be sure," replied Roland, somewhat surprised at the

* This same bag, like every thing belonging to falconry, was esteemed an honourable distinction, and worn often by the nobility and gentry. One of the Sommervilles of Camnethan was called *Sir John with the red bag* because it was his wont to wear his hawking pouch covered with satin of that colour.

hesitation with which Adam Woodcock asked a question apparently so simple.

"With leather, lad?" said Woodcock; "ay, and with silver to the boot of that. See here," he said, showing a secret slit in the lining of his bag of office—"here they are, thirty good Harry groats as ever were struck in bluff old Hal's time, and ten of them are right heartily at your service; and now the murder is out."

Roland's first idea was to refuse his assistance; but he recollected the vows of humility which he had just taken upon him, and it occurred that this was the opportunity to put his new-formed resolution to the test. Assuming a strong command of himself, he answered Adam Woodcock with as much frankness as his nature permitted him to wear, in doing what was so contrary to his inclinations, that he accepted thankfully of his kind offer, while, to soothe his own reviving pride, he could not help adding, "he hoped soon to requite the obligation."

"That as you list—that as you list, young man," said the falconer, with glee, counting out and delivering to his young friend the supply he had so generously offered, and then adding, with great cheerfulness,—"Now you may go through the world; for he that can back a horse, wind a horn, hollow a greyhound, fly a hawk, and play at sword and buckler, with a whole pair of shoes, a green jacket, and ten lily-white groats in his pouch, may bid Father Care hang himself in his own jesses. Farewell, and God be with you!"

So saying, and as if desirous to avoid the thanks of his companion, he turned hastily round, and left Roland Græme to pursue his journey alone.

Chapter the Eighth.

The sacred tapers lights are gone,
Gray moss has clad the altar stone,
The holy image is o'erthrown,
The bell has ceased to toll,
The long ribb'd aisles are burst and shrunk,
The holy shrines to ruin sunk,
Departed is the pious monk,
God's blessing on his soul!

REDIVIVA.

The cell of Saint Cuthbert, as it was called, marked, or was supposed to mark, one of those resting-places, which that venerable saint was pleased to assign to his monks, when his convent, being driven from Lindisfern by the Danes, became a peripatetic society of religionists, and bearing their patron's body on their shoulders, transported him from place to place through Scotland and the borders of England, until he was pleased at length to spare them the pain of carrying him farther, and to choose his ultimate place of rest in the lordly towers of Durham. The odour of his sanctity remained behind him at each place where he had granted the monks a transient respite from their labours; and proud were those who could assign, as his temporary resting-place, any spot within their vicinity. There were few cells more celebrated and honoured than that of Saint Cuthbert, to which Roland Græme now bent his way, situated considerably to the north-west of the great Abbey of Kennaquhair, on which it was dependent. In the neighbourhood were some of those recommendations which weighed with the experienced priesthood of Rome, in choosing their sites for places of religion.

There was a well, possessed of some medicinal qualities, which, of course, claimed the saint for its guardian and patron, and occasionally produced some advantage to the recluse who inhabited his cell, since none could reasonably expect to benefit by the fountain who did not extend their bounty to the saint's chaplain. A few rods of fertile land afforded the monk his plot of garden ground; an eminence well clothed with trees rose behind the cell, and sheltered it from the north and the east, while the front, opening to the south-west, looked up a wild but pleasant valley, down which wandered a lively brook, which battled with every stone that interrupted its passage.

The cell itself was rather plainly than rudely constructed — a low Gothic building with two small apartments, one of which served the priest for his dwelling-place, the other for his chapel. As there were few of the secular clergy who durst venture to reside so near the Border, the assistance of this monk in spiritual affairs had not been useless to the community, while the Catholic religion retained the ascendancy; as he could marry, christen, and administer the other sacraments of the Roman church. Of late, however, as the Protestant doctrines gained ground, he had found it convenient to live in close retirement, and to avoid, as much as possible, drawing upon himself observation or animadversion. The appearance of his habitation, however, when Roland Græme came before it in the close of the evening, plainly showed that his caution had been finally ineffectual.

The page's first movement was to knock at the door, when he observed, to his surprise, that it was open, not from being left unlatched, but because, beat off its upper hinge, it was only fastened to the door-post by the lower, and could therefore no longer perform its functions. Somewhat alarmed at this, and receiving no answer when he knocked and called, Roland began to look more at leisure upon the exterior of the little dwelling before he ventured to enter it. The flowers, which had been trained with care against the walls, seemed to have been recently torn down, and trailed their dishonoured garlands on the earth; the latticed window was broken and dashed in. The garden, which the monk had maintained by his constant labour in the highest order and beauty, bore marks of having been lately trod down and destroyed by the hoofs of animals, and the feet of men.

The sainted spring had not escaped. It was wont to rise beneath a canopy of ribbed arches, with which the devotion of elder times had secured and protected its healing waters. These arches were now almost entirely demolished, and the stones of which they were built were tumbled into the well, as if for the purpose of choking up and destroying the fountain, which, as it had shared in other days the honour of the saint, was, in the present, doomed to partake his unpopularity. Part of the roof had been pulled down from the house itself, and an attempt had been made with crows and levers upon one of the angles, by which several large corner-stones had been forced out of their place; but the solidity of ancient mason-work had proved too great for the time or patience of the assailants, and they had relinquished their task of destruction. Such dilapidated buildings, after the lapse of years, during which nature has gradually covered the effects of violence with creeping plants, and with weather-stains, exhibit, amid their decay, a melancholy beauty. But when the visible effects of violence appear raw and recent, there is no feeling to mitigate the sense of devastation with which they impress the spectators; and such was now the scene on which the youthful page gazed, with the painful feelings it was qualified to excite.

When his first momentary surprise was over, Roland Græme was at no loss to conjecture the cause of these ravages. The destruction of the Popish edifices did not take place at once throughout Scotland, but at different times, and according to the spirit which actuated the reformed clergy; some of whom instigated their hearers to these acts of demolition, and others, with better taste and feeling, endeavoured to protect the ancient shrines, while they desired to see them purified from the objects which had attracted idolatrous devotion. From time to time, therefore, the populace of the Scottish towns and villages, when instigated either by their own feelings of abhorrence for Popish superstition, or by the doctrines of the more zealous preachers, resumed the work of destruction, and exercised it upon some sequestered church, chapel, or cell, which had escaped the first burst of their indignation against the religion of Rome. In many places, the vices of the Catholic clergy, arising out of the wealth and the corruption of that tremendous hierarchy, furnished too good an apology for wreaking vengeance upon the splendid edifices which they inhabited; and of this an old Scottish historian gives a remarkable instance.

"Why mourn ye," said an aged matron, seeing the discontent of some of the citizens, while a stately convent was burnt by the multitude, — "why mourn ye for its destruction? If you knew half the flagitious wickedness which has been perpetrated within that house, you would rather bless the divine judgment, which permits not even the senseless walls that screened such profligacy, any longer to cumber Christian ground."

But although, in many instances, the destruction of the Roman Catholic buildings might be, in the matron's way of judging, an act of justice, and in others an act of policy, there is no doubt that the humour of demolishing monuments of ancient piety and munificence, and that in a poor country like Scotland, where there was no chance of their being replaced, was both useless, mischievous, and barbarous.

In the present instance, the unpretending and quiet seclusion of the monk of Saint Cuthbert's had hitherto saved him from the general wreck; but it would seem ruin had now at length reached him. Anxious to discover if he had at least escaped personal harm, Roland Græme entered the half ruined cell.

The interior of the building was in a state which fully justified the opinion he had formed from its external injuries. The few rude utensils of the solitary's hut were broken down, and lay scattered on the floor, where it seemed as if a fire had been made with some of the fragments to destroy the rest of his property, and to consume, in particular, the rude old image of Saint Cuthbert, in its episcopal habit, which lay on the hearth like Dagon of yore, shattered with the axe and scorched with the flames, but only partially destroyed. In the little apartment which served as a chapel, the altar was overthrown, and the four huge stones of which it had been once composed lay scattered around the floor. The large stone crucifix which occupied the niche behind the altar, and fronted the supplicant while he paid his devotion there, had been pulled down and dashed by its own weight into three fragments. There were marks of sledge-hammers on each of these; yet the image had been saved from utter demolition by the size and strength of the remaining fragments, which, though much injured, retained enough of the original sculpture to show what it had been intended to represent.*

Roland Græme, secretly nursed in the tenets of Rome, saw with horror the profanation of the most sacred emblem, according to his creed, of our holy religion.

"It is the badge of our redemption," he said, "which the felons have

---

* I may here observe, that this is entirely an ideal scene. Saint Cuthbert, a person of established sanctity, had, no doubt, several places of worship on the Borders, where he flourished whilst living; but Tillmouth Chapel is the only one which bears some resemblance to the hermitage described in the text. It has, indeed, a well, famous for gratifying three wishes for every worshipper who shall quaff the fountain with sufficient belief in its efficacy. At this spot the Saint is said to have landed in his stone coffin, in which he sailed down the Tweed from Melrose, and here the stone coffin long lay, in evidence of the fact. The late Sir Francis Blake Delaval is said to have taken the exact measure of the coffin, and to have ascertained, by hydrostatic principles, that it might have actually swum. A profane farmer in the neighborhood announced his intention of converting this last bed of the Saint into a trough for his swine; but the profanation was rendered impossible, either by the Saint, or by some pious votary in his behalf, for on the following morning the stone sarcophagus was found broken in two fragments.

Tillmouth Chapel, with these points of resemblance, lies, however, in exactly the opposite direction as regards Melrose, which the supposed cell of St. Cuthbert is said to have borne towards Kennaquhair

dared to violate — would to God my weak strength were able to replace it my humble strength, to atone for the sacrilege!"

He stooped to the task he first meditated, and with a sudden, and to himself almost an incredible exertion of power, he lifted up the one extremity of the lower shaft of the cross, and rested it upon the edge of the large stone which served for its pedestal. Encouraged by this success, he applied his force to the other extremity, and, to his own astonishment, succeeded so far as to erect the lower end of the limb into the socket, out of which it had been forced, and to place this fragment of the image upright.

While he was employed in this labour, or rather at the very moment when he had accomplished the elevation of the fragment, a voice, in thrilling and well-known accents, spoke behind him these words:—"Well done, thou good and faithful servant! Thus would I again meet the child of my love — the hope of my aged eyes."

Roland turned round in astonishment, and the tall commanding form of Magdalen Græme stood beside him. She was arrayed in a sort of loose habit, in form like that worn by penitents in Catholic countries, but black in colour, and approaching as near to a pilgrim's cloak as it was safe to wear in a country where the suspicion of Catholic devotion in many places endangered the safety of those who were suspected of attachment to the ancient faith. Roland Græme threw himself at her feet. She raised and embraced him, with affection indeed, but not unmixed with gravity which amounted almost to sternness.

"Thou hast kept well," she said, "the bird in thy bosom.* As a boy, as a youth, thou hast held fast thy faith amongst heretics—thou hast kept thy secret and mine own amongst thine enemies. I wept when I parted from you — I who seldom weep, then shed tears, less for thy death than for thy spiritual danger — I dared not even see thee to bid thee a last farewell — my grief, my swelling grief, had betrayed me to these heretics. But thou hast been faithful — down, down on thy knees before the holy sign, which evil men injure and blaspheme; down, and praise saints and angels for the grace they have done thee, in preserving thee from the leprous plague which cleaves to the house in which thou wert nurtured!"

"If, my mother — so I must ever call you," replied Græme, — "if I am returned such as thou wouldst wish me, thou must thank the care of the pious father Ambrose, whose instructions confirmed your early precepts, and taught me at once to be faithful and to be silent."

"Be he blessed for it," said she; "blessed in the cell and in the field, in the pulpit and at the altar — the saints rain blessings on him! — they are just, and employ his pious care to counteract the evils which his detested brother works against the realm and the church, — but he knew not of thy lineage?"

"I could not myself tell him that," answered Roland. "I knew but darkly from your words, that Sir Halbert Glendinning holds mine inheritance, and that I am of blood as noble as runs in the veins of any Scottish Baron — these are things not to be forgotten, but for the explanation I must now look to you."

"And when time suits, thou shalt not look for it in vain. But men say, my son, that thou art bold and sudden; and those who bear such tempers are not lightly to be trusted with what will strongly move them."

"Say rather, my mother," returned Roland Græme, "that I am laggard and cold-blooded — what patience or endurance can you require of which *he* is not capable, who for years has heard his religion ridiculed and insulted, yet failed to plunge his dagger into the blasphemer's bosom!"

"Be contented, my child," replied Magdalen Græme; "the time, which then and even now demands patience, will soon ripen to that of effort and

* An expression used by Sir Ralph Percy, slain in the battle of Hedgly-moor in 1464, when dying, to express his having preserved unstained his fidelity to the house of Lancaster

action—great events are on the wing, and thou,—thou shalt have thy share in advancing them. Thou hast relinquished the service of the Lady of Avenel?"

"I have been dismissed from it, my mother—I have lived to be dismissed, as if I were the meanest of the train."

"It is the better, my child," replied she; "thy mind will be the more hardened to undertake that which must be performed."

"Let it be nothing, then, against the Lady of Avenel," said the page, "as thy look and words seem to imply. I have eaten her bread — I have experienced her favour — I will neither injure nor betray her."

"Of that hereafter, my son," said she; "but learn this, that it is not for thee to capitulate in thy duty, and to say this will I do, and that will I leave undone—No, Roland! God and man will no longer abide the wickedness of this generation. Seest thou these fragments — knowest thou what they represent? — and canst thou think it is for thee to make distinctions amongst a race so accursed by Heaven, that they renounce, violate, blaspheme, and destroy, whatsoever we are commanded to believe in, whatsoever we are commanded to reverence?"

As she spoke, she bent her head towards the broken image, with a countenance in which strong resentment and zeal were mingled with an expression of ecstatic devotion; she raised her left hand aloft as in the act of making a vow, and thus proceeded; "Bear witness for me, blessed symbol of our salvation, bear witness, holy saint, within whose violated temple we stand, that as it is not for vengeance of my own that my hate pursues these people, so neither, for any favour or earthly affection towards any amongst them, will I withdraw my hand from the plough, when it shall pass through the devoted furrow! Bear witness, holy saint, once thyself a wanderer and fugitive as we are now—bear witness, Mother of Mercy, Queen of Heaven —bear witness, saints and angels!"

In this high train of enthusiasm, she stood, raising her eyes through the fractured roof of the vault, to the stars which now began to twinkle through the pale twilight, while the long gray tresses which hung down over her shoulders waved in the night-breeze, which the chasm and fractured windows admitted freely.

Roland Græme was too much awed by early habits, as well as by the mysterious import of her words, to ask for farther explanation of the purpose she obscurely hinted at. Nor did she farther press him on the subject; for, having concluded her prayer or obtestation, by clasping her hands together with solemnity, and then signing herself with the cross, she again addressed her grandson, in a tone more adapted to the ordinary business of life.

"Thou must hence," she said, "Roland, thou must hence, but not till morning — And now, how wilt thou shift for thy night's quarters? — thou hast been more softly bred than when we were companions in the misty hills of Cumberland and Liddesdale."

"I have at least preserved, my good mother, the habits which I then learned — can lie hard, feed sparingly, and think it no hardship. Since I was a wanderer with thee on the hills, I have been a hunter, and fisher, and fowler, and each of these is accustomed to sleep freely in a worse shelter than sacrilege has left us here."

"Than sacrilege has left us here!" said the matron, repeating his words, and pausing on them. "Most true, my son; and God's faithful children are now worst sheltered, when they lodge in God's own house and the demesne of his blessed saints. We shall sleep cold here, under the night-wind, which whistles through the breaches which heresy has made. They shall lie warmer who made them—ay, and through a long hereafter."

Notwithstanding the wild and singular expression of this female, she appeared to retain towards Roland Græme, in a strong degree, that affectionate and sedulous love which women bear to their nurslings, and the children dependent on their care. It seemed as if she would not permit him to do aught for himself which in former days her attention had been used to do for him, and that she considered the tall stripling before her as being equally dependent on her careful attention as when he was the orphan child, who had owed all to her affectionate solicitude.

"What hast thou to eat now?" she said, as, leaving the chapel, they went into the deserted habitation of the priest; "or what means of kindling a fire, to defend thee from this raw and inclement air? Poor child! thou hast made slight provision for a long journey; nor hast thou skill to help thyself by wit, when means are scanty. But Our Lady has placed by thy side one to whom want, in all its forms, is as familiar as plenty and splendour have formerly been. And with want, Roland, come the arts of which she is the inventor."

With an active and officious diligence, which strangely contrasted with her late abstracted and high tone of Catholic devotion, she set about her domestic arrangements for the evening. A pouch, which was hidden under her garment, produced a flint and steel, and from the scattered fragments around (those pertaining to the image of Saint Cuthbert scrupulously excepted) she obtained splinters sufficient to raise a sparkling and cheerful fire on the hearth of the deserted cell.

"And now," she said, "for needful food."

"Think not of it, mother," said Roland, "unless you yourself feel hunger. It is a little thing for me to endure a night's abstinence, and a small atonement for the necessary transgression of the rules of the Church upon which I was compelled during my stay in the castle."

"Hunger for myself!" answered the matron—"Know, youth, that a mother knows not hunger till that of her child is satisfied." And with affectionate inconsistency, totally different from her usual manner, she added, "Roland, you must not fast; you have dispensation; you are young, and to youth food and sleep are necessaries not to be dispensed with. Husband your strength, my child,—your sovereign, your religion, your country, require it. Let age macerate by fast and vigil a body which can only suffer; let youth, in these active times, nourish the limbs and the strength which action requires."

While she thus spoke, the scrip, which had produced the means of striking fire, furnished provision for a meal; of which she herself scarce partook, but anxiously watched her charge, taking a pleasure, resembling that of an epicure, in each morsel which he swallowed with a youthful appetite which abstinence had rendered unusually sharp. Roland readily obeyed her recommendations, and ate the food which she so affectionately and earnestly placed before him. But she shook her head when invited by him in return to partake of the refreshment her own cares had furnished; and when his solicitude became more pressing, she refused him in a loftier tone of rejection.

"Young man," she said, "you know not to whom or of what you speak. They to whom Heaven declares its purpose must merit its communication by mortifying the senses; they have that within which requires not the superfluity of earthly nutriment, which is necessary to those who are without the sphere of the Vision. To them the watch spent in prayer is a refreshing slumber, and the sense of doing the will of Heaven is a richer banquet than the tables of monarchs can spread before them!—But do thou sleep soft, my son," she said, relapsing from the tone of fanaticism into that of maternal affection and tenderness; "do thou sleep sound while life is but young with thee, and the cares of the day can be drowned in the slumbers of the evening. Different is thy duty and mine, and as different the means by which we must qualify and strengthen ourselves to perform it. From thee is demanded strength of body—from me, strength of soul."

When she thus spoke, she prepared with ready address a pallet-couch, composed partly of the dried leaves which had once furnished a bed to the solitary, and the guests who occasionally received his hospitality, and which, neglected by the destroyers of his humble cell, had remained little disturbed in the corner allotted for them. To these her care added some of the vestures which lay torn and scattered on the floor. With a zealous hand she selected all such as appeared to have made any part of the sacerdotal vestments, laying them aside as sacred from ordinary purposes, and with the rest she made, with dexterous promptness, such a bed as a weary man might willingly stretch himself on; and during the time she was preparing it, rejected, even with acrimony, any attempt which the youth made to assist her, or any entreaty which he urged, that she would accept of the place of rest for her own use. "Sleep thou," said she, "Roland Græme, sleep thou — the persecuted, the disinherited orphan — the son of an ill-fated mother—sleep thou! I go to pray in the chapel beside thee."

The manner was too enthusiastically earnest, too obstinately firm, to permit Roland Græme to dispute her will any farther. Yet he felt some shame in giving way to it. It seemed as if she had forgotten the years that had passed away since their parting; and expected to meet, in the tall, indulged, and wilful youth, whom she had recovered, the passive obedience of the child whom she had left in the Castle of Avenel. This did not fail to hurt her grandson's characteristic and constitutional pride. He obeyed, indeed, awed into submission by the sudden recurrence of former subordination, and by feelings of affection and gratitude. Still, however, he felt the yoke.

"Have I relinquished the hawk and the hound," he said, "to become the pupil of her pleasure, as if I were still a child?—I, whom even my envious mates allowed to be superior in those exercises which they took most pains to acquire, and which came to me naturally, as if a knowledge of them had been my birthright? This may not, and must not be. I will be no reclaimed sparrow-hawk, who is carried hooded on a woman's wrist, and has his quarry only shown to him when his eyes are uncovered for his flight. I will know her purpose ere it is proposed to me to aid it."

These, and other thoughts, streamed through the mind of Roland Græme; and although wearied with the fatigues of the day, it was long ere he could compose himself to rest.

Chapter the Ninth.

Kneel with me—swear it—'tis not in words I trust,
Save when they're fenced with an appeal to Heaven.
OLD PLAY

AFTER passing the night in that sound sleep for which agitation and fatigue had prepared him, Roland was awakened by the fresh morning air, and by the beams of the rising sun. His first feeling was that of surprise; for, instead of looking forth from a turret window on the Lake of Avenel, which was the prospect his former apartment afforded, an unlatticed aperture gave him the view of the demolished garden of the banished anchorite. He sat up on his couch of leaves, and arranged in his memory, not without wonder, the singular events of the preceding day, which appeared the more surprising the more he considered them. He had lost the protectress of his youth, and, in the same day, he had recovered the guide and guardian of his childhood. The former deprivation he felt ought to be matter of unceasing regret, and it seemed as if the latter could hardly be the subject of unmixed self-congratulation. He remembered this person, who had stood to him in the relation of a mother, as equally affectionate in her attention, and absolute in her authority. A singular mixture of love and fear attended upon his early remembrances as they were connected with her; and the fear that she might desire to resume the same absolute control over his motions—a fear which her conduct of yesterday did not tend much to dissipate—weighed heavily against the joy of this second meeting.

"She cannot mean," said his rising pride, "to lead and direct me as a pupil, when I am at the age of judging of my own actions?—this she cannot mean, or meaning it, will feel herself strangely deceived."

A sense of gratitude towards the person against whom his heart thus rebelled, checked his course of feeling. He resisted the thoughts which involuntarily arose in his mind, as he would have resisted an actual instigation of the foul fiend; and, to aid him in his struggle, he felt for his beads. But, in his hasty departure from the Castle of Avenel, he had forgotten and left them behind him.

"This is yet worse," he said; "but two things I learned of her under the most deadly charge of secrecy—to tell my beads, and to conceal that I did so; and I have kept my word till now; and when she shall ask me for the rosary, I must say I have forgotten it! Do I deserve she should believe me when I say I have kept the secret of my faith, when I set so light by its symbol?"

He paced the floor in anxious agitation. In fact, his attachment to his faith was of a nature very different from that which animated the enthusiastic matron, but which, notwithstanding, it would have been his last thought to relinquish.

The early charges impressed on him by his grandmother, had been instilled into a mind and memory of a character peculiarly tenacious. Child as he was, he was proud of the confidence reposed in his discretion, and resolved to show that it had not been rashly intrusted to him. At the same time, his resolution was no more than that of a child, and must, necessarily, have gradually faded away under the operation both of precept and example, during his residence at the Castle of Avenel, but for the exhortations of Father Ambrose, who, in his lay estate, had been called Edward Glendinning. This zealous monk had been apprized, by an unsigned letter placed in his hand by a pilgrim, that a child educated in the Catholic faith was now in the Castle of Avenel, perilously situated, (so was the scroll expressed,) as ever the three children who were cast into the fiery furnace of persecution. The letter threw upon Father Ambrose the fault, should this solitary lamb, unwillingly left within the demesnes of the prowling wolf, become his final prey. There needed no farther exhortation to the monk than the idea that a soul might be endangered, and that a Catholic might become an apostate; and he made his visits more frequent than usual to the castle of Avenel, lest, through want of the private encouragement and instruction which he always found some opportunity of dispensing, the church should lose a proselyte, and, according to the Romish creed, the devil acquire a soul.

Still these interviews were rare; and though they encouraged the solitary boy to keep his secret and hold fast his religion, they were neither frequent nor long enough to inspire him with any thing beyond a blind attachment to the observances which the priest recommended. He adhered to the forms of his religion rather because he felt it would be dishonourable to change that of his fathers, than from any rational conviction or sincere belief of its mysterious doctrines. It was a principal part of the distinction which, in his own opinion, singled him out from those with whom he lived, and gave him an additional, though an internal and concealed reason, for contemning those of the household who showed an undisguised dislike of him, and for hardening himself against the instructions of the chaplain, Henry Warden.

"The fanatic preacher," he thought within himself, during some one of the chaplain's frequent discourses against the Church of Rome, "he little knows whose ears are receiving his profane doctrine, and with what contempt and abhorrence they hear his blasphemies against the holy religion by which kings have been crowned, and for which martyrs have died!"

But in such proud feelings of defiance of heresy, as it was termed, and of its professors, which associated the Catholic religion with a sense of generous independence, and that of the Protestants with the subjugation of his mind and temper to the direction of Mr. Warden, began and ended the faith of Roland Græme, who, independently of the pride of singularity, sought not to understand, and had no one to expound to him, the peculiarities of the tenets which he professed. His regret, therefore, at missing the rosary which had been conveyed to him through the hands of Father Ambrose, was rather the shame of a soldier who has dropped his cockade, or badge of service, than that of a zealous votary who had forgotten a visible symbol of his religion.

His thoughts on the subject, however, were mortifying, and the more so from apprehension that his negligence must reach the ears of his relative. He felt it could be no one but her who had secretly transmitted these beads to Father Ambrose for his use, and that his carelessness was but an indifferent requital of her kindness.

"Nor will she omit to ask me about them," said he to himself; "for hers is a zeal which age cannot quell; and if she has not quitted her wont, my answer will not fail to incense her."

While he thus communed with himself, Magdalen Græme entered the apartment. "The blessing of the morning on your youthful head, my son," she said, with a solemnity of expression which thrilled the youth to the heart, so sad and earnest did the benediction flow from her lips, in a tone where devotion was blended with affection. "And thou hast started thus early from thy couch to catch the first breath of the dawn? But it is not well, my Roland. Enjoy slumber while thou canst; the time is not far behind when the waking eye must be thy portion, as well as mine."

She uttered these words with an affectionate and anxious tone, which showed, that devotional as were the habitual exercises of her mind, the thoughts of her nursling yet bound her to earth with the cords of human affection and passion.

But she abode not long in a mood which she probably regarded as a momentary dereliction of her imaginary high calling—"Come," she said, "youth, up and be doing—It is time that we leave this place."

"And whither do we go?" said the young man; "or what is the object of our journey?"

The matron stepped back, and gazed on him with surprise, not unmingled with displeasure.

"To what purpose such a question?" she said; "is it not enough that I lead the way? Hast thou lived with heretics till thou hast learned to instal the vanity of thine own private judgment in place of due honour and obedience?"

"The time," thought Roland Græme within himself, "is already come, when I must establish my freedom, or be a willing thrall for ever—I feel that I must speedily look to it."

She instantly fulfilled his foreboding, by recurring to the theme by which her thoughts seemed most constantly engrossed, although, when she pleased, no one could so perfectly disguise her religion.

"Thy beads, my son—hast thou told thy beads?"

Roland Græme coloured high; he felt the storm was approaching, but scorned to avert it by a falsehood.

"I have forgotten my rosary," he said, "at the Castle of Avenel."

"Forgotten thy rosary!" she exclaimed; "false both to religion and to natural duty, hast thou lost what was sent so far, and at such risk, a token of the truest affection, that should have been, every bead of it, as dear to thee as thine eyeballs?"

"I am grieved it should have so chanced, mother," replied the youth, "and much did I value the token, as coming from you. For what remains, I trust to win gold enough, when I push my way in the world; and till then, beads of black oak, or a rosary of nuts, must serve the turn."

"Hear him!" said his grandmother; "young as he is, he hath learned already the lessons of the devil's school! The rosary, consecrated by the Holy Father himself, and sanctified by his blessing, is but a few knobs of gold, whose value may be replaced by the wages of his profane labour, and whose virtue may be supplied by a string of hazel-nuts!—This is heresy—So Henry Warden, the wolf who ravages the flock of the Shepherd, hath taught thee to speak and to think."

"Mother," said Roland Græme, "I am no heretic; I believe and I pray according to the rules of our church—This misfortune I regret, but I cannot amend it."

"Thou canst repent it, though," replied his spiritual directress, "repent it in dust and ashes, atone for it by fasting, prayer, and penance, instead of looking on me with a countenance as light as if thou hadst lost but a button from thy cap."

"Mother," said Roland, "be appeased; I will remember my fault in the next confession which I have space and opportunity to make, and will do whatever the priest may require of me in atonement. For the heaviest fault I can do no more.—But, mother," he added, after a moment's pause, "let me not incur your farther displeasure, if I ask whither our journey is bound, and what is its object. I am no longer a child, but a man, and at my own disposal, with down upon my chin, and a sword by my side—I will go to the end of the world with you to do your pleasure; but I owe it to myself to inquire the purpose and direction of our travels."

"You owe it to yourself, ungrateful boy?" replied his relative, passion rapidly supplying the colour which age had long chased from her features,—"to yourself you owe nothing—you can owe nothing—to me you owe every thing—your life when an infant—your support while a child—the means of instruction, and the hopes of honour—and, sooner than thou shouldst abandon the noble cause to which I have devoted thee, would I see thee lie a corpse at my feet!"

Roland was alarmed at the vehement agitation with which she spoke, and which threatened to overpower her aged frame; and he hastened to reply,—"I forget nothing of what I owe to you, my dearest mother—show me how my blood can testify my gratitude, and you shall judge if I spare it. But blindfold obedience has in it as little merit as reason."

"Saints and angels!" replied Magdalen, "and do I hear these words from the child of my hopes, the nursling by whose bed I have kneeled, and for whose weal I have wearied every saint in heaven with prayers? Roland, by obedience only canst thou show thy affection and thy gratitude. What avails it that you might perchance adopt the course I propose to thee, were it to be fully explained? Thou wouldst not then follow my command, but thine own judgment; thou wouldst not do the will of Heaven, communicated through thy best friend, to whom thou owest thine all; but thou wouldst observe the blinded dictates of thine own imperfect reason. Hear me, Roland! a lot calls thee—solicits thee—demands thee—the proudest to which man can be destined, and it uses the voice of thine earliest, thy best, thine only friend—Wilt thou resist it? Then go thy way—leave me here—my hopes on earth are gone and withered—I will kneel me down before yonder profaned altar, and when the raging heretics return, they shall dye it with the blood of a martyr."

"But, my dearest mother," said Roland Græme, whose early recollections of her violence were formidably renewed by these wild expressions of reckless passion, "I will not forsake you—I will abide with you—worlds shall not force me from your side—I will protect—I will defend you—I will live with you, and die for you!"

"One word, my son, were worth all these—say only, 'I will obey you.'"

"Doubt it not, mother," replied the youth, "I will, and that with all my heart; only——"

"Nay, I receive no qualifications of thy promise," said Magdalen Græme, catching at the word, "the obedience which I require is absolute; and a blessing on thee, thou darling memory of my beloved child, that thou hast power to make a promise so hard to human pride! Trust me well, that in the design in which thou dost embark, thou hast for thy partners the mighty and the valiant, the power of the church, and the pride of the noble. Succeed or fail, live or die, thy name shall be among those with whom success or failure is alike glorious, death or life alike desirable. Forward, then, forward! life is short, and our plan is laborious—Angels, saints, and the whole blessed host of heaven, have their eyes even now on this barren and blighted land of Scotland—What say I? on Scotland?—their eye is on *us*, Roland—on the frail woman, on the inexperienced youth, who, amidst the ruins which sacrilege hath made in the holy place, devote themselves to God's cause, and that of their lawful Sovereign. Amen, so be it! The blessed eyes of saints and martyrs, which see our resolve, shall witness the execution; or their ears, which hear our vow, shall hear our death-groan drawn in the sacred cause!"

While thus speaking, she held Roland Græme firmly with one hand, while she pointed upward with the other, to leave him, as it were, no means of protest against the obtestation to which he was thus made a party. When she had finished her appeal to Heaven, she left him no leisure for farther hesitation, or for asking any explanation of her purpose; but passing with the same ready transition as formerly, to the solicitous attentions of an anxious parent, overwhelmed him with questions concerning his residence in the Castle of Avenel, and the qualities and accomplishments he had acquired.

"It is well," she said, when she had exhausted her inquiries, "my gay goss-hawk* hath been well trained, and will soar high; but those who bred him will have cause to fear as well as to wonder at his flight.—Let us now," she said, "to our morning meal, and care not though it be a scanty one. A few hours' walk will bring us to more friendly quarters."

They broke their fast accordingly, on such fragments as remained of their yesterday's provision, and immediately set out on their farther journey. Magdalen Græme led the way, with a firm and active step much beyond her years, and Roland Græme followed, pensive and anxious, and far from satisfied with the state of dependence to which he seemed again to be reduced.

"Am I for ever," he said to himself, "to be devoured with the desire of independence and free agency, and yet to be for ever led on, by circumstances, to follow the will of others?"

* The comparison is taken from some beautiful verses in an old ballad, entitled Fause Foodrage, published in the "Minstrelsy of the Scottish Border." A deposed queen, to preserve her infant son from the traitors who have slain his father, exchanges him with the female offspring of a faithful friend, and goes on to direct the education of the children, and the private signals by which the parents are to hear news each of her own offspring.

"And you shall learn my gay goss-hawk
Right well to breast a steed;
And so will I your turtle dow,
As well to write and read.

And ye shall learn my gay goss-hawk
To wield both bow and brand;
And so will I your turtle dow,
To lay gowd with her hand.

At kirk or market when we meet,
We'll dare make no avow,
But, 'Dame, how does my gay goss-hawk?'
'Madame, how does my dow?'"

Chapter the Tenth.

She dwelt unnoticed and alone,
Beside the springs of Dove:
A maid whom there was none to praise,
And very few to love.

WORDSWORTH.

In the course of their journey the travellers spoke little to each other. Magdalen Græme chanted, from time to time, in a low voice, a part of some one of those beautiful old Latin hymns which belong to the Catholic service, muttered an Ave or a Credo, and so passed on, lost in devotional contemplation. The meditations of her grandson were more bent on mundane matters; and many a time, as a moor-fowl arose from the heath, and shot along the moor, uttering his bold crow of defiance, he thought of the jolly Adam Woodcock, and his trusty goss-hawk; or, as they passed a thicket where the low trees and bushes were intermingled with tall fern, furze, and broom, so as to form a thick and intricate cover, his dreams were of a roebuck and a brace of gaze-hounds. But frequently his mind returned to the benevolent and kind mistress whom he had left behind him, offended justly, and unreconciled by any effort of his.

"My step would be lighter," he thought, "and so would my heart, could I but have returned to see her for one instant, and to say, Lady, the orphan boy was wild, but not ungrateful!"

Travelling in these divers moods, about the hour of noon they reached a small straggling village, in which, as usual, were seen one or two of those predominating towers, or peel houses, which, for reasons of defence elsewhere detailed, were at that time to be found in every Border hamlet. A brook flowed beside the village, and watered the valley in which it stood. There was also a mansion at the end of the village, and a little way separated from it, much dilapidated, and in very bad order, but appearing to have been the abode of persons of some consideration. The situation was agreeable, being an angle formed by the stream, bearing three or four large sycamore trees, which were in full leaf, and served to relieve the dark appearance of the mansion, which was built of a deep red stone. The house itself was a large one, but was now obviously too big for the inmates; several windows were built up, especially those which opened from the lower story; others were blockaded in a less substantial manner. The court before the door, which had once been defended with a species of low outer-wall, now ruinous, was paved, but the stones were completely covered with long gray nettles, thistles, and other weeds, which, shooting up betwixt the flags, had displaced many of them from their level. Even matters demanding more peremptory attention had been left neglected, in a manner which argued sloth or poverty in the extreme. The stream, undermining a part of the bank near an angle of the ruinous wall, had brought it down, with a corner turret, the ruins of which lay in the bed of the river. The current, interrupted by the ruins which it had overthrown, and turned yet nearer to the site of the tower, had greatly enlarged the breach it had made, and was in the process of undermining the ground on which the house itself stood, unless it were speedily protected by sufficient bulwarks.

All this attracted Roland Græme's observation, as they approached the dwelling by a winding path, which gave them, at intervals, a view of it from different points.

"If we go to yonder house," he said to his mother, "I trust it is but for a short visit. It looks as if two rainy days from the north-west would send the whole into the brook."

"You see but with the eyes of the body," said the old woman; "God will defend his own, though it be forsaken and despised of men. Better to dwell on the sand, under his law, than fly to the rock of human trust."

As she thus spoke, they entered the court before the old mansion, and Roland could observe that the front of it had formerly been considerably ornamented with carved work, in the same dark-coloured freestone of which it was built. But all these ornaments had been broken down and destroyed, and only the shattered vestiges of niches and entablatures now strewed the place which they had once occupied. The larger entrance in front was walled up, but a little footpath, which, from its appearance, seemed to be rarely trodden, led to a small wicket, defended by a door well clenched with iron-headed nails, at which Magdalen Græme knocked three times, pausing betwixt each knock, until she heard an answering tap from within. At the last knock, the wicket was opened by a pale thin female, who said, "*Benedicti qui venient in nomine Domini.*" They entered, and the portress hastily shut behind them the wicket, and made fast the massive fastenings by which it was secured.

The female led the way through a narrow entrance, into a vestibule of some extent, paved with stone, and having benches of the same solid material ranged around. At the upper end was an oriel window, but some of the intervals formed by the stone shafts and mullions were blocked up, so that the apartment was very gloomy.

Here they stopped, and the mistress of the mansion, for such she was, embraced Magdalen Græme, and greeting her by the title of sister, kissed her with much solemnity, on either side of the face.

"The blessing of Our Lady be upon you, my sister," were her next words; and they left no doubt upon Roland's mind respecting the religion of their hostess, even if he could have suspected his venerable and zealous guide of resting elsewhere than in the habitation of an orthodox Catholic. They spoke together a few words in private, during which he had leisure to remark more particularly the appearance of his grandmother's friend.

Her age might be betwixt fifty and sixty; her looks had a mixture of melancholy and unhappiness that bordered on discontent, and obscured the remains of beauty which age had still left on her features. Her dress was of the plainest and most ordinary description, of a dark colour, and, like Magdalen Græme's, something approaching to a religious habit. Strict neatness and cleanliness of person, seemed to intimate, that if poor, she was not reduced to squalid or heart-broken distress, and that she was still sufficiently attached to life to retain a taste for its decencies, if not its elegancies. Her manner, as well as her features and appearance, argued an original condition and education far above the meanness of her present appearance. In short, the whole figure was such as to excite the idea, "That female must have had a history worth knowing." While Roland Græme was making this very reflection, the whispers of the two females ceased, and the mistress of the mansion, approaching him, looked on his face and person with much attention, and, as it seemed, some interest.

"This, then," she said, addressing his relative, "is the child of thine unhappy daughter, sister Magdalen; and him, the only shoot from your ancient tree, you are willing to devote to the Good Cause?"

"Yes, by the rood," answered Magdalen Græme, in her usual tone of resolved determination, "to the good cause I devote him, flesh and fell, sinew and limb, body and soul."

"Thou art a happy woman, sister Magdalen," answered her companion, "that, lifted so high above human affection and human feeling, thou canst bind such a victim to the horns of the altar. Had I been called to make such a sacrifice — to plunge a youth so young and fair into the plots and bloodthirsty dealings of the time, not the patriarch Abraham, when he led Isaac up the mountain, would have rendered more melancholy obedience."

She then continued to look at Roland with a mournful aspect of compassion, until the intentness of her gaze occasioned his colour to rise, and he was about to move out of its influence, when he was stopped by his grandmother with one hand, while with the other she divided the hair upon his forehead, which was now crimson with bashfulness, while she added, with a mixture of proud affection and firm resolution, — "Ay, look at him well, my sister, for on a fairer face thine eye never rested. I too, when I first saw him, after a long separation, felt as the worldly feel, and was half shaken in my purpose. But no wind can tear a leaf from the withered tree which has long been stripped of its foliage, and no mere human casualty can awaken the mortal feelings which have long slept in the calm of devotion."

While the old woman thus spoke, her manner gave the lie to her assertions, for the tears rose to her eyes while she added, "But the fairer and the more spotless the victim, is it not, my sister, the more worthy of acceptance?"

She seemed glad to escape from the sensations which agitated her, and instantly added, "He will escape, my sister — there will be a ram caught in the thicket, and the hand of our revolted brethren shall not be on the youthful Joseph. Heaven can defend its own rights, even by means of babes and sucklings, of women and beardless boys."

"Heaven hath left us," said the other female; "for our sins and our fathers' the succours of the blessed Saints have abandoned this accursed land. We may win the crown of Martyrdom, but not that of earthly triumph. One, too, whose prudence was at this deep crisis so indispensable, has been called to a better world. The Abbot Eustatius is no more."

"May his soul have mercy!" said Magdalen Græme, "and may Heaven, too, have mercy upon us, who linger behind in this bloody land! His loss is indeed a perilous blow to our enterprise; for who remains behind possessing his far-fetched experience, his self-devoted zeal, his consummate wisdom, and his undaunted courage! He hath fallen with the church's standard in his hand, but God will raise up another to lift the blessed banner. Whom have the Chapter elected in his room?"

"It is rumoured no one of the few remaining brethren dare accept the office. The heretics have sworn that they will permit no future election, and will heavily punish any attempt to create a new Abbot of Saint Mary's. *Conjuraverunt inter se principes, dicentes, Projiciamus laqueos ejus.*"

"*Quousque, Domine!*" — ejaculated Magdalen; "this, my sister, were indeed a perilous and fatal breach in our band; but I am firm in my belief, that another will arise in the place of him so untimely removed. Where is thy daughter Catharine?"

"In the parlour," answered the matron, "but"——She looked at Roland Græme, and muttered something in the ear of her friend.

"Fear it not," answered Magdalen Græme, "it is both lawful and necessary — fear nothing from him — I would he were as well grounded in the faith by which alone comes safety, as he is free from thought, deed, or speech of villany. Therein is the heretics' discipline to be commended, my sister, that they train up their youth in strong morality, and choke up every inlet to youthful folly."

"It is but a cleansing the outside of the cup," answered her friend, "a whitening of the sepulchre; but he shall see Catharine, since you, sister, judge it safe and meet. — Follow us, youth," she added, and led the way from the apartment with her friend. These were the only words which the matron had addressed to Roland Græme, who obeyed them in silence. As they paced through several winding passages and waste apartments with a very slow step, the young page had leisure to make some reflections on his situation, — reflections of a nature which his ardent temper considered as specially disagreeable. It seemed he had now got two mistresses, or tutoresses, instead of one, both elderly women, and both, it would seem, in league to direct his motions according to their own pleasure, and for the accomplishment of plans to which he was no party. This, he thought, was too much; arguing reasonably enough, that whatever right his grandmother and benefactress had to guide his motions, she was neither entitled to transfer her authority or divide it with another, who seemed to assume, without ceremony, the same tone of absolute command over him.

"But it shall not long continue thus," thought Roland; "I will not be all my life the slave of a woman's whistle, to go when she bids, and come when she calls. No, by Saint Andrew! the hand that can hold the lance is above the control of the distaff. I will leave them the slipp'd collar in their hands on the first opportunity, and let them execute their own devices by their own proper force. It may save them both from peril, for I guess what they meditate is not likely to prove either safe or easy—the Earl of Murray and his heresy are too well rooted to be grubbed up by two old women."

As he thus resolved, they entered a low room, in which a third female was seated. This apartment was the first he had observed in the mansion which was furnished with moveable seats, and with a wooden table, over which was laid a piece of tapestry. A carpet was spread on the floor, there was a grate in the chimney, and, in brief, the apartment had the air of being habitable and inhabited.

But Roland's eyes found better employment than to make observations on the accommodations of the chamber; for this second female inhabitant of the mansion seemed something very different from any thing he had yet seen there. At his first entry, she had greeted with a silent and low obeisance the two aged matrons, then glancing her eyes towards Roland, she adjusted a veil which hung back over her shoulders, so as to bring it over her face; an operation which she performed with much modesty, but without either affected haste or embarrassed timidity.

During this manœuvre Roland had time to observe, that the face was that of a girl apparently not much past sixteen, and that the eyes were at once soft and brilliant. To these very favourable observations was added the certainty that the fair object to whom they referred possessed an excellent shape, bordering perhaps on *enbonpoint*, and therefore rather that of a Hebe than of a Sylph, but beautifully formed, and shown to great advantage by the close jacket and petticoat which she wore after a foreign fashion, the last not quite long enough to conceal a very pretty foot, which rested on a bar of the table at which she sate; her round arms and taper fingers very busily employed in repairing the piece of tapestry which was spread on it, which exhibited several deplorable fissures, enough to demand the utmost skill of the most expert seamstress.

It is to be remarked, that it was by stolen glances that Roland Græme contrived to ascertain these interesting particulars; and he thought he could once or twice, notwithstanding the texture of the veil, detect the damsel in the act of taking similar cognizance of his own person. The matrons in the meanwhile continued their separate conversation, eyeing from time to time the young people, in a manner which left Roland in no doubt that they were the subject of their conversation. At length he distinctly heard Magdalen Græme say these words—"Nay, my sister, we must give them opportunity to speak together, and to become acquainted; they must be personally known to each other, or how shall they be able to execute what they are intrusted with?"

It seemed as if the matron, not fully satisfied with her friend's reasoning, continued to offer some objections; but they were borne down by her more dictatorial friend.

"It must be so," she said, "my dear sister; let us therefore go forth on the balcony, to finish our conversation.—And do you," she said, addressing Roland and the girl, "become acquainted with each other."

With this she stepped up to the young woman, and raising her veil, discovered features which, whatever might be their ordinary complexion, were now covered with a universal blush.

"*Licitum sit,*" said Magdalen, looking at the other matron.

"*Vix licitum,*" replied the other, with reluctant and hesitating acquiescence; and again adjusting the veil of the blushing girl, she dropped it so as to shade, though not to conceal her countenance, and whispered to her, in a tone loud enough for the page to hear, "Remember, Catharine, who thou art, and for what destined."

The matron then retreated with Magdalen Græme through one of the casements of the apartment, that opened on a large broad balcony, which, with its ponderous balustrade, had once run along the whole south front of the building which faced the brook, and formed a pleasant and commodious walk in the open air. It was now in some places deprived of the balustrade, in others broken and narrowed; but, ruinous as it was, could still be used as a pleasant promenade. Here then walked the two ancient dames, busied in their private conversation; yet not so much so, but that Roland could observe the matrons, as their thin forms darkened the casement in passing or repassing before it, dart a glance into the apartment, to see how matters were going on there.

Chapter the Eleventh.

Life hath its May, and is mirthful then:
The woods are vocal, and the flowers all odour;
Its very blast has mirth in't,—and the maidens,
The while they don their cloaks to screen their kirtles,
Laugh at the rain that wets them.

OLD PLAY.

CATHERINE was at the happy age of innocence and buoyancy of spirit, when, after the first moment of embarrassment was over, a situation of awkwardness, like that in which she was suddenly left to make acquaintance with a handsome youth, not even known to her by name, struck her, in spite of herself, in a ludicrous point of view. She bent her beautiful eyes upon the work with which she was busied, and with infinite gravity sate out the two first turns of the matrons upon the balcony; but then, glancing her deep blue eye a little towards Roland, and observing the embarrassment under which he laboured, now shifting on his chair, and now dangling his cap, the whole man evincing that he was perfectly at a loss how to open the conversation, she could keep her composure no longer, but after a vain struggle broke out into a sincere, though a very involuntary fit of laughing, so richly accompanied by the laughter of her merry eyes, which actually glanced through the tears which the effort filled them with, and by the waving of her rich tresses, that the goddess of smiles herself never looked more lovely than Catherine at that moment. A court page would not have left her long alone in her mirth; but Roland was country-bred, and, besides, having some jealousy as well as bashfulness, he took it into his head that he was himself the object of her inextinguishable laughter. His endeavours to sympathize with Catherine, therefore, could carry him no farther than a forced giggle, which had more of displeasure than of mirth in it, and which so much enhanced that of the girl, that it seemed to render it impossible for her ever to bring her laughter to an end, with whatever anxious pains she laboured to do so. For every one has felt, that when a paroxysm of laughter has seized him at a misbecoming time and place, the efforts which he made to suppress it, nay, the very sense of the impropriety of giving way to it, tend only to augment and prolong the irresistible impulse.

It was undoubtedly lucky for Catherine, as well as for Roland, that the latter did not share in the excessive mirth of the former. For, seated as she was, with her back to the casement, Catherine could easily escape the observation of the two matrons during the course of their promenade; whereas Græme was so placed, with his side to the window, that his mirth, had he shared that of his companion, would have been instantly visible, and could not have failed to give offence to the personages in question. He sate, however, with some impatience, until Catherine had exhausted either her power or her desire of laughing, and was returning with good grace to the exercise of her needle, and then he observed with some dryness, that "there seemed no great occasion to recommend to them to improve their acquaintance, as it seemed, that they were already tolerably familiar."

Catherine had an extreme desire to set off upon a fresh score, but she repressed it strongly, and fixing her eyes on her work, replied by asking his pardon, and promising to avoid future offence.

Roland had sense enough to feel, that an air of offended dignity was very much misplaced, and that it was with a very different bearing he ought to meet the deep blue eyes which had borne such a hearty burden in the laughing scene. He tried, therefore, to extricate himself as well as he could from his blunder, by assuming a tone of correspondent gaiety, and requesting to know of the nymph, "how it was her pleasure that they should proceed in improving the acquaintance which had commenced so merrily."

"That," she said, "you must yourself discover; perhaps I have gone a step too far in opening our interview."

"Suppose," said Roland Græme, "we should begin as in a tale-book, by asking each other's names and histories?"

"It is right well imagined," said Catherine, "and shows an argute judgment. Do you begin, and I will listen, and only put in a question or two at the dark parts of the story. Come, unfold then your name and history, my new acquaintance."

"I am called Roland Græme, and that tall woman is my grandmother."

"And your tutoress? — good. Who are your parents?"

"They are both dead," replied Roland.

"Ay, but who were they? you *had* parents, I presume?"

"I suppose so," said Roland, "but I have never been able to learn much of their history. My father was a Scottish knight, who died gallantly in his stirrups — my mother was a Græme of Hathergill, in the Debateable Land — most of her family were killed when the Debateable country was burned by Lord Maxwell and Herries of Caerlaverock."

"Is it long ago?" said the damsel.

"Before I was born," answered the page.

"That must be a great while since," said she, shaking her head gravely; "look you, I cannot weep for them."

"It needs not," said the youth, "they fell with honour."

"So much for your lineage, fair sir," replied his companion, "of whom I like the living specimen (a glance at the casement) far less than those that are dead. Your much honoured grandmother looks as if she could make one weep in sad earnest. And now, fair sir, for your own person — if you tell not the tale faster, it will be cut short in the middle; Mother Bridget pauses longer and longer every time she passes the window, and with her there is as little mirth as in the grave of your ancestors."

"My tale is soon told — I was introduced into the castle of Avenel to be page to the lady of the mansion."

"She is a strict Huguenot, is she not?" said the maiden.

"As strict as Calvin himself. But my grandmother can play the puritan when it suits her purpose, and she had some plan of her own, for quartering me in the Castle — it would have failed, however, after we had remained several weeks at the hamlet, but for an unexpected master of ceremonies ——"

"And who was that?" said the girl.

"A large black dog, Wolf by name, who brought me into the castle one day in his mouth, like a hurt wild-duck, and presented me to the lady."

"A most respectable introduction, truly," said Catherine; "and what might you learn at this same castle? I love dearly to know what my acquaintances can do at need."

"To fly a hawk, hollow to a hound, back a horse, and wield lance, bow, and brand."

"And to boast of all this when you have learned it," said Catherine, "which, in France at least, is the surest accomplishment of a page. But proceed, fair sir; how came your Huguenot lord and your no less Huguenot lady to receive and keep in the family so perilous a person as a Catholic page?"

"Because they knew not that part of my history, which from infancy I have been taught to keep secret—and because my grand-dame's former zealous attendance on their heretic chaplain, had laid all this suspicion to sleep, most fair Callipolis," said the page; and in so saying, he edged his chair towards the seat of the fair querist.

"Nay, but keep your distance, most gallant sir," answered the blue-eyed maiden, "for, unless I greatly mistake, these reverend ladies will soon interrupt our amicable conference, if the acquaintance they recommend shall seem to proceed beyond a certain point—so, fair sir, be pleased to abide by your station, and reply to my questions.— By what achievements did you prove the qualities of a page, which you had thus happily acquired?"

Roland, who began to enter into the tone and spirit of the damsel's conversation, replied to her with becoming spirit.

"In no feat, fair gentlewoman, was I found inexpert, wherein there was mischief implied. I shot swans, hunted cats, frightened serving-women, chased the deer, and robbed the orchard. I say nothing of tormenting the chaplain in various ways, for that was my duty as a good Catholic."

"Now, as I am a gentlewoman," said Catherine, "I think these heretics have done Catholic penance in entertaining so all-accomplished a serving-man! And what, fair sir, might have been the unhappy event which deprived them of an inmate altogether so estimable?"

"Truly, fair gentlewoman," answered the youth, "your real proverb says that the longest lane will have a turning, and mine was more — it was, in fine, a turning off."

"Good!" said the merry young maiden, "it is an apt play on the word —and what occasion was taken for so important a catastrophe?—Nay, start not for my learning, I do know the schools—in plain phrase, why were you sent from service?"

The page shrugged his shoulders while he replied, — "A short tale is soon told—and a short horse soon curried. I made the falconer's boy taste of my switch—the falconer threatened to make me brook his cudgel—he is a kindly clown as well as a stout, and I would rather have been cudgelled by him than any man in Christendom to choose — but I knew not his qualities at that time—so I threatened to make him brook the stab, and my Lady made me brook the 'Begone;' so adieu to the page's office and the fair Castle of Avenel — I had not travelled far before I met my venerable parent—And so tell your tale, fair gentlewoman, for mine is done."

"A happy grandmother," said the maiden, "who had the luck to find the stray page just when his mistress had slipped his leash, and a most lucky page that has jumped at once from a page to an old lady's gentleman-usher!"

All this is nothing of your history," answered Roland Græme, who began to be much interested in the congenial vivacity of this facetious young gentlewoman,—"tale for tale is fellow-traveller's justice."

"Wait till we are fellow-travellers, then," replied Catherine.

"Nay, you escape me not so," said the page; "if you deal not justly by me, I will call out to Dame Bridget, or whatever your dame be called, and proclaim you for a cheat."

"You shall not need," answered the maiden—"my history is the counterpart of your own; the same words might almost serve, change but dress and name. I am called Catherine Seyton, and I also am an orphan."

"Have your parents been long dead?"

"This is the only question," said she, throwing down her fine eyes with a sudden expression of sorrow, "that is the only question I cannot laugh at."

"And Dame Bridget is your grandmother?"

The sudden cloud passed away like that which crosses for an instant the summer sun, and she answered with her usual lively expression, "Worse by twenty degrees—Dame Bridget is my maiden aunt."

"Over gods forbode!" said Roland—"Alas! that you have such a tale to tell! and what horror comes next?"

"Your own history, exactly. I was taken upon trial for service——"

"And turned off for pinching the duenna, or affronting my lady's waiting-woman?"

"Nay, our history varies there," said the damsel—"Our mistress broke up house, or had her house broke up, which is the same thing, and I am a free woman of the forest."

"And I am as glad of it as if any one had lined my doublet with cloth of gold," said the youth.

"I thank you for your mirth," said she, "but the matter is not likely to concern you."

"Nay, but go on," said the page, "for you will be presently interrupted; the two good dames have been soaring yonder on the balcony, like two old hooded crows, and their croak grows hoarser as night comes on; they will wing to roost presently.—This mistress of yours, fair gentlewoman, who was she, in God's name?"

"Oh, she has a fair name in the world," replied Catherine Seyton. "Few ladies kept a fairer house, or held more gentlewomen in her household; my aunt Bridget was one of her housekeepers. We never saw our mistress's blessed face, to be sure, but we heard enough of her; were up early and down late, and were kept to long prayers and light food."

"Out upon the penurious old beldam!" said the page.

"For Heaven's sake, blaspheme not!" said the girl, with an expression of fear.—"God pardon us both! I meant no harm. I speak of our blessed Saint Catherine of Sienna!—may God forgive me that I spoke so lightly, and made you do a great sin and a great blasphemy. This was her nunnery, in which there were twelve nuns and an abbess. My aunt was the abbess, till the heretics turned all adrift."

"And where are your companions?" asked the youth.

"With the last year's snow," answered the maiden; "east, north, south, and west—some to France, some to Flanders, some, I fear, into the world and its pleasures. We have got permission to remain, or rather our remaining has been connived at, for my aunt has great relations among the Kerrs, and they have threatened a death-feud if any one touches us; and bow and spear are the best warrant in these times."

"Nay, then, you sit under a sure shadow," said the youth; "and I suppose you wept yourself blind when Saint Catherine broke up housekeeping before you had taken arles* in her service?"

* *Anglice*—Earnest-money.

"Hush! for Heaven's sake," said the damsel, crossing herself; "no more of that! but I have not quite cried my eyes out," said she, turning them upon him, and instantly again bending them upon her work. It was one of those glances which would require the threefold plate of brass around the heart, more than it is needed by the mariners, to whom Horace recommends it. Our youthful page had no defence whatever to offer.

"What say you, Catherine," he said, "if we two, thus strangely turned out of service at the same time, should give our two most venerable duennas the torch to hold, while we walk a merry measure with each other over the floor of this weary world?"

"A goodly proposal, truly," said Catherine, "and worthy the mad-cap brain of a discarded page!—And what shifts does your worship propose we should live by?—by singing ballads, cutting purses, or swaggering on the highway? for there, I think, you would find your most productive exchequer."

"Choose, you proud peat!" said the page, drawing off in huge disdain at the calm and unembarrassed ridicule with which his wild proposal was received. And as he spoke the words, the casement was again darkened by the forms of the matrons—it opened, and admitted Magdalen Græme and the Mother Abbess, so we must now style her, into the apartment.

Chapter the Twelfth.

Nay, hear me, brother—I am elder, wiser,
And holier than thou—And age, and wisdom,
And holiness, have peremptory claims,
And will be listen'd to.

OLD PLAY.

WHEN the matrons re-entered, and put an end to the conversation which we have detailed in the last chapter, Dame Magdalen Græme thus addressed her grandson and his pretty companion: "Have you spoke together, my children?—Have you become known to each other as fellow-travellers on the same dark and dubious road, whom chance hath brought together, and who study to learn the tempers and dispositions of those by whom their perils are to be shared?"

It was seldom the light-hearted Catharine could suppress a jest, so that she often spoke when she would have acted more wisely in holding her peace.

"Your grandson admires the journey which you propose so very greatly, that he was even now preparing for setting out upon it instantly."

"This is to be too forward, Roland," said the dame, addressing him, "as yesterday you were over slack—the just mean lies in obedience, which both waits for the signal to start, and obeys it when given.—But once again, my children, have you so perused each other's countenances, that when you meet, in whatever disguise the times may impose upon you, you may recognize each in the other the secret agent of the mighty work in which you are to be leagued?—Look at each other, know each line and lineament of each other's countenance. Learn to distinguish by the step, by the sound of the voice, by the motion of the hand, by the glance of the eye, the partner whom Heaven hath sent to aid in working its will.—Wilt thou know that maiden, whensoever, or wheresoever you shall again meet her, my Roland Græme?"

As readily as truly did Roland answer in the affirmative. "And thou, my daughter, wilt thou again remember the features of this youth?"

"Truly, mother," replied Catherine Seyton, "I have not seen so many men of late, that I should immediately forget your grandson, though I mark not much about him that is deserving of especial remembrance."

"Join hands, then, my children," said Magdalen Græme; but, in saying so, was interrupted by her companion, whose conventual prejudices had been gradually giving her more and more uneasiness, and who could remain acquiescent no longer.

"Nay, my good sister, you forget," said she to Magdalen, "Catharine is the betrothed bride of Heaven—these intimacies cannot be."

"It is in the cause of Heaven that I command them to embrace," said Magdalen, with the full force of her powerful voice; "the end, sister, sanctifies the means we must use."

"They call me Lady Abbess, or Mother at the least, who address me," said Dame Bridget, drawing herself up, as if offended at her friend's authoritative manner—"the Lady of Heathergill forgets that she speaks to the Abbess of Saint Catherine."

"When I was what you call me," said Magdalen, "you indeed were the Abbess of Saint Catherine, but both names are now gone, with all the rank that the world and that the church gave to them; and we are now, to the eye of human judgment, two poor, despised, oppressed women, dragging our dishonoured old age to a humble grave. But what are we in the eye of Heaven?—Ministers, sent forth to work his will,—in whose weakness the strength of the church shall be manifested—before whom shall be humbled the wisdom of Murray, and the dark strength of Morton,—And to such wouldst thou apply the narrow rules of thy cloistered seclusion?—or, hast thou forgotten the order which I showed thee from thy Superior, subjecting thee to me in these matters?"

"On thy head, then, be the scandal and the sin," said the Abbess, sullenly.

"On mine be they both," said Magdalen. "I say, embrace each other, my children."

But Catherine, aware, perhaps, how the dispute was likely to terminate, had escaped from the apartment, and so disappointed the grandson, at least as much as the old matron.

"She is gone," said the Abbess, "to provide some little refreshment. But it will have little savour to those who dwell in the world; for I, at least, cannot dispense with the rules to which I am vowed, because it is the will of wicked men to break down the sanctuary in which they wont to be observed."

"It is well, my sister," replied Magdalen, "to pay each even the smallest tithes of mint and cummin which the church demands, and I blame not thy scrupulous observance of the rules of thine order. But they were established by the church, and for the church's benefit; and reason it is that they should give way when the salvation of the church herself is at stake."

The Abbess made no reply.

One more acquainted with human nature than the inexperienced page, might have found amusement in comparing the different kinds of fanaticisms which these two females exhibited. The Abbess, timid, narrow-minded, and discontented, clung to ancient usages and pretensions which were ended by the Reformation; and was in adversity, as she had been in prosperity, scrupulous, weak-spirited, and bigoted. While the fiery and more lofty spirit of her companion suggested a wider field of effort, and would not be limited by ordinary rules in the extraordinary schemes which were suggested by her bold and irregular imagination. But Roland Græme, instead of tracing these peculiarities of character in the two old dames, only waited with great anxiety for the return of Catherine, expecting probably that the proposal of the fraternal embrace would be renewed, as his grand mother seemed disposed to carry matters with a high hand.

His expectations, or hopes, if we may call them so, were, however, disappointed; for, when Catherine re-entered on the summons of the Abbess, and placed on the table an earthen pitcher of water, and four wooden platters, with cups of the same materials, the Dame of Heathergill, satisfied with the arbitrary mode in which she had borne down the opposition of the Abbess, pursued her victory no farther—a moderation for which her grandson, in his heart, returned her but slender thanks.

In the meanwhile, Catherine continued to place upon the table the slender preparations for the meal of a recluse, which consisted almost entirely of colewort, boiled and served up in a wooden platter, having no better seasoning than a little salt, and no better accompaniment than some coarse barley-bread, in very moderate quantity. The water-pitcher, already mentioned, furnished the only beverage. After a Latin grace, delivered by the Abbess, the guests sat down to their spare entertainment. The simplicity of the fare appeared to produce no distaste in the females, who ate of it moderately, but with the usual appearance of appetite. But Roland Græme had been used to better cheer. Sir Halbert Glendinning, who affected even an unusual degree of nobleness in his housekeeping, maintained it in a style of genial hospitality, which rivalled that of the Northern Barons of England. He might think, perhaps, that by doing so, he acted yet more completely the part for which he was born — that of a great Baron and a leader. Two bullocks, and six sheep, weekly, were the allowance when the Baron was at home, and the number was not greatly diminished during his absence. A boll of malt was weekly brewed into ale, which was used by the household at discretion. Bread was baked in proportion for the consumption of his domestics and retainers; and in this scene of plenty had Roland Græme now lived for several years. It formed a bad introduction to lukewarm greens and spring-water; and probably his countenance indicated some sense of the difference, for the Abbess observed, "It would seem, my son, that the tables of the heretic Baron, whom you have so long followed, are more daintily furnished than those of the suffering daughters of the church; and yet, not upon the most solemn nights of festival, when the nuns were permitted to eat their portion at mine own table, did I consider the cates, which were then served up, as half so delicious as these vegetables and this water, on which I prefer to feed, rather than do aught which may derogate from the strictness of my vow. It shall never be said that the mistress of this house made it a house of feasting, when days of darkness and of affliction were hanging over the Holy Church, of which I am an unworthy member."

"Well hast thou said, my sister," replied Magdalen Græme; "but now it is not only time to suffer in the good cause, but to act in it. And since our pilgrim's meal is finished, let us go apart to prepare for our journey tomorrow, and to advise on the manner in which these children shall be employed, and what measures we can adopt to supply their thoughtlessness and lack of discretion."

Notwithstanding his indifferent cheer, the heart of Roland Græme bounded high at this proposal, which he doubted not would lead to another *tête-à-tête* betwixt him and the pretty novice. But he was mistaken. Catherine, it would seem, had no mind so far to indulge him; for, moved either by delicacy or caprice, or some of those indescribable shades betwixt the one and the other, with which women love to tease, and at the same time to captivate, the ruder sex, she reminded the Abbess that it was necessary she should retire an hour before vespers; and, receiving the ready and approving nod of her Superior, she arose to withdraw. But before leaving the apartment, she made obeisance to the matrons, bending herself till her hands touched her knees, and then made a lesser reverence to Roland, which consisted in a slight bend of the body and gentle depression of the head. This she performed very demurely; but the party on whom the salutation was conferred, thought he could discern in her manner an arch and mischievous exultation over his secret disappointment.—"The devil take the saucy girl," he thought in his heart, though the presence of the Abbess should have repressed all such profane imaginations,—"she is as hard-hearted as the laughing hyæna that the story-books tell of—she has a mind that I shall not forget her this night at least."

The matrons now retired also, giving the page to understand that he was on no account to stir from the convent, or to show himself at the windows, the Abbess assigning as a reason, the readiness with which the rude heretics caught at every occasion of scandalizing the religious orders.

"This is worse than the rigour of Mr. Henry Warden, himself," said the page, when he was left alone; "for, to do him justice, however strict in requiring the most rigid attention during the time of his homilies, he left us to the freedom of our own wills afterwards—ay, and would take a share in our pastimes, too, if he thought them entirely innocent. But these old women are utterly wrapt up in gloom, mystery and self-denial.—Well, then, if I must neither stir out of the gate nor look out at window, I will at least see what the inside of the house contains that may help to pass away one's time—peradventure I may light on that blue-eyed laugher in some corner or other.

Going, therefore, out of the chamber by the entrance opposite to that through which the two matrons had departed, (for it may be readily supposed that he had no desire to intrude on *their* privacy,) he wandered from one chamber to another, through the deserted edifice, seeking, with boyish eagerness, some source of interest and amusement. Here he passed through a long gallery, opening on either hand into the little cells of the nuns, all deserted, and deprived of the few trifling articles of furniture which the rules of the order admitted.

"The birds are flown," thought the page; "but whether they will find themselves worse off in the open air than in these damp narrow cages, I leave my Lady Abbess and my venerable relative to settle betwixt them. I think the wild young lark whom they have left behind them, would like best to sing under God's free sky."

A winding stair, strait and narrow, as if to remind the nuns of their duties of fast and maceration, led down to a lower suite of apartments, which occupied the ground story of the house. These rooms were even more ruinous than those which he had left; for, having encountered the first fury of the assailants by whom the nunnery had been wasted, the windows had been dashed in, the doors broken down, and even the partitions betwixt the apartments, in some places, destroyed. As he thus stalked from desolation to desolation, and began to think of returning from so uninteresting a research to the chamber which he had left, he was surprised to hear the low of a cow very close to him. The sound was so unexpected at the time and place, that Roland Græme started as if it had been the voice of a lion, and laid his hand on his dagger, while at the same moment the light and lovely form of Catherine Seyton presented itself at the door of the apartment from which the sound had issued.

"Good even to you, valiant champion!" said she: "since the days of Guy of Warwick, never was one more worthy to encounter a dun cow."

"Cow?" said Roland Græme, "by my faith, I thought it had been the devil that roared so near me. Who ever heard of a convent containing a cow-house?"

"Cow and calf may come hither now," answered Catherine, "for we have no means to keep out either. But I advise you, kind sir, to return to the place from whence you came."

"Not till I see your charge, fair sister," answered Roland, and made his way into the apartment, in spite of the half serious half laughing remonstrances of the girl.

The poor solitary cow, now the only severe recluse within the nunnery, was quartered in a spacious chamber, which had once been the refectory of the convent. The roof was graced with groined arches, and the wall with niches, from which the images had been pulled down. These remnants of architectural ornaments were strangely contrasted with the rude crib constructed for the cow in one corner of the apartment, and the stack of fodder which was piled beside it for her food.*

"By my faith," said the page, "Crombie is more lordly lodged than any one here!"

"You had best remain with her," said Catherine, "and supply by your filial attentions the offspring she has had the ill luck to lose."

"I will remain, at least, to help you to prepare her night's lair, pretty Catherine," said Roland, seizing upon a pitch-fork.

"By no means," said Catherine; "for, besides that you know not in the least how to do her that service, you will bring a chiding my way, and I get enough of that in the regular course of things."

"What! for accepting my assistance?" said the page,—"for accepting *my* assistance, who am to be your confederate in some deep matter of import? That were altogether unreasonable—and, now I think on it, tell me if you can, what is this mighty emprise to which I am destined?"

"Robbing a bird's nest, I should suppose," said Catherine, "considering the champion whom they have selected."

"By my faith," said the youth, "and he that has taken a falcon's nest in the Scaurs of Polmoodie, has done something to brag of, my fair sister.—But that is all over now—a murrain on the nest, and the eyases and their food, washed or unwashed, for it was all anon of cramming these worthless kites that I was sent upon my present travels. Save that I have met with you, pretty sister, I could eat my dagger-hilt for vexation at my own folly. But, as we are to be fellow-travellers——"

"Fellow-labourers! not fellow-travellers!" answered the girl; "for to your comfort be it known, that the Lady Abbess and I set out earlier than you and your respected relative to-morrow, and that I partly endure your company at present, because it may be long ere we meet again."

"By Saint Andrew, but it shall not though," answered Roland; "I will not hunt at all unless we are to hunt in couples."

"I suspect, in that and in other points, we must do as we are bid," replied the young lady.—"But, hark! I hear my aunt's voice."

The old lady entered in good earnest, and darted a severe glance at her niece, while Roland had the ready wit to busy himself about the halter of the cow.

"The young gentleman," said Catherine, gravely, "is helping me to tie the cow up faster to her stake, for I find that last night when she put her head out of window and lowed, she alarmed the whole village; and we shall be suspected of sorcery among the heretics, if they do not discover the cause of the apparition, or lose our cow if they do."

"Relieve yourself of that fear," said the Abbess, somewhat ironically; "the person to whom she is now sold, comes for the animal presently."

---

* This, like the cell of Saint Cuthbert, is an imaginary scene, but I took one or two ideas of the desolation of the interior from a story told me by my father. In his youth—it may be near eighty years since, as he was born in 1729—he had occasion to visit an old lady who resided in a Border castle of considerable renown. Only one very limited portion of the extensive ruins sufficed for the accommodation of the inmates, and my father amused himself by wandering through the part that was untenanted. In a dining apartment, having a roof richly adorned with arches and drops, there was deposited a large stack of hay, to which calves were helping themselves from opposite sides. As my father was scaling a dark ruinous turnpike staircase, his greyhound ran up before him, and probably was the means of saving his life, for the animal fell through a trap door, or aperture in the stair, thus warning the owner of the danger of the ascent. As the dog continued howling from a great depth, my father got the old butler, who alone knew most of the localities about the castle, to unlock a sort of stable, in which Kill-buck was found safe and sound, the place being filled with the same commodity which littered the stalls of Augeas, and which had rendered the dog's fall an easy one.

"Good night, then, my poor companion," said Catherine, patting the animal's shoulders; "I hope thou hast fallen into kind hands, for my happiest hours of late have been spent in tending thee — I would I had been born to no better task!"

"Now, out upon thee, mean-spirited wench!" said the Abbess; "is that a speech worthy of the name of Seyton, or of the mouth of a sister of this house, treading the path of election — and to be spoken before a stranger youth, too?—Go to my oratory, minion—there read your Hours till I come thither, when I will read you such a lecture as shall make you prize the blessings which you possess."

Catherine was about to withdraw in silence, casting a half sorrowful half comic glance at Roland Græme, which seemed to say — "You see to what your untimely visit has exposed me," when, suddenly changing her mind, she came forward to the page, and extended her hand as she bid him good evening. Their palms had pressed each other ere the astonished matron could interfere, and Catherine had time to say — "Forgive me, mother; it is long since we have seen a face that looked with kindness on us. Since these disorders have broken up our peaceful retreat, all has been gloom and malignity. I bid this youth kindly farewell, because he has come hither in kindness, and because the odds are great, that we may never again meet in this world. I guess better than he, that the schemes on which you are rushing are too mighty for your management, and that you are now setting the stone a-rolling, which must surely crush you in its descent. I bid farewell," she added, "to my fellow-victim!"

This was spoken with a tone of deep and serious feeling, altogether different from the usual levity of Catherine's manner, and plainly showed, that beneath the giddiness of extreme youth and total inexperience, there lurked in her bosom a deeper power of sense and feeling, than her conduct had hitherto expressed.

The Abbess remained a moment silent after she had left the room. The proposed rebuke died on her tongue, and she appeared struck with the deep and foreboding tone in which her niece had spoken her good-even. She led the way in silence to the apartment which they had formerly occupied, and where there was prepared a small refection, as the Abbess termed it, consisting of milk and barley-bread. Magdalen Græme, summoned to take share in this collation, appeared from an adjoining apartment, but Catherine was seen no more. There was little said during the hasty meal, and after was finished, Roland Græme was dismissed to the nearest cell, where some preparations had been made for his repose.

The strange circumstances in which he found himself, had their usual effect in preventing slumber from hastily descending on him, and he could distinctly hear, by a low but earnest murmuring in the apartment which he had left, that the matrons continued in deep consultation to a late hour. As they separated he heard the Abbess distinctly express herself thus: "In a word, my sister, I venerate your character and the authority with which my Superiors have invested you; yet it seems to me, that, ere entering on this perilous course, we should consult some of the Fathers of the Church."

"And how and where are we to find a faithful Bishop or Abbot at whom to ask counsel? The faithful Eustatius is no more — he is withdrawn from a world of evil, and from the tyranny of heretics. May Heaven and our Lady assoilzie him of his sins, and abridge the penance of his mortal infirmities! — Where shall we find another, with whom to take counsel?"

"Heaven will provide for the Church," said the Abbess; "and the faithful fathers who yet are suffered to remain in the house of Kennaquhair, will proceed to elect an Abbot. They will not suffer the staff to fall down, or the mitre to be unfilled, for the threats of heresy."

"That will I learn to-morrow," said Magdalen Græme; "yet who now takes the office of an hour, save to partake with the spoilers in their work of plunder? — to-morrow will tell us if one of the thousand saints who are sprung from the House of Saint Mary's continues to look down on it in its misery. — Farewell, my sister — we meet at Edinburgh."

"Benedicite!" answered the Abbess, and they parted.

"To Kennaquhair and to Edinburgh we bend our way," thought Roland Græme. "That information have I purchased by a sleepless hour—it suits well with my purpose. At Kennaquhair I shall see Father Ambrose; — at Edinburgh I shall find the means of shaping my own course through this bustling world, without burdening my affectionate relation—at Edinburgh, too, I shall see again the witching novice, with her blue eyes and her provoking smile." — He fell asleep, and it was to dream of Catherine Seyton.

Chapter the Thirteenth.

> What, Dagon up again!—I thought we had hurl'd him
> Down on the threshold, never more to rise.
> Bring wedge and axe; and, neighbours, lend your hands
> And rive the idol into winter fagots!
>
> ATHELSTANE, OR THE CONVERTED DANE.

ROLAND GRÆME slept long and sound, and the sun was high over the horizon, when the voice of his companion summoned him to resume their pilgrimage; and when, hastily arranging his dress, he went to attend her call, the enthusiastic matron stood already at the threshold, prepared for her journey. There was in all the deportment of this remarkable woman, a promptitude of execution, and a sternness of perseverance, founded on the fanaticism which she nursed so deeply, and which seemed to absorb all the ordinary purposes and feelings of mortality. One only human affection gleamed through her enthusiastic energies, like the broken glimpses of the sun through the rising clouds of a storm. It was her maternal fondness for her grandson—a fondness carried almost to the verge of dotage, in circumstances where the Catholic religion was not concerned, but which gave way instantly when it chanced either to thwart or come in contact with the more settled purpose of her soul, and the more devoted duty of her life. Her life she would willingly have laid down to save the earthly object of her affection; but that object itself she was ready to hazard, and would have been willing to sacrifice, could the restoration of the Church of Rome have been purchased with his blood. Her discourse by the way, excepting on the few occasions in which her extreme love of her grandson found opportunity to display itself in anxiety for his health and accommodation, turned entirely on the duty of raising up the fallen honours of the Church, and replacing a Catholic sovereign on the throne. There were times at which she hinted, though very obscurely and distantly, that she herself was foredoomed by Heaven to perform a part in this important task; and that she had more than mere human warranty for the zeal with which she engaged in it. But on this subject she expressed herself in such general language, that it was not easy to decide whether she made any actual pretensions to a direct and supernatural call, like the celebrated Elizabeth Barton, commonly called the Nun of Kent;* or whether she dwelt upon the general duty which was

* A fanatic nun, called the Holy Maid of Kent, who pretended to the gift of prophecy and power of miracles. Having denounced the doom of speedy death against Henry VIII. for his marriage with Anne Boleyn, the prophetess was attainted in Parliament, and executed with her accomplices. Her imposture was for a time so successful, that even Sir Thomas More was disposed to be a believer.

incumbent on all Catholics of the time, and the pressure of which she felt in an extraordinary degree.

Yet though Magdalen Græme gave no direct intimation of her pretensions to be considered as something beyond the ordinary class of mortals, the demeanour of one or two persons amongst the travellers whom they occasionally met, as they entered the more fertile and populous part of the valley, seemed to indicate their belief in her superior attributes. It is true, that two clowns, who drove before them a herd of cattle—one or two village wenches, who seemed bound for some merry-making—a strolling soldier, in a rusted morion, and a wandering student, as his threadbare black cloak and his satchel of books proclaimed him — passed our travellers without observation, or with a look of contempt; and, moreover, that two or three children, attracted by the appearance of a dress so nearly resembling that of a pilgrim, joined in hooting and calling "Out upon the mass-monger!" But one or two, who nourished in their bosoms respect for the downfallen hierarchy — casting first a timorous glance around, to see that no one observed them—hastily crossed themselves—bent their knee to Sister Magdalen, by which name they saluted her — kissed her hand, or even the hem of her dalmatique — received with humility the Benedicite with which she repaid their obeisance; and then starting up, and again looking timidly round to see that they had been unobserved, hastily resumed their journey. Even while within sight of persons of the prevailing faith, there were individuals bold enough, by folding their arms and bending their head, to give distant and silent intimation that they recognized Sister Magdalen, and honoured alike her person and her purpose.

She failed not to notice to her grandson these marks of honour and respect which from time to time she received. "You see," she said, "my son, that the enemies have been unable altogether to suppress the good spirit, or to root out the true seed. Amid heretics and schismatics, spoilers of the church's lands, and scoffers at saints and sacraments, there is left a remnant."

"It is true, my mother," said Roland Græme; "but methinks they are of a quality which can help us but little. See you not all those who wear steel at their side, and bear marks of better quality, ruffle past us as they would past the meanest beggars? for those who give us any marks of sympathy, are the poorest of the poor, and most outcast of the needy, who have neither bread to share with us, nor swords to defend us, nor skill to use them if they had. That poor wretch that last kneeled to you with such deep devotion, and who seemed emaciated by the touch of some wasting disease within, and the grasp of poverty without — that pale, shivering, miserable caitiff, how can he aid the great schemes you meditate?"

"Much, my son," said the Matron, with more mildness than the page perhaps expected. "When that pious son of the church returns from the shrine of Saint Ringan, whither he now travels by my counsel, and by the aid of good Catholics, — when he returns, healed of his wasting malady, high in health, and strong in limb, will not the glory of his faithfulness, and its miraculous reward, speak louder in the ears of this besotted people of Scotland, than the din which is weekly made in a thousand heretical pulpits?"

"Ay, but, mother, I fear the Saint's hand is out. It is long since we have heard of a miracle performed at St. Ringan's."

The matron made a dead pause, and, with a voice tremulous with emotion, asked, "Art thou so unhappy as to doubt the power of the blessed Saint?"

"Nay, mother," the youth hastened to reply, "I believe as the Holy Church commands, and doubt not Saint Ringan's power of healing; but, be it said with reverence, he hath not of late showed the inclination."

"And has this land deserved it?" said the Catholic matron, advancing hastily while she spoke, until she attained the summit of a rising ground, over which the path led, and then standing again still. "Here," she said, "stood the Cross, the limits of the Halidome of Saint Mary's — here — on this eminence — from which the eye of the holy pilgrim might first catch a view of that ancient monastery, the light of the land, the abode of Saints, and the grave of monarchs — Where is now that emblem of our faith? It lies on the earth—a shapeless block, from which the broken fragments have been carried off, for the meanest uses, till now no semblance of its original form remains. Look towards the east, my son, where the sun was wont to glitter on stately spires — from which crosses and bells have now been hurled, as if the land had been invaded once more by barbarous heathens.— Look at yonder battlements, of which we can, even at this distance, descry the partial demolition; and ask if this land can expect from the blessed saints, whose shrines and whose images have been profaned, any other miracles but those of vengeance? How long," she exclaimed, looking upward, "How long shall it be delayed?" She paused, and then resumed with enthusiastic rapidity, "Yes, my son, all on earth is but for a period — joy and grief, triumph and desolation, succeed each other like cloud and sunshine; — the vineyard shall not be forever trodden down, the gaps shall be amended, and the fruitful branches once more dressed and trimmed. Even this day — ay, even this hour, I trust to hear news of importance. Dally not—let us on—time is brief, and judgment is certain."

She resumed the path which led to the Abbey — a path which, in ancient times, was carefully marked out by posts and rails, to assist the pilgrim in his journey — these were now torn up and destroyed. A half-hour's walk placed them in front of the once splendid Monastery, which, although the church was as yet entire, had not escaped the fury of the times. The long range of cells and of apartments for the use of the brethren, which occupied two sides of the great square, were almost entirely ruinous, the interior having been consumed by fire, which only the massive architecture of the outward walls had enabled them to resist. The Abbot's house, which formed the third side of the square, was, though injured, still inhabited, and afforded refuge to the few brethren, who yet, rather by connivance than by actual authority, were permitted to remain at Kennaquhair. Their stately offices — their pleasant gardens — the magnificent cloisters constructed for their recreation, were all dilapidated and ruinous; and some of the building materials had apparently been put into requisition by persons in the village and in the vicinity, who, formerly vassals of the Monastery, had not hesitated to appropriate to themselves a part of the spoils. Roland saw fragments of Gothic pillars richly carved, occupying the place of door-posts to the meanest huts; and here and there a mutilated statue, inverted or laid on its side, made the door-post, or threshold, of a wretched cow-house. The church itself was less injured than the other buildings of the Monastery. But the images which had been placed in the numerous niches of its columns and buttresses, having all fallen under the charge of idolatry, to which the superstitious devotion of the Papists had justly exposed them, had been broken and thrown down, without much regard to the preservation of the rich and airy canopies and pedestals on which they were placed; nor, if the devastation had stopped short at this point, could we have considered the preservation of these monuments of antiquity as an object to be put in the balance with the introduction of the reformed worship.

Our pilgrims saw the demolition of these sacred and venerable representations of saints and angels — for as sacred and venerable they had been taught to consider them — with very different feelings. The antiquary may be permitted to regret the necessity of the action, but to Magdalen Græme it seemed a deed of impiety, deserving the instant vengeance of heaven, — a sentiment in which her relative joined for the moment as cordially as herself. Neither, however, gave vent to their feelings in words, and uplifted hands and eyes formed their only mode of expressing them. The page was about to approach the great eastern gate of the church, but was prevented by his guide. "That gate," she said, "has long been blockaded, that the heretical rabble may not know there still exist among the brethren of Saint Mary's men who dare worship where their predecessors prayed while alive, and were interred when dead — follow me this way, my son."

Roland Græme followed accordingly; and Magdalen, casting a hasty glance to see whether they were observed, (for she had learned caution from the danger of the times,) commanded her grandson to knock at a little wicket which she pointed out to him. "But knock gently," she added, with a motion expressive of caution. After a little space, during which no answer was returned, she signed to Roland to repeat his summons for admission; and the door at length partially opening, discovered a glimpse of the thin and timid porter, by whom the duty was performed, skulking from the observation of those who stood without; but endeavouring at the same time to gain a sight of them without being himself seen. How different from the proud consciousness of dignity with which the porter of ancient days offered his important brow, and his goodly person, to the pilgrims who repaired to Kennaquhair! His solemn "*Intrate, mei filii,*" was exchanged for a tremulous "You cannot enter now — the brethren are in their chambers." But, when Magdalen Græme asked, in an under tone of voice, "Hast thou forgotten me, my brother?" he changed his apologetic refusal to "Enter, my honoured sister, enter speedily, for evil eyes are upon us."

They entered accordingly, and having waited until the porter had, with jealous haste, barred and bolted the wicket, were conducted by him through several dark and winding passages. As they walked slowly on, he spoke to the matron in a subdued voice, as if he feared to trust the very walls with the avowal which he communicated.

"Our Fathers are assembled in the Chapter-house, worthy sister — yes, in the Chapter-house — for the election of an Abbott.—Ah, Benedicite! there must be no ringing of bells — no high mass — no opening of the great gates now, that the people might see and venerate their spiritual Father! Our Fathers must hide themselves rather like robbers who choose a leader, than godly priests who elect a mitred Abbot."

"Regard not that, my brother," answered Magdalen Græme; "the first successors of Saint Peter himself were elected, not in sunshine, but in tempests — not in the halls of the Vatican, but in the subterranean vaults and dungeons of heathen Rome — they were not gratulated with shouts and salvos of cannon-shot and of musketry, and the display of artificial fire — no, my brother — but by the hoarse summons of Lictors and Prætors, who came to drag the Fathers of the Church to martyrdom. From such adversity was the Church once raised, and by such will it now be purified.—And mark me, brother! not in the proudest days of the mitred Abbey, was a Superior ever chosen, whom his office shall so much honour, as *he* shall be honoured, who now takes it upon him in these days of tribulation. On whom, my brother, will the choice fall?"

"On whom can it fall — or, alas! who would dare to reply to the call, save the worthy pupil of the Sainted Eustatius—the good and valiant Father Ambrose?"

"I know it," said Magdalen; "my heart told me long ere your lips had uttered his name. Stand forth, courageous champion, and man the fatal breach! — Rise, bold and experienced pilot, and seize the helm while the tempest rages! — Turn back the battle, brave raiser of the fallen standard! —Wield crook and slang, noble shepherd of a scattered flock!"

"I pray you, hush, my sister!" said the porter, opening a door which led into the great church, "the brethren will be presently here to celebrate their election with a solemn mass — I must marshal them the way to the high altar—all the offices of this venerable house have now devolved on one poor decrepit old man."

He left the church, and Magdalen and Roland remained alone in that great vaulted space, whose style of rich, yet chaste architecture, referred its origin to the early part of the fourteenth century, the best period of Gothic building. But the niches were stripped of their images in the inside as well as the outside of the church; and in the pell-mell havoc, the tombs of warriors and of princes had been included in the demolition of the idolatrous shrines. Lances and swords of antique size, which had hung over the tombs of mighty warriors of former days, lay now strewed among relics, with which the devotion of pilgrims had graced those of their peculiar saints; and the fragments of the knights and dames, which had once lain recumbent, or kneeled in an attitude of devotion, where their mortal relics were reposed, were mingled with those of the saints and angels of the Gothic chisel, which the hand of violence had sent headlong from their stations.

The most fatal symptom of the whole appeared to be, that, though this violence had now been committed for many months, the Fathers had lost so totally all heart and resolution, that they had not adventured even upon clearing away the rubbish, or restoring the church to some decent degree of order. This might have been done without much labour. But terror had overpowered the scanty remains of a body once so powerful, and, sensible they were only suffered to remain in this ancient seat by connivance and from compassion, they did not venture upon taking any step which might be construed into an assertion of their ancient rights, contenting themselves with the secret and obscure exercise of their religious ceremonial, in as unostentatious a manner as was possible.

Two or three of the more aged brethren had sunk under the pressure of the times, and the ruins had been partly cleared away to permit their interment. One stone had been laid over Father Nicholas, which recorded of him in special, that he had taken the vows during the incumbency of Abbot Ingelram, the period to which his memory so frequently recurred. Another flag-stone, yet more recently deposited, covered the body of Philip the Sacristan, eminent for his aquatic excursion with the phantom of Avenel, and a third, the most recent of all, bore the outline of a mitre, and the words *Hic jacet Eustatius Abbas;* for no one dared to add a word of commendation in favour of his learning, and strenuous zeal for the Roman Catholic faith.

Magdalen Græme looked at and perused the brief records of these monuments successively, and paused over that of Father Eustace. "In a good hour for thyself," she said, "but oh! in an evil hour for the Church, wert thou called from us. Let thy spirit be with us, holy man — encourage thy successor to tread in thy footsteps — give him thy bold and inventive capacity, thy zeal and thy discretion—even *thy* piety exceeds not his." As she spoke, a side door, which closed a passage from the Abbot's house into the church, was thrown open, that the Fathers might enter the choir, and conduct to the high altar the Superior whom they had elected.

In former times, this was one of the most splendid of the many pageants which the hierarchy of Rome had devised to attract the veneration of the faithful. The period during which the Abbacy remained vacant, was a state of mourning, or, as their emblematical phrase expressed it, of widowhood; a melancholy term, which was changed into rejoicing and triumph when a new Superior was chosen. When the folding doors were on such solemn occasions thrown open, and the new Abbot appeared on the threshold in full-blown dignity, with ring and mitre, and dalmatique and crosier, his hoary standard-bearers and his juvenile dispensers of incense preceding him, and the venerable train of monks behind him, with all besides which could announce the supreme authority to which he was now raised, his appearance was a signal for the magnificent *jubilate* to rise from the organ and music-loft, and to be joined by the corresponding bursts of Alleluiah from the whole assembled congregation. Now all was changed. In the midst of rubbish and desolation, seven or eight old men, bent and shaken as much by grief and fear as by age, shrouded hastily in the proscribed dress of their order, wandered like a procession of spectres, from the door which had been thrown open, up through the encumbered passage, to the high altar, there to instal their elected Superior a chief of ruins. It was like a band of bewildered travellers choosing a chief in the wilderness of Arabia; or a shipwrecked crew electing a captain upon the barren island on which fate has thrown them.

They who, in peaceful times, are most ambitious of authority among others, shrink from the competition at such eventful periods, when neither ease nor parade attend the possession of it, and when it gives only a painful pre-eminence both in danger and in labour, and exposes the ill-fated chieftain to the murmurs of his discontented associates, as well as to the first assault of the common enemy. But he on whom the office of the Abbot of Saint Mary's was now conferred, had a mind fitted for the situation to which he was called. Bold and enthusiastic, yet generous and forgiving—wise and skilful, yet zealous and prompt—he wanted but a better cause than the support of a decaying superstition, to have raised him to the rank of a truly great man. But as the end crowns the work, it also forms the rule by which it must be ultimately judged; and those who, with sincerity and generosity, fight and fall in an evil cause, posterity can only compassionate as victims of a generous but fatal error. Amongst these, we must rank Ambrosius, the last Abbot of Kennaquhair, whose designs must be condemned, as their success would have riveted on Scotland the chains of antiquated superstition and spiritual tyranny; but whose talents commanded respect, and whose virtues, even from the enemies of his faith, extorted esteem.

The bearing of the new Abbot served of itself to dignify a ceremonial which was deprived of all other attributes of grandeur. Conscious of the peril in which they stood, and recalling, doubtless, the better days they had seen, there hung over his brethren an appearance of mingled terror, and grief, and shame, which induced them to hurry over the office in which they were engaged, as something at once degrading and dangerous.

But not so Father Ambrose. His features, indeed, expressed a deep melancholy, as he walked up the centre aisle, amid the ruin of things which he considered as holy, but his brow was undejected, and his step firm and solemn. He seemed to think that the dominion which he was about to receive, depended in no sort upon the external circumstances under which it was conferred; and if a mind so firm was accessible to sorrow or fear, it was not on his own account, but on that of the Church to which he had devoted himself.

At length he stood on the broken steps of the high altar, barefooted, as was the rule, and holding in his hand his pastoral staff, for the gemmed ring and jewelled mitre had become secular spoils. No obedient vassals came, man after man, to make their homage, and to offer the tribute which should provide their spiritual Superior with palfrey and trappings. No Bishop assisted at the solemnity, to receive into the higher ranks of the Church nobility a dignitary, whose voice in the legislature was as potential as his own. With hasty and maimed rites, the few remaining brethren stepped forward alternately to give their new Abbot the kiss of peace, in token of fraternal affection and spiritual homage. Mass was then hastily performed, but in such precipitation as if it had been hurried over rather to satisfy the scruples of a few youths, who were impatient to set out on a hunting party, than as if it made the most solemn part of a solemn ordination. The officiating priest faltered as he spoke the service, and often looked around, as if he expected to be interrupted in the midst of his office;

and the brethren listened to that which, short as it was, they wished yet more abridged.*

These symptoms of alarm increased as the ceremony proceeded, and, as it seemed, were not caused by mere apprehension alone; for, amid the pauses of the hymn, there were heard without sounds of a very different sort, beginning faintly and at a distance, but at length approaching close to the exterior of the church, and stunning with dissonant clamour those engaged in the service. The winding of horns, blown with no regard to harmony or concert; the jangling of bells, the thumping of drums, the squeaking of bagpipes, and the clash of cymbals — the shouts of a multitude, now as in laughter, now as in anger—the shrill tones of female voices, and of those of children, mingling with the deeper clamour of men, formed a Babel of sounds, which first drowned, and then awed into utter silence, the official hymns of the Convent. The cause and result of this extraordinary interruption will be explained in the next chapter.

Chapter the Fourteenth.

Not the wild billow, when it breaks its barrier—
Not the wild wind, escaping from its cavern—
Not the wild fiend, that mingles both together,
And pours their rage upon the ripening harvest,
Can match the wild freaks of this mirthful meeting—
Comic, yet fearful—droll, and yet destructive.
THE CONSPIRACY.

THE monks ceased their song, which, like that of the choristers in the legend of the Witch of Berkley, died away in a quaver of consternation; and, like a flock of chickens disturbed by the presence of the kite, they at first made a movement to disperse and fly in different directions, and then, with despair, rather than hope, huddled themselves around their new Abbot; who, retaining the lofty and undismayed look which had dignified him through the whole ceremony, stood on the higher step of the altar, as if desirous to be the most conspicuous mark on which danger might discharge itself, and to save his companions by his self-devotion, since he could afford them no other protection.

Involuntarily, as it were, Magdalen Græme and the page stepped from the station which hitherto they had occupied unnoticed, and approached to the altar, as desirous of sharing the fate which approached the monks, whatever that might be. Both bowed reverently low to the Abbot; and while Magdalen seemed about to speak, the youth, looking towards the main entrance, at which the noise now roared most loudly, and which was at the same time assailed with much knocking, laid his hand upon his dagger.

The Abbot motioned to both to forbear: "Peace, my sister," he said, in a low tone, but which, being in a different key from the tumultuary sounds without, could be distinctly heard, even amidst the tumult; — "Peace," he said, "my sister; let the new Superior of Saint Mary's himself receive and reply to the grateful acclamations of the vassals, who come to celebrate his installation.—And thou, my son, forbear, I charge thee, to touch thy earthly weapon;—if it is the pleasure of our protectress, that her shrine be this day

* In Catholic countries, in order to reconcile the pleasures of the great with the observances of religion, it was common, when a party was bent for the chase, to celebrate mass, abridged and maimed of its rites, called a hunting-mass, the brevity of which was designed to correspond with the impatience of the audience.

desecrated by deeds of violence, and polluted by blood-shedding, let it not, I charge thee, happen through the deed of a Catholic son of the church."

The noise and knocking at the outer gate became now every moment louder; and voices were heard impatiently demanding admittance. The Abbot, with dignity, and with a step which even the emergency of danger rendered neither faltering nor precipitate, moved towards the portal, and demanded to know, in a tone of authority, who it was that disturbed their worship, and what they desired?

There was a moment's silence, and then a loud laugh from without. At length a voice replied, "We desire entrance into the church; and when the door is opened you will soon see who we are."

"By whose authority do you require entrance?" said the Father.

"By authority of the right reverend Lord Abbot of Unreason," * replied

---

* We learn from no less authority than that of Napoleon Bonaparte, that there is but a single step between the sublime and ridiculous; and it is a transition from one extreme to another; so very easy, that the vulgar of every degree are peculiarly captivated with it. Thus the inclination to laugh becomes uncontrollable, when the solemnity and gravity of time, place, and circumstances, render it peculiarly improper. Some species of general license, like that which inspired the ancient Saturnalia, or the modern Carnival, has been commonly indulged to the people at all times and in almost all countries. But it was, I think, peculiar to the Roman Catholic Church, that while they studied how to render their church rites imposing and magnificent, by all that pomp, music, architecture, and external display could add to them, they nevertheless connived, upon special occasions, at the frolics of the rude vulgar, who, in almost all Catholic countries, enjoyed, or at least assumed, the privilege of making some Lord of the revels, who, under the name of the Abbot of Unreason, the Boy Bishop, or the President of Fools, occupied the churches, profaned the holy places by a mock imitation of the sacred rites, and sung indecent parodies on hymns of the church. The indifference of the clergy, even when their power was greatest, to the indecent exhibitions which they always tolerated, and sometimes encouraged, forms a strong contrast to the sensitiveness with which they regarded any serious attempt, by preaching or writing, to impeach any of the doctrines of the church. It could only be compared to the singular apathy with which they endured, and often admired the gross novels which Chaucer, Dunbar, Boccacio, Bandello, and others, composed upon the bad morals of the clergy. It seems as if the churchmen in both instances had endeavoured to compromise with the laity, and allowed them occasionally to gratify their coarse humour by indecent satire, provided they would abstain from any grave question concerning the foundation of the doctrines on which was erected such an immense fabric of ecclesiastical power.

But the sports thus licensed assumed a very different appearance, so soon as the Protestant doctrines began to prevail; and the license which their forefathers had exercised in mere gaiety of heart, and without the least intention of dishonouring religion by their frolics, were now persevered in by the common people as a mode of testifying their utter disregard for the Roman priesthood and its ceremonies.

I may observe, for example, the case of an apparitor sent to Borthwick from the Primate of Saint Andrews, to cite the lord of that castle, who was opposed by an Abbot of Unreason, at whose command the officer of the spiritual court was appointed to be ducked in a mill-dam, and obliged to eat up his parchment citation.

The reader may be amused with the following whimsical details of this incident, which took place in the castle of Borthwick, in the year 1547. It appears, that in consequence of a process betwixt Master George Hay de Minzeane and the Lord Borthwick, letters of excommunication had passed against the latter, on account of the contumacy of certain witnesses. William Langlands, an apparitor or macer (*bacularius*) of the See of St Andrews, presented these letters to the curate of the church of Borthwick, requiring him to publish the same at the service of high mass. It seems that the inhabitants of the castle were at this time engaged in the favourite sport of enacting the Abbot of Unreason, a species of high jinks, in which a mimic prelate was elected, who, like the Lord of Misrule in England, turned all sort of lawful authority, and particularly the church ritual, into ridicule. This frolicsome person with his retinue, notwithstanding of the apparitor's character, entered the church, seized upon the primate's officer without hesitation, and, dragging him to the mill-dam on the south side of the castle, compelled him to leap into the water. Not contented with this partial immersion, the Abbot of Unreason pronounced, that Mr. William Langlands was not yet sufficiently bathed, and therefore caused his assistants to lay him on his back in the stream, and duck him in the most satisfactory and perfect manner. The unfortunate apparitor was then conducted back to the church, where, for his refreshment after his bath, the letters of excommunication were torn to pieces, and steeped in a bowl of wine; the mock abbot being probably of opinion that a tough parchment was but dry eating, Langlands was compelled to eat the letters, and swallow the wine, and dismissed by the Abbot of Unreason, with the comfortable assurance, that if any more such letters should arrive during the continuance of his office, "they should a' gang the same gate," *i. e.* go the same road.

A similar scene occurs betwixt a sumner of the Bishop of Rochester, and Harpool, the servant of Lord Cobham, in the old play of Sir John Oldcastle, when the former compels the church-officer to eat his citation. The dialogue, which may be found in the note, contains most of the jests which may be supposed ppropriate to such an extraordinary occasion: *

* *Harpool.* Marry, sir, is this process parchment?

Sumner. Yes, marry is it.

Harpool. And this seal wax?

Sumner. It is so.

Harpool. If this be parchment, and this be wax, eat you this parchment and wax, or I will make parchment of your skin, and beat your brains into wax. Sirrah Sumner, despatch—devour, sirrah, devour.

Sumner. I am my Lord of Rochester's sumner; I came to do my office, and thou shalt answer it.

Harpool. Sirrah, no railing, but betake thyself to thy teeth. Thou shalt eat no worse than thou bringest with thee. Thou bringest it for my lord; and wilt thou bring my lord worse than thou wilt eat thyself?

Sumner. Sir, I brought it not my lord to eat.

Harpool. O, do you *Sir* me now? All's one for that; I'll make you eat it for bringing it.

Sumner. I cannot eat it.

Harpool. Can you not? 'Sblood, I'll beat you till you have a stomach! (*Beats him.*)

Sumner. Oh, hold, hold, good Mr. Servingman; I will eat it.

Harpool. Be champing, be chewing, sir, or I will chew you, you rogue. Tough wax is the purest of the honey.

Sumner. The purest of the honey?—O Lord, sir, oh! oh!

Harpool. Feed, feed; 'tis wholesome, rogue, wholesome. Cannot you, like an honest sumner, walk with the devil your brother, to fetch in your bailiff's rents, but you must come to a nobleman's house with process? If the seal were broad as the lead which covers Rochester Church, thou shouldst eat it.

the voice from without; and, from the laugh which followed, it seemed as if there was something highly ludicrous couched under this reply.

"I know not, and seek not to know, your meaning," replied the Abbot, "since it is probably a rude one. But begone, in the name of God, and leave his servants in peace. I speak this, as having lawful authority to command here."

"Open the door," said another rude voice, "and we will try titles with you, Sir Monk, and show you a superior we must all obey."

"Break open the doors if he dallies any longer," said a third, "and down with the carrion monks who would bar us of our privilege!" A general shout followed. "Ay, ay, our privilege! our privilege! down with the doors, and with the lurdane monks, if they make opposition!"

The knocking was now exchanged for blows with great hammers, to which the doors, strong as they were, must soon have given way. But the Abbot, who saw resistance would be in vain, and who did not wish to incense the assailants by an attempt at offering it, besought silence earnestly, and with difficulty obtained a hearing. "My children," said he, "I will save you from committing a great sin. The porter will presently undo the gate—he is gone to fetch the keys—meantime I pray you to consider with yourselves, if you are in a state of mind to cross the holy threshold."

"Tillyvally for your papistry!" was answered from without; "we are in the mood of the monks when they are merriest, and that is when they sup beef-brewis for lanten-kail. So, if your porter hath not the gout, let him come speedily, or we heave away readily.—Said I well, comrades?"

"Bravely said, and it shall be as bravely done," said the multitude; and had not the keys arrived at that moment, and the porter in hasty terror performed his office, throwing open the great door, the populace would have saved him the trouble. The instant he had done so, the affrighted janitor fled, like one who has drawn the bolts of a flood-gate, and expects to be overwhelmed by the rushing inundation. The monks, with one consent, had withdrawn themselves behind the Abbot, who alone kept his station, about three yards from the entrance, showing no signs of fear or perturbation. His brethren—partly encouraged by his devotion, partly ashamed to desert him, and partly animated by a sense of duty—remained huddled close together, at the back of their Superior. There was a loud laugh and huzza when the doors were opened; but, contrary to what might have been expected, no crowd of enraged assailants rushed into the church. On the contrary, there was a cry of "A halt!—a halt—to order, my masters! and let the two reverend fathers greet each other, as beseems them."

The appearance of the crowd who were thus called to order, was grotesque in the extreme. It was composed of men, women, and children, ludicrously disguised in various habits, and presenting groups equally diversified and grotesque. Here one fellow with a horse's head painted before him, and a tail behind, and the whole covered with a long foot-cloth, which was supposed to hide the body of the animal, ambled, caracoled, pranced, and plunged, as he performed the celebrated part of the hobby-horse,* so often

---

Sumner. Oh, I am almost choked—I am almost choked!
Harpool. Who's within there? Will you shame my lord? Is there no beer in the house? Butler, I say.

Enter BUTLER.

Butler. Here, here.
Harpool. Give him beer. Tough old sheep skin's but dry meat.

First Part of Sir John Oldcastle, Act II. Scene I.

* This exhibition, the play-mare of Scotland, stood high among holyday gambols. It must be carefully separated from the wooden chargers which furnish out our nurseries. It gives rise to Hamlet's ejaculation,—

But oh, but oh, the hobby-horse is forgot!

There is a very comic scene in Beaumont and Fletcher's play of "Woman Pleased," where Hope-on-high Bombye, a puritan cobbler, refuses to dance with the hobby-horse. There was much difficulty and great variety in the motions which the hobby-horse was expected to exhibit.

The learned Mr. Douce, who has contributed so much to the illustration of our theatrical antiquities, has given us a full account of this pageant, and the burlesque horsemanship which it practised.

"The hobby-horse," says Mr. Douce, "was represented by a man equipped with as much pasteboard as was sufficient to form the head and hinder parts of a horse, the quadrupedal defects being concealed by a long

alluded to in our ancient drama; and which still flourishes on the stage in the battle that concludes Bayes's tragedy. To rival the address and agility displayed by this character, another personage advanced in the more formidable character of a huge dragon, with gilded wings, open jaws, and a scarlet tongue, cloven at the end, which made various efforts to overtake and devour a lad, dressed as the lovely Sabæa, daughter of the King of Egypt, who fled before him; while a martial Saint George, grotesquely armed with a goblet for a helmet, and a spit for a lance, ever and anon interfered, and compelled the monster to relinquish his prey. A bear, a wolf, and one or two other wild animals, played their parts with the discretion of Snug the joiner; for the decided preference which they gave to the use of their hind legs, was sufficient, without any formal annunciation, to assure the most timorous spectators that they had to do with habitual bipeds. There was a group of outlaws with Robin Hood and Little John at their head*—the best repre-

---

mantle or footcloth that nearly touched the ground. The former, on this occasion, exerted all his skill in burlesque horsemanship. In Sympson's play of the Law-breakers, 1636, a miller personates the hobby-horse, and being angry that the Mayor of the city is put in competition with him, exclaims, 'Let the mayor play the hobby-horse among his brethren, an he will; I hope our town-lads cannot want a hobby-horse. Have I practised my reins, my careers, my prankers, my ambles, my false trots, my smooth ambles, and Canterbury paces, and shall master mayor put me beside the hobby-horse? Have I borrowed the fore-horse bells, his plumes, his braveries; nay, had his mane new shorn and frizzled, and shall the mayor put me beside the hobby-horse?"—*Douce's Illustrations*, vol. II. p 468.

* The representation of Robin Hood was the darling Maygame both in England and Scotland, and doubtless the favourite personification was often revived, when the Abbot of Unreason, or other pretences of frolic, gave an unusual degree of license.

The Protestant clergy, who had formerly reaped advantage from the opportunities which these sports afforded them of directing their own satire and the ridicule of the lower orders against the Catholic church, began to find that, when these purposes were served, their favourite pastimes deprived them of the wish to attend divine worship, and disturbed the frame of mind in which it can be attended to advantage. The celebrated Bishop Latimer gives a very *naive* account of the manner in which, bishop as he was, he found himself compelled to give place to Robin Hood and his followers.

"I came once myselfe riding on a journey homeward from London, and I sent word over night into the towne that I would preach there in the morning, because it was holiday, and me thought it was a holidayes worke. The church stood in my way, and I took my horse and my company, and went thither, (I thought I should have found a great company in the church,) and when I came there the church doore was fast locked. I tarryed there halfe an houre and more. At last the key was found, and one of the parish comes to me and said,—'Sir, this is a busie day with us, we cannot hear you; it is Robin Hood's day. The parish are gone abroad to gather for Robin Hood. I pray you let them not.' I was faine there to give place to Robin Hood. I thought my rochet should have been regarded, though I were not: but it would not serve, it was faine to give place to Robin Hood's men. It is no laughing matter, my friends, it is a weeping matter, a heavie matter, a heavie matter. Under the pretence for gathering for Robin Hood, a traytour, and a theif, to put out a preacher; to have his office lesse esteemed; to preferre Robin Hood before the ministration of God's word; and all this hath come of unpreaching prelates. This realme hath been ill provided for, that it hath had such corrupt judgments in it, to prefer Robin Hood to God's word."—*Bishop Latimer's sixth Sermon before King Edward.*

While the English Protestants thus preferred the outlaw's pageant to the preaching of their excellent Bishop, the Scottish calvinistic clergy, with the celebrated John Knox at their head, and backed by the authority of the magistrates of Edinburgh, who had of late been chosen exclusively from this party, found it impossible to control the rage of the populace, when they attempted to deprive them of the privilege of presenting their pageant of Robin Hood.

(561.) "Vpon the xxi day of Junij, Archibalde Dowglas of Kilspindie, Provest of Edr., David Symmer and Adame Fullartoun, baillies of the samyne, causit ane cordinare servant, callit James Gillion, takin of befoir, for playing in Edr. with Robene Hude, to wnderly the law, and put him to the knawlege of ane assyize qlk yaij haid electit of yair favoraris, quha with schort deliberatioun condemnit him to be hangit for ye said cryme. And the deaconis of ye craftismen fearing vproare, maid great solistatnis at ye handis of ye said provost and baillies, and als requirit John Knox, minister, for eschewing of tumult, to superceid ye execution of him, vnto ye tyme yai suld adverteis my Lord Duke yairof. And yan, if it wes his mynd and will yat he should be disponit vpoun, ye said deaconis and craftismen sould convey him yaire; quha answerit, yat yai culd na way stope ye executioun of justice. Quhan ye time of ye said pouer mans hanging approchit, and yat ye hangman wes cum to ye jibbat with ye ledder, vpoune ye qlk ye said cordinare should have bene hangit, ane certaine and remanent craftischilder, quha wes put to ye horne with ye said Gillione, ffor ye said Robene Hiude's *playes*, and vyris yair assistaris and favoraris, past to wappinis, and yai brak down ye said jibbat, and yan chacit ye said provest, baillies, and Alexr. Guthrie, in ye said Alexander's writing buith, and held yame yairin; and yairefter past to ye tolbuyt, and becaus the samyne was steiket, and onnawayes culd get the keyes thairof, thai brak the said tolbuith dore with foure harberis, per force, (the said provest and baillies luckand thairon,) and not onlie put thar the said Gillione to fredome and libertie, and brocht him furth of the said tolbuit, bot alsua the remanent presonaris being thairintill; and this done, the said craftismen's servands, with the said condempnit cordonar, past doun to the Netherbow, to have past furth thairat; bot becaus the samyne on thair coming thairto wes closet, thai past vp agane the Hie streit of the said bourghe to the Castellhill, and in this menetymne the saidis provest and baillies, and thair assistaris being in the writing buith of the said Alexr. Guthrie, past and enterit in the said tolbuyt, and in the said servandes passage vp the Hie streit, then schote furth thairof at thame ane dog, and hurt ane servand of the said childer. This being done, thair wes nathing vthir but the one partie schuteand out and castand stanes furth of the said tolbuyt, and the vther pairtie schuteand hagbuttis in the same agane. Aund sua the craftismen's servandis, aboue written, held and inclosit the said provest and baillies continewallie in the said tolbuyth, frae three houris efternone, quhill aught houris at even, and na man of the said town prensit to relieve their said provest and baillies. And than thai send to the maisters of the Castell, to caus tham if thai mycht stay the said servandis, quha maid ane maner to do the same, bot thai could not bring the same to ane finall end, ffor the said servands wold on noways stay fra, quhill thai had revengit the hurting of ane of them; and thairefter the constable of the castell come down thairfra, and he with the said maisters treatet betwix the said ptios in this maner:—That the said provost and baillies sall remit to the said craftischilder, all actioun, cryme, and offens that thai had committit aganes thame in any tyme bygane; and band and oblast thame never to pursew them thairfor

sentation exhibited at the time; and no great wonder, since most of the actors were, by profession, the banished men and thieves whom they presented. Other masqueraders there were, of a less marked description. Men were disguised as women, and women as men — children wore the dress of aged people, and tottered with crutch-sticks in their hands, furred gowns on their little backs, and caps on their round heads — while grandsires assumed the infantine tone as well as the dress of children. Besides these, many had their faces painted, and wore their shirts over the rest of their dress; while coloured pasteboard and ribbons furnished out decorations for others. Those who wanted all these properties, blacked their faces, and turned their jackets inside out; and thus the transmutation of the whole assembly into a set of mad grotesque mummers, was at once completed.

The pause which the masqueraders made, waiting apparently for some person of the highest authority amongst them, gave those within the Abbey Church full time to observe all these absurdities. They were at no loss to comprehend their purpose and meaning.

Few readers can be ignorant, that at an early period, and during the plenitude of her power, the Church of Rome not only connived at, but even encouraged, such Saturnalian licenses as the inhabitants of Kennaquhair and the neighbourhood had now in hand, and that the vulgar, on such occasions, were not only permitted but encouraged by a number of gambols, sometimes puerile and ludicrous, sometimes immoral and profane, to indemnify themselves for the privations and penances imposed on them at other seasons. But, of all other topics for burlesque and ridicule, the rites and ceremonial of the church itself were most frequently resorted to; and, strange to say, with the approbation of the clergy themselves.

While the hierarchy flourished in full glory, they do not appear to have dreaded the consequences of suffering the people to become so irreverently familiar with things sacred; they then imagined the laity to be much in the condition of the labourer's horse, which does not submit to the bridle and the whip with greater reluctance, because, at rare intervals, he is allowed to frolic at large in his pasture, and fling out his heels in clumsy gambols at the master who usually drives him. But, when times changed — when doubt of the Roman Catholic doctrine, and hatred of their priesthood, had possessed the reformed party, the clergy discovered, too late, that no small inconvenience arose from the established practice of games and merry-makings, in which they themselves, and all they held most sacred, were made the subject of ridicule. It then became obvious to duller politicians than the Romish churchmen, that the same actions have a very different tendency when done in the spirit of sarcastic insolence and hatred, than when acted merely in exuberance of rude and uncontrollable spirits. They, therefore, though of the latest, endeavoured, where they had any remaining influence, to discourage the renewal of these indecorous festivities. In this particular, the Catholic clergy were joined by most of the reformed preachers, who were more shocked at the profanity and immorality of many of these exhibitions, than disposed to profit by the ridiculous light in which they placed the Church of Rome and her observances. But it was long ere these scandalous and immoral sports could be abrogated; — the rude multitude continued attached to their favourite pastimes, and, both in England and Scotland, the mitre of the Catholic — the rochet of the reformed bishop — and the cloak and band of the Calvinistic divine — were, in turn, compelled

---

and als commandit thair maisters to resaue them agane in thair services, as thai did befoir. And this being proclamit at the mercat cross, thai scalit, and the said provest and bailies come furth of the same tolbouyth." &c. &c. &c.

John Knox, who writes at large upon this tumult, informs us it was inflamed by the deacons of craftes, who, resenting the superiority assumed over them by the magistrates, would yield no assistance to put down the tumult. "They will be magistrates alone," said the recusant deacons, "e'en let them rule the populace alone;" and accordingly they passed quietly to take *their four-hours penny*, and left the magistrates to help themselves as they could. Many persons were excommunicated for this outrage, and not admitted to church ordinances till they had made satisfaction.

to give place to those jocular personages, the Pope of Fools, the Boy-Bishop, and the Abbot of Unreason.*

It was the latter personage who now, in full costume, made his approach to the great door of the church of St. Mary's, accoutred in such a manner as to form a caricature, or practical parody, on the costume and attendants of the real Superior, whom he came to beard on the very day of his installation, in the presence of his clergy, and in the chancel of his church. The mock dignitary was a stout-made under-sized fellow, whose thick squab form had been rendered grotesque by a supplemental paunch, well stuffed. He wore a mitre of leather, with the front like a grenadier's cap, adorned with mock embroidery, and trinkets of tin. This surmounted a visage, the nose of which was the most prominent feature, being of unusual size, and at least as richly gemmed as his head-gear. His robe was of buckram, and his cope of canvass, curiously painted, and cut into open work. On one shoulder was fixed the painted figure of an owl; and he bore in the right hand his pastoral staff, and in the left a small mirror having a handle to it, thus resembling a celebrated jester, whose adventures, translated into English, were whilom extremely popular, and which may still be procured in black letter, for about one sterling pound per leaf.

The attendants of this mock dignitary had their proper dresses and equipage, bearing the same burlesque resemblance to the officers of the Convent which their leader did to the Superior. They followed their leader in regular procession, and the motley characters, which had waited his arrival, now crowded into the church in his train, shouting as they came,—"A hall, a hall! for the venerable Father Howleglas, the learned Monk of Misrule, and the Right Reverend Abbot of Unreason!"

The discordant minstrelsy of every kind renewed its din; the boys shrieked and howled, and the men laughed and hallooed, and the women giggled and screamed, and the beasts roared, and the dragon wallopped and hissed, and the hobby-horse neighed, pranced, and capered, and the rest frisked and frolicked, clashing their hobnailed shoes against the pavement, till it sparkled with the marks of their energetic caprioles.

It was, in fine, a scene of ridiculous confusion, that deafened the ear, made the eyes giddy, and must have altogether stunned any indifferent spectator; the monks, whom personal apprehension and a consciousness that much of the popular enjoyment arose from the ridicule being directed against them, were, moreover, little comforted by the reflection, that, bold in their disguise, the mummers who whooped and capered around them, might, on slight provocation, turn their jest into earnest, or at least proceed to those practical pleasantries, which at all times arise so naturally out of the frolicsome and mischievous disposition of the populace. They looked to their Abbot amid the tumult, with such looks as landsmen cast upon the pilot when the storm is at the highest—looks which express that they are devoid of all hope arising from their own exertions, and not very confident in any success likely to attend those of their Palinurus.

The Abbot himself seemed at a stand; he felt no fear, but he was sensible of the danger of expressing his rising indignation, which he was scarcely able to suppress. He made a gesture with his hand as if commanding silence, which was at first only replied to by redoubled shouts, and peals of wild laughter. When, however, the same motion, and as nearly in the same manner, had been made by Howleglas, it was immediately obeyed by his riotous companions, who expected fresh food for mirth in the conversation betwixt the real and mock Abbot, having no small confidence in the vulgar wit and impudence of their leader. Accordingly, they began to shout, "To it, fathers—to it!"—"Fight monk, fight madcap—Abbot against Abbot is fair play, and so is reason against unreason, and malice against monkery!"

* From the interesting novel entitled Anastasius, it seems the same burlesque ceremonies were practised in the Greek Church.

"Silence, my mates!" said Howleglas; "cannot two learned Fathers of the Church hold communion together, but you must come here with your bear-garden whoop and hollo, as if you were hounding forth a mastiff upon a mad bull? I say silence! and let this learned Father and me confer, touching matters affecting our mutual state and authority."

"My children"—said Father Ambrose.

"*My* children too, — and happy children they are!" said his burlesque counterpart; "many a wise child knows not its own father, and it is well they have two to choose betwixt."

"If thou hast aught in thee, save scoffing and ribaldry," said the real Abbot, "permit me, for thine own soul's sake, to speak a few words to these misguided men."

"Aught in me but scoffing, sayest thou?" retorted the Abbot of Unreason; "why, reverend brother, I have all that becomes mine office at this time a-day—I have beef, ale, and brandy-wine, with other condiments not worth mentioning; and for speaking, man—why, speak away, and we will have turn about, like honest fellows."

During this discussion the wrath of Magdalen Græme had risen to the uttermost; she approached the Abbot, and placing herself by his side, said in a low and yet distinct tone—"Wake and arouse thee, Father—the sword of Saint Peter is in thy hand—strike and avenge Saint Peter's patrimony! —Bind them in the chains which, being riveted by the church on earth, are riveted in Heaven——"

"Peace, sister!" said the Abbot; "let not their madness destroy our discretion—I pray thee, peace, and let me do mine office. It is the first, peradventure it may be the last time, I shall be called on to discharge it."

"Nay, my holy brother!" said Howleglas, "I rede you, take the holy sister's advice—never throve convent without woman's counsel."

"Peace, vain man!" said the Abbot; "and you, my brethren——"

"Nay, nay!" said the Abbot of Unreason, "no speaking to the lay people, until you have conferred with your brother of the cowl. I swear by bell, book, and candle, that no one of my congregation shall listen to one word you have to say; so you had as well address yourself to me who will."

To escape a conference so ludicrous, the Abbot again attempted an appeal to what respectful feelings might yet remain amongst the inhabitants of the Halidome, once so devoted to their spiritual Superiors. Alas! the Abbot of Unreason had only to flourish his mock crosier, and the whooping, the hallooing, and the dancing, were renewed with a vehemence which would have defied the lungs of Stentor.

"And now, my mates," said the Abbot of Unreason, "once again dight your gabs and be hushed—let us see if the Cock of Kennaquhair will fight or flee the pit."

There was again a dead silence of expectation, of which Father Ambrose availed himself to address his antagonist, seeing plainly that he could gain an audience on no other terms. "Wretched man!" said he, "hast thou no better employment for thy carnal wit, than to employ it in leading these blind and helpless creatures into the pit of utter darkness?"

"Truly, my brother," replied Howleglas, "I can see little difference betwixt your employment and mine, save that you make a sermon of a jest, and I make a jest of a sermon."

"Unhappy being," said the Abbot, "who hast no better subject of pleasantry than that which should make thee tremble—no sounder jest than thine own sins, and no better objects for laughter than those who can absolve thee from the guilt of them!"

"Verily, my reverend brother," said the mock Abbot, "what you say might be true, if, in laughing at hypocrites, I meant to laugh at religion.— Oh, it is a precious thing to wear a long dress, with a girdle and a cowl—

we become a holy pillar of Mother Church, and a boy must not play at ball against the walls for fear of breaking a painted window!"

"And will you, my friends," said the Abbot, looking round and speaking with a vehemence which secured him a tranquil audience for some time — "will you suffer a profane buffoon, within the very church of God, to insult his ministers? Many of you — all of you, perhaps — have lived under my holy predecessors, who were called upon to rule in this church where I am called upon to suffer. If you have worldly goods, they are their gift; and, when you scorned not to accept better gifts — the mercy and forgiveness of the church—were they not ever at your command?—did we not pray while you were jovial—wake while you slept?"

"Some of the good wives of the Halidome were wont to say so," said the Abbot of Unreason; but his jest met in this instance but slight applause, and Father Ambrose, having gained a moment's attention, hastened to improve it.

"What!" said he; "and is this grateful — is it seemly—is it honest — to assail with scorn a few old men, from whose predecessors you hold all, and whose only wish is to die in peace among these fragments of what was once the light of the land, and whose daily prayer is, that they may be removed ere that hour comes when the last spark shall be extinguished, and the land left in the darkness which it has chosen rather than light? We have not turned against you the edge of the spiritual sword, to revenge our temporal persecution; the tempest of your wrath hath despoiled us of land, and deprived us almost of our daily food, but we have not repaid it with the thunders of excommunication — we only pray your leave to live and die within the church which is our own, invoking God, our Lady, and the Holy Saints to pardon your sins, and our own, undisturbed by scurril buffoonery and blasphemy."

This speech, so different in tone and termination from that which the crowd had expected, produced an effect upon their feelings unfavourable to the prosecution of their frolic. The morris-dancers stood still — the hobby-horse surceased his capering—pipe and tabor were mute, and "silence, like a heavy cloud," seemed to descend on the once noisy rabble. Several of the beasts were obviously moved to compunction; the bear could not restrain his sobs, and a huge fox was observed to wipe his eyes with his tail. But in especial the dragon, lately so formidably rampant, now relaxed the terror of his claws, uncoiled his tremendous rings, and grumbled out of his fiery throat in a repentant tone, "By the mass, I thought no harm in exercising our old pastime, but an I had thought the good Father would have taken it so to heart, I would as soon have played your devil, as your dragon."

In this momentary pause, the Abbot stood amongst the miscellaneous and grotesque forms by which he was surrounded, triumphant as Saint Anthony, in Callot's Temptations; but Howleglas would not so resign his purpose.

"And how now, my masters!" said he, "is this fair play or no? Have you not chosen me Abbot of Unreason, and is it lawful for any of you to listen to common sense to-day? Was I not formally elected by you in solemn chapter, held in Luckie Martin's change-house, and will you now desert me, and give up your old pastime and privilege? Play out the play —and he that speaks the next word of sense or reason, or bids us think or consider, or the like of that, which befits not the day, I will have him solemnly ducked in the mill-dam!"

The rabble, mutable as usual, huzzaed, the pipe and tabor struck up, the hobby-horse pranced, the beasts roared, and even the repentant dragon began again to coil up his spires, and prepare himself for fresh gambols. But the Abbot might still have overcome, by his eloquence and his entreaties, the malicious designs of the revellers, had not Dame Magdalen Græme given loose to the indignation which she had long suppressed.

"Scoffers," she said, "and men of Belial—Blasphemous heretics, and truculent tyrants——"

"Your patience, my sister, I entreat and I command you!" said the Abbot; "let me do my duty—disturb me not in mine office!"

But Dame Magdalen continued to thunder forth her threats in the name of Popes and Councils, and in the name of every Saint, from St. Michael downward.

"My comrades!" said the Abbot of Unreason, "this good dame hath not spoken a single word of reason, and therein may esteem herself free from the law. But what she spoke was meant for reason, and, therefore, unless she confesses and avouches all which she has said to be nonsense, it shall pass for such, so far as to incur our statutes. Wherefore, holy dame, pilgrim, or abbess, or whatever thou art, be mute with thy mummery or beware the mill-dam. We will have neither spiritual nor temporal scolds in our Diocese of Unreason!"

As he spoke thus, he extended his hand towards the old woman, while his followers shouted, "A doom—a doom!" and prepared to second his purpose, when lo! it was suddenly frustrated. Roland Græme had witnessed with indignation the insults offered to his old spiritual preceptor, but yet had wit enough to reflect he could render him no assistance, but might well, by ineffective interference, make matters worse. But when he saw his aged relative in danger of personal violence, he gave way to the natural impetuosity of his temper, and, stepping forward, struck his poniard into the body of the Abbot of Unreason, whom the blow instantly prostrated on the pavement.

Chapter the Fifteenth.

As when in tumults rise the ignoble crowd,
Mad are their motions, and their tongues are loud,
And stones and brands in rattling furies fly,
And all the rustic arms which fury can supply—
Then if some grave and pious man appear,
They hush their noise, and lend a listening ear.

DRYDEN'S VIRGIL.

A DREADFUL shout of vengeance was raised by the revellers, whose sport was thus so fearfully interrupted; but for an instant, the want of weapons amongst the multitude, as well as the inflamed features and brandished poniard of Roland Græme, kept them at bay, while the Abbot, horror-struck at the violence, implored, with uplifted hands, pardon for bloodshed committed within the sanctuary. Magdalen Græme alone expressed triumph in the blow her descendant had dealt to the scoffer, mixed, however, with a wild and anxious expression of terror for her grandson's safety. "Let him perish," she said, "in his blasphemy—let him die on the holy pavement which he has insulted!"

But the rage of the multitude, the grief of the Abbot, the exultation of the enthusiastic Magdalen, were all mistimed and unnecessary. Howleglas, mortally wounded as he was supposed to be, sprung alertly up from the floor, calling aloud, "A miracle, a miracle, my masters! as brave a miracle as ever was wrought in the kirk of Kennaquhair. And I charge you, my masters, as your lawfully chosen Abbot, that you touch no one without my command—You, wolf and bear, will guard this pragmatic youth, but without hurting him — And you, reverend brother, will, with your comrades, withdraw to your cells; for our conference has ended like all conferences, leaving each of his own mind, as before; and if we fight, both you, and your brethren, and the Kirk, will have the worst on't—Wherefore, pack up you pipes and begone."

The hubbub was beginning again to awaken, but still Father Ambrose hesitated, as uncertain to what path his duty called him, whether to face out the present storm, or to reserve himself for a better moment. His brother of Unreason observed his difficulty, and said, in a tone more natural and less affected than that with which he had hitherto sustained his character, "We came hither, my good sir, more in mirth than in mischief—our bark is worse than our bite — and, especially, we mean you no personal harm — wherefore, draw off while the play is good; for it is ill whistling for a hawk when she is once on the soar, and worse to snatch the quarry from the ban-dog — Let these fellows once begin their brawl, and it will be too much for madness itself, let alone the Abbot of Unreason, to bring them back to the lure."

The brethren crowded around Father Ambrosius, and joined in urging him to give place to the torrent. The present revel was, they said, an ancient custom which his predecessors had permitted, and old Father Nicholas himself had played the dragon in the days of the Abbot Ingelram.

"And we now reap the fruit of the seed which they have so unadvisedly sown," said Ambrosius; "they taught men to make a mock of what is holy, what wonder that the descendants of scoffers become robbers and plunderers? But be it as you list, my brethren—move towards the dortour — And you, dame, I command you, by the authority which I have over you, and by your respect for that youth's safety, that you go with us without farther speech—Yet, stay—what are your intentions towards that youth whom you detain prisoner?—Wot ye," he continued, addressing Howleglas in a stern tone of voice, "that he bears the livery of the House of Avenel? They who fear not the anger of Heaven, may at least dread the wrath of man."

"Cumber not yourself concerning him," answered Howleglas, "we know right well who and what he is."

"Let me pray," said the Abbot, in a tone of entreaty, "that you do him no wrong for the rash deed which he attempted in his imprudent zeal."

"I say, cumber not yourself about it, father," answered Howleglas, "but move off with your train, male and female, or I will not undertake to save yonder she-saint from the ducking-stool—And as for bearing of malice, my stomach has no room for it; it is," he added, clapping his hand on his portly belly, "too well bumbasted out with straw and buckram—gramercy to them both — they kept out that madcap's dagger as well as a Milan corslet could have done."

In fact, the home-driven poniard of Roland Græme had lighted upon the stuffing of the fictitious paunch, which the Abbot of Unreason wore as a part of his characteristic dress, and it was only the force of the blow which had prostrated that reverend person on the ground for a moment.

Satisfied in some degree by this man's assurances, and compelled to give way to superior force, the Abbot Ambrosius retired from the Church at the head of the monks, and left the court free for the revellers to work their will. But, wild and wilful as these rioters were, they accompanied the retreat of the religionists with none of those shouts of contempt and derision with which they had at first hailed them. The Abbot's discourse had affected some of them with remorse, others with shame, and all with a transient degree of respect. They remained silent until the last monk had disappeared through the side-door which communicated with their dwelling-place, and even then it cost some exhortations on the part of Howleglas, some caprioles of the hobby-horse, and some wallops of the dragon, to rouse once more the rebuked spirit of revelry.

"And how now, my masters?" said the Abbot of Unreason; "and wherefore look on me with such blank Jack-a-Lent visages? Will you lose your old pastime for an old wife's tale of saints and purgatory? Why, I thought you would have made all split long since — Come, strike up, tabor and harp, strike up, fiddle and rebeck—dance and be merry to-day, and let care come to-morrow. Bear and wolf, look to your prisoner — prance, hobby — hiss, dragon, and halloo, boys — we grow older every moment we stand idle, and life is too short to be spent in playing mumchance."

This pithy exhortation was attended with the effect desired. They fumigated the Church with burnt wool and feathers instead of incense, put foul water into the holy-water basins, and celebrated a parody on the Church-service, the mock Abbot officiating at the altar; they sung ludicrous and indecent parodies, to the tunes of church hymns; they violated whatever vestments or vessels belonging to the Abbey they could lay their hands upon; and, playing every freak which the whim of the moment could suggest to their wild caprice, at length they fell to more lasting deeds of demolition, pulled down and destroyed some carved wood-work, dashed out the painted windows which had escaped former violence, and in their rigorous search after sculpture dedicated to idolatry, began to destroy what ornaments yet remained entire upon the tombs, and around the cornices of the pillars.

The spirit of demolition, like other tastes, increases by indulgence; from these lighter attempts at mischief, the more tumultuous part of the meeting began to meditate destruction on a more extended scale — "Let us heave it down altogether, the old crow's nest," became a general cry among them; "it has served the Pope and his rooks too long;" and up they struck a ballad which was then popular among the lower classes.*

"The Paip, that pagan full of pride,
Hath blinded us ower lang,
For where the blind the blind doth lead,
No marvel baith gae wrang.
Like prince and king,
He led the ring
Of all iniquity.
Sing hay trix, trim-go-trix,
Under the greenwood tree.

"The Bishop rich, he could not preach
For sporting with the lasses;
The silly friar behoved to fleech
For awmous as he passes:
The curate his creed
He could not read,—
Shame fa' the company!
Sing hay trix, trim-go-trix,
Under the greenwood tree."

Thundering out this chorus of a notable hunting song, which had been pressed into the service of some polemical poet, the followers of the Abbot of Unreason were turning every moment more tumultuous, and getting beyond the management even of that reverend prelate himself, when a knight in full armour, followed by two or three men-at-arms, entered the church, and in a stern voice commanded them to forbear their riotous mummery.

His visor was up, but if it had been lowered, the cognizance of the holly-branch sufficiently distinguished Sir Halbert Glendinning, who, on his homeward road, was passing through the village of Kennaquhair; and moved, perhaps, by anxiety for his brother's safety, had come directly to the church on hearing of the uproar.

"What is the meaning of this," he said, "my masters? are ye Christian men, and the king's subjects, and yet waste and destroy church and chancel like so many heathens?"

All stood silent, though doubtless there were several disappointed and surprised at receiving chiding instead of thanks from so zealous a protestant.

* These rude rhymes are taken, with some trifling alterations, from a ballad called Trim-go-trix. It occurs in a singular collection, entitled, "A Compendious Book of Godly and Spiritual Songs, collected out of sundrie parts of the Scripture, with sundry of other ballatis changed out of prophane sanges, for avoyding of sin and harlotrie, with Augmentation of sundrie Gude and Godly Ballates. Edinburgh, printed by Andro Hart." This curious collection has been reprinted in Mr. John Grahame Dalyell's Scottish Poems of the 16th century Edin. 1801, 2 vols.

The dragon, indeed, did at length take upon him to be spokesman, and growled from the depth of his painted maw, that they did but sweep Popery out of the church with the besom of destruction.

"What! my friends," replied Sir Halbert Glendinning, "think you this mumming and masking has not more of Popery in it than have these stone walls? Take the leprosy out of your flesh, before you speak of purifying stone walls—abate your insolent license, which leads but to idle vanity and sinful excess; and know, that what you now practise, is one of the profane and unseemly sports introduced by the priests of Rome themselves, to mislead and to brutify the souls which fell into their net."

"Marry come up—are you there with your bears?" muttered the dragon, with a draconic sullenness, which was in good keeping with his character, "we had as good have been Romans still, if we are to have no freedom in our pastimes!"

"Dost thou reply to me so?" said Halbert Glendinning; "or is there any pastime in grovelling on the ground there like a gigantic kail-worm?—Get out of thy painted case, or, by my knighthood, I will treat you like the beast and reptile you have made yourself."

"Beast and reptile?" retorted the offended dragon, "setting aside your knighthood, I hold myself as well a born man as thyself."

The Knight made no answer in words, but bestowed two such blows with the butt of his lance on the petulant dragon, that had not the hoops which constituted the ribs of the machine been pretty strong, they would hardly have saved those of the actor from being broken. In all haste the masker crept out of his disguise, unwilling to abide a third buffet from the lance of the enraged Knight. And when the ex-dragon stood on the floor of the church, he presented to Halbert Glendinning the well-known countenance of Dan of the Howlet-hirst, an ancient comrade of his own, ere fate had raised him so high above the rank to which he was born. The clown looked sulkily upon the Knight, as if to upbraid him for his violence towards an old acquaintance, and Glendinning's own good-nature reproached him for the violence he had acted upon him.

"I did wrong to strike thee," he said, "Dan; but in truth, I knew thee not—thou wert ever a mad fellow—come to Avenel Castle, and we shall see how my hawks fly."

"And if we show him not falcons that will mount as merrily as rockets," said the Abbot of Unreason, "I would your honour laid as hard on my bones as you did on his even now."

"How now, Sir Knave," said the Knight, "and what has brought you hither?"

The Abbot, hastily ridding himself of the false nose which mystified his physiognomy, and the supplementary belly which made up his disguise, stood before his master in his real character, of Adam Woodcock, the falconer of Avenel.

"How, varlet!" said the Knight; "hast thou dared to come here and disturb the very house my brother was dwelling in?"

"And it was even for that reason, craving your honour's pardon, that I came hither—for I heard the country was to be up to choose an Abbot of Unreason, and sure, thought I, I that can sing, dance, leap backwards over a broadsword, and am as good a fool as ever sought promotion, have all chance of carrying the office; and if I gain my election, I may stand his honour's brother in some stead, supposing things fall roughly out at the Kirk of Saint Mary's."

"Thou art but a cogging knave," said Sir Halbert, "and well I wot, that love of ale and brandy, besides the humour of riot and frolic, would draw thee a mile, when love of my house would not bring thee a yard. But, go to—carry thy roisterers elsewhere—to the alehouse if they list, and there are crowns to pay your charges—make out the day's madness without doing more mischief, and be wise men to-morrow — and hereafter learn to serve a good cause better than by acting like buffoons or ruffians."

Obedient to his master's mandate, the falconer was collecting his discouraged followers, and whispering into their ears—" Away, away—*tace* is Latin for a candle—never mind the good Knight's puritanism—we will play the frolic out over a stand of double ale in Dame Martin the Brewster's barn-yard—draw off, harp and tabor—bagpipe and drum—mum till you are out of the church-yard, then let the welkin ring again—move on, wolf and bear—keep the hind legs till you cross the kirk-stile, and then show yourselves beasts of mettle — what devil sent him here to spoil our holiday!—but anger him not, my hearts; his lance is no goose-feather, as Dan's ribs can tell."

" By my soul," said Dan, " had it been another than my ancient comrade, I would have made my father's old fox* fly about his ears!"

" Hush! hush! man," replied Adam Woodcock, " not a word that way, as you value the safety of your bones—what man? we must take a clink as it passes, so it is not bestowed in downright ill-will."

" But I will take no such thing," said Dan of the Howlet-hirst, suddenly resisting the efforts of Woodcock, who was dragging him out of the church; when the quick military eye of Sir Halbert Glendinning detecting Roland Græme betwixt his two guards, the Knight exclaimed, " So ho! falconer,—Woodcock,—knave, hast thou brought my Lady's page in mine own livery, to assist at this hopeful revel of thine, with your wolves and bears? Since you were at such mummings, you might, if you would, have at least saved the credit of my household, by dressing him up as a jackanapes—bring him hither, fellows!"

Adam Woodcock was too honest and downright, to permit blame to light upon the youth, when it was undeserved. " I swear," he said, " by Saint Martin of Bullions†——"

" And what hast thou to do with Saint Martin?"

" Nay, little enough, sir, unless when he sends such rainy days that we cannot fly a hawk — but I say to your worshipful knighthood, that as I am a true man——"

" As you are a false varlet, had been the better obtestation."

" Nay, if your knighthood allows me not to speak," said Adam, " I can hold my tongue—but the boy came not hither by my bidding, for all that."

" But to gratify his own malapert pleasure, I warrant me," said Sir Halbert Glendinning — " Come hither, young springald, and tell me whether you have your mistress's license to be so far absent from the castle, or to dishonour my livery by mingling in such a May-game?"

" Sir Halbert Glendinning," answered Roland Græme with steadiness, " I have obtained the permission, or rather the commands, of your lady, to dispose of my time hereafter according to my own pleasure. I have been a most unwilling spectator of this May-game, since it is your pleasure so to call it; and I only wear your livery until I can obtain clothes which bear no such badge of servitude."

" How am I to understand this, young man?" said Sir Halbert Glendinning; " speak plainly, for I am no reader of riddles.—That my lady favoured thee, I know. What hast thou done to disoblige her, and occasion thy dismissal?"

" Nothing to speak of," said Adam Woodcock, answering for the boy — " a foolish quarrel with me, which was more foolishly told over again to my honoured lady, cost the poor boy his place. For my part, I will say freely, that I was wrong from beginning to end, except about the washing of the eyas's meat. There I stand to it that I was right."

* *Fox*, An old-fashioned broadsword was often so called.

† The Saint Swithin, or weeping Saint of Scotland. If his festival (fourth July) prove wet, forty days of rain are expected.

With that, the good-natured falconer repeated to his master the whole history of the squabble which had brought Roland Græme into disgrace with his mistress, but in a manner so favourable for the page, that Sir Halbert could not but suspect his generous motive.

"Thou art a good-natured fellow," he said, "Adam Woodcock."

"As ever had falcon upon fist," said Adam; "and, for that matter, so is Master Roland; but, being half a gentleman by his office, his blood is soon up, and so is mine."

"Well," said Sir Halbert, "be it as it will, my lady has acted hastily, for this was no great matter of offence to discard the lad whom she had trained up for years; but he, I doubt not, made it worse by his prating — it jumps well with a purpose, however, which I had in my mind. Draw off these people, Woodcock, — and you, Roland Græme, attend me."

The page followed him in silence into the Abbot's house, where, stepping into the first apartment which he found open, he commanded one of his attendants to let his brother, Master Edward Glendinning, know that he desired to speak with him. The men-at-arms went gladly off to join their comrade, Adam Woodcock, and the jolly crew whom he had assembled at Dame Martin's, the hostler's wife, and the Page and Knight were left alone in the apartment. Sir Halbert Glendinning paced the floor for a moment in silence and then thus addressed his attendant—

"Thou mayest have remarked, stripling, that I have but seldom distinguished thee by much notice; — I see thy colour rises, but do not speak till thou hearest me out. I say I have never much distinguished thee, not because I did not see that in thee which I might well have praised, but because I saw something blameable, which such praises might have made worse. Thy mistress, dealing according to her pleasure in her own household, as no one had better reason or title, had picked thee from the rest, and treated thee more like a relation than a domestic; and if thou didst show some vanity and petulance under such distinction, it were injustice not to say that thou hast profited both in thy exercises and in thy breeding, and hast shown many sparkles of a gentle and manly spirit. Moreover, it were ungenerous, having bred thee up freakish and fiery, to dismiss thee to want or wandering, for showing that very peevishness and impatience of discipline which arose from thy too delicate nurture. Therefore, and for the credit of my own household, I am determined to retain thee in my train, until I can honourably dispose of thee elsewhere, with a fair prospect of thy going through the world with credit to the house that brought thee up."

If there was something in Sir Halbert Glendinning's speech which flattered Roland's pride, there was also much that, according to his mode of thinking, was an alloy to the compliment. And yet his conscience instantly told him that he ought to accept, with grateful deference, the offer which was made him by the husband of his kind protectress; and his prudence, however slender, could not but admit he should enter the world under very different auspices as a retainer of Sir Halbert Glendinning, so famed for wisdom, courage, and influence, from those under which he might partake the wanderings, and become an agent in the visionary schemes, for such they appeared to him, of Magdalen, his relative. Still, a strong reluctance to re-enter a service from which he had been dismissed with contempt, almost counterbalanced these considerations.

Sir Halbert looked on the youth with surprise, and resumed—"You seem to hesitate, young man. Are your own prospects so inviting, that you should pause ere you accept those which I should offer to you? or, must I remind you that, although you have offended your benefactress, even to the point of her dismissing you, yet I am convinced, the knowledge that you have gone unguided on your own wild way, into a world so disturbed as ours of Scotland, cannot, in the upshot, but give her sorrow and pain; from which it is, in gratitude, your duty to preserve her, no less than it is in common wisdom your duty to accept my offered protection, for your own sake, where body and soul are alike endangered, should you refuse it."

Roland Græme replied in a respectful tone, but at the same time with some spirit, "I am not ungrateful for such countenance as has been afforded me by the Lord of Avenel, and I am glad to learn, for the first time, that I have not had the misfortune to be utterly beneath his observation, as I had thought — And it is only needful to show me how I can testify my duty and my gratitude towards my early and constant benefactress with my life's hazard, and I will gladly peril it." He stopped.

"These are but words, young man," answered Glendinning, "large protestations are often used to supply the place of effectual service. I know nothing in which the peril of your life can serve the Lady of Avenel; I can only say, she will be pleased to learn you have adopted some course which may ensure the safety of your person, and the weal of your soul — What ails you, that you accept not that safety when it is offered you?"

"My only relative who is alive," answered Roland, "at least the only relative whom I have ever seen, has rejoined me since I was dismissed from the Castle of Avenel, and I must consult with her whether I can adopt the line to which you now call me, or whether her increasing infirmities, or the authority which she is entitled to exercise over me, may not require me to abide with her."

"Where is this relation?" said Sir Halbert Glendinning.

"In this house," answered the page.

"Go then, and seek her out," said the Knight of Avenel; "more than meet it is that thou shouldst have her approbation, yet worse than foolish would she show herself in denying it."

Roland left the apartment to seek for his grandmother; and, as he retreated, the Abbot entered.

The two brothers met as brothers who loved each other fondly, yet meet rarely together. Such indeed was the case. Their mutual affection attached them to each other; but in every pursuit, habit or sentiment, connected with the discords of the times, the friend and counsellor of Murray stood opposed to the Roman Catholic priest; nor, indeed, could they have held very much society together, without giving cause of offence and suspicion to their confederates on each side. After a close embrace on the part of both, and a welcome on that of the Abbot, Sir Halbert Glendinning expressed his satisfaction that he had come in time to appease the riot raised by Howleglas and his tumultuous followers.

"And yet," he said, "when I look on your garments, brother Edward, I cannot help thinking there still remains an Abbot of Unreason within the bounds of the Monastery."

"And wherefore carp at my garments, brother Halbert?" said the Abbot; "it is the spiritual armour of my calling, and, as such, beseems me as well as breastplate and baldric becomes your own bosom."

"Ay, but there were small wisdom, methinks, in putting on armour where we have no power to fight; it is but a dangerous temerity to defy the foe whom we cannot resist."

"For that, my brother, no one can answer," said the Abbot, "until the battle be fought; and, were it even as you say, methinks a brave man, though desperate of victory, would rather desire to fight and fall, than to resign sword and shield on some mean and dishonourable composition with his insulting antagonist. But, let not you and I make discord of a theme on which we cannot agree, but rather stay and partake, though a heretic, of my admission feast. You need not fear, my brother, that your zeal for restoring the primitive discipline of the church will, on this occasion, be offended with the rich profusion of a conventual banquet. The days of our old friend Abbot Boniface are over; and the Superior of Saint Mary's has neither forests nor fishings, woods nor pastures, nor corn-fields; — neither flocks nor herds, bucks nor wild-fowl — granaries of wheat, nor storehouses of oil and wine, of ale and of mead. The refectioner's office is ended; and such a meal as a hermit in romance can offer to a wandering knight, is all we have to set before you. But, if you will share it with us, we shall eat it with a cheerful heart, and thank you, my brother, for your timely protection against these rude scoffers."

"My dearest brother," said the Knight, "it grieves me deeply I cannot abide with you; but it would sound ill for us both were one of the reformed congregation to sit down at your admission feast; and, if I can ever have the satisfaction of affording you effectual protection, it will be much owing to my remaining unsuspected of countenancing or approving your religious rites and ceremonies. It will demand whatever consideration I can acquire among my own friends, to shelter the bold man, who, contrary to law and the edicts of parliament, has dared to take up the office of Abbot of Saint Mary's."

"Trouble not yourself with the task, my brother," replied Father Ambrosius. "I would lay down my dearest blood to know that you defended the church for the church's sake; but, while you remain unhappily her enemy, I would not that you endangered your own safety, or diminished your own comforts, for the sake of my individual protection. — But who comes hither to disturb the few minutes of fraternal communication which our evil fate allows us?"

The door of the apartment opened as the Abbot spoke, and Dame Magdalen entered.

"Who is this woman?" said Sir Halbert Glendinning, somewhat sternly, "and what does she want?"

"That you know me not," said the matron, "signifies little; I come by your own order, to give my free consent that the stripling, Roland Græme, return to your service; and, having said so, I cumber you no longer with my presence. Peace be with you!" She turned to go away, but was stopped by inquiries of Sir Halbert Glendinning.

"Who are you? — what are you? — and why do you not await to make me answer?"

"I was," she replied, "while yet I belonged to the world, a matron of no vulgar name; now I am Magdalen, a poor pilgrimer, for the sake of Holy Kirk."

"Yea," said Sir Halbert, "art thou a Catholic? I thought my dame said that Roland Græme came of reformed kin."

"His father," said the matron, "was a heretic, or rather one who regarded neither orthodoxy or heresy — neither the temple of the church or of antichrist. I, too, for the sins of the times make sinners, have seemed to conform to your unhallowed rites — but I had my dispensation and my absolution."

"You see, brother," said Sir Halbert, with a smile of meaning towards his brother, "that we accuse you not altogether without grounds of mental equivocation."

"My brother, you do us injustice," replied the Abbot; "this woman, as her bearing may of itself warrant you, is not in her perfect mind. Thanks, I must needs say, to the persecution of your marauding barons, and of your latitudinarian clergy."

"I will not dispute the point," said Sir Halbert; "the evils of the time are unhappily so numerous, that both churches may divide them, and have enow to spare." So saying, he leaned from the window of the apartment, and winded his bugle.

"Why do you sound your horn, my brother?" said the Abbot; "we have spent but few minutes together."

"Alas!" said the elder brother, "and even these few have been sullied by disagreement. I sound to horse, my brother — the rather that, to avert the consequences of this day's rashness on your part, requires hasty efforts on mine.—Dame, you will oblige me by letting your young relative know that we mount instantly. I intend not that he shall return to Avenel with me—it would lead to new quarrels betwixt him and my household; at least to taunts which his proud heart could ill brook, and my wish is to do him kindness. He shall, therefore, go forward to Edinburgh with one of my retinue, whom I shall send back to say what has chanced here.—You seem rejoiced at this?" he added, fixing his eyes keenly on Magdalen Græme, who returned his gaze with calm indifference.

"I would rather," she said, "that Roland, a poor and friendless orphan, were the jest of the world at large, than of the menials at Avenel."

"Fear not, dame—he shall be scorned by neither," answered the Knight.

"It may be," she replied—"it may well be—but I will trust more to his own bearing than to your countenance." She left the room as she spoke.

The Knight looked after her as she departed, but turned instantly to his brother, and expressing, in the most affectionate terms, his wishes for his welfare and happiness, craved his leave to depart. "My knaves," he said, "are too busy at the ale-stand, to leave their revelry for the empty breath of a bugle-horn."

"You have freed them from higher restraint, Halbert," answered the Abbot, "and therein taught them to rebel against your own."

"Fear not that, Edward," exclaimed Halbert, who never gave his brother his monastic name of Ambrosius; "none obey the command of real duty so well as those who are free from the observance of slavish bondage."

He was turning to depart, when the Abbot said,—"Let us not yet part, my brother—here comes some light refreshment. Leave not the house which I must now call mine, till force expel me from it, until you have at least broken bread with me."

The poor lay brother, the same who acted as porter, now entered the apartment, bearing some simple refreshment, and a flask of wine. "He had found it," he said with officious humility, "by rummaging through every nook of the cellar."

The Knight filled a small silver cup, and, quaffing it off, asked his brother to pledge him, observing, the wine was Bacharac, of the first vintage, and great age.

"Ay," said the poor lay brother, "it came out of the nook which old brother Nicholas, (may his soul be happy!) was wont to call Abbot Ingelram's corner; and Abbot Ingelram was bred at the Convent of Wurtzburg, which I understand to be near where that choice wine grows."

"True, my reverend sir," said Sir Halbert; "and therefore I entreat my brother and you to pledge me in a cup of this orthodox vintage."

The thin old porter looked with a wishful glance towards the Abbot. "*Do veniam*," said his Superior; and the old man seized, with a trembling hand, a beverage to which he had been long unaccustomed; drained the cup with protracted delight, as if dwelling on the flavour and perfume, and set it down with a melancholy smile and shake of the head, as if bidding adieu in future to such delicious potations. The brothers smiled. But when Sir Halbert motioned to the Abbot to take up his cup and do him reason, the Abbot, in turn, shook his head, and replied—"This is no day for the Abbot of Saint Mary's to eat the fat and drink the sweat. In water from our Lady's well," he added, filling a cup with the limpid element, "I wish you, brother, all happiness, and above all, a true sight of your spiritual errors."

"And to you, my beloved Edward," replied Glendinning, "I wish the free exercise of your own free reason, and the discharge of more important duties than are connected with the idle name which you have so rashly assumed."

The brothers parted with deep regret; and yet, each confident in his opinion, felt somewhat relieved by the absence of one whom he respected so much, and with whom he could agree so little.

Soon afterwards the sound of the Knight of Avenel's trumpets was heard, and the Abbot went to the top of the tower, from whose dismantled battlements he could soon see the horsemen ascending the rising ground in the direction of the drawbridge. As he gazed, Magdalen Græme came to his side.

"Thou art come," he said, "to catch the last glimpse of thy grandson, my sister. Yonder he wends, under the charge of the best knight in Scotland, his faith ever excepted."

"Thou canst bear witness, my father, that it was no wish either of mine or of Roland's," replied the matron, "which induced the Knight of Avenel, as he is called, again to entertain my grandson in his household — Heaven, which confounds the wise with their own wisdom, and the wicked with their own policy, hath placed him where, for the services of the Church, I would most wish him to be."

"I know not what you mean, my sister," said the Abbot.

"Reverend father," replied Magdalen, "hast thou never heard that there are spirits powerful to rend the walls of a castle asunder when once admitted, which yet cannot enter the house unless they are invited, nay, dragged over the threshold?* Twice hath Roland Græme been thus drawn into the household of Avenel by those who now hold the title. Let them look to the issue."

So saying she left the turret; and the Abbot, after pausing a moment on her words, which he imputed to the unsettled state of her mind, followed down the winding stair to celebrate his admission to his high office by fast and prayer instead of revelling and thanksgiving.

---

* There is a popular belief respecting evil spirits, that they cannot enter an inhabited house unless invited, nay, dragged over the threshold. There is an instance of the same superstition in the Tales of the Genii, where an enchanter is supposed to have intruded himself into the Divan of the Sultan.

"'Thus,' said the illustrious Misnar, 'let the enemies of Mahomet be dismayed! but inform me, O ye sages! under the semblance of which of your brethren did that foul enchanter gain admittance here?'—'May the lord of my heart,' answered Balihu, the hermit of the faithful from Queda, 'triumph over all his foes! As I travelled on the mountains from Queda, and saw neither the footsteps of beasts, nor the flight of birds, behold, I chanced to pass through a cavern, in whose hollow sides I found this accursed sage, to whom I unfolded the invitation of the Sultan of India, and we, joining, journeyed towards the Divan; but ere we entered, he said unto me, 'Put thy hand forth, and pull me towards thee into the Divan, calling on the name of Mahomet, for the evil spirits are on me, and vex me.'"

I have understood that many parts of these fine tales, and in particular that of the Sultan Misnar, were taken from genuine Oriental sources by the editor, Mr. James Ridley.

But the most picturesque use of this popular belief occurs in Coleridge's beautiful and tantalizing fragment of Christabel. Has not our own imaginative poet cause to fear that future ages will desire to summon him from his place of rest, as Milton longed

"To call him up, who left half told
The story of Cambuscan bold?"

The verses I refer to are when Christabel conducts into her father's castle a mysterious and malevolent being, under the guise of a distressed female stranger.

"They cross'd the moat, and Christabel
Took the key that fitted well;
A little door she open'd straight,
All in the middle of the gate;
The gate that was iron'd within and without,
Where an army in battle array had march'd out.

"The lady sank, belike through pain,
And Christabel with might and main
Lifted her up, a weary weight,
Over the threshold of the gate:
Then the lady rose again,
And moved as she were not in pain.

"So free from danger, free from fear,
They cross'd the court;—right glad they were,
And Christabel devoutly cried
To the lady by her side:
'Praise we the Virgin, all divine,
Who hath rescued thee from this distress.'
'Alas, alas!' said Geraldine,
'I cannot speak from weariness.'
So free from danger, free from fear,
They cross'd the court: right glad they were

Chapter the Sixteenth.

Youth! thou wear'st to manhood now,
Darker lip and darker brow,
Statelier step, more pensive mien,
In thy face and gate are seen:
Thou must now brook midnight watches,
Take thy food and sport by snatches;
For the gambol and the jest,
Thou wert wont to love the best,
Graver follies must thou follow,
But as senseless, false, and hollow.
LIFE, A POEM.

YOUNG Roland Græme now trotted gaily forward in the train of Sir Halbert Glendinning. He was relieved from his most galling apprehension, — the encounter of the scorn and taunt which might possibly hail his immediate return to the Castle of Avenel. "There will be a change ere they see me again," he thought to himself; "I shall wear the coat of plate, instead of the green jerkin, and the steel morion for the bonnet and feather. They will be bold that may venture to break a gibe on the man-at-arms for the follies of the page; and I trust, that ere we return I shall have done something more worthy of note than hallooing a hound after a deer, or scrambling a crag for a kite's nest." He could not, indeed, help marvelling that his grandmother, with all her religious prejudices, leaning, it would seem, to the other side, had consented so readily to his re-entering the service of the House of Avenel; and yet more, at the mysterious joy with which she took leave of him at the Abbey.

"Heaven," said the dame, as she kissed her young relation, and bade him farewell, "works its own work, even by the hands of those of our enemies who think themselves the strongest and the wisest. Thou, my child, be ready to act upon the call of thy religion and country; and remember, each earthly bond which thou canst form is, compared to the ties which bind thee to them, like the loose flax to the twisted cable. Thou hast not forgot the face or form of the damsel Catherine Seyton?"

Roland would have replied in the negative, but the word seemed to stick in his throat and Magdalen continued her exhortations.

"Thou must not forget her, my son; and here I intrust thee with a token, which I trust thou wilt speedily find an opportunity of delivering with care and secrecy into her own hand."

She put here into Roland's hand a very small packet, of which she again enjoined him to take the strictest care, and to suffer it to be seen by no one save Catherine Seyton, who, she again (very unnecessarily) reminded him, was the young lady he had met on the preceding day. She then bestowed on him her solemn benediction, and bade God speed him.

There was something in her manner and her conduct which implied mystery; but Roland Græme was not of an age or temper to waste much time in endeavoring to decipher her meaning. All that was obvious to his perception in the present journey, promised pleasure and novelty. He rejoiced that he was travelling towards Edinburgh, in order to assume the character of a man, and lay aside that of a boy. He was delighted to think that he would have an opportunity of rejoining Catherine Seyton, whose bright eyes and lively manners had made so favourable an impression on his imagination; and, as an experienced, yet high-spirited youth, entering for the first time upon active life, his heart bounded at the thought, that he was about to see all those scenes of courtly splendour and warlike adventures, of which the followers of Sir Halbert used to boast on their occasional visits to Avenel, to the wonderment and envy of those who, like Roland, knew courts and camps only by hearsay, and were condemned to the solitary sports and almost monastic seclusion of Avenel, surrounded by its lonely lake, and embossed among its pathless mountains. "They shall mention my name," he said to himself, "if the risk of my life can purchase me opportunities of distinction, and Catherine Seyton's saucy eye shall rest with more respect on the distinguished soldier, than that with which she laughed to scorn the raw and inexperienced page."—There was wanting but one accessary to complete the sense of rapturous excitation, and he possessed it by being once more mounted on the back of a fiery and active horse, instead of plodding along on foot, as had been the case during the preceding days.

Impelled by the liveliness of his own spirits, which so many circumstances tended naturally to exalt, Roland Græme's voice and his laughter were soon distinguished amid the trampling of the horses of the retinue, and more than once attracted the attention of the leader, who remarked with satisfaction, that the youth replied with good-humoured raillery to such of the train as jested with him on his dismissal and return to the service of the House of Avenel.

"I thought the holly-branch in your bonnet had been blighted, Master Roland?" said one of the men-at-arms.

"Only pinched with half an hour's frost; you see it flourishes as green as ever."

"It is too grave a plant to flourish on so hot a soil as that headpiece of thine, Master Roland Græme," retorted the other, who was an old equerry of Sir Halbert Glendinning.

"If it will not flourish alone," said Roland, "I will mix it with the laurel and the myrtle — and I will carry them so near the sky, that it shall make amends for their stinted growth."

Thus speaking, he dashed his spurs into his horse's sides, and, checking him at the same time, compelled him to execute a lofty caracole. Sir Halbert Glendinning looked at the demeanour of his new attendant with that sort of melancholy pleasure with which those who have long followed the pursuits of life, and are sensible of their vanity, regard the gay, young, and buoyant spirits to whom existence, as yet, is only hope and promise.

In the meanwhile, Adam Woodcock, the falconer, stripped of his masquing habit, and attired, according to his rank and calling, in a green jerkin, with a hawking-bag on the one side, and a short hanger on the other, a glove on his left hand which reached half way up his arm, and a bonnet and feather upon his head, came after the party as fast as his active little galloway-nag could trot, and immediately entered into parley with Roland Græme.

"So, my youngster, you are once more under shadow of the holly-branch?"

"And in case to repay you, my good friend," answered Roland, "your ten groats of silver."

"Which, but an hour since," said the falconer, "you had nearly paid me with ten inches of steel. On my faith, it is written in the book of our destiny, that I must brook your dagger after all."

"Nay, speak not of that, my good friend," said the youth, "I would rather have broached my own bosom than yours; but who could have known you in the mumming dress you wore?"

"Yes," the falconer resumed,—for both as a poet and actor he had his own professional share of self-conceit,—"I think I was as good a Howleglas as ever played part at a Shrovetide revelry, and not a much worse Abbot of Unreason. I defy the Old Enemy to unmask me when I choose to keep my vizard on. What the devil brought the Knight on us before we had the game out? You would have heard me hollo my own new ballad with a voice should have reached to Berwick. But I pray you, Master Roland, be less free of cold steel on slight occasions; since, but for the stuffing of my reverend doublet, I had only left the kirk to take my place in the kirkyard."

"Nay, spare me that feud," said Roland Græme, "we shall have no time to fight it out; for, by our lord's command, I am bound for Edinburgh."

"I know it," said Adam Woodcock, "and even therefore we shall have time to solder up this rent by the way, for Sir Halbert has appointed me your companion and guide."

"Ay? and with what purpose?" said the page.

"That," said the falconer, "is a question I cannot answer; but I know, that be the food of the eyases washed or unwashed, and, indeed, whatever becomes of perch and mew, I am to go with you to Edinburgh, and see you safely delivered to the Regent at Holyrood."

"How, to the Regent?" said Roland, in surprise.

"Ay, by my faith, to the Regent," replied Woodcock; "I promise you, that if you are not to enter his service, at least you are to wait upon him in the character of a retainer of our Knight of Avenel."

"I know no right," said the youth, "which the Knight of Avenel hath to transfer my service, supposing that I owe it to himself."

"Hush, hush!" said the falconer; "that is a question I advise no one to stir in until he has the mountain or the lake, or the march of another kingdom, which is better than either, betwixt him and his feudal superior."

"But Sir Halbert Glendinning," said the youth, "is not my feudal superior; nor has he aught of authority——"

"I pray you, my son, to rein your tongue," answered Adam Woodcock; "my lord's displeasure, if you provoke it, will be worse to appease than my lady's. The touch of his least finger were heavier than her hardest blow. And, by my faith, he is a man of steel, as true and as pure, but as hard and as pitiless. You remember the Cock of Capperlaw, whom he hanged over his gate for a mere mistake — a poor yoke of oxen taken in Scotland, when he thought he was taking them in English land? I loved the Cock of Capperlaw; the Kerrs had not an honester man in their clan, and they have had men that might have been a pattern to the Border — men that would not have lifted under twenty cows at once, and would have held themselves dishonoured if they had taken a drift of sheep, or the like, but always managed their raids in full credit and honour.—But see, his worship halts, and we are close by the bridge. Ride up — ride up — we must have his last instructions."

It was as Adam Woodcock said. In the hollow way descending towards the bridge, which was still in the guardianship of Peter Bridgeward, as he was called, though he was now very old, Sir Halbert Glendinning halted his retinue, and beckoned to Woodcock and Græme to advance to the head of the train.

"Woodcock," said he, "thou knowest to whom thou art to conduct this youth. And thou, young man, obey discreetly and with diligence the orders that shall be given thee. Curb thy vain and peevish temper. Be just, true, and faithful; and there is in thee that which may raise thee many a degree above thy present station. Neither shalt thou — always supposing thine efforts to be fair and honest — want the protection and countenance of Avenel."

Leaving them in front of the bridge, the centre tower of which now began to cast a prolonged shade upon the river, the Knight of Avenel turned to the left, without crossing the river, and pursued his way towards the chain of hills within whose recesses are situated the Lake and Castle of Avenel. There remained behind, the falconer, Roland Græme, and a domestic of the Knight, of inferior rank, who was left with them to look after their horses while on the road, to carry their baggage, and to attend to their convenience.

So soon as the more numerous body of riders had turned off to pursue their journey westward, those whose route lay across the river, and was directed towards the north, summoned the Bridgeward, and demanded a free passage.

"I will not lower the bridge," answered Peter, in a voice querulous with age and ill-humour.—"Come Papist, come Protestant, ye are all the same. The Papist threatened us with Purgatory, and fleeched us with pardons—the Protestant mints at us with his sword, and cuttles us with the liberty of conscience; but never a one of either says, 'Peter, there is your penny.' I am well tired of all this, and for no man shall the bridge fall that pays me not ready money; and I would have you know I care as little for Geneva as for Rome—as little for homilies as for pardons; and the silver pennies are the only passports I will hear of."

"Here is a proper old chuff!" said Woodcock to his companion; then raising his voice, he exclaimed, "Hark thee, dog—Bridgeward, villain, dost thou think we have refused thy namesake Peter's pence to Rome, to pay thine at the bridge of Kennaquhair? Let thy bridge down instantly to the followers of the house of Avenel, or by the hand of my father, and that handled many a bridle rein, for he was a bluff Yorkshireman—I say, by my father's hand, our Knight will blow thee out of thy solan-goose's nest there in the middle of the water, with the light falconet which we are bringing southward from Edinburgh to-morrow."

The Bridgeward heard, and muttered, "A plague on falcon and falconet, on cannon and demicannon, and all the barking bull-dogs whom they halloo against stone and lime in these our days! It was a merry time when there was little besides handy blows, and it may be a flight of arrows that harmed an ashler wall as little as so many hailstones. But we must jouk and let the jaw gang by." Comforting himself in his state of diminished consequence with this pithy old proverb, Peter Bridgeward lowered the drawbridge, and permitted them to pass over. At the sight of his white hair, albeit it discovered a visage equally peevish through age and misfortune, Roland was inclined to give him an alms, but Adam Woodcock prevented him. "E'en let him pay the penalty of his former churlishness and greed," he said; "the wolf, when he has lost his teeth, should be treated no better than a cur."

Leaving the Bridgeward to lament the alteration of times, which sent domineering soldiers and feudal retainers to his place of passage, instead of peaceful pilgrims, and reduced him to become the oppressed, instead of playing the extortioner, the travellers turned them northward; and Adam Woodcock, well acquainted with that part of the country, proposed to cut short a considerable portion of the road, by traversing the little vale of Glendearg, so famous for the adventures which befell therein during the earlier part of the Benedictine's manuscript. With these, and with the thousand commentaries, representations, and misrepresentations, to which they had given rise, Roland Græme was, of course, well acquainted; for in the Castle of Avenel, as well as in other great establishments, the inmates talked of nothing so often, or with such pleasure, as of the private affairs of their lord and lady. But while Roland was viewing with interest these haunted scenes, in which things were said to have passed beyond the ordinary laws of nature, Adam Woodcock was still regretting in his secret soul the unfinished revel and the unsung ballad, and kept every now and then breaking out with some such verses as these:—

"The Friars of Fail drank berry-brown ale,
The best that e'er was tasted;
The Monks of Melrose made gude kale
On Fridays, when they fasted.
Saint Monance' sister,
The gray priest kist her—
Fiend save the company!
Sing hay trix, trim-go-trix,
Under the greenwood tree."

"By my hand, friend Woodcock," said the page, "though I know you for a hardy gospeller, that fear neither saint nor devil, yet, if I were you, I would not sing your profane songs in this valley of Glendearg, considering what has happened here before our time."

"A straw for your wandering spirits!" said Adam Woodcock; "I mind them no more than an earn cares for a string of wild-geese — they have all fled since the pulpits were filled with honest men, and the people's ears with sound doctrine. Nay, I have a touch at them in my ballad, an I had but had the good luck to have it sung to end;" and again he set off in the same key:

From haunted spring and grassy ring,
Troop goblin, elf, and fairy;
And the kelpie must flit from the black bog-pit,
And the brownie must not tarry;
To Limbo-lake,
Their way they take,
With scarce the pith to flee.
Sing hay trix, trim-go-trix,
Under the greenwood tree.

I think," he added, "that could Sir Halbert's patience have stretched till we came that length, he would have had a hearty laugh, and that is what he seldom enjoys."

"If it be all true that men tell of his early life," said Roland, "he has less right to laugh at goblins than most men."

"Ay, *if* it be all true," answered Adam Woodcock; "but who can ensure us of that? Moreover, these were but tales the monks used to gull us simple laymen withal; they knew that fairies and hobgoblins brought aves and paternosters into repute; but, now we have given up worship of images in wood and stone, methinks it were no time to be afraid of bubbles in the water, or shadows in the air."

"However," said Roland Græme, "as the Catholics say they do not worship wood or stone, but only as emblems of the holy saints, and not as things holy in themselves——"

"Pshaw! pshaw!" answered the falconer; "a rush for their prating. They told us another story when these baptized idols of theirs brought pike-staves and sandalled shoon from all the four winds, and whillied the old women out of their corn and their candle ends, and their butter, bacon, wool, and cheese, and when not so much as a gray groat escaped tithing."

Roland Græme had been long taught, by necessity, to consider his form of religion as a profound secret, and to say nothing whatever in its defence when assailed, lest he should draw on himself the suspicion of belonging to the unpopular and exploded church. He therefore suffered Adam Woodcock to triumph without farther opposition, marvelling in his own mind whether any of the goblins, formerly such active agents, would avenge his rude raillery before they left the valley of Glendearg. But no such consequences followed. They passed the night quietly in a cottage in the glen, and the next day resumed their route to Edinburgh.

Chapter the Seventeenth.

Edina! Scotia's darling seat,
All hail thy palaces and towers,
Where once, beneath a monarch's feet,
Sate legislation's sovereign powers.
BURNS.

"THIS, then, is Edinburgh?" said the youth, as the fellow-travellers arrived at one of the heights to the southward, which commanded a view of the great northern capital — "This is that Edinburgh of which we have heard so much!"

"Even so," said the falconer; "yonder stands Auld Reekie — you may see the smoke hover over her at twenty miles' distance, as the gosshawk hangs over a plump of young wild-ducks — ay, yonder is the heart of Scotland, and each throb that she gives is felt from the edge of Solway to Duncan's-bay-head. See, yonder is the old Castle; and see to the right, on yon rising ground, that is the Castle of Craigmillar, which I have known a merry place in my time."

"Was it not there," said the page in a low voice, "that the Queen held her court?"

"Ay, ay," replied the falconer, "Queen she was then, though you must not call her so now. Well, they may say what they will — many a true heart will be sad for Mary Stewart, e'en if all be true men say of her; for look you, Master Roland — she was the loveliest creature to look upon that I ever saw with eye, and no lady in the land liked better the fair flight of a falcon. I was at the great match on Roslin Moor betwixt Bothwell — he was a black sight to her that Bothwell — and the Baron of Roslin, who could judge a hawk's flight as well as any man in Scotland — a butt of Rhenish and a ring of gold was the wager, and it was flown as fairly for as ever was red gold and bright wine. And to see her there on her white palfrey, that flew as if it scorned to touch more than the heather blossom; and to hear her voice, as clear and sweet as the mavis's whistle, mix among our jolly whooping and whistling; and to mark all the nobles dashing round her; happiest he who got a word or a look — tearing through moss and hagg, and venturing neck and limb to gain the praise of a bold rider, and the blink of a bonny Queen's bright eye! — she will see little hawking where she lies now — ay, ay, pomp and pleasure pass away as speedily as the wap of a falcon's wing."

"And where is this poor Queen now confined?" said Roland Græme, interested in the fate of a woman whose beauty and grace had made so strong an impression even on the blunt and careless character of Adam Woodcock.

"Where is she now imprisoned?" said honest Adam; "why, in some castle in the north, they say—I know not where, for my part, nor is it worth while to vex one's sell anent what cannot be mended — An she had guided her power well whilst she had it, she had not come to so evil a pass. Men say she must resign her crown to this little baby of a prince, for that they will trust her with it no longer. Our master has been as busy as his neighbours in all this work. If the Queen should come to her own again, Avenel Castle is like to smoke for it, unless he makes his bargain all the better."

"In a castle in the north Queen Mary is confined?" said the page.

"Why, ay — they say so, at least — In a castle beyond that great river which comes down yonder, and looks like a river but it is a branch of the sea, and as bitter as brine."

"And amongst all her subjects," said the page, with some emotion, "is there none that will adventure anything for her relief?"

"That is a kittle question," said the falconer; "and if you ask it often, Master Roland, I am fain to tell you that you will be mewed up yourself in some of those castles, if they do not prefer twisting your head off, to save farther trouble with you — Adventure any thing? Lord, why, Murray has the wind in his poop now, man, and flies so high and strong, that the devil a wing of them can match him — No, no; there she is, and there she must lie, till Heaven send her deliverance, or till her son has the management of all — But Murray will never let her loose again, he knows her too well. — And hark thee, we are now bound for Holyrood, where thou wilt find plenty of news, and of courtiers to tell it—But, take my counsel, and keep a calm sough, as the Scots say — hear every man's counsel, and keep your own. And if you hap to learn any news you like, leap not up as if you were to put on armour direct in the cause — Our old Mr. Wingate says — and he knows court-cattle well — that if you are told old King Coul is come alive again, you should turn it off with, 'And is he in truth?—I heard not of it,' and should seem no more moved, than if one told you, by way of novelty, that old King Coul was dead and buried. Wherefore, look well to your bearing, Master Roland, for, I promise you, you come among a generation that are keen as a hungry hawk — And never be dagger out of sheath at every wry word you hear spoken; for you will find as hot blades as yourself, and then will be letting of blood without advice either of leech or almanack."

"You shall see how staid I will be, and how cautious, my good friend," said Græme; "but, blessed Lady, what goodly house is that which is lying all in ruins so close to the city? Have they been playing at the Abbot of Unreason here, and ended the gambol by burning the church?"

"There again now," replied his companion, "you go down the wind like a wild haggard, that minds neither lure nor beck — that is a question you should have asked in as low a tone as I shall answer it."

"If I stay here long," said Roland Græme, "it is like I shall lose the natural use of my voice—but what are the ruins then?"

"The Kirk of Field," said the falconer, in a low and impressive whisper, laying at the same time his finger on his lip; "ask no more about it — somebody got foul play, and somebody got the blame of it; and the game began there which perhaps may not be played out in our time.—Poor Henry Darnley! to be an ass, he understood somewhat of a hawk; but they sent him on the wing through the air himself one bright moonlight night."

The memory of this catastrophe was so recent, that the page averted his eyes with horror from the scathed ruins in which it had taken place; and the accusations against the Queen, to which it had given rise, came over his mind with such strength as to balance the compassion he had begun to entertain for her present forlorn situation.

It was, indeed, with that agitating state of mind which arises partly from horror, but more from anxious interest and curiosity, that young Græme found himself actually traversing the scene of those tremendous events, the report of which had disturbed the most distant solitudes in Scotland, like the echoes of distant thunder rolling among the mountains.

"Now," he thought, "now or never shall I become a man, and bear my part in those deeds which the simple inhabitants of our hamlets repeat to each other, as if they were wrought by beings of a superior order to their own. I will know now, wherefore the Knight of Avenel carries his crest so much above those of the neighbouring baronage, and how it is that men, by valour and wisdom, work their way from the hoddin-gray coat to the cloak of scarlet and gold. Men say I have not much wisdom to recommend me; and if that be true, courage must do it; for I will be a man amongst living men, or a dead corpse amongst the dead."

From these dreams of ambition he turned his thoughts to those of pleasure, and began to form many conjectures, when and where he should see Catherine Seyton, and in what manner their acquaintance was to be renewed. With such conjectures he was amusing himself, when he found that they had entered the city, and all other feelings were suspended in the sensation of giddy astonishment with which an inhabitant of the country is affected, when, for the first time, he finds himself in the streets of a large and populous city, a unit in the midst of thousands.

The principal street of Edinburgh was then, as now, one of the most spacious in Europe. The extreme height of the houses, and the variety of Gothic gables and battlements, and balconies, by which the sky-line on each side was crowned and terminated, together with the width of the street itself, might have struck with surprise a more practised eye than that of young Græme. The population, close packed within the walls of the city, and at this time increased by the number of the lords of the King's party who had thronged to Edinburgh to wait upon the Regent Murray, absolutely swarmed like bees on the wide and stately street. Instead of the shop-windows, which are now calculated for the display of goods, the traders had their open booths projecting on the street, in which, as in the fashion of the modern bazaars, all was exposed which they had upon sale. And though the commodities were not of the richest kinds, yet Græme thought he beheld the wealth of the whole world in the various bales of Flanders cloths, and the specimens of tapestry; and, at other places, the display of domestic utensils and pieces of plate struck him with wonder. The sight of cutlers' booths, furnished with swords and poniards, which were manufactured in Scotland, and with pieces of defensive armour, imported from Flanders, added to his surprise; and, at every step, he found so much to admire and gaze upon, that Adam Woodcock had no little difficulty in prevailing on him to advance through such a scene of enchantment.

The sight of the crowds which filled the streets was equally a subject of wonder. Here a gay lady, in her muffler, or silken veil, traced her way delicately, a gentleman-usher making way for her, a page bearing up her train, and a waiting gentlewoman carrying her Bible, thus intimating that her purpose was towards the church—There he might see a group of citizens bending the same way, with their short Flemish cloaks, wide trowsers, and high-caped doublets, a fashion to which, as well as to their bonnet and feather, the Scots were long faithful. Then, again, came the clergyman himself, in his black Geneva cloak and band, lending a grave and attentive ear to the discourse of several persons who accompanied him, and who were doubtless holding serious converse on the religious subject he was about to treat of. Nor did there lack passengers of a different class and appearance.

At every turn, Roland Græme might see a gallant ruffle along in the newer or French mode, his doublet slashed, and his points of the same colours with the lining, his long sword on one side, and his poniard on the other, behind him a body of stout serving men, proportioned to his estate and quality, all of whom walked with the air of military retainers, and were armed with sword and buckler, the latter being a small round shield, not unlike the Highland target, having a steel spike in the centre. Two of these parties, each headed by a person of importance, chanced to meet in the very centre of the street, or, as it was called, "the crown of the causeway," a post of honour as tenaciously asserted in Scotland, as that of giving or taking the wall used to be in the more southern part of the island. The two leaders being of equal rank, and, most probably, either animated by political dislike, or by recollection of some feudal enmity, marched close up to each other, without yielding an inch to the right or the left; and neither showing the least purpose of giving way, they stopped for an instant, and then drew their swords. Their followers imitated their example; about a score of weapons at once flashed in the sun, and there was an immediate clatter of swords and bucklers, while the followers on either side cried their master's name; the one shouting "Help, a Leslie! a Leslie!" while the others answered with shouts of "Seyton! Seyton!" with the additional punning slogan, "Set on, set on—bear the knaves to the ground!"

If the falconer found difficulty in getting the page to go forward before, it was now perfectly impossible. He reined up his horse, clapped his hands, and, delighted with the fray, cried and shouted as fast as any of those who were actually engaged in it.

The noise and cries thus arising on the Highgate, as it was called, drew into the quarrel two or three other parties of gentlemen and their servants, besides some single passengers, who, hearing a fray betwixt these two distinguished names, took part in it, either for love or hatred.

The combat became now very sharp, and although the sword-and-buckler men made more clatter and noise than they did real damage, yet several good cuts were dealt among them; and those who wore rapiers, a more formidable weapon than the ordinary Scottish swords, gave and received dangerous wounds. Two men were already stretched on the causeway, and the party of Seyton began to give ground, being much inferior in number to the other, with which several of the citizens had united themselves, when young Roland Græme, beholding their leader, a noble gentleman, fighting bravely, and hard pressed with numbers, could withhold no longer. "Adam Woodcock," he said, "an you be a man, draw, and let us take part with the Seyton." And, without waiting a reply, or listening to the falconer's earnest entreaty, that he would leave alone a strife in which he had no concern, the fiery youth sprung from his horse, drew his short sword, and shouting like the rest, "A Seyton! a Seyton! Set on! set on!" thrust forward into the throng, and struck down one of those who was pressing hardest upon the gentleman whose cause he espoused. This sudden reinforcement gave spirit to the weaker party, who began to renew the combat with much alacrity, when four of the magistrates of the city, distinguished by their velvet cloaks and gold chains, came up with a guard of halberdiers and citizens, armed with long weapons, and well accustomed to such service, thrust boldly forward, and compelled the swordsmen to separate, who immediately retreated in different directions, leaving such of the wounded on both sides, as had been disabled in the fray, lying on the street.

The falconer, who had been tearing his beard for anger at his comrade's rashness, now rode up to him with the horse which he had caught by the bridle, and accosted him with "Master Roland — master goose — master mad-cap — will it please you to get on horse, and budge? or will you remain here to be carried to prison, and made to answer for this pretty day's work?"

The page, who had begun his retreat along with the Seytons, just as if he had been one of their natural allies, was by this unceremonious application made sensible that he was acting a foolish part; and, obeying Adam Woodcock with some sense of shame, he sprung actively on horseback, and upsetting with the shoulder of the animal a city-officer, who was making towards him, he began to ride smartly down the street, along with his companion, and was quickly out of the reach of the hue and cry. In fact, rencounters of the kind were so common in Edinburgh at that period, that the disturbance seldom excited much attention after the affray was over, unless some person of consequence chanced to have fallen, an incident which imposed on his friends the duty of avenging his death on the first convenient opportunity. So feeble, indeed, was the arm of the police, that it was not unusual for such skirmishes to last for hours, where the parties were numerous and well matched. But at this time the Regent, a man of great strength of character, aware of the mischief which usually arose from such acts of violence, had prevailed with the magistrates to keep a constant guard on foot for preventing or separating such affrays as had happened in the present case.

The falconer and his young companion were now riding down the Canongate, and had slackened their pace to avoid attracting attention, the rather that there seemed to be no appearance of pursuit. Roland hung his head as one who was conscious his conduct had been none of the wisest, whilst his companion thus addressed him:

"Will you be pleased to tell me one thing, Master Roland Græme, and that is, whether there be a devil incarnate in you or no?"

"Truly, Master Adam Woodcock," answered the page, "I would fain hope there is not."

"Then," said Adam, "I would fain know by what other influence or instigation you are perpetually at one end or the other of some bloody brawl? What, I pray, had you to do with these Seytons and Leslies, that you never heard the names of in your life before?"

"You are out there, my friend," said Roland Græme, "I have my own reasons for being a friend to the Seytons."

"They must have been very secret reasons then," answered Adam Woodcock, "for I think I could have wagered, you had never known one of the name; and I am apt to believe still, that it was your unhallowed passion for that clashing of cold iron, which has as much charm for you as the clatter of a brass pan hath for a hive of bees, rather than any care either for Seyton or for Leslie, that persuaded you to thrust your fool's head into a quarrel that no ways concerned you. But take this for a warning, my young master, that if you are to draw sword with every man who draws sword on the Highgate here, it will be scarce worth your while to sheathe bilbo again for the rest of your life, since, if I guess rightly, it will scarce endure on such terms for many hours — all which I leave to your serious consideration."

"By my word, Adam, I honour your advice; and I promise you, that I will practise by it as faithfully as if I were sworn apprentice to you, to the trade and mystery of bearing myself with all wisdom and safety through the new paths of life that I am about to be engaged in."

"And therein you will do well," said the falconer; "and I do not quarrel with you, Master Roland, for having a grain over much spirit, because I know one may bring to the hand a wild hawk which one never can a dunghill hen — and so betwixt two faults you have the best on't. But besides your peculiar genius for quarrelling and lugging out your side companion, my dear Master Roland, you have also the gift of peering under every woman's muffler and screen, as if you expected to find an old acquaintance. Though were you to spy one, I should be as much surprised at it, well wotting how few you have seen of these same wild-fowl, as I was at your taking so deep an interest even now in the Seyton."

"Tush, man! nonsense and folly," answered Roland Græme, "I but sought to see what eyes these gentle hawks have got under their hood."

"Ay, but it's a dangerous subject of inquiry," said the falconer; "you had better hold out your bare wrist for an eagle to perch upon.—Look you, Master Roland, these pretty wild-geese cannot be hawked at without risk—they have as many divings, boltings, and volleyings, as the most gamesome quarry that falcon ever flew at — And besides, every woman of them is manned with her husband, or her kind friend, or her brother, or her cousin, or her sworn servant at the least — But you heed me not, Master Roland, though I know the game so well — your eye is all on that pretty damsel who trips down the gate before us — by my certes, I will warrant her a blithe dancer either in reel or revel — a pair of silver morisco bells would become these pretty ankles as well as the jesses would suit the fairest Norway hawk."

"Thou art a fool, Adam," said the page, "and I care not a button about the girl or her ankles — But, what the foul fiend, one must look at something!"

"Very true, Master Roland Græme," said his guide, "but let me pray you to choose your objects better. Look you, there is scarce a woman walks this High-gate with a silk screen or a pearlin muffler, but, as I said before, she has either gentleman-usher before her, or kinsman, or lover, or husband, at her elbow, or it may be a brace of stout fellows with sword and buckler, not so far behind but what they can follow close — But you heed me no more than a goss-hawk minds a yellow yoldring."

"O yes, I do — I do mind you indeed," said Roland Græme; "but hold my nag a bit—I will be with you in the exchange of a whistle." So saying, and ere Adam Woodcock could finish the sermon which was dying on his tongue, Roland Græme, to the falconer's utter astonishment, threw him the bridle of his jennet, jumped off horseback, and pursued down one of the closes or narrow lanes, which, opening under a vault, terminate upon the main-street, the very maiden to whom his friend had accused him of showing so much attention, and who had turned down the pass in question.

"Saint Mary, Saint Magdalen, Saint Benedict, Saint Barnabas!" said the poor falconer, when he found himself thus suddenly brought to a pause in the midst of the Canongate, and saw his young charge start off like a madman in quest of a damsel whom he had never, as Adam supposed, seen in his life before,—"Saint Satan and Saint Beelzebub—for this would make one swear saint and devil — what can have come over the lad, with a wanion! And what shall I do the whilst! — he will have his throat cut, the poor lad, as sure as I was born at the foot of Roseberry-Topping. Could I find some one to hold the horses! but they are as sharp here northaway as in canny Yorkshire herself, and quit bridle, quit titt, as we say. An I could but see one of our folks now, a holly-sprig were worth a gold tassel; or could I but see one of the Regent's men—but to leave the horses to a stranger, that I cannot — and to leave the place while the lad is in jeopardy, that I wonot."

We must leave the falconer, however, in the midst of his distress, and follow the hot-headed youth who was the cause of his perplexity.

The latter part of Adam Woodcock's sage remonstrance had been in a great measure lost upon Roland, for whose benefit it was intended; because, in one of the female forms which tripped along the street, muffled in a veil of striped silk, like the women of Brussels at this day, his eye had discerned something which closely resembled the exquisite shape and spirited bearing of Catherine Seyton. — During all the grave advice which the falconer was dinning in his ears, his eye continued intent upon so interesting an object of observation; and at length, as the damsel, just about to dive under one of the arched passages which afforded an outlet to the Canongate from the houses beneath, (a passage, graced by a projecting shield of arms, supported by two huge foxes of stone,) had lifted her veil for the purpose perhaps of descrying who the horseman was who for some time had eyed her so closely, young Roland saw, under the shade of the silken plaid, enough of the bright azure eyes, fair locks, and blithe features, to induce him, like an inexperienced and rash madcap, whose wilful ways never had been traversed by contradiction, nor much subjected to consideration, to throw the bridle of his horse into Adam Woodcock's hand, and leave him to play the waiting gentleman, while he dashed down the paved court after Catherine Seyton—all as aforesaid.

Women's wits are proverbially quick, but apparently those of Catherine suggested no better expedient than fairly to betake herself to speed of foot, in hopes of baffling the page's vivacity, by getting safely lodged before he could discover where. But a youth of eighteen, in pursuit of a mistress, is not so easily outstripped. Catherine fled across a paved court, decorated with large formal vases of stone, in which yews, cypresses, and other evergreens, vegetated in sombre sullenness, and gave a correspondent degree of solemnity to the high and heavy building in front of which they were placed as ornaments, aspiring towards a square portion of the blue hemisphere, corresponding exactly in extent to the quadrangle in which they were stationed, and all around which rose huge black walls, exhibiting windows in rows of five stories, with heavy architraves over each, bearing armorial and religious devices.

Through this court Catherine Seyton flashed like a hunted doe, making the best use of those pretty legs which had attracted the commendation even of the reflective and cautious Adam Woodcock. She hastened towards a large door in the centre of the lower front of the court, pulled the bobbin till the latch flew up, and ensconced herself in the ancient mansion. But, if she fled like a doe, Roland Græme followed with the speed and ardour of a youthful stag-hound, loosed for the first time on his prey. He kept her in view in spite of her efforts; for it is remarkable what an advantage, in such a race, the gallant who desires to see, possesses over the maiden who wishes not to be seen—an advantage which I have known counterbalance a great start in point of distance. In short, he saw the waving of her screen, or veil, at one corner, heard the tap of her foot, light as that was, as it crossed the court, and caught a glimpse of her figure just as she entered the door of the mansion.

Roland Græme, inconsiderate and headlong as we have described him, having no knowledge of real life but from the romances which he had read, and not an idea of checking himself in the midst of any eager impulse; possessed, besides, of much courage and readiness, never hesitated for a moment to approach the door through which the object of his search had disappeared. He, too, pulled the bobbin, and the latch, though heavy and massive, answered to the summons, and arose. The page entered with the same precipitation which had marked his whole proceeding, and found himself in a large hall, or vestibule, dimly enlightened by latticed casements of painted glass, and rendered yet dimmer through the exclusion of the sunbeams, owing to the height of the walls of those buildings by which the court-yard was enclosed. The walls of the hall were surrounded with suits of ancient and rusted armour, interchanged with huge and massive stone scutcheons, bearing double tressures, fleured and counter-fleured, wheat-sheaves, coronets, and so forth, things to which Roland Græme gave not a moment's attention.

In fact, he only deigned to observe the figure of Catherine Seyton, who, deeming herself safe in the hall, had stopped to take breath after her course, and was reposing herself for a moment on a large oaken settle which stood at the upper end of the hall. The noise of Roland's entrance at once disturbed her; she started up with a faint scream of surprise, and escaped through one of the several folding-doors which opened into this apartment as a common centre. This door, which Roland Græme instantly approached, opened on a large and well-lighted gallery, at the upper end of which he could hear several voices, and the noise of hasty steps approaching towards the hall or vestibule. A little recalled to sober thought by an appearance of serious danger, he was deliberating whether he should stand fast or retire, when Catherine Seyton re-entered from a side door, running towards him with as much speed as a few minutes since she had fled from him.

"Oh, what mischief brought you hither?" she said; "fly—fly, or you are a dead man,—or stay—they come—flight is impossible—say you came to ask for Lord Seyton."

She sprung from him and disappeared through the door by which she had made her second appearance; and, at the same instant, a pair of large folding-doors at the upper end of the gallery flew open with vehemence, and six or seven young gentlemen, richly dressed, pressed forward into the apartment, having, for the greater part, their swords drawn.

"Who is it," said one, "dare intrude on us in our own mansion?"

"Cut him to pieces," said another; "let him pay for this day's insolence and violence — he is some follower of the Rothes."

"No, by Saint Mary," said another; "he is a follower of the arch-fiend and ennobled clown Halbert Glendinning, who takes the style of Avenel — once a church-vassal, now a pillager of the church."

"It is so," said a fourth; "I know him by the holly-sprig, which is their cognizance. Secure the door, he must answer for this insolence."

Two of the gallants, hastily drawing their weapons, passed on to the door by which Roland had entered the hall, and stationed themselves there as if to prevent his escape. The others advanced on Græme, who had just sense enough to perceive that any attempt at resistance would be alike fruitless and imprudent. At once, and by various voices, none of which sounded amicably, the page was required to say who he was, whence he came, his name, his errand, and who sent him hither. The number of the questions demanded of him at once, afforded a momentary apology for his remaining silent, and ere that brief truce had elapsed, a personage entered the hall, at whose appearance those who had gathered fiercely around Roland, fell back with respect.

This was a tall man, whose dark hair was already grizzled, though his high and haughty features retained all the animation of youth. The upper part of his person was undressed to his Holland shirt, whose ample folds were stained with blood. But he wore a mantle of crimson, lined with rich fur, cast around him, which supplied the deficiency of his dress. On his head he had a crimson velvet bonnet, looped up on one side with a small golden chain of many links, which, going thrice around the hat, was fastened by a medal, agreeable to the fashion amongst the grandees of the time.

"Whom have you here, sons and kinsmen," said he, "around whom you crowd thus roughly? — Know you not that the shelter of this roof should secure every one fair treatment, who shall come hither either in fair peace, or in open and manly hostility?"

"But here, my lord," answered one of the youths, "is a knave who comes on treacherous espial!"

"I deny the charge!" said Roland Græme, boldly, "I came to inquire after my Lord Seyton."

"A likely tale," answered his accusers, "in the mouth of a follower of Glendinning."

"Stay, young men," said the Lord Seyton, for it was that nobleman himself, "let me look at this youth — By heaven, it is the very same who came so boldly to my side not very many minutes since, when some of my own knaves bore themselves with more respect to their own worshipful safety than to mine! Stand back from him, for he well deserves honour and a friendly welcome at your hands, instead of this rough treatment."

They fell back on all sides, obedient to Lord Seyton's commands, who, taking Roland Græme by the hand, thanked him for his prompt and gallant assistance, adding, that he nothing doubted, "the same interest which he had taken in his cause in the affray, brought him hither to inquire after his hurt."

Roland bowed low in acquiescence.

"Or is there any thing in which I can serve you, to show my sense f your ready gallantry?"

But the page, thinking it best to abide by the apology for his visit which the Lord Seyton had so aptly himself suggested, replied, "that to be assured of his lordship's safety, had been the only cause of his intrusion. He judged," he added, "he had seen him receive some hurt in the affray."

"A trifle," said Lord Seyton; "I had but stripped my doublet, that the chirurgeon might put some dressing on the paltry scratch, when these rash boys interrupted us with their clamour."

Roland Græme, making a low obeisance, was now about to depart, for, relieved from the danger of being treated as a spy, he began next to fear, that his companion, Adam Woodcock, whom he had so unceremoniously quitted, would either bring him into some farther dilemma, by venturing into the hotel in quest of him, or ride off and leave him behind altogether. But Lord Seyton did not permit him to escape so easily.—"Tarry," he said, "young man, and let me know thy rank and name. The Seyton has of late been more wont to see friends and followers shrink from his side, than to receive aid from strangers—but a new world may come around, in which he may have the chance of rewarding his well-wishers."

"My name is Roland Græme, my lord," answered the youth, "a page, who, for the present, is in the service of Sir Halbert Glendinning."

"I said so from the first," said one of the young men; "my life I will wager, that this is a shaft out of the heretic's quiver—a stratagem from first to last, to injeer into your confidence some espial of his own. They know how to teach both boys and women to play the intelligencers."

"That is false, if it be spoken of me," said Roland; "no man in Scotland should teach me such a foul part!"

"I believe thee, boy," said Lord Seyton, "for thy strokes were too fair to be dealt upon an understanding with those that were to receive them. Credit me, however, I little expected to have help at need from one of your master's household; and I would know what moved thee in my quarrel, to thine own endangering?"

"So please you, my lord," said Roland, "I think my master himself would not have stood by, and seen an honourable man borne to earth by odds, if his single arm could help him. Such, at least, is the lesson we were taught in chivalry, at the Castle of Avenel."

"The good seed hath fallen into good ground, young man," said Seyton; "but, alas! if thou practise such honourable war in these dishonourable days, when right is every where borne down by mastery, thy life, my poor boy, will be but a short one."

"Let it be short, so it be honourable," said Roland Græme; "and permit me now, my lord, to commend me to your grace, and to take my leave. A comrade waits with my horse in the street."

"Take this, however, young man," said Lord Seyton,* undoing from his bonnet the golden chain and medal, "and wear it for my sake."

---

* George, fifth Lord Seton, was immovably faithful to Queen Mary during all the mutabilities of her fortune. He was grand master of the household, in which capacity he had a picture painted of himself, with his official baton, and the following motto:—

In adversitate, patiens;
In prosperitate, benevolus.
Hazard, yet forward.

On various parts of his castle he inscribed, as expressing his religious and political creed, the legend,

UN DIEU, UN FOY, UN ROY, UN LOY.

He declined to be promoted to an earldom, which Queen Mary offered him at the same time when she advanced her natural brother to be Earl of Mar, and afterwards of Murray.

On his refusing this honour, Mary wrote, or caused to be written, the following lines in Latin and French:—

Sunt comites, ducesque alii; sunt denique reges;
Sethom dominum sit satis esse mihi.

Il y a des comptes, des roys, des ducs; ainsi
C'est assez pour moy d'estre Seigneur de Seton.

Which may be thus rendered:—

Earl, duke, or king, be thou that list to be:
Seton, thy lordship is enough for me.

This distich reminds us of the "pride which aped humility," in the motto of the house of Couci:

Je suis ni roy, ni prince aussi;
Je suis le Seigneur de Coucy.

After the battle of Langside, Lord Seton was obliged to retire abroad for safety, and was an exile for two years, during which he was reduced to the necessity of driving a waggon in Flanders for his subsistence. He rose to favour in James VI.'s reign, and assuming his paternal property, had himself painted in his waggoner's dress, and in the act of driving a wain with four horses, on the north end of a stately gallery at Seton Castle

With no little pride Roland Græme accepted the gift, which he hastily fastened around his bonnet, as he had seen gallants wear such an ornament, and renewing his obeisance to the Baron, left the hall, traversed the court, and appeared in the street, just as Adam Woodcock, vexed and anxious at his delay, had determined to leave the horses to their fate, and go in quest of his youthful comrade. "Whose barn hast thou broken next?" he exclaimed, greatly relieved by his appearance, although his countenance indicated that he had passed through an agitating scene.

"Ask me no questions," said Roland, leaping gaily on his horse; "but see how short time it takes to win a chain of gold," pointing to that which he now wore.

"Now, God forbid that thou hast either stolen it, or reft it by violence," said the falconer; "for, otherwise, I wot not how the devil thou couldst compass it. I have been often here, ay, for months at an end, and no one gave me either chain or medal."

"Thou seest I have got one on shorter acquaintance with the city," answered the page, "but set thine honest heart at rest; that which is fairly won and freely given, is neither reft nor stolen."

"Marry, hang thee, with thy fanfarona* about thy neck!" said the falconer; "I think water will not drown, nor hemp strangle thee. Thou hast been discarded as my lady's page, to come in again as my lord's squire; and for following a noble young damsel into some great household, thou gettest a chain and medal, where another would have had the baton across his shoulders, if he missed having the dirk in his body.—But here we come in front of the old Abbey. Bear thy good luck with you when you cross these paved stones, and, by our Lady, you may brag Scotland."

As he spoke, they checked their horses, where the huge old vaulted entrance to the Abbey or Palace of Holyrood crossed the termination of the street down which they had proceeded. The court-yard of the palace opened within this gloomy porch, showing the front of an irregular pile of monastic buildings, one wing of which is still extant, forming a part of the modern palace, erected in the days of Charles I.

At the gate of the porch the falconer and page resigned their horses to the serving-man in attendance; the falconer commanding him with an air of authority, to carry them safely to the stables.—"We follow," he said, "the Knight of Avenel.—We must bear ourselves for what we are here," said he in a whisper to Roland, "for every one here is looked on as they demean themselves; and he that is too modest must to the wall, as the proverb says; therefore cock thy bonnet, man, and let us brook the causeway bravely."

Assuming, therefore, an air of consequence, corresponding to what he supposed to be his master's importance and quality, Adam Woodcock led the way into the court-yard of the Palace of Holyrood.

He appears to have been fond of the arts; for there exists a beautiful family-piece of him in the centre of his family. Mr. Pinkerton, in his Scottish Iconographia, published an engraving of this curious portrait. The original is the property of Lord Somerville, nearly connected with the Seton family, and is at present at his lordship's fishing villa of the Pavilion, near Melrose.

* A name given to the gold chains worn by the military men of the period It is of Spanish origin; for the fashion of wearing these costly ornaments was much followed amongst the conquerers of the New World.

Chapter the Eighteenth.

—The sky is clouded, Gaspard,
And the vexed ocean sleeps a troubled sleep,
Beneath a lurid gleam of parting sunshine.
Such slumber hangs o'er discontented lands,
While factions doubt, as yet, if they have strength
To front the open battle.

ALBION — A POEM.

THE youthful page paused on the entrance of the court-yard, and implored his guide to give him a moment's breathing space. "Let me but look around me, man," said he; "you consider not I have never seen such a scene as this before.—And this is Holyrood — the resort of the gallant and gay, and the fair, and the wise, and the powerful!"

"Ay, marry, is it!" said Woodcock; "but I wish I could hood thee as they do the hawks, for thou starest as wildly as if you sought another fray or another fanfarona. I would I had thee safely housed, for thou lookest wild as a goss-hawk."

It was indeed no common sight to Roland, the vestibule of a palace traversed by its various groups,—some radiant with gaiety — some pensive, and apparently weighed down by affairs concerning the state, or concerning themselves. Here the hoary statesman, with his cautious yet commanding look, his furred cloak and sable pantoufles; there the soldier in buff and steel, his long sword jarring against the pavement, and his whiskered upper lip and frowning brow, looking an habitual defiance of danger, which perhaps was not always made good; there again passed my lord's serving-man, high of heart, and bloody of hand, humble to his master and his master's equals, insolent to all others. To these might be added, the poor suitor, with his anxious look and depressed mien — the officer, full of his brief authority, elbowing his betters, and possibly his benefactors, out of the road—the proud priest, who sought a better benefice—the proud baron, who sought a grant of church lands — the robber chief, who came to solicit a pardon for the injuries he had inflicted on his neighbors — the plundered franklin, who came to seek vengeance for that which he had himself received. Besides there was the mustering and disposition of guards and soldiers — the despatching of messengers, and the receiving them—the trampling and neighing of horses without the gate — the flashing of arms, and rustling of plumes, and jingling of spurs, within it. In short, it was that gay and splendid confusion, in which the eye of youth sees all that is brave and brilliant, and that of experience much that is doubtful, deceitful, false, and hollow — hopes that will never be gratified — promises which will never be fulfilled — pride in the disguise of humility—and insolence in that of frank and generous bounty.

As, tired of the eager and enraptured attention which the page gave to a scene so new to him, Adam Woodcock endeavoured to get him to move forward, before his exuberance of astonishment should attract the observation of the sharp-witted denizens of the court, the falconer himself became an object of attention to a gay menial in a dark-green bonnet and feather, with a cloak of a corresponding colour, laid down, as the phrase then went, by six broad bars of silver lace, and welted with violet and silver. The words of recognition burst from both at once. "What! Adam Woodcock at court!" and "What! Michael Wing-the-wind—and how runs the hackit greyhound bitch now?"

"The waur for the wear, like ourselves, Adam — eight years this grass —no four legs will carry a dog forever; but we keep her for the breed, and so she 'scapes Border doom—But why stand you gazing there? I promise you my lord has wished for you, and asked for you."

"My Lord of Murray asked for me, and he Regent of the kingdom too!" said Adam. "I hunger and thirst to pay my duty to my good lord;—but I fancy his good lordship remembers the day's sport on Carnwath-moor; and my Drummelzier falcon, that beat the hawks from the Isle of Man, and won his lordship a hundred crowns from the Southern baron whom they called Stanley."

"Nay, not to flatter thee, Adam," said his court-friend, "he remembers nought of thee, or of thy falcon either. He hath flown many a higher flight since that, and struck his quarry too. But come, come hither away; I trust we are to be good comrades on the old score."

"What!" said Adam, "you would have me crush a pot with you; but I must first dispose of my eyas, where he will neither have girl to chase, nor lad to draw sword upon."

"Is the youngster such a one?" said Michael.

"Ay, by my hood, he flies at all game," replied Woodcock.

"Then had he better come with us," said Michael Wing-the-wind; "for we cannot have a proper carouse just now, only I would wet my lips, and so must you. I want to hear the news from Saint Mary's before you see my lord, and I will let you know how the wind sits up yonder."

While he thus spoke, he led the way to a side door which opened into the court; and threading several dark passages with the air of one who knew the most secret recesses of the palace, conducted them to a small matted chamber, where he placed bread and cheese and a foaming flagon of ale before the falconer and his young companion, who immediately did justice to the latter in a hearty draught, which nearly emptied the measure. Having drawn his breath, and dashed the froth from his whiskers, he observed, that his anxiety for the boy had made him deadly dry.

"Mend your draught," said his hospitable friend, again supplying the flagon from a pitcher which stood beside. "I know the way to the buttery-bar. And now, mind what I say—this morning the Earl of Morton came to my lord in a mighty chafe."

"What! they keep the old friendship, then?" said Woodcock.

"Ay, ay, man, what else?" said Michael; "one hand must scratch the other. But in a mighty chafe was my Lord of Morton, who, to say truth, looketh on such occasions altogether uncanny, and, as it were, fiendish; and he says to my lord,—for I was in the chamber taking orders about a cast of hawks that are to be fetched from Darnoway—they match your long-winged falcons, friend Adam."

"I will believe that when I see them fly as high a pitch," replied Woodcock, this professional observation forming a sort of parenthesis.

"However," said Michael, pursuing his tale, "my Lord of Morton, in a mighty chafe, asked my Lord Regent whether he was well dealt with—'for my brother,' said he, 'should have had a gift to be Commendator of Kennaquhair, and to have all the temporalities erected into a lordship of regality for his benefit; and here,' said he, 'the false monks have had the insolence to choose a new Abbot to put his claim in my brother's way; and moreover, the rascality of the neighbourhood have burnt and plundered all that was left in the Abbey, so that my brother will not have a house to dwell in, when he hath ousted the lazy hounds of priests.' And my lord, seeing him chafed, said mildly to him, 'These are shrewd tidings, Douglas, but I trust they be not true; for Halbert Glendinning went southward yesterday, with a band of spears, and assuredly, had either of these chances happened, that the monks had presumed to choose an Abbot, or that the Abbey had been burnt, as you say, he had taken order on the spot for the punishment of such insolence, and had despatched us a messenger.' And the Earl of Morton replied—now I pray you, Adam, to notice, that I say this out of love to you and your lord, and also for old comradeship, and also because Sir Halbert hath done me good, and may again — and also because I love not the Earl of Morton, as indeed more fear than like him—so then it were a foul deed in you to betray me.—'But,' said the Earl to the Regent, 'take heed, my lord, you trust not this Glendinning too far—he comes of churl's blood, which was never true to the nobles'— by Saint Andrew, these were his very words. — 'And besides,' he said, 'he hath a brother, a monk in Saint Mary's, and walks all by his guidance, and is making friends on the Border with Buccleuch and with Ferniehirst,* and will join hand with them, were there likelihood of a new world.' And my lord answered, like a free noble lord as he is; 'Tush! my Lord of Morton, I will be warrant for Glendinning's faith; and for his brother, he is a dreamer, that thinks of nought but book and breviary — and if such hap have chanced as you tell of, I look to receive from Glendinning the cowl of a hanged monk, and the head of a riotous churl, by way of sharp and sudden justice.' — And my Lord of Morton left the place, and, as it seemed to me, somewhat malecontent. But since that time, my lord has asked me more than once whether there has arrived no messenger from the Knight of Avenel. And all this I have told you, that you may frame your discourse to the best purpose, for it seems to me that my lord will not be well-pleased, if aught has happened like what my Lord of Morton said, and if your lord hath not ta'en strict orders with it."

There was something in this communication which fairly blanked the bold visage of Adam Woodcock, in spite of the reinforcement which his natural hardihood had received from the berry-brown ale of Holyrood.

"What was it he said about a churl's head, that grim Lord of Morton?" said the discontented falconer to his friend.

"Nay, it was my Lord Regent, who said that he expected, if the Abbey was injured, your Knight would send him the head of the ringleader among the rioters."

"Nay, but is this done like a good Protestant," said Adam Woodcock, "or a true Lord of the Congregation? We used to be their white-boys and darlings when we pulled down the convents in Fife and Perthshire."

"Ay, but that," said Michael, "was when old mother Rome held her own, and our great folks were determined she should have no shelter for her head in Scotland. But, now that the priests are fled in all quarters, and their houses and lands are given to our grandees, they cannot see that we are working the work of reformation in destroying the palaces of zealous Protestants."

"But I tell you Saint Mary's is not destroyed!" said Woodcock, in increasing agitation; "some trash of painted windows there were broken — things that no nobleman could have brooked in his house—some stone saints were brought on their marrow-bones, like old Widdrington at Chevy-Chase; but as for fire-raising, there was not so much as a lighted lunt amongst us, save the match which the dragon had to light the burning tow withal, which he was to spit against Saint George; nay, I had caution of that."

"How! Adam Woodcock," said his comrade, "I trust thou hadst no hand in such a fair work? Look you, Adam, I were loth to terrify you, and you just come from a journey; but I promise you, Earl Morton hath brought you down a Maiden from Halifax, you never saw the like of her—and she'll clasp you round the neck, and your head will remain in her arms."

"Pshaw!" answered Adam, "I am too old to have my head turned by any maiden of them all. I know my Lord of Morton will go as far for a buxom lass as an yone; but what the devil took him to Halifax all the way? and if he has got a gamester there, what hath she to do with my head?"

* Both these Border Chieftains were great friends of Queen Mary.

"Much, much!" answered Michael. "Herod's daughter, who did such execution with her foot and ankle, danced not men's heads off more cleanly than this maiden of Morton.* 'Tis an axe, man, — an axe which falls of itself like a sash window, and never gives the headsmen the trouble to wield it."

"By my faith, a shrewd device," said Woodcock; "heaven keep us free on't!"

The page, seeing no end to the conversation betwixt these two old comrades, and anxious from what he had heard, concerning the fate of the Abbot, now interrupted their conference.

"Methinks," he said, "Adam Woodcock, thou hadst better deliver thy master's letter to the Regent; questionless he hath therein stated what has chanced at Kennaquhair, in the way most advantageous for all concerned."

"The boy is right," said Michael Wing-the-wind, "my lord will be very impatient."

"The child hath wit enough to keep himself warm," said Adam Woodcock, producing from his hawking-bag his lord's letter, addressed to the Earl of Murray, "and for that matter so have I. So, Master Roland, you will e'en please to present this yourself to the Lord Regent; his presence will be better graced by a young page than by an old falconer."

"Well said, canny Yorkshire!" replied his friend; "and but now you were so earnest to see our good lord! — Why, wouldst thou put the lad into the noose that thou mayst slip tether thyself? — or dost thou think the maiden will clasp his fair young neck more willingly than thy old sunburnt weasand?"

"Go to," answered the falconer; "thy wit towers high an it could strike the quarry. I tell thee, the youth has nought to fear — he had nothing to do with the gambol — a rare gambol it was, Michael, as mad-caps ever played; and I had made as rare a ballad, if we had had the luck to get it sung to an end. But mum for that — *tace*, as I said before, is Latin for a candle. Carry the youth to the presence, and I will remain here, with bridle in hand, ready to strike the spurs up to the rowel-heads, in case the hawk flies my way.—I will soon put Soltraedge, I trow, betwixt the Regent and me, if he means me less than fair play."

"Come on then, my lad," said Michael, "since thou must needs take the spring before canny Yorkshire." So saying, he led the way through winding passages, closely followed by Roland Græme, until they arrived at a large winding stone stair, the steps of which were so long and broad, and at the same time so low, as to render the ascent uncommonly easy. When they had ascended about the height of one story, the guide stepped aside, and pushed open the door of a dark and gloomy antechamber; so dark, indeed, that his youthful companion stumbled, and nearly fell down upon a low step, which was awkwardly placed on the very threshold.

"Take heed," said Michael Wing-the-wind, in a very low tone of voice, and first glancing cautiously round to see if any one listened—"Take heed, my young friend, for those who fall on these boards seldom rise again — Seest thou that," he added, in a still lower voice, pointing to some dark crimson stains on the floor, on which a ray of light, shot through a small aperture, and traversing the general gloom of the apartment, fell with mottled radiance — "Seest thou that, youth? — walk warily, for men have fallen here before you."

"What mean you?" said the page, his flesh creeping, though he scarce knew why; "Is it blood?"

"Ay, ay," said the domestic, in the same whispering tone, and dragging the youth on by the arm—"Blood it is,—but this is no time to question, or

* *Maiden of Morton*—a species of Guillotine which the Regent Morton brought down from Halifax, certainly at a period considerably later than intimated in the tale. He was himself the first who suffered by the engine.

even to look at it. Blood it is, foully and fearfully shed, as foully and fearfully avenged. The blood," he added, in a still more cautious tone, "of Seignior David."

Roland Græme's heart throbbed when he found himself so unexpectedly in the scene of Rizzio's slaughter, a catastrophe which had chilled with horror all even in that rude age, which had been the theme of wonder and pity through every cottage and castle in Scotland, and had not escaped that of Avenel. But his guide hurried him forward, permitting no farther question, and with the manner of one who has already tampered too much with a dangerous subject. A tap which he made at a low door at one end of the vestibule, was answered by a huissier or usher, who, opening it cautiously, received Michael's intimation that a page waited the Regent's leisure, who brought letters from the Knight of Avenel.

"The Council is breaking up," said the usher; "but give me the packet; his Grace the Regent will presently see the messenger."

"The packet," replied the page, "must be delivered into the Regent's own hands; such were the orders of my master."

The usher looked at him from head to foot, as if surprised at his boldness, and then replied, with some asperity, "Say you so, my young master? Thou crowest loudly to be but a chicken, and from a country barn-yard too."

"Were it a time or place," said Roland, "thou shouldst see I can do more than crow; but do your duty, and let the Regent know I wait his pleasure."

"Thou art but a pert knave to tell me of my duty," said the courtier in office; "but I will find a time to show you you are out of yours; meanwhile, wait there till you are wanted." So saying, he shut the door in Roland's face.

Michael Wing-the-wind, who had shrunk from his youthful companion during this altercation, according to the established maxim of courtiers of all ranks, and in all ages, now transgressed their prudential line of conduct so far as to come up to him once more. "Thou art a hopeful young springald," said he, "and I see right well old Yorkshire had reason in his caution. Thou hast been five minutes in the court, and hast employed thy time so well, as to make a powerful and a mortal enemy out of the usher of the council-chamber. Why, man, you might almost as well have offended the deputy butler!"

"I care not what he is," said Roland Græme; "I will teach whomever I speak with to speak civilly to me in return. I did not come from Avenel to be browbeaten in Holyrood."

"Bravo, my lad!" said Michael; "it is a fine spirit if you can but hold it—but see, the door opens."

The usher appeared, and, in a more civil tone of voice and manner, said, that his Grace the Regent would receive the Knight of Avenel's message; and accordingly marshalled Roland Græme the way into the apartment, from which the Council had been just dismissed, after finishing their consultations. There was in the room a long oaken table, surrounded by stools of the same wood, with a large elbow chair, covered with crimson velvet, at the head. Writing materials and papers were lying there in apparent disorder; and one or two of the privy counsellors who had lingered behind, assuming their cloaks, bonnets, and swords, and bidding farewell to the Regent, were departing slowly by a large door, on the opposite side to that through which the page entered. Apparently the Earl of Murray had made some jest, for the smiling countenances of the statesmen expressed that sort of cordial reception which is paid by courtiers to the condescending pleasantries of a prince.

The Regent himself was laughing heartily as he said, "Farewell, my lords, and hold me remembered to the Cock of the North."

He then turned slowly round towards Roland Græme, and the marks of gaiety, real or assumed, disappeared from his countenance, as completely as the passing bubbles leave the dark mirror of a still profound lake into which a traveller has cast a stone; in the course of a minute his noble features had assumed their natural expression of deep and even melancholy gravity.

This distinguished statesman, for as such his worst enemies acknowledged him, possessed all the external dignity, as well as almost all the noble qualities, which could grace the power that he enjoyed; and had he succeeded to the throne as his legitimate inheritance, it is probable he would have been recorded as one of Scotland's wisest and greatest kings. But that he held his authority by the deposition and imprisonment of his sister and benefactress, was a crime which those only can excuse who think ambition an apology for ingratitude. He was dressed plainly in black velvet, after the Flemish fashion, and wore in his high-crowned hat a jewelled clasp, which looped it up on one side, and formed the only ornament of his apparel. He had his poniard by his side, and his sword lay on the council table.

Such was the personage before whom Roland Græme now presented himself, with a feeling of breathless awe, very different from the usual boldness and vivacity of his temper. In fact, he was, from education and nature, forward, but not impudent, and was much more easily controlled by the moral superiority, arising from the elevated talents and renown of those with whom he conversed, than by pretensions founded only on rank or external show. He might have braved with indifference the presence of an earl, merely distinguished by his belt and coronet; but he felt overawed in that of the eminent soldier and statesman, the wielder of a nation's power, and the leader of her armies.—The greatest and wisest are flattered by the deference of youth — so graceful and becoming in itself; and Murray took, with much courtesy, the letter from the hands of the abashed and blushing page, and answered with complaisance to the imperfect and half-muttered greeting, which he endeavoured to deliver to him on the part of Sir Halbert of Avenel. He even paused a moment ere he broke the silk with which the letter was secured, to ask the page his name — so much he was struck with his very handsome features and form.

"Roland Græme," he said, repeating the words after the hesitating page. What! of the Grahams of the Lennox?"

"No, my lord," replied Roland; "my parents dwelt in the Debateable Land."

Murray made no further inquiry, but proceeded to read his dispatches; during the perusal of which his brow began to assume a stern expression of displeasure, as that of one who found something which at once surprised and disturbed him. He sat down on the nearest seat, frowned till his eyebrows almost met together, read the letter twice over, and was then silent for several minutes. At length, raising his head, his eye encountered that of the usher, who in vain endeavoured to exchange the look of eager and curious observation with which he had been perusing the Regent's features, for that open and unnoticing expression of countenance, which, in looking at all, seems as if it saw and marked nothing — a cast of look which may be practised with advantage by all those, of whatever degree, who are admitted to witness the familiar and unguarded hours of their superiors. Great men are as jealous of their thoughts as the wife of King Candaules was of her charms, and will as readily punish those who have, however involuntarily, beheld them in mental déshabillé and exposure.

"Leave the apartment, Hyndman," said the Regent, sternly, "and carry your observation elsewhere. You are too knowing, sir, for your post, which, by special order, is destined for men of blunter capacity. So! now you look more like a fool than you did," — (for Hyndman, as may easily be supposed, was not a little disconcerted by this rebuke) — "keep that confused stare, and it may keep your office. Begone, sir!"

The usher departed in dismay, not forgetting to register, amongst his other causes of dislike to Roland Græme, that he had been the witness of this disgraceful chiding. When he had left the apartment, the Regent again addressed the page.

"Your name, you say, is Armstrong?"

"No," replied Roland, "my name is Græme, so please you — Roland Græme, whose forbears were designated of Heathergill, in the Debateable Land."

"Ay, I knew it was a name from the Debateable Land. Hast thou any acquaintance in Edinburgh?"

"My lord," replied Roland, willing rather to evade this question than to answer it directly, for the prudence of being silent with respect to Lord Seyton's adventure immediately struck him, "I have been in Edinburgh scarce an hour, and that for the first time in my life."

"What! and thou Sir Halbert Glendinning's page?" said the Regent.

"I was brought up as my Lady's page," said the youth, "and left Avenel Castle for the first time in my life — at least since my childhood — only three days since."

"My Lady's page!" repeated the Earl of Murray, as if speaking to himself; "it was strange to send his Lady's page on a matter of such deep concernment — Morton will say it is of a piece with the nomination of his brother to be Abbot; and yet in some sort an inexperienced youth will best serve the turn. — What hast thou been taught, young man, in thy doughty apprenticeship?"

"To hunt, my lord, and to hawk," said Roland Græme.

"To hunt coneys, and to hawk at ouzels!" said the Regent, smiling; "for such are the sports of ladies and their followers."

Græme's cheek reddened deeply as he replied, not without some emphasis, "To hunt red-deer of the first head, and to strike down herons of the highest soar, my lord, which, in Lothian speech, may be termed, for aught I know, coneys and ouzels;—also I can wield a brand and couch a lance, according to our Border meaning; in inland speech these may be termed water-flags and bulrushes."

"Thy speech rings like metal," said the Regent, "and I pardon the sharpness of it for the truth. — Thou knowest, then, what belongs to the duty of a man-at-arms?"

"So far as exercise can teach it without real service in the field," answered Roland Græme; "but our Knight permitted none of his household to make raids, and I never had the good fortune to see a stricken field."

"The good fortune!" repeated the Regent, smiling somewhat sorrowfully, "take my word, young man, war is the only game from which both parties rise losers."

"Not always, my lord!" answered the page, with his characteristic audacity, "if fame speaks truth."

"How, sir?" said the Regent, colouring in his turn, and perhaps suspecting an indiscreet allusion to the height which he himself had attained by the hap of civil war.

"Because, my lord," said Roland Græme, without change of tone, "he who fights well, must have fame in life, or honour in death; and so war is a game from which no one can rise a loser."

The Regent smiled and shook his head, when at that moment the door opened, and the Earl of Morton presented himself.

"I come somewhat hastily," he said, "and I enter unannounced because my news are of weight—It is as I said; Edward Glendinning is named Abbot, and——"

"Hush, my lord!" said the Regent, "I know it, but——"

"And perhaps you knew it before I did, my Lord of Murray," answered Morton, his dark red brow growing darker and redder as he spoke.

"Morton," said Murray, "suspect me not — touch not mine honour — I have to suffer enough from the calumnies of foes, let me not have to contend with the unjust suspicions of my friends.—We are not alone," said he, recollecting himself, "or I could tell you more."

He led Morton into one of the deep embrasures which the windows formed in the massive wall, and which afforded a retiring place for their conversing apart. In this recess, Roland observed them speak together with much earnestness, Murray appearing to be grave and earnest, and Morton having a jealous and offended air, which seemed gradually to give way to the assurances of the Regent.

As their conversation grew more earnest, they became gradually louder in speech, having perhaps forgotten the presence of the page, the more readily as his position in the apartment placed him out of sight, so that he found himself unwillingly privy to more of their discourse than he cared to hear. For, page though he was, a mean curiosity after the secrets of others had never been numbered amongst Roland's failings; and moreover, with all his natural rashness, he could not but doubt the safety of becoming privy to the secret discourse of these powerful and dreaded men. Still he could neither stop his ears, nor with propriety leave the apartment; and while he thought of some means of signifying his presence, he had already heard so much, that, to have produced himself suddenly would have been as awkward, and perhaps as dangerous, as in quiet to abide the end of their conference. What he overheard, however, was but an imperfect part of their communication; and although an expert politician, acquainted with the circumstances of the times, would have had little difficulty in tracing the meaning, yet Roland Græme could only form very general and vague conjectures as to the import of their discourse.

"All is prepared," said Murray, "and Lindsay is setting forward — She must hesitate no longer—thou seest I act by thy counsel, and harden myself against softer considerations."

"True, my lord," replied Morton, "in what is necessary to gain power, you do not hesitate, but go boldly to the mark. But are you as careful to defend and preserve what you have won? — Why this establishment of domestics around her? — has not your sister men and maidens enough to tend her, but you must consent to this superfluous and dangerous retinue?"

"For shame, Morton! — a Princess, and my sister, could I do less than allow her due attendance?"

"Ay," replied Morton, "even thus fly all your shafts — smartly enough loosened from the bow, and not unskilfully aimed — but a breath of foolish affection ever crosses in the mid volley, and sways the arrow from the mark."

"Say not so, Morton," replied Murray, "I have both dared and done——"

"Yes, enough to gain, but not enough to keep — reckon not that she will think and act thus — you have wounded her deeply, both in pride and in power — it signifies nought, that you would tent now the wound with unavailing salves — as matters stand with you, you must forfeit the title of an affectionate brother, to hold that of a bold and determined statesman."

"Morton!" said Murray, with some impatience, "I brook not these taunts—what I have done I have done—what I must farther do, I must and will — but I am not made of iron like thee, and I cannot but remember—Enough of this—my purpose holds."

"And I warrant me," said Morton, "the choice of these domestic consolations will rest with——"

Here he whispered names which escaped Roland Græme's ear. Murray replied in a similar tone, but so much raised towards the conclusion of the sentence, that the page heard these words—"And of him I hold myself secure, by Glendinning's recommendation."

"Ay, which may be as much trustworthy as his late conduct at the Abbey of Saint Mary's—you have heard that his brother's election has taken place. Your favourite Sir Halbert, my Lord of Murray, has as much fraternal affection as yourself."

"By heaven, Morton, that taunt demanded an unfriendly answer, but I pardon it, for your brother also is concerned; but this election shall be annulled. I tell you, Earl of Morton, while I hold the sword of state in my royal nephew's name, neither Lord nor Knight in Scotland shall dispute my authority; and if I bear with insults from my friends, it is only while I know them to be such, and forgive their follies for their faithfulness."

Morton muttered what seemed to be some excuse, and the Regent answered him in a milder tone, and then subjoined, "Besides, I have another pledge than Glendinning's recommendation, for this youth's fidelity—his nearest relative has placed herself in my hands as his security, to be dealt withal as his doings shall deserve."

"That is something," replied Morton; "but yet in fair love and good-will, I must still pray you to keep on your guard. The foes are stirring again, as horse-flies and hornets become busy so soon as the storm-blast is over. George of Seyton was crossing the causeway this morning with a score of men at his back, and had a ruffle with my friends of the house of Leslie—they met at the Tron, and were fighting hard, when the provost, with his guard of partisans, came in thirdsman, and staved them asunder with their halberds, as men part dog and bear."

"He hath my order for such interference," said the Regent—"Has any one been hurt?"

"George of Seyton himself, by black Ralph Leslie—the devil take the rapier that ran not through from side to side! Ralph has a bloody cox-comb, by a blow from a messan-page whom nobody knew—Dick Seyton of Windygowl is run through the arm, and two gallants of the Leslies have suffered phlebotomy. This is all the gentle blood which has been spilled in the revel; but a yeoman or two on both sides have had bones broken and ears chopped. The ostlere-wives, who are like to be the only losers by their miscarriage, have dragged the knaves off the street, and are crying a drunken coronach over them."

"You take it lightly, Douglas," said the Regent; "these broils and feuds would shame the capital of the great Turk, let alone that of a Christian and reformed state. But, if I live, this gear shall be amended; and men shall say, when they read my story, that if it were my cruel hap to rise to power by the dethronement of a sister, I employed it, when gained, for the benefit of the commonweal."

"And of your friends," replied Morton; "wherefore I trust for your instant order annulling the election of this lurdane Abbot, Edward Glendinning."

"You shall be presently satisfied," said the Regent; and stepping forward, he began to call, "So ho, Hyndman!" when suddenly his eye lighted on Roland Græme—"By my faith, Douglas," said he, turning to his friend, "here have been three at counsel!"

"Ay, but only two can keep counsel," said Morton; "the galliard must be disposed of."

"For shame, Morton—an orphan boy!—Hearken thee, my child—Thou hast told me some of thy accomplishments—canst thou speak truth?"

"Ay, my lord, when it serves my turn," replied Græme.

"It shall serve thy turn now," said the Regent; "and falsehood shall be thy destruction. How much hast thou heard or understood of what we two have spoken together?"

"But little, my lord," replied Roland Græme boldly, "which met my apprehension, saving that it seemed to me as if in something you doubted the faith of the Knight of Avenel, under whose roof I was nurtured."

"And what hast thou to say on that point, young man?" continued the Regent, bending his eyes upon him with a keen and strong expression of observation.

"That," said the page, "depends on the quality of those who speak against his honour whose bread I have long eaten. If they be my inferiors, I say they lie, and will maintain what I say with my baton; if my equals, still I say they lie, and will do battle in the quarrel, if they list, with my sword; if my superiors"—he paused.

"Proceed boldly," said the Regent—"What if thy superiors said aught that nearly touched your master's honour?"

"I would say," replied Græme, "that he did ill to slander the absent, and that my master was a man who could render an account of his actions to any one who should manfully demand it of him to his face."

"And it were manfully said," replied the Regent—"what thinkest thou, my Lord of Morton?"

"I think," replied Morton, "that if the young galliard resemble a certain ancient friend of ours, as much in the craft of his disposition as he does in eye and in brow, there may be a wide difference betwixt what he means and what he speaks."

"And whom meanest thou that he resembles so closely?" said Murray.

"Even the true and trusty Julian Avenel," replied Morton.

"But this youth belongs to the Debateable Land," said Murray.

"It may be so; but Julian was an outlaying striker of venison, and made many a far cast when he had a fair doe in chase."

"Pshaw!" said the Regent, "this is but idle talk—Here, thou Hyndman—thou curiosity," calling to the usher, who now entered,—"conduct this youth to his companion—You will both," he said to Græme, "keep yourselves in readiness to travel on short notice."—And then motioning to him courteously to withdraw, he broke up the interview.

Chapter the Nineteenth.

It is and is not—'tis the thing I sought for,
Have kneel'd for, pray'd for, risk'd my fame and life for,
And yet it is not—no more than the shadow
Upon the hard, cold, flat, and polished mirror,
Is the warm, graceful, rounded, living substance
Which it presents in form and lineament.

OLD PLAY.

THE usher, with gravity which ill concealed a jealous scowl, conducted Roland Græme to a lower apartment, where he found his comrade the falconer. The man of office then briefly acquainted them that this would be their residence till his Grace's farther orders; that they were to go to the pantry, to the buttery, to the cellar, and to the kitchen, at the usual hours, to receive the allowances becoming their station,—instructions which Adam Woodcock's old familiarity with the court made him perfectly understand—"For your beds," he said, "you must go to the hostelry of Saint Michael's, in respect the palace is now full of the domestics of the greater nobles."

No sooner was the usher's back turned than Adam exclaimed, with all the glee of eager curiosity, "And now, Master Roland, the news—the news—come unbutton thy pouch, and give us thy tidings—What says the Regent?

asks he for Adam Woodcock?—and is all soldered up, or must the Abbot of Unreason strap for it?"

"All is well in that quarter," said the page; "and for the rest—But, hey-day, what! have you taken the chain and medal off from my bonnet?"

"And meet time it was, when yon usher, vinegar-faced rogue that he is, began to inquire what Popish trangam you were wearing—By the mass, the metal would have been confiscated for conscience-sake, like your other rattle-trap yonder at Avenel, which Mistress Lilias bears about on her shoes in the guise of a pair of shoe-buckles—This comes of carrying Popish nick-nackets about you."

"The jade!" exclaimed Roland Græme, "has she melted down my rosary into buckles for her clumsy hoofs, which will set off such a garnish nearly as well as a cow's might?—But, hang her, let her keep them—many a dog's trick have I played old Lilias, for want of having something better to do, and the buckles will serve for a remembrance. Do you remember the verjuice I put into the comfits, when old Wingate and she were to breakfast together on Easter morning?"

"In troth do I, Master Roland—the major-domo's mouth was as crooked as a hawk's beak for the whole morning afterwards, and any other page in your room would have tasted the discipline of the porter's lodge for it. But my Lady's favour stood between your skin and many a jerking—Lord send you may be the better for her protection in such matters!"

"I am least grateful for it, Adam! and I am glad you put me in mind of it."

"Well, but the news, my young master," said Woodcock, "spell me the tidings—what are we to fly at next?—what did the Regent say to you?"

"Nothing that I am to repeat again," said Roland Græme, shaking his head.

"Why, hey-day," said Adam, "how prudent we are become all of a sudden! You have advanced rarely in brief space, Master Roland. You have well nigh had your head broken, and you have gained your gold chain, and you have made an enemy, Master Usher to wit, with his two legs like hawks' perches, and you have had audience of the first man in the realm, and bear as much mystery in your brow, as if you had flown in the court-sky ever since you were hatched. I believe, in my soul, you would run with a piece of the egg-shell on your head like the curlews, which (I would we were after them again) we used to call whaups in the Halidome and its neighbourhood. But sit thee down, boy; Adam Woodcock was never the lad to seek to enter into forbidden secrets—sit thee down, and I will go and fetch the vivers—I know the butler and the pantler of old."

The good-natured falconer set forth upon his errand, busying himself about procuring their refreshment; and, during his absence, Roland Græme abandoned himself to the strange, complicated, and yet heart-stirring reflections, to which the events of the morning had given rise. Yesterday he was of neither mark nor likelihood, a vagrant boy, the attendant on a relative, of whose sane judgment he himself had not the highest opinion; but now he had become, he knew not why, or wherefore, or to what extent, the custodier, as the Scottish phrase went, of some important state secret, in the safe keeping of which the Regent himself was concerned. It did not diminish from, but rather added to the interest of a situation so unexpected, that Roland himself did not perfectly understand wherein he stood committed by the state secrets, in which he had unwittingly become participator. On the contrary, he felt like one who looks on a romantic landscape, of which he sees the features for the first time, and then obscured with mist and driving tempest. The imperfect glimpse which the eye catches of rocks, trees, and other objects around him, adds double dignity to these shrouded mountains and darkened abysses, of which the height, depth, and extent, are left to imagination.

But mortals, especially at the well-appetized age which precedes twenty years, are seldom so much engaged either by real or conjectural subjects of speculation, but that their earthly wants claim their hour of attention. And with many a smile did our hero, so the reader may term him if he will, hail the re-appearance of his friend Adam Woodcock, bearing on one platter a tremendous portion of boiled beef, and on another a plentiful allowance of greens, or rather what the Scotch call lang-kale. A groom followed with bread, salt, and the other means of setting forth a meal; and when they had both placed on the oaken table what they bore in their hands, the falconer observed, that since he knew the court, it had got harder and harder every day to the poor gentlemen and yeoman retainers, but that now it was an absolute flaying of a flea for the hide and tallow. Such thronging to the wicket, and such churlish answers, and such bare beef-bones, such a shouldering at the buttery-hatch and cellarage, and nought to be gained beyond small insufficient single ale, or at best with a single straike of malt to counterbalance a double allowance of water—"By the mass, though, my young friend," said he, while he saw the food disappearing fast under Roland's active exertions, "it is not so well to lament for former times as to take the advantage of the present, else we are like to lose on both sides."

So saying, Adam Woodcock drew his chair towards the table, unsheathed his knife, (for every one carried that minister of festive distribution for himself,) and imitated his young companion's example, who for the moment had lost his anxiety for the future in the eager satisfaction of an appetite sharpened by youth and abstinence.

In truth, they made, though the materials were sufficiently simple, a very respectable meal, at the expense of the royal allowance; and Adam Woodcock, notwithstanding the deliberate censure which he had passed on the household beer of the palace, had taken the fourth deep draught of the black jack ere he remembered him that he had spoken in its dispraise. Flinging himself jollily and luxuriously back in an old danske elbow-chair, and looking with careless glee towards the page, extending at the same time his right leg, and stretching the other easily over it, he reminded his companion that he had not yet heard the ballad which he had made for the Abbot of Unreason's revel. And accordingly he struck merrily up with

"The Pope, that pagan full of pride,
Has blinded us full lang"——

Roland Græme, who felt no great delight, as may be supposed, in the falconer's satire, considering its subject, began to snatch up his mantle, and fling it around his shoulders, an action which instantly interrupted the ditty of Adam Woodcock.

"Where the vengeance are you going now," he said, "thou restless boy? —Thou hast quicksilver in the veins of thee to a certainty, and canst no more abide any douce and sensible communing, than a hoodless hawk would keep perched on my wrist!"

"Why, Adam," replied the page, "if you must needs know, I am about to take a walk and look at this fair city. One may as well be still mewed up in the old castle of the lake, if one is to sit the live-long night between four walls, and hearken to old ballads."

"It is a new ballad—the Lord help thee!" replied Adam, "and that one of the best that ever was matched with a rousing chorus."

"Be it so," said the page, "I will hear it another day, when the rain is dashing against the windows, and there is neither steed stamping, nor spur jingling, nor feather waving in the neighbourhood to mar my marking it well. But, even now, I want to be in the world, and to look about me."

"But the never a stride shall you go without me," said the falconer, "until the Regent shall take you whole and sound off my hand; and so, if you will, we may go to the hostelrie of Saint Michael's, and there you will see company enough, but through the casement, mark you me; for as to rambling through the street to seek Seytons and Leslies, and having a dozen holes drilled in your new jacket with rapier and poniard, I will yield no way to it."

"To the hostelrie of Saint Michael's, then, with all my heart," said the page; and they left the palace accordingly, rendered to the sentinels at the gate, who had now taken their posts for the evening, a strict account of their names and business, were dismissed through a small wicket of the close-barred portal, and soon reached the inn or hostelrie of Saint Michael, which stood in a large court-yard, off the main street, close under the descent of the Calton-hill. The place, wide, waste, and uncomfortable, resembled rather an Eastern caravansary, where men found shelter indeed, but were obliged to supply themselves with every thing else, than one of our modern inns;

> Where not one comfort shall to those be lost,
> Who never ask, or never feel, the cost.

But still, to the inexperienced eye of Roland Græme, the bustle and confusion of this place of public resort, furnished excitement and amusement. In the large room, into which they had rather found their own way than been ushered by mine host, travellers and natives of the city entered and departed, met and greeted, gamed or drank together, forming the strongest contrast to the stern and monotonous order and silence with which matters were conducted in the well-ordered household of the Knight of Avenel. Altercation of every kind, from brawling to jesting, was going on amongst the groups around them, and yet the noise and mingled voices seemed to disturb no one and indeed to be noticed by no others than by those who composed the group to which the speaker belonged.

The falconer passed through the apartment to a projecting latticed window, which formed a sort of recess from the room itself; and having here ensconced himself and his companion, he called for some refreshments; and a tapster, after he had shouted for the twentieth time, accommodated him with the remains of a cold capon and a neat's tongue, together with a pewter stoup of weak French vin-de-pays. "Fetch a stoup of brandy-wine, thou knave—We will be jolly to-night, Master Roland," said he, when he saw himself thus accommodated, "and let care come to-morrow."

But Roland had eaten too lately to enjoy the good cheer; and feeling his curiosity much sharper than his appetite, he made it his choice to look out of the lattice, which overhung a large yard, surrounded by the stables of the hostelrie, and fed his eyes on the busy sight beneath, while Adam Woodcock, after he had compared his companion to the "Laird of Macfarlane's geese, who liked their play better than their meat," disposed of his time with the aid of cup and trencher, occasionally humming the burden of his birth-strangled ballad, and beating time to it with his fingers on the little round table. In this exercise he was frequently interrupted by the exclamations of his companion, as he saw something new in the yard beneath, to attract and interest him.

It was a busy scene, for the number of gentlemen and nobles who were now crowded into the city, had filled all spare stables and places of public reception with their horses and military attendants. There were some score of yeomen, dressing their own or their masters' horses in the yard, whistling, singing, laughing, and upbraiding each other, in a style of wit which the good order of Avenel Castle rendered strange to Roland Græme's ears. Others were busy repairing their own arms, or cleaning those of their masters. One fellow, having just bought a bundle of twenty spears, was sitting in a corner, employed in painting the white staves of the weapons with yellow and vermillion. Other lacqueys led large stag-hounds, or wolf-dogs, of noble race, carefully muzzled to prevent accidents to passengers. All came and went, mixed together and separated, under the delighted eye of the page, whose imagination had not even conceived a scene so gaily diversified with the objects he had most pleasure in beholding; so that he was perpetually breaking the quiet reverie of honest Woodcock, and the mental progress which he was making in his ditty, by exclaiming, "Look here, Adam — look at the bonny bay horse — Saint Anthony, what a gallant forehand he hath got! — and see the goodly gray, which yonder fellow in the frieze-jacket is dressing as awkwardly as if he had never touched aught but a cow—I would I were nigh him to teach him his trade! — And lo you, Adam, the gay Milan armour that the yeoman is scouring, all steel and silver, like our Knight's prime suit, of which old Wingate makes such account — And see to yonder pretty wench, Adam, who comes tripping through them all with her milk-pail—I warrant me she has had a long walk from the loaning; she has a stammel waistcoat, like your favourite Cicely Sunderland, Master Adam!"

"By my hood, lad," answered the falconer, "it is well for thee thou wert brought up where grace grew. Even in the Castle of Avenel thou wert a wild-blood enough, but hadst thou been nurtured here, within a flight-shot of the Court, thou hadst been the veriest crack-hemp of a page that ever wore feather in thy bonnet or steel by thy side: truly, I wish it may end well with thee."

"Nay, but leave thy senseless humming and drumming, old Adam, and come to the window ere thou hast drenched thy senses in the pint-pot there. See here comes a merry minstrel with his crowd, and a wench with him, that dances with bells at her ankles; and see, the yeomen and pages leave their horses and the armour they were cleaning, and gather round, as is very natural, to hear the music. Come, old Adam, we will thither too."

"You shall call me cutt if I do go down," said Adam; "you are near as good minstrelsy as the stroller can make, if you had but the grace to listen to it."

"But the wench in the stammel waistcoat is stopping too, Adam — by heaven, they are going to dance! Frieze-jacket wants to dance with stammel waistcoat, but she is coy and recusant."

Then suddenly changing his tone of levity into one of deep interest and surprise, he exclaimed, "Queen of Heaven! what is it that I see!" and then remained silent.

The sage Adam Woodcock, who was in a sort of languid degree amused with the page's exclamations, even while he professed to despise them, became at length rather desirous to set his tongue once more a-going, that he might enjoy the superiority afforded by his own intimate familiarity with all the circumstances which excited in his young companion's mind so much wonderment.

"Well, then," he said at last, "what is it you do see, Master Roland, that you have become mute all of a sudden?"

Roland returned no answer.

"I say, Master Roland Græme," said the falconer, "it is manners in my country for a man to speak when he is spoken to."

Roland Græme remained silent.

"The murrain is in the boy," said Adam Woodcock, "he has stared out his eyes, and talked his tongue to pieces, I think."

The falconer hastily drank off his can of wine, and came to Roland, who stood like a statue, with his eyes eagerly bent on the court-yard, though Adam Woodcock was unable to detect amongst the joyous scenes which it exhibited aught that could deserve such devoted attention.

"The lad is mazed!" said the falconer to himself.

But Roland Græme had good reasons for his surprise, though they were not such as he could communicate to his companion.

The touch of the old minstrel's instrument, for he had already begun to play, had drawn in several auditors from the street when one entered the gate of the yard, whose appearance exclusively arrested the attention of Roland Græme. He was of his own age, or a good deal younger, and from his dress and bearing might be of the same rank and calling, having all the air of coxcombry and pretension, which accorded with a handsome, though slight and low figure, and an elegant dress, in part hid by a large purple cloak. As he entered, he cast a glance up towards the windows, and, to his extreme astonishment, under the purple velvet bonnet and white feather, Roland recognized the features so deeply impressed on his memory, the bright and clustered tresses, the laughing full blue eyes, the well-formed eyebrows, the nose, with the slightest possible inclination to be aquiline, the ruby lip, of which an arch and half-suppressed smile seemed the habitual expression — in short, the form and face of Catherine Seyton; in man's attire, however, and mimicking, as it seemed, not unsuccessfully, the bearing of a youthful but forward page.

"Saint George and Saint Andrew!" exclaimed the amazed Roland Græme to himself, "was there ever such an audacious quean! — she seems a little ashamed of her mummery too, for she holds the lap of her cloak to her face, and her colour is heightened—but Santa Maria, how she threads the throng, with as firm and bold a step as if she had never tied petticoat round her waist!—Holy Saints! she holds up her riding-rod as if she would lay it about some of their ears, that stand most in her way—by the hand of my father! she bears herself like the very model of pagehood.—Hey! what! sure she will not strike frieze-jacket in earnest?" But he was not long left in doubt; for the lout whom he had before repeatedly noticed, standing in the way of the bustling page, and maintaining his place with clownish obstinacy or stupidity, the advanced riding-rod was, without a moment's hesitation, sharply applied to his shoulders, in a manner which made him spring aside, rubbing the part of the body which had received so unceremonious a hint that it was in the way of his betters. The party injured growled forth an oath or two of indignation, and Roland Græme began to think of flying down stairs to the assistance of the translated Catherine; but the laugh of the yard was against frieze-jacket, which indeed had, in those days, small chance of fair play in a quarrel with velvet and embroidery; so that the fellow, who was menial in the inn, slunk back to finish his task of dressing the bonny gray, laughed at by all, but most by the wench in the stammel waist-coat, his fellow-servant, who, to crown his disgrace, had the cruelty to cast an applauding smile upon the author of the injury, while, with a freedom more like the milk-maid of the town than she of the plains, she accosted him with — "Is there any one you want here, my pretty gentleman, that you seem in such haste?"

"I seek a sprig of a lad," said the seeming gallant, "with a sprig of holly in his cap, black hair, and black eyes, green jacket, and the air of a country coxcomb—I have sought him through every close and alley in the Canongate, the fiend gore him!"

"Why, God-a-mercy, Nun!" muttered Roland Græme, much bewildered.

"I will inquire him presently out for your fair young worship," said the wench of the inn.

"Do," said the gallant squire, "and if you bring me to him, you shall have a groat to-night, and a kiss on Sunday when you have on a cleaner kirtle."

"Why, God-a-mercy, Nun!" again muttered Roland, "this is a note above E La."

In a moment after, the servant entered the room, and ushered in the object of his surprise.

While the disguised vestal looked with unabashed brow, and bold and rapid glance of her eye, through the various parties in the large old room, Roland Græme, who felt an internal awkward sense of bashful confusion, which he deemed altogether unworthy of the bold and dashing character to which he aspired, determined not to be browbeaten and put down by this singular female, but to meet her with a glance of recognition so sly, sc penetrating, so expressively humorous, as should show her at once he was in possession of her secret and master of her fate, and should compel her to humble herself towards him, at least into the look and manner of respectful and deprecating observance.

This was extremely well planned; but just as Roland had called up the knowing glance, the suppressed smile, the shrewd intelligent look, which was to ensure his triumph, he encountered the bold, firm, and steady gaze of his brother or sister-page, who, casting on him a falcon glance, and recognizing him at once as the object of his search, walked up with the most unconcerned look, the most free and undaunted composure, and hailed him with "You, Sir Holly-top, I would speak with you."

The steady coolness and assurance with which these words were uttered, although the voice was the very voice he had heard at the old convent, and although the features more nearly resembled those of Catharine when seen close than when viewed from a distance, produced, nevertheless, such a confusion in Roland's mind, that he became uncertain whether he was not still under a mistake from the beginning; the knowing shrewdness which should have animated his visage faded into a sheepish bashfulness, and the half-suppressed but most intelligible smile, became the senseless giggle of one who laughs to cover his own disorder of ideas.

"Do they understand a Scotch tongue in thy country, Holly-top?" said this marvellous specimen of metamorphosis. "I said I would speak with thee."

"What is your business with my comrade, my young chick of the game?" said Adam Woodcock, willing to step in to his companion's assistance, though totally at a loss to account for the sudden disappearance of all Roland's usual smartness and presence of mind.

"Nothing to you, my old cock of the perch," replied the gallant; "go mind your hawk's castings. I guess by your bag and your gauntlet that you are squire of the body to a sort of kites."

He laughed as he spoke, and the laugh reminded Roland so irresistibly of the hearty fit of risibility, in which Catherine had indulged at his expense when they first met in the old nunnery, that he could scarce help exclaiming, "Catherine Seyton, by Heavens!"—He checked the exclamation, however, and only said, "I think, sir, we two are not totally strangers to each other."

"We must have met in our dreams then," said the youth; "and my days are too busy to remember what I think on at nights."

"Or apparently to remember upon one day those whom you may have seen on the preceding eve," said Roland Græme.

The youth in his turn cast on him a look of some surprise, as he replied, "I know no more of what you mean than does the horse I ride on—if there be offence in your words, you shall find me ready to take it as any lad in Lothian."

"You know well," said Roland, "though it pleases you to use the language of a stranger, that with you I have no purpose to quarrel."

"Let me do mine errand, then, and be rid of you," said the page. "Step hither this way, out of that old leathern fist's hearing."

They walked into the recess of the window, which Roland had left upon the youth's entrance into the apartment. The messenger then turned his back on the company, after casting a hasty and sharp glance around to see if they were observed. Roland did the same, and the page in the purple mantle thus addressed him, taking at the same time from under his cloak a short but beautifully wrought sword, with the hilt and ornaments upon the sheath of silver, massively chased and over-gilded—"I bring you this weapon from a friend, who gives it you under the solemn condition, that you will not unsheath it until you are commanded by your rightful Sovereign. For your warmth of temper is known, and the presumption with which you intrude yourself into the quarrels of others; and, therefore, this is laid upon you as a penance by those who wish you well, and whose hand will influence your destiny for good or for evil. This is what I was charged to tell you. So if you will give a fair word for a fair sword, and pledge your promise, with hand and glove, good and well; and if not, I will carry back Caliburn to those who sent it."

"And may I not ask who these are?" said Roland Græme, admiring at the same time the beauty of the weapon thus offered him.

"My commission in no way leads me to answer such a question," said he of the purple mantle.

"But if I am offended," said Roland, "may I not draw to defend myself?"

"Not *this* weapon," answered the sword-bearer; "but you have your own at command, and, besides, for what do you wear your poniard?"

"For no good," said Adam Woodcock, who had now approached close to them, "and that I can witness as well as any one."

"Stand back, fellow," said the messenger, "thou hast an intrusive curious face, that will come by a buffet if it is found where it has no concern."

"A buffet, my young Master Malapert?" said Adam, drawing back, however; "best keep down fist, or, by Our Lady, buffet will beget buffet!"

"Be patient, Adam Woodcock," said Roland Græme; "and let me pray you, fair sir, since by such addition you choose for the present to be addressed, may I not barely unsheathe this fair weapon, in pure simplicity of desire to know whether so fair a hilt and scabbard are matched with a befitting blade?"

"By no manner of means," said the messenger; "at a word, you must take it under the promise that you never draw it until you receive the commands of your lawful Sovereign, or you must leave it alone."

"Under that condition, and coming from your friendly hand, I accept of the sword," said Roland, taking it from his hand; "but credit me, if we are to work together in any weighty emprise, as I am induced to believe, some confidence and openness on your part will be necessary to give the right impulse to my zeal — I press for no more at present, it is enough that you understand me."

"I understand you!" said the page, exhibiting the appearance of unfeigned surprise in his turn, — "Renounce me if I do! — here you stand jiggeting, and sniggling, and looking cunning, as if there were some mighty matter of intrigue and common understanding betwixt you and me, whom you never set your eyes on before!"

"What!" said Roland Græme, "will you deny that we have met before?"

"Marry that I will, in any Christian court," said the other page.

"And will you also deny," said Roland, "that it was recommended to us to study each other's features well, that in whatever disguise the time might impose upon us, each should recognize in the other the secret agent of a mighty work? Do not you remember, that Sister Magdalen and Dame Bridget——"

The messenger here interrupted him, shrugging up his shoulders, with a look of compassion, "Bridget and Magdalen! why, this is madness and dreaming! Hark ye, Master Holly-top, your wits are gone on wool-gathering; comfort yourself with a caudle, and thatch your brain-sick noddle with a woollen night-cap, and so God be with you!"

As he concluded this polite parting address, Adam Woodcock, who was again seated by the table on which stood the now empty can, said to him, "Will you drink a cup, young man, in the way of courtesy, now you have done your errand, and listen to a good song?" and without waiting for an answer, he commenced his ditty,—

"The Pope, that pagan full of pride,
Hath blinded us full lang——"

It is probable that the good wine had made some innovation in the falconer's brain, otherwise he would have recollected the danger of introducing any thing like political or polemical pleasantry into a public assemblage at a time when men's minds were in a state of great irritability. To do him justice, he perceived his error, and stopped short so soon as he saw that the word Pope had at once interrupted the separate conversations of the various parties which were assembled in the apartment; and that many began to draw themselves up, bridle, look big, and prepare to take part in the impending brawl; while others, more decent and cautious persons, hastily paid down their lawing, and prepared to leave the place ere bad should come to worse.

And to worse it was soon likely to come; for no sooner did Woodcock's ditty reach the ear of the stranger page, than, uplifting his riding-rod, he exclaimed, "He who speaks irreverently of the Holy Father of the church in my presence, is the cub of a heretic wolf-bitch, and I will switch him as I would a mongrel-cur."

"And I will break thy young pate," said Adam, "if thou darest to lift a finger to me." And then, in defiance of the young Drawcansir's threats, with a stout heart and dauntless accent, he again uplifted the stave.

"The Pope, that pagan full of pride,
Hath blinded——"

But Adam was able to proceed no farther, being himself unfortunately blinded by a stroke of the impatient youth's switch across his eyes. Enraged at once by the smart and the indignity, the falconer started up, and darkling as he was, for his eyes watered too fast to permit his seeing any thing, he would soon have been at close grips with his insolent adversary, had not Roland Græme, contrary to his nature, played for once the prudent man and the peacemaker, and thrown himself betwixt them, imploring Woodcock's patience. "You know not," he said, "with whom you have to do.—And thou," addressing the messenger, who stood scornfully laughing at Adam's rage, "get thee gone, whoever thou art; if thou be'st what I guess thee, thou well knowest there are earnest reasons why thou shouldst."

"Thou hast hit it right for once, Holly-top," said the gallant, "though I guess you drew your bow at a venture.—Here, host, let this yeoman have a pottle of wine to wash the smart out of his eyes—and there is a French crown for him." So saying, he threw the piece of money on the table, and left the apartment, with a quick yet steady pace, looking firmly at right and left, as if to defy interruption: and snapping his fingers at two or three respectable burghers, who, declaring it was a shame that any one should be suffered to rant and ruffle in defence of the Pope, were labouring to find the hilts of their swords, which had got for the present unhappily entangled in the folds of their cloaks. But, as the adversary was gone ere any of them had reached his weapon, they did not think it necessary to unsheath cold iron, but merely observed to each other, "This is more than masterful violence, to see a poor man stricken in the face just for singing a ballad against the whore of Babylon! If the Pope's champions are to be bangsters in our very change-houses, we shall soon have the old shavelings back again."

"The provost should look to it," said another, "and have some five or six armed with partisans, to come in upon the first whistle, to teach these gallants their lesson. For, look you, neighbour Lugleather, it is not for decent householders like ourselves to be brawling with the godless grooms and pert pages of the nobles, that are bred up to little else save bloodshed and blasphemy."

"For all that, neighbour," said Lugleather, "I would have curried that youngster as properly as ever I curried a lamb's hide, had not the hilt of my bilboo been for the instant beyond my grasp; and before I could turn my girdle, gone was my master!"

"Ay," said the others, "the devil go with him, and peace abide with us — I give my rede, neighbours, that we pay the lawing, and be stepping homeward, like brother and brother; for old Saint Giles's is tolling curfew, and the street grows dangerous at night."

With that the good burghers adjusted their cloaks, and prepared for their departure, while he that seemed the briskest of the three, laying his hand on his Andrea Ferrara, observed, "that they that spoke in the praise of the Pope on the High-gate of Edinburgh, had best bring the sword of Saint Peter to defend them."

While the ill-humour excited by the insolence of the young aristocrat was thus evaporating in empty menace, Roland Græme had to control the far more serious indignation of Adam Woodcock. "Why, man, it was but a switch across the mazzard—blow your nose, dry your eyes, and you will see all the better for it."

"By this light, which I cannot see," said Adam Woodcock, "thou hast been a false friend to me, young man — neither taking up my rightful quarrel, nor letting me fight it out myself."

"Fy for shame, Adam Woodcock," replied the youth, determined to turn the tables on him, and become in turn the counsellor of good order and peaceable demeanour — "I say, fy for shame! — Alas, that you will speak thus! Here are you sent with me, to prevent my innocent youth getting into snares——"

"I wish your innocent youth were cut short with a halter, with all my heart," said Adam, who began to see which way the admonition tended.

—"And instead of setting before me," continued Roland, "an example of patience and sobriety becoming the falconer of Sir Halbert Glendinning, you quaff me off I know not how many flagons of ale, besides a gallon of wine, and a full measure of strong waters."

"It was but one small pottle," said poor Adam, whom consciousness of his own indiscretion now reduced to a merely defensive warfare.

"It was enough to pottle you handsomely, however," said the page — "And then, instead of going to bed to sleep off your liquor, must you sit singing your roistering songs about popes and pagans, till you have got your eyes almost switched out of your head; and but for my interference, whom your drunken ingratitude accuses of deserting you, yon galliard would have cut your throat, for he was whipping out a whinger as broad as my hand, and as sharp as a razor — And these are lessons for an inexperienced youth!—Oh, Adam! out upon you! out upon you!"

"Marry, amen, and with all my heart," said Adam; "out upon my folly for expecting any thing but impertinent raillery from a page like thee, that if he saw his father in a scrape, would laugh at him, instead of lending him aid."

"Nay, but I will lend you aid," said the page, still laughing, "that is, I will lend thee aid to thy chamber, good Adam, where thou shalt sleep off wine and ale, ire and indignation, and awake the next morning with as much fair wit as nature has blessed thee withal. Only one thing I will warn thee, good Adam, that henceforth and for ever, when thou railest at me for being somewhat hot at hand, and rather too prompt to out with poniard or so, thy admonition shall serve as a prologue to the memorable adventure of the switching of Saint Michael's."

With such condoling expressions he got the crest-fallen falconer to his bed, and then retired to his own pallet, where it was some time ere he could fall asleep. If the messenger whom he had seen were really Catherine Seyton, what a masculine virago and termagant must she be! and stored with what an inimitable command of insolence and assurance!—The brass on her brow would furbish the front of twenty pages; "and I should know," thought Roland, "what that amounts to — And yet, her features, her look, her light gait, her laughing eye, the art with which she disposed the mantle to show no more of her limbs than needs must be seen — I am glad she had at least that grace left — the voice, the smile — it must have been Catherine Seyton, or the devil in her likeness! One thing is good, I have silenced the eternal predications of that ass, Adam Woodcock, who has set up for being a preacher and a governor over me, so soon as he has left the hawks' mew behind him."

And with this comfortable reflection, joined to the happy indifference which youth hath for the events of the morrow, Roland Græme fell fast asleep.

Chapter the Twentieth.

> Now have you reft me from my staff, my guide,
> Who taught my youth, as men teach untamed falcons,
> To use my strength discreetly — I am reft
> Of comrade and of counsel.
>
> OLD PLAY.

In the gray of the next morning's dawn, there was a loud knocking at the gate of the hostelrie; and those without, proclaiming that they came in the name of the Regent, were instantly admitted. A moment or two afterwards, Michael Wing-the-wind stood by the bedside of our travellers.

"Up! up!" he said, "there is no slumber where Murray hath work ado."

Both sleepers sprung up, and began to dress themselves.

"You, old friend," said Wing-the-wind to Adam Woodcock, "must to horse instantly, with this packet to the Monks of Kennaquhair; and with this," delivering them as he spoke, "to the Knight of Avenel."

"As much as commanding the monks to annul their election, I'll warrant me, of an Abbot," quoth Adam Woodcock, as he put the packets into his bag, "and charging my master to see it done — To hawk at one brother with another, is less than fair play, methinks."

"Fash not thy beard about it, old boy," said Michael, "but betake thee to the saddle presently; for if these orders are not obeyed, there will be bare walls at the Kirk of Saint Mary's, and it may be at the Castle of Avenel to boot; for I heard my Lord of Morton loud with the Regent, and we are at a pass that we cannot stand with him anent trifles."

"But," said Adam, "touching the Abbot of Unreason — what say they to that outbreak — An they be shrewishly disposed, I were better pitch the packets to Satan, and take the other side of the Border for my bield."

"Oh, that was passed over as a jest, since there was little harm done.— But, hark thee, Adam," continued his comrade, "if there was a dozen vacant abbacies in your road, whether of jest or earnest, reason or unreason, draw thou never one of their mitres over thy brows — The time is not fitting, man! — besides, our Maiden longs to clip the neck of a fat churchman."

"She shall never sheer mine in that capacity," said the falconer, while he knotted the kerchief in two or three double folds around his sunburnt bull-neck, calling out at the same time, "Master Roland, Master Roland, make haste! we must back to perch and mew, and, thank Heaven, more than our own wit, with our bones whole, and without a stab in the stomach."

"Nay, but," said Wing-the-wind, "the page goes not back with you; the Regent has other employment for him."

"Saints and sorrows!" exclaimed the falconer—"Master Roland Græme to remain here, and I to return to Avenel!—Why, it cannot be—the child cannot manage himself in this wide world without me, and I question if he will stoop to any other whistle than mine own; there are times I myself can hardly bring him to my lure."

It was at Roland's tongue's end to say something concerning the occasion they had for using mutually each other's prudence, but the real anxiety which Adam evinced at parting with him, took away his disposition to such ungracious raillery. The falconer did not altogether escape, however, for, in turning his face towards the lattice, his friend Michael caught a glimpse of it, and exclaimed, "I prithee, Adam Woodcock, what hast thou been doing with these eyes of thine? They are swelled to the starting from the socket!"

"Nought in the world," said he, after casting a deprecating glance at Roland Græme, "but the effect of sleeping in this d——d truckle without a pillow."

"Why, Adam Woodcock, thou must be grown strangely dainty," said his old companion; "I have known thee sleep all night with no better pillow than a bush of ling, and start up with the sun, as glegg as a falcon; and now thine eyes resemble——"

"Tush, man, what signifies how mine eyes look now?" said Adam—"let us but roast a crab-apple, pour a pottle of ale on it, and bathe our throats withal, thou shalt see a change in me."

"And thou wilt be in heart to sing thy jolly ballad about the Pope," said his comrade.

"Ay, that I will," replied the falconer, "that is, when we have left this quiet town five miles behind us, if you will take your hobby and ride so far on my way."

"Nay, that I may not," said Michael—"I can but stop to partake your morning draught, and see you fairly to horse—I will see that they saddle them, and toast the crab for thee, without loss of time."

During his absence the falconer took the page by the hand—"May I never hood hawk again," said the good-natured fellow, "if I am not as sorry to part with you as if you were a child of mine own, craving pardon for the freedom—I cannot tell what makes me love you so much, unless it be for the reason that I loved the vicious devil of a brown galloway nag whom my master the Knight called Satan, till Master Warden changed his name to Seyton; for he said it was over boldness to call a beast after the King of Darkness——"

"And," said the page, "it was over boldness in him, I trow, to call a vicious brute after a noble family."

"Well," proceeded Adam, "Seyton or Satan, I loved that nag over every other horse in the stable—There was no sleeping on his back—he was for ever fidgeting, bolting, rearing, biting, kicking, and giving you work to do, and maybe the measure of your back on the heather to the boot of it all. And I think I love you better than any lad in the castle, for the self-same qualities."

"Thanks, thanks, kind Adam. I regard myself bound to you for the good estimation in which you hold me."

"Nay, interrupt me not," said the falconer—"Satan was a good nag—But I say I think I shall call the two eyases after you, the one Roland, and the other Græme; and while Adam Woodcock lives, be sure you have a friend—Here is to thee, my dear son."

Roland most heartily returned the grasp of the hand, and Woodcock, having taken a deep draught, continued his farewell speech.

"There are three things I warn you against, Roland, now that you art to tread this weary world without my experience to assist you. In the first place, never draw dagger on slight occasion—every man's doublet is not so well stuffed as a certain abbot's that you wot of. Secondly, fly not at every pretty girl, like a merlin at a thrush—you will not always win a gold chain for your labour — and, by the way, here I return to you your fanfarona — keep it close, it is weighty, and may benefit you at a pinch more ways than one. Thirdly, and to conclude, as our worthy preacher says, beware of the pottle-pot — it has drenched the judgment of wiser men than you. I could bring some instances of it, but I dare say it needeth not; for if you should forget your own mishaps, you will scarce fail to remember mine — And so farewell, my dear son."

Roland returned his good wishes, and failed not to send his humble duty to his kind Lady, charging the falconer, at the same time, to express his regret that he should have offended her, and his determination so to bear him in the world that she would not be ashamed of the generous protection she had afforded him.

The falconer embraced his young friend, mounted his stout, round-made, trotting-nag, which the serving-man, who had attended him, held ready at the door, and took the road to the southward. A sullen and heavy sound echoed from the horse's feet, as if indicating the sorrow of the good-natured rider. Every hoof-tread seemed to tap upon Roland's heart as he heard his comrade withdraw with so little of his usual alert activity, and felt that he was once more alone in the world.

He was roused from his reverie by Michael Wing-the-wind, who reminded him that it was necessary they should instantly return to the palace, as my Lord Regent went to the Sessions early in the morning. They went thither accordingly, and Wing-the-wind, a favourite old domestic, who was admitted nearer to the Regent's person and privacy, than many whose posts were more ostensible, soon introduced Græme into a small matted chamber, where he had an audience of the present head of the troubled State of Scotland. The Earl of Murray was clad in a sad-coloured morning-gown, with a cap and slippers of the same cloth, but, even in this easy déshabillé, held his sheathed rapier in his hand, a precaution which he adopted when receiving strangers, rather in compliance with the earnest remonstrances of his friends and partisans, than from any personal apprehensions of his own. He answered with a silent nod the respectful obeisance of the page, and took one or two turns through the small apartment in silence, fixing his keen eye on Roland, as if he wished to penetrate into his very soul. At length he broke silence.

"Your name is, I think, Julian Græme?"

"Roland Græme, my lord, not Julian," replied the page.

"Right — I was misled by some trick of my memory — Roland Græme, from the Debateable Land. — Roland, thou knowest the duties which belong to a lady's service?"

"I should know them, my lord," replied Roland, "having been bred so near the person of my Lady of Avenel; but I trust never more to practise them, as the Knight hath promised——"

"Be silent, young man," said the Regent, "I am to speak, and you to hear and obey. It is necessary that, for some space at least, you shall again enter into the service of a lady, who, in rank, hath no equal in Scotland; and this service accomplished, I give thee my word as Knight and Prince, that it shall open to you a course of ambition, such as may well gratify the aspiring wishes of one whom circumstances entitle to entertain much higher views than thou. I will take thee into my household and near to my person, or, at your own choice, I will give you the command of a foot-company — either is a preferment which the proudest laird in the land might be glad to ensure for a second son."

"May I presume to ask, my lord," said Roland, observing the Earl paused for a reply, "to whom my poor services are in the first place destined?"

"You will be told hereafter," said the Regent; and then, as if overcoming some internal reluctance to speak farther himself, he added, "or why should I not myself tell you, that you are about to enter into the service of a most illustrious — most unhappy lady — into the service of Mary of Scotland."

"Of the Queen, my lord!" said the page, unable to suppress his surprise.

"Of her who was the Queen!" said Murray, with a singular mixture of displeasure and embarrassment in his tone of voice. "You must be aware, young man, that her son reigns in her stead."

He sighed from an emotion, partly natural, perhaps, and partly assumed.

"And am I to attend upon her Grace in her place of imprisonment, my lord?" again demanded the page, with a straightforward and hardy simplicity, which somewhat disconcerted the sage and powerful statesman.

"She is not imprisoned," answered Murray, angrily; "God forbid she should — she is only sequestered from state affairs, and from the business of the public, until the world be so effectually settled, that she may enjoy her natural and uncontrolled freedom, without her royal disposition being exposed to the practices of wicked and designing men. It is for this purpose," he added, "that while she is to be furnished, as right is, with such attendance as may befit her present secluded state, it becomes necessary that those placed around her, are persons on whose prudence I can have reliance. You see, therefore, you are at once called on to discharge an office most honourable in itself, and so to discharge it that you may make a friend of the Regent of Scotland. Thou art, I have been told, a singularly apprehensive youth; and I perceive by thy look, that thou dost already understand what I would say on this matter. In this schedule your particular points of duty are set down at length — but the sum required of you is fidelity — I mean fidelity to myself and to the state. You are, therefore, to watch every attempt which is made, or inclination displayed, to open any communication with any of the lords who have become banders in the west — with Hamilton, Seyton, with Fleming, or the like. It is true that my gracious sister, reflecting upon the ill chances that have happened to the state of this poor kingdom, from evil counsellors who have abused her royal nature in time past, hath determined to sequestrate herself from state affairs in future. But it is our duty, as acting for and in the name of our infant nephew, to guard against the evils which may arise from any mutation or vacillation in her royal resolutions. Wherefore, it will be thy duty to watch, and report to our lady mother, whose guest our sister is for the present, whatever may infer a disposition to withdraw her person from the place of security in which she is lodged, or to open communication with those without. If, however, your observation should detect any thing of weight, and which may exceed mere suspicion, fail not to send notice by an especial messenger to me directly, and this ring shall be thy warrant to order horse and men on such service. — And now begone. If there be half the wit in thy head that there is apprehension in thy look, thou fully comprehendest all that I would say — Serve me faithfully, and sure as I am belted earl, thy reward shall be great."

Roland Græme made an obeisance, and was about to depart.

The Earl signed to him to remain. "I have trusted thee deeply," he said, "young man, for thou art the only one of her suite who has been sent to her by my own recommendation. Her gentlewomen are of her own nomination — it were too hard to have barred her that privilege, though some there were who reckoned it inconsistent with sure policy. Thou art young and handsome. Mingle in their follies, and see they cover not deeper designs under the appearance of female levity — if they do mine, do thou countermine. For the rest, bear all decorum and respect to the person of thy mistress — she is a princess, though a most unhappy one, and hath been a queen! though now, alas! no longer such! Pay, therefore, to her all honour and respect, consistent with thy fidelity to the King and me — and now, farewell. — Yet stay — you travel with Lord Lindesay, a man of the old world, rough and honest, though untaught; see that thou offend him not, for he is not patient of raillery, and thou, I have heard, art a crack-halter." This he said with a smile, then added, "I could have wished the Lord Lindesay's mission had been intrusted to some other and more gentle noble."

"And wherefore should you wish that, my lord?" said Morton, who even then entered the apartment; "the council have decided for the best — we have had but too many proofs of this lady's stubbornness of mind, and the oak that resists the sharp steel axe, must be riven with the rugged iron wedge. — And this is to be her page? — My Lord Regent hath doubtless instructed you, young man, how you shall guide yourself in these matters; I will add but a little hint on my part. You are going to the castle of a Douglas, where treachery never thrives — the first moment of suspicion will be the last of your life. My kinsman, William Douglas, understands no raillery, and if he once have cause to think you false, you will waver in the wind from the castle battlements ere the sun set upon his anger.—And is the lady to have an almoner withal?"

"Occasionally, Douglas," said the Regent; "it were hard to deny the spiritual consolation which she thinks essential to her salvation."

"You are ever too soft hearted, my lord — What! a false priest to communicate her lamentations, not only to our unfriends in Scotland, but to the Guises, to Rome, to Spain, and I know not where!"

"Fear not," said the Regent, "we will take such order that no treachery shall happen."

"Look to it then," said Morton; "you know my mind respecting the wench you have consented she shall receive as a waiting-woman — one of a family, which, of all others, has ever been devoted to her, and inimical to us. Had we not been wary, she would have been purveyed of a page as much to her purpose as her waiting-damsel. I hear a rumour that an old mad Romish pilgrimer, who passes for at least half a saint among them, was employed to find a fit subject."

"We have escaped that danger at least," said Murray, "and converted it into a point of advantage, by sending this boy of Glendinning's — and for her waiting-damsel, you cannot grudge her one poor maiden instead of her four noble Marys and all their silken train?"

"I care not so much for the waiting-maiden," said Morton, "but I cannot brook the almoner — I think priests of all persuasions are much like each other — Here is John Knox, who made such a noble puller-down, is ambitious of becoming a setter-up, and a founder of schools and colleges out of the Abbey lands, and bishops' rents, and other spoils of Rome, which the nobility of Scotland have won with their sword and bow, and with which he would endow new hives to sing the old drone."

"John is a man of God," said the Regent, "and his scheme is a devout imagination."

The sedate smile with which this was spoken, left it impossible to conjecture whether the words were meant in approbation, or in derision, of the plan of the Scottish Reformer. Turning then to Roland Græme, as if he thought he had been long enough a witness of this conversation, he bade him get him presently to horse, since my Lord of Lindesay was already mounted. The page made his reverence, and left the apartment.

Guided by Michael Wing-the-wind, he found his horse ready saddled and prepared for the journey, in front of the palace porch, where hovered about a score of men-at-arms, whose leader showed no small symptoms of surly impatience.

"Is this the jackanape page for whom we have waited thus long?" said he to Wing-the-wind. — "And my Lord Ruthven will reach the castle long before us."

Michael assented, and added, that the boy had been detained by the Regent to receive some parting instructions. The leader made an inarticulate sound in his throat, expressive of sullen acquiescence, and calling to one of his domestic attendants, "Edward," said he, "take the gallant into your charge, and let him speak with no one else."

He then addressed, by the title of Sir Robert, an elderly and respectable-looking gentleman, the only one of the party who seemed above the rank of a retainer or domestic, and observed, that they must get to horse with all speed.

During this discourse, and while they were riding slowly along the street of the suburb, Roland had time to examine more accurately the looks and figure of the Baron, who was at their head.

Lord Lindesay of the Byres was rather touched than stricken with years. His upright stature and strong limbs, still showed him fully equal to all the exertions and fatigues of war. His thick eyebrows, now partially grizzled, lowered over large eyes full of dark fire, which seemed yet darker from the uncommon depth at which they were set in his head. His features, naturally strong and harsh, had their sternness exaggerated by one or two scars received in battle. These features, naturally calculated to express the harsher passions, were shaded by an open steel cap, with a projecting front, but having no visor, over the gorget of which fell the black and grizzled beard of the grim old Baron, and totally hid the lower part of his face. The rest of his dress was a loose buff-coat, which had once been lined with silk and adorned with embroidery, but which seemed much stained with travel, and damaged with cuts, received probably in battle. It covered a corslet, which had once been of polished steel, fairly gilded, but was now somewhat injured with rust. A sword of antique make and uncommon size, framed to be wielded with both hands, a kind of weapon which was then beginning to go out of use, hung from his neck in a baldrick, and was so disposed as to traverse his whole person, the huge hilt appearing over his left shoulder, and the point reaching well-nigh to the right heel, and jarring against his spur as he walked. This unwieldy weapon could only be unsheathed by pulling the handle over the left shoulder — for no human arm was long enough to draw it in the usual manner. The whole equipment was that of a rude warrior, negligent of his exterior even to misanthropical sullenness; and the short, harsh, haughty tone, which he used towards his attendants, belonged to the same unpolished character.

The personage who rode with Lord Lindesay, at the head of the party, was an absolute contrast to him, in manner, form, and features. His thin and silky hair was already white, though he seemed not above forty-five or fifty years old. His tone of voice was soft and insinuating—his form thin, spare, and bent by an habitual stoop — his pale cheek was expressive of shrewdness and intelligence — his eye was quick though placid, and his whole demeanour mild and conciliatory. He rode an ambling nag, such as were used by ladies, clergymen, or others of peaceful professions — wore a riding habit of black velvet, with a cap and feather of the same hue, fastened up by a golden medal—and for show, and as a mark of rank rather than for use, carried a walking-sword, (as the short light rapiers were called,) without any other arms, offensive or defensive.

The party had now quitted the town, and proceeded, at a steady trot, towards the west.—As they prosecuted their journey, Roland Græme would gladly have learned something of its purpose and tendency, but the countenance of the personage next to whom he had been placed in the train, discouraged all approach to familiarity. The Baron himself did not look more grim and inaccessible than his feudal retainer, whose grisly beard fell over his mouth like the portcullis before the gate of a castle, as if for the purpose of preventing the escape of any word, of which absolute necessity did not demand the utterance. The rest of the train seemed under the same taciturn influence, and journeyed on without a word being exchanged amongst them—more like a troop of Carthusian friars than a party of military retainers. Roland Græme was surprised at this extremity of discipline; for even in the household of the Knight of Avenel, though somewhat distinguished for the accuracy with which decorum was enforced, a journey was a period of license, during which jest and song, and every thing within the limits of becoming mirth and pastime were freely permitted. This unusual silence was, however, so far acceptable, that it gave him time to bring any shadow of judgment which he possessed to council on his own situation and prospects, which would have appeared to any reasonable person in the highest degree dangerous and perplexing.

It was quite evident that he had, through various circumstances not under his own control, formed contradictory connexions with both the contending factions, by whose strife the kingdom was distracted, without being properly an adherent of either. It seemed also clear, that the same situation in the household of the deposed Queen, to which he was now promoted by the influence of the Regent, had been destined to him by his enthusiastic grandmother, Magdalen Græme; for on this subject, the words which Morton had dropped had been a ray of light; yet it was no less clear that these two persons, the one the declared enemy, the other the enthusiastic votary, of the Catholic religion,—the one at the head of the King's new government, the other, who regarded that government as a criminal usurpation—must have required and expected very different services from the individual whom they had thus united in recommending. It required very little reflection to foresee that these contradictory claims on his services might speedily place him in a situation where his honour as well as his life might be endangered. But it was not in Roland Græme's nature to anticipate evil before it came, or to prepare to combat difficulties before they arrived. "I will see this beautiful and unfortunate Mary Stewart," said he, "of whom we have heard so much, and then there will be time enough to determine whether I will be kingsman or queensman. None of them can say I have given word or promise to either of their factions; for they have led me up and down like a blind Billy, without giving me any light into what I was to do. But it was lucky that grim Douglas came into the Regent's closet this morning, otherwise I had never got free of him without plighting my troth to do all the Earl would have me, which seemed, after all, but foul play to the poor imprisoned lady, to place her page as an espial on her."

Skipping thus lightly over a matter of such consequence, the thoughts of the hare-brained boy went a wool-gathering after more agreeable topics. Now he admired the Gothic towers of Barnbougle, rising from the sea-beaten rock, and overlooking one of the most glorious landscapes in Scotland—and now he began to consider what notable sport for the hounds and the hawks must be afforded by the variegated ground over which they travelled—and now he compared the steady and dull trot at which they were then prosecuting their journey, with the delight of sweeping over hill and dale in pursuit of his favourite sports. As, under the influence of these joyous recollections, he gave his horse the spur, and made him execute a gambade, he instantly incurred the censure of his grave neighbour, who hinted to him to keep the pace, and move quietly and in order, unless he wished such notice to be taken of his eccentric movements as was likely to be very displeasing to him.

The rebuke and the restraint under which the youth now found himself, brought back to his recollection his late good-humoured and accommodating associate and guide, Adam Woodcock; and from that topic his imagination made a short flight to Avenel Castle, to the quiet and unconfined life of its inhabitants, the goodness of his early protectress, not forgetting the denizens of its stables, kennels, and hawk-mews. In a brief space, all these subjects of meditation gave way to the resemblance of that riddle of womankind, Catherine Seyton, who appeared before the eye of his mind—now in her female form, now in her male attire—now in both at once—like some strange dream, which presents to us the same individual under two different characters at the same instant. Her mysterious present also recurred to his recollection—the sword which he now wore at his side, and which he was not to draw save by command of his legitimate Sovereign! But the key of this mystery he judged he was likely to find in the issue of his present journey.

With such thoughts passing through his mind, Roland Græme accompanied the party of Lord Lindesay to the Queen's-Ferry, which they passed in vessels that lay in readiness for them. They encountered no adventure whatever in their passage, excepting one horse being lamed in getting into the boat, an accident very common on such occasions, until a few years ago, when the ferry was completely regulated. What was more peculiarly characteristic of the olden age, was the discharge of a culverin at the party from the battlements of the old castle of Rosythe, on the north side of the Ferry, the lord of which happened to have some public or private quarrel with the Lord Lindesay, and took this mode of expressing his resentment. The insult, however, as it was harmless, remained unnoticed and unavenged, nor did any thing else occur worth notice until the band had come where Lochleven spread its magnificent sheet of waters to the beams of a bright summer's sun.

The ancient castle, which occupies an island nearly in the centre of the lake, recalled to the page that of Avenel, in which he had been nurtured. But the lake was much larger, and adorned with several islets besides that on which the fortress was situated; and instead of being embosomed in hills like that of Avenel, had upon the southern side only a splendid mountainous screen, being the descent of one of the Lomond hills, and on the other was surrounded by the extensive and fertile plain of Kinross. Roland Græme looked with some degree of dismay on the water-girdled fortress, which then, as now, consisted only of one large donjon-keep, surrounded with a court-yard, with two round flanking-towers at the angles, which contained within its circuit some other buildings of inferior importance. A few old trees, clustered together near the castle, gave some relief to the air of desolate seclusion; but yet the page, while he gazed upon a building so sequestrated, could not but feel for the situation of a captive Princess doomed to dwell there, as well as for his own. "I must have been born," he thought, "under the star that presides over ladies and lakes of water, for I cannot by any means escape from the service of the one, or from dwelling in the other. But if they allow me not the fair freedom of my sport and exercise, they shall find it as hard to confine a wild-drake, as a youth who can swim like one."

The band had now reached the edge of the water, and one of the party advancing displayed Lord Lindesay's pennon, waving it repeatedly to and fro, while that Baron himself blew a clamorous blast on his bugle. A banner was presently displayed from the roof of the castle in reply to these signals, and one or two figures were seen busied as if unmooring a boat which lay close to the islet.

"It will be some time ere they can reach us with the boat," said the companion of Lord Lindesay; "should we not do well to proceed to the town, and array ourselves in some better order, ere we appear before——"

"You may do as you list, Sir Robert," replied Lindesay, "I have neither time nor temper to waste on such vanities. She has cost me many a hard ride, and must not now take offence at the threadbare cloak and soiled doublet that I am arrayed in. It is the livery to which she has brought all Scotland."

"Do not speak so harshly," said Sir Robert; "if she hath done wrong, she hath dearly abied it; and in losing all real power, one would not deprive her of the little external homage due at once to a lady and a princess."

"I say to you once more, Sir Robert Melville," replied Lindesay, "do as you will—for me, I am now too old to dink myself as a gallant to grace the bower of dames."

"The bower of dames, my lord!" said Melville, looking at the rude old tower—"is it yon dark and grated castle, the prison of a captive Queen, to which you give so gay a name?"

"Name it as you list," replied Lindesay; "had the Regent desired to send an envoy capable to speak to a captive Queen, there are many gallants in his court who would have courted the occasion to make speeches out of Amadis of Gaul, or the Mirror of Knighthood. But when he sent blunt old Lindesay, he knew he would speak to a misguided woman, as her former misdoings and her present state render necessary. I sought not this employment—it has been thrust upon me; and I will not cumber myself with more form in the discharge of it, than needs must be tacked to such an occupation."

So saying, Lord Lindesay threw himself from horseback, and wrapping his riding-cloak around him, lay down at lazy length upon the sward, to await the arrival of the boat, which was now seen rowing from the castle towards the shore. Sir Robert Melville, who had also dismounted, walked at short turns to and fro upon the bank, his arms crossed on his breast, often looking to the castle, and displaying in his countenance a mixture of sorrow and of anxiety. The rest of the party sate like statues on horseback, without moving so much as the points of their lances, which they held upright in the air.

As soon as the boat approached a rude quay or landing-place, near to which they had stationed themselves, Lord Lindesay started up from his recumbent posture, and asked the person who steered, why he had not brought a larger boat with him to transport his retinue.

"So please you," replied the boatman, "because it is the order of our lady, that we bring not to the castle more than four persons."

"Thy lady is a wise woman," said Lindesay, "to suspect me of treachery! —Or, had I intended it, what was to hinder us from throwing you and your comrades into the lake, and filling the boat with my own fellows?"

The steersman, on hearing this, made a hasty signal to his men to back their oars, and hold off from the shore which they were approaching.

"Why, thou ass," said Lindesay, "thou didst not think that I meant thy fool's head serious harm? Hark thee, friend—with fewer than three servants I will go no whither—Sir Robert Melville will require at least the attendance of one domestic; and it will be at your peril and your lady's to refuse us admission, come hither as we are, on matters of great national concern."

The steersman answered with firmness, but with great civility of expression, that his orders were positive to bring no more than four into the island, but he offered to row back to obtain a revisal of his orders.

"Do so, my friend," said Sir Robert Melville, after he had in vain endeavoured to persuade his stubborn companion to consent to a temporary abatement of his train, "row back to the castle, sith it will be no better, and obtain thy lady's orders to transport the Lord Lindesay, myself, and our retinue hither."

"And hearken," said Lord Lindesay, "take with you this page, who comes as an attendant on your lady's guest. — Dismount, sirrah," said he, addressing Roland, "and embark with them in that boat."

"And what is to become of my horse?" said Græme; "I am answerable for him to my master."

"I will relieve you of the charge," said Lindesay; "thou wilt have little enough to do with horse, saddle, or bridle, for ten years to come — Thou mayst take the halter an thou wilt — it may stand thee in a turn."

"If I thought so," said Roland — but he was interrupted by Sir Robert Melville, who said to him good-humouredly, "Dispute it not, young friend — resistance can do no good, but may well run thee into danger."

Roland Græme felt the justice of what he said, and, though neither delighted with the matter or manner of Lindesay's address, deemed it best to submit to necessity, and to embark without farther remonstrance. The men plied their oars. The quay, with the party of horse stationed near it, receded from the page's eyes — the castle and the islet seemed to draw near in the same proportion, and in a brief space he landed under the shadow of a huge old tree which overhung the landing place. The steersman and Græme leaped ashore; the boatmen remained lying on their oars ready for farther service.

Chapter the Twenty-First.

Could valour aught avail or people's love,
France had not wept Navarre's brave Henry slain;
If wit or beauty could compassion move,
The rose of Scotland had not wept in vain.
Elegy in a Royal Mausoleum.—LEWIS.

AT the gate of the court-yard of Lochleven appeared the stately form of the Lady Lochleven, a female whose early charms had captivated James V., by whom she became mother of the celebrated Regent Murray. As she was of noble birth (being a daughter of the house of Mar) and of great beauty, her intimacy with James did not prevent her being afterwards sought in honourable marriage by many gallants of the time, among whom she had preferred Sir William Douglas of Lochleven. But well has it been said

——"Our pleasant vices
Are made the whips to scourge us"—

The station which the Lady of Lochleven now held as the wife of a man of high rank and interest, and the mother of a lawful family, did not prevent her nourishing a painful sense of degradation, even while she was proud of the talents, the power, and the station of her son, now prime ruler of the state, but still a pledge of her illicit intercourse. "Had James done to her," she said, in her secret heart, "the justice he owed her, she had seen in her son, as a source of unmixed delight and of unchastened pride, the lawful monarch of Scotland, and one of the ablest who ever swayed the sceptre. The House of Mar, not inferior in antiquity or grandeur to that of Drummond, would then have also boasted a Queen among its daughters, and escaped the stain attached to female frailty, even when it has a royal lover for its apology. While such feelings preyed on a bosom naturally proud and severe, they had a corresponding effect on her countenance, where, with the remains of great beauty, were mingled traits of inward discontent and peevish melancholy. It perhaps contributed to increase this habitual temperament, that the Lady Lochleven had adopted uncommonly rigid and severe views of religion, imitating in her ideas of reformed faith the very worst errors of the Catholics, in limiting the benefit of the gospel to those who profess their own speculative tenets.

In every respect, the unfortunate Queen Mary, now the compulsory guest, or rather prisoner, of this sullen lady, was obnoxious to her hostess. Lady Lochleven disliked her as the daughter of Mary of Guise, the legal possessor of those rights over James's heart and hand, of which she conceived herself to have been injuriously deprived; and yet more so as the professor of a religion which she detested worse than Paganism.

Such was the dame, who, with stately mien, and sharp yet handsome features, shrouded by her black velvet coif, interrogated the domestic who steered her barge to the shore, what had become of Lindesay and Sir Robert Melville. The man related what had passed, and she smiled scornfully as she replied, "Fools must be flattered, not foughten with. — Row back — make thy excuse as thou canst — say Lord Ruthven hath already reached this castle, and that he is impatient for Lord Lindesay's presence. Away with thee, Randal—yet stay—what galopin is that thou hast brought hither?"

"So please you, my lady, he is the page who is to wait upon——"

"Ay, the new male minion," said the Lady Lochleven; "the female attendant arrived yesterday. I shall have a well-ordered house with this lady and her retinue; but I trust they will soon find some others to undertake such a charge. Begone, Randal — and you" (to Roland Græme) "follow me to the garden."

She led the way with a slow and stately step to the small garden, which, enclosed by a stone wall ornamented with statues, and an artificial fountain in the centre, extended its dull parterres on the side of the court-yard, with which it communicated by a low and arched portal. Within the narrow circuit of its formal and limited walks, Mary Stewart was now learning to perform the weary part of a prisoner, which, with little interval, she was doomed to sustain during the remainder of her life. She was followed in her slow and melancholy exercise by two female attendants; but in the first glance which Roland Græme bestowed upon one so illustrious by birth, so distinguished by her beauty, accomplishments, and misfortunes, he was sensible of the presence of no other than the unhappy Queen of Scotland.

Her face, her form, have been so deeply impressed upon the imagination, that even at the distance of nearly three centuries, it is unnecessary to remind the most ignorant and uninformed reader of the striking traits which characterize that remarkable countenance, which seems at once to combine our ideas of the majestic, the pleasing, and the brilliant, leaving us to doubt whether they express most happily the queen, the beauty, or the accomplished woman. Who is there, that, at the very mention of Mary Stewart's name, has not her countenance before him, familiar as that of the mistress of his youth, or the favourite daughter of his advanced age? Even those who feel themselves compelled to believe all, or much, of what her enemies laid to her charge, cannot think without a sigh upon a countenance expressive of anything rather than the foul crimes with which she was charged when living, and which still continue to shade, if not to blacken, her memory. That brow, so truly open and regal — those eyebrows, so regularly graceful, which yet were saved from the charge of regular insipidity by the beautiful effect of the hazel eyes which they overarched, and which seem to utter a thousand histories — the nose, with all its Grecian precision of outline—the mouth, so well proportioned, so sweetly formed, as if designed to speak nothing but what was delightful to hear — the dimpled chin—the stately swan-like neck, form a countenance, the like of which we know not to have existed in any other character moving in that class of life, where the actresses as well as the actors command general and undivided attention. It is in vain to say that the portraits which exist of this remarkable woman are not like each other; for, amidst their discrepancy, each possesses general features which the eye at once acknowledges as peculiar to the vision which our imagination has raised while we read her history for the first time, and which has been impressed upon it by the numerous prints and pictures which we have seen. Indeed we cannot look on the worst of them, however deficient in point of execution, without saying that it is meant for Queen Mary; and no small instance it is of the power of beauty, that her charms should have remained the subject not merely of admiration, but of warm and chivalrous interest, after the lapse of such a length of time. We know that by far the most acute of those who, in latter days, have adopted the unfavourable view of Mary's character, longed, like the executioner before his dreadful task was performed, to kiss the fair hand of her on whom he was about to perform so horrible a duty.

Dressed, then, in a deep mourning robe, and with all those charms of face, shape, and manner, with which faithful tradition has made each reader familiar, Mary Stewart advanced to meet the Lady of Lochleven, who, on her part, endeavoured to conceal dislike and apprehension under the appearance of respectful indifference. The truth was, that she had experienced repeatedly the Queen's superiority in that species of disguised yet cutting sarcasm, with which women can successfully avenge themselves, for real and substantial injuries. It may be well doubted, whether this talent was not as fatal to its possessor as the many others enjoyed by that highly gifted, but most unhappy female; for, while it often afforded her a momentary triumph over her keepers, it failed not to exasperate their resentment; and the satire and sarcasm in which she had indulged were frequently retaliated by the deep and bitter hardships which they had the power of inflicting. It is well known that her death was at length hastened by a letter which she wrote to Queen Elizabeth, in which she treated her jealous rival, and the Countess of Shrewsbury, with the keenest irony and ridicule.

As the ladies met together, the Queen said, bending her head at the same time, in return to the obeisance of the Lady Lochleven, "We are this day fortunate — we enjoy the company of our amiable hostess at an unusual hour, and during a period which we have hitherto been permitted to give to our private exercise. But our good hostess knows well she has at all times access to our presence, and need not observe the useless ceremony of requiring our permission."

"I am sorry my presence is deemed an intrusion by your Grace," said the Lady of Lochleven. "I came but to announce the arrival of an addition to your train," motioning with her hand towards Roland Græme; "a circumstance to which ladies are seldom indifferent."

"Oh! I crave your ladyship's pardon; and am bent to the earth with obligations for the kindness of my nobles — or my sovereigns, shall I call them?—who have permitted me such a respectable addition to my personal retinue."

"They have indeed studied, Madam," said the Lady of Lochleven, "to show their kindness towards your Grace—something at the risk perhaps of sound policy, and I trust their doings will not be misconstrued."

"Impossible!" said the Queen; "the bounty which permits the daughter of so many kings, and who yet is Queen of the realm, the attendance of two waiting-women and a boy, is a grace which Mary Stewart can never sufficiently acknowledge. Why! my train will be equal to that of any country dame in this your kingdom of Fife, saving but the lack of a gentleman-usher, and a pair or two of blue-coated serving-men. But I must not forget, in my selfish joy, the additional trouble and charges to which this magnificent augmentation of our train will put our kind hostess, and the whole house of Lochleven. It is this prudent anxiety, I am aware, which clouds your brows, my worthy lady. But be of good cheer; the crown of Scotland has many a fair manor, and your affectionate son, and my no less affectionate brother, will endow the good knight your husband with the best of them, ere Mary should be dismissed from this hospitable castle from your ladyship's lack of means to support the charges."

"The Douglasses of Lochleven, madam," answered the lady, "have known for ages how to discharge their duty to the State, without looking for reward, even when the task was both irksome and dangerous."

"Nay! but, my dear Lochleven," said the Queen, "you are over scrupulous—I pray you accept of a goodly manor; what should support the Queen of Scotland in this her princely court, saving her own crown-lands — and who should minister to the wants of a mother, save an affectionate son like the Earl of Murray, who possesses so wonderfully both the power and inclination?—Or said you it was the danger of the task which clouded your smooth and hospitable brow? — No doubt, a page is a formidable addition to my body-guard of females; and I bethink me it must have been for that reason that my Lord of Lindesay refused even now to venture within the reach of a force so formidable, without being attended by a competent retinue."

The Lady Lochleven started, and looked something surprised; and Mary suddenly changing her manner from the smooth ironical affectation of mildness to an accent of austere command, and drawing up at the same time her fine person, said, with the full majesty of her rank, "Yes! Lady of Lochleven; I know that Ruthven is already in the castle, and that Lindesay waits on the bank the return of your barge to bring him hither along with Sir Robert Melville. For what purpose do these nobles come — and why am I not in ordinary decency apprised of their arrival?"

"Their purpose, madam," replied the Lady of Lochleven, "they must themselves explain — but a formal annunciation were needless, where your Grace hath attendants who can play the espial so well."

"Alas! poor Fleming," said the Queen, turning to the elder of the female attendants, "thou wilt be tried, condemned, and gibbeted, for a spy in the garrison, because thou didst chance to cross the great hall while my good Lady of Lochleven was parleying at the full pitch of her voice with her pilot Randal. Put black wool in thy ears, girl, as you value the wearing of them longer. Remember, in the Castle of Lochleven, ears and tongues are matters not of use, but for show merely. Our good hostess can hear, as well as speak, for us all. We excuse your farther attendance, my lady hostess," she said, once more addressing the object of her resentment, "and retire to prepare for an interview with our rebel lords. We will use the ante-chamber of our sleeping apartment as our hall of audience. You, young man," she proceeded, addressing Roland Græme, and at once softening the ironical sharpness of her manner into good-humoured raillery, "you, who are all our male attendance, from our Lord High Chamberlain down to our least galopin, follow us to prepare our court."

She turned, and walked slowly towards the castle. The Lady of Lochleven folded her arms, and smiled in bitter resentment, as she watched her retiring steps.

"The whole male attendance!" she muttered, repeating the Queen's last words, "and well for thee had it been had thy train never been larger;" then turning to Roland, in whose way she had stood while making this pause, she made room for him to pass, saying at the same time, "Art thou already eaves-dropping? follow thy mistress, minion, and, if thou wilt, tell her what I have now said."

Roland Græme hastened after his royal mistress and her attendants, who had just entered a postern-gate communicating betwixt the castle and the small garden. They ascended a winding-stair as high as the second story, which was in a great measure occupied by a suite of three rooms, opening into each other, and assigned as the dwelling of the captive Princess. The outermost was a small hall or ante-room, within which opened a large parlour, and from that again the Queen's bedroom. Another small apartment, which opened into the same parlour, contained the beds of the gentlewomen in waiting.

Roland Græme stopped, as became his station, in the outermost of these apartments, there to await such orders as might be communicated to him. From the grated window of the room he saw Lindesay, Melville, and their followers disembark; and observed that they were met at the castle gate by a third noble, to whom Lindesay exclaimed, in his loud harsh voice, "My Lord of Ruthven, you have the start of us!"

At this instant, the page's attention was called to a burst of hysterical sobs from the inner apartment, and to the hurried ejaculations of the terrified females, which led him almost instantly to hasten to their assistance. When he entered, he saw that the Queen had thrown herself into the large chair which stood nearest the door, and was sobbing for breath in a strong fit of hysterical affection. The elder female supported her in her arms, while the younger bathed her face with water and with tears alternately.

"Hasten, young man!" said the elder lady, in alarm, "fly — call in assistance — she is swooning!"

But the Queen ejaculated in a faint and broken voice, "Stir not, I charge you! — call no one to witness — I am better — I shall recover instantly." And, indeed, with an effort which seemed like that of one struggling for life, she sate up in her chair, and endeavoured to resume her composure, while her features yet trembled with the violent emotion of body and mind which she had undergone. "I am ashamed of my weakness, girls," she said, taking the hands of her attendants; "but it is over — and I am Mary Stewart once more. The savage tone of that man's voice — my knowledge of his insolence — the name which he named — the purpose for which they come—may excuse a moment's weakness, and it shall be a moment's only." She snatched from her head the curch or cap, which had been disordered during her hysterical agony, shook down the thick clustered tresses of dark brown which had been before veiled under it — and, drawing her slender fingers across the labyrinth which they formed, she arose from the chair, and stood like the inspired image of a Grecian prophetess in a mood which partook at once of sorrow and pride, of smiles and of tears. "We are ill appointed," she said, "to meet our rebel subjects; but, as far as we may, we will strive to present ourselves as becomes their Queen. Follow me, my maidens," she said; "what says thy favourite song, my Fleming?

'My maids, come to my dressing-bower,
And deck my nut-brown hair;
Where'er ye laid a plait before,
Look ye lay ten times mair.'

Alas!" she added, when she had repeated with a smile these lines of an old ballad, "violence has already robbed me of the ordinary decorations of my rank; and the few that nature gave me have been destroyed by sorrow and by fear." Yet while she spoke thus, she again let her slender fingers stray through the wilderness of the beautiful tresses which veiled her kingly neck and swelling bosom, as if, in her agony of mind, she had not altogether lost the consciousness of her unrivalled charms. Roland Græme, on whose youth, inexperience, and ardent sense of what was dignified and lovely, the demeanour of so fair and high-born a lady wrought like the charm of a magician, stood rooted to the spot with surprise and interest, longing to hazard his life in a quarrel so fair as that which Mary Stewart's must needs be. She had been bred in France — she was possessed of the most distinguished beauty — she had reigned a Queen and a Scottish Queen, to whom knowledge of character was as essential as the use of vital air. In all these capacities, Mary was, of all women on the earth, most alert at perceiving and using the advantages which her charms gave her over almost all who came within the sphere of their influence. She cast on Roland a glance which might have melted a heart of stone. "My poor boy," she said, with a feeling partly real, partly politic, "thou art a stranger to us—sent to this doleful captivity from the society of some tender mother, or sister, or maiden, with whom you had freedom to tread a gay measure round the Maypole. I grieve for you; but you are the only male in my limited household — wilt thou obey my orders?"

"To the death, madam," said Græme, in a determined tone.

"Then keep the door of mine apartment," said the Queen; "keep it till they offer actual violence, or till we shall be fitly arrayed to receive these intrusive visiters."

"I will defend it till they pass over my body," said Roland Græme; any hesitation which he had felt concerning the line of conduct he ought to pursue being completely swept away by the impulse of the moment.

"Not so, my good youth," answered Mary; "not so, I command. If I have one faithful subject beside me, much need, God wot, I have to care for his safety. Resist them but till they are put to the shame of using actual violence, and then give way, I charge you. Remember my commands." And, with a smile expressive at once of favour and of authority, she turned from him, and, followed by her attendants, entered the bedroom.

The youngest paused for half a second ere she followed her companion, and made a signal to Roland Græme with her hand. He had been already long aware that this was Catherine Seyton — a circumstance which could not much surprise a youth of quick intellects, who recollected the sort of mysterious discourse which had passed betwixt the two matrons at the deserted nunnery, and on which his meeting with Catherine in this place seemed to cast so much light. Yet such was the engrossing effect of Mary's presence, that it surmounted for the moment even the feelings of a youthful lover; and it was not until Catherine Seyton had disappeared, that Roland began to consider in what relation they were to stand to each other. "She held up her hand to me in a commanding manner," he thought; "perhaps she wanted to confirm my purpose for the execution of the Queen's commands; for I think she could scarce purpose to scare me with the sort of discipline which she administered to the groom in the frieze-jacket, and to poor Adam Woodcock. But we will see to that anon; meantime, let us do justice to the trust reposed in us by this unhappy Queen. I think my Lord of Murray will himself own that it is the duty of a faithful page to defend his lady against intrusion on her privacy."

Accordingly, he stepped to the little vestibule, made fast, with lock and bar, the door which opened from thence to the large staircase, and then sat himself down to attend the result. He had not long to wait — a rude and strong hand first essayed to lift the latch, then pushed and shook the door with violence, and, when it resisted his attempt to open it, exclaimed, "Undo the door there, you within!"

"Why, and at whose command," said the page, "am I to undo the door of the apartments of the Queen of Scotland?"

Another vain attempt, which made hinge and bolt jingle, showed that the impatient applicant without would willingly have entered altogether regardless of his challenge; but at length an answer was returned.

"Undo the door, on your peril — the Lord Lindesay comes to speak with the Lady Mary of Scotland."

"The Lord Lindesay, as a Scottish noble," answered the page, "must await his Sovereign's leisure."

An earnest altercation ensued amongst those without, in which Roland distinguished the remarkable harsh voice of Lindesay in reply to Sir Robert Melville, who appeared to have been using some soothing language—"No! no! no! I tell thee, no! I will place a petard against the door rather than be baulked by a profligate woman, and bearded by an insolent footboy."

"Yet, at least," said Melville, "let me try fair means in the first instance. Violence to a lady would stain your scutcheon for ever. Or await till my Lord Ruthven comes."

"I will await no longer," said Lindesay; "it is high time the business were done, and we on our return to the council. But thou mayest try thy fair play, as thou callest it, while I cause my train to prepare the petard. I came hither provided with as good gunpowder as blew up the Kirk of Field."

"For God's sake, be patient," said Melville; and, approaching the door, he said, as speaking to those within, "Let the Queen know, that I, her faithful servant, Robert Melville, do entreat her, for her own sake, and to prevent worse consequences, that she will undo the door, and admit Lord Lindesay, who brings a mission from the Council of State."

"I will do your errand to the Queen," said the page, "and report to you her answer."

He went to the door of the bedchamber, and tapping against it gently, it was opened by the elderly lady, to whom he communicated his errand, and returned with directions from the Queen to admit Sir Robert Melville and Lord Lindesay. Roland Græme returned to the vestibule, and opened the door accordingly, into which the Lord Lindesay strode, with the air of a soldier who has fought his way into a conquered fortress; while Melville, deeply dejected, followed him more slowly.

"I draw you to witness, and to record," said the page to this last, "that, save for the especial commands of the Queen, I would have made good the entrance, with my best strength, and my best blood, against all Scotland."

"Be silent, young man," said Melville, in a tone of grave rebuke; "add not brands to fire — this is no time to make a flourish of thy boyish chivalry."

"She has not appeared even yet," said Lindesay, who had now reached the midst of the parlour or audience-room; "how call you this trifling?"

"Patience, my lord," replied Sir Robert, "time presses not — and Lord Ruthven hath not as yet descended."

At this moment the door of the inner apartment opened, and Queen Mary presented herself, advancing with an air of peculiar grace and majesty, and seeming totally unruffled, either by the visit, or by the rude manner in which it had been enforced. Her dress was a robe of black velvet; a small ruff, open in front, gave a full view of her beautifully formed chin and neck, but veiled the bosom. On her head she wore a small cap of lace, and a transparent white veil hung from her shoulders over the long black robe, in large loose folds, so that it could be drawn at pleasure over the face and person. She wore a cross of gold around her neck, and had her rosary of gold and ebony hanging from her girdle. She was closely followed by her two ladies, who remained standing behind her during the conference. Even Lord Lindesay, though the rudest noble of that rude age, was surprised into something like respect by the unconcerned and majestic mien of her, whom he had expected to find frantic with impotent passion, or dissolved in useless and vain sorrow, or overwhelmed with the fears likely in such a situation to assail fallen royalty.

"We fear we have detained you, my Lord of Lindesay," said the Queen, while she curtsied with dignity in answer to his reluctant obeisance; "but a female does not willingly receive her visiters without some minutes spent at the toilette. Men, my lord, are less dependant on such ceremonies."

Lord Lindesay, casting his eye down on his own travel-stained and disordered dress, muttered something of a hasty journey, and the Queen paid her greeting to Sir Robert Melville with courtesy, and even, as it seemed, with kindness. There was then a dead pause, during which Lindesay looked towards the door, as if expecting with impatience the colleague of their embassy. The Queen alone was entirely unembarrassed, and, as if to break the silence, she addressed Lord Lindesay, with a glance at the large and cumbrous sword which he wore, as already mentioned, hanging from his neck.

"You have there a trusty and a weighty travelling companion, my lord. I trust you expected to meet with no enemy here, against whom such a formidable weapon could be necessary? it is, methinks, somewhat a singular ornament for a court, though I am, as I well need to be, too much of a Stuart to fear a sword."

"It is not the first time, madam," replied Lindesay, bringing round the weapon so as to rest its point on the ground, and leaning one hand on the huge cross-handle, "it is not the first time that this weapon has intruded itself into the presence of the House of Stewart."

"Possibly, my lord," replied the Queen, "it may have done service to my ancestors — Your ancestors were men of loyalty."

"Ay, madam," replied he, "service it hath done; but such as kings love neither to acknowledge nor to reward. It was the service which the knife renders to the tree when trimming it to the quick, and depriving it of the superfluous growth of rank and unfruitful suckers, which rob it of nourishment."

"You talk riddles, my lord," said Mary; "I will hope the explanation carries nothing insulting with it."

"You shall judge, madam," answered Lindesay. "With this good sword was Archibald Douglas, Earl of Angus, girded on the memorable day when he acquired the name of Bell-the-Cat, for dragging from the presence of your great grandfather, the third James of the race, a crew of minions, flatterers, and favourites whom he hanged over the bridge of Lauder, as a warning to such reptiles how they approach a Scottish throne. With this same weapon, the same inflexible champion of Scottish honour and nobility slew at one blow Spens of Kilspindie, a courtier of your grandfather, James the fourth, who had dared to speak lightly of him in the royal presence. They fought near the brook of Fala; and Bell-the-Cat, with this blade, sheared through the thigh of his opponent, and lopped the limb as easily as a shepherd's boy slices a twig from a sapling."

"My lord," replied the Queen, reddening, "my nerves are too good to be alarmed even by this terrible history—May I ask how a blade so illustrious passed from the House of Douglas to that of Lindesay?—Methinks it should have been preserved as a consecrated relic, by a family who have held all that they could do against their king, to be done in favour of their country."

"Nay, madam," said Melville, anxiously interfering, "ask not that question of Lord Lindesay — And you, my lord, for shame — for decency — forbear to reply to it."

"It is time that this lady should hear the truth," replied Lindesay.

"And be assured," said the Queen, "that she will be moved to anger by none that you can tell her, my lord. There are cases in which just scorn has always the mastery over just anger."

"Then know," said Lindesay, "that upon the field of Carberry-hill, when that false and infamous traitor and murderer, James, sometime Earl of Bothwell, and nicknamed Duke of Orkney, offered to do personal battle with any of the associated nobles who came to drag him to justice, I accepted his challenge, and was by the noble Earl of Morton gifted with his good sword that I might therewith fight it out — Ah! so help me Heaven, had his presumption been one grain more, or his cowardice one grain less, I should have done such work with this good steel on his traitorous corpse, that the hounds and carrion-crows should have found their morsels daintily carved to their use!"

The Queen's courage well-nigh gave way at the mention of Bothwell's name — a name connected with such a train of guilt, shame, and disaster. But the prolonged boast of Lindesay gave her time to rally herself, and to answer with an appearance of cold contempt—"It is easy to slay an enemy who enters not the lists. But had Mary Stewart inherited her father's sword as well as his sceptre, the boldest of her rebels should not upon that day have complained that they had no one to cope withal. Your lordship will forgive me if I abridge this conference. A brief description of a bloody fight is long enough to satisfy a lady's curiosity; and unless my Lord of Lindesay has something more important to tell us than of the deeds which old Bell-the-Cat achieved, and how he would himself have emulated them, had time and tide permitted, we will retire to our private apartment, and you, Fleming, shall finish reading to us yonder little treatise *Des Rodomontades Espagnolles.*"

"Tarry, madam," said Lindesay, his complexion reddening in his turn, "I know your quick wit too well of old to have sought an interview that you might sharpen its edge at the expense of my honour. Lord Ruthven and myself, with Sir Robert Melville as a concurrent, come to your Grace on the part of the Secret Council, to tender to you what much concerns the safety of your own life and the welfare of the State."

"The Secret Council?" said the Queen; "by what powers can it subsist or act, while I, from whom it holds its character, am here detained under unjust restraint? But it matters not — what concerns the welfare of Scotland shall be acceptable to Mary Stewart, come from whatever quarter it will — and for what concerns her own life, she has lived long enough to be weary of it, even at the age of twenty-five. — Where is your colleague, my lord? — why tarries he?"

"He comes, madam," said Melville, and Lord Ruthven entered at the instant, holding in his hand a packet. As the Queen returned his salutation she became deadly pale, but instantly recovered herself by dint of strong and sudden resolution, just as the noble, whose appearance seemed to excite such emotions in her bosom, entered the apartment in company with George Douglas, the youngest son of the Knight of Lochleven, who, during the absence of his father and brethren, acted as Seneschal of the Castle, under the direction of the elder Lady Lochleven, his father's mother.

Chapter the Twenty-Second.

I give this heavy weight from off my head,
And this unwieldy sceptre from my hand;
With mine own tears I wash away my balm,
With mine own hand I give away my crown,
With mine own tongue deny my sacred state,
With mine own breath release all duteous oaths.

RICHARD II.

LORD RUTHVEN had the look and bearing which became a soldier and a statesman, and the martial cast of his form and features procured him the popular epithet of Greysteil, by which he was distinguished by his intimates, after the hero of a metrical romance then generally known. His dress, which was a buff-coat embroidered, had a half-military character, but exhibited nothing of the sordid negligence which distinguished that of Lindesay. But the son of an ill-fated sire, and the father of a yet more unfortunate family, bore in his look that cast of inauspicious melancholy, by which the physiognomists of that time pretended to distinguish those who were predestined to a violent and unhappy death.

The terror which the presence of this nobleman impressed on the Queen's mind, arose from the active share he had borne in the slaughter of David Rizzio; his father having presided at the perpetration of that abominable crime, although so weak from long and wasting illness, that he could not endure the weight of his armour, having arisen from a sick-bed to commit a murder in the presence of his Sovereign. On that occasion his son also had attended and taken an active part. It was little to be wondered at, that the Queen, considering her condition when such a deed of horror was acted in her presence, should retain an instinctive terror for the principal actors in the murder. She returned, however, with grace the salutation of Lord Ruthven, and extended her hand to George Douglas, who kneeled, and kissed it with respect; the first mark of a subject's homage which Roland Græme had seen any of them render to the captive Sovereign. She returned his greeting in silence, and there was a brief pause, during which the steward of the castle, a man of a sad brow and a severe eye, placed, under George Douglas's directions, a table and writing materials; and the page, obedient to his mistress's dumb signal, advanced a large chair to the side on which the Queen stood, the table thus forming a sort of bar which divided the Queen and her personal followers from her unwelcome visiters. The steward then withdrew after a low reverence. When he had closed the door behind him, the Queen broke silence—"With your favour, my lords, I will sit—my walks are not indeed extensive enough at present to fatigue me greatly, yet I find repose something more necessary than usual."

She sat down accordingly, and, shading her cheek with her beautiful hand, looked keenly and impressively at each of the nobles in turn. Mary Fleming applied her kerchief to her eyes, and Catherine Seyton and Roland Græme exchanged a glance, which showed that both were too deeply engrossed with sentiments of interest and commiseration for their royal mistress, to think of any thing which regarded themselves.

"I wait the purpose of your mission, my lords," said the Queen, after she had been seated for about a minute without a word being spoken,—"I wait your message from those you call the Secret Council.—I trust it is a petition of pardon, and a desire that I will resume my rightful throne, without using with due severity my right of punishing those who have dispossessed me of it."

"Madam," replied Ruthven, "it is painful for us to speak harsh truths to a Princess who has long ruled us. But we come to offer, not to implore, pardon. In a word, madam, we have to propose to you on the part of the Secret Council, that you sign these deeds, which will contribute greatly to the pacification of the State, the advancement of God's word, and the welfare of your own future life."

"Am I expected to take these fair words on trust, my lord? or may I hear the contents of these reconciling papers, ere I am asked to sign them?"

"Unquestionably, madam; it is our purpose and wish, you should read what you are required to sign," replied Ruthven.

"Required?" replied the Queen, with some emphasis; "but the phrase suits well the matter—read, my lord."

The Lord Ruthven proceeded to read a formal instrument, running in the Queen's name, and setting forth that she had been called, at an early age, to the administration of the crown and realm of Scotland, and had toiled diligently therein, until she was in body and spirit so wearied out and disgusted, that she was unable any longer to endure the travail and pain of State affairs; and that since God had blessed her with a fair and hopeful son, she was desirous to ensure to him, even while she yet lived, his succession to the crown, which was his by right of hereditary descent. "Wherefore," the instrument proceeded, "we, of the motherly affection we bear to our said son, have renounced and demitted, and by these our letters of free good-will, renounce and demit, the Crown, government, and guiding of the realm of Scotland, in favour of our said son, that he may succeed to us as native Prince thereof, as much as if we had been removed by disease, and not by our own proper act. And that this demission of our royal authority may have the more full and solemn effect, and none pretend ignorance, we give, grant, and commit, full and free and plain power to our trusty cousins, Lord Lindesay of the Byres, and William Lord Ruthven, to appear in our name before as many of the nobility, clergy, and burgesses, as may be assembled at Stirling, and there, in our name and behalf, publicly, and in their presence, to renounce the Crown, guidance, and government of this our kingdom of Scotland."

The Queen here broke in with an air of extreme surprise. "How is this, my lords?" she said: "Are my ears turned rebels, that they deceive me with sounds so extraordinary? — And yet it is no wonder that, having conversed so long with rebellion, they should now force its language upon my understanding. Say I am mistaken, my lords — say, for the honour of yourselves and the Scottish nobility, that my right trusty cousins of Lindesay and Ruthven, two barons of warlike fame and ancient line, have not sought the prison-house of their kind mistress for such a purpose as these words seem to imply. Say, for the sake of honour and loyalty, that my ears have deceived me."

"No, madam," said Ruthven gravely, "your ears do *not* deceive you—they deceived you when they were closed against the preachers of the evangele, and the honest advice of your faithful subjects; and when they were ever open to flattery of pickthanks and traitors, foreign cubiculars and domestic minions. The land may no longer brook the rule of one who cannot rule herself; wherefore, I pray you to comply with the last remaining wish of your subjects and counsellors, and spare yourself and us the farther agitation of matter so painful."

"And is this *all* my loving subjects require of me, my lord?" said Mary, in a tone of bitter irony. "Do they really stint themselves to the easy boon that I should yield up the crown, which is mine by birthright, to an infant which is scarcely more than a year old — fling down my sceptre, and take up a distaff — Oh no! it is too little for them to ask — That other roll of parchment contains something harder to be complied with, and which may more highly task my readiness to comply with the petitions of my lieges."

"This parchment," answered Ruthven, in the same tone of inflexible gravity, and unfolding the instrument as he spoke, "is one by which your grace constitutes your nearest in blood, and the most honourable and trustworthy of your subjects, James, Earl of Murray, Regent of the kingdom during the minority of the young King. He already holds the appointment from the Secret Council.

The Queen gave a sort of shriek, and, clapping her hands together, exclaimed, "Comes the arrow out of his quiver? — out of my brother's bow? — Alas! I looked for his return from France as my sole, at least my readiest, chance of deliverance. — And yet, when I heard he had assumed the government, I guessed he would shame to wield it in my name."

"I must pray your answer, madam," said Lord Ruthven, "to the demand of the Council."

"The demand of the Council!" said the Queen; "say rather the demand of a set of robbers, impatient to divide the spoil they have seized. To such a demand, and sent by the mouth of a traitor, whose scalp, but for my womanish mercy, should long since have stood on the city gates, Mary of Scotland has no answer."

"I trust, madam," said Lord Ruthven, "my being unacceptable to your presence will not add to your obduracy of resolution. It may become you to remember that the death of the minion, Rizzio, cost the house of Ruthven its head and leader. My father, more worthy than a whole province of such vile sycophants, died in exile, and broken-hearted."

The Queen clasped her hands on her face, and, resting her arms on the table, stooped down her head and wept so bitterly, that the tears were seen to find their way in streams between the white and slender fingers with which she endeavoured to conceal them.

"My lords," said Sir Robert Melville, "this is too much rigour. Under your lordship's favour, we came hither, not to revive old griefs, but to find the mode of avoiding new ones."

"Sir Robert Melville," said Ruthven, "we best know for what purpose we were delegated hither, and wherefore you were somewhat unnecessarily sent to attend us."

"Nay, by my hand," said Lord Lindesay, "I know not why we were cumbered with the good knight, unless he comes in place of the lump of sugar which pothicars put into their wholesome but bitter medicaments, to please a froward child — a needless labour, methinks, where men have the means to make them swallow the physic otherwise."

"Nay, my lords," said Melville, "ye best know your own secret instructions. I conceive I shall best obey mine in striving to mediate between her Grace and you."

"Be silent, Sir Robert Melville," said the Queen, arising, and her face still glowing with agitation as she spoke. "My kerchief, Fleming — I shame that traitors should have power to move me thus. — Tell me, proud lords," she added, wiping away the tears as she spoke, "by what earthly warrant can liege subjects pretend to challenge the rights of an anointed Sovereign — to throw off the allegiance they have vowed, and to take away the crown from the head on which Divine warrant hath placed it?"

"Madam," said Ruthven, "I will deal plainly with you. Your reign, from the dismal field of Pinkie-cleugh, when you were a babe in the cradle, till now that ye stand a grown dame before us, hath been such a tragedy of losses, disasters, civil dissensions, and foreign wars, that the like is not to be found in our chronicles. The French and English have, with one consent, made Scotland the battle-field on which to fight out their own ancient quarrel. — For ourselves every man's hand hath been against his brother, nor hath a year passed over without rebellion and slaughter, exile of nobles, and oppressing of the commons. We may endure it no longer, and therefore, as a prince, to whom God hath refused the gift of hearkening to wise counsel, and on whose dealings and projects no blessing hath ever descended, we pray you to give way to other rule and governance of the land, that a remnant may yet be saved to this distracted realm."

"My lord," said Mary, "it seems to me that you fling on my unhappy and devoted head those evils, which, with far more justice, I may impute to your own turbulent, wild, and untameable dispositions — the frantic violence with which you, the Magnates of Scotland, enter into feuds against each other, sticking at no cruelty to gratify your wrath, taking deep revenge for the slightest offences, and setting at defiance those wise laws which your ancestors made for stanching of such cruelty, rebelling against the lawful authority, and bearing yourselves as if there were no king in the land; or rather as if each were king in his own premises. And now you throw the blame on me — on me, whose life has been embittered — whose sleep has been broken — whose happiness has been wrecked by your dissensions. Have I not myself been obliged to traverse wilds and mountains, at the head of a few faithful followers, to maintain peace and put down oppression? Have I not worn harness on my person, and carried pistols at my saddle; fain to lay aside the softness of a woman, and the dignity of a Queen, that I might show an example to my followers?"

"We grant, madam," said Lindesay, "that the affrays occasioned by your misgovernment, may sometimes have startled you in the midst of a masque or galliard; or it may be that such may have interrupted the idolatry of the mass, or the jesuitical counsels of some French ambassador. But the longest and severest journey which your Grace has taken in my memory, was from Hawick to Hermitage Castle; and whether it was for the weal of the state, or for your own honour, rests with your Grace's conscience."

The Queen turned to him with inexpressible sweetness of tone and manner, and that engaging look which Heaven had assigned her, as if to show that the choicest arts to win men's affections may be given in vain. "Lindesay," she said, "you spoke not to me in this stern tone, and with such scurril taunt, yon fair summer evening, when you and I shot at the butts against the Earl of Mar and Mary Livingstone, and won of them the evening's collation, in the privy garden of Saint Andrews. The Master of Lindesay was then my friend, and vowed to be my soldier. How I have offended the Lord of Lindesay I know not, unless honours have changed manners."

Hardhearted as he was, Lindesay seemed struck with this unexpected appeal, but almost instantly replied, "Madam, it is well known that your Grace could in those days make fools of whomever approached you. I pretend not to have been wiser than others. But gayer men and better courtiers soon jostled aside my rude homage, and I think your Grace cannot but remember times, when my awkward attempts to take the manners that pleased you, were the sport of the court-popinjays, the Marys and the Frenchwomen."

"My lord, I grieve if I have offended you through idle gaiety," said the Queen; "and can but say it was most unwittingly done. You are fully revenged; for through gaiety," she said with a sigh, "will I never offend any one more."

"Our time is wasting, madam," said Lord Ruthven; "I must pray your decision on this weighty matter which I have submitted to you."

"What, my lord!" said the Queen, "upon the instant, and without a moment's time to deliberate?—Can the Council, as they term themselves, expect this of me?"

"Madam," replied Ruthven, "the Council hold the opinion, that since the fatal term which passed betwixt the night of King Henry's murder and the day of Carberry-hill, your Grace should have held you prepared for the measure now proposed, as the easiest escape from your numerous dangers and difficulties."

"Great God!" exclaimed the Queen; "and is it as a boon that you propose to me, what every Christian king ought to regard as a loss of honour equal to the loss of life!—You take from me my crown, my power, my subjects, my wealth, my state. What, in the name of every saint, can you offer, or do you offer, in requital of my compliance?"

"We give you pardon," answered Ruthven, sternly—"we give you space and means to spend your remaining life in penitence and seclusion—we give you time to make your peace with Heaven, and to receive the pure Gospel, which you have ever rejected and persecuted."

The Queen turned pale at the menace which this speech, as well as the rough and inflexible tones of the speaker, seemed distinctly to infer—"And if I do not comply with your request so fiercely urged, my lord, what then follows?"

She said this in a voice in which female and natural fear was contending with the feelings of insulted dignity.—There was a pause, as if no one cared to return to the question a distinct answer. At length Ruthven spoke: "There is little need to tell to your Grace, who are well read both in the laws and in the chronicles of the realm, that murder and adultery are crimes for which ere now queens themselves have suffered death."

"And where, my lord, or how, found you an accusation so horrible, against her who stands before you?" said Queen Mary. "The foul and odious calumnies which have poisoned the general mind of Scotland, and have placed me a helpless prisoner in your hands, are surely no proof of guilt?"

"We need look for no farther proof," replied the stern Lord Ruthven, "than the shameless marriage betwixt the widow of the murdered and the leader of the band of murderers! — They that joined hands in the fated month of May, had already united hearts and counsel in the deed which preceded that marriage but a few brief weeks."

"My lord, my lord!" said the Queen, eagerly, "remember well there were more consents than mine to that fatal union, that most unhappy act of a most unhappy life. The evil steps adopted by sovereigns are often the suggestion of bad counsellors; but these counsellors are worse than fiends who tempt and betray, if they themselves are the first to call their unfortunate princes to answer for the consequences of their own advice. — Heard ye never of a bond by the nobles, my lords, recommending that ill-fated union to the ill-fated Mary? Methinks, were it carefully examined, we should see that the names of Morton and of Lindesay, and of Ruthven, may be found in that bond, which pressed me to marry that unhappy man. —Ah! stout and loyal Lord Herries, who never knew guile or dishonour, you bent your noble knee to me in vain, to warn me of my danger, and wert yet the first to draw thy good sword in my cause when I suffered for neglecting thy counsel! Faithful knight and true noble, what a difference betwixt thee and those counsellors of evil, who now threaten my life for having fallen into the snares they spread for me!"

"Madam," said Ruthven, "we know that you are an orator; and perhaps for that reason the Council has sent hither men, whose converse hath been more with the wars, than with the language of the schools or the cabals of state. We but desire to know if, on assurance of life and honour, ye will demit the rule of this kingdom of Scotland?"

"And what warrant have I," said the Queen, "that ye will keep treaty with me, if I should barter my kingly estate for seclusion, and leave to weep in secret?"

"Our honour and our word, madam," answered Ruthven.

"They are too slight and unsolid pledges, my lord," said the Queen; "add at least a handful of thistle-down to give them weight in the balance."

"Away, Ruthven," said Lindesay; "she was ever deaf to counsel, save of slaves and sycophants; let her remain by her refusal, and abide by it!"

"Stay, my lord," said Sir Robert Melville, "or rather permit me to have but a few minutes' private audience with her Grace. If my presence with you could avail aught, it must be as a mediator — do not, I conjure you, leave the castle, or break off the conference, until I bring you word how her Grace shall finally stand disposed."

"We will remain in the hall," said Lindesay, "for half an hour's space; but in despising our words and our pledge of honour, she has touched the honour of my name — let her look herself to the course she has to pursue. If the half hour should pass away without her determining to comply with the demands of the nation, her career will be brief enough."

With little ceremony the two nobles left the apartment, traversed the vestibule, and descended the winding-stairs, the clash of Lindesay's huge sword being heard as it rang against each step in his descent. George Douglas followed them, after exchanging with Melville a gesture of surprise and sympathy.

As soon as they were gone, the Queen, giving way to grief, fear, and agitation, threw herself into the seat, wrung her hands, and seemed to abandon herself to despair. Her female attendants, weeping themselves, endeavoured yet to pray her to be composed, and Sir Robert Melville, kneeling at her feet, made the same entreaty. After giving way to a passionate burst of sorrow, she at length said to Melville, "Kneel not to me, Melville—mock me not with the homage of the person, when the heart is far away—Why stay you behind with the deposed, the condemned? her who has but few hours perchance to live? You have been favoured as well as the rest; why do you continue the empty show of gratitude and thankfulness any longer than they?"

"Madam," said Sir Robert Melville, "so help me Heaven at my need, my heart is as true to you as when you were in your highest place."

"True to me! true to me!" repeated the Queen, with some scorn; "tush, Melville, what signifies the truth which walks hand in hand with my enemies' falsehood?—thy hand and thy sword have never been so well acquainted that I can trust thee in aught where manhood is required—Oh, Seyton, for thy bold father, who is both wise, true, and valiant!"

Roland Græme could withstand no longer his earnest desire to offer his services to a princess so distressed and so beautiful. "If one sword," he said, "madam, can do any thing to back the wisdom of this grave counsellor, or to defend your rightful cause, here is my weapon, and here is my hand ready to draw and use it." And raising his sword with one hand, he laid the other upon the hilt.

As he thus held up the weapon, Catherine Seyton exclaimed, "Methinks I see a token from my father, madam;" and immediately crossing the apartment, she took Roland Græme by the skirt of the cloak, and asked him earnestly whence he had that sword.

The page answered with surprise, "Methinks this is no presence in which to jest—Surely, damsel, you yourself best know whence and how I obtained the weapon."

"Is this a time for folly?" said Catherine Seyton; "unsheathe the sword instantly!"

"If the Queen commands me," said the youth, looking towards his royal mistress.

"For shame, maiden!" said the Queen; "wouldst thou instigate the poor boy to enter into useless strife with the two most approved soldiers in Scotland?"

"In your Grace's cause," replied the page, "I will venture my life upon them!" And as he spoke, he drew his weapon partly from the sheath, and a piece of parchment, rolled around the blade, fell out and dropped on the floor. Catherine Seyton caught it up with eager haste.

"It is my father's hand-writing," she said, "and doubtless conveys his best duteous advice to your Majesty; I know that it was prepared to be sent in this weapon, but I expected another messenger."

"By my faith, fair one," thought Roland, "and if you knew not that I had such a secret missive about me, I was yet more ignorant."

The Queen cast her eye upon the scroll, and remained a few minutes wrapped in deep thought. "Sir Robert Melville," she at length said, "this scroll advises me to submit myself to necessity, and to subscribe the deeds these hard men have brought with them, as one who gives way to the natural fear inspired by the threats of rebels and murderers. You, Sir Robert, are a wise man, and Seyton is both sagacious and brave. Neither, I think, would mislead me in this matter."

"Madam," said Melville, "if I have not the strength of body of the Lord Herries or Seyton, I will yield to neither in zeal for your Majesty's service. I cannot fight for you like these lords, but neither of them is more willing to die for your service."

"I believe it, my old and faithful counsellor," said the Queen, "and believe me, Melville, I did thee but a moment's injustice. Read what my Lord Seyton hath written to us, and give us thy best counsel."

He glanced over the parchment, and instantly replied,—"Oh! my dear and royal mistress, only treason itself could give you other advice than Lord Seyton has here expressed. He, Herries, Huntly, the English ambassador Throgmorton, and others, your friends, are all alike of opinion, that whatever deeds or instruments you execute within these walls, must lose all force and effect, as extorted from your Grace by duresse, by sufferance of present evil, and fear of men, and harm to ensue on your refusal. Yield, therefore, to the tide, and be assured, that in subscribing what parchments they present to you, you bind yourself to nothing, since your act of signature wants that which alone can make it valid, the free will of the granter."

"Ay, so says my Lord Seyton," replied Mary; "yet methinks, for the daughter of so long a line of sovereigns to resign her birthright, because rebels press upon her with threats, argues little of royalty, and will read ill for the fame of Mary in future chronicles. Tush! Sir Robert Melville, the traitors may use black threats and bold words, but they will not dare to put their hands forth on our person."

"Alas! madam, they have already dared so far and incurred such peril by the lengths which they have gone, that they are but one step from the worst and uttermost."

"Surely," said the Queen, her fears again predominating, "Scottish nobles would not lend themselves to assassinate a helpless woman?"

"Bethink you, madam," he replied, "what horrid spectacles have been seen in our day; and what act is so dark, that some Scottish hand has not been found to dare it? Lord Lindesay, besides his natural sullenness and hardness of temper, is the near kinsman of Henry Darnley, and Ruthven has his own deep and dangerous plans. The Council, besides, speak of proofs by writ and word, of a casket with letters — of I know not what."

"Ah! good Melville," answered the Queen, "were I as sure of the even-handed integrity of my judges, as of my own innocence — and yet ——"

"Oh! pause, madam," said Melville; "even innocence must sometimes for a season stoop to injurious blame. Besides, you are here ——"

He looked round, and paused.

"Speak out, Melville," said the Queen, "never one approached my person who wished to work me evil; and even this poor page, whom I have to-day seen for the first time in my life, I can trust safely with your communication."

"Nay, madam," answered Melville, "in such emergence, and he being the bearer of Lord Seyton's message, I will venture to say, before him and these fair ladies, whose truth and fidelity I dispute not—I say I will venture to say, that there are other modes besides that of open trial, by which deposed sovereigns often die; and that, as Machiavel saith, there is but one step betwixt a king's prison and his grave."

"Oh! were it but swift and easy for the body," said the unfortunate Princess, "were it but a safe and happy change for the soul, the woman lives not that would take the step so soon as I — But, alas! Melville, when we think of death, a thousand sins, which we have trod as worms beneath our feet, rise up against us as flaming serpents. Most injuriously do they accuse me of aiding Darnley's death; yet, blessed Lady! I afforded too open occasion for the suspicion — I espoused Bothwell."

"Think not of that now, madam," said Melville, "think rather of the immediate mode of saving yourself and son. Comply with the present unreasonable demands, and trust that better times will shortly arrive."

"Madam," said Roland Græme, "if it pleases you that I should do so, I will presently swim through the lake, if they refuse me other conveyance to the shore; I will go to the courts successively of England, France, and Spain, and will show you have subscribed these vile instruments from no stronger impulse than the fear of death, and I will do battle against them that say otherwise."

The Queen turned her round, and with one of those sweet smiles which, during the era of life's romance, overpay every risk, held her hand towards Roland, but without speaking a word. He kneeled reverently, and kissed it, and Melville again resumed his plea.

"Madam," he said, "time presses, and you must not let those boats, which I see they are even now preparing, put forth on the lake. Here are enough of witnesses — your ladies — this bold youth — myself, when it can serve your cause effectually, for I would not hastily stand committed in this matter — but even without me here is evidence enough to show, that you have yielded to the demands of the Council through force and fear, but from no sincere and unconstrained assent. Their boats are already manned for their return — oh! permit your old servant to recall them."

"Melville," said the Queen, "thou art an ancient courtier — when didst thou ever know a Sovereign Prince recall to his presence subjects who had parted from him on such terms as those on which these envoys of the Council left us, and who yet were recalled without submission or apology?— Let it cost me both life and crown, I will not again command them to my presence."

"Alas! madam, that empty form should make a barrier! If I rightly understand, you are not unwilling to listen to real and advantageous counsel — but your scruple is saved — I hear them returning to ask your final resolution. Oh! take the advice of the noble Seyton, and you may once more command those who now usurp a triumph over you. But hush! I hear them in the vestibule."

As he concluded speaking, George Douglas opened the door of the apartment, and marshalled in the two noble envoys.

"We come, madam," said the Lord Ruthven, "to request your answer to the proposal of the Council."

"Your final answer," said Lord Lindesay; "for with a refusal you must couple the certainty that you have precipitated your fate, and renounced the last opportunity of making peace with God, and ensuring your longer abode in the world."

"My lords," said Mary, with inexpressible grace and dignity, "the evils we cannot resist we must submit to—I will subscribe these parchments with such liberty of choice as my condition permits me. Were I on yonder shore, with a fleet jennet and ten good and loyal knights around me, I would subscribe my sentence of eternal condemnation as soon as the resignation of my throne. But here, in the Castle of Lochleven, with deep water around me—and you, my lords, beside me,—I have no freedom of choice.—Give me the pen, Melville, and bear witness to what I do, and why I do it."

"It is our hope your Grace will not suppose yourself compelled by any apprehensions from us," said the Lord Ruthven, "to execute what must be your own voluntary deed."

The Queen had already stooped towards the table, and placed the parchment before her, with the pen between her fingers, ready for the important act of signature. But when Lord Ruthven had done speaking, she looked up, stopped short, and threw down the pen. "If," she said, "I am expected to declare I give away my crown of free will, or otherwise than because I am compelled to renounce it by the threat of worse evils to myself and my subjects, I will not put my name to such an untruth — not to gain full possession of England, France, and Scotland!—all once my own, in possession, or by right."

"Beware, madam," said Lindesay, and, snatching hold of the Queen's arm with his own gauntleted hand, he pressed it, in the rudeness of his passion, more closely, perhaps, than he was himself aware of, — "beware how you contend with those who are the stronger, and have the mastery of your fate!"

He held his grasp on her arm, bending his eyes on her with a stern and intimidating look, till both Ruthven and Melville cried shame; and Douglas, who had hitherto remained in a state of apparent apathy, had made a stride from the door, as if to interfere. The rude Baron then quitted his hold, disguising the confusion which he really felt at having indulged his passion to such extent, under a sullen and contemptuous smile.

The Queen immediately began, with an expression of pain, to bare the arm which he had grasped, by drawing up the sleeve of her gown, and it appeared that his gripe had left the purple marks of his iron fingers upon her flesh — "My lord," she said, "as a knight and gentleman, you might have spared my frail arm so severe a proof that you have the greater strength on your side, and are resolved to use it — But I thank you for it — it is the most decisive token of the terms on which this day's business is to rest.—I draw you to witness, both lords and ladies," she said, "showing the marks of the grasp on her arm, "that I subscribe these instruments in obedience to the sign manual of my Lord of Lindesay, which you may see imprinted on mine arm."*

Lindesay would have spoken, but was restrained by his colleague Ruthven, who said to him, "Peace, my lord. Let the Lady Mary of Scotland ascribe her signature to what she will, it is our business to procure it, and carry it to the Council. Should there be debate hereafter on the manner in which it was adhibited, there will be time enough for it."

Lindesay was silent accordingly, only muttering within his beard, "I meant not to hurt her; but I think women's flesh be as tender as new-fallen snow."

The Queen meanwhile subscribed the rolls of parchment with a hasty indifference, as if they had been matters of slight consequence, or of mere formality. When she had performed this painful task, she arose, and, having curtsied to the lords, was about to withdraw to her chamber. Ruthven and Sir Robert Melville made, the first a formal reverence, the second an obeisance, in which his desire to acknowledge his sympathy was obviously checked by the fear of appearing in the eyes of his colleagues too partial to his former mistress. But Lindesay stood motionless, even when they were preparing to withdraw. At length, as if moved by a sudden impulse, he walked round the table which had hitherto been betwixt them and the Queen, kneeled on one knee, took her hand, kissed it, let it fall, and arose— "Lady," he said, "thou art a noble creature, even though thou hast abused God's choicest gifts. I pay that devotion to thy manliness of spirit, which I would not have paid to the power thou hast long undeservedly wielded—I kneel to Mary Stewart, not to the Queen."

"The Queen and Mary Stewart pity thee alike, Lindesay," said Mary — "alike thee pity, and they forgive thee. An honoured soldier hadst thou been by a king's side—leagued with rebels, what art thou but a good blade in the hands of a ruffian? — Farewell, my Lord Ruthven, the smoother but the deeper traitor.—Farewell, Melville—Mayest thou find masters that can understand state policy better, and have the means to reward it more richly, than Mary Stewart. — Farewell, George of Douglas — make your respected grand-dame comprehend that we would be alone for the remainder of the day — God wot, we have need to collect our thoughts."

All bowed and withdrew; but scarce had they entered the vestibule, ere Ruthven and Lindesay were at variance. "Chide not with me, Ruthven,"

* The details of this remarkable event are, as given in the preceding chapter, imaginary; but the outline of the events is historical. Sir Robert Lindesay, brother to the author of the Memoirs, was at first intrusted with the delicate commission of persuading the imprisoned queen to resign her crown. As he flatly refused to interfere, they determined to send the Lord Lindesay, one of the rudest and most violent of their own faction, with instructions, first to use fair persuasions, and if these did not succeed, to enter into harder terms Knox associates Lord Ruthven with Lindesay in this alarming commission. He was the son of that Lord Ruthven who was prime agent in the murder of Rizzio; and little mercy was to be expected from his conjunction with Lindesay.

The employment of such rude tools argued a resolution on the part of those who had the Queen's person in their power, to proceed to the utmost extremities, should they find Mary obstinate. To avoid this pressing danger, Sir Robert Melville was despatched by them to Lochleven, carrying with him, concealed in the scabbard of his sword, letters to the Queen from the Earl of Athole, Maitland of Lethington, and even from Throgmorton, the English Ambassador, who was then favourable to the unfortunate Mary, conjuring her to yield to the necessity of the times, and to subscribe such deeds as Lindesay should lay before her, without being startled by their tenor: and assuring her that her doing so, in the state of captivity under which she was placed, would neither, in law, honour, nor conscience, be binding upon her when she should obtain her liberty. Submitting by the advice of one part of her subjects to the menace of the others, and learning that Lindesay was arrived in a boasting, that is, threatening humour, the Queen, "with some reluctancy, and with tears," saith Knox, subscribed one deed resigning her crown to her infant son, and another establishing the Earl of Murray regent. It seems agreed by historians that Lindesay behaved with great brutality on the occasion. The deeds were signed 24th July, 1567.

Lindesay was heard to say, in answer to something more indistinctly urged by his colleague — "Chide not with me, for I will not brook it! You put the hangman's office on me in this matter, and even the very hangman hath leave to ask some pardon of those on whom he does his office. I would I had as deep cause to be this lady's friend as I have to be her enemy — thou shouldst see if I spared limb and life in her quarrel."

"Thou art a sweet minion," said Ruthven, "to fight a lady's quarrel, and all for a brent brow and a tear in the eye! Such toys have been out of thy thoughts this many a year."

"Do me right, Ruthven," said Lindesay. "You are like a polished corslet of steel; it shines more gaudily, but it is not a whit softer — nay, it is five times harder than a Glasgow breastplate of hammered iron. Enough. We know each other."

They descended the stairs, were heard to summon their boats, and the Queen signed to Roland Græme to retire to the vestibule, and leave her with her female attendants.

Chapter the Twenty-Third.

Give me a morsel on the greensward rather,
Coarse as you will the cooking—Let the fresh spring
Bubble beside my napkin—and the free birds
Twittering and chirping, hop from bough to bough,
To claim the crumbs I leave for perquisites—
Your prison feasts I like not.

THE WOODSMAN, A DRAMA.

A RECESS in the vestibule was enlightened by a small window, at which Roland Græme stationed himself to mark the departure of the lords. He could see their followers mustering on horseback under their respective banners — the western sun glancing on their corslets and steel-caps as they moved to and fro, mounted or dismounted, at intervals. On the narrow space betwixt the castle and the water, the Lords Ruthven and Lindesay were already moving slowly to their boats, accompanied by the Lady of Lochleven, her grandson, and their principal attendants. They took a ceremonious leave of each other, as Roland could discern by their gestures, and the boats put off from their landing-place; the boatmen stretched to their oars, and they speedily diminished upon the eye of the idle gazer, who had no better employment than to watch their motions. Such seemed also the occupation of the Lady Lochleven and George Douglas, who, returning from the landing-place, looked frequently back to the boats, and at length stopped as if to observe their progress under the window at which Roland Græme was stationed. — As they gazed on the lake, he could hear the lady distinctly say, "And she has bent her mind to save her life at the expense of her kingdom?"

"Her life, madam!" replied her son; "I know not who would dare to attempt it in the castle of my father. Had I dreamt that it was with such purpose that Lindesay insisted on bringing his followers hither, neither he nor they should have passed the iron gate of Lochleven castle."

"I speak not of private slaughter, my son, but of open trial, condemnation, and execution; for with such she has been threatened, and to such threats she has given way. Had she not more of the false Gusian blood than of the royal race of Scotland in her veins, she had bidden them defiance to their teeth — But it is all of the same complexion, and meanness is the natural companion of profligacy.—I am discharged, forsooth, from intruding on her gracious presence this evening. Go thou, my son, and render the usual service of the meal to this unqueened Queen."

"So please you, lady mother," said Douglas, "I care not greatly to approach her presence."

"Thou art right, my son; and therefore I trust thy prudence, even because I have noted thy caution. She is like an isle on the ocean, surrounded with shelves and quicksands; its verdure fair and inviting to the eye, but the wreck of many a goodly vessel which hath approached it too rashly. But for thee, my son, I fear nought; and we may not, with our honour, suffer her to eat without the attendance of one of us. She may die by the judgment of Heaven, or the fiend may have power over her in her despair; and then we would be touched in honour to show that in our house, and at our table, she had had all fair play and fitting usage."

Here Roland was interrupted by a smart tap on the shoulders, reminding him sharply of Adam Woodcock's adventure of the preceding evening. He turned round, almost expecting to see the page of Saint Michael's hostelry. He saw, indeed, Catherine Seyton; but she was in female attire, differing, no doubt, a great deal in shape and materials from that which she had worn when they first met, and becoming her birth as the daughter of a great baron, and her rank as the attendant on a princess. "So, fair page," said she, "eaves-dropping is one of your page-like qualities, I presume."

"Fair sister," answered Roland, in the same tone, "if some friends of mine be as well acquainted with the rest of our mystery as they are with the arts of swearing, swaggering, and switching, they need ask no page in Christendom for farther insight into his vocation."

"Unless that pretty speech infer that you have yourself had the discipline of the switch since we last met, the probability whereof I nothing doubt, I profess, fair page, I am at a loss to conjecture your meaning. But there is no time to debate it now—they come with the evening meal. Be pleased, Sir Page, to do your duty."

Four servants entered bearing dishes, preceded by the same stern old steward whom Roland had already seen, and followed by George Douglas, already mentioned as the grandson of the Lady of Lochleven, and who, acting as seneschal, represented, upon this occasion, his father, the Lord of the Castle. He entered with his arms folded on his bosom, and his looks bent on the ground. With the assistance of Roland Græme, a table was suitably covered in the next or middle apartment, on which the domestics placed their burdens with great reverence, the steward and Douglas bending low when they had seen the table properly adorned, as if their royal prisoner had sat at the board in question. The door opened, and Douglas, raising his eyes hastily, cast them again on the earth, when he perceived it was only the Lady Mary Fleming who entered.

"Her Grace," she said, "will not eat to-night."

"Let us hope she may be otherwise persuaded," said Douglas; "meanwhile, madam, please to see our duty performed."

A servant presented bread and salt on a silver plate, and the old steward carved for Douglas a small morsel in succession from each of the dishes presented, which he tasted, as was then the custom at the tables of princes, to which death was often suspected to find its way in the disguise of food.

"The Queen will not then come forth to-night?" said Douglas.

"She has so determined," replied the lady.

"Our farther attendance then is unnecessary—we leave you to your supper, fair ladies, and wish you good even."

He retired slowly as he came, and with the same air of deep dejection, and was followed by the attendants belonging to the castle. The two ladies sate down to their meal, and Roland Græme, with ready alacrity, prepared to wait upon them. Catherine Seyton whispered to her companion, who replied with the question spoken in a low tone, but looking at the page — "Is he of gentle blood and well nurtured?"

The answer which she received seemed satisfactory, for she said to Roland, "Sit down, young gentleman, and eat with your sisters in captivity."

"Permit me rather to perform my duty in attending them," said Roland, anxious to show he was possessed of the high tone of deference prescribed by the rules of chivalry towards the fair sex, and especially to dames and maidens of quality.

"You will find, Sir Page," said Catherine, "you will have little time allowed you for your meal; waste it not in ceremony, or you may rue your politeness ere to-morrow morning."

"Your speech is too free, maiden," said the elder lady; "the modesty of the youth may teach you more fitting fashions towards one whom to-day you have seen for the first time."

Catherine Seyton cast down her eyes, but not till she had given a single glance of inexpressible archness towards Roland, whom her more grave companion now addressed in a tone of protection.

"Regard her not, young gentleman — she knows little of the world, save the forms of a country nunnery — take thy place at the board-end, and refresh thyself after thy journey."

Roland Græme obeyed willingly, as it was the first food he had that day tasted; for Lindesay and his followers seemed regardless of human wants. Yet, notwithstanding the sharpness of his appetite, a natural gallantry of disposition, the desire of showing himself a well-nurtured gentleman, in all courtesies towards the fair sex, and, for aught I know, the pleasure of assisting Catherine Seyton, kept his attention awake, during the meal, to all those nameless acts of duty and service which gallants of that age were accustomed to render. He carved with neatness and decorum, and selected duly whatever was most delicate to place before the ladies. Ere they could form a wish, he sprung from the table, ready to comply with it — poured wine — tempered it with water — removed the exchanged trenchers, and performed the whole honours of the table, with an air at once of cheerful diligence, profound respect, and graceful promptitude.

When he observed that they had finished eating, he hastened to offer to the elder lady the silver ewer, basin, and napkin, with the ceremony and gravity which he would have used towards Mary herself. He next, with the same decorum, having supplied the basin with fair water, presented it to Catherine Seyton. Apparently, she was determined to disturb his self-possession, if possible; for, while in the act of bathing her hands, she contrived, as it were by accident, to flirt some drops of water upon the face of the assiduous assistant. But if such was her mischievous purpose she was completely disappointed; for Roland Græme, internally piquing himself on his self-command, neither laughed nor was discomposed; and all that the maiden gained by her frolic was a severe rebuke from her companion, taxing her with mal-address and indecorum. Catherine replied not, but sat pouting, something in the humour of a spoilt child, who watches the opportunity of wreaking upon some one or other its resentment for a deserved reprimand.

The Lady Mary Fleming, in the meanwhile, was naturally well pleased with the exact and reverent observance of the page, and said to Catherine, after a favourable glance at Roland Græme, — "You might well say, Catherine, our companion in captivity was well born and gentle nurtured. I would not make him vain by my praise, but his services enable us to dispense with those which George Douglas condescends not to afford us, save when the Queen is herself in presence."

"Umph! I think hardly," answered Catherine. "George Douglas is one of the most handsome gallants in Scotland, and 'tis pleasure to see him even still, when the gloom of Lochleven Castle has shed the same melancholy over him, that it has done over every thing else. When he was at Holyrood who would have said the young sprightly George Douglas would have been contented to play the locksman here in Lochleven, with no gayer amusement than that of turning the key on two or three helpless women? — a strange office for a Knight of the Bleeding Heart — why does he not leave it to his father or his brothers?"

"Perhaps, like us, he has no choice," answered the Lady Fleming. "But, Catherine, thou hast used thy brief space at court well, to remember what George Douglas was then."

"I used mine eyes, which I suppose was what I was designed to do, and they were worth using there. When I was at the nunnery, they were very useless appurtenances; and now I am at Lochleven, they are good for nothing, save to look over that eternal work of embroidery."

"You speak thus, when you have been but a few brief hours amongst us — was this the maiden who would live and die in a dungeon, might she but have permission to wait on her gracious Queen?"

"Nay, if you chide in earnest, my jest is ended," said Catherine Seyton. "I would not yield in attachment to my poor god-mother, to the gravest dame that ever had wise saws upon her tongue, and a double-starched ruff around her throat — you know I would not, Dame Mary Fleming, and it is putting shame on me to say otherwise."

"She will challenge the other court lady," thought Roland Græme; "she will to a certainty fling down her glove, and if Dame Mary Fleming hath but the soul to lift it, we may have a combat in the lists!"—but the answer of Lady Mary Fleming was such as turns away wrath.

"Thou art a good child," she said, "my Catherine, and a faithful; but Heaven pity him who shall have one day a creature so beautiful to delight him, and a thing so mischievous to torment him — thou art fit to drive twenty husbands stark mad."

"Nay," said Catherine, resuming the full career of her careless good-humour, "he must be half-witted beforehand, that gives me such an opportunity. But I am glad you are not angry with me in sincerity," casting herself as she spoke into the arms of her friend, and continuing, with a tone of apologetic fondness, while she kissed her on either side of the face; "you know, my dear Fleming, that I have to contend with both my father's lofty pride, and with my mother's high spirit — God bless them! they have left me these good qualities, having small portion to give besides, as times go — and so I am wilful and saucy; but let me remain only a week in this castle, and oh, my dear Fleming, my spirit will be as chastised and humble as thine own."

Dame Mary Fleming's sense of dignity, and love of form, could not resist this affectionate appeal. She kissed Catherine Seyton in her turn affectionately; while, answering the last part of her speech, she said, "Now Our Lady forbid, dear Catherine, that you should lose aught that is beseeming of what becomes so well your light heart and lively humour. Keep but your sharp wit on this side of madness, and it cannot but be a blessing to us. But let me go, mad wench — I hear her Grace touch her silver call." And, extricating herself from Catherine's grasp, she went towards the door of Queen Mary's apartment, from which was heard the low tone of a silver whistle, which, now only used by the boatswains in the navy, was then, for want of bells, the ordinary mode by which ladies, even of the very highest rank, summoned their domestics. When she had made two or three steps towards the door, however, she turned back, and advancing to the young couple whom she left together, she said, in a very serious though a low tone, "I trust it is impossible that we can, any of us, or in any circumstances, forget, that, few as we are, we form the household of the Queen of Scotland; and that, in her calamity, all boyish mirth and childish jesting can only serve to give a great triumph to her enemies, who have already found their account in objecting to her the lightness of every idle folly, that the young and the gay practised in her court." So saying, she left the apartment.

Catherine Seyton seemed much struck with this remonstrance — She suffered herself to drop into the seat which she had quitted when she went to embrace Dame Mary Fleming, and for some time rested her brow upon her hands; while Roland Græme looked at her earnestly, with a mixture of emotions which perhaps he himself could neither have analysed nor explained. As she raised her face slowly from the posture to which a momentary feeling of self-rebuke had depressed it, her eyes encountered those of Roland, and became gradually animated with their usual spirit of malicious drollery, which not unnaturally excited a similar expression in those of the equally volatile page. They sat for the space of two minutes, each looking at the other with great seriousness on their features, and much mirth in their eyes, until at length Catherine was the first to break silence.

"May I pray you, fair sir," she began, very demurely, "to tell me what you see in my face to arouse looks so extremely sagacious and knowing as those with which it is your worship's pleasure to honour me? It would seem as if there were some wonderful confidence and intimacy betwixt us, fair sir, if one is to judge from your extremely cunning looks; and so help me, Our Lady, as I never saw you but twice in my life before."

"And where were those happy occasions," said Roland, "if I may be bold enough to ask the question?"

"At the nunnery of St. Catherine's," said the damsel, "in the first instance; and, in the second, during five minutes of a certain raid or foray which it was your pleasure to make into the lodging of my lord and father, Lord Seyton, from which, to my surprise, as probably to your own, you returned with a token of friendship and favour, instead of broken bones, which were the more probable reward of your intrusion, considering the prompt ire of the house of Seyton. I am deeply mortified," she added, ironically, "that your recollection should require refreshment on a subject so important; and that my memory should be stronger than yours on such an occasion, is truly humiliating."

"Your own memory is not so exactly correct, fair mistress," answered the page, "seeing you have forgotten meeting the third, in the hostelrie of St. Michael's, when it pleased you to lay your switch across the face of my comrade, in order, I warrant, to show that, in the house of Seyton, neither the prompt ire of its descendants, nor the use of the doublet and hose, are subject to Salique law, or confined to the use of the males."

"Fair sir," answered Catherine, looking at him with great steadiness, and some surprise, "unless your fair wits have forsaken you, I am at a loss what to conjecture of your meaning."

"By my troth, fair mistress," answered Roland, "and were I as wise a warlock as Michael Scott, I could scarce riddle the dream you read me. Did I not see you last night in the hostelrie of St. Michael's?—Did you not bring me this sword, with command not to draw it save at the command of my native and rightful Sovereign? And have I not done as you required me? Or is the sword a piece of lath—my word a bulrush—my memory a dream — and my eyes good for nought — espials which corbies might pick out of my head?"

"And if your eyes serve you not more truly on other occasions than in your vision of St. Michael," said Catherine, "I know not, the pain apart, that the corbies would do you any great injury in the deprivation —But hark, the bell — hush, for God's sake, we are interrupted.——"

The damsel was right; for no sooner had the dull toll of the castle bell begun to resound through the vaulted apartment, than the door of the vestibule flew open, and the steward, with his severe countenance, his gold chain, and his white rod, entered the apartment, followed by the same train of domestics who had placed the dinner on the table, and who now, with the same ceremonious formality, began to remove it.

The steward remained motionless as some old picture, while the domestics did their office; and when it was accomplished, every thing removed from the table, and the board itself taken from its tressels and disposed against the wall, he said aloud, without addressing any one in particular, and somewhat in the tone of a herald reading a proclamation, "My noble lady, Dame Margaret Erskine, by marriage Douglas, lets the Lady Mary of Scotland and her attendants to wit, that a servant of the true evangele, her reverend chaplain, will to-night, as usual, expound, lecture, and catechise, according to the forms of the congregation of gospellers."

"Hark you, my friend, Mr. Dryfesdale," said Catherine, "I understand this announcement is a nightly form of yours. Now, I pray you to remark, that the Lady Fleming and I—for I trust your insolent invitation concerns us only—have chosen Saint Peter's pathway to Heaven, so I see no one whom your godly exhortation, catechise, or lecture, can benefit, excepting this poor page, who, being in Satan's hand as well as yourself, had better worship with you than remain to cumber our better-advised devotions."

The page was well-nigh giving a round denial to the assertions which this speech implied, when, remembering what had passed betwixt him and the Regent, and seeing Catherine's finger raised in a monitory fashion, he felt himself, as on former occasions at the Castle of Avenel, obliged to submit to the task of dissimulation, and followed Dryfesdale down to the castle chapel, where he assisted in the devotions of the evening.

The chaplain was named Elias Henderson. He was a man in the prime of life, and possessed of good natural parts, carefully improved by the best education which those times afforded. To these qualities were added a faculty of close and terse reasoning; and, at intervals, a flow of happy illustration and natural eloquence. The religious faith of Roland Græme, as we have already had opportunity to observe, rested on no secure basis, but was entertained rather in obedience to his grandmother's behests, and his secret desire to contradict the chaplain of Avenel Castle, than from any fixed or steady reliance which he placed on the Romish creed. His ideas had been of late considerably enlarged by the scenes he had passed through; and feeling that there was shame in not understanding something of those political disputes betwixt the professors of the ancient and the reformed faith, he listened with more attention than it had hitherto been in his nature to yield on such occasions, to an animated discussion of some of the principal points of difference betwixt the churches. So passed away the first day in the Castle of Lochleven; and those which followed it were, for some time, of a very monotonous and uniform tenor.

Chapter the Twenty-Fourth.

'Tis a weary life this——
Vaults overhead, and grates and bars around me,
And my sad hours spent with as sad companions,
Whose thoughts are brooding o'er their own mischances,
Far, far too deeply to take part in mine.

THE WOODSMAN.

THE course of life to which Mary and her little retinue were doomed, was in the last degree secluded and lonely, varied only as the weather permitted or rendered impossible the Queen's usual walk in the garden or on the battlements. The greater part of the morning she wrought with her ladies at those pieces of needlework, many of which still remain proofs of her indefatigable application. At such hours the page was permitted the freedom of the castle and islet; nay, he was sometimes invited to attend George Douglas when he went a-sporting upon the lake, or on its margin; opportunities of diversion which were only clouded by the remarkable melancholy which always seemed to brood on that gentleman's brow, and to mark his whole demeanour, — a sadness so profound, that Roland never observed him to smile, or to speak any word unconnected with the immediate object of their exercise.

The most pleasant part of Roland's day, was the occasional space which he was permitted to pass in personal attendance on the Queen and her ladies, together with the regular dinner-time, which he always spent with Dame Mary Fleming and Catharine Seyton. At these periods, he had frequent occasion to admire the lively spirit and inventive imagination of the latter damsel, who was unwearied in her contrivances to amuse her mistress, and to banish, for a time at least, the melancholy which preyed on her bosom. She danced, she sung, she recited tales of ancient and modern times, with that heartfelt exertion of talent, of which the pleasure lies not in the vanity of displaying it to others, but in the enthusiastic consciousness that we possess it ourselves. And yet these high accomplishments were mixed with an air of rusticity and harebrained vivacity, which seemed rather to belong to some village maid, the coquette of the ring around the Maypole, than to the high-bred descendant of an ancient baron. A touch of audacity, altogether short of effrontery, and far less approaching to vulgarity, gave as it were a wildness to all that she did; and Mary, while defending her from some of the occasional censures of her grave companion, compared her to a trained singing-bird escaped from a cage, which practises in all the luxuriance of freedom, and in full possession of the greenwood bough, the airs which it had learned during its earlier captivity.

The moments which the page was permitted to pass in the presence of this fascinating creature, danced so rapidly away, that, brief as they were, they compensated the weary dulness of all the rest of the day. The space of indulgence, however, was always brief, nor were any private interviews betwixt him and Catharine permitted, or even possible. Whether it were some special precaution respecting the Queen's household, or whether it were her general ideas of propriety, Dame Fleming seemed particularly attentive to prevent the young people from holding any separate correspondence together, and bestowed, for Catharine's sole benefit in this matter, the full stock of prudence and experience which she had acquired, when mother of the Queen's maidens of honour, and by which she had gained their hearty hatred. Casual meetings, however, could not be prevented, unless Catherine had been more desirous of shunning, or Roland Græme less anxious in watching for them. A smile, a gibe, a sarcasm, disarmed of its severity by the arch look with which it was accompanied, was all that time permitted to pass between them on such occasions. But such passing interviews neither afforded means nor opportunity to renew the discussion of the circumstances attending their earlier acquaintance, nor to permit Roland to investigate more accurately the mysterious apparition of the page in the purple velvet cloak at the hostelrie of Saint Michael's.

The winter months slipped heavily away, and spring was already advanced, when Roland Græme observed a gradual change in the manners of his fellow-prisoners. Having no business of his own to attend to, and being, like those of his age, education, and degree, sufficiently curious concerning what passed around, he began by degrees to suspect, and finally to be convinced, that there was something in agitation among his companions in captivity, to which they did not desire that he should be privy. Nay, he became almost certain that, by some means unintelligible to him, Queen Mary held correspondence beyond the walls and waters which surrounded her prison-house, and that she nourished some secret hope of deliverance oı escape. In the conversations betwixt her and her attendants, at which he was necessarily present, the Queen could not always avoid showing that she was acquainted with the events which were passing abroad in the world, and which he only heard through her report. He observed that she wrote more and worked less than had been her former custom, and that, as if desirous to lull suspicion asleep, she changed her manner towards the Lady Lochleven into one more gracious, and which seemed to express a resigned submission to her lot. "They think I am blind," he said to himself, "and that I am unfit to be trusted because I am so young, or it may be because I was sent hither by the Regent. Well! — be it so — they may be glad to confide in me in the long run; and Catherine Seyton, for as saucy as she is, may find me as safe a confidant as that sullen Douglas, whom she is always running after. It may be they are angry with me for listening to Master Elias Henderson; but it was their own fault for sending me there, and if the man speaks truth and good sense, and preaches only the word of God, he is as likely to be right as either Pope or Councils."

It is probable that in this last conjecture, Roland Græme had hit upon the real cause why the ladies had not intrusted him with their councils. He had of late had several conferences with Henderson on the subject of religion, and had given him to understand that he stood in need of his instructions, although he had not thought there was either prudence or necessity for confessing that hitherto he had held the tenets of the Church of Rome.

Elias Henderson, a keen propagator of the reformed faith, had sought the seclusion of Lochleven Castle, with the express purpose and expectation of making converts from Rome amongst the domestics of the dethroned Queen, and confirming the faith of those who already held the Protestant doctrines. Perhaps his hopes soared a little higher, and he might nourish some expectation of a proselyte more distinguished in the person of the deposed Queen. But the pertinacity with which she and her female attendants refused to see or listen to him, rendered such hope, if he nourished it, altogether abortive.

The opportunity, therefore, of enlarging the religious information of Roland Græme, and bringing him to a more due sense of his duties to Heaven, was hailed by the good man as a door opened by Providence for the salvation of a sinner. He dreamed not, indeed, that he was converting a Papist, but such was the ignorance which Roland displayed upon some material points of the reformed doctrine, that Master Henderson, while praising his docility to the Lady Lochleven and her grandson, seldom failed to add, that his venerable brother, Henry Warden, must be now decayed in strength and in mind, since he found a catechumen of his flock so ill-grounded in the principles of his belief. For this, indeed, Roland Græme thought it was unnecessary to assign the true reason, which was his having made it a point of honour to forget all that Henry Warden taught him, as soon as he was no longer compelled to read it over as a lesson acquired by rote. The lessons of his new instructor, if not more impressively delivered, were received by a more willing ear, and a more awakened understanding, and the solitude of Lochleven Castle was favourable to graver thoughts than the page had hitherto entertained. He wavered yet, indeed, as one who was almost persuaded; but his attention to the chaplain's instructions procured him favour even with the stern old dame herself; and he was once or twice, but under great precaution, permitted to go to the neighbouring village of Kinross, situated on the mainland, to execute some ordinary commission of his unfortunate mistress.

For some time Roland Græme might be considered as standing neuter betwixt the two parties who inhabited the water-girdled Tower of Lochleven; but, as he rose in the opinion of the Lady of the Castle and her chaplain, he perceived, with great grief, that he lost ground in that of Mary and her female allies.

He came gradually to be sensible that he was regarded as a spy upon their discourse, and that, instead of the ease with which they had formerly conversed in his presence, without suppressing any of the natural feelings of anger, of sorrow, or mirth, which the chance topic of the moment happened to call forth, their talk was now guardedly restricted to the most indifferent subjects, and a studied reserve observed even in their mode of treating these. This obvious want of confidence was accompanied with a correspondent change in their personal demeanor towards the unfortunate page. The Queen, who had at first treated him with marked courtesy, now scarce spoke to him, save to convey some necessary command for her service. The Lady Fleming restricted her notice to the most dry and distant expressions of civility, and Catherine Seyton became bitter in her pleasantries, and shy, cross, and pettish, in any intercourse they had together. What was yet more provoking, he saw, or thought he saw, marks of intelligence betwixt George Douglas and the beautiful Catherine Seyton; and, sharpened by jealousy, he wrought himself almost into a certainty, that the looks which they exchanged, conveyed matters of deep and serious import. "No wonder," he thought, "if, courted by the son of a proud and powerful baron, she can no longer spare a word or look to the poor fortuneless page."

In a word, Roland Græme's situation became truly disagreeable, and his heart naturally enough rebelled against the injustice of this treatment, which deprived him of the only comfort which he had received for submitting to a confinement in other respects irksome. He accused Queen Mary and Catherine Seyton (for concerning the opinion of Dame Fleming he was indifferent) of inconsistency in being displeased with him on account of the natural consequences of an order of their own. Why did they send him to hear this overpowering preacher? The Abbot Ambrosius, he recollected, understood the weakness of their Popish cause better, when he enjoined him to repeat within his own mind, *aves*, and *credos*, and *paters*, all the while old Henry Warden preached or lectured, that so he might secure himself against lending even a momentary ear to his heretical doctrine. "But I will endure this life no longer," said he to himself, manfully; "do they suppose I would betray my mistress, because I see cause to doubt of her religion?—that would be a serving, as they say, the devil for God's sake. I will forth into the world—he that serves fair ladies, may at least expect kind looks and kind words; and I bear not the mind of a gentleman, to submit to cold treatment and suspicion, and a life-long captivity besides. I will speak to George Douglas to-morrow when we go out a-fishing."

A sleepless night was spent in agitating this magnanimous resolution, and he arose in the morning not perfectly decided in his own mind whether he should abide by it or not. It happened that he was summoned by the Queen at an unusual hour, and just as he was about to go out with George Douglas. He went to attend her commands in the garden; but as he had his angling-rod in his hand, the circumstance announced his previous intention, and the Queen, turning to the Lady Fleming, said, "Catherine must devise some other amusement for us, *ma bonnie amie;* our discreet page has already made his party for the day's pleasure."

"I said from the beginning," answered the Lady Fleming, "that your Grace ought not to rely on being favoured with the company of a youth who has so many Huguenot acquaintances, and has the means of amusing himself far more agreeably than with us."

"I wish," said Catherine, her animated features reddening with mortification, "that his friends would sail away with him for good, and bring us in return a page (if such a thing can be found) faithful to his Queen and to his religion."

"One part of your wishes may be granted, madam," said Roland Græme, unable any longer to restrain his sense of the treatment which he received on all sides; and he was about to add, "I heartily wish you a companion in my room, if such can be found, who is capable of enduring women's caprices without going distracted." Luckily, he recollected the remorse which he had felt at having given way to the vivacity of his temper upon a similar occasion; and, closing his lips, imprisoned, until it died on his tongue, a reproach so misbecoming the presence of majesty.

"Why do you remain there," said the Queen, "as if you were rooted to the parterre?"

"I but attend your Grace's commands," said the page.

"I have none to give you — Begone, sir!"

As he left the garden to go to the boat, he distinctly heard Mary upbraid one of her attendants in these words:—"You see to what you have exposed us!"

This brief scene at once determined Roland Græme's resolution to quit the castle, if it were possible, and to impart his resolution to George Douglas without loss of time. That gentleman, in his usual mood of silence, sate in the stern of the little skiff which they used on such occasions, trimming his fishing-tackle, and, from time to time, indicating by signs to Græme, who pulled the oars, which way he should row. When they were a furlong or two from the castle, Roland rested on the oars, and addressed his companion somewhat abruptly,—"I have something of importance to say to you, under your pleasure, fair sir."

The pensive melancholy of Douglas's countenance at once gave way to the eager, keen, and startled look of one who expects to hear something of deep and alarming import.

"I am wearied to the very death of this Castle of Lochleven," continued Roland.

"Is that all?" said Douglas; "I know none of its inhabitants who are much better pleased with it."

"Ay, but I am neither a native of the house, nor a prisoner in it, and so I may reasonably desire to leave it."

"You might desire to quit it with equal reason," answered Douglas, "if you were both the one and the other."

"But," said Roland Græme, "I am not only tired of living in Lochleven Castle, but I am determined to quit it."

"That is a resolution more easily taken than executed," replied Douglas.

"Not if yourself, sir, and your Lady Mother, choose to consent," answered the page.

"You mistake the matter, Roland," said Douglas; "you will find that the consent of two other persons is equally essential—that of the Lady Mary your mistress, and that of my uncle the Regent, who placed you about her person, and who will not think it proper that she should change her attendants so soon."

"And must I then remain whether I will or no?" demanded the page, somewhat appalled at a view of the subject, which would have occurred sooner to a person of more experience.

"At least," said George Douglas, "you must will to remain till my uncle consents to dismiss you."

"Frankly," said the page, "and speaking to you as a gentleman who is incapable of betraying me, I will confess, that if I thought myself a prisoner here, neither walls nor water should confine me long."

"Frankly," said Douglas, "I could not much blame you for the attempt; yet, for all that, my father, or uncle, or the earl, or any of my brothers, or in short any of the king's lords into whose hands you fell, would in such a case hang you like a dog, or like a sentinel who deserts his post; and I promise you that you will hardly escape them. But row towards Saint

Serf's island—there is a breeze from the west, and we shall have sport, keeping to windward of the isle, where the ripple is strongest. We will speak more of what you have mentioned when we have had an hour's sport."

Their fishing was successful, though never did two anglers pursue even that silent and unsocial pleasure with less of verbal intercourse.

When their time was expired, Douglas took the oars in his turn, and by his order Roland Græme steered the boat, directing her course upon the landing-place at the castle. But he also stopped in the midst of his course, and, looking around him, said to Græme, "There is a thing which I could mention to thee; but it is so deep a secret, that even here, surrounded as we are by sea and sky, without the possibility of a listener, I cannot prevail on myself to speak it out."

"Better leave it unspoken, sir," answered Roland Græme, "if you doubt the honour of him who alone can hear it."

"I doubt not your honour," replied George Douglas; "but you are young, imprudent, and changeful."

"Young," said Roland, "I am, and it may be imprudent—but who hath informed you that I am changeful?"

"One that knows you, perhaps, better than you know yourself," replied Douglas.

"I suppose you mean Catherine Seyton," said the page, his heart rising as he spoke; "but she is herself fifty times more variable in her humour than the very water which we are floating upon."

"My young acquaintance," said Douglas, "I pray you to remember that Catherine Seyton is a lady of blood and birth, and must not be lightly spoken of."

"Master George of Douglas," said Græme, "as that speech seemed to be made under the warrant of something like a threat, I pray you to observe, that I value not the threat at the estimation of a fin of one of these dead trouts; and, moreover, I would have you to know that the champion who undertakes the defence of every lady of blood and birth, whom men accuse of change of faith and of fashion, is like to have enough of work on his hands."

"Go to," said the Seneschal, but in a tone of good-humour, "thou art a foolish boy, unfit to deal with any matter more serious than the casting of a net, or the flying of a hawk."

"If your secret concern Catherine Seyton," said the page, "I care not for it, and so you may tell her if you will. I wot she can shape you opportunity to speak with her, as she has ere now."

The flush which passed over Douglas's face, made the page aware that he had alighted on a truth, when he was, in fact, speaking at random; and the feeling that he had done so, was like striking a dagger into his own heart. His companion, without farther answer, resumed the oars, and pulled lustily till they arrived at the island and the castle. The servants received the produce of their spoil, and the two fishers, turning from each other in silence, went each to his several apartment.

Roland Græme had spent about an hour in grumbling against Catherine Seyton, the Queen, the Regent, and the whole house of Lochleven, with George Douglas at the head of it, when the time approached that his duty called him to attend the meal of Queen Mary. As he arranged his dress for this purpose, he grudged the trouble, which, on similar occasions, he used, with boyish foppery, to consider as one of the most important duties of his day; and when he went to take his place behind the chair of the Queen, it was with an air of offended dignity, which could not escape her observation, and probably appeared to her ridiculous enough, for she whispered something in French to her ladies, at which the lady Fleming laughed, and Catherine appeared half diverted and half disconcerted. This pleasantry, of which the subject was concealed from him, the unfortunate page received, of course, as a new offence, and called an additional degree of sullen dignity into his mien, which might have exposed him to farther raillery, but that Mary appeared disposed to make allowance for and compassionate his feelings.

With the peculiar tact and delicacy which no woman possessed in greater perfection, she began to soothe by degrees the vexed spirit of her magnanimous attendant. The excellence of the fish which he had taken in his expedition, the high flavour and beautiful red colour of the trouts, which have long given distinction to the lake, led her first to express her thanks to her attendant for so agreeable an addition to her table, especially upon a *jour de jeune;* and then brought on inquiries into the place where the fish had been taken, their size, their peculiarities, the times when they were in season, and a comparison between the Lochleven trouts and those which are found in the lakes and rivers of the south of Scotland. The ill humour of Roland Græme was never of an obstinate character. It rolled away like mist before the sun, and he was easily engaged in a keen and animated dissertation about Lochleven trout, and sea trout, and river trout, and bull trout, and char, which never rise to a fly, and par, which some suppose infant salmon, and *herlings*, which frequent the Nith, and *vendisses*, which are only found in the Castle-Loch of Lochmaben; and he was hurrying on with the eager impetuosity and enthusiasm of a young sportsman, when he observed that the smile with which the Queen at first listened to him died languidly away, and that, in spite of her efforts to suppress them, tears rose to her eyes. He stopped suddenly short, and, distressed in his turn, asked, "If he had the misfortune unwittingly to give displeasure to her Grace?"

"No, my poor boy," replied the Queen; "but as you numbered up the lakes and rivers of my kingdom, imagination cheated me, as it will do, and snatched me from these dreary walls away to the romantic streams of Nithsdale, and the royal towers of Lochmaben.—O land, which my fathers have so long ruled! of the pleasures which you extend so freely, your Queen is now deprived, and the poorest beggar, who may wander free from one landward town to another, would scorn to change fates with Mary of Scotland!"

"Your highness," said the Lady Fleming, "will do well to withdraw."

"Come with me, then, Fleming," said the Queen, "I would not burden hearts so young as these are, with the sight of my sorrows."

She accompanied these words with a look of melancholy compassion towards Roland and Catherine, who were now left alone together in the apartment.

The page found his situation not a little embarrassing; for, as every reader has experienced who may have chanced to be in such a situation, it is extremely difficult to maintain the full dignity of an offended person in the presence of a beautiful girl, whatever reason we may have for being angry with her. Catherine Seyton, on her part, sate still like a lingering ghost, which, conscious of the awe which its presence imposes, is charitably disposed to give the poor confused mortal whom it visits, time to recover his senses, and comply with the grand rule of demonology by speaking first. But as Roland seemed in no hurry to avail himself of her condescension, she carried it a step farther, and herself opened the conversation.

"I pray you, fair sir, if it may be permitted me to disturb your august reverie by a question so simple,—what may have become of your rosary?"

"It is lost, madam—lost some time since," said Roland, partly embarrassed and partly indignant.

"And may I ask farther, sir," said Catherine, "why you have not replaced it with another?—I have half a mind," she said, taking from her pocket a string of ebony beads adorned with gold, "to bestow one upon you, to keep for my sake, just to remind you of former acquaintance."

There was a little tremulous accent in the tone with which these words were delivered, which at once put to flight Roland Græme's resentment, and brought him to Catherine's side; but she instantly resumed the bold and firm accent which was more familiar to her. "I did not bid you," she said, "come and sit so close by me; for the acquaintance that I spoke of, has been stiff and cold, dead and buried, for this many a day."

"Now Heaven forbid!" said the page, "it has only slept, and now that you desire it should awake, fair Catherine, believe me that a pledge of your returning favour——"

"Nay, nay," said Catherine, withholding the rosary, towards which, as he spoke, he extended his hand, "I have changed my mind on better reflection. What should a heretic do with these holy beads, that have been blessed by the father of the church himself?"

Roland winced grievously, for he saw plainly which way the discourse was now likely to tend, and felt that it must at all events be embarrassing. "Nay, but," he said, "it was as a token of your own regard that you offered them."

"Ay, fair sir, but that regard attended the faithful subject, the loyal and pious Catholic, the individual who was so solemnly devoted at the same time with myself to the same grand duty; which, you must now understand, was to serve the church and Queen. To such a person, if you ever heard of him, was my regard due, and not to him who associates with heretics, and is about to become a renegado."

"I should scarce believe, fair mistress," said Roland, indignantly, "that the vane of your favour turned only to a Catholic wind, considering that it points so plainly to George Douglas, who, I think, is both kingsman and Protestant."

"Think better of George Douglas," said Catherine, "than to believe——" and then checking herself, as if she had spoken too much, she went on, "I assure you, fair Master Roland, that all who wish you well are sorry for you."

"Their number is very few, I believe," answered Roland, "and their sorrow, if they feel any, not deeper than ten minutes' time will cure."

"They are more numerous, and think more deeply concerning you, than you seem to be aware," answered Catherine. "But perhaps they think wrong—You are the best judge in your own affairs; and if you prefer gold and church-lands to honour and loyalty, and the faith of your fathers, why should you be hampered in conscience more than others?"

"May Heaven bear witness for me," said Roland, "that if I entertain any difference of opinion—that is, if I nourish any doubts in point of religion, they have been adopted on the conviction of my own mind, and the suggestion of my own conscience!"

"Ay, ay, your conscience—your conscience!" repeated she with satiric emphasis; "your conscience is the scape-goat; I warrant it an able one—it will bear the burden of one of the best manors of the Abbey of Saint Mary of Kennaquhair, lately forfeited to our noble Lord the King, by the Abbot and community thereof, for the high crime of fidelity to their religious vows, and now to be granted by the High and Mighty Traitor, and so forth, James Earl of Murray, to the good squire of dames Roland Græme, for his loyal and faithful service as under-espial, and deputy-turnkey, for securing the person of his lawful sovereign, Queen Mary."

"You misconstrue me cruelly," said the page; "yes, Catherine, most cruelly—God knows I would protect this poor lady at the risk of my life, or with my life; but what can I do—what can any one do for her?"

"Much may be done—enough may be done—all may be done—if men will be but true and honourable, as Scottish men were in the days of Bruce and Wallace. Oh, Roland, from what an enterprise you are now withdrawing your heart and hand, through mere fickleness and coldness of spirit!"

"How can I withdraw," said Roland, "from an enterprise which has never been communicated to me?—Has the Queen, or have you, or has any one, communicated with me upon any thing for her service which I have refused? Or have you not, all of you, held me at such distance from your counsels, as if I were the most faithless spy since the days of Ganelon?"*

"And who," said Catherine Seyton, "would trust the sworn friend, and pupil, and companion, of the heretic preacher Henderson? ay—a proper tutor you have chosen, instead of the excellent Ambrosius, who is now turned out of house and homestead, if indeed he is not languishing in a dungeon, for withstanding the tyranny of Morton, to whose brother the temporalities of that noble house of God have been gifted away by the Regent."

"Is it possible?" said the page; "and is the excellent Father Ambrose in such distress?"

"He would account the news of your falling away from the faith of your fathers," answered Catherine, "a worse mishap than aught that tyranny can inflict on himself."

"But why," said Roland, very much moved, "why should you suppose that—that—that it is with me as you say?"

"Do you yourself deny it?" replied Catherine; "do you not admit that you have drunk the poison which you should have dashed from your lips?—Do you deny that it now ferments in your veins, if it has not altogether corrupted the springs of life?—Do you deny that you have your doubts, as you proudly term them, respecting what popes and councils have declared it unlawful to doubt of?—Is not your faith wavering, if not overthrown?—Does not the heretic preacher boast his conquest?—Does not the heretic woman of this prison-house hold up thy example to others?—Do not the Queen and the Lady Fleming believe in thy falling away?—And is there any except one—yes, I will speak it out, and think as lightly as you please of my good-will—is there one except myself that holds even a lingering hope that you may yet prove what we once all believed of you?"

"I know not," said our poor page, much embarrassed by the view which was thus presented to him of the conduct he was expected to pursue, and by a person in whom he was not the less interested that, though long a resident in Lochleven Castle, with no object so likely to attract his undivided attention, no lengthened interview had taken place since they had first met,—"I know not what you expect of me, or fear from me. I was sent hither to attend Queen Mary, and to her I acknowledge the duty of a servant through life and death. If any one had expected service of another kind, I was not the party to render it. I neither avow nor disclaim the doctrines of the reformed church.—Will you have the truth?—It seems to me that the profligacy of the Catholic clergy has brought this judgment on their own heads, and, for aught I know, it may be for their reformation. But, for betraying this unhappy Queen, God knows I am guiltless of the thought. Did I even believe worse of her, than as her servant I wish—as her subject I dare to do—I would not betray her—far from it—I would aid her in aught which could tend to a fair trial of her cause."

"Enough! enough!" answered Catherine, clasping her hands together; "then thou wilt not desert us if any means are presented, by which, placing our Royal Mistress at freedom, this case may be honestly tried betwixt her and her rebellious subjects?"

"Nay—but, fair Catherine," replied the page, "hear but what the Lord of Murray said when he sent me hither."—

"Hear but what the devil said," replied the maiden, "rather than what a false subject, a false brother, a false counsellor, a false friend, said! A man raised from a petty pensioner on the crown's bounty, to be the coun-

* Gan, Gano, or Ganelon of Mayence, is, in the Romances on the subject of Charlemagne and his Paladins, always represented as the traitor by whom the Christian champions are betrayed.

sellor of majesty, and the prime distributor of the bounties of the state;—one with whom rank, fortune, title, consequence, and power, all grew up like a mushroom, by the mere warm good-will of the sister, whom, in requital, he hath mewed up in this place of melancholy seclusion—whom, in farther requital, he has deposed, and whom, if he dared, he would murder!"

"I think not so ill of the Earl of Murray," said Roland Græme; "and sooth to speak," he added, with a smile, "it would require some bribe to make me embrace, with firm and desperate resolution, either one side or the other."

"Nay, if that is all," replied Catherine Seyton, in a tone of enthusiasm, "you shall be guerdoned with prayers from oppressed subjects—from dispossessed clergy—from insulted nobles—with immortal praise by future ages—with eager gratitude by the present—with fame on earth, and with felicity in heaven! Your country will thank you—your Queen will be debtor to you—you will achieve at once the highest from the lowest degree in chivalry—all men will honour, all women will love you—and I, sworn with you so early to the accomplishment of Queen Mary's freedom, will—yes, I will—love you better than—ever sister loved brother!"

"Say on—say on!" whispered Roland, kneeling on one knee, and taking her hand, which, in the warmth of exhortation, Catherine held towards him.

"Nay," said she, pausing, "I have already said too much—far too much, if I prevail not with you—far too little if I do. But I prevail," she continued, seeing that the countenance of the youth she addressed returned the enthusiasm of her own—"I prevail; or rather the good cause prevails through its own strength—thus I devote thee to it." And as she spoke she approached her finger to the brow of the astonished youth, and, without touching it, signed the cross over his forehead—stooped her face towards him, and seemed to kiss the empty space in which she had traced the symbol; then starting up, and extricating herself from his grasp, darted into the Queen's apartment.

Roland Græme remained as the enthusiastic maiden had left him, kneeling on one knee, with breath withheld, and with eyes fixed upon the space which the fairy form of Catherine Seyton had so lately occupied. If his thoughts were not of unmixed delight, they at least partook of that thrilling and intoxicating, though mingled sense of pain and pleasure, the most overpowering which life offers in its blended cup. He rose and retired slowly; and although the chaplain Mr. Henderson preached on that evening his best sermon against the errors of Popery, I would not engage that he was followed accurately through the train of his reasoning by the young proselyte, with a view to whose especial benefit he had handled the subject.

Chapter the Twenty-Fifth.

And when love's torch hath set the heart in flame,
Comes Seignor Reason with his saws and cautions,
Giving such aid as the old gray-beard Sexton,
Who from the church-vault drags the crazy engine,
To ply its dribbling ineffectual streamlet
Against a conflagration.

OLD PLAY.

IN a musing mood, Roland Græme upon the ensuing morning betook himself to the battlements of the Castle, as a spot where he might indulge the course of his thick-coming fancies with least chance of interruption.

But his place of retirement was in the present case ill chosen, for he was presently joined by Mr. Elias Henderson.

"I sought you, young man," said the preacher, "having to speak of something which concerns you nearly."

The page had no pretence for avoiding the conference which the chaplain thus offered, though he felt that it might prove an embarrassing one.

"In teaching thee, as far as my feeble knowledge hath permitted, thy duty towards God," said the chaplain, "there are particulars of your duty towards man, upon which I was unwilling long or much to insist. You are here in the service of a lady, honourable as touching her birth, deserving of all compassion as respects her misfortunes, and garnished with even but too many of those outward qualities which win men's regard and affection. Have you ever considered your regard to this Lady Mary of Scotland, in its true light and bearing?"

"I trust, reverend sir," replied Roland Græme, "that I am well aware of the duties a servant in my condition owes to his royal mistress, especially in her lowly and distressed condition."

"True," answered the preacher; "but it is even that honest feeling which may, in the Lady Mary's case, carry thee into great crime and treachery."

"How so, reverend sir?" replied the page; "I profess I understand you not."

"I speak to you not of the crimes of this ill-advised lady," said the preacher; "they are not subjects for the ears of her sworn servant. But it is enough to say, that this unhappy person hath rejected more offers of grace, and more hopes of glory, than ever were held out to earthly princes; and that she is now, her day of favour being passed, sequestered in this lonely castle, for the common weal of the people of Scotland, and it may be for the benefit of her own soul."

"Reverend sir," said Roland, somewhat impatiently, "I am but too well aware that my unfortunate mistress is imprisoned, since I have the misfortune to share in her restraint myself—of which, to speak sooth, I am heartily weary."

"It is even of that which I am about to speak," said the chaplain, mildly; "but, first, my good Roland, look forth on the pleasant prospect of yonder cultivated plain. You see, where the smoke arises, yonder village standing half hidden by the trees, and you know it to be the dwelling-place of peace and industry. From space to space, each by the side of its own stream, you see the gray towers of barons, with cottages interspersed; and you know that they also, with their household, are now living in unity; the lance hung upon the wall, and the sword resting in its sheath. You see, too, more than one fair church, where the pure waters of life are offered to the thirsty, and where the hungry are refreshed with spiritual food.—What would he deserve, who should bring fire and slaughter into so fair and happy a scene — who should bare the swords of the gentry and turn them against each other—who should give tower and cottage to the flames, and slake the embers with the blood of the indwellers? — What would he deserve who should lift up again that ancient Dagon of Superstition, whom the worthies of the time have beaten down, and who should once more make the churches of God the high places of Baal?"

"You have limned a frightful picture, reverend sir," said Roland Græme; "yet I guess not whom you would charge with the purpose of effecting a change so horrible."

"God forbid," replied the preacher, "that I should say to thee, Thou art the man. — Yet beware, Roland Græme, that thou, in serving thy mistress, hold fast the still higher service which thou owest to the peace of thy country, and the prosperity of her inhabitants; else, Roland Græme, thou mayest be the very man upon whose head will fall the curses and assured punishment due to such work. If thou art won by the song of these sirens to aid that unhappy lady's escape from this place of penitence and security, it is over with the peace of Scotland's cottages, and with the prosperity of her palaces — and the babe unborn shall curse the name of the man who gave inlet to the disorder which will follow the war betwixt the mother and the son."

"I know of no such plan, reverend sir," answered the page, "and therefore can aid none such. — My duty towards the Queen has been simply that of an attendant; it is a task, of which, at times, I would willingly have been freed; nevertheless——"

"It is to prepare thee for the enjoyment of something more of liberty," said the preacher, "that I have endeavoured to impress upon you the deep responsibility under which your office must be discharged. George Douglas hath told the Lady Lochleven that you are weary of this service, and my intercession hath partly determined her good ladyship, that, as your discharge cannot be granted, you shall, instead, be employed in certain commissions on the mainland, which have hitherto been discharged by other persons of confidence. Wherefore, come with me to the lady, for even to-day such duty will be imposed on you."

"I trust you will hold me excused, reverend sir," said the page, who felt that an increase of confidence on the part of the Lady of the Castle and her family would render his situation in a moral view doubly embarrassing, "one cannot serve two masters—and I much fear that my mistress will not hold me excused for taking employment under another."

"Fear not that," said the preacher; "her consent shall be asked and obtained. I fear she will yield it but too easily, as hoping to avail herself of your agency to maintain correspondence with her friends, as those falsely call themselves, who would make her name the watchword for civil war."

"And thus," said the page, "I shall be exposed to suspicion on all sides; for my mistress will consider me as a spy placed on her by her enemies, seeing me so far trusted by them; and the Lady Lochleven will never cease to suspect the possibility of my betraying her, because circumstances put it into my power to do so—I would rather remain as I am."

There followed a pause of one or two minutes, during which Henderson looked steadily in Roland's countenance, as if desirous to ascertain whether there was not more in the answer than the precise words seemed to imply. He failed in this point, however; for Roland, bred a page from childhood, knew how to assume a sullen pettish cast of countenance, well enough calculated to hide all internal emotions.

"I understand thee not, Roland," said the preacher, "or rather thou thinkest on this matter more deeply than I apprehended to be in thy nature. Methought, the delight of going on shore with thy bow, or thy gun, or thy angling-rod, would have borne away all other feelings."

"And so it would," replied Roland, who perceived the danger of suffering Henderson's half-raised suspicions to become fully awake,—"I would have thought of nothing but the gun and the oar, and the wild water-fowl that tempt me by sailing among the sedges yonder so far out of flight-shot, had you not spoken of my going on shore as what was to occasion burning of town and tower, the downfall of the evangele, and the upsetting of the mass."

"Follow me, then," said Henderson, "and we will seek the Lady Lochleven."

They found her at breakfast with her grandson George Douglas.—"Peace be with your ladyship!" said the preacher, bowing to his patroness; "Roland Græme awaits your order."

"Young man," said the lady, "our chaplain hath warranted for thy fidelity, and we are determined to give you certain errands to do for us in our town of Kinross."

"Not by my advice," said Douglas, coldly.

"I said not that it was," answered the lady, something sharply. "The mother of thy father may, I should think, be old enough to judge for herself in a matter so simple. — Thou wilt take the skiff, Roland, and two of my people, whom Dryfesdale or Randal will order out, and fetch off certain stuff of plate and hangings, which should last night be lodged at Kinross by the wains from Edinburgh."

"And give this packet," said George Douglas, "to a servant of ours, whom you will find in waiting there. — It is the report to my father," he added, looking towards his grandmother, who acquiesced by bending her head.

"I have already mentioned to Master Henderson," said Roland Græme, "that as my duty requires my attendance on the Queen, her Grace's permission for my journey ought to be obtained before I can undertake your commission."

"Look to it, my son," said the old lady, "the scruple of the youth is honourable."

"Craving your pardon, madam, I have no wish to force myself on her presence thus early," said Douglas, in an indifferent tone; "it might displease her, and were no way agreeable to me."

"And I," said the Lady Lochleven, "although her temper hath been more gentle of late, have no will to undergo, without necessity, the rancour of her wit."

"Under your permission, madam," said the chaplain, "I will myself render your request to the Queen. During my long residence in this house she hath not deigned to see me in private, or to hear my doctrine; yet so may Heaven prosper my labours, as love for her soul, and desire to bring her into the right path, was my chief desire for coming hither."

"Take care, Master Henderson," said Douglas, in a tone which seemed almost sarcastic, "lest you rush hastily on an adventure to which you have no vocation — you are learned, and know the adage, *Ne accesseris in consilium nisi vocatus.*—Who hath required this at your hand?"

"The Master to whose service I am called," answered the preacher, looking upward,—"He who hath commanded me to be earnest in season and out of season."

"Your acquaintance hath not been much, I think, with courts or princes," continued the young Esquire.

"No, sir," replied Henderson, "but like my Master Knox, I see nothing frightful in the fair face of a pretty lady."

"My son," said the Lady of Lochleven, "quench not the good man's zeal — let him do the errand to this unhappy Princess."

"With more willingness than I would do it myself," said George Douglas. Yet something in his manner appeared to contradict his words.

The minister went accordingly, followed by Roland Græme, and, demanding an audience of the imprisoned Princess, was admitted. He found her with her ladies engaged in the daily task of embroidery. The Queen received him with that courtesy, which, in ordinary cases, she used towards all who approached her, and the clergyman, in opening his commission, was obviously somewhat more embarrassed than he had expected to be. — "The good Lady of Lochleven — may it please your Grace——"

He made a short pause, during which Mary said, with a smile, "My Grace would, in truth, be well pleased, were the Lady Lochleven our *good* lady — But go on — what is the will of the good Lady of Lochleven?"

"She desires, madam," said the chaplain, "that your Grace will permit this young gentleman, your page, Roland Græme, to pass to Kinross, to look after some household stuff and hangings, sent hither for the better furnishing your Grace's apartments."

"The Lady of Lochleven," said the Queen, "uses needless ceremony, in requesting our permission for that which stands within her own pleasure.

We well know that this young gentleman's attendance on us had not been so long permitted, were he not thought to be more at the command of that good lady than at ours.—But we cheerfully yield consent that he shall go on her errand—with our will we would doom no living creature to the captivity which we ourselves must suffer."

"Ay, madam," answered the preacher, "and it is doubtless natural for humanity to quarrel with its prison-house. Yet there have been those, who have found, that time spent in the house of temporal captivity may be so employed as to redeem us from spiritual slavery."

"I apprehend your meaning, sir," replied the Queen, "but I have heard your apostle—I have heard Master John Knox; and were I to be perverted, I would willingly resign to the ablest and most powerful of heresiarchs, the poor honour he might acquire by overcoming my faith and my hope."

"Madam," said the preacher, "it is not to the talents or skill of the husbandman that God gives the increase — the words which were offered in vain by him whom you justly call our apostle, during the bustle and gaiety of a court, may yet find better acceptance during the leisure for reflection which this place affords. God knows, lady, that I speak in singleness of heart, as one who would as soon compare himself to the immortal angels, as to the holy man whom you have named. Yet would you but condescend to apply to their noblest use, those talents and that learning which all allow you to be possessed of — would you afford us but the slightest hope that you would hear and regard what can be urged against the blinded superstition and idolatry in which you are brought up, sure am I, that the most powerfully-gifted of my brethren, that even John Knox himself, would hasten hither, and account the rescue of your single soul from the nets of Romish error——"

"I am obliged to you and to them for their charity," said Mary; "but as I have at present but one presence-chamber, I would reluctantly see it converted into a Huguenot synod."

"At least, madam, be not thus obstinately blinded in your errors! Hear one who has hungered and thirsted, watched and prayed, to undertake the good work of your conversion, and who would be content to die the instant that a work so advantageous for yourself and so beneficial to Scotland were accomplished — Yes, lady, could I but shake the remaining pillar of the heathen temple in this land — and that permit me to term your faith in the delusions of Rome — I could be content to die overwhelmed in the ruins!"

"I will not insult your zeal, sir," replied Mary, "by saying you are more likely to make sport for the Philistines than to overwhelm them — your charity claims my thanks, for it is warmly expressed and may be truly purposed — But believe as well of me as I am willing to do of you, and think that I may be as anxious to recall you to the ancient and only road, as you are to teach me your new by-ways to paradise."

"Then, madam, if such be your generous purpose," said Henderson, eagerly, "what hinders that we should dedicate some part of that time, unhappily now too much at your Grace's disposal, to discuss a question so weighty? You, by report of all men, are both learned and witty; and I, though without such advantages, am strong in my cause as in a tower of defence. Why should we not spend some space in endeavouring to discover which of us hath the wrong side in this important matter?"

"Nay," said Queen Mary, "I never alleged my force was strong enough to accept of a combat *en champ clos*, with a scholar and a polemic. Besides, the match is not equal. You, sir, might retire when you felt the battle go against you, while I am tied to the stake, and have no permission to say the debate wearies me. — I would be alone."

She curtsied low to him as she uttered these words; and Henderson, whose zeal was indeed ardent, but did not extend to the neglect of delicacy, bowed in return, and prepared to withdraw.

"I would," he said, "that my earnest wish, my most zealous prayer, could procure to your Grace any blessing or comfort, but especially that in which alone blessing or comfort is, as easily as the slightest intimation of your wish will remove me from your presence."

He was in the act of departing, when Mary said to him with much courtesy, "Do me no injury in your thoughts, good sir; it may be, that if my time here be protracted longer — as surely I hope it will not, trusting that either my rebel subjects will repent of their disloyalty, or that my faithful lieges will obtain the upper hand — but if my time be here protracted, it may be I shall have no displeasure in hearing one who seems so reasonable and compassionate as yourself, and I may hazard your contempt by endeavouring to recollect and repeat the reasons which schoolmen and councils give for the faith that is in me, — although I fear that, God help me! my Latin has deserted me with my other possessions. This must, however, be for another day. Meanwhile, sir, let the Lady of Lochleven employ my page as she lists — I will not afford suspicion by speaking a word to him before he goes. — Roland Græme, my friend, lose not an opportunity of amusing thyself — dance, sing, run, and leap — all may be done merrily on the mainland; but he must have more than quicksilver in his veins who would frolic here."

"Alas! madam," said the preacher, "to what is it you exhort the youth, while time passes, and eternity summons? Can our salvation be insured by idle mirth, or our good work wrought out without fear and trembling?"

"I cannot fear or tremble," replied the Queen; "to Mary Stewart such emotions are unknown. But if weeping and sorrow on my part will atone for the boy's enjoying an hour of boyish pleasure, be assured the penance shall be duly paid."

"Nay, but, gracious lady," said the preacher, "in this you greatly err; —our tears and our sorrows are all too little for our own faults and follies, nor can we transfer them, as your church falsely teaches, to the benefit of others."

"May I pray you, sir," answered the Queen, "with as little offence as such a prayer may import, to transfer yourself elsewhere? We are sick at heart, and may not now be disposed with farther controversy — and thou, Roland, take this little purse;" (then, turning to the divine, she said, showing its contents,) "Look, reverend sir, —it contains only these two or three gold testoons, a coin which, though bearing my own poor features, I have ever found more active against me than on my side, just as my subjects take arms against me, with my own name for their summons and signal.—Take this purse, that thou mayest want no means of amusement. Fail not—fail not to bring me back news from Kinross; only let it be such as, without suspicion or offence, may be told in the presence of this reverend gentleman, or of the good Lady Lochleven herself."

The last hint was too irresistible to be withstood; and Henderson withdrew, half mortified, half pleased, with his reception; for Mary, from long habit, and the address which was natural to her, had learned, in an extraordinary degree, the art of evading discourse which was disagreeable to her feelings or prejudices, without affronting those by whom it was proffered.

Roland Græme retired with the chaplain, at a signal from his lady; but it did not escape him, that as he left the room, stepping backwards, and making the deep obeisance due to royalty, Catherine Seyton held up her slender forefinger, with a gesture which he alone could witness, and which seemed to say, "Remember what has passed betwixt us."

The young page had now his last charge from the Lady of Lochleven. "There are revels," she said, "this day at the village — my son's authority is, as yet, unable to prevent these continued workings of the ancient leaven of folly which the Romish priests have kneaded into the very souls of the Scottish peasantry. I do not command thee to abstain from them — that would be only to lay a snare for thy folly, or to teach thee falsehood; but enjoy these vanities with moderation, and mark them as something thou must soon learn to renounce and contemn. Our chamberlain at Kinross, Luke Lundin,—Doctor, as he foolishly calleth himself,—will acquaint thee what is to be done in the matter about which thou goest. Remember thou art trusted—show thyself, therefore, worthy of trust."

When we recollect that Roland Græme was not yet nineteen, and that he had spent his whole life in the solitary Castle of Avenel, excepting the few hours he had passed in Edinburgh, and his late residence at Lochleven, (the latter period having very little served to enlarge his acquaintance with the gay world,) we cannot wonder that his heart beat high with hope and curiosity, at the prospect of partaking the sport even of a country wake. He hastened to his little cabin, and turned over the wardrobe with which (in every respect becoming his station) he had been supplied from Edinburgh, probably by order of the Earl of Murray. By the Queen's command he had hitherto waited upon her in mourning, or at least in sad-coloured raiment. Her condition, she said, admitted of nothing more gay. But now he selected the gayest dress his wardrobe afforded; composed of scarlet slashed with black satin, the royal colours of Scotland—combed his long curled hair—disposed his chain and medal round a beaver hat of the newest block; and with the gay falchion which had reached him in so mysterious a manner, hung by his side in an embroidered belt, his apparel, added to his natural frank mien and handsome figure, formed a most commendable and pleasing specimen of the young gallant of the period. He sought to make his parting reverence to the Queen and her ladies, but old Dryfesdale hurried him to the boat.

"We will have no private audiences," he said, "my master; since you are to be trusted with somewhat, we will try at least to save thee from the temptation of opportunity. God help thee, child," he added, with a glance of contempt at his gay clothes, "an the bear-ward be yonder from Saint Andrews, have a care thou go not near him."

"And wherefore, I pray you?" said Roland.

"Lest he take thee for one of his runaway jackanapes," answered the steward, smiling sourly.

"I wear not my clothes at thy cost," said Roland indignantly.

"Nor at thine own either, my son," replied the steward, "else would thy garb more nearly resemble thy merit and thy station."

Roland Græme suppressed with difficulty the repartee which arose to his lips, and, wrapping his scarlet mantle around him, threw himself into the boat, which two rowers, themselves urged by curiosity to see the revels, pulled stoutly towards the west end of the lake. As they put off, Roland thought he could discover the face of Catherine Seyton, though carefully withdrawn from observation, peeping from a loophole to view his departure. He pulled off his hat, and held it up as a token that he saw and wished her adieu. A white kerchief waved for a second across the window, and for the rest of the little voyage, the thoughts of Catherine Seyton disputed ground in his breast with the expectations excited by the approaching revel. As they drew nearer and nearer the shore, the sounds of mirth and music, the laugh, the halloo, and the shout, came thicker upon the ear, and in a trice the boat was moored, and Roland Græme hastened in quest of the chamberlain, that, being informed what time he had at his own disposal, he might lay it out to the best advantage.

Chapter the Twenty-Sixth.

Room for the master of the ring, ye swains,
Divide your crowded ranks—before him march
The rural minstrelsy, the rattling drum,
The clamorous war-pipe, and far-echoing horn.
Rural Sports.— SOMERVILLE.

No long space intervened ere Roland Græme was able to discover among the crowd of revellers, who gambolled upon the open space which extends betwixt the village and the lake, a person of so great importance as Dr. Luke Lundin, upon whom devolved officially the charge of representing the lord of the land, and who was attended for support of his authority by a piper, a drummer, and four sturdy clowns armed with rusty halberds, garnished with party-coloured ribbons; myrmidons who, early as the day was, had already broken more than one head in the awful names of the Laird of Lochleven and his chamberlain.*

As soon as this dignitary was informed that the castle skiff had arrived, with a gallant, dressed like a lord's son at the least, who desired presently to speak to him, he adjusted his ruff and his black coat, turned round his girdle till the garnished hilt of his long rapier became visible, and walked with due solemnity towards the beach. Solemn indeed he was entitled to be, even on less important occasions, for he had been bred to the venerable study of medicine, as those acquainted with the science very soon discovered from the aphorisms which ornamented his discourse. His success had not been equal to his pretensions; but as he was a native of the neighbouring kingdom of Fife, and bore distant relation to, or dependence upon, the ancient family of Lundin of that Ilk, who were bound in close friendship with the house of Lochleven, he had, through their interest, got planted comfortably enough in his present station upon the banks of that beautiful lake. The profits of his chamberlainship being moderate, especially in those unsettled times, he had eked it out a little with some practice in his original profession; and it was said that the inhabitants of the village and barony of Kinross were not more effectually thirled (which may be translated enthralled) to the baron's mill, than they were to the medical monopoly of the chamberlain. Wo betide the family of the rich boor, who presumed to depart this life without a passport from Dr. Luke Lundin! for if his representatives had aught to settle with the baron, as it seldom happened otherwise, they were sure to find a cold friend in the chamberlain. He was considerate enough, however, gratuitously to help the poor out of their ailments, and sometimes out of all their other distresses at the same time.

Formal, in a double proportion, both as a physician and as a person in office, and proud of the scraps of learning which rendered his language almost universally unintelligible, Dr. Luke Lundin approached the beach, and hailed the page as he advanced towards him.—"The freshness of the morning upon you, fair sir—You are sent, I warrant me, to see if we observe here the regimen which her good ladyship hath prescribed, for eschewing all

* At Scottish fairs, the bailie, or magistrate, deputed by the lord in whose name the meeting is held, attends the fair with his guard, decides trifling disputes, and punishes on the spot any petty delinquencies. His attendants are usually armed with halberds, and sometimes, at least, escorted by music. Thus, in the "Life and Death of Habbie Simpson," we are told of that famous minstrel,—

"At fairs he play'd before the spear-men,
And gaily graithed in their gear-men;—
Steel bonnets, jacks, and swords shone clear then,
Like ony bead;
Now wha shall play before sic weir-men,
Since Habbie's dead!

superstitious observances and idle anilities in these our revels. I am aware that her good ladyship would willingly have altogether abolished and abrogated them—But as I had the honour to quote to her from the works of the learned Hercules of Saxony, *omnis curatio est vel canonica vel coacta,*— that is, fair sir, (for silk and velvet have seldom their Latin *ad unguem,*) every cure must be wrought either by art and induction of rule, or by constraint; and the wise physician chooseth the former. Which argument her ladyship being pleased to allow well of, I have made it my business so to blend instruction and caution with delight—*fiat mixtio,* as we say — that I can answer that the vulgar mind will be defecated and purged of anile and Popish fooleries by the medicament adhibited, so that the *primæ viæ* being cleansed, Master Henderson, or any other able pastor, may at will throw in tonics, and effectuate a perfect moral cure, *tuto, cito, jucunde.*"

"I have no charge, Dr. Lundin," replied the page——

"Call me not doctor," said the chamberlain, "since I have laid aside my furred gown and bonnet, and retired me into this temporality of chamberlainship."

"Oh, sir," said the page, who was no stranger by report to the character of this original, "the cowl makes not the monk, neither the cord the friar—we have all heard of the cures wrought by Dr. Lundin."

"Toys, young sir—trifles," answered the leech with grave disclamation of superior skill; "the hit-or-miss practice of a poor retired gentleman, in a short cloak and doublet—Marry, Heaven sent its blessing—and this I must say, better fashioned mediciners have brought fewer patients through — *lunga roba corta scienzia,* saith the Italian — ha, fair sir, you have the language?"

Roland Græme did not think it necessary to expound to this learned Theban whether he understood him or no; but, leaving that matter uncertain, he told him he came in quest of certain packages which should have arrived at Kinross, and been placed under the chamberlain's charge the evening before.

"Body o' me!" said Doctor Lundin, "I fear our common carrier, John Auchtermuchty, hath met with some mischance, that he came not up last night with his wains—bad land this to journey in, my master; and the fool will travel by night too, although, (besides all maladies from your *tussis* to your *pestis,* which walk abroad in the night-air,) he may well fall in with half a dozen swash-bucklers, who will ease him at once of his baggage and his earthly complaints. I must send forth to inquire after him, since he hath stuff of the honourable household on hand—and, by our Lady, he hath stuff of mine too—certain drugs sent me from the city for composition of my alexipharmics — this gear must be looked to.—Hodge," said he, addressing one of his redoubted body-guard, "do thou and Toby Telford take the mickle brown aver and the black cut-tailed mare, and make out towards the Kerry-craigs, and see what tidings you can have of Auchtermuchty and his wains—I trust it is only the medicine of the pottle-pot, (being the only *medicamentum* which the beast useth,) which hath caused him to tarry on the road. Take the ribbons from your halberds, ye knaves, and get on your jacks, plate-sleeves, and knapskulls, that your presence may work some terror if you meet with opposers." He then added, turning to Roland Græme, "I warrant me, we shall have news of the wains in brief season. Meantime it will please you to look upon the sports; but first to enter my poor lodging and take your morning's cup. For what saith the school of Salerno?

Poculum, mane haustum,
Restaurat naturam exhaustam."

"Your learning is too profound for me," replied the page; "and so would your draught be likewise, I fear."

"Not a whit, fair sir — a cordial cup of sack, impregnated with wormwood, is the best anti-pestilential draught; and, to speak truth, the pestilential miasmata are now very rife in the atmosphere. We live in a happy time, young man," continued he, in a tone of grave irony, "and have many blessings unknown to our fathers — Here are two sovereigns in the land, a regnant and a claimant—that is enough of one good thing—but if any one wants more, he may find a king in every peel-house in the country; so if we lack government, it is not for want of governors. Then have we a civil war to phlebotomize us every year, and to prevent our population from starving for want of food — and for the same purpose we have the Plague proposing us a visit, the best of all recipes for thinning a land, and converting younger brothers into elder ones. Well, each man in his vocation. You young fellows of the sword desire to wrestle, fence, or so forth, with some expert adversary; and for my part, I love to match myself for life or death against that same Plague."

As they proceeded up the street of the little village towards the Doctor's lodgings, his attention was successively occupied by the various personages whom he met, and pointed out to the notice of his companion.

"Do you see that fellow with the red bonnet, the blue jerkin, and the great rough baton in his hand? — I believe that clown hath the strength of a tower — he has lived fifty years in the world, and never encouraged the liberal sciences by buying one penny-worth of medicaments. — But see you that man with the *facies hippocratica?*" said he, pointing out a thin peasant, with swelled legs, and a most cadaverous countenance; "that I call one of the worthiest men in the barony—he breakfasts, luncheons, dines, and sups by my advice, and not without my medicine; and, for his own single part, will go farther to clear out a moderate stock of pharmaceutics, than half the country besides.—How do you, my honest friend?" said he to the party in question, with a tone of condolence.

"Very weakly, sir, since I took the electuary," answered the patient; "it neighboured ill with the two spoonfuls of pease-porridge and the kirnmilk."

"Pease-porridge and kirnmilk! Have you been under medicine these ten years, and keep your diet so ill? — the next morning take the electuary by itself, and touch nothing for six hours." — The poor object bowed, and limped off.

The next whom the Doctor deigned to take notice of, was a lame fellow, by whom the honour was altogether undeserved, for at sight of the mediciner, he began to shuffle away in the crowd as fast as his infirmities would permit.

"There is an ungrateful hound for you," said Doctor Lundin; "I cured him of the gout in his feet, and now he talks of the chargeableness of medicine, and makes the first use of his restored legs to fly from his physician. His *podagra* hath become a *chiragra*, as honest Martial hath it — the gout has got into his fingers, and he cannot draw his purse. Old saying and true,

Præmia cum poscit medicus, Sathan est.

We are angels when we come to cure—devils when we ask payment—but I will administer a purgation to his purse I warrant him. There is his brother too, a sordid chuff.—So ho, there! Saunders Darlet! you have been ill, I hear?"

"Just got the turn, as I was thinking to send to your honour, and I am brawly now again—it was nae great thing that ailed me."

"Hark you, sirrah," said the Doctor, "I trust you remember you are owing to the laird four stones of barleymeal, and a bow of oats; and I would have you send no more such kain-fowls as you sent last season, that looked as wretchedly as patients just dismissed from a plague-hospital; and there is hard money owing besides."

"I was thinking, sir," said the man, *more Scotico*, that is, returning no direct answer on the subject on which he was addressed, "my best way would be to come down to your honour, and take your advice yet, in case my trouble should come back."

"Do so, then, knave," replied Lundin, "and remember what Ecclesiasticus saith—'Give place to the physician—let him not go from thee, for thou hast need of him.'"

His exhortation was interrupted by an apparition, which seemed to strike the doctor with as much horror and surprise, as his own visage inflicted upon sundry of those persons whom he had addressed.

The figure which produced this effect on the Esculapius of the village, was that of a tall old woman, who wore a high-crowned hat and muffler. The first of these habiliments added apparently to her stature, and the other served to conceal the lower part of her face, and as the hat itself was slouched, little could be seen besides two brown cheek-bones, and the eyes of swarthy fire, that gleamed from under two shaggy gray eyebrows. She was dressed in a long dark-coloured robe of unusual fashion, bordered at the skirts, and on the stomacher, with a sort of white trimming resembling the Jewish phylacteries, on which were wrought the characters of some unknown language. She held in her hand a walking staff of black ebony.

"By the soul of Celsus," said Doctor Luke Lundin, "it is old Mother Nicneven herself—she hath come to beard me within mine own bounds, and in the very execution of mine office! Have at thy coat, Old Woman, as the song says—Hob Anster, let her presently be seized and committed to the tolbooth; and if there are any zealous brethren here who would give the hag her deserts, and duck her, as a witch, in the loch, I pray let them in no way be hindered."

But the myrmidons of Dr. Lundin showed in this case no alacrity to do his bidding. Hob Anster even ventured to remonstrate in the name of himself and his brethren. "To be sure he was to do his honour's bidding; and for a' that folks said about the skill and witcheries of Mother Nicneven, he would put his trust in God, and his hand on her collar, without dreadour. But she was no common spaewife, this Mother Nicneven, like Jean Jopp that lived in the Brierie-baulk. She had lords and lairds that would ruffle for her. There was Moncrieff of Tippermalloch, that was Popish, and the laird of Carslogie, a kend Queen's man, were in the fair, with wha kend how mony swords and bucklers at their back; and they would be sure to make a break-out if the officers meddled with the auld Popish witch-wife, who was sae weel friended; mair especially as the laird's best men, such as were not in the castle, were in Edinburgh with him, and he doubted his honour the Doctor would find ower few to make a good backing, if blades were bare."

The doctor listened unwillingly to this prudential counsel, and was only comforted by the faithful promise of his satellite, that "the old woman should," as he expressed it, "be ta'en canny the next time she trespassed on the bounds."

"And in that event," said the Doctor to his companion, "fire and fagot shall be the best of her welcome."

This he spoke in hearing of the dame herself, who even then, and in passing the Doctor, shot towards him from under her gray eyebrows a look of the most insulting and contemptuous superiority.

"This way," continued the physician, "this way," marshalling his guest into his lodging,—"take care you stumble not over a retort, for it is hazardous for the ignorant to walk in the ways of art."

The page found all reason for the caution; for besides stuffed birds, and lizards, and snakes bottled up, and bundles of simples made up, and other parcels spread out to dry, and all the confusion, not to mention the mingled and sickening smells, incidental to a druggist's stock in trade, he had also to avoid heaps of charcoal crucibles, bolt-heads, stoves, and the other furniture of a chemical laboratory.

Amongst his other philosophical qualities, Doctor Lundin failed not to be a confused sloven, and his old dame housekeeper, whose life, as she said, was spent in "redding him up," had trotted off to the mart of gaiety with other and younger folks. Much chattering and jangling therefore there was among jars, and bottles, and vials, ere the Doctor produced the salutiferous potion which he recommended so strongly, and a search equally long and noisy followed, among broken cans and cracked pipkins, ere he could bring forth a cup out of which to drink it. Both matters being at length achieved, the Doctor set the example to his guest, by quaffing off a cup of the cordial, and smacking his lips with approbation as it descended his gullet.—Roland, in turn, submitted to swallow the potion which his host so earnestly recommended, but which he found so insufferably bitter, that he became eager to escape from the laboratory in search of a draught of fair water to expel the taste. In spite of his efforts, he was nevertheless detained by the garrulity of his host, till he gave him some account of Mother Nicneven.

"I care not to speak of her," said the Doctor, "in the open air, and among the throng of people; not for fright, like yon cowardly dog Anster, but because I would give no occasion for a fray, having no leisure to look to stabs, slashes, and broken bones. Men call the old hag a prophetess—I do scarce believe she could foretell when a brood of chickens will chip the shell—Men say she reads the heavens—my black bitch knows as much of them when she sits baying the moon—Men pretend the ancient wretch is a sorceress, a witch, and what not—*Inter nos*, I will never contradict a rumour which may bring her to the stake which she so justly deserves; but neither will I believe that the tales of witches which they din into our ears are aught but knavery, cozenage, and old women's fables."

"In the name of Heaven, what is she then," said the page, "that you make such a stir about her?"

"She is one of those cursed old women," replied the Doctor, "who take currently and impudently upon themselves to act as advisers and curers of the sick, on the strength of some trash of herbs, some rhyme of spells, some julap or diet, drink or cordial."

"Nay, go no farther," said the page; "if they brew cordials, evil be their lot and all their partakers!"

"You say well, young man," said Dr. Lundin; "for mine own part, I know no such pests to the commonwealth as these old incarnate devils, who haunt the chambers of the brain-sick patients, that are mad enough to suffer them to interfere with, disturb, and let, the regular process of a learned and artificial cure, with their sirups, and their julaps, and diascordium, and mithridate, and my Lady What-shall-call'um's powder, and worthy Dame Trashem's pill; and thus make widows and orphans, and cheat the regular and well-studied physician, in order to get the name of wise women and skeely neighbours, and so forth. But no more on't—Mother Nicneven* and I will meet one day, and she shall know there is danger in dealing with the Doctor."

"It is a true word, and many have found it," said the page; "but under your favour, I would fain walk abroad for a little, and see these sports."

"It is well moved," said the Doctor, "and I too should be showing myself abroad. Moreover the play waits us, young man—to-day, *totus mundus agit histrionem.*"—And they sallied forth accordingly into the mirthful scene.

---

* This was the name given to the grand Mother Witch, the very Hecate of Scottish popular superstition. Her name was bestowed, in one or two instances, upon sorceresses, who were held to resemble her by their superior skill in "Hell's black grammar."

Chapter the Twenty-Seventh.

See on yon verdant lawn, the gathering crowd
Thickens amain; the buxom nymphs advance,
Usher'd by jolly clowns; distinctions cease,
Lost in the common joy, and the bold slave
Leans on his wealthy master unreproved.
Rural Games.—SOMERVILLE.

THE re-appearance of the dignified Chamberlain on the street of the village was eagerly hailed by the revellers, as a pledge that the play, or dramatic representation, which had been postponed owing to his absence, was now full surely to commence. Any thing like an approach to this most interesting of all amusements, was of recent origin in Scotland, and engaged public attention in proportion. All other sports were discontinued. The dance around the Maypole was arrested — the ring broken up and dispersed, while the dancers, each leading his partner by the hand, tripped off to the silvan theatre. A truce was in like manner achieved betwixt a huge brown bear and certain mastiffs, who were tugging and pulling at his shaggy coat, under the mediation of the bear-ward and half a dozen butchers and yeomen, who, by dint of *staving and tailing*, as it was technically termed, separated the unfortunate animals, whose fury had for an hour past been their chief amusement. The itinerant minstrel found himself deserted by the audience he had collected, even in the most interesting passage of the romance which he recited, and just as he was sending about his boy, with bonnet in hand, to collect their oblations. He indignantly stopped short in the midst of *Rosewal and Lilian*, and, replacing his three-stringed fiddle, or rebeck, in its leathern case, followed the crowd, with no good-will, to the exhibition which had superseded his own. The juggler had ceased his exertions of emitting flame and smoke, and was content to respire in the manner of ordinary mortals, rather than to play gratuitously the part of a fiery dragon. In short, all other sports were suspended, so eagerly did the revellers throng towards the place of representation.

They would err greatly, who should regulate their ideas of this dramatic exhibition upon those derived from a modern theatre; for the rude shows of Thespis were far less different from those exhibited by Euripides on the stage of Athens, with all its magnificent decorations and pomp of dresses and of scenery. In the present case, there were no scenes, no stage, no machinery, no pit, box, and gallery, no box-lobby; and, what might in poor Scotland be some consolation for other negations, there was no taking of money at the door. As in the devices of the magnanimous Bottom, the actors had a greensward plot for a stage, and a hawthorn bush for a green-room and tiring-house; the spectators being accommodated with seats on the artificial bank which had been raised around three-fourths of the play-ground, the remainder being left open for the entrance and exit of the performers. Here sate the uncritical audience, the Chamberlain in the centre, as the person highest in office, all alive to enjoyment and admiration, and all therefore dead to criticism.

The characters which appeared and disappeared before the amused and interested audience, were those which fill the earlier stage in all nations — old men, cheated by their wives and daughters, pillaged by their sons, and imposed on by their domestics, a braggadocia captain, a knavish pardoner or quæstionary, a country bumpkin and a wanton city dame. Amid all these, and more acceptable than almost the whole put together, was the all-licensed fool, the Gracioso of the Spanish drama, who, with his cap fashioned into the resemblance of a coxcomb, and his bauble, a truncheon terminated by a carved figure wearing a fool's cap, in his hand, went, came, and returned, mingling in every scene of the piece, and interrupting the business, without having any share himself in the action, and ever and anon transferring his gibes from the actors on the stage to the audience who sate around, prompt to applaud the whole.

The wit of the piece, which was not of the most polished kind, was chiefly directed against the superstitious practices of the Catholic religion; and the stage artillery had on this occasion been levelled by no less a person than Doctor Lundin, who had not only commanded the manager of the entertainment to select one of the numerous satires which had been written against the Papists, (several of which were cast in a dramatic form,) but had even, like the Prince of Denmark, caused them to insert, or according to his own phrase, to infuse here and there, a few pleasantries of his own penning, on the same inexhaustible subject, hoping thereby to mollify the rigour of the Lady of Lochleven towards pastimes of this description. He failed not to jog Roland's elbow, who was sitting in state behind him, and recommend to his particular attention these favourite passages. As for the page, to whom the very idea of such an exhibition, simple as it was, was entirely new, he beheld it with the undiminished and ecstatic delight with which men of all ranks look for the first time on dramatic representation, and laughed, shouted, and clapped his hands as the performance proceeded. An incident at length took place, which effectually broke off his interest in the business of the scene.

One of the principal personages in the comic part of the drama was, as we have already said, a quæstionary or pardoner, one of those itinerants who hawked about from place to place relics, real or pretended, with which he excited the devotion at once, and the charity of the populace, and generally deceived both the one and the other. The hypocrisy, impudence, and profligacy of these clerical wanderers, had made them the subject of satire from the time of Chaucer down to that of Heywood. Their present representative failed not to follow the same line of humour, exhibiting pig's bones for relics, and boasting the virtues of small tin crosses, which had been shaken in the holy porringer at Loretto, and of cockleshells, which had been brought from the shrine of Saint James of Compostella, all which he disposed of to the devout Catholics at nearly as high a price as antiquaries are now willing to pay for baubles of similar intrinsic value. At length the pardoner pulled from his scrip a small phial of clear water, of which he vaunted the quality in the following verses:—

Listneth, gode people, everiche one
For in the londe of Babylone,
Far eastward I wot it lyeth,
And is the first londe the sonne espieth,
Ther, as he cometh fro out the sé;
In this ilk londe, as thinketh me,
Right as holie legendes tell,
Snottreth from a roke a well,
And falleth into ane bath of ston,
Where chaste Susanne, in times long gon,
Was wont to wash her bodie and lim
Mickle vertue hath that streme,
As ye shall se er that ye pas,
Ensample by this little glas—
Through nightés cold and dayés hote
Hiderward I have it brought;
Hath a wife made slip or side,
Or a maiden stepp'd aside,
Putteth this water under her nese,
Wold she nold she, she shall snese.

The jest, as the reader skilful in the antique language of the drama must at once perceive, turned on the same pivot as in the old minstrel tales of the Drinking Horn of King Arthur, and the Mantle made Amiss. But the audience were neither learned nor critical enough to challenge its want of originality. The potent relic was, after such grimace and buffoonery as befitted the subject, presented successively to each of the female personages of the drama, not one of whom sustained the supposed test of discretion; but, to the infinite delight of the audience, sneezed much louder and longer than perhaps they themselves had counted on. The jest seemed at last worn threadbare, and the pardoner was passing on to some new pleasantry, when the jester or clown of the drama, possessing himself secretly of the phial which contained the wondrous liquor, applied it suddenly to the nose of a young woman, who, with her black silk muffler, or screen drawn over her face, was sitting in the foremost rank of the spectators, intent apparently upon the business of the stage. The contents of the phial, well calculated to sustain the credit of the pardoner's legend, set the damsel a-sneezing violently, an admission of frailty which was received with shouts of rapture by the audience. These were soon, however, renewed at the expense of the jester himself, when the insulted maiden extricated, ere the paroxysm was well over, one hand from the folds of her mantle, and bestowed on the wag a buffet, which made him reel fully his own length from the pardoner, and then acknowledge the favour by instant prostration.

No one pities a jester overcome in his vocation, and the clown met with little sympathy, when, rising from the ground, and whimpering forth his complaints of harsh treatment, he invoked the assistance and sympathy of the audience. But the Chamberlain, feeling his own dignity insulted, ordered two of his halberdiers to bring the culprit before him. When these official persons first approached the virago, she threw herself into an attitude of firm defiance, as if determined to resist their authority; and from the sample of strength and spirit which she had already displayed, they showed no alacrity at executing their commission. But on half a minute's reflection, the damsel changed totally her attitude and manner, folded her cloak around her arms in modest and maiden-like fashion, and walked of her own accord to the presence of the great man, followed and guarded by the two manful satellites. As she moved across the vacant space, and more especially as she stood at the footstool of the Doctor's judgment-seat, the maiden discovered that lightness and elasticity of step, and natural grace of manner, which connoisseurs in female beauty know to be seldom divided from it. Moreover, her neat russet-coloured jacket, and short petticoat of the same colour, displayed a handsome form and a pretty leg. Her features were concealed by the screen; but the Doctor, whose gravity did not prevent his pretensions to be a connoisseur of the school we have hinted at, saw enough to judge favourably of the piece by the sample.

He began, however, with considerable austerity of manner.—"And how now, saucy quean!" said the medical man of office; "what have you to say why I should not order you to be ducked in the loch, for lifting your hand to the man in my presence?"

"Marry," replied the culprit, "because I judge that your honour will not think the cold bath necessary for my complaints."

"A pestilent jade," said the Doctor, whispering to Roland Græme; "and I'll warrant her a good one—her voice is as sweet as sirup.—But, my pretty maiden," said he, "you show us wonderful little of that countenance of yours — be pleased to throw aside your muffler."

"I trust your honour will excuse me till we are more private," answered the maiden; "for I have acquaintance, and I should like ill to be known in the country as the poor girl whom that scurvy knave put his jest upon."

"Fear nothing for thy good name, my sweet little modicum of candied manna," replied the Doctor, "for I protest to you, as I am Chamberlain of Lochleven, Kinross, and so forth, that the chaste Susanna herself could not have snuffed that elixir without sternutation, being in truth a curious distillation of rectified *acetum*, or vinegar of the sun, prepared by mine own hands — Wherefore, as thou sayest thou wilt come to me in private, and express thy contrition for the offence whereof thou hast been guilty, I command that all for the present go forward as if no such interruption of the prescribed course had taken place."

The damsel curtsied and tripped back to her place. The play proceeded, but it no longer attracted the attention of Roland Græme.

The voice, the figure, and what the veil permitted to be seen of the neck and tresses of the village damsel, bore so strong a resemblance to those of Catherine Seyton, that he felt like one bewildered in the mazes of a changeful and stupifying dream. The memorable scene of the hostelrie rushed on his recollection, with all its doubtful and marvellous circumstances. Were the tales of enchantment which he had read in romances realized in this extraordinary girl? Could she transport herself from the walled and guarded Castle of Lochleven, moated with its broad lake, (towards which he cast back a look as if to ascertain it was still in existence,) and watched with such scrupulous care as the safety of a nation demanded?—Could she surmount all these obstacles, and make such careless and dangerous use of her liberty, as to engage herself publicly in a quarrel in a village fair? Roland was unable to determine whether the exertions which it must have cost her to gain her freedom, or the use to which she had put it, rendered her the most unaccountable creature.

Lost in these meditations, he kept his gaze fixed on the subject of them; and in every casual motion, discovered, or thought he discovered, something which reminded him still more strongly of Catherine Seyton. It occurred to him more than once, indeed, that he might be deceiving himself by exaggerating some casual likeness into absolute identity. But then the meeting at the hostelrie of Saint Michael's returned to his mind, and it seemed in the highest degree improbable, that, under such various circumstances, mere imagination should twice have found opportunity to play him the self-same trick. This time, however, he determined to have his doubts resolved, and for this purpose he sate during the rest of the play like a greyhound in the slip, ready to spring upon the hare the instant that she was started. The damsel, whom he watched attentively lest she should escape in the crowd when the spectacle was closed, sate as if perfectly unconscious that she was observed. But the worthy Doctor marked the direction of his eyes, and magnanimously suppressed his own inclination to become the Theseus to this Hippolyta, in deference to the rights of hospitality, which enjoined him to forbear interference with the pleasurable pursuits of his young friend. He passed one or two formal gibes upon the fixed attention which the page paid to the unknown, and upon his own jealousy; adding, however, that if both were to be presented to the patient at once, he had little doubt she would think the younger man the sounder prescription. "I fear me," he added, "we shall have no news of the knave Auchtermuchty for some time, since the vermin whom I sent after him seem to have proved corbie-messengers. So you have an hour or two on your hands, Master Page; and as the minstrels are beginning to strike up, now the play is ended, why, an you incline for a dance, yonder is the green, and there sits your partner—I trust you will hold me perfect in my diagnostics, since I see with half an eye what disease you are sick of, and have administered a pleasing remedy.

"*Discernit sapiens res* (as Chambers hath it) *quas confundit asellus.*"

The page hardly heard the end of the learned adage, or the charge which the Chamberlain gave him to be within reach, in case of the wains arriving suddenly, and sooner than expected—so eager he was at once to shake himself free of his learned associate, and to satisfy his curiosity regarding the unknown damsel. Yet in the haste with which he made towards her he found time to reflect, that, in order to secure an opportunity of conversing with her in private, he must not alarm her at first accosting her. He therefore composed his manner and gait, and advancing with becoming self-confidence before three or four country-fellows who were intent on the same design, but knew not so well how to put their request into shape, he acquainted her that he, as the deputy of the venerable Chamberlain, requested the honour of her hand as a partner.

"The venerable Chamberlain," said the damsel frankly, reaching the page her hand, "does very well to exercise this part of his privilege by deputy; and I suppose the laws of the revels leave me no choice but to accept of his faithful delegate."

"Provided, fair damsel," said the page, "his choice of a delegate is not altogether distasteful to you."

"Of that, fair sir," replied the maiden, "I will tell you more when we have danced the first measure."

Catherine Seyton had admirable skill in gestic lore, and was sometimes called on to dance for the amusement of her royal mistress. Roland Græme had often been a spectator of her skill, and sometimes, at the Queen's command, Catherine's partner on such occasions. He was, therefore, perfectly acquainted with Catherine's mode of dancing; and observed that his present partner, in grace, in agility, in quickness of ear, and precision of execution, exactly resembled her, save that the Scottish jig, which he now danced with her, required a more violent and rapid motion, and more rustic agility, than the stately pavens, lavoltas, and courantoes, which he had seen her execute in the chamber of Queen Mary. The active duties of the dance left him little time for reflection, and none for conversation; but when their *pas de deux* was finished, amidst the acclamations of the villagers, who had seldom witnessed such an exhibition, he took an opportunity, when they yielded up the green to another couple, to use the privilege of a partner and enter into conversation with the mysterious maiden, whom he still held by the hand.

"Fair partner, may I not crave the name of her who has graced me thus far?"

"You may," said the maiden; "but it is a question whether I shall answer you."

"And why?" asked Roland.

"Because nobody gives anything for nothing — and you can tell me nothing in return which I care to hear."

"Could I not tell you my name and lineage, in exchange for yours?" returned Roland.

"No!" answered the maiden, "for you know little of either."

"How?" said the page, somewhat angrily.

"Wrath you not for the matter," said the damsel; "I will show you in an instant that I know more of you than you do of yourself."

"Indeed," answered Græme; "for whom then do you take me?"

"For the wild falcon," answered she, "whom a dog brought in his mouth to a certain castle, when he was but an unfledged eyas — for the hawk whom men dare not fly, lest he should check at game, and pounce on carrion — whom folk must keep hooded till he has the proper light of his eyes, and can discover good from evil."

"Well — be it so," replied Roland Græme; "I guess at a part of your parable, fair mistress mine — and perhaps I know as much of you as you do of me, and can well dispense with the information which you are so niggard in giving."

"Prove that," said the maiden, "and I will give you credit for more penetration than I judged you to be gifted withal."

"It shall be proved instantly," said Roland Græme. "The first letter of your name is S, and the last N."

"Admirable," said his partner, "guess on."

"It pleases you to-day," continued Roland, "to wear the snood and kirtle, and perhaps you may be seen to-morrow in hat and feather, hose and doublet."

"In the clout! in the clout! you have hit the very white," said the damsel, suppressing a great inclination to laugh.

"You can switch men's eyes out of their heads, as well as the heart out of their bosoms."

These last words were uttered in a low and tender tone, which, to Roland's great mortification, and somewhat to his displeasure, was so far from allaying, that it greatly increased, his partner's disposition to laughter. She could scarce compose herself while she replied, "If you had thought my hand so formidable," extricating it from his hold, "you would not have grasped it so hard; but I perceive you know me so fully, that there is no occasion to show you my face."

"Fair Catherine," said the page, "he were unworthy ever to have seen you, far less to have dwelt so long in the same service, and under the same roof with you, who could mistake your air, your gesture, your step in walking or in dancing, the turn of your neck, the symmetry of your form — none could be so dull as not to recognize you by so many proofs; but for me, I could swear even to that tress of hair that escapes from under your muffler."

"And to the face, of course, which that muffler covers," said the maiden, removing her veil, and in an instant endeavouring to replace it. She showed the features of Catherine; but an unusual degree of petulant impatience inflamed them, when, from some awkwardness in her management of the muffler, she was unable again to adjust it with that dexterity which was a principal accomplishment of the coquettes of the time.

"The fiend rive the rag to tatters!" said the damsel, as the veil fluttered about her shoulders, with an accent so earnest and decided, that it made the page start. He looked again at the damsel's face, but the information which his eyes received, was to the same purport as before. He assisted her to adjust her muffler, and both were for an instant silent. The damsel spoke first, for Roland Græme was overwhelmed with surprise at the contrarieties which Catherine Seyton seemed to include in her person and character.

"You are surprised," said the damsel to him, "at what you see and hear — But the times which make females men, are least of all fitted for men to become women; yet you yourself are in danger of such a change."

"I in danger of becoming effeminate!" said the page.

"Yes, you, for all the boldness of your reply," said the damsel. "When you should hold fast your religion, because it is assailed on all sides by rebels, traitors, and heretics, you let it glide out of your breast like water grasped in the hand. If you are driven from the faith of your fathers from fear of a traitor, is not that womanish?—If you are cajoled by the cunning arguments of a trumpeter of heresy, or the praises of a puritanic old woman, is not that womanish? — If you are bribed by the hope of spoil and preferment, is not that womanish? — And when you wonder at my venting a threat or an execration, should you not wonder at yourself, who, pretending to a gentle name and aspiring to knighthood, can be at the same time cowardly, silly, and self-interested!"

"I would that a man would bring such a charge," said the page; "he should see, ere his life was a minute older, whether he had cause to term me coward or no."

"Beware of such big words," answered the maiden; "you said but anon that I sometimes wear hose and doublet."

"But remain still Catharine Seyton, wear what you list," said the page, endeavouring again to possess himself of her hand.

"You indeed are pleased to call me so," replied the maiden, evading his intention, "but I have many other names besides."

"And will you not reply to that," said the page, "by which you are distinguished beyond every other maiden in Scotland?"

The damsel, unallured by his praises, still kept aloof, and sung with gaiety a verse from an old ballad,

"Oh, some do call me Jack, sweet love,
And some do call me Gill;
But when I ride to Holyrood,
My name is Wilful Will."

'Wilful Will!" exclaimed the page, impatiently; "say rather Will o' the Wisp—Jack with the Lantern — for never was such a deceitful or wandering meteor!"

"If I be such," replied the maiden, "I ask no fools to follow me—If they do so, it is at their own pleasure, and must be on their own proper peril."

"Nay, but, dearest Catherine," said Roland Græme, "be for one instant serious."

"If you will call me your dearest Catherine, when I have given you so many names to choose upon," replied the damsel, "I would ask you how, supposing me for two or three hours of my life escaped from yonder tower, you have the cruelty to ask me to be serious during the only merry moments I have seen perhaps for months?"

"Ay, but, fair Catherine, there are moments of deep and true feeling, which are worth ten thousand years of the liveliest mirth; and such was that of yesterday, when you so nearly——"

"So nearly what?" demanded the damsel, hastily.

"When you approached your lips so near to the sign you had traced on my forehead."

"Mother of Heaven!" exclaimed she, in a yet fiercer tone, and with a more masculine manner than she had yet exhibited,—"Catherine Seyton approach her lips to a man's brow, and thou that man!—vassal, thou liest!"

The page stood astonished; but, conceiving he had alarmed the damsel's delicacy by alluding to the enthusiasm of a moment, and the manner in which she had expressed it, he endeavoured to falter forth an apology. His excuses, though he was unable to give them any regular shape, were accepted by his companion, who had indeed suppressed her indignation after its first explosion—"Speak no more on't," she said. "And now let us part; our conversation may attract more notice than is convenient for either of us."

"Nay, but allow me at least to follow you to some sequestered place."

"You dare not," replied the maiden.

"How," said the youth, "dare not? where is it you dare go, where I dare not follow?"

"You fear a Will o' the Wisp," said the damsel; "how would you face a fiery dragon, with an enchantress mounted on its back?"

"Like Sir Eger, Sir Grime, or Sir Greysteil," said the page; "but be there such toys to be seen here?"

"I go to Mother Nicneven's," answered the maid; "and she is witch enough to rein the horned devil, with a red silk thread for a bridle, and a rowan-tree switch for a whip."

"I will follow you," said the page.

"Let it be at some distance," said the maiden.

And wrapping her mantle round her with more success than on her former attempt, she mingled with the throng, and walked towards the village, heedfully followed by Roland Græme at some distance, and under every precaution which he could use to prevent his purpose from being observed.

Chapter the Twenty-Eighth.

Yes, it is he whose eyes look'd on thy childhood,
And watch'd with trembling hope thy dawn of youth,
That now, with these same eyeballs dimm'd with age,
And dimmer yet with tears, sees thy dishonour.

Old Play.

At the entrance of the principal, or indeed, so to speak, the only street in Kinross, the damsel, whose steps were pursued by Roland Græme, cast a glance behind her, as if to be certain he had not lost trace of her and then plunged down a very narrow lane which ran betwixt two rows of poor and ruinous cottages. She paused for a second at the door of one of those miserable tenements, again cast her eye up the lane towards Roland, then lifted the latch, opened the door, and disappeared from his view.

With whatever haste the page followed her example, the difficulty which he found in discovering the trick of the latch, which did not work quite in the usual manner, and in pushing open the door, which did not yield to his first effort, delayed for a minute or two his entrance into the cottage. A dark and smoky passage led, as usual, betwixt the exterior wall of the house, and the *hallan*, or clay wall, which served as a partition betwixt it and the interior. At the end of this passage, and through the partition, was a door leading into the *ben*, or inner chamber of the cottage, and when Roland Græme's hand was upon the latch of this door, a female voice pronounced, "*Benedictus qui veniat in nomine Domini, damnandus qui in nomine inimici.*" On entering the apartment, he perceived the figure which the chamberlain had pointed out to him as Mother Nicneven, seated beside the lowly hearth. But there was no other person in the room. Roland Græme gazed around in surprise at the disappearance of Catherine Seyton, without paying much regard to the supposed sorceress, until she attracted and riveted his regard by the tone in which she asked him — "What seekest thou here?"

"I seek," said the page, with much embarrassment; "I seek ——"

But his answer was cut short, when the old woman, drawing her huge gray eyebrows sternly together, with a frown which knitted her brow into a thousand wrinkles, arose, and erecting herself up to her full natural size, tore the kerchief from her head, and seizing Roland by the arm, made two strides across the floor of the apartment to a small window through which the light fell full on her face, and showed the astonished youth the countenance of Magdalen Græme.—"Yes, Roland," she said, "thine eyes deceive thee not; they show thee truly the features of her whom thou hast thyself deceived, whose wine thou hast turned into gall, her bread of joyfulness into bitter poison, her hope into the blackest despair — it is she who now demands of thee, what seekest thou here?—She whose heaviest sin towards Heaven hath been, that she loved thee even better than the weal of the whole church, and could not without reluctance surrender thee even in the cause of God — she now asks you, what seekest thou here?"

While she spoke, she kept her broad black eye riveted on the youth's face, with the expression with which the eagle regards his prey ere he tears it to pieces. Roland felt himself at the moment incapable either of reply or evasion. This extraordinary enthusiast had preserved over him in some measure the ascendency which she had acquired during his childhood; and, besides, he knew the violence of her passions and her impatience of contradiction, and was sensible that almost any reply which he could make, was likely to throw her into an ecstasy of rage. He was therefore silent; and Magdalen Græme proceeded with increasing enthusiasm in her apostrophe —"Once more, what seek'st thou, false boy?—seek'st thou the honour thou hast renounced, the faith thou hast abandoned, the hopes thou hast destroyed? — Or didst thou seek me, the sole protectress of thy youth, the only parent whom thou hast known, that thou mayest trample on my gray hairs, even as thou hast already trampled on the best wishes of my heart?"

"Pardon me, mother," said Roland Græme; "but, in truth and reason, I deserve not your blame. I have been treated amongst you — even by yourself, my revered parent, as well as by others — as one who lacked the common attributes of free-will and human reason, or was at least deemed unfit to exercise them. A land of enchantment have I been led into, and spells have been cast around me—every one has met me in disguise—every one has spoken to me in parables — I have been like one who walks in a weary and bewildering dream; and now you blame me that I have not the sense, and judgment, and steadiness of a waking, and a disenchanted, and a reasonable man, who knows what he is doing, and wherefore he does it. If one must walk with masks and spectres, who waft themselves from place to place as it were in vision rather than reality, it might shake the soundest faith and turn the wisest head. I sought, since I must needs avow my folly, the same Catherine Seyton with whom you made me first acquainted, and whom I most strangely find in this village of Kinross, gayest among the revellers, when I had but just left her in the well-guarded castle of Lochleven, the sad attendant of an imprisoned Queen—I sought her, and in her place I find you, my mother, more strangely disguised than even she is."

"And what hadst thou to do with Catherine Seyton?" said the matron, sternly; "is this a time or a world to follow maidens, or to dance around a Maypole? When the trumpet summons every true-hearted Scotsman around the standard of the true sovereign, shalt thou be found loitering in a lady's bower?"

"No, by Heaven, nor imprisoned in the rugged walls of an island castle!" answered Roland Græme: "I would the blast were to sound even now, for I fear that nothing less loud will dispel the chimerical visions by which I am surrounded."

"Doubt not that it will be winded," said the matron, "and that so fearfully loud, that Scotland will never hear the like until the last and loudest blast of all shall announce to mountain and to valley that time is no more. Meanwhile, be thou but brave and constant—Serve God and honour thy sovereign—Abide by thy religion—I cannot—I will not—I dare not ask thee the truth of the terrible surmises I have heard touching thy falling away—perfect not that accursed sacrifice—and yet, even at this late hour, thou mayest be what I have hoped for the son of my dearest hope—what say I? the son of *my* hope—thou shalt be the hope of Scotland, her boast and her honour!—Even thy wildest and most foolish wishes may perchance be fulfilled—I might blush to mingle meaner motives with the noble guerdon I hold out to thee—It shames me, being such as I am, to mention the idle passions of youth, save with contempt and the purpose of censure. But we must bribe children to wholesome medicine by the offer of cates, and youth to honourable achievement with the promise of pleasure. Mark me, therefore, Roland. The love of Catherine Seyton will follow him only who shall achieve the freedom of her mistress; and believe, it may be one day in thine own power to be that happy lover. Cast, therefore, away doubt and fear, and prepare to do what religion calls for, what thy country demands of thee, what thy duty as a subject and as a servant alike require at your hand; and be assured, even the idlest or wildest wishes of thy heart will be most readily attained by following the call of thy duty."

As she ceased speaking, a double knock was heard against the inner door. The matron hastily adjusting her muffler, and resuming her chair by the hearth, demanded who was there.

"*Salve in nomine sancto*," was answered from without.

"*Salvete et vos*," answered Magdalen Græme.

And a man entered in the ordinary dress of a nobleman's retainer, wearing at his girdle a sword and buckler—"I sought you," said he, "my mother, and him whom I see with you." Then addressing himself to Roland Græme, he said to him, "Hast thou not a packet from George Douglas?"

"I have," said the page, suddenly recollecting that which had been committed to his charge in the morning, "but I may not deliver it to any one without some token that they have a right to ask it."

"You say well," replied the serving-man, and whispered into his ear, "The packet which I ask is the report to his father—will this token suffice?"

"It will," replied the page, and taking the packet from his bosom, gave it to the man.

"I will return presently," said the serving-man, and left the cottage.

Roland had now sufficiently recovered his surprise to accost his relative in turn, and request to know the reason why he found her in so precarious a disguise, and a place so dangerous — "You cannot be ignorant," he said, "of the hatred that the Lady of Lochleven bears to those of your — that is of our religion — your present disguise lays you open to suspicion of a different kind, but inferring no less hazard; and whether as a Catholic, or as a sorceress, or as a friend to the unfortunate Queen, you are in equal danger, if apprehended within the bounds of the Douglas; and in the chamberlain who administers their authority, you have, for his own reasons, an enemy, and a bitter one."

"I know it," said the matron, her eyes kindling with triumph; "I know that, vain of his school-craft, and carnal wisdom, Luke Lundin views with jealousy and hatred the blessings which the saints have conferred on my prayers, and on the holy relics, before the touch, nay, before the bare presence of which, disease and death have so often been known to retreat. —I know he would rend and tear me; but there is a chain and a muzzle on the ban dog that shall restrain his fury, and the Master's servant shall not be offended by him until the Master's work is wrought. When that hour comes, let the shadows of the evening descend on me in thunder and in tempest; the time shall be welcome that relieves my eyes from seeing guilt, and my ears from listening to blasphemy. Do thou but be constant — play thy part as I have played and will play mine, and my release shall be like that of a blessed martyr whose ascent to heaven angels hail with psalm and song, while earth pursues him with hiss and with execration."

As she concluded, the serving-man again entered the cottage, and said, "All is well! the time holds for to-morrow night."

"What time? what holds?" exclaimed Roland Græme; "I trust I have given the Douglas's packet to no wrong——"

"Content yourself, young man," answered the serving-man; "thou hast my word and token."

"I know not if the token be right," said the page; "and I care not much for the word of a stranger."

"What," said the matron, "although thou mayest have given a packet delivered to thy charge by one of the Queen's rebels into the hand of a loyal subject — there were no great mistake in that, thou hot-brained boy!"

"By Saint Andrew, there were foul mistake, though," answered the page; "it is the very spirit of my duty, in this first stage of chivalry, to be faithful to my trust; and had the devil given me a message to discharge, I would not (so I had plighted my faith to the contrary) betray his counsel to an angel of light."

"Now, by the love I once bore thee," said the matron, "I could slay thee with mine own hand, when I hear thee talk of a dearer faith being due to rebels and heretics, than thou owest to thy church and thy prince!"

"Be patient, my good sister," said the serving-man; "I will give him such reasons as shall counterbalance the scruples which beset him — the spirit is honourable, though now it may be mistimed and misplaced. — Follow me, young man."

"Ere I go to call this stranger to a reckoning," said the page to the matron, "is there nothing I can do for your comfort and safety?"

"Nothing," she replied, "nothing, save what will lead more to thine own honour; — the saints who have protected me thus far, will lend me succour as I need it. Tread the path of glory that is before thee, and only think of me as the creature on earth who will be most delighted to hear of thy fame. — Follow the stranger — he hath tidings for you that you little expect."

The stranger remained on the threshold as if waiting for Roland, and as soon as he saw him put himself in motion, he moved on before at a quick pace. Diving still deeper down the lane, Roland perceived that it was now bordered by buildings upon the one side only, and that the other was fenced by a high old wall, over which some trees extended their branches. Descending a good way farther, they came to a small door in the wall. Roland's guide paused, looked around an instant to see if any one were within sight, then taking a key from his pocket, opened the door and entered, making a sign to Roland Græme to follow him. He did so, and the stranger locked the door carefully on the inside. During this operation the page had a moment to look around, and perceived that he was in a small orchard very trimly kept.

The stranger led him through an alley or two, shaded by trees loaded with summer-fruit, into a pleached arbour, where, taking the turf-seat which was on the one side, he motioned to Roland to occupy that which was opposite to him, and, after a momentary silence, opened the conversation as follows: "You have asked a better warrant than the word of a mere stranger, to satisfy you that I have the authority of George of Douglas for possessing myself of the packet intrusted to your charge."

"It is precisely the point on which I demand reckoning of you," said Roland. "I fear I have acted hastily; if so, I must redeem my error as I best may."

"You hold me then as a perfect stranger?" said the man. "Look at my face more attentively, and see if the features do not resemble those of a man much known to you formerly."

Roland gazed attentively; but the ideas recalled to his mind were so inconsistent with the mean and servile dress of the person before him, that he did not venture to express the opinion which he was irresistibly induced to form.

"Yes, my son," said the stranger, observing his embarrassment, "you do indeed see before you the unfortunate Father Ambrosius, who once accounted his ministry crowned in your preservation from the snares of heresy, but who is now condemned to lament thee as a castaway!"

Roland Græme's kindness of heart was at least equal to his vivacity of temper — he could not bear to see his ancient and honoured master and spiritual guide in a situation which inferred a change of fortune so melancholy, but throwing himself at his feet, grasped his knees and wept aloud.

"What mean these tears, my son?" said the Abbot; "if they are shed for your own sins and follies, surely they are gracious showers, and may avail thee much — but weep not, if they fall on my account. You indeed see the Superior of the community of Saint Mary's in the dress of a poor swerder, who gives his master the use of his blade and buckler, and, if needful, of his life, for a coarse livery coat and four marks by the year. But such a garb suits the time, and, in the period of the church militant, as well becomes her prelates, as staff, mitre, and crosier, in the days of the church's triumph.

"By what fate," said the page — "and yet why," added he, checking himself, "need I ask? Catherine Seyton in some sort prepared me for this. But that the change should be so absolute — the destruction so complete!"——

"Yes, my son," said the Abbot Ambrosius, "thine own eyes beheld, in my unworthy elevation to the Abbot's stall, the last especial act of holy solemnity which shall be seen in the church of Saint Mary's, until it shall please Heaven to turn back the captivity of the church. For the present, the shepherd is smitten — ay, well-nigh to the earth — the flock are scattered, and the shrines of saints and martyrs, and pious benefactors to the church, are given to the owls of night, and the satyrs of the desert."

"And your brother, the Knight of Avenel — could he do nothing for your protection?"

"He himself hath fallen under the suspicion of the ruling powers," said the Abbot, "who are as unjust to their friends as they are cruel to their enemies. I could not grieve at it, did I hope it might estrange him from his cause; but I know the soul of Halbert, and I rather fear it will drive him to prove his fidelity to their unhappy cause, by some deed which may be yet more destructive to the church, and more offensive to Heaven. Enough of this; and now to the business of our meeting.—I trust you will hold it sufficient if I pass my word to you that the packet of which you were lately the bearer, was designed for my hands by George of Douglas?"

"Then," said the page, "is George of Douglas——"

"A true friend to his Queen, Roland; and will soon, I trust, have his eyes opened to the errors of his (miscalled) church."

"But what is he to his father, and what to the Lady of Lochleven, who has been as a mother to him?" said the page impatiently.

"The best friend to both, in time and through eternity," said the Abbot, "if he shall prove the happy instrument for redeeming the evil they have wrought, and are still working."

"Still," said the page, "I like not that good service which begins in breach of trust."

"I blame not thy scruples, my son," said the Abbot; "but the time which has wrenched asunder the allegiance of Christians to the church, and of subjects to their king, has dissolved all the lesser bonds of society; and, in such days, mere human ties must no more restrain our progress, than the brambles and briers which catch hold of his garments, should delay the path of a pilgrim who travels to pay his vows."

"But, my father,"—said the youth, and then stopt short in a hesitating manner.

"Speak on, my son," said the Abbot; "speak without fear."

"Let me not offend you then," said Roland, "when I say, that it is even this which our adversaries charge against us; when they say that, shaping the means according to the end, we are willing to commit great moral evil in order that we may work out eventual good."

"The heretics have played their usual arts on you, my son," said the Abbot; "they would willingly deprive us of the power of acting wisely and secretly, though their possession of superior force forbids our contending with them on terms of equality. They have reduced us to a state of exhausted weakness, and now would fain proscribe the means by which weakness, through all the range of nature, supplies the lack of strength and defends itself against its potent enemies. As well might the hound say to the hare, use not these wily turns to escape me, but contend with me in pitched battle, as the armed and powerful heretic demand of the down-trodden and oppressed Catholic to lay aside the wisdom of the serpent, by which alone they may again hope to raise up the Jerusalem over which they weep, and which it is their duty to rebuild—But more of this hereafter. And now, my son, I command thee on thy faith to tell me truly and particularly what has chanced to thee since we parted, and what is the present state of thy conscience. Thy relation, our sister Magdalen, is a woman of excellent gifts, blessed with a zeal which neither doubt nor danger can quench; but yet it is not a zeal altogether according to knowledge; wherefore, my son, I would willingly be myself thy interrogator, and thy counsellor, in these days of darkness and stratagem."

With the respect which he owed to his first instructor, Roland Græme went rapidly through the events which the reader is acquainted with; and while he disguised not from the prelate the impression which had been made on his mind by the arguments of the preacher Henderson, he accidentally and almost involuntarily gave his Father Confessor to understand the influence which Catherine Seyton had acquired over his mind.

"It is with joy I discover, my dearest son," replied the Abbot, "that I have arrived in time to arrest thee on the verge of the precipice to which thou wert approaching. These doubts of which you complain, are the weeds which naturally grow up in a strong soil, and require the careful hand of the husbandman to eradicate them. Thou must study a little volume, which I will impart to thee in fitting time, in which, by Our Lady's grace, I have placed in somewhat a clearer light than heretofore, the points debated betwixt us and these heretics, who sow among the wheat the same tares which were formerly privily mingled with the good seed by the Albigenses and the Lollards. But it is not by reason alone that you must hope to conquer these insinuations of the enemy: It is sometimes by timely resistance, but oftener by timely flight. You must shut your ears against the arguments of the heresiarch, when circumstances permit you not to withdraw the foot from his company. Anchor your thoughts upon the service of Our Lady, while he is expending in vain his heretical sophistry. Are you unable to maintain your attention on heavenly objects—think rather on thine own earthly pleasures, than tempt Providence and the Saints by giving an attentive ear to the erring doctrine—think of thy hawk, thy hound, thine angling rod, thy sword and buckler—think even of Catherine Seyton, rather than give thy soul to the lessons of the tempter. Alas! my son, believe not that, worn out with woes, and bent more by affliction than by years, I have forgotten the effect of beauty over the heart of youth. Even in the watches of the night, broken by thoughts of an imprisoned Queen, a distracted kingdom, a church laid waste and ruinous, come other thoughts than these suggest, and feelings which belonged to an earlier and happier course of life. Be it so—we must bear our load as we may: and not in vain are these passions implanted in our breast, since, as now in thy case, they may come in aid of resolutions founded upon higher grounds. Yet beware, my son—this Catherine Seyton is the daughter of one of Scotland's proudest, as well as most worthy barons; and thy state may not suffer thee, as yet, to aspire so high. But thus it is—Heaven works its purposes through human folly; and Douglas's ambitious affection, as well as thine, shall contribute alike to the desired end."

"How, my father," said the page, "my suspicions are then true!—Douglas loves——"

"He does; and with a love as much misplaced as thine own; but beware of him—cross him not—thwart him not."

"Let him not cross or thwart me," said the page; "for I will not yield him an inch of way, had he in his body the soul of every Douglas that has lived since the time of the Dark Gray Man."*

"Nay, have patience, idle boy, and reflect that your suit can never interfere with his.—But a truce with these vanities, and let us better employ the little space which still remains to us to spend together. To thy knees, my son, and resume the long-interrupted duty of confession, that, happen what may, the hour may find in thee a faithful Catholic, relieved from the guilt of his sins by authority of the Holy Church. Could I but tell thee, Roland, the joy with which I see thee once more put thy knee to its best and fittest use! *Quid dicis, mi fili?*"

"*Culpas meas,*" answered the youth; and according to the ritual of the Catholic Church, he confessed and received absolution, to which was annexed the condition of performing certain enjoined penances.

When this religious ceremony was ended, an old man, in the dress of a peasant of the better order, approached the arbour, and greeted the Abbot. —"I have waited the conclusion of your devotions," he said, "to tell you the youth is sought after by the chamberlain, and it were well he should appear without delay. Holy Saint Francis, if the halberdiers were to seek him here, they might sorely wrong my garden-plot—they are in office, and

* By an ancient, though improbable tradition, the Douglasses are said to have derived their name from a champion who had greatly distinguished himself in an action. When the king demanded by whom the battle had been won, the attendants are said to have answered, "Sholto Douglas, sir;" which is said to mean, "Yonder dark gray man." But the name is undoubtedly territorial, and taken from Douglas river and vale.

reck not where they tread, were each step on jessamine and clovegilly flowers."

"We will speed him forth, my brother," said the Abbot; "but alas! is it possible that such trifles should live in your mind at a crisis so awful as that which is now impending?"

"Reverend father," answered the proprietor of the garden, for such he was, "how oft shall I pray you to keep your high counsel for high minds like your own? What have you required of me, that I have not granted unresistingly, though with an aching heart?"

"I would require of you to be yourself, my brother," said the Abbot Ambrosius; "to remember what you were, and to what your early vows have bound you."

"I tell thee, Father Ambrosius," replied the gardener, "the patience of the best saint that ever said pater-noster, would be exhausted by the trials to which you have put mine—What I have been, it skills not to speak at present—no one knows better than yourself, father, what I renounced, in hopes to find ease and quiet during the remainder of my days—and no one better knows how my retreat has been invaded, my fruit-trees broken, my flower-beds trodden down, my quiet frightened away, and my very sleep driven from my bed, since ever this poor Queen, God bless her, hath been sent to Lochleven.—I blame her not; being a prisoner, it is natural she should wish to get out from so vile a hold, where there is scarcely any place even for a tolerable garden, and where the water-mists, as I am told, blight all the early blossoms—I say, I cannot blame her for endeavouring for her freedom; but why I should be drawn into the scheme—why my harmless arbours, that I planted with my own hands, should become places of privy conspiracy—why my little quay, which I built for my own fishing boat, should have become a haven for secret embarkations—in short, why I should be dragged into matters where both heading and hanging are like to be the issue, I profess to you, reverend father, I am totally ignorant."

"My brother," answered the Abbot, "you are wise, and ought to know——"

"I am not—I am not—I am not wise," replied the horticulturist, pettishly, and stopping his ears with his fingers—"I was never called wise but when men wanted to engage me in some action of notorious folly."

"But, my good brother," said the Abbot——

"I am not good neither," said the peevish gardener; "I am neither good nor wise—Had I been wise, you would not have been admitted here; and were I good, methinks I should send you elsewhere to hatch plots for destroying the quiet of the country. What signifies disputing about queen or king, when men may sit at peace—*sub umbra vitis sui?* and so would I do, after the precept of Holy Writ, were I, as you term me, wise or good. But such as I am, my neck is in the yoke, and you make me draw what weight you list.—Follow me, youngster. This reverend father, who makes in his jackman's dress nearly as reverend a figure as I myself, will agree with me in one thing at least, and that is, that you have been long enough here."

"Follow the good father, Roland," said the Abbot, "and remember my words—a day is approaching that will try the temper of all true Scotsmen—may thy heart prove faithful as the steel of thy blade!"

The page bowed in silence, and they parted; the gardener, notwithstanding his advanced age, walking on before him very briskly, and muttering as he went, partly to himself, partly to his companion, after the manner of old men of weakened intellects—"When I was great," thus ran his maundering, "and had my mule and my ambling palfrey at command, I warrant you I could have as well flown through the air as have walked at this pace. I had my gout and my rheumatics, and an hundred things besides, that hung fetters on my heels; and now, thanks to Our Lady, and honest labour,

I can walk with any good man of my age in the kingdom of Fife—Fy upon it, that experience should be so long in coming!"

As he was thus muttering, his eye fell upon the branch of a pear-tree which drooped down for want of support, and at once forgetting his haste, the old man stopped and set seriously about binding it up. Roland Græme had both readiness, neatness of hand, and good nature in abundance; he immediately lent his aid, and in a minute or two the bough was supported, and tied up in a way perfectly satisfactory to the old man, who looked at it with great complaisance. "They are bergamots," he said, "and if you will come ashore in autumn, you shall taste of them — the like are not in Lochleven Castle — the garden there is a poor pin-fold, and the gardener, Hugh Houkham, hath little skill of his craft — so come ashore, Master Page, in autumn, when you would eat pears. But what am I thinking of — ere that time come, they may have given thee sour pears for plums. Take an old man's advice, youth, one who hath seen many days, and sat in higher places than thou canst hope for — bend thy sword into a pruning-hook, and make a dibble of thy dagger—thy days shall be the longer, and thy health the better for it, — and come to aid me in my garden, and I will teach thee the real French fashion of *imping*, which the Southron call graffing. Do this, and do it without loss of time, for there is a whirlwind coming over the land, and only those shall escape who lie too much beneath the storm to have their boughs broken by it."

So saying, he dismissed Roland Græme, through a different door from that by which he had entered, signed a cross, and pronounced a benedicite as they parted, and then, still muttering to himself, retired into the garden, and locked the door on the inside.

Chapter the Twenty-Ninth.

Pray God she prove not masculine ere long!
KING HENRY VI.

DISMISSED from the old man's garden, Roland Græme found that a grassy paddock, in which sauntered two cows, the property of the gardener, still separated him from the village. He paced through it, lost in meditation upon the words of the Abbot. Father Ambrosius had, with success enough, exerted over him that powerful influence which the guardians and instructors of our childhood possess over our more mature youth. And yet, when Roland looked back upon what the father had said, he could not but suspect that he had rather sought to evade entering into the controversy betwixt the churches, than to repel the objections and satisfy the doubts which the lectures of Henderson had excited. "For this he had no time," said the page to himself, "neither have I now calmness and learning sufficient to judge upon points of such magnitude. Besides, it were base to quit my faith while the wind of fortune sets against it, unless I were so placed, that my conversion, should it take place, were free as light from the imputation of self-interest. I was bred a Catholic — bred in the faith of Bruce and Wallace — I will hold that faith till time and reason shall convince me that it errs. I will serve this poor Queen as a subject should serve an imprisoned and wronged sovereign — they who placed me in her service have to blame themselves—who sent me hither, a gentleman trained in the paths of loyalty and honour, when they should have sought out some truckling, cogging, double-dealing knave, who would have been at once the observant page of the Queen, and the obsequious spy of her enemies. Since I must choose betwixt aiding and betraying her, I will decide as becomes her servant and her subject; but Catherine Seyton—Catherine Seyton, beloved by Douglas, and holding me on or off as the intervals of her leisure or caprice will permit—how shall I deal with the coquette?—By heaven, when I next have an opportunity, she shall render me some reason for her conduct, or I will break with her for ever!"

As he formed this doughty resolution, he crossed the stile which led out of the little enclosure, and was almost immediately greeted by Dr. Luke Lundin.

"Ha! my most excellent young friend," said the Doctor, "from whence come you? — but I note the place. — Yes, neighbour Blinkhoolie's garden is a pleasant rendezvous, and you are of the age when lads look after a bonny lass with one eye, and a dainty plum with another. But hey! you look subtriste and melancholic — I fear the maiden has proved cruel, or the plums unripe; and surely I think neighbour Blinkhoolie's damsons can scarcely have been well preserved throughout the winter — he spares the saccharine juice on his confects. But courage, man, there are more Kates in Kinross; and for the immature fruit, a glass of my double distilled *aqua mirabilis—probatum est.*"

The page darted an ireful glance at the facetious physician; but presently recollecting that the name Kate, which had provoked his displeasure, was probably but introduced for the sake of alliteration, he suppressed his wrath, and only asked if the wains had been heard of?

"Why, I have been seeking for you this hour, to tell you that the stuff is in your boat, and that the boat waits your pleasure. Auchtermuchty had only fallen into company with an idle knave like himself, and a stoup of aquavitæ between them. Your boatmen lie on their oars, and there have already been made two wefts from the warder's turret to intimate that those in the castle are impatient for your return. Yet there is time for you to take a slight repast; and, as your friend and physician, I hold it unfit you should face the water-breeze with an empty stomach."

Roland Græme had nothing for it but to return, with such cheer as he might, to the place where his boat was moored on the beach, and resisted all offer of refreshment, although the Doctor promised that he should prelude the collation with a gentle appetizer — a decoction of herbs, gathered and distilled by himself. Indeed, as Roland had not forgotten the contents of his morning cup, it is possible that the recollection induced him to stand firm in his refusal of all food, to which such an unpalatable preface was the preliminary. As they passed towards the boat, (for the ceremonious politeness of the worthy Chamberlain would not permit the page to go thither without attendance,) Roland Græme, amidst a group who seemed to be assembled around a party of wandering musicians, distinguished, as he thought, the dress of Catherine Seyton. He shook himself clear from his attendant, and at one spring was in the midst of the crowd, and at the side of the damsel. "Catherine," he whispered, "is it well for you to be still here? — will you not return to the castle?"

"To the devil with your Catherines and your castles!" answered the maiden, snappishly; "have you not had time enough already to get rid of your follies? Begone! I desire not your farther company, and there will be danger in thrusting it upon me."

"Nay — but if there be danger, fairest Catherine," replied Roland; "why will you not allow me to stay and share it with you?"

"Intruding fool," said the maiden, "the danger is all on thine own side —the risk in, in plain terms, that I strike thee on the mouth with the hilt of my dagger." So saying, she turned haughtily from him, and moved through the crowd, who gave way in some astonishment at the masculine activity with which she forced her way among them.

As Roland, though much irritated, prepared to follow, he was grappled on the other side by Doctor Luke Lundin, who reminded him of the loaded boat, of the two wefts, or signals with the flag, which had been made from the tower, of the danger of the cold breeze to an empty stomach, and of the vanity of spending more time upon coy wenches and sour plums. Roland was thus, in a manner, dragged back to his boat, and obliged to lanch her forth upon his return to Lochleven Castle.

That little voyage was speedily accomplished, and the page was greeted at the landing-place by the severe and caustic welcome of old Dryfesdale. "So, young gallant, you are come at last, after a delay of six hours, and after two signals from the castle? But, I warrant, some idle junketing hath occupied you too deeply to think of your service or your duty. Where is the note of the plate and household stuff?—Pray Heaven it hath not been diminished under the sleeveless care of so young a gad-about!"

"Diminished under my care, Sir Steward!" retorted the page angrily; "say so in earnest, and by Heaven your gray hair shall hardly protect your saucy tongue!"

"A truce with your swaggering, young esquire," returned the steward; "we have bolts and dungeons for brawlers. Go to my lady, and swagger before her, if thou darest — she will give thee proper cause of offence, for she has waited for thee long and impatiently."

"And where then is the Lady of Lochleven?" said the page; "for I conceive it is of her thou speakest."

"Ay — of whom else?" replied Dryfesdale; "or who besides the Lady of Lochleven hath a right to command in this castle?"

"The Lady of Lochleven is thy mistress," said Roland Græme; "but mine is the Queen of Scotland."

The steward looked at him fixedly for a moment, with an air in which suspicion and dislike were ill concealed by an affectation of contempt. "The bragging cock-chicken," he said, "will betray himself by his rash crowing. I have marked thy altered manner in the chapel of late — ay, and your changing of glances at meal-time with a certain idle damsel, who, like thyself, laughs at all gravity and goodness. There is something about you, my master, which should be looked to. But, if you would know whether the Lady of Lochleven, or that other lady, hath a right to command thy service, thou wilt find them together in the Lady Mary's anteroom."

Roland hastened thither, not unwilling to escape from the ill-natured penetration of the old man, and marvelling at the same time what peculiarity could have occasioned the Lady of Lochleven's being in the Queen's apartment at this time of the afternoon, so much contrary to her usual wont. His acuteness instantly penetrated the meaning. "She wishes," he concluded, "to see the meeting betwixt the Queen and me on my return, that she may form a guess whether there is any private intelligence or understanding betwixt us — I must be guarded."

With this resolution he entered the parlour, where the Queen, seated in her chair, with the Lady Fleming leaning upon the back of it, had already kept the Lady of Lochleven standing in her presence for the space of nearly an hour, to the manifest increase of her very visible bad humour. Roland Græme, on entering the apartment, made a deep obeisance to the Queen, and another to the Lady, and then stood still as if to await their farther question. Speaking almost together, the Lady Lochleven said, "So, young man, you are returned at length?"

And then stopped indignantly short, while the Queen went on without regarding her — "Roland, you are welcome home to us — you have proved the true dove and not the raven — Yet I am sure I could have forgiven you, if, once dismissed from this water-circled ark of ours, you had never again returned to us. I trust you have brought back an olive-branch, for our kind and worthy hostess has chafed herself much on account of your long absence, and we never needed more some symbol of peace and reconciliation."

"I grieve I should have been detained, madam," answered the page; "but from the delay of the person intrusted with the matters for which I was sent, I did not receive them till late in the day."

"See you there now," said the Queen to the Lady Lochleven; "we could not persuade you, our dearest hostess, that your household goods were in all safe keeping and surety. True it is, that we can excuse your anxiety, considering that these august apartments are so scantily furnished, that we have not been able to offer you even the relief of a stool during the long time you have afforded us the pleasure of your society."

"The will, madam," said the lady, "the will to offer such accommodation was more wanting than the means."

"What!" said the Queen, looking round, and affecting surprise, "there are then stools in this apartment — one, two — no less than four, including the broken one—a royal garniture!—We observed them not—will it please your ladyship to sit?"

"No, madam, I will soon relieve you of my presence," replied the Lady Lochleven; "and while with you, my aged limbs can still better brook fatigue, than my mind stoop to accept of constrained courtesy."

"Nay, Lady of Lochleven, if you take it so deeply," said the Queen, rising and motioning to her own vacant chair, "I would rather you assumed my seat—you are not the first of your family who has done so."

The Lady of Lochleven curtsied a negative, but seemed with much difficulty to suppress the angry answer which rose to her lips.

During this sharp conversation, the page's attention had been almost entirely occupied by the entrance of Catherine Seyton, who came from the inner apartment, in the usual dress in which she attended upon the Queen, and with nothing in her manner which marked either the hurry or confusion incident to a hasty change of disguise, or the conscious fear of detection in a perilous enterprise. Roland Græme ventured to make her an obeisance as she entered, but she returned it with an air of the utmost indifference, which, in his opinion, was extremely inconsistent with the circumstances in which they stood towards each other. — "Surely," he thought, "she cannot in reason expect to bully me out of the belief due to mine own eyes, as she tried to do concerning the apparition in the hostelry of Saint Michael's — I will try if I cannot make her feel that this will be but a vain task, and that confidence in me is the wiser and safer course to pursue."

These thoughts had passed rapidly through his mind, when the Queen, having finished her altercation with the Lady of the castle, again addressed him — "What of the revels at Kinross, Roland Græme? Methought they were gay, if I may judge from some faint sounds of mirth and distant music, which found their way so far as these grated windows, and died when they entered them, as all that is mirthful must — But thou lookest as sad as if thou hadst come from a conventicle of the Huguenots!"

"And so perchance he hath, madam," replied the Lady of Lochleven, at whom this side-shaft was lanched. "I trust, amid yonder idle fooleries, there wanted not some pouring forth of doctrine to a better purpose than that vain mirth, which, blazing and vanishing like the crackling of dry thorns, leaves to the fools who love it nothing but dust and ashes."

"Mary Fleming," said the Queen, turning round and drawing her mantle about her, "I would that we had the chimney-grate supplied with a fagot or two of these same thorns which the Lady of Lochleven describes so well. Methinks the damp air from the lake, which stagnates in these vaulted rooms, renders them deadly cold."

"Your Grace's pleasure shall be obeyed," said the Lady of Lochleven; "yet may I presume to remind you that we are now in summer?"

"I thank you for the information, my good lady," said the Queen; "for prisoners better learn their calender from the mouth of their jailor, than from any change they themselves feel in the seasons.—Once more, Roland Græme, what of the revels?"

"They were gay, madam," said the page, "but of the usual sort, and little worth your Highness's ear."

"Oh, you know not," said the Queen, "how very indulgent my ear has become to all that speaks of freedom and the pleasures of the free. Methinks I would rather have seen the gay villagers dance their ring round the Maypole, than have witnessed the most stately masques within the precincts of a palace. The absence of stone-wall—the sense that the green turf is under the foot which may tread it free and unrestrained, is worth all that art or splendour can add to more courtly revels."

"I trust," said the Lady Lochleven, addressing the page in her turn, "there were amongst these follies none of the riots or disturbances to which they so naturally lead?"

Roland gave a slight glance to Catherine Seyton, as if to bespeak her attention, as he replied,—"I witnessed no offence, madam, worthy of marking—none indeed of any kind, save that a bold damsel made her hand somewhat too familiar with the cheek of a player-man, and ran some hazard of being ducked in the lake."

As he uttered these words he cast a hasty glance at Catherine; but she sustained, with the utmost serenity of manner and countenance, the hint which he had deemed could not have been thrown out before her without exciting some fear and confusion.

"I will cumber your Grace no longer with my presence," said the Lady Lochleven, "unless you have aught to command me."

"Nought, our good hostess," answered the Queen, "unless it be to pray you, that on another occasion you deem it not needful to postpone your better employment to wait so long upon us."

"May it please you," added the Lady Lochleven, "to command this your gentleman to attend us, that I may receive some account of these matters which have been sent hither for your Grace's use?"

"We may not refuse what you are pleased to require, madam," answered the Queen. "Go with the lady, Roland, if our commands be indeed necessary to thy doing so. We will hear to-morrow the history of thy Kinross pleasures. For this night we dismiss thy attendance."

Roland Græme went with the Lady of Lochleven, who failed not to ask him many questions concerning what had passed at the sports, to which he rendered such answers as were most likely to lull asleep any suspicions which she might entertain of his disposition to favour Queen Mary, taking especial care to avoid all allusion to the apparition of Magdalen Græme, and of the Abbot Ambrosius. At length, after undergoing a long and somewhat close examination, he was dismissed with such expressions, as, coming from the reserved and stern Lady of Lochleven, might seem to express a degree of favour and countenance.

His first care was to obtain some refreshment, which was more cheerfully afforded him by a good-natured pantler than by Dryfesdale, who was, on this occasion, much disposed to abide by the fashion of Pudding-burn House, where

> They who came not the first call,
> Gat no more meat till the next meal.

When Roland Græme had finished his repast, having his dismissal from the Queen for the evening, and being little inclined for such society as the castle afforded, he stole into the garden, in which he had permission to spend his leisure time, when it pleased him. In this place, the ingenuity of the contriver and disposer of the walks had exerted itself to make the most of little space, and by screens, both of stone ornamented with rude sculpture, and hedges of living green, had endeavoured to give as much intricacy and variety as the confined limits of the garden would admit.

Here the young man walked sadly, considering the events of the day, and comparing what had dropped from the Abbot with what he had himself noticed of the demeanour of George Douglas. "It must be so," was the painful but inevitable conclusion at which he arrived. "It must be by his aid that she is thus enabled, like a phantom, to transport herself from place to place, and to appear at pleasure on the mainland or on the islet.—It must be so," he repeated once more; "with him she holds a close, secret, and intimate correspondence, altogether inconsistent with the eye of favour which she has sometimes cast upon me, and destructive to the hopes which she must have known these glances have necessarily inspired." And yet (for love will hope where reason despairs) the thought rushed on his mind, that it was possible she only encouraged Douglas's passion so far as might serve her mistress's interest, and that she was of too frank, noble, and candid a nature, to hold out to himself hopes which she meant not to fulfil. Lost in these various conjectures, he seated himself upon a bank of turf which commanded a view of the lake on the one side, and on the other of that front of the castle along which the Queen's apartments were situated.

The sun had now for some time set, and the twilight of May was rapidly fading into a serene night. On the lake, the expanded water rose and fell, with the slightest and softest influence of a southern breeze, which scarcely dimpled the surface over which it passed. In the distance was still seen the dim outline of the island of Saint Serf, once visited by many a sandalled pilgrim, as the blessed spot trodden by a man of God — now neglected or violated, as the refuge of lazy priests, who had with justice been compelled to give place to the sheep and the heifers of a Protestant baron.

As Roland gazed on the dark speck, amid the lighter blue of the waters which surrounded it, the mazes of polemical discussion again stretched themselves before the eye of the mind. Had these men justly suffered their exile as licentious drones, the robbers, at once, and disgrace, of the busy hive? or had the hand of avarice and rapine expelled from the temple, not the ribalds who polluted, but the faithful priests who served the shrine in honour and fidelity? The arguments of Henderson, in this contemplative hour, rose with double force before him, and could scarcely be parried by the appeal which the Abbot Ambrosius had made from his understanding to his feelings, — an appeal which he had felt more forcibly amid the bustle of stirring life, than now when his reflections were more undisturbed. It required an effort to divert his mind from this embarrassing topic; and he found that he best succeeded by turning his eyes to the front of the tower, watching where a twinkling light still streamed from the casement of Catherine Seyton's apartment, obscured by times for a moment as the shadow of the fair inhabitant passed betwixt the taper and the window. At length the light was removed or extinguished, and that object of speculation was also withdrawn from the eyes of the meditative lover. Dare I confess the fact, without injuring his character for ever as a hero of romance? These eyes gradually became heavy; speculative doubts on the subject of religious controversy, and anxious conjectures concerning the state of his mistress's affections, became confusedly blended together in his musings; the fatigues of a busy day prevailed over the harassing subjects of contemplation which occupied his mind, and he fell fast asleep.

Sound were his slumbers, until they were suddenly dispelled by the iron tongue of the castle-bell, which sent its deep and sullen sounds wide over the bosom of the lake, and awakened the echoes of Bennarty, the hill which descends steeply on its southern bank. Roland started up, for this bell was always tolled at ten o'clock, as the signal for locking the castle gates, and placing the keys under the charge of the seneschal. He therefore hastened to the wicket by which the garden communicated with the building, and had the mortification, just as he reached it, to hear the bolt leave its sheath with a discordant crash, and enter the stone groove of the door-lintel.

"Hold, hold," cried the page, "and let me in ere you lock the wicket."

The voice of Dryfesdale replied from within, in his usual tone of embittered sullenness, "The hour is passed, fair master—you like not the inside of these walls — even make it a complete holiday, and spend the night as well as the day out of bounds."

"Open the door," exclaimed the indignant page, "or by Saint Giles I will make thy gold chain smoke for it!"

"Make no alarm here," retorted the impenetrable Dryfesdale, "but keep thy sinful oaths and silly threats for those that regard them — I do mine office, and carry the keys to the seneschal. — Adieu, my young master! the cool night air will advantage your hot blood."

The steward was right in what he said; for the cooling breeze was very necessary to appease the feverish fit of anger which Roland experienced, nor did the remedy succeed for some time. At length, after some hasty turns made through the garden, exhausting his passion in vain vows of vengeance, Roland Græme began to be sensible that his situation ought rather to be held as matter of laughter than of serious resentment. To one bred a sportsman, a night spent in the open air had in it little of hardship, and the poor malice of the steward seemed more worthy of his contempt than his anger. "I would to God," he said, "that the grim old man may always have contented himself with such sportive revenge. He often looks as he were capable of doing us a darker turn." Returning, therefore, to the turf-seat which he had formerly occupied, and which was partially sheltered by a trim fence of green holly, he drew his mantle around him, stretched himself at length on the verdant settle, and endeavoured to resume that sleep which the castle bell had interrupted to so little purpose.

Sleep, like other earthly blessings, is niggard of its favours when most courted. The more Roland invoked her aid, the farther she fled from his eyelids. He had been completely awakened, first, by the sounds of the bell, and then by his own aroused vivacity of temper, and he found it difficult again to compose himself to slumber. At length, when his mind was wearied out with a maze of unpleasing meditation, he succeeded in coaxing himself into a broken slumber. This was again dispelled by the voices of two persons who were walking in the garden, the sound of whose conversation, after mingling for some time in the page's dreams, at length succeeded in awaking him thoroughly. He raised himself from his reclining posture in the utmost astonishment, which the circumstance of hearing two persons at that late hour conversing on the outside of the watchfully guarded Castle of Lochleven, was so well calculated to excite. His first thought was of supernatural beings; his next, upon some attempt on the part of Queen Mary's friends and followers; his last was, that George of Douglas, possessed of the keys, and having the means of ingress and egress at pleasure, was availing himself of his office to hold a rendezvous with Catherine Seyton in the castle garden. He was confirmed in this opinion by the tone of the voice, which asked in a low whisper, "whether all was ready?"

Chapter the Thirtieth.

In some breasts passion lies conceal'd and silent,
Like war's swart powder in a castle vault,
Until occasion, like the linstock, lights it:
Then comes at once the lightning and the thunder,
And distant echoes tell that all is rent asunder.
OLD PLAY.

ROLAND GRÆME, availing himself of a breach in the holly screen, and of the assistance of the full moon, which was now arisen, had a perfect opportunity, himself unobserved, to reconnoitre the persons and the motions of those by whom his rest had been thus unexpectedly disturbed; and his observations confirmed his jealous apprehensions. They stood together in close and earnest conversation within four yards of the place of his retreat, and he could easily recognize the tall form and deep voice of Douglas, and the no less remarkable dress and tone of the page at the hostelry of Saint Michael's.

"I have been at the door of the page's apartment," said Douglas, "but he is not there, or he will not answer. It is fast bolted on the inside, as is the custom, and we cannot pass through it—and what his silence may bode I know not."

"You have trusted him too far," said the other; "a feather-headed coxcomb, upon whose changeable mind and hot brain there is no making an abiding impression."

"It was not I who was willing to trust him," said Douglas, "but I was assured he would prove friendly when called upon — for ——" Here he spoke so low that Roland lost the tenor of his words, which was the more provoking, as he was fully aware that he was himself the subject of their conversation.

"Nay," replied the stranger, more aloud, "I have on my side put him off with fair words, which make fools vain—but now, if you distrust him at the push, deal with him with your dagger, and so make open passage."

"That were too rash," said Douglas; "and besides, as I told you, the door of his apartment is shut and bolted. I will essay again to waken him."

Græme instantly comprehended, that the ladies, having been somehow made aware of his being in the garden, had secured the door of the outer room in which he usually slept, as a sort of sentinel upon that only access to the Queen's apartments. But then, how came Catherine Seyton to be abroad, if the Queen and the other lady were still within their chambers, and the access to them locked and bolted?—"I will be instantly at the bottom of these mysteries," he said, "and then thank Mistress Catherine, if this be really she, for the kind use which she exhorted Douglas to make of his dagger—they seek me, as I comprehend, and they shall not seek me in vain."

Douglas had by this time re-entered the castle by the wicket, which was now open. The stranger stood alone in the garden walk, his arms folded on his breast, and his eyes cast impatiently up to the moon, as if accusing her of betraying him by the magnificence of her lustre. In a moment Roland Græme stood before him—"A goodly night," he said, "Mistress Catherine, for a young lady to stray forth in disguise, and to meet with men in an orchard!"

"Hush!" said the stranger page, "hush, thou foolish patch, and tell us in a word if thou art friend or foe."

"How should I be friend to one who deceives me by fair words, and who would have Douglas deal with me with his poniard?" replied Roland.

"The fiend receive George of Douglas and thee too, thou born madcap and sworn marplot!" said the other; "we shall be discovered, and then death is the word."

"Catherine," said the page, "you have dealt falsely and cruelly with me, and the moment of explanation is now come—neither it nor you shall escape me."

"Madman!" said the stranger, "I am neither Kate nor Catherine—the moon shines bright enough surely to know the hart from the hind."

"That shift shall not serve you, fair mistress," said the page, laying hold on the lap of the stranger's cloak; "this time, at least, I will know with whom I deal."

"Unhand me," said she, endeavouring to extricate herself from his grasp; and in a tone where anger seemed to contend with a desire to laugh, "use you so little discretion towards a daughter of Seyton?"

But as Roland, encouraged perhaps by her risibility to suppose his violence was not unpardonably offensive, kept hold on her mantle, she said, in a sterner tone of unmixed resentment,—"Madman! let me go!—there is life and death in this moment—I would not willingly hurt thee, and yet beware!"

As she spoke she made a sudden effort to escape, and, in doing so, a pistol, which she carried in her hand or about her person, went off.

This warlike sound instantly awakened the well-warded castle. The warder blew his horn, and began to toll the castle bell, crying out at the same time, "Fie, treason! treason! cry all! cry all!"

The apparition of Catherine Seyton, which the page had let loose in the first moment of astonishment, vanished in darkness; but the plash of oars was heard, and, in a second or two, five or six harquebuses and a falconet were fired from the battlements of the castle successively, as if levelled at some object on the water. Confounded with these incidents, no way for Catherine's protection (supposing her to be in the boat which he had heard put from the shore) occurred to Roland, save to have recourse to George of Douglas. He hastened for this purpose towards the apartment of the Queen, whence he heard loud voices and much trampling of feet. When he entered, he found himself added to a confused and astonished group, which, assembled in that apartment, stood gazing upon each other. At the upper end of the room stood the Queen, equipped as for a journey, and attended not only by the Lady Fleming, but by the omnipresent Catherine Seyton, dressed in the habit of her own sex, and bearing in her hand the casket in which Mary kept such jewels as she had been permitted to retain. At the other end of the hall was the Lady of Lochleven, hastily dressed, as one startled from slumber by the sudden alarm, and surrounded by domestics, some bearing torches, others holding naked swords, partisans, pistols, or such other weapons as they had caught up in the hurry of a night alarm. Betwixt these two parties stood George of Douglas, his arms folded on his breast, his eyes bent on the ground, like a criminal who knows not how to deny, yet continues unwilling to avow, the guilt in which he has been detected.

"Speak, George of Douglas," said the Lady of Lochleven; "speak, and clear the horrid suspicion which rests on thy name. Say, 'A Douglas was never faithless to his trust, and I am a Douglas.' Say this, my dearest son, and it is all I ask thee to say to clear thy name, even under such a foul charge. Say it was but the wile of these unhappy women, and this false boy, which plotted an escape so fatal to Scotland—so destructive to thy father's house."

"Madam," said old Dryfesdale the steward, "this much do I say for this silly page, that he could not be accessary to unlocking the doors, since I myself this night bolted him out of the castle. Whoever limned this night-piece, the lad's share in it seems to have been small"

"Thou liest, Dryfesdale," said the Lady, "and wouldst throw the blame on thy master's house, to save the worthless life of a gipsy boy."

"His death were more desirable to me than his life," answered the steward, sullenly; "but the truth is the truth."

At these words Douglas raised his head, drew up his figure to its full height, and spoke boldly and sedately, as one whose resolution was taken. "Let no life be endangered for me. I alone——"

"Douglas," said the Queen, interrupting him, "art thou mad? Speak not, I charge you."

"Madam," he replied, bowing with the deepest respect, "gladly would I obey your commands, but they must have a victim, and let it be the true one.—Yes, madam," he continued, addressing the Lady of Lochleven, "I alone am guilty in this matter. If the word of a Douglas has yet any weight with you, believe me that this boy is innocent; and on your conscience I charge you, do him no wrong; nor let the Queen suffer hardship for embracing the opportunity of freedom which sincere loyalty—which a sentiment yet deeper—offered to her acceptance. Yes! I had planned the escape of the most beautiful, the most persecuted of women; and far from regretting that I, for a while, deceived the malice of her enemies, I glory in it, and am most willing to yield up life itself in her cause."

"Now may God have compassion on my age," said the Lady of Lochleven, "and enable me to bear this load of affliction! O Princess, born in a luckless hour, when will you cease to be the instrument of seduction and of ruin to all who approach you? O ancient house of Lochleven, famed so long for birth and honour, evil was the hour which brought the deceiver under thy roof!"

"Say not so, madam," replied her grandson; "the old honours of the Douglas line will be outshone, when one of its descendants dies for the most injured of queens—for the most lovely of women."

"Douglas," said the Queen, "must I at this moment—ay, even at this moment, when I may lose a faithful subject for ever, chide thee for forgetting what is due to me as thy Queen?"

"Wretched boy," said the distracted Lady of Lochleven, "hast thou fallen even thus far into the snare of this Moabitish woman?—hast thou bartered thy name, thy allegiance, thy knightly oath, thy duty to thy parents, thy country, and thy God, for a feigned tear, or a sickly smile, from lips which flattered the infirm Francis—lured to death the idiot Darnley—read luscious poetry with the minion Chastelar—mingled in the lays of love which were sung by the beggar Rizzio—and which were joined in rapture to those of the foul and licentious Bothwell?"

"Blaspheme not, madam!" said Douglas;—"nor you, fair Queen, and virtuous as fair, chide at this moment the presumption of thy vassal!—Think not that the mere devotion of a subject could have moved me to the part I have been performing. Well you deserve that each of your lieges should die for you; but I have done more—have done that to which love alone could compel a Douglas—I have dissembled. Farewell, then, Queen of all hearts, and Empress of that of Douglas!—When you are freed from this vile bondage—as freed you shall be, if justice remains in Heaven—and when you load with honours and titles the happy man who shall deliver you, cast one thought on him whose heart would have despised every reward for a kiss of your hand—cast one thought on his fidelity, and drop one tear on his grave." And throwing himself at her feet, he seized her hand, and pressed it to his lips.

"This before my face!" exclaimed the Lady of Lochleven—"wilt thou court thy adulterous paramour before the eyes of a parent?—Tear them asunder, and put him under strict ward! Seize him, upon your lives!" she added, seeing that her attendants looked at each other with hesitation.

"They are doubtful," said Mary. "Save thyself, Douglas, I command thee!"

He started up from the floor, and only exclaiming, "My life or death are yours, and at your disposal!"—drew his sword, and broke through those who stood betwixt him and the door. The enthusiasm of his onset was too sudden and too lively to have been opposed by any thing short of the most decided opposition; and as he was both loved and feared by his father's vassals, none of them would offer him actual injury.

The Lady of Lochleven stood astonished at his sudden escape—"Am I surrounded," she said, "by traitors? Upon him, villains!—pursue, stab, cut him down!"

"He cannot leave the island, madam," said Dryfesdale, interfering; "I have the key of the boat-chain."

But two or three voices of those who pursued from curiosity, or command of their mistress, exclaimed from below, that he had cast himself into the lake.

"Brave Douglas still!" exclaimed the Queen—"Oh, true and noble heart, that prefers death to imprisonment!"

"Fire upon him!" said the Lady of Lochleven; "if there be here a true servant of his father, let him shoot the runagate dead, and let the lake cover our shame!"

The report of a gun or two was heard, but they were probably shot rather to obey the Lady, than with any purpose of hitting the mark; and Randal immediately entering, said that Master George had been taken up by a boat from the castle, which lay at a little distance.

"Man a barge, and pursue them!" said the Lady.

"It were quite vain," said Randal; "by this time they are half way to shore, and a cloud has come over the moon."

"And has the traitor then escaped?" said the Lady, pressing her hands against her forehead with a gesture of despair; "the honour of our house is for ever gone, and all will be deemed accomplices in this base treachery."

"Lady of Lochleven," said Mary, advancing towards her, "you have this night cut off my fairest hopes—You have turned my expected freedom into bondage, and dashed away the cup of joy in the very instant I was advancing it to my lips—and yet I feel for your sorrow the pity that you deny to mine—Gladly would I comfort you if I might; but as I may not, I would at least part from you in charity."

"Away, proud woman!" said the Lady; "who ever knew so well as thou to deal the deepest wounds under the pretence of kindness and courtesy?—Who, since the great traitor, could ever so betray with a kiss?"

"Lady Douglas of Lochleven," said the Queen, "in this moment thou canst not offend me—no, not even by thy coarse and unwomanly language, held to me in the presence of menials and armed retainers. I have this night owed so much to one member of the house of Lochleven, as to cancel whatever its mistress can do or say in the wildness of her passion."

"We are bounden to you, Princess," said Lady Lochleven, putting a strong constraint on herself, and passing from her tone of violence to that of bitter irony; "our poor house hath been but seldom graced with royal smiles, and will hardly, with my choice, exchange their rough honesty for such court-honour as Mary of Scotland has now to bestow."

"They," replied Mary, "who knew so well how to *take*, may think themselves excused from the obligation implied in receiving. And that I have now little to offer, is the fault of the Douglasses and their allies."

"Fear nothing, madam," replied the Lady of Lochleven, in the same bitter tone, "you retain an exchequer which neither your own prodigality can drain, nor your offended country deprive you of. While you have fair words and delusive smiles at command, you need no other bribes to lure youth to folly."

The Queen cast not an ungratified glance on a large mirror, which, hanging on one side of the apartment, and illuminated by the torch-light, reflected her beautiful face and person. "Our hostess grows complaisant," she said, "my Fleming; we had not thought that grief and captivity had left us so well stored with that sort of wealth which ladies prize most dearly."

"Your Grace will drive this severe woman frantic," said Fleming, in a low tone. "On my knees I implore you to remember she is already dreadfully offended, and that we are in her power."

"I will not spare her, Fleming," answered the Queen; "it is against my nature. She returned my honest sympathy with insult and abuse, and I will gall her in return, — if her words are too blunt for answer, let her use her poniard if she dare!"

"The Lady Lochleven," said the Lady Fleming aloud, "would surely do well now to withdraw, and to leave her Grace to repose."

"Ay," replied the Lady, "or to leave her Grace, and her Grace's minions, to think what silly fly they may next wrap their meshes about. My eldest son is a widower—were he not more worthy the flattering hopes with which you have seduced his brother? — True, the yoke of marriage has been already thrice fitted on — but the church of Rome calls it a sacrament, and its votaries may deem it one in which they cannot too often participate."

"And the votaries of the church of Geneva," replied Mary, colouring with indignation, "as they deem marriage *no* sacrament, are said at times to dispense with the holy ceremony."—Then, as if afraid of the consequences of this home allusion to the errors of Lady Lochleven's early life, the Queen added, "Come, my Fleming, we grace her too much by this altercation; we will to our sleeping apartment. If she would disturb us again to-night, she must cause the door to be forced." So saying, she retired to her bed-room, followed by her two women.

Lady Lochleven, stunned as it were by this last sarcasm, and not the less deeply incensed that she had drawn it upon herself, remained like a statue on the spot which she had occupied when she received an affront so flagrant. Dryfesdale and Randal endeavoured to rouse her to recollection by questions.

"What is your honourable Ladyship's pleasure in the premises?"

"Shall we not double the sentinels, and place one upon the boats and another in the garden?" said Randal.

"Would you that despatches were sent to Sir William at Edinburgh, to acquaint him with what has happened?" demanded Dryfesdale; "and ought not the place of Kinross to be alarmed, lest there be force upon the shores of the lake?"

"Do all as thou wilt," said the Lady, collecting herself, and about to depart. "Thou hast the name of a good soldier, Dryfesdale, take all precautions. — Sacred Heaven! that I should be thus openly insulted!"

"Would it be your pleasure," said Dryfesdale, hesitating, "that this person — this Lady — be more severely restrained?"

"No, vassal!" answered the Lady, indignantly, "my revenge stoops not to so low a gratification. But I will have more worthy vengeance, or the tomb of my ancestors shall cover my shame!"

"And you shall have it, madam," replied Dryfesdale — "ere two suns go down, you shall term yourself amply revenged."

The Lady made no answer — perhaps did not hear his words, as she presently left the apartment. By the command of Dryfesdale, the rest of the attendants were dismissed, some to do the duty of guard, others to their repose. The steward himself remained after they had all departed; and Roland Græme, who was alone in the apartment, was surprised to see the old soldier advance towards him with an air of greater cordiality than he had ever before assumed to him, but which sat ill on his scowling features.

"Youth," he said, "I have done thee some wrong — it is thine own fault, for thy behaviour hath seemed as light to me as the feather thou wearest in thy hat; and surely thy fantastic apparel, and idle humour of mirth and folly, have made me construe thee something harshly. But I saw this night from my casement, (as I looked out to see how thou hadst disposed of thyself in the garden,) I saw, I say, the true efforts which thou didst make to detain the companion of the perfidy of him who is no longer worthy to be called by his father's name, but must be cut off from his house like a rotten branch. I was just about to come to thy assistance when the pistol went off; and the warder (a false knave, whom I suspect to be bribed for the nonce) saw himself forced to give the alarm, which, perchance, till then he had wilfully withheld. To atone, therefore, for my injustice towards you, I would willingly render you a courtesy, if you would accept of it from my hands."

"May I first crave to know what it is?" replied the page.

"Simply to carry the news of this discovery to Holyrood, where thou mayest do thyself much grace, as well with the Earl of Morton and the Regent himself, as with Sir William Douglas, seeing thou hast seen the matter from end to end, and borne faithful part therein. The making thine own fortune will be thus lodged in thine own hand, when I trust thou wilt estrange thyself from foolish vanities, and learn to walk in this world as one who thinks upon the next."

"Sir Steward," said Roland Græme, "I thank you for your courtesy, but I may not do your errand. I pass that I am the Queen's sworn servant, and may not be of counsel against her. But, setting this apart, methinks it were a bad road to Sir William of Lochleven's favour, to be the first to tell him of his son's defection — neither would the Regent be over well pleased to hear the infidelity of his vassal, nor Morton to learn the falsehood of his kinsman."

"Um!" said the steward, making that inarticulate sound which expresses surprise mingled with displeasure. "Nay, then, even fly where ye list; for, giddy-pated as ye may be, you know how to bear you in the world."

"I will show you my esteem is less selfish than ye think for," said the page; "for I hold truth and mirth to be better than gravity and cunning— ay, and in the end to be a match for them.—You never loved me less, Sir Steward, than you do at this moment. I know you will give me no real confidence, and I am resolved to accept no false protestations as current coin. Resume your old course — suspect me as much and watch me as closely as you will, I bid you defiance — you have met with your match."

"By Heaven, young man," said the steward, with a look of bitter malignity, "if thou darest to attempt any treachery towards the House of Lochleven, thy head shall blacken in the sun from the warder's turret!"

"He cannot commit treachery who refuses trust," said the page; "and for my head, it stands as securely on my shoulders, as on any turret that ever mason built."

"Farewell, thou prating and speckled pie," said Dryfesdale, "that art so vain of thine idle tongue and variegated coat! Beware trap and lime-twig."

"And fare thee well, thou hoarse old raven," answered the page; "thy solemn flight, sable hue, and deep croak, are no charms against bird-bolt or hail-shot, and that thou mayst find — it is open war betwixt us, each for the cause of our mistress, and God show the right!"

"Amen, and defend his own people!" said the steward. "I will let my mistress know what addition thou hast made to this mess of traitors. Good night, Monsieur Featherpate."

"Good-night, Seignior Sowersby," replied the page; and, when the old man departed, he betook himself to rest.

Chapter the Thirty-First

Poison'd — ill fare! — dead, forsook, cast off! —
KING JOHN.

HOWEVER weary Roland Græme might be of the Castle of Lochleven — however much he might wish that the plan for Mary's escape had been perfected, I question if he ever awoke with more pleasing feelings than on the morning after George Douglas's plan for accomplishing her deliverance had been frustrated. In the first place, he had the clearest conviction that he had misunderstood the innuendo of the Abbot, and that the affections of Douglas were fixed, not on Catherine Seyton, but on the Queen; and in the second place, from the sort of explanation which had taken place betwixt the steward and him, he felt himself at liberty, without any breach of honour towards the family of Lochleven, to contribute his best aid to any scheme which should in future be formed for the Queen's escape; and, independently of the good-will which he himself had to the enterprise, he knew he could find no surer road to the favour of Catherine Seyton. He now sought but an opportunity to inform her that he had dedicated himself to this task, and fortune was propitious in affording him one which was unusually favourable.

At the ordinary hour of breakfast, it was introduced by the steward with his usual forms, who, as soon as it was placed on the board in the inner apartment, said to Roland Græme, with a glance of sarcastic import, "I leave you, my young sir, to do the office of sewer — it has been too long rendered to the Lady Mary by one belonging to the house of Douglas."

"Were it the prime and principal who ever bore the name," said Roland, "the office were an honour to him."

The steward departed without replying to this bravade, otherwise than by a dark look of scorn. Græme, thus left alone, busied himself as one engaged in a labour of love, to imitate, as well as he could, the grace and courtesy with which George of Douglas was wont to render his ceremonial service at meals to the Queen of Scotland. There was more than youthful vanity—there was a generous devotion in the feeling with which he took up the task, as a brave soldier assumes the place of a comrade who has fallen in the front of battle. "I am now," he said, "their only champion: and, come weal, come wo, I will be, to the best of my skill and power, as faithful, as trustworthy, as brave, as any Douglas of them all could have been."

At this moment Catherine Seyton entered alone, contrary to her custom; and not less contrary to her custom, she entered with her kerchief at her eyes. Roland Græme approached her with beating heart and with down cast eyes, and asked her, in a low and hesitating voice, whether the Queen were well?

"Can you suppose it?" said Catherine. "Think you her heart and body are framed of steel and iron, to endure the cruel disappointment of yester even, and the infamous taunts of yonder puritanic hag?—Would to God that I were a man, to aid her more effectually!"

"If those who carry pistols, and batons, and poniards," said the page, "are not men, they are at least Amazons; and that is as formidable."

"You are welcome to the flash of your wit, sir," replied the damsel; "I am neither in spirits to enjoy, nor to reply to it."

"Well, then," said the page, "list to me in all serious truth. And, first, let me say, that the gear last night had been smoother, had you taken me into your counsels."

"And so we meant; but who could have guessed that Master Page should choose to pass all night in the garden, like some moon-stricken knight in a Spanish romance—instead of being in his bed-room, when Douglas came to hold communication with him on our project."

"And why," said the page, "defer to so late a moment so important a confidence?"

"Because your communications with Henderson, and—with pardon—the natural impetuosity and fickleness of your disposition, made us dread to entrust you with a secret of such consequence, till the last moment."

"And why at the last moment?" said the page, offended at this frank avowal; "why at that, or any other moment, since I had the misfortune to incur so much suspicion?"

"Nay — now you are angry again," said Catherine; "and to serve you aright I should break off this talk; but I will be magnanimous, and answer your question. Know, then, our reason for trusting you was twofold. In the first place, we could scarce avoid it, since you slept in the room through which we had to pass. In the second place——"

"Nay," said the page, "you may dispense with a second reason, when the first makes your confidence in me a case of necessity."

"Good now, hold thy peace," said Catherine. "In the second place, as I said before, there is one foolish person among us, who believes that Roland Græme's heart is warm, though his head is giddy—that his blood is pure, though it boils too hastily—and that his faith and honour are true as the load-star, though his tongue sometimes is far less than discreet."

This avowal Catherine repeated in a low tone, with her eye fixed on the floor, as if she shunned the glance of Roland while she suffered it to escape her lips — "And this single friend," exclaimed the youth in rapture; "this only one who would do justice to the poor Roland Græme, and whose own generous heart taught her to distinguish between follies of the brain and faults of the heart—Will you not tell me, dearest Catherine, to whom I owe my most grateful, my most heartfelt thanks?"

"Nay," said Catherine, with her eyes still fixed on the ground, "if your own heart tell you not——"

"Dearest Catherine!" said the page, seizing upon her hand, and kneeling on one knee.

"If your own heart, I say, tell you not," said Catherine, gently disengaging her hand, "it is very ungrateful; for since the maternal kindness of the Lady Fleming——"

The page started on his feet. "By Heaven, Catherine, your tongue wears as many disguises as your person! But you only mock me, cruel girl. You know the Lady Fleming has no more regard for any one, than hath the forlorn princess who is wrought into yonder piece of old figured court tapestry."

"It may be so," said Catherine Seyton, "but you should not speak so loud."

"Pshaw!" answered the page, but at the same time lowering his voice, "she cares for no one but herself and the Queen. And you know, besides, there is no one of you whose opinion I value, if I have not your own. No —not that of Queen Mary herself."

"The more shame for you, if it be so," said Catherine, with great composure.

"Nay, but, fair Catherine," said the page, "why will you thus damp my ardour, when I am devoting myself, body and soul, to the cause of your mistress?"

"It is because in doing so," said Catherine, "you debase a cause so noble, by naming along with it any lower or more selfish motive. Believe me," she said, with kindling eyes, and while the blood mantled on her cheek, "they think vilely and falsely of women — I mean of those who deserve the name — who deem that they love the gratification of their vanity, or the mean purpose of engrossing a lover's admiration and affection, better than they love the virtue and honour of the man they may be brought to prefer. He that serves his religion, his prince, and his country, with ardour and devotion, need not plead his cause with the commonplace rant of romantic passion — the woman whom he honours with his love becomes his debtor, and her corresponding affection is engaged to repay his glorious toil."

"You hold a glorious prize for such toil," said the youth, bending his eyes on her with enthusiasm.

"Only a heart which knows how to value it," said Catherine. "He that should free this injured Princess from these dungeons, and set her at liberty among her loyal and warlike nobles, whose hearts are burning to welcome her — where is the maiden in Scotland whom the love of such a hero would not honour, were she sprung from the blood royal of the land, and he the offspring of the poorest cottager that ever held a plough?"

"I am determined," said Roland, "to take the adventure. Tell me first, however, fair Catherine, and speak it as if you were confessing to the priest — this poor Queen, I know she is unhappy — but, Catherine, do you hold her innocent? She is accused of murder."

"Do I hold the lamb guilty, because it is assailed by the wolf?" answered Catherine; "do I hold yonder sun polluted, because an earth-damp sullies his beams?"

The page sighed and looked down. "Would my conviction were as deep as thine! But one thing is clear, that in this captivity she hath wrong — She rendered herself up, on a capitulation, and the terms have been refused her—I will embrace her quarrel to the death!"

"Will you — will you, indeed?" said Catherine, taking his hand in her turn. "Oh, be but firm in mind, as thou art bold in deed and quick in resolution; keep but thy plighted faith, and after ages shall honour thee as the saviour of Scotland!"

"But when I have toiled successfully to win that Leah, Honour, thou wilt not, my Catherine," said the page, "condemn me to a new term of service for that Rachel, Love?"

"Of that," said Catherine, again extricating her hand from his grasp, "we shall have full time to speak; but Honour is the elder sister, and must be won the first."

"I may not win her," answered the page; "but I will venture fairly for her, and man can do no more. And know, fair Catherine, — for you shall see the very secret thought of my heart,—that not Honour only — not only that other and fairer sister, whom you frown on me for so much as mentioning — but the stern commands of duty also, compel me to aid the Queen's deliverance."

"Indeed!" said Catherine; "you were wont to have doubts on that matter."

"Ay, but her life was not then threatened," replied Roland.

"And is it now more endangered than heretofore?" asked Catherine Seyton, in anxious terror.

"Be not alarmed," said the page; "but you heard the terms on which your royal mistress parted with the Lady of Lochleven?"

"Too well — but too well," said Catherine; "alas! that she cannot rule her princely resentment, and refrain from encounters like these!"

"That hath passed betwixt them," said Roland, "for which woman never forgives woman. I saw the Lady's brow turn pale, and then black, when, before all the menzie, and in her moment of power, the Queen humbled her to the dust by taxing her with her shame. And I heard the oath of deadly resentment and revenge which she muttered in the ear of one, who by his answer will, I judge, be but too ready an executioner of her will."

"You terrify me," said Catherine.

"Do not so take it — call up the masculine part of your spirit — we will counteract and defeat her plans, be they dangerous as they may. Why do you look upon me thus, and weep?"

"Alas!" said Catherine, "because you stand there before me a living and breathing man, in all the adventurous glow and enterprise of youth, yet still possessing the frolic spirits of childhood — there you stand, full alike of generous enterprise and childish recklessness; and if to-day, or to-morrow, or some such brief space, you lie a mangled and lifeless corpse upon the floor of these hateful dungeons, who but Catherine Seyton will be the cause of your brave and gay career being broken short as you start from the goal? Alas! she whom you have chosen to twine your wreath, may too probably have to work your shroud!"

"And be it so, Catherine," said the page, in the full glow of youthful enthusiasm; "and *do* thou work my shroud! and if thou grace it with such tears as fall now at the thought, it will honour my remains more than an earl's mantle would my living body. But shame on this faintness of heart! the time craves a firmer mood—Be a woman, Catherine, or rather be a man —thou canst be a man if thou wilt."

Catherine dried her tears, and endeavoured to smile.

"You must not ask me," she said, "about that which so much disturbs your mind; you shall know all in time—nay, you should know all now, but that——Hush! here comes the Queen."

Mary entered from her apartment, paler than usual, and apparently exhausted by a sleepless night, and by the painful thoughts which had ill supplied the place of repose; yet the languor of her looks was so far from impairing her beauty, that it only substituted the frail delicacy of the lovely woman for the majestic grace of the Queen. Contrary to her wont, her toilette had been very hastily despatched, and her hair, which was usually dressed by Lady Fleming with great care, escaping from beneath the head-tire, which had been hastily adjusted, fell in long and luxuriant tresses of Nature's own curling, over a neck and bosom which were somewhat less carefully veiled than usual.

As she stepped over the threshold of her apartment, Catherine, hastily drying her tears, ran to meet her royal mistress, and having first kneeled at her feet, and kissed her hand, instantly rose, and placing herself on the other side of the Queen, seemed anxious to divide with the Lady Fleming the honour of supporting and assisting her. The page, on his part, advanced and put in order the chair of state, which she usually occupied, and having placed the cushion and footstool for her accommodation, stepped back, and stood ready for service in the place usually occupied by his predecessor, the young Seneschal. Mary's eye rested an instant on him, and could not but remark the change of persons. Hers was not the female heart which could refuse compassion, at least, to a gallant youth who had suffered in her cause, although he had been guided in his enterprise by a too presumptuous passion; and the words "Poor Douglas!" escaped from her lips, perhaps unconsciously, as she leant herself back in her chair, and put the kerchief to her eyes.

"Yes, gracious madam," said Catherine, assuming a cheerful manner, in order to cheer her sovereign, "our gallant Knight is indeed banished — the adventure was not reserved for him; but he has left behind him a youthful Esquire, as much devoted to your Grace's service, and who, by me, makes you tender of his hand and sword."

"If they may in aught avail your Grace," said Roland Græme, bowing profoundly.

"Alas!" said the Queen, "what needs this, Catherine?—why prepare new victims to be involved in, and overwhelmed by, my cruel fortune?—were we not better cease to struggle, and ourselves sink in the tide without farther resistance, than thus drag into destruction with us every generous heart which makes an effort in our favour?—I have had but too much of plot and intrigue around me, since I was stretched an orphan child in my very cradle, while contending nobles strove which should rule in the name of the unconscious innocent. Surely time it were that all this busy and most dangerous coil should end. Let me call my prison a convent, and my seclusion a voluntary sequestration of myself from the world and its ways."

"Speak not thus, madam, before your faithful servants," said Catherine, "to discourage their zeal at once, and to break their hearts. Daughter of Kings, be not in this hour so unkingly—Come, Roland, and let us, the youngest of her followers, show ourselves worthy of her cause—let us kneel before her footstool, and implore her to be her own magnanimous self." And leading Roland Græme to the Queen's seat, they both kneeled down before her. Mary raised herself in her chair, and sat erect, while, extending one hand to be kissed by the page, she arranged with the other the clustering locks which shaded the bold yet lovely brow of the high-spirited Catherine.

"Alas! *ma mignóne*," she said, for so in fondness she often called her young attendant, "that you should thus desperately mix with my unhappy fate the fortune of your young lives!—Are they not a lovely couple, my Fleming? and is it not heart-rending to think that I must be their ruin?"

"Not so," said Roland Græme, "it is we, gracious Sovereign, who will be your deliverers."

"*Ex oribus parvulorum!*" said the Queen, looking upward; "if it is by the mouth of these children that Heaven calls me to resume the stately thoughts which become my birth and my rights, thou wilt grant them thy protection, and to me the power of rewarding their zeal!"—Then turning to Fleming, she instantly added,—"Thou knowest, my friend, whether to make those who have served me happy, was not ever Mary's favourite pastime. When I have been rebuked by the stern preachers of the Calvinistic heresy—when I have seen the fierce countenances of my nobles averted from me, has it not been because I mixed in the harmless pleasures of the young and gay, and rather for the sake of their happiness than my own, have mingled in the masque, the song, or the dance, with the youth of my household? Well, I repent not of it—though Knox termed it sin, and Morton degradation—I was happy, because I saw happiness around me; and woe betide the wretched jealousy that can extract guilt out of the overflowings of an unguarded gaiety!—Fleming, if we are restored to our throne, shall we not have one blithesome day at a blithesome bridal, of which we must now name neither the bride nor the bridegroom? but that bridegroom shall have the barony of Blairgowrie, a fair gift even for a Queen to give, and that bride's chaplet shall be twined with the fairest pearls that ever were found in the depths of Lochlomond; and thou thyself, Mary Fleming, the best dresser of tires that ever busked the tresses of a Queen, and who would scorn to touch those of any woman of lower rank,—thou thyself shalt, for my love, twine them into the bride's tresses.—Look, my Fleming, suppose them such clustered locks as those of our Catherine, they would not put shame upon thy skill."

So saying, she passed her hand fondly over the head of her youthful favourite, while her more aged attendant replied despondently, "Alas! madam, your thoughts stray far from home."

"They do, my Fleming," said the Queen; "but is it well or kind in you to call them back?—God knows, they have kept the perch this night but too closely—Come, I will recall the gay vision, were it but to punish them. Yes, at that blithesome bridal, Mary herself shall forget the weight of sorrows, and the toil of state, and herself once more lead a measure.—At whose wedding was it that we last danced, my Fleming? I think care has troubled my memory — yet something of it I should remember — canst thou not aid me?—I know thou canst."

"Alas! madam," replied the lady——

"What!" said Mary, "wilt thou not help us so far? this is a peevish adherence to thine own graver opinion, which holds our talk as folly. But thou art court-bred, and wilt well understand me when I say, the Queen *commands* Lady Fleming to tell her where she led the last *branle*."

With a face deadly pale, and a mien as if she were about to sink into the earth, the court-bred dame, no longer daring to refuse obedience, faltered out—"Gracious Lady—if my memory err not—it was at a masque in Holyrood—at the marriage of Sebastian."

The unhappy Queen, who had hitherto listened with a melancholy smile, provoked by the reluctance with which the Lady Fleming brought out her story, at this ill-fated word interrupted her with a shriek so wild and loud that the vaulted apartment rang, and both Roland and Catherine sprung to their feet in the utmost terror and alarm. Meantime, Mary seemed, by the train of horrible ideas thus suddenly excited, surprised not only beyond self-command, but for the moment beyond the verge of reason.

"Traitress!" she said to the Lady Fleming, "thou wouldst slay thy sovereign—Call my French guards—*a moi! a moi! mes Français!*—I am beset with traitors in mine own palace—they have murdered my husband—Rescue! rescue for the Queen of Scotland!" She started up from her chair—her features, late so exquisitely lovely in their paleness, now inflamed with the fury of frenzy, and resembling those of a Bellona. "We will take the field ourself," she said; "warn the city — warn Lothian and Fife — saddle our Spanish barb, and bid French Paris see our petronel be charged!—Better to die at the head of our brave Scotsmen, like our grandfather at Flodden, than of a broken heart, like our ill-starred father!"

"Be patient—be composed, dearest Sovereign," said Catherine: and then addressing Lady Fleming angrily, she added, "How could you say aught that reminded her of her husband?"

The word reached the ear of the unhappy Princess, who caught it up, speaking with great rapidity. "Husband!—what husband?—Not his most Christian Majesty—he is ill at ease—he cannot mount on horseback.—Not him of the Lennox—but it was the Duke of Orkney thou wouldst say."

"For God's love, madam, be patient!" said the Lady Fleming.

But the Queen's excited imagination could by no entreaty be diverted from its course. "Bid him come hither to our aid," she said, "and bring with him his lambs, as he calls them—Bowton, Hay of Talla, Black Ormiston, and his kinsman Hob — Fie! how swart they are, and how they smell of sulphur! What! closeted with Morton? Nay, if the Douglas and the Hepburn hatch the complot together, the bird, when it breaks the shell, will scare Scotland. Will it not, my Fleming?"

"She grows wilder and wilder," said Fleming; "we have too many hearers for these strange words."

"Roland," said Catherine, "in the name of God, begone! You cannot aid us here—Leave us to deal with her alone—Away—away!"

She thrust him to the door of the anteroom; yet even when he had entered that apartment, and shut the door, he could still hear the Queen talk in a loud and determined tone, as if giving forth orders, until at length the voice died away in a feeble and continued lamentation.

At this crisis Catherine entered the anteroom. "Be not too anxious," she said, "the crisis is now over; but keep the door fast—let no one enter until she is more composed."

"In the name of God, what does this mean?" said the page; "or what was there in the Lady Fleming's words to excite so wild a transport?"

"Oh, the Lady Fleming, the Lady Fleming," said Catherine, repeating the words impatiently; "the Lady Fleming is a fool—she loves her mistress, yet knows so little how to express her love, that were the Queen to ask her for very poison, she would deem it a point of duty not to resist her commands. I could have torn her starched head-tire from her formal head—The Queen should have as soon had the heart out of my body, as the word Sebastian out of my lips — That that piece of weaved tapestry should be a woman, and yet not have wit enough to tell a lie!"

"And what was this story of Sebastian?" said the page. "By Heaven, Catherine, you are all riddles alike!"

"You are as great a fool as Fleming," returned the impatient maiden; "know ye not, that on the night of Henry Darnley's murder, and at the blowing up of the Kirk of Field, the Queen's absence was owing to her attending on a masque at Holyrood, given by her to grace the marriage of this same Sebastian, who, himself a favoured servant, married one of her female attendants, who was near to her person?"

"By Saint Giles," said the page, "I wonder not at her passion, but only marvel by what forgetfulness it was that she could urge the Lady Fleming with such a question."

"I cannot account for it," said Catherine; "but it seems as if great and violent grief and horror sometimes obscure the memory, and spread a cloud like that of an exploding cannon, over the circumstances with which they are accompanied. But I may not stay here, where I came not to moralize with your wisdom, but simply to cool my resentment against that unwise Lady Fleming, which I think hath now somewhat abated, so that I shall endure her presence without any desire to damage either her curch or vasquine. Meanwhile, keep fast that door—I would not for my life that any of these heretics saw her in the unhappy state, which, brought on her as it has been by the success of their own diabolical plottings, they would not stick to call, in their snuffling cant, the judgment of Providence."

She left the apartment just as the latch of the outward door was raised from without. But the bolt which Roland had drawn on the inside, resisted the efforts of the person desirous to enter. "Who is there?" said Græme aloud.

"It is I," replied the harsh and yet slow voice of the steward Dryfesdale.

"You cannot enter now," returned the youth.

"And wherefore?" demanded Dryfesdale, "seeing I come but to do my duty, and inquire what mean the shrieks from the apartment of the Moabitish woman. Wherefore, I say, since such is mine errand, can I not enter?"

"Simply," replied the youth, "because the bolt is drawn, and I have no fancy to undo it. I have the right side of the door to-day, as you had last night."

"Thou art ill-advised, thou malapert boy," replied the steward, "to speak to me in such fashion; but I shall inform my Lady of thine insolence."

"The insolence," said the page, "is meant for thee only, in fair guerdon of thy discourtesy to me. For thy Lady's information, I have answer more courteous—you may say that the Queen is ill at ease, and desires to be disturbed neither by visits nor messages."

"I conjure you, in the name of God," said the old man, with more solemnity in his tone than he had hitherto used, "to let me know if her malady really gains power on her!"

"She will have no aid at your hand, or at your Lady's — wherefore, begone, and trouble us no more—we neither want, nor will accept of, aid at your hands."

With this positive reply, the steward, grumbling and dissatisfied, returned down stairs.

Chapter the Thirty-Second.

It is the curse of kings to be attended
By slaves, who take their humours for a warrant
To break into the bloody house of life,
And on the winking of authority
To understand a law.

KING JOHN.

The Lady of Lochleven sat alone in her chamber, endeavouring with sincere but imperfect zeal, to fix her eyes and her attention on the black-lettered Bible which lay before her, bound in velvet and embroidery, and adorned with massive silver clasps and knosps. But she found her utmost efforts unable to withdraw her mind from the resentful recollection of what had last night passed betwixt her and the Queen, in which the latter had with such bitter taunt reminded her of her early and long-repented transgression.

"Why," she said, "should I resent so deeply that another reproaches me with that which I have never ceased to make matter of blushing to myself? and yet, why should this woman, who reaps—at least, has reaped—the fruits of my folly, and has jostled my son aside from the throne, why should she, in the face of all my domestics, and of her own, dare to upbraid me with my shame? Is she not in my power? Does she not fear me? Ha! wily tempter, I will wrestle with thee strongly, and with better suggestions than my own evil heart can supply!"

She again took up the sacred volume, and was endeavouring to fix her attention on its contents, when she was disturbed by a tap at the door of the room. It opened at her command, and the steward Dryfesdale entered, and stood before her with a gloomy and perturbed expression on his brow.

"What has chanced, Dryfesdale, that thou lookest thus?" said his mistress—"Have there been evil tidings of my son, or of my grandchildren?"

"No, Lady," replied Dryfesdale, "but you were deeply insulted last night, and I fear me thou art as deeply avenged this morning—Where is the chaplain?"

"What mean you by hints so dark, and a question so sudden? The chaplain, as you well know, is absent at Perth upon an assembly of the brethren."

"I care not," answered the steward; "he is but a priest of Baal."

"Dryfesdale," said the Lady, sternly, "what meanest thou? I have ever heard, that in the Low Countries thou didst herd with the Anabaptist preachers, those boars which tear up the vintage.—But the ministry which suits me and my house must content my retainers."

"I would I had good ghostly counsel, though," replied the steward, not attending to his mistress's rebuke, and seeming to speak to himself. "This woman of Moab——"

"Speak of her with reverence," said the Lady; "she is a king's daughter."

"Be it so," replied Dryfesdale; "she goes where there is little difference betwixt her and a beggar's child—Mary of Scotland is dying."

"Dying, and in my castle!" said the Lady, starting up in alarm; "of what disease, or by what accident?"

"Bear patience, Lady. The ministry was mine."

"Thine, villain and traitor!—how didst thou dare——"

"I heard you insulted, Lady—I heard you demand vengeance—I promised you should have it, and I now bring tidings of it."

"Dryfesdale, I trust thou ravest?" said the Lady.

"I rave not," replied the steward. "That which was written of me a million of years ere I saw the light, must be executed by me. She hath that in her veins that, I fear me, will soon stop the springs of life."

"Cruel villain," exclaimed the Lady, "thou hast not poisoned her?"

"And if I had," said Dryfesdale, "what does it so greatly merit? Men bane vermin—why not rid them of their enemies so? in Italy they will do it for a cruizuedor."

"Cowardly ruffian, begone from my sight!"

"Think better of my zeal, Lady," said the steward, "and judge not without looking around you. Lindesay, Ruthven, and your kinsman Morton, poniarded Rizzio, and yet you now see no blood on their embroidery — the Lord Semple stabbed the Lord of Sanquhar — does his bonnet sit a jot more awry on his brow? What noble lives in Scotland who has not had a share, for policy or revenge, in some such dealing? — and who imputes it to them? Be not cheated with names — a dagger or a draught work to the same end, and are little unlike — a glass phial imprisons the one, and a leathern sheath the other — one deals with the brain, the other sluices the blood — Yet, I say not I gave aught to this lady."

"What dost thou mean by thus dallying with me?" said the Lady; "as thou wouldst save thy neck from the rope it merits, tell me the whole truth of this story — thou hast long been known a dangerous man."

"Ay, in my master's service I can be cold and sharp as my sword. Be it known to you, that when last on shore, I consulted with a woman of skill and power, called Nicneven, of whom the country has rung for some brief time past. Fools asked her for charms to make them beloved, misers for means to increase their store; some demanded to know the future—an idle wish, since it cannot be altered; others would have an explanation of the past — idler still, since it cannot be recalled. I heard their queries with scorn, and demanded the means of avenging myself of a deadly enemy, for I grow old, and may trust no longer to Bilboa blade. She gave me a packet —'Mix that,' said she, 'with any liquid, and thy vengeance is complete.'"

"Villain! and you mixed it with the food of this imprisoned Lady, to the dishonour of thy master's house?"

"To redeem the insulted honour of my master's house, I mixed the contents of the packet with the jar of succory-water: They seldom fail to drain it, and the woman loves it over all."

"It was a work of hell," said the Lady Lochleven, "both the asking and the granting. — Away, wretched man, let us see if aid be yet too late!"

"They will not admit us, madam, save we enter by force — I have been twice at the door, but can obtain no entrance."

"We will beat it level with the ground, if needful — And, hold — summon Randal hither instantly. — Randal, here is a foul and evil chance befallen — send off a boat instantly to Kinross, the Chamberlain Luke Lundin is said to have skill — Fetch off, too, that foul witch Nicneven; she shall first counteract her own spell, and then be burned to ashes in the island of Saint Serf. Away, away — Tell them to hoist sail and ply oar, as ever they would have good of the Douglas's hand!"

"Mother Nicneven will not be lightly found, or fetched hither on these conditions," answered Dryfesdale.

"Then grant her full assurance of safety — Look to it, for thine own life must answer for this lady's recovery."

"I might have guessed that," said Dryfesdale, sullenly; "but it is my comfort I have avenged mine own cause, as well as yours. She hath scoffed and scripped at me, and encouraged her saucy minion of a page to ridicule my stiff gait and slow speech. I felt it borne in upon me that I was to be avenged on them."

"Go to the western turret," said the Lady, "and remain there in ward until we see how this gear will terminate. I know thy resolved disposition — thou wilt not attempt escape."

"Not were the walls of the turret of egg-shells, and the lake sheeted with ice," said Dryfesdale. "I am well taught, and strong in belief, that man does nought of himself; he is but the foam on the billow, which rises, bubbles, and bursts, not by its own effort, but by the mightier impulse of fate which urges him. Yet, Lady, if I may advise, amid this zeal for the life of the Jezebel of Scotland, forget not what is due to thine own honour, and keep the matter secret as you may."

So saying, the gloomy fatalist turned from her, and stalked off with sullen composure to the place of confinement allotted to him.

His lady caught at his last hint, and only expressed her fear that the prisoner had partaken of some unwholesome food, and was dangerously ill. The castle was soon alarmed and in confusion. Randal was dispatched to the shore to fetch off Lundin, with such remedies as could counteract poison; and with farther instructions to bring mother Nicneven, if she could be found, with full power to pledge the Lady of Lochleven's word for her safety.

Meanwhile the Lady of Lochleven herself held parley at the door of the Queen's apartment, and in vain urged the page to undo it.

"Foolish boy!" she said, "thine own life and thy Lady's are at stake — Open, I say, or we will cause the door to be broken down."

"I may not open the door without my royal mistress's orders," answered Roland; "she has been very ill, and now she slumbers — if you wake her by using violence, let the consequence be on you and your followers."

"Was ever woman in a strait so fearful!" exclaimed the Lady of Lochleven — "At least, thou rash boy, beware that no one tastes the food, but especially the jar of succory-water."

She then hastened to the turret, where Dryfesdale had composedly resigned himself to imprisonment. She found him reading, and demanded of him, "Was thy fell potion of speedy operation?"

"Slow," answered the steward. "The hag asked me which I chose — I told her I loved a slow and sure revenge. 'Revenge,' said I, 'is the highest-flavoured draught which man tastes upon earth, and he should sip it by little and little — not drain it up greedily at once.'"

"Against whom, unhappy man, couldst thou nourish so fell a revenge?"

"I had many objects, but the chief was that insolent page."

"The boy! — thou inhuman man!" exclaimed the lady; "what could he do to deserve thy malice?"

"He rose in your favour, and you graced him with your commissions — that was one thing. He rose in that of George Douglas's also — that was another. He was the favourite of the Calvinistic Henderson, who hated me because my spirit disowns a separated priesthood. The Moabitish Queen held him dear — winds from each opposing point blew in his favour — the old servitor of your house was held lightly among ye — above all, from the first time I saw his face, I longed to destroy him."

"What fiend have I nurtured in my house!" replied the Lady. "May God forgive me the sin of having given thee food and raiment!"

"You might not choose, Lady," answered the steward. "Long ere this castle was builded — ay, long ere the islet which sustains it reared its head above the blue water, I was destined to be your faithful slave, and you to be my ungrateful mistress. Remember you not when I plunged amid the victorious French, in the time of this lady's mother, and brought off your husband, when those who had hung at the same breasts with him dared not attempt the rescue? — Remember how I plunged into the lake when your grandson's skiff was overtaken by the tempest, boarded, and steered her safe to the land. Lady — the servant of a Scottish baron is he who regards not his own life, or that of any other, save his master. And, for the death of the woman, I had tried the potion on her sooner, had not Master George been her taster. Her death — would it not be the happiest news that

Scotland ever heard? Is she not of the bloody Guisian stock, whose sword was so often red with the blood of God's saints? Is she not the daughter of the wretched tyrant James, whom Heaven cast down from his kingdom, and his pride, even as the king of Babylon was smitten?"

"Peace, villain!" said the Lady — a thousand varied recollections thronging on her mind at the mention of her royal lover's name; "Peace, and disturb not the ashes of the dead — of the royal, of the unhappy dead. Read thy Bible; and may God grant thee to avail thyself better of its contents than thou hast yet done!" She departed hastily, and as she reached the next apartment, the tears rose in her eyes so hastily, that she was compelled to stop and use her kerchief to dry them. "I expected not this," she said, "no more than to have drawn water from the dry flint, or sap from a withered tree. I saw with a dry eye the apostacy and shame of George Douglas, the hope of my son's house — the child of my love; and yet I now weep for him who has so long lain in his grave — for him to whom I owe it that his daughter can make a scoffing and a jest of my name! But she is *his* daughter — my heart, hardened against her for so many causes, relents when a glance of her eye places her father unexpectedly before me — and as often her likeness to that true daughter of the house of Guise, her detested mother, has again confirmed my resolution. But she must not — must not die in my house, and by so foul a practice. Thank God, the operation of the potion is slow, and may be counteracted. I will to her apartment once more. But oh! that hardened villain, whose fidelity we held in such esteem, and had such high proof of! What miracle can unite so much wickedness and so much truth in one bosom!"

The Lady of Lochleven was not aware how far minds of a certain gloomy and determined cast by nature, may be warped by a keen sense of petty injuries and insults, combining with the love of gain, and sense of self-interest, and amalgamated with the crude, wild, and indigested fanatical opinions which this man had gathered among the crazy sectaries of Germany; or how far the doctrines of fatalism, which he had embraced so decidedly, sear the human conscience, by representing our actions as the result of inevitable necessity.

During her visit to the prisoner, Roland had communicated to Catherine the tenor of the conversation he had had with her at the door of the apartment. The quick intelligence of that lively maiden instantly comprehended the outline of what was believed to have happened, but her prejudices hurried her beyond the truth.

"They meant to have poisoned us," she exclaimed in horror, "and there stands the fatal liquor which should have done the deed!—Ay, as soon as Douglas ceased to be our taster, our food was likely to be fatally seasoned. Thou, Roland, who shouldst have made the essay, wert readily doomed to die with us. Oh, dearest Lady Fleming, pardon, pardon, for the injuries I said to you in my anger—your words were prompted by Heaven to save our lives, and especially that of the injured Queen. But what have we now to do? that old crocodile of the lake will be presently back to shed her hypocritical tears over our dying agonies.—Lady Fleming, what shall we do?"

"Our Lady help us in our need!" she replied; "how should I tell?—unless we were to make our plaint to the Regent."

"Make our plaint to the devil," said Catherine impatiently, "and accuse his dam at the foot of his burning throne!—The Queen still sleeps—we must gain time. The poisoning hag must not know her scheme has miscarried; the old envenomed spider has but too many ways of mending her broken web. The jar of succory-water," said she—"Roland, if thou be'st a man, help me—empty the jar on the chimney or from the window—make such waste among the viands as if we had made our usual meal, and leave the fragments on cup and porringer, but taste nothing as thou lovest thy life. I will sit by the Queen, and tell her at her waking, in what a fearful pass we stand. Her sharp wit and ready spirit will teach us what is best to be done. Meanwhile, till farther notice, observe, Roland, that the Queen is in a state of torpor—that Lady Fleming is indisposed—that character" (speaking in a lower tone) "will suit her best, and save her wits some labour in vain. I am not so much indisposed, thou understandest."

"And I?" said the page——

"You?" replied Catherine, "you are quite well—who thinks it worth while to poison puppy-dogs or pages?"

"Does this levity become the time?" asked the page.

"It does, it does," answered Catherine Seyton; "if the Queen approves, I see plainly how this disconcerted attempt may do us good service."

She went to work while she spoke, eagerly assisted by Roland. The breakfast table soon displayed the appearance as if the meal had been eaten as usual; and the ladies retired as softly as possible into the Queen's sleeping apartment. At a new summons of the Lady Lochleven, the page undid the door, and admitted her into the anteroom, asking her pardon for having withstood her, alleging in excuse, that the Queen had fallen into a heavy slumber since she had broken her fast.

"She has eaten and drunken, then?" said the Lady of Lochleven.

"Surely," replied the page, "according to her Grace's ordinary custom, unless upon the fasts of the church."

"The jar," she said, hastily examining it, "it is empty—drank the Lady Mary the whole of this water?"

"A large part, madam; and I heard the Lady Catherine Seyton jestingly upbraid the Lady Mary Fleming with having taken more than a just share of what remained, so that but little fell to her own lot."

"And are they well in health?" said the Lady of Lochleven.

"Lady Fleming," said the page, "complains of lethargy, and looks duller than usual; and the Lady Catherine of Seyton feels her head somewhat more giddy than is her wont."

He raised his voice a little as he said these words, to apprise the ladies of the part assigned to each of them, and not, perhaps, without the wish of conveying to the ears of Catherine the page-like jest which lurked in the allotment.

"I will enter the Queen's bedchamber," said the Lady of Lochleven; "my business is express."

As she advanced to the door, the voice of Catherine Seyton was heard from within—"No one can enter here—the Queen sleeps."

"I will not be controlled, young lady," replied the Lady of Lochleven; "there is, I wot, no inner bar, and I will enter in your despite."

"There is, indeed, no inner bar," answered Catherine, firmly, "but there are the staples where that bar should be; and into those staples have I thrust mine arm, like an ancestress of your own, when, better employed than the Douglasses of our days, she thus defended the bedchamber of her sovereign against murderers. Try your force, then, and see whether a Seyton cannot rival in courage a maiden of the house of Douglas."

"I dare not attempt the pass at such risk," said the Lady of Lochleven: "Strange, that this Princess, with all that justly attaches to her as blameworthy, should preserve such empire over the minds of her attendants.—Damsel, I give thee my honour that I come for the Queen's safety and advantage. Awaken her, if thou lovest her, and pray her leave that I may enter—I will retire from the door the whilst."

"Thou wilt not awaken the Queen?" said the Lady Fleming.

"What choice have we?" said the ready-witted maiden, "unless you deem it better to wait till the Lady Lochleven herself plays lady of the bedchamber. Her fit of patience will not last long, and the Queen must be prepared to meet her."

"But thou wilt bring back her Grace's fit by thus disturbing her."

"Heaven forbid!" replied Catherine; "but if so, it must pass for an effect of the poison. I hope better things, and that the Queen will be able when she wakes to form her own judgment in this terrible crisis. Meanwhile, do thou, dear Lady Fleming, practise to look as dull and heavy as the alertness of thy spirit will permit."

Catherine kneeled by the side of the Queen's bed, and, kissing her hand repeatedly, succeeded at last in awakening without alarming her. She seemed surprised to find that she was ready dressed, but sate up in her bed, and appeared so perfectly composed, that Catherine Seyton, without farther preamble, judged it safe to inform her of the predicament in which they were placed. Mary turned pale, and crossed herself again and again, when she heard the imminent danger in which she had stood. But, like the Ulysses of Homer,

—Hardly waking yet,
Sprung in her mind the momentary wit,

and she at once understood her situation, with the dangers and advantages that attended it.

"We cannot do better," she said, after her hasty conference with Catherine, pressing her at the same time to her bosom, and kissing her forehead; "we cannot do better than to follow the scheme so happily devised by thy quick wit and bold affection. Undo the door to the Lady Lochleven—She shall meet her match in art, though not in perfidy. Fleming, draw close the curtain, and get thee behind it—thou art a better tire-woman than an actress; do but breathe heavily, and, if thou wilt, groan slightly, and it will top thy part. Hark! they come. Now, Catherine of Medicis, may thy spirit inspire me, for a cold northern brain is too blunt for this scene!"

Ushered by Catherine Seyton, and stepping as light as she could, the Lady Lochleven was shown into the twilight apartment, and conducted to the side of the couch, where Mary, pallid and exhausted from a sleepless night, and the subsequent agitation of the morning, lay extended so listlessly as might well confirm the worst fears of her hostess.

"Now, God forgive us our sins!" said the Lady of Lochleven, forgetting her pride, and throwing herself on her knees by the side of the bed; "It is too true—she is murdered!"

"Who is in the chamber?" said Mary, as if awaking from a heavy sleep. "Seyton, Fleming, where are you? I heard a strange voice. Who waits? —Call Courcelles."

"Alas! her memory is at Holyrood, though her body is at Lochleven.—Forgive, madam," continued the Lady, "if I call your attention to me—I am Margaret Erskine, of the house of Mar, by marriage Lady Douglas of Lochleven."

"Oh, our gentle hostess," answered the Queen, "who hath such care of our lodgings and of our diet—We cumber you too much and too long, good Lady of Lochleven; but we now trust your task of hospitality is well-nigh ended."

"Her words go like a knife through my heart," said the Lady of Lochleven—"With a breaking heart, I pray your Grace to tell me what is your ailment, that aid may be had, if there be yet time."

"Nay, my ailment," replied the Queen, "is nothing worth telling, or worth a leech's notice—my limbs feel heavy—my heart feels cold—a prisoner's limbs and heart are rarely otherwise—fresh air, methinks, and freedom, would soon revive me; but as the Estates have ordered it, death alone can break my prison-doors."

"Were it possible, madam," said the Lady, "that your liberty could restore your perfect health, I would myself encounter the resentment of the Regent—of my son, Sir William—of my whole friends, rather than you should meet your fate in this castle."

"Alas! madam," said the Lady Fleming, who conceived the time propi tious to show that her own address had been held too lightly of; "it is but trying what good freedom may work upon us; for myself, I think a free walk on the greensward would do me much good at heart."

The Lady of Lochleven rose from the bedside, and darted a penetrating look at the elder valetudinary. "Are you so evil-disposed, Lady Fleming?"

"Evil-disposed indeed, madam," replied the court dame, "and more especially since breakfast."

"Help! help!" exclaimed Catherine, anxious to break off a conversation which boded her schemes no good; "help! I say, help! the Queen is about to pass away. Aid her, Lady Lochleven, if you be a woman!"

The Lady hastened to support the Queen's head, who, turning her eyes towards her with an air of great languor, exclaimed, "Thanks, my dearest Lady of Lochleven — notwithstanding some passages of late, I have never misconstrued or misdoubted your affection to our house. It was proved, as I have heard, before I was born."

The Lady Lochleven sprung from the floor, on which she had again knelt, and, having paced the apartment in great disorder, flung open the lattice, as if to get air.

"Now, Our Lady forgive me!" said Catherine to herself. "How deep must the love of sarcasm be implanted in the breasts of us women, since the Queen, with all her sense, will risk ruin rather than rein in her wit!" She then adventured, stooping over the Queen's person, to press her arm with her hand, saying, at the same time, "For God's sake, madam, restrain yourself!"

"Thou art too forward, maiden," said the Queen; but immediately added, in a low whisper, "Forgive me, Catherine; but when I felt the hag's murderous hands busy about my head and neck, I felt such disgust and hatred, that I must have said something, or died. But I will be schooled to better behaviour—only see that thou let her not touch me."

"Now, God be praised!" said the Lady Lochleven, withdrawing her head from the window, "the boat comes as fast as sail and oar can send wood through water. It brings the leech and a female — certainly, from the appearance, the very person I was in quest of. Were she but well out of this castle, with our honour safe, I would that she were on the top of the wildest mountain in Norway; or I would I had been there myself, ere I had undertaken this trust."

While she thus expressed herself, standing apart at one window, Roland Græme, from the other, watched the boat bursting through the waters of the lake, which glided from its side in ripple and in foam. He, too, became sensible, that at the stern was seated the medical Chamberlain, clad in his black velvet cloak; and that his own relative, Magdalen Græme, in her assumed character of Mother Nicneven, stood in the bow, her hands clasped together, and pointed towards the castle, and her attitude, even at that distance, expressing enthusiastic eagerness to arrive at the landing-place. They arrived there accordingly, and while the supposed witch was detained in a room beneath, the physician was ushered to the Queen's apartment, which he entered with all due professional solemnity. Catherine had, in the meanwhile, fallen back from the Queen's bed, and taken an opportunity to whisper to Roland, "Methinks, from the information of the threadbare velvet cloak and the solemn beard, there would be little trouble in haltering yonder ass. But thy grandmother, Roland — thy grandmother's zeal will ruin us, if she get not a hint to dissemble."

Roland, without reply, glided towards the door of the apartment, crossed the parlour, and safely entered the antechamber; but when he attempted to pass farther, the word "Back! Back!" echoed from one to the other, by two men armed with carabines, convinced him that the Lady of Lochleven's suspicions had not, even in the midst of her alarms, been so far lulled to sleep as to omit the precaution of stationing sentinels on her prisoners. He was compelled, therefore, to return to the parlour, or audience-chamber, in which he found the Lady of the castle in conference with her learned leech.

"A truce with your cant phrase and your solemn foppery, Lundin," in such terms she accosted the man of art, "and let me know instantly, if thou canst tell, whether this lady hath swallowed aught that is less than wholesome?"

"Nay, but, good lady—honoured patroness—to whom I am alike bondsman in my medical and official capacity, deal reasonably with me. If this, mine illustrious patient, will not answer a question, saving with sighs and moans—if that other honourable lady will do nought but yawn in my face when I inquire after the diagnostics—and if that other young damsel, who I profess is a comely maiden——"

"Talk not to me of comeliness or of damsels," said the Lady of Lochleven, "I say, are they evil-disposed?—In one word, man, have they taken poison, ay or no?"

"Poisons, madam," said the learned leech, "are of various sorts. There is your animal poison, as the lepus marinus, as mentioned by Dioscorides and Galen — there are mineral and semi-mineral poisons, as those compounded of sublimate regulus of antimony, vitriol, and the arsenical salts —there are your poisons from herbs and vegetables, as the aqua cymbalariæ, opium, aconitum, cantharides, and the like—there are also——"

"Now, out upon thee for a learned fool! and I myself am no better for expecting an oracle from such a log," said the Lady.

"Nay, but if your ladyship will have patience—if I knew what food they have partaken of, or could see but the remnants of what they have last eaten —for as to the external and internal symptoms, I can discover nought like; for, as Galen saith in his second book *de Antidotis*——"

"Away, fool!" said the Lady; "send me that hag hither; she shall avouch what it was that she hath given to the wretch Dryfesdale, or the pilniewinks and thumbikins shall wrench it out of her finger joints!"

"Art hath no enemy unless the ignorant," said the mortified Doctor; veiling, however, his remark under the Latin version, and stepping apart into a corner to watch the result.

In a minute or two Magdalen Græme entered the apartment, dressed as we have described her at the revel, but with her muffler thrown back, and all affectation of disguise. She was attended by two guards, of whose presence she did not seem even to be conscious, and who followed her with an air of embarrassment and timidity, which was probably owing to their belief in her supernatural power, coupled with the effect produced by her bold and undaunted demeanour. She confronted the Lady of Lochleven, who seemed to endure with high disdain the confidence of her air and manner.

"Wretched woman!" said the Lady, after essaying for a moment to bear her down, before she addressed her, by the stately severity of her look, "what was that powder which thou didst give to a servant of this house, by name Jasper Dryfesdale, that he might work out with it some slow and secret vengeance? — Confess its nature and properties, or, by the honour of Douglas, I give thee to fire and stake before the sun is lower!"

"Alas!" said Magdalen Græme in reply, "and when became a Douglas or a Douglas's man so unfurnished in his revenge, that he should seek them at the hands of a poor and solitary woman? The towers in which your captives pine away into unpitied graves, yet stand fast on their foundation — the crimes wrought in them have not yet burst their vaults asunder — your men have still their cross-bows, pistolets, and daggers — why need you seek to herbs or charms for the execution of your revenges?"

"Hear me, foul hag," said the Lady Lochleven, — "but what avails speaking to thee? — Bring Dryfesdale hither, and let them be confronted together."

"You may spare your retainers the labour," replied Magdalen Græme. "I came not here to be confronted with a base groom, nor to answer the interrogatories of James's heretical leman—I came to speak with the Queen of Scotland — Give place there!"

And while the Lady Lochleven stood confounded at her boldness, and at the reproach she had cast upon her, Magdalen Græme strode past her into the bedchamber of the Queen, and, kneeling on the floor, made a salutation as if, in the Oriental fashion, she meant to touch the earth with her forehead.

"Hail, Princess!" she said, "hail, daughter of many a King, but graced above them all in that thou art called to suffer for the true faith — hail to thee, the pure gold of whose crown has been tried in the seven-times heated furnace of affliction — hear the comfort which God and Our Lady send thee by the mouth of thy unworthy servant.—But first"—and stooping her head she crossed herself repeatedly, and, still upon her knees, appeared to be rapidly reciting some formula of devotion.

"Seize her, and drag her to the massy-more! — to the deepest dungeon with the sorceress, whose master, the Devil, could alone have inspired her with boldness enough to insult the mother of Douglas in his own castle!"

Thus spoke the incensed Lady of Lochleven, but the physician presumed to interpose.

"I pray of you, honoured madam, she be permitted to take her course without interruption. Peradventure we shall learn something concerning the nostrum she hath ventured, contrary to law and the rules of art, to adhibit to these ladies, through the medium of the steward Dryfesdale."

"For a fool," replied the Lady of Lochleven, "thou hast counselled wisely — I will bridle my resentment till their conference be over."

"God forbid, honoured Lady," said Doctor Lundin, "that you should suppress it longer — nothing may more endanger the frame of your honoured body; and truly, if there be witchcraft in this matter, it is held by the vulgar, and even by solid authors on Demonology, that three scruples of the ashes of the witch, when she hath been well and carefully burned at a stake, is a grand Catholicon in such matter, even as they prescribe *crinis canis rabidi*, a hair of the dog that bit the patient, in cases of hydrophobia. I warrant neither treatment, being out of the regular practice of the schools; but, in the present case, there can be little harm in trying the conclusion upon this old necromancer and quacksalver —*fiat experimentum* (as we say) *in corpore vili*."

"Peace, fool!" said the Lady, "she is about to speak."

At that moment Magdalen Græme arose from her knees, and turned her countenance on the Queen, at the same time advancing her foot, extending her arm, and assuming the mien and attitude of a Sibyl in frenzy. As her gray hair floated back from beneath her coif, and her eye gleamed fire from under its shaggy eyebrow, the effect of her expressive though emaciated features, was heightened by an enthusiasm approaching to insanity, and her appearance struck with awe all who were present. Her eyes for a time glanced wildly around as if seeking for something to aid her in collecting her powers of expression, and her lips had a nervous and quivering motion, as those of one who would fain speak, yet rejects as inadequate the words which present themselves. Mary herself caught the infection as if by a sort of magnetic influence, and raising herself from her bed, without being able to withdraw her eyes from those of Magdalen, waited as if for the oracle of a Pythoness. She waited not long, for no sooner had the enthusiast collected herself, than her gaze became instantly steady, her features assumed a determined energy, and when she began to speak, the words flowed from her with a profuse fluency, which might have passed for inspiration, and which, perhaps, she herself mistook for such.

"Arise," she said, "Queen of France and of England! Arise, Lioness of Scotland, and be not dismayed though the nets of the hunters have encircled thee! Stoop not to feign with the false ones, whom thou shall soon meet in the field. The issue of battle is with the God of armies, but by battle thy cause shall be tried. Lay aside, then, the arts of lower mortals, and assume those which become a Queen! True defender of the only true faith, the armoury of heaven is open to thee! Faithful daughter of the Church, take the keys of St. Peter, to bind and to loose! — Royal Princess of the land, take the sword of St. Paul, to smite and to shear! There is darkness in thy destiny; — but not in these towers, not under the rule of their haughty mistress, shall that destiny be closed.— In other lands the lioness may crouch to the power of the tigress, but not in her own — not in Scotland shall the Queen of Scotland long remain captive — nor is the fate of the royal Stuart in the hands of the traitor Douglas. Let the Lady of Lochleven double her bolts and deepen her dungeons, they shall not retain thee — each element shall give thee its assistance ere thou shalt continue captive — the land shall lend its earthquakes, the water its waves, the air its tempests, the fire its devouring flames, to desolate this house, rather than it shall continue the place of thy captivity. — Hear this, and tremble, all ye who fight against the light, for she says it, to whom it hath been assured!"

She was silent, and the astonished physician said, "If there was ever an *Energumene*, or possessed demoniac, in our days, there is a devil speaking with that woman's tongue!"

"Practice," said the Lady of Lochleven, recovering her surprise; "here is all practice and imposture — To the dungeon with her!"

"Lady of Lochleven," said Mary, arising from her bed, and coming forward with her wonted dignity, "ere you make arrest on any one in our presence, hear me but one word. I have done you some wrong — I believed you privy to the murderous purpose of your vassal, and I deceived you in suffering you to believe it had taken effect. I did you wrong, Lady of Lochleven, for I perceive your purpose to aid me was sincere. We tasted not of the liquid, nor are we now sick, save that we languish for our freedom."

"It is avowed like Mary of Scotland," said Magdalen Græme; "and know, besides, that had the Queen drained the drought to the dregs, it was harmless as the water from a sainted spring. Trow ye, proud woman," she added, addressing herself to the Lady of Lochleven, "that I — I — would have been the wretch to put poison into the hands of a servant or vassal of the house of Lochleven, knowing whom that house contained? as soon would I have furnished drug to slay my own daughter!"

"Am I thus bearded in mine own castle?" said the Lady; "to the dungeon with her! — she shall abye what is due to the vender of poisons and practiser of witchcraft."

"Yet hear me for an instant, Lady of Lochleven," said Mary; "and do you," to Magdalen, "be silent at my command.—Your steward, lady, has by confession attempted my life, and those of my household, and this woman hath done her best to save them, by furnishing him with what was harmless, in place of the fatal drugs which he expected. Methinks I propose to you but a fair exchange when I say I forgive your vassal with all my heart, and leave vengeance to God, and to his conscience, so that you also forgive the boldness of this woman in your presence; for we trust you do not hold it as a crime, that she substituted an innocent beverage for the mortal poison which was to have drenched our cup."

"Heaven forfend, madam," said the Lady, "that I should account that a crime which saved the house of Douglas from a foul breach of honour and hospitality! We have written to our son touching our vassal's delict, and he must abide his doom, which will most likely be death. Touching this woman, her trade is damnable by Scripture, and is mortally punished by the wise laws of our ancestry—she also must abide her doom."

"And have I then," said the Queen, "no claim on the house of Lochleven for the wrong I have so nearly suffered within their walls? I ask but in requital, the life of a frail and aged woman, whose brain, as yourself may judge, seems somewhat affected by years and suffering."

"If the Lady Mary," replied the inflexible Lady of Lochleven, "hath been menaced with wrong in the house of Douglas, it may be regarded as some compensation, that her complots have cost that house the exile of a valued son."

"Plead no more for me, my gracious Sovereign," said Magdalen Græme, "nor abase yourself to ask so much as a gray hair of my head at her hands. I knew the risk at which I served my Church and my Queen, and was ever prompt to pay my poor life as the ransom. It is a comfort to think, that in slaying me, or in restraining my freedom, or even in injuring that single gray hair, the house, whose honour she boasts so highly, will have filled up the measure of their shame by the breach of their solemn written assurance of safety."—And taking from her bosom a paper, she handed it to the Queen.

"It is a solemn assurance of safety in life and limb," said Queen Mary, "with space to come and go, under the hand and seal of the Chamberlain of Kinross, granted to Magdalen Græme, commonly called Mother Nicneven, in consideration of her consenting to put herself, for the space of twenty-four hours, if required, within the iron gate of the Castle of Lochleven."

"Knave!" said the Lady, turning to the Chamberlain, "how dared you grant her such a protection?"

"It was by your Ladyship's orders, transmitted by Randal, as he can bear witness," replied Doctor Lundin; "nay, I am only like the pharmacopolist, who compounds the drugs after the order of the mediciner."

"I remember—I remember," answered the Lady; "but I meant the assurance only to be used in case, by residing in another jurisdiction, she could not have been apprehended under our warrant."

"Nevertheless," said the Queen, "the Lady of Lochleven is bound by the action of her deputy in granting the assurance."

"Madam," replied the Lady, "the house of Douglas have never broken their safe-conduct, and never will—too deeply did they suffer by such a breach of trust, exercised on themselves, when your Grace's ancestor, the second James, in defiance of the rights of hospitality, and of his own written assurance of safety, poniarded the brave Earl of Douglas with his own hand, and within two yards of the social board, at which he had just before sat the King of Scotland's honoured guest."

"Methinks," said the Queen, carelessly, "in consideration of so very recent and enormous a tragedy, which I think only chanced some six-score years agone, the Douglasses should have shown themselves less tenacious of the company of their sovereigns, than you, Lady of Lochleven, seem to be of mine."

"Let Randal," said the Lady, "take the hag back to Kinross, and set her at full liberty, discharging her from our bounds in future, on peril of her head.—And let your wisdom," to the Chamberlain, "keep her company. And fear not for your character, though I send you in such company; for, granting her to be a witch, it would be a waste of fagots to burn you for a wizard."

The crest-fallen Chamberlain was preparing to depart; but Magdalen Græme, collecting herself, was about to reply, when the Queen interposed, saying, "Good mother, we heartily thank you for your unfeigned zeal towards our person, and pray you, as our liege-woman, that you abstain from whatever may lead you into personal danger; and, farther, it is our will that you depart without a word of farther parley with any one in this castle. For thy present guerdon, take this small reliquary—it was given to us by our uncle the Cardinal, and hath had the benediction of the Holy Father himself;—and now depart in peace and in silence.—For you, learned sir," continued the Queen, advancing to the Doctor, who made his reverence in a manner doubly embarrassed by the awe of the Queen's presence, which made him fear to do too little, and by the apprehension of his lady's displeasure, in case he should chance to do too much — "for you, learned sir, as it was not your fault, though surely our own good fortune, that we did not need your skill at this time, it would not become us, however circumstanced, to suffer our leech to leave us without such guerdon as we can offer."

With these words, and with the grace which never forsook her, though, in the present case, there might lurk under it a little gentle ridicule, she offered a small embroidered purse to the Chamberlain, who, with extended hand and arched back, his learned face stooping until a physiognomist might have practised the metoposcopical science upon it, as seen from behind betwixt his gambadoes, was about to accept of the professional recompense offered by so fair as well as illustrious a hand. But the Lady interposed, and, regarding the Chamberlain, said aloud, "No servant of our house, without instantly relinquishing that character, and incurring withal our highest displeasure, shall dare receive any gratuity at the hand of the Lady Mary."

Sadly and slowly the Chamberlain raised his depressed stature into the perpendicular attitude, and left the apartment dejectedly, followed by Magdalen Græme, after, with mute but expressive gesture, she had kissed the reliquary with which the Queen had presented her, and, raising her clasped hands and uplifted eyes towards Heaven, had seemed to entreat a benediction upon the royal dame. As she left the castle, and went towards the quay where the boat lay, Roland Græme, anxious to communicate with her if possible, threw himself in her way, and might have succeeded in exchanging a few words with her, as she was guarded only by the dejected Chamberlain and his halberdiers, but she seemed to have taken, in its most strict and literal acceptation, the command to be silent which she had received from the Queen; for, to the repeated signs of her grandson, she only replied by laying her finger on her lip. Dr. Lundin was not so reserved. Regret for the handsome gratuity, and for the compulsory task of self-denial imposed on him, had grieved the spirit of that worthy officer and learned mediciner — "Even thus, my friend," said he, squeezing the page's hand as he bade him farewell, "is merit rewarded. I came to cure this unhappy Lady — and I profess she well deserves the trouble, for, say what they will of her, she hath a most winning manner, a sweet voice, a gracious smile, and a most majestic wave of her hand. If she was not poisoned, say, my dear Master Roland, was that fault of mine, I being ready to cure her if she had? — and now I am denied the permission to accept my well-earned honorarium — O Galen! O Hippocrates! is the graduate's cap and doctor's scarlet brought to this pass! *Frustra fatigamus remediis ægros!*"

He wiped his eyes, stepped on the gunwale, and the boat pushed off from the shore, and went merrily across the lake, which was dimpled by the summer wind.*

* A romancer, to use a Scottish phrase, wants but a hair to make a tether of. The whole detail of the steward's supposed conspiracy against the life of Mary, is grounded upon an expression in one of her letters, which affirms, that Jasper Dryfesdale, one of the Laird of Lochleven's servants, had threatened to murder William Douglas, (for his share in the Queen's escape,) and averred that he would plant a dagger in Mary's own heart.—CHALMER'S *Life of Queen Mary*, vol. i. p. 278.

Chapter the Thirty-Third.

Death distant?—No, alas! he's ever with us,
And shakes the dart at us in all our actings:
He lurks within our cup, while we're in health;
Sits by our sick-bed, mocks our medicines;
We cannot walk, or sit, or ride, or travel,
But Death is by to seize us when he lists.

THE SPANISH FATHER.

FROM the agitating scene in the Queen's presence-chamber, the Lady of Lochleven retreated to her own apartment, and ordered the steward to be called before her.

"Have they not disarmed thee, Dryfesdale?" she said, on seeing him enter, accoutred, as usual, with sword and dagger.

"No!" replied the old man; "how should they? — Your ladyship, when you commanded me to ward, said nought of laying down my arms; and, I think none of your menials, without your order, or your son's, dare approach Jasper Dryfesdale for such a purpose. — Shall I now give up my sword to you? — it is worth little now, for it has fought for your house till it is worn down to old iron, like the pantler's old chipping knife."

"You have attempted a deadly crime — poison under trust."

"Under trust?—hem!—I know not what your ladyship thinks of it, but the world without thinks the trust was given you even for that very end; and you would have been well off had it been so ended as I proposed, and you neither the worse nor the wiser."

"Wretch!" exclaimed the lady, "and fool as well as villain, who could not even execute the crime he had planned!"

"I bid as fair for it as man could," replied Dryfesdale; "I went to a woman—a witch and a Papist—If I found not poison, it was because it was otherwise predestined. I tried fair for it; but the half-done job may be clouted, if you will."

"Villain! I am even now about to send off an express messenger to my son, to take order how thou shouldst be disposed of. Prepare thyself for death, if thou canst."

"He that looks on death, Lady," answered Dryfesdale, "as that which he may not shun, and which has its own fixed and certain hour, is ever prepared for it. He that is hanged in May will eat no flaunes* in midsummer — so there is the moan made for the old serving-man. But whom, pray I, send you on so fair an errand?"

"There will be no lack of messengers," answered his mistress.

"By my hand, but there will," replied the old man; "your castle is but poorly manned, considering the watches that you must keep, having this charge—There is the warder, and two others, whom you discarded for tampering with Master George; then for the warder's tower, the bailie, the donjon — five men mount each guard, and the rest must sleep for the most part in their clothes. To send away another man, were to harass the sentinels to death—unthrifty misuse for a household. To take in new soldiers were dangerous, the charge requiring tried men. I see but one thing for it —I will do your errand to Sir William Douglas myself."

"That were indeed a resource! — And on what day within twenty years would it be done?" said the Lady.

"Even with the speed of man and horse," said Dryfesdale; "for though I care not much about the latter days of an old serving-man's life, yet I

* Pancakes.

would like to know as soon as may be, whether my neck is mine own or the hangman's."

"Holdest thou thy own life so lightly?" said the Lady.

"Else I had reckoned more of that of others," said the predestinarian — "What is death?—it is but ceasing to live—And what is living?—a weary return of light and darkness, sleeping and waking, being hungered and eating. Your dead man needs neither candle nor can, neither fire nor feather-bed; and the joiner's chest serves him for an eternal frieze-jerkin."

"Wretched man! believest thou not that after death comes the judgment?"

"Lady," answered Dryfesdale, "as my mistress, I may not dispute your words; but, as spiritually speaking, you are still but a burner of bricks in Egypt, ignorant of the freedom of the saints; for, as was well shown to me by that gifted man, Nicolaus Schœfferbach, who was martyred by the bloody Bishop of Munster, he cannot sin who doth but execute that which is predestined, since——"

"Silence!" said the Lady, interrupting him,—"Answer me not with thy bold and presumptuous blasphemy, but hear me. Thou hast been long the servant of our house——"

"The born servant of the Douglas — they have had the best of me — I served them since I left Lockerbie: I was then ten years old, and you may soon add the threescore to it."

"Thy foul attempt has miscarried, so thou art guilty only in intention. It were a deserved deed to hang thee on the warder's tower; and yet in thy present mind, it were but giving a soul to Satan. I take thine offer, then—Go hence — here is my packet — I will add to it but a line, to desire him to send me a faithful servant or two to complete the garrison. Let my son deal with you as he will. If thou art wise, thou wilt make for Lockerbie so soon as thy foot touches dry land, and let the packet find another bearer; at all rates, look it miscarries not."

"Nay, madam," replied he — "I was born, as I said, the Douglas's servant, and I will be no corbie-messenger in mine old age — your message to your son shall be done as truly by me as if it concerned another man's neck. I take my leave of your honour."

The Lady issued her commands, and the old man was ferried over to the shore, to proceed on his extraordinary pilgrimage. It is necessary the reader should accompany him on his journey, which Providence had determined should not be of long duration.

On arriving at the village, the steward, although his disgrace had transpired, was readily accommodated with a horse, by the Chamberlain's authority; and the roads being by no means esteemed safe, he associated himself with Auchtermuchty, the common carrier, in order to travel in his company to Edinburgh.

The worthy waggoner, according to the established customs of all carriers, stage-coachmen, and other persons in public authority, from the earliest days to the present, never wanted good reasons for stopping upon the road, as often as he would; and the place which had most captivation for him as a resting-place was a change-house, as it was termed, not very distant from a romantic dell, well known by the name of Keirie Craigs. Attractions of a kind very different from those which arrested the progress of John Auchtermuchty and his wains, still continue to hover round this romantic spot, and none has visited its vicinity without a desire to remain long and to return soon.

Arrived near his favourite *howff*, not all the authority of Dryfesdale (much diminished indeed by the rumours of his disgrace) could prevail on the carrier, obstinate as the brutes which he drove, to pass on without his accustomed halt, for which the distance he had travelled furnished little or no pretence. Old Keltie, the landlord, who had bestowed his name on a bridge in the neighbourhood of his quondam dwelling, received the carrier with his usual festive cordiality, and adjourned with him into the house, under pretence of important business, which, I believe, consisted in their emptying together a mutchkin stoup of usquebaugh. While the worthy host and his guest were thus employed, the discarded steward, with a double portion of moroseness in his gesture and look, walked discontentedly into the kitchen of the place, which was occupied but by one guest. The stranger was a slight figure, scarce above the age of boyhood, and in the dress of a page, but bearing an air of haughty aristocratic boldness and even insolence in his look and manner, that might have made Dryfesdale conclude he had pretensions to superior rank, had not his experience taught him how frequently these airs of superiority were assumed by the domestics and military retainers of the Scottish nobility. — "The pilgrim's morning to you, old sir," said the youth; "you come, as I think, from Lochleven Castle — What news of our bonny Queen? — a fairer dove was never pent up in so wretched a dovecot."

"They that speak of Lochleven, and of those whom its walls contain," answered Dryfesdale, "speak of what concerns the Douglas; and they who speak of what concerns the Douglas, do it at their peril."

"Do you speak from fear of them, old man, or would you make a quarrel for them? — I should have deemed your age might have cooled your blood."

"Never, while there are empty-pated coxcombs at each corner to keep it warm."

"The sight of thy gray hairs keeps mine cold," said the boy, who had risen up and now sat down again.

"It is well for thee, or I had cooled it with this holly-rod," replied the steward. "I think thou be'st one of those swash-bucklers, who brawl in alehouses and taverns; and who, if words were pikes, and oaths were Andrew Ferraras, would soon place the religion of Babylon in the land once more, and the woman of Moab upon the throne."

"Now, by Saint Bennet of Seyton," said the youth, "I will strike thee on the face, thou foul-mouthed old railing heretic!"

"Saint Bennet of Seyton," echoed the steward; "a proper warrant is Saint Bennet's, and for a proper nest of wolf-birds like the Seytons! — I will arrest thee as a traitor to King James and the good Regent.——Ho! John Auchtermuchty, raise aid against the King's traitor!"

So saying, he laid his hand on the youth's collar, and drew his sword. John Auchtermuchty looked in, but, seeing the naked weapon, ran faster out than he entered. Keltie, the landlord, stood by and helped neither party, only exclaiming, "Gentlemen! gentlemen! for the love of Heaven!" and so forth. A struggle ensued, in which the young man, chafed at Dryfesdale's boldness, and unable, with the ease he expected, to extricate himself from the old man's determined grasp, drew his dagger, and with the speed of light, dealt him three wounds in the breast and body, the least of which was mortal. The old man sunk on the ground with a deep groan, and the host set up a piteous exclamation of surprise.

"Peace, ye brawling hound!" said the wounded steward; "are dagger-stabs and dying men such rarities in Scotland, that you should cry as if the house were falling? — Youth, I do not forgive thee, for there is nought betwixt us to forgive. Thou hast done what I have done to more than one — And I suffer what I have seen them suffer — it was all ordained to be thus and not otherwise. But if thou wouldst do me right, thou wilt send this packet safely to the hands of Sir William Douglas; and see that my memory suffer not, as if I would have loitered on mine errand for fear of my life."

The youth, whose passion had subsided the instant he had done the deed, listened with sympathy and attention, when another person, muffled in his cloak, entered the apartment, and exclaimed—"Good God! Dryfesdale, and expiring!"

"Ay, and Dryfesdale would that he had been dead," answered the wounded man, "rather than that his ears had heard the words of the only Douglas that ever was false — but yet it is better as it is. Good my murderer, and the rest of you, stand back a little, and let me speak with this unhappy apostate. — Kneel down by me, Master George — You have heard that I failed in my attempt to take away that Moabitish stumbling-block and her retinue—I gave them that which I thought would have removed the temptation out of thy path — and this, though I had other reasons to show to thy mother and others, I did chiefly purpose for love of thee."

"For the love of me, base poisoner!" answered Douglas, "wouldst thou have committed so horrible, so unprovoked a murder, and mentioned my name with it?"

"And wherefore not, George of Douglas?" answered Dryfesdale. "Breath is now scarce with me, but I would spend my last gasp on this argument. Hast thou not, despite the honour thou owest to thy parents, the faith that is due to thy religion, the truth that is due to thy king, been so carried away by the charms of this beautiful sorceress, that thou wouldst have helped her to escape from her prison-house, and lent her thine arm again to ascend the throne, which she had made a place of abomination?—Nay, stir not from me—my hand, though fast stiffening, has yet force enough to hold thee—What dost thou aim at?—to wed this witch of Scotland?—I warrant thee, thou mayest succeed — her heart and hand have been oft won at a cheaper rate, than thou, fool that thou art, would think thyself happy to pay. But, should a servant of thy father's house have seen thee embrace the fate of the idiot Darnley, or of the villain Bothwell — the fate of the murdered fool, or of the living pirate — while an ounce of ratsbane would have saved thee?"

"Think on God, Dryfesdale," said George Douglas, "and leave the utterance of those horrors — Repent, if thou canst—if not, at least be silent. — Seyton, aid me to support this dying wretch, that he may compose himself to better thoughts, if it be possible."

"Seyton!" answered the dying man; "Seyton! Is it by a Seyton's hand that I fall at last? — There is something of retribution in that — since the house had nigh lost a sister by my deed." Fixing his fading eyes on the youth, he added, "He hath her very features and presence! — Stoop down, youth, and let me see thee closer — I would know thee when we meet in yonder world, for homicides will herd together there, and I have been one." He pulled Seyton's face, in spite of some resistance, closer to his own, looked at him fixedly, and added, "Thou hast begun young—thy career will be the briefer — ay, thou wilt be met with, and that anon — a young plant never throve that was watered with an old man's blood.—Yet why blame I thee? Strange turns of fate," he muttered, ceasing to address Seyton; "I designed what I could not do, and he has done what he did not perchance design.— Wondrous, that our will should ever oppose itself to the strong and uncontrollable tide of destiny — that we should strive with the stream when we might drift with the current! My brain will serve me to question it no farther—I would Schœfferbach were here—yet why?—I am on a course which the vessel can hold without a pilot. — Farewell, George of Douglas — I die true to thy father's house." He fell into convulsions at these words, and shortly after expired.

Seyton and Douglas stood looking on the dying man, and when the scene was closed, the former was the first to speak. "As I live, Douglas, I meant not this, and am sorry; but he laid hands on me, and compelled me to defend my freedom, as I best might, with my dagger. If he were ten times thy friend and follower, I can but say that I am sorry."

"I blame thee not, Seyton," said Douglas, "though I lament the chance.

There is an overruling destiny above us, though not in the sense in which it was viewed by that wretched man, who, beguiled by some foreign mystagogue, used the awful word as the ready apology for whatever he chose to do — we must examine the packet."

They withdrew into an inner room, and remained deep in consultation, until they were disturbed by the entrance of Keltie, who, with an embarrassed countenance, asked Master George Douglas's pleasure respecting the disposal of the body. "Your honour knows," he added, "that I make my bread by living men, not by dead corpses; and old Mr. Dryfesdale, who was but a sorry customer while he was alive, occupies my public room now that he is deceased, and can neither call for ale nor brandy."

"Tie a stone round his neck," said Seyton, "and when the sun is down, have him to the Loch of Ore, heave him in, and let him alone for finding out the bottom."

"Under your favour, sir," said George Douglas, "it shall not be so.— Keltie, thou art a true fellow to me, and thy having been so shall advantage thee. Send or take the body to the chapel at Scotland's wall, or to the church of Ballanry, and tell what tale thou wilt of his having fallen in a brawl with some unruly guests of thine. Auchtermuchty knows nought else, nor are the times so peaceful as to admit close-looking into such accounts."

"Nay, let him tell the truth," said Seyton, "so far as it harms not our scheme. — Say that Henry Seyton met with him, my good fellow; — I care not a brass bodle for the feud."

"A feud with the Douglas was ever to be feared, however," said George, displeasure mingling with his natural deep gravity of manner.

"Not when the best of the name is on my side," replied Seyton.

"Alas! Henry, if thou meanest me, I am but half a Douglas in this emprize — half head, half heart, and half hand. — But I will think on one who can never be forgotten, and be all, or more, than any of my ancestors was ever. — Keltie, say it was Henry Seyton did the deed; but beware, not a word of me! — Let Auchtermuchty carry this packet" (which he had re-sealed with his own signet) "to my father at Edinburgh; and here is to pay for the funeral expenses, and thy loss of custom."

"And the washing of the floor," said the landlord, "which will be an extraordinary job; for blood they say, will scarcely ever cleanse out."

"But as for your plan," said George of Douglas, addressing Seyton, as if in continuation of what they had been before treating of, "it has a good face; but, under your favour, you are yourself too hot and too young, besides other reasons which are much against your playing the part you propose."

"We will consult the Father Abbot upon it," said the youth. "Do you ride to Kinross to-night?"

"Ay — so I purpose," answered Douglas; "the night will be dark, and suits a muffled man.* — Keltie, I forgot, there should be a stone laid on that man's grave, recording his name, and his only merit, which was being a faithful servant to the Douglas."

"What religion was the man of?" said Seyton; "he used words, which make me fear I have sent Satan a subject before his time."

"I can tell you little of that," said George Douglas; "he was noted for disliking both Rome and Geneva, and spoke of lights he had learned among the fierce sectaries of Lower Germany — an evil doctrine it was, if we judge by the fruits. God keep us from presumptuously judging of Heaven's secrets!"

---

* Generally, a disguised man; originally one who wears the cloak or mantle muffled round the lower part of the face to conceal his countenance. I have on an ancient piece of iron the representation of a robber thus accoutred, endeavouring to make his way into a house, and opposed by a mastiff, to whom he in vain offers food. The motto is *spernit dona fides.* It is part of a fire-grate said to have belonged to Archbishop Sharpe.

"Amen!" said the young Seyton, "and from meeting any encounter this evening."

"It is not thy wont to pray so," said George Douglas.

"No! I leave that to you," replied the youth, "when you are seized with scruples of engaging with your father's vassals. But I would fain have this old man's blood off these hands of mine ere I shed more — I will confess to the Abbot to-night, and I trust to have light penance for ridding the earth of such a miscreant. All I sorrow for is, that he was not a score of years younger — He drew steel first, however, that is one comfort."

Chapter the Thirty-Fourth.

Ay, Pedro,—Come you here with mask and lantern,
Ladder of ropes and other moonshine tools—
Why, youngster, thou mayst cheat the old Duenna,
Flatter the waiting-woman, bribe the valet;
But know, that I her father play the Gryphon,
Tameless and sleepless, proof to fraud or bribe,
And guard the hidden treasure of her beauty.

THE SPANISH FATHER.

THE tenor of our tale carries us back to the Castle of Lochleven, where we take up the order of events on the same remarkable day on which Dryfesdale had been dismissed from the castle. It was past noon, the usual hour of dinner, yet no preparations seemed made for the Queen's entertainment. Mary herself had retired into her own apartment, where she was closely engaged in writing. Her attendants were together in the presence-chamber, and much disposed to speculate on the delay of the dinner; for it may be recollected that their breakfast had been interrupted. "I believe in my conscience," said the page, "that having found the poisoning scheme miscarry, by having gone to the wrong merchant for their deadly wares, they are now about to try how famine will work upon us."

Lady Fleming was somewhat alarmed at this surmise, but comforted herself by observing that the chimney of the kitchen had reeked that whole day in a manner which contradicted the supposition. — Catherine Seyton presently exclaimed, "They were bearing the dishes across the court, marshalled by the Lady Lochleven herself, dressed out in her highest and stiffest ruff, with her partlet and sleeves of cyprus, and her huge old-fashioned farthingale of crimson velvet."

"I believe on my word," said the page, approaching the window also, "it was in that very farthingale that she captivated the heart of gentle King Jamie, which procured our poor Queen her precious bargain of a brother."

"That may hardly be, Master Roland," answered the Lady Fleming, who was a great recorder of the changes of fashion, "since the farthingales came first in when the Queen Regent went to Saint Andrews, after the battle of Pinkie, and were then called *Vertugardins* ——"

She would have proceeded farther in this important discussion, but was interrupted by the entrance of the Lady of Lochleven, who preceded the servants bearing the dishes, and formally discharged the duty of tasting each of them. Lady Fleming regretted, in courtly phrase, that the Lady of Lochleven should have undertaken so troublesome an office."

"After the strange incident of this day, madam," said the Lady, "it is necessary for my honour and that of my son, that I partake whatever is offered to my involuntary guest. Please to inform the Lady Mary that I attend her commands."

"Her Majesty," replied Lady Fleming, with due emphasis on the word, "shall be informed that the Lady Lochleven waits."

Mary appeared instantly, and addressed her hostess with courtesy, which even approached to something more cordial. "This is nobly done, Lady Lochleven," she said; "for though we ourselves apprehend no danger under your roof, our ladies have been much alarmed by this morning's chance, and our meal will be the more cheerful for your presence and assurance. Please you to sit down."

The Lady Lochleven obeyed the Queen's commands, and Roland performed the office of carver and attendant as usual. But, notwithstanding what the Queen had said, the meal was silent and unsocial; and every effort which Mary made to excite some conversation, died away under the solemn and chill replies of the Lady of Lochleven. At length it became plain that the Queen, who had considered these advances as a condescension on her part, and who piqued herself justly on her powers of pleasing, became offended at the repulsive conduct of her hostess. After looking with a significant glance at Lady Fleming and Catherine, she slightly shrugged her shoulders, and remained silent. A pause ensued, at the end of which the Lady Douglas spoke:—"I perceive, madam, I am a check on the mirth of this fair company. I pray you to excuse me—I am a widow—alone here in a most perilous charge—deserted by my grandson—betrayed by my servant—I am little worthy of the grace you do me in offering me a seat at your table, where I am aware that wit and pastime are usually expected from the guests."

"If the Lady Lochleven is serious," said the Queen, "we wonder by what simplicity she expects our present meals to be seasoned with mirth. If she is a widow, she lives honoured and uncontrolled, at the head of her late husband's household. But I know at least of one widowed woman in the world, before whom the words desertion and betrayal ought never to be mentioned, since no one has been made so bitterly acquainted with their import."

"I meant not, madam, to remind you of your misfortunes, by the mention of mine," answered the Lady Lochleven, and there was again a deep silence.

Mary at length addressed Lady Fleming. "We can commit no deadly sins here, *ma bonne*, where we are so well warded and looked to; but if we could, this Carthusian silence might be useful as a kind of penance. If thou hast adjusted my wimple amiss, my Fleming, or if Catherine hath made a wry stitch in her broidery, when she was thinking of something else than her work, or if Roland Græme hath missed a wild-duck on the wing, and broke a quarrel-pane* of glass in the turret window, as chanced to him a week since, now is the time to think on your sins and to repent of them."

"Madam, I speak with all reverence," said the Lady Lochleven; "but I am old, and claim the privilege of age. Methinks your followers might find fitter subjects for repentance than the trifles you mention, and so mention—once more, I crave your pardon—as if you jested with sin and repentance both."

"You have been our taster, Lady Lochleven," said the Queen, "I perceive you would eke out your duty with that of our Father Confessor—and since you choose that our conversation should be serious, may I ask you why the Regent's promise—since your son so styles himself—has not been kept to me in that respect? From time to time this promise has been renewed, and as constantly broken. Methinks those who pretend themselves to so much gravity and sanctity, should not debar from others the religious succours which their consciences require."

* Diamond-shaped; literally, formed like the head of a *quarrel*, or arrow for the crossbow

"Madam, the Earl of Murray was indeed weak enough," said the Lady Lochleven, "to give so far way to your unhappy prejudices, and a religioner of the Pope presented himself on his part at our town of Kinross. But the Douglass is Lord of his own castle, and will not permit his threshold to be darkened, no not for a single moment, by an emissary belonging to the Bishop of Rome."

"Methinks it were well, then," said Mary, "that my Lord Regent would send me where there is less scruple and more charity."

"In this, madam," answered the Lady Lochleven, "you mistake the nature both of charity and of religion. Charity giveth to those who are in delirium the medicaments which may avail their health, but refuses those enticing cates and liquors which please the palate, but augment the disease."

"This your charity, Lady Lochleven, is pure cruelty, under the hypocritical disguise of friendly care. I am oppressed amongst you as if you meant the destruction both of my body and soul; but Heaven will not endure such iniquity for ever, and they who are the most active agents in it may speedily expect their reward."

At this moment Randal entered the apartment, with a look so much perturbed, that the Lady Fleming uttered a faint scream, the Queen was obviously startled, and the Lady of Lochleven, though too bold and proud to evince any marked signs of alarm, asked hastily what was the matter?

"Dryfesdale has been slain, madam," was the reply; "murdered as soon as he gained the dry land by young Master Henry Seyton."

It was now Catherine's turn to start and grow pale—"Has the murderer of the Douglas's vassal escaped?" was the Lady's hasty question.

"There was none to challenge him but old Keltie, and the carrier Auchtermuchty," replied Randal; "unlikely men to stay one of the frackest* youths in Scotland of his years, and who was sure to have friends and partakers at no great distance."

"Was the deed completed?" said the Lady.

"Done, and done thoroughly," said Randal; "a Seyton seldom strikes twice—But the body was not despoiled, and your honour's packet goes forward to Edinburgh by Auchtermuchty, who leaves Keltie-Bridge early to-morrow—marry, he has drunk two bottles of aquavitæ to put the fright out of his head, and now sleeps them off beside his cart-avers."†

There was a pause when this fatal tale was told. The Queen and Lady Douglas looked on each other, as if each thought how she could best turn the incident to her own advantage in the controversy, which was continually kept alive betwixt them—Catherine Seyton kept her kerchief at her eyes and wept.

"You see, madam, the bloody maxims and practice of the deluded Papists," said Lady Lochleven.

"Nay, madam," replied the Queen, "say rather you see the deserved judgment of Heaven upon a Calvinistical poisoner."

"Dryfesdale was not of the Church of Geneva, or of Scotland," said the Lady of Lochleven, hastily.

"He was a heretic, however," replied Mary; "there is but one true and unerring guide; the others lead alike into error."

"Well, madam, I trust it will reconcile you to your retreat, that this deed shows the temper of those who might wish you at liberty. Blood-thirsty tyrants, and cruel men-quellers are they all, from the Clan-Ranald and Clan-Tosach in the north, to the Fernihérst and Buccleuch in the south—the murdering Seytons in the east, and——"

"Methinks, madam, you forget that I am a Seyton?" said Catherine, withdrawing her kerchief from her face, which was now coloured with indignation.

---

* Boldest—most forward. † Cart-horses.

"If I had forgot it, fair mistress, your forward bearing would have reminded me," said Lady Lochleven.

"If my brother has slain the villain that would have poisoned his Sovereign, and his sister," said Catherine, "I am only so far sorry that he should have spared the hangman his proper task. For aught farther, had it been the best Douglas in the land, he would have been honoured in falling by the Seyton's sword."

"Farewell, gay mistress," said the Lady of Lochleven, rising to withdraw; "it is such maidens as you, who make giddy-fashioned revellers and deadly brawlers. Boys must needs rise, forsooth, in the grace of some sprightly damsel, who thinks to dance through life as through a French galliard." She then made her reverence to the Queen, and added, "Do you also, madam, fare you well, till curfew time, when I will make, perchance, more bold than welcome in attending upon your supper board.—Come with me, Randal, and tell me more of this cruel fact."

"'Tis an extraordinary chance," said the Queen, when she had departed; "and, villain as he was, I would this man had been spared time for repentance. We will cause something to be done for his soul, if we ever attain our liberty, and the Church will permit such grace to a heretic.—But, tell me, Catherine, *ma mignóne*—this brother of thine, who is so *frack*, as the fellow called him, bears he the same wonderful likeness to thee as formerly?"

"If your Grace means in temper, you know whether I am so *frack* as the serving-man spoke him."

"Nay, thou art prompt enough in all reasonable conscience," replied the Queen; "but thou art my own darling notwithstanding—But I meant, is this thy twin-brother as like thee in form and features as formerly? I remember thy dear mother alleged it as a reason for destining thee to the veil, that, were ye both to go at large, thou wouldst surely get the credit of some of thy brother's mad pranks."

"I believe, madam," said Catherine, "there are some unusually simple people even yet, who can hardly distinguish betwixt us, especially when, for diversion's sake, my brother hath taken a female dress,"—and as she spoke, she gave a quick glance at Roland Græme, to whom this conversation conveyed a ray of light, welcome as ever streamed into the dungeon of a captive through the door which opened to give him freedom.

"He must be a handsome cavalier this brother of thine, if he be so like you," replied Mary. "He was in France, I think, for these late years, so that I saw him not at Holyrood."

"His looks, madam, have never been much found fault with," answered Catherine Seyton; "but I would he had less of that angry and heady spirit which evil times have encouraged amongst our young nobles. God knows, I grudge not his life in your Grace's quarrel; and love him for the willingness with which he labours for your rescue. But wherefore should he brawl with an old ruffianly serving-man, and stain at once his name with such a broil, and his hands with the blood of an old and ignoble wretch?"

"Nay, be patient, Catherine; I will not have thee traduce my gallant young knight. With Henry for my knight, and Roland Græme for my trusty squire, methinks I am like a princess of romance, who may shortly set at defiance the dungeons and the weapons of all wicked sorcerers.—But my head aches with the agitation of the day. Take me *La Mer Des Histoires*, and resume where we left off on Wednesday.—Our Lady help thy head, girl, or rather may she help thy heart!—I asked thee for the Sea of Histories, and thou hast brought *La Cronique d'Amour*."

Once embarked upon the Sea of Histories, the Queen continued her labours with her needle, while Lady Fleming and Catherine read to her alternately for two hours.

As to Roland Græme, it is probable that he continued in secret intent upon the Chronicle of Love, notwithstanding the censure which the Queen seemed to pass upon that branch of study. He now remembered a thousand circumstances of voice and manner, which, had his own prepossession been less, must surely have discriminated the brother from the sister; and he felt ashamed, that, having as it were by heart every particular of Catherine's gestures, words, and manners, he should have thought her, notwithstanding her spirits and levity, capable of assuming the bold step, loud tones, and forward assurance, which accorded well enough with her brother's hasty and masculine character. He endeavoured repeatedly to catch a glance of Catherine's eye, that he might judge how she was disposed to look upon him since he had made the discovery, but he was unsuccessful; for Catherine, when she was not reading herself, seemed to take so much interest in the exploits of the Teutonic knights against the Heathens of Esthonia and Livonia, that he could not surprise her eye even for a second. But when, closing the book, the Queen commanded their attendance in the garden, Mary, perhaps of set purpose, (for Roland's anxiety could not escape so practised an observer,) afforded him a favourable opportunity of accosting his mistress. The Queen commanded them to a little distance, while she engaged Lady Fleming in a particular and private conversation; the subject whereof we learn, from another authority, to have been the comparative excellence of the high standing ruff and the falling band. Roland must have been duller, and more sheepish than ever was youthful lover, if he had not endeavoured to avail himself of this opportunity.

"I have been longing this whole evening to ask of you, fair Catherine," said the page, "how foolish and unapprehensive you must have thought me, in being capable to mistake betwixt your brother and you?"

"The circumstance does indeed little honour to my rustic manners," said Catherine, "since those of a wild young man were so readily mistaken for mine. But I shall grow wiser in time; and with that view I am determined not to think of your follies, but to correct my own."

"It will be the lighter subject of meditation of the two," said Roland.

"I know not that," said Catherine, very gravely; "I fear we have been both unpardonably foolish."

"I have been mad," said Roland, "unpardonably mad. But you, lovely Catherine——"

"I," said Catherine, in the same tone of unusual gravity, "have too long suffered you to use such expressions towards me—I fear I can permit it no longer, and I blame myself for the pain it may give you."

"And what can have happened so suddenly to change our relation to each other, or alter, with such sudden cruelty, your whole deportment to me?"

"I can hardly tell," replied Catherine, "unless it is that the events of the day have impressed on my mind the necessity of our observing more distance to each other. A chance similar to that which betrayed to you the existence of my brother, may make known to Henry the terms you have used to me; and, alas! his whole conduct, as well as his deed this day, makes me too justly apprehensive of the consequences."

"Fear nothing for that, fair Catherine," answered the page; "I am well able to protect myself against risks of that nature."

"That is to say," replied she, "that you would fight with my twin-brother to show your regard for his sister? I have heard the Queen say, in her sad hours, that men are, in love or in hate, the most selfish animals of creation; and your carelessness in this matter looks very like it. But be not so much abashed — you are no worse than others."

"You do me injustice, Catherine," replied the page, "I thought but of being threatened with a sword, and did not remember in whose hand your fancy had placed it. If your brother stood before me, with his drawn weapon in his hand, so like as he is to you in word, person, and favour, he might shed my life's blood ere I could find in my heart to resist him to his injury."

"Alas!" said she, "it is not my brother alone. But you remember only the singular circumstances in which we have met in equality, and I may say in intimacy. You think not, that whenever I re-enter my father's house, there is a gulf between us you may not pass, but with peril of your life.—Your only known relative is of wild and singular habits, of a hostile and broken clan*—the rest of your lineage unknown—forgive me that I speak what is the undeniable truth."

"Love, my beautiful Catherine, despises genealogies," answered Roland Græme.

"Love may, but so will not the Lord Seyton," rejoined the damsel.

"The Queen, thy mistress and mine, she will intercede. Oh! drive me not from you at the moment I thought myself most happy!—and if I shall aid her deliverance, said not yourself that you and she would become my debtors?"

"All Scotland will become your debtors," said Catherine; "but for the active effects you might hope from our gratitude, you must remember I am wholly subjected to my father; and the poor Queen is, for a long time, more likely to be dependant on the pleasure of the nobles of her party, than possessed of power to control them."

"Be it so," replied Roland; "my deeds shall control prejudice itself—it is a bustling world, and I will have my share. The Knight of Avenel, high as he now stands, rose from as obscure an origin as mine."

"Ay!" said Catherine, "there spoke the doughty knight of romance, that will cut his way to the imprisoned princess, through fiends and fiery dragons!"

"But if I can set the princess at large, and procure her the freedom of her own choice," said the page, "where, dearest Catherine, will that choice alight?"

"Release the princess from duresse, and she will tell you," said the damsel; and breaking off the conversation abruptly, she joined the Queen so suddenly, that Mary exclaimed, half aloud—

"No more tidings of evil import—no dissension, I trust, in my limited household?"—Then looking on Catherine's blushing cheek, and Roland's expanded brow and glancing eye—"No—no," she said, "I see all is well—*Ma petite mignóne*, go to my apartment and fetch me down—let me see—ay, fetch my pomander box."

And having thus disposed of her attendant in the manner best qualified to hide her confusion, the Queen added, speaking apart to Roland, "I should at least have two grateful subjects of Catherine and you; for what sovereign but Mary would aid true love so willingly?—Ay, you lay your hand on your sword—your *petite flamberge à rien* there—Well, short time will show if all the good be true that is protested to us—I hear them toll curfew from Kinross. To our chamber—this old dame hath promised to be with us again at our evening meal. Were it not for the hope of speedy deliverance, her presence would drive me distracted. But I will be patient."

"I profess," said Catherine, who just then entered, "I would I could be Henry, with all a man's privileges, for one moment—I long to throw my plate at that confect of pride and formality, and ill-nature."

The Lady Fleming reprimanded her young companion for this explosion of impatience; the Queen laughed, and they went to the presence-chamber, where almost immediately entered supper, and the Lady of the castle. The Queen, strong in her prudent resolutions, endured her presence with great fortitude and equanimity, until her patience was disturbed by a new form, which had hitherto made no part of the ceremonial of the castle. When

* A broken clan was one who had no chief able to find security for their good behaviour—a clan of outlaws; and the Græmes of the Debateable Land were in that condition.

the other attendant had retired, Randal entered, bearing the keys of the castle fastened upon a chain, and, announcing that the watch was set, and the gates locked, delivered the keys with all reverence to the Lady of Lochleven.

The Queen and her ladies exchanged with each other a look of disappointment, anger, and vexation; and Mary said aloud, "We cannot regret the smallness of our court, when we see our hostess discharge in person so many of its offices. In addition to her charges of principal steward of our household and grand almoner, she has to-night done duty as captain of our guard."

"And will continue to do so in future, madam," answered the Lady Lochleven, with much gravity; "the history of Scotland may teach me how ill the duty is performed, which is done by an accredited deputy — We have heard, madam, of favourites of later date, and as little merit, as Oliver Sinclair."*

"Oh, madam," replied the Queen, "my father had his female as well as his male favourites — there were the Ladies Sandilands and Olifaunt,† and some others, methinks; but their names cannot survive in the memory of so grave a person as you."

The Lady Lochleven looked as if she could have slain the Queen on the spot, but commanded her temper and retired from the apartment, bearing in her hand the ponderous bunch of keys.

"Now God be praised for that woman's youthful frailty!" said the Queen. "Had she not that weak point in her character, I might waste my words on her in vain — But that stain is the very reverse of what is said of the witch's mark — I can make her feel there, though she is otherwise insensible all over. — But how say you, girls — here is a new difficulty. — How are these keys to be come by? — there is no deceiving or bribing this dragon, I trow."

"May I crave to know," said Roland, "whether, if your Grace were beyond the walls of the castle, you could find means of conveyance to the firm land, and protection when you are there?"

"Trust us for that, Roland," said the Queen; "for to that point our scheme is indifferent well laid."

"Then if your Grace will permit me to speak my mind, I think I could be of some use in this matter."

"As how, my good youth? — speak on," said the Queen, "and fearlessly."

"My patron the Knight of Avenel used to compel the youth educated in his household to learn the use of axe and hammer, and working in wood and iron — he used to speak of old northern champions, who forged their own weapons, and of the Highland Captain, Donald nan Ord, or Donald of the Hammer, whom he himself knew, and who used to work at the anvil with a sledge-hammer in each hand. Some said he praised this art, because he was himself of churl's blood. However, I gained some practice in it, as the Lady Catherine Seyton partly knows; for since we were here, I wrought her a silver brooch."

"Ay," replied Catharine, "but you should tell her Grace that your workmanship was so indifferent that it broke to pieces next day, and I flung it away."

"Believe her not, Roland," said the Queen; "she wept when it was broken, and put the fragments into her bosom. But for your scheme — could your skill avail to forge a second set of keys?"

"No, madam, because I know not the wards. But I am convinced I could make a set so like that hateful bunch which the Lady bore off even now, that could they be exchanged against them by any means, she would never dream she was possessed of the wrong."

---

* A favourite, and said to be an unworthy one, of James V.

† The names of these ladies, and a third frail favourite of James, are preserved in an epigram too *gaillard* for quotation.

"And the good dame, thank Heaven, is somewhat blind," said the Queen; "but then for a forge, my boy, and the means of labouring unobserved?"

"The armourer's forge, at which I used sometimes to work with him, is the round vault at the bottom of the turret—he was dismissed with the warder for being supposed too much attached to George Douglas. The people are accustomed to see me work there, and I warrant I shall find some excuse that will pass current with them for putting bellows and anvil to work."

"The scheme has a promising face," said the Queen; "about it, my lad, with all speed, and beware the nature of your work is not discovered."

"Nay, I will take the liberty to draw the bolt against chance visiters, so that I will have time to put away what I am working upon, before I undo the door."

"Will not that of itself attract suspicion, in a place where it is so current already?" said Catherine.

"Not a whit," replied Roland; "Gregory the armourer, and every good hammerman, locks himself in when he is about some master piece of craft. Besides, something must be risked."

"Part we then to-night," said the Queen, "and God bless you my children!—If Mary's head ever rises above water, you shall all rise along with her."

Chapter the Thirty-Fifth.

It is a time of danger, not of revel,
When churchmen turn to masquers.

SPANISH FATHER.

THE enterprise of Roland Græme appeared to prosper. A trinket or two, of which the work did not surpass the substance, (for the materials were silver, supplied by the Queen,) were judiciously presented to those most likely to be inquisitive into the labours of the forge and anvil, which they thus were induced to reckon profitable to others and harmless in itself. Openly, the page was seen working about such trifles. In private, he forged a number of keys resembling so nearly in weight and in form those which were presented every evening to the Lady Lochleven, that, on a slight inspection, it would have been difficult to perceive the difference. He brought them to the dark rusty colour by the use of salt and water; and, in the triumph of his art, presented them at length to Queen Mary in her presence-chamber, about an hour before the tolling of the curfew. She looked at them with pleasure, but at the same time with doubt.—"I allow," she said, "that the Lady Lochleven's eyes, which are not of the clearest, may be well deceived, could we pass those keys on her in place of the real implements of her tyranny. But how is this to be done, and which of my little court dare attempt this *tour de jongleur* with any chance of success? Could we but engage her in some earnest matter of argument—but those which I hold with her, always have been of a kind which make her grasp her keys the faster, as if she said to herself—Here I hold what sets me above your taunts and reproaches—And even for her liberty, Mary Stuart could not stoop to speak the proud heretic fair.—What shall we do? Shall Lady Fleming try her eloquence in describing the last new head-tire from Paris?—alas! the good dame has not changed the fashion of her head-gear since Pinkie-field, for aught that I know. Shall my *mignóne* Catherine sing to her one of those touching airs, which draw the very souls out of me and Roland Græme?—Alas! Dame Margaret Douglas would rather hear a Huguenot psalm of Clement Marrot, sung to the tune of *Réveillez vous, belle endormie.*—Cousins and liege counsellors, what is to be done, for our wits are really astray in this matter?—Must our man-at-arms and the champion of our body, Roland Græme, manfully assault the old lady, and take the keys from her *par voie du fait?*"

"Nay! with your Grace's permission," said Roland, "I do not doubt being able to manage the matter with more discretion; for though, in your Grace's service, I do not fear——"

"A host of old women," interrupted Catherine, "each armed with rock and spindle, yet he has no fancy for pikes and partisans, which might rise at the cry of *Help! a Douglas, a Douglas!*"

"They that do not fear fair ladies' tongues," continued the page, "need dread nothing else.—But, gracious Liege, I am well-nigh satisfied that I could pass the exchange of these keys on the Lady Lochleven; but I dread the sentinel who is now planted nightly in the garden, which, by necessity, we must traverse."

"Our last advices from our friends on the shore have promised us assistance in that matter," replied the Queen.

"And is your Grace well assured of the fidelity and watchfulness of those without?"

"For their fidelity, I will answer with my life, and for their vigilance, I will answer with my life—I will give thee instant proof, my faithful Roland, that they are ingenuous and trusty as thyself. Come hither—Nay, Catherine, attend us; we carry not so deft a page into our private chamber alone. Make fast the door of the parlour, Fleming, and warn us if you hear the least step—or stay, go thou to the door, Catherine," (in a whisper, "thy ears and thy wits are both sharper.)—Good Fleming, attend us thyself"—(and again she whispered, "her reverend presence will be as safe a watch on Roland as thine can—so be not jealous, *mignóne.*")

Thus speaking, they were lighted by the Lady Fleming into the Queen's bedroom, a small apartment enlightened by a projecting window.

"Look from that window, Roland," she said; "see you amongst the several lights which begin to kindle, and to glimmer palely through the gray of the evening from the village of Kinross—seest thou, I say, one solitary spark apart from the others, and nearer it seems to the verge of the water?—It is no brighter at this distance than the torch of the poor glow-worm, and yet, my good youth, that light is more dear to Mary Stuart, than every star that twinkles in the blue vault of heaven. By that signal, I know that more than one true heart is plotting my deliverance; and without that consciousness, and the hope of freedom it gives me, I had long since stooped to my fate, and died of a broken heart. Plan after plan has been formed and abandoned, but still the light glimmers; and while it glimmers, my hope lives.—Oh! how many evenings have I sat musing in despair over our ruined schemes, and scarce hoping that I should again see that blessed signal; when it has suddenly kindled, and, like the lights of Saint Elmo in a tempest, brought hope and consolation, where there was only dejection and despair!"

"If I mistake not," answered Roland, "the candle shines from the house of Blinkhoolie, the mail-gardener."

"Thou hast a good eye," said the Queen; "it is there where my trusty lieges—God and the saints pour blessings on them!—hold consultation for my deliverance. The voice of a wretched captive would die on these blue waters, long ere it could mingle in their councils; and yet I can hold communication—I will confide the whole to thee—I am about to ask those faithful friends if the moment for the great attempt is nigh.—Place the lamp in the window, Fleming."

She obeyed, and immediately withdrew it. No sooner had she done so, than the light in the cottage of the gardener disappeared.

"Now count," said Queen Mary, "for my heart beats so thick that I cannot count myself."

The Lady Fleming began deliberately to count one, two, three, and when she had arrived at ten, the light on the shore showed its pale twinkle.

"Now, our Lady be praised!" said the Queen; "it was but two nights since, that the absence of the light remained while I could tell thirty. The hour of deliverance approaches. May God bless those who labour in it with such truth to me! — alas! with such hazard to themselves — and bless you, too, my children! — Come, we must to the audience-chamber again. Our absence might excite suspicion, should they serve supper."

They returned to the presence-chamber, and the evening concluded as usual.

The next morning, at dinner-time, an unusual incident occurred. While Lady Douglas of Lochleven performed her daily duty of assistant and taster at the Queen's table, she was told a man-at-arms had arrived, recommended by her son, but without any letter or other token than what he brought by word of mouth.

"Hath he given you that token?" demanded the Lady.

"He reserved it, as I think, for your Ladyship's ear," replied Randal.

"He doth well," said the Lady; "tell him to wait in the hall—But no—with your permission, madam," (to the Queen) "let him attend me here."

"Since you are pleased to receive your domestics in my presence," said the Queen, "I cannot choose ——"

"My infirmities must plead my excuse, madam," replied the Lady; "the life I must lead here ill suits with the years which have passed over my head, and compels me to waive ceremonial."

"Oh, my good Lady," replied the Queen, "I would there were nought in this your castle more strongly compulsive than the cobweb chains of ceremony; but bolts and bars are harder matters to contend with."

As she spoke, the person announced by Randal entered the room, and Roland Græme at once recognized in him the Abbot Ambrosius.

"What is your name, good fellow?" said the Lady.

"Edward Glendinning," answered the Abbot, with a suitable reverence.

"Art thou of the blood of the Knight of Avenel?" said the Lady of Lochleven.

"Ay, madam, and that nearly," replied the pretended soldier.

"It is likely enough," said the Lady, "for the Knight is the son of his own good works, and has risen from obscure lineage to his present high rank in the Estate — But he is of sure truth and approved worth, and his kinsman is welcome to us. You hold, unquestionably, the true faith?"

"Do not doubt of it, madam," said the disguised churchman.

"Hast thou a token to me from Sir William Douglas?" said the Lady.

"I have, madam," replied he; "but it must be said in private."

"Thou art right," said the Lady, moving towards the recess of a window; "say in what does it consist?"

"In the words of an old bard," replied the Abbot.

"Repeat them," answered the Lady; and he uttered, in a low tone, the lines from an old poem, called The Howlet,—

"O Douglas! Douglas!
Tender and true."

"Trusty Sir John Holland!"* said the Lady Douglas, apostrophizing the poet, "a kinder heart never inspired a rhyme, and the Douglas's honour was ever on thy heart-string! We receive you among our followers, Glendin-

* Sir John Holland's poem of the Howlet is known to collectors by the beautiful edition presented to the Bannatyne Club, by Mr. David Laing.

ning—But, Randal, see that he keep the outer ward only, till we shall hear more touching him from our son.—Thou fearest not the night air, Glendinning?"

"In the cause of the Lady before whom I stand, I fear nothing, madam," answered the disguised Abbot.

"Our garrison, then, is stronger by one trustworthy soldier," said the matron—"Go to the buttery, and let them make much of thee."

When the Lady Lochleven had retired, the Queen said to Roland Græme, who was now almost constantly in her company, "I spy comfort in that stranger's countenance; I know not why it should be so, but I am well persuaded he is a friend."

"Your Grace's penetration does not deceive you," answered the page; and he informed her that the Abbot of St. Mary's himself played the part of the newly arrived soldier.

"The Queen crossed herself and looked upwards. "Unworthy sinner that I am," she said, "that for my sake a man so holy, and so high in spiritual office, should wear the garb of a base sworder, and run the risk of dying the death of a traitor!"

"Heaven will protect its own servant, madam," said Catherine Seyton; "his aid would bring a blessing on our undertaking, were it not already blest for its own sake."

"What I admire in my spiritual father," said Roland, "was the steady front with which he looked on me, without giving the least sign of former acquaintance. I did not think the like was possible, since I have ceased to believe that Henry was the same person with Catherine."

"But marked you not how astuciously the good father," said the Queen, "eluded the questions of the woman Lochleven, telling her the very truth, which yet she received not as such?"

Roland thought in his heart, that when the truth was spoken for the purpose of deceiving, it was little better than a lie in disguise. But it was no time to agitate such questions of conscience.

"And now for the signal from the shore," exclaimed Catherine; "my bosom tells me we shall see this night two lights instead of one gleam from that garden of Eden—And then, Roland, do you play your part manfully, and we will dance on the greensward like midnight fairies!"

Catherine's conjecture misgave not, nor deceived her. In the evening two beams twinkled from the cottage, instead of one; and the page heard, with beating heart, that the new retainer was ordered to stand sentinel on the outside of the castle. When he intimated this news to the Queen, she held her hand out to him—he knelt, and when he raised it to his lips in all dutiful homage, he found it was damp and cold as marble. "For God's sake, madam, droop not now,—sink not now!"

"Call upon our Lady, my Liege," said the Lady Fleming—"call upon your tutelar saint."

"Call the spirits of the hundred kings you are descended from," exclaimed the page; "in this hour of need, the resolution of a monarch were worth the aid of a hundred saints."

"Oh! Roland Græme," said Mary, in a tone of deep despondency, "be true to me—many have been false to me. Alas! I have not always been true to myself. My mind misgives me that I shall die in bondage, and that this bold attempt will cost all our lives. It was foretold me by a soothsayer in France, that I should die in prison, and by a violent death, and here comes the hour—Oh, would to God it found me prepared!"

"Madam," said Catherine Seyton, "remember you are a Queen. Better we all died in bravely attempting to gain our freedom, than remained here to be poisoned, as men rid them of the noxious vermin that haunt old houses."

"You are right, Catherine," said the Queen; "and Mary will bear her like herself. But alas! your young and buoyant spirit can ill spell the causes which have broken mine. Forgive me, my children, and farewell for a while—I will prepare both mind and body for this awful venture."

They separated, till again called together by the tolling of the curfew. The Queen appeared grave, but firm and resolved; the Lady Fleming, with the art of an experienced courtier, knew perfectly how to disguise her inward tremors; Catherine's eye was fired, as if with the boldness of the project, and the half smile which dwelt upon her beautiful mouth seemed to contemn all the risk and all the consequences of discovery; Roland, who felt how much success depended on his own address and boldness, summoned together his whole presence of mind, and if he found his spirits flag for a moment, cast his eye upon Catherine, whom he thought he had never seen look so beautiful. — "I may be foiled," he thought, "but with this reward in prospect, they must bring the devil to aid them ere they cross me." Thus resolved, he stood like a greyhound in the slips, with hand, heart, and eye intent upon making and seizing opportunity for the execution of their project.

The keys had, with the wonted ceremonial, been presented to the Lady Lochleven. She stood with her back to the casement, which, like that of the Queen's apartment, commanded a view of Kinross, with the church, which stands at some distance from the town, and nearer to the lake, then connected with the town by straggling cottages. With her back to this casement, then, and her face to the table, on which the keys lay for an instant while she tasted the various dishes which were placed there, stood the Lady of Lochleven, more provokingly intent than usual — so at least it seemed to her prisoners — upon the huge and heavy bunch of iron, the implements of their restraint. Just when, having finished her ceremony as taster of the Queen's table, she was about to take up the keys, the page, who stood beside her, and had handed her the dishes in succession, looked sideways to the churchyard, and exclaimed he saw corpse-candles in the churchyard. The Lady of Lochleven was not without a touch, though a slight one, of the superstitions of the time; the fate of her sons made her alive to omens, and a corpse-light, as it was called, in the family burial-place boded death. She turned her head towards the casement — saw a distant glimmering — forgot her charge for one second, and in that second were lost the whole fruits of her former vigilance. The page held the forged keys under his cloak, and with great dexterity exchanged them for the real ones. His utmost address could not prevent a slight clash as he took up the latter bunch. "Who touches the keys?" said the Lady; and while the page answered that the sleeve of his cloak had stirred them, she looked round, possessed herself of the bunch which now occupied the place of the genuine keys, and again turned to gaze on the supposed corpse-candles.

"I hold these gleams," she said, after a moment's consideration, "to come, not from the churchyard, but from the hut of the old gardener Blinkhoolie. I wonder what thrift that churl drives, that of late he hath ever had light in his house till the night grew deep. I thought him an industrious, peaceful man — If he turns resetter of idle companions and night-walkers, the place must be rid of him."

"He may work his baskets perchance," said the page, desirous to stop the train of her suspicion.

"Or nets, may he not?" answered the Lady.

"Ay, madam," said Roland, "for trout and salmon."

"Or for fools and knaves," replied the Lady: "but this shall be looked after to-morrow. — I wish your Grace and your company a good evening. — Randal, attend us." And Randal, who waited in the antechamber after having surrendered his bunch of keys, gave his escort to his mistress as usual, while, leaving the Queen's apartments, she retired to her own.

"To-morrow," said the page, rubbing his hands with glee as he repeated the Lady's last words, "fools look to-morrow, and wise folk use to-night.—May I pray you, my gracious Liege, to retire for one half hour, until all the castle is composed to rest? I must go and rub with oil these blessed implements of our freedom. Courage and constancy, and all will go well, provided our friends on the shore fail not to send the boat you spoke of."

"Fear them not," said Catherine, "they are true as steel—if our dear mistress do but maintain her noble and royal courage." *

"Doubt not me, Catherine," replied the Queen; "a while since I was overborne, but I have recalled the spirit of my earlier and more sprightly days, when I used to accompany my armed nobles, and wish to be myself a man, to know what life it was to be in the fields with sword and buckler, jack, and knapscap."

"Oh, the lark lives not a gayer life, nor sings a lighter and gayer song than the merry soldier," answered Catherine. "Your Grace shall be in the midst of them soon, and the look of such a liege Sovereign will make each of your host worth three in the hour of need:—but I must to my task."

"We have but brief time," said Queen Mary; "one of the two lights in the cottage is extinguished—that shows the boat is put off."

"They will row very slow," said the page, "or kent where depth permits, to avoid noise.—To our several tasks—I will communicate with the good Father."

At the dead hour of midnight, when all was silent in the castle, the page put the key into the lock of the wicket which opened into the garden, and which was at the bottom of a staircase which descended from the Queen's apartment. "Now, turn smooth and softly, thou good bolt," said he, "if ever oil softened rust!" and his precautions had been so effectual, that the bolt revolved with little or no sound of resistance. He ventured not to cross the threshold, but exchanging a word with the disguised Abbot, asked if the boat were ready?

"This half hour," said the sentinel. "She lies beneath the wall, too close under the islet to be seen by the warder, but I fear she will hardly escape his notice in putting off again."

"The darkness," said the page, "and our profound silence, may take her off unobserved, as she came in. Hildebrand has the watch on the tower—a heavy-headed knave, who holds a can of ale to be the best headpiece upon a night-watch. He sleeps, for a wager."

"Then bring the Queen," said the Abbot, "and I will call Henry Seyton to assist them to the boat."

On tiptoe, with noiseless step and suppressed breath, trembling at every rustle of their own apparel, one after another the fair prisoners glided down the winding stair, under the guidance of Roland Græme, and were received at the wicket-gate by Henry Seyton and the churchman. The former seemed instantly to take upon himself the whole direction of the enterprise. "My Lord Abbot," he said, "give my sister your arm—I will conduct the Queen—and that youth will have the honour to guide Lady Fleming."

This was no time to dispute the arrangement, although it was not that

---

* In the dangerous expedition to Aberdeenshire, Randolph, the English Ambassador, gives Cecil the following account of Queen Mary's demeanour:—

"In all those garbulles, I assure your honour, I never saw the Queen merrier, never dismayed; nor never thought I that stomache to be in her that I find. She repented nothing but, when the Lords and others, at Inverness, came in the morning from the watches, that she was not a man, to know what life it was to lye all night in the fields, or to walk upon the causeway with a jack and a knaps-cap, a Glasgow buckler, and a broadsword."—RANDOLPH *to* CECIL, *September* 18, 1562.

The writer of the above letter seems to have felt the same impression which Catherine Seyton, in the text, considered as proper to the Queen's presence among her armed subjects.

"Though we neither thought nor looked for other than on that day to have fought or never—what desperate blows would not have been given, when every man should have fought in the sight of so noble a Queen, and so many fair ladies, our enemies to have taken them from us, and we to save our honours, not to be reft of them, your honour can easily judge."—*The same to the same, September* 24, 1562.

which Roland Græme would have chosen. Catherine Seyton, who well knew the garden path, tripped on before like a sylph, rather leading the Abbot than receiving assistance — the Queen, her native spirit prevailing over female fear, and a thousand painful reflections, moved steadily forward, by the assistance of Henry Seyton — while the Lady Fleming, encumbered with her fears and her helplessness Roland Græme, who followed in the rear, and who bore under the other arm a packet of necessaries belonging to the Queen. The door of the garden, which communicated with the shore of the islet, yielded to one of the keys of which Roland had possessed himself, although not until he had tried several, — a moment of anxious terror and expectation. The ladies were then partly led, partly carried, to the side of the lake, where a boat with six rowers attended them, the men couched along the bottom to secure them from observation. Henry Seyton placed the Queen in the stern; the Abbot offered to assist Catherine, but she was seated by the Queen's side before he could utter his proffer of help; and Roland Græme was just lifting Lady Fleming over the boat-side, when a thought suddenly occurred to him, and exclaiming, "Forgotten, forgotten! wait for me but one half-minute," he replaced on the shore the helpless Lady of the bed-chamber, threw the Queen's packet into the boat, and sped back through the garden with the noiseless speed of a bird on the wing.

"By Heaven, he is false at last!" said Seyton; "I ever feared it!"

"He is as true," said Catherine, "as Heaven itself, and that I will maintain."

"Be silent, minion," said her brother, "for shame, if not for fear — Fellows, put off, and row for your lives!"

"Help me, help me on board!" said the deserted Lady Fleming, and that louder than prudence warranted.

"Put off — put off!" cried Henry Seyton; "leave all behind, so the Queen is safe."

"Will you permit this, madam?" said Catherine, imploringly; "you leave your deliverer to death."

"I will not," said the Queen.—"Seyton I command you to stay at every risk."

"Pardon me, madam, if I disobey," said the intractable young man; and with one hand lifting in Lady Fleming, he began himself to push off the boat.

She was two fathoms' length from the shore, and the rowers were getting her head round, when Roland Græme, arriving, bounded from the beach, and attained the boat, overturning Seyton, on whom he lighted. The youth swore a deep but suppressed oath, and stopping Græme as he stepped towards the stern, said, "Your place is not with high-born dames — keep at the head and trim the vessel — Now give way — give way — Row, for God and the Queen!"

The rowers obeyed, and began to pull vigorously.

"Why did ye not muffle the oars?" said Roland Græme; "the dash must awaken the sentinel — Row, lads, and get out of reach of shot; for had not old Hildebrand, the warder, supped upon poppy-porridge, this whispering must have waked him."

"It was all thine own delay," said Seyton; "thou shalt reckon with me hereafter for that and other matters."

But Roland's apprehension was verified too instantly to permit him to reply. The sentinel, whose slumbering had withstood the whispering, was alarmed by the dash of the oars. His challenge was instantly heard. "A boat — a boat! — bring to, or I shoot!" And, as they continued to ply their oars, he called aloud, "Treason! treason!" rung the bell of the castle, and discharged his harquebuss at the boat. The ladies crowded on each other like startled wild foul, at the flash and report of the piece, while the men urged the rowers to the utmost speed. They heard more than one ball whiz along the surface of the lake, at no great distance from their little bark; and from the lights, which glanced like meteors from window to window, it was evident the whole castle was alarmed, and their escape discovered.

"Pull!" again exclaimed Seyton; "stretch to your oars, or I will spur you to the task with my dagger — they will launch a boat immediately."

"That is cared for," said Roland; "I locked gate and wicket on them when I went back, and no boat will stir from the island this night, if doors of good oak and bolts of iron can keep men within stone-walls.—And now I resign my office of porter of Lochleven, and give the keys to the Kelpie's keeping."

As the heavy keys plunged in the lake, the Abbot, who till then had been repeating his prayers, exclaimed, "Now, bless thee, my son! for thy ready prudence puts shame on us all."*

"I knew," said Mary, drawing her breath more freely, as they were now out of reach of the musketry — "I knew my squire's truth, promptitude, and sagacity. — I must have him my dear friends with my no less true knights, Douglas and Seyton — but where, then, is Douglas?"

"Here, madam," answered the deep and melancholy voice of the boatman who sat next her, and who acted as steersman.

"Alas! was it you who stretched your body before me," said the Queen, "when the balls were raining around us?"

"Believe you," said he, in a low tone, "that Douglas would have resigned to any one the chance of protecting his Queen's life with his own?"

The dialogue was here interrupted by a shot or two from one of those small pieces of artillery called falconets, then used in defending castles. The shot was too vague to have any effect, but the broader flash, the deeper sound, the louder return which was made by the midnight echoes of Bennarty, terrified and imposed silence on the liberated prisoners. The boat was alongside of a rude quay or landing-place, running out from a garden

---

* It is well known that the escape of Queen Mary from Lochleven was effected by George Douglas, the youngest brother of Sir William Douglas, the lord of the castle; but the minute circumstances of the event have been a good deal confused, owing to two agents having been concerned in it who bore the same name. It has been always supposed that George Douglas was induced to abet Mary's escape by the ambitious hope that, by such service, he might merit her hand. But his purpose was discovered by his brother Sir William, and he was expelled from the castle. He continued, notwithstanding, to hover in the neighbourhood, and maintain a correspondence with the royal prisoner and others in the fortress.

If we believe the English ambassador Drury, the Queen was grateful to George Douglas, and even proposed a marriage with him; a scheme which could hardly be serious, since she was still the wife of Bothwell, but which, if suggested at all, might be with a purpose of gratifying the Regent Murray's ambition, and propitiating his favour; since he was, it must be remembered, the brother uterine of George Douglas, for whom such high honour was said to be designed.

The proposal, if seriously made, was treated as inadmissible, and Mary again resumed her purpose of escape. Her failure in her first attempt has some picturesque particulars, which might have been advantageously introduced in fictitious narrative. Drury sends Cecil the following account of the matter:—

"But after, upon the 25th of the last, (April 1567,) she interprised an escape, and was the rather near effect, through her accustomed long lying in bed all the morning. The manner of it was thus: there cometh in to her the laundress early as other times before she was wanted, and the Queen according to such a secret practice putteth on her the hood of the laundress, and so with the fardel of clothes and the muffler upon her face, passeth out and entereth the boat to pass the Loch; which, after some space, one of them that rowed said merrily, 'Let us see what manner of dame this is,' and therewith offered to pull down her muffler, which to defend, she put up her hands, which they spied to be very fair and white; wherewith they entered into suspicion whom she was, beginning to wonder at her enterprise. Whereat she was little dismayed, but charged them, upon danger of their lives, to row her over to the shore, which they nothing regarded, but eftsoons rowed her back again, promising her it should be secreted, and especially from the lord of the house, under whose guard she lyeth. It seemeth she knew her refuge, and where to have found it if she had once landed; for there did, and yet do linger, at a little village called Kinross, hard at the Loch side, the same George Douglas, one Sempel and one Beton, the which two were sometime her trusty servants, and, as yet appeareth, they mind her no less affection."—*Bishop Keith's History of the Affairs of Church and State in Scotland*, p. 490.

Notwithstanding this disappointment, little spoke of by historians, Mary renewed her attempts to escape. There was in the Castle of Lochleven a lad, named William Douglas, some relation probably of the baron, and about eighteen years old. This youth proved as accessible to Queen Mary's prayers and promises, as was the brother of his patron, George Douglas, from whom this William must be carefully kept distinct. It was young William who played the part commonly assigned to his superior, George, stealing the keys of the castle from the table on which they lay, while his lord was at supper. He let the Queen and a waiting woman out of the apartment where they were secured, and out of the tower itself, embarked with them in a small skiff, and rowed them to the shore. To prevent instant pursuit, he, for precaution's sake, locked the iron grated door of the tower, and threw the keys into the lake. They found George Douglas and the Queen's servant, Beton, waiting for them, and Lord Seyton and James Hamilton of Orbeiston in attendance, at the head of a party of faithful followers, with whom they fled to Niddrie Castle, and from thence to Hamilton.

In narrating this romantic story, both history and tradition confuse the two Douglasses together, and confer on George the successful execution of the escape from the castle, the merit of which belongs, in reality, to the boy called William, or, more frequently, the Little Douglas, either from his youth or his slight stature. The reader will observe, that in the romance, the part of the Little Douglas has been assigned to Roland Græme. In another case, it would be tedious to point out in a work of amusement such minute points of historical fact; but the general interest taken in the fate of Queen Mary, renders every thing of consequence which connects itself with her misfortunes

of considerable extent, ere any of them again attempted to speak. They landed, and while the Abbot returned thanks aloud to Heaven, which had thus far favoured their enterprise, Douglas enjoyed the best reward of his desperate undertaking, in conducting the Queen to the house of the gardener. Yet, not unmindful of Roland Græme even in that moment of terror and exhaustion, Mary expressly commanded Seyton to give his assistance to Fleming, while Catherine voluntarily, and without bidding, took the arm of the page. Seyton presently resigned Lady Fleming to the care of the Abbot, alleging, he must look after their horses; and his attendants, disencumbering themselves of their boat-cloaks, hastened to assist him.

While Mary spent in the gardener's cottage the few minutes which were necessary to prepare the steeds for their departure, she perceived, in a corner, the old man to whom the garden belonged, and called him to approach. He came as it were with reluctance.

"How, brother," said the Abbot, "so slow to welcome thy royal Queen and mistress to liberty and to her kingdom!"

The old man, thus admonished, came forward, and, in good terms of speech, gave her Grace joy of her deliverance. The Queen returned him thanks in the most gracious manner, and added, "It will remain to us to offer some immediate reward for your fidelity, for we wot well your house has been long the refuge in which our trusty servants have met to concert measures for our freedom." So saying, she offered gold, and added, "We will consider your services more fully hereafter."

"Kneel, brother," said the Abbot, "kneel instantly, and thank her Grace's kindness."

"Good brother, that wert once a few steps under me, and art still many years younger," replied the gardener, pettishly, "let me do mine acknowledgments in my own way. Queens have knelt to me ere now, and in truth my knees are too old and stiff to bend even to this lovely-faced lady. May it please your Grace, if your Grace's servants have occupied my house, so that I could not call it mine own — if they have trodden down my flowers in the zeal of their midnight comings and goings, and destroyed the hope of the fruit season, by bringing their war-horses into my garden, I do but crave of your Grace in requital, that you will choose your residence as far from me as possible. I am an old man who would willingly creep to my grave as easily as I can, in peace, good-will, and quiet labour."

"I promise you fairly, good man," said the Queen, "I will not make yonder castle my residence again, if I can help it. But let me press on you this money — it will make some amends for the havoc we have made in your little garden and orchard."

"I thank your Grace, but it will make me not the least amends," said the old man. "The ruined labours of a whole year are not so easily replaced to him who has perchance but that one year to live; and besides, they tell me I must leave this place and become a wanderer in mine old age — I that have nothing on earth saving these fruit-trees, and a few old parchments and family secrets not worth knowing. As for gold, if I had loved it, I might have remained Lord Abbot of St. Mary's — and yet, I wot not — for, if Abbot Boniface be but the poor peasant Blinkhoolie, his successor, the Abbot Ambrosius, is still transmuted for the worse into the guise of a sword-and-buckler-man."

"Is this indeed the Abbot Boniface of whom I have heard?" said the Queen. "It is indeed I who should have bent the knee for your blessing, good Father."

"Bend no knee to me, Lady! The blessing of an old man, who is no longer an Abbot, go with you over dale and down — I hear the trampling of your horses."

"Farewell, Father," said the Queen. "When we are once more seated at Holyrood, we will neither forget thee nor thine injured garden."

"Forget us both," said the Ex-Abbot Boniface, "and may God be with you!"

As they hurried out of the house, they heard the old man talking and muttering to himself, as he hastily drew bolt and bar behind them.

"The revenge of the Douglasses will reach the poor old man," said the Queen. "God help me, I ruin every one whom I approach!"

"His safety is cared for," said Seyton; "he must not remain here, but will be privately conducted to a place of greater security. But I would your Grace were in the saddle. — To horse! to horse!"

The party of Seyton and of Douglas were increased to about ten by those attendants who had remained with the horses. The Queen and her ladies, with all the rest who came from the boat, were instantly mounted; and holding aloof from the village, which was already alarmed by the firing from the castle, with Douglas acting as their guide, they soon reached the open ground and began to ride as fast as was consistent with keeping together in good order.

Chapter the Thirty-Sixth.

He mounted himself on a coal-black steed,
And her on a freckled gray,
With a bugelet horn hung down from his side,
And roundly they rode away.
OLD BALLAD.

THE influence of the free air, the rushing of the horses over high and low, the ringing of the bridles, the excitation at once arising from a sense of freedom and of rapid motion, gradually dispelled the confused and dejected sort of stupefaction by which Queen Mary was at first overwhelmed. She could not at last conceal the change of her feelings to the person who rode at her rein, and who she doubted not was the Father Ambrosius; for Seyton, with all the heady impetuosity of a youth, proud, and justly so, of his first successful adventure, assumed all the bustle and importance of commander of the little party, which escorted, in the language of the time, the Fortune of Scotland. He now led the van, now checked his bounding steed till the rear had come up, exhorted the leaders to keep a steady, though rapid pace, and commanded those who were hindmost of the party to use their spurs, and allow no interval to take place in their line of march; and anon he was beside the Queen, or her ladies, inquiring how they brooked the hasty journey, and whether they had any commands for him. But while Seyton thus busied himself in the general cause with some advantage to the regular order of the march, and a good deal of personal ostentation, the horseman who rode beside the Queen gave her his full and undivided attention, as if he had been waiting upon some superior being. When the road was rugged and dangerous, he abandoned almost entirely the care of his own horse, and kept his hand constantly upon the Queen's bridle; if a river or larger brook traversed their course, his left arm retained her in the saddle, while his right held her palfrey's rein.

"I had not thought, reverend Father," said the Queen, when they reached the other bank, "that the convent bred such good horsemen."—The person she addressed sighed, but made no other answer.—"I know not how it is," said Queen Mary, "but either the sense of freedom, or the pleasure of my favourite exercise, from which I have been so long debarred, or both combined, seem to have given wings to me—no fish ever shot through the water, no bird through the air, with the hurried feeling of liberty and rapture with which I sweep through this night-wind, and over these wolds. Nay, such is the magic of feeling myself once more in the saddle, that I could almost swear I am at this moment mounted on my own favourite Rosabelle, who was never matched in Scotland for swiftness, for ease of motion, and for sureness of foot."

"And if the horse which bears so dear a burden could speak," answered the deep voice of the melancholy George of Douglas, "would she not reply, who but Rosabelle ought at such an emergence as this to serve her beloved mistress, or who but Douglas ought to hold her bridle-rein?"

Queen Mary started; she foresaw at once all the evils like to arise to herself and him from the deep enthusiastic passion of this youth; but her feelings as a woman, grateful at once and compassionate, prevented her assuming the dignity of a Queen, and she endeavoured to continue the conversation in an indifferent tone.

"Methought," she said, "I heard that, at the division of my spoils, Rosabelle had become the property of Lord Morton's paramour and ladye-love Alice."

"The noble palfrey had indeed been destined to so base a lot," answered Douglas; "she was kept under four keys, and under the charge of a numerous crew of grooms and domestics—but Queen Mary needed Rosabelle, and Rosabelle is here."

"And was it well, Douglas," said Queen Mary, "when such fearful risks of various kinds must needs be encountered, that you should augment their perils to yourself for a subject of so little moment as a palfrey?"

"Do you call that of little moment," answered Douglas, "which has afforded you a moment's pleasure? — Did you not start with joy when I first said you were mounted on Rosabelle?—And to purchase you that pleasure, though it were to last no longer than the flash of lightning doth, would not Douglas have risked his life a thousand times?"

"Oh, peace, Douglas, peace," said the Queen, "this is unfitting language; and, besides, I would speak," said she, recollecting herself, "with the Abbot of Saint Mary's—Nay, Douglas, I will not let you quit my rein in displeasure."

"Displeasure, lady!" answered Douglas: "alas! sorrow is all that I can feel for your well-warranted contempt—I should be as soon displeased with Heaven for refusing the wildest wish which mortal can form."

"Abide by my rein, however," said Mary, "there is room for my Lord Abbot on the other side; and, besides, I doubt if his assistance would be so useful to Rosabelle and me as yours has been, should the road again require it."

The Abbot came up on the other side, and she immediately opened a conversation with him on the topic of the state of parties, and the plan fittest for her to pursue in consequence of her deliverance. In this conversation Douglas took little share, and never but when directly applied to by the Queen, while, as before, his attention seemed entirely engrossed by the care of Mary's personal safety. She learned, however, she had a new obligation to him, since, by his contrivance, the Abbot, whom he had furnished with the family pass-word, was introduced into the castle as one of the garrison.

Long before daybreak they ended their hasty and perilous journey before the gates of Niddrie, a castle in West Lothian, belonging to Lord Seyton. When the Queen was about to alight, Henry Seyton, preventing Douglas, received her in his arms, and, kneeling down, prayed her Majesty to enter the house of his father, her faithful servant.

"Your Grace," he added, "may repose yourself here in perfect safety—it is already garrisoned with good men for your protection; and I have sent a post to my father, whose instant arrival, at the head of five hundred men, may be looked for. Do not dismay yourself, therefore, should your sleep be broken by the trampling of horse; but only think that here are some scores more of the saucy Seytons come to attend you."

"And by better friends than the Saucy Seytons, a Scottish Queen cannot be guarded," replied Mary. "Rosabelle went fleet as the summer breeze, and well-nigh as easy; but it is long since I have been a traveller, and I feel that repose will be welcome. — Catherine, *ma mignône*, you must sleep in my apartment to-night, and bid me welcome to your noble father's castle. — Thanks, thanks to all my kind deliverers — thanks, and a good night is all I can now offer; but if I climb once more to the upper side of Fortune's wheel, I will not have her bandage. Mary Stewart will keep her eyes open, and distinguish her friends. — Seyton, I need scarcely recommend the venerable Abbot, the Douglas, and my page, to your honour able care and hospitality."

Henry Seyton bowed, and Catherine and Lady Fleming attended the Queen to her apartment; where, acknowledging to them that she should have found it difficult in that moment to keep her promise of holding her eyes open, she resigned herself to repose, and awakened not till the morning was advanced.

Mary's first feeling when she awoke, was the doubt of her freedom; and the impulse prompted her to start from bed, and hastily throwing her mantle over her shoulders, to look out at the casement of her apartment. Oh, sight of joy! instead of the crystal sheet of Lochleven, unaltered save by the influence of the wind, a landscape of wood and moorland lay before her, and the park around the castle was occupied by the troops of her most faithful and most favourite nobles.

"Rise, rise, Catherine," cried the enraptured Princess; "arise and come hither! — here are swords and spears in true hands, and glittering armour on loyal breasts. Here are banners, my girl, floating in the wind, as lightly as summer clouds — Great God! what pleasure to my weary eyes to trace their devices — thine own brave father's — the princely Hamilton's — the faithful Fleming's — See — see — they have caught a glimpse of me, and throng towards the window!"

She flung the casement open, and with her bare head, from which the tresses flew back loose and dishevelled, her fair arm slenderly veiled by her mantle, returned by motion and sign the exulting shouts of the warriors, which echoed for many a furlong around. When the first burst of ecstatic joy was over, she recollected how lightly she was dressed, and, putting her hands to her face, which was covered with blushes at the recollection, withdrew abruptly from the window. The cause of her retreat was easily conjectured, and increased the general enthusiasm for a Princess, who had forgotten her rank in her haste to acknowledge the services of her subjects. The unadorned beauties of the lovely woman, too, moved the military spectators more than the highest display of her regal state might; and what might have seemed too free in her mode of appearing before them, was more than atoned for by the enthusiasm of the moment, and by the delicacy evinced in her hasty retreat. Often as the shouts died away, as often were they renewed, till wood and hill rung again; and many a deep oath was made that morning on the cross of the sword, that the hand should not part with the weapon, till Mary Stewart was restored to her rights. But what are promises, what the hopes of mortals? In ten days, these gallant and devoted votaries were slain, were captives, or had fled.

Mary flung herself into the nearest seat, and still blushing, yet half smiling, exclaimed, "*Ma mignône*, what will they think of me? — to show myself to them with my bare feet, hastily thrust into the slippers—only this loose mantle about me—my hair loose on my shoulders—my arms and neck so bare—Oh, the best they can suppose is, that her abode in yonder dungeon has turned their Queen's brain! But my rebel subjects saw me exposed when I was in the depth of affliction, why should I hold colder ceremony with these faithful and loyal men?—Call Fleming, however—I trust she has not forgotten the little mail with my apparel—We must be as brave as we can, *mignône.*"

"Nay, madam, our good Lady Fleming was in no case to remember any thing."

"You jest, Catherine," said the Queen, somewhat offended; "it is not in her nature surely, to forget her duty so far as to leave us without a change of apparel?"

"Roland Græme, madam, took care of that," answered Catherine; "for he threw the mail, with your highness's clothes and jewels, into the boat, ere he ran back to lock the gate—I never saw so awkward a page as that youth—the packet well-nigh fell on my head."

"He shall make thy heart amends, my girl," said Queen Mary, laughing, "for that and all other offences given. But call Fleming, and let us put ourselves into apparel to meet our faithful lords."

Such had been the preparations, and such was the skill of Lady Fleming, that the Queen appeared before her assembled nobles in such attire as became, though it could not enhance, her natural dignity. With the most winning courtesy, she expressed to each individual her grateful thanks, and dignified not only every noble, but many of the lesser barons by her particular attention.

"And whither now, my lords?" she said; "what way do your counsels determine for us?"

"To Draphane Castle," replied Lord Arbroath, "if your Majesty is so pleased; and thence to Dunbarton, to place your Grace's person in safety, after which we long to prove if these traitors will abide us in the field."

"And when do we journey?"

"We propose," said Lord Seyton, "if your Grace's fatigue will permit, to take horse after the morning's meal."

"Your pleasure, my Lords, is mine," replied the Queen; "we will rule our journey by your wisdom now, and hope hereafter to have the advantage of governing by it our kingdom.—You will permit my ladies and me, my good lords, to break our fasts along with you—We must be half soldiers ourselves, and set state apart."

Low bowed many a helmeted head at this gracious proffer, when the Queen, glancing her eyes through the assembled leaders, missed both Douglas and Roland Græme, and inquired for them in a whisper to Catherine Seyton.

"They are in yonder oratory, madam, sad enough," replied Catherine; and the Queen observed that her favourite's eyes were red with weeping.

"This must not be," said the Queen. "Keep the company amused—I will seek them, and introduce them myself."

She went into the oratory, where the first she met was George Douglas, standing, or rather reclining, in the recess of a window, his back rested against the wall, and his arms folded on his breast. At the sight of the Queen he started, and his countenance showed, for an instant, an expression of intense delight, which was instantly exchanged for his usual deep melancholy.

"What means this?" she said; "Douglas, why does the first deviser and bold executor of the happy scheme for our freedom, shun the company of his fellow-nobles, and of the Sovereign whom he has obliged?"

"Madam," replied Douglas, "those whom you grace with your presence bring followers to aid your cause, wealth to support your state,—can offer you halls in which to feast, and impregnable castles for your defence. I am a houseless and landless man—disinherited by my mother, and laid under her malediction—disowned by my name and kindred—who bring nothing to your standard but a single sword, and the poor life of its owner."

"Do you mean to upbraid me, Douglas," replied the Queen, "by showing what you have lost for my sake?"

"God forbid, madam!" interrupted the young man, eagerly; "were it to do again, and had I ten times as much rank and wealth, and twenty times as many friends to lose, my losses would be overpaid by the first step you made, as a free princess, upon the soil of your native kingdom."

"And what then ails you, that you will not rejoice with those who rejoice upon the same joyful occasion?" said the Queen.

"Madam," replied the youth, "though exheridated and disowned, I am yet a Douglas: with most of yonder nobles my family have been in feud for ages—a cold reception amongst them were an insult, and a kind one yet more humiliating."

"For shame, Douglas," replied the Queen, "shake off this unmanly gloom!—I can make thee match for the best of them in title and fortune, and, believe me, I will.—Go then amongst them, I command you."

"That word," said Douglas, "is enough—I go. This only let me say, that not for wealth or title would I have done that which I have done—Mary Stewart will not, and the Queen cannot, reward me."

So saying, he left the oratory, mingled with the nobles, and placed himself at the bottom of the table. The Queen looked after him, and put her kerchief to her eyes.

"Now, Our Lady pity me," she said, "for no sooner are my prison cares ended, than those which beset me as a woman and a Queen again thicken around me.—Happy Elizabeth! to whom political interest is every thing, and whose heart never betrays thy head.—And now must I seek this other boy, if I would prevent daggers-drawing betwixt him and the young Seyton."

Roland Græme was in the same oratory, but at such a distance from Douglas, that he could not overhear what passed betwixt the Queen and him. He also was moody and thoughtful, but cleared his brow at the Queen's question, "How now, Roland? you are negligent in your attendance this morning. Are you so much overcome with your night's ride?"

"Not so, gracious madam," answered Græme; "but I am told the page of Lochleven is not the page of Niddrie Castle; and so Master Henry Seyton hath in a manner been pleased to supersede my attendance."

"Now, Heaven forgive me," said the Queen, "how soon these cock-chickens begin to spar!—with children and boys, at least, I may be a queen.—I will have you friends.—Some one send me Henry Seyton hither." As she spoke the last words aloud, the youth whom she had named entered the apartment. "Come hither," she said, "Henry Seyton—I will have you give your hand to this youth, who so well aided in the plan of my escape."

"Willingly, madam," answered Seyton, "so that the youth will grant me, as a boon, that he touch not the hand of another Seyton whom he knows of. My hand has passed current for hers with him before now—and to win my friendship, he must give up thoughts of my sister's love."

"Henry Seyton," said the Queen, "does it become you to add any condition to my command?"

"Madam," said Henry, "I am the servant of your Grace's throne, son to the most loyal man in Scotland. Our goods, our castles, our blood, are yours: Our honour is in our own keeping. I could say more, but——"

"Nay, speak on, rude boy," said the Queen; "what avails it that I am released from Lochleven, if I am thus enthralled under the yoke of my pretended deliverers, and prevented from doing justice to one who has deserved as well of me as yourself?"

"Be not in this distemperature for me, sovereign Lady," said Roland; "this young gentleman, being the faithful servant of your Grace, and the brother of Catherine Seyton, bears that about him which will charm down my passion at the hottest."

"I warn thee once more," said Henry Seyton, haughtily, "that you make no speech which may infer that the daughter of Lord Seyton can be aught to thee beyond what she is to every churl's blood in Scotland."

The Queen was again about to interfere, for Roland's complexion rose, and it became somewhat questionable how long his love for Catherine would suppress the natural fire of his temper. But the interposition of another person, hitherto unseen, prevented Mary's interference. There was in the oratory a separate shrine, enclosed with a high screen of pierced oak, within which was placed an image of Saint Bennet, of peculiar sanctity. From this recess, in which she had been probably engaged in her devotions, issued suddenly Magdalen Græme, and addressed Henry Seyton, in reply to his last offensive expressions—"And of what clay, then, are they moulded these Seytons, that the blood of the Græmes may not aspire to mingle with theirs? Know, proud boy, that when I call this youth my daughter's child, I affirm his descent from Malise Earl of Strathern, called Malise with the Bright Brand; and I trow the blood of your house springs from no higher source."

"Good mother," said Seyton, "methinks your sanctity should make you superior to these worldly vanities; and indeed it seems to have rendered you somewhat oblivious touching them, since, to be of gentle descent, the father's name and lineage must be as well qualified as the mother's."

"And if I say he comes of the blood of Avenel by the father's side," replied Magdalen Græme, "name I not blood as richly coloured as thine own?"

"Of Avenel?" said the Queen; "is my page descended of Avenel?"

"Ay, gracious Princess, and the last male heir of that ancient house—Julian Avenel was his father, who fell in battle against the Southron."

"I have heard the tale of sorrow," said the Queen; "it was thy daughter, then, who followed that unfortunate baron to the field, and died on his body? Alas! how many ways does woman's affection find to work out her own misery! The tale has oft been told and sung in hall and bower—And thou, Roland, art that child of misfortune, who was left among the dead and dying? Henry Seyton, he is thine equal in blood and birth."

"Scarcely so," said Henry Seyton, "even were he legitimate; but if the tale be told and sung aright, Julian Avenel was a false knight, and his leman a frail and credulous maiden."

"Now, by Heaven, thou liest!" said Roland Græme, and laid his hand on his sword. The entrance of Lord Seyton, however, prevented violence.

"Save me, my lord," said the Queen, "and separate these wild and untamed spirits."

"How, Henry," said the Baron, "are my castle, and the Queen's presence, no checks on thine insolence and impetuosity?—And with whom art thou brawling?—unless my eyes spell that token false, it is with the very youth who aided me so gallantly in the skirmish with the Leslies—Let me look, fair youth, at the medal which thou wearest in thy cap. By Saint Bennet, it is the same!—Henry, I command thee to forbear him, as thou lovest my blessing——"

"And as you honour my command," said the Queen; "good service hath he done me."

"Ay, madam," replied young Seyton, "as when he carried the billet enclosed in the sword-sheath to Lochleven—marry, the good youth knew no more than a pack-horse what he was carrying."

"But I who dedicated him to this great work," said Magdalen Græme—"I, by whose advice and agency this just heir hath been unloosed from her thraldom—I, who spared not the last remaining hope of a falling house in this great action—I, at least, knew and counselled; and what merit may be mine, let the reward, most gracious Queen, descend upon this youth. My ministry here is ended; you are free—a sovereign Princess, at the head of a gallant army, surrounded by valiant barons—My service could avail you no farther, but might well prejudice you; your fortune now rests upon men's hearts and men's swords—May they prove as trusty as the faith of women!"

"You will not leave us, mother," said the Queen—"you whose practices in our favour were so powerful, who dared so many dangers, and wore so many disguises, to blind our enemies and to confirm our friends—you will not leave us in the dawn of our reviving fortunes, ere we have time to know and to thank you?"

"You cannot know her," answered Magdalen Græme, "who knows not herself—there are times, when, in this woman's frame of mine, there is the strength of him of Gath—in this overtoiled brain, the wisdom of the most sage counsellor—and again the mist is on me, and my strength is weakness, my wisdom folly. I have spoken before princes and cardinals—ay, noble Princess, even before the princes of thine own house of Lorraine; and I know not whence the words of persuasion came which flowed from my lips, and were drunk in by their ears.—And now, even when I most need words of persuasion, there is something which chokes my voice, and robs me of utterance."

"If there be aught in my power to do thee pleasure," said the Queen, "the barely naming it shall avail as well as all thine eloquence."

"Sovereign Lady," replied the enthusiast, "it shames me that at this high moment something of human frailty should cling to one, whose vows the saints have heard, whose labours in the rightful cause Heaven has prospered. But it will be thus while the living spirit is shrined in the clay of mortality—I will yield to the folly," she said, weeping as she spoke, "and it shall be the last." Then seizing Roland's hand, she led him to the Queen's feet, kneeling herself upon one knee, and causing him to kneel on both. "Mighty Princess," she said, "look on this flower—it was found by a kindly stranger on a bloody field of battle, and long it was ere my anxious eyes saw, and my arms pressed, all that was left of my only daughter. For your sake, and for that of the holy faith we both profess, I could leave this plant, while it was yet tender, to the nurture of strangers—ay, of enemies, by whom, perchance, his blood would have been poured forth as wine, had the heretic Glendinning known that he had in his house the heir of Julian Avenel. Since then I have seen him only in a few hours of doubt and dread, and now I part with the child of my love—for ever—for ever!—Oh, for every weary step I have made in your rightful cause, in this and in foreign lands, give protection to the child whom I must no more call mine!"

"I swear to you, mother," said the Queen, deeply affected, "that, for your sake and his own, his happiness and fortunes shall be our charge!"

"I thank you, daughter of princes," said Magdalen, and pressed her lips, first to the Queen's hand, then to the brow of her grandson. "And now," she said, drying her tears, and rising with dignity, "Earth has had its own, and Heaven claims the rest.—Lioness of Scotland, go forth and conquer! and if the prayers of a devoted votaress can avail thee, they will rise in many a land, and from many a distant shrine. I will glide like a ghost from land to land, from temple to temple; and where the very name of my country is unknown, the priests shall ask who is the Queen of that distant northern land, for whom the aged pilgrim was so fervent in prayer. Farewell! Honour be thine, and earthly prosperity, if it be the will of God—if not, may the penance thou shalt do here ensure thee happiness hereafter! —Let no one speak or follow me—my resolution is taken—my vow cannot be cancelled."

She glided from their presence as she spoke, and her last look was upon her beloved grandchild. He would have risen and followed, but the Queen and Lord Seyton interfered.

"Press not on her now," said Lord Seyton, "if you would not lose her for ever. Many a time have we seen the sainted mother, and often at the most needful moment; but to press on her privacy, or to thwart her purpose, is a crime which she cannot pardon. I trust we shall yet see her at her need—a holy woman she is for certain, and dedicated wholly to prayer and penance; and hence the heretics hold her as one distracted, while true Catholics deem her a saint."

"Let me then hope," said the Queen, "that you, my lord, will aid me in the execution of her last request."

"What! in the protection of my young second?—cheerfully—that is, in all that your majesty can think it fitting to ask of me. — Henry, give thy hand upon the instant to Roland Avenel, for so I presume he must now be called."

"And shall be Lord of the Barony," said the Queen, "if God prosper our rightful arms."

"It can only be to restore it to my kind protectress, who now holds it," said young Avenel. "I would rather be landless, all my life, than she lost a rood of ground by me."

"Nay," said the Queen, looking to Lord Seyton, "his mind matches his birth — Henry, thou hast not yet given thy hand."

"It is his," said Henry, giving it with some appearance of courtesy, but whispering Roland at the same time, — "For all this, thou hast not my sister's."

"May it please your Grace," said Lord Seyton, "now that these passages are over, to honour our poor meal. Time it were that our banners were reflected in the Clyde. We must to horse with as little delay as may be."

Chapter the Thirty-Seventh.

Ay, sir — our ancient crown, in these wild times,
Oft stood upon a cast — the gamester's ducat,
So often staked, and lost, and then regain'd,
Scarce knew so many hazards.

THE SPANISH FATHER.

It is not our object to enter into the historical part of the reign of the ill-fated Mary, or to recount how, during the week which succeeded her flight from Lochleven, her partisans mustered around her with their followers, forming a gallant army, amounting to six thousand men. So much light has been lately thrown on the most minute details of the period, by Mr. Chalmers, in his valuable history of Queen Mary, that the reader may be safely referred to it for the fullest information which ancient records afford concerning that interesting time. It is sufficient for our purpose to say, that while Mary's head-quarters were at Hamilton, the Regent and his adherents had, in the King's name, assembled a host at Glasgow, inferior indeed to that of the Queen in numbers, but formidable from the military talents of Murray, Morton, the Laird of Grange, and others, who had been trained from their youth in foreign and domestic wars.

In these circumstances, it was the obvious policy of Queen Mary to avoid a conflict, secure that were her person once in safety, the number of her adherents must daily increase; whereas, the forces of those opposed to her must, as had frequently happened in the previous history of her reign, have diminished, and their spirits become broken. And so evident was this to her counsellors, that they resolved their first step should be to place the Queen in the strong castle of Dunbarton, there to await the course of events, the arrival of succours from France, and the levies which were made by her adherents in every province of Scotland. Accordingly, orders were given, that all men should be on horseback or on foot, apparelled in their armour, and ready to follow the Queen's standard in array of battle, the avowed determination being to escort her to the Castle of Dunbarton in defiance of her enemies.

The muster was made upon Hamilton-Moor, and the march commenced in all the pomp of feudal times. Military music sounded, banners and pennons waved, armour glittered far and wide, and spears glanced and twinkled like stars in a frosty sky. The gallant spectacle of warlike parade was on this occasion dignified by the presence of the Queen herself, who, with a fair retinue of ladies and household attendants, and a special guard of gentlemen, amongst whom young Seyton and Roland were distinguished, gave grace at once and confidence to the army, which spread its ample files before, around, and behind her. Many churchmen also joined the cavalcade, most of whom did not scruple to assume arms, and declare their intention of wielding them in defence of Mary and the Catholic faith. Not so the Abbot of Saint Mary's. Roland had not seen this prelate since the night of their escape from Lochleven, and he now beheld him, robed in the dress of his order, assume his station near the Queen's person. Roland hastened to pull off his basnet, and beseech the Abbot's blessing.

"Thou hast it, my son!" said the priest; "I see thee now under thy true name, and in thy rightful garb. The helmet with the holly branch befits your brows well—I have long waited for the hour thou shouldst assume it."

"Then you knew of my descent, my good father!" said Roland.

"I did so, but it was under seal of confession from thy grandmother; nor was I at liberty to tell the secret, till she herself should make it known."

"Her reason for such secrecy, my father?" said Roland Avenel.

"Fear, perchance of my brother—a mistaken fear, for Halbert would not, to ensure himself a kingdom, have offered wrong to an orphan; besides that, your title, in quiet times, even had your father done your mother that justice which I well hope he did, could not have competed with that of my brother's wife, the child of Julian's elder brother."

"They need fear no competition from me," said Avenel. "Scotland is wide enough, and there are many manors to win, without plundering my benefactor. But prove to me, my reverend father, that my father was just to my mother — show me that I may call myself a legitimate Avenel, and make me your bounden slave for ever."

"Ay," replied the Abbot, "I hear the Seytons hold thee cheap for that stain on thy shield. Something, however, I have learnt from the late Abbot Boniface, which, if it prove sooth, may redeem that reproach."

"Tell me that blessed news," said Roland, "and the future service of my life——"

"Rash boy!" said the Abbot, "I should but madden thine impatient temper, by exciting hopes that may never be fulfilled — and is this a time for them? Think on what perilous march we are bound, and if thou hast a sin unconfessed, neglect not the only leisure which Heaven may perchance afford thee for confession and absolution."

"There will be time enough for both, I trust, when we reach Dunbarton," answered the page.

"Ay," said the Abbot, "thou crowest as loudly as the rest — but we are not yet at Dunbarton, and there is a lion in the path."

"Mean you Murray, Morton, and the other rebels at Glasgow, my reverend father? Tush! they dare not look on the royal banner."

"Even so," replied the Abbot, "speak many of those who are older, and should be wiser, than thou. — I have returned from the southern shires, where I left many a chief of name arming in the Queen's interest — I left the lords here wise and considerate men — I find them madmen on my return—they are willing, for mere pride and vain-glory, to brave the enemy, and to carry the Queen, as it were in triumph, past the walls of Glasgow, and under the beards of the adverse army.—Seldom does Heaven smile on such mistimed confidence. We shall be encountered, and that to the purpose "

"And so much the better," replied Roland; "the field of battle was my cradle."

"Beware it be not thy dying bed," said the Abbot. "But what avails it whispering to young wolves the dangers of the chase? You will know, perchance, ere this day is out, what yonder men are, whom you hold in rash contempt."

"Why, what are they?" said Henry Seyton, who now joined them: "have they sinews of wire, and flesh of iron?—Will lead pierce and steel cut them?—If so, reverend father, we have little to fear."

"They are evil men," said the Abbot, "but the trade of war demands no saints.—Murray and Morton are known to be the best generals in Scotland. No one ever saw Lindesay's or Ruthven's back—Kirkaldy of Grange was named by the Constable Montmorency the first soldier in Europe—My brother, too good a name for such a cause, has been far and wide known for a soldier."

"The better, the better!" said Seyton, triumphantly; "we shall have all these traitors of rank and name in a fair field before us. Our cause is the best, our numbers are the strongest, our hearts and limbs match theirs—Saint Bennet, and set on!"

The Abbot made no reply, but seemed lost in reflection; and his anxiety in some measure communicated itself to Roland Avenel, who ever, as their line of march led over a ridge or an eminence, cast an anxious look towards the towers of Glasgow, as if he expected to see symptoms of the enemy issuing forth. It was not that he feared the fight, but the issue was of such deep import to his country, and to himself, that the natural fire of his spirit burned with a less lively, though with a more intense glow. Love, honour, fame, fortune, all seemed to depend on the issue of one field, rashly hazarded perhaps, but now likely to become unavoidable and decisive.

When, at length, their march came to be nearly parallel with the city of Glasgow, Roland became sensible that the high grounds before them were already in part occupied by a force, showing, like their own, the royal banner of Scotland, and on the point of being supported by columns of infantry and squadrons of horse, which the city gates had poured forth, and which hastily advanced to sustain those troops who already possessed the ground in front of the Queen's forces. Horseman after horseman galloped in from the advanced guard, with tidings that Murray had taken the field with his whole army; that his object was to intercept the Queen's march, and his purpose unquestionable to hazard a battle. It was now that the tempers of men were subjected to a sudden and a severe trial; and that those who had too presumptuously concluded that they would pass without combat, were something disconcerted, when, at once, and with little time to deliberate, they found themselves placed in front of a resolute enemy.—Their chiefs immediately assembled around the Queen, and held a hasty council of war. Mary's quivering lip confessed the fear which she endeavoured to conceal under a bold and dignified demeanour. But her efforts were overcome by painful recollections of the disastrous issue of her last appearance in arms at Carberry-hill; and when she meant to have asked them their advice for ordering the battle, she involuntarily inquired whether there were no means of escaping without an engagement?

"Escaping?" answered the Lord Seyton; "when I stand as one to ten of your Highness's enemies, I may think of escape—but never while I stand with three to two!"

"Battle! battle!" exclaimed the assembled lords; "we will drive the rebels from their vantage ground, as the hound turns the hare on the hill side."

"Methinks, my noble lords," said the Abbot, "it were as well to prevent his gaining that advantage.—Our road lies through yonder hamlet on the brow, and whichever party hath the luck to possess it, with its little gardens and enclosures, will attain a post of great defence."

"The reverend father is right," said the Queen. "Oh, haste thee, Seyton, haste, and get thither before them—they are marching like the wind."

Seyton bowed low, and turned his horse's head.—"Your Highness honours me," he said; "I will instantly press forward, and seize the pass."

"Not before me, my lord, whose charge is the command of the vanguard," said the Lord of Arbroath.

"Before you, or any Hamilton in Scotland," said the Seyton, "having the Queen's command—Follow me, gentlemen, my vassals and kinsmen—Saint Bennet, and set on!"

"And follow me," said Arbroath, "my noble kinsmen, and brave mentenants, we will see which will first reach the post of danger. For God and Queen Mary!"

"Ill-omened haste, and most unhappy strife," said the Abbot, who saw them and their followers rush hastily and emulously to ascend the height without waiting till their men were placed in order.—"And you, gentlemen," he continued, addressing Roland and Seyton, who were each about to follow those who hastened thus disorderly to the conflict, "will you leave the Queen's person unguarded?"

"Oh, leave me not, gentlemen!" said the Queen—"Roland and Seyton, do not leave me—there are enough of arms to strike in this fell combat—withdraw not those to whom I trust for my safety."

"We may not leave her Grace," said Roland, looking at Seyton, and turning his horse.

"I ever looked when thou wouldst find out that," rejoined the fiery youth.

Roland made no answer, but bit his lip till the blood came, and spurring his horse up to the side of Catherine Seyton's palfrey, he whispered in a low voice, "I never thought to have done aught to deserve you; but this day I have heard myself upbraided with cowardice, and my sword remained still sheathed, and all for the love of you."

"There is madness among us all," said the damsel; "my father, my brother, and you, are all alike bereft of reason. Ye should think only of this poor Queen, and you are all inspired by your own absurd jealousies—The monk is the only soldier and man of sense amongst you all.—My lord Abbot," she cried aloud, "were it not better we should draw to the westward, and wait the event that God shall send us, instead of remaining here in the highway, endangering the Queen's person, and cumbering the troops in their advance?"

"You say well, my daughter," replied the Abbot; "had we but one to guide us where the Queen's person may be in safety—Our nobles hurry to the conflict, without casting a thought on the very cause of the war."

"Follow me," said a knight, or man-at-arms, well mounted, and attired completely in black armour, but having the visor of his helmet closed, and bearing no crest on his helmet, or device upon his shield.

"We will follow no stranger," said the Abbot, "without some warrant of his truth."

"I am a stranger and in your hands," said the horseman; "if you wish to know more of me, the Queen herself will be your warrant."

The Queen had remained fixed to the spot, as if disabled by fear, yet mechanically smiling, bowing, and waving her hand, as banners were lowered and spears depressed before her, while, emulating the strife betwixt Seyton and Arbroath, band on band pressed forward their march towards the enemy. Scarce, however, had the black rider whispered something in her ear, than she assented to what he said; and when he spoke aloud, and with an air of command, "Gentlemen, it is the Queen's pleasure that you should follow me," Mary uttered, with something like eagerness, the word "Yes."

All were in motion in an instant; for the black horseman, throwing off a sort of apathy of manner, which his first appearance indicated, spurred his horse to and fro, making him take such active bounds and short turns, as showed the rider master of the animal; and getting the Queen's little retinue in some order for marching, he led them to the left, directing his course towards a castle, which, crowning a gentle yet commanding eminence, presented an extensive view over the country beneath, and in particular, commanded a view of those heights which both armies hastened to occupy, and which it was now apparent must almost instantly be the scene of struggle and dispute.

"Yonder towers," said the Abbot, questioning the sable horseman, "to whom do they belong?—and are they in the hands of friends?"

"They are untenanted," replied the stranger, "or, at least, they have no hostile inmates.—But urge these youths, Sir Abbot, to make more haste—this is but an evil time to satisfy their idle curiosity, by peering out upon the battle in which they are to take no share."

"The worse luck mine," said Henry Seyton, who overheard him—"I would rather be under my father's banner at this moment than be made Chamberlain of Holyrood, for this my present duty of peaceful ward well and patiently discharged."

"Your place under your father's banner will shortly be right dangerous," said Roland Avenel, who, pressing his horse towards the westward, had still his look reverted to the armies; "for I see yonder body of cavalry, which presses from the eastward, will reach the village ere Lord Seyton can gain it."

"They are but cavalry," said Seyton, looking attentively; "they cannot hold the village without shot of harquebuss."

"Look more closely," said Roland; "you will see that each of these horseman who advance so rapidly from Glasgow, carries a footman behind him."

"Now, by Heaven, he speaks well!" said the black cavalier; "one of you two must go carry the news to Lord Seyton and Lord Arbroath, that they hasten not their horsemen on before the foot, but advance more regularly."

"Be that my errand," said Roland, "for I first marked the stratagem of the enemy."

"But, by your leave," said Seyton, "yonder is my father's banner engaged, and it best becomes me to go to the rescue."

"I will stand by the Queen's decision," said Roland Avenel.

"What new appeal?—what new quarrel?" said Queen Mary—"Are there not in yonder dark host enemies enough to Mary Stewart, but must her very friends turn enemies to each other?"

"Nay, madam," said Roland, "the young master of Seyton and I did but dispute who should leave your person to do a most needful message to the host. He thought his rank entitled him, and I deemed that the person of least consequence, being myself, were better perilled——"

"Not so," said the Queen; "if one must leave me, be it Seyton."

Henry Seyton bowed till the white plumes on his helmet mixed with the flowing mane of his gallant war-horse, then placed himself firm in the saddle, shook his lance aloft with an air of triumph and determination, and striking his horse with the spurs, made towards his father's banner, which was still advancing up the hill, and dashed his steed over every obstacle that occurred in his headlong path.

"My brother! my father!" exclaimed Catherine, with an expression of agonized apprehension—"they are in the midst of peril, and I in safety!"

"Would to God," said Roland, "that I were with them, and could ransom every drop of their blood by two of mine!"

"Do I not know thou dost wish it?" said Catherine—"Can a woman say to a man what I have well-nigh said to thee, and yet think that he could harbour fear or faintness of heart?—There is that in yon distant sound of approaching battle that pleases me even while it affrights me. I would I were a man, that I might feel that stern delight, without the mixture of terror!"

"Ride up, ride up, Lady Catherine Seyton," cried the Abbot, as they still swept on at a rapid pace, and were now close beneath the walls of the castle—"ride up, and aid Lady Fleming to support the Queen—she gives way more and more."

They halted and lifted Mary from the saddle, and were about to support her towards the castle, when she said faintly, "Not there—not there—these walls will I never enter more!"

"Be a Queen, madam," said the Abbot, "and forget that you are a woman."

"Oh, I must forget much, much more," answered the unfortunate Mary, in an under tone, "ere I can look with steady eyes on these well-known scenes!—I must forget the days which I spent here as the bride of the lost—the murdered——"

"This is the Castle of Crookstone," said the Lady Fleming, "in which the Queen held her first court after she was married to Darnley."

"Heaven," said the Abbot, "thy hand is upon us!—Bear yet up, madam—your foes are the foes of Holy Church, and God will this day decide whether Scotland shall be Catholic or heretic."

A heavy and continued fire of cannon and musketry, bore a tremendous burden to his words, and seemed far more than they to recall the spirits of the Queen.

"To yonder tree," she said, pointing to a yew-tree which grew on a small mount close to the castle; "I know it well—from thence you may see a prospect wide as from the peaks of Schehallion."

And freeing herself from her assistants, she walked with a determined, yet somewhat wild step, up to the stem of the noble yew. The Abbot, Catherine, and Roland Avenel followed her, while Lady Fleming kept back the inferior persons of her train. The black horseman also followed the Queen, waiting on her as closely as the shadow upon the light, but ever remaining at the distance of two or three yards—he folded his arms on his bosom, turned his back to the battle, and seemed solely occupied by gazing on Mary, through the bars of his closed visor. The Queen regarded him not, but fixed her eyes upon the spreading yew."

"Ay, fair and stately tree," she said, as if at the sight of it she had been rapt away from the present scene, and had overcome the horror which had oppressed her at the first approach to Crookstone, "there thou standest, gay and goodly as ever, though thou hearest the sounds of war, instead of the vows of love. All is gone since I last greeted thee—love and lover—vows and vower—king and kingdom.—How goes the field, my Lord Abbot?—with us, I trust—yet what but evil can Mary's eyes witness from this spot?"

Her attendants eagerly bent their eyes on the field of battle, but could discover nothing more than that it was obstinately contested. The small enclosures and cottage gardens in the village, of which they had a full and commanding view, and which shortly before lay, with their lines of sycamore and ash-trees, so still and quiet in the mild light of a May sun, were now each converted into a line of fire, canopied by smoke; and the sustained and constant report of the musketry and cannon, mingled with the shouts of meeting combatants, showed that as yet neither party had given ground.

"Many a soul finds its final departure to heaven or hell, in these awful thunders," said the Abbot; "let those that believe in the Holy Church, join me in orisons for victory in this dreadful combat."

"Not here — not here," said the unfortunate Queen; "pray not here, father, or pray in silence — my mind is too much torn between the past and the present, to dare to approach the heavenly throne — Or, if we will pray, be it for one whose fondest affections have been her greatest crimes, and who has ceased to be a queen, only because she was a deceived and a tender-hearted woman."

"Were it not well," said Roland, "that I rode somewhat nearer the hosts, and saw the fate of the day?"

"Do so, in the name of God," said the Abbot; "for if our friends are scattered, our flight must be hasty—but beware thou approach not too nigh the conflict; there is more than thine own life depends on thy safe return."

"Oh, go not too nigh," said Catherine; "but fail not to see how the Seytons fight, and how they bear themselves."

"Fear nothing, I will be on my guard," said Roland Avenel; and without waiting farther answer, rode towards the scene of conflict, keeping, as he rode, the higher and unenclosed ground, and ever looking cautiously around him, for fear of involving himself in some hostile party. As he approached, the shots rung sharp and more sharply on his ear, the shouts came wilder and wilder, and he felt that thick beating of the heart, that mixture of natural apprehension, intense curiosity, and anxiety for the dubious event, which even the bravest experience when they approach alone to a scene of interest and of danger.

At length he drew so close, that from a bank, screened by bushes and underwood, he could distinctly see where the struggle was most keenly maintained. This was in a hollow way, leading to the village, up which the Queen's vanguard had marched, with more hasty courage than well-advised conduct, for the purpose of possessing themselves of that post of advantage. They found their scheme anticipated, and the hedges and enclosures already occupied by the enemy, led by the celebrated Kirkaldy of Grange and the Earl of Morton; and not small was the loss which they sustained while struggling forward to come to close with the men-at-arms on the other side. But, as the Queen's followers were chiefly noblemen and barons, with their kinsmen and followers, they had pressed onward, con temning obstacles and danger, and had, when Roland arrived on the ground, met hand to hand at the gorge of the pass with the Regent's vanguard, and endeavoured to bear them out of the village at the spear-point; while their foes, equally determined to keep the advantage which they had attained, struggled with the like obstinacy to drive back the assailants.

Both parties were on foot, and armed in proof; so that, when the long lances of the front ranks were fixed in each other's shields, corslets, and breastplates, the struggle resembled that of two bulls, who fixing their frontlets hard against each other, remain in that posture for hours, until the superior strength or obstinacy of the one compels the other to take to flight, or bears him down to the earth. Thus locked together in the deadly struggle, which swayed slowly to and fro, as one or other party gained the advantage, those who fell were trampled on alike by friends and foes; those whose weapons were broken, retired from the front rank, and had their place supplied by others; while the rearward ranks, unable otherwise to share in the combat, fired their pistols, and hurled their daggers, and the points and truncheons of the broken weapons, like javelins against the enemy.

"God and the Queen!" resounded from the one party; "God and the King!" thundered from the other; while, in the name of their sovereign, fellow-subjects on both sides shed each other's blood, and, in the name of their Creator, defaced his image. Amid the tumult was often heard the voices of the captains, shouting their commands; of leaders and chiefs, crying their gathering words; of groans and shrieks from the falling and the dying.

The strife had lasted nearly an hour. The strength of both parties seemed exhausted; but their rage was unabated, and their obstinacy unsubdued, when Roland, who turned eye and ear to all around him, saw a column of infantry, headed by a few horsemen, wheel round the base of the bank where he had stationed himself, and, levelling their long lances, attack the Queen's vanguard, closely engaged as they were in conflict on their front. The very first glance showed him that the leader who directed this movement was the Knight of Avenel, his ancient master; and the next convinced him, that its effects would be decisive. The result of the attack of fresh and unbroken forces upon the flank of those already wearied with a long and obstinate struggle, was, indeed, instantaneous.

The column of the assailants, which had hitherto shown one dark, dense, and united line of helmets, surmounted with plumage, was at once broken and hurled in confusion down the hill, which they had so long endeavoured to gain. In vain were the leaders heard calling upon their followers to stand to the combat, and seen personally resisting when all resistance was evidently vain. They were slain, or felled to the earth, or hurried backwards by the mingled tide of flight and pursuit. What were Roland's feelings on beholding the rout, and feeling that all that remained for him was to turn bridle, and endeavour to ensure the safety of the Queen's person! Yet, keen as his grief and shame might be, they were both forgotten, when, almost close beneath the bank which he occupied, he saw Henry Seyton forced away from his own party in the tumult, covered with dust and blood, and defending himself desperately against several of the enemy who had gathered around him, attracted by his gay armour. Roland paused not a moment, but pushing his steed down the bank, leaped him amongst the hostile party, dealt three or four blows amongst them, which struck down two, and made the rest stand aloof; then reaching Seyton his hand, he exhorted him to seize fast on his horse's mane.

"We live or die together this day," said he; "keep but fast hold till we are out of the press, and then my horse is yours."

Seyton heard and exerted his remaining strength, and, by their joint efforts, Roland brought him out of danger, and behind the spot from whence he had witnessed the disastrous conclusion of the fight. But no sooner were they under shelter of the trees, than Seyton let go his hold, and, in spite of Roland's efforts to support him, fell at length on the turf. "Trouble yourself no more with me," he said; "this is my first and my last battle —and I have already seen too much to wish to see the close. Hasten to save the Queen—and commend me to Catherine—she will never more be mistaken for me nor I for her—the last sword-stroke has made an eternal distinction."

"Let me aid you to mount my horse," said Roland, eagerly, "and you may yet be saved—I can find my own way on foot—turn but my horse's head westward, and he will carry you fleet and easy as the wind."

"I will never mount steed more," said the youth; "farewell—I love thee better dying, than ever I thought to have done while in life—I would that old man's blood were not on my hand!—*Sancte Benedicte, ora pro m.*—Stand not to look on a dying man, but haste to save the Queen!"

These words were spoken with the last effort of his voice, and scarce were they uttered ere the speaker was no more. They recalled Roland to a sense of the duty which he had well-nigh forgotten, but they did not reach his ears only.

"The Queen — where is the Queen?" said Halbert Glendinning, who, followed by two or three horsemen, appeared at this instant. Roland made no answer, but, turning his horse, and confiding in his speed, gave him at once rein and spur, and rode over height and hollow towards the Castle of Crookstone. More heavily armed, and mounted upon a horse of less speed, Sir Halbert Glendinning followed with couched lance, calling out as he rode, "Sir, with the holly-branch, halt, and show your right to bear that badge—

fly not thus cowardly, nor dishonour the cognizance thou deservest not to wear!—Halt, sir coward, or by Heaven, I will strike thee with my lance on the back, and slay thee like a dastard—I am the Knight of Avenel—I am Halbert Glendinning."

But Roland, who had no purpose of encountering his old master, and who, besides, knew the Queen's safety depended on his making the best speed he could, answered not a word to the defiances and reproaches which Sir Halbert continued to throw out against him; but making the best use of his spurs, rode yet harder than before, and had gained about a hundred yards upon his pursuer, when, coming near to the yew-tree where he had left the Queen, he saw them already getting to horse, and cried out as loud as he could, "Foes! foes!—Ride for it, fair ladies—Brave gentlemen, do your devoir to protect them!"

So saying, he wheeled his horse, and avoiding the shock of Sir Halbert Glendinning, charged one of that Knight's followers, who was nearly on a line with him, so rudely with his lance, that he overthrew horse and man. He then drew his sword and attacked the second, while the black man-at-arms, throwing himself in the way of Glendinning, they rushed on each other so fiercely, that both horses were overthrown, and the riders lay rolling on the plain. Neither was able to arise, for the black horseman was pierced through with Glendinning's lance, and the Knight of Avenel, oppressed with the weight of his own horse and sorely bruised besides, seemed in little better plight than he whom he had mortally wounded.

"Yield thee, Sir Knight of Avenel, rescue or no rescue," said Roland, who had put a second antagonist out of condition to combat, and hastened to prevent Glendinning from renewing the conflict.

"I may not choose but yield," said Sir Halbert, "since I can no longer fight; but it shames me to speak such a word to a coward like thee!"

"Call me not coward," said Roland, lifting his visor, and helping his prisoner to rise, "since but for old kindness at thy hands, and yet more at thy lady's, I had met thee as a brave man should."

"The favourite page of my wife!" said Sir Halbert, astonished; "Ah! wretched boy, I have heard of thy treason at Lochleven."

"Reproach him not, my brother," said the Abbot, "he was but an agent in the hands of Heaven."

"To horse, to horse!" said Catherine Seyton; "mount and begone, or we are all lost. I see our gallant army flying for many a league—To horse, my Lord Abbot—To horse, Roland—my gracious Liege, to horse! Ere this, we should have ridden many a mile."

"Look on these features," said Mary, pointing to the dying knight, who had been unhelmed by some compassionate hand; "look there, and tell me if she who ruins all who love her, ought to fly a foot farther to save her wretched life!"

The reader must have long anticipated the discovery which the Queen's feelings had made before her eyes confirmed it. It was the features of the unhappy George Douglas, on which death was stamping his mark.

"Look—look at him well," said the Queen, "thus has it been with all who loved Mary Stewart!—The royalty of Francis, the wit of Chastelar, the power and gallantry of the gay Gordon, the melody of Rizzio, the portly form and youthful grace of Darnley, the bold address and courtly manners of Bothwell—and now the deep-devoted passion of the noble Douglas—nought could save them!—they looked on the wretched Mary, and to have loved her was crime enough to deserve early death! No sooner had the victim formed a kind thought of me, than the poisoned cup, the axe and block, the dagger, the mine, were ready to punish them for casting away affection on such a wretch as I am!—Importune me not—I will fly no farther—I can die but once, and I will die here."

While she spoke, her tears fell fast on the face of the dying man, who continued to fix his eyes on her with an eagerness of passion, which death itself could hardly subdue.—"Mourn not for me," he said faintly, "but care for your own safety—I die in mine armour as a Douglas should, and I die pitied by Mary Stewart!"

He expired with these words, and without withdrawing his eyes from her face; and the Queen, whose heart was of that soft and gentle mould, which in domestic life, and with a more suitable partner than Darnley, might have made her happy, remained weeping by the dead man, until recalled to herself by the Abbot, who found it necessary to use a style of unusual remonstrance. "We also, madam," he said, "we, your Grace's devoted followers, have friends and relatives to weep for. I leave a brother in imminent jeopardy—the husband of the Lady Fleming—the father and brothers of the Lady Catherine, are all in yonder bloody field, slain, it is to be feared, or prisoners. We forget the fate of our nearest and dearest, to wait on our Queen, and she is too much occupied with her own sorrows to give one thought to ours."

"I deserve not your reproach, father," said the Queen, checking her tears; "but I am docile to it—where must we go—what must we do?"

"We must fly, and that instantly," said the Abbot; "whither is not so easily answered, but we may dispute it upon the road—Lift her to her saddle, and set forward."*

---

* I am informed in the most polite manner, by D. MacVean, Esq. of Glasgow, that I have been incorrect in my locality, in giving an account of the battle of Langside. Crookstone Castle, he observes, lies four miles west from the field of battle, and rather in the rear of Murray's army. The real place from which Mary saw the rout of her last army, was Cathcart Castle, which, being a mile and a half east from Langside, was situated in the rear of the Queen's own army. I was led astray in the present case, by the authority of my deceased friend, James Grahame the excellent and amiable author of the Sabbath, in his drama on the subject of Queen Mary; and by a traditionary report of Mary having seen the battle from the Castle of Crookstone, which seemed so much to increase the interest of the scene, that I have been unwilling to make, in this particular instance, the fiction give way to the fact, which last is undoubtedly in favour of Mr. MacVean's system.

It is singular how tradition, which is sometimes a sure guide to truth, is, in other cases, prone to mislead us. In the celebrated field of battle at Killiecrankie, the traveller is struck with one of those rugged pillars of rough stone, which indicate the scenes of ancient conflict. A friend of the author, well acquainted with the circumstances of the battle, was standing near this large stone, and looking on the scene around, when a highland shepherd hurried down from the hill to offer his services as cicerone, and proceeded to inform him, that Dundee was slain at that stone, which was raised to his memory. "Fie, Donald," answered my friend, "how can you tell such a story to a stranger? I am sure you know well enough that Dundee was killed at a considerable distance from this place, near the house of Fascally, and that this stone was here long before the battle, in 1688."—"Oich! oich!" said Donald, no way abashed, "and your honour's in the right, and I see you ken a' about it. And he wasna killed on the spot neither, but lived till the next morning; but a' the Saxon gentlemen like best to hear he was killed at the great stane." It is on the same principle of pleasing my readers, that I retain Crookstone Castle instead of Cathcart.

If, however, the author has taken a liberty in removing the actual field of battle somewhat to the eastward, he has been tolerably strict in adhering to the incidents of the engagement, as will appear from a comparison of events in the novel, with the following account from an old writer.

"The Regent was out on foot and all his company, except the Laird of Grange, Alexander Hume of Manderston, and some borderers to the number of two hundred. The Laird of Grange had already viewed the ground, and with all imaginable diligence caused every horseman to take behind him a footman of the Regent's, to guard behind them, and rode with speed to the head of Langside-hill, and set down the footmen with their culverings at the head of a straight lane, where there were some cottage houses and yards of great advantage. Which soldiers with their continual shot killed divers of the vaunt guard, led by the Hamiltons, who, courageously and fiercely ascending up the hill, were already out of breath, when the Regent's vaunt guard joined with them Where the worthy Lord Hume fought on foot with his pike in his hand very manfully, assisted by the Laird of Cessford, his brother-in-law, who helped him up again when he was strucken to the ground by many strokes upon his face, through the throwing pistols at him after they had been discharged. He was also wounded with staves, and had many strokes of spears through his legs; for he and Grange, at the joining, cried to let their adversaries first lay down their spears, to bear up theirs; which spears were so thick fixed in the others' jacks, that some of the pistols and great staves that were thrown by them which were behind, might be seen lying upon the spears.

"Upon the Queen's side the Earl of Argyle commanded the battle, and the Lord of Arbroth the vaunt guard. But the Regent committed to the Laird of Grange the special care, as being an experimented captain, to oversee every danger, and to ride to every wing, to encourage and make help where greatest need was. He perceived, at the first joining, the right wing of the Regent's vaunt guard put back and like to fly, whereof the greatest part were commons of the barony of Renfrew; whereupon he rode to them, and told them that their enemy was already turning their backs, requesting them to stay and debate till he should bring them fresh men forth of the battle. Whither at full speed he did ride alone, and told the Regent that the enemy were shaken and flying away behind the little village, and desired a few number of fresh men to go with him. Where he found enough willing, as the Lord Lindesay, the Laird of Lochleven, Sir James Balfour, and all the Regent's servants, who followed him with diligence, and reinforced that wing which was beginning to fly; which fresh men with their loose weapons struck the enemies in their flank and faces, which forced them incontinent to give place and turn back after long fighting and pushing others to and fro with their spears. There were not many horsemen to pursue after them, and the Regent cried to save and not to kill, and Grange was never cruel, so that there were few slain and taken. And the only slaughter was at the first rencounter by the shot of the soldiers, which Grange had planted at the lane head behind some dikes."

It is remarkable that, while passing through the small town of Renfrew, some partisans, adherents of the House of Lennox, attempting to arrest Queen Mary and her attendants, were obliged to make way for her not without slaughter.

They set off accordingly—Roland lingered a moment to command the attendants of the Knight of Avenel to convey their master to the Castle of Crookstone, and to say that he demanded from him no other condition of liberty, than his word, that he and his followers would keep secret the direction in which the Queen fled. As he turned his rein to depart, the honest countenance of Adam Woodcock stared upon him with an expression of surprise, which, at another time, would have excited his hearty mirth. He had been one of the followers who had experienced the weight of Roland's arm, and they now knew each other, Roland having put up his visor, and the good yeoman having thrown away his barret-cap, with the iron bars in front, that he might the more readily assist his master. Into this barret-cap, as it lay on the ground, Roland forgot not to drop a few gold pieces, (fruits of the Queen's liberality,) and with a signal of kind recollection and enduring friendship, he departed at full gallop to overtake the Queen, the dust raised by her train being already far down the hill.

"It is not fairy-money," said honest Adam, weighing and handling the gold—"And it was Master Roland himself, that is a certain thing—the same open hand, and, by our Lady!" (shrugging his shoulders)—"the same ready fist!—My Lady will hear of this gladly, for she mourns for him as if he were her son. And to see how gay he is! But these light lads are as sure to be uppermost as the froth to be on the top of the quart-pot—Your man of solid parts remains ever a falconer." So saying, he went to aid his comrades, who had now come up in greater numbers, to carry his master into the Castle of Crookstone.

Chapter the Thirty-Eighth.

My native land, good night!

BYRON.

MANY a bitter tear was shed, during the hasty flight of Queen Mary, over fallen hopes, future prospects, and slaughtered friends. The deaths of the brave Douglas, and of the fiery but gallant young Seyton, seemed to affect the Queen as much as the fall from the throne, on which she had so nearly been again seated. Catherine Seyton devoured in secret her own grief, anxious to support the broken spirits of her mistress; and the Abbot, bending his troubled thoughts upon futurity, endeavoured in vain to form some plan which had a shadow of hope. The spirit of young Roland—for he also mingled in the hasty debates held by the companions of the Queen's flight—continued unchecked and unbroken.

"Your Majesty," he said, "has lost a battle—Your ancestor, Bruce, lost seven successively, ere he sat triumphant on the Scottish throne, and proclaimed with the voice of a victor, in the field of Bannockburn, the independence of his country. Are not these heaths, which we may traverse at will, better than the locked, guarded, and lake-moated Castle of Lochleven?—We are free—in that one word there is comfort for all our losses."

He struck a bold note, but the heart of Mary made no response.

"Better," she said, "I had still been in Lochleven, than seen the slaughter made by rebels among the subjects who offered themselves to death for my sake. Speak not to me of farther efforts—they would only cost the lives of you, the friends who recommend them! I would not again undergo what I felt, when I saw from yonder mount the swords of the fell horsemen of Morton raging among the faithful Seytons and Hamiltons, for their loyalty to their Queen — I would not again feel what I felt when Douglas's life-blood stained my mantle for his love to Mary Stewart — not to be empress of all that Britain's seas enclose. Find for me some place where I can hide my unhappy head, which brings destruction on all who love it—it is the last favour that Mary asks of her faithful followers."

In this dejected mood, but still pursuing her flight with unabated rapidity, the unfortunate Mary, after having been joined by Lord Herries and a few followers, at length halted, for the first time, at the Abbey of Dundrennan, nearly sixty miles distant from the field of battle. In this remote quarter of Galloway, the Reformation not having yet been strictly enforced against the monks, a few still lingered in their cells unmolested; and the Prior, with tears and reverence, received the fugitive Queen at the gate of his convent.

"I bring you ruin, my good father," said the Queen, as she was lifted from her palfrey.

"It is welcome," said the Prior, "if it comes in the train of duty."

Placed on the ground, and supported by her ladies, the Queen looked for an instant at her palfrey, which, jaded and drooping its head, seemed as if it mourned the distresses of its mistress.

"Good Roland," said the Queen, whispering, "let Rosabelle be cared for — ask thy heart, and it will tell thee why I make this trifling request even in this awful hour."

She was conducted to her apartment, and in the hurried consultation of her attendants, the fatal resolution of the retreat to England was finally adopted. In the morning it received her approbation, and a messenger was despatched to the English warden, to pray him for safe-conduct and hospitality, on the part of the Queen of Scotland. On the next day the Abbot Ambrose walked in the garden of the Abbey with Roland, to whom he expressed his disapprobation of the course pursued. "It is madness and ruin," he said; "better commit herself to the savage Highlanders or wild Bordermen, than to the faith of Elizabeth. A woman to a rival woman — a presumptive successor to the keeping of a jealous and childless Queen! — Roland, Herries is true and loyal, but his counsel has ruined his mistress."

"Ay, ruin follows us every where," said an old man, with a spade in his hand, and dressed like a lay-brother, of whose presence, in the vehemence of his exclamation, the Abbot had not been aware — "Gaze not on me with such wonder!—I am he who was the Abbot Boniface at Kennaquhair, who was the gardener Blinkhoolie at Lochleven, hunted round to the place in which I served my noviciate, and now ye are come to rouse me up again! — A weary life I have had for one to whom peace was ever the dearest blessing!"

"We will soon rid you of our company, good father," said the Abbot; "and the Queen will, I fear, trouble your retreat no more."

"Nay, you said as much before," said the querulous old man, "and yet I was put forth from Kinross, and pillaged by troopers on the road. — They took from me the certificate that you wot of — that of the Baron — ay, he was a moss-trooper like themselves—You asked me of it, and I could never find it, but they found it—it showed the marriage of—of—my memory fails me — Now see how men differ! Father Nicholas would have told you an hundred tales of the Abbot Ingelram, on whose soul God have mercy! — He was, I warrant you, fourscore and six, and I am not more than — let me see——"

"Was not Avenel the name you seek, my good father?" said Roland, impatiently, yet moderating his tone for fear of alarming or offending the infirm old man.

"Ay, right — Avenel, Julian Avenel — You are perfect in the name — I kept all the special confessions, judging it held with my vow to do so — I could not find it when my successor, Ambrosius, spoke on't—but the troopers found it, and the Knight who commanded the party struck his breast, till the target clattered like an empty watering-can."

"Saint Mary!" said the Abbot, "in whom could such a paper excite such interest! What was the appearance of the knight, his arms, his colours?"

"Ye distract me with your questions—I dared hardly look at him—they charged me with bearing letters for the Queen, and searched my mail—This was all along of your doings at Lochleven."

"I trust in God," said the Abbot to Roland, who stood beside him, shivering and trembling with impatience, "the paper has fallen into the hands of my brother—I heard he had been with his followers on the scout betwixt Stirling and Glasgow.—Bore not the Knight a holly-bough on his helmet?—Canst thou not remember?"

"Oh, remember—remember," said the old man pettishly; "count as many years as I do, if your plots will let you, and see what, and how much, you remember.—Why, I scarce remember the pear-mains which I graffed here with my own hands some fifty years since."

At this moment a bugle sounded loudly from the beach.

"It is the death-blast to Queen Mary's royalty," said Ambrosius; "the English warden's answer has been received, favourable doubtless, for when was the door of the trap closed against the prey which it was set for?—Droop not, Roland—this matter shall be sifted to the bottom—but we must not now leave the Queen—follow me—let us do our duty, and trust the issue with God—Farewell, good Father—I will visit thee again soon."

He was about to leave the garden, followed by Roland, with half-reluctant steps. The Ex-Abbot resumed his spade.

"I could be sorry for these men," he said, "ay, and for that poor Queen, but what avail earthly sorrows to a man of fourscore?—and it is a rare dropping morning for the early colewort."

"He is stricken with age," said Ambrosius, as he dragged Roland down to the sea-beach; "we must let him take his time to collect himself—nothing now can be thought on but the fate of the Queen."

They soon arrived where she stood, surrounded by her little train, and by her side the sheriff of Cumberland, a gentleman of the house of Lowther, richly dressed and accompanied by soldiers. The aspect of the Queen exhibited a singular mixture of alacrity and reluctance to depart. Her language and gestures spoke hope and consolation to her attendants, and she seemed desirous to persuade even herself that the step she adopted was secure, and that the assurance she had received of kind reception was altogether satisfactory; but her quivering lip, and unsettled eye, betrayed at once her anguish at departing from Scotland, and her fears of confiding herself to the doubtful faith of England.

"Welcome, my Lord Abbot," she said, speaking to Ambrosius, "and you, Roland Avenel, we have joyful news for you—our loving sister's officer proffers us, in her name, a safe asylum from the rebels who have driven us from our home—only it grieves me we must here part from you for a short space."

"Part from us, madam!" said the Abbot. "Is your welcome in England, then, to commence with the abridgment of your train, and dismissal of your counsellors?"

"Take it not thus, good Father," said Mary; "the Warden and the Sheriff, faithful servants of our Royal Sister, deem it necessary to obey her instructions in the present case, even to the letter, and can only take upon them to admit me with my female attendants. An express will instantly be despatched from London, assigning me a place of residence; and I will speedily send to all of you whenever my Court shall be formed."

"Your Court formed in England! and while Elizabeth lives and reigns?"

said the Abbot—"that will be when we shall see two suns in one heaven!"

"Do not think so," replied the Queen; "we are well assured of our sister's good faith. Elizabeth loves fame—and not all that she has won by her power and her wisdom will equal that which she will acquire by extending her hospitality to a distressed sister!—not all that she may hereafter do of good, wise, and great, would blot out the reproach of abusing our confidence.—Farewell, my page—now my knight—farewell for a brief season. I will dry the tears of Catherine, or I will weep with her till neither of us can weep longer." She held out her hand to Roland, who flinging himself on his knees, kissed it with much emotion. He was about to render the same homage to Catherine, when the Queen, assuming an air of sprightliness, said, "Her lips, thou foolish boy! and, Catherine, coy it not—these English gentlemen should see, that, even in our cold clime, Beauty knows how to reward Bravery and Fidelity!"

"We are not now to learn the force of Scottish beauty, or the mettle of Scottish valour," said the Sheriff of Cumberland, courteously—"I would it were in my power to bid these attendants upon her who is herself the mistress of Scottish beauty, as welcome to England as my poor cares would make them. But our Queen's orders are positive in case of such an emergence, and they must not be disputed by her subject.—May I remind your Majesty that the tide ebbs fast?"

The Sheriff took the Queen's hand, and she had already placed her foot on the gangway, by which she was to enter the skiff, when the Abbot, starting from a trance of grief and astonishment at the words of the Sheriff, rushed into the water, and seized upon her mantle.

"She foresaw it!—She foresaw it!"—he exclaimed—"she foresaw your flight into her realm; and, foreseeing it, gave orders you should be thus received. Blinded, deceived, doomed Princess! your fate is sealed when you quit this strand.—Queen of Scotland, thou shalt not leave thine heritage!" he continued, holding a still firmer grasp upon her mantle; "true men shall turn rebels to thy will, that they may save thee from captivity or death. Fear not the bills and bows whom that gay man has at his beck—we will withstand him by force. Oh, for the arm of my warlike brother!—Roland Avenel, draw thy sword."

The Queen stood irresolute and frightened; one foot upon the plank, the other on the sand of her native shore, which she was quitting for ever.

"What needs this violence, Sir Priest?" said the Sheriff of Cumberland; "I came hither at your Queen's command, to do her service; and I will depart at her least order, if she rejects such aid as I can offer. No marvel is it if our Queen's wisdom foresaw that such chance as this might happen amidst the turmoils of your unsettled State; and, while willing to afford fair hospitality to her Royal Sister, deemed it wise to prohibit the entrance of a broken army of her followers into the English frontier."

"You hear," said Queen Mary, gently unloosing her robe from the Abbot's grasp, "that we exercise full liberty of choice in leaving this shore; and, questionless, the choice will remain free to us in going to France, or returning to our own dominions, as we shall determine—Besides, it is too late—Your blessing, Father, and God speed thee!"

"May He have mercy on thee, Princess, and speed thee also!" said the Abbot, retreating. "But my soul tells me I look on thee for the last time!"

The sails were hoisted, the oars were plied, the vessel went freshly on her way through the firth, which divides the shores of Cumberland from those of Galloway; but not till the vessel diminished to the size of a child's frigate, did the doubtful, and dejected, and dismissed followers of the Queen cease to linger on the sands; and long, long could they discern the kerchief of Mary, as she waved the oft-repeated signal of adieu to her faithful adherents, and to the shores of Scotland.

If good tidings of a private nature could have consoled Roland for parting with his mistress, and for the distresses of his sovereign, he received such comfort some days subsequent to the Queen's leaving Dundrennan. A breathless post—no other than Adam Woodcock—brought despatches from Sir Halbert Glendinning to the Abbot, whom he found with Roland, still residing at Dundrennan, and in vain torturing Boniface with fresh interrogations. The packet bore an earnest invitation to his brother to make Avenel Castle for a time his residence. "The clemency of the Regent," said the writer, "has extended pardon both to Roland and to you, upon condition of your remaining a time under my wardship. And I have that to communicate respecting the parentage of Roland, which not only you will willingly listen to, but which will be also found to afford me, as the husband of his nearest relative, some interest in the future course of his life."

The Abbot read this letter, and paused, as if considering what were best for him to do. Meanwhile, Woodcock took Roland side, and addressed him as follows:—"Now, look, Mr. Roland, that you do not let any papestrie nonsense lure either the priest or you from the right quarry. See you, you ever bore yourself as a bit of a gentleman. Read that, and thank God that threw old Abbot Boniface in our way, as two of the Seyton's men were conveying him towards Dundrennan here.—We searched him for intelligence concerning that fair exploit of yours at Lochleven, that has cost many a man his life, and me a set of sore bones—and we found what is better for your purpose than ours."

The paper which he gave, was, indeed, an attestation by Father Philip, subscribing himself unworthy Sacristan, and brother of the House of Saint Mary's, stating, "that under a vow of secrecy he had united, in the holy sacrament of marriage, Julian Avenel and Catherine Græme; but that Julian having repented of his union, he, Father Philip, had been sinfully prevailed on by him to conceal and disguise the same, according to a complot devised betwixt him and the said Julian Avenel, whereby the poor damsel was induced to believe that the ceremony had been performed by one not in holy orders, and having no authority to that effect. Which sinful concealment the undersigned conceived to be the cause why he was abandoned to the misguiding of a water-fiend, whereby he had been under a spell, which obliged him to answer every question, even touching the most solemn matters, with idle snatches of old songs, besides being sorely afflicted with rheumatic pains ever after. Wherefore he had deposited this testificate and confession with the day and date of the said marriage, with his lawful superior Boniface, Abbot of Saint Mary's, *sub sigillo confessionis*."

It appeared by a letter from Julian, folded carefully up with the certificate, that the Abbot Boniface had, in effect, bestirred himself in the affair, and obtained from the Baron a promise to avow his marriage; but the death of both Julian and his injured bride, together with the Abbot's resignation, his ignorance of the fate of their unhappy offspring, and above all, the good father's listless and inactive disposition, had suffered the matter to become totally forgotten, until it was recalled by some accidental conversation with the Abbot Ambrosius concerning the fortunes of the Avenel family. At the request of his successor, the quondam Abbot made search for it; but as he would receive no assistance in looking among the few records of spiritual experiences and important confessions, which he had conscientiously treasured, it might have remained for ever hidden amongst them, but for the more active researches of Sir Halbert Glendinning.

"So that you are like to be heir of Avenel at last, Master Roland, after my lord and lady have gone to their place," said Adam; "and as I have but one boon to ask, I trust you will not nick me with nay."

"Not if it be in my power to say yes, my trusty friend."

"Why then, I must needs, if I live to see that day, keep on feeding the eyases with unwashed flesh," said Woodcock sturdily, as if doubting the reception that his request might meet with.

"Thou shalt feed them with what you list for me," said Roland, laughing; "I am not many months older than when I left the Castle, but I trust I have gathered wit enough to cross no man of skill in his own vocation."

"Then I would not change places with the King's falconer," said Adam Woodcock, "nor with the Queen's neither—but they say she will be mewed up and never need one.—I see it grieves you to think of it, and I could grieve for company; but what help for it?—Fortune will fly her own flight, let a man hollo himself hoarse."

The Abbot and Roland journeyed to Avenel, where the former was tenderly received by his brother, while the lady wept for joy to find that in her favourite orphan she had protected the sole surviving branch of her own family. Sir Halbert Glendinning and his household were not a little surprised at the change which a brief acquaintance with the world had produced in their former inmate, and rejoiced to find, in the pettish, spoiled, and presuming page, a modest and unassuming young man, too much acquainted with his own expectations and character, to be hot or petulant in demanding the consideration which was readily and voluntarily yielded to him. The old Major Domo Wingate was the first to sing his praises, to which Mistress Lilias bore a loud echo, always hoping that God would teach him the true gospel.

To the true gospel the heart of Roland had secretly long inclined, and the departure of the good Abbot for France, with the purpose of entering into some house of his order in that kingdom, removed his chief objection to renouncing the Catholic faith. Another might have existed in the duty which he owed to Magdalen Græme, both by birth and from gratitude. But he learned, ere he had been long a resident in Avenel, that his grandmother had died at Cologne, in the performance of a penance too severe for her age, which she had taken upon herself in behalf of the Queen and Church of Scotland, as soon as she heard of the defeat at Langside. The zeal of the Abbot Ambrosius was more regulated; but he retired into the Scottish convent of——, and so lived there, that the fraternity were inclined to claim for him the honours of canonization. But he guessed their purpose, and prayed them, on his death-bed, to do no honours to the body of one as sinful as themselves; but to send his body and his heart to be buried in Avenel burial-aisle, in the monastery of Saint Mary's, that the last Abbot of that celebrated house of devotion might sleep among its ruins.*

---

* This was not the explanation of the incident of searching for the heart, mentioned in the introduction to the tale, which the author originally intended. It was designed to refer to the heart of Robert Bruce. It is generally known that that great monarch, being on his death-bed, bequeathed to the good Lord James of Douglas, the task of carrying his heart to the Holy Land, to fulfil in a certain degree his own desire to perform a crusade. Upon Douglas's death, fighting against the Moors in Spain, a sort of military *hors d'œuvre* to which he could have pleaded no regular call of duty, his followers brought back the Bruce's heart, and deposited it in the Abbey church of Melrose, the Kennaquhair of the tale.

This Abbey has been always particularly favoured by the Bruce. We have already seen his extreme anxiety that each of the reverend brethren should be daily supplied with a service of boiled almonds, rice and milk, pease, or the like, to be called the King's mess, and that without the ordinary service of their table being either disturbed in quantity or quality. But this was not the only mark of the benignity of good King Robert towards the monks of Melrose, since, by a charter of the date 29th May, 1326, he conferred on the Abbot of Melrose the sum of two thousand pounds sterling, for rebuilding the church of St. Mary's, ruined by the English; and there is little or no doubt that the principal part of the remains which now display such exquisite specimens of Gothic architecture, at its very purest period, had their origin in this munificent donation. The money was to be paid out of crown lands, estates forfeited to the King, and other property or demesnes of the crown.

A very curious letter written to his son about three weeks before his death, has been pointed out to me by my friend Mr. Thomas Thomson, Deputy-Register for Scotland. It enlarges so much on the love of the royal writer to the community of Melrose, that it is well worthy of being inserted in a work connected in some degree with Scottish History.

LITERA DOMINI REGIS ROBERTI AD FILIUM SUUM DAVID.

"Robertus dei gratia Rex Scottorum, David precordialissimo filio suo, ac ceteris successoribus suis; Salutem, et sic ejus precepta tenere, ut cum sua benedictione possint regnare. Fili carissime, digne censeri videtur filius, qui, paternos in bonis mores imitans, piam ejus nititur exequi voluntatem; nec proprie sibi sumit nomen heredis, qui salubribus predecessoris affectibus non adherit: Cupientes igitur, ut piam affectionem et scinceram delectionem, quam erga monasterium de Melros, ubi cor nostrum ex speciali devotione disposuimus tumulandum, et erga Religiosos ibidem Deo servientes, ipsorum vita sanctissima nos ad hoc excitante, concepimus; Tu ceterique successores mei pia scinceritate prosequammi, ut, ex vestre dilectionis affectu dictis Religiosis nostri causa post mortem nostram ostenso, ipsi pro nobis ad orandum fervencius et forcius animen-

Long before that period arrived, Roland Avenel was wedded to Catherine Seyton, who, after two years' residence with her unhappy mistress, was dismissed upon her being subjected to closer restraint than had been at first exercised. She returned to her father's house, and as Roland was acknowledged for the successor and lawful heir of the ancient house of Avenel, greatly increased as the estate was by the providence of Sir Halbert Glendinning, there occurred no objections to the match on the part of her family. Her mother was recently dead when she first entered the convent; and her father, in the unsettled times which followed Queen Mary's flight to England, was not averse to an alliance with a youth, who, himself loyal to Queen Mary, still held some influence, through means of Sir Halbert Glendinning, with the party in power.

Roland and Catherine, therefore, were united, spite of their differing faiths; and the White Lady, whose apparition had been infrequent when the house of Avenel seemed verging to extinction, was seen to sport by her haunted well, with a zone of gold around her bosom as broad as the baldrick of an Earl.

---

tur: Vobis precipimus quantum possumus, instanter supplicamus, et ex toto corde injungimus, Quatinus assignacionibus quas eisdem viris Religiosis et fabrica Ecclesie sue de novo fecimus ac eciam omnibus aliis donacionibus nostris, ipsos libere gaudere permittatis, Easdem potius si necesse fuerit augmentantes quam diminuentes, ipsorum peticiones auribus benevolis admittentes, ac ipsos contra suos invasores et emulos pia defensione protegentes. Hanc autem exhortacionem supplicacionem et preceptum tu, fili ceterique successores nostri, prestanti animo complere curetis, si nostram benedictionem habere velitis, una cum benedictione filii summi Regis, qui filios docuit patrum voluntates in bono perficere, asserens in mundum se venisse non ut suam voluntatem faceret sed paternam. In testimonium autem nostre devotionis erga locum predictum sic a nobis dilectum et electum concepte, presentem literam Religiosis predictis dimittimus, nostris successoribus in posterum ostendendam. Data apud Cardros, undecimo die Maij, Anno Regni nostri vicesimo quarto."

If this charter be altogether genuine, and there is no appearance of forgery, it gives rise to a curious doubt in Scottish History. The letter announces that the King had already destined his heart to be deposited at Melrose. The resolution to send it to Palestine, under the charge of Douglas, must have been adopted betwixt 11th May 1329, the date of the letter, and 7th June of the same year, when the Bruce died; or else we must suppose that the commission of Douglas extended not only to taking the Bruce's heart to Palestine, but to bring it safe back to its final place of deposit in the Abbey of Melrose.

It would not be worth inquiring by what caprice the author was induced to throw the incident of the Bruce's heart entirely out of the story, save merely to say, that he found himself unable to fill up the canvass he had sketched, and indisposed to prosecute the management of the supernatural machinery with which his plan, when it was first rough-hewn, was connected and combined.

END OF THE ABBOT.

www.ingramcontent.com/pod-product-compliance
Lightning Source LLC
LaVergne TN
LVHW021259110826
845150LV00003B/431

* 9 7 8 1 4 2 5 5 6 0 5 1 5 *